The Concise Garland Encyclopedia of

WORLD MUSIC

VOLUME 1

The Garland Encyclopedia of World Music

Volume 1
Africa
edited by Ruth M. Stone

Volume 2
South America, Mexico, Central America, and the Caribbean
edited by Dale A. Olsen and Daniel E. Sheehy

Volume 3
The United States and Canada
edited by Ellen Koskoff

Volume 4
Southeast Asia
edited by Terry E. Miller and Sean Williams

Volume 5
South Asia: The Indian Subcontinent
edited by Alison Arnold

Volume 6
The Middle East
edited by Virginia Danielson, Scott Marcus, and Dwight Reynolds

Volume 7
East Asia: China, Japan, and Korea
edited by Robert C. Provine, Yosihiko Tokumaru, and J. Lawrence Witzleben

Volume 8
Europe
edited by Timothy Rice, James Porter, and Chris Goertzen

Volume 9
Australia and the Pacific Islands
edited by Adrienne L. Kaeppler and J. Wainwright Love

Volume 10
The World's Music: General Perspectives and Reference Tools
edited by Ruth M. Stone

Advisory Editors
Bruno Nettl and Ruth M. Stone

Founding Editors
James Porter and Timothy Rice

The Concise Garland Encyclopedia of

WORLD MUSIC

Volume 1

Africa

*South America, Mexico, Central America,
and the Caribbean*

The United States and Canada

Europe

Oceania

Routledge
Taylor & Francis Group

NEW YORK AND LONDON

First published 2008
by Routledge
270 Madison Ave, New York, NY 10016

Simultaneously published in the UK
by Routledge
2 Park Square, Milton Park, Abingdon, Oxon OX14 4RN

Routledge is an imprint of the Taylor & Francis Group, an informa business

© 2008 Taylor & Francis

Typeset in Times New Roman by RefineCatch Limited, Bungay, Suffolk
Printed and bound in the United States of America on acid-free paper by
Sheridan Books, Inc.

Library of Congress Cataloging in Publication Data
The concise Garland encyclopedia of world music / advisory board, Ellen Koskoff . . . [et al.].
    p. cm.
  1. World music—Encyclopedias.   I. Koskoff, Ellen, 1943–
ML100.C69 2008
780.3—dc22

                                                                    2008019670

ISBN10: 0–415–97293–0 (2 vol. set hbk)
ISBN10: 0–415–99403–9 (vol. 1 hbk)

ISBN13: 978–0–415–97293–2 (2 vol. set hbk)
ISBN13: 978–0–415–99403–3 (vol. 1 hbk)

Contents

VOLUME 1

Contents

VOLUME 2

Contents

x

Contents

Foreword

Beyond the Borders of World Music

PHILIP V. BOHLMAN

*Mary Werkman Distinguished Service Professor of the
Humanities and of Music
University of Chicago
President of the Society of Ethnomusicology, 2005–2007*

The expressive force that joined music to voice in song lived in the ear of the people, on the lips and in the harp of the living singer. It sang of history, daily events, secrets, and miracles—of the very signs of humanity. It was the flower of the uniqueness of every people, its language and its land, everything it did and all its prejudices, a people's passions and all that made them distinctive: It was the measure of its music and soul.

Johann Gottfried Herder, *Volkslieder* (1779)

The *Concise Garland Encyclopedia of World Music* inherits a long and distinguished history, which springs in its foundational moment from the two-volume work of the great Enlightenment thinker Johann Gottfried Herder, *The Voices of the People in Song* and *Folk Songs* (1778–1779). Herder ascribed to song—he actually coined the word *Volkslied,* or "folk song," for the phenomenon—the potential to conjoin music and language, empowering them to bear witness to all that was human, so clearly evident in the epigraph opening this foreword. Herder, who wrote philosophy, poetry, libretti for musical works, and the diverse tracts on religion appropriate for his professional life as a theologian, returned to the music of the people throughout his life, expanding at each encounter the concepts he had formulated while hearing the music of peasants during his childhood and early adulthood in what is today Lithuania and Latvia, and adding layer upon layer of musical experience from what we might call fieldwork during travels through the North Sea, Alsace, Italy, and the provinces of eastern Germany, where he settled in Weimar, home to the great intellectual and artistic giants of his day, among them Goethe and Schiller.

Herder deserves a position in the foreword to the two volumes that now draw the endeavors of the many authors and editors who have contributed to the most ambitious world-music publication of our own day not because he established a canon for world music or charted a global geography with immutable borders containing similarities and excluding differences. Rather, Herder's own two volumes and his return to them again and again revealed the persistent need to redraw the borders of world music and to realize the ways in which they recognized difference as the response of human societies, indeed, of the subaltern, those without power, who employed music to give voice to their aspirations. As Herder was preparing the final edition of his volumes, which appeared only posthumously four years after his death in 1903, he expanded the scope of what had clearly become a global landscape for world music by confronting the question of colonial encounter, particularly the destruction of indigenous peoples in Africa and South America.

The study of world music raises the most important questions of the modern era, and it was this realization, first given voice by Herder, that underlies the endeavors gathered in the two volumes of the *Concise Garland Encyclopedia of World Music*. With renewed vigor and with a sense of commitment to hearing the "voices of the people in songs," the legacy of Herder, the authors and editors in the concise edition have set out once again to reexamine and re-draw the borders of world music, and to ensure that they are inclusive rather than exclusive. Herder's historical influence notwithstanding, there is a new heritage that resonates in these twenty-first-century voices, that of ethnomusicology. Just as the original ten-volume *Garland Encyclopedia* gathered the many voices of ethnomusicologists from throughout the world in unprecedented fashion, the concise edition draws them together with even greater resonance—and relevance—in a field dedicated not only to understanding globalization but encountering it head-on. The legacy of world music is born of ethical responsibility and moral imperative, which join in common purpose in the ethnomusicology that provides the context for the present two volumes.

The *Concise Garland Encyclopedia of World Music* bears witness to a comprehensive rethinking of the history and historiography of world music. That rethinking first began to take shape in the wake of World War II, when the hegemonic parsing of the world—and by extension its musics—began to collapse, together with the colonial empires that fostered it. Not insignificantly at the same historical moment, ethnomusicology as an international field emerged as a collective discipline dedicated to the study of all musics in their cultural contexts. From its formative moments—the establishment of the International Folk Music Council (today, the International Council for Traditional Music) in the late 1940s and the Society for Ethnomusicology in 1955—the field of ethnomusicology insisted on the need for disciplinary realignments that took seriously the need to examine world musics in the historical contexts of a post-colonial world. The ethnomusicologists of the post-World War II generation consciously sought ways to combine the aesthetic and the political, the musical and the cultural, indeed the two components in the underlying subject of these volumes: world music.

The emergence of modern ethnomusicology in the mid-twentieth century and its transformation to a post-disciplinary ethnomusicology in the twenty-first century, nonetheless, sustained a long history of charting the aesthetic and political territories immanent in world music. As we have already witnessed in Herder's seminal writings, the concepts and constructs of world music were born of encounter. Encounter, inevitably, both resulted from and contributed to unequal distributions of power. It is in the contexts of these unequal distributions of power, however, that the challenge of rethinking world music really emerges.

Throughout the *Garland Encyclopedia* the critical importance of past for the present—of music histories in local and global forms—asserts itself. The history of world music, as each chapter makes clear, is one of critical moments and paradigm shifts. The reader would do well to remember the most global of these as she or he engages in the challenge of rethinking world music. With the sixteenth century comes the so-called Age of Discovery, a re-settling of many parts of the world with subsequent appropriation of resources, material and musical, for use in the West. Empires expanded in the seventeenth century, even as Europe and the world upon which it had imposed its borders descended into the chaos of the Thirty Years War. Enlightenment, with its national and religious idiolects, followed in the eighteenth century, with dictionaries (e.g., Diderot) and world music anthologies (e.g., Herder) attempting to ascribe order to world music. Political paradigms shifted radically in the nineteenth century, with the onset of various colonialisms, which then in the twentieth century shifted, often violently, to the nationalisms that shaped modernity. We cannot think about world music, historically or ethnomusicologically, without recognizing the critical presence of music as a measure of these moments in which cultural and political power on a global scale often led to destructive ends. Rethinking world music in the twenty-first century possesses, for ethnomusicology, a profound ethical significance and moral imperative.

The borders of world music in the twenty-first century intersect with those of a post-disciplinary ethnomusicology, and accordingly they become capacious and inclusive. The post-disciplinary character of ethnomusicology was crucial to the concept and conception of the *Garland Encyclopedia,* for the authors who contribute to it bring multiple perspectives to their entries, from the fields in which they primarily work as well as those beyond primary fields. National entries, for example, not only transcend bounded notions of national styles, repertories, and styles, but they also grow from an interactive scholarship that relies on musicians, scholars, and institutions within nations, not just universities and academies of science, but also archives, museums, and non-governmental organizations. National historiography and folklore studies, ensembles and research institutions both private and state-supported, musical subject positions contingent upon indigenous recording and broadcast media, all these are tapped to give new meaning to the musics of a nation or, for that matter, the musics of peoples without nations.

Ethnomusicology's interdisciplinarity during the past generation has been crucial to its expansion, in both academic and public sectors, and surely in the ways these several sectors interact. The chapters in the *Concise Garland Encyclopedia of World Music,* too, reveal the ways in which ethnomusicology, throughout its considerable history, has always broken distinctive paths for interdisciplinarity. Anthropology, historical musicology, and folklore have together afforded the field its methodological foundations. In theory and practice, the truly fundamental question is not whether ethnomusicology belongs to one discipline or another. Whether it is really anthropology or musicology. Whether it belongs in the academy or the agencies and NGOs that act within the public sphere. Ethnomusicologists draw upon and work in all of these areas. They resolutely refuse to exclude approaches on disciplinary grounds, and they consciously realize new possibilities for collaboration and interdisciplinarity.

The post-disciplinarity of twenty-first-century ethnomusicology does not and could not abandon music. Quite the contrary, music assumes a new, even a privileged, position in the post-disciplinarity of the field. Above all, music becomes much more than a sonic product, reducible to unambiguous representation and restricted to a metaphysics determined by self-sustained musical identities. Music shifts from object to subject, from stasis to process. Whereas the object music was far too often imagined to exist apart from those who created it and gave it meaning through performance and the functions it acquired in society. By generating multiple subject positions music powerfully generates agency for those who perform and consume it, and situate it at the center of society and culture, ritual and history.

The shift from object to subject that is so crucial to a post-disciplinary ethnomusicology has transformed the ways in which we consider musical identity in its multiple dimensions, not least in the ways such identities extend to world music in these volumes. In earlier approaches to world music identity assumed concentrated forms: Folk song and folk music, for example, belonged to one nation or another—Polish, Brazilian, Japanese, American—as if such identities expressed themselves in straightforward attributes. Language was one of these. So, too, were the cultural functions of remote villages and the restrictions of oral tradition.

Social and ideological hierarchies, too, were part of an ethnomusicology predicated on simple identities. If a nation or people had folk music, by necessity it also had art music, as well as identifiable religious musics and popular musics. Classical musics depended on some manner of literacy. Folk and popular musics in contrast were independent of literacy. Literacy or lack thereof, however, was hardly the issue, for the limited identities espoused in earlier approaches to world music simply failed to include film music or religious music, in which orality and literacy were more often than not in tension, each dependent on the other. World musics, it often followed, contained identities that were in certain ways mere versions and variants of each other.

The musical and cultural identities of world music in a post-disciplinary ethnomusicology insistently reveal themselves as hybrids, affording musicians and social groups many identities, some of them highly individual, others growing from the many choices about making music with others. Individuals and music-making communities exhibit a tendency to draw from more rather than fewer musical repertories. It is not surprising that globalization, as it so often shapes the world musics in these volumes, has contributed profoundly to this proliferation of the identities now critical to the methods of a post-disciplinary ethnomusicology.

The publication of the *Concise Garland Encyclopedia of World Music* marks the beginning of a new age of ethnomusicology and world music in the twenty-first century. Even as it does so, it resonates with the echoes of the long legacy of encounter with music in its local and global contexts. Just as Herder and the generations that followed him struggled with the complicated questions of canon and discipline, so too do the authors and editors of these volumes struggle with the implications of identifying and claiming world music in the generations that preceded them. In the twenty-first century, there are new contexts for experiencing music close to home and on a global landscape, and technology and the seemingly infinite possibility of mediation engender new forms of encounter, making them virtually quotidian. As these new contexts resituate the borders of world music, they also challenge us to reexamine what world music really is, that is, whether we can fully perceive and engage with its new ontologies. When we encounter world music in the twenty-first century, we realize that the old borders of nations, languages, genres, and social collectivity have been supplanted by the processes of globalization, hybridity, revival, embodiment, and decolonization. Popular music and sacred music no longer lurk at the peripheries but they remix the center. Aesthetics and politics no longer occupy separate territories but cohabit the everyday world of all musical experience.

Johann Gottfried Herder, in many ways, got it right, but he did so only because he recognized the need relentlessly to push the borders of music so that they would include more and more. The legacy of the volumes to which the reader now turns is therefore not one of claiming categories and canons from the world into which Herder's successors were moving, but rather the challenge to move beyond them. This is the legacy that fills the pages of the *Concise Garland Encyclopedia of World Music.*

Chicago, April 2008

Preface

The *Concise Garland Encyclopedia of World Music* is an adaptation of the respected ten-volume *Garland Encyclopedia of World Music* that has become a staple for ethnomusicologists. The new *Concise* edition was conceived with broader goals. It is directed to a more general audience and well-suited for small libraries. Furthermore, libraries housing the original ten-volume set will appreciate the *Concise* version as a supplement to the existing material. In the effort to consolidate ten volumes to two, essays were revised, summarized, added or removed, and brought up-to-date in the process.

We have adapted the content to the needs of a more general audience: articles intended primarily for a specialized audience—those on previous scholarship and research, on the archaeology of instruments, and on the discipline of ethnomusicology itself—have been excluded. Certain terms are replaced by or supplemented with more familiar ones; for example, *wind instrument* is used for *aerophone*, *stringed instrument* for *chordophone*, *self-sounding instrument* for *idiophone*, and *drum* or *percussion instrument* for *membranophone*. (Explanations as to why the Hornbostel-Sachs terms are preferable to these appear in Dale A. Olsen and Anthony Seeger's introduction to section 2, in the glossary, and elsewhere.) In-text references have been removed, except for direct quotes, attributions in musical figures, and a few other instances. The lists of references to bibliographies have been changed and supplemented with works from the literature guides appearing at the end of the original volumes. Fundamental musical terms—*tone*, *harmony*, *melody*—are added to the glossary, and many existing definitions have been expanded.

Numerous resources were consulted, in addition to the ten-volume encyclopedia set, including: *Grove Music Online*, *Encyclopedia Britannica Online*, *The Harvard Dictionary of Music* edited by Don Michael Randel (Harvard, 2003), *The Encyclopedia of Popular Music* edited by Colin Larkin (Oxford, 2006), *The CIA Factbook*, and many monographs and journals. The maps have been reviewed and revised using the Perry-Castañeda Library Map Collection of the University of Texas at Austin, *Encyclopedia Britannica Online*, Indiana University Graphic Services and Google Map.

Organization

The *Concise Garland* adopts the geographic approach of the original set: the nine sections correspond to the regions covered in the nine volumes, though their order differs. Each section begins with an introduction, which covers the region's culture and music. The introductions to several sections lead into an additional article or articles discussing other unifying aspects of a region's music, especially its instruments, genres, or theories. The remainder (and bulk) of a section is devoted to articles on some of the region's individual music cultures.

The articles within a section overlap only minimally; each section can be read in its entirety as an introduction to the region's music and culture. In general, the introductory articles focus on culture and history, and the individual articles focus on music. Those interested in reading an article on a specific music—i.e., Sam-Ang Sam's "Cambodia" in the Southeast Asia section—will find cultural and historical context for it in Terry Miller and Sean Williams' introductory articles: "Southeast Asian Musics: An Overview" and "Waves of Cultural Influence." Several sections have introductions to the region *and* introductions to geographic areas within the region. For example, context for Christian Poché's "Musical Life in Aleppo, Syria" in the Middle East section is found in Stephen Blum's "Hearing the Music of the Middle East" and A. J. Racy's "Overview of Music in the Mashriq." The Table of Contents serves as a guide to finding the historical and cultural background for a particular article.

Acknowledgments

More than one hundred scholars wrote, reviewed and revised articles, contributed photographs, and provided advice. Jacob W. Love, Terry E. Miller, Dale A. Olsen, and Sean Williams deserve special recognition. Alison Arnold, Stephen Blum, Virginia Danielson, Robin Elliott, Ron Emoff, Keith Howard, Adrienne L. Kaeppler, Ellen Koskoff, Gayathri Rajapur Kassebaum, Theodore Levin, Portia K. Maultsby, James Porter, A. J. Racy, N. Scott Robinson, Jonathan Shannon, Daniel Sheehy, Ruth M. Stone, and Dale Wilson also made helpful contributions. Some scholars substantially revised articles or authored new ones, particularly Michael Birenbaum Quintero, David Coplan, Veronica Doubleday, Ron Emoff, Oliver Greene, Clare Jones, Jean Kidula, Jacob W. Love, Irene Markoff, Daniel Neely, Dale A. Olsen, Gordon Thompson, Sean Williams, Dale Wilson, and Holly Wissler.

Douglas Puchowski managed the process of compiling the two *Concise* volumes, adapting them from the original ten-volume edition. Jessie Reiswig, Tony Coulter, Dacus Thompson, Daniel Webb and R. Brian Smith are acknowledged for their assistance.

Routledge Editorial and Production extend grateful thanks to all involved with this project. Following are listed the editors, contributors and reviewers whose work is reflected in the *Concise Garland Encyclopedia of World Music*.

Editorial Board

Contributing Authors

Volume 1

Africa

Laura Arntson
Public Health Institute,
USAID Nigeria
Abuja, Nigeria

Fremont E. Besmer
City College of the City University of
New York
New York, New York, U.S.A.

David B. Coplan
University of the Witwatersrand
Johannesburg, South Africa

Jacqueline Cogdell DjeDje
University of California at
Los Angeles
Los Angeles, California, U.S.A.

Ron Emoff
Ohio State University-Newark
Newark, Ohio, U.S.A.

Angela Impey
School of Oriental and African
Studies, University of London
London, England

John William Johnson
Indiana University
Bloomington, Indiana, U.S.A.

John Kaemmer
DePauw University
Greencastle, Indiana, U.S.A.

Paul N. Kavyu (deceased)
Kenyatta University
Nairobi, Kenya

Jean Ngoya Kidula
University of Georgia
Athens, Georgia, U.S.A.

Gerhard Kubik
University of Vienna
Vienna, Austria

Ruth M. Stone
Indiana University
Bloomington, Indiana, U.S.A.

Christopher A. Waterman
University of California at Los
Angeles
Los Angeles, California, U.S.A.

Caroline Card Wendt
Noblesville, Indiana, U.S.A.

South America, Mexico, Central America, and the Caribbean

Olavo Alén Rodríguez
Center for Research and Development
of Cuban Music (CIDMUC)
Havana, Cuba

Gage Averill
University of Toronto
Toronto, Canada

Gerard Béhague (deceased)
University of Texas,
Austin, Texas, U.S.A.

Michael Birenbaum Quintero
New York University
New York, New York, U.S.A.

Max H. Brandt
University of Pittsburgh
Pittsburgh, Pennsylvania, U.S.A.

Arturo Chamorro
Universidad de Guadalajara
Guadalajara, Mexico

John Cohen
Putnam Valley, New York, U.S.A.

Larry Crook
University of Florida
Gainesville, Florida, U.S.A.

Martha Ellen Davis
University of Florida
Gainesville, Florida, U.S.A.

Monique Desroches
Université de Montréal
Montréal, Québec, Canada

Oliver Greene
Georgia State University
Atlanta, Georgia, U.S.A.

Olive Lewin
Kingston, Jamaica

Lorna McDaniel
University of Michigan
Ann Arbor, Michigan, U.S.A.

Ercilia Moreno Chá
Instituto Nacional de Antropología
Buenos Aires, Argentina

Helen Myers
Bristol, Connecticut, U.S.A.

Daniel Tannehill Neely
New York University
New York, New York, U.S.A.

Linda O'Brien-Rothe
San Pedro, California, U.S.A.

Dale A. Olsen
The Florida State University
Tallahassee, Florida, U.S.A.

Suzel Ana Reily
The Queen's University of Belfast
Belfast, Northern Ireland

Raúl R. Romero
Pontífica Universidad Católica del
Perú
Lima, Perú

Anthony Seeger
University of California at Los
Angeles
Los Angeles, California, U.S.A.

Daniel E. Sheehy
Smithsonian Institute
Washington, D.C., U.S.A.

Ronald R. Smith (deceased)
Indiana University
Bloomington, Indiana, U.S.A.

William David Tompkins
University of Calgary
Calgary, Alberta, Canada

Holly Wissler
The Florida State University
Tallahassee, Florida, U.S.A.

Vivian Nina Michelle Wood
Davie, Florida, U.S.A.

The United States and Canada

Nicole Beaudry
University of Québec at Montréal
Montréal, Québec, Canada

Jody Berland
York University
North York, Ontario, Canada

Rob Bowman
York University
Toronto, Ontario, Canada

Mellonee V. Burnim
Indiana University
Bloomington, Indiana, U.S.A.

Steven Cornelius
Bowling Green State University
Bowling Green, Ohio, U.S.A.

Beverley Diamond
Memorial University of
Newfoundland
St. John's, Newfoundland and
Labrador, Canada

Robin Elliott
University of Toronto
Toronto, Canada

David Evans
University of Memphis
Memphis, Tennessee, U.S.A.

Annemarie Gallaugher
York University
Toronto, Ontario, Canada

Chris Goertzen
University of Southern Mississippi
Hattiesburg, Mississippi, U.S.A.

Erik D. Gooding
Minnesota State University,
Moorhead, Minnesota, U.S.A.

Judith A. Gray
American Folklife Center, Library of
Congress
Washington, D.C., U.S.A.

J. Richard Haefer
Arizona State University
Tempe, Arizona, U.S.A.

Charlotte Heth
University of California at Los
Angeles
Los Angeles, California, U.S.A.

Elaine Keillor
Carleton University
Ottawa, Ontario, Canada

Ellen Koskoff
University of Rochester
Rochester, New York, U.S.A.

Anne Lederman
Toronto, Canada

Mark Levy
University of Oregon
Eugene, Oregon, U.S.A.

Steven Loza
University of California at Los
Angeles
Los Angeles, California, U.S.A.

Claire Martin
School of Oriental and African
Studies
London, England

Rebecca S. Miller
Hampshire College
Amherst, Massachusetts, U.S.A.

Terry E. Miller
Kent State University
Kent, Ohio, U.S.A.

Ingrid Monson
Harvard University
Cambridge, Massachusetts, U.S.A.

Val Morrison
University of Québec
Montréal, Québec, Canada

Dawn M. Norfleet
Los Angeles, California, U.S.A.

Carl Rahkonen
Indiana University of Pennsylvania
Indiana, Pennsylvania, U.S.A.

José R. Reyna
California State University at
Bakersfield
Bakersfield, California, U.S.A.

Brenda M. Romero
University of Colorado
Boulder, Colorado, U.S.A.

Neil V. Rosenberg
Memorial University of
Newfoundland
St. John's, Newfoundland, Canada

Daniel E. Sheehy
Smithsonian Institute
Washington, D.C., U.S.A.

Mark Slobin
Wesleyan University
Middletown, Connecticut, U.S.A.

Gordon E. Smith
Queen's University
Kingston, Ontario, Canada

Robert Witmer
York University
Toronto, Ontario, Canada

Charles K. Wolfe (deceased)
Middle Tennessee State University
Murfreesboro, Tennessee, U.S.A.

Europe

Valeriu Apan
Los Angeles, California, U.S.A.

Wim Bosmans
Muziekinstrumentenmuseum
Brussels, Belgium

Salwa El-Shawan Castelo-Branco
Universidade Nova de Lisboa
Lisbon, Portugal

Loren Chuse
Oakland, California, U.S.A.

Jane K. Cowan
University of Sussex
Brighton, England

Ewa Dahlig
Institute of Arts, Polish Academy of
Sciences
Warsaw, Poland

Silvia Delorenzi-Schenkel
Biasca, Switzerland

Brian Patrick Fox
University of California at Los
Angeles
Los Angeles, California, U.S.A.

Judit Frigyesi
Bar-Ilan University
Ramat-Gan, Israel

Vic Gammon
Newcastle University
Newcastle upon Tyne, England

Paulette Gershen
Van Nuys, California, U.S.A.

Chris Goertzen
University of Southern Mississippi
Hattiesburg, Mississippi, U.S.A.

Johanna Hoffman
University of California at Los
Angeles
Los Angeles, California, U.S.A.

Pandora Hopkins
Brooklyn City College of the City
University of New York
Brooklyn, New York, U.S.A.

Erik Kjellberg
Uppsala Universitet
Uppsala, Sweden

Denis Laborde
Centre National de la Recherche
Scientifique
Paris, France

Edward Larkey
University of Maryland, Baltimore
County
Baltimore, Maryland, U.S.A.

Timo Leisiö
University of Tampere
Tampere, Finland

Jan Ling
Göteborg University
Göteborg, Sweden

Elizabeth Miles
Palo Alto, California, U.S.A.

Svend Nielsen
Dansk Folkminde samling
Copenhagen, Denmark

William Noll
Center for the Study of Oral History
and Culture
Kyiv, Ukraine

Edward J. P. O'Connor
University of Connecticut
Storrs, Connecticut, U.S.A.

James Porter
University of Aberdeen
Aberdeen, Scotland

Timothy Rice
University of California at Los
Angeles
Los Angeles, California, U.S.A.

Owe Ronström
Gotland University
Visby, Sweden

Wilhelm Schepping
University of Cologne
Institut für Musikalische Volkskunde
Cologne, Germany

Hugh Shields
Trinity College
Dublin, Ireland

Carol Silverman
University of Oregon
Eugene, Oregon, U.S.A.

Marcello Sorce Keller
Monash University
Melbourne, Australia

Gordon R. Thompson
Skidmore College
Saratoga Springs, New York, U.S.A.

Magda Ferl Želinská
Hollywood, California, U.S.A.

Izaly Zemtsovsky
Stanford University
Palo Alto, California, U.S.A.

Oceania

Te Ahukaramū Charles Royal
Otaki, New Zealand

Raymond Ammann
University of Basel
Basel, Switzerland

Linda Barwick
University of Sydney
Sydney, New South Wales, Australia

Jean-Michel Beaudet
Musée de l'Homme
Paris, France

Paul W. Brennan
East-West Center
Honolulu, Hawai'i, U.S.A.

Mary E. Lawson Burke
Framingham State College
Framingham, Massachusetts, U.S.A.

Vida Chenoweth
Wharton College
Wheaton, Illinois, U.S.A.

Peter Russell Crowe (deceased)
Toulouse, France

Tamsin Donaldson
The Australian National University
Canberra, ACT, Australia

Catherine J. Ellis (deceased)
University of New England
Armidale, New South Wales,
Australia

David Goldsworthy
University of New England
Armidale, New South Wales,
Australia

Margaret Gummow
University of Sydney
Sydney, New South Wales, Australia

Michael Gunn
Saint Louis Art Museum
Saint Louis, Missouri, U.S.A.

Takiora Ingram
Cremorne, New South Wales,
Australia

Jon Tikivanotau M. Jonassen
Brigham Young University of Hawai'i
Laie, Hawai'i, U.S.A.

Adrienne L. Kaeppler
Smithsonian Institute
Washington, D.C., U.S.A.

Grace Koch
Australian Institute of Aboriginal and
Torres Strait Islander Studies
Canberra, ACT, Australia

Jacob Wainwright Love
The George Washington University
Washington, D.C., U.S.A.

Lamont Lindstrom
University of Tulsa
Tulsa, Oklahoma, U.S.A.

Allan Marett
University of Sydney
Sydney, New South Wales, Australia

Deirdre Marshall
Stratford, Victoria, Australia

Gerald Florian Messner
SBS Radio News
Artarmon, New South Wales,
Australia

Jane Freeman Moulin
University of Hawai'i
Honolulu, Hawai'i, U.S.A.

Don Niles
Institute for Papua New Guinea
Studies
Boroko, Papua New Guinea

JoAnne Page
University of Sydney
Sydney, New South Wales, Australia

Herbert Patten
Glen Iris, Victoria, Australia

Eve C. Pinsker
University of Illinois
Chicago, Illinois, U.S.A.

Alice Pomponio
St. Lawrence University
Canton, New York, U.S.A.

Jacqueline Pugh-Kitingan
Universiti Malaysia Sabah
Kota Kinabalu, Sabah, Malaysia

Robin Ryan
Glen Iris, Victoria, Australia

Richard Scaglion
University of Pittsburgh
Pittsburgh, Pennsylvania, U.S.A.

Jennifer Shennan
Wellington, New Zealand

Artur Simon
Museum für Völkerkunde
Berlin, Germany

Barbara B. Smith
University of Hawai'i
Honolulu, Hawai'i, U.S.A.

Amy Ku'uleialoha Stillman
University of Michigan
Ann Arbor, Michigan, U.S.A.

Andrew J. Strathern
University of Pittsburgh
Pittsburgh, Pennsylvania, U.S.A.

Allan Thomas
Victoria University of Wellington
Wellington, New Zealand

Kathleen Van Arsdale
Denver Christian High School
Denver, Colorado, U.S.A.

Virginia Whitney
Waxhaw, North Carolina, U.S.A.

Stephen A. Wild
The Australian National University
Canberra, ACT, Australia

Hugo Zemp
Musée de l'Homme
Paris, France

Reviewers

Volume 1

Africa

Laura Arntson
Public Health Institute, USAID
Nigeria
Abuja, Nigeria

David B. Coplan
University of the Witwatersrand
Johannesburg, South Africa

Jacqueline Cogdell DjeDje
University of California at Los
Angeles
Los Angeles, California, U.S.A.

Ron Emoff
Ohio State University-Newark
Newark, Ohio, U.S.A.

John William Johnson
Indiana University
Bloomington, Indiana, U.S.A.

Claire Jones
Seattle, Washington, U.S.A.

John Kaemmer
DePauw University
Greencastle, Indiana, U.S.A.

Jean Kidula
University of Georgia
Athens, Georgia, U.S.A.

Ruth M. Stone
Indiana University
Bloomington, Indiana, U.S.A.

Christopher A. Waterman
University of California at Los
Angeles
Los Angeles, California, U.S.A.

Caroline Card Wendt
Noblesville, Indiana, U.S.A.

South America, Mexico, Central America, and the Caribbean

Olavo Alén Rodríguez
Center for Research and Development
of Cuban Music (CIDMUC)
Havana, Cuba

Kenneth M. Bilby
Center for Black Music Research,
Columbia College
Chicago, Illinois, U.S.A.

Max H. Brandt
University of Pittsburgh
Pittsburgh, Pennsylvania, U.S.A.

John Cohen
Putnam Valley, New York, U.S.A.

Larry Crook
University of Florida
Gainesville, Florida, U.S.A.

Martha Ellen Davis
University of Florida
Gainesville, Florida, U.S.A.

Monique Desroches
Université de Montréal
Montréal, Québec, Canada

Jane Florine
Chicago State University
Chicago, Illinois, U.S.A.

Oliver Greene
Georgia State University
Atlanta, Georgia, U.S.A.

Colleen M. Haas
University of Indiana
Bloomington, Indiana, U.S.A.

Xilonen Luna Ruiz
Comisión Nacional para el Desarrollo
de los Pueblos Indígenas
Mexico City, Mexico

Linda O'Brien-Rothe
San Pedro, California

Dale A. Olsen
The Florida State University
Tallahassee, Florida, U.S.A.

Suzel Ana Reily
The Queen's University of Belfast
Belfast, Northern Ireland

Daniel E. Sheehy
Smithsonian Institute
Washington, D.C., U.S.A.

Peter Wade
University of Manchester
Manchester, England

Vivian Nina Michelle Wood
Davie, Florida, U.S.A.

The United States and Canada

Rob Bowman
York University,
North York, Ontario, Canada

Patrick Burke
Washington University in St. Louis
St. Louis, Missouri, U.S.A.

Mellonee V. Burnim
Indiana University
Bloomington, Indiana, U.S.A.

Robin Elliott
University of Toronto
Toronto, Canada

David Evans
University of Memphis
Memphis, Tennessee, U.S.A.

Charlotte J. Frisbie
Southern Illinois University
Edwardsville
Edwardsville, Illinois, U.S.A.

Ellen Koskoff
University of Rochester
Rochester, New York, U.S.A.

Terry E. Miller
Kent State University
Kent, Ohio, U.S.A.

Dawn M. Norfleet
Los Angeles, California

Daniel E. Sheehy
Smithsonian Institute
Washington, D.C., U.S.A.

Europe

Valeriu Apan
Los Angeles, California, U.S.A.

Wim Bosmans
Muziekinstrumentenmuseum
Brussels, Belgium

Ann Briegleb-Schuutsma
UCLA, California, U.S.A.

Jane K. Cowan
University of Sussex
Brighton, England

Salwa El-Shawan Castelo-Branco
Universidade Nova de Lisboa
Lisbon, Portugal

Ewa Dahlig
Institute of Arts, Polish Academy of
Sciences
Warsaw, Poland

Silvia Delorenzi-Schenkel
Biasca, Switzerland

Vic Gammon
Newcastle University
Newcastle upon Tyne, England

Chris Goertzen

University of Southern Mississippi
Hattiesburg, Mississippi, U.S.A.

Allan Kozinn
New York Times
New York, New York, U.S.A.

Timo Leisiö
University of Tampere
Tampere, Finland

Irene Markoff
York University
Toronto, Ontario, Canada

Erin Mulligan
University of Pittsburgh
Pittsburgh, Pennsylvania, U.S.A.

William Noll
Center for the Study of Oral History
and Culture, Kyiv, Ukraine

Edward J. P. O'Connor
University of Connecticut
Storrs, Connecticut, U.S.A

James Porter
University of Aberdeen
Aberdeen, Scotland

Owe Ronström
Gotland University
Visby, Sweden

Wilhelm Schepping
University of Cologne
Institut für Musikalische Volkskunde
Cologne, Germany

Carol Silverman
University of Oregon
Eugene, Oregon, U.S.A.

Marcello Sorce Keller
Monash University
Melbourne, Australia

Sean Williams
The Evergreen State College
Olympia, Washington, U.S.A.

Izaly Zemtsovsky
Stanford University
Palo Alto, California, U.S.A.

Oceania

Adrienne L. Kaeppler
Smithsonian Institute
Washington, D.C., U.S.A.

Jacob Wainwright Love
The George Washington University
Washington, D.C., U.S.A.

Audio Examples

Volume 1

The following examples are included on the accompanying audio compact disc packaged with this volume. Track numbers are also indicated on the pages listed below for easy reference to text discussions. Complete notes on each example may be found on pages 1387–1392.

1. Africa

Africa astounds with its geographic expanse and its regional diversities. The richness of its cultural heritage includes an extraordinary vitality in its performing arts. This section begins with a profile of Africa and an introduction to these arts, and then presents representative studies of the musics of each region—west, north, east, central, and south. These studies give us insights into the factors that contribute to the diversity of Africa's cultural traditions; at the same time, we see elements and processes that cross regional boundaries and create distinctly African musical flavors.

A modern Asante *kete* drum troupe performs at a funeral, Kumase, Ghana, 2001. *Photo by Joseph S. Kaminski.*

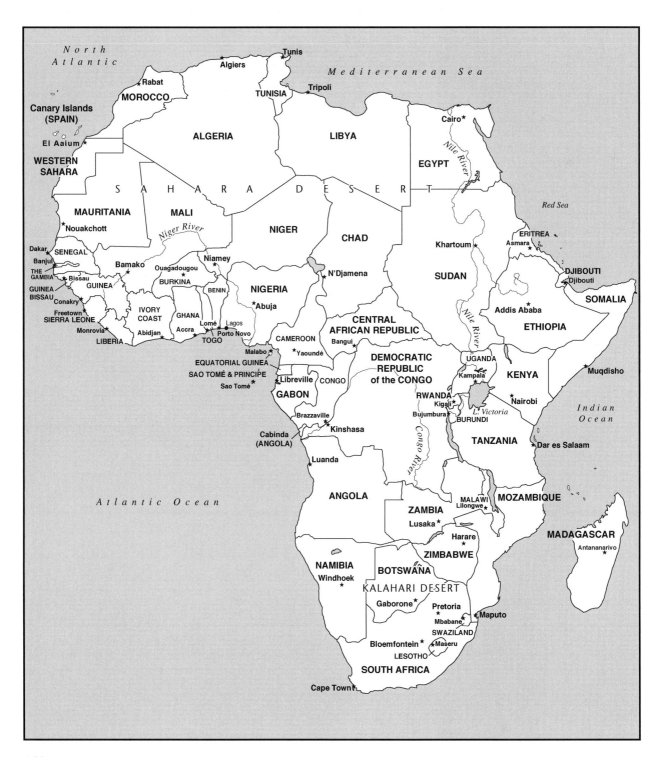

Africa

Profile of Africa

The African continent first impresses by its size: the second-largest of the continents of the world, it contains more than 28 million square kilometers, spanning 8000 kilometers from north to south and 7400 kilometers from east to west. Islands dot the coasts, with Madagascar in the southeast being the largest.

Bisected by the equator and lying predominantly within the tropics, where thick rainforests grow, the continent consists of a plateau that rises from rather narrow coastal plains. Vast expanses of grassland characterize its inland areas. The Sahara Desert dominates the north, and the Kalahari Desert the south. Vast mineral resources—of iron, gold, diamonds, oil—and deep tropical forests enrich the continent.

Peoples and Languages

The population of Africa constitutes only one-tenth of the world's people, though many urban areas and countries (like Nigeria) have a high density, counterbalancing extensive tracts of sparse population. Large urban areas have sprung up in nearly every country of Africa, with high-rise office buildings and computers part of the milieu. People cluster into nearly three thousand ethnic groups, each of which shares aspects of social identity. The most widely known reference work that classifies these groups is George Peter Murdock's *Africa: Its People and Their Culture History* (1959).

About one thousand distinct indigenous languages are spoken throughout Africa. They can be classified into four major families: Niger-Kordofanian, Nilo-Saharan, Hamito-Semitic, and Khoisan. The Niger-Kordofanian is the largest and most widespread of these, extending from West Africa to the southern tip of Africa; its geographical distribution points to the rapid movement of people from West Africa eastward and southward beginning about 2000 B.C.E. and extending into the 1600s of the common era.

Swahili, an East African trade language (with a Bantu grammar and much Arabic vocabulary), reflects the movements of peoples within Africa and to and from Arabia. Bambara and Hausa, other trade languages (spoken across wide areas of West Africa), are but a few of the languages that show Arabic influence. In addition, the Austronesian family is represented by Malagasy, spoken on the

Orthography

ε or ẹ	=	"eh" as in **bet**
ɔ or ọ	=	"aw" as in **awful**
ŋ or ṇ	=	"ng" as in **sing**
γ or yg	=	"ch" as in German **ach**
ʃ or ṣ	=	"sh" as in **shout**
ɗ	=	implosive "d"
ƙ	=	implosive "k"
!	=	click sound
´	=	high tone
`	=	low tone
∧	=	high-low tone
~	=	nasalized sound

island of Madagascar, and the Indo-European family by Afrikaans, spoken by descendants of seventeenth-century Dutch settlers in South Africa.

Following colonial rule in many countries, English, French, and Portuguese still serve as languages of commerce and education in the former colonies. Several languages of the Indian subcontinent are spoken by members of Asian communities that have arisen in many African countries, and numerous Lebanese traders throughout Africa speak a dialect of Arabic.

From the 1500s to the 1800s, trade in slaves produced a great outward movement of perhaps 10 million people from West and Central Africa to the Americas, and from East Africa to Arabia. A token return of ex-slaves and their descendants to Liberia during the 1800s represented a further disruption, as African-American settlers displaced portions of local populations. The long-term effects of this loss of human potential, and the attendant suffering it produced, have yet to be adequately understood. The movement of peoples contributed to the formation of new languages, such as Krio of Sierra Leone and Liberian English of Liberia—hybrids of indigenous and foreign tongues.

Though indigenous systems of writing were not widespread in Africa, some peoples invented their own scripts. These peoples included some of the Tuareg and Berber groups in the Sahara and more than fifteen groups in West Africa, including the Vai and the Kpelle of Liberia.

Subsistence and Industry

A majority of Africans engage in farming. In many areas, farmers use shifting cultivation, in which they plant a portion of land for a time and then leave it to regenerate, moving to another plot. This form of agriculture is characteristically tied to a system of communal ownership; increasingly, however, people and corporations, by acquiring exclusive ownership of large areas of arable land, are changing African land-use patterns.

International commerce has resulted in a shift from subsistence to cash crops: cocoa, coffee, palm oil, rubber, sugarcane, tea, tobacco. The wage laborers who work with these crops migrate from their home villages and settle on large farms. Grasslands throughout the continent support flocks of camels, cattle, goats, and sheep, and people there are predominantly herders, who spend much of their lives as nomads to find the best grazing for their animals.

In many areas of Africa, processing coal, copper, diamonds, gold, iron, oil, uranium, and other natural resources provides employment for notable numbers of people. Processing these materials provides wages for workers and exports for the resource-rich nations.

Transport and Trade

For trade and travel, people have long moved across African deserts and savannas, and through African forests, but the intensity and speed of their movement increased with the building of roads, railways, and airports, particularly since the 1950s in many parts of the continent.

Suddenly, perishable fruits and vegetables could be shipped from interior farms to coastal urban areas. Taxis and buses built a lively trade shuttling people and goods from local markets to urban areas and back again. Manufactured goods were more readily available from petty traders and shopkeepers alike, and foods like frozen fish augmented daily diets.

Among all that activity, cassettes of the latest popular music of local nations and the world became part of the goods available for purchase. Feature films of East Asian karate, Indian love stories, and American black heroes became available, first from itinerant film projectionists, by the 1980s from video clubs, and now on DVDs. On a weekly and sometimes daily basis, maritime shipping is now supplemented with air travel to Europe and the rest of the world.

Social and Political Formations

Several African kingdoms with large centralized governments emerged in the Middle Ages. Among these were Ghana in the West African grasslands around the Niger River (C.E. 700–1200); Mali, which succeeded Ghana and became larger (1200–1500); and Songhai (1350–1600), which took over the territory of ancient Mali. Kanem-Bornu flourished further east in the interior (800–1800). In forested areas, Benin developed in parts of present-day Nigeria (1300–1800); Asante, in the area of contemporary Ghana (1700–1900); Kongo, along the Congo River (1400–1650); Luba-Lunda, in the Congo–Angola–Zambia grasslands (1400–1700); Zimbabwe, in southern Africa (1400–1800); and Buganda, in the area of present-day Uganda (1700–1900).

Archaeological evidence provides information about the indigenous African empires that were fueled by long-distance trade in gold, ivory, salt, and other commodities. Typical of these kingdoms were large retinues of royal musicians, who enhanced state occasions and provided musical commentary on current events. Benin bronze plaques, preserving visual images of some of these musicians, are in museums around the world.

Alongside large-scale political formations have been much smaller political units, known as stateless societies. Operating in smaller territories, inhabited by smaller numbers of people, these societies may have several levels in a hierarchy of chiefs, who in turn owe allegiance to a national government. At the lowest level in these societies, government is consensual; at the upper levels, chiefs, in consultation with elders and ordinary citizens, make decisions.

Some communities in West Africa support Poro and Sande, organizations—called secret societies by Westerners—to which adults belong, and through which they are enculturated about social mores and customs. Children of various ages leave the village and live apart in the forest, in enclosures known as Poro (for men) and Sande (for women). There, they learn dances and songs that they will perform upon emergence at the closing ceremonies. Required parts of their education, these songs and dances are displayed for community appreciation at the end of the educational period. It is during this seclusion that promising young soloists in dance and drumming may be identified and specially tutored.

Kinship, though long studied by anthropologists in Africa, has proved complex and often hard to interpret. Ancestors are listed in formal lineages, which may be recited in praise singing and often reinterpreted to fit an occasion and its exigencies. Residence may be patrilocal or matrilocal, depending on local customs, and the extended families that are ubiquitous in Africa become distanced through urban relocation and labor migration, even if formal ties continue.

Settlements may take the form of nomadic camps (moving with the season and pasture), cities, towns, or dispersed homesteads along motor roads. They may develop around mines, rubber plantations, and other worksites. Camps for workers who periodically travel home may become permanent settlements, where families also reside.

Religious Beliefs and Practices

Indigenous religious beliefs and practices exhibit many varieties, but they share some common themes. A high, supreme, and often distant, creator-god rules. Intermediate deities become the focus of worship, divination, and sacrificial offerings. Spirits live in water, trees, rocks, and other places, and these become the beings through whose mediation people maintain contact with the creator-god.

Indigenous religious practices in Africa have been influenced and overlaid by Christian, Islamic, and other practices. New religious movements, such as *aladura* groups, have skillfully linked Christian religious practices with indigenous ones.

Elsewhere, Islam penetrated the forested areas and brought changes to local practices, even as it, too, underwent change. The observance of Ramadan, the month of fasting, was introduced, certain musical practices were banned, and altered indigenous practices remained as compromises.

—Adapted from an article by Ruth M. Stone

Bibliography

Davidson, Basil. 1966. *African Kingdoms*. New York: Time-Life Books.

Greenberg, Joseph H. 1970. *The Languages of Africa*. Bloomington, Ind.: Research Center for the Language Sciences.

Murdock, George P. 1959. *Africa: Its People and Their Culture History*. New York: McGraw-Hill.

Murray, Jocelyn, ed. 1981. *Cultural Atlas of Africa*. Oxford: Elsevier Publishers.

African Music in a Constellation of Arts

African performance is a tightly wrapped bundle of arts that are sometimes difficult to separate, even for analysis. Singing, playing instruments, dancing, masquerading, and dramatizing are part of a conceptual package that many Africans think of as one and the same (figure 1). The Kpelle people of Liberia use a single word, *sang*, to describe a well-danced movement, a well-sung phrase, or especially fine drumming. For them, the expressive acts that give rise to these media are related and interlinked. The visual arts, the musical arts, the dramatic arts—all work together in the same domain and are conceptually treated as intertwined. To describe the execution of a sequence of dances, a Kpelle drummer might speak of "the dance that she spoke."

Concepts of Music

Honest observers are hard pressed to find a single indigenous group in Africa that has a term congruent with the usual Western notion of "music." There are terms for more specific acts like singing, playing instruments, and more broadly performing (dance, games, music); but the isolation of musical sound from other arts proves to be a Western abstraction.

The arts maintain close links to the rest of African social and political life, which they reflect upon and create in performance. Highlife songs are famous for having been employed in political campaigns in Ghana, poetry in Somalia has influenced political history [see MUSIC AND POETRY IN SOMALIA], and work in many areas is coordinated and enhanced as bush-clearers follow the accompaniment of an instrumental ensemble. The arts are not an extra or separate expression to be enjoyed apart from the social and political ebb and flow: they emerge centrally in the course of life, vital to normal conduct.

Musical specialists in the West have often used notions of "folk," "popular," and "art" to categorize music, but these concepts prove problematic in African settings. They often indicate more of the social formations associated with music than of musical sound. "Folk" is often equated with "traditional," or music performed in rural areas, "popular" is commonly associated with mass audiences and urban areas, and "art" is associated with elite, upper-class, written notation. These terms imply a prejudicial tilt toward things written and reserved for a few—but in African settings, aural traditions are highly developed and thoroughly practiced forms of transmission, no less competent or effective in artistic creation.

Figure 1 An Asante *adowa* troupe performs at a royal funeral, Kumase, Ghana 2001. Musicians play *atumpan* talking drums and other instruments as people sing and dance.
Photo by Joseph S. Kaminski.

A further complication is that African practices often mingle musics from apparently disparate idioms. For example, Djimo Kouyate (1946–2004), performed on the twenty-one-stringed harp-lute (*kora*) of Senegal and with Mamaya African Jazz, an eight-member ensemble, which performs a fusion of African music and worldbeat, the latter a form of international popular music. The West African superstar Baaba Maal (b. 1953; figure 2) recorded the album *Firin' in Fouta* (1994) in three phases, each reflecting a different kind of music. He began by returning to his ancestral village (Podor, northern Senegal), where he recorded instruments and songs of everyday life. In Dakar, the capital, his band, Dande Lenol, transformed these sounds into rhythm tracks. Finally, he took those tracks to England, where he added vocals, synthesizers, and Celtic instruments. The resultant album draws on local African music to inform high-tech Western dance music.

Concepts of Performance

Some generalizations can be drawn about performance in Africa, emphasizing the perspectives of the performers and their ideas about creating that performance; however, we must bear in mind that great variation exists, even about fundamental ideas.

Performers

Most people in African communities are expected to perform music and dance at a basic level; performing is considered as normal as speaking. In many areas, social puberty is marked by singing and dancing, as young people display their accomplishments in token of their maturation. Solo performers may be trained to excel because they have shown aptitude for an instrument, or they may be selected because they come from a family whose occupation is to be musicians, as often occurs among the *griots* of West Africa.

Soloists may believe that a tutelary spirit or some form of supernatural assistance aids them in developing their skills. At musical performances, they believe spirits are sometimes present, forming an elusive audience, which certain human participants will sense. Spirits can make a singer's voice particularly fine; they make high demands, however, and fame does not come easily. For aiding a singer, a spirit may exact much, even a singer's life.

Performance as an Engine of National Policy

Ensembles perform within a local area, often traveling to neighboring towns, but some ensembles have been formed to represent contemporary nation-states. These ensembles may meld performers from various locations and teach them to adapt their performances to meet the requirements of Western stages.

Some African countries have set up national training centers where musicians and dancers work together to create ensembles. These performers are often paid by national governments. They travel around the country or tour the world, representing a blend of musics from the particular area, adapted to outsiders' expectations for performance.

Figure 2 Baaba Maal (center) performs with his group at Royal Festival Hall in London, 2006. *Photo by UrbanImage.tv/Adrian Boot.*

Figure 3 The Asante *nkofe* trumpet ensemble performs, Kumase, Ghana, 2001. The trumpets are made from elephant tusks, some are bound in black tape to seal cracks.
Photo by Joseph S. Kaminski.

Figure 4 A Tuareg *tende* singing group performs in Niamey, Niger, accompanied by the *tende* mortar drum (played by the woman third from left) and an *assakalabu* (played by the woman at left), which is a half-calabash upturned in a basin of water and struck with a stick beater.
Photo by Caroline Card Wendt, 1976.

Musical Instruments as Human Extensions

The people of Africa make and use a vast array of musical instruments (figures 3, 4, 5, and 6). Beyond an expected variety of drums, musicians play harps, harp-lutes, lutes, lyres, zithers, and guitars, to name but a few of the stringed instruments found across the continent.

Within African contexts, instruments are more than material objects: they frequently take on human features and qualities. Certain solo instruments may have personal names, be kept in special houses, receive special sacrificial food or other offerings, and be regarded as quasi-human. To a musician playing them, they provide power and sometimes special aid. A close, humanlike partnership sometimes develops between musician and instrument.

Ethnomusicologists use categories such as aerophones (bullroarers, flutes, horns, oboes), chordophones (harps, lutes, zithers), membranophones (drums), and idiophones (rattles, lamellaphones, xylophones), but African peoples frequently employ other ways of grouping instruments. Among the Kpelle of Liberia, instruments are blown (*fɛɛ*) or struck (*ngale*); all wind instruments fit into the

Figure 5 The *mbira dzavadzimu* 'mbira of the ancestral spirits' is a lamellaphone of the Shona of Zimbabwe that is played widely in Africa and abroad. Its keys are plucked with the thumbs and forefingers. To increase the volume, it is often played inside a gourd resonator.
Photo by N. Scott Robinson, 2007.

Figure 6 The ethnomusicologist Jean Ngoya Kidula demonstrates the *nyatiti*, a lyre of the Luo people of Kenya. Kidula holds the instrument in a manner that was developed in the late twentieth century to better suit female musicians. Traditionally, a *nyatiti* player sits on a low stool and rests the instrument on the ground at his side.
Photo by Becky Dewald, 2007.

former category, and all other instruments fit into the latter. All Kpelle stringed instruments are plucked, and so the finger, from a Kpelle conception, "strikes" the string.

Exchange among Voices
Ethnomusicologists often describe musical sounds according to scalar tones (labeled with numbers or letters of the alphabet), but peoples in Africa often conceive of these sounds as voices. People, instruments, and birds all employ voices, which, in performance, musicians imitate. Performers conceive of one voice singing a part and another voice responding, in a call-and-response dialogue.

In the idea of call and response, the conversational metaphor captures many exchanges that are the fabric of the performance. Kpelle choral singing always has a counterpart to the solo or the first part. A master drummer may create the first part, and a vocal soloist may become the counterpart to the drum; but then, when the chorus members come in as a response to the soloist, the vocalist and master drummer function as a pair, which the chorus answers. A web of balances is created, and interchanges abound at many levels. The voices that create these exchanges are frequently described in terms

like *large* or *small*, implying certain aspects of pitch, timbre, and dynamics.

Some peoples stress the primacy of the transaction between paired performing parts. Two players of the *mangwilo*, a xylophone of southeast Africa, sit at the same instrument facing one another. One is called the starting one (*opachera*) and the other the responding one (*wakulela*). Similarly, among the Shona of Zimbabwe, a solo mbira player designates one part he or she plays as *kushaura* 'to lead the piece, to take the solo part' and the second as *kutsinhira* 'to exchange parts of a song, to interweave a second interlocking part'.

Motoric Patterns in Performance
In the early twentieth century, the ethnomusicologist Erich M. von Hornbostel (1877–1935) called for the

9

study of patterns of human movement to aid our understanding of African rhythm. Though many scholars have found fault with his conclusions, some, taking leads from his work, have explored issues of bodily movement.

The ethnomusicologist Gerhard Kubik (b. 1934) has underscored the importance of the acoustic, kinetic, and visual elements of rhythm. Moses Serwadda and Hewitt Pantaleoni have shown how drumming and dancing link: "A drummer will indicate the dance motions sometimes as a way of explaining and teaching a [drum] pattern" (1968:52).

In multipart textures, individual parts may interweave or interlock in short, repetitive motives (ostinatos), which become layered in complex ways. Certain of these motives are invariant; others subtly transform in variation as the performance develops. A sense of multiple layering emerges as the density increases, ideally with contrasting timbres among parts.

Historical Preservation of African Music

Documentation of African performances predates the arrival of the Europeans or sound recordings. Oral traditions served to preserve in dynamic ways the aspects of performance that people wanted to remember. Myths, legends, epics, oral histories, and life histories were only a few of the genres that embodied memories of performances.

Almost a thousand years before the phonograph was invented, Arab travelers wrote about their impressions of African music. Perhaps the most famous, Mohammed ibn Abdullah ibn Battuta, vividly described court music scenes in the kingdom of Mali in the 1100s. When first the Portuguese, and then other Europeans, arrived in Africa, Arabs had long been active in exploring the continent. We should beware of assuming that the "dark continent" (as nineteenth-century Europeans unsubtly dubbed it) suddenly came to life with the arrival of the Europeans. African contacts with the outside world—especially with West, South, and Southeast Asia—were lively long before Europeans "discovered" the continent.

As Europeans began to study Africa, and in particular its music, their interpretations emphasized a music of rather monotonous stasis and inaction, discovered by ever-adventurous Europeans, who, conversely, associated themselves with music of change and development. Such interpretations are especially curious when we note that motion and action are central to the aesthetic principles of many African groups. The most charitable assessment is that European misperceptions came from a lack of appreciation of African musical subtleties, including the language of performance.

Before the twentieth century, African music was preserved for Western posterity in verbal descriptions and musical notation. These forms of writing froze and isolated moving sounds into static forms. As wax cylinders were etched with sound (beginning in Africa in the early 1900s), they opened up new horizons while fixing sound images, though perhaps not to the same extent (or in the same way) as written musical transcription.

Western adventurers collected examples of African sounds in much the same manner as they collected samples of African flora and fauna. These examples were transported back to archives and museums to be sorted, duplicated, and catalogued. Africans, in contrast, have over the years been more concerned with continuing their live performance traditions, and have paid less attention to acquiring and preserving samples of sounds.

—Adapted from an article by Ruth M. Stone

Bibliography

Berliner, Paul. 1978. *The Soul of Mbira: Music and Traditions of the Shona People of Zimbabwe*. Berkeley and Los Angeles: University of California Press.

Gibb, H. A. R. 1929. *lbn Battuta, Travels in Asia and Africa*. London: Darf.

Hornbostel, Erich M. von. 1928. "African Negro Music." *Africa* 1:30–62.

Kubik, Gerhard. 1972. "Transcription of African Music from Silent Film: Theory and Methods." *African Music* 5(1):28–39.

———. 1977. "Patterns of Body Movement in the Music of Boys' Initiation in South-East Angola." In *The Anthropology of the Body*, edited by John Blacking, 253–274. London: Academic Press.

Serwadda, Moses, and Hewitt Pantaleoni. 1968. "A Possible Notation for African Dance Drumming." *African Music* 4(2):47–52.

Stone, Ruth. 1982. *Let the Inside Be Sweet: The Interpretation of Music Event among the Kpelle of Liberia*. Bloomington: Indiana University Press.

———. 1985. "In Search of Time in African Music." *Music Theory Spectrum* 7:139–158.

Stone, Ruth, and Frank J. Gillis. 1976. *African Music and Oral Data: A Catalog of Field Recordings, 1902–1975*. Bloomington and London: Indiana University Press.

West Africa

West Africa

West Africa most clearly exhibits the polyrhythmic, multiple layered aspects of music in Africa. With a wide variety of musical instruments, performances here reflect the heritage of cultural interchange with North African traditions, especially in the savannas and deserts. It is in the west that several early kingdoms and nation-states of Africa developed.

To offer a sense of the musics in this region, we present an introductory article, an article on Yorùbá popular music, and an article on praise singing in northern Sierra Leone.

Members of the Maninka Bala Ensemble, featuring Pa Sanasi Kuyateh on *bala*, perform in Sierra Leone, 1987.
Photo by Laura Arntson. Courtesy of Indiana University, Archives of Traditional Music.

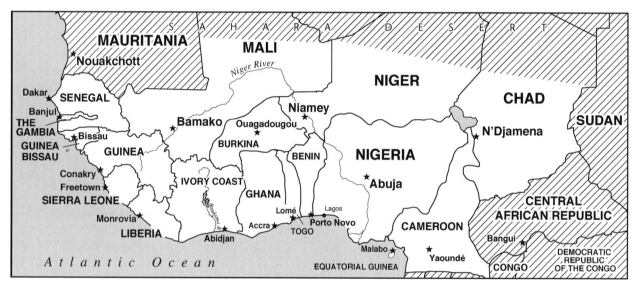

West Africa

West Africa: An Introduction

West Africa extends roughly from 5 degrees to 17 degrees north latitude, and from 17 degrees west to 15 degrees east longitude. It includes all or portions of Senegal, The Gambia, Guinea, Guinea Bissau, Mali, Burkina Faso, Niger, Nigeria, Benin, Togo, Ghana, Côte d'Ivoire (Ivory Coast), Liberia, and Sierra Leone.

The environment, which varies from forest in the south to grasslands and desert in the north, has dramatically affected local history and culture. The Sahel savanna, an area of low rainfall and short grasses, directly south of the Sahara desert and north of the Guinea savanna, has been an area of significant population movements and political developments. The invention of agriculture in Africa may have occurred among ancestors of the Manding people, who live in the western part of the savanna belt of West Africa, around the headwaters of the Niger River. Much of the Guinea savanna (an area directly north of the forest) is sparsely populated, but some of the most densely settled areas are in the forest belt, which migrant peoples settled from the north, displacing or absorbing indigenous peoples.

The languages of peoples that inhabit West Africa belong to three families: Niger-Congo, Songhai, and Chad. Differences in environment and culture divide West Africa into two geographical subregions: savanna and forest.

The Savanna

Several peoples in the savanna have played a large role in the history of West Africa, for some have established empires and nation-states. By the eleventh century, the Mande had organized a small state, Mali; by the 1300s, it had become an empire, which dominated most of West Africa—from the edge of the tropical forest in the south, to Senegal in the northwest and the Aïr Mountains of Niger in the northeast; in the 1400s, it went into decline; and by the late 1900s, Manding-speakers had dispersed widely. Most peoples in the savanna have felt influence from North Africa, and have to some degree adopted Islam. Many are agriculturalists, and several participate in herding cattle and trading; a few produce textiles and leatherworks.

The musical culture of societies in the savanna displays much uniformity, particularly in social organization, musicians' role and status, types of instruments, and styles of performance. Despite the history of interaction, important differences among peoples require a subregional division into three clusters: the Western Sudanic, the Central Sudanic, and the Voltaic. The Western Sudanic cluster is represented in the article Praise Singing in Northern Sierra Leone. The Central Sudanic cluster is represented by the Hausa; the Voltaic cluster, by the Mossi-Bariba.

The Hausa of the Central Sudanic Cluster

The peoples of this cluster include the Songhai, the Fulani (Fulbe), the Djerma, the Dendi, the Kanuri, the Jukun, the Tiv, and the Hausa. Most inhabit northern Nigeria, Niger, Mali, and Burkina Faso; some inhabit scattered locations in Benin, Togo, and Ghana. Continuing contacts have ensured much uniformity in the music of peoples of this cluster. Influence from North Africa is most apparent in ceremonial music and types of instruments. The Songhai began to dominate large parts of Sudanic Africa during the 1200s, and the Songhai Empire reached its height in the early 1500s. It extended from close to the Atlantic in the west to include most of the Hausa states of northern Nigeria in the east.

The Hausa, now a predominantly Muslim people, were probably not a homogeneous ethnic group. The word *Hausa* was once used to refer to peoples for whom Hausa was a mother tongue. Their language, Chadic in origin, is spoken widely—in markets from western to central Africa. For a while, they lived within the Songhai Empire, though they paid tribute to the king of Bornu, a Muslim state mostly in northeastern Nigeria. Since the early 1800s, the Hausa have associated themselves with the Fulani, who conquered the Hausa (a conquest called the Fulani jihad) and organized their territory into emirates. After this conquest, the Hausa adopted musical traits from the Songhai and the Fulani, but the resultant Hausa music dominates the Central Sudanic cluster with influences that extend to central and southwest Nigeria, the Guinea coast, and Voltaic peoples.

Ethnographic Context

The Hausa used to live in walled city-states ruled by an emir, a royal court, and a bureaucracy of ranked, titled officials. At present, the city walls in such places as Kano in northern Nigeria are a reminder of a glorious past—which people partly relive every time the emir and his mounted horsemen, musketeers, musicians, retainers, and vassal chiefs and headmen ride in parade, and when, in front of the palace, the emir accepts the charge of his horsemen and other loyal followers. The emir and his royal kin hold mandated positions on a local government council, part of a federalized state government system enforced by the national army. Many minor functionaries have lost positions that depended on the largesse of a potentate authorized to collect taxes and administer a sizable budget; but such people as court musicians (instrumentalists, vocalists, panegyrists, praise shouters), whose activities were never a formal part of that budget, have managed to continue, dependent on institutionalized generosity and networks of obligations.

The Hausa social system is highly stratified, and the most important criterion for placing people in it is occupation. The hierarchical ranking of traditional political offices is part of this system, in which the emir holds the highest political and social position. No single hierarchy covers all the traditional occupations, and other considerations—ethnic membership, kinship, lineage, sex—often affect individual cases. All authorities agree that *maròokaa*—musicians and praise singers or praise shouters—stand at the same level as *griots* and bards in their societies, in the broadly lowest rank. Royal musicians, perhaps because of their association with the highest strata in the traditional social system, rank near the top of the *maròokii* class; and *bòorii* musicians, because of their association with widely recognized social deviants—gamblers, trancers, card players, drinkers, courtesans, transvestites—rank at the bottom. Islam is another factor in this ranking. Royal musicians are outwardly devout Muslims in a society in which a performer's faith is frequently more important as a question for social placement than his genetic background; and while *bòorii* musicians describe themselves as Muslims, their association with deviants and the *bòorii* pantheon makes their respectability difficult to defend. Other groups of professional musicians are not usually identified as non-Muslims, but their status is still in the lowest strata of Hausa society.

The Hausa do not have a single word for the Western concept of "music," nor do they use a single word for "musician." They speak of activities—drumming (*kiɗàa*), singing (*waakàa*), and blowing (*buusàa*)—and add to the list such "nonmusical" activities as begging (*ròokoo*), praise shouting, and celebratory ululating. People commonly call the men who practice these crafts *those who beg*, placing emphasis on the social status of the craft, rather than its

aural aspect. Terms are sex-specific, so a woman who "begs" is called *maròokìyaa* or *zaabìyaa*.

Certain royal courtiers who practice this craft are classified as *maròokaa*, while others are described as "slaves" (*baayii*; masc. sing, *baawàa*). Royal beggar-minstrels have a status much lower than that of royal slaves, whose positions at court are hereditary, subject to the emir's confirmation; they were formerly one of the ways emirs protected their kingdoms and personal safety from the treachery of their patrilineal relatives.

The Social Organization of Musicians' Groups

Maròokaa, praise singers, and praise shouters—all of them professional musicians—divide into five categories: (a) the musicians of such craft groups as blacksmiths, hunters, and farmers; (b) musicians in political life, who consist mainly of royal musicians and famous (recording-star) musicians; (c) musicians of recreational music, who play for many different craft groups and social classes, in contexts not restricted by ceremony or religious ritual; (d) musician-entertainers and musician-comedians; and (e) musicians for *bòorii*. Some praise shouters and panegyrists are not musicians in the English sense, but some royal slaves who play ceremonial drums are.

Musical Contexts

Professional specializations in Hausa culture involve ceremonial music, court praise songs, general praise songs, entertainment music, music associated with spirits, and vocal acclamations. State ceremonial music (*rok'on fada*), court praise (*yabon sarakai*), and rural folk music or popular music stem from nineteenth-century practices.

Ceremonial music, probably the most esteemed form of music in Hausa society, is the symbol of traditional power. Two kinds of praise songs exist: urban classical and popular. Professional musicians who serve a single patron perform urban classical traditions of the past; the music has set stylistic and textual characteristics. Freelance musicians, who may have many patrons, perform popular music of a more recent origin. It rivals court praise song because it appeals to the same audience and resembles praise song in its leading exponents' artistry. The instruments used in popular music—*kalangu* (double-membrane hourglass tension drum), *goge* (one-stringed bowed lute), *kukuma* (smaller one-stringed bowed lute), and *kuntigi* (one-stringed plucked lute)—distinguish it from court praise singing, as does musicians' freedom to praise and ridicule anyone, including rulers.

The emir controls the occasions for the performance of state ceremonial music, which occurs mostly during *sara*, a weekly statement of authority on Fridays outside the emir's palace; Babbar Salla or K'aramar Salla, religious festivals at which the emir rides in procession to and from the mosque; *nad'in sarauta*, the installation of the emir and his officials; the emir's departure and return from a journey; visits from other emirs or important people; and weddings and births within the emir's family. The performance of court praise songs occurs at similar occasions and whenever there is a gathering.

Royal musicians divide into groups on the basis of the instruments they play, or the kinds of "music" (including praise singing and shouting, panegyrizing, eulogizing) they perform. In recognition of their position, the emir gives the heads of groups of royal *maròokii* a title and a turban. Their instruments, the songs they perform, and the praises they shout, are governed by strict rules, which emphasize that their use belongs, not to individual musicians or title-holders, but to the offices they hold. The *kàakàakii* (long metal trumpet, made from the metal of a kerosene tin, or thin brass) may be played only for a first-class or paramount chief (for example, the emir), but the *kòotsoo* (single-membrane, snared, hourglass drum, played with the hand) may in addition be played for senior titleholders.

Hausa music and dance, except for *bòorii*, have no associations with religion. Music other than the call to prayer is rarely heard in the mosque or during Islamic ritual. *Bòorii*, a pre-Islamic religion, makes much use of music, which communicates with spirits during the possession ceremony. Freelance musicians perform popular music in all contexts: at work, for entertainment at beer bars and nightclubs, for life-cycle events, or at any gathering.

Musical Instruments
The Hausa and all other peoples in the Central Sudanic cluster traditionally used no stringed instruments except plucked and bowed lutes. This avoidance suggests that stringed instruments entered the area from outside. The Hausa use a one-stringed bowed lute (*goge*), which has the resonating hole on its membrane, rather than on the resonator, and a smaller one-stringed bowed lute (*kukuma*). Bowed lutes in the Central Sudanic cluster have associations with spirit possession entertainment, praise, and politics. The Hausa use a two- or three-stringed plucked lute (*móló*) and a one-stringed plucked lute (*kuntigi*). Predecessors of the *móló*, known as *gurmi* (hemispherical calabash) and *garaya* (oval wood) among the Hausa, date back to the 1300s in the Western Sudanic cluster.

The Hausa prominently use double-membrane hourglass tension drums in various sizes (*jauje*,

kalangu, *'dan kar'bi*). The Hausa reserve the *jauje* for royalty, and they associate the *kalangu* and *'dan kar'bi* with butchers and recreation, though in some areas court musicians use them. Whether the single-membrane hourglass tension drum (*kotso*) has as wide a distribution as the double-membrane prototype is unknown. The Hausa associate the *kotso* with royalty, and regard it as a Fulani instrument.

Hausa wind instruments include a flute (*sarewa*), a horn (*k'aho*), and several kinds of pipes (*bututu*, *damalgo*, *farai*, *til'boro*), constructed from guinea corn, wood, and reed. The Songhai use a clarinet (*dilliara*).

Musical Style
In Hausa music, and that of the Central Sudanic cluster in general, men and women favor a tense vocal style, and melodies are usually melismatic. Songforms depend on the text and the language, and because Hausa is a tonal language, Hausa textual meaning depends on syllabic pitch. Instruments often imitate speech. Hausa

> In a **tonal language** differences of pitch distinguish words that otherwise sound alike.

vocal and instrumental music, melodically and sometimes rhythmically, depends on syllabic tones and quantities. The text is sung or vocally declaimed, or performed nonverbally by instruments. Instrumental music is predominantly for drums or strings, with rhythmic accompaniment by an idiophone. In nonprofessional music, the text dominates the reading and recitation of poems and incantations and the calling of praises. Songs are freer, though somewhat dependent on verbal patterns, chants, and acclamations.

The Mossi-Bariba of the Voltaic Cluster
Ethnic groups in the Voltaic cluster have not built empires comparable to those of their neighbors. As a result, the Voltaic cluster consists, not of a few homogeneous nations, but of many culturally distinct peoples—a fact reflected in the diversity of local musical traditions. These peoples are dispersed within Burkina Faso, Mali, and northern areas of Côte d'Ivoire, Ghana, Togo, and Benin. Throughout the cluster, the impact of Islam and Christianity is slight, though certain peoples are increasingly adopting Islam. Most Voltaic peoples are agriculturalists, and all their languages belong to the Voltaic-Gur subfamily of the Niger-Congo family.

Mossi-Bariba
The Mossi-Bariba subcluster includes these ethnic groups: Mossi (a complex encompassing the Mam-

prussi, Dagbamba, and Nanumba), Konkomba, Gourmantché (also called Gurma), Bariba, Kusasi, Frafra, Namnam, some Gonja, and Yarse. Because of common origins, the existence of centralized political structures, and historical links with northern and southern neighbors, societies in the Mossi complex are similar to each other. During the 1400s and 1500s, when the Mossi kingdoms rose to power, the Mossi fought several times with the Songhai over control of the Niger Bend in Mali. In their campaign against peoples in the south, they met the Gourmantché and the Kusasi. By the late 1600s and early 1700s, the growing acceptance of Islam opened communication between the Mossi kingdoms and those in the Western and Central Sudanic clusters, and the isolation that characterized the earlier phases of Islam in the area began to break down.

The Bariba are distinct because of their location. In the Benin Gap (an area covering roughly present-day Benin, Togo, and southeast Ghana), the savanna breaks through the tropical forest zone and extends to the Atlantic seaboard. Navigable rivers and coastal lagoons facilitated human movement and generated contacts and connections that stimulated cultural interchange between the forest and the savanna. During the 1500s, the Bariba occupied the land of Borgu (northwest of Yorùbáland) in the present-day country of Benin, and their kingdom reached its height in the 1700s. The Mande and Songhai of the Western and Central Sudanic clusters, respectively, exercised considerable influence on them; in turn, the Bariba had a strong formative influence on northern Yorùbá groups.

Musical Instruments
Influences from peoples in the Western and Central Sudanic clusters are clear in the music of Mossi-Bariba peoples. Professional musicians belonging to a distinct social class dominate musical life. Because of their attachment to royalty or important persons, most have high status. Instruments associated with North Africa (hourglass tension drum, bowed and plucked lutes, metal trumpets) occur in most cultures. As with the Hausa, these instruments symbolize power. The Bariba associate kettledrums, long metal trumpets, and hourglass tension drums with traditional power; but the Dagbamba associate both the hourglass tension drum (*lunga*, pl. *lunsi*) and the bowed lute (*gonje*; also *gondze* and *goondze*) with royalty. There is no evidence that any Mossi people has adopted metal trumpets. The use of the harp and the xylophone reflects Mande influence.

Mossi-Bariba stringed instruments are the musical bow, bowed and plucked lutes, and various zithers and flutes. Their wind instruments include an ocarina, a clarinet, a trumpet made from wood and animal horn, a whirled slat (bullroarer), a whirled disc, and a mirliton. Their drums are made of gourd, wood, and clay, in several shapes: square frame, cylindrical, conical, hourglass, and barrel. Their idiophones include gourd rattles, sticks, lamellaphones, and water drums. The Bariba use rock gongs and leg xylophones.

> A **mirliton** is an object or membrane made to sound by the indirect action of the vibration of the instrument to which it is attached; its sound is often described as a buzz.

> A **lamellaphone** is a musical instrument whose sound is the vibration of a long, thin, movable plate or plates affixed to one end.

Musical Style
The use of a high tessitura is widespread and closely related to the range of melodic instruments that accompany singing. The range of Dagbamba vocal and instrumental music appears narrower in comparison to the range of music performed by peoples of the Western and Central Sudanic clusters, where Islamic influence is heavier. Vocal quality is tense, as in other Islamic areas. Most scales are pentatonic, and slight ornamentation occurs in vocal and instrumental styles.

Musical Contexts
In the context of performing for royalty and other patrons, specialists usually emphasize praise singing. Praise songs honoring royalty reinforce the importance of history. Many include references to important moral values. As with other peoples of the Voltaic cluster, occasions for making music include lifecycle events, work, harvest celebrations, religious rites, and festivals. So much Dagbamba music and dramatic display occurs at funerals that they seem to be festive events. Unlike the Western and Central Sudanic clusters, societies within the Mossi-Bariba subcluster prominently integrate traditional African music at Islamic events. At Islamic occasions in Dagbon in northern Ghana, drummers and fiddlers commonly perform historical or genealogy songs.

The Forest

Savanna dwellers have had contact with each other through the development of empires, the movement of populations, and the influence of North Africa. As a result, their cultures are similar to each other. In contrast, the cultures of the forest and coast are diverse. The forest has provided refuge from peoples of the grasslands. Extreme ethnic fragmentation, among more than five hundred ethnic groups, has led to extreme differentiation in political and social organization. Several originally small-scale societies evolved into complex nation-states; others remained small, but joined loosely organized confederacies. No forest societies have matched the scope or size of empires in the Western and Central Sudanic cluster.

For subsistence, the people of most forest-belt cultures participate in agriculture and hunting; those of a few rely on fishing and livestock grazing. Generally, secret societies and age-grade associations have served as important institutions. External influences apparently resulted from contacts with savanna dwellers and Europeans. Indigenous African religions are prominent; however, members of some societies have adopted Islam or Christianity.

Differences within the sociopolitical organization of societies are reflected in music. Elaborate traditions of court music and masquerades are important. Features that characterize forest-belt music include the use of percussive instruments and an emphasis on complex rhythms. Because similarities and differences exist in how features are manifested and music is socially organized, forest-belt music falls into two clusters: eastern and western, divided by the Bandama River, in Côte d'Ivoire.

The Akan of the Eastern Forest Cluster

The languages of ethnic groups in the east belong to the Kwa and Benue-Congo divisions of the Niger-Congo family. An extensive amount of musical research has been done on peoples of this area. The music of groups living in the Eastern Forest most often serve as a model to represent the music of West Africa as a whole. Because of cultural diversity, the area subdivides into several subclusters: the Igbo, the Yorùbá, the Aja, the Gã, and the Akan.

Akan-speaking peoples (Asante, Brong, Akim, Kwahu, Akwapim, Akwamu, Wasa, Asen, Agona, Fante, Baoulé) inhabit widely dispersed areas in modern Ghana and Côte d'Ivoire. The basis of their social organization is rule by matrilineal descent. Political organization, particularly among the Asante, is diffuse. The Asantehene is paramount ruler of a confederation of provincial chiefs, and the chiefs in turn exercise authority over subchiefs and headmen of villages under their jurisdiction. The king is not an absolute ruler: a council—the queen mother, the chiefs of the most important provinces, the general of the army—controls him. The symbol of national solidarity is the Golden Stool, which came into being in the time of Osei Tutu (1700–1730), the fourth known king of the Asante, and the founder of the empire. Asante religion acknowledges belief in an earth spirit and a supreme god, but lesser gods and ancestor spirits attract popular worship and propitiation.

Performances at the Asante royal court are one of the most important contexts for musicmaking (figure 1). Royal musicians permanently attach themselves to the Asantehene and other chiefs, and oral tradition attributes certain chiefs with the introduction of musical instruments, orchestras, musical types, and styles of singing. Such traditions appear in all Akan areas. The number of musicians, variety of instruments, and musical types are indicators of a king's

Figure 1 An *adzewa* group performs at a funeral at the Asante court in Kumase, Ghana, 2001. The *adzewa* player is seated at left. The woman at right plays the *donno* drum. The other women play various percussive instruments and sing.
Photo by Joseph S. Kaminski.

greatness. Chiefs with a higher status may keep drums and other instruments that lesser chiefs may not.

Territorial expansion by conquest, and contact with peoples to the north and west of the Akan area, have led to the adoption of new traditions and musical instruments. Interaction with other peoples also pushed Akan influences into other areas. Many groups in Ghana use the Asante talking drum (*atumpan*), and play it in the Akan language, interactions between Asante and the Dahomey kingdom have resulted in common musical types and instruments. Besides the use of music for royalty (*atumpan, kete, ntahera, kwadwom*), religion (*akom*), events of the lifecycle (no music occurs at births or marriages), and recreation, there are occupational associations and an elaborate military structure with a highly organized repertory of traditional songs and drum music.

Akan instrumental types most commonly include drums, as in ensembles of *fontomfrom, kete,* and *atumpan*. Rattles and bells accompany drumming, either at court, at events of the lifecycle, or during religious and recreational activities. Percussion logs accompany *asonko* recreational music, but percussion vessels occur only sporadically. Drums indigenous to the area are usually single-headed and open-ended, but as a result of interaction with neighbors, the Akan have adopted drums from the north: gourd drums (*bentere, pentre*) and the hourglass tension drum (*donno*). Two wind instruments have associations with royalty: the *mmεn* (*abεn,* singular), ivory trumpets, played in groups at the court of paramount chiefs (figure 2); and the *odurugya,* a notched flute, made of cane husk, played at the Asantehene's court. Other wind instruments include the *atenteben* (played solo and in ensembles) and the *taletenga* (an idioglot reed pipe). There are few stringed instruments. Among them are the *seperewa* (a six-stringed harp) and the *benta* (a mouth bow). The Baoulé, who live in Côte d'Ivoire, use a wider variety of melodic instruments: the lamellaphone, xylophone (with keys laid over the trunks of two banana trees), and harps. Their use of these instruments may reflect their close contact with neighbors to the north and west.

Use of the seven-tone scale and singing in thirds is distinctive to the Akan. "Clearcut short phrases," phrases of a standard duration, and "longer fluid patterns" can occur within one composition (Nketia 1980:330). Phrasal variation is also apparent in Gā and Ewe drum ensembles.

Kpelle of the Western Forest Cluster

Of the indigenous peoples that live west of the Bandama River in Liberia, Sierra Leone, and western Côte d'Ivoire, none evolved into kingdoms or states comparable to the political structures that arose among some forest dwellers in the east. Before about 1400, peoples in this area, particularly those in Liberia and Côte d'Ivoire, felt little influence from the savanna empires of Ghana and Mali. This isolation permitted the development of small and widely scattered states, with enough contact to form

Figure 2 The *nkofe* ivory trumpet ensemble of the Asantehene performs at an ancestor veneration outside the ancestral shrine, Kumase, Ghana, 2001.
Photo by Joseph. S. Kaminski.

confederations for defense and trade; however, in the 1400s, with the disintegration of the Mali Empire, Mande traders and warriors began to move from the savanna into the kola plantations of the forest, bringing merchandise and Islam. Migrations from the north, continuing until the 1800s, resulted in the invention of an indigenous alphabet among the Vai, and in secret societies (Poro for men, Sande for women) that were vehicles for transmitting culture over time.

As a result of migrations from the savanna, the music of peoples who inhabit the Western Forest cluster shows a unity that distinguishes local music from that of the Eastern Forest, but unlike the eastern area, only a few societies in the western area have been the focus of intensive musical research. Though detailed information about all ethnic groups is lacking, enough is known for a discussion of the typical features of some societies. This cluster divides into three subclusters, based on linguistic families (Mande, West Atlantic, and Kwa subfamilies of the Niger-Congo family); only the Kwa are probably indigenous to the area.

The musical traditions of Mande speakers (Kpelle, Susu, Lokko, Koranko, Kono, Krim, Yalunka, Kondi, Gallina, Mende, Vai, Belle, Loma, Mano, Gbandi, Gio, Dan, Guere, Gouro) have had the most dramatic impact on this cluster. Being in the majority, they have heavily affected local social and political institutions.

Kpelle migrations into the area known as Liberia occurred between the 1400s and the 1800s. Most professional musicians nowadays work as subsistence farmers or laborers. Known as Kpelle singers, *ngulei-sîyge-nuu* 'the song-raising person', achieve renown for performing at festivals, funerals, and receptions: "Solo singers are often women, but male professional storytellers, and instrumentalists playing the pluriarc, the lamellaphone, and the triangular frame zither, are also singers" (Stone 1980:716).

The Kpelle use two words to classify musical instruments: *fée* 'blown' and *ygále* 'struck'. Among blown instruments are a flute (*boo*) and a side-blown horn (*túru*) made of wood, ivory, or horn. Struck instruments include idiophones, drums (membranophones), and stringed instruments (chordophones). The Kpelle use a variety of melodic and rhythmic idiophones, including lamellaphones (*gbèlee, kónkoma*); a xylophone (*bala*), which consists of free logs resting on banana stalks; struck logs (*kóno, kéleng*); rattles; and bells. Drums may be single-headed or double-headed, and are goblet- and hourglass-shaped. Some drums have feet. Stringed instruments include a triangular frame zither (*konîng*), a multiple bow-lute (*gbegbetêle*), a single-stringed bow-lute (*gbee-kee*), a musical bow (*kòn-kpàla*), and a harp (*kerân-non-konîng*).

The organization of ensembles reflects the social structure of Kpelle culture. The largest and lowest-pitched instrument in a struck log ensemble is the 'mother' (*kóno-lee*), and the medium-sized and smallest are the 'middle' (*kóno-sama*) and the 'child' (*kóno-long*), respectively.

The Kpelle play music on many different occasions. Activities associated with puberty—initiation into Poro and Sande—include more music than other lifecycle events. The Kpelle have music associated with holidays, work, harvest, games, and masked dancing.

Kpelle melody is syllabic and percussive. Repetition is common, and in some traditions hocketing occurs. The scale usually has five tones. Ensembles include a combination of pitches with different timbres—voices, drums, rattles, and metal idiophones: "Entries are usually staggered, giving an accumulation of textures" (Stone 1980:718). Men sing in an upper vocal register, but women sing in a lower one.

> A piece of music played in **hocket** has its melody distributed among several voices so that each voice performs only intermittent notes.

Percussive instruments usually accompany singing and dancing. Accompaniments "range in form from the accent of the cutlass striking the bush at regular intervals, as in agricultural labor songs, to the drumming of a professional musician" at masked dances (Monts 1982:106). One instrument usually provides the basic pulse, while another instrument supplies intricate rhythmic patterns. Most songs, particularly those associated with communal activities (social institutions, occupational groups, lifecycle events) have one- and two-part structures. Songs performed in unison have the one-part structure. Songs based on a two-part structure may have a call-and-response pattern between a solo and a chorus, or between one chorus and another. Occupational groups that have a recognized leader normally make use of the solo-chorus format, but divisions based on sex, age, or no recognizable leader employ the chorus-chorus format.

—Adapted from articles by Jacqueline Cogdell DjeDje and Fremont E. Besmer

Bibliography

Besmer, Fremont E. 1972. *Hausa Court Music in Kano, Nigeria*. Ann Arbor, Mich.: University Microfilms.
———. 1974. *Kídàn Dárán Sállà: Music for the Muslim Festivals of Id al-Fitr and Id al-Kabir in Kano, Nigeria*. Indiana

University Monographs. Bloomington; African Studies Program, Indiana University.

——. 1983. *Horses, Musicians, and Gods: The Hausa Cult of Possession-Trance*. South Hadley, Mass.: Bergin and Garvey.

Charry, Eric. 2000. *Mande Music: Traditional and Modern Music of the Maninka and Mandinka of Western Africa*. Chicago: University of Chicago Press.

DjeDje, Jacqueline Cogdell. 2008. *Fiddling in West Africa: Touching the Spirit in Fulbe, Hausa, and Dagbamba Cultures*. Bloomington: University of Indiana Press.

Monts, Lester P. 1982. "Musical Clusteral Relationships in a Liberian–Sierra Leonean Region: A Preliminary Analysis." *Journal of African Studies* 9(3):101–115.

Nketia, J. H. Kwabena. 1963. *African Music in Ghana*. Evanston, Ill.: Northwestern University Press.

——. 1980. "Ghana." *The New Grove Dictionary of Music and Musicians*, edited by Stanley Sadie. London: Macmillan.

Stone, Ruth. 1980. "Liberia." *The New Grove Dictionary of Music and Musicians*, edited by Stanley Sadie. London: Macmillan.

Thieme, Darius. 1970. "Music in Yorùbá Society." In *Development of Materials for a One Year Course in African Music for the General Undergraduate Student (Project in African Music)*, edited by Vada E. Butcher, 107–111. Washington, D.C.: Howard University Press.

Yorùbá Popular Music

About 30 million Yorùbá live in southwestern Nigeria and parts of Benin and Togo. The term *Yariba* appears in written form in the early 1700s, in Hausa-Fulani clerics' accounts of the kingdom of Ọyọ, one of a series of some twenty independent polities (including Ile-Ifẹ, Ọyọ, Ibadan, Ilọrin, Ẹgba, Egbado, Ijẹbu, Ilesa, Ondo, Ekiti). Expansion of the Ọyọ Empire and its successor state, Ibadan, encouraged the application of this term to a larger population. The spread of certain musical instruments and genres—including the *dùndún*, an hourglass-shaped pressure drum ("talking drum"), now among the most potent symbols of pan-Yorùbá identity, and the *bàtá*, an ensemble of conical, two-headed drums, associated with the thunder god Shango—played a role in Ọyọ's attempt to establish a cultural underpinning for imperial domination.

Inter-Yorùbá wars of the 1700s and 1800s encouraged the dispersal of musicians, especially praise singers and talking drummers. We might regard such performers as predecessors of today's popular musicians, since their survival as craft specialists depended largely upon creating broadly comprehensible and appealing styles. Some performers, linked exclusively to particular communities, kin groups, or religious organizations, were responsible for mastering secret knowledge, protected by supernatural sanctions; other, more mobile musicians, exploiting regional economic networks, had to develop a broader and shallower corpus of musical techniques and verbal texts.

In the late 1800s and early 1900s, a pan-Yorùbá popular culture emerged, but perceptions of cultural differences among regional subgroups survived. Dialect and musical style continued to play a role in maintaining local identities and allegiances, providing a framework for criticism of regional and national politics. Yorùbá popular musicians have often drawn upon the traditions of their natal communities to create distinctive "sounds," intended to give them a competitive edge in the marketplace.

In the early 1900s, in and around Lagos (port and colonial capital), syncretic cultural forms—including religious movements and traditions of theater, dance, and music—reinforced Yorùbá identity. By 1900, the population of Lagos included culturally diverse groups: a local Yorùbá community; Sierra Leonean, Brazilian, and Cuban repatriates; Yorùbá immigrants from the west African hinterland; and a sprinkling of other migrants from Nigeria and farther afield. Interaction among these groups was a crucial factor in the development of Yorùbá popular culture during the early 1900s. Lagos was a locus for importing new musical technology and, beginning in 1928, for commercial recording by European firms. Since the late 1800s, continual flows of people, techniques, and technologies between Lagos and hinterland communities have shaped Yorùbá popular music.

General Features

Performances of most genres of Yorùbá popular music occur at elaborate parties; after rites of passage, such as naming ceremonies, weddings, and funerals; and at urban nightspots ("hotels"). Recorded music of local and foreign origin is played, often at high volume, in patrilineal compounds, taxicabs, barbershops, and kiosks. Some genres of popular music are associated with Islam, and others with syncretic Christianity; some praise the powerful, and others critique social inequalities; some have texts in Yorùbá, and others in pidgin English; some are fast, vigorous, and youthful in spirit, and others are slow and solemn, "music for the elders."

Yorùbá popular music fuses the role of song (a medium for praise, criticism, and moralizing) and the role of rhythmic coordination in sound and physical movement (an expression of sociability and sensory pleasure). As tradition is important to Yorùbá musicians and listeners, so are the transnational forces that shape Yorùbá lives. Yorùbá popular culture—not only music, but also styles of dancing, televised comedies and dramas, tabloids, sports, gambling, slang, and fashion in clothing and hair—incorporates imported technologies and exotic styles, providing Yorùbá listeners with an experiential bridge between local and global cultures.

The organization of instruments in Yorùbá popular music generally follows the pattern of traditional drumming: an *iyá'lù* "mother drum" leads the ensemble, and one or more *omele* "supporting drums" play ostinatos, which interlock rhythmically. In *jùjú*, electric guitars are organized on this pattern. Another practice associated with deep Yorùbá tradition is the use of musical instruments to "speak." Yorùbá is a tonal language, in which distinctions of pitch and timbre play important roles in determining the meaning of words, and *jùjú*, *fújì*, and most other popular genres employ some variant of the *dùndún*, which articulates stereotyped contours of pitch, representing verbal formulas such as proverbs (*òwe*) and praise poetry (*oríkì*). Imported instruments—such as congas, electric guitars, and drum synthesizers—can articulate proverbs and epithets of praise, though Yorùbá musicians say such instruments are less "talkative" than the traditional pressure drums.

In most genres, the bandleader (often called a captain) is a praise singer who initiates solo vocal phrases (*dá orin* 'creates song alone'), segments of which a chorus doubles. He sings responsorial sequences, in which his improvised solo phrases alternate with a fixed phrase, sung by the chorus. His calls are *elé*, the nominal form of the verb *lé* 'to drive something away from or into something else'. The choral responses and the vocalists who sing them are *ègbè* (from *gbè* 'to support, side with, or protect someone'). The social structure of popular music ensembles is closely linked to traditional ideals of social organization, which simultaneously stress the "naturalness" of hierarchy and the mutual dependency of leaders and supporters.

The practice of "spraying"—in which a satisfied praisee dances up to the bandleader or praise singer and pastes money to his forehead—provides the bulk of musicians' profits. Cash advances, guaranteed minimums, and record royalties, except in the case of a handful of superstars, are minor sources of income. The dynamics of remuneration are linked to the musical form, which is often modular or serial. Performances of *jùjú* and *fújì* typically consist of a series of expressive strategies—proverbs and praise names, slang, melodic quotations, and satisfying dance grooves—unreeled with an eye toward pulling in the maximum amount of cash from patrons.

Songtexts

Some genres—and even segments of particular performances—are weighted more toward the text–song side of the spectrum, others more to the instrument–dance side. Colloquial aesthetic terminology suggests a developed appreciation of certain aural qualities: dense, buzzing textures, vibrant contrasts in tone color, and rhythmic energy and flow. Nevertheless, Yorùbá listeners usually concentrate most carefully on the words of a performance. One of the most damning criticisms listeners can level against a singer or drummer is that he speaks incoherently, or does not choose his words to suit the occasion.

Yorùbá songtexts are centrally concerned with competition, fate (*orí* 'head'), and the limits of human knowledge in an uncertain universe.

Invidious comparison—between the bandleader and competing musicians (who seek to trip him up), or between the patron whose praises are sung and his or her enemies—is the rhetorical linchpin of Yorùbá popular music. Advertisements for business concerns are common in live performance and on commercial recordings. Musicians praise brands of beer and cigarettes, hotels, rugmakers, football pools, and patent medicines.

Prayers for protection—offered to Jesus, Allah, or the creator deity Elédùmarè—are another common rhetorical strategy. *Ayé* 'life, the world' is portrayed as a transitory and precarious condition, a conception evoked by phrases like *ayé fèlè 'fèlè* 'flimsy world' and *ayé gbègi* 'world that chips like wood or pottery'. Songtexts continually evoke the conceptual dialectic of *ayíniké* and *ayínipadà*—the reality that can be perceived (and, if one is clever and lucky, manipulated) and the unseen, potentially menacing underside of things. Competition for access to patrons and touring overseas is fierce, and sometimes involves the use of magical medicines and curses. Yorùbá pop music stars have often carried out bitter rhetorical battles on a series of recordings.

Another major theme of the lyrics of popular songs is sensual enjoyment (*igbádùn* 'sweetness perception'). Singers and talking drummers often switch from themes of religious piety and deep moral philosophy to flirtatious teasing, focused on references to dancers' bodily exertions. Many musicians have adopted good-timing honorifics, such as "minister of enjoyment," "father of good order," "ikebe [butt] king." The images of pleasure projected in *jùjú* and *fújì* are related to themes of praise and the search for certainty. The subject of praise singing is rhetorically encased in a warm web of social relationships: surrounded by supporters and shielded from enemies, her head "swells" with pride as she sways to "rolling" rhythms.

Yorùbá Highlife

The tradition of highlife dance bands originated in the early 1900s in Accra, capital of Gold Coast (present-day Ghana). Before the 1940s, Ghanaian bands (such as the Cape Coast Sugar Babies) had traveled to Lagos, where they left a lasting impression on local musicians. In the 1920s and 1930s, Lagos was home to the Calabar Brass Band, which recorded for Parlophone as the Lagos Mozart Orchestra. The core of the band consisted of clarinets, trumpets and cornets, baritones, trombones, tuba, and parade drums. The band played a proto-highlife style, a transitional phase between the colonial martial band and the African dance orchestra.

During the 1930s and 1940s, Lagos supported several African ballroom-dance orchestras, including the Chocolate Dandies, the Lagos City Orchestra, the Rhythm Brothers, the Deluxe Swing Rascals, and the Harlem Dynamites. These bands played for the city's African élites, a social formation comprised largely of Sierra Leonean and Brazilian repatriates, whose grandparents had returned to Lagos in the 1800s. Their repertory included foxtrots, waltzes, Latin dances, and arrangements of popular Yorùbá songs.

The 1950s are remembered as the Golden Age of Yorùbá highlife. Scores of highlife bands played at hotels in Lagos and the major Yorùbá towns. Bobby Benson's Jam Session Orchestra (founded in 1948) exerted a particularly strong influence on Yorùbá highlife. A guitarist who had worked as a dance-band musician in England, Benson (1920–1983) brought the first electric guitar to Lagos (1948), opened his own nightclub (Caban Bamboo), and employed many of the best musicians in Nigeria. His 1960 recording of "Taxi Driver, I Don't Care" (Philips P 82019), was the biggest hit of the highlife era in Nigeria. During the 1950s and 1960s, many of his apprentices—Victor Ọlaiya ("the evil genius of high-life"), Roy Chicago, Edy Okonta, Fela Ransome-Kuti—went on to form their own bands.

The typical highlife band included three to five winds, a string bass, a guitar, bongos, a conga, and maracas. Though the sound of British and American dance bands influenced African bands, the emphasis was on Latin American repertory, rather than on swing arrangements. Unlike *jùjú* bands, highlife bands often included non-Yorùbá members, and typically performed songs in several languages, including Yorùbá, English, and pidgin English.

By the mid-1960s, highlife was declining in Yorùbáland, partly as a result of competition from *jùjú*. Some highlife bandleaders, including Roy Chicago, incorporated the *dùndún*, and in an attempt to compete with *jùjú* began to use more deep Yorùbá verbal materials. Musicians such as Dele Ojo, who had apprenticed with Victor Ọlaiya, forged hybrid *jùjú*-highlife styles. Soul, popular among urban youth from around 1966, attacked highlife from another angle. The Nigerian civil war (1967–1970), which caused many of the best Igbo musicians to leave Lagos, delivered the final blow. By the 1980s, highlife bands had become rare in Yorùbáland.

Jùjú

This genre, named for the tambourine (*jùjú*), emerged in Lagos around 1932. The typical *jùjú* group in the 1930s was a trio: a leader (who sang and played banjo), a *ṣèkèrè*, and *jùjú*. Some groups operated as quartets, adding a second vocalist. The basic framework was drawn from palm-wine guitar music, played by a mobile population of African workers in Lagos: sailors, railway men, truck drivers.

The rhythms of early *jùjú* were strongly influenced by *aṣíkò*, a dance-drumming style, performed mainly by Christian boys' clubs. Many early *jùjú* bandleaders began their careers as *aṣíkò* musicians. Played on square frame drums and a carpenter's saw, *aṣíkò* drew upon the traditions of two communities of Yorùbá-speaking repatriates who had settled in Lagos during the 1800s: the Amaro were emancipados of Brazilian or Cuban descent, and the Saro were Sierra Leonean repatriates (who formed a majority of the educated black élite in Lagos). *Aṣíkò* rhythms came from the Brazilian samba (many older Nigerians use the terms *aṣíkò* and *sámbà* interchangeably), and the associated style of dancing was influenced by the *caretta* 'fancy dance', a Brazilian version of the contredanse. The square *sámbà* drum may have been introduced by the Brazilians (known for their carpentry), or from the British West Indies, perhaps via Sierra Leone. Though identifying a single source for the introduction of the frame drum is impossible, this drum was clearly associated with immigrant black Christian identity.

Early Styles

The first star of *jùjú* was Tunde King, born in 1910 into the Saro community. Though a member of the Muslim minority, he learned Christian hymns while attending primary school. He made the first recordings with the term *jùjú* on the label, recorded by Parlophone in 1936. Ayinde Bakare, a Yorùbá migrant who recorded for His Master's Voice beginning in 1937, began as an *aṣíkò* musician, and went on to become one of the most influential figures in postwar *jùjú*. Musical style was an important idiom for the expression of competitive relationships between neighborhoods. During the 1930s, each quarter in Lagos had its favorite *jùjú* band.

The melodies of early *jùjú*, modeled on *aṣíkò* and palm-wine songs and Christian hymns, were diatonic, often harmonized in parallel thirds. The vocal style used the upper range of the male full-voice tessitura, and was nasalized and moderately tense, with no vibrato. The banjo—including a six-stringed guitar-banjo and a mandolin-banjo—played a role similar to that of the fiddle in *sákárà* music, often introducing or bridging between vocal segments, and providing heterophonic accompaniment for the vocal line. *Jùjú* banjoists used a technique of thumb and forefinger plucking introduced to Lagos by Liberian sailors.

After the mid-1940s, *jùjú* underwent a rapid transformation. The first major change was the introduction, in 1948, of the *gángan* talking drum, a change attributed to bandleader Akanbi Ege. Another change was the availability of electronic amplifiers, microphones, and pickups. Portable public-address systems had been introduced during the war and were in regular use by Yorùbá musicians by the late 1940s. The first *jùjú* musician to adopt the amplified guitar was Ayinde Bakare, who experimented with a contact microphone in 1949, switching from ukulele-banjo to "box guitar" (acoustic), because there was no place to attach the device to the body of the banjo. Electronic amplification of voices and guitar catalyzed an expansion of *jùjú* ensembles during the 1950s. In particular, it enabled musicians to incorporate more percussion instruments without upsetting the aural balance they wanted between singing and instrumental accompaniment.

In the postwar period, *jùjú* bands began to use the *agídìgbo* (a box-resonated lamellaphone) and various conga drums (*àkúbà, ògìdo*), reflecting the influence of a genre called mambo music, a Yorùbá version of *konkoma* music, brought to Lagos from Ghana by Ewe and Fanti migrant workers. According to *jùjú* musicians active at the time, the *agídìgbo* and *ògìdo* (bass conga) provided a bass counterbalance for the electric guitar and *gángan*.

The instrumentation of Bakare's group shifted from one stringed instrument and two percussion instruments (before the war), to one stringed instrument and five percussion instruments (in 1954). By 1966, most *jùjú* bands had eight or nine musicians. Expansion and reorganization of the ensemble occurred simultaneously with a slowing of tempos. Slower tempos and expanded ensembles in turn reflected changes in aural textures. Western technology was put into the service of indigenous aesthetics: the channeling of singing and guitar through cheap and infrequently serviced tube amplifiers and speakers augmented the density and buzzing of the music.

Many bandleaders produced records with a song in standard Yorùbá dialect and mainstream *jùjú* style on the A side, and a local Yorùbá dialect and style on the B side. Most *jùjú* singing shifted from the high-tessitura, nasalized style of the 1930s and 1940s to a lower, more relaxed sound, closer to the traditional secular male vocal style and the imported model of the crooner. Tunde King's distinctive style of singing was extended by Tunde Western Nightingale, "the bird that sings at night," a popular Lagosian bandleader of the 1950s and 1960s.

Later Styles

The birth of later *jùjú* can be traced to the innovations of Isiah Kehinde Dairo (1930–1996), an Ijeṣa Yorùbá musician, who had a series of hit records around the time of Nigerian independence (1960). His recordings for the British company Decca were so successful that the British government in 1963 designated him a member of the Order of the British Empire. In 1967, he joined *àpàlà* star Haruna Iṣọla (1919–1983) to found Star Records. His hits of the early 1960s, recorded on two-track tape at Decca Studios in Lagos, reveal his mastery of the three-minute recording. Most of his records from this period begin with an accordion or guitar introduction and the main lyric, sung once or twice. This leads into a middle section, in which the *dùndún* predominates, playing proverbs and slogans, which in turn a chorus repeats. The final section usually reprises the main text.

The vocal style on Dairo's records was influenced by Christian hymnody. (Dairo was pastor of a syncretic church in Lagos.) It reflects the polyphonic singing of eastern Yorùbáland (Ileṣa, Ekiti). His lyrics—in Standard Yorùbá, Ijeṣa dialect, and various other Nigerian and Ghanaian languages—were carefully composed. By his own account, he made special efforts to research traditional poetic idioms. Many of his songs consist of philosophical advice and prayers for himself and his patrons.

Jùjú continued to develop along lines established by Bakare and Dairo. The oil boom of the 1970s led to a rapid expansion of the Nigerian economy. Many individuals earned enough money from trade and entrepreneurial activity to hire musicians for lifecycle celebrations, and the number and size of *jùjú* bands increased concomitantly. By the mid-1970s, the ideal *jùjú* ensemble had expanded beyond the ten-piece bands of Bakare and Dairo to include fifteen or more musicians. Large bands helped boost the reputation of the patrons who hired them to perform at parties, and helped sustain an idealized image of Yorùbá society as a flexible hierarchy.

Jùjú Stars

A noteworthy star of *jùjú* is King Sunny Adé. Born in Ondo, Nigeria, in 1946, he started his musical career playing a *sámbà* drum with a *jùjú* band. He formed his own ensemble, the Green Spot Band, in 1966. He modeled his style on that of Tunde Nightingale, and his vocal sound represents an extension of the high-tessitura, slightly nasalized sound established by Tunde King in the 1930s. His first big hit was "Challenge Cup" (1968), a praise song for a football team, released on a local label, African Songs. In

1970, he added electric bass guitar (displacing the *agídìgbo*), and began to record with imported instruments, purchased for him by his patron, Chief Bọlatinwa Abioro. Adé quickly developed a reputation as a technically skilled musician, and his fans gave him the informal title *Àlùjànun Onígítà* 'The Wizard of Guitar'.

In 1972, splitting with Chief Abioro, Adé changed the name of his band to the "African Beats." The LP *Synchro System Movement* (1976) artfully blended the vocal style he had adopted from Tunde Nightingale with aspects of Afro-Beat (see below), including minor tonalities, slower tempos, and a langorous electric bass part. This LP featured a continuous thirty-minute performance, a move away from the three-minute limit of most previous recordings, and toward the typical extended forms of live performances. By the end of the 1970s, Adé had expanded his band to include sixteen performers, including two tenor guitars, a rhythm guitar, a Hawaiian (pedal steel) guitar, a bass guitar, two talking drummers, a *sèkèrè*, a conga (*àkúbà*), a drumset, a synthesizer, and four choral vocalists.

Chief Commander Ebenezer Obey is another star of *jùjú*. Born in the Ẹgbado area of western Yorùbáland in 1942, he formed his first band, the International Brothers, in 1964. His early style, strongly influenced by I. K. Dairo, incorporated elements of highlife, Congolese guitar style, soul, and country. His band expanded during the years of the oil boom. In 1964, he started with seven players; by the early 1970s, he was employing thirteen; and by the early 1980s, he was touring with eighteen. He is praised for his voice, and for the philosophical depth of his Yorùbá lyrics. Like Dairo, he is a devout Christian, and many of his songs derive from the melodies of hymns.

During the early 1980s, a few top *jùjú* bands began to tour Europe and the United States. In 1982, Sunny Adé scored an international success with the LP *Juju Music*, released on Island Records (the label Bob Marley recorded for), which rose to number 111 on the *Billboard* album chart. Adé and Obey's only serious competitor during that period was Sir Shina Peters (b. 1958), whose 1989 album, *Ace*, incorporated rhythms from *fújì* music and was a big hit in Nigeria.

The *jùjú* music scene in Nigeria never recovered from the economic decline and currency devaluations of the 1990s, which put many bands out of business. In recent years, Ebenezer Obey has retired from the *jùjú* music field and has turned to church music. Sunny Adé's career as a bandleader continues, though his major international successes are behind him.

Afro-Beat

Centered on the charismatic figure Fela Anikulapo-Kuti (1938–1997, born in Abeokuta, Nigeria), Afro-Beat began in the late 1960s as a mix of dance-band highlife, jazz, and soul. Though in style and content it stands somewhat apart from the mainstream of Yorùbá popular music, it has influenced *jùjú* and *fùjì*.

Fela was the grandson of the Reverend J. J. Ransome-Kuti, a prominent educator, who played a major role in indigenizing Christian hymns. His mother was Funmilayo Ransome-Kuti, a political activist and founder of the Nigerian Women's Union. It is said that he received his musicality from his father's family and his temperament from his mother's. In the mid-1950s, he played with Bobby Benson's and Victor Olaiya's highlife orchestras. In 1958, he traveled to London to study trumpet at Trinity College of Music. While there, he joined with J. K. Braimah to form Koola Lobitos, a band that played a jazz–highlife hybrid. Fela returned to Lagos in 1963, and by 1966 had been voted the top jazz performer in a readers' poll held by *Spear Magazine*. Though his reputation grew among musicians in Lagos, his music appealed primarily to an audience of collegians and professionals.

The popularity of soul among young people in Lagos during the late 1960s strongly influenced Fela. In particular, the success of Geraldo Pino, a Sierra Leonean imitator of James Brown, caused him to incorporate aspects of soul into his style. A 1969 trip to the United States, where he met black activists, changed his political orientation and his concept of the goals of musical performance. In 1970, on returning to Lagos, he formed a new group, Africa '70, and began to develop Afro-Beat, a mixture of highlife and soul, with infusions of deep Yorùbá verbal materials.

In the early 1970s, Fela's style featured Tony Allen's drumming, Maurice Ekpo's electric-bass playing, and Peter Animaṣaun's percussive rhythm-guitar style (influenced by Jimmy Nolen (1934–1983), longtime guitarist for James Brown). The band included three congas, percussion sticks, *sèkèrè*, and a four-piece horn section (two trumpets, tenor sax, baritone sax). Jazz-influenced solos were provided by trumpeter Tunde Williams and the brilliant tenor saxophonist Igo Chico. Like many Lagos highlife bands of the 1950s, Fela's early bands included Ghanaians and non-Yorùbá Nigerians. The original Africa '70 stayed together until the mid-1970s, when Fela's increasingly autocratic behavior led Allen and Chico to quit.

For more than twenty years, the organizational principles of Afro-Beat remained remarkably constant. The basic rhythm-section pattern divides into complementary strata: a bottom layer, made up of interlocking patterns on the electric bass and the bass drum; a middle layer, with a rhythm guitar, congas, and a snare back beat; and a top layer, with percussion sticks and ṣèkèrè playing ostinatos. The horn section provides riffs in support of Fela's singing, and its members play extended solos.

Fela died of AIDS in 1997. He remains one of the most influential figures in the history of African popular music, remembered for his charismatic personality, political convictions, and musical innovations.

Fújì

This genre, the most popular one in the early 1990s, grew out of ajísáàrì, music customarily performed before dawn during Ramadan by young men associated with neighborhood mosques. Ajísáàrì groups, made up of a lead singer, a chorus, and drummers, walk through their neighborhood, stopping at patrilineal compounds to wake the faithful for their early-morning meal (sáàrì). Fújì emerged as a genre and marketing label in the late 1960s, when former ajísáàrì-singers Sikiru Ayinde Barrister (b. 1948) and Ayinla Kollington (b. 1952) were discharged from the Nigerian Army, made their first recordings, and began a periodically bitter rivalry. In the early 1970s, fújì succeeded àpàlà as the most popular genre among Yorùbá Muslims, and has since gained a substantial Christian audience.

The instrumentation of fújì bands features drums. Most important are various sizes of talking-drum: dùndún, àdàmọ, and sometimes a smaller hourglass-shaped drum, the kànàngó, two or three of which may be played by a single drummer. Bands often include sàkàrà drums (still associated with Muslim identity), plus the conga-type drums used in àpàlà and jùjú. Commonly, they also use ṣèkèrè, maracas, and a set of agogo attached to a metal rack. In the mid-1980s, fújì musicians borrowed the drumset from jùjú. The wealthiest bands use electronic drum pads connected to synthesizers.

Other experiments represent an attempt to forge symbolic links with deep Yorùbá traditions. In the early 1980s, Barrister introduced into his style the bàtá drum, associated with the Yorùbá thunder god Shango. He named the drum "Fújì Bàtá Reggae." He dropped the bàtá after influential Muslim patrons complained about his using a quintessentially pagan instrument. On other recordings, he employed the kàkàkì, an indigenous trumpet, used for saluting the kings of northern Yorùbá towns.

Later appropriations of Western instruments—the Hawaiian (pedal steel) guitar, keyboard synthesizers, and drum machines—have largely been filtered through jùjú. Some jùjú musicians complain that fújì musicians, whom they regard as musical illiterates, have no idea what to do with such instruments. In fact, imported high-tech instruments are usually used in fújì recordings to play melodic sequences without harmonic accompaniment, to signal changes of rhythm or subject, and to add coloristic effects—techniques consistent with the norms of the genre.

Fújì has to a large degree been secularized, but it is still associated with Muslims, and record companies time the release of certain fújì recordings to coincide with holy days, such as Id-al-Fitr and Id-al-Kabir. Segments of Qur'ānic text are frequently deployed in performance, and many fújì recordings open with a prayer in Yorùbá Arabic: "La ilaha illa llahu; Mohamudu ya asuru lai 'There is no god but Allah; Mohammed is his prophet'."

Fújì music is an intensively syncretic style, incorporating aspects of Muslim recitations, Christian hymns, highlife classics, jùjú songs, Indian film-music themes, and American pop, within a rhythmic framework based on Yorùbá social-dance drumming. To demonstrate knowledge of Yorùbá tradition, fújì musicians make use of folkloric idioms, like proverbs and praise names.

"Traditional" and "Popular" Styles

To draw a sharp boundary between "traditional" and "popular" music in Yorùbá society is impossible. The criteria most commonly invoked in attempts to formulate a cross-cultural definition of popular music—openness to change, syncretism, intertexuality, urban provenience, commodification—are characteristic even of genres that Yorùbá musicians and audiences identify as deeply traditional. The penetration of indigenous economies by international capital and the creation of local markets for recorded music have shaped Yorùbá conceptions of music as a commodity, but musical commodification did not originate with colonialism and mass reproduction: Yorùbá musicians have long conceived of performance as a form of labor, a marketable product. The notion of the market as a microcosm of life—captured in the aphorism ayé l'ọjà 'the world is a market'—and a competitive arena, fraught with danger and ripe with possibilities, guides the strategies of musicians, who struggle to make a living under unpredictable economic conditions.

If Yorùbá popular music is partly a product of markets, it is also, in important ways, unlike other commodities. Many Yorùbá musicians and audiences still regard music as a potent force, with material and spiritual effects.

Though the foregoing genres of music vary in instrumentation, style, and social context, each invokes deep Yorùbá tradition while connecting listeners to the world of transnational commerce. Taken as a whole, Yorùbá popular music provides a complex commentary on the relationship between local traditions and foreign influence in an epoch of profound change.

—*Adapted from an article by*
Christopher A. Waterman

Bibliography

Euba, Akin. 1990. *Yorùbá Drumming: The Dùndún Tradition*. Bayreuth African Studies, 21–22. Bayreuth: Bayreuth University.

Stewart, Gary. 1992. *Breakout: Profiles in African Rhythm*. Chicago: University of Chicago Press.

Thieme, Darius. 1969. "A Descriptive Catalog of Yorùbá Musical Instruments." Ph.D. dissertation, Catholic University of America.

Waterman, Christopher A. 1990. *Jùjú: A Social History and Ethnography of an African Popular Music*. Chicago: University of Chicago Press.

Praise Singing in Northern Sierra Leone

Praise singing holds special significance for people who share the heritage of Manden, the political and economic center of the Mali Empire, formerly situated in the area of modern-day Mali and Guinea. Since the thirteenth century, individuals, families, and clans have emigrated from Manden. Several ethnic groups (Maninka, Koranko, Yalunka, Mandinka, Malinké, Bamana, Dyula) say their ancestors came from there. These groups share linguistic and cultural traits, and bear the collective name *Mande*. People from these groups have dispersed throughout West Africa—into Burkina Faso, Ivory Coast, The Gambia, Guinea, Liberia, Mali, Senegal, and Sierra Leone.

Manden represents a historical and mythic past, whose heritage endures in epics, extended narratives, and praise songs. In particular, performances of the *bolo gbili* repertory can recreate, through musical and verbal allusion, the history and myths surrounding the creation of, conflicts within, and migration from, Manden. These songs (singular, *bolo gbili*; plural, *bololu gbili*) are considered the oldest in a praise singer's repertory. They are "heavier" or "weightier" than *tulon bololu* 'play songs'.

Praise singing involves instrumental performance, singing, and speech. Praise songs most often compliment and challenge an individual or individuals present at a performance. The vehicle for praise, and advice or challenges offered in the guise of praise, take the form of a song in praise of a historical or mythical person. Praise singing offers more than mere praise: it invokes the heritage of Manden and its lineages; it publicly musters social roles and expectations related to this heritage, and to contemporary contexts.

Among the Maninka (Mandingo) and the Koranko of Sierra Leone, a verbal and musical specialist is known as a *jeli* or *yeli* (/j/ and /y/ are interchangeable; *jelilu* is the plural form), also called a bard or griot by some scholars. In a typical performance, a specialist begins by singing text from a praise song or playing a recognizable pattern on a musical instrument, such as the *bala*, the instrument most often included in praise-song performances. Praise singing may be accompanied by other instruments: the guitar (figure 1), often amplified through an altered tape deck or other apparatus; the *kora*, a twenty-one-stringed harp-lute, popular in Mali, Senegal, and The Gambia; or drums, the *jènbe* (which has a single stretched-skin drumhead, fastened with sinew or twine to a conical-bore log) and the *ban* (a small kettledrum, played with one stick). The *bala*, also known as the *balafon* or *balanji*, is played almost exclusively by *jelikèlu* 'male praise singers' (female praise singers are *jelimusolu*).

Figure 1 Sayon Kamara, a *jeliba* from Kondembaia, plays guitar, Maninka, 1987.
Photo by Laura Arntson. Courtesy of Indiana University, Archives of Traditional Music.

The *bala* has wooden keys or bars (figure 2), arranged in consecutive order of pitch, and fastened to a frame to which gourds are attached as resonators. Pieces of spider-egg casing or cigarette paper cover small holes in each gourd; they add a buzz to the sound. To add another texture, a *bala* player may tie rattles to the backs of his hands. The keys of most *balas* are tuned so the octave divides into seven pitches, approximately in equidistant tuning. The keys, which number from sixteen to twenty-one, lie in relation to one another in consecutive order of pitch, at a distance of about one and a half semi-tones. The latitude of a pitch area is greater than transcriptions in Western notation show; and variations in the tuning, whether intentional or the result of accidental chipping or splitting of the keys, occur. The sounding of pitches that deviate from absolute consonance (for example, an octave pair at a distance larger or smaller than 1200 cents) sets up a musical tension that people consider aesthetically desirable, not aberrant.

For a praise song, a *bala* player (or *jeliba*) plays, varies, and improvises on a basic pattern, the *balabolo*. While maintaining a recognizable kinesic and rhythmic contour, he may interject descending runs or sequences into it; he may vary the rhythms or selected pitches within it; and he may play a vocal song line, in more or less parallel octaves. When a performance includes several *jelilu*, most *bala* players maintain the basic pattern while a recognized master in the group improvises more. At a large gathering, such as a wedding or an initiation, all the *bala* players, *jelimusolu*, and drummers play or sing simultaneously—which, with the crowd's singing, dancing, handclapping, and talking, creates a dense texture. Throughout the variation and improvisation, a *jeli* maintains a single rhythmic impetus or drive, which helps shape the rhythms of the text. As he calls out praisewords (*fola*), a *bala* player may suspend his playing. The texts of *fola* include proverbs or references to proverbs; a brief narration or description of the current situation; commentary, advice, or criticism; bits of text drawn from a much longer narrative, to which the praise song alludes; or a praise name for a patron or the receiver of the praise at that moment. In performance, a *jeliba* intersperses instrumental playing with *fola*, and a praise singer (of either sex) guides a performance into singing (*donkilila la*), then back to *fola*, and so on. When a female specialist is not speaking or singing, she may play rhythmic patterns on the *karinyan*, a cylindrical iron bell suspended by a string or cloth from a finger of one hand and struck with an iron beater held in the other hand. When women present know the choral response, a female specialist may lead a song; if no one is present to sing a choral response, she may do all the singing.

For each song or piece in the repertory, the verbal text and the musical patterns performed on the *bala* are equally capable of calling to mind a larger text, a shared area of knowledge, or a storyline—a text envelope that includes bits of textual and musical information, with distinctive conventions of performance. It is a fluid set of descriptive phrases, praise names, proverbs, songs, and instrumental patterns, which all feed into a storyline, or collection of deeds, actions, events, attributes, and social mores. It can be expanded, embellished, or condensed.

Figure 2 Pa Sanasi Kuyateh plays *bala* with the Maninka Bala Ensemble, Sukurala, 1987. *Photo by Laura Arntson. Courtesy of Indiana University, Archives of Traditional Music.*

Through verbal and musical reference or allusion, a praise singer can emphasize certain of its aspects, and augment or reshape listeners' notions of it.

The way a *jeli* praises someone is, in the midst of performing a *balabolo*, to sing or play formulaic phrases, or other phrases from the text envelope, and to call out the name or praise names of the patron or recipient of the praise. When a *jeli* praises someone with a song from the *bolo gbili* repertory, he aligns that person with a past hero or leader, or with an idealized occupation: warrior (*kèlèkè*), hunter (*simbon*), farmer (*konkoba*).

By calling to mind the achievements and salient qualities of famous hunters of the past (real or mythical), a *jeli* likens the person receiving the praise to a larger-than-life character or an ideal. He attributes various qualities to a contemporary individual, and people expect the praised person to embody those ideals, or at least to respond with a gift. While alluding to a much larger vocabulary of references, praise singing steers public attention, praise, advice, and criticism. It calls attention not only to a contemporary individual, but to a historical or mythical character, his deeds and attributes, and the expectations or assigned attributes of members of the patrilineage to which both individuals belong or are aligned.

Form

Textual Aspects

Heightened speech, a primary characteristic of praise singing, involves rhythmic and dynamic elements that are not a part of everyday speech, whose primary function is communication. The poetic or musical qualities of speech that are out of the ordinary are self-conscious and performative. In heightened speech, rhythm and accentuation serve an aesthetic value over communicative function.

Musical Aspects

When a *jeli* introduces into the rhythmic texture additional rhythmic ideas and impetuses, he creates aesthetic tension; he thus displays his mastery of the form and its prosody. By introducing an additional rhythmic impetus drawn from rhythmic ideas available to and suggested by verbal performance, he often works against instrumental rhythms. In performance, the spoken rhythms deviate from the "natural" linguistic rhythms: they introduce nonphonemic accents, altered tempos, and nonlinguistic melodic contours. The languages spoken by the Bamana (Bambara), the Dyula, and to a lesser extent the Maninka and the Koranko, are tonal languages; in praise singing, other melodic contours may alter or obscure linguistic tonal patterns.

One technique a *jeli* uses to create a rhythmic tension is to deliver, in a fast stream (which pulls a listener away from an established pulse or rhythmic impetus), a verbal phrase such as a proverb, a praise name, or a bit of narration. A rush of words obscures expected accents and the sense of release or repose that comes with the end of a rhythmic pattern or phrase.

Another technique that creates aesthetic tension is the addition of a word or verbal rhythm at the end of a phrase—a technique that by complicating the rhythmic focus again deceives the listener's expectations of repose.

The Emergence of Form

During a praise-song performance, a *jeliba* varies or improvises on the basic *bala* pattern. When the performance moves into song, he may parallel the *donkili* (song) melody, continue with the *bala* pattern, or improvise further. By continually returning to or reinforcing important aspects of a pattern, he maintains its rhythmic impetus.

Bala patterns hold clues to the structure or musical organization of praise-song performance. They are sets of rhythmic ideas or motifs with particular kinesic contours and sometimes emergent melodies. What Western audiences recognize as a melodic contour in a *bala* pattern is more appropriately represented as a tonal-kinesic contour, since the Maninka do not perceive pitches as high or low: rather, they think of the keys (or pitches) of the *bala* in a right-left relationship. Depending on which side of a *bala* a *jeli* sits, notes elsewhere conceived as "lower" will be to the right or to the left. The contour of a *bala* pattern, then, is a contour of the hand-and-mallet movement over the keys. Furthermore, some pitches within a pattern may vary, while the kinesic contour remains the same. The contours of the lower register (represented in the lower staff in transcriptions) are tied to certain keys of the *bala* for each *bala* pattern, though particular intervals within a contour may vary. The kinesic contour is represented here at the point of the articulation, since the goal of hand-and-mallet movement is the articulation of sound.

The nature of the genre allows for extensive variation in text and form. Motivic elements such as praise names, proverbs, and truisms, and thematic or narrative elements of the text envelope, make up the text of a performance. Since a text envelope exists as a collection of ideas or an area of knowledge, rather than a sequence of details and events, elements may be invoked outside a chronological order. The bits of text capture and contribute to qualities and perceptions of the larger text. For a reference to the text envelope to be successful, they do not have to appear in a set order; it is a thematic area, rather than a thematic form, that holds significance for appreciation and analysis.

The text of a Mansareh *bolo* praise-song performance may successfully evoke heroic qualities and myths surrounding Sunjata (see textbox), though it may not be extensive, contain narration, or have a fixed form.

Since a *jeli* improvises and addresses an individual or individuals, the form and length of the performance are shaped by context. If the praise singing moves a person, he or she will give a gift to the *jeli*. Praise singers continue to praise someone until they feel they have received an appropriate gift for the praise, or until a point in the implied but tacit negotiation has been reached, so the specifically directed praise in a performance will come to an end or shift to a more generic, undirected performance.

Function

The ability to obtain property through praise singing and patronage is only one aspect of a *jeli*'s praise. In Maninka and Koranko culture and society, the praise itself has many functions. In the *tulon bolo* and *bolo gbili* repertories, the singing has value as entertainment, which can make people happy. Songs in the *tulon bolo* repertory "can make people forget about death and fighting"; when a *jeli* sings "adult songs, the ones adults enjoy, when they are together with their girlfriends," and sings of things they like, it will "make the young men's minds get up and move" (Harris 1987–1988:120-A). Others will enjoy hearing the *bala* and the words because it reminds them of past times and of other occasions for praise singing.

Because praise singing occurs most frequently during parties, celebrations, or other events that call for entertainment, a *jeli* carries a certain immunity from blame, and can therefore criticize and advise others, all in the guise of praise. When people mistreat their spouses, siblings, other family members, or friends, a *jeli* may offer advice about social behavior, as praise to someone else—and in so doing, he may draw a favorable or unfavorable comparison to others in a group. Through proverbs, truisms, and other references to social mores and shared stories or text envelopes, a *jeli* presents and reinforces shared ideals of behavior and personality. In praise songs, the portrayal of ideals and the references to behaviors serve to criticize and challenge others.

Another important aspect of praise singing is the receipt or acknowledgment of praise beyond simply giving something to a *jeli*. A gift may deflect or mediate the power in a specialist's words or music, but it does not do away with the fact that the *jeli* has directed praise toward an individual; and by accepting praise, a person takes on a debt. The *bolo gbili* praise songs are heavier with obligation than the *tulon bololu* because they are older and therefore contain more historical references. Praise within the *bolo gbili* repertory is dense with layers of associations and references to mythic and historical personalities and events. By virtue of membership in or affiliation with a particular patrilineage, an individual can accept praise, and can dance (figuratively and literally) to certain *bololu gbili*. Each major patrilineage has its own pattern, employed when praising those with an identical or affiliated surname. Thus, the *bolo gbili* repertory contains not only the Mansareh *bolo*, but also the Kondeh *bolo*, the Koroman *bolo*, the Kamara *bolo*, and so on. This repertory contains songs in praise of certain occupations, such as *Duwa* (for warriors), *Simba* (for hunters), and *Konkoba* (for farmers). By accepting the praise from one of the patterns (for instance, by dancing), a person takes on a mantle of attributes and expectations. In this way, he or she can gather strength and followers. Such praise may function to prepare and carry someone into battle or adversity; however, not everyone can accept the praise of certain *bololu gbili* or meet the power and obligation particular patterns carry with them.

The Song Duwa

The praise name and praise song *Duwa* praises warriors. It has accumulated layers of references to Sunjata—which may show it has been played a long time, as praise for Sunjata in his role of warrior. *Duwa* is a *bolo gbili*, specifically a *kèlèbolo* or "warrior pattern." It carries a mantle of power. It may have some relation to the most powerful of the men's secret associations in the area of West Africa under the influence of Manden. In performance, it becomes an agent, because people credit it with the ability to prepare a warrior for battle and supply him with strength, power, and followers. It carries a strong association with death, since it praises those who are such fierce warriors that the vultures (*duwa* or *duba*) will never go hungry in their path, and because the collected references to deadly conflicts are many.

Different warriors have different strengths: some are bigger and stronger than others; some have prepared for battle, while others have not. A warrior

SUNJATA

Sunjata, also known as Keita Manden Sumaworo Maramagan Jata, is known as the grandfather of the Mansareh clan. Oral traditions credit him with founding the Mali Empire, and credit the Mansareh clan, through patronage (since the Mansareh belong to a lineage of landowners and leaders, not musicians) with the development of the *jeli*'s art, and with *bala* playing in particular.

The Sunjata text envelope includes accounts and references to Sunjata's background (including mythic origins), plus the battles that led to the formation of the Mali Empire. During the eleventh and twelfth centuries, the Mansareh clan unified several kingdoms of the Upper Niger, but clans continued to compete for power. The unified clans of Manden eventually rose against Sumanguru, a Susu ruler, who had consolidated an area west of Manden; under Sunjata's leadership, they defeated Sumanguru about the year 1235. Because of its ties to the origins of the Mali Empire and praise singing, many consider the Mansareh *bolo* the oldest *bala* pattern and the first praise song. When it is performed, the *bala* part is likely to contain a version of the recognizable melody from "*Nyin min nyama, nyama*" (figures 3 and 4). In translation, the text of figure 3 is

> That which is Nyama,
> All things are hidden under Nyama,
> Nyama is not hidden under anything.

DISC
1
TRACK
1

Figure 3 Excerpt from "*Nyin min nyama, nyama*," a famous song, which appears in many performances of the Sunjata epic.

Figure 4 Excerpt from the Mansareh *bolo*, with a version of the melody of "*Nyin min nyama, nyama*" included in the *bala* improvisation.
From a performance by Pa Sanasi Kuyateh (Harris 1987–1988:112-B).

34

who has prepared properly for battle is one who has caused his "heart to come forth," making his flesh impenetrable to bullets or arrows. Such a warrior is said to have bitten the *jala* tree in his anger at having been fired upon; the bite caused the bark and flesh of the tree to become bitter. The text of *Duwa* alludes to the differences between warriors, and to the tie between fierce warriors and the *jala*. A coward (*kèbajito*) can never accept the praise, or take on the weight of obligations and attributes a performance of *Duwa* carries, because he could not live up to cultural expectations about a true warrior.

Content

The *bolo gbili* repertory captures the past in characterizations of, or references to, historical characters. These songs allude to and, in a sense, reshape the personal attributes, deeds, exploits, and circumstances surrounding the origins and lives of heroes, leaders, and warriors of Manden. Individuals have inspired fear and admiration over the centuries because their individuality and unique leadership, or other real or attributed qualities, have set them apart. A *jeli*'s portrayal of cultural heroes or of other significant characters makes them larger than life. In addition, mythical elements, drawn from indigenous and Islamic beliefs, attach to them. Mythical and historical time collapses into a hero's own time. The hero is not just a human being, but a larger-than-life representation of cultural beliefs and ideals. This character, his deeds, and the circumstances surrounding his existence, become a motto for his lineage and the lineages aligned with him.

A *jeli*'s repertory reflects the impact of certain cultural characters and occupations. A Gambian (Mandinka) *jali*'s repertory, for example, can differ from that of a Sierra Leonean *jeli*. (*Jali* is the pronunciation for *jeli* in Gambia.) Sunjata holds central importance in the world made by Manden because of his role in the founding of the Mali Empire, his promotion of artistic specialization (notably his patronage of *jelilu*), and the origins of clans or lineage names traced to the text envelope surrounding him. The Maninka of Sierra Leone place such personages as Kondeh Buraima, Fakoli, Jirikaranani, and Almamy Samori in roles that are important to their heritage.

—*Adapted from an article by Laura Arntson*

Bibliography

Bird, Charles S. 1971. "Oral Art in the Mande." In *Papers on the Manding*, edited by Carleton Hodge, 15–25. Bloomington: Indiana University Press.

——. 1976. "Poetry in the Mande: Its Form and Meaning." *Poetics* 5:89–100.

Harris, Laura A[rntson]. 1987–1988. Field tapes recorded in Sukurala, Northern Sierra Leone. Deposited at the Archives of Traditional Music, Indiana University, Bloomington, Indiana.

——. 1992. "The Play of Ambiguity in Praise-Song Performance: A Definition of the Genre through an Examination of its Practice in Northern Sierra Leone." Ph.D. dissertation, Indiana University, Bloomington, Indiana.

Johnson. John W. 1986. *The Epic of Son-Jara: A West African Tradition*. Bloomington: Indiana University Press.

Knight, Roderic. 1984a. "Music in Africa: The Manding Contexts." In *Performance Practice: Ethnomusicological Perspectives*, edited by Gerard Béhague, 53–90. Westport, Conn.: Greenwood Press.

——. 1984b. "The Style of Mandinka Music: A Study Extracting Theory from Practice." In *Studies in African Music*, edited by J. H. Kwabena Nketia and Jacqueline Cogdell DjeDje, 2–66. Los Angeles: Program in Ethnomusicology, University of California at Los Angeles.

North Africa

The music of North Africa—played by Arabs, Berbers, and black Africans—combines elements from the Middle East with those from sub-Saharan cultures. Blends of northern and southern musical practice are common throughout this region. To give readers a sense of North African music, we present an introductory article and one on the music of the Tuareg.

Jima (Ajo) wult Emini plays an *anzad*, Niger, 1978.
Photo by Caroline Card Wendt.

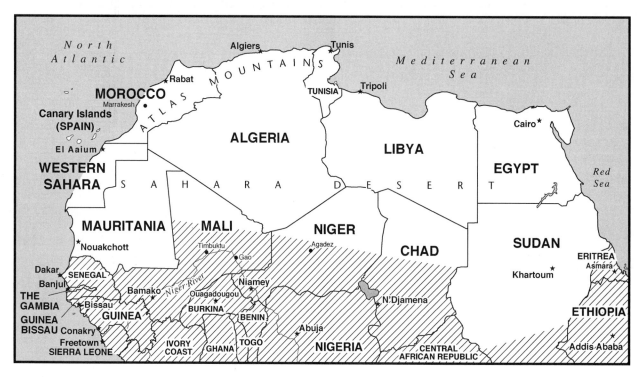

North Africa

North Africa: An Introduction

North Africa extends eastward from the Atlantic coast to encompass the Mediterranean nations of Morocco, Algeria, Tunisia, and Libya, known as the Maghrib, to the western desert of Egypt. The region reaches southward into the Sahara to include Mauritania and northern sections of Mali, Niger, Chad, and the Sudan. The Atlas Mountains, which extend from Morocco to Tunisia, divide a narrow stretch of fertile and densely populated agricultural land along the Mediterranean coast from the sparsely populated, arid expanses of the Sahara. Major elements unifying the peoples of this region are the religion of Islam and the Arabic language—the official language of each country except Mali and Niger. All the countries were formerly subject to one or another of the European powers, which in varying degrees influenced their present economies, educational systems, and development. Because political boundaries are often inconsistent with ethnic distributions, some peoples (such as the Tuareg) divide into several different nationalities.

The People

The population consists principally of Caucasoid Arabs and Berbers, and of black Africans, known in the Maghrib as Gnawa. The Arabs are descendants of Muslim invaders from the Arabian Peninsula and of native Berber inhabitants long assimilated into their society and culture. The Berbers, whose ancestors may be the earliest inhabitants of Mediterranean North Africa, comprise numerous groups who speak related dialects of a Hamito-Semitic language and exhibit similar cultural traits. The largest Berber populations live in Morocco and Algeria. The black Africans are descendants of indigenous Saharans and immigrants from the broad intermediate zone at the southern edge of the Sahara, known as the Sahel or the Sudan. Though black Africans are a minority in the Maghrib, they form a noticeable portion of the population of Mauritania and the Saharan areas of the other countries. The musical traditions of the Arabs, Berbers, and black Africans, though not untouched by acculturation, stem from different cultural heritages, which merit separate consideration. Of relevance, also, are patterns of nomadic, village, and urban ways of living that often cut across ethnic and areal categories. As the Arab musical traditions of the Maghrib are the focus of NORTH AFRICA of the Middle East section in volume 2, the focus here is on the musical traditions of the Berbers and black Africans.

Culture History

Berber tribes dwelled on the coast until Phoenician traders arrived, about 1200 B.C.E. Together, the Phoenicians and Berbers built Carthage and a civilization that spread across western North Africa and the Mediterranean, from Sicily to Spain. In 202 B.C.E., a Roman army took Carthage. By C.E. 40, Rome controlled an area from the Atlantic coast to present-day eastern Libya. About six hundred years of Roman rule ended with the invasion of Vandals from Scandinavia, soon followed by Christian Byzantines. In 688, at the time of the first Muslim Arab invasion, North Africa was widely, though superficially, Christian. Within a century, the Arabs were masters of all Mediterranean North Africa and Spain, and though their empire eventually receded, most of the lands and peoples they subjugated were irreversibly changed, in language, religion, and culture. Subsequent European conquests hardly affected Arabic cultural patterns.

The character that distinguishes North Africa from the Arabic-speaking Muslim Near East arises in large measure from its Berber subculture. Urban Berbers were receptive to the culture of their conquerors, but rural and nomadic Berbers were much less so. Withdrawing into mountain villages or retreating deep into the desert, they remained resistant and hostile to foreign intrusion. As a result, Berber language, culture, and tribal patterns have persisted in the Moroccan Atlas, in the Algerian high plateaus, in desert towns in Mauritania and Libya, and in oasis communities and nomadic encampments across the Sahara. In remote areas, Islam and the accompanying Arab traditions penetrated slowly, forming a veneer of Muslim culture over local customs and beliefs. In the Ahaggar area of the Sahara in southern Algeria, long an impenetrable mountain stronghold of warrior Berber Tuareg tribes, Muslim religion and culture had little effect until after the mid-1800s.

Gradually, the Arab culture of the Maghrib filtered southward to give the Sahara an Islamic character. Over centuries, the trans-Saharan trade routes, mainly under control of the Berber Tuareg, carried Mediterranean arts and technology southward. The northern Berbers introduced methods of irrigation, fertilization, and animal husbandry that enabled Sahelian cultivators to grow crops farther north into the arid zone. In varying degrees, many Sahelian cultivators were incorporated into Tuareg society and culture, and elements of sub-Saharan music became part of Tuareg traditions.

In cultivation centers throughout the Sahara, rhythms, vocal styles, and dances of sub-Saharan origin predominate. In the Maghrib, black Muslim brotherhoods perform Sahelian-style music for exorcisms, curing rituals, and Muslim celebrations and festivals. Blends of northern and southern musical practices are clear too in the Mauritanian bardic tradition, which combines modal structures akin to Arab music with rhythmic patterns related to those of West Africa; musicians refer to the varying styles as "white and black ways." Since the 1960s, recurring drought, increasing population, and political strife have prompted migrations in many directions: herders drive their animals farther in search of water and pasture, and pastoralists and cultivators abandon rural areas for employment in towns and cities. The musical result of these migrations is the rapid evolution of new genres from older and borrowed sources. For source material and inspiration, composers of urban music have turned increasingly to rural repertories and foreign music. Radio broadcasts and cassette recordings convey a wide range of musical styles to the remotest areas.

The musics of the region do not form ready categories. As modern composers and arrangers adapt old traditions to new situations, the distinctions among classical, folk, and popular genres often become blurred. Broadcast media have spread repertories once specific to particular villages or areas. Conversely, urban styles and instrumentation, with their special appeal to youth, increasingly influence the performance of traditional musics in rural communities. Distinctions between religious and secular genres are equally unclear, for the texts of many songs sung for secular purposes have religious content or sentiment, and some religious music collectively performed exhibits folk-genre traits. Some genres performed exclusively by traditional specialists at folklife celebrations straddle the categories of folk and professional, and of religious and secular. Musical styles, subject-matter, and performance practices continually interplay with the social contexts and histories that underlie and inform the musical cultures.

Music and Islam

The Muslim call to prayer (*adhan*), intoned five times daily, is a familiar sound in local towns and cities. Its style varies according to local tradition and the personal style of the muezzin (*mu'adhdhin* 'caller'). Calls range from stylized recitation on one or two tones to highly melismatic renditions, based on specific melodic formulas (*maqamat*) of the Middle Eastern Arab tradition. Familiar too are the sounds of children intoning memorized verses from the Koran at neighborhood mosques and religious schools. Children receive rewards for precise and artful recitation, which may follow, depending on local custom, any of several established methods of Qur'ānic chanting. Calls to prayer and scriptural recitations are performed in Arabic, the language of the Qur'ān. Whether simply spoken or elaborately sung, they emphasize clarity of pronunciation and strict adherance to the grammatical rules of Arabic. Devout Muslims deny that these chants are music.

Music occupies an ambiguous position in Muslim life. Since the beginning of Islam, Muslim authorities have disputed whether music should be permitted in worship. Because music, especially instrumental music, was associated with pagan practices and sensual entertainments, early authorities declared the act of listening to music "unworthy" of a Muslim. The debate continues. To avoid secular associations, references to music are usually avoided in connection with calls to prayer, Qur'ānic recitations, and other forms of religious expression. Some communities discourage making music of any kind, religious or secular; a few forbid music altogether, as do members of the Mozabite sect of Algeria. Nevertheless, the sung praise of Allah and the Prophet Muhammad is standard practice in most of the region.

The annual departure and return of pilgrims to Mecca (*hajj*), a journey every Muslim tries to make at least once, are occasions for singing religious songs. Muhammad's birthday (Mawlid) is celebrated with hymns of praise and epic songs depicting events in his life. The best known of these is *el-burda* 'the Prophet's mantle'. Religious music is mainly vocal, but instruments are used in certain contexts, as in the ceremonial Thursday evening proclamations of the holy day in Morocco, with trumpet (*nfir*) or oboe (*ghaita*) accompaniment. In the holy month of Ramadan, during which the faithful fast in the daylight hours, families sing religious songs as they gather for the evening and predawn meals. Ramadan songs may occur in street processions. Pairs of oboes or trumpets, in ensemble with drums, such as the double-headed cylindrical types (*gangatan*; sing.

ganga) played in Niger, herald the beginning and end of Ramadan.

Pre-Islamic beliefs and unorthodox practices of Sufi mystics have mingled with canonic precepts to produce a unique form of Islam, in which the veneration of saints (*marabutin*; sing, *marabut*) is a feature. The concept of saints as mediators between divinity and humanity and as sources of good health and fortune, became a feature of Islamic worship in western North Africa after about the year 1200. Religious brotherhoods (sing, *zawiya*) arose around legendary holy figures, often revered as patron saints or village founders. The activities of the brotherhoods center on small mosques, which enclose the saints' tombs. Some of these structures contain facilities for lodging and teaching. Each year, thousands of worshipers make pilgrimages to the tombs of locally revered saints.

Hymns are regularly sung at the tombs. In Tunisia, canticles of praise are performed to the accompaniment of *mizwid* (bagpipe) and *bendir* (single-headed frame drum). In the Atlas Mountains of Morocco, Friday, the holy day, is celebrated weekly at the tomb with a procession of oboes and drums. The musicians, by virtue of their close identification with the saint, are believed to possess some of the holy man's spiritual power (*baraka*), enabling them to aid the sick and offer protection to the community.

Featured in the rituals of the religious brotherhoods are songs and recitations of Sufi origin, known collectively as *zikr* (or *dhikr*), meaning "in recollection" of Allah. Though *zikr* are usually sung in Arabic, vernaculars are occasionally used, as by the Berber Tuareg. Some practices include the repetition of raspy, gutteral utterances on the syllable *he*. As these increase in intensity, they may lead participants into states of trance.

On Muhammad's birthday or other occasions deemed appropriate, *zikr* may be part of a larger ceremony known as *hadra*, a term meaning 'in the presence of', with allusion to the supernatural. Though the *hadra* takes many forms, it typically includes special songs and rhythms, rigorous dancing, and altered states of consciousness. In trance, a participant may become possessed or may express emotional fervor with acts demonstrating extraordinary strength or oblivion to pain. In other instances, participants seek exorcism of unwanted spirits believed to be the cause of illness or misfortune. In Libya, where the *hadra* is a curing ceremony, a ritual specialist performs exorcisms to an accompaniment of songs and drums—a procedure that, if the illness is severe, may be repeated for seven days or more. In Morocco, professional musicians play music for the *hadra* on the *ghaita* (oboe) and the *tbel* (kettledrum). In Algeria, use of melodic instruments is rare. In the *hadra*, Islamic concepts of spirits (*jinn*), as described in the Qur'ān, merge with pre-Islamic beliefs and practices.

The Gnawa brotherhoods specialize in the manipulation of spirits, and are much in demand for exorcisms, curing rites, circumcision ceremonies, and purification rituals after funerals. Their ceremonies appear to consist mainly of a blend of Islamic and pre-Islamic black African beliefs and practices. Prominent is their use of the *qarqabu* (or *qarqaba*), an instrument, likely of Sudanic origin, that is played in Hausa communities in much of North Africa. It consists of two pairs of iron castanets joined by a connecting bar; the player uses two of these instruments, one in each hand. The Gnawa also play a *gumbri*, a three-stringed plucked lute, known by different names to black musicians throughout North and West Africa. The possession and curing ceremonies of the Gnawa, in particular, resemble those of Sudanic practice, though cultural elements from other sources may be present. At annual celebrations of the Tunisian Gnawa in honor of their patron saint, Sidi Marzuk, the ritual texts are sung in a language (*Ajmi*) apparently neither of Arabic nor Berber derivation and unknown to the present participants.

The Tuareg of Niger conduct curing ceremonies (*tende n-guma*), in which men's raspy, guttural sounds, uttered on the syllable *he*, mingle with women's songs and the rhythms of a mortar drum (*tende*) and handclapping. The men's vocal sounds are similar to those heard in *zikr* performances, to which they may be related. Sudanese Sufi orders practice an African form of *zikr*, in which repetitions of certain syllables, including the breathy *he*, appear to have replaced most of the original texts. The Tuareg deny, however, that the curing ceremonies are religious. Secular songs are sung, though always in duple meter and in slower than normal tempo to accommodate the swaying movements of entranced patients—a behavioral feature also of Sudanese *zikr*. Though local Muslim leaders denounce the rituals as pagan and contrary to the teachings of Islam, the Tuareg view them as psychotherapeutic, and exhibit no conflict between their concepts of a spirit-filled world and their Islamic faith. If these rituals once had religious associations, they are unknown.

Music in Folklife

Religious festivals, national holidays, and lifecycle celebrations are major occasions for making folk music. The Muslim holidays, local saints' festivals, and political or national holidays are the most important annual events; weddings and circumcisions are the most celebrated lifecycle moments.

Annual Events

Muslim festivals follow a lunar calendar, containing about 354 days. Because the annual cycle is shorter than that of the 365-day year, the religious holidays rotate through the seasons, arriving about eleven days earlier each year. The religious observances normally contain no music, but the accompanying festivities are occasions for music and dance. On ʿAid el-Fitr (Id al-Fitr), the festival marking the end of Ramadan, the townspeople of Agadez, Niger, gather in the courtyard of the Sultan's palace to hear the ceremonial oboes and kettledrums played by the court musicians. When this ceremony is over, the musicians, mounted on horseback, lead the Sultan's parade through the streets, playing the oboes and large cylindrical drums suspended from their shoulders. On the tenth day of the twelfth month occurs the feast of ʿAid el-Adha (also known as ʿAid-el-Kbir and Tafaski), which commemorates Abraham's sacrifice of a sheep in place of his son. This holiday provides an occasion for Algerian Tuareg women to gather around a mortar drum to sing from a repertory of festival songs. The community crowds around them, emitting shouts and shrill cries of approval while clapping rhythms in synchrony or in hemiolic contrast with those of the drum. On Mawlid (the twelfth day of the third month), townspeople in Libya have musical gatherings and fireworks after the religious observances.

Saints' festivals (*moussem* or *ziara*, sing.) are often linked to dates in the Muslim lunar calendar. The tomb of Mouley Abdallah is located in the desert, near the village of Abalessa in southern Algeria; an annual pilgrimage is made to it fifteen days after ʿAid el-Fitr. In the Moroccan Rif, the Aith Waryaghar make an annual pilgrimage to the tomb of Sidi Bu Khiyar on the day before ʿAid-el Adha. Such events, which often draw thousands of people, typically last two days. In hope of obtaining personal good health and fortune through exposure to the spiritual power of the saint and the precincts of his tomb, people say prayers and perform rituals. Social reunions, feasting, and music follow the ritual observances.

Many saints' festivals follow a seasonal schedule, occurring regularly during the summer months. Some of them have an economic role. The *moussem* of Imilchil in central Morocco, held annually at the autumnal equinox, attracts thousands of pilgrims to the tomb of Sidi Mohamed el-Merheni. After devotions, the participants turn to bartering goods and animals, performing music, dancing, and carrying on courtships. Tazzʾunt, a Berber festival in the Moroccan High Atlas, occurs on 31 July, in accordance with the Julian calendar (12 August by the Gregorian). Though the functions of this festival resemble those of a *moussem*, the event is limited to the inhabitants of neighboring villages who share bonds of lineage. The rituals performed are for the collective well-being of the community, rather than for individuals.

Political or patriotic celebrations follow a solar calendar. Each country in the region commemorates its independence and important historical moments with annual holidays featuring military parades and the singing of patriotic songs. Public presentations of local music and dance that highlight the nation's ethnic heritage often have a part.

Lifecycle Celebrations

Weddings normally occur during favorable periods in agricultural or pastoral cycles, which govern the people's lives. In the Moroccan Atlas, Berber weddings usually occur during the festival season in late summer, after the first harvest. The pastoral Tuareg of Niger customarily hold weddings after summer rains, when they assemble their camels on the plains near In-Gall (west of Agadez)—an event known in French as the *cure salée*.

The sequence of rituals constituting a traditional Muslim wedding gives rise to several kinds of music, some of it performed or led by professionals. Special wedding songs are sung by women to the bride and by men to the groom, seeking blessings on the union and instructing each in the duties of marriage. Ritual verses are sung during the ceremonial application of henna to the bride's and groom's hands and feet. Professional praise singers extol the virtues of the couple and comment on the guests' generosity. Musicians with tambourines, oboes or flutes, and drums—the sizes and shapes varying with local custom—lead the bride and groom in processions. Separate musical entertainments are provided for male and female guests. A professional bard may sing traditional poetry to the men on religious, heroic, or romantic themes, while female specialists lead the

hemiola Two notes of equal value in the time occupied by three metrical pulses, or three notes of equal value in the time occupied by two metrical pulses.

For the feast of ʿAid el-Adha, the women drum in duple meter with alternating duple and ternary subdivisions. The men occasionally clap in ternary meter—three claps spanning two measures of the women's duple meter—thereby producing, at times, two or more layers of hemiolic rhythm.

women in lively songs and dances to their accompaniment of handheld drums or tambourines.

Circumcision is regarded as a young boy's first step toward manhood. As a rite of passage, it is a sacred and festive occasion. Though the preferred age is four or five or younger, the event is often postponed because of the cost of the ceremony and its attendant feast. To minimize expenses, several families with boys of an appropriate age may collaborate in a collective ceremony, or a family may choose to perform the rituals as part of an annual festival. In Algerian tradition, the event consists of several stages: a ceremonial haircut (*tahfifa*), attended by men only; a ritual application of henna and the bestowal of gifts, attended by women only; a ceremonial feast for relatives and guests; and finally, the surgical operation. During the henna ritual, the women sing the child's praises, and exhort the nervous mother to be joyous and proud. Their songs and activities are interspersed with shrill ululations of approval. The henna ceremony concludes with singing, which may last for hours, of songs dedicated to Muhammad. Moroccan village custom contains similar elements, but in a different order. The surgery, which precedes the feast, is announced with intermittent volleys of gunfire. During the operation, men recite prayers and women sing special ritual songs, similar to those sung for marriage, but with other texts. Ceremonies for circumcision may include the services of Gnawa musicians, who perform special ritual songs and dances of mystical or magical significance.

Musical Specialists

The professional singer-poets, ritual specialists, praise singers, and instrumentalists who perform at festivals and family celebrations are commonly members of hereditary musician clans or artisanal castes who specialize in particular traditions. Gifted singer-poets were formerly attached to the courts of tribal chiefs or other persons of power and wealth. Their heroic ballads and songs of praise enhanced their patrons' status and imbued the surrounding community with a sense of shared history and identity. Though the patronage system has almost disappeared, the traditions and functions of praise and epic singing are perpetuated by musicians who perform at weddings, religious festivals, and private parties.

In Mauritania, professional, hereditary poet-musicians (*griots*) sing panegyric poetry to the accompaniment of an elongated four-stringed lute (*tidinit*), played by men, and a harp-lute (*ardin*), played by women. In addition, a large, hand-struck kettledrum (*tbel*), played by women, is occasionally used. The tradition is sometimes termed *classical*, as it demands not only instrumental virtuosity and a command of classical Arabic and Moorish poetry, but also mastery of an elaborate and complex body of theory. In Mali, Niger, and southern Algeria, Tuareg *griots* of the artisanal caste practice a related tradition. Known to the Tuareg as *aggutan* (figure 1), they typically entertain at weddings, celebrations for births, and small, private parties. Their repertory similarly consists of heroic legends and praise poetry, sung to the accompaniment of a *tahardent*, a three-stringed lute similar to the Mauritanian *tidinit*. Their tradition embraces a system of rhythms and modes, serving as the material for improvisation, and a set of rules (though less explicit than the Mauritanian) that govern composition and performance. In the late 1960s, the *tahardent* tradition of the Malian Tuareg

Figure 1 Hattaye ag Muhammed Ahmed, an *aggu*, plays a *tahardent* in Agadez, Niger, 1978. Typically musicians use the right hand to pluck the instrument and the left hand to finger it.
Photo by Caroline Card Wendt.

began to spread to urban centers throughout the Sahara as musicians driven by drought migrated to new locations.

During the festival months of late summer, the professional musicians (*imdyazn*) of the eastern parts of Morocco travel in small bands through the villages of the High Atlas. A typical ensemble consists of a singer-poet and several accompanists, whose instruments include a double clarinet (*zammar*) or a flute (*talawat*), one or two frame drums (sing., *daf*), and an alto fiddle (*lkmnza*), similar to a European viola. The *rways*, itinerant musicians of southern Morocco, wander throughout the country performing an acculturated music derived from Arab-Andalusian, European, Arab-popular, and West African styles; they often perform at Djemma el Fna, the grand square in the heart of Marrakesh, which for centuries has been a center for traditional musical entertainments.

For sedentary performers, music is often a part-time activity, supplemented by some other line of work, and payment for services is frequently in gifts, rather than in money. In this category are the women who as ritual specialists perform at weddings, births, and circumcisions; some of them are professional mourners and singers of funeral laments. In Morocco, female entertainers (*haddarat*) accompany their songs with *bendir* (a single-headed frame drum), *tbel* (a kettledrum), and the clay cylindrical drum *ta'riya*. In Algeria, urban female professionals (*msam'at*) accompany their songs and dances with *derbuka*, a single-headed goblet-shaped drum, and *tar*, a handheld frame drum with attached cymbals. Tuareg singers, traditionally members of artisanal clans, employ small, double-headed, handheld drums (*gangatan*; sing, *ganga*) or a kettledrum (in Algeria, *tegennewt*, in Niger, *tazawai*).

Poetry and Song

Vocal music, except when used for dancing, functions primarily as a vehicle for poetry, a highly developed and esteemed art in North Africa. The singer-poet, usually male, draws material from a traditional repertory, setting it to one of several musical meters that correspond with the rhythm of the text. Frequent topics are love (always in allusive or idealized form) and recent or historical events. Topics pertaining to valor in battle, actual or allegorical, form an important part of *tesîwit*, a solo repertory sung by pastoral Tuareg men. The texts are interspersed with praises and evocations of Allah, or exclamations such as "O my soul!" or "O my mother!" [see TUAREG MUSIC]. Both men and women sing; those much in demand can set to a familiar melody a spontaneously com-

posed, rhyming text concerning persons and events of immediate local interest. These songs can serve a journalistic function. Songs for ritual purposes vary little in melody or text from one performance to the next. In this category are the Berber *urar* (also *ural*) verses, sung usually by women at weddings and at circumcision ceremonies.

Songs for dancing belong to a separate category. Instruments, infrequently used with other vocal genres, hold an important role in dance music. They typically include the *bendir* drum, the *tabl*, and the *ghaita*. The texts, of secondary importance, usually consist of formulaic verses, often with ostinato or vocable responses.

The characteristics of songs vary by territory, ethnic group, genre, and occasion. Melodies range from little-ornamented, repetitive forms, to complex and highly melismatic structures. Much of the local character derives from the rhythms, which adhere closely to the meters of local poetry. The repertories of village and nomadic Berbers are possibly the least acculturated of local traditions. Pentatonicism of various types is common, and melodic use of an augmented fourth above the tonic is often prominent. Microtonicism in melodic structure and ornamentation occurs in Berber song, but is more characteristic of Arab styles. The songs of the Gnawa, like those of black cultivators in the Sahara, make occasional use of thirds and fourths, intervals rarely heard in Arab or Berber music. The vocal styles and repertories characteristic of sedentary and nomadic groups often cut across ethnic and areal divisions. Agricultural and other types of worksongs are prominent among sedentarists, but songs for caravans and ballads about warriors are characteristic of nomads. Within the same group, the vocal styles of men often differ from those of women.

Instrumental Music

Instrumental music, played primarily for listening, is uncommon in the folklife of towns and villages. Instruments serve mainly for dances and ceremonial purposes, such as wedding processions and the proclamation of a holy day or the onset of Ramadan. Instrumental improvisations serve as interludes between verses sung by professional bards, but they rarely occur apart from vocal contexts. It is principally in the traditions of pastoral groups that purely instrumental music has a prominent place.

Music for solo flute is common among herdsmen and others in lonely occupations. An end-blown flute, held in oblique position, with fingerholes arranged in two sets, is played by Arab shepherds in the Maghrib and Mauritania, and by Tuareg herders in Algeria and Niger. The Arab *gasba* (or *qasaba*), made of a hollow reed, has five or more fingerholes; the four-hole *zaowzaya* of Mauritania is made from an acacia root or bark; the four-hole Tuareg *tazammart* is made from a reed or a metal tube. *Tazammart* players in the Algerian Sahara sometimes accompany their melodies with a vocal drone produced in the throat while blowing into and fingering the instrument; the drone functions as a pedal point to the melody. Flute music, though traditionally played for solitary pleasure or the entertainment of a few companions, is now heard by a wider audience through recordings and radio broadcasts of accomplished performers.

Local traditions often bear the imprint of a celebrated performer, whose personal style is much emulated. In the late twentieth century, such influence intensified, resulting in a trend toward stylistic homogeneity, constrained only by the strength of local traditions. The rise of recordings has reduced the number of persons engaged in live performance.

Dance

The most widely known Berber dances of Morocco are the *ahidus* (also *haidous*) of the middle and eastern High Atlas, and the *ahwash* of the western High Atlas. Dancers stand shoulder to shoulder in a circle or in two incurved, facing lines; musicians, who both accompany and direct the dances, stand in the center. Musicians for the *ahidus* include a singer-poet (*ammessad*), one or more assisting singers, and drummers with instruments of diverse sizes and pitches. The rhythms, which include solo improvisa-tions, are frequently in quintuple meter. The songs (*izlan*, sing., *izli*) contain short verses with choral responses, sung to melodies composed of small intervals within a narrow range. The structure of the *ahwash* is more complex. The drumming begins slowly, in duple or quadruple meter, but is transformed at midpoint into a rapid, asymmetric rhythm. The songs, sung to pentatonic melodies, consist of two-line verses, exchanged between the men and women. The *ahwash*, involving an entire village, is a highlight of festivals. Care is lavished on a performance, for its quality is said to determine the success or failure of the festival. Another Moroccan Berber dance is the *tamghra*, specific to weddings. To a men's accompaniment of *bendir*, it is performed for or by the bride and her attendants. The rhythms are similar to those of *ahidus*, but include no solo improvisations.

Movements emulating the gestures of battle are a part of many local dances. Popular among North African Arabs is the gun dance (*baroud*, also *berzana*). In its Algerian form, male dancers armed with loaded muskets arrange themselves in a circle or facing lines. The dancers turn shoulder against shoulder, taking small steps in response to the melody of the *ghaita* and rhythms of the *qallal* or *dendun*. Alternating vocal soloists chant invocations of Muhammad in the form of brief couplets with choral responses. On cue, the participants point their muskets to the earth and fire in synchrony, bringing the dance to a smoky, noisy climax. Other battle dances are performed with swords and sticks: in Tunisia, pairs of men perform the saber dance

Figure 2 Preparation for a Tuareg *ilugan* at a festival in the Ahaggar region of Algeria, 1972.
Photo by Caroline Card Wendt.

(*zagara*); in the Algerian Sahara, men perform a similar stick dance (*'lawi*). In southeastern Algeria, the costumed inhabitants of an entire town, representing two separate lineages, engage annually in a choreographed battle spectacle (*sebiba*): the musicians and dance leaders are women, who sing and play small drums struck with curved beaters.

Dance in North Africa is not limited to human beings. The Arab fantasy (*fantaziya*) of the Maghrib is a choreographed spectacle involving horses and men. To an accompaniment of drums, mounted riders armed with swords maneuver and race their horses. The maneuvers culminate in elaborate displays of horsemanship and swordplay. The *fantaziya* symbolically reenacts battles waged by the warriors who established Islam in North Africa. A similar spectacle is the Berber Tuareg *ilugan* (*ilujan*), sometimes called a "camel fantasy" (figure 2). To the accompaniment of women's *tende* singing and drumming, the camels, under their riders' direction, perform a series of stylized movements. The rhythms of the women's songs, usually in duple meter with ternary subdivisions, are said to imitate the gait of the camels. The warrior elements, infused with Tuareg concepts of gallantry, often lead to flirtatious exchanges between the men and the women.

Popular Music

In the late 1960s, *tahardent* music of the Malian Tuareg began to move eastward with the migration of drought refugees into Niger. Among the migrants were artisanal specialists (*aggutan*) whose former patrons could no longer support them. Finding little success in singing Tuareg legends of Mali to mixed urban audiences in Niger, they turned their talents to more marketable material. Most successful was the setting of new strophic texts with romantic and risqué themes to *takumba*, an existing rhythmic-modal formula of Malian origin. Many *aggutan* augmented their opportunities by learning to sing in local languages. The instrumental interludes between strophes—a traditional practice—provided displays

of virtuosity that attracted urban audiences. Astute performers emphasized stylistic elements common to several related traditions, making their music more accessible to audiences of diverse ethnic backgrounds. Itinerant musicians carried the music across Niger into southern Algeria. Though verses of heroism and praise continue to be sung for those who request them, *takumba* and its stylistic successors are the mainstay of modern Tuareg professionals.

—*Adapted from an article by Caroline Card Wendt*

Bibliography

Anderson, Lois Ann. 1971. "The Interrelation of African and Arab Musics: Some Preliminary Considerations." In *Essays in Music and History in Africa*, edited by Klaus P. Wachsmann, 143–169. Evanston, Ill.: Northwestern University Press.

Card, Caroline. 1982. "Tuareg Music and Social Identity." Ph.D. dissertation, Indiana University.

Danielson, Virginia. 1988. "The Arab Middle East." In *Popular Musics of the Non-Western World*, edited by Peter Manuel, 141–160. New York: Oxford University Press.

Murdock, George Peter. 1959. *Africa: Its People and Their Culture History*. New York: McGraw-Hill.

Nicolaisen, Johannes. 1963. *Ecology and Culture of the Pastoral Tuareg*. Copenhagen: National Museum.

Nikiprowetzky, Tolia. 1961. *La musique de la Mauritanie*. Paris: Radiodiffusion Outre-Mer Sorafom.

Pacholczyk, Jozef M. 1980. "Secular Classical Music in the Arabic Near East." In *Music of Many Cultures*, edited by Elizabeth May, 253–268. Berkeley: University of California Press.

Rouget, Gilbert. 1985. *Music and Trance: A Theory of the Relations between Music and Possession*. Chicago: University of Chicago Press.

Schuyler, Philip. 1983. "The Master Musicians of Jahjouka." *Natural History*, October, 60–69.

———. 1984. "Moroccan Andalusian Music." In *Maqam: Music of the Islamic World and its Influences*, edited by Robert H. Browning, 14–17. New York: Alternative Museum.

Trimingham, John Spencer. 1965. *Islam in the Sudan*. London: Frank Cass.

Wendt, Caroline Card. 1994. "Regional Style in Tuareg *Anzad* Music." In *To the Four Corners*, edited by Ellen Leichtman. Warren, Michigan: Harmonie Park Press.

Tuareg Music

For more than a thousand years, Saharan travelers have reported encounters with the Tuareg people. From the pens of Arab and European explorers come tales of tall, veiled, camel-riding warriors, who once commanded the trade routes from the Mediterranean to sub-Saharan Africa. Most of the reports dwell on the warriors' appearance and ferocity, but observers who looked more closely noted distinctive cultural traits, such as matrilineal kinship and high status among unveiled women, rarities in the Muslim world. As Saharan travel became easier, observers from many backgrounds—missionaries, militaries, colonial administrators, traders, scholars, tourists—ventured among the Tuareg and reported their findings. The result is a large, varied, and often contradictory, body of literature.

The name *Tuareg*, a term outsiders conferred on the people, suggests a sociopolitical unity that has probably never existed. The people constitute eight large units or confederations, each composed of peoples and tribal groups with varying degrees of autonomy. These groups and their locations are: Kel Ahaggar (Ahaggar mountains and surrounding area in southern Algeria, southward to the plains of Tamesna in northern Niger); Kel Ajjer (Tassili n-Ajjer area of southeastern Algeria, eastward into southwestern Libya); Kel Aïr (Aïr mountains of northern Niger, and plains to the west and south); Kel Geres (southern Niger, south of Aïr); Kel Adrar (Adrar n-Foras mountains of Mali, southwest of Ahaggar); Iwllimmedan Kel Dennek, "eastern Iwllimmedan" (plains between Tawa and In-Gal in western Niger); Iwllimmedan Kel Ataram, "western Iwllimmedan" (along the Niger River, southwestern Niger); and Kel Tademaket (along the bend of the Niger River, between Timbuktu and Gao, Mali). The word *Kel* denotes sovereign status.

Tuareg musical traditions and other cultural traits vary by locale. The dialects of the Berber language spoken by the Tuareg—*tamabaq* (north), *tamajag* (south), *tamashaq* (west)—are so different as to be mutually unintelligible to many speakers.

Countering the cultural diversity is the cohesion generated by a set of ancient ideals and values flowing from the nomadic traditions that form the society's cultural core. The heroic images reach outward from their source, endowing on all within their sphere a shared identity and the legacy of a glorious past. The perseverance of the Tuareg as a people has been due less, perhaps, to the prowess of its warriors than to the ability of the dominant groups to impose their culture on others. Thus, Tuareg identity endures, only slightly diminished by the cessation of warfare and raiding, economic hardship, and loss of sovereignty. Ancient values, expressed in modified forms, continue to give Tuareg culture its character.

Musical Culture

Music occupies a prominent position in Tuareg social, political, and ceremonial life. It plays an important role in celebrations of birth, adulthood, and marriage, and in religious festivals, customs of courtship, and curing rituals. It is the focus of many informal social gatherings. Tuareg music and poetry are well-developed arts. The Tuareg highly esteem the verbal arts, of which they consider music an extension, and they recognize and respect outstanding composers and performers. They look down on professionalism, in the sense of a livelihood earned from musical performance, which is limited to specialized members within the artisanal caste; they do, however, recognize musical ability wherever it emerges, and they admire skillful musicians of all social ranks.

Most Tuareg music is vocal; but much includes instruments, primarily a one-stringed fiddle (*anzad*), a mortar drum (*tende*), and a three-stringed plucked lute (*tahardent*). Though few in kind and number, these instruments have greater cultural significance than their quantity might suggest, for each has an association with specific poetic genres and styles of performance, and each serves as the focal point of particular social events.

The *Anzad*

The one-stringed fiddle (*imzad* in northern dialect, *anzad* in southern, *anzhad* in western), played only by women, is basic to the traditional culture (figure 1). Its use has declined markedly since about 1900, but it continues to enjoy a symbolic place in the culture. The Tuareg have long believed it a mighty force for good, a power capable of giving strength to men and of inspiring them to heroic deeds. Its playing formerly encouraged men in battle and ensured their safe return; today, women play it, though much less

Figure 1 Bouchet, a Tuareg noblewomen, plays an *anzad*, Tamanrasset, Algeria, 1972.
Photo by Caroline Card Wendt.

often, for the benefit of men working or studying in distant places. For all Tuareg listeners, its music evokes images of love and beauty.

Much of its power was in reality the power of the women who played it. Tuareg society required repeated recognition of heroic acts and constant revalidation of the behavioral ideals that motivated them; the women's melodies and accompanying songs of praise were a potent force toward that end. In 1864, warriors in combat strove always to act courageously, lest their women deprive them of music: the prospect of silent fiddles on their return renewed their courage in the face of defeat (Duvéyrier 1864:450).

To play the *anzad* well requires years of practice. The Tuareg say a woman cannot acquire the necessary skill under the age of about thirty. Formerly, a mature woman of talent and imagination could command respect, and if she combined these endowments with noble lineage, she would enjoy high status. Tuareg women of all social levels have been known to play the instrument, but it was mainly those of the camel-herding warrior aristocracy with slaves to attend them who had the leisure to learn to

play the instrument well. In the early 1900s, during the economic decline that followed defeat by the French and the abolition of slavery, most women of noble lineage lost this advantage over their lower-born sisters; and consequently, the number of highly accomplished fiddlers diminished. The end of warfare as a noble occupation probably reduced some of the incentive to play, for the Tuareg look upon most types of modern work as degrading and little worthy of celebration in music and poetry.

In addition to its significance in the ethos of warfare, the *anzad* symbolizes youthfulness and romantic love. Musical evenings with it usually continue to function as occasions for unattached young people's courting. A courtship gathering (*ahal*) features love songs, poetical recitations, jokes, and games of wit. Presiding over the event is an *anzad* player, whose renown may attract visitors from far away. So closely associated is the *anzad* with the *ahal* that "the name of one brings to mind the other." Attendance at an *ahal* carries no shame, but discretion requires that young people not mention the word *ahal* in the presence of their elders. For similar reasons, they must speak the word *anzad* discreetly (Foucauld 1951–1952:1270–71).

According to context and viewpoint, the *anzad* has diverse meanings. It symbolizes intellectual and spiritual purity and traditional behavioral ideals. It connotes gallantry, love, sensuousness, and youth. It evokes images of a distant, pre-Islamic past. The traditions surrounding it reflect the status of Tuareg women, unusual in the Muslim world, yet within this diversity there is no contradiction: the *anzad* is a multifaceted symbol of Tuareg culture and identity.

Techniques of Construction and Playing

The *anzad* is a one-stringed bowed fiddle. The name, glossable as 'hair', refers to the substance of the string. The body of the instrument is a hollow gourd 25 to 40 centimeters in diameter, cut to form a bowl. Tightly stretched leather, usually goatskin, covers the opening; leather lacings usually attach it to the gourd. A slender stick, inserted under the leather top at opposite edges, extends 30 to 36 centimeters beyond the body on one side, and serves as a neck. One or two large soundholes, the number varying with local tradition, are cut into the leather near the perimeter of the gourd. The string, formed of about forty strands of horsehair, is attached at each end of the inserted stick. Short twigs, crossed and bound with leather, positioned beneath the string near the center of the skin surface, form a bridge. As the string tightens, the neck arches forward. The bow consists of a slender stick, held in an arc by the tension of the attached hair. To improve contact, people rub resin on bow hair and string. Players tune the instrument by moving a leather strip that binds the string to the neck near the tip, thereby adjusting the length of the vibrating portion of the string. Players vary in choosing a tuning pitch, but from one performance to another, the tuning pitch of an individual player is usually consistent.

The player sits, holding the fiddle in her lap, with the neck in her left hand. Rarely during the performance of a single piece does she change the position of her hand, though she may do so to prepare for another piece, using her thumb as a stop to effect a new tuning without changing the tension of the string. She fingers the string with a light touch. (Women do not try to press the string to the neck, which does not function as a fingerboard.) By extension of the little finger, the performer can readily gain access to the secondary harmonic, which sounds an octave above the open string. A few performers employ additional harmonics: by exerting light pressure at nodal points on the string, they produce brilliant tones, and can increase the pitch range beyond an octave. The result is a rich musical texture, a kaleidoscope of tone colors.

To exploit the instrument's imitative possibilities, a skillful fiddler may vary the speed and length of the bow strokes. Slow strokes combined with rapidly fingered notes can suggest a melismatic singing-style, and short strokes paired with single notes can produce a syllabic effect. Short, light strokes coupled with harmonics may simulate the tones of a flute; rapid use of the bow in tremolo style may depict animals in flight; halting, interrupted strokes may portray a limping straggler. Storytellers use these techniques, which can support a singer's text or vocal style.

Anzad n-Asak: *Music for Fiddle and Voice*

A large portion of the *anzad* repertory involves the voice. When accompanying a vocalist, the fiddler reinforces the vocal line with a heterophonic rendering of the melody. Each performer conveys a personal style, emphasizing different aspects of the melody or rhythm, and each makes little effort to synchronize the lines. Interludes between the strophes of the texts provide opportunities for instrumental display and for improvization on thematic material. If accompanying herself, a woman may play a single drone, reserving for the instrumental interludes a display of her musicianship. Men are the preferred vocalists, and if male singers are available at a gathering, women seldom sing. Women may once have sung more in mixed company, for there are many references in the older literature to women's songs of praise and encouragement for warriors.

The texts constitute a genre known as *tesîwit*, the highest achievement in Tuareg poetic arts. The principal subjects are love and heroism. In diction rich in imagery, the poems extol the virtues of courage in battle and gallantry in love, ever confirming the ideals of the warrior aristocracy. People may sing *tesîwit* alone, or to the accompaniment of the *anzad*; but they never sing it with any other instrument. The *anzad*, in turn, is rarely heard with other poetic genres. A *tesîwit* may take any of several meters traditional to an area; composers then set it to a new or existing melody that corresponds with the meter. New texts and melodies are constantly being created, subject to the constraints of the poetic meters. Old texts are kept in the repertory as long as they are of interest, the names of the composers usually remaining with them.

The male vocal style in singing *tesîwit* is typically high-pitched, tense, and much ornamented with mordents, shakes, and other graces, unlike the usual male singing of other genres. The nomadic Tuareg admire high-pitched male singing, produced with high tension of the throat muscles, and singers often strain to attain the ideal. A range extending to an octave above middle C is common. When women sing *tesîwit*, they do so at a more relaxed midrange, exhibiting none of the piercing quality that characterizes male singers' style.

The *Tende*

The word *tende* (*tindi*, in northern dialect) refers to a mortar drum, the music performed to its accompaniment, and the social event that features it. Though the Tuareg hold *anzad* music in higher esteem, *tende* is the music they more often perform. It is central to Tuareg camel festivals and curing ceremonies, and is a part of certain dance traditions. In addition to drumming, men and women take part—by singing, dancing, clapping, and shouting. Unlike the *anzad*, the mortar drum does not require years to learn acceptable skills, and the person who plays it, unless unusually gifted, receives little special attention. A *tende* singer occasionally gains recognition (figure 2), but most performers are nonspecialists. *Tende* is a music of ordinary people; its appeal is immediate and communal. Residents of urban areas increasingly employ its forms, but it remains a music of the bush, a symbol of earthy values.

Figure 2 Lalla bint Salem (*left*), a popular *tende* singer in Tamanrasset performs, as an audience claps in appreciation, 1976. Salem sings the traditional *tende* camel songs, but is especially admired for her ability to improvise texts that serve a journalistic function and often contain caustic social commentary. She sings of current events, recent disputes, and small intrigues, and of her longings to return to her native Mali. The women's dress and jewelry are typical of Algerian Tuareg. *Photo by Caroline Card Wendt.*

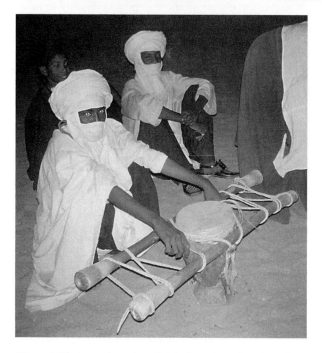

Figure 3 Two men have just finished constructing a *tende*, Tchin-Tabizgen, Niger, 1977. *Photo by Caroline Card Wendt.*

Construction

The *tende* is a single-headed mortar drum, named for the wooden vessel from which people make it. Because it is constructed of a mortar and pestles—items used daily in the preparation of food—it appears only on festive occasions, when people assemble it for a few hours of use (figure 3). Its construction requires a footed wooden mortar, two heavy wooden pestles about 1¼ meters long, a piece of moistened goatskin, and a length of rope. The ends of dampened goatskin are initially wrapped around the pestles, which serve as grips for stretching the skin over the opening of the mortar. In some traditions, people discard the pestles as soon as they have secured the skin with rope; commonly, however, they attach the pestles in parallel to the drumhead as part of the instrument, providing for later tuning and adjustment. To hold the ends of the pestles parallel, people lace rope between the ends of the pestles, forming "seats" on which women usually sit. Their weight on the pestles increases the tension on the attached drumhead, thus tuning it: the heavier the weight, the higher the pitch. This form of mortar drum is unique to the Tuareg.

Camel-festival Tende

The mortar-drum music most often mentioned in the literature is *tende n-ǝmnas* 'mortar drum of the camels'. These events celebrate weddings, births, honored visits, and other joyous occasions. Featured are camel races and dances. In its classic form, women sing and play the drum, while men parade or race their camels around them, in a fashion sometimes described as a "fantasy," and known in Tuareg dialects as *ilugan*, *ilujan*, and *ilaguan*. The races and displays of precision riding, combined with the men's flirting with the women, evoke the traditional virtues of male prowess and gallantry. In the late twentieth century, as nomadic herders were becoming urbanized, the music of *tende n-ǝmnas* was increasingly performed out of context; and on some occasions, male artisan-specialists played the drum.

The texts of *tende n-ǝmnas* burgeon with personalized references to camels, extolling them with esteem and affection. Mere ownership of a superb riding camel is often sufficient for a man's commemoration in song, and texts praise good riders for their skill and rapport with their animals, but though the references to camels are numerous, the real subjects are people. Songs of love and praise form a large portion of the traditional repertory, but criticism and scorn have their place too. Nearly any topic of interest is fitting subject-matter. Some texts, set to familiar tunes, develop extemporaneously, and include the singer's commentary on local persons and current events. Such songs function in a journalistic capacity, and performers skilled in this kind of improvization attract an appreciative following.

Dance Tende

In Niger, people perform *tende n-tagbast* 'dance tende' (figure 4), at many birth and marriage celebrations, and at other special events. Only artisans, sedentary blacks, and (to a lesser extent) vassals dance it. Traditionally, noble Tuareg do not dance. The word *tagbast* is the nominal form of the verb *egbas* 'circle the waist with a belt'. By extension, it bears the sense of "elegant attire" or "stylish dress," and with *tende*, denotes a musical occasion celebrated with fine clothes and dancing. Dancers perform within a circle of spectators. Dancers, alone or in groups, enter the circle and perform for a few steps, then retreat, to be followed by others. Men's shouts and women's flutter-tongued cries of approval reward expert exhibitions.

Women sing the texts, but the *tende* is usually played by men of the artisanal caste, whom women accompany on the *assakalabu* (a gourd upturned in a basin of water). The instrumental ensemble may also include a frame drum, *əkänzam*, which men or women play. The use of instruments with the dance

may be a recent addition to a formerly unaccompanied dance tradition; and if instruments are not readily available, the dances take an accompaniment of singing and handclapping only. Dance music without instruments is known as *ezele n-tagbast*. Artisan-musicians familiar with the tradition of *tende n-əmnas* may have introduced a mortar drum into the dance. The texts praise and commemorate good dancers, much as texts of *tende n-əmnas* praise good riders; and many of the texts similarly speak of love.

Duple meter with duple subdivisions, occasionally syncopated, is characteristic of the genre. The pulse, strongly marked and accompanied by handclapping, receives further reinforcement from steady, equal beats struck on the *assakalabu*. Though slower than *tende n-əmnas*, the tempos of *tende n-tagbast* vary according to the dance.

The *Tahardent*

A popular music and dance associated with the three-stringed lute (*tahardent*) is performed in urban centers across the Sahara from Mali to Algeria. Men of the artisanal caste, many of whom earn their living as professional musicians (*aggu*; pl. *aggutan*), perform the music. Such men once performed as bards in the chiefs' courts, singing the praises of their noble patrons and reciting tales of battles and heroes of local Tuareg legend to the accompaniment of the plucked lute. The *tahardent* repertory that is now popular among urban Tuareg is not the heroic music of the past: it is music for entertainment, which friends and acquaintances of diverse ethnic backgrounds can share.

Figure 4 The *tende n-tagbast* is performed, Aouderas, Niger, 1976. An *assakalabu* can be seen in the lower left. The *tende* is not visible. *Photo by Frederick and Eileen Kaarsemaker.*

The *tahardent* has long been a part of Tuareg traditions in Mali, but not until the late 1960s did the instrument begin to spread into other Tuareg areas. The movement of *tahardent* music from its source (between Timbuktu and Gao) began about 1968, when Malian Tuareg suffering from drought began to seek relief across the border, in Niger. Among the refugees were many artisan-musicians whose traditional patrons could no longer support them. To increase their opportunities, the itinerants quickly altered their repertories to appeal to more diverse, multiethnic audiences. Crowded conditions in the refugee centers forced many to continue their migration northeastward. By 1971, *tahardent* music began to be heard in Agadez, Niger; in 1974, it reached Tamanrasset, in southern Algeria. Since 1976, Malian *tahardent* players have been active in most urban centers across the Sahara and Sahelian borderlands, and recordings of *tahardent* music are in wide circulation throughout West Africa.

DISC
1
TRACK
2

The new genre, popularly known as *takəmba*, consists of accompanied songs and instrumental solos. Seated listeners, male and female, respond by making undulating movements of the upper torso and outstretched arms. People exchange prized recordings of star performers and hit songs, and copy them from one tape to another. The texts are often sensuous. At vital moments, people express approval in rhapsodic exclamations of "ush-sh-sh!"

Songs of this type appeal most to Tuareg who have accepted urban life and contemporary values. Those who adhere to traditional ways are often vehement in their disdain for the instrument, the music, and its devotees: they denounce the music as a corrupt, urban product, and not a true Tuareg art. To them, it matters little that the *tahardent* represents an old and respected Tuareg tradition in Mali. Their attitudes toward it highlight an emerging division between conservatives and progressives.

Construction and Playing

The instrument has an oblong body covered with cowhide or goatskin. Artisans carve the body from a single block of wood, and cover it with cowhide or goatskin, which they attach with tacks or lacings. A length of bamboo, inserted under the skin and extending beyond the body, serves as a neck. A large soundhole is cut into the skin just below the bridge. The instrument comes in two sizes. The larger (and more commonly used) has a body length of about 51 to 53 centimeters, a width of about 18 to 20, and a neck of about 30. Three strings, of differing lengths and thicknesses, are attached to a mounting just above the soundhole. They stretch over the bridge, where they are fastened to the end of the neck with leather bindings that are adjustable for tuning. The strings, formerly made of horsehair, are now commonly made of nylon. The two lower strings are tuned to a perfect fourth or perfect fifth, depending on the music. The upper string—occasionally plucked, but not fingered—sounds an octave above the lowest; its principal function is sympathetic vibration. A metal resonator dangles from the end of the neck, where it buzzes sympathetically.

The player sits cross-legged, and normally holds the neck in his left hand. On his right index finger he wears a plectrum, made of bone and leather. He plucks the middle string with an index finger; the lower, with a thumb. With the other fingers he taps accompanying rhythms on the instrument's surface. With his left-hand fingers he stops the strings against the (unfretted) neck. As the melodic range rarely exceeds an octave, hand-shifts during the course of a composition are unnecessary. A player may occasionally slide a finger along the string to produce a glissando, but normally the fingering is crisp, and the pitches clearly articulated. Esteemed performers exhibit virtuosity in their improvizations on the basic rhythmic patterns, particularly in the instrumental interludes between vocal strophes. People do not perform separately or with other instruments, the poetry they sing or recite to the accompaniment of the *tahardent*, whether of the old tradition or the new.

Musical Styles

Many Tuareg, unaware of historical and stylistic distinctions, refer to all *tahardent* music as *takəmba*. To the performers, however, *takəmba* is but one of several compositional formulas, which they call "rhythms." Each rhythm has a name, is suitable for a specific context, and may bear distinctive modal and rhythmic characteristics. The rhythms *n-geru* and *yalli* serve only in the performance of heroic ballads, a tradition that may be several hundred years old; both have five-pulse rhythms, but different tonal (or modal) structures. The rhythms *abakkabuk*, *ser-i*, *jabâ*, and *takəmba* serve for light entertainment and dancing. All rely on twelve-pulse patterns in various configurations. *Abakkabuk* is an old rhythm unique to the Tuareg. *Ser-i* 'toward me' is a traditional pattern played for the enjoyment of members of the artisanal caste, to which the musicians belong. *Jabâ* and *takəmba*, of more recent origin, are rhythms that praise youth and youthful pleasures; according to performers, *jabâ* is the product of a commission in 1960 by wealthy patrons of the Kel Tamoulayt; similarly, *takəmba* is a rhythm composed for the chief of the Malian village of that name near Bourem, northwest of Gao.

Few outsiders have studied *tahardent* music, and older recordings are scarce. Newer recordings are increasingly available as *tahardent* music comes to the attention of Western musicians seeking new material for their own compositions. Comparison of the limited historical data with those of similar neighboring traditions points to relationships between the Tuareg heroic forms (*yalli, n-geru*) and Arabic music of North Africa and the Middle East, particularly in tonal structures and sociomusical meanings. The dance music, with its twelve-pulse horizontal hemiolas, shows greater affinity with sub-Saharan Africa. The *tahardent* tradition of the Tuareg thus reflects the interculturality of its artisan-creators, who, more than other musicians, have drawn freely upon Middle Eastern and sub-Saharan sources.

—*Adapted from an article by Caroline Card Wendt*

Bibliography

Briggs, Lloyd Cabot. 1960. *Tribes of the Sahara*. Cambridge, Mass.: Harvard University Press.

Card, Caroline. 1982. "Tuareg Music and Social Identity." Ph.D. dissertation, Indiana University.

Duvéyrier, Henri. [1864] 1973. *Les Touareg du nord*. New York: Krauss.

Foucauld, Charles de. 1951–1952. *Dictonnaire touareg-français: dialect de l'Ahaggar*. 4 vols. Paris: Imprimerie national de France.

Keenan, Jeremy H. 1977. *The Tuareg: People of Ahaggar*. London: Allen Lane.

Murdock, George Peter. 1959. *Africa: Its Peoples and Their Culture History*. New York: McGraw-Hill.

Nicolaisen, Johannes. 1963. *Ecology and Culture of the Pastoral Tuareg*. Copenhagen: National Museum.

Wendt, Caroline Card. 1994. "Regional Style in Tuareg *Anzad* Music." In *To the Four Corners*, edited by Ellen Leichtman. Warren, Mich.: Harmonie Park Press.

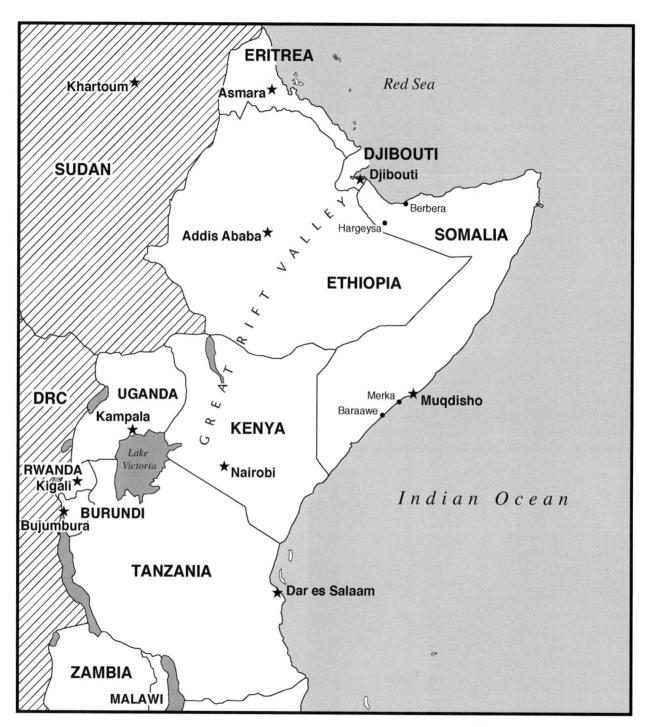

East Africa

East Africa

East Africa ranges from the dry scrubland of northern Mozambique to the empty deserts of Sudan and Eritrea, and from the seasonally dry savanna bordering the Indian Ocean to the mountain-rainforest mosaic of Rwanda and Burundi. Roughly 200 million people live in this region, and their lifestyles and origins vary as much as anywhere else in Africa. About 118 different languages have been identified in the Sudan alone, and almost as many in Ethiopia; and since language and musical style are often closely related, it is not surprising to find that musical traditions vary as much as languages and dialects. To offer a sense of this diversity, we present articles on the musics of Somalia and Kenya.

Music and Poetry in Somalia

Uniquely in Africa, the people of Somalia constitute a single ethnic group, though divided into clan families, with lineages and subgroups based on descent in male lines, which often have problematic relations with each other. In 2006, the national population, which can only be estimated, was about 5.7 to 6 million. During the colonial period (late 1800s and early 1900s), political decisions severed from the main body another one-and-a-half to two million Somalis, who live on the frontiers of Djibouti, Ethiopia, and Kenya. Today, other Somalis live in North America, Western Europe, and the Middle East. The overwhelming majority of Somalis share one religion (Islam), one language, and one ethnic identity; until 1991, one central administration governed the country.

The Somali language is in the Eastern Cushitic branch of the Afroasiatic family. The spelling of Somali words here follows the alphabet devised for the language and put into general use in 1972. Because non-Somalis do not commonly recognize indigenous spelling conventions, alternate spellings of certain words in this article parenthetically follow their first occurrence.

Several socioeconomic traditions distinguish the country. The main ones are nomadic herding (camel, sheep, goats, cattle), settled farming, and urban dwellers' mercantile pursuits. At independence (1960), 75 to 80 percent of the people participated in nomadic animal husbandry; by 1987, however, only an estimated 44 percent were still nomads. Since 1900, Somalia has seen an increase in urbanization, though the mercantile cities of Berbera in the north, and Muqdisho (Mogadishu), Marka (Merka), and Barawa or Baraawe (Brava) in the south, have had permanent settlements for centuries. Since 1900, a portion of the populace has shifted from nomadism to agriculture.

Musical Instruments

Socioeconomic diversity leads to local differences in Somali cultural expression, including music. Important differences exist in the use of instrumental musical accompaniment with the songs and poems of northern nomads, southern farmers, and urban populations, of both ancient and recent origin. Until the late 1940s, northern nomads used no musical instrument except a drum, beaten by women. Hand-clapping and footstamping as rhythmic accompaniment are common throughout Somalia.

In performing oral genres, people in agricultural and older mercantile cities employ various musical instruments. In southern areas, they use three drums (*durbaan*, *yoome*, *nasar*) and handheld clappers. Some clappers are of carved wood (*shanbaal*). Some, with resonating chambers whittled from their centers, have little decoration, unlike their West African counterparts; though not so large (about a third of a meter in length), they resemble eighteenth-century European military officers' cocked hats. Other clappers (*sharaq*, *biro*), with a flat, triangular shape, are of metal. They resemble metal hoeheads and axheads, and hoeing may actually be their primary function; in fact, one Somali lineage calls the clapper and the hoe by the same term (*yaambo*).

For musical accompaniment and signaling, coastal Somalis use *Bursa*, *Turbinella*, and other gastropod seashells (*buun*, *caroog*). By buzzing their lips into a hole drilled in the apex, or on the side of the spire of the shell, skilled performers can produce a loud sound. For the same purpose, southern Somalis use the horns of antelopes (*gees*, *gees-goodir*), plus a variety of horns carved from wood and cane (*siimbaar*, *malakata*, *sumari*, *parapanda*). They play a six-stringed lyre (*shareero*).

Some Somali instruments have a wide geographical range, and appear among other groups in eastern Africa. Between 1950 and 1960, musicians in Somalia began to play the principal instruments of Western orchestras and bands.

Innovation of Musical Forms

The history of music in Somalia from the early 1940s reflects artistic innovation, which brought about important changes. Scholars often call older forms of Somali music and poetry traditional, and newer forms modern; but it may be more useful to view the process of Somali musical and poetic traditions as continuous, with a multiplicity of aspects. Some pieces are older, some newer, some indigenous, some foreign, some conservative, and some more open to change. Perceiving older forms as "traditional" gives a false sense of their cultural stagnation, and tends to deny that they too were once innovative. Some of them show the influence of foreign modes of expression, as some newer Somali forms do.

Certain aspects of Somali musical behavior have widespread representation among other Cushitic peoples of East Africa, such as the Oromo in Ethiopia and the Beja in the Sudan. An alternative view is to call the older forms nonprofessional and the newer ones professional. Nonprofessional Somali genres are still composed and performed by men and women who, though skilled musicians and poets, do not make a living from musical performance. People who receive government support (through bureaucratic agencies such as the National Theater) and public support (through the sale of tickets to privately produced performances and mass-produced cassettes) create professional forms.

Until the 1990s, Somali oral expression made no dynamic distinction between music and poetry. All forms of poetry can be sung, and some are always sung. The domestic classification of the forms of Somali oral performance rests on a combination of structures, only one of which relates to music. To differentiate one genre from another, four criteria—prosody, melody, topic, function—act together. If any criterion changes, the genre may change. Two forms may have the same prosody, the same melody, and the same subject matter, but be different in function. Most of the time, more than one criterion actually differentiates genres. Somalis group genres into larger classes, according to function and social context.

Linguistic Traits of Somali Prosody

The prosody of Somali poetry takes a patterned configuration of long and short vowels. The temporal duration of a short vowel, a mora, occupies an amount of time analysts call a seme. In a given poem, a monoseme contains a short vowel of one mora, and a diseme contains two moras.

> **Prosody** is the traditional term used for the theory of versification in the patterning of sound, especially through meter, rhyme, and stanza.

Three principles characterize the relationship between moras and syllables. First, a closed-set morosyllabic relationship allows only long vowels to fill disemes, resulting in an identical number of syllables and vowels (long or short) in each line, with a fixed number of moras. Second, an open-set morosyllabic relationship allows one long or two short vowels to fill disemes. Since there are two moras in a diseme, the number of syllables varies according to how many vowels occur. Finally, in a semiopen-set morosyllabic relationship, with a specified number of disemes and a specified number of syllables, there are always more disemes than long-vowel requirements,

so some disemes must contain two short vowels, while others must contain long vowels. Poetic license allows composers to choose which disemes to fill with long vowels, and which to fill with short vowels.

All Somali genres have specific rules about the arrangement of disemic and monosemic patterns in a line of poetry. Such arrangements sometimes result in units comparable to feet. In some cases, the line is the smallest recurrent pattern of semes. Terms like *foot*, *line*, *mora*, and *seme*, used here for convenience, do not represent indigenous Somali vocabulary. Much of the local understanding of these rules is implicit, and critical terminology, when it occurs, tends to be metaphoric, not systematic.

> A **foot** is a basic metrical unit of prosody.

> A **mora** is the temporal duration of a short vowel.

> A **seme** is the amount of time occupied by a mora; a monoseme contains one mora, and a diseme contains two moras.

Musical Traits of Somali Prosody

Somali music—both the older, nonprofessional, and the newer, post-1945 professional—uses a pentatonic scale, the tones of which are not standardized by pitch. The resulting intervals are also not standardized; but relative to the pitches on either side of them, they are more predictable.

Melody helps differentiate Somali genres. Subservient to language-internal constraints, indigenous Somali musical traits are predictable from the prosody of the poetry. A small number of melodies belong to each genre, and a musician can utilize any of them to sing any poem in the genre; but each of these melodies is subservient to the prosody of the genre. Hearing a Somali whistling, one might guess the genre, but not the poem. Conversely, Somali professional poetry reflects language-external constraints. Each poem within a genre has its own melody, which sets up a rhythm that supersedes linguistic prosody: "the movement of speech through poetry to song is in fact a continuum" of ever-increasing constraints (Bird 1976:95).

The interaction between music and words represents a polyrhythmic relationship in Somali prosody. Because Somali prosody is quantitative, its perception—through short and long durations of vowels—is rhythmic. Duration in music is also quantitative, and its perception—through short and long sung vowels—is the element that gives music its rhythm. Simultaneously, audiences and poets alike can perceive the poetic and musical rhythms, and can follow their interrelationships. At the same time, in the same stream of speech, a performer recites two parallel systems of rhythm. This kind of polyrhythm is unique to Somali. A different sort of polyrhythm is found elsewhere in Africa.

The Classes of Genres

Somalis combine groups of genres into classes, determined mainly by function and context and reflected topically. Three of these classes are pre-eminent. Scholars have labeled them from two points of view: students of literature call them classical poetry, work poetry, and recreational poetry; students of music call them poetry, song, and dance. Somalis call them *gabay*, *hees*, and *cayaar* (or *ciyaar*), respectively. These terms are easy to gloss ('poetry', 'song', 'play'), but researchers have difficulty understanding how Somalis view the concepts the terms convey. To Somalis, each class is both poetic and musical, but the newer, professional form is not, and the duality of names Somalis give to it bears witness to their problem of integrating it into their poetic-musical tradition. By naming the form *heello*, they emphasize its poetic origins. *Heello, heellooy*, and *heelleellooy*, are the vocables of an introductory formula, the main function of which is to set the meter of a poem. Other linked vocables (such as *hobaale*, *hobeeye*, and *balwooy*) serve the same purpose (figure 1). Sometimes, the same genre is called *hees*, 'song', a term that emphasizes its musical characteristics. Each *heello-hees* has a unique melody and does not employ a generic one—which may account for the duality of nomenclature and the confusion.

Classical Poetry (Gabay)

This class includes the genres *gabay*, *geeraar*, *jiifto*, and *buraambur*. The most prestigious genre in it is also called *gabay*. The class is known as *guurow* in the south, where a variant name, *masafo*, exists for the *jiifto*, especially when it covers religious topics. Except for the *buraambur* (reserved for women), these poems are composed and recited by men. Topics these genres deal with include politics, war, peace, social debate, interclan negotiations, and philosophy. Their performance, which occurs only in serious contexts, functions similarly to newspaper editorials, political speeches, and philosophical exegeses.

For each genre, the prosody is tight and unified. A poem in poor prosody elicits severe criticism, and its composer often fails to persuade. Except for the *buraambur*, alliteration involves only one consonant per poem, which may have as many as seventy or eighty lines—a mental feat few can manage. Alternately, all the vowels alliterate together, so a poem

may alliterate with words that begin with any vowel. The rules tax memory so strenuously that some poets limit their repertories to a few consonants for alliteration.

Poets compose classical poems in private, and memorize them for public performance. Some people have skill in composing classical poetry, but others specialize in memorizing and reciting. People often remember composers by name, as creators of specific poems. Though some variation occurs between the recitations of the same poem by different people, evidence suggests that, from one performance to another, individuals do not vary much in their own recitation of a given poem.

Worksongs (Hees)

Worksongs are differentiated mainly by function and performer's gender. Each socially defined form of work is represented by a genre. Work associated with camels, for example, inspires separate genres: people sing *heesaha aroorka* when driving camels to watering points; *heesaha shubaaha*, for watering them; *heesaha rakaadda*, for rewatering them; *heesaha fulinta*, for driving them to grazing areas; *heesaha carraabada*, for driving them to corrals; and *heesaha raridda*, for loading goods onto their backs. Similarly, poems exist for watering cattle, watering sheep and goats, herding sheep and goats, herding lambs and kids, weaving the mats used as inner and outer walls of the portable nomadic house (*aqal*), churning milk, pounding grain, and comforting and rocking children. This list is only a partial one.

The prosody of some genres in this class is so complex that they may have been memorized for public performance, as matweaving *heeso* are, but other genres, like the *heeso* for pounding grain and churning milk, are simpler in structure and rhythm. So much repetition occurs that composition is formulaic, but different singers repeat so many words exactly that memory obviously plays a role.

Dance Songs (Cayaar)

This class is musically the most complex. It contains many genres, whose musical performance researchers have little explored. The names of these genres may not always indicate a set pattern of prosody, and much regional variation complicates analysis: a *dhaanto* in one part of the country, for example, is not the same as a poem with that name in another part; a term that represents a genre to one singer sometimes represents a larger generic set to another, even to a person from the same region. One poet used the word *dhaanto* synonymously with the larger class of *cayaar*. Some of the most common dance

Ho— bey ho— beey, hoo—beey ho— beey

Ho— bey ho— beey, saw—laa— la— cooy,

Heey. ho— beey, ma lays— ka qu— bo!?

Figure 1 Excerpt from a *hees maqasha* 'lamb- or kid-watering song', by Cibaado Jaamac Faarax (Ibado Jama Farah), composed in 1987. Translation: "*Hobey hobeey, hoobeey hobeey,* / *Hobey hobeey*, O you who scamper about, . . . / *Heey hobeey*, why are they [not] cast out?" Triangular noteheads show short vowels sung to long notes; square noteheads show long vowels sung to short notes; regular, elliptical noteheads show the use of short notes with short vowels and long notes with long vowels.

genres from different regions of Somalia are *gaaleysi, saar-lugeed, saddexley, saar-mooye, wale-saqo, ceeri-gaabo, bariyo, jaan-dheer, guuxo, dawladamiin, shaba-shabaay, gabley-shimbir, balwo, hirwo, dhaanto, wiglo, shirib, balaqley, tur,* and *jiib*.

Unlike the other classes of Somali genres, dance poems are not composed once and memorized. Their topics often deal specifically with activities surrounding the performance. There is so little refrain in their lines that they may not be formulaically composed, though composition is simultaneous with performance.

The description of one session will shed light on composition in performance. On 29 May 1987, dancers from all over Somalia attended a street festival in Muqdisho (Mogadishu), the capital. As usual at national festivals, groups competed for public attention, starting about four o'clock in the afternoon, and continuing until sundown. In one group, Cabdillaahi Xirsi "Baarleex" (Abdillahi Hirsi Barleh), a singer from the Ogaadeeniya (Ogaden) area of Ethiopia—the far western area, where Somalis live—performed a poem he called a *dhaanto*. The rest of his company surrounded him in a circle. In his verses, he maintained a consistent prosody, and sang eight to fifteen lines of solo at a time; but enjambment obscured where one line ended and another began—a phenomenon unknown in *gabay* and *hees*. He did not maintain a consistent rhythm. The lines of figure 2 illustrate the style of the solo part. A micron symbolizes short vowels, and a macron symbolizes long values; vertical lines separate semes, and double vertical lines separate feet.

At a certain point, Baarleex began singing a two-line rhythmic refrain. During this performance, he taught this refrain to two choirs (one male and one female), which quickly learned their parts and sang them antiphonally. After several solo performances (all followed by choral refrains), Baarleex changed the refrain, which did not scan identically with the previous one. After he started each refrain, the second choir began singing with the first choir at the caesura of the second line, and would then sing both lines, joined by the first choir during the second hemistich of the second line. So it proceeded, until a cue from Baarleex allowed him to begin another set of solo lines. Figure 3 illustrates one of the choral refrains.

The solo-choral refrain repeated about a dozen times; and then suddenly, untaught by the soloist, the choirs began singing a different chorus, in a different

Ummadday garabaysee,

Intee baan arladayda,

Afeef maansiyo heelliyo,

Ku dhawaaqay afkayga,

Ilaah baygu abuuree.

DISC
1
TRACK
3

Figure 2 Excerpt from a *dhaanto* by Cabdillaahi Xirsi "Baarleex" (Abdillahi Hirsi Barleh), from the Ogaden region, 29 May 1987. Translation: "The nation knows me: / How often have I, in my country, / Great literature and song / Performed in my language! / God created it in me."

rhythm. This time, the lines were twice as long as before, but again each choir antiphonally sang two lines of refrain. This rhythm cued dancers to enter the center circle. When they finished dancing, the entire process would repeat. Each performance (soloist, choral refrain, dance refrain) lasted from twenty to thirty minutes, and the singers and dancers would then rest for a while.

Somali Professional Music

The *heello-hees* originated immediately after 1945, when foreign influence caused Somali musical behavior to change. During World War II, the introduction of radio had exposed Somalis to English, Italian, Arabic, and Indian musics. Somali men in the northwestern city of Hargeysa, capital of the then British Somaliland Protectorate, formed a theatrical company, the Brothers of Hargeysa (Walaalo Hargeysa), whose innovations included use of the newly emerging *heello-hees*, with the introduction of a small orchestra (flute, violin, tambourine, drum). Because this company's productions included political themes (topics earlier reserved for classical *gabayo*), the new form rapidly gained popularity in the drive toward independence.

Change from the older forms included the accelerating introduction of foreign musical instruments. In distinction to nonprofessional genres (which drew from a common stock of melodies), the *heello-hees* had melodies unique to each newly composed poem. The new distinctions of composer of poetry, composer of music, professional singer, and professional musician, joined the composer-reciter distinction of

nonprofessional poetry. Like its foreign models, the earliest of which was Indian, the new form made extensive use of patterned refrains, sometimes sung by male and female choirs. Much of this innovation stems from the British practice of paying royalties to Somali composers of poems broadcast on radio. Because the British paid more for longer poems, refrains became popular among Somali *heello-hees* composers and musicians.

After about 1943, more and more musical innovations came into being, in style and instrumentation (electric guitars, electric organs, Western drumsets). Radio stations in Muqdisho and Hargeysa became the principal medium of diffusion for the new genre, but stations abroad began to play Somali music and poetry too: by the 1970s, radio stations in Addis Ababa, Djibouti, Cairo, London, Moscow, and Peking featured Somali music and poetry. With radio, the burgeoning Somali theater continued its use of the new poetry and music. In Muqdisho, an Italian military conductor formed an orchestra, which performed on radio and at military parades and special public events. During this period, private ensembles playing Somali music and foreign music began to emerge. In both these spheres of support (government and private), the new genre began to gain in prestige alongside the classical genres, because it began to include political topics.

Another innovation in the public use of this poetry helps clarify the relationship of music and poetry to social structures on the Horn of Africa. Nonprofessional poetry represents a more gerontocractic hierarchy of control in the composition,

Figure 3 The choral refrain in a *dhaanto*; Parliament Square, Muqdisho, 29 May 1987. Translation: "I have fallen for you. Do you feel the same?"

performance, and sociopolitical use of serious poetry; but the *heello-hees* allows younger men—and even more radically, women—to have a voice in politics. To be taken seriously, the classical genres of *gabay, jiifto,* and *geeraar,* which hold the highest prestige in nomadic life, have to be composed by elderly men. A description of the Somali tradition of *silsilaad* 'poetic chain combat' illustrates this fact. Somali poets challenge each other to poetic duels in the classical genres. The most admired poem composed in answer to another is not only in the same genre, but also in the same alliteration. The D-alliteration in one such poem of the 1980s dominated some sixty-seven *jiiftos* before it changed. Only poets of equal reputation may contribute to the chain. Violations of this rule, and debates on the abilities of specific poets and on political issues, result in lively arguments and disagreements about the levels of prestige surrounding poems in the same chain; but Somali youths may not participate in this tradition.

Unlike veiled political and social commentary in worksongs and recreational poetry (where younger men and women of all ages have found an outlet for expressing their views in the context of Somali nomadic life), the *heello-hees* class of professional poetry has always been a medium under the control of youth. Participation of younger Somalis in political life is an innovation in Somalia. That the first major political party in the southern regions of the country bore the name Somali Youth League is no accident. Beginning in the 1950s, many *heello-hees* treated political themes; hence, Somali nomadic elders held professional poetry in contempt. Including political topics in this genre placed it in an ambiguous position.

A skillful Somali may participate in all three of these traditions. A young man growing up around people who sing worksongs may learn to compose worksongs while laboring among his livestock. As a youth, he may learn to compose dance songs during their performance at festivals. When he becomes an elder, he may refuse to compose dance songs because of the lowliness of their social prestige, and may then turn his creative abilities solely to the composition of poetry in the classical genres.

—Adapted from an article by
John William Johnson

Bibliography

Ahmed Ali Abokor. 1990. "Somali Pastoral Work Songs: The Poetic Voice of the Politically Powerless." M.A. thesis, Indiana University.

Andrzejewski, Bogumil Witalis, and I. M. Lewis. 1964. *Somali Poetry: An Introduction.* Oxford: Oxford University Press.

Bird, Charles S. 1976. "Poetry in the Mande: Its Form and Meaning." *Poetics* 5:89–100.

Giannattasio, Francesco. 1988 "The Study of Somali Music: Present State." In *Proceedings of the Third International Congress of Somali Studies,* edited by Annarita Puglielli, 158–167. Rome: II Pensiero Scientifico Editore.

Johnson, John William. 1972. *Heellooy Heelleellooy: The Development of the Genre Heello in Modern Somali Poetry.* Bloomington, Ind.: Research Center for the Language Sciences.

——. 1980. "Somalia." *The New Grove Dictionary of Music and Musicians,* edited by Stanley Sadie. London: Macmillan.

——. 1993. "Somali Poetry." *The New Princeton Encyclopedia of Poetry and Poetics,* edited by Alex Preminger and T. V. F. Brogan, 1164–65. Princeton, N. J.: Princeton University Press.

Music in Kenya

The Republic of Kenya, independent since 1963, lies along the East African coast. It shares boundaries with Tanzania to the south, Uganda and Sudan to the west and northwest, and Ethiopia and Somalia to the north and northeast. Important lakes—Victoria to the west, Turkana to the north—partly define its boundaries. The eastern Rift Valley runs through it. Its coastal areas and this valley receive abundant rainfall, but the rest of it is dry. The coastal plains rise to the Nyika Plateau, and then gradually to highlands. The peak of Mount Kenya rises more than 5,000 meters above sea level.

Kenya's climate is largely tropical, with two rainy seasons: short rains from November to December, and long rains between March and June. Agriculture is its chief export. Its climate, beaches, and wild animals draw more tourists than do the attractions of any other African country.

Kenya is multilingual. Its indigenous languages belong to four major families: Bantu, Paranilotic, Nilotic, and Kushitic. Typical speakers of these languages are the Kikuyu (the largest), the Nandi, the Luo, and the Somali peoples. Kiswahili and English are official languages for national and international communication and business.

Kenya is the regional base for many nongovernmental organizations that operate in Africa. Similarly, regional representatives of multinational organizations have made it their continental headquarters.

Cultural Zones

Kenya has three main cultural zones: semiarid, savanna-grassland, and rainy. The semiarid and savanna-grassland zones support pastoral com-

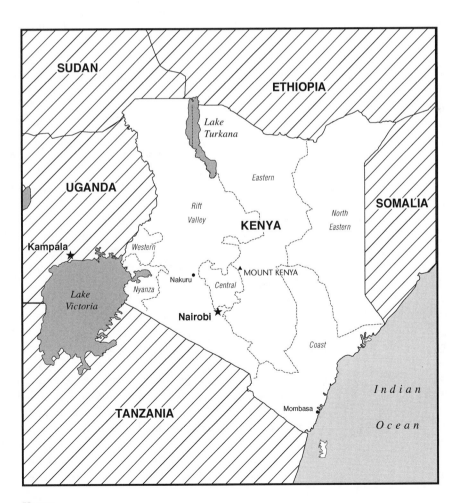

Kenya

munities of Paranilotic and Kushitic peoples. The savanna-grassland and rainy zones support Bantus (including the Akamba, the Kikuyu, and the Taita) and Nilotics. Local musics reflect local ecological systems and subsistence practices and record popular responses to two political periods: colonial and postcolonial.

The musics of pastoral communities of Paranilotic and Kushitic peoples of Kenya's North Eastern and Rift Valley provinces (including the Maasai, the Nandi, and the Somali) have structures and performance practices that differ from those of Bantu-speakers (Kikuyu and Luyia) and Nilotic-speakers (Luo) of Western, Eastern, Central, and Nyanza provinces. However, even among the Bantu-speakers, each music has distinctive features and instruments. Because of contact with Arabic and Indic populations before the time of modern European colonization, the musics of the Bantu of the Coast Province differ from those of the rest of the country. Intraethnic contact before, during, and after colonialism further eased the fusion of disparate cultural musics.

Musical instruments and performance practices reflect local ecological environments, subsistence practices, and sociocultural norms. Nationally, however, English and Kiswahili, the media, religion, and other unifying forces have led to the creation of national popular and religious forms, such as *benga* (originally associated with the Luo of western Kenya), *makwaya* (rooted in Christian religious choirs), and *taarab* (originally located in coastal Kenya and associated with Islamization).

Vocal Music
Vocal music—solo and choral response performance without instrumental accompaniment—is a feature of the Nilotic and other pastoral communities. The Akamba and Ameru of the eastern slopes of Mount Kenya sing unaccompanied, solo or in call-response; they also sing with accompaniment on idiophones.

People in semiarid areas display specific vocal styles. In the Rift Valley, large groups of men (as among the Pokot, the Maasai, and their neighbors the Samburu) typically perform together. In long melodies, they praise their cattle or country, mostly in free rhythm. Maasai men may sing an underlying ostinato against a solo line. Commonly, the responding group repeats the syllables *ho-la-le-i-yo* in unison. From that pattern, they form an interlude to the performance: *laleiyo laleiyo, laleiyo*. As the soloist approaches the end of his phrase, he prepares the choral group, either by transposing to an octave above, or by giving a certain word as a cue.

Musician-composers who practice the art of solo singing comment on the social, political, and economic dimensions of life. In the 1950s, many songs composed during the "emergency days"—seven years of armed resistance against British colonial rule—were major sources of information. During the colonial period, some songs provided a kind of eyewitness that disputed the written colonial documents.

Singing revolves around daily occupations. The popular music of agricultural people accompanies cultivating, threshing, and grinding cereals. In pastoral communities, animal themes dominate vocal music: performers cite cattle as an important store of wealth, or praise the finest bulls in the herd.

Areas of Instrumental Music Prominence
The variety and distribution of musical instruments in Kenya reflects local vegetation, the primary occupation of its people, their migratory patterns, and the contact they have had with outsiders. In semiarid areas, as in the northeast, people play few instruments, which tend to be small. In wet, fertile areas, as in Western Province, people play large and small instruments, solo and in ensembles. Adults exclusively play some, and children play others. This variety offers numerous forms of accompaniment for vocal music.

Bantu communities have more kinds of instruments than Nilotic and Kushitic peoples. These instruments include idiophones, membranophones, chordophones, and aerophones. The distribution of lyres is related to the migration of peoples along the Rift Valley. The Nilotic communities, specifically the Luo, are known for their lyres. The Luo, the Kalenjin, and their Bantu neighbors (the Abaluhya, the Kisii, the Abakuria) have similar lyres, but with different numbers of strings and a different repertoire. These groups have two styles of playing: plucking the strings (Luo and Abaluhya) and strumming with the right thumb and index finger (Kalenjin). In the latter style, the fingers of the left hand touch strings to change their pitches. Singing and performance on rhythmic idiophones may accompany performance on the lyre.

Bantu communities in Kenya favor drums. Those of the western highlands (Luhya and Abakuria) play sets of three drums, the most famous of which are the *sukuti* of the Abaluyha. Coastal Bantu play sets of five: the Digo and Duruma people use a tuned set, accompanied by a flute (*chivoti*), an oboe (*nzumari*), and several percussive instruments; the Giriama, the Chonyi, and other communities of the northern coast of Kenya use an untuned set of drums.

Figure 1 A *kilumi* ceremony with dancing, drumming, and singing, Kitui District, Eastern Province, 2005. *Kilumi*, a religious dance of the Akamba people, is performed as a healing ritual, for initiation ceremonies, and for entertainment. The drummers play *kithembe* drums. *Photo by Muriithi Kigunda.*

The coastal Bantus play two instruments popular elsewhere in Africa: the xylophone (*rimba*) and the lamellaphone (*karimba*). Musicians may play these instruments solo, but they also play the xylophone in the instrumental ensemble of the *kiringongo* (a boys' and girls' dance, accompanied by vocal and instrumental music), or in an ensemble of light idiophones (instruments that do not weigh much, and are easy to carry).

Some dances contain instrumental motifs, repeated throughout a performance, as in the *kilumi* (a dance of the Akamba people; figure 1) and the *kishavi* (a dance of the Taita people). In other dances (such as the *mwinjiro* of the Mbeere people, and the *mwanzele* of the Rabai people), short rhythms form phrases and regulate performances. The movements of other dances, such as the *sengenya* and *gonda* of the Mijikenda, duplicate the rhythms of the drums. Certain instruments replicate the rhythmic grouping of syllables. Among the most commonly used instruments in replicating vocal rhythm are the drum and the *kayamba*, a rectangular stone- or seed-filled reed box, played by all coastal communities. The Mbeere people of Mount Kenya dance the *nguchu* with leg bells (*igamba*) and a horn (*coro*). In the central highlands, the Kikuyu people dance the *muchungwa* with idiophones attached to dancers' legs. Some dances, such as the *sukuti* of the Abaluhya, are named after instruments that accompany the dance; or the instrumental ensemble itself is considered a dance, as with the *kayamba* of the Giriama,

because of the spectacle provided by the choreography of the instrumental techniques.

Idiophones ("Self-sounders")

Idiophones, the most widespread instruments in Kenya, include the *kayamba*, a raft rattle of the Mijikenda people; gourd rattles; *kigamba*, a tin rattle of the Agikuyu; and *gara*, metal bells of the Luo, attached to dancers' legs. Melodic idiophones include the xylophones and lamellaphones originating from the coastal peoples and groups that straddle the Kenya–Uganda border, such as the Iteso.

Membranophones (Drums)

Drums are played alone or as a set, and are used for signaling and for accompanying songs, dances, rituals, and events. Drums can be played alone, or accompanied by other instruments, with or without singing. The most famous drum set is the *sukuti* (figure 2), played by the Luhya; it is made up of two or more drums of different sizes, each with its own musical function. The Akamba play multiple drums, but in unison; their style was popularized at nationalistic gatherings for folkloristic cultural memory, but it plays a seminal role in indigenous therapeutic sessions (*kilumi*). Other drums include those played for *ngoma* sessions by the Digo and other Mijikenda of coastal Kenya; these drums accompany such dances as the *sengenya*.

Drumming involves three techniques: the hand technique, the stick technique, and the stick-and-hand technique with the armpit controlling the pitch.

The style of hitting varies with the drum, the mode of drumming, and the purpose of the performance. No drummer uses two sticks. The right hand serves for hitting the drumhead; the left hand mutes the sound and produces various tones. Musicians in Christian churches commonly use the stick-and-hand technique, a transformation of Luhya traditional drumming, which involves mainly the hand technique. The shapes and sizes of drums used for sacred performance differ from the shapes and sizes of those used for secular performances. In outdoor performances, musicians prefer the stick technique for its amplitude.

Not every Kenyan indigenous culture had drums before colonial times. The Agikuyu borrowed the side drum from Christian churches and military and police bands. They call this drum *ndarama*, an appropriation of the word drum. Another popular drumset is the Luo *ohangla*, which has a history of appropriation from the Luhya *sukuti* because of precolonial intercultural contact. An earlier drum of the *ohangla* set was called *sukuti*.

Figure 2 Sukuti drums.
Photo by Jean Ngoya Kidula.

Chordophones (Stringed Instruments)

Chordophones, including lyres and fiddles, set the pitch, double the melody of songs, and provide ostinato accompaniment and melodic interludes and responses. These instruments include the one-stringed lute-fiddle (Aembu *wandidi*, Luhya *shiriri* [figure 3], Luo *orutu*) and the seven- and eight-stringed lyres of the Luo (*nyatiti*; figure 4) and Gusii (*obukano*). Other stringed instruments include the Iteso harp (*adeudeu*). Among the stringed instruments, innovation occurred in the Abaluhya seven-stringed *litungu*, which became an eight-stringed

Figure 3 The *shiriri* (one-string fiddle) is played by William Ingotsi of the Tiriki people, a subgroup of the Luhya. He is accompanied by a *sukuti* player, Nairobi, ca. 1990s.
Photo by David O. Akombo.

fast: one is a small, cylindrical, military-shaped drum (closed on both ends), played in most churches during Sunday services; the other is a rattle (*kayamba*). Played for the articulation of rhythm, these instruments have spread inland from the coast through festivals sponsored by churches and schools. Two instruments used in festivals and competitions are a one-stringed fiddle (found throughout Kenya) and a xylophone (formerly used only along the coast).

Several imported instruments have joined traditional ensembles. Waswahili, Luo, and Kikuyu communities play the accordion. Each group has developed a new way of using it: the Waswahili use it for melodic accompaniment; the Luo, for harmonic purposes. Without melodic or harmonic emphasis, but with frequent polyrhythmic effects between it and singers, the Kikuyu create a rhythmic dialogue between it and the voice.

Other national influences include the use of the Kiswahili language for lyrics, abetting intraethnic musics that show the influence of music from outside Kenya, as reflected in popular musics of the 1950s and 1960s. These new musics led to the popularity of such musicians as Daudi Kabaka (1939–2001), who created fusions with 1960s rock to popularize a style of music called twist, and Fadhili William (ca. 1938–2001), who recorded the song "*Malaika*" (the song's authorship is disputed), which later became internationally popular.

Figure 4 The *nyatiti* lyre played by Everett Igobwa, 2007. The ring on his toe (*oduong'o*) is used to keep a steady rhythm. The striking of the *oduong'o* against the lower arm of the *nyatiti* causes the metal bells (*gara*) on his ankle to sound and the strings of the *nyatiti* to vibrate.
Photo by Sarah Macharia.

instrument with a heptatonic inventory of tones, and in the Kikuyu single-stringed *wandindi*, which acquired a second string, tuned a fourth below the original string so as to function as a drone. In cultures with stringed instruments, the guitar was easily appropriated in the 1950s and 1960s and played with the techniques resembling those used for indigenous instruments.

Aerophones (Wind Instruments)

Aerophones, less widespread in Kenya than other instruments, include grass whistles, animal horns, and seashells. The most popular and well-known wind instruments are a side-blown flute (*chivoti*) and an oboe (*nzumari*), which shares features with South and West Asian oboes and clarinets. These wind instruments are found primarily on the Kenyan coast.

National Influences

Some local instruments have crossed ethnic boundaries. Two instruments from the coast have spread

The Colonial Period

The colonial contribution to late nineteenth-century musical taste in Kenya in some cases started with suppression of certain sociocultural institutions: traditional initiations, religious activities, military institutions, and others. In some areas, these institutions died out because they could not compete with those supported by the colonial system. Some musicians, however, fulfilled a traditional duty by singing praise songs to indigenous politicians, whom they made into heroes of the struggle against colonialism.

With the arrival of European music, styles unrelated to local traditional music in content and form came into existence. Christianity introduced congregational hymn singing, four-part harmony, and Western instruments, including the piano and brasses.

New venues began replacing older ones. Popular band music developed through the support of mass media. The beginning of popular music, however, goes back to the settlement of freed slaves around Mombasa, in Freetown and Rabai. From this seaport, popular music spread in towns along the railway routes up to Nyanza and Western Kenya. People employed on railways and in post offices along the line were among the first to have gramophones, on which their children heard the popular music of the day.

New forms of music spread fast between the urban centers and the countryside, often carried by migrant workers. Urbanization then married the tonal organization of traditional music with that of churches and schools. Foreign musical instruments became popular for accompanying newly created dance forms. Compositional themes came from issues such as landholding, reduction of livestock, and freedom of movement to urban centers.

Servicemen returning from the world wars increased the pace of musical change. Some of them had learned to play Western musical instruments; on their return home, they simply continued playing. Where the authentic instruments were lacking, Kenyans manufactured imitations. For playing in the *beni* a newly invented dance, they devised a wooden version of the trumpet.

In the early 1960s, just before independence, many songs praised local political leaders, encouraged political movements, and voiced disdain for the colonial system. Some songs spread over wide areas.

> *Beni ngoma* is a music and dance that arose in East Africa in the late 1890s and remained popular until the 1960s. The music was created after Africans adopted the instruments of European military bands. The dance was derived from European military drills. The form was reinvigorated after each world war and became a major social and political force.

Troupes and Venues

In Kenya, many troupes of musicians have spread from large urban areas to small rural ones and have achieved national recognition. At any soccer stadium whenever the Abaluhya-dominated team is playing, hired dancers and club supporters perform "*Mwana wa mberi*," a song for the *sukuti*, a dance from western Kenya. In urban areas, the *hukabe humze* (a dance from the coast), the acrobatic *mukanda* or *beni* (an Akamba dance), the *sengenya* (a dance of the Digo), and the *muchungwa* (a dance of the Kikuyu) are popular.

The Ministry of Education and the Ministry of Culture organize performances of national music festivals in the country. During national days, the provincial administration of the Office of the President coordinates and supervises performances of music and dance. Public and private organizations and individuals support musical groups of three sorts: (1) private choirs, composed of people with common interests, such as business or school; (2) institutional groups, supported by churches, states, local communities, and private firms; and (3) professional groups under private management, including popular bands and dance groups.

Groups of the first sort practice and usually perform in members' homes. Singing hymns and anthems, married couples perform the vocal parts they performed during their school days. Occasionally, by invitation, groups perform in a church that has invited one of their members to give a sermon.

Groups of the second sort practice and perform at work, during office hours, even if they have additional obligations in the evening. As musicians, they have access to the benefits enjoyed by other workers in the organization. They also perform for political and social events and at religious services and festivals.

The third sort includes the self-employed. Bandleaders, unemployed youths, and owners of bars organize some groups, which perform for fees in restaurants, nightclubs, and big hotels. When they play in small, rural bars, the patrons of the bar or the owner pays them.

A growing number of musicians in Kenya earn a living by playing music. Particularly in the Nyanza and Western provinces, some play in their home villages, where they entertain guests. They accompany their performances with the lyre, a single-stringed lute, and more rarely a drum. They may perform for hire at a wedding, where they play dances, as in the Digo and Giriama communities; at a funeral, where they perform ritual and secular dances (including war dances) in Luo and Abaluhya communities; and at beer parties in Luo, Kikuyu, and other areas, where they praise generous individuals. At weddings and funerals, musicians attend by invitation and play for a fixed fee. For a beer party, they simply appear, and individuals pay a fee if they want a song played for them, or if they want an improvised song to praise them. Alcoholic beverages are an extra reward for playing.

Musicians travel from one market to another in Nyanza and in the western, central, and coastal areas. Musicians in Nyanza and western Kenya usually play the lyre and the fiddle. Those in the central highlands usually play the accordion (*kinanda*), accompanied by a motor-engine flywheel (*karing'a-ringa*) used as an idiophone: the inside of the wheel is struck by a nail or other iron piece to produce a sound that is onomatopoeic to the name of the instrument. Musicians from the coast play drums, xylophones, or an ensemble of drums, *kayambas*, and other instruments found in the area.

In the cities, low-cost residential areas and slums become another venue of performances by semi-professional musicians, invited by the proprietor or visiting the premises on their own initiative. Residential areas with a majority of people from the same ethnic origin will be frequented by musicians of that ethnic group, though groups with broad ethnic composition and repertory can reach wider audiences. Kaloleni Estate in Nairobi, predominantly the home of Luo people, is the main venue for Luo musicians. In the same way, at Bahati Estate, which has a high concentration of Kikuyu people, Kikuyu musicians often entertain bar patrons.

Street performances are another form of entertainment. In large towns (Nairobi, Mombasa, Nakuru, and others), musicians stage spontaneous performances at bus stops, the entrances of shops, and other busy locations. In Nairobi, these musicians often perform near major hotels and banks in and around the central business district in downtown Nairobi. In Mombasa, they play along Kenyatta Avenue, Digo Road, and Moi Avenue. After attracting an audience, they ask people to put coins into a hat or a container.

Since the late 1980s, secondary schools have invited musicians who play indigenous instruments to train students preparing for national music examinations; the schools invite the musicians to teach students the instrument prescribed for examination. Each province encourages students to play instruments known to be particularly popular in it or those popularized nationally. For example, students from western Kenya are encouraged to play the *siriri*, a tube fiddle of the Abaluhya people. The Luo lyre and the *kayamba* have gained such national prominence that students in schools which admit students from all parts of the country or in schools in urban areas with a mixture of ethnic groups can opt to learn to play these instruments. Musicians receive a fee to maintain themselves during their period of residence at a school. Those who visit several schools a week can make a comfortable living. If the instruments the musicians play are not among those prescribed for examination, their income from the schools may be low.

Some musicians work in the Department of Music at Kenyatta University, where they give practical tuition to students of African instruments. Not regular employees of the University, they often scrounge for additional income. During scholastic vacations, they earn money by playing music in the tourist hotels of Nairobi.

Once in a while, broadcasters invite musicians to perform on radio or television. They do so mainly during music festivals, when prominent musicians are in Nairobi. After recording a program, musicians receive a fee, but get no royalties when the station airs the performance.

Local and international mass media aggressively market local and international musical hits. After rural electrification was achieved (from the mid-1970s), jukebox and disco music became rural entertainments. Since developmental aid is mainly technological, the population is gradually changing from traditionally based to technologically based entertainment.

Musical Organizations

There are several musical organizations in Kenya, and each one has specific goals. The Permanent Presidential Music Commission, founded in 1988, is responsible for promoting, developing, and protecting musicians and all forms of music in the country. The Nairobi Music Society, founded in 1938, and the Kenya Music Trust, established in 1977, devote themselves exclusively in promoting Western symphonic and vocal music. The Kenya Music Festival for Education Institutions, founded in 1927, encourages the creation and performance of local and global music. The Kenya Music Festival for Non-Educational Institutions and Clubs, founded in 1988, promotes local talent in folk music and other styles.

Music in Schools

Kenyan schoolchildren know a mixed repertory of songs—from ethnic groups other than their own, and even from areas outside the country. Lessons and activities provide them with opportunities for performing (figure 5). Classroom music includes songs used as aids by teachers, songs performed during games and physical-education activities, songs mastered for festivals of drama and music, and songs absorbed as part of religious worship. Outside school, children sing songs learned in these contexts.

Throughout Kenya, choirs of children from neighboring primary schools form choirs of up to a thousand voices. These choirs sing mainly on public holidays and national days. Musicians compose some songs specifically for them, and borrow other songs from other choirs. In sound and movement, children show their determination to participate in national issues.

Schools sponsored by religious organizations, which most Kenyan school-age children attend, teach Christian songs or have Islamic religious classes

Figure 5 Schoolgirls dance the *sukuti*, a dance associated with the *sukuti* drums, Western Kenya, 1983. The students playing the drums kneel in a circle behind the dancers at left.
Photo by Iris Scheel.

(*madrasa*) that include chants and other Arabic musics. Teaching music in schools has led to the creation of folkloristic genres that celebrate the past. Schools provide a place for the fusing of European and African musical ideas. For one of the commonest choral forms, professional and amateur musicians adapt Kenyan and other African tunes (folk and popular) to a new environment and context and arrange them in two-, three-, or four-part harmony to preserve the African source and to innovate using European practices.

Music in Churches

Christian churches in Kenya have a strong influence on the development and performance of music. The church has played a key role in nationalizing Kenyans and their musics. Originally, many Christian churches banned the use of African music and instruments in Christian worship, and introduced new performance practices, such as congregational singing. Churches introduced such instruments as the organ, the piano, and brasses, depending on the denomination. Eventually, drumming was accepted in mission churches, though it had already been accepted in African Initiated Christian groups.

A main reason for banning drums was that they stimulated movement. Many Euro-American churches introduced drumming to maintain the tempo or as a feature of Africanization. With independence and greater liberalization of the African contribution to Christian worship, drums have become a mainstay in Christian churches, with or without other instruments. Large churches sponsor music festivals and maintain groups for the improvement of congregational singing.

As required by law, religious denominations and sects—more than 200 of them—have registered in the offices of the Registrar of Societies. Each has its own songbook. Some of their songs are arrangements or adaptations of local songs, with Western harmonization.

Continuity and change distinguish performances in these churches. In the Abaluhya, Akikuyu, Luo, and other communities, traditional singing combines with congregational hymn singing to create new musical styles. Drums, several indigenous idiophones, and Western instruments became features of worship in the early twentieth century.

In some independent churches, garments and associated objects are defining parts of worship services. For example, congregation members of the Africa Israeli Nineveh Church wear white robes with red and green stripes on their headscarves or hats, as a sign of nationalism (the Kenyan flag is red, green, black, and white). Some congregations of this sect processionally carry flags, which they plant in the place of worship. Some meet for worship under a tree, in a social hall, or at a school compound. Processions—accompanied by singing, drumming, stamping, and clapping—are essential to the worship. Four elders start a procession. Behind them follow drummers, leading two lines: one for men, and the other for women. Energetic music and dance progressively intensify all stages of worship: people sing loudly and dance vigorously, starting slowly and building to a climax.

Perhaps the most diverse musics are found in urban churches, which draw on international, national, and local music resources for their repertoire and styles. Some churches founded by male and female African cosmopolitans—such as Margaret Wanjiru, of the famed Jesus Is Alive Ministries—incorporate classic Euro-American hymns (performed in a variety of styles), Kenyan indigenous songs, and contemporary compositions by their members.

By far the most lucrative commercial music in Kenya is religious music known generically as gospel. This music includes as many variants as there are ethnic groups and Christian denominations, integrated with former and current popular styles. This music is performed not only in Christian religious gatherings, but also in political and social venues.

Music in Swahili Communities

In Swahili communities (heavily influenced by Islam) certain musical occasions are exclusively for women or exclusively for men. Showing the influence of Arabic and Islamic practices, Swahili women perform *tumbuizo*, *nyimbo*, and other types of sung poetry. Many Swahili songs fall into the genre known as *tumbuizo*, deriving from a word that can be translated as 'soothe by singing'. Women perform in this genre by creating texts to suit the occasion, like this worksong (collected in 1992 by Geoffrey K. King'ei):

Banat ndugu wa kike, mwatupa shauri gani?
Yafaa tuzitundike, nguo za usichanani,
Tena majembe tuyashikem twendeni tukalime.

Women, our sisters, what advice do you give us?
We should hang up our maiden robes,
Then get hold of hoes and go dig the land.

The singing of worksongs (*tumbuizo za kazi*) lightens tedious jobs, like cultivating, pounding, and grinding grain into flour. For a woman in labor, other women sing such songs "to comfort pain," as they say; women also sing songs that pray for the safety of fishermen at sea.

Weddings are among the most prominent events of Swahili communities. In large towns, participants commonly dance *chakacha*, *lelemama*, and *vugo*. In rural areas along the coast, songs of the first and last of these genres accompany circumcision celebrations (*kutahiri*).

Swahili Taarab

Taarab, Arab-influenced music, has been popular on the East African coast since the 1930s. Kenyans recognize two main styles by their location, instrumentation, and even poetic structure: the classical style and the modern style. The classical style dates to nineteenth-century Egypt and uses the *'ūd* and modern versions of North African strings, such as violins, cellos, and double basses. Mombasa *taarab* is well-known for its appropriation of the harmonium from India. Modern *taarab* uses some of the aforementioned instruments, but it also employs electric and electronic instruments, like guitars and organs. Actors prominent in India frequently visit and entertain the Indian communities of East Africa. In the 1980s, *taarab* introduced the vocal styles of Bollywood music [see FILM MUSIC IN INDIA in the South Asia section of volume 2].

Taarab has often been associated with and performed at Swahili weddings, but its lyrical scope is broad, as it embraces, reiterates, and questions local happenings, values, and so on. It increasingly voices political views. Thus, it has become an important vehicle for disseminating national cultural values and aspirations. This political song, collected in 1992 by King'ei, reproaches dishonest politicians:

Mwalikitumia khila, na urongo mkiapa.
Sasa hamba lahaula, na mmekuwa lutanda.
Pesa zenu cumekula, na von hatuku wapa.

You used tricks, and swore any lies.
Now you curse your luck, and have become desperate.
We have eaten your money, but we did not vote for you.

Taarab plays an important role in the life of Kenya and other East African coastal communities.

Professional Popular Music

Contemporary popular music by Kenyans began to gain ground after 1945. At first, the market was saturated by Cuban rumba and its appropriations by Kenyans and other Africans, especially the Congolese. Country music was marketed and Kenyanized in the early 1950s by people like Julia Lucy and later Joseph Kamaru and others. In the 1960s, Kenyan popular music gained pan-African prominence with musicians such as Daudi Kabaka and John Mwale, who invigorated a two-finger technique popular in most of Africa, fused with music styles from their language groups and international musics, such as rumba and rock and roll.

The 1970s were a period of transition. Many Kenyan dance bands preoccupied themselves with Congo-Zaïre covers, African-American soul, and international pop, a new style, called *benga*, began to emerge. Developed among the Luo in the western areas, it has come to be seen as the definitive Kenyan pop, played by most musicians regardless of language or local identification. Probably the best exponent of the genre is D. O. Misiani and his Shirati Jazz, whose style is characterized by soft, flowing two-part harmonies and hard, pulsating rhythm section.

Alongside the development of these styles, there has been a revival of older styles and interest in Kenyan musicians and Tanzanian national and Congolese international stars who lived or worked in Kenya. Kenyan groups such as Kayamba Africa are reworking folksongs for urban audiences. *Taarab*, in its amalgamation of African, Indian, and Arabian and other west Asian influences, has moved beyond its association with Islam and Arabism to become a major popular genre in secular and folk arenas and in popular Christian and national musics. Popular music continues to be an avenue for social, educational, and political dialogue as much as it is recreation and entertainment for its makers and patrons.

—*Adapted from an article by Paul N. Kavyu and Jean Ngoya Kidula*

Bibliography

Gearhart, Rebecca. 2005. "*Ngoma* Memories: How Ritual Music and Dance Shaped the Northern Kenya Coast." *African Studies Review* 48(3):21–47.

Hyslop, Graham. 1975. *Musical Instruments of East Africa.* Nairobi: Nelson.

Kavyu, Paul N. 1977. *An Introduction to Akamba Music.* Nairobi: Kenya Literature Bureau.

——. 1978. "The Development of Guitar Music in Kenya." *Jazzforschung* 10:111–120.

——. 1990. "The Development of New Intercultural Music in East Africa: A Preliminary Survey." *Proceedings of the Intercultural Music International Symposium and Festival, London.*

Kidula, Jean. 2000. "Polishing the Luster of the Stars: Music Professionalism Made Workable in Kenya." *Ethnomusicology* 44:408–428.

Kigunda, Muriithi. 2007. "Music and Health in Kenya: Sound, Spirituality, and Altered Consciousness Juxtaposed with Emotions." Ph.D. dissertation, Otto-von-Guericke-Universität Magdeburg.

King'ei, Geoffrey K. 1992. "Language, Culture and Communication: The Role of Swahili Taarab Songs in Kenya, 1963–1990." Ph.D. dissertation, Howard University.

Kubik, Gerhard. 1981. "Neo-Traditional Popular Music in East Africa since 1945." *Popular Music* 1:83–104.

Ntarangwi, Mwenda. 2001. "A Socio-Historical and Contextual Analysis of the Popular Musical Performances among the Swahili of Mombasa, Kenya." *Cultural Analysis* 2:1–37.

Nyairo, Joyce, and James Ogude. 2005. "Popular Music, Popular Politics: *Unbwogable* and the Idioms of Freedom in Kenyan Popular Music." *African Affairs* 104(415):225–249.

Ranger, Terence O. 1975. *Dance and Society in Eastern Africa, 1890–1970: the Beni Ngoma.* Berkeley: University of California Press.

Roberts, John. 1965. "Kenya's Pop Music." *Transition* 19:40–43.

Stapleton, Chris, and Chris May. 1990. *African Rock: The Pop Music of a Continent.* New York: Dutton.

Varnum, John P. 1971 "The Obukano of the Gusii: A Bowl Lyre of East Africa." *Ethnomusicology* 15(2):242–248.

Wilson, James A. 2006. "Political Songs, Collective Memories and Kikuyu *Indi* Schools." *History in Africa* 33:363–388.

Zake, W. G. S. 1986. *Folk Music of Kenya.* Nairobia: Uzima Press.

Central Africa

Central Africa

Central Africa

In Central Africa, music reflects interchanges with styles from such distant sources as Portugal and Latin America. Within the area, the polyphonic singing of the Pygmies has influenced—and been influenced by—the music of their neighbors. Royal chiefdoms, secret societies, migrant laborers, European Christian evangelization, and the electric guitar have all added to the richness of the musical palette.

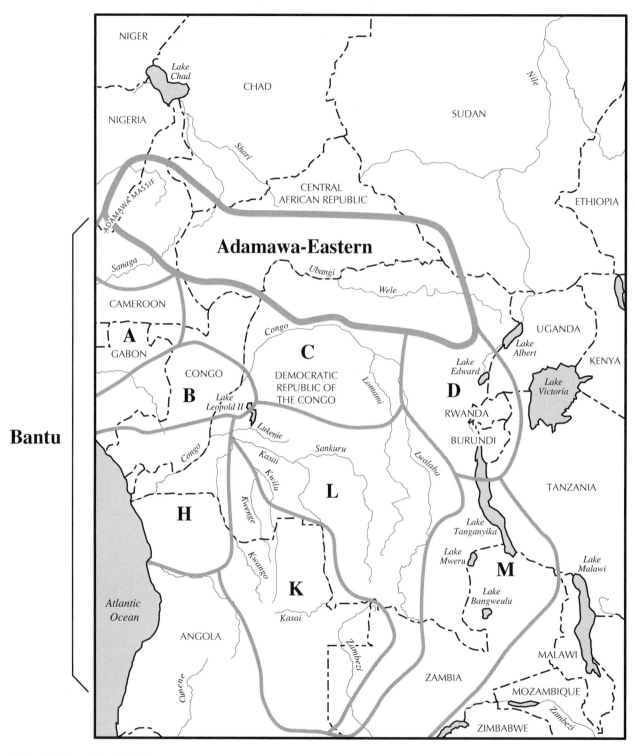

Central African Linguistic Zones

Central Africa: An Introduction

We can think of Central Africa as comprising most of the Democratic Republic of Congo (DRC), all of Gabon, Equatorial Guinea, the islands of São Tome and Principe, Congo, most of the Central African Republic, and large parts of Cameroon, Angola, and the northern parts of Zambia. This grouping acknowledges a combination of linguistic and cultural affinities, patterns of migration, and musical styles. Because of a historical migration of pastoral peoples from the East African Horn, and the presence of specific patterns of political organization in the interlacustrine area, Rwanda and Burundi are properly perceived as belonging to East Africa, rather than to Central Africa. Similar grounds exclude the southwestern part of Angola (particularly the province of Huila), which includes the cultures of the Nkhumbi, the Handa, and others.

> The **interlacustrine area** of Central Africa is the area bounded by Lakes Victoria, Kyoga, Albert, Edward, Kivu, and Tanganyika.

So defined, Central Africa is a vast region, diverse in musical cultures. In large expanses of the rainforest, the musical cultures of Bantu-speakers have supplanted an ancient culture, which survives in pockets, dispersed from southern Cameroon across the Congo to the Ituri Forest: that of Pygmy hunter-gatherers. Though the Pygmies adopted Bantu languages long ago, their musical culture retained distinctive traits, which influenced the later arrivals. The region has three ethnic-linguistic entities—Adamawa-Eastern-speakers, Bantu-speakers, and Pygmy-speakers. Wherever contact occurred among them, cultural exchange and adaptation followed. In addition, cultures from outside Central Africa repeatedly made inroads into the region.

On the linguistic map of Central Africa, the line between the Adamawa-Eastern languages and Bantu languages of zones A, B, C, H, L, K, and (in part) D and M, marks a stylistic divide between Central African musical subregions.

Musical Cultures in the Adamawa-Eastern Subregion

This subregion lies north of the equator and extends from the border of northeastern Nigeria, across Cameroon and the Central African Republic, into parts of the southern Sudan, including northern DRC (see Adamawa-Eastern area on the map).

The people who settled in this subregion can be classed in the following cultural clusters, proceeding from west to east.

(a) Chamba-Yungur, in the west, with individual peoples such as the Chamba, the Kutin, the Longuda, the Yungur, the Ndongo, and the Vere.
(b) Adamawa, also in the west, including the Mundanga, the Fali, the Mumuye, the Mbum, the Lakka, and the Namshi.
(c) Banda-Gbaya, including the Gbaya, the Banda, the Manja, and the Ngbandi.
(d) Azande, including the Azande with their subdivisions, plus the (related) Nzakara.

The ecology of this subregion draws on a uniform savanna, which supports a small population. Intermittently mountainous areas, especially the Adamawa massif, have often served as a retreat for invaded indigenous peoples.

Certain stylistic and structural traits in music occur saliently throughout this subregion, as an extensive sample of recordings, obtained during the mid-1960s by the musicologist Gerhard Kubik shows (Kubik 1963–1964). These traits encompass tonal systems, singing in parts, patterns of movement, and instrumental resources. Some of them occur in the whole subregion, and some only in parts of it.

Possibly all these peoples use pentatonic tonal systems. In western areas, the typical scale is often a plain anhemitonic pentatonic one, with seconds and minor thirds. In eastern areas, narrower intervals

> An **anhemitonic pentatonic** scale has five tones, but no half-steps or minor seconds.

occur, as in some forms of Azande music. In several cultures, this scale combines with a homophonic two-part style of singing with a predilection for simultaneous fourths and fifths. Despite differences in the intervals actually preferred in different areas—even within a homogeneous musical culture, like that of the Azande—simultaneous fourths and fifths are perfect (that is, aimed at 498 and 702 cents, respectively). In this subregion, no evidence for the use of a tempered tonal system has turned up.

Some cultural anthropologists have thought the peoples of the western highlands or mountains of this subregion represented an old Sudanic or paleonegritic stratum: these peoples are the descendants of long-established agriculturalists of the savanna. Significantly, we here find evidence of the presence of kinetic patterns combined in interlocking style. Musicians play two double iron bells (*toŋ ito*) of the Central African flange-welded type, with bow grip. The bells are individually called *toŋ senwa* 'the higher', and *toŋ deni* 'the lower'. Positioned with their openings toward the chest, they are played in a two-tone pattern with a softwood beater, held in the right hand. The patterns interlock. By varying the distance between the opening and the chest, the musicians modify the timbre of the bells. Both these techniques of structuring are probably ancient in African music; they also grace the instrumental music of other areas, as in the *mvet* of zone A (see map).

Among the Chamba, who are related to the Kutin, evidence of tripartite interlocking appears in the organization of women's millet-pounding strokes. Three women, pestles in hand, stand around a mortar. They strike in turn into the mortar, to produce an interlocking beat. Sometimes, between the main working strokes, each woman lightly taps her pestle on the rim of the mortar to create accents and rhythmic patterns within a twelve-pulse cycle. From time to time, with lips, palate, and tongue, the women add sucking and clicking sounds, forming another timbral-melodic line.

From northernmost Cameroon across the Central African Republic into southern Sudan stretches what can be called Africa's most cohesive harp territory. The harp, an ancient Egyptian-Saharan heritage, found widespread footholds in the savannas at the northern fringes of the rainforest. From the specimens played by the Ngbaka, south of Bangui, to those of the Nzakara and the Azande, most of the peoples mentioned under (c) and (d) above, except for the Gbaya in the west, play harps.

Ancient connections are audible in harp music across this subregion, including nomenclature, with the frequently heard term *kundi* (Azande, Nzakara) and its variants, like *kundeŋ* (Karre at Bozoum). In the northwesternmost areas of the Adamawa-Eastern division of languages, harps accompany iron smelting, and are played by associates—often close family members or junior apprentices—of a blacksmith working at a furnace. In the southeastern areas, harps have spread into the land of the Mangbetu, speakers of a Central Sudanic language, whom outsiders have often erroneously associated with the Azande. In the early 1900s, Mangbetu carvers, exploiting the beginnings of a lucrative colonial trade in touristic art, produced thousands of ivory harps with carved motifs and body coverings made of reptile skin. (A large collection lives in the Musikinstrumentenmuseum in Munich.) European tourists bought these specimens of Mangbetu harps, which ended up in the international trade of African art, or in public collections.

Older styles of Azande harp music include asymmetric patterns within a regularly cyclical number, such as twelve or twenty-four pulses. Harmony in Zande harp music includes sequences of four bichords, which also appear in Azande vocal harmony. The tonal-harmonic system of Azande music strictly regulates the occurrence of each of these bichords. The scale is a descending pentatonic one, which musicians memorize with the aid of a text they often play to check the tuning at the beginning of a piece (figure 1); here is its translation.

Little by little, that's work.
One must play the harp, and sing its song.
The ancient things implicate work.

The harp is not the only prominent Azande instrument: they have numerous instrumental resources, including three types of xylophone: the *manza*, the *longo*, and the *kponingbo*. The first of these, associated with Azande royalty, has a pentatonic tuning, in two large intervals, one medium interval, and two small intervals. A specimen documented in DRC had gourd resonators (Kremser 1982). Another, found at Chief Zekpio's place in Dembia, southeastern Central African Republic, had five logs placed over banana stems; a chief's relative played it to accompany the chief's harp music. The term *manza* may connect with other xylophone terminology in northern Central Africa. No evidence of Indonesian origins has turned up, but relationships with xylophone names west of the Azande are likely: *mɛndzãŋ* in Ewondo (southern Cameroon), and *mɛntʃaɲà* in Mpyɛmɔ̃ (southwestern Central African Republic). These cognates imply historical relationships in the distribution of xylophones in this subregion. The *longo* (also pronounced /rongo/) is a portable, gourd-resonated xylophone. The specimen documented among the Azande at Dembia resembles types found in Chad, and falls clearly within the northernmost area of gourd-resonated xylophones in Africa. The Azande *kponingbo*, a twelve- or thirteen-key log xylophone, accompanied by a slit drum (*guru*) and a double-skin drum in the *kponingbo* circle dance, is likely an import from farther south. Pieces for *kponingbo* suggest this origin by a rhythmic pattern that seems to be a remolding of a timeline associated with music in Katanga and eastern Angola (zones L and K). Characteristically, Azande

Figure 1 An Azande phrase for checking the tuning of the harp (*kundi*). It is performed in free-speech rhythm.

xylophones are not played in interlocking style, though those of Uganda and northern Mozambique are.

The instrumental resources of the Azande include one flute ensemble: a set of notched flutes, with four fingerholes each, accompanied by marching-style drums. Based in Rafai (Central African Republic), it survived as late as 1964. Evidence available suggests it was a late-nineteenth-century adaptation of military music that bands had performed on expeditions in the southern Sudan during the Mahdi rebellion.

Musical Cultures in the Bantu Subregion

Pygmy Cultures

The linguistic and cultural map of the tropical-rainforest areas of Central Africa of the early twenty-first century differs distinctly from that of thousands of years ago. Before about 1000 to 500 B.C.E., when speakers of early Bantu languages from the Bantu Nucleus (a zone embracing parts of western Cameroon and eastern Nigeria) migrated to western parts of Central Africa, the equatorial forest was inhabited by bands of hunter-gatherers, who differed genetically from other speakers of Niger-Congo languages, namely the Pygmies. All remaining Pygmies speak Bantu languages believed to be adaptations of the Bantu tongues spoken by the first migrants with whom the Pygmies had contact. In music, however, a pre-Bantu Pygmy musical culture may have survived. Pygmy music distinctively combines a polyphonic style of singing with an extremely developed technique of yodeling. These traits appear in the music of Pygmy groups in widely separated areas, as shown by a comparison of recordings: in the Ituri Forest, which lies on the northeastern tip of the Congo River basin in DRC; among the Bangombe and Bambenjele of the Upper Sangha River, southwestern Central African Republic; and among the Bambenjele (Ba-Bénzélé) and the Aka, south of Bangui. Even outposts of Pygmy culture prove the persistence of a Pygmy musical style, as witness recordings by barely a dozen individuals staying at Ngambe, in the Cameroon grasslands, and associating with the Tikar chief of that town (Kubik 1963–1964: B 8650).

The strength of Pygmy musical culture shows in the fact that the Pygmies' neighbors have almost invariably borrowed, however imperfectly, the Pygmies' vocal polyphony. In one musical genre or another, these neighbors adopt a Pygmy style of singing, which quite often associates with hunting songs. Bantu-speakers such as the Mpyɛmɔ̃ and Mpompo, in the southwestern Central African Republic and southeastern Cameroon, have adopted Pygmy musical traits; but so have semi-Bantu-speakers, such as the Tikar, notably in a dance called *ngbãnya* and in hunting songs called *nswẽ*. The Mangbetu, speakers of a Central Sudanic language in northeastern DRC, have also adopted elements of Pygmy polyphony. Therefore, on finding Pygmy-style vocal polyphony among any sedentary population in Central Africa, a listener can conclude there has been Pygmy contact in the past, even if none occurs at present.

Similarly, Pygmies have adopted musical traits from their neighbors, with whom they have long economically associated themselves. These traits include playing reed pipes, such as the *luma*, popular among the Ituri Forest Pygmies; playing various types of drums, and even the polyidiochord stick zither, used by the Pygmies of the Upper Sangha (and borrowed from Bantu speakers of zones A and B); and performing pieces drawn from the expressive repertory of secret societies, such as the *jenge*. Practiced in the area of the Ogowe River, Congo, *jenge* was first documented and recorded by André Didier and Gilbert Rouget (1946); it was later studied extensively by Maurice Djenda. Among the Bangombe Pygmies (along the Sangha River), *jenge* is a men's society, which centers on a masked monster (also *jenge*). The mask boasts strips of raffia leaves and resembles a moving bell or robe. In public performance, accompanied by drums, it performs rapidly twisting movements in front of women and children. Noninitiates believe the monster lives in the forest, where it controls hunters' luck. The people consider the monster the ancestor of one of the oldest members of the group in the camp. The songs sung at public *jenge* performances correspond in style with general Upper Sangha Pygmy traits (as in dances like *wunga* or *moyaya*), but an unusual song for rituals in homophonic harmony uses simultaneous fifths: members of the secret society sing it while they carry raffia leaves back from the river to build the mask. The members run through the village, where they end the song with shouts.

Bantu Musical Cultures in Zones H, L, K

These musical cultures exhibit diversity that is partly explained by successive migrations, cultural divergence, and cultural convergence, during the past two thousand years. The tentative division of the Bantu languages into zones is a useful yardstick, because it reflects, if only imperfectly, cultural dividing lines.

Zone H

Thanks to early contacts established between Portugal and the kingdoms of Congo, Ndongo, and Matamba, zone H is unique on the map of Central African musical cultures: a large amount of written and pictorial sources date from the 1500s on. If nowhere else, music history can be partially reconstructed there for the last four hundred years.

The major language of the zone is Kikoongo, including related languages such as Yombe and Sundi, spoken in southwestern DRC. Kimbundu is the most important language spoken in Luanda (Angola), and in the hinterland into the province of Malanji. The zone includes southwestern DRC, southern Congo, Cabinda (with the Loango coast), and northwestern Angola.

European Influences and Research The kingdom of Congo was an area of early Christian evangelization. Whether by the 1600s missionaries had affected the music of Kikoongo-speaking peoples is difficult to assess, but there were probably considerable influences from Christian religious music and European military and ceremonial music. European wind instruments came into local use at that time, and their knowledge spread into the interior, where wooden trumpets still figure among the paraphernalia of secret societies. Smaller ones have a separate mouthpiece, similar in size and bore to sixteenth-century European trombones. The introduction of church bells into the kingdom of Congo spawned an industry that produced small clapper bells with local metallurgical techniques.

During the late 1600s, detailed accounts of Congo music, musical instruments, organology, and musical sociology, appear in works by two Capuchin missionaries: António Giovanni Cavazzi and Girolamo Merolla. Cavazzi went to what is now northern Angola in 1654; for thirteen years, he lived and traveled in the kingdom of Congo and adjoining areas. Many of the illustrations in his book *Istorica Descrizione de 'tre' Regni Congo, Matamba et Angola* (1687) depict musical scenes. One shows warriors playing a bell and a "double bell." Since the discovery of his original paintings, new sources on the music of the Congo and neighboring kingdoms have opened up.

Merolla traveled to Luanda from Naples in 1682; he worked for five years in the town of Sonyo, traveled up the Congo River, and visited Cabinda. His testimony, written with obvious love of African music, rivals that of Cavazzi. A famous etching shows several musical instruments: a gourd-resonated xylophone (*marimba*), a pluriarc (*nsamhi*), two types of scraper (*kasuto, kilondo*), a double bell (*longa*), a goblet-shaped single-skin drum (*ngamba*), and an end-blown horn (*epungu*).

Referring to the kingdom of Congo and neighboring areas, Merolla describes some of these instruments:

> One of the most common instruments is the *marimba*. Sixteen calabashes act as resonators and are supported lengthwise by two bars. Above the calabashes little boards of red wood, somewhat longer than a span, are placed, called *taculla*. The instrument is hung round the neck and the boards (keys) are beaten with small sticks. Mostly four *marimbas* play together; if six want to play, the *cassuto* is added—a hollowed piece of wood four spans long, with ridges in it. The bass of this orchestra is the *quilondo*, a roomy, big-bellied instrument two and a half to three spans in height which looks like a bottle towards the end and is rubbed in the same way as the *cassuto*. When all the instruments are played together, a truly harmonic effect is produced from a distance; nearby one can hear the sticks rattling, which causes a great noise. The *nsambi* is a stringed instrument consisting of a resonator and five small bows strung with strings of bark fiber, which are made to vibrate with the index finger. The instrument is supported on the chest for playing. The notes sound weak but not unpleasant. (Hirschberg 1969:16, 18)

The four-piece xylophone ensemble described by Merolla does not survive in the territory of the former kingdom of Congo; in fact, xylophones seem to have disappeared from there. Some people have thought, therefore, that Cavazzi and Merolla were describing xylophones from one of the neighboring kingdoms, possibly Matamba, in the present Malanji Province of Angola, where large, gourd-resonated xylophones appear in association with chiefs; however, present-day Malanji xylophones, played on the ground and not carried on a strap around the musicians' shoulders, are probably not related historically to the depicted seventeenth-century specimens.

Survivals The xylophone tradition seen by Cavazzi and Merolla does survive—not in the kingdom of Congo, but farther north, where, in organology, attitude of playing, and other traits, including the fact that four xylophones play together, the xylophones of southern Cameroon provide the closest parallel to what Merolla described. This situation exemplifies a pattern frequently met in cultural history: a tradition migrates away from its original center of distribution, but survives in lands on the periphery, while it disappears from its original home.

In zone H, particularly among Kimbundu-speakers in Angola, scrapers (*cassuto*) survive. In Luanda, scrapers (*dikanza*) have served particularly in novel twentieth-century ballroom dance traditions, such as the *rebita* and *semba*, dances characterized by the belly bounce, a light abdominal touch. In Angola, scrapers accompany military-music-inspired dances, such as *kalukuta*.

Not much of the sixteenth-to-seventeenth-century tradition has probably survived in zone H. Extensive contact with the outside world—via sea links to West Africa, Europe, and Brazil; and via trade links to the interior of Africa, from the 1700s on, especially by *pombeiros* (Portuguese-African traders who crossed Africa from Luanda to Mozambique)—has many times remodeled the musical cultures of the zone.

Bell-resonator Lamellaphones Among the traditions of the Loango coast (Cabinda and adjacent areas), a tradition that has aroused considerable interest is the "Loango-sanza," (Laurenty 1962) a lamellaphone in the broad category classed by Hugh Tracey as having a bell-type resonator, made of wood, hollowed out from below. In Loango lamellaphones, the cavity usually has a half-moon shape. The number of tones it can produce is usually seven; in contrast to many other African lamellaphones, the tones lie in ascending scalar order from left to right.

Loango lamellaphones have a small distribution area: mainly along the Loango coast. By chance, however, the oldest specimen preserved in collections is of the Loango type; it was collected in Brazil, where it was undoubtedly made by a slave from the Loango coast, not later than 1820. It has a carved head—a trait that must have been common in the 1800s, because Stephen Chauvet (1929) printed a photograph of another specimen with a carved figure on top, in contrast to many later-collected specimens, which have only a somewhat extended top. The head and the shape of the cavity of the resonator imply strong cultural contacts with zones A and B.

There could be a historical sequence from the Loango-type lamellaphones to a later (and possibly mid-nineteenth-century) development in the lower

Congo-DRC area: the *likembe* (with a box resonator), though this type has a V-shaped or N-shaped arrangement of the lamellae. The *likembe* originated in zone H. With Belgian colonial penetration up the Congo River, it spread rapidly: by the 1920s, it had reached all of DRC and Congo, most of Uganda and northeastern Angola, and areas beyond.

Instrumental Innovations Widespread innovations in instrumental technology and musical style have their origins in zone H, which has absorbed and modified many traditions outside the area. The two-stringed bowed lute (*kakoxa*) took inspiration from seventeenth- or eighteenth-century Iberian stringed instruments. The gourd-resonated xylophones (*madimba*) found in Malanji Province probably derive from southeast African models, whose techniques of playing and manufacture were carried to northern Angola by personnel who regularly traveled with *pombeiros*, traders who followed the route from Luanda to Malanji, the Lunda Empire, and Kazembe near Lake Mweru, and down south through the Maravi Empire to the Portuguese trading posts Tete and Sena, on the Zambezi River in Mozambique.

Musical innovations that emerged from zone H include developments in urban music, around the twin cities of Brazzaville (Congo) and Kinshasa (DRC). After the 1940s, these municipalities, separated only by the Congo River, witnessed the rise of the guitar-based music called *musique moderne zaïreoise* and *musique moderne congolèse*. It is thought that guitars first came to Matadi and Kinshasa (then Léopoldville) in the 1930s, brought by Kru sailors from West Africa.

Local music for solo guitar, with performers such as Polo Kamba singing in Lingala (the Congolese trade language), was recorded on the Ngoma label by the Firme Jeronimidis, based in Kinshasa. An ensemble style of music for guitar also developed; it was heavily influenced by Latin American records, which brought to Central Africa African-American music from Latin America and the Caribbean.

This infusion culminated in the development of electric-guitar styles in the 1960s, advanced by bands that achieved international renown: OK Jazz, Rochereau Tabu Ley and his African Fiesta, and others [see POPULAR MUSIC IN THE CONGOS]. Some bands, such as that of Jean Bokilo, with his celebrated "Mwambe" series of recordings of many versions of one song, tried to integrate into the new styles supposedly traditional patterns—in Bokilo's case, harmonic patterns. Though these styles originated in zone H, they cannot be considered extensions of Kikoongo traditional music, because they include elements from many regions of DRC and the Congo, in reflection of the ethnic mix in cities like Kinshasa and Brazzaville.

Zone L and (in part) Zone M

This area extends from central parts of DRC, across Katanga in southeast DRC, and into northwestern Zambia; it includes languages of the Pende, the Luba, the Kaonde, the Lunda, and the Mbweraŋkoya. It has been well researched, particularly by musicologists associated with the Musée Royal de l'Afrique Centrale at Tervuren, Belgium. It is one of the rare areas in Central Africa where archaeological evidence of musical practices is available. South of the equatorial forest, several Iron Age cultures produced a surplus population, which, beginning about C.E. 1000 to 1100, began the third Bantu dispersal, from a wide area in northern Katanga, to the southwest (Angola), south (Zambia), and southeast (Malawi, Mozambique). From graves at Sanga and Katoto (in Katanga), single iron bells and other iron objects have been dated to about A.D. 800, and coincide in time with findings farther south, especially at the site of Ingombe Ilede.

> The **Bantu dispersals** were a widespread migration of peoples that began in West Africa 3,000 to 4,000 years ago, moving east and south.

Iron bells in this area, as elsewhere in Central Africa, figure among the regalia of chiefs and other officials of centralized states. Other musical instruments associated with chieftainship or kingship in this area include the double-skin hourglass drums (*mukupela*) of the Luba–Lunda; because their materials are wood and skin, there is little chance any can be recovered from archaeological deposits.

In precolonial times, trade routes going through Katanga from west and southeast left their mark on the music of zones L and M. Small, board-shaped lamellaphones known in Shiluba as *cisanji* probably developed from southeast African models that had been reduced in size for use by long-distance porters coming up the Zambezi. The Maravi Empire (1600s and 1700s), through which the trade route passed, was the source of single-note xylophones called *limba*, used in religious contexts that similarly became known farther north. East African trade routes ending in Katanga led to the rise of a sizable Swahili-speaking population there (speaking Kingwana, a Swahili dialect) and the introduction of instruments such as the flatbar zither (Shiluba *luzenze*) and the board zither (*ngyela*), played in "vamping style" with a pendular motion of the right index finger.

The presence of centralized political structures among the peoples of zones L and M found expression in royal music associated with traditional rulers, such as the drums called *cinkumbi* by the peoples of Mwata Kazembe, in the Lwapula Valley near Lake Mweru. The importance of music for initiations in this zone, particularly for the initiations of girls—such as the *cisungu* rites among the Lenje, the Soli, and others in Zambia—stresses the continuation of a social structure with a matrilineal system of descent.

Christian Evangelization

In the twentieth century, southern DRC and northeastern Zambia proved fertile ground for Christian missions. The result was two byproducts that have affected the musical cultures of these areas: scientific research by Christian missionaries, and indigenous acquaintance with Christian hymnody.

The effort of missionaries who interested themselves in local musical cultures led to the study and development of the music. A. M. Jones worked from 1929 to 1950 as a missionary and principal of St. Mark's College in Mapanza, Zambia; he studied the musical cultures of the Bemba, the Nsenga, and other groups. Also in Zambia, Father Jean Jacques Corbeil collected musical instruments, which remain in the University of Zambia.

Introducing Christian hymns and school music had many effects and stimulated the emergence of a new ecclesiastical music, both in the established churches (for example, the work of Joseph Kiwele, who in the 1950s composed *Messe Katangaise*), and in separatist ones.

Zones L and M have also seen the emergence of a guitar-based, popular music for dancing, in response to multiple factors, including urbanization and migrant labor. This process started in the 1930s, particularly along the copper belt on both sides of the DRC–Zambia border, an area that attracted miners from many parts of Central Africa. A township culture soon developed around the emerging major centers, where a Katanga guitar style arose. In the 1950s and 1960s, Mwenda-Jean Bosco (1930–1990), alias Mwenda wa Bayeke, a Luba–Sanga guitar composer, rose to be one of Africa's foremost guitarists.

Zone K

This zone covers all of eastern Angola, northwestern Zambia, and adjacent areas in DRC. Musicologically, it is one of the most thoroughly studied parts of Central Africa, and it has been one of the most attractive to fine-arts researchers because of the formal intimacies of music, masked dancing, and visual art. It is a zone of highly institutionalized music connected with initiation schools and secret societies. Included in it are the following languages: Cokwe, Lwena, Luchazi, Mbwela, Nkhangala; Lozi; Luyana; and Totela. The latter two groups have perhaps more links with southern Africa than to Central Africa.

Within zone K, the cultures of the Cokwe, the Lwena, and the so-called Ngangela peoples (including the Lucazi, the Mbwela, the Nkhangala, the Nyemba, and others), show ancient affinities with the Luba–Lunda cultural cluster (zone L). Migration of the Cokwe to new lands continued until late in the twentieth century. In the 1800s, Cokwe families penetrated farther and farther south from northeastern Angola, and they settled on riverine grasslands in the Kwandu-Kuvangu Province of Angola. They have culturally influenced the Ngangela-speaking peoples, with whom they developed close relationships. Cokwe masks, such as *Cikūza* or *Kalelwa*—the latter depicting a nineteenth-century Cokwe king, Mwene Ndumba wa Tembo—appear all over eastern Angola and in northwestern Zambia. In musical performances, these masks proceed to the public dance place (*cilende*) in a village, stop in front of the set of long, goblet-shaped drums (*vipwali* or *zing'oma*), and perform a recitation (*kutangesa*), which drum strokes guide, cue, and interrupt.

In zone K, most music is performed within the traditional institutions of education for the young, the secret societies, and the context of royalty. Among the Lozi or "Barotse" on the Zambezi River, the paramount chief presides over the *kuomboka* ceremony, a picturesque festival, marked yearly by a procession with boats. Every year, when the Zambezi inundates the plains up to the highlands, the Lozi people migrate ceremonially to the dry places, accompanied by instrumental music and dancing. Their music stands stylistically apart from most of the music in zone K because of the historical links of the Lozi with the south, and because of their proximity to Ndebele culture in Zimbabwe. In contrast to the multipart singing style of the Luchazi, Cokwe, Lwena, their style emphasizes fourths and fifths as simultaneous intervals, structured in a manner comparable to Shona-Nsenga harmonic patterns. The tunings and chords of Lozi gourd-resonated xylophones (*silimba*) reflect this tonal system.

Among the Luchazi, Cokwe, and Lwena peoples, the performance of certain musical works marks royal events, especially a chief's death or installation. The chiefs of these peoples keep in their assortment of regalia the *mukupele* or *mukupela*, a double-headed hourglass drum and sometimes a double bell. The *mukupele* is played only at a royal

death or installation. It has a penetrating sound that owes its loudness to an ingenious device, a small piece of calabash neck covered with a mirliton (a spider's-nest covering), and inserted into a hole on its side.

Megaphones Another ritual for dead kings or chiefs is in the Ngangela languages called *vandumbu*, a term that refers to the principal musical instrument of the occasion, a megaphone, whose sound is not considered *mwaso* 'song, music' (pl. *myaso*), though it represents the dead kings' voices. Its production is a secret, whose knowledge is reserved to those who have passed an initiation ceremony; those persons keep it under water all year long, in a shallow place in riverine marshlands. Individual megaphones, up to 4 meters long, consist of wooden tubes with a round mouthpiece, cut from tall trees; the orifice often takes the shape of a crocodile's mouth, or that of some other ferocious riverine animal. The body of each tube is wrapped with plant fiber.

In the dark of night, men of the secret society bring the tubes up to the village and emit into the mouthpiece fearful vocal sounds, which the tubes seemingly amplify. Three megaphones are normally used. In front of them, as in a procession, walk the players of three trumpets (*nyavikali*), about 1.5 meters long; by overblowing, the players can produce the tones of the harmonic series. During the event, people make a sacrifice of millet beer: they dip one of the horns into a mortar and pour the beer onto its teeth. The ceremony tries to guarantee the fertility of the village by gaining the dead kings' goodwill. The salient aspects of this procession resemble those of royal receptions in the kingdom of Congo in the 1600s, as described by seventeenth-century authors.

Initiations Other Luchazi, Cokwe, and Lwena musical performances highlight the public aspects of age-grade initiations. Every year during the dry season, from about May to October, circumcision schools (*mikanda*) for boys aged six to twelve are held outside the villages. In that season, one can probably find a *mukanda* (sing.) every six to twelve miles through the more-densely populated areas of eastern Angola, northwestern Zambia, and adjacent border areas in DRC.

The circumcising surgery marks the beginning of a *mukanda*, and precedes the building of the lodge in which the recuperant boys will stay in seclusion for several months. Music and dance instruction play an important role. In a Luchazi *mukanda*, three kinds of musical instruction occur.

1. *myaso yatundanda* 'songs of the initiates', performed with the *kuhunga* and *kawali* dance-actions, accompanied by *vipwali* drums. There are also songs for the initiates to perform on specific occasions—when receiving food, at sunrise, and at sunset.
2. *kutangesa* 'recitations by the initiates'. The music teacher, sitting astride a *vipwali* drum, cues the group of initiates, who recite long texts, sometimes with historical content.
3. *myaso yakukuwa* 'songs performed at night by initiates' (and their teachers and guardians), accompanied with concussion sticks.

The songs performed at night are in three- or four-part harmony. Cokwe, Lwena, and Luchazi vocal music is homophonic in a hexa- or heptatonic system, which emphasizes simultaneous triads, in thirds plus fifths, or in fourths plus thirds.

A Song for Circumcision Voices interrelate in parallel, oblique, or contrary motion; they characteristically proceed stepwise, as in a song that expresses the secluded initiates' yearning for their return home, at the beginning of the rainy season.

In this song, singers accompany themselves on concussion sticks in two groups. Each person holds two sticks, one in each hand, and by turns, uses the right-hand stick to strike the left-hand stick from above and the left-hand stick to strike the right-hand stick from above. This pattern is achieved by an even and regular left-right, up-down alternation of both hands. The sticks hit each other at a point in the middle of the path described by the hands. Each group plays a distinctive rhythm.

Some performances include a third rhythmic part: two or three *tutanga* players hold in the left hand a wooden slat about 6 decimeters long, and strike it with a stick held in the right.

The text of the song below expresses yearning for the village. A *mukanda* normally ends with the dry season, when trees begin to sprout. So the boys in seclusion, and their guardians and teachers, are looking forward to that day:

LEADER Tangwa ilombela mity'e—Tangwa ilombela miti, lelo tukuya kwimbo.
CHORUS Tangwa ilombela mity'e.
LEADER Ee!
CHORUS Tangwa ilombela miti, lelo tukuya kwimbo. Tangwa ilombela mity'e.
LEADER Ee!
CHORUS Oo! Mwaka uk'e?

LEADER The day the trees will sprout—The day the trees will sprout, that day we return to the village.
CHORUS The day the trees will sprout.
LEADER Ee!
CHORUS The day the trees will sprout, that day we return to the village. The day the trees will sprout.
LEADER Ee!
CHORUS Oo! Which year?

As in this song, each singer can form his own vocal part by choosing any of several notes within a particular range, and he can vary it from one repetition to another. Each singer must follow a basic rule: the melody of any voice line must move strictly stepwise.

The relationship of aural, visual, and kinetic arts informs masked dancing, by women's masks (*makisi a vampwevo*), in which body paint is used, and men's masks (*makisi a vamala*). Every year, men construct individual masked characters. Most masks depict a human form; some, an animal form. All are made in a *mukanda* by the guardians of the secluded initiates, and it is the guardians who appear disguised as masks in front of the women, to reassure them of their children's well-being. During the *mukanda* season, many maskfests take place. A performance late in the evening, after supper, may feature appearances of the court fool (*cileya*), or of the young woman (*mwanaphwo*), a famous Cokwe mask.

Recent innovations, such as the wig (*ciwiki*), with its Afro hairstyle, can also appear. These masks appear singly; but in contrast, a dramatic masquerade takes place in the daytime, at the village dance-place (*cilende*). It features a dozen masked characters in succession, until the feast closes with the appearance of the madman, a spectacular mask, taking the highest rank; it is called *mpumpu* (in Mbwela), *lipumpu* (in Lucazi), and *cizaluke* (in Lwena-Luvale). In southeastern Angola, the person wearing it sports a simulated penis, which he wags during his performance. The madman represents an ancient king, Mwene Nyumbu, who after his sister insulted him is said to have instituted circumcision by circumcising himself.

All masked performances are accompanied by the standard *vipwali* or *zing'oma* drums, sometimes three of them played by one person, when the set of instruments is called *tumboi* by the Mbwela and Nkhangala of southeastern Angola.

Musical Instruments Zone K is characterized by the predominance of struck idiophones and membranophones. Stringed instruments include only the friction bow (*kawayawaya*), imports such as the *kalyalya* (two- or three-stringed bowed lute,

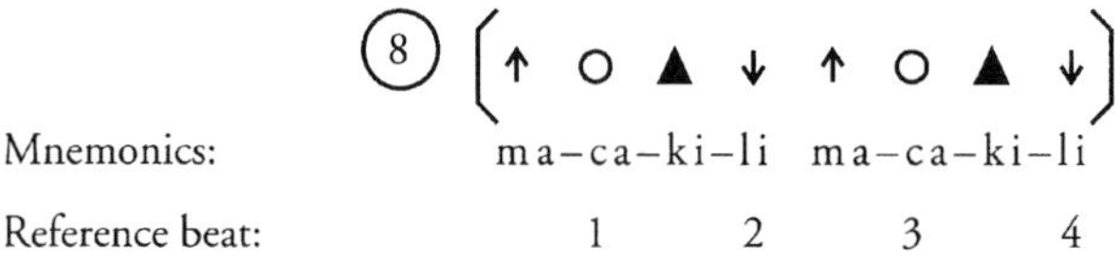

⑧ ⎡ ↑ ○ ▲ ↓ ↑ ○ ▲ ↓ ⎤

Mnemonics: ma–ca–ki–li   ma–ca–ki–li

Reference beat: 1   2   3   4

Figure 2 A Ngangela mnemonic pattern (*macakili macakili* for rattles).

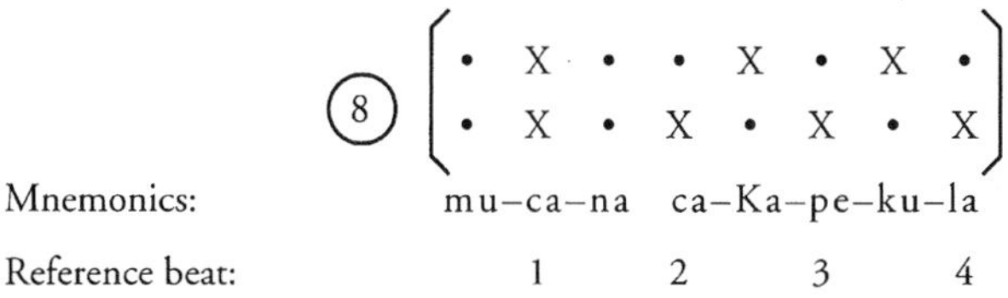

⑧ ⎡ • X • • X • X • ⎤
     ⎣ • X • X • X • X ⎦

Mnemonics: mu–ca–na   ca–Ka–pe–ku–la

Reference beat: 1   2   3   4

Figure 3 A Ngangela mnemonic pattern (*mu cana ca Kapekula*, struck on any object with two sticks). For the symbols, see figure 2.

based on the *kakoxa* of zone H), and, beginning in the mid-1900s, homemade banjos and guitars.

Mnemonic Patterns Rhythmic patterns are taught by syllabic or verbal mnemonics, such as *macakili, macakili, kuvamba kuli masika* 'in the circumcision lodge there is coldness', and *mu cana ca Kapekula* 'in the river grasslands of Kapekula'. These mnemonics are almost notations of the accentual, rhythmic, and conceptual characteristics associated with the patterns they represent. Plosive sounds, such as /p/, /t/, and /k/, represent accented strokes, the affricate sound /tʃ/ (orthographically spelled "c," and pronounced as in English "church") usually shows the position of the referential beat, while nasal sounds tend to represent silent or unaccented pulse-units. The mnemonics transcribed in figures 2 and 3 come from the Ngangela repertory of eastern Angola, where these patterns

serve as accompaniment and timeline in several genres of music and dance.

Timelines Two standard asymmetric timelines (figures 4 and 5) are most prominent for steering performances with drums, lamellaphones, or other instruments. In Luvale, they are called *kachacha* or *muse
lemeka*, respectively, because of their association with the kinetic pattern of dances of the same name. The Lwena–Luvale *kachacha* is a dance accompanied by a set of single-skin goblet-shaped drums (*jing'oma*), and sometimes a two-note xylophone (*jinjimba*).

Both timelines in zone K are usually struck with two sticks on the body of a drum. When accompanying a *likembe*, a second performer strikes the sticks against the body of the *likembe*; when accompanying some other types of lamellaphones, the second performer strikes the resonator. When a friction drum (*pwita*) plays with other drums, the timeline is struck on the body of the *pwita*. The friction stick is rubbed with wet hands; performers wet their hands intermittently from a water vessel beside them.

Among the instrumental resources within zone K, lamellaphones have played an important role; five different Cokwe types are distinguishable.

1. *cisaji cakele* often refers to lamellaphones with a board-shaped composite body, made of material from the raffia palm, from which the keys also derive.
2. *cisaji cakakolondondo* has a board-shaped body, with ten iron keys arranged in a V-shape. Tuning is often achieved by attaching differently sized lumps of black wax to the underside of the playing-ends of each lamella.

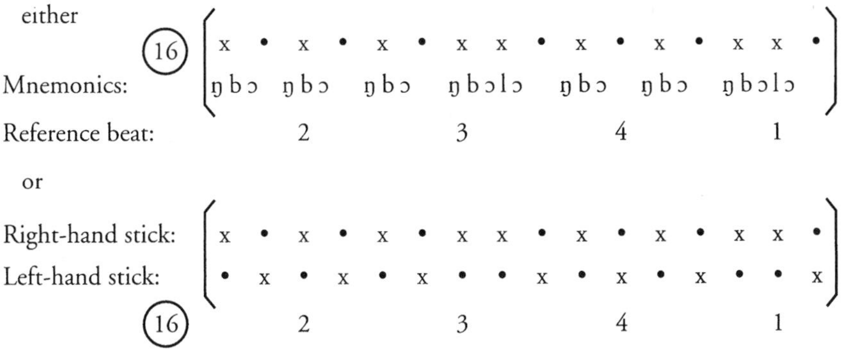

either

⑯ ⎡ x • x • x • x x • x • x • x x • ⎤

Mnemonics: ŋ b ɔ   ŋ b ɔ   ŋ b ɔ   ŋ b ɔ l ɔ   ŋ b ɔ   ŋ b ɔ   ŋ b ɔ l ɔ

Reference beat: 2   3   4   1

or

Right-hand stick: ⎡ x • x • x • x x • x • x • x x • ⎤

Left-hand stick: • x • x • x • • x • x • x • x

⑯   2   3   4   1

Figure 4 The *kachacha* timeline. The referential beat starts on the stroke over the numeral 1, but the pattern begins on the first stroke of the mnemonics as written. This notation captures both concepts: top line, in mnemonics; bottom line, in the pattern's relationship with the referential beat. ŋ is equivalent to "ng" as in sing. ɔ is equal to "aw" as in awful.

⑫ ⎡ x • x • x x • x • x x • ⎤

Mnemonics: ŋ b ɔ   ŋ b ɔ   ŋ b ɔ l ɔ   ŋ b ɔ   ŋ b ɔ l ɔ

Reference beat: 2   3   4   1

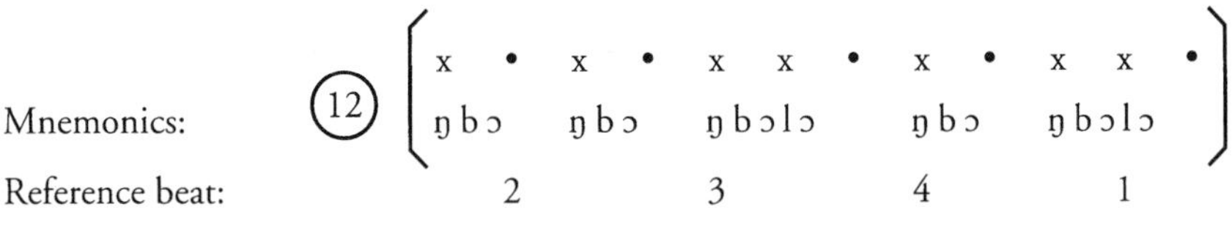

Figure 5 The *museleme
ka* timeline, transcribed in mnemonics with a referential beat. ŋ is equivalent to "ng" as in sing. ɔ is equal to "aw" as in awful.

3. *cisaji calungandu* has a board-shaped body, with two interspersed ranks of keys, six in each, in ascending order from left to right. Tuning is with wax, as above.

4. *mucapata* has 17, 19, or more, iron keys, arranged in sections according to tonality. The body is hollowed out from the end facing the player (the "bell-shaped" resonator). Tuning exclusively involves adjusting the length of the keys that extend over the bridge.

5. *likembe* has a box resonator, normally (in this area) with tongues that produce eight tones, arranged in an N-shape—that is, with two deep tones, one in the middle and one on the right, as seen from the player's viewpoint. A trait of the playing technique of this type of lamellaphone is the extensive use of the soundhole at the back of the box: opening and closing it makes a "wow" effect.

The history of these lamellaphones, like the history of Central African music in general, involves forces of diffusion, adaptation, and innovation. The *likembe* is a twentieth-century introduction to zone K. The raffia lamellaphones are either ancient, and linked with cultures across Central Africa (such as central Cameroon, where they play a prominent role), or imitative of lamellaphone types with iron lamellae, now found among the Cokwe. The *cisaji cakakolondondo* and *cisaji calungandu* may have remote connections with the Lower Zambezi Valley; and from the 1700s, the ideas leading to their invention may have spread from there to Angola. Alternatively, *mucapata*—undoubtedly an original Cokwe or Cokwe-Mbangala invention—may have some historical connection with the Loango-type lamellaphones. This possibility is suggested by the shape of the top part (where the backrest is often missing), the presence of a bell-type resonator, and certain patterns in the arrangement of the notes.

—*Adapted from an article by Gerhard Kubik*

Bibliography

Cavazzi, Giovanni António. 1687. *Istorica Descrizione de 'tre' Regni Congo, Matamba et Angola*. Bologna: Giacomo Monti.

Chauvet, Stephen. 1929. *Musique Nègre*. Paris: Société d'éditions géographiques, maritimes et coloniales.

Djenda, Maurice. 1968. "Les Pygmées de la Haute Sangha." *Geographica* 14:26–43.

Hirschberg, Walter. 1969. "Early Illustrations of West and Central African Music." *African Music* 4(3):6–18.

Jones, Arthur M. 1959. *Studies in African Music*. 2 vols. London: Oxford University Press.

Kazadi wa Mukuna. 1980. "The Origin of Zaïrean Modern Music: A Socio-Economic Aspect." *African Urban Studies* 6:77–78.

Kremser, Manfred. 1982. "Die Musikinstrumente der Azande: Ein Beitrag zur Musikgeschichte Zentralafrikas." In *Bericht über den 15. Österreichischen Historikertag in Salzburg, 14. bis 18. September 1981*, Referate und Protokolle der Sektion 7, 295–300.

Kubik, Gerhard. 1963–1964. *Field-Research Notes: Nigeria, Cameroon, Central African Republic, Congo, Gabon*. Vienna: Phonogrammarchiv.

———. 1964. "Harp Music of the Azande and Related Peoples in the Central African Republic." *African Music* 3(3):37–76.

Laurenty, Jean-Sebastien. 1962. *Les Sanza du Congo*. Tervuren: Musée Royal de l'Afrique Centrale.

Low, John. 1982. *Shaba Diary: A Trip to Rediscover the 'Katanga' Guitar Styles and Songs of the 1950's and 60's*. Acta Ethnologica et Linguistica, 54. Vienna: Föhrenau.

Mapoma, Mwesa I. 1974. "Ingomba: The Royal Musicians of the Bembe People of the Luapula and Northern Provinces of Zambia." Ph.D. dissertation, University of California, Los Angeles.

———. 1980. "Zambia." *The New Grove Dictionary of Music and Musicians*, edited by Stanley Sadie. London: Macmillan.

Merolla, Girolamo. 1692. *Breve, e Succinta Relazione del Viaggio nel Regno di Congo nell' Africa Meridionale*, edited by Angelo Piccardo. Napoli: Per F. Mollo.

Murray, Jocelyn, ed. 1981. *Cultural Atlas of Africa*. Oxford: Elsevier.

Tracey, Hugh. 1948. *Handbook for Librarians*. Roodepoort: African Music Society.

———. 1973. *Catalogue of the Sound of Africa Recordings*. Roodepoort: International Library of African Music.

Popular Music in the Congos

The popular music of Congo and the Democratic Republic of Congo (DRC) has had the most widespread and lasting impact on commercial music in sub-Saharan Africa, where Kinshasa–Brazzaville, the twin capitals on the Congo River, have been the undisputed musical trendsetters.

This electric band music, known locally by the names of numerous dancestyles, has become known outside the two Congos as rumba. Rumba has inspired artists across the continent since the 1960s with its interlocking rhythmic patterns, commanding guitar solos, and smooth vocals, usually delivered in Lingala (one of the four national languages in Congo). Its defining traits are multilayered cyclical guitar riffs, which roll relentlessly above a rhythm section of electric bass and drums; and the *sebene*, a second section that is the inspirational takeoff part for guitarists and exhorting vocalist *animateurs*, and the raison-d'être for dancers.

With the introduction of the gramophone in the 1920s, African-American and Caribbean music—especially the Cuban *son*—found their way into Congolese urban music. Other important influences came from Christian hymnody, with its characteristic harmonic constructions based on triads, and from military bands, which stimulated an interest in brass instruments. Later, European jazz musicians living in the two capitals became heavily influential in the nascent recording scene.

During World War II, the establishment of Radio Congo Belge provided an important promotional outlet for local music. After the war, Greek entrepreneurs who recognized the commercial potential of local music set up recording studios in Kinshasa. This period marked the heyday of rumba and is often referred to as La Belle Époque. Star dance bands featuring electric guitars and horns were the first commercial rumba bands to become publicly acclaimed in the 1950s and 1960s; they included groups such as African Jazz, OK Success, and Bantou Jazz.

The singer-composer Joseph "Le Grand Kalle" Kabasele (1930–1983) is considered the founding father of Congo rumba. He and his band, African Jazz, attracted a huge following abroad. His success was matched by guitar genius Luambo Makiadi "Franco" (1938–1989) and his OK Jazz. Franco, one of the most widely loved artists, was popularly referred to as the grand master of rumba, the Balzac

of Zaïrean music, and the godfather of African music. He was a prolific composer and claimed to have recorded more than a thousand songs during his forty-year career.

In the 1970s, a bold and streamlined rendering of rumba solidified and came to be known internationally as *soukous*. (*Soukous* itself was the name given to one of many competing dance styles of the time.) A new generation of young musicians emerged, led by such ensembles as Zaiko Langa Langa, Choc Stars, Stukas and their many permutations, this music blended local sounds with pop attitudes of the time. Perhaps the most internationally renowned among these was Papa Wemba (b. 1949) who used state-of-the-art production techniques merged with traditional folk forms to surround his beautiful, high-pitched voice. He also became a leader of *sapeur* fashion. *Sapeurs* ('members' of the Society of Ambienceurs and Persons of Elegance) were inextricably linked with Congolese music, and were distinguished by their parading of 1950s Paris fashions and flamboyant designer-label dandyism. Wemba established his own fashion trends, including three-quarter-length trousers, colonial pith helmets, leather suits, and eight stylish ways of walking. By this time, Paris and Brussels had become centers of the spreading recording industry, indicating new political moments and new opportunities for the artists and the music.

Though women's roles in popular music in Congo have been limited, the establishment of recording studios in Kinshasa afforded women the opportunity to record from the 1950s.

In the 1970s, Abeti Masekini (1951–1994) became the first female artist to lead her own band, Les Redoutables. One of her protégées, Mbilia Bel (b. 1959), began her career as a dancer with them. She was subsequently recruited by the superstar singer and bandleader Tabu Ley Rochereau (b. 1940), with whom she performed in the only male-female duo on the continent at the time. In the 1990s, she separated from Ley and achieved the status of first female superstar of Congo.

Bel was closely followed by the much-admired M'pongo Love (1956–1990), who became known as *la voix la plus limpide du Zaïre*: 'the clearest voice of Zaïre'. She achieved international renown in the early 1980s when she moved to Paris and recorded with some of the period's best West African musicians. She was a role model for young female artists, most notably Tshala Mwana (b. 1958) and the postpunk-styled Deyess Mukangi. In an industry dominated by male artists, Mbilia Bel, M'pongo Love, Tshala Mwana, and Deyess Mukangi have used their position to challenge some of the formulaic male-led musical conventions, and thus to innovate as they wish. Tshala Mwana—drawing on the *mutuashi* 12/8 roots rhythm that was to become her trademark—was instrumental in highlighting the so-called *folklore* (a sonic and cultural presence that acknowledges the many ethnic groups which found their way into the urban world of Kinshasa and Brazzaville), thus heralding the "tradi-moderne" trend of gritty distortion and full-on folklore internationalized in the twenty-first century by bands such as Konono No. 1 and the Kasaï Allstars.

Dancefloor styles have always driven the musicians and their innovations in the Congos: the contemporary dancestyle *ndombolo* is to the current generation what *rumba* and *soukous* were to previous ones.

—Adapted from an article by Angela Impey

Bibliography

Ewens, Graeme. 1991. *Africa Oye! A Celebration of African Music*. London: Sango Publications.
——. 1994. *Congo Colossus: Life and Legacy of Franco and OK Jazz*. Baku Press.
——. 2006. "Congo: Heart of Danceness" in *The Rough Guide to World Music: Africa and Middle East*, vol.1, edited by Simon Broughton, Mark Ellingham, and Jon Lusk, 74–90. London: Rough Guides.
Stewart, Gary. 2000. *Rumba on the River: A History of the Popular Music of the Two Congos*. London: Verso.
Wrong, Michela. 2001. *In the Footsteps of Mr. Kurtz: Living on the Brink of Disaster in Mobuto's Congo*. HarperCollins.

Southern Africa

Southern Africa

Music in southern Africa, as elsewhere on the continent, has long been associated with political power and royal musicians. During the colonial and apartheid eras, music provided a crucial means of expression for people. The articles that follow aim to offer a sense of the region's traditional and popular musics and some of their social and political implications.

Frank Gomba plays the *chipendani* mouthbow, Harare, Zimbabwe, 1990. A mbira is visible in the gourd resonator next to him.
Photo by Claire Jones.

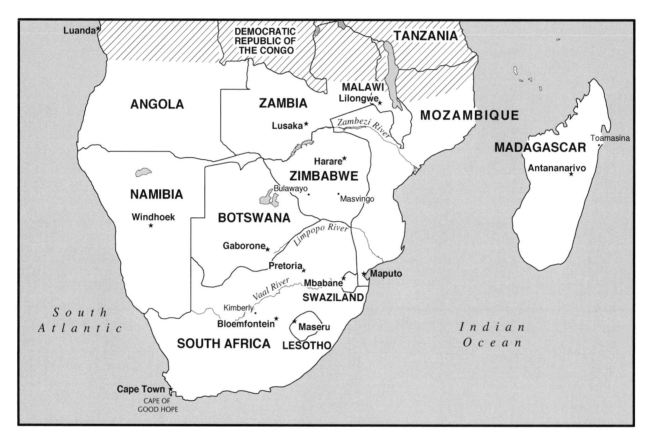

Southern Africa

Indigenous Music of Southern Africa

Southern Africa shares with much of central Africa a history of hierarchical societies with similar traits. In southern Africa, as elsewhere on the continent, music has been important as a symbol of political power. The symbols by which kings maintained power included ritual fires, an important female secondary ruler, and the sponsorship of royal musicians. The history of these kingdoms is in part the history of colonialism. Many of these kingdoms were destroyed during interethnic fighting and the impact of Europeans in the last two hundred years, but many headmen of small groups maintain symbolic drums or xylophones. Music has played an important part in areas with puberty initiation rites, particularly where control of the rituals is a mark of political strength.

Many peoples in southern Africa define music in terms of the presence of metered rhythm. This means that drumming alone is considered music, and chanting or speaking words is singing, so long as it is metrical. When the singing voice is used without rhythm, the resulting vocalization is not usually considered singing. Many groups have no word that would accurately be glossed as 'music'; most of them have distinct words for singing, for playing an instrument, and for dancing.

Languages are an important and fascinating part of the story of southern African music, but they are dealt with here only as they affect music. Like other African languages, those of southern Africa are tonal, so the nature of the speech tones may restrict melodies to some degree. The languages of southern Africa are not so highly dependent upon tones as are the languages of West Africa, so the match of speech tone with melody is more a matter of aesthetics than comprehension. Among the Venda of the southeastern part of the region, singing adheres to the speech tones most closely at the beginning of phrases, and with rising more than falling melodic intervals; adherence to speech tones is stronger in the beginning line of a song than in later ones.

A feature that distinguishes southern Africa is that the musical bow is the major stringed instrument (figure 1). A few general comments on musical bows will enable the reader to follow more easily the discussions of bows found in the subregions. Musical bows commonly have one string, fastened with tension at each end of a curved stick, so the string makes a sound when put into motion. One of the basic differences among musical bows is how the string is

Figure 1 A man plays a musical bow, Zimbabwe. *Photo by John E. Kaemmer.*

caused to vibrate. It can be struck by something, usually a small stick, or it can be plucked by one finger, or by the thumb and index finger together. It can be vibrated by indirect action, as by scraping a stick across notches carved into the bow (friction bow), or by blowing onto a feather attached to a bow (*gora* or *lesiba*). Scraping the string, as in bowing any stringed instrument, has been practiced in the region.

The sound of a bow is resonated in different ways. With a mouthbow, part of the bow is inserted in the player's mouth, and movements of the player's mouth and throat emphasize different overtones. With a gourd bow, the resonator is a gourd fastened to or held against the bow; the player can produce tunes by moving the gourd against his or her body, emphasizing different overtones by varying the volume of air resonating in the gourd.

Musical bows are made so that they can produce more than one fundamental tone. Sometimes, as with a braced bow, a thread links the string to the bow somewhere along the length of the string, making the string vibrate in two sections. Other bows produce different fundamentals as the player stops the string with a finger or an object.

Southern African societies exchanged cultural and musical features far back in the past. The most accurate term for referring to this music is *indigenous*—a term applicable, for example, to the Khoisan adoption of Bantu lamellaphones, but not to their use of the guitar. Though the following treatment of different groups gives the impression of distinct differences, ethnic boundaries in the region are often fuzzy. The same is true of differences between musical traditions.

Khoisan Peoples

At the end of the 1400s, when Europeans first found the southern tip of Africa, that area was inhabited by diverse peoples. The pastoral groups around the Cape of Good Hope were called Hottentots by the Europeans; the hunter-gatherers farther north were called Bushmen. Both of these peoples differ physically from other Africans. Their languages, which exploit several clicking sounds, have been classified as click languages and Khoisan languages. The latter term comes from the names these people use for themselves: Khoi or Khoikhoi for the Hottentots, and San for the Bushmen.

In the late 1400s, the people who spoke Bantu languages were living farther to the north and east of the cape, and were interacting with the Khoisan peoples. Archaeological and linguistic evidence indicates that the Bantu-speaking peoples of southern Africa arrived there from the north within the last thousand years, overrunning or displacing the indigenous peoples. Many Khoikhoi were enslaved by European settlers, and eventually mixed with Europeans and workers brought from Asia to form what are now called the Coloured people of South Africa. Though the San were traditionally hunters and gatherers, they are increasingly becoming cattleherders and farmers.

The Khoikhoi

The Khoikhoi included four major groups: the Cape Hottentots, the Eastern Hottentots, the Nama (or Namaqua), and the Korana. These groups no longer survive; most of these people disappeared or became assimilated into the Coloured population. A few groups speaking dialects of Khoi languages remain in Namibia. The musical practices of the Khoikhoi as recorded in early documents are important because of their influence on later developments. Many of their songs were reportedly based on a descending four-note scale, intervallically equivalent to D–C–A–G.

Among the major instruments of the Khoikhoi were musical bows, of which they played several types. Men played a braced mouthbow. Women played a longer bow, *kha:s*. Seated, a woman secured the instrument by one foot, resting its center on a hollow object serving as a resonator; she held the upper part of the bow near her face, touching it with her chin to vary the fundamental tone, which she could modify by touching the center of the string.

The most notable Khoikhoi bow, the *gora*, was used to accompany cattleherding. It consisted of a string that the player put into motion by forcefully inhaling and exhaling over a feather connecting the string to one end of the bow. Variations in the blowing would make the instrument bring out different tones of the harmonic series. The *gora* was borrowed by neighboring Bantu speakers.

Single-tone flutes were important to the Khoikhoi, especially the Nama and the Korana. These flutes were about 40 centimeters long, made from reeds with all the nodes removed, or from the bark of a particular root. In either case, a plug inserted in the bottom could be raised or lowered to modify the pitch. Flutes were played in ensembles for dancing, with each man sounding his note as needed to create a melody in hocket. Seventeenth-century descriptions indicate that men and women danced in separate, concentric circles; which sex danced on the inside varied from one group to another.

The Khoikhoi made drums by placing skins over their pots. The Europeans called this instrument a *rommelpot*, though the *rommelpot* in Europe is a type of friction drum.

The San

The San live in scattered places in Botswana, Namibia, and southern Angola. As hunter-gatherers, they did not have complex musical institutions. Much of their music was for self-expression, dealing with everyday topics, such as the success of the hunt. Songs accompanied curative dances, in which men would go into a quivering trance, representing internal heat.

In the 1960s, the San in the Cuito-Cuanavale area of southeastern Angola and nearby areas of Namibia were the only ones who could give a clear idea of their indigenous musical styles. Their most widely used indigenous instrument was the bow, classifiable in four musical-bow complexes, of which three used the common hunting bow. The player resonated the bow by putting one end in his or her mouth, resting the other on the ground. By changing the shape of the mouth, the player emphasized certain overtones, creating melodic interest; by stopping the string, the player obtained different fundamental tones. Because the bows were long, they were stopped near the end, producing two fundamental tones, separated by intervals of a second, a minor third, or a major third. The bows were also played with a gourd resonator, not fastened to the bow, but held against it; the gourd was moved in contact with the bare chest, causing a variety of overtones to resonate.

A third tradition, the group bow, required three individuals to play one bow. The bow was laid with one end on the ground, with the center resting on an upended pan or gourd, serving as a resonator. The first player (A) secured the bow with his foot, and held a piece of gourd with which he stopped the string at either of two places, depending on the song; with a short stick, he beat the string in steady triplets. The second performer (B), at the upper end of the bow, played an irregular rhythm with his stick, with duplets on one part of the string and triplets on another. The third player (C), sitting between the other two, beat the stick in duple rhythms. The name of the instrument when used this way was *kambulumbumba*. The same technique was used by children among surrounding Bantu-speakers. For several reasons, including the name of the instrument, it is probable that this bow was originally a Bantu instrument. The San have a tradition of mouth-resonated friction bows made especially for musical purposes with a palm-leaf ribbon, rather than with a string.

The musical bow produces multipart music in the interplay between the fundamental tone and overtones. San vocal multipart music becomes a type of counterpoint as singers are encouraged to sing individual variants on a basic line. Singers employ techniques of canon and imitation, singing with few words.

In San multipart music, tones that can be used interchangeably or occur simultaneously are always in the same harmonic series. Many San songs have a tetrachordal structure, in which two tones at the interval of a fifth are used with another fifth, placed a second or a third above the first pair. The commonest occurrence of this involves the use of the first, second, fifth, and sixth scalar tones (*do, re, sol, la*). This structure would naturally result from playing two bows together if they were tuned a second or a third apart.

The San played a stamping tube (*bavugu*) made of three gourds or mock oranges set one above the other and held together with wax. A hole was cut through all three, which were struck against the upper thigh with the top of the instrument struck with the hand. This instrument was played only by women, who were reticent about showing it to the researchers. It probably had something to do with female initiation or fertility.

The San play raft zithers (*kuma*), and are using more and more of the musical resources of the peoples surrounding them. In addition to the group bow, they have adopted the plucked lamellaphone (*likembe* or mbira).

The San sing with multipart and hocket techniques. Their singing differs from responsorial singing elsewhere in Africa because San soloists in a group interweave their singing without necessarily responding to each other. When players of a mouthbow begin to sing, they must temporarily stop bringing out melodic overtones with the mouth, so the alternation of vocal and instrumental sections results in a kind of two-part form. Both Khoikhoi and San yodeled as they sang.

Nguni Peoples

Nguni is a term scholars use to denote the southernmost Bantu-speaking people in Africa. That they interacted extensively with earlier non-Bantu inhabitants of southern Africa is shown by the fact that unlike Bantu farther north, they have clicks in their languages.

Two Nguni groups, the Xhosa and Zulu, constitute a major part of the indigenous population of South Africa. The Xhosa were closer to the Cape of Good Hope, and at least some of them settled among Khoisan peoples and mixed with them. They were the first Bantu-speakers to come into conflict with Europeans. These conflicts weakened them, so they did not form strong kingdoms, as did the Zulu and Swazi, their neighbors to the northeast. The Zulu are descendants of clans united into a nation by Chaka, who ruled from 1816 to 1828; they fought the Boers and the British, and were finally defeated in 1879. The Swazi were organized as a kingdom, which eventually became a British protectorate, and later the independent nation of Swaziland.

During the early 1800s, the Boers emigrated north to escape the English, and the indigenous peoples became involved in wars with the whites and with each other. Various groups separated themselves from the Zulu kingdom and fled, conquering others as they went. A branch of the Nguni went north, to become the Ndebele of northern Transvaal (now Limpopo Province) and Zimbabwe. People now called Ngoni invaded what is now Malawi, mixing with other peoples there. The Shangaan (or Shangana) in Mozambique, and along its border with Zimbabwe and South Africa, are also descendants of the Zulu

The **Transvaal** is a former province of South Africa that occupied the area between the Limpopo and the Vaal Rivers in the northeastern part of the country.

95

dispersion. Thus, the ethnic configuration in these countries is complex, with traits of Nguni culture often appearing in non-Nguni contexts.

General Traits of Nguni Music

Several features typify Nguni musical culture. In communal musical events, choral singing is the most important form of music. Singing is considered best when done with an open voice, "like the lowing of cattle" (Tracey 1948b:46). Singing is polyphonic and responsorial, with the divergence of parts occurring as phrases begin and end at different points.

Another typical feature is the traditional prominence of the musical bow. Scales are based on its natural tones, often omitting the seventh. Nguni musical cultures have diverse scalar systems; the seventh is often missing, and perfect fourths and fifths are often important. The use of semitones may reflect traits of the bow.

Though drums are not commonly used in many Nguni traditions, they are known. The friction drum and double-headed drum are used in some rituals. The friction drum is a drum that has a leather or fiber thong inserted through it and fastened; the thong is rubbed or scraped when held tightly, passing the vibrations on to the drumhead.

The major form of Zulu communal music consists of choral dance songs. This form of music graces many rituals, including puberty ceremonies, weddings, and divinations. Drinking songs and worksongs are also in this style. Men's praise poetry is performed unmetrically; therefore, it is not considered music, though the clearly pitched singing voice is used.

Individualistic forms of song, such as lullabies and songs for personal enjoyment, were traditionally accompanied on the musical bow—a practice that has long been declining. One musical bow used by the Zulu was the *ugubhu*, an unbraced gourd-resonated bow more than a meter long. Another, the *umakhweyana*, was braced near the center and gourd resonated; it is thought to have been borrowed from the Tsonga, to the north. Braced bows have the main string divided in different ways, so the differences in the fundamental tones range from a whole tone to a minor third.

Xhosa women and girls have a form of overtone singing, *umngqokolo*. This technique involves singing a low fundamental tone while shaping the mouth to emphasize different overtones. It is said to sound somewhat like a performance on the *umrhubhe*, a bow played by scraping a string with a stick. The style may have developed from a practice of small boys: they impale a beetle on a thorn, put it in their

mouths, and isolate various overtones produced by the insect's buzzing.

The Xhosa have a quivering dance, which calls to mind the curative dances of the San.

Single-tone flutes are found among the Zulu and Swazi. The latter use them during their firstfruits rituals. These flutes are long and tuned by means of plugs—as was the practice among the Khoikhoi.

Sotho Peoples

Three major Sotho groups regularly appear in the ethnomusicological literature: those living in Lesotho (the southern Sotho), those living in Botswana (the Tswana or Chwana, or western Sotho), and those living in South Africa (the Pedi, or eastern Sotho). The Sotho of Lesotho are a mixture of refugees who in the mid-1800s united into a state. Their leader, Moshoeshoe I, asked for missionaries in 1833, and sought status for his kingdom as a British protectorate in 1868. This action led to strong European influence and to Lesotho's becoming politically, but not economically, separate from South Africa. This branch of Sotho is the only one whose language incorporates clicks from the Khoisan languages.

The Sotho peoples share many musical features with the Nguni, such as the importance of choral singing (*mahobelo*) and the use of one-stringed instruments and reed flutes. The Tswana, who originally lived on open plains with few trees, have a strong tradition of choral singing. Their vocal music is primarily pentatonic. Unlike Nguni musical textures, Sotho responsorial parts do not overlap often.

Dancing to instrumental sounds may be a twentieth-century development in Lesotho, but not with other Sotho peoples. The Sotho outside Lesotho have customarily performed flute dances. Perhaps the people of Lesotho lacked such dances because they came from many ethnic backgrounds. Reed-flute dances occurred among the Tswana, possibly adopted from the Khoikhoi. Reed-flute ensembles are among a chief's prerogatives. Though the Sotho in Lesotho do not have the flute dances, they do have flutes, which resemble those of the Nguni. Pedi boys use a one-tone flute, but when they play it, they whistle with their lips while they inhale.

The southern Sotho have adapted a Khoi bow (*gora*), which they call *lisiba*, from their word *siba* 'feather'; it may well be called an air-activated stick zither. Both inhaling and exhaling, players cause air to move past the feather; they produce most overtones while inhaling. Exhaling often produces laryngeal sounds, except during an expert's performance. Changes of pitch can be caused by changes in breath pressure and changes in the shape of the oral cavity.

The songs the southern Sotho sing with the *lesiba* have a special name, *linon'*. The instrument is connected with cattleherding, as it was among the Khoikhoi, and the Sotho use its sounds to control their cattle. The feather from the instrument ideally comes from the cape vulture, the bird the instrument represents.

Sotho peoples use rattles made from cocoons and animal skins, but not from gourds (as used by people farther north). Pedi cocoon rattles are worn by women only; their dance skirts, made of reeds, rattle during dancing.

Southeastern African Peoples

Several groups in southeastern Africa appear to have lived in the same area for several hundred years. These include the Venda in the northern Transvaal, the Chopi in southern Mozambique, and the Shona between the Limpopo and Zambezi rivers in Zimbabwe and Mozambique. The Thonga include several groups formed when the Zulu wars of the early 1800s sent conquerors and refugees eastward into the coastal lowlands; these groups include the Tswa, the Ronga, the Tsonga, and the Shangaan.

Because the Zulu dispersion brought many Zulu-speakers into southeastern Africa, the area is now characterized by a mixture of languages. Many of these languages (and Shona) pronounce sibilant fricatives, /z/ or /s/, with something of a whistle. The Venda have been influenced by the Sotho, but they share many linguistic and cultural traits with the Shona.

The musical cultures of southeastern Africa emphasize instruments, rather than choral singing. The separation between the two parts of responsorial forms is more distinct, and polyrhythms occur in accompaniment and its relation to singing. Musical bows among the San and the Nguni are usually played with fundamentals a second or a third apart, but Shona and Tsonga bows usually have fundamentals a fourth or fifth apart. Southeast African single-toned flutes are played in hocket, but they are constructed differently from those of the San and Nguni. Instead of having plugs for tuning, the nodes are retained in the bamboo or the reeds, and the instruments are tuned by being shortened or by receiving extra sections.

The musical cultures of southeast Africa have several instruments in common, including a variety of drums, mbiras (lamellaphones), and xylophones. Since the Shona are the subject of a full article

later in this section (see MUSIC OF THE SHONA OF ZIMBABWE), only the Venda and the Chopi are covered here.

The Venda

The Venda, living in mountains of northeastern South Africa, submitted to European rule in 1899. When John Blacking did research among them (in the 1950s), they were still performing many of their traditional musical events.

The Venda are believed to have crossed the Limpopo River from the north several hundred years ago; their language and culture closely resemble those of the Karanga branch of Shona. Though Venda musical skills are widespread, public performances require some form of payment. The Venda assume that any normal person is capable of performing music well.

The national music of the Venda is the *tshikona*, an ensemble of one-pitch pipes played in hocket. Traditionally men played pipes, and women played drums. Each chief had his *tshikona*, which would perform on important occasions, such as firstfruits ceremonies. The chiefs vied with each other to create the best ensemble, sometimes using it to further their own political ends. Venda men working in the mines of South Africa perform the dance there, doing their own drumming. The tonalities of *tshikona* music are the most important feature of Venda tonal organization.

Tshikona is not the only music sponsored by chiefs. The Venda share with the Tsonga the practice whereby each chief sends youthful performers on collective visits to other chiefs to perform and bring back gifts. Thus, each chief succeeds in building up a corps of devoted followers. Among the Tsonga, such performing groups are competitive.

The nature of musical sponsorship means that little social commentary is expressed through song; however, in individual musical performances, people may express their feelings and frustrations, including criticism of others, without fear of negative consequences.

The Venda have many kinds of instruments. Differential tuning—some instruments using heptatonic scales, and others using pentatonic scales—indicates different origins for different instruments. The pipes used in *tshikona* are ideally made from bamboo from a secret grove in eastern Venda country, and are heptatonic within a range of three octaves; metal and plastic pipes are also used. The Venda also play reed pipes, pentatonically covering two octaves.

Venda instruments include a twenty-one-key xylophone, the *mbila mutondo* (nearly obsolete), plus a twenty-seven-key lamellaphone, the *mbila dzamadeza*. The Venda have a friction bow (*tshizambi*), obtained from the Tsonga, and the *dende*, a braced gourd-resonated bow. The *ng'oma* is a huge pegged drum with four handles, played with *tshikona* and in rainmaking rituals.

The Venda have borrowed some of their musical practices from neighboring peoples. Circumcision schools, with their related music, have come from the Sotho. These schools are sponsored by individuals, who gain financial and political advantages from them. Venda possession cults have come from the Karanga, a Shona group to the north.

An important feature of Venda music is the "principle of harmonic equivalence" (Blacking 1967:168). Though the rise and fall of tones in various verses may differ objectively, the Venda consider them the same, so long as the tones involved are within the same harmonic series. By substituting pitches in this way, the Venda can allow for variations in the rise and fall of linguistic tones in different parts of the text.

The Chopi

One of the most important musical traditions in southern Africa is that of the Chopi, who seem to have inhabited their lands, in present-day Mozambique, just east of the mouth of the Limpopo River, since the early 1500s; they were not subjugated by the Zulu invasions of the 1800s. To accompany dance cycles (*ngodo*), they use large ensembles of xylophones.

The ideal Chopi ensemble consists of xylophones (*timbila*) in five sizes, covering a range of four octaves. The slats are fixed to the framework, each with a resonator attached below it. Originally the resonators were gourds, each matched to resonate best with the slat to which it was attached. Carefully checking the tuning of these xylophones by using a set of tuning forks and asking the players which fork most closely matched each slat, the musicologist Hugh Tracey found that the scale approximated an equidistant heptatonic one.

Each chief formerly sponsored a xylophone ensemble. The lyrics often related to popular social concerns, and could criticize wrongdoing. To keep the messages up to date, new compositions were created every few years, with the lyrics created before the music. A complete dance cycle, lasting about forty-five minutes, had nine to eleven movements.

Middle Zambezi Peoples

To the north of the Zambezi River in Zambia are several ethnic groups culturally considered a part of southern Africa: the Tonga live in the area bordering the river to the east of Victoria Falls; the Ila live farther to the northwest, along the Kafue River; still farther west are the Lozi and the Nkoya, groups that have consistently maintained stratified societies, with kings and royal musical ensembles. The music of the latter two groups is described below.

The Lozi and the Nkoya

The Lozi (also called Barotse, formerly Luya) and the Nkoya are neighbors along the Zambezi near the Zambian border with Angola. Each has a strong monarchy, whose leaders are thought to have come from the Lunda kingdoms in the Democratic Republic of Congo. The Lozi inhabit the floodplain, where annual runoff from the rainy season brings silt that enriches the soil; the Nkoya inhabit the hills, depending less on agriculture and more on livestock and hunting. The richness of the soil has led to differences in the wealth of the two groups—differences that influence the relationship of their royal families and their musical practices.

In 1840, the Lozi were conquered by the Kololo, a Sotho group; they freed themselves in 1868. In the late 1800s, their king negotiated for his kingdom status as a British protectorate. This status helped keep the kingdom intact; in fact, both the king and the royal musicians received salaries from the colonial government. The Lozi language is a mixture, basically Southern Bantu Luyana with heavy borrowing from Sotho. The Nkoya have a Central Bantu language.

In both groups, royal music is distinct from commoners' music. Royal ensembles, consisting of a xylophone and three drums, accompany the king and symbolize his status. Only the chiefs can use double bells (*ngongi*)—a usage common in West Africa, but usually found farther south only in archaeological excavations. Unlike most xylophones, Lozi and Nkoya xylophones are played by one person each. To facilitate being carried in processions, each instrument is secured by straps around its performer's neck, held away from his body by a bowed piece of wood. The drums in royal ensembles include the *ng'oma* (the most important one), which has tuning paste added to the head to deepen its sound. The other two drums are double-headed pegged drums, which have higher pitches than the *ng'oma*, with a buzzer arrangement; the *ng'oma* player does the major improvizations.

Instruments are not the only feature that distinguishes royal music from commoners' music: linguistic distinctions are important: Lozi royal musicians sing in Luyana, the archaic language, but commoners sing in Lozi. Nkoya beliefs concerning sources of music help strengthen the differences of status between royalty and commonalty: the Nkoya believe that spirits taught the people royal music, but not nonroyal music. Royal dances are more restrained than those of commoners.

Music highlights differences between the Lozi and the Nkoya: Nkoya instruments are pitched higher. The Lozi have a special kind of music, *lisboma*, which they consider their national music. Lozi songs concern cattle, including raids and conquest; Nkoya royal songs emphasize death and dying. Lozi texts are more detailed and organized.

Lozi xylophones usually have eleven keys, with the lower three separated by thirds. The other keys approximate the diatonic scale, but with a flat third and no seventh. The vocal range may be a fourth or less. Songs are polyrhythmic: some have sixteen-pulse units, and others have twelve-pulse units; the latter pattern readily allows duple and triple rhythmic mixes.

Music plays a big part in an important Lozi ritual, the *kuomboka*, a ceremony that occurs while the people retreat from the floodplain to higher ground as the river rises. An important feature of this ceremony is the royal barge, which carries the king to his palace on higher ground. In his entourage is the *maoma*, the national drum. It is unusually large, about a meter in diameter. Its head is painted with dots, and its side bears carvings of human and animal figures. Only royal men play it. During the *kuomboka*, the ancient Luyana language is used. After it comes two days of dances: the *liwale* for women and the *ng'omalume* for men. The latter includes dancing to drumming without singing. Because the Nkoya do not live on a floodplain, their major ritual is a firstfruits ceremony, the *mukanda*.

Lozi music is not limited to royal ensembles. Music called *makwasha* is sung by everyone. It deals with various subjects, including hunting, and serves for paddling canoes. It is played on fifteen-key lamellaphones (*kahanzi*), with lower keys tuned like royal xylophones.

Impact of the Wider World

Though interethnic borrowing of cultural features has occurred in southern Africa as long ago as can be determined, it is only in the last three hundred fifty years that the impact of non-African societies is clear and overwhelming. The impact of non-African societies comes partly from the musical practices themselves, but the impact of social and cultural changes brought about by European conquest has been paramount.

The musical practices of all of southern Africa have been heavily influenced by unique factors emanating from the Republic of South Africa, which has the largest proportion of Europeans of any country in Africa, largely because of the temperateness of its climate and the wealth of its minerals. Settlers sent by the Dutch East India Company landed in Cape Town in 1652. Before long, they had brought in Asians to help work their farms. English settlers arrived after armed forces had defeated the Dutch. All these immigrants brought musical traditions with them.

Mining

In the 1800s, with the discovery of diamonds in Kimberley and gold in the Transvaal, the European influence in southern Africa intensified. Conflict developed between English and Dutch settlers, who had precipitated devastating wars by moving into areas occupied by Africans. The impact of the British spread with the colonization of Southern Rhodesia (now Zimbabwe) and the discovery of copper in Northern Rhodesia (now Zambia). The explorations of David Livingstone brought Malawi into the British orbit, leaving Angola and Mozambique to the Portuguese and Southwest Africa (now Namibia) to the Germans.

The wealth in the mines lured many African men from their communities. Most had no choice but to leave their wives and families behind. Their absence from home meant that village rituals, with their associated music, had to be adapted to weekends or holidays, or else they died out. The communities that grew up around the mines provided meeting places where people of many ethnic groups heard each other's music, including that of Africans of European descent.

The companies that ran the mines often sponsored indigenous African dances as entertainment on Sundays, the miners' day off. These dances helped maintain differences of ethnic identity among the men, and gave them an outlet for entertainment and self-expression. The dances catered to tourists, providing outsiders with convenient views of exotic music and dance.

In nonmining areas, Africans educated in Western knowledge became clerks and household help, and others worked on plantations. Many who worked in the big mining centers were not Western-educated, but became permanently urban. They sought to become recognized as city dwellers, rather than "tribesmen," and used skills in European music to demonstrate their claims.

Apartheid

South Africa was unique in having such strong European influence so early. In most of southern Africa, intensive European domination did not occur until after the Treaty of Berlin (1885). Major wars of colonial conquest occurred in Namibia, Zimbabwe, and South Africa. Africans were subject not only to military activity, but also to the presence of military bands, with instruments that seemed new and exciting to them. Since African tradition viewed musical spectacles as an important symbol of political power, military bands were seen as a new type of power, and were often imitated as a new kind of dance.

The policy of apartheid—strict racial separation—heavily influenced music in South Africa and Namibia, which from 1915 to 1990 was under South African control. Racial separation was a continentwide practice; but in South Africa in 1948, after the Afrikaner party had taken electoral power, it became official policy. Until then, musical events mixed Africans and Europeans, with Africans often providing the music.

Under apartheid, Africans were forbidden to perform at European nightclubs, and they thus missed out on opportunities for economic improvement and interracial communication [see BLACK POPULAR MUSIC IN SOUTH AFRICA]. The lack of resources devoted to African education meant that African schoolchildren had less formal training in music than European schoolchildren. Songs in African theatrical performances became a major form of social commentary in South Africa, where theater was seen as a form of communication, rather than an aesthetic activity.

Missions and Education

An important feature of musical change in southern Africa was the activity of Christian missionaries, both as proponents of new religious doctrines, and as purveyors of European education. Most missionaries did not distinguish between Christian doctrine and European culture. They disparaged African customs and African music, which they believed not only inferior, but even sinful.

Many Africans viewed religion as a form of power that equaled spears and guns. Consequently, they viewed Christianity as an important reason for European domination and thus a more effective religion. Converts who accepted the rituals adopted the music that accompanied them. They turned away from indigenous forms of music, accepting the notion that they were sinful and inferior. Missionaries often translated their hymns into African languages, unaware of the importance of linguistic tones to the understandability and aesthetic quality of the music.

Some missionary agencies, recognizing the importance of indigenous forms of expression to their converts, created hymns and songs in indigenous styles. The Livingstonia mission in northern Malawi did so from the beginning. In the 1960s, the Methodist mission in Zimbabwe began a program of using indigenous musical idioms in church, but older people had already formed negative opinions about them. Workshops on indigenization of the arts have been held regularly since then, with many churches cooperating. After the second Vatican Council (1962–1965), the Roman Catholic Church began using vernacular languages in services—a change that afforded an opportunity to adopt indigenous musical styles to accommodate the new languages of worship.

Education, fostered by the missions until the various countries became independent, was oriented to European culture. Its aim was preparing workers for government and business; training in music played only a small part in it. The curriculum used in the schools of the colonial power was taught in Africa, including the songs. Being related to the missions, schools usually promoted choral singing.

One type of music became popular all over southern Africa: the *makwaya*, from the English word *choir*. It involved singing, complex marching routines, and special costumes. Adaptations of jazz in responsorial form, accompanied by drumming and dancing, have become popular with young people. [See BLACK POPULAR MUSIC IN SOUTH AFRICA.]

In Anglophone areas of southern Africa, schools commonly sponsored musical contests. The judges were usually Europeans, who formed their judgments on the basis of European musical criteria. Having African judges was avoided in South Africa, for fear that African judges would be biased in favor of their kinsmen.

Sociopolitical Factors

In the twentieth century, during struggles for political liberation, songs served to politicize people and motivate fighters. In Zimbabwe's struggle, composers and performers emphasized the indigenous aspects of culture; during the 1960s and 1970s, the mbira became more popular than the guitar among young people, but since independence, the situation seems to have reversed.

The stigma attached to Africans and their culture by European racism and ethnocentrism directly influenced musical practices in many ways. In most of southern Africa, the mastery of European music was seen as prestigious—resulting in considerable decline of indigenous traditions. The Venda of South Africa, however, refused to perform European music. In most parts of the country, the performance of indigenous music was often seen as implying support of "separate development" (that is, apartheid), and was thus avoided.

That socioeconomic factors play an important role in musical change does not mean that musical interest is irrelevant in itself. From the earliest days of European settlement, the Khoikhoi at the cape were utilizing Malay and Dutch musical idioms. Black vaudeville entertainers from the United States helped improve Africans' self-respect, and served as musical models for African musical entertainers. As early as 1890, African-American choirs traveled to South Africa to perform. That the Nguni peoples valued choral singing helped them relate to African-American singing. The improvisational nature of African-American music also struck a responsive chord with them.

Musical Instruments

The adoption or imitation of European instruments has strongly affected southern African music, but merely adopting the instruments has not necessarily meant that Africans have played European music on them. Double-headed drums are common in southern Africa, especially in separatist religious groups. The use of round metal tins in the manufacture of these drums and their style of playing indicate that they were copied from the European bass drums used in military bands. In the early days of the Cape Colony, the Khoikhoi were copying violins and guitars to create the *ramkie*, a homemade lute.

Commercially produced European instruments were found to be louder and more versatile than indigenous instruments. The most important of these was the guitar, which became a major instrument all over southern Africa. Acoustic guitars were popular for many years, but electric guitars have taken their place. Guitars have often supplanted musical bows because the latter are quiet, and much of their appeal is only to the performer. Among Xhosa girls, imported lamellaphones took the place of bows. Pennywhistles experienced a surge of popularity in the 1950s in South Africa because they were versatile and cheap.

Independence and International Relations

Independence has changed the situation in many southern African countries. A major development has been in the amount of readily available modern education. The curriculum has not usually covered music in depth, but the increasing consciousness brought about by Western education has carried over into music. Many traditional African musicians can perform superbly on their instruments, but cannot explain, in Western terms, what they are doing and how they are doing it; younger musicians who have been to school, however, have become aware of what is happening in their musical traditions—such as young Shona mbira players, able to explain the four sections of a cycle of their music.

Increased contacts with the outside world have led young people to see the possibility of producing recordings as a way of building a successful career. With some exceptions, young musicians imitate the popular music stars they hear, apparently shunning the music of their elders. Both South Africa and Zimbabwe have active recording industries, serving local and international markets; however, much of the control of production is in the hands of international corporations, which seek to market worldbeat on the basis of technical simplicity and exotic appeal. European producers and technicians in South Africa tend to impose their own values and criteria on African performers, whom they have often considered mere laborers. Some studios pay the performers royalties instead of a onetime fee.

—*Adapted from an article by John E. Kaemmer*

Bibliography

Blacking, John. 1965. "The Role of Music in the Culture of the Venda of the Northern Transvaal." In *Studies in Ethnomusicology*, edited by Mieczeslaw Kolinski, 2:20–53. New York: Oak Publications.

——. 1967. *Venda Children's Songs: A Study in Ethnomusicological Analysis*. Johannesburg: Witwatersrand University Press.

——. 1972. *How Musical Is Man?* Seattle: University of Washington Press.

Erlmann, Veit. 1991. *African Stars: Studies in Black South African Performance*. Chicago: University of Chicago Press.

Kaemmer, John. E. 1993. *Music in Human Life: Anthropological Perspectives on Music*. Austin: University of Texas Press.

Tracey, Hugh. 1948a. *Chopi Musicians: Their Music, Poetry, and Instruments*. London: International Africa Institute.

——. 1948b. *Ngoma: An Introduction to Music for Southern Africans*. New York: Longmans, Green.

Music of the Shona of Zimbabwe

The Shona, a population of about 8.5 million Bantu-speakers, live mostly in Zimbabwe and partly in Mozambique and Zambia. They speak five major dialects—Zezuru, Korekore, Manyika, Ndau and Karanga—which have been standardized to a single chiShona orthography. The source of the term *Shona* is unknown, but it has referred to these groups since the mid-nineteenth century. Shona peoples still recognize the areas of linguistic difference, which partly coincide with variation in traditional music.

The early Shona speakers who settled on the plateau between the Zambezi and Limpopo rivers practiced subsistence agriculture, living on lands spiritually connected with family and chiefly ancestors. Independent chiefdoms formed the basis of political and social organization, but several lineages were able to establish centralized bases of power from the twelfth century onward. The resulting succession of states varied in their extent and capacity to exert authority over outlying areas. Great Zimbabwe, centered in what are now stone ruins near the town of Masvingo, was the earliest-known plateau state (ca. 1150–1450). Ecological pressures may have led to its collapse. Its successor, the Munhumutapa Empire (ca. 1400–1902), was based in the northern Zimbabwean region of Dande. Both kingdoms carried on maritime trade. At one time the Munhumutapa state held dominion over territory stretching as far eastward as the Indian Ocean, and effectively controlled the lower Zambezi trade route. In the early 1800s, as European influence expanded in southern Africa, Nguni-speaking peoples began migrating northward. A group led by Mzilikazi settled in southwestern Zimbabwe and established the powerful Ndebele state. Save for occasional raiding, however, Ndebele domination did not extend very far into Shona territory. In 1890, European settlers set up a colonial state that lasted ninety years. For the Shona peoples, the settler regime represented a major discontinuity with the previous states and decentralized chieftaincies.

Little of the early development of Shona music is known. The Shona practice of yodeling suggests influences from Pygmies, who probably inhabited the area before the arrival of Bantu-speakers. Scattered among archaeological excavations in Zimbabwe, remains of metal lamellae (prongs) indicate the early importance of the mbira. Tonal harmony among the Shona and neighboring peoples possibly relates to the musical system of the San, who presumably inhabited the area before the Shona arrived. Since the San share several cultural features with the Bantu of the area, they may share musical features with them. The Shona, however, have not adopted the clicks of San languages, as have some Bantu-speaking populations in South Africa. The musical system of the San may reflect the harmonic series created by the two fundamental tones a musical bow produces as the string is stopped in two segments. We may never know whether Shona music actually arose from playing musical bows, but the affinities between the harmonics of a musical bow and the structure of Shona mbira music are unmistakable.

Musical Instruments and Performance

Mbira

The most distinctive feature of Shona music is the use of the mbira, a lamellaphone plucked by thumbs and forefingers. The instrument is widespread in Africa, but the Shona have developed several of the largest instruments, and use them the most frequently in rituals. The mbira may have arisen as a portable version of a xylophone, but evidence to prove this origin may never appear. The *mbira dzavadzimu* 'mbira of the ancestral spirits', which the Shona recognize as the mbira of the Zezuru people, has become the most prevalent version of the instrument domestically and the best-known worldwide (figure 1). Players of the *mbira dzavadzimu* or *nhare* (iron) strike or pluck the twenty-two or more wide keys with the forefinger of the right hand and both thumbs. The Korekore people have traditionally used a form of mbira variously termed *hera, munyonga, matepe,* and *madhebhe*. This form has about twenty-nine narrow keys, played with both thumbs and both forefingers. In comparison with other forms of mbira, its music is much faster, it has lower bass notes but a "lighter" sound, and its rhythms are more complex. The *njari* form came from the Zambezi River Valley in the 1700s, and has served in rituals involving tutelary spirits (*mashave*); in the late twentieth century, old men played it, mostly to accompany non-ritual singing. The *karimba* (in some areas, *kalimba*) with eight to twenty-three keys is usually smaller than the others, and traditionally does not have ritual uses. It often serves as a novice's instrument.

Figure 1 A *mbira dzavadzimu* inside a *deze* (gourd resonator).
Photo by Claire Jones.

All mbira consist primarily of a soundboard and an assortment of prongs or keys, hammered from metal. The board—hollow in the *hera*, but not in the other forms—is usually about 19 centimeters wide, and slightly larger from front to back. In pre-European times, blacksmiths forged keys from smelted iron; contemporary mbira makers may pound them from nails, or from the wire found in the springs of seats of bicycles and cars. Longer, lower-pitched keys lie near the center of the instrument; shorter ones, on the outside edges. One end of each key rests on wood at the upper edge of the board, and a metal bridge passes under all the keys about 5 centimeters from the same end. Above the key, between the wood and the bridge, a pressure bar holds the key tightly in place; the other end of the key is free for plucking. For tuning, a player can move a key back and forth. Like the English word *sheep*, the Shona word *mbira* is both singular and plural: in the singular, it denotes one of the metal prongs; and when referring to the instrument, the Shona use the plural forms of verbs and modifiers.

The mbira has a subdued sound, often amplified by a resonator and a buzzing device. For personal entertainment or practice, players often omit the resonator. To produce the desired volume of sound in rituals and public performances, the player puts the instrument inside a gourd resonator. The gourds, which have to be uncommonly large, require for sufficient growth either virgin soil or fertilizer; they may serve as containers for water or beer before musicians make them into resonators by cutting off their tops. Mbira players increasingly use resonators made from large fiberglass "gourds." The buzzing comes from a series of rattles, strung along the rim; formerly pieces of landsnail shell, the rattles are now usually bottle caps. The *hera* and related types have metal rattles placed in the hollow part of the board, but the *mbira dzavadzimu* has them attached to the outside of the board. For the buzzing, the *njari* type of mbira relies only on the rattles on the resonator.

As the piano provides a conceptual basis for the Western musical system, so the mbira provides a conceptual basis for the Shona, which is primarily an improvizational tradition, with vocal and instrumental performances based on recurring harmonic and rhythmic cycles. The harmonic cycles involve a succession of fifths (bichords), whose lower notes move in prescribed ways. The most common pattern consists of the movement of fifths in groups of three, with each group only slightly different from the group preceding it. Many mbira songs follow this pattern, but other patterns of harmonic progression are common (figures 2 and 3).

Shona harmony is based upon ascending thirds and fourths and descending seconds. To maintain important kinetic and rhythmic patterns, musicians sometimes insert extraneous notes into the basic harmonic pattern, despite an incomplete keyboard. These notes often include a third, which gives the outside observer the impression the Shona are using triads. These principles of harmony are important, because they relate closely to Shona rhythm. In the literature on Shona rhythms, as on African rhythms in general, different usages of the words *pulse* and *beat* have led to confusion. Sometimes, authors use them interchangeably, but carefully distinguishing them helps to explain this music more clearly. In Shona music, the term *pulse* is best reserved for the rapid and equal rhythmic units often heard in fast drumming. The term *beat* more effectively refers to the somewhat slower rhythmic units that are

Figure 2 The standard harmonic pattern on the mbira. In this example and the next, the staff represents a treble clef, but the absence of the clef serves as a reminder the tuning is different.

Figure 3 Potential tones for the standard harmonic progression.

combinations of pulses and are not always even; the beat often coincides with dance steps.

In the performance of a typical mbira song, the four harmonic segments repeat constantly, with variations. In most songs, each harmonic segment becomes a twelve-pulse rhythmic segment, to produce forty-eight pulses in each cycle. In each segment, the progression from one bichord to the next produces a distinctive harmonic rhythm. Using an eighth note to signal each pulse, the harmonic rhythm is often even, with each segment containing three beats (figure 4a). Four-beat segments are common, forming an uneven harmonic rhythm (figures 4b and 4c), which usually serves as the basis for dance steps. Sometimes the change from one chord to another is ambiguous, because the third tone in one chord anticipates the jump of a third in the root tones. This ambiguity permits two forms of harmonic rhythm to combine to produce rhythmic complexity.

The rhythms within each twelve-pulse group are subject to extensive variation. When two mbirists play together, one may follow a triple meter while the other follows a duple or quadruple one, thus creating polyrhythm. Duple pulse patterns on the mbira result from interlocking the actions of the right and left hands; this interlocking produces an even harmonic rhythm, or patterns of triple beats. The triplet pulse patterns often vary. Asymmetrical pulse patterns can contrast with the basic beats, particularly on the *hera*.

All major mbira songs have two parts, in contrasting and complementary rhythms. The lead (*kushaura*) plays the melodic and higher notes; the following (*kutsinhira*) part emphasizes the root movements of the harmonic patterns. Ideally, one person is available to play each part; people expect a soloist to play something of each part, and they judge his competence accordingly. In one improvizational technique, the *kushaura* starts the changes from one mode of playing to another, and the *kutsinhira* follows. Not every cycle of forty-eight pulses varies, but people play several cycles one way before making a change

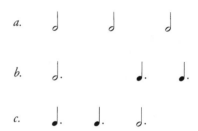

Figure 4 Harmonic rhythms.

to another. The *munyonga* tradition of northeastern Zimbabwe reserves simplified versions of the songs (*dambatimbu*) for use in learning.

Mbira players or *gwenyambira* (one who scratches the mbira keys) often change the harmonic and rhythmic relationships by playing certain patterns of notes louder, and then changing to emphasize other notes. By changing the loudness of certain notes, performers emphasize different rhythmic features. Other perceived differences come randomly from the shapes of the resonators and the positions of the instruments inside the resonators. Though people often play the mbira solo, in some areas they accompany it (particularly the *hera*) with drums. Rattles or *hosho* are generally required to complete an mbira ensemble.

Other Instrumental and Vocal Genres

The mbira is a harmonic and rhythmic instrument; melody comes from the human voice, and popular evaluation of mbirists often rests on their skill in singing. Shona singing includes yodeling, responsorial form, and improvisation. When people are singing without the mbira, vocal sounds still follow the instrumental harmonies. Bass singing (*mahon'era*) consists primarily of the roots of the bichords, with ornamentation such as yodeling. This kind of singing, frequently hummed, can accompany mbira music or stand alone.

In songs in responsorial form, the group-response parts are usually fixed, but the sung lead (*kushaura*) has considerable leeway in improvising text and tune. Certain textual fragments are appropriate only for specific songs, which they serve to identify. In many songs, other textual fragments serve interchangeably. Singers are free to invent new words to fit new occasions. A sung phrase often starts on a high note and descends; the sound of the high notes affects the configuration of the rhythms.

In addition to the mbira, the Shona play many instruments, of which drums are the most important. Drums alone often accompany singing and dancing. A number of regionally associated dance styles are linked with distinct drum and percussion patterns. The names and features of drums vary notably by district. In their primary dance and drum ensemble, Shona of the northeast have three types of traditional drums, all of which are open-ended, with pegs that fasten the head to the body. The smallest, the *mhito*, is about 30 centimeters high and 18 to 20 centimeters in diameter; often beaten with sticks, it maintains the basic rhythm. The *dandi* is 30 to 36 centimeters high, with a diameter as large as 30 centimeters. The *dandi* player performs with hands, sticks, or a combination of both; he is the principal player of improvised variations. The performer on the *mutumba* (a low-pitched, waist-high drum) plays a limited amount of variation; he straddles the drum as it lies on the ground, leans it against his knees when sitting, or stands beside the upright drum.

In northeastern Zimbabwe, panpipe (*ngororombe*) groups, now quite rare, play for entertainment and a dance of the same name (figure 5). Each performer blows two or three pipes in hocket with the other performers, and intersperses vocables with blown notes; they sometimes even break into song.

Most other traditional Shona instruments, including various musical bows, flutes, horns and whistles, are played solo rather than in groups. The *chipendani*, a mouth-resonated bow, has a single string divided into two unequal parts, but is capable of producing extremely complex music through the use of overtones. It was commonly played by herdboys to while away the time. Many of the bows and flutes are disappearing as precolonial activities associated with music such as herding are fading away.

Rattles (*hosho*) are extremely important because they accompany singing, mbira, panpipes and drum and dance ensembles. The most popular type is a knobby gourd, cleaned out and filled with seeds. People use loud rattles made from tin cans and stones because they are easy to prepare. When played with the *mbira dzavadzimu*, two rattles are shaken, one in each hand. The Shona preference is for each to have a distinct sound, which readily comes from instruments of different sizes. The *hosho* are played in contrasting rhythms, often two against three. In some districts, leg rattles accompany dancing: large rattles (*magavhu*) employ three 9-centimeter-diameter gourds on each leg; smaller ones (*tswawo*) employ

Figure 5 The Muzimu Uripo Ngororombe Dance Club, from Murehwa district (east of Harare), performs for the opening of the Murehwa Culture House, 1988. The men play panpipes and dance with *maghavu* rattles on their legs; the women sing, dance, and play handheld *hosho* rattles.
Photo by Claire Jones.

eight 4-centimeter-diameter gourds. The two sets of leg rattles have different timbres.

Shona Concepts of Music

In the chiShona language, no word precisely translates the Western concept of "music." The Shona have separate words for singing (*kuimba*) and playing an instrument (*kuridza* 'cause to cry out'). Since dancing includes instruments and songs, the word for dancing (*kutamba* 'play') implies the combination of these three elements.

Shona people value music highly, and ascribe power to it. Many folktales include songs that so charm or distract the characters that they follow someone's wishes. A particularly good musical performance is described as causing people to run off and allow their cooking pots to boil over.

Traditionally, the Shona believe music implies supernatural power. The ability to play the mbira is said to come to young men in dreams, from ancestral spirits, often those of grandfathers. Special ability in drumming or dancing is a sign of these spirits' favor, and such talents are perceived to be a sign of mediumistic potential.

Shona beliefs assume that their ritual songs, including those for the mbira, take forms set by the ancestors. Creative activity in singing and playing the mbira consist of inventing new ways of playing an existing song, rather than making new songs. Mbira songs have many ways of playing (*miridziro*), which pass in and out of fashion while the songs themselves retain popularity. The differences in forms of mbira correlate with views of repertory. Some songs belong to certain kinds of mbira, and not to others. This distinction relates to the common expression that songs are "in the mbira," and the player simply brings them out.

A song's identity is not always clear, even to many Shona, who group together songs that follow the same harmonic progression. Because the location of the basic pitch of a harmonic pattern can be on any key of the mbira, listeners can confuse songs. To listeners, particularly those unfamiliar with the mbira, the difference in pitch is sometimes vague. Many times, a line of text will provide a clue to the identity of a song, but the mbira itself does not provide such guidance. The place in the harmonic progression where the singing begins is another clue. Mbira songs are often differentiated by characteristic patterns of melody or rhythm played on the mbira.

The Shona classify songs as being modern (*chimanjemanje*) and traditional (*nziyo dzepasi* 'songs of the earth'). The former stand apart from songs of church and school. The latter are classified primarily by use: play songs, hunting songs, death songs, children's songs, and songs of ancestral spirits (*mudzimu*) and tutelary spirits (*mashave*).

Uses and Functions of Shona Music

In pre-European Shona society, music served purposes beyond mere entertainment. One of the most important of these was the enhancement of chieftainship-related rituals. Traditionally, a chief had at his headquarters a set of drums reserved for official purposes. In the past, worksongs were particularly important. The most popular types accompanied the threshing and grinding of grain. Songs served to express social criticism, improvised through their texts. On occasions of exchange labor, people sang threshing songs; the texts, often ribald, held wrongdoers up to public criticism and ridicule. Grinding songs, usually sung solo by women, served to air domestic grievances without fear of reprisal.

Songs are an integral part of many rituals, which, though structurally simple, often follow a night of dancing and singing. Many songs concern death, burial, and the activities of the spirit of the deceased. Burials usually follow a wake, when relatives and friends of the deceased maintain a nocturnal watch over the body. Older people sometimes sing traditional songs inside the hut where the body rests, and younger people sing modern dance songs outdoors. Carrying the body to the grave is accompanied by a special class of songs (*ngondo* or *dendende*). Traditional Shona belief holds that the deceased will hover about the gravesite for months, and will then be ready to find a medium through whom to speak. The *kurova guva* ceremony shows that the descendants have not forgotten the deceased, and frees the spirit from the grave. It involves a night of singing, dancing, and beer drinking, often accompanied by spirit possession on the part of several mediums. At dawn, mourners sing burial songs as they proceed to the gravesite, which they clean; they then offer a sacrifice to show that the spirit is free to seek a medium.

The ordinary spirit-possession ceremony (*bira*) provides an opportunity for members of the community to beg guidance and assistance from their deceased ancestors. Various members of the community are known as spirit mediums—meaning that a particular spirit permanently inhabits their bodies. Because of ritual restrictions, life as a medium may be onerous, but the traditional community highly respects persons having this status. There is no idea of exorcising a spirit from the individual, but the Shona intend the rituals to cause the spirit to come out (*kubuda*), appearing to the community. When it

DISC
1
TRACK
4

Figure 6 At a *bira* in Highfield Township, Harare, people sing, clap, play *hosho* rattles, and drum (not in photo) to make the spirit come out, 1990. Gwenyambira Mondrek Muchena (at right) began the ceremony playing mbira before switching to the *hosho*. *Photo by Claire Jones.*

does, the medium goes into a trance, and the Shona consider whatever he or she says to be the spirit's voice. Mbira music or drumming is usually essential for bringing on the trance or state of possession (figure 6). In theory, each spirit has a favorite song or musical genre that he or she enjoyed while alive; a performance of this song or genre brings the spirit out (the medium goes into trance). At a *bira*, mediums often begin a song that they know will put them into trance.

The course of a *bira* follows a standard format. As the crowd assembles, singing and dancing spontaneously break out, but the proceedings officially begin with a song begun by the drummers or *gwenyambira*(s). Then, the principal medium sits on a mat and receives a pot of water and several cloths. To the spirit within the medium, the organizer tells the purpose of the event, after which the music resumes. During this period, people expect the principal medium and other mediums in attendance to go into trance. As the mediums show signs of possession, they put on special black and white cloths, and the music stops, so the participants can greet and converse with the spirits. The remainder of the night, the mediums and the participants dance and sing together.

Change in Shona Music

During the twentieth century, Shona musical practices changed markedly, mainly because of the impact of European colonization and urbanization. In the central plateau, where most of the European immigrants established themselves, many features of traditional Shona music began to fall away, and indigenous styles survived only through the knowledge and continued practice of a few traditionalists. Where the European population was not abundant, traditional practices continued.

Instruments of non-African origin appeared in Zimbabwe from the beginning of European contact, brought by migrant laborers as well as colonial settlers. The autoharp was one of the first to arrive, followed by the guitar, banjo and harmonica. At first, foreign styles were associated with the imported instruments, but in time, Shona musicians began to adapt their own styles to them. The 1930s saw a new phenomenon: the appearance of itinerant musicians playing for money. These performers, emerging from a culture in which everyone participates musically, can be regarded the first professional Shona musicians.

A major factor that caused changes in Shona musical life was the growth of churches and schools. Schools taught European music and enabled young people to find work in the towns and cities, where contacts with Europeans led to changes in musical idioms. A few Shona people learned to appreciate various kinds of European music, but by far the most popular kinds of music in the towns were syncretic or hybrid musical styles. Before the 1950s, a style that frequently appeared in school activities was the *makwaya* (from English word *choir*), with choral singing in the South African style, frequently accompanied by displays of marching. Dance songs for youth passed regularly through cycles of popularity. In the 1970s, rural middle-aged people enjoyed dancing to *jocho*, a type of song that showed little European influence; youths, however, preferred styles called *jiti* or *jez* (jazz), which combined African

107

drumming and simple European harmonies in songs with responsorial form.

After World War II, several European-led organizations affected the development of musical style in Zimbabwe. The Church Music Service, organized by Methodist missionaries, sought to encourage the use of traditional-style music in churches and conducted workshops encouraging African composers. In Bulawayo in the early 1960s, the Kwanongoma College of Music undertook the training of music teachers for African schools and taught the appreciation of traditional African music. It taught skills in mbira and introduced marimbas. The Kwanongoma marimbas were designed to be flexible enough to play all sorts of music, and soon began spreading to schools, community centers, and tourist spots.

Another major factor that caused changes in Shona music has been the development of electronic media and the music industry, which developed in tandem with the spread of radio, since the latter disseminated new types of songs that became extremely popular. The radio originally broadcast foreign music, including European and American popular music, and songs from Zaïre (now Democratic Republic of the Congo) and South Africa. In the early 1950s, the Rhodesia Broadcasting Corporation began recording traditional music in the rural areas, to broadcast for Shona people who had gone to the cities to find jobs.

Urban Shona people heard much foreign music and began to copy it, using inexpensive or handmade instruments. The locally produced music in foreign styles first served for radio commercials; later, people engaged local troupes to play dance music for urban nightclubs, beer halls, and hotels.

Many of these troupes sprang up because people saw producing live music as a means of making money when jobs were neither plentiful nor gratifying. By the 1970s, popular bands required expensive foreign instruments and amplifiers. Therefore, many of the bands sought the sponsorship of wealthy businessmen, who provided instruments and equipment in exchange for a share of the profits from the performances. Such arrangements frequently involved blatant exploitation. Many such bands found it more profitable to tour the countryside, where they built up a following. In the 1970s, companies began recording popular Shona bands and selling their records. One reason for this trend was that the Shona people preferred records with texts in Shona, rather than in unknown languages. Bands experimenting with adaptations of traditional music played on electric guitars were widely seen as affirming cultural heritage, and began to gain popularity in the decade before independence.

Music and the Uprising

Near the end of the colonial period, indigenous music, particularly that of the mbira, became an important symbol of Shona identity. In the 1970s, the mbira and related ancestral-spirit rites helped politicize rural people, who resented the conditions of their lives, but were not so politically aware as urban people. Instead of taking part in rituals in their home area, some spirit mediums would go from area to area. The occasion of a *bira* brought many people together and provided an opportunity for discussing political matters. Many of the songs sung had subtle political connotations. People called the war the uprising or struggle (*chimurenga*), the same term that in the mid-1890s had referred to a rebellion against white settlers: it now became a common term to describe any song related to the uprising, or to modern Shona political processes. Educated urban Africans, who preferred hybrid musical styles, organized the struggle for independence; in rural areas, indigenous styles still appealed to many people. *Chimurenga* songs were stylistically eclectic. They included *makwaya*, *jocho*, *jiti*, Ndebele songs, modern rock, mbira, and hymns; all received words related to the war.

In the 1970s, freedom fighters used a radio station in Mozambique to broadcast opposition to the propaganda given by the Rhodesia Broadcasting Corporation. In Zimbabwe, the popularity of bands that broadcast and sold records of Shona songs provided additional opportunities for African nationalists to use music to politicize the African population. At first, the studios concerned themselves with limiting their production to songs with nonpolitical topics, but Shona words were often extremely subtle, so many political songs seemed to be innocent.

Thomas Mapfumo (b. 1945), a popular singer and songwriter, created many *chimurenga* songs. The Teal Record Company put many of his songs on disk and changed some of the lyrics so the songs would be acceptable to the government. Thus, it became possible to disseminate Mapfumo's songs by selling his records, though the government banned the songs from radio. Mapfumo was once taken into custody, but a public outcry effected his release.

Mapfumo's songs were not the only ones sending political messages. Some songs used traditional imagery of fighting or hunting, such as "*Baya wabaya*" ('Spear those who spear'). Songs related to the 1896 uprising against the settlers included references to tribal and ancestral spirits, which, people believed, provided help in the struggle.

Figure 7 Members of the Mhembero Dance Company perform for a private party, Harare, 2000. The troupe is led by a former member of the National Dance Company. Marimbas were added to its lineup in the mid-1990s. *Photo by Claire Jones.*

Shona Music in Independent Zimbabwe

Zimbabwe achieved independence in April 1980 after a long and bitter fight. The new majority-ruled government instituted cultural programs to promote traditional music and represent the nation at home and abroad. Their National Dance Company (NDC) included expert men and women performers of a number of different regional Shona and Ndebele dances. *Mbira dzavadzimu* was the featured instrument alongside the drums and rattles used to accompany dances. The NDC ceased to exist in the 1990s because of funding problems, but aspiring musicians have formed similar troupes. These professional groups help to preserve standardized forms of the dances by putting them to new uses for display and entertainment.

The Zimbabwean educational system expanded exponentially after independence, and the Kwanongoma-designed marimbas became extremely popular in urban schools. By the late 1980s, Shona musicians began to include the instruments in their professional bands (figure 7), sometimes alongside western instruments such as guitars. A generation of Zimbabweans has grown up with these instruments and considers them part of their musical heritage. The modern marimbas have also spread to other countries of southern Africa and to the United States, where Shona musician Dumisani Maraire taught for many years.

In the popular music industry, local musicians face competition from international stars and imported styles. Young urbanites often prefer music from England, America, and Jamaica; hip hop has been popular since the 1990s. The most consistently popular local genres, especially among rural Shona, are the Congolese-influenced Zimbabwean rumba and *sungura* styles. By 2000, however, gospel music—in Zimbabwe, any foreign or indigenous style of music with Christian lyrics qualifies as gospel music—was leading local music sales.

The growth in worldwide visibility and popularity of mbira music has been a significant musical development in post-independence Zimbabwe. Bands led by Thomas Mapfumo and mbira player Stella Chiweshe integrated the *mbira dzavadzimu* with western instrumentation in the late 1980s. Both these musicians now make their homes outside Zimbabwe and are popular with world music audiences. Within the country, unemployed traditional and popular musicians struggle to earn a living in the difficult economic and political climate of Zimbabwe in the twenty-first century. Yet mbira seems to be alive and well. The group Mbira DzeNharira (from the rural Nharira area) became a hit in 1999 with its innovative all-mbira orchestra. The ongoing popularity of this group and its offshoots attests to the relevance and vitality of the ancestral mbira tradition in Zimbabwe.

—Adapted from an article by John E. Kaemmer

Bibliography

Berliner, Paul F. [1978] 1993. *The Soul of Mbira: Music and Traditions of the Shona People of Zimbabwe*. Chicago: University of Chicago Press.

Jones, Claire. 1992. *Making Music: Musical Instruments in Zimbabwe Past and Present*. Harare: Academic Books.

Frederikse, Julie. 1982. *None but Ourselves: Masses vs. Media in the Making of Zimbabwe*. New York: Penguin Books.

Tracey Andrew. 1961. "The Mbira Music of Jege Tapera." *African Music* 4(2):44–63.

———. 1970a. *How to Play the Mbira*. Roodepoort, Transvaal: International Library of African Music.

———. 1970b. "The Matepe Mbira Music of Rhodesia." *African Music* 4(4):37–61.

———. 1972. "The Original African Mbira?" *African Music* 5(2):85–104.

Turino, Thomas. 2000. *Nationalists, Cosmopolitans, and Popular Music in Zimbabwe*. Chicago: University of Chicago Press.

Zindi, Fred. 1985. *Roots Rocking in Zimbabwe*. Gweru: Mambu Press.

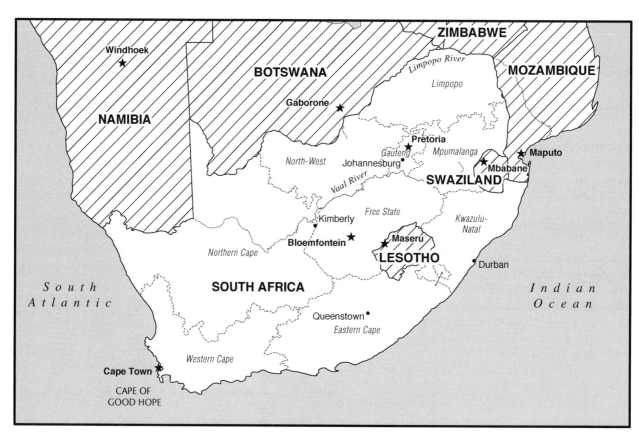

South Africa

Black Popular Music in South Africa

The study of popular musical traditions in South Africa stretches over three and a half centuries of cultural turbulence, across linguistic and political boundaries, to the far reaches of the subcontinent and the capitals and colleges of Europe and America. It encompasses the contributions made by South Africans of African, European, and Asian origin, and by Americans of African descent.

From the late 1600s, increasingly dominant European colonists overwhelmed the cultures of the majority population. Popular musical forms emerged and spread within colonial contexts: European settlers, mainly from the Netherlands and Britain, developed an industrialized economy, based on exploiting an indigenous, conscripted labor force. Since the 1860s, the growth of urban centers accompanied that development and produced environments where intensive interethnic and interracial contacts occurred, amid institutionalized racial segregation and the processes of class formation.

In the late 1800s and early 1900s, South African mining and manufacturing grew prodigiously and created a demand for labor that reached nearly to the equator and transformed the face of southern Africa. The African communities most affected by Christian missionization responded readily to the prospect of better employment in Kimberley and Johannesburg, yet colonial taxes and seductive labor recruiters drew to the mines thousands of cattlekeepers and farmers. So it was that black people arriving with circumscribed provincial patterns of African and Afro-Western (African Christian) culture found themselves at once enmeshed, not only in what people described as "a welter of the tribes," but in a welter of races, values, customs, languages, nationalities, social conditions, levels of education, and worldviews.

These conditions provided contexts for the development of a stylistically diverse, but strongly interactive, popular-performance culture. The genres that appeared reflected the expressive and recreational preferences of a given ethnic, regional, or class-based audience, yet coexisted with new styles and performance venues, designed by their managers and performers to attract an unrestricted clientele. Audiences and the influences involved in developing particular music-and-dance genres usually varied more than popular stereotypes supposed. In rural areas, new forms often evolved in the context of changing realities, but urban spaces—"black locations," mine compounds, factory hostels, schools, churches, welfare centers, union halls—became the crucibles of creativity and dissemination. The cities, in particular Johannesburg, became the centers of local recording and broadcasting industries—from the end of World War II, the largest in Africa. So it is appropriate that this description of the country's indigenous popular music begins with the cultural history of Johannesburg.

Johannesburg

In 1886, the discovery of the world's largest known gold deposits in the South African Republic of the Transvaal upstaged the diamond lode discovered in Kimberley more than a decade earlier. Workers from all over southern Africa gravitated to the spot, soon to be the "Golden City" of Johannesburg, which by about 1900 sheltered at least fifty thousand whites, forty thousand urbanized blacks, and one hundred thousand black miners. To Johannesburg flocked educated African professionals, frustrated by the limited opportunities, low pay, and isolation of smaller communities; by 1904, the census reported 25 percent of the permanent black population was literate. The regional, ethnic, class, and educational backgrounds that crowded together within the black communities created a musical mix that became the basis for black show business in South Africa.

Like other towns in South Africa, turn-of-the-century Johannesburg was racially segregated as much by custom as by law. The city's atmosphere, duplicating that of Kimberley a quarter-century before, gave blacks opportunities to circulate more freely than in the older, settled towns of the Cape, Orange Free State (now Free State), Natal (now KwaZulu-Natal), and Transvaal (a former province in the northeast). Some poorer residential areas on the eastern and western fringes of the city supported a racial mixture of Africans, Coloureds (racially mixed), Whites, Indians, and Chinese. In addition to canteens frequented by blacks only, musical entertainment was available at many of the city's 118 unsegregated canteens. The harshness and insecurity of black life was accompanied by cultural disorientation. In response, musical performances became workshops in which musicians fashioned new models of urban African and African-Western culture, and devised new patterns of social identity and practice. In the context of recreational socialization, interpersonal and community relationships formed and strengthened, and people enacted and celebrated the process of collective self-definition.

Probably the most familiar setting for *informal* music was the *shebeen*, an unlicensed business (usually a private residence), whose owners illegally brewed and sold beer and liquor. The origins of this institution apparently go back to seventeenth-century Cape Town, where Dutch colonists sold liquor to black servants and slaves, and sometimes provided rooms to drink it in. The term *shebeen* 'little shop' apparently came from the Gaelic slang of immigrant Irish vice police in early-twentieth-century Cape Town. Transvaal law decreed prohibition for blacks in 1896, but government-run distilleries continued to produce cheap brandy for them. In addition to African home-brewed beer, the supply of strong drink led to the illegal sale of several near-lethal concoctions. Different shebeens attracted different kinds of patrons, as people sought each other's company on the basis of ethnic or geographical origins, occupational and class affiliations, neighborhood and friendship ties, shared styles of self-expression and aspiration, and the forms of dance and music with which they were associated.

A group of Basotho migrants at a shebeen might hold an impromptu performance of young men's *mangae* manhood initiation songs or male-bonding *mohobelo* dances, or listen to the improvisations of a concertina virtuoso; Zulu domestics and manual workers enjoyed guitar and violin duos and songs for walking and courting; Shangaans (Batsonga from Mozambique) displayed their (Portuguese-influenced) solo guitar styles; and the Bapedi excelled at accompanying melodies on the autoharp, or dancing in a circle to the beat of rhythms on rubber or oxhide stretched over the top of a 44-gallon petrol drum. Much of that music was what can be called neotraditional, as rural-born musicians discovered what they could do with trade-store instruments. The instruments themselves provided a natural vehicle for importing American, British, and even Afrikaans songs, rhythms, and styles of playing.

Christian Religious Music

European Christian hymnody first became a factor in the development of black South African music in the early 1800s. Strife between white settlers and Xhosa pastoralists led to the uprooting of many African communities in the Eastern Cape as early as 1816, when Ntsikana, a Xhosa prophet and visionary, prescribed for the cultural reformulation of Xhosa society a blend of African and Christian religious beliefs, values, and practices. For his congregation, he composed several Afro-Christian hymns, which choirs performed and transmitted orally. In 1876, a mission newspaper published in tonic sol-fa notation his hymn "*Ulo Tixo Mkulu*" 'Thou, Great God'. In 1884, John Knox Bokwe (1855–1922), a renowned Xhosa composer and Presbyterian choirmaster, republished it, with three of Ntsikana's other hymns. Ntsikana's style strikingly infuses Protestant hymnody with the stateliness of Xhosa melody, harmony, and rhythm.

> **tonic sol-fa** is a pedagogic and sight-singing system of verbal syllables that represent relative pitches; for example, *do, re, mi, fa, sol, la, ti, do*.

On mission stations, refugees from successive frontier wars in the Eastern Cape and from the rapid expansion of the Zulu kingdom to the north found shelter, farms, work, and access to the religious and educational requirements of life in colonial society. There, the choral part singing that became the foundation of all indigenous southern Bantu music achieved a fit with Christian hymnody.

Blacks thought congregational singing one of the most attractive aspects of Christian ritual. African choirs made harmonies, not on the basis of a dominant melodic line, but by polyphonically embellishing a bass ostinato. Though Western concepts of tonality were foreign, blacks enshrined as a choral set piece Handel's *Hallelujah* chorus (from *Messiah*, an oratorio premiered in 1742). More importantly, the melodic direction of southern Bantu part songs tends to follow the tonal patterns of the words. To Bantu-speakers' ears, the violation of traditional tone–tune relationships and patterns of syllabic stress made many of the early translations of European hymns unlovely, even incomprehensible, but converts eventually got used to it.

By the 1880s, a movement toward cultural revitalization and nationalism was growing among mission blacks disappointed with their lack of social advancement John Bokwe, a leader in the movement, preserved semantic tones while achieving a high musical and literary quality—a happy marriage of African and European compositional principles. His efforts pioneered a new black South African choral style, widely known as *makwaya* (from the English word *choir*), which he used in Scotland to support his studies for the ministry, and to gain for black South African Christians a sympathetic hearing. Since then, many illustrious figures in black South African choral music—Benjamin Tyamzashe (1890–1978), A. A. Khumalo (1879–1966), Hamilton

Figure 1 Enoch Sontonga, composer of *"Nkosi Sikelel'*
iAfrika" ('God Bless Africa').
From the collection of David B. Coplan.

Masiza (1894–1955), Reuben Caluza (1895–1969),
Joshua Mohapeloa (1908–1982), Michael Moerane
(1904–1980)—have appeared.

Several outstanding songs exemplify the *makwaya*
style. One is *"Nkosi Sikelel' iAfrika"* ('God Bless
Africa'), composed in Xhosa in 1897 by a Johannesburg teacher, Enoch Sontonga (1860–1904; figure
1); S. E. K. Mqhayi (1875–1945), the Xhosa national
poet, later added more stanzas. In the early 1900s,
Reuben Caluza's Ohlange Institute Choir popularized this song, which in 1925 became the anthem of
the African National Congress, South Africa's most
important organization fighting for the rights of
black South Africans; it is now the national anthem
of Tanzania and Zambia. Though rhythmically
stolid, its perceived combination of melancholic
yearning and spiritual grandeur made it a musical
embodiment of the thirst for freedom.

Makwaya must be considered popular music
because of its distribution among choirs, civic and
political organizations, unions, and wedding parties,
in community concerts, and on television, radio, and
other media. In evolving contexts, it supported the
traditional attachment of black South Africans to
choral song. Reflecting the secular use of the emotional and spiritual catharsis provided in sacred
pieces (such as Methodist hymns), it influenced other
forms of vocal and instrumental music, including
working-class choral forms—the sonorous *ingoma
ebusuku* (Zulu) 'night music', more recently known
as *isicathamiya* 'sneaking up', and lighter school
songs, known as *mbholoho*—and South African ragtime and early jazz, plus the rearrangement of
indigenous folksongs for choral performance in
four-part harmony.

Jazz, *Marabi*

For new arrivals from the countryside, the ability to
incorporate black American and European elements
and items into performances expressed knowledge of,
and a certain mastery over, the dominant exogenous
culture and the new social environment. Africans
returning home injected urban tunes, rhythms, and
steps into rural dances. Laborers who set their sights
on permanent urban residence began buying
American-style clothes, sending their families to
church and school, and seeking popular music at
neighborhood concerts and shebeens. All black
people in the towns lived close together—well off and
poor, educated and illiterate, Christian and animist,
Zulu and Basotho, Coloured and African. Ethnic
musical traditions began to blend with Afro-Western
and Western ones. An early generation of professional and semiprofessional black musicians, who
by supplying musical modes of adaptation intended
to earn good money, syncretized the new styles.

In the vanguard of that generation were solo
pianomen, primarily from the Cape, but not uncommonly from other towns in Natal, the Free State,
and the Transvaal. In the early 1900s, American ragtime, dixieland, and jazz became popular among
Westernizing Coloureds and Africans, whether
educated or not. Queenstown, in the Cape midlands,
produced so many leading players (like Meekly
"Fingertips" Matshikiza, brother of legendary composer and writer Todd Matshikiza) that it earned the
nickname "Little Jazz Town." Whether pianomen
performed at school and community concerts and
élite social affairs, or in rough canteens at railway
junctions and in periurban shantytowns, they soon
found they could lessen or cut their dependence on
pay from menial jobs, provided they kept moving

and played a variety of popular styles for diverse audiences. The shebeens belonged mostly to women, who had transformed their traditional skill at brewing into a profitable business. "Shebeen queens" often bought their own instruments and vied for the services of popular pianists and organists, who attracted patrons to parties. In Johannesburg, their competition produced an unstable stylistic blend of Xhosa melodies, ragtime, and *tickey draai*, a dance accompanied by the guitar, popular until the 1940s. This was *thula n'divile* 'keep quiet, I've heard it', a three-chord harmonic format, which served as an exhortation for others to cease their noise, so the player might flaunt something new.

Whenever black people tried to create stable, ordered communities with functioning social institutions and viable patterns of urban culture, the government moved in to destroy them. By the 1920s, authorities scheduled the "black spots" ("locations") for removal, yet these places, which in Johannesburg included Doornfontein, Prospect Township, and Malay Camp–Vrededorp, and in Pretoria included Marabastad and Lady Selbourne, were centers of social and cultural inventiveness. Though slums, they were the settings for professional black stage entertainment and the birth of an indigenous kind of jazz.

In the dancehalls and shebeens, the pianomen's efforts at devising a musical formula that would please a diverse patronage led them to work the melodies and rhythms of black ethnic groups into a repetitive three-chord version of American ragtime and jazz. By the late 1920s, that music was known in the Transvaal towns as *marabi*, a term whose origins are uncertain, but whose incorporative flexibility and lively danceability gave listeners the sense of a music at once indigenous, urbanized, African, up to date, and worldly. *Marabi* often has a four-bar progression of chords ending on the dominant: $I–IV–I_4^6–V^7$. In it, a recurrent sequence of chords, offset with varying melodic phrases, simulates indigenous as well as African Christian choral part songs. Fingertips Matshikiza and others were renowned *marabi* pianists, but in Johannesburg the most famous was Tebetjane, whose 1932 composition "*uTebetjana Ufana ne'Mfene*" ('Tebetjane looks like a baboon') became the emblem of the style. In accordance with African holistic concepts of performance and the close identification of performance genres with their practitioners and social settings, *marabi* was not merely a hybrid instrumental music, but a dance-form, a social occasion, and a category of participants—urbanizing proletarians. So pervasive a part of life did it become that Todd Matshikiza (1920 or 1921–1968) proclaimed it "the name of an epoch."

True to its inclusivity, its rhythmic and chordal structure was rigid, and there was little of the "free" improvisation that characterized American jazz; but because it fed so many streams of indigenous music into the river of American honkytonk, it became the reservoir of a uniquely South African jazz.

Pianomen and pedal organists were not the only instrumentalists who spawned *marabi*: the brass and fife-and-drum bands of British forces sent to South Africa during the Boer War (1899–1902) had much impressed Africans. Later, African brass and reed players trained in the marching bands of the Native Military Corps and the Salvation Army began to form their own ensembles. They played at weddings and church festivals, and for women's neighborhood and religious organizations and the coins of outsiders seeking excitement in the "locations." Theirs was a process that added to European marches African polyrhythm and polyphonic improvisation. Soon, however, untrained bandsmen, especially Bapedi domestic servants exposed to brass by the Lutheran missions of the Transvaal, joined trained players. Their method was to repeat short segments of European tunes in combination with African melodies, worked out by trial and error on the new instruments, and orchestrated polyphonically by ear. During the 1920s and 1930s, *marabi*—including the famous *tamatie saus* (Afrikaans) 'ketchup', and the antipolice satire "Pick-Up Van"—became staples of marching band repertories. In time, small ensembles of piano, brass, reed, violin, banjo, and drums began to play at shebeens and neighborhood social occasions, leading to the emergence of *marabi* dance bands, like the Japanese Express.

Stylistic exchange between rural neotraditional African music on the one hand and *marabi* on the other took place in both directions. Rural dances (like Xhosa *mabokwe*), neotraditional forms (like the Zulu guitar songs of roving *abaqhafi* 'street cowboys'), and incipient syncretic urban styles (like Xhosa *itswari* 'soirée' and *thula n'divile*), all flowed into *marabi*, which in turn contributed new rhythms and inventive, often deliberately comical, footwork. In Johannesburg, *famo*, a wild and risqué version of *marabi*, appeared among Basotho migrants and proletarians; combined with neotraditional Basotho dance, it became a staple of working-class entertainment in the towns and rural villages of the Orange Free State and Lesotho. Zulu guitar and violin players quickly assimilated *marabi*'s vamp into their walking, courting, and wedding songs. In Durban, workers danced to a Zulu piano vamp style of *marabi* called *indunduma* 'mine dumps'—a reference to Johannesburg, where people disappeared amid mountains of slag.

For people trying to maintain traditional family systems and codes of social behavior, or to construct new Afro-Western Christian ones, *marabi* represented the dangers and the depths of urban immorality and hedonism; but the children of the "locations," loving the ragtime love songs and *marabi* favorites of the day, sneaked to the parties and dances with many a joy-seeking husband or wife. Rural-oriented traditionalists, urbanized elitists, and those trying to keep one foot in both social environments developed self-defining styles and occasions of performance.

Jazz: The "Respectable Response"

Through Christian preparatory schools, teachers' colleges and associations, membership in churches, urban professional employment, and even newspapers (such as *Isigidimi sama Xhosa, Ilanga lase Natal, Imvo Zabantsundu,* and *Tsala ea Bechuana*), educated African élites had long possessed social institutions and networks connecting rural areas, small towns, and "locations." By the 1920s, their culture was a century old. During the years between the world wars, several important developments occurred in it, in conscious opposition to ragtime, jazz, and *marabi*. First, a generation of *makwaya* composers arose, more innovative and influential than before. Benjamin Tyamzashe enhanced the contribution of Xhosa folksong to *makwaya*. Joshua Mohapeloa, a talented tunesmith, used his facility with tonic sol-fa notation to arrange Basotho folksongs for Western four-part choral performance and to compose choral songs that stretched the rules of Western harmony to fit Basotho ideals of polyphony. A choirleader himself, Mohapeloa helped perfect the local method, whereby choirs are led, rather than conducted: the leader sets up a melody in the bass, and the other three parts enter above, in polyphonic relation to the bass, though not necessarily to each other. For the representation of African part songs, Mohapeloa saw he could turn the rigidity and insufficiency of tonic sol-fa to his advantage. While encouraging the free use of African tonality, ornamentation, timbre, and polyphonic "part agreement," choral leaders used tonic sol-fa as a skeletal sign of the general direction and organization of parts.

The greatest composer of *makwaya* was Reuben T. Caluza, of Natal. His promotion of music as a fundraiser for the Ohlange Institute, a trade school, led him to experiment with a range of ensembles and styles. He went so far as to found student pennywhistle-and-drum bands, which paraded in the streets of small towns around Natal. More important was the Ohlange choir, whose performances under his direction became, before the Great War, major cultural events in Durban, Johannesburg, and elsewhere. Caluza composed in tonic sol-fa dozens of songs, many of which had social and political themes, such as "*iLand Act*" (to protest the Land Act of 1913); "*Influenza*" (to mourn deaths in the flu epidemic of 1918), and "*Ingoduso*" (to deplore a perceived loss of moral responsibility among young Zulu immigrants to Johannesburg). By combining indigenous Zulu melodies, ragtime, and hymnodic *makwaya*, he objectified three distinct categories of Afro-Western choral song: *isiZulu*, traditional folksongs arranged in four-part harmony; *imusic*, strongly Westernized "classical" *makwaya*; and ragtime (*ukureka*). In 1932, for His Master's Voice (London), he recorded more than one hundred twenty of his arrangements and compositions; Lovedale Press published several in tonic sol-fa. He had no hesitation about performing for working-class audiences, or for any audience that cared to hire him; and he was not, despite his status, above composing a choral *marabi* or two. What apparently astonished audiences was his ability to synchronize voices, onstage movements, and keyboard. He earned musical degrees at Hampton Institute (Virginia) and Columbia University (New York), and spent the later part of his musical career as director of the music school at Adams College (Amanzimtoti, Natal). His influence on popular composition and performance in Zulu was lasting and profound, from school concerts to élite and workers' choral competitions to jazz bands like J. C. P. Mavimbela's Rhythm Kings, which in the late 1930s specialized in swing-jazz arrangements of Caluza songs.

Another major development in élite performance was the development of polished semiprofessional variety-song-and-dance companies (still called minstrels) out of the school and neighborhood amateur concerts of the 1920s. Minstrel companies like the Erie Lads, Darktown Negroes, Africans Own Entertainers, Hiver Hyvas, and Darktown Strutters, drew on British "concert-party" and black American vaudeville, made available through films, recordings, and sheet music. Their performers offered a mix of ragtime and dixieland vocals in African languages, American popular standards (like "Can't Help Lovin' Dat Man"), *makwaya*, step-dancing, tap-dancing, comic turns, and dramatic sketches—all wearing matching tuxedos.

By the 1940s, ballroom and swing-jazz orchestras on the American big-band model dominated black show business in the cities, especially Johannesburg. Despite laws that did not recognize "musician" as a legitimate category of employment for blacks, dozens of such bands toured the country, often teaming up for concert and dance performances with variety troupes. Once begun, shows had to carry on until at least four or five in the morning, since curfew laws and an absence of public transportation made it impossible for black concertgoers to go home at night. Some bands, like the Jazz Maniacs and Harlem Swingsters, avoided touring by securing regular engagements around Johannesburg, but few musicians could manage exclusively on their musical earnings. For example, Wilson "King Force" Silgee, saxophonist and leader of the Jazz Maniacs, was for a lengthy period a "tea boy" in the Johannesburg municipal clerk's office. The Jazz Maniacs were among those bands that for many years refused to make recordings, stating that the flat fees of a few pounds per side weren't worth the effort, and helped competing bands copy their compositions and style. Others, especially the top vocal soloists and groups, viewed records as a useful medium for increasing their audience. People commonly attended shows expressly to hear their favorite recording artists perform current hits. In the late 1940s, The Band in Blue, starring virtuoso clarinetist and alto saxophonist Kippie Moeketsi (1925–1983), backed an all-black ensemble in Ike Brooks's musical variety film *Zonk* (unreleased, in private hands).

Among the most popular vocal groups were the male close-harmony quartets (patterned after the Mills Brothers and the Inkspots), such as the Manhattan Brothers, the African Inkspots, and the Woody Woodpeckers. Similar female soloists included Dolly Rathebe (1928–2004; figure 2), Dorothy Masuku (b. 1935), and Susan Gabashane (b. 1939). In the 1950s and early 1960s, female quartets, such as the Dark City Sisters and Miriam Makeba's Skylarks, sang jazz with a local flavor. Much of the jazz the singers and bands popularized was arrangements of American songs and local compositions in the American swing idiom, with lyrics in African languages. Local music made its mark in jazz orchestrations of African folksongs and *marabi*, and in the use of African rhythms in original compositions.

Many songs engagingly combined American and African melodic and rhythmic motifs. An important aspect of this process occurred in the late hours of live shows, when players would put away their American sheet music and "let go." A more *marabi*-based, African jazz took over, and the brass, reeds, and piano took improvised solo choruses over a pulsating beat. Not all audiences adored American popular culture, and many patrons demanded from the bandsmen a more local jazz idiom. Some bands, like the Chisa Ramblers, specialized in "backyard" party engagements, for which they supplied *marabi*.

Figure 2 Cameron Pinocchio Mokgaleng, founder of the Sophiatown Modern Jazz Club, and vocalist Dolly Rathebe, in the 1950s.
From the collection of David B. Coplan.

From that kind of playing and the vocals that accompanied it arose *mbaqanga*, a Zulu name for a stiff corn porridge, which jazzmen regarded as their professional staple, a musical daily bread. The dance of the period was the *tsaba-tsaba*, a big-band successor to the *marabi*. The best-known song in this style was "*Skokiaan*" (named after a deadly drink), composed in the late 1940s by a Rhodesian, August Musarurwa, and first recorded by his African Dance Band of the Cold Storage Commission of Southern Rhodesia (later the Bulawayo Sweet Rhythm Band). This hit was eventually released as sheet music in seventeen European and African languages; in the United States, it topped the Lucky Strike Hit Parade in 1954, in a rendition by Louis Armstrong (1901–1971) titled "Happy Africa." As for *mbaqanga*, South Africa's own jazz, there is no more characteristic a composition than Miriam Makeba's "*Patha Patha*" ('Touch Touch'), the signature tune of a popular and playfully sexy dance of the 1950s.

As the example of *marabi* proves, much of what was African in local jazz was bubbling up from the music of migrants, urban workers, and people of the "locations"—music performed in shebeens, in workers' hostels, in community halls, at backyard feasts, at weddings. At least as early as the Great War, Zulu workers arriving in Durban from smaller communities in Natal formed male choirs, modeled on church and school concerts, amateur coon variety shows (*isikunzi*), and Caluza's ensembles. The music of these choirs, a blend of ragtime and indigenous part singing, was first known as *ingoma ebusuku* 'night music', after all-night competitions among choirs. Performers wore matching blazers and sharply pressed trousers, and made synchronous movements with their arms, torsos, and bodies. Their step-dancing styles—*isicatamiya*, and later *cothoza 'mfana* (Zulu) 'sneak up, boy'—became standard terms for the music and dance of Zulu workers' choirs. By the 1940s, a range of styles within that idiom had evolved. The most traditional were the *mbombing* choirs, named after loud, high-pitched, choral yells, sung antiphonally with low-pitched parts, said to imitate the whine of bombs falling from airplanes in newsreels of World War II. The most sophisticated were the songs of Solomon Linda (1909–1962), a brilliant composer and arranger, whose Original Evening Birds were the acknowledged champions of *isicatamiya*. Under the title "Wimoweh" (a mnemonic for the guitar vamp, which survived American transformation), Pete Seeger and the Weavers later rearranged and recorded a hit song "*Mbube*" ("Lion"). Because of its popularity, *mbube* survived for many years as a term for a style of Zulu male singing. On the other side of the Atlantic, "Wimoweh," reworked by arranger George Weiss for the Tokens as "The Lion Sleeps Tonight" (1961), became one of the most popular and widely distributed songs of all time, earning untold millions of dollars for its American publishers. Legal battles over these revenues ceased only in 2006, with a settlement for Linda's heirs.

The same rhythm that found its way to America in "Wimoweh" put a characteristic stamp on South African jazz through the interposition of *kwela*, a style of street jazz that sprang up in the 1940s. Several etymologies compete in explaining this term, but there is a clear association with petty criminality, youth gangs, and other forms of socially resistant street life. The central instrument of a *kwela* ensemble, the pennywhistle (a six-hole fipple metal recorder or flageolet), has antecedants in the Zulu *umtshingo* (a one-hole reed pipe) and other indigenous wind instruments. Its most noticeable early appearance in South Africa seems to have been with fife-and-drum corps of Scottish regiments, which paraded in Johannesburg and Pretoria during the Second Boer War. Early in the 1900s, groups of young Northern Sotho domestics and street toughs

Figure 3 Little Lemmy Mabaso, pennywhistler in *King Kong*, performing on the streets of Johannesburg, late 1950s. *From the collection of David B. Coplan.*

known as *amalaita* formed their own pennywhistle-and-drum bands; on weekends, they marched in the streets. Later, the pennywhistle became the favored instrument of proletarian hustlers and crapshooters, who, whenever the police pickup van (known as a *kwela-kwela*) passed by, would hide their dice and take out their pennywhistles for an innocent-looking jam session.

"Our Kind of Jazz": *Mbaqanga*

During the 1940s and 1950s, for the coins of admiring passersby, aspiring young musicians (many only ten years old), formed street bands to play pennywhistles, acoustic guitars, and one-stringed washtub basses. Their music was *kwela*, a blend of American swing and the African melodies and guitar-vamp rhythms of the "locations." *Kwela* became a popular downscale version of *mbaqanga*, and several of its most talented pennywhistle soloists found their way into recording studios. Since no system for paying royalties to black musicians existed in South Africa until 1964, they made little money; but they did achieve publicity. Famous pennywhistle virtuosos included Spokes Mashiyane (1933–1972) (whose

117

revenues from recording helped build Gallo into South Africa's largest recording company), and Little Lemmy Mabaso (b. 1949 or 1950; figure 3) (who, when, in 1960, the black musical *King Kong* toured to London, played for Queen Elizabeth II). *Kwela* featured an ostinato vamp sequence of chords (C–F–C–G^7) on guitar, under a pennywhistle melody divided into an antiphonal AABB phrase pattern. This pattern also occurs in *mbaqanga*; its phrasing originates in traditional Nguni songs, which consist of a single musical sentence divided into two phrases. *Kwela* studio bands typically featured a soloist backed by four pennywhistles playing the theme in unison, plus bass and drums. Many studio reed players got their start as pennywhistlers, and even the famous virtuosos wound up in the studios playing saxophone *mbaqanga*. In the early 1990s, Mambaso still made a living that way. Spokes Mashiyane said the simplicity of the pennywhistle allowed him greater freedom to bend and blend notes in the near-vocalized African manner. Improvised jazz solos on recordings such as "Kwela Kong" attest to Spokes' genius for making an aesthetic virtue out of technical limitations: he acrobatically shaded, warped, and vocalized a torrent of timbres and tones.

Black studio musicians had at first little respect for the street pennywhistlers, but the latter's popularity forced acceptance and encouraged musical exchange. By the late 1950s, a blend of *kwela, mbaqanga*, and American big-band jazz, had emerged in recordings such as "Baby Come Duze" by Ntemi Piliso (1925–2000) and the Alexandra Allstar Band. That form of *mbaqanga*, sometimes known as *majuba* (after the Jazz Maniacs' recording of the same name), characterized South African jazz at its popular height. American jazz was also popular, especially among sophisticates. In the United States, the big bands were dying out, and jazz as a broadly popular music was in decline.

These developments influenced black South African jazzmen profoundly, and the honor roll of local musical giants—such as Kippie "Morolong" Moeketsi, Dollar Brand (b. 1934), Mackay Davashe (1920–1972), Elijah Nkonyane, Sol Klaaste, Hugh Masekela (b. 1939), Jonas Gwangwa (b. 1941), Chris McGregor (1936–1990; a white pianist and leader of a multiracial band), and Gideon Nxumalo (1929–1970)—is too lengthy to summarize here. Female singers—such as Miriam Makeba (b. 1932), Dolly Rathebe, Abigail Kubekha (b. 1941), Peggy Phango (1928–1998), and Thandi Klaasens (b. 1931)—and close-harmony quartets (such as the Manhattan Brothers and LoSix) helped maintain the popularity and compositional productivity of *mbaqanga* and American-style vocal jazz in local languages.

A series of jam sessions organized at the Odin Cinema (figure 4) by the Modern Jazz Club in Sophiatown, a vigorous black freehold suburb known as Johannesburg's "Little Harlem," epitomized and energized interest in American mainstream jazz. As in the United States, smaller units, such as Mackay Davashe's Shantytown Sextet and the King Force Quintet (Wilson Silgee's successor to the Jazz Maniacs), were replacing big bands. Those ensembles

Figure 4 Jazz at the Odin, *from left*: Kippie Moeketsi, Skip Phahlane, Ntemi Piliso, David Mtimkulu, Mackay Davashe, and Elijah Nkonyane, circa 1955. *From the collection of David B. Coplan.*

played bebop *mbaqanga*, combining the melodic and rhythmic motifs and two-part, two-repeat phrasing of the latter with the virtuosic improvising of the former. Almost indistinguishable from their American counterparts were the Jazz Epistles, featuring Dollar Brand on piano, Hugh Masekela on trumpet (figure 5), Jonas Gwangwa on trombone, and Kippie Moeketsi on clarinet and alto saxophone. Except for Moeketsi, who toured to London only with Mackay Davashe's Jazz Dazzlers Orchestra and *King Kong* in 1960–1961, these players, and a good many others of South Africa's most prominent musicians, fled from apartheid into exile, where they enjoyed outstanding careers overseas. Most of the Jazz Epistles, Miriam Makeba, all four of the Manhattan Brothers, drummer Louis Moholo (b. 1940), singer Letta Mbulu (b. 1942), composer and author Todd Matshikiza, and countless other stars settled outside South Africa. Their decision to leave the country was not based on the declining popularity of jazz. Despite their departure, the 1960s saw spirited developments in South African jazz. During the first half of the decade, a series of major "Cold Castle" jazz festivals, sponsored by South African Breweries in Soweto, helped focus urban blacks' attention on established and rising vocalists and players.

Black Show Business under Apartheid

Voluntary exile was a response to increasingly restrictive conditions imposed by the Nationalist Party government, which came to power in 1948 and implemented a system of rigid measures to enforce the separation of the races. Under "separate-amenities" legislation, black and white musicians could not perform together, or play for multiracial audiences, without special permits. To make way for white settlement, the government removed black suburbs close to urban centers, which had often served as centers of black cultural life. The residents relocated to distant new townships. In the late 1950s, Sophiatown, home of African jazz, was bulldozed out of existence—at its cultural and political height. In 1960, the musical *King Kong*, based on the downfall of black heavyweight boxing champion Ezekial "King Kong" Dhlamini, appeared. It was a result of collaboration between African performers and composers and white directors, choreographers, and producers. It featured the music of Todd Matshikiza, with arrangements by Stanley Glasser, Mackay Davashe's swinging Jazz Dazzlers Orchestra, Miriam Makeba, and the Manhattan Brothers' Nathan Mdledle (1923–1995) in the leading roles, and a host of Johannesburg's top black performers. It was a big success with black and white audiences in Johannesburg; it defined an era, in opposition to the government's good-fences-make-good-neighbors vision of apartheid. When the show toured in London, many members of the cast chose to stay abroad, and returnees found the basis of black show business had severely eroded. Cut off from the city, the black communities like Soweto turned inward, and dissention and violence plagued concert and dancehall stages. Beginning in the 1960s, community halls, and even the black cinemas in Johannesburg, where African music was staged, instituted a no-dancing policy, lest high spirits lead to physical violence.

Frustrated in one direction, black popular musicians turned their energies in others. Neotraditionalists were as active as ever, and electric amplification of their favored instruments provided opportunities for increased technical sophistication, a broader range of outside influences, and access to a wider popular audience. In the 1960s, the guitar became the dominant instrument in all Western popular music. In West and Central Africa, syncretic styles of guitar playing, such as highlife and Congo beat, dominated local scenes. In South Africa, a new electrified-guitar *mbaqanga* (accordion, violin, pennywhistle-cum-saxophone, backed by electric bass and drumset) emerged, also known by the American loanword *jive*. Musically, *mbaqanga* jive borrowed from the old *mbaqanga* and *tsaba-tsaba* to create a new up-tempo rhythm, played in 8/8 time on high hat, but with a strong internal feeling of 2/4 and syncopated accents on offbeats. The melodic theme was in the bass, which, with the backup vocalists, became the lead instrument, representing the chorus in traditional

Figure 5 A young Hugh Masekela.
From the collection of David B. Coplan.

vocal music. The lead guitar, saxophone, violin, accordion, and solo vocal took the upper parts in antiphonal fashion. The phrase structure was the familiar AABB repeat of the old *mbaqanga*. Hence, the sound of *mbaqanga* jive derived more from traditional and neotraditional African music than from the earlier, more Western and jazz-influenced *mbaqanga* of the 1950s. The leading figures in its innovation and development were Simon Nkabinde (1937–1999), a Swazi composer and vocalist (known as Indoda Mahlathini), and John Bhengu (b. 1930), a Zulu guitarist (known as Phuzushukela).

The audience for this music was not the sophisticated, English-speaking, urbanized, American-jazz and popular-ballad fans of "Little Harlem," but the thousands of semiliterate domestic servants, industrial workers, and mineworkers who retained rural connections. With the clearing of the "locations" under the group-areas legislation of the early 1950s, influx-control regulations reinforced the migrant-labor system, and denied most recent arrivals the right to bring their relatives, or to settle permanently in urban areas. In the same decade, the Land Acts of 1913, 1936, and 1945, which had reserved 87 percent of South Africa's territory for white ownership, uprooted and impoverished rural life. The remaining 13 percent became the basis for the infamous "Bantustans" or homelands, which South Africa began to declare independent, starting in 1963 with the Transkei. The government pursued on a new level the policy of preventing the formation of a stable urban workforce or a landed rural peasantry. By law, many black South Africans found themselves citizens of reserves they had never seen.

In such an atmosphere, urban workers turned their eyes and ears from the ecological devastation, poverty, and hopelessness of their rural districts. In sound, text, and choreography, the music they preferred, *mbaqanga* jive, provided symbolic images of once independent African cultures, in which men and women possessed their full *ubuntu* (Zulu) 'humanity'. Indoda Mahlathini had a thrilling bass register, which he employed to develop the role of solo male "groaner" in front of a chorus of four female voices, the legendary Mahotella Queens. Mahlathini and his Queens developed a kind of variety show, which included fast changes among traditional dance movements in beads, feathers, and skins; athletic turns in shorts, sneakers, and baseball caps; and svelte ballads in evening dress. This format for *mbaqanga* became known as *simanjemanje* ('now-now things'), a form that at once celebrated and burlesqued Western manners, material culture, and indigenous heritage.

The texts of Mahlathini's songs created a vision of an autonomous rural African past, when people daily honored cohesive moral and political values, not just in the breach, but in the observance. The songs favorably compared these values to the supposed individualism and immorality of "now-now," but the comparison was less important than Mahlathini's presentation of forceful images of a heroic, independent African past, and of a self-sufficient African idyll. In the face of dependency and dehumanization, these images contributed to a sense of resistant nationalism and self-regard, and were less a mystification of African tradition than a mobilization of its remaining psychocultural resources. By the late 1960s, the major recording companies had recruited or formed dozens of *simanjemanje* ensembles, which sang in a variety of local languages, each with a groaner and a chorus. Until the mid 1970s, *simanjemanje* dominated sales of locally made recordings and the airwaves of the African-language services of the South African Broadcasting Corporation ("Radio Bantu"). Concerts and extended tours of groups like Mahlathini's, sponsored by their recording companies, were among the most frequent professional performance events for blacks. Educated Africans cared little for these events and preferred jazz or the rock and soul arriving from North America and England.

During the 1970s, township-jazz musical theater expanded to become the preeminent local showcase for new black talent. The *simanjemanje* style of *mbaqanga* or *mqhashiyo* (Zulu) 'fly off, like chips from the ax', as people then called it, continued to command a large following, rivaled only by imported Anglo-American popular hits, and by the latest and most professionally polished and talented of the *cothoz' mfana* or *isicatamiya* groups, Ladysmith Black Mambazo. People consider the leader of that group, Joseph Shabalala (b. 1941), a masterful composer and singer. Ladysmith Black Mambazo, who usually performed unaccompanied and in Zulu, were among the top-selling groups in South Africa, more than a decade before the American musician Paul Simon recruited them for his *Graceland* album and tour of 1986. In 1987, they won a Grammy, for best folk album (*Shaka Zulu*), and repeated that feat in 2005 (*Raise Your Spirit Higher*).

By the end of the 1970s the folk-electric *mbaqanga* of Mahlathini and Phuzushukela was in sharp decline. By the time Mahlathini and the Queens emerged from retirement to make their historic and brilliantly successful tours of newly reopened Europe and North America in the early 1990s, *mbaqanga* jive was an extinct genre in South Africa, but their successors brought electric "popular-traditional" music to new heights of creativity and popularity. The Soul Brothers, led by keyboardist Moses Ngwenya, developed a genre of Zulu male close-harmony song-and-dance jive, derived from both Mahlathini and the old *isicatamiya* choirs, and developed a loyal fan base that still buys their albums and attends their performances. The style they pioneered has become a staple, in several languages, on neotraditional music television programs, such as the perennially popular *Ezodumo* and its replacement, *Roots.*

Phuzushukela, for his part, inspired not only nearly every Zulu folksinging guitarist in the land, but also Johnny Clegg (b. 1953) and Sipho Mchunu, who blended 1970s soft rock and Zulu guitar *mbaqanga* song and dance and attained international stardom. More profound and extensive was the institutionalization of Phuzushukela's Zulu guitar *mbaqanga* as *maskanda*, a Zulu electric popular traditional guitar-band style, featuring male and female folk dancers. *Maskanda* owed as much to Zulu folk guitar music as to *Mbaqanga*, and today passes, along with the *isicatamiya* male choral music of Ladysmith Black Mambazo, for what is universally understood as "Zulu traditional music." No broadcast of *Roots* seems complete without it and exponents such as Phushukemisi, Ihashi Elimhlophe, Bhekumuzi Luthuli, or Nothembi Mkhwebane (a female Ndebele singer-guitarist and band leader). Some of these *maskanda* artists, most notably Bheki Khoza and Madala Kunene (b. 1951) among the men

and Tu Nokwe and Busi Mhlongo (b. 1947) among the women, have taken this structured form beyond its seemingly rigid boundaries into blends with a wide range of contemporary musical styles.

Another phenomenon of the late 1960s and 1970s whose popularity lasted two decades was the group Malombo, a unique fusion of the indigenous African musics of northern South Africa and progressive, "free" jazz and rock influences from North America. Malombo began with Philip Tabane (ca. 1940) on guitar, Abbie Cindi on flute, and Julian Bahula (b. 1938) on African drums; but the band soon divided. For ten years, Thabane, the guiding genius of the group, and originator of its style, teamed up with Gabriel Mabee Thobejane, percussionist and dancer (figure 6). They derived their vocals, melody, and percussion from the Northern Sotho, Amandebele, and Venda cultures of the Transvaal; and they took guitar arrangements and improvisatory style from such Americans as Wes Montgomery and John McLaughlin. Their music, though not explicitly political, came to occupy a special place in the vanguard of local progressive music, where it embodied a blend of African cultural nationalism and modernism known as the Black Consciousness Movement. Other groups that performed in the Malombo style, such as Dashiki, were explicitly political; they played at rallies of the South African Students Organization. Curiously, Malombo established a loyal following among young white listeners. They probably spent more time touring in

Figure 6 Malombo guitarist Philip Tabane and percussionist Gabriel Thobejane perform with the author, David B. Coplan, at the Market Café (now Kippie's) in Johannesburg, 1976.
From the collection of the author.

the United States than did any other South African band.

The years immediately following the "Soweto Uprising" of 1976–1977 were dominated by African-American music in a range of styles, but by the mid-1980s there arose a new form of "township jive" or "township soul," one that ended this dominance and expressed musically the new political consciousness that would fuel the victory over apartheid. Among its exponents were Sipho Mabuse (b. 1950), a founder of the unique and enormously successful Soweto Zulu rock band Harari, Sello "Chicco" Twala, Condry Ziqhubu, Steve Kekana, Johnny Clegg, Ray Phiri (b. 1950), and the legendary pop diva and the bestselling South African recording artist of all time, Brenda Fassie (1964–2004). Oddly misnamed "bubblegum," this genre, including songs like "Chant of the Marching" (Mabuse), "Confusion" (Ziqhubu), "We Miss You Manelo [aka Mandela]" (Twala), "Black President" (Fassie), "Whispers in the Deep" (Phiri), and *Asimbonanga* (Clegg) provided—with the famous choral "freedom songs"—musical anthems for the political struggle, combining explicit political texts with the irresistible danceability of jive.

Johnny Clegg, the famous "white Zulu," was the most visible avatar of the phenomenon of "crossover," a hybrid musical movement that crossed the deeply ingrained divisions of race, class, and age during the 1980s. Fusing African melody and rhythm with rock, funk, and jazz, these groups included Bayete, Sakhile, Sankomota, Ringo Madlingozi, and Cape Town's Tananas. Crossover as a movement gave musical expression to the increasing awareness of South African youth (of all ethnic backgrounds) that they ought to embrace one another sufficiently to avoid destroying the country in the process of liberating it.

By 1990, when Nelson Mandela (b. 1918) and others were released from prison, "bubblegum" had lost its flavor and favor, and American house and rhythm and blues once again dominated the local industry, as local artists responded to the fall of apartheid and the liberating aftermath. Combining the beat of American house, slowed down a bit and blended with local African vocal tonalities, with rapping in mixed African and township argots, the new style, called *kwaito*, took the youth-music market by storm. The Struggle had been miraculously won and black youth were ready, understandably, to celebrate. Performative embodiments of the early *kwaito* spirit included Boom Shaka ("It's About Time"), Arthur ("Don't Call Me Kaffir"), and Abashante ("Come and Get Me").

Elders disliked *kwaito* for its overt materialism, explicit sexuality, gangster Americanism, and overall hedonism; nor did its simple, repetitive lyrics encourage youth to face the challenges of society: but to black youth, *kwaito* was an assertion of their right to possess the present and future while shedding the burden of the past. In answer to the new black elite's appropriation of the spoils of victory, and the fears—ultimately unfounded—of black middle-class flight to the "white" suburbs, *kwaito* was an assertion by the majority of youth who still struggled along in the townships that they, and not their suburban peers, would set the cultural agenda. In time, *kwaito*'s performers and audience matured, and recent releases by remaining exponents, such as Kabelo, deal directly with the social deficits plaguing urban black communities.

A decade and a half since the advent of *kwaito*, the form has become absorbed into the South African musical mainstream. American hip-hop has arrived in local linguistic guise, but has not managed to replace it. This is in part because historically, black South Africans will not long remain loyal to a form that lacks strong singing. This has been provided by the emergence of a new generation of primarily female vocalists, exponents of every style from local language rhythm and blues to gospel to jazz, and most notably Afropop, a style that harks back to the classics of Sophiatown and township jive. One Afropop group, Mafikizolo, performs on stage in retro 1950s Sophiatown high fashion. Their lead vocalist, Nhlanhla Mafu, rivals the great popular divas of the past, but she is not alone, and must compete with Freshly Ground's Zolani Mahola, Malaika's Matshediso Mpholo, and black techno-rave ensemble Kwani Experience's Nosisi Ngakane. The most influential of all the Afropop divas, however, is Thandiswa Mazwai, who has taken long-lived eclectic *kwaito* icons Bongo Maffin into new creative territory.

—Adapted from an article by David B. Coplan

Bibliography

Andersson, Muff. 1981. *Music in the Mix*. Johannesburg: Ravan Press.

Coplan, David. "Musical Understanding: The Ethnoacoustics of Migrant Workers' Poetic Song in Lesotho." *Ethnomusicology* 32:337–368.

——. 2008. *In Township Tonight! South Africa's Black City Music and Theatre*. 2nd edition. Chicago: Chicago University Press; Johannesburg: Jacana Books.

Erlmann, Veit. 1991. *African Stars*. Chicago: University of Chicago Press.

Music of Madagascar: An Overview

Madagascar, the world's fourth-largest island, is situated in the Indian Ocean southeast of Africa. Its dimensions extend approximately 1000 miles from northern to southern tip, and 350 miles from west to east at its widest point. It supports distinct climatic zones, including rainforest (which has vastly receded since the colonial era), savannah, high plateau, and dry spiny forest.

Human settlement of Madagascar is thought to have occurred 1500 to 2000 years ago; recent estimates support the earlier end of this range. The first inhabitants were Southeast Asians, who likely sailed from what is now Malaysia or Indonesia. Waves of Bantu speakers from the south of Africa arrived shortly thereafter. Arab settlements on the island date from approximately the ninth century, and first European contact occurred in 1500 with the arrival of Portuguese explorers; French explorers arrived soon thereafter. Indian (largely Muslim), Chinese, and European explorers, traders, and settlers flowed into the island, often by way of its east coast, where the port of Tamatave (Toamasina in the Malagasy language) developed. By the late seventeenth century, European pirates had established settlements up and down this coast. By the early nineteenth century, the London Missionary Society had attained an influential presence, especially in the central Haut Plateau area, where the capital, Antananarivo, is located. In 1896, France claimed Madagascar as a colony, which it remained until 1960, when it became independent. Since the 1970s, its government has gradually shifted from promoting socialist policies to promoting democratic ones, including holding free elections. Though Madagascar has experienced a culturally heterogeneous past, its musical practices cannot be accurately conceived as simply Southeast Asian, African, Arabic, or European (though European-like instruments, such as the accordion, are prevalent). Rather, varied musical practices and instruments throughout the island are distinctively Malagasy.

There are commonly eighteen to twenty different groups of people designated throughout Madagascar. Differentiations between groups are often based largely upon linguistic, historical, and musical traits, upon means of subsistence, and in some cases even upon imagined degree of cultural or historical connection to Africa or Southeast Asia. Some of these "ethnic" delineations reflect French colonial conceptions and actions more than the actual perceptions and beliefs of Malagasy people. Though these groups share some cultural consciousness and experiences, considerable musical diversity and other modes of cultural distinctiveness thrive among them. Therefore, only an overview of select genres, instruments, styles, musicians, contexts, and explanations of musical significance, can be represented in this article.

Musical Instruments

Chordophones

Valiha is a Malagasy term that refers both to a specific stringed instrument as well as to a family of stringed instruments of variable structure and tuning that are constructed from different materials throughout the island. The earliest *valiha* were made of a length of bamboo often three to four feet long and three to four inches in diameter. The strings were made from the body of the instrument: long slivers of the bamboo were incised, yet left attached at their endpoints. Then, small wooden bridges were placed under these slivers (strings) to allow them to vibrate away from the body of the instrument. The bridges served as tuning devices: when one bridge was moved closer to the other, the pitch of the string would rise; this remains the tuning method on most current *valiha*. Later, with European contact and the appearance of European industrial materials, the bamboo strings on the *valiha* were replaced with individual unwound strands of bicycle brake cable. These metal-stringed instruments were louder than earlier *valiha*, while they resounded with greatly enhanced low- and high-end frequencies. Nowadays, musicians who can perform a few compositions on a bamboo-strung *valiha* are rare, but not unknown.

The bamboo-body *valiha* (figure 1) is especially popular with Merina, the people in the central Haut Plateau and is occasionally found elsewhere on the island such as in Sakalava territory in the northwest. The number of strings on a Merina *valiha* varies according to its player's preference (it often has 20 to 24). And throughout Madagascar, the form, structure, and tuning of *valiha* vary by the preference of the musician. Musical scales also vary, though European equal temperament appears to have had a strong influence, as stringed instruments throughout Madagascar are commonly tuned to mirror the

Figure 1 Bamboo *valiha* with bicycle brake-cable strands for strings.
Photo by Ron Emoff, 2007.

Figure 2 Betsimisaraka *tôle valiha.*
Photo by Ron Emoff, 1994.

equal-tempered major mode (sometimes minor mode) diatonic scale. On many instruments in the *valiha* family, scalar order tends to alternate between left and right halves or planes of the instrument, so that one string is often adjacent to a string tuned a third above or below it.

On the east coast of Madagascar in the Tamatave area, musicians of the Betsimisaraka group prefer a *valiha* whose resonant chamber is constructed from corrugated roofing sheet metal (*tôle*) (figure 2). The metal is pounded into a rectangular shape, and bicycle brake-cable strands are strung in two courses on either length of the instrument; each hand of the player accesses its own separate course of strings. Again, the precise number of strings and scalar tuning order (and tunings themselves) vary by the musician's preference, yet repertoires are shared among Betsimisaraka as well as other Malagasy musicians; tunings can therefore vary only within limits that allow specific bodies of compositions to be performed. The metal body of the resonant chamber yields timbres quite distinct from those produced by a bamboo *valiha.*

Antandroy, a southern group of Malagasy known for their prowess in spiritual matters, and some others primarily from the south of Madagascar, call their version of the *valiha, maro vany* 'many strings' (figure 3). Young Antandroy who have migrated to Tamatave in search of wage labor sometimes call their instrument *maro tady* (also 'many strings'). Antandroy commonly build their *valiha* from pine

Figure 3 Antandroy *maro vany.*
Photo by Ron Emoff, 2007.

planks, which they nail together into a rectangular form. Antandroy in Tamatave commonly make the strings of their *maro vany* (often 21 or 22 in number) from unraveled strands of a much thicker industrial metal cable. The combination of wooden resonant chamber and thicker gauge strings gives the Antandroy *maro vany* a distinctive voice. Timbral differences in *valiha* sound production are significant to Malagasy people, for only specific sound qualities are efficacious in communicating with a particular people's ancestral spirits, most of whom they believe are extremely sensitive to sound and specifically to music.

Other Chordophones
The term *kabosy* designates another family of stringed instruments found throughout Madagascar and characterized by general shape—a small-body guitar-like instrument, often semirectangular—and by the rapid-strumming technique with which it is played. Performance on the *kabosy* tends to accentuate a harmonic pattern based more upon rhythmic accentuation than upon linear melodic development. The Merina construct a *kabosy* with a fret pattern that uniquely incorporates partial frets (figure 4). This construction allows one to play a barred major or minor triad without complex fingering (the six strings are tuned to a major triad on this type of *kabosy*; the bass string is tonic, the next highest-pitched string an octave above tonic, the next two strings a pair tuned in unison to the major third, and the highest-pitched two strings another pair tuned in unison to the fifth). This combination of frets and tuning may have been developed so that this type of

kabosy could be played while walking; it has a history of use by boys and elders while tending cattle. The Merina *kabosy* might utilize geared tuning pegs if they were available, but many other *kabosy* throughout the island are made with friction tuning pegs, like the pegs used on a violin.

In the south, the *kabosy* is commonly called *mandolina*. It often has moveable frets made of fishing line, and only the upper part of the neck (near the peghead) is commonly fretted. Unlike the Merina *kabosy*, which has metallic strings (again, often bicycle brake-cable strands), the *mandolina* is usually strung with nylon strings. In some parts of the island, the *kabosy* is made with the curved body shape of a guitar, though still in miniature.

A bowed instrument called *lokanga* is popular in the south, primarily with Bara and Antandroy people. It likely displays influence from the Arabic *rabāb* (a vertically held bowed instrument) and the European violin. It typically has three metal strings, the tuning for which can vary; one string commonly serves as a drone. [For more on the *rabāb*, see MUSICAL INSTRUMENTS IN THE ARAB WORLD in The Middle East section of volume 2. The violin is covered in numerous articles in the Europe section of this volume.]

Aerophones
In the twentieth century, accordions became immensely popular throughout Madagascar. The accordion was invented in the mid-nineteenth century [see GERMANY in the Europe section], and some accordions likely arrived in Madagascar with traders and explorers before the twentieth century;

Figure 4 Merina *kabosy*.
Photo by Ron Emoff, 2007.

Figure 5 Two-row diatonic button accordion.
Photo by Ron Emoff, 1994.

however, the instrument was not exported to the French colonies for commercial sale until the 1910s. The accordion most commonly played in Madagascar is the two-row diatonic button accordion (figure 5); though a few piano-key chromatic accordions are found. Some Malagasy play their accordions in the factory tuning; others deconstruct them and completely alter their tunings and voicings. The chosen timbre of an accordion commonly correlates with beliefs in communicability with ancestral spirits. The timbral distinctiveness of a group's accordion also contributes significantly to a shared collective consciousness. Though the accordion was once considered a colonial instrument, most Malagasy now consider it a distinctively Malagasy instrument. Because the cost of new instruments is prohibitive and replacement parts are unavailable, Malagasy accordions are often quite old and worn.

The *sodina*, a well-known Malagasy wind instrument, was initially a bamboo end-blown flute with six fingerholes and one thumbhole. Recently, *sodina* have been constructed from metal or plastic piping, which is less affected by changes in humidity and temperature than bamboo. The instrument has no mouthpiece of any sort: sound is created by forcing air at an angle across the open tube—a difficult technique to master. Merina musicians often play *sodina* in ensemble to create a polyphonic texture.

Other Malagasy wind instruments include the *kabiro*, a reed instrument from the north of the island, likely with Arabic roots (by way of the Comoros Islands); the *kiloloka*, a bamboo whistle played in hocket syle; and the *antsiva*, a conch shell. European-like clarinets and trumpets are commonly employed in Merina *hira gasy* performance (see below), though in Malagasy versions, which are distinctive in structure and in performance practice.

Idiophones

Malagasy music, particularly ceremonial music, is most often accompanied by a rattle known widely as *kaiamba*. Other names for rattles include *tsikatrehana* in the east and *katsa* in the south. Rattles are often seed-filled short lengths of bamboo, or metal cans that vary in size and contain seeds, small pebbles, or broken glass; local forms of rattle also exist. The *masevy* is a foot rattle, worn by dancers among the Makoa people in the north.

Membranophones

Malagasy drums, some of which have evolved through the influence of colonial military bands, include *amponga*, *langoroana*, *hazolahy*, and *dabalava*. More recently, some Malagasy musicians have adopted the West African *djembe*, a goblet-shaped drum.

Other Instruments

Some Malagasy instruments have seen a decline in use, or are now used in specific areas only. These include the *jejilava* or *jejolava*, a musical bow; the *katiboky*, a wooden-key xylophone, played across the legs of the performer and often requiring more than one player; the *tsikaretika* or *tsipetrika* (and other names), a bamboo tube struck with wooden sticks; and the *jejy voatavo*, a fretted stringed instrument with a calabash resonator.

Principles of Musical Process

In Malagasy ceremonial performance, only one accordion, *valiha*, or *kabosy* is typically played at a time. These instruments are not played in ensemble, nor is one played simultaneously with another. Numerous *kaiamba* shakers often accompany the *valiha*, accordion, or *kabosy*. Most Malagasy spirit-related ceremonial music is based upon a tripartite rhythmic structure (figure 6), similar to what is described elsewhere as hemiola. In performance, participants may clap any of these rhythms individually; any two or all three of the rhythms might be clapped simultaneously by various participants.

The structure of an individual *tromba* composition (see below) usually consists of a short-duration melodic or rhythmic motive that is replicated indefinitely. Instrumentalists improvise upon this motive, varying its enunciation as the composition progresses. *Kaiamba* pulses do not necessarily or consistently align with the beginning or the ending of the melodic phrase played, for instance, by the accordion. The result can create a sense that the accordion and the *kaiamba* move in, and then out, of metrical phase with one another. Musics for occasions other than *tromba* often follow these principles too.

Performance Contexts

A prominent occasion for musical performance in Madagascar is in *tromba* ceremony, which involves ancestor reverence, worship, and possession of spirit mediums by ancestral spirits. The spirits of kings and queens that once ruled the island are the most revered *tromba* spirits. Before the late nineteenth century, powerful Malagasy kingdoms emanated from the Merina group in the central part of the island and the Sakalava in the north and west. Thus, Malagasy royal ancestral spirits embody a mode of empowerment that predates colonial control of Madagascar. Recollections of and sentiments toward colonization and France are sometimes dramatically (and musically) expressed through *tromba* practice.

Each *tromba* spirit has her or his own favored musical composition; thus, *tromba* musicians must retain a sizeable repertoire. These musicians must also be able to perform with the proper amount of improvisational acuity, or the *tromba* spirits, who have human personalities and temperaments, will not arrive in the present. Music, thus, is vitally powerful in Madagascar—it calls ancestral spirits believed to be capable of healing illness, resolving disputes among the living, offering advice, and ameliorating everyday problems.

Kaiamba accompaniment to the accordion, *valiha*, or *kabosy* (*mandolina*) in *tromba* performance is

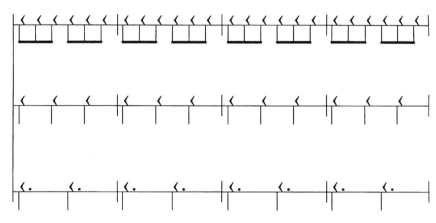

Figure 6 The rhythmic structure of most Malagasy ceremonial music. The interweaving of pulses from the distinct rhythms can create a syncopated inner rhythm, making the beat often difficult or impossible for an unaccustomed listener to perceive.

essential in creating the *maresaka*, the combination of sounds that appeals to *tromba* spirits. The choice of instrumentalist may depend upon the preference of the *tromba* spirit needed at a particular ceremony. The musicians exert considerable control over a *tromba* ceremony, as they orchestrate or greatly influence ancestral spirits' comings, goings, and actions.

Another important context for ceremonial music in Madagascar is the *tsaboraha*, a ceremony in which a zébu (a kind of humpbacked cattle) is slaughtered. While spirit possession may not be an integral component of a *tsaboraha*, these ceremonies involve sentiments toward and interaction with ancestral spirits known collectively as the *razana*. An accordion, a *valiha*, or a *kabosy* is commonly used in *tsaboraha*, but *tsaboraha* repertoires are often distinct from those performed for a *tromba*.

The *hira gasy*, a mode of musical theater performed primarily in the central highland area, is performed by large troupes of musicians, dancers, singers, and acrobats. The texts of *hira gasy* songs commonly offer political and social critique, humor, and proverbial or ethical advice. Instrumentation for performances includes numerous *amponga* drums, both basslike and snarelike, and an array of clarinets and trumpets, or *sodina* flutes. The musicians of a *hira gasy* ensemble commonly perform at a Merina *famadihana*, a ceremony at which ancestors' bones are unearthed, and after much celebration, placed into a familial tomb.

In the west of Madagascar, the Sakalava Menabe, descendants of a great precolonial kingdom, practice a ceremony called *fitampoha*, in which the relics of ancient kings are ritually bathed, to music supplied commonly by *hazolahy* and *dabalava* drums, and group singing. Circumcision ceremonies throughout the island typically call for musical performance, the style of which varies areally.

Vocal Music

A variety of vocal styles exist across Madagascar, from heterophonic harmonizing in thirds, to call-and-response singing, to the complex polyphonic singing and vocalizing performed by Antandroy in their healing songs. In these healing songs, a technique called *ndrimotra* (from the Malagasy verb 'to heal') is employed, in which a raspy deep-diaphragm breath-chant adds to a polyphonic mix of voices and other sounds, such as whistle-blowing and handclapping.

In *tromba* ceremony, singing and other vocalizations (such as *tsodrano* 'benedictions to ancestral spirits') can occur spontaneously when a singer or vocalizer is compelled to give voice to emotion. Often

it is the *tromba* spirit itself that sings, chants, or speaks. *Kabary*, an important ceremonial speech mode, involves formulaic speech commonly addressed to the living and the ancestors, and often made at the outset of a ceremony. *Kabary* often occurs as a dialogic speech event between groups of elders. Varied funerary songs integral to ancestor reverence and worship are performed throughout the island.

There exist throughout Madagascar Protestant and Lutheran hymns that have been translated into the Malagasy language (and into local versions of Malagasy). These hymns are often sung unaccompanied by church congregations; in the mid-nineteenth century, the London Missionary Society purportedly prohibited the use of Malagasy instruments in the church. Currently, the Jesosy Mamonjy (Jesus Saves) Church encourages the use of traditional instruments, such as the *valiha*, to accompany hymns, as an incentive for people to attend services. Through missionary efforts in the nineteenth-century, royal choirs were established, under royal patronage. This contributed to the establishment of a social élite, centered in the capital area and based in part upon musical knowledge. Malagasy Christians usually maintain some belief in ancestral spirits, sometimes emergent in their fear of such spirits. It is also common for Christian Malagasy to continue to perform and participate in ancestor-related ceremonies, such as *famadihana*.

During the 1960s and 1970s, *vakisoava*, a call-and-response choral genre sung by groups of boys on street corners in Antananarivo, was popular, but it has declined in popularity. *Kalon'ny fahiny*, also from the central area, represents efforts by Merina in the years immediately after World War I to create a Malagasy élite musical form based largely upon European opera, yet *kalon'ny fahiny* was still distinctively Malagasy, using dramatic themes from everyday experience, and incorporating a unique and highly exaggerated vocal vibrato, especially in the upper register of women's voices. *Kalon'ny fahiny* songs have regained some popularity since the late 1980s.

Popular Music

The term *popular* is used here to designate music that is commercially produced (intended to be recorded and sold, or performed before an audience that makes some financial contribution to the performance), usually electronically amplified, and intended for leisure, rather than for use in sacred ritual. Perhaps the most familiar Malagasy popular music is *salegy*, which originated in the north of the island, but can currently be heard in most parts of the country. A favorite *salegy* star is Jaojoby, from Diégo-Suarez in the north. Not currently so prominent in stature as *salegy*, the east-coast *basesa* remains quite popular among Betsimisaraka. Jean Freddy, from Fénérive-Est in the Tamatave area, was a popular *basesa* star in the 1970s and 1980s. *Tsapiky* is a fast-paced dance music from the south that owes much to the accessibility of African music transmitted on radio to this area in the 1970s. All these popular musics rely on what might be conceived as a 6/8 meter (see figure 6 above), and all have roots in the ceremonial music used throughout the island for ancestral veneration. In 2004, Canadian Sean Whittaker, who had worked on environmental conservation projects in Madagascar, organized a pan-Malagasy recording project entitled *Vakoka*, which mixed Malagasy musicians from diverse musical backgrounds (including jazz) and various parts of the island.

—*By Ron Emoff*

Bibliography

Edkvist, Ingela. 1997. *The Performance of Tradition: An Ethnography of* Hira Gasy *Popular Theatre in Mada-gascar*. Uppsala Studies in Cultural Anthropology, 23. Uppsala: Department of Cultural Anthropology and Ethnology, Uppsala University.

Emoff, Ron. 2002a. "Alterations in Accordion Structure on the East Coast of Madagascar." *Musical Performance* 3(2–4):243–257. London: Harwood Academic Publishers, Taylor and Francis Group.

——. 2002b. *Recollecting from the Past: Musical Practice and Spirit Possession on the East Coast of Madagascar.* Music and Culture Series. Middletown, Conn.: Wesleyan University Press.

Mallet, Julien. 2002. "Histoire de vies, histoire d'une vie: Damily, musicien de 'tsapik'." *Cahiers de musiques traditionelles* 15:113–132.

McLeod, Norma. 1977. "Musical Instruments and History in Madagascar." In *Essays for a Humanist: An Offering to Klaus Wachsmann.* Spring Valley, New York: The Townhouse Press.

Rakotomalala, Mireille. 1998. "Performance in Madagascar." In *Africa*, edited by Ruth Stone, 781–792. *The Garland Encyclopedia of World Music*, 1. New York and London: Garland Publishing.

Schmidhofer, August. 1994. "Kabôsy, mandoliny, gitara: Zur Entwicklung neuerer Popularmusikformen in Madagaskar." In *For Gerhard Kubik: Festschrift on the Occasion of his 60th Birthday*, edited by August Schmidhofer and Dietrich Schüller, 179–191. Frankfurt: Peter Lang.

——. 1995. *Das Xylophonspiel der Mädchen: Zum afrikanischen Erbe in der Musik Madagaskars.* Frankfurt: Peter Lang.

2. South America, Mexico, Central America, and the Caribbean

Cumbia, merengue, tango; carnival, fiesta, shamanic curing; mariachi, samba school, steelband; Bob Marley, Tom Jobim, Astor Piazzolla—these genres, contexts, bands, and musicians conjure up sinuous rhythms, lyrical melodies, pensive moods, ideological power, and above all unforgettable music. Music, dance, and music-related behavior are of great importance to the people of the countries south of the Río Grande (the river that separates the United States and Mexico), the island countries south and east of Florida, and many native American cultures that thrive within these politically determined regions.

Señor Antonio Sulca, a blind Quechua Indian musician of Peru, wears a European-designed suit as he plays a Spanish-derived harp. His music tells of his people from Ayacucho, and his harp is adorned with a lute-playing siren, possibly an indigenous protective and amorous figure. *Photo by Dale Olsen, 1979.*

South America, Mexico, Central America, and the Caribbean

A Profile of the Lands, Peoples, and Musics of South America, Mexico, Central America, and the Caribbean

The articles in this section cover the music of peoples from a vast area of the Western Hemisphere. Here you will find descriptions of music from Mexico and from countries in South America, Central America, and the Caribbean. You will also find descriptions of the music of several of the Amerindian cultures that thrive as autochthonous and somewhat homogenous entities within these countries.

Geography

Political and cultural history makes geographic and cultural classifications in this area difficult. Furthermore, Central and South America include topographies of extreme contrast. In South America are the world's largest tropical forest (Amazon) and one of its driest deserts (the Atacama in Chile). There are many lowland basins (Orinoco, La Plata, Amazon) and frigid highlands and glacial peaks (the Andes, including Aconcagua in Argentina, the highest mountain in the Western Hemisphere). The country of Chile is, in reverse, a compressed version of the span from coastal Alaska to Baja California: its land goes from a northern dry desert, fertile central valleys, and lush southern pine forests, to extreme southern, rugged, canyonlike estuaries studded with glaciers, terminating in frigid mountains and waters of the part of the world that is the closest to Antarctica. Because of such topographies, most of the urban centers of South America are on or near the coasts of the Atlantic, Caribbean, or Pacific. All these considerations have affected the music of Central and South America.

Demography

Demography, the description of human populations, is more than a statistical science. When joined with cultural studies, it becomes more complex than mere calculation of numbers and migration of people. There is probably no place on earth as racially and culturally diverse and complex as the Americas, especially the Americas covered in this volume.

As a way of explaining the complexity of a

particular area, George List (1983) tried to fit certain regions of Latin America within the framework of a tricultural heritage—Amerindian, African, and Iberian (i.e., Spanish or Portuguese). But within each of these areas there could be dozens of subareas of influence: which Amerindian culture? which African culture? and even which Iberian culture? These are questions that must be asked.

Likewise, terms such as *mestizaje* 'miscegenation' (a mixing of race and culture, usually assumed between indigenous American and Spanish or Portuguese) and *criolismo* 'creolism' (usually a mixing of African and European, or referring to European descendants born in the New World; usage depends on the country; in Haiti, creole refers to the language) have been used to categorize people and cultures in Mexico, Central America, South America, and the Caribbean. The terms *mestizo* and *criollo* are used throughout these areas by the people themselves, but they are perhaps less useful today, with the amounts of urban migration taking place, the increasing possibilities of upward mobility, and the influx of postcolonial immigrants and their descendants from Asia (China, India, Indonesia, Japan, Korea, and so on), Europe (England, Germany, Italy, and so on), and elsewhere. Each country has its own ways of using the terms *mestizo* and *criollo*, or uses other terms to accommodate its unique demographic mixture.

Cultural Settings

Ethnomusicology is the study of music made by people for themselves, their gods, and other people. The peoples of South America, Mexico, Central America, and the Caribbean are diverse, the countries are pluralistic, and their musical styles and other cultural attributes are equally so. When a person is making music, rarely is he or she completely alone: someone—a family member, a friend, a community—is listening, enjoying, crying, singing along. When music is made for God or the gods, rarely is it done in isolation: people are listening, learning the songs, perhaps praying or thinking spiritual thoughts. When music is made by a group of people or for a group of people, rarely does the musical event exist without dancing and the participation of members of a family or a village. Music is an affair, an experience, an event to be shared.

Musical Instruments

Sounds are transmitted via waves that travel from their sources through air or other medium, strike the receiver's eardrums, and register in the receiver's brain. The shape of the wave determines whether what is received is music (and what kind of music), speech, noise, or whatever a culture calls it. The sources that produce what we may call music are what we call musical instruments (it could be argued that the human voice and whistling are also musical instruments). These points are important because what we call music or musical instruments may not always be considered music or musical instruments by the people of the cultures themselves.

Musical instruments (other than a voice or whistling) tell us much about cultures, not so much as items in themselves, but as tokens of meaning—what they signify to their cultures and how they came to mean what they mean. Musical instruments are artifacts and "ethnofacts"—the former because they

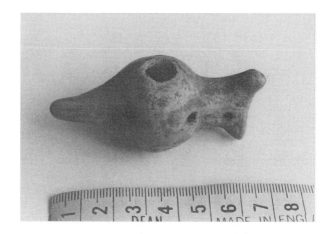

Figure 1 A ceramic dog-shaped ocarina or globular flute with a cross-blown mouthpiece on its stomach (it was photographed upside down to show the mouthpiece) and two fingerholes. Ancient Moche culture, Peru. *Photo by Dale A. Olsen, 1996.*

are objects created by humans, and the latter because they have meaning, often of a symbolic kind.

The musical instruments found in South America, Mexico, Central America, and the Caribbean are diverse, and their number is large. From the Encounter in 1492 until the present, about two thousand languages have been spoken by Amerindians, not including those of North America. If an average of three musical instruments per language group existed, that means that the names of probably six thousand instruments were once being used. The Spanish, Portuguese, Africans, and all the other foreigners who came after the Encounter and up to the present probably introduced another thousand names for musical instruments. Because of the disappearance of many Amerindian cultures, assimilation, modernization, and other forces of culture change, a much smaller quantity exists today. Nevertheless, we are still dealing with a vast number, and diversity is still a hallmark of these instruments.

Wind instruments (aerophones) make up the largest and most complex group of instruments in the Americas, and numerous subgroups can be included within it. Because of diversity, it would perhaps be prudent to refrain from employing terms derived from the classification of Western European orchestral instruments. For example, such terms as *edge aerophone* for *flute* or *single-reed-concussion aerophone* for *clarinet*, would be organologically clear. Common sense, however, suggests that for most readers, terms like *flute* and *clarinet* are easier to understand. In all cases, when the common European terms are used in this section, they never mean the European form of the instrument unless carefully

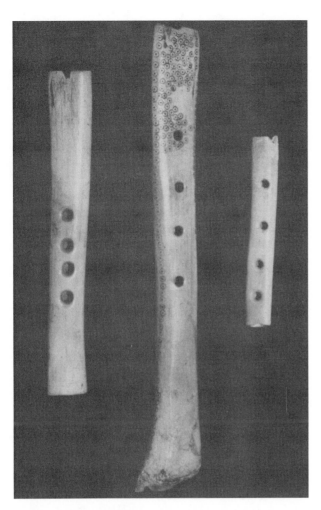

Figure 2 Three bone flutes with notched mouthpieces and four fingerholes: *left and right*, the ancient Nasca culture; *middle*, the Chancay culture, Peru.
Photo by Dale A. Olsen, 1973.

Figure 3 The *tres*, a guitar-type instrument with six strings strung into three courses, common in Cuba and the Dominican Republic. This man plays with a Dominican merengue quartet.
Photo by Dale A. Olsen, 1977.

stated so. Other terms, such as *ocarina* for *globular flute* (figure 1) and *panpipe* for a multitubed flute without holes, may be used. In addition, the terms *duct* (like the mouthpiece of a recorder) and *ductless* (like the mouthpiece of a Western flute, a single tube of a panpipe, or the Andean notched flute, figure 2) here serve to clarify the subcategory of flute.

Idiophones "self-sounders" are another huge category because of the cultural diversity of the geographic areas. Because of forced and unforced immigration, idiophones essentially include instruments from (or inspired by) Africa, Europe, and Asia, in addition to those of Amerindians. Examples of idiophones, using some common and general terms, range from dancers' ankle-tied bells to maracas (*maráka*, from the Tupí language), rhythm sticks, triangles, steel drums, marimbas, gongs, scrapers, and many more.

A membranophone "skin sounder" is an instrument in which a skin (or skins) stretched tightly over a rigid support vibrates, sending off sound waves. Skin instruments are often called drums, a term otherwise used for the body or chamber. Confusion arises when *drum* is used for items without a skin, such as oil drums or steel drums—the former not a musical instrument, the latter an idiophone. Cone-shaped drums, barrel-shaped drums, and cylindrical drums are the most common in the area; drums of African origin are the most diverse.

Most stringed instruments (chordophones) derive from Iberian prototypes, and their names are most often here given in their English forms, rather than their Spanish or Portuguese forms (*guitar* for *guitarra*, *harp* for *arpa*, *mandolin* for *mandolina*, and *violin* for *violín*, for example). Exceptions are the *tres* (figure 3) and the *cuatro*, whose names are determined by the numbers of strings or string courses they have or once had.

Musical Genres and Contexts

Music is being played or listened to almost everywhere and most of the time in Mexico, Central America, South America, and the Caribbean. Ranging from the sound of a single flute played by a lonely shepherd in a high mountain valley, to privately performed curing ceremonies witnessed only by the curers and the ill, to radios playing in millions of homes, to massive celebrations mobilizing hundreds of thousands of participants packed into the broad avenues and civic squares of densely populated cities, the richness and diversity of the musical traditions seem almost to defy description.

This musical diversity has underlying patterns that enable observers to speak about the music of the entire region. The remainder of this article presents some of the significant general features of the musical genres performed and the contexts in which music is played, drawing on the material from the entries on specific societies and nations, where these processes are described with more attention to local histories and the specifics of social processes, cultures, and styles.

The principal contexts of which music is a part in the Americas include religious activities, lifecycle celebrations, leisure, tourism, and to a lesser degree work. Some of these categories are general throughout the lands covered in this section, but in other cases (such as tourism), music is more heavily involved in some areas than in others.

Many are the contexts for musical performance in the Americas. Though some new contexts replace older ones, what appears to happen more often is that new contexts are added to older ones, which after a generation they may eventually replace. The music changes, but the contexts often remain, and music itself goes on: work, lifecycle rituals, religious events, urban entertainment, tourism, and mass media all include musical performances of significance to their participants. [For a sense of how a change of context affected the musical traditions of Latin America and the Caribbean, see the relevant articles in PART 3: UNITED STATES AND CANADA.]

Sounds and Movements

Music and movement are closely intertwined in South America, Mexico, Central America, and the Caribbean. Some native South American communities use the same word for both, arguing that appropriate movements are as much a part of a performance as the sounds themselves. Stylized movements are often an important part of musicians' performances; dancing has been an important part

Figure 4 At the Fiesta de San Pedro, La Plata, Huila, Colombia, couples dance the *sanjuanero,* a courtship dance. Traditional attire, including the woman's full skirt and the man's neckerchief and hat, is essential to the choreography. *Photo by William J. Gradante, 1976.*

of secular music for centuries, and the name of a rhythm or a dance may define a genre—such as the waltz, the tango, and the samba. Also found throughout the region are dance-dramas, in which music, speech, and movement combine to depict a story (such as a battle between Moors and Christians, or the crucifixion of Jesus), often performed in association with the religious calendar, and occasionally with civic and national holidays. Body movements, like the sounds with which they may be associated, are endowed with meaning and convey attitudes, values, and individual and shared emotions.

Ritualized movements throughout the region include children's games, musicians' movements while performing, processions, and solo, couple (figure 4), and group dances. Though common features can be discerned, dances of Amerindian, African, and European origins have distinctive features, often combined today in popular traditions. Traditional Amerindian dances tend to involve stamping or moving the legs and arms to a fairly regular rhythm, with the rest of the trunk and head fairly straight and rigid. Dances in circles and lines are common, usually with the genders separated; dancing in couples was extremely rare, if found at all. In European dance traditions, the trunk and head are fairly motionless, the legs usually move to a simple rhythm, and dancing in couples (and combinations of couples) is often a defining feature. Dances that originated in Africa frequently involve moving different parts of the body to different rhythms— resembling the polyrhythmic patterns of the music itself. Formations by individuals and in lines and circles are more common than dances in couples.

During the past five hundred years, whatever distinctness the dances of different ethnic groups once had has been blurred by adaptations of existing styles and creations of new ones. This situation is especially true of twentieth-century popular dances, which have often drawn heavily on African-descended traditions. Amerindian and African religious traditions reveal their origins with greater clarity than secular dances. European religions have had an ambivalent attitude toward music and dance altogether—often banning the performance of secular music and dance and discouraging dancing in religious services. Whereas music and dance open communication with spirits in many Amerindian and African-based religions, silent prayer is considered the most effective communication with the deity in many Christian churches.

Dancehalls, nightclubs, and lifecycle celebrations in which dancing in couples is a part (birthday parties and weddings, for example) are important performance locations that provide a livelihood for many musicians. The importance of these locations may have influenced the development of musical technology (in favor of louder instruments that can be played for many hours), and technology has influenced the development of these venues. Several articles in this section touch on the importance of secular social dancing in the musical environments of different areas and describe specific dances that were, and are, popular. It is important to remember that rhythms for dancing usually involve distinctive body movements, and that the challenge, pleasure, exhilaration, and meaning of moving the body are an important part of musical events almost everywhere.

Religious Music

Amerindian Belief Systems

Before the colonization of the Americas by Europe beginning in 1492, it is quite likely that most musical events were part of religious or state-sponsored events. Where states were based on religion, it is difficult to separate the concepts of religion and politics. The elaborate ceremonies described by the Maya and the Inca for their Spanish conquerors included musical performances by specialists. The religious rituals of the coastal Tupi-Guaraní in Brazil and the island-dwelling Arawak and Carib communities in the Caribbean featured unison singing, shouts, dancing, and the sound of flutes and rattles. The archaeological record is replete with examples of clay wind instruments; in the humid areas, little else has survived.

Intensive investigation of Amerindian music in the twentieth century has been restricted to areas where such groups survive and continue to practice what appear to be traditional religions and musical forms. They are often found living in "refuge areas"— remote locations, away from non-Indian settlements, in areas of relatively little economic importance to the national society, and where missionization is recent, tolerant, or ineffective. With small populations and facing the effects of new diseases and economic changes, these groups cannot serve for generalizing about the musical situation in the pre-Columbian empires. Their music, however, reveals striking similarities to descriptions written in the 1500s and 1600s of performances in the nonstate societies. In these refuge areas, music continues to be closely related to religious events, and to direct communications with spirits and interactions with spirits of animals (such as jaguars, deer, and vultures) or ancestors. In some cases, musical sounds are themselves the voices of spirits; the performers may or may not be hybrid humans or spirits, and the instruments themselves spirits. Dale Olsen, in his discussion of communication with spirits among the Warao, describes a feature that reappears throughout South America [see WARAO].

European-introduced Christianity

Most countries in Mexico, Central America, South America, and the Caribbean are nominally Christian, and most of their people are Roman Catholic. This situation is the result of extensive colonization by Spain and Portugal. Amerindians and enslaved African populations were converted to Christianity, and under colonial rule, the Roman Catholic Church influenced their beliefs and social institutions tremendously. The mass itself was seldom elaborated musically, and then for special occasions only, and the singing of hymns is a recent introduction, but Roman Catholic missionaries were quite concerned with the musical development of the Amerindians they encountered. They set up music schools in several countries, and introduced their own music in part to replace the "diabolical" traditions they encountered. Some enslaved Africans were similarly taught to play European instruments and participated in many kinds of musical events.

The church supported the establishment of social groups called brotherhoods (Portuguese *irmandades*, Spanish *cofradías*), which had been organized in Europe but in the New World came to be one of the few organizations available to enslaved Africans and their descendants. These institutions had social and religious features and often included the performance of music and dancing on religious occasions. Voluntary religious organizations, continued by the descendants of these brotherhoods, survive in many parts of Mexico, Central America, South America, and the Caribbean, where they perform on saints' days and around Christmas.

For many communities of Amerindian, African, and European descent alike, the Christian religious calendar has structured the most important public musical events of the year. The birth of Jesus is celebrated in the end of December, at Christmas. Local community celebrations frequently extend to 6 January, with pageantlike wanderings of kings bearing gifts. Jesus' crucifixion and resurrection, celebrated during Holy Week (culminating in Easter), are preceded by a penitential period called Lent, which itself is preceded by enthusiastic celebrations of carnival during the final days before Ash Wednesday and the beginning of Lent. Carnival celebrations, not always welcomed by the church, are considered to be a kind of last chance for fleshly excesses before Lent, and music often plays an important role in the events. The most famous of these may be in the Caribbean, in Rio de Janeiro, and in New Orleans, but carnival celebrations and restrictions on musical performances during Lent are found in many communities throughout the area.

In addition to these religious events, the days of many different saints are celebrated in different areas. In some cases, a country may celebrate a saint (as Mexico does the Virgin of Guadalupe); in others, a certain saint may be celebrated as the patron of a particular city, a particular trade, or a particular ethnic group. Often saints' days are occasions for competitions in music and dance. Communities with populations of African and Amerindian descent have often combined elements of previous beliefs with Roman Catholic ones—which has led to a multiplicity of traditions throughout the region.

In the twentieth century, evangelical Protestant groups have made considerable inroads into Roman Catholicism and African spirit-based religions. Hymns, sung in Spanish, Portuguese, English, and Amerindian languages, are a common musical form. Among the Protestant sects are Hallelujah groups, in which possession by spirits is common, often to the accompaniment of some form of participatory music. In some communities, considerable conflict occurs between religious groups, expressed in musical events, theology, and church rituals.

African-introduced Religions

Africans were enslaved and brought to the Americas from widely variant societies and regions. They therefore had no unifying language, religion, or musical tradition. Many, however, shared general musical traits that transcended particular African communities—among them collective participation in making music, call-and-response singing, and dense and often interlocking rhythms played on drums.

Slaves of African descent turned to, and were in some cases encouraged to turn to, Christian churches for worship. They brought to these churches a musical tradition that persisted despite systematic efforts to suppress some of its African elements, such as the playing of drums (repeatedly outlawed in different countries). Important, too, were brotherhoods where slaves and free people of African descent could meet to socialize and to prepare ritual events. These have continued in such places as St. Lucia, Brazil, and Panama, where their members perform on certain religious occasions. Important among the performances are *congos*, dramatic presentations of stories, combining special forms of speech, music, and highly coordinated dancing.

Among the later waves of peoples brought to the New World were Yorùbá-speaking populations from West Africa, whose religion included the worship of spirits that would possess adepts and speak through them. These religions have persisted throughout the Caribbean and along Brazil's east coast into Argentina, under various names and using various musical forms. Called Santería in Cuba, Vodou in Haiti, Candomblé in northeastern Brazil, and other names in other countries, they usually employ three sacred drums and other instruments whose rhythms are specific to specific gods. Called by the rhythms, the gods descend and "ride" the bodies of specific worshipers. Though formerly persecuted in some countries, these religions are expanding to new audiences.

The Music Industry

Mass media—radio, television, cassettes, compact discs, videotapes, the Internet—have transformed the musical environment at an ever-increasing rate. The entertainment industry creates an important venue for performance and an influential conduit for new styles. Musical performance is no longer a face-to-face event, and new genres, styles, and audiences have been created through this transformation.

Technology has at times influenced musical performances in concrete ways. The standard three-minute length for recorded songs was determined in part by the playing-time of a wax cylinder, and later by that of a ten-inch 78-rpm record. The difficulty of controlling radio emissions across national boundaries has led to exchange of musical ideas despite local laws and import restrictions. The possibility of creating certain sounds in a studio affects the way live performances are evaluated. The impact of these media is so widespread that it is difficult to imagine musical life without them.

Live performances often include topical songs and local references, but broadcast restrictions in many countries have limited which kinds of ideas can be expressed in music or image.

—Adapted from articles by Dale A. Olsen and Anthony Seeger

Bibliography

Arguedas, José María. 1977. *Nuestra Música Pópular y sus Intérpretes.* Lima: Mosca Azul & Horizonte.

Béhague, Gérard. 1979. *Music in Latin America: An Introduction.* Englewood Cliffs, N.J.: Prentice-Hall.

Bergman, Billy. 1985. *Hot Sauces: Latin and Caribbean Pop.* New York: Quarto Books.

Cobo, Father Bernabé. 1979. *History of the Inca Empire.* Edited and translated by Roland Hamilton. Austin: University of Texas Press.

Garcilaso de la Vega, El Inca. [1609] 1966. *The Incas: The Royal Commentaries of the Inca.* 2nd ed., edited by Alain Gheerbrant. Translated by Maria Jolas. New York: Avon Books, Orion Press.

List, George. 1983. *Music and Poetry in a Colombian Village: A Tri-Cultural Heritage.* Bloomington: Indiana University Press.

Olsen, Dale A. 1996. *Music of the Warao of Venezuela. The Song People of the Rain Forest.* Gainesville: University Press of Florida. Book and compact disc.

Music of Native South Americans: Q'eros and Warao

Since the Encounter of 1492, hundreds of cultures in South America have become absorbed by the dominant cultures of Spanish, Portuguese, British, Dutch, and French heritage. Nevertheless, many indigenous "nations" remain. Neither acculturated nor traditional native people of South America are completely constrained by the political boundaries of countries, but inhabit broader geographic areas. One way of grouping the native peoples of South America focuses on ecosystems, including tropical forest, desert, mountain, and perhaps others. Of these, the tropical forest is so vast that many regions in the geography-based plan belong to it.

Here we offer coverage of groups from two of these regions: the Andean Q'eros, the only such group that bears a resemblance to Inca and pre-Incan societies; and the Warao, who live deep within the tropical forest of the Orinoco River Delta in eastern Venezuela.

In the Orinoco Delta of Venezuela, a Warao man tests his newly crafted deer-bone flute. *Photo by Dale A. Olsen, 1972.*

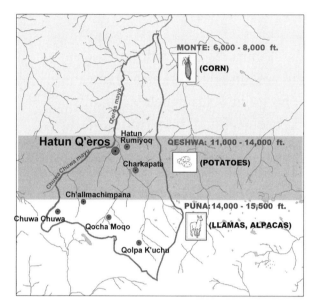

Hatun Q'eros

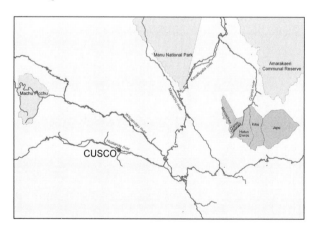

Nación Q'eros

Peru

Maps composed by Sandro Arias Loayza of the Asociación para la Conservacion de la Cuenca Amazónica.

Q'eros

The Q'eros are a Quechua-speaking people living high in the Andes Mountains, east of Cusco, Peru. Though it is tempting to see the Q'eros as an Inca survival, their unique musical practices probably reflect an even earlier Andean diversity with an Inca overlay. All past orthographies refer to this group as "Q'ero," but today it is common for the people to call themselves Q'eros. The term Q'eros refers to the entire cultural region that comprises eight Q'eros communities, located approximately 100 miles east of the ancient Incan capital of Cusco, in the province of Paucartambo. This region includes the communities of Kiku, Hapu, Totorani, Marcachea, Pucara, K'allacancha, Kachupata, and (Hatun) Q'eros, all of which have their own corresponding annexes, or hamlets, consisting of small isolated clusters of houses. In response to current political developments in Peru, five of these communities recently banded together as a statement of solidarity to form "the Nación Q'eros."

In population, Hatun Q'eros is the largest of these communities, consisting of approximately 24 percent of all Q'eros. It is the most remote of all Q'eros cultural communities, and therefore the most traditional and least acculturated. For these reasons, this article focuses on it, and presents the names and language in use by the Q'eros people today, though these may differ from previous orthographies and descriptions.

Q'eros ceremonial music is heard throughout seasonal cycles. Centered on flocks of llamas and alpacas, music is an integral part of Q'eros rituals. The Q'eros share many social, economic, and cultural ties with their Andean neighbors, but they have been sufficiently isolated to have preserved their own cultural and musical traits in coexistence with contemporary elements.

The Q'eros exploit every local ecological zone from the mountaintops to the jungle. Living at an elevation of approximately 14,200 feet, the Q'eros are herders near their homes. They raise potatoes in the middle ecological zone (11,000–14,000 feet), and corn, squash, and peppers in the high jungle farther down (6000–7500 feet). Each family has temporary wood shelters in the jungle, large stone houses in the ceremonial center at an elevation of 11,200 feet, and small stone houses located in isolated clusters in the high valleys. The total population is about one hundred and twenty families (about nine hundred people), distributed in six hamlets. This is a major increase when compared to forty families counted in 1922 and eighty-two in 1970.

The Q'eros share certain musical traditions with the entire region of Cusco, but they have distinctly emblematic songs and music, heard only in their highland home. Their major festivals coincide with Spanish calendrical festivals, but with little or no European or colonial elements. Each of their festivals has songs and instruments specifically associated with it, but the emblematic and uniquely recognizable Q'eros style consists of descending three-note melodies sung and played on the indigenous flute (*pinkuyllu*). Their songs serve many functions, including celebrating carnival, venerating animals in fertility rituals, and enlivening Christian-influenced festivals. The music associated with each ritual varies from endogenous to exogenous musical styles. For this reason, it cannot be characterized by a single style, musical scale, or musical function. This diversity within the music of a single community is inherent in Andean cultural life.

Musical Instruments

Q'eros autochthonous music is not influenced by European elements: it uses neither instruments introduced by the Spanish, nor any of the stringed instruments (like the *charango* and the *bandurria*) or the brass instruments that evolved in the Andes in the colonial era. Though the Q'eros have had transistor radios since about 1980 and can hear Andean radio programs of *huayno* (*wayno*) music broadcast from Cusco, they still use only musical instruments extant at the time of the Incas: end-blown and side-blown flutes, panpipes, conch trumpets, and drums. Two Q'eros musical styles consist of distinct musical instruments found only in Q'eros territory: Q'eros-style panpipes and *pinkuyllu*, an end-blown flute.

Panpipes

The Q'eros have single-unit raft panpipes that are two bound rows of seven reed tubes each. One row is never played, yet holding two sets is representative of *yanantin*, the Andean system of duality. Each instrument has three names: *qanchis sipas* 'seven young unmarried women', *qori phukuna* 'golden blow-pipe', and *choqewanka* 'golden song of echo'. The women sing pentatonic songs to sheep, cows, and alpacas, and about the Apu (mountain deities) who protect these animals, while the men play the pipes. The sheep and cows are venerated in a ritual known as Sinalay (from the Spanish *señalar* 'to mark animals'). This festival is also called Santos since the ritual is performed in October just before the Christian festivity of Todos Los Santos (All Saints), which occurs on November 1. The alpacas are venerated soon after, before the end of the year. These rituals are performed much less today than a few decades ago. In one song, women sing:

> Because you eat, we eat.
> Because you drink, we drink.
> Because you are, we are.

In the department of Cusco, panpipes are rare, but they are common in the altiplano (high plateau) around Lake Titicaca. The presence of these pan-pipes and the Q'eros use of four-stake looms suggest an earlier cultural connection to the Titicaca basin.

Flutes

The *pinkuyllu* (figure 1), an end-blown notched flute, produces music uniquely associated with Q'eros. It is

Figure 1 Man playing *pinkuyllu* in Hatun Q'eros on Ash Wednesday of Carnival, 2006.
Photo by Holly Wissler.

played in conjunction with women's singing in two fertility rituals: during Aqhata Ukyachichis (for the male llamas) and Phallchay (for alpacas and female llamas). It is also played to accompany carnival songs (*Pukllay taki*) composed of subject-matter in the Q'eros world—songs such as "*Phallcha*," a gentian flower that grows at an elevation of 14,000 feet and blooms in February and March; "*Wallata*," Andean geese; "Sirena," a mythical mermaid who lives in waterfalls; and "*Thurpa*," a high-altitude flower used for healing coughs. The translation of some Q'eros words to "*Thurpa*" goes: "*Panti thurpa*, why have you come to these desolate ravines?" Older *Pukllay taki* are no longer sung, and are slowly dying with the generation of Q'eros who remember them.

Pinkuyllus are made from hollow reeds obtained in the jungle that range from 15 to 71 centimeters long. Four rectangular fingerholes are evenly spaced toward the distal end of each tube to be made into a flute, with no thumbhole. Four-hole flutes of this description have not been found in other parts of the Andes.

The outline of the *pinkuyllu* rhythm and melody follows that of the sung melody. The sung melody is based roughly on the three pitches of a major triad (in Western musical terms), which is considered an ancient scale in the Andes. The *pinkuyllu* shares the upper pitches of the vocal melody line but adds another higher pitch. In this way, they share the central two notes of the melody, then the woman's voice goes lower, while the *pinkuyllu* goes higher. In this sense, the two parts together make a melody consisting of four notes. This combination of flute and voice, male and female, is consistent with the Andean sense of *yanantin* (duality), and introduces a dimension of gender into the musical structure.

Always in connection with animals, shepherds play the *pinkuyllu* in pastures while herding. Usually, several such flutes can be heard playing independently of each other across the high pastures (*puna*). The music directs and comforts the animals by locating their shepherd in space. This custom of playing *pinkuyllu* while herding is giving way to portable radios.

A person plays the *pinkuyllu* by uncovering the four holes in sets of two and sometimes three fingers rather than one finger for each tone. The timbre is breathy, composed of many overtones. Sometimes only the outline of the melody is heard, with segments conceived under the breath without being audibly played (the musician plays mentally, silently). In addition, coloration is sometimes given to the music when the flutist overblows on the notch, producing short and high overtones or octaves. A technique frequently used in transitions from one note to another is to touch two fingers rapidly down, covering and uncovering two holes, producing a sound akin to a trill. *Pinkuyllus* are not tuned to each other, and are not played together in unison, nor do people necessarily sing in unison, though they may. For example, three men playing in the same room will play the same tune together, and three women will sing the same song, though not in the same pitches, and not with shared points of starting or stopping. In this way the music is both communal and individual.

Other Musical Instruments

The Q'eros use musical instruments found in other Andean communities. Of these instruments, the *pututu* is a conch trumpet, played by communal authorities as a sign of their position. The conch produces a blast of sound to announce the beginning of an event or a ceremony. *Pututus* are an old instrument, dating back to Inca and pre-Inca times. The shells come from the sea, hundreds of kilometers away, and originally were traded for and carried to the mountaintops. Though this instrument is commonly called *pututu* elsewhere in the Andes, it is called *pusunis* by the Q'eros, possibly a loanword based on the Spanish *bocina* (horn, trumpet).

A side-blown six-note flute, *pitu*, is used principally for melodies of the *ch'unchu*, a pre-Hispanic dance that represents Amazonian jungle culture. This music is played with drums during the pilgrimage to Qoyllur Rit'i, southeast Peru's largest pilgrimage festival, a day's walk from Q'eros, where hundreds of troupes worship a combination of Christian and Andean elements through colorfully costumed dance and song. The *ch'unchu* melody is a pentatonic tune that sometimes ends with a sequence of notes unrelated to the tonal center of the melody. Dancers representing the *ch'unchu* dress in brightly colored feather headdresses, carrying long pieces of jungle wood (from a bow), festooned with short feathers. The *ch'unchu* as a visual motif is also seen in Q'eros weaving. After Qoyllur Rit'i, the Q'eros continue the *ch'unchu* music and dance in Hatun Q'eros for their own celebration of Corpus Christi. In addition, the *pitus* and drums are used to play *huaynos* (examples of a popular Andean dance genre) at Easter, also held in Hatun Q'eros.

Musical Genres and Contexts

The Q'eros celebrate their annual festivals in their hamlets or at a lower elevation at the ceremonial center, Hatun Q'eros, where the entire community gathers several times a year for major feasts. In addition, they make a pilgrimage to Qoyllur Rit'i the Sunday before Corpus Christi. In sequence, the major festivals are Chayampuy, Phallchay, Carnival (with Tinkuy), Pascuas (Easter), Corpus Christi, Aqhata Ukyachichis (Santiago, Saint James), and Sinalay (Santos).

The most unusual and emblematic Q'eros festivals are the ones for venerating animals: Phallchay, Aqhata Ukyachichis, and Sinalay. Phallchay focuses on alpacas and llamas, Aqhata Uyachichis is for the male llamas that successfully carried the corn harvest from the high jungle to the homes above, and Sinalay is for the cows and sheep. Each animal type has its own song, and there are no specialized musicians: all women sing the songs, and all men play the *pinkuyllu* and sing.

At Phallchay (occurring on the Monday before Ash Wednesday, based on the Christian calendar), individual Q'eros families hold rituals in their houses. Starting in the morning, the woman of the house sings, and the man plays *pinkuyllu*. They pour corn beer (*aqha*) onto grass from the pasture, and onto little statues of the animals. Then several families join together outside and throw flowers (*phallcha*) over their gathered herd of llamas and alpacas while singing and playing *pinkuyllu*. Five or more women sing the song for the animals at the same time, sometimes interspersing ritual phrases (usually song refrains) with improvised complaints about their daily lives. Each tells her own story in song. At times, the musical texture consists of different people singing personalized songs simultaneously. Only occasionally do they meet on ritual phrases or on final notes.

The following day, Tuesday, many elements come together. For Carnival, the entire community descends (figure 2) from the isolated mountain hamlets and gathers at Hatun Q'eros, overlooking the jungle. Each family has a large house here, used only for community rituals. The male authorities are greeted with exchanges of conch trumpets in the central plaza in front of the church, while other men play *pinkuyllu* and do a stomping dance. Groups of families or friends do rounds to many houses, singing and playing the year's chosen Carnival song all night long. Thirty people may be packed together inside, drinking, dancing, and singing all at once with a "wide" overlapping melodic line and conch trumpets blasting. Sometimes, late in the night, the individual qualities become less apparent, as people find common accord and reach a degree of musical consensus. At this point, the sustained final note of a phrase provides a drone beneath the individual voices, yet the wide overlapping of voices and *pinkuyllu* creates a dense, complex texture.

On the principal day of Carnival, Ash Wednesday,

Figure 2 Q'eros men play *pinkuyllu* in the center plaza of Hatun Q'eros, 2006. They are dressed in Carnival garb with hats (*monteras*) and balloons attached.
Photo by Holly Wissler.

everyone gathers at the plaza. While the men dance, sing, and play *pinkuyllu*, the women sing separately or in unison in groups. In this way, many groups of women sing the same song in overlapping disregard for each other. The women arrange themselves in a single line, which arcs around the men. This event has a rich, pulsating, dense sonic texture. This kind of dense overlapping of voices and *pinkuyullu* does not occur elsewhere in the Andes, but it resembles celebrations in the Amazon basin. The structure of the music may therefore suggest a cultural connection between the Andes and the Amazon.

The prevalent song at Carnival is chosen by the *carguyoq* (*cargo* holder, or main organizer of carnival for a particular year) and his *regidores* (officials and assistants elected from all six hamlets) two weeks before Carnival during the ritual known as Chayampuy, held in Hatun Q'eros. After officially receiving their authority, these men stay up all night in a type of song competition, in which they sing Carnival songs (*Pukllay taki*) for one another. These songs are then sung by the entire community for two nights until one emerges as this year's Carnival song. Formerly, before Q'eros had their own town council and needed to walk one day to Paucartambo (district capital) to receive their authority, the *carguyoq* would compose a new song by "reading the landscape," and this song became the song of the year. Today, there is an existing body of *Pukllay taki* from which one is chosen, and no new songs are composed. "*Thurpa*" was the chosen song in 2005, and "*Phallcha*" in 2006.

Similar celebrations with music are held at the hamlets in the high valleys. From late August into September, individual families thank the gods for the strength and fertility of their male llamas. In the *mullucancha* (sacred, chosen corral for this ceremony), they mark the male animals by putting tassels in their ears and force them to drink corn beer (*aqha*). This festival is known as Aqhata Ukyachichis (Let's Water with Corn Beer, referring to the act of sharing their corn beer with the llamas). Each family's ritual differs slightly from that of its neighbors. Though families celebrate on separate days, they all employ similar ritual items. A special cloth, the *unkhuña,* is set on the ground as an altar on which ritual objects are placed. These are special ritual versions of items used in daily life: ropes, bells, and offerings of corn beer and coca leaves. The women sing and men play *pinkuyllu* in the *mullucancha* among the male llamas, creating a dense and rich texture of overlapping sound and activity (as at carnival): singing, playing *pinkuyllu*, dancing with the lead llama's bells, "inviting" the llamas to drink corn beer, putting tassels on their ears, drinking, talking, laughing, crying, all simultaneously.

The ritual then moves from the corral into the house. As it progresses through the night, the men increasingly mimic the animals, shaking llama bells and ropes, hitting each other with whips as if they themselves were llamas, and whistling as they do when they drive the animals along. Some men sing in a low, forced growl, in imitation of the humming of the llamas. Often the women sing intensely, and some men play *pinkuyllu*.

The music goes on continuously, but individuals start and stop as they please, sometimes not completing a phrase. After the ritual items are put away, the celebration becomes an expression of human fertility as couples go off to bed. This musical style allows for expression of the individual while retaining a distinctive communal identity.

Social Structure, Ideology, Aesthetics

Because Q'eros music functions as an integral part of ritual, considering music a separate entity may be a mistaken notion. The Q'eros explain music this way: "It's always like this, we sing this song of the Incas. We compose the songs from all things. Every song comes on its appropriate date. If there is no song, there is no fiesta; and without the fiesta, there is no song."

Q'eros songs reflect a complex cosmology, which moves freely between mountain spirits (Awki and Apu) and personal events from daily life. The texts speak of parallels between the lineage of animals and humans; they include metaphorical references to flowers as symbols of love and representatives of the gods. They portray wild birds and animals as representatives of mountain spirits, whereas they associate domesticated animals (llamas and alpacas) with human counterparts. Songs that celebrate the fertility of the animals are mixtures of courtship, floral symbols, and giving thanks to the gods; the songs may contain calendrical and landscape references.

Though men and women know and sing the songs, women are the primary singers; only men play the accompanying *pinkuyllu* or panpipes. (As with indigenous Andean tradition, Q'eros women do not play instruments.) At rituals for the fertility of the animals, gender differences in singing-styles are defined in terms of the animals: men imitate the sound of male alpacas; women imitate the sound of female alpacas.

Often the flute serves as a prod to initiate women's participation, and the flutist sounds a melody in anticipation of the singing, which is more involving and intense than the playing of the flute. At communal gatherings, the maximal female vocal qualities find fullest expression: their singing becomes emotional and intense rather than formal or dutiful, and often they express loss and grief spontaneously through song. Men's singing can become an expression of a constrained explosion, a forceful assertion of local conceptions of maleness, complete with growls and explosive yelps.

The general Q'eros musical aesthetic allows different pitches, texts, and rhythms to sound at the same time. Though the Q'eros sometimes sing in perfect unison, their songs are structured to be sung individually. There is no sense of choral singing or harmony. A family, or extended group may be singing and playing the same song at the same time, but each singer sets her or his own pace, pattern of breathing, and point of starting and stopping. The melodies sung at communal occasions have a sustained note at the end of phrases, permitting singers to catch up and share this prolongation, which serves as a drone. When the new verse starts, the overlapping begins anew.

—*By John Cohen and Holly Wissler*

Bibliography

Cohen, John, and Ann Pollard Rowe. 2002. *Hidden Threads of Peru: Q'ero Textiles*. London: Merrell Publishers Ltd.

Wissler, Holly. 2005. "Tradición y Modernización en la Música de las dos Principales Festividades Anuales de Q'eros: Qoyllurit'i (con Corpus Christi) y Carnaval." In *Q'ero: El Ultimo Ayllu Inca*, 2nd ed., edited by Jorge Flores Ochoa and Juan Nuñez del Prado, 375–413. Lima, Peru: National Institute of Culture.

——. 2007. *From Grief and Joy We Sing: The Musical Rituals of Q'eros, Peru*. Video documentary. Produced and directed by Holly Wissler. Albuquerque, N.M.: The Mountain Fund.

——. Forthcoming. "Musical Tradition and Change in the Quechua Community of Q'eros, Peru" (working title). Ph.D. dissertation, Florida State University.

Yábar Palacios, Luis. 1922. "El Ayllu de Q'eros." *Revista Universitario* 38:3–26. Universidad Nacional del Cusco.

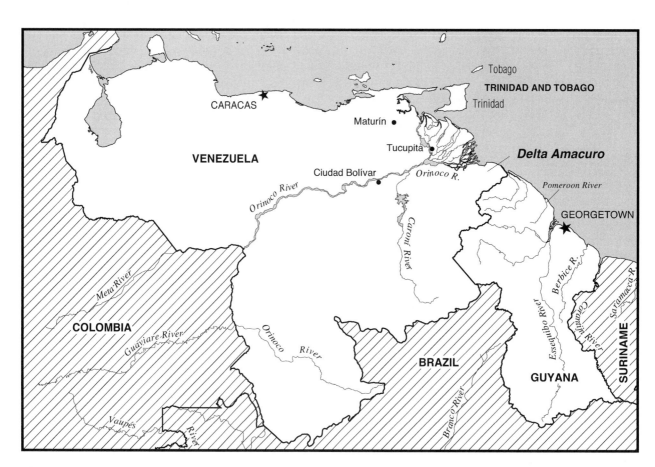

The Warao live in the Orinoco River Delta of eastern Venezuela

Warao

"Tropical-forest spirits singing with beautiful voices, fruit scattering on the forest floor, a scissors-tailed kite circling high above the forest canopy—it's time to sing a magical protection *hoa* song, or you'll die!" So believe the Warao of eastern Venezuela, deep within the tropical forest of the Orinoco River Delta. "And so many Warao die because they do not know the songs," says Jaime, a Warao elder and religious leader.

The Warao (also spelled Warrau, Guarao, Guarauno) are the "canoe people" (*wa* 'canoe', *arao* 'owners of'). We can think of them as the "song people" (*wara* 'ritual song communication', *arao* 'owners of'), because magical singing is as essential to them as canoeing. They speak and sing in a language believed to belong to the Chibchan-Paezan phylum, making them related to the Yanomamö, Kogi, Kuna, and other Amerindians in northwestern South America.

The traditional Warao world is the swamp of the Orinoco River Delta, known politically as the Delta Amacuro Federal Territory. Most Warao live in houses built on pilings over the water, where members of each extended family share a cluster of houses. Because the delta is a web of rivers and streams, constituting about 26,500 square kilometers, the Warao are a riverine fishing people, though they were not always so. In ancient times, they lived in the jungle, and built their villages next to groves of *moriche* palms, which, then as today, provided essentials of life, including mortal food for the people and spiritual food for their patronal being, Kanobo ('Our Grandfather'). Anciently, the Warao were primarily gatherers and occasionally hunters; today, they include horticulture in their food-quest activities. They have always needed to travel through swampy jungles, by land as well as by water, in search of food or cosmological sustenance.

Until about the 1950s, isolation kept the Warao relatively free from contact with European- and African-derived cultures. For this reason, they are numerous and rich in traditional culture. Their population is more than twenty-five thousand individuals, settled in about 250 villages. Extensive missionization began in 1925, when Spanish Capuchín missionaries founded mission schools in the delta. Even into the twenty-first century, these missionaries control the area, and Protestant missionization, common in other parts of the South American tropical forest, has not been possible.

Other locally acculturative forces of the twenty-first century are creole-owned sawmills, with their attraction of outside traders, adventurers, and frontiersmen; exploration for oil; the building of roads and dikes; and research by anthropologists and other scientists. An additional but much smaller number of Warao, the "Spanish Warao," inhabit the swampy coasts of Guyana between the Orinoco Delta and the Pomeroon River; they have mixed with Spanish settlers and are an acculturated group.

The Warao live closer to the Caribbean Islands than the people of any other native South American culture. Trinidad is a short distance by sea, north of the delta. Some musical traits of extant Warao culture resemble those noted in historical accounts of indigenous Caribbeans, especially the Taino or Island Arawak; the most important of these traits involve musical instruments, festivals, and shamanic tools common to the Warao and the Taino. These peoples share some religious and musical similarities with the Yanomamö, a thousand kilometers to the southwest.

Musical Instruments

The Warao use ten traditional musical and noise-making instruments in shamanistic rituals, other ceremonies and musical occasions, and signaling. They play two borrowed instruments for entertainment and retain knowledge of three other instruments, the latter belonging to an extinct part of their culture and no longer used.

The ten surviving traditional instruments are four idiophones, the *sewei* (strung rattle), *habi sanuka* (small container rattle), *hebu mataro* (large container rattle), and a small woven wicker container rattle; one membranophone, the *ehuru* (double-headed drum); and five aerophones, the *muhusemoi* (deer-bone notched vertical flute), *hekunukabe* (cane vertical flute), *isimoi* (clarinet), *heresemoi* (conch trumpet), and *bakohi* (bamboo or cowhorn trumpet). The recently borrowed instruments are two chordophones: *sekeseke* (violin) and *wandora* (Venezuelan *cuatro*).

The following classification, based on the production of sounds, serves for an objective study. The Warao themselves suit their instruments to cultural contexts, such as religious rituals and dance, shamanism, traveling in the jungle or on water in search of food, entertainment, and tourism. Some of these contexts cause the overlapping use of certain instruments.

Rattles (Idiophones)

The religious dances known as *habi sanuka* (for fertility) and *nahanamu* (for harvest) are occasions for attaching *sewei* to male dancers' right ankles. Consisting of numerous small hoofs, seeds, nuts, fruits, or beetle wings threaded on a string, these rattles are sacred, though their sounds simply enhance the rhythms of the dancing. Women never use them. As gifts from the Kanobo, they have great value, and only village chiefs or shamans own them.

The *habi sanuka* is used by Warao men (and occasionally women) during the fertility festival also called *habi sanuka* (see below). It is made from the fruit of the calabash tree known as *mataro* or *totuma* in the delta. Filled with small stones, pieces of shells, or black seeds, the fruit (the container) is pierced by a wooden handle. The total length of this rattle is 23 centimeters.

The *hebu mataro* is a huge calabash container rattle about 70 centimeters long. It serves for the festival of *nahanamu* and in *wisiratu* shamanism (see below). No instrument among the Warao is more important than this rattle, whose size, sound, symbolism, and supernatural power are unsurpassable. When not used, it is stored in a *torotoro* basket (figure 1). The Warao believe it capable of providing profound spiritual help as a "head-spirit." The handle (the leg), which pierces the calabash (the head), is made from a stick of wood, and the stones (the voice) are small quartz pebbles, which are not found in the central delta, but must be brought from Tucupita, the territorial capital. When the *hebu mataro* belongs to a powerful *wisiratu* priest-shaman elder (as opposed to a less powerful younger *wisiratu* shaman, who has not yet inherited the position of priest), the instrument is adorned with feathers (the hair) where the handle protrudes from the top of the calabash. Selected red and yellow tail feathers from a *cotorra* parrot are sewn into a long sash wound around the tip of the shaft. Two vertical and two horizontal slits (the mouth) always appear in the sides of the container, and geometric designs (the teeth) often adorn the slits. The shaft symbolizes fertility, an obvious power symbol for the festival of *nahanamu* and curing rituals, in which male and female power unite to restore a patient's health.

The *hebu mataro* is usually gripped and shaken with both hands while the player dances during the festival of *nahanamu* and while he cures illnesses. For curing, a *wisiratu* shaman usually begins by sitting on a bench, singing, and shaking his *hebu mataro*

Figure 1 A Warao *wisiratu* shaman's *hebu mataro* rattle in a *torotoro* basket.
Photo by Dale A. Olsen, 1972.

(figure 2). He will later stand to lean over his patient and shake it with all his strength. At this time, the *hebu mataro* often produces a fiery glow, seen only by the shaman and the patient during a nighttime curing séance. When the *wisiratu* shaman vigorously shakes his rattle during the transitional part of the séance, the quartz pebbles repeatedly strike against the wooden handle, producing a fine dust. This dust, which has a low flashpoint, is in turn ignited by the heat produced by the concussion of pieces of quartz. Seeing a glow through the slits of the rattle has a psychological effect on the patient, reinforcing his or her belief in the shaman's curative powers.

Tourism accounts for the existence of one Warao musical instrument: a small, finely woven, wicker rattle, about the same size as the *habi sanuka*. It is simply a toy, most often made for sale to tourists in the Venezuelan towns of Tucupita and Barrancas.

Figure 2 Bernardo Jiménez Tovar, a *wisiratu* shaman, uses his *hebu mataro* rattle in an attempt to cure a girl. *Photo by Dale A. Olsen, 1972.*

Drum (Membranophone)

The Warao play a double-headed skin drum known as *ehuru* (or *eruru*) while traveling through the jungle in quest of food and to the *morichal* (grove of *moriche* palms) to prepare for the *nahanamu*. In those contexts, it often accompanies singing; it has the secondary function of letting those behind the drummer and those ahead at the destination know where they are. Additionally, the Warao use it to frighten off jaguars and evil spirits that lurk in the jungle.

A hollowed log cut into the shape of an hourglass, the *ehuru* has heads usually made from the skins of howler monkeys. The player strikes one end with a single stick; the other end has a snare made of twisted *moriche*-fiber string and toothpick-sized thorns.

Stringed Instruments (Chordophones)

Solely for entertainment, the Warao use two stringed instruments: *sekeseke* (a violin) and *wandora* (a small, four-stringed guitar, like the Venezuelan *cuatro*). The *sekeseke* is an often crude copy of a European violin, especially of the Renaissance prototype of the modern violin. A bow, slightly arched at each end, is made from a branch with several dozen loose strands of cotton fibers attached. Warao bowing especially resembles European Renaissance bowed-lute technique. According to Warao lore, the *sekeseke* was first fabricated and transported to the Warao in a ship captained by Nakurao, a man-monkey from a far-off land. This creature, which had the upper torso of a man and the lower torso of a monkey, learned how to make the violin in a dream.

Wind Instruments (Aerophones)

The *muhusemoi* (*muhu* 'bone', *semoi* 'wind instrument') is a bone flute made from the tibia of a deer (figure 3). Its mouthpiece consists of a wide, obliquely cut notch, against which the flutist focuses a stream of air; the flute's body has three fingerholes. The Warao flutist has a unique way of fingering his *muhusemoi*: he opens only one hole at a time, producing a musical scale quite unlike any Western example. No two *muhusemoi* are alike, because no two deer's tibias are exactly the same size—and more importantly, each maker uses his own fingers as rulers for placing the holes.

During the *nahanamu* festival, several *muhusemoi* are played in ensemble with two *isimoi* clarinets, several strung rattles, and *hebu mataro*. Men may play several bone flutes with the *ehuru* drum while traveling by foot in the jungle. If a man does not own a *muhusemoi*, he may fabricate a *hekunakabe*, a disposable plant-stalk flute with the same proportions as the bone flute. After the travelers have reached their destination, the men play their instruments again while women collect and prepare *moriche* palm starch (*yuruma*) for Kanobo—a process undertaken in preparation for the *nahanamu*.

The most sacred wind instrument played during the festival is the *isimoi*, a heteroglot clarinet without fingerholes, made and played by the musical leader of the festival, the *isimoi arotu* 'owner of the *isimoi*'. The Warao believe that, according to the ancients, the *isimoi* has a spirit that is the same as Kanobo.

The owner of the *isimoi* plays his instrument in duet with an *isimoi* played by an apprentice (the owner's instrument has a lower pitch). The *isimoi* does not have fingerholes, but by increasing and

Figure 3 Juan Bustillo Calderón plays a *muhusemoi* deerbone flute.
Photo by Dale A. Olsen, 1972.

decreasing the air pressure, a skillful player can produce two distinct notes at the interval of a minor third, plus limited microtonal glissandi. Like the first interval produced by most *muhusemoi* flutes, and like the basic interval of Warao shamanistic music for curing, an approximate minor third is the interval that fundamentally identifies most Warao music.

An end-blown conch trumpet, *heresemoi*, is an important Warao instrument, though it is associated primarily with canoeing during the crabbing season. Basically a signaling instrument, used for giving directions to canoes at night and to signal the departure and arrival of the crabbing canoes, it can be blown to announce a tribal member's death, to signal the annual trek to the *morichal* in preparation for *nahanamu*, to announce the completion of a newly made canoe, and "to herald each new phase in the process of building a canoe" from a living *cachicamo* tree (Wilbert 1993:55).

Electronic Sound Devices
Modern Venezuelan material culture has had little effect on Warao music. A transistor radio may occasionally appear in a village, but the lack of receivable broadcasts and the expense of batteries work against its use and survival. In Warao villages next to Roman Catholic missions, small phonographs were once found, and children could occasionally be seen dancing to Venezuelan creole music from scratchy 45-rpm records.

Musical Contexts and Genres

By far the most important Warao context for making music is theurgy (supernatural communication), and the most common kind is healing. Sickness and accidents abound, and though their causes are always attributed to the supernatural, some require a shaman's help; song, however, is always the most powerful medium for curing.

Music and Shamans' Work
The Warao worldview specifies three types of cosmological practitioners loosely classifiable as shamans: *wisiratu*, who oversee the apex of the Warao celestial dome and communicate with ancestral spirits; *bahanarotu*, who communicate with the eastern part of the cosmos, where the sun rises (a good place); and *hoarotu*, who appease the spirits of the dead in the west, where the sun sets (a bad place).

One of the most important duties of these specialists is curing illnesses caused by the intrusions of foreign essences. Through an ecstatic technique, culturally induced with the aid of music and tobacco smoke, shamans transform themselves into powerful entities, able to sustain contact with the spiritual world to determine the illness-causing essences and how they got into their patients. Each kind of shaman has a melodically and textually distinct set of songs for curing.

In all cases, the curer must name the illness-causing spiritual essence. When properly named within a descending melody, the malevolent essence is removed, and the patient recovers. While curing, *hoarotu* shamans sing alone, or in twos or threes (as do, to a lesser degree, *wisiratu* shamans). Singing together, prescribed when the patient is an important person, results in a complex, multipart texture like a free round.

The Wisiratu *Shaman*
Only the *wisiratu* regularly rattles a large *hebu mataro* while curing illnesses. With this tool and its powerful properties, he is the most commonly consulted Warao doctor, primarily in charge of curing everyday respiratory and febrile diseases. As the mediator between man and ancestors, he can communicate

with the major Warao supreme beings, known as Kanobotuma ('Our Grandfathers'). In addition to his role as a curer, he therefore functions as a priest in charge of Kanoboism, a Warao temple-idol religion, in which the patron, Kanobo, is represented by a stone; as a person in direct communication with the ancestors, he is greatly admired by all Warao.

The *wisiratu* shaman has three melodically and textually differentiated sections in his curing-song cycle. These respectively function to release and communicate with the helping spirits that reside within his chest, to name the illness-causing essence, and to communicate with the spirit essence after it has been removed and before it is blown off into the cosmos.

The first of these musical sections, characterized by masking of the voice, has the narrowest melodic range, consisting of two or three notes cadencing in the interval of a minor third (such as fourth, minor third, tonic). This section of his curing song is accompanied throughout by the *hebu mataro*, which is at times vigorously shaken as a means to punish the illness-causing *hebu*.

The second is the naming section, in which the shaman seeks out the illness-causing spirit within the patient. It does not include masking of the voice, and in it the rattle is only minimally played. Guided by the patient's symptoms, the *wisiratu* names animate and inanimate objects from the Warao physical, vegetable, or cosmic world—objects that he suspects are causing the illness. The naming section is characterized by the widest melodic range, again terminating in a minor third (such as fifth, fourth, minor third, tonic). In the naming excerpt transcribed in figure 4, the shaman begins by establishing rapport with his patient as he sings, "My friend, my friend, my friend, my friend, you are sad; my friend, you are sad."

The third section of the *wisiratu* curing-song cycle, when the shaman communicates with the illness-causing spirit, is an unmasked, high-pitched, one-note recitation.

The Bahanarotu Shaman

The *bahanarotu* shaman cures gastrointestinal and gynecological illnesses caused by the intrusion of essences of material objects (believed to be the material objects themselves) that living or ancestral malevolent *bahanarotu* shamans have placed into a victim via magical arrows. He is the ritual specialist pertaining to *hokonemu*, the misty, easternmost part of the Warao cosmos and the tobacco-smoke home of Mawari, the supreme *bahana* bird.

Like the *wisiratu*, the *bahanarotu* sings musical sections that differ melodically and functionally. The first, in which he communicates and releases his

Figure 4 A naming section of a *wisiratu* shamanistic curing-song cycle.
Transcription by Dale A. Olsen.

helping spirits from his chest, is characterized by masking of the voice, and has a narrow range, which emphasizes major-second and minor-third cadential intervals in about equal proportion. This section is followed by a second, similar to the first, except that the voice is not masked, and the performance includes dialogues with helping and malevolent spirits.

When the *bahanarotu* finishes the second part of his ritual, he begins to suck on the patient's body where the illness is believed to be located, removing the illness-causing material object. Accompanied by noisy slurps and gagging sounds, the shaman produces a saliva-covered object from his mouth, such as a thorn, a nail, or a piece of rope. This, he says, was causing the illness.

If the *bahanarotu* shaman does not detect and remove an object, or if the removal causes no relief, he will continue singing a third section, in which he names what he believes to be the illness-causing object itself and its supernatural cause. This third part, the naming section, which has the widest melodic range of his curing ritual and melodically resembles the naming section of *wisiratu* curing, is used only when an object has been placed within the patient via the magical arrows of the supernatural *bahana* wizards living in *hokonemu*. The curing wizard names as many objects as he can, until the patient's body begins to vibrate, when he once again applies suction to extract the pathogen.

The Hoarotu *Shaman*

The third type of Warao shaman, the *hoarotu*, sings in his attempt to cure deadly diarrheal or hemorrhagic illnesses, believed to be caused by the supreme deity of the western part of the Warao cosmos. This cosmic place, where the sun dies, is the abode of Hoebo (symbolically represented by a scarlet macaw) and his accomplices, the living-dead *hoarotu* shamans of eternity. Hoebo and his court, who feast on human flesh and drink human blood from human bones, must be fed by living *hoarotu* shamans. Through dreams, a living *hoarotu* receives a message to provide food for his supernatural leaders, which he accomplishes through inflicting songs ("sung" mentally) for killing other Warao, especially children. (Warao cite this practice in explanation of high infant mortality.) This inflicting genre employs an ascending two-note melody based on a major second, sung aloud only when being taught to an apprentice, in which the shaman names the essences that he will place into his victim.

Living *hoarao* (plural form) are called upon by the families of the patients to cure what are believed to be *hoa* illnesses. Through performing a curing ritual

characterized by singing a descending naming melody similar to those employed by the *wisiratu* and *bahanarotu* shamans, but with different words and spiritual intent, a *hoarotu* tries to effect a cure; masking the voice does not occur. Inspired by the patient's symptoms, a curing *hoarotu* names anything he can think of, from any aspect of the Warao tangible or intangible, mortal or immortal world. Many Warao die, it is said, because of the nearly impossible task of naming the correct intruding spiritual essence that is causing the *hoa* illness.

Songs of Utility

Another common Warao context for music is utility, including lullabies and songs for working and traveling in the jungle, often with drum accompaniment.

Lullabies are sung by men and women, and often have texts that teach older children about Warao life and beliefs, including the dangers of ogres and animals. "Go to sleep, little child, or the jaguar-ogre which has no bones will think you are a deer and eat you" is a common theme. The educative aspect of the lullabies is an important form of Warao enculturation.

Worksongs once had an entertainment context. Known as *dakoho*, they are dance songs whose dance context is obsolete. They are more commonly sung to ease the work of men and women, to accompany the paddling of canoes, to augment drinking, or just for relaxing around the house.

Unlike theurgical songs and the other songs of utility, most worksongs have Western melodic traits. Many of them can effectively be accompanied with standard tonic, dominant, and subdominant harmonies, though the most common practice is to sing them unaccompanied. They are occasionally played on the *seke-seke*, or less often accompanied on the *wandora*. When and how this aspect of acculturation occurred is unknown.

When the Warao walk through the forest to get to the *morichal* to find large *cachicamo* trees, to visit neighboring villages not easily accessible by canoe, and to gather food, they sing songs. Led by a male player of the *ehuru* drum, the songs keep the group together and help maintain the walking pace.

Performers and Performances

Most Warao musicians are adults, from whom children, because of the constancy and closeness of family and village contact, informally learn all kinds of songs. Occasionally children will sing a prayerful song (*hoa*) to themselves to ease their pain from cuts, stings, or bruises. Likewise, some children, especially those who attend Roman Catholic mission schools in the delta, sing dance songs and popular Venezuelan songs.

Though women have been shamans, most singers of theurgical songs are men. The older the male adult, the more likely he knows the important theurgical songs, whether he is a shaman or some other leader of his village. Because Warao male elders are highly respected as leaders of families, knowledge of the songs increases the opportunity to sing them.

All Warao men must have a role within their society. Without a social position—as shaman, basketmaker, canoemaker, keeper of the *isimoi*, and so forth—men would have no place to go with their wives after death except to the western part of the cosmos, the place of eternal death, and nearly all Warao roles, from shaman to artisan, include songs of power.

The underlying structure of Warao theurgical music is not an aesthetic one: it is based on the proper knowledge of melodic formulas determined by context, and on the ability to choose words that will effectively communicate with the proper supernatural entities for accomplishing the appropriate tasks. This lack of aesthetic concern is typical of lullabies and other secular songs. The Warao sometimes, however, comment that someone is a good singer of *dakoho*— a reference to knowledge and ability. Other than the knowledge of *dakoho* or Venezuelan popular songs, there is no musical creolization or miscegenation between the Warao and African- or Spanish-derived Venezuelans—a factor caused by the Warao's physical isolation.

—Adapted from an article by Dale A. Olsen

Bibliography

Greenberg, Joseph H. 1987. *Language in the Americas*. Stanford: Stanford University Press.

Olsen, Dale A. 1996. *Music of the Warao of Venezuela: The Song People of the Rain Forest*. Gainesville: University Press of Florida. Book and compact disc.

Wilbert, Johannes. 1993. *Mystic Endowment: Religious Ethnography of the Warao Indians*. Cambridge, Mass.: Harvard University Press.

——. 1996. *Mindful of Famine: Religious Climatology of the Warao Indians*. Cambridge, Mass.: Harvard University Press.

South America

What is the essence of South American music? Many will think of the guitar and its dozens of relatives. Others may think of skin-covered drums or handheld rattles, like maracas. South American music includes these instruments and many others, as it is a region of many heritages and great musical diversity. We think immediately of Spanish and Portuguese, African, and native American backgrounds, but we must also think of other Europeans, the great diversity of Africans forcibly brought to the New World, and the multitude of other immigrants whose musics have become part of the cultural mosaic of South America. To give a sense of this great diversity, we offer coverage of the tango in Argentina, of *cumbia*, *vallenato*, *currulao*, and other popular music in Colombia, and of a range of musics in Brazil, Peru, and Venezuela.

Pipe-and-tabor player, Yungay, Peru, 1979.
Photo by Dale A. Olsen.

Argentina

Argentina: Tango

Located in the southern "cone" of South America, the Republic of Argentina is the southeast extreme of the Americas. It covers about 2.77 million square kilometers of continental land, which extends westward to the Andes and Chile, eastward to the Atlantic Ocean, Uruguay, and Brazil, northward to the borders with Bolivia and Paraguay, and southward to Chile and the Atlantic Ocean. Its territory has a varied topography, in which several cultural areas can be distinguished: Patagonia (Chubut, Neuquén, Río Negro, Santa Cruz, and Tierra del Fuego Provinces), the area of the pampa (Buenos Aires, La Pampa, Santa Fe, the south of Córdoba), the area of Cuyo (Mendoza, San Juan, San Luis), the northwestern area (Catamarca, Jujuy, La Rioja, Salta, Tucumán), the central area (Santiago del Estero, the center and north of Córdoba), the area of Chaco (Chaco, Formosa, the east of Salta), and the littoral area (Corrientes, Entre Ríos, Misiones).

Argentina's population is about 39.9 million persons, the majority of whom are of European descent. Natives and mestizos have been pushed aside or absorbed. A famous character, immortalized in literature, is a kind of mestizo called gaucho, an Argentine cowboy, synonymous with the interior or the country.

Tango

The tango, one of the best-known musical genres of Argentina, is a popular dance for couples, with sensual and complex choreography. It is music of nostalgia and melancholy, centered on one city: Buenos Aires. Its popularity peaked in the 1940s and then declined, but in the 1980s it began to rise again, nationally and internationally. It is a form of music and dance that in the late 1800s began to make its way through cafés, academies, dancehalls, sites for dancing at carnival, theaters, variety shows, cabarets, and early recordings. It continues to be danced in halls and clubs, and is heard in *tanguerías*, a recent name for tango clubs given by its fans.

In its first stage of development, the tango did not reach the central locales of Buenos Aires, but remained marginalized among lower-middle-class people and seedy characters. Beginning in 1912, political and social changes brought together various social classes in Buenos Aires. With the opening of cabarets downtown, the tango encountered more-demanding venues, where it won not only new audiences, but new musicians, who, being better trained, could make a living by playing it.

The early instrumentation of tangos included one *bandoneón* (a concertina, whose popularity was spread by the tango) and two guitars; or a *bandoneón*, a violin, a flute, and a guitar; or a clarinet, a violin, and a piano; or a violin, a piano, and a *bandoneón*; or a similar trio or quartet. The 1920s saw the appearance of solo performers and the formation of the typical ensemble (*orquesta típica*): two violins, two *bandoneones*, a piano, and a string bass.

During the heyday of tango, different genres and expressions developed within the idiom. These included sung tangos (*tango canción* and *tango característico*), instrumental tangos (*tango romanza*, *milonga*, and others, performed by virtuosic ensembles), important lyrics, the appearance of prolific writers, such as Pascual Contursi (1888–1932) and Celedonio Flores (1896–1947), and male and female singers who acquired tremendous popularity, of whom the most important was Carlos Gardel (1887 or 1890–1935).

The most prominent musicians of this time were Julio De Caro (1899–1980), an icon in the development of the composition, arrangement, and performance of instrumental tangos, and Osvaldo Fresedo (1897–1984), who singlehandedly did away with the tango's chamber-music character (in which solo instruments were important) by consolidating the orchestra, so groups of instruments were treated as single voices.

The Tango in the 1930s and Later

The beginning of the 1930s was a difficult time for the tango and its musicians. Since most tango performances accompanied silent films, the arrival of movies with sound took away much of the market. From 1935 to 1950, however, the tango recovered its popularity and gained a new audience, particularly through the media of film and radio. Cabarets attracted a new audience, the middle class, which adopted the tango as its favorite dance because it acquired a stronger rhythm and became easier to dance. Instrumental parts continued to be treated homophonically (like voices in a chorus), and solos decreased.

Figure 1 Two of the most outstanding tango dancers—Milena Plebs and Miguel Angel Zotto—in their show "Perfume de Tango" as performed at Sadler's Wells Theatre, London, 1993.

The great orchestras of the 1930s and 1940s were those of Miguel Caló (1907–1972), Carlos Di Sarli (1903–1960), Enrique Mario Francini (1916–1978), Osmar Maderna (1918–1951), and Osvaldo Pugliese (1905–1995); major figures were Alfredo Gobbi (1912–1965), Horacio Salgán (b. 1916), and Aníbal Troilo (1914–1975). Singers acquired a new importance as soloists, because they began to sing all the lyrics, rather than just the refrains. The vocalists Roberto Goyeneche (1926–1994) and Edmundo Rivero (1911–1986) became highly popular.

The 1950s marked the end of the tango's greatest creativity and popularity. The genre became associated with closed intellectual circles, which did not dance to it, but listened to it and studied it as a relic of earlier times. Beginning in 1955, however, a new stage began. It was headed by Astor Piazzolla (1921–1992) and his octet: two *bandoneones*, two violins, piano, and electric guitar. New venues where the tango could be heard opened. These included Gotán 676, La Noche, and other clubs, frequented mainly by upper-middle-class *porteños* (people of the port, Buenos Aires) and international tourists.

The 1960s marked the appearance of Editorial Freeland, dedicated to the publication of the lyrics from the "golden age" of tango. Academic studies on the subject appeared, and the Academia Porteña del Lunfardo opened. It was a center for the study of the dialect (*lunfardo*) used by the social classes among which the tango originated and which is still used in some lyrics.

During the 1970s and especially in the 1980s, the tango had a resurgence, not so much in terms of new compositions, but in the appearance of new singers and small instrumental ensembles—trios, quartets, sextets. The principal reason for this resurgence was tango's recovery as a dance. The success of tango shows abroad, especially *Tango Argentina* (Paris, 1983; Paris and Venice, 1984; Broadway, 1985), brought a renaissance of the dance in middle and upper classes, especially in big Argentine cities; however, much of the tango's popularity in Europe resulted from the international activity of Astor Piazzolla, Osvaldo Pugliese, Horacio Salgán, the Sexteto Mayor, and the singer Susana Rinaldi (b. 1935).

Since the 1970s, tango as a dance has attracted the attention of important choreographers, including Maurice Béjart (Belgium; b. 1927) and Pina Bausch (Germany; b. 1940), and outstanding dancers, including Mikhail Baryshnikov (United States; b. 1948), Julio Bocca (Argentina; b. 1967), Milena Plebs (b. 1961), and Miguel Angel Zotto (b. 1958) (figure 1).

Since the 1980s, tango has been going through another phase of splendor, and it has occupied prominent places in such countries as Japan, Germany, and Finland. In Argentina, it has been preserved by some sectors of Buenos Aires that never abandoned it and transmitted it by tradition. It began to obtain more visibility through films, literature, and research, and by embracing new audiences, which came from abroad and from the Argentine middle and upper classes, especially young people, eager to learn from professional dancers called *maestros*.

—Adapted from an article by Ercilia Moreno Chá
Translated by Timothy D. Watkins

Bibliography

Castro, Donald S. 1991. *The Argentine Tango as Social History, 1880–1955: The Soul of the People.* Lewiston, Maine: E. Mellen Press.

Ferrer, Horacio. 1977. *El libro del tango.* 2 vols. Buenos Aires: Galerna.

Labraña, Luis, and Ana Sebsatián. 1992. *Tango, una historia.* Buenos Aires: Ediciones Corregidor.

Savigliano, Marta E. 1995. *Tango and the Political Economy of Passion.* Boulder, San Francisco, Oxford: Westview Press.

Brazil

Brazil: Central and Southern Areas

The music of central and southern Brazil is as diverse as the 110,000,000 people that populate the area. Gross topological contrasts occur throughout the rural areas of central and southern Brazil, which cover about 2,224,000 square kilometers, and an equally wide range of musical activities occur in Rio de Janeiro and São Paulo. These and other cities provide opportunities for hearing many kinds of Brazilian musics, including Brazilian popular musical genres that have become known all over the world; traditional southeastern rural genres of medieval origin and their later developments; and a wide variety of Afro-Brazilian traditions.

Historical Overview

Little is known of the music of central and southern Brazil before its first encounter with Portuguese explorers, on 22 April 1500, and information is scant on the three hundred years that followed. During the colonial period, documents detail the musical activities of the major Roman Catholic cathedrals and upper-class parlors, but data about musical life outside these domains are sparse.

In the first years of colonization, the goals of Portugal were seemingly congruent with those of the church, but the crown's greater interest in gold than in souls had important consequences. About 250 years after the first encounter, Portugal had scarcely fulfilled its part of the bargain; there were but eight dioceses in the colony, and only a few thousand priests to serve a population of 1.4 million freemen and others. Most of the priests were employed on northeastern plantations to administer the sacraments to owners and their families.

Central and southern Brazil were especially affected by official neglect. Unlike the northeast, where sugarcane started generating profits almost immediately after the Portuguese had arrived, the southern areas had little economic importance to the metropolis. The land was settled by Portuguese subsistence farmers, who moved farther and farther into the hinterland, displacing indigenous peoples. They formed small, scattered communities (*bairros*) of around ten to fifteen households each, which helped one another with tasks that a single family could not complete. These circumstances led to the emergence of a peasant ethos, marked by nomadism, community solidarity, and an emphasis on personalized social interaction.

In these communities, Christian festivities were the primary contexts for social interaction. In the absence of priests, colonists developed devotional forms based on rituals brought from Portugal, many rooted in late medieval musical traditions. Households alternated in promoting popular religious festivities. It was up to the host of the festival (*festeiro*) to invite musicians to lead the ritual proceedings at his house. The only leadership roles in these communities were those of popular Roman Catholic traditions. In rural areas, in such traditions as the baptism of Saint John the Baptist, the Saint Gonçalo dance, and the *folia de reis*, the legacy of the household forms of popular Christianity can still be observed.

In the early 1800s, coffee had become popular in Europe and the Americas. Coffee plants could be cultivated profitably in the soil of the Paraíba Valley, an area soon taken over by large landholdings, modeled on the northeastern plantation system. Around 1860, coffee moved westward to the areas around Campinas and into Ribeirão Preto. By 1900, the state of São Paulo was producing nearly 75 percent of the world's supply. In the mid-1940s, northern Paraná became the locus of the new boom.

As coffee made its westward march, rural communities were absorbed as sharecroppers into the plantation lifestyle. The coffee economy brought vast numbers of African slaves and their descendants, mostly of Bantu origin, plus European and other immigrant groups. The musical traditions of these social groups existed side by side, but in time they began to borrow from one another.

As in rural communities, sociability on plantations centered on Roman Catholic festivities. On special saints' days, landowners provided a hefty meal and entertainment for their workers. At these festivals, the landowners congregated in the parlor of the plantation house for European-style couple dancing; sharecroppers participated in the *cateretê* in the front patio of the house; and slaves enjoyed *batuques* near the slave quarters (*senzalas*). In the *batuque*, individual dancers entered a circle to perform acrobatic steps to other participants' singing, clapping, and percussive accompaniment; each soloist ended his or her performance with a belly bump (*umbigada*) against someone in the circle, transferring the role of soloist to that person.

As the population increased, patronal festivals became common in towns throughout the coffee-producing areas. The hosts of these festivals were mostly large landholders. To confront labor shortages, they competed to produce ever grander festivals, demonstrating their benevolence toward their workers. As the festivals became more and more elaborate, new musical styles emerged to enhance them. Many communities founded brass bands, derived from the European military-band tradition, to lead their processions, and Afro-Brazilian dramatic traditions of dance and music emerged, amalgamating Portuguese and African musics and rituals.

These ensembles still perform for patronal festivals throughout central and southern Brazil. In many rural communities, the patronal festival is the most important event of the calendar, bringing crowds of people to the streets, where they are bombarded with sounds, music, dancing, sights, and smells.

Musical Traits of Central and Southern Brazil

Contemporary musical traditions in central and southern Brazil resonate with the processes of interaction of the social groups in the area. Though Portuguese material has been substantially re-invented over the centuries, the solidarity that united peasant communities before the invasion of coffee culture has guaranteed the persistence of a marked Lusitanian-Hispanic legacy in the area. Iberian stylistic traits include arched melodies, conjunct melodic movement, parallel thirds and sixths, tonality, strophic forms with stanza-refrain alternation, and the extensive use of stringed instruments.

Many contemporary musical traditions associated with blacks and mulattos evince the influence of the *batuque*. These traditions often involve responsorial singing, syncopated rhythms (irregular accentuation and anticipation), and the extensive use of percussive accompaniment organized around an eight-pulse timeline (3+3+2).

In the process of acculturation, unique musical styles developed, reflecting the amalgamation of European and African musical practices. Many African traditions incorporated parallel thirds, functional harmony, and stringed instruments of European origin; likewise, the eight-pulse timeline became ubiquitous in the traditions of the Portuguese peasantry.

Some forms (*embolada*, *moda-de-viola*, *xácara*, others) have fixed texts, but many genres—particularly those involving musical duels, including *cururu*, *paulista*, and *porfia* of the extreme south, known as *cantoria* in the northeast [see BRAZIL: NORTHEAST AREA]—involve textual improvisation within the form of the Iberian four-line stanza. In these genres, two singers take turns improvising versified insults about each other until one is declared the winner.

Musical Instruments

Numerous musical instruments are used during central and southern Brazilian social events; the rhythmic percussion instruments are used in ensembles, and the melodic instruments are played solo or in ensembles. The former include a great variety of idiophones and drums; the latter include wind instruments, many influenced by use in military bands, and stringed instruments derived from colonial times. Only the commonest musical instruments are included here.

Percussion Instruments (Idiophones)

The idiophones of central and southern Brazil are mostly small percussion instruments used to give timbral diversity to various ensembles. The *ganzá* (also *guaiá*, cylindrical shaker), *melê* (also *afoxé*, friction rattle), *rêco-rêco* (spring or bamboo scraper), and triangle are used in many settings in urban and rural contexts. The double bell (*agogô*) is used exclusively in Afro-Brazilian urban traditions such as Candomblé (an Afro-Brazilian possession cult; see AFRO-BRAZILIAN TRADITIONS) and the carnival associations known as samba schools (*escolas de samba*). Knee-tied bells (*paiás*) are unique to certain rural Afro-Brazilian dances, especially the *moçambique* of the Paraíba Valley. Large cymbals are an integral part of the percussion section of town bands.

Drums (Membranophones)

Drums of various shapes and sizes are common throughout central and southern Brazil. Like idiophones, some are used in numerous traditions; others are only found in specific contexts. The tambourine (*pandeiro*, often known as *adufo* in some rural areas), and the *caixa* (a medium-sized double-headed drum, with or without snare) are the most versatile drums in the area, found in such diverse traditions as samba ensembles, *choros*, and popular Roman Catholic rural traditions of Portuguese or African influence.

Afro-Brazilian traditions, which use several drums of different sizes, often have distinct names for the different drums. In the popular traditions of Roman Catholic dramatic music and dance, the three commonest are a small drum (*repico*), a medium-size drum (*caixa*), and a large drum (*bumbo*). *Baterias*, the percussion ensembles of samba schools, may have any number of small, single-headed frame drum (*tamborim*), *caixa*, *repique* (also *repinique*) (medium-size single-headed drum), *atabaque* (large narrow single-headed conical drum), *cuíca* (single-headed friction drum), and *surdo* (large double-headed bass drum). In these traditions, each kind of drum has its own basic rhythmic pattern, often in a polymetric relation to the other parts.

Wind Instruments (Aerophones)

One of the most popular aerophones in Brazil is the accordion. Throughout the country, it is known as *sanfona*, but in the extreme south, it is called *gaita*. It was introduced into the country by German immigrants in the early 1800s, but it became popular with the population at large only after 1870. In southern Brazil, it is commonly associated with the fandango, a social dance; in southeastern and central Brazil, it often accompanies the *quadrilha*, danced during festivities in honor of Saint John the Baptist.

Military bands have left their legacy throughout central and southern Brazil, and many small towns maintain bands that perform for patronal and civic festivities. The wind instruments used in these ensembles often include flutes, clarinets, alto and tenor saxophones, cornets, trombones, saxhorns, tubas (*bombardinos*), and sousaphones (*baixos*). They primarily play *dobrados* (marches in 2/4 time), appropriate for processions. Flutes, clarinets, and saxophones serve as melodic instruments in *chorinhos*. In many percussive ensembles of African influence, the leader uses a whistle to cue stops and transitions.

Stringed Instruments (Chordophones)

Two of the commonest stringed instruments in the area are the *viola* (a guitar with five single or double courses of strings) and the *violão* (the ordinary Portuguese term for guitar).

The *viola*, the Brazilian descendant of the Spanish *vihuela*, is the most important instrument of central and southern Brazil, and it exists in a variety of types. A form of the instrument found in Mato Grosso do Sul is known as a *viola de cocho* 'trough guitar'. The body of the instrument, dug out of a single trunk of soft wood, is covered with a thin layer of wood. It has five single courses of strings, made of animal gut or fishing line. It produces a deep, hollow sound, more percussive than harmonic.

In southeastern Brazil, the most common *viola* is the *viola caipira* 'country guitar'. It is smaller than a guitar, and has five double courses of metal strings. In contrast with the *viola de cocho*, it has a full, metallic timbre. It can be tuned in many ways, the commonest being the *cebolão* 'big onion' (b–b^1,

e^1–e^2, g♯^{1}–g♯^{2}, b^1–b^1, e^2–e^2) and the *rio abaixo* 'down-river' (g–g^1, d^1–d^2, g^1–g^2, b^1–b^1, d^2–d^2). Currently, the *viola dinâmica* is gaining popularity; though larger than a *viola caipira*, it can be tuned in the same way, and it produces a louder sound.

A *violeiro* (*viola* player) must be competent to play in a tonality other than the one in which the instrument has been tuned. *Música sertaneja* (the Brazilian equivalent of North American country music) is accompanied by a *viola* and a *violão*, an instrumental configuration that has come to be known as *o casal* 'the couple'. Since the 1960s, however, the *violão* has been taking the place of the *viola*, since it is considered more modern and versatile.

Though the *viola* is the quintessential instrument of the Brazilian lower classes, the *violão* epitomizes the popular musical traditions of the upper and middle classes. It was celebrated in many pieces by Heitor Villa-Lobos (1887–1959), and it was the primary instrument of the bossa nova movement. Nonetheless, it is used in popular Roman Catholic traditions in rural areas, just as it is included in samba styles of the urban underprivileged.

Music within Popular Roman Catholicism

Musical activities in rural areas are associated with religious events, and many popular rituals still take place with little or no ecclesiastical intervention. Many saints who have become the objects of popular devotion—the Virgin Mary, Saint John the Baptist, Saint Sebastian, and many others—are depicted with all-too-human traits, and quite frequently they are fun-loving musicians and dancers. Devotion to these saints typically involves making merry, eating heavily, performing music, and dancing.

Ternos

In central and southern Brazil, ensembles of dramatic music and dance known as *caboclinhos*, *caiapós*, *congadas*, *moçambiques*, and others are collectively called *ternos*. They often perform in the streets during patronal festivals. They are usually dedicated to the Virgin Mary in her capacity as Our Lady of the Rosary, and to Saint Benedict the Moor (d. 1589), but they may come out for festivals in honor of other saints.

Their typical choreography consists of a symbolic battle—between Christians and Moors, or Africans and slavers, or Indians and Portuguese—enacted through dialogues (*embaixadas*) and manipulated batons. Symbolically, good (or the oppressed group) prevails over evil (or the oppressing group), thanks to the honored saint's intervention.

At large festivals, several *ternos*—some local, and others from neighboring municipalities—roam the streets. Each ensemble has unique uniforms and a unique combination of colors, and all the ensembles compete with one another, beating their instruments as loudly as possible.

Ternos are voluntary associations, but members are almost exclusively male; women may participate as banner-bearers (*porta-bandeiras*), who lead the procession of musicians and dancers. The ensembles perform in two parallel lines, in which the leaders stay behind the instruments, in front of the dancers (*soldados* 'soldiers'), organized in pairs according to their ages, with elders in front.

The musical performances of these ensembles begin with a slow tune sung in parallel thirds by the captain (*capitão*) and his helper (*ajudante*), immediately answered by the responder (*resposta*) and his helper (also *ajudante*). The first singers then break into a faster tune, which, once presented, is repeated by the responder and his helper. Finally, the dancers behind them take it up. Once the singing is under way, the captain blows his whistle, and the dancers begin to strike their batons in choreographed routines.

Music in Urban Contexts

Around 1900, musical activities in the urban centers of central and southern Brazil were clearly defined along class lines: elites congregated in enclosed spaces (parlors, concert halls, ballrooms) to participate in events involving European and national art music and couple dancing; the middle classes were associated with *chorões*, musician-seranaders that performed in the street, though in respectable places; and the lower classes, who were restricted to the hills overlooking Rio and poor peripheral neighborhoods, were recreating musical forms that had developed in *batuque* circles during the slave era. By the 1930s, however, samba had become a national phenomenon, crosscutting class-drawn barriers.

Samba

Samba is the best-known of Brazil's musical expressive forms. Almost an international synonym for Brazilian music, it has become something of an umbrella term to designate a range of popular styles, including *samba carnavalesca* (carnival samba), *samba-enredo* (theme samba), *samba baiana* (Bahian samba), *samba-lenço* (handkerchief samba), *samba rural* (rural samba), *samba de morro* (hill samba), *samba da cidade* (city samba), *samba de terreiro* (yard samba), *samba de breque* (break samba), *samba de*

partido-alto (specialist samba), and *samba corrido* (verse samba), *samba-canção* (song samba), *samba-choro* (*choro* samba). All these genres have elements that at some level can be traced to African origins, particularly to Bantu traditions organized in eight- and sixteen-pulse timelines.

These timelines generate some rhythmic patterns (*batucadas*) played by several instruments in the percussion ensembles of the samba schools (figure 1). Other instruments, such as the *surdo*, the *ganzá*, and the *cuíca*, are accented on offbeats, creating a rich, polyrhythmic texture.

Samba first became associated with carnival in Rio de Janeiro. At carnival around 1900, mobile associations (*ranchos*, also *blocos*), made up of blacks, mulattoes, and unskilled white laborers danced down the streets to the rhythm of percussive instruments, singing responsorially to the short improvised verses of a leader. In Rio, this samba style became known as *samba baiana* or *samba carnavalesca*.

The new 2/4 rhythm proved particularly suitable for keeping unity in the movements of the mobile associations while allowing each dancer to move freely. By appearing to be more organized, these ensembles were less likely to attract official repression. Soon the samba became extremely popular among the lower-class inhabitants of Rio de Janeiro (*cariocas*), displacing practically all other musical

Figure 1 A rhythmic pattern played by a samba school's percussion ensemble.
Transcription Suzel Ana Reily.

genres. Samba and carnival would remain linked from then on, each lending its prestige to the other.

One afternoon in 1928, a group of samba musicians (*sambistas*) belonging to an association known as Deixa Falar ('Let Them Speak') was rehearsing in a field in front of a teacher-training college. Inspired by this situation, they decided to call their own association a samba school (*escola de samba*). Thereafter, other carnival associations adopted the term, and samba schools began turning up in Rio neighborhoods.

Samba-enredo

During the 1930s, samba schools began presenting themes (*enredos*) in their parades, and these presentations soon led to the development of the *samba-enredo*, samba with a narrative text. Uniformed dancers (*alas*) became clearly demarcated, each representing part of the story of the *samba-enredo*. Floats carrying *destaques* (people in special outfits placed on the floats) were added, also relating to the theme.

Local politicians quickly perceived the social utility of the samba schools, for these were among the few associations capable of organizing the urban popular masses. In 1930, Getúlio Vargas came to power, and by 1937 he had instituted a nationalist regime, the new state (*estado novo*), modeled on Mussolini's Italy. His government quickly coopted Rio's samba schools, incorporating them into its nationalist project.

In 1934, carnival in Rio was made official, and only legally registered schools could receive public funds to help cover the costs of their exhibitions. By 1937, these groups had to develop themes that would stimulate nationalist feelings among the participants by glorifying patriotic symbols and national heroes. National glorification remained a dominant thematic trait of samba-school performances long after the Vargas era, which ended in 1954. In the mid-1960s, literary figures and Brazilian folklore became dominant themes.

With the onset of the 1980s, as the country faced redemocratization, many samba schools began to use the parades as a venue for addressing national issues, such as direct presidential elections, inflation, poverty, ecological devastation, discrimination against minorities, and other social and economic problems that afflict Brazil's people.

Hill Samba and City Samba

The distinction between hill samba and city samba emerged in the 1930s, when members of the ascending middle classes within urban contexts took to the new rhythm. Styles classed as sambas from the hills were those used by the lower classes, which lived in shantytowns (*favelas*) overlooking the respectable neighborhoods. These included the carnival sambas (*samba carnavalesco*, *samba baiana*, and *samba-enredo*), *samba de terreiro* (sambas played by samba school musicians outside the carnival period), *samba de partido-alto* (sambas in which prominent musicians improvised long verses between refrains), and *samba corrido* (a style of samba without refrains). City sambas catered to middle-class tastes; they emphasized melody and text, and their composers had better access to recording studios. Their dominant form was song samba (*samba-canção*), but break samba and *choro* samba were also included in this category.

The first recording of a samba, made in 1917, was of the composition "*Pelo Telefone*" ('By Telephone'). Only in the 1930s, when radios were more widespread, did samba become a quasi-national phenomenon. With the popularization of the genre, the demand for it was no longer restricted to carnival and composers of sambas responded by creating a new modality: *samba-canção*, samba for any time of the year. Performers and composers such as Ary Barroso (1903–1964), Araci Cortes (1904–1985), Ataúlfo Alves (1909–1969), Carmen Miranda (1909–1955), Noel Rosa (1910–1937), and many others could be heard year-round, all over the country.

In the 1980s, new forms of samba, such as *pagode* and *samba de gafieira*, became popular. The *pagode* grew out of the intimate, backyard forms of samba, but added new instruments, such as banjo and the tan-tan, to the mix. The lyrics of *pagode* tend to be clever and humorous, suggesting solutions to life on the margins of society. *Gafieiras*, on the other hand, are large dancehalls patronized by the urban working class, and *samba de gafieira* is the style of samba used in these establishments.

Bossa Nova

After more than two decades of *samba-canção*, Brazilian audiences in the late 1950s welcomed the change brought by bossa nova. While drawing on traditions, the mellow sound of the guitar and the soft percussion highlighted complex principles of rhythmic organization, rather than visceral qualities; the vocal timidity and quietue of bossa nova negated the stereotype of Brazilians as an over-emotional, exuberant people, to portray them as contemplative, intimate, and sophisticated.

The first recording of a bossa nova was made in 1958. The song was "*Chega de Saudade*" ('No More Longing'), which united the heavyweights of the movement, epitomizing their individual contributions. Antônio Carlos Jobim (1927–1994) wrote the music, which had a modal feeling set against altered and compact chords; the lyrics, by Vinícius de Moraes (1913–1980), had a colloquial ethos, crafted to make full use of the timbre of each word, in a manner reminiscent of the symbolist poets of the late 1800s. João Gilberto's (b. 1931) nasal, speech-like vocal style, was ideally suited to bossa-nova aesthetics.

Gilberto's guitar technique attracted special attention: he slotted the chords between the syncopations of the melody, avoiding coincidences—a style that became known as the stuttering guitar. He derived the upper snaps of his beat from the rhythms of the *tamborim*, while the thumb reproduced the thump of the *surdo*. He produced chords with up to five tones by using the little finger of his right hand to pluck the highest string.

Classics of the bossa nova repertoire, such as "*Desafinado*" ('Off-Key', Antônio Carlos Jobim and Newton Mendonça), "*Samba de Uma Nota So*" ('The One-Note Samba', Jobim and Mendonça), "*Garota de Ipanema*" ('The Girl from Ipanema', Jobim and Vinícius de Moraes), "*Insensatez*" ('How Insensitive', Jobim and de Moraes), "*Corcovado*" ('Quiet Night of Quiet Stars', Jobim), and "Wave" (Jobim), became known internationally.

Popular Music after Bossa Nova

After bossa nova, Brazilian popular music (*música popular brasileira*, MPB) took many directions. The 1960s saw the rise of a protest movement, in which musicians Carlos Lyra (b. 1935), Geraldo Vandré (b. 1935), Chico Buarque (b. 1944), and others somewhat naively proposed to use their music for "raising the consciousness" of the underprivileged masses.

Local styles were reformulated within the bossa-nova framework, and musical texts moved away from love, sun, and beaches to depict the harshness of life, especially for poor people. Though too distant from the reality of the lower classes to have any effect

on them, these songs helped incite intellectualized sectors of the upper classes, who began to organize in opposition to the military dictatorship, but the 1960s was the decade of the young guard (*jovem guarda*), a romantic and alienated movement, which helped set the foundations for Brazilian rock (*roque brasileiro*). Trying to place Brazilian popular music back onto its "evolutionary track" (an expression used by Caetano Veloso (b. 1942) in an interview with Augusto de Campos [1986:63] in 1966), the *tropicália* movement of the late 1960s depicted Brazilian society as an amalgam of diverse and contradictory elements. In text and music, *tropicália* exposed the contradictions of this diversity, but the movement was cut short with a new law, Institutional Act No. 5 (1968), which led to the imprisonment of Veloso and Gilberto Gil (b. 1942) and their subsequent exile in London.

The 1970s saw a series of revivalist and locally oriented movements. With the recognition that the national repertoire was made up of more than sambas, Brazilian popular music in the 1980s became particularly heterogeneous: it was the decade of the independents. Alongside Brazilian rock, the *mineiros*, led by Milton Nascimento (b. 1942), were reinventing their local styles; the nativist (*nativista*) festivals of Rio Grande do Sul were reviving the cowboy-derived traditions; and various reformalized northeastern tendencies found niches in the southern commercial recording market.

—*Adapted from an article by Suzel Ana Reily*

Bibliography

Appleby, David P. 1983. *The Music of Brazil.* Austin: University of Texas Press.

Béhague, Gerard. 1979. *Music in Latin America: An Introduction.* Englewood Cliffs, N.J.: Prentice Hall.

Campos, Augusto de. 1986. "Boa Palavra sobre a Músic Popular." In *Balanço da Bossa e Outras Bossas,* 4th edition, edited by Augusto de Campos, 59–65. São Paulo: Perspectiva.

Perrone, Charles. 1989. *Masters of Contemporary Brazilian Song: MPB 1965–1985.* Austin: University of Texas Press.

Brazil: Northeast Area

Northeast Brazil comprises all or parts of nine states—Alagoas, Bahia, Ceará, Maranhão, Paraíba, Pernambuco, Piauí, Rio Grande do Norte, Sergipe—with an area covering roughly 20 percent of Brazil [see map in BRAZIL: CENTRAL AND SOUTHERN AREAS]. This region can be divided into three ecological-geographic zones: the *zona da mata*, a heavily populated, humid, coastal strip, running from Bahia through Rio Grande do Norte; the *agreste*, the zone mediating a wet coastal strip and a dry interior; and the *sertão*, a sparsely populated, drought-prone hinterland.

In size and population, the northeast is larger than most Latin American countries. It contains a mix of three principal cultural heritages: African, European, and Amerindian. Portuguese-descended people are found throughout the region; the *zona da mata* has the largest concentration of Brazilians of African descent and the most pronounced degree of African cultural manifestations. Also in the *zona da mata*, the mix of Portuguese and African populations is most evident. In the hinterlands, in the *agreste* and the *sertão*, live pockets of Amerindian groups, but the bulk of the population consists of *caboclos*, bronze-colored mestizos of Portuguese and Amerindian bloodlines, with a smaller degree of African heritage. Common history, economic hardships, and the blending of cultural traditions have helped northeasterners develop a strong regional identity.

For the present discussion, the musical traditions of the northeast are divided into two categories: music of the interior and music of the coast. Traditions associated strongly with African heritage or African-Brazilian identity are discussed in AFRO-BRAZILIAN TRADITIONS.

Musical Traditions of the Interior

The music that dominates rural areas, towns, and small cities of the *sertão* and the *agreste* (and migrant neighborhoods in coastal cities) is the result of ethnic diversity and the historical processes of colonialization and nation-building. Closely identified with mestizo (*caboclo*) populations, *caboclo* music is conceptualized as "folklore" by state-sponsored cultural institutions and the private culture industry. *Caboclo* musical traditions include *cantoria*, a repertoire of secular songs performed by singer-bards; religious songs, mainly those associated with Roman

Catholicism; the music of instrumental ensembles, accompanying various occasions; and social dance-music known generically as *forró*.

Brazilian scholars have noted some Amerindian influences (speech inflections, the importance of flutes) in *caboclo* music, but they find it hard to link these to specific Amerindian musical practices. Iberian influences are more easily distinguished. The catechistic practices of Roman Catholic missionaries during Brazil's colonial period included medieval European modes, Gregorian chant, and Iberian musical elements. African influences are generally stronger in coastal areas.

Cantoria

DISC 1 TRACK 5

Cantoria, the generic term for the sung poetry and singing-contests of bards in the northeast, represents one of the richest forms of improvised poetry in Latin America. A singer-poet tradition related to medieval Iberian minstrelsy, it dates to Brazilian colonial times, when bards served as primary sources of news for rural populations. Today, *cantoria* is found throughout the northeast and in Brazilian cities where northeasterners have migrated, especially São Paulo, Brasília, and Rio de Janeiro. It is performed in homes; on street corners; at parks, fairs, and rodeos; in bars; on radio programs; in concert halls; at political rallies; and even on television. Most of its practitioners and audiences come from lower classes, but some are ranchers, lawyers, and politicians.

The subjects of the songs come from history, current affairs, myths, legends, political criticism, and especially the concerns of the marginalized poor: homelessness, poverty, misery, and a desire for agrarian reform. The function of *cantoria* as political criticism is particularly evident during election seasons, when singers align with political candidates and perform at their public rallies, praising them and criticizing their opponents.

Local radio programs devoted to *cantoria* are found throughout the northeast. Public and privately sponsored competitions, concerts, and festivals have become increasingly common since 1970. *Cantoria* singers are evaluated primarily for verbal, rather than musical, skills. *Cantoria* typically involves improvised song duels (*desafios*), performed by two singers accompanying themselves on a *viola* (10-string folk guitar) or percussion instruments such as a *pandeiro* (tambourine) or *ganzá* (metal shaker).

Prosodic Forms of the Poetry

Numerous prosodic forms are employed in *viola*-accompanied *cantoria* (*cantoria de viola*). The *desafio* involves two singers, who alternately improvise verses utilizing a series of fixed forms. *Desafios* begin with *sextilhas* (six-line heptasyllabic stanzas) featuring a rhyme scheme of *abcbdb*; in the past, they also featured four-line stanzas rhyming *abcb*. After the first verse, each singer must begin his stanza with a rhyme (*deixa*) that matches the last line of the preceding stanza.

The singing has many repeated notes, syllabic execution of the text, a steady stream of equal note values, and a high, tense tessitura with strong nasalization. As with *caboclo* music in general, modal structures with lowered sevenths are common. Melodies are constructed out of simple motives, sequences, and melodic cadences. The cadential rising or falling of a major third is typical (figure 1*a*).

Sextilhas are usually sung in a quasi-duple meter. Some other poetic forms used in *cantoria de viola*, especially those based on the *décima*, tend to be unmetered.

During a *desafio*, *sextilhas* are followed by any of a variety of poetic forms, including *gemedeira*, a *sextilha* with the insertion of the call *ay-ay-ui-ui* between the fifth and sixth lines; *mourã o-de-sete-pés*, a dialogic seven-line stanza, which one singer initiates and ends and the other singer provides lines three and four; *mourão-de-você-cai*, a dialogic twelve-line stanza with a fixed ninth line, including the words *você cai* 'you will fall'; *oito-pés a quadrão*, eight-line stanzas with an *aaabbccb* rhyme scheme, ending with the word *quadrão*; and *martelo*, primarily in ten-line stanzas featuring the rhyme scheme *abbaaccddc*.

Throughout a *desafio*, the *viola* supplies a harmonic-rhythmic drone (open fifths and octaves are typical), and fills in between stanzas with a syncopated ostinato known as a *rojão* or *baião de viola* (figure 1*b*). This interlude gives the next singer a moment to formulate his or her thoughts into the proper poetic-musical structure.

Contexts of Performances

The several forms of *cantoria*, accompanied by *pandeiro* or *ganzá* (or both together), are typically performed on street corners, in parks, at fairs, and in other outdoor public spaces. For instance, *emboladores* (song duelers specializing in tongue twisters, known as *emboladas*) accompanying themselves on *pandeiros* perform six days a week at a public square in the center of Recife. Their perform-

ances include put-downs, appeals for money, and comical jibes at onlookers. Audiences consist of clerks, taxi drivers, maids, street vendors, night watchmen, and other members of the working class, or tourists. The singing-style is nasal, staccato, and rapid-fire, with many repeated notes within a small melodic range. The *pandeiros* give out syncopated patterns resembling the *rojão* ostinato.

Religious Songs

The Roman Catholicism practiced by *caboclos* includes acts of public and private devotion to saints and popular religious figures, such as making pilgrimages to holy sites, participating in religious processions, and hosting ritualized prayer sessions. In these activities, devotional singing is ubiquitous. Women take active and dominant roles in religious life in general and in singing in particular. Loosely structured groups of female specialists (*turmas de mulheres* 'groups of women'), which often lead praying and singing at domestic religious rituals, have extensive repertoires of hymns, praise-songs (*benditos*), funerary songs (*excelências*), and prayers (*rezas*). The whole month of May, they organize nightly prayer sessions involving a sung rendition of the rosary with hymns and praise-songs honoring the Virgin Mary. Female specialists take leading roles in religious pilgrimages (*romarias*) to sacred locations, such as Juazeiro do Norte in Ceará, where hundreds of thousands of devotees of Padre Cícero (1844–1934), a priest from Ceará, travel each year to fulfill religious obligations. These pilgrimages involve hours of nonstop singing.

Songs praising God, the Virgin Mary, Padre Cícero, saints, and other important religious figures exhibit the modal traits of *caboclo* music (flatted sevenths, augmented fourths), but make use of the major mode. They are strophic, and the text is usually set syllabically. The singing-style is smooth in a flexible and fluid tempo. Unison or parallel octaves are typical, as are improvised harmonies at the third and sixth. Occasional harmonies of fourths and fifths occur.

Forró

The most popular form of social dance-music among *caboclos* is performed by accordion-based groups with a core instrumentation of accordion, triangle, and *zabumba* (double-headed bass drum), to which other instruments—*cavaquinho* (small 4-string guitar), *agogô* (metal double bell), *ganzá*, bamboo scraper, *violão*—are freely added. Such groups are known as regional bands (*conjuntos regionais*) or northeastern bands (*conjuntos nordestinos*). This

♩ = 92

a

Quem con— he— ceu o nor— des— te Hà mui— tos a— nos a trás

No tem— po dos meus a— vós E da in— sân— cia dos meus pais

Ho—je o— b— ser— va que e— le es—tá di— fer— en— te de— mais.

b

Figure 1 *Desafio* melody and *viola* accompaniment pattern: *a*, from a *setilha* (transcribed by Larry Crook from Laurentino and da Silva 1978:A1); *b*, rhythmic pattern (*rojão*) played on the *viola*.

tradition dates to the 1800s and has developed into the northeastern popular music known as *forró*, which has spread throughout Brazil. The standardization of the trio format is attributed to the popular musician Luiz Gonzaga (1912–1989).

Accordion-based groups are particularly active every June, when a series of winter festivals celebrates three Christian saints: Saint Anthony, Saint John, and Saint Joseph. To hold dances, rural communities and working-class neighborhoods in towns and cities decorate their streets with paper flags, build bonfires, and construct temporary huts (*palhoças*) with thatched roofs and dirt floors. Accordion-based groups provide accompaniment for satirical plays about the marriage of a country bumpkin (*casamento de matuto*), square dancing (*quadrilhas*), social dancing for couples in the huts, and other activities. The dancing and partying in the huts is collectively called *forró*.

The main social dances of *forró* include the *arrasta-pé* (a fast, foot-dragging dance), the *baião* (a syncopated dance), the *forró* (a syncopated modern hybrid of the *baião*), and the *xote* (a northeastern version of the schottische). Most of the music stresses a driving syncopated rhythm, exciting improvisation, and verbal double-entendres, sometimes pornographic. Though this music is seasonally associated with the June celebrations, it has been popularized throughout Brazil via broadcast media and commercial *forró* clubs that operate year-round.

Northeastern accordion music was first popularized nationally in the 1940s by Luiz Gonzaga, "King of the *Baião*," regarded as the creator of the genre.

He claims he took the guitarists' rhythmic pattern, *baião de viola*, and mixed it with *zabumba* patterns common to fife-and-drum bands. The musical basis of the *baião* is thus a syncopated rhythm performed on the *zabumba* featuring two interlocking parts played on the top skin of the drum with a soft mallet and on the bottom skin with a thin stick.

Between 1946 and 1956, northeastern music was a national fad, and the *baião* even made an international splash. By the mid-1950s, working-class *forró* dancehalls featuring accordion trios emerged in Rio de Janeiro and São Paulo, catering to homesick migrant laborers from the northeast. In the late 1950s or early 1960s, *zabumba* drummers began deleting the stroke that fell on beat two of the *baião*. This change produced a new, more syncopated *baião*. Further experimentations yielded another variant, which came to be called *forró*. The rhythmic basis of the *forró* is a syncopated interlocking pattern performed with variously muffled and open strokes on the *zabumba*, featuring continual variations and improvisations.

In Campina Grande in Paraíba, in Caruaru in Pernambuco, and in other cities, June celebrations became huge commercial affairs, rivaling carnival and drawing thousands of tourists. Commercial *forró* clubs evolved in conjunction with these celebrations and now bring nationally and regionally famous *forró* musicians (*forroizeiros*) to perform as part of three weeks of activities. Caruaru, the self-titled capital of *forró*, claims the largest *forró* club in Brazil, aptly named the Forrozão (Big Forró); it can accommodate more than four thousand people.

Musical Traditions of the Coast

Music of the northeastern coast is largely a mix of African and European traditions. The establishment of sugarcane plantations and the introduction of enslaved Africans during colonial times left indelible marks on musical life. European erudite traditions were sustained by the Portuguese upper class (often by training slaves to play European music), while vernacular African and Iberian traditions were maintained and mixed by the lower classes. Historical documentation shows that European-style erudite musical activities existed in the major urban centers of Pernambuco (Recife) and Bahia (Salvador) from the 1500s. During the colonial period, art music was primarily related to activities of the Roman Catholic Church, as local chapel masters and organists composed and organized music for daily services and special rituals. Formalized music instruction was given to blacks and mulattoes as early as 1600, and some excelled as instrumentalists, singers, and composers. Private orchestras and choruses of slave musicians existed on large sugar plantations, and concert life and opera houses first appeared in the 1700s in Bahia and Pernambuco.

In addition to these activities, marching bands and concert bands have a long history in the cities and towns of the area and still serve for religious processions, ceremonies of state, public concerts, and other community functions. In the 1800s, communal bands helped disseminate European social dances of the day. The abolition of slavery (1888) and the subsequent urbanization and proletarianization of former slaves had an important impact on the vernacular musical traditions of the area, and on the formation of urban popular musics that developed in the 1900s. The two most important coastal traditions are dramatic dances and carnival music.

Dramatic Dances

The northeastern coast is the center of the danced folkplays that Mário de Andrade (1982) termed dramatic dances. These dances were introduced mostly by Jesuit priests during colonial times to instruct non-Christian Indians and Africans in religious matters. They present stories of conversion or death and resurrection, divided into two parts: a procession and a sequence of choreographed scenes. Both parts are danced, involve stock characters and a cycle of songs, and are usually accompanied by a small instrumental ensemble. Though based loosely on religious themes, most dramatic dances include an abundance of secular action. They can be divided into three broad categories: the *baile pastoril*, a Christmas cycle; *cheganças*, recounting Portuguese maritime exploits and battles between Christians and infidels; and *reisados*, cyclic dances associated with Christmas and Epiphany.

Baile Pastoril

In numerous forms, the *baile pastoril* occurs during the Christmas season, when it presents the story of the birth of Jesus Christ. It is particularly popular in Alagoas, Pernambuco, Paraíba, and Rio Grande do Norte, where teenage girls dressed as shepherdesses form two lines, blue and red, and perform a series of danced segments (*jornadas*) that include songs and spoken dialogue accompanied by *pandeiros* and maracas. Small ensembles of string, wind, and brasses may accompany their singing.

Chegança *and Other Dances*

Portuguese maritime exploits are presented in *cheganças*, dances including the *chegança de marujo* (of Alagoas), the *barca* (of Paraíba), the *nau catarineta* (of Paraíba), and the fandango (of Pernambuco, Paraíba, Rio Grande do Norte, and Maranhão). Epic stories of seafaring are told through a series of songs sung by men dressed as sailors, accompanying themselves on tambourines.

Dances involving battle scenes between two opposing groups—commonly Christians against infidels, or blacks against Indians—include the *quilombo* (from Alagoas), which symbolically enacts a battle between blacks and Indians. It is accompanied by a band of fifes that plays dance-music specific to each group.

Reisado

The *reisado*, a cycle of dances associated with Christmastide, features human and animal figures presented in short scenes. The last dance in the cycle, *bumba-meu-boi*, has many regional variants in the northeast and throughout Brazil, such as *boi-surubi* (of Ceará), *boi-de-matraca*, *boi-de-zabumba*, and *boi de orquestra* (of Maranhão and Piauí).

Carnival Music

The northeast coast is renowned for its participatory traditions of carnival (*carnaval*). Though carnival is officially confined to the five days before Ash Wednesday, carnival season in major cities involves months of preparation and six to eight weeks of intense activity. All cities and most towns sponsor carnival celebrations. The major carnivals in the northeast occur in Pernambuco (Recife/Olinda) and Bahia (Salvador) and feature a variety of musical traditions unique to those cities.

Carnival season is a busy period for amateur and professional musicians, hired to play for a variety of activities. In addition to municipally sanctioned public parades, presentations, and competitions, they perform at masked balls in private social clubs of the middle and upper class, are employed by carnival associations, and give presentations in restaurants and other commercial establishments.

Frevo

The most characteristic carnival music from Pernambuco is the *frevo*, a term likely derived from the Portuguese verb *ferver* 'boil over.' It has three main types: *frevo de rua*, *frevo de bloco*, and *frevo-canção*. The earliest of these, *frevo de rua* 'street *frevo*', originated in the early 1900s in carnival clubs of urban laborers in Recife; these clubs used military marching bands to accompany their parades. Inter-club competition involved violent encounters between capoeira groups, which paraded in front of the clubs. From the bands' repertoires (especially the marches and polkas) and the choreographic movements of *capoeira* (game-dance) [see AFRO-BRAZILIAN TRADITIONS] developed the aggressive dance and syncopated music that came to be known as *frevo*.

The earliest composers of *frevo* were mainly band-leaders and instrumentalists of the marching bands. In contrast to semierudite salon music, cultivated by the more educated composers of the day, the *frevo de rua* was a loud, street-band music, heavy on brasses, winds, and percussion. Typical instrumentation included clarinets, saxophones (combinations of alto, tenor, and baritone), trumpets, trombones, tubas, a snare drum (*tarol*), a tambourine (*pandeiro*), and two tenor drums (*surdos*).

The music of a *frevo de rua* is typically in a fast duple meter, organized into two repeated sections of sixteen measures each, separated by a short bridge or interlude. Highly syncopated melodies and counter-melodies played by the brasses and woodwinds are accented and punctuated by the percussion. Compositions are strung together with drum cadences and rolloffs, allowing for nonstop music and dancing while the band marches down the street, with dancers and revelers in tow. The instrumental *frevo de rua* continues to be an important part of *frevo* clubs (*clubes de frevo*) in Recife and Olinda, which hire bands to accompany their parades.

Because encounters between carnival clubs around 1900 often became violent and most of the revelers were from the lower strata of Recife society, the *frevo de rua* acquired an unfavorable reputation among the middle and upper classes. Around 1915, new carnival associations (called *blocos*), which

catered to middle-class tastes, emerged in Recife. Among these groups developed the *frevo de bloco*, which featured songs sung by a female chorus accompanied by supposedly soft instruments: the flute, the clarinet, the *bandolín* (similar to a man-dolin), the banjo, the *cavaquinho*, the violin, the *violão*, and a few percussion instruments. The *frevo de bloco* is distinguished from the *frevo de rua* by lighter instrumentation, the inclusion of a female chorus, a slower tempo, frequent use of the minor mode, and lyrical sentimentality of the words.

To animate middle-class carnival balls held indoors in private clubs, the *frevo* song (*frevo-canção*) was first cultivated by popular composers in the 1930s in Recife. It is a solo song with choral refrains, featuring an instrumental introduction (inspired by the *frevo de rua*), followed by a song. Two major composers of this genre were Capiba (Lourenço Barbosa; 1904–1997) and Nelson Ferreira (1902–1976), who led popular jazz orchestras in Recife. In addition to writing for the three types of *frevo*, these composers experimented with a stylized version of the *maracatú*, an Afro-Brazilian carnival genre from Recife, and composed in other popular Brazilian and international genres.

The three main types of *frevo* are the primary moving forces behind the carnival in Recife and Olinda. Annual competitions for new *frevos* are sponsored by the city of Recife, and the winners are recorded on commemorative albums. Popular *frevo* singers such as Claudionor Germano (b. 1932) (specializing in *frevo-canção*), backed up by professional bands, release seasonal records each year in conjunction with carnival. Other popular musicians from Recife—Alceu Valença (b. 1946), for instance—include *frevos* in their repertoires.

—Adapted from an article by Larry Crook

Bibliography

Almeida. Renato. 1942. *História da música brasileira*. 2nd ed. Rio de Janeiro: Briguiet.

Alvarenga, Oneyda. 1982. *Música popular brasileira*. São Paulo: Livraria Duas Cidades.

Andrade, Mário de. 1982. *Danças dramáticas do Basil*. 2nd ed. 3 vols. Belo Horizonte, Brazil: Editorial Itatiaia.

Béhague, Gerard. 1979. *Music in Latin America: An Introduction*. Englewood Cliffs, N.J.: Prentice Hall.

Crook, Larry. 2001. "Turned-Around Beat: *Maracatu de Baque Virado* and Chico Science." In *Brazilian Popular Music and Globalization*, edited by Charles A. Perrone and Christopher Dunn, 233–244. Gainesville: University of Florida Press.

———. 2005. *Brazilian Music: Northeastern Traditions and the Heartbeat of a Modern Nation*. Santa Barbara: ABC-CLIO, Inc.

Kazadi wa Mukuna. 1994. "Sotaques: Style and Ethnicity in a Brazilian Folk Drama." In *Music and Black Ethnicity:*

The Caribbean and South America, edited by Gerard Behague, 207–224. Miami: North-South Center, University of Miami.

Laurentino, Moacir, and Sebastião da Silva. 1978. *Violas da minha terra*. Chantecler LP 2–04–405–075. LP disk.

McGowan, Chris, and Ricardo Pessanha. 1998. *The Brazilian Sound: Samba, Bossa Nova, and the Popular Music of Brazil*. Philadelphia: Temple University Press.

Mello, Luiz Gonzaga de. 1990. *O pastoril profano de Pernambuco*. Recife, Brazil: Fundação Joaquim Nabuco, Editora Massangana.

Murphy, John Patrick. 2001. "Self-Discovery in Brazilian Popular Music: Mestre Ambrósio." In *Brazilian Popular Music and Globalization*, edited by Charles A. Perrone and Christopher Dunn, 245–257. Gainesville: University of Florida Press.

——. 2006. *Music in Brazil: Experiencing Music, Expressing Culture*. New York: Oxford University Press.

Oliveira, Valdemar de. 1985. *Frevo, Capoeira, e "Passo."* Recife, Brazil: Editôra de Pernambuco.

Real, Katarina. 1990. *O folclore no carnaval do*. 2nd ed. Recife, Brazil: Fundação Joaquim Nabuco, Editora Massangana.

Slater, Candace. 1982. *Stories on a String*. Berkeley: University of California Press.

Teles, José. 2000. *Do Frevo ao Manguebeat*. São Paulo: Editora 34.

Tinhorã, José Ramos. 1986. *Pequena história da música popular—da modinha ao tropicalismo*. 5th ed. São Paulo: Art Editora.

Afro-Brazilian Traditions

Nationally and internationally, the iconic music of Brazil comes from Afro-Brazilian traditions. For its true meanings to be understood, it must be viewed in its historical and regional contexts. A multiplicity of black identities emerges from the ambiguity of ethnic self-identities and the complexities of Brazilian social stratification.

Afro-Brazilians have historically remained at the lowest of the social strata, and discrimination against them continues at certain levels, but Brazil saw deep racial integration throughout the twentieth century. Official segregation never became a reality after slavery. All of this eased the true nationalization of certain originally Afro-Brazilian popular musical expressions.

The history of African cultural transfers to Brazil is imprecise and often confused. The aftermath of the abolition of slavery brought such an overwhelming sense of national shame on the part of some governmental officials that in 1891 the minister of finances, Rui Barbosa, ordered the destruction of a large amount of archival documents relating to slavery in the naive hope that such negative aspects of national history would be forgotten. Our knowledge of early Afro-Brazilian musical traditions therefore comes primarily from oral, written, and iconographic sources dating mainly from the 1800s and throughout the twentieth century.

Traditional Afro-Brazilian musical manifestations are centered in three parts of the country: the northeastern and northern states of Alagoas, Bahia, Maranhão, Pará, Paraíba, Pernambuco, and Sergipe; the southeastern area of Espírito Santo, Minas Gerais, and Rio de Janeiro; and parts of São Paulo [see map in BRAZIL: CENTRAL AND SOUTHERN AREAS]. As far south as Rio Grande do Sul, religious worship of African gods, as in the Batuque of Pôrto Alegre, survives. Afro-Brazilian traditions are an integral part of some of the most important genres of Brazilian popular music of the twentieth century.

After a period of sociopolitical vindication since the late 1970s, and especially after the centenary of the Brazilian abolition of slavery, the position of Afro-Brazilian musicians in the national market of the late 1990s remained ambivalent. In Bahia, these musicians have come of age in their involvement, freedom in, and control over their activities; in other areas, their future is uncertain. Nationwide, at the start of the twenty-first century, Afro-Brazilian musics commanded an unprecedented recognition and respect.

Religious Musical Traditions

The stylistic continuity observable in Afro-Brazilian religious music is most probably a case of cultural resistance during centuries of cultural confrontations—centuries that involved cultural sharing. Afro-Brazilian religions present a complex configuration of dogmas and practices resulting from the local adaptation and transformation of belief-systems inherited from Africa and Europe, encapsulating the historical national experience.

The most nationally acknowledged popular religion, Umbanda, is found almost everywhere. Other religions, such as Candomblé (Candomblé Gêge-Nagô, Congo-Angola, de Caboclo in Bahia and Sergipe, and Macumba in Rio de Janeiro), Xangô (Pernambuco), Tambor de Mina (Maranhão), Batuque (Pará), Pajelança (Amazonas), and others, are specific to certain areas. In varying degrees, they recognize aspects of the African Yorùbá and Fon pantheon and the basic beliefs and practices of traditional African religions.

Animism, divination, initiation, ancestor worship, offerings to deities, ritual use of sacred plants, ritual music and dance, and specific social hierarchical organization prevail in all Afro-Brazilian religious communities. In Brazil, African religions underwent multiple transformations: on the one hand, Yorùbá-Fon religions (of the *orixá* / *vodun* complex) exerted considerable influence on Bantu (Congo-Angola) religions; on the other hand, Roman Catholicism, imposed on slaves, blended in varying degrees with African beliefs—which explains the so-called syncretism of Afro-Brazilian religions.

Candomblé

In Candomblé, the leader, known as *babalorixá* or *pai de santo* if a man, or *ialorixá* or *mãe de santo* if a woman, assumes full responsibility in general liturgical matters and in the musical and choreographic training of the initiates and their subsequent position in the center. As the ultimate authority in the knowledge of music and dance, he or she usually leads the performance of the proper sequence of songs. This power emanates primarily from ritual knowledge, including music and dance, in addition to a complex of esoteric knowledge of the precepts operating in the ceremonies.

The music of the Gêge-Nagô groups retains a strongly Yorùbá style, both in the pentatonic and hexatonic melodic structures and in the rhythmic organization of the accompaniment. Overlapping responsorial singing prevails, with solo vocal lines performed in general by the cult leader, the master drummer, or less frequently by any of the official civil protectors of the group, known as *ogans*. Monophonic choral responses are provided by the initiates and any members of the congregation, male and female, who may wish to participate. The lyrics and most ritual speech are still in the Yorùbá and Fon languages, though these languages are not spoken in Brazil as a rule, and few participants can give a word-for-word translation of the texts, though they know the overall meaning and function of the songs. Portuguese dominates in Candomblé de Caboclo and Umbanda.

The musical repertoires originate from the association of specific songs with specific deities, with all private and public ceremonies, and within each ceremony with a rigorous sequence of ritual events. Each event or gesture has its corresponding songs. Repertoires are classified according to their ritual functions: botanical songs, sacrificial songs, songs of offering, songs for calling the gods, songs for sending them away, and so on. The ritual power of musical sounds, combined with the liturgical significance of lyrics as components of myths, explains the length and complexity of Candomblé ritual songs.

The rhythmic structure of Candomblé music reveals a typically African sense of rhythm, one whereby regular motoric, unchangeable parts are contrasted with improvised parts. Ritual drumming occurs with sung performances and in solos. Specific rhythmic patterns are associated with specific gods, such as *alujá* for Xangô (god of thunder and fire), *bravum* for Ogum (warrior deity and god of metal tools), and *igbim* for Oxalá (god of creation). To each rhythm corresponds a given choreography, associated with a specific god. The interlocking rhythmic organization common in traditional West African and Afro-Cuban religious music does not prevail in Brazil; however, the African type of hemiola is quite frequent. Cone-shaped, single-headed drums, known in Bahia as *atabaques*, are played in a battery of three sizes (figure 1). The largest, *rum*, is played with a stick and a bare hand by the master drummer, who, by improvising, shapes the ritual dance. The middle-sized drum (the *rumpi*) and the smallest (the *lê*), played with sticks in Gêge-Nagô music, perform standard, unchanging patterns. The double bell (*agogô*), played with a metal stick, completes the accompanying ensemble. As a symbol of communication with the *orixás* (deities), the drums must go through a sort of baptism before they can be used in ritual contexts. The sacred role of drummers (*alabês*) is recognized by means of a ceremony of confirmation. The drummers' primary function is to call gods, hence to bring about initiates' spirit possession, but drummers themselves never fall into trance while drumming.

Figure 1 Atabaques drums for Candomblé: *from left,* the *rum,* the *rumpi,* and the *lê.* These drums are from an Angolan ceremony, celebrating a woman's seven years of training as a medium for *lansa* (*orixá*) and her installation into the community.
Photo by Colleen M. Haas, 2006.

Umbanda

Since the 1950s, Brazilian religious music has gained a greater following as a result of the countrywide popularity of Umbanda, the religion that combines Candomblé beliefs, popular Roman Catholicism, spiritualism, and Kardecism, a Brazilian spiritualist movement, based on the writings of Allan Kardec. Umbanda music displays stylistic changes that illustrate how completely national values permeate strong regional and urban cultural settings. It caters to all segments of urban society, especially the lower middle class, by relying on a nationally omnipresent and familiar style, the folk-urban type of dance-music most readily associated with the samba [see BRAZIL: CENTRAL AND SOUTHERN AREAS].

In contrast to traditional Candomblé religions, the repertoire of Umbanda music is in constant elaboration, albeit stylistically restricted, but this stylistic limitation appears effective in attracting worshippers from all social strata. In effect, Caboclo, Umbanda, and their expressive means, mostly music and dance, may be the most important factors contributing to the cultural and regional integration of Brazil after the 1960s.

Secular Musical Traditions

The ancestry of secular traditions is not always easily established whenever the elements of a given musical genre and of specific sociocultural contexts of performance cannot be unequivocally related to an African derivation. Regardless of origin, one should consider traditions that are fully integrated in contemporary musicmaking among self-defined Afro-Brazilian communities. Criteria of use, function, origin, and structure define the identification of traditions.

"Sacred" and "secular" are relative concepts, especially in Afro-Brazilian culture, in which songs and dances functioning outside a religious context frequently refer to sacred topics. As in Africa, religion sustains expressive culture in all its dimensions.

Capoeira

The game-dance known as *capoeira* (figure 2) is considered by some to have come from Angola, and by others to have been the creation of Brazilian slaves. Most probably, it is a local elaboration of some African model. From a game-fight believed to have been practiced by slaves during resting periods in the fields, it developed into a martial art with subtle choreographic movements and rules—a well-defined musical repertoire of songs and accompanimental rhythms. It originated in Bahia, but has reached other major coastal cities, especially since the 1940s, and it has become a martial art taught in military schools. The traditional dance is known as *capoeira Angola*—a term that gives a linguistic justification to believers in the Angolese origin. The choreographic development involves a series of figures known as *golpes*, in which a swaying motion (*ginga*) is fundamental. Pairs of male dancer-fighters (*capoeiristas*) perform figures that simulate motions of attack and defense (using the feet only), plus head-over-heels turns. The synchronization of movements between the attack of one dancer and the defense of the other, and vice versa, can be remarkable.

Capoeira is accompanied by an ensemble of a musical bow (*berimbau de barriga*), a tambourine (*pandeiro*), a double bell (*agogô*), and at least one drum (*atabaque*); the singing is responsorial. The main instrument, the *berimbau*, has a calabash resonator and is played by a wooden stick with a basket rattle (*caxixí*). By using a coin as a bridge, the player of the *berimbau* can produce two distinct pitches (usually a second apart), but the simultaneous performance of several bows of different sizes allows multipart and harmonic textures. Specific rhythmic patterns (*toques*) include the *São Bento grande*, the *São Bento pequeno*, the *lúna*, the *Santa Maria*, the *Angola*, and the *cavalaria*, with specific functions and references to the dance. They differ mostly in tempo, rather than in structure.

Capoeira songs—some 139 have been collected—constitute a rich source of Afro-Bahian expressive culture relating to slavery, the local lingo, and poetics. Except for the "hymn of the *capoeira*" and litanies (*ladainhas*), the repertoire of *capoeira* songs borrows a great deal from other repertoires, such as children's game songs. Other songs, such as "*Santa Maria, mãe de Deus*" ('St. Mary, mother of God'), invoke religious themes and figures.

Dramatic Dances

Originating in missionaries' activities during the early colonization of the country, dramatic dances (*bailados*) have survived in many Brazilian communities of the Northeast. These dances include processions and actual dramatic representation, with numerous characters, spoken dialogues, songs, and dances, accompanied by small instrumental ensembles. The major themes of such dramatic dances relate to the Iberian medieval catechistic theater, including conversion, resurrection, and battle scenes between Christians and infidels (Moors).

The Bumba-meu-boi

The *bumba-meu-boi*, perhaps the most popular of all folk dramas, is known and practiced in various styles

Figure 2 A *capoeira* group performs, Salvador, Bahia,1996. *Photo by Max Brandt.*

in several parts of the country, north and south; it has its origins in the triethnic heritage, but its Afro-Brazilian elements are prominent in the northeastern and northern states. The main character is the bull (*boi*), representing for some an African totemic survival. The dramatic action enacts regional variants of a legend concerning characters of the colonial period: the Portuguese master; the black slave (variously named Mateus or Francisco); his wife, Catarina; the captain (*cavalo marinho*); and others. Fantastic figures and animals participate, but only human characters sing. According to Mário de Andrade (1982), the dance includes fixed and variable elements, the former consisting of the main characters' entrances and dances, the latter involving the secondary characters. Most of the songs exhibit characteristic elements of mestizo folk music, including the style of cattle-herding songs known as *aboios*.

Documentation of the dance in Maranhão (Kazadi wa Mukuna 1994) reveals the presence of three distinct styles: the *boi de zabumba* (*zabumba* is a double-headed bass drum), the *boi de matraca* (*matraca* is a type of wooden rattle), and the *boi de orquestra* (mostly brass-band instruments). Of these, the first is considered to represent a truly Afro-Brazilian tradition, not only in its instrumentation (including, besides the *zabumba*, the friction drum [*tambor onça*] and other percussion instruments), but also in its musical and choreographic structures. The criticism of the dominating characters, hence of the ruling class, evidenced in the comic scenes of the bull's death and resurrection, is a clue that the drama originated in slave culture.

Social Dances

Dance music from Afro-Brazilian traditions includes a variety of genres and instrumental ensembles. Quite frequently, collective singing is part of such genres, often combined with dancing. The performance of this music occurs on numerous social occasions, from spontaneous, informal performances in party gatherings to formal contexts associated with cyclical celebrations of life.

The Afro-Brazilian contribution to and influence on Brazilian folk dances is reflected in the number of specific Afro-Brazilian dances and the Brazilianization—that is, Afro-Brazilianization—of European dances, an important aspect of Brazilian urban popular music. The commonest traits of African-derived choreographic structures in folkloric dance are circular formation, frequently with solo dancers, and the presence of *umbigada* (from Portuguese *umbigo* 'navel'), the bumping of dancers' navels, signifying an invitation to the dance or challenge.

In African culture, music and dance are often inseparable—which might explain why the name of a dance is used to refer to the music it accompanies. Among the dances of predominantly Brazilian blacks are the *batuque* and the samba, the *caxambu*, the *jongo*, the *côco*, the *baiano* (*baião*), and the former *lundu* and *sarambeque*, all with numerous regional names. Two are considered here.

The Samba

Many regional and temporal varieties of samba exist. As a folk dance, it was formerly meaningful, but its salience has diminished in most of the country because of the popularity of other types of urban samba styles. In southern-central areas, the folk samba is known as *samba-lenço*, *samba da roda*, and *samba campineiro*. The choreographic arrangement of the *samba-lenço*—dancers with a kerchief (*lenço*) in their hand—resembles the old *batuque*, again in circular formation. With texts in quatrains, the songs are performed in parallel thirds with snare drum and tambourine accompaniment. Melodies are usually eight bars long, in duple meter with an anacrusis, and have a range of up to an octave, a descending motion with repeated notes, and isometric rhythm. The accompaniment exhibits typical Afro-Brazilian syncopation.

The dance itself stresses collectivity—which explains the absence of the *umbigada*. Besides the instrumentalists (who also dance), the main participants are women. The *samba de roda* has lost its former importance in São Paulo, but in the Northeast, especially in Bahia, it remains the most popular social dance. As a round dance involving soloists, it is usually performed responsorially, with frequent overlapping between the vocal soloist and the choral response.

The Bahian *samba de viola* is a *samba de roda* from a choreographic standpoint, but *violas* (various sizes of guitars, with five double-stringed courses as a rule) are the central instruments of the ensemble, completed by a *prato-e-faca* 'plate and knife,' a *pandeiro*, a triangle, an occasional *atabaque*, and handclapping. The lyrics set this samba apart from others, in their extreme eclecticism in form and subject. In the 1980s and 1990s, the tradition of *samba de viola* lost its former importance and was known and performed by only a handful of older musicians.

The Coconut

The coconut (*côco*) is a dance of poorer people in the North and Northeast. Its name derives from the fact that the dance is commonly accompanied by clapping with hands cupped to create a low-pitched sound, like that of a coconut shell. Sometimes a drum or a rattle may be used, in which case the dance is named after the instrument: *côco-de-ganzá* (shaker), *côco-de-mugonguê* (drum), and so on. In the northern states, different names refer to the type of song associated with the coconut, such as *côco-de-décima*, *côco-de-embolada*, and *côco-desafio*. The choreographic structure dictates the alternation of stanza and refrain in the song: a solo dancer in the middle of the circle improvises a stanza and is answered by the other dancers. A frequent feature of coconut-song melodies (also present in *côco-de-embolada*) is the peculiar rhythm of short durations (usually sixteenth notes in 2/4 time) repeated continually, resulting in exciting ostinatos.

Urban Popular Music in Bahia

Urban popular music found its most famous early cultivators in Rio de Janeiro [see BRAZIL: CENTRAL AND SOUTHERN AREAS], but the state of Bahia has produced its share of popular musicians and styles. As early as the mid-1950s, the Afro-Bahian Dorival Caymmi, through his fisherman or beach songs (*canções praieiras*) and his sambas (even before the advent of bossa nova), created an innovative style based on direct, empathetic references to Afro-Bahian folklore and music. For decades, his popularity throughout the country remained high, perhaps because he conveyed even to listeners alien to Bahia the essence of his cultural experience as an Afro-Bahian practitioner of Candomblé and a cultivator of the most modern popular genres and styles. In addition, his lyrics, deeply rooted in the African linguistic and emotional tradition of his native state, represent a chief asset of his creativity.

The city of Salvador, Bahia (figure 3), the traditional bastion of Afro-Brazilian artistic expression, has become a stronghold of popular-music developments since the 1960s. Besides the avant-garde movement of *tropicália*, whose members were mostly Bahians, a new carnival music appeared in the 1970s and 1980s, when the Afro-Bahian phenomena of *afoxé*, *carnaval ijexá*, and *bloco afro* had significant sociopolitical and economic repercussions and the traditional music and culture of Candomblé played an important role as a creative source and force in the concept of Afro-Brazilian ethnicity. The emergence of an African consciousness among young people of African descent represents a social and human history of great significance, in which traditional music has had a fundamental function in the movement of ethnic and political vindication. Local black and mestizo young people have contributed to the re-Africanization of carnival. The new black-consciousness movement, though it has much to do with the ideology of negritude, was never based on the cultural incorporation of contemporary African elements; rather, it originated in a new interpretation and rendition of the most traditional elements of Afro-Bahian culture. It would appear more accurate, therefore, to refer to a re-Afro-Brazilianization within a new concern for validating contemporary black culture and expressing a new ethnicity.

In the 1970s, the revitalization of the Afro-Bahian carnival associations called *afoxés* gave the new black movement a reference point. *Afoxés* whose members were devotees of Candomblé represented the first attempts in Bahia to transfer to the street, during carnival, the aura of the mythical world. The name

Figure 3 The Pelourinho, the historic district of Salvador, is a hotbed for music, especially the newest styles coming out of Bahia. The *bloco* Olodum has been based here since its founding, as have Cortejo Afro and Banda Didá.
Photo by Colleen M. Haas, 2006.

of the oldest practicing *afoxé*, Filhos de Gandhi (Sons of Gandhi), paid homage to the great statesman a few months after his assassination (1948) and revealed the ideological affinity of the group with Gandhi's anticolonialism, philosophy of nonviolence, and activism against European domination. Traditionally, the music performed in the carnival *afoxé* groups was actually Candomblé music, specifically *ijexá* songs and rhythms. Filhos de Gandhi developed its own music, but retained key stylistic features of *ijexá* music.

By extension, the new carnival of the 1970s and 1980s became known as *carnaval ijexá*, primarily to establish a direct relationship with some of the most essential aspects of Afro-Brazilian culture. In a general sense, the word *ijexá* implied at that time Afro-Bahian culture associated with Candomblé, as the term, *ijexá* designates a specific body of musical patterns for particular *orixas* and musically moves in a slow, stately fashion. Several lyrics composed for *afoxés* reference *ijexá* as a rhythm, a style, and/or a dance.

Beginning in the mid-1970s, new carnival organizations called *blocos afro* began to appear. The first one, founded in 1974, bore the linguistically and politically significant name Ilê Aiyê (from Yorùbá *ilê* 'house, temple' and *aiyê* 'real world' in Yorùbá cosmovision and mythology, as opposed to Yorùbá *orum* 'supernatural world'). At first, Ilê Aiyê barred white people's participation, and its compositions constantly mentioned the *aiyê* as the living, exciting, beautiful world of black people. The themes "black is beautiful" and "the living world is the black

world" became part of the ideological manifesto of *blocos afro* (figure 4). Perhaps reinforced by the appearance of the militant political group known as Movimento Negro Unificado (MNU), *blocos afro* took on the form of grassroots activism in the 1980s. Their support of the MNU, however, was more a symbol of black identity and power than a direct political militancy or affiliation. The songs of *blocos afro* evoked the Afrocentricity of their origins, and addressed issues of racism and socioeconomic injustice. The creation of a new aesthetic involved the imitation and transformation of African and Afro-Caribbean models of music, dance, and dressing, real or imagined. The choice of instruments was limited to drums—several *surdos* (low pitched), *repiques* (high pitched), and *tarols* (snare drums)—and other percussion, supporting a responsorial vocal structure. At first, the basic rhythmic organization, known as the *toque afro-primitivo*, or *samba-afro* consisted of a slow-to-moderate-tempo samba in a rich and forceful percussive texture. *Bloco afro* songs referred to Afro-Brazilian and other Afro-diasporal subjects, always expressing the black world, its history, and its problems and accomplishments.

With the new *afoxés* and *blocos afro*, the direct relationship to Candomblé diminished considerably, since the young leaders were no longer Candomblé priests, the musicians were not necessarily Candomblé drummers, and the songs no longer came from liturgical repertoires. The members of the new groups, however, did not fail to recognize and adhere to some aspects of Candomblé traditions, as some members are Candomblé devotees or grew up in

Figure 4 Ilê Aiyê perform at Carnival in Salvador, Bahia, 2006. Founded in the mid-1970s in the Liberdade neighborhood of Bahia, the group has long incorporated a "black is beautiful" theme into its work. *Photo by Colleen M. Haas.*

these religious communities. Before celebrating an important festivity (such as carnival), people sometimes perform rituals of offering to the *orixás* in the name of the groups. Some Candomblé rhythms have been incorporated into *bloco afro*'s rhythmic sections. In general, though, whether or not they are close to the Afro-Bahian religions, leaders of *blocos afro* are aware of and in tune with Candomblé s traditional function as a center of cultural resistance and of social and ethnic identity.

Among the Afro groups that emerged in the 1980s (including Araketu, Badauê, Ebony, Malê Debalê, and Muzenza) the most commercially successful *bloco afro* undoubtedly has been Olodum, founded in 1979 by former members of Ilê Aiyê. Musically innovative, Olodum had by the mid-1980s introduced different patterns into its fundamental samba beat. These patterns recalled Afro-Caribbean rhythms (merengue, salsa), but the influence of Jamaican reggae was so strong that, the new patterns of drumming having acquired the interlocking structure of samba and Afro-Caribbean rhythms, Olodum's sound became known as samba-reggae. Cuban *timbales* were incorporated into Olodum. Ideologically, the reference to Jamaica claimed affinity and solidarity with the Afro-Bahian movement. Through reggae and Rastafarianism, Jamaican black culture had been recognized the world over, and Bob Marley and Jimmy Cliff were idols of Afro-Bahian youths. Eventually Olodum created its own Banda Reggae (Reggae Band), which continues to tour extensively. The success of Olodum's sociopolitical program—schools, shelters and jobs for street children, community services—reflected the vision and determination of the group's leaders, and has been financially supported by Olodum's participation in the world music industry. Though its first musical success was local, its international popularity, translated into multimillion-dollar activity in a few years, has caused disputes among many regarding their loyalty or departure from their ideological beginnings. Nevertheless, Olodum continues its social work and musical performing, and is internationally recognized as a marker of contemporary Brazilian popular music.

—Adapted from an article by Gerard Béhague

Bibliography

Almeida, Renato. 1942. *História da música brasileira.* 2nd ed. Rio de Janeiro: F. Briguiet.

Andrade, Mário de. 1982. *Danças dramáticas do Brasil.* 3 vols. Belo Horizonte, Brazil: Itatiaia.

Béhague, Gerard. 1979. *Music in Latin America: An Introduction.* Englewood Cliffs, N.J.: Prentice Hall.

Carvalho, José Jorge de. 1994. *The Multiplicity of Black Identities in Brazilian Popular Music.* Brasilia: Universidade de Brasilia.

Kazadi wa Mukuna. 1994. "Sotaques: Style and Ethnicity in a Brazilian Folk Drama." In *Music and Black Ethnicity: The Caribbean and South America,* edited by Gerard Behague, 207–224. Miami: North-South Center, University of Miami.

Perrone, Charles. 1989. *Masters of Contemporary Brazilian Song: MPB 1965–1985.* Austin: University of Texas Press.

Risério, Antonio. 1981. *Carnaval Ijexá: notas sobre afoxés e blocos do novo carnaval afrobaiano.* Salvador: Editora Corrupio.

Colombia

Afro-Colombian Popular Music

Afro-Colombians have contributed extensively to Colombian popular music. Of a population of 44 million in Colombia, an estimated 16 to 24 percent are of African descent, and Colombia thus has the third largest black population in the Western Hemisphere, after the United States and Brazil. Africans have long been in Colombia: Hispanified blacks accompanied the conquistadors in their first explorations of the country, and the importation of enslaved Africans had become widespread by 1600. The majority of these people came to Colombia from western and central Africa. They arrived in the Caribbean port of Cartagena, and were put to work on cattle ranches and plantations throughout the Caribbean, as boatsmen on the Cauca and Magdalena rivers, and as gold miners along the Pacific coast. Also, an English-speaking, Protestant black population inhabits the Caribbean islands of San Andrés and Providencia, Colombian possessions originally settled by the English.

The traditional musics that arose in these areas show strong African influence, with varying degrees of influence from European and indigenous musical forms. Musics such as *currulao*, from the mostly black Pacific coast, and the *lumbalú*, from San Basilio de Palenque (a village founded by runaway slaves), are markedly African; forms such as *gaita*, from the Caribbean coast, have an African rhythmic base and indigenous-derived flutes; the *chirimía* of the northern Pacific Chocó Province is essentially a black appropriation of the European brass band; and Andean *bambuco* is a mestizo stringband tradition that many scholars believe developed from an Afro-Colombian rhythmic base.

Of present-day Afro-Colombian musics, some are modernizations of traditional music styles; others are adoptions of international black musical forms into Colombian contexts; still others are innovative, self-conscious fusions of traditional and modern, local and cosmopolitan, black and nonblack musical forms.

Urbanized Traditional Forms

Cumbia

Cumbia, the best-known Afro-Colombian popular music, is a modernized traditional musical style, a synthesis of Caribbean traditional musics such as *porro*, *gaita*, and folkloric *cumbia*. These genres feature complex polyrhythms played on a hand drum called *alegre*, a timekeeping drum called *llamador*, and a bass drum called *tambora*, accompanied by a large maraca called *maracón* or a tubular shaker called *guache*, voices, and flutes such as the *gaita* or the *caña de millo*. The raucous brass bands of the Caribbean coast, a major element in local *fiestas* since the late nineteenth century, adopted some of these genres into their repertoire. These genres were arranged for a large-band format (based on the big bands of the swing era) in the mid-twentieth century by Lucho Bermúdez (1912–1994; known as "the Colombian Benny Goodman"), Pacho Galán (1906–1988), and others, with instruments such as drumsets and congas replacing the traditional percussion, and with clarinet-led winds replacing the melodic instruments. This period saw the introduction of the *merecumbé*, a fusion of cumbia with Dominican *merengue*. *Cumbia* was further modernized in the 1970s, with the replacement of the winds with electric pianos and keyboards, and in some cases with the borrowing of the accordion from *vallenato* music. This modern *cumbia*, exemplified by the Sonora Dinamita and other groups, has proved immensely popular in other Latin American countries, particularly Mexico, the Andean nations, and Argentina.

Vallenato

Vallenato, dating from around 1900, is associated with the town of Valledupar, from which it gets its name, although the site of its origin is disputed. With a lyrical style inherited from archaic Spanish oral poetry and worksongs, its black roots are crystallized in the *paseo*, *merengue*, *son*, and *puya* (all subgenres of *vallenato*) and the rhythmic interactions among a small drum (*vallenato caja*), the scraper called *guacharaca*, and an accordion (or in some early versions, a guitar). The more African-derived subgenres, *merengue* and *puya*, have largely disappeared from the modern *vallenato* repertoire as the music has become more urbanized—a process in which local themes have yielded to the more universal subject of love, and the instrumentation has come to include the electric bass and sometimes keyboards. Nonetheless, *vallenato* is enormously popular among black and nonblack Colombians, particularly in the Caribbean. Several well-known modern *vallenato* performers, such as Diomedes Díaz (b. 1957) and Kaleth Morales (1984–2005), and artists of the older generation such as Alejo Durán (1919–1989), are of black ancestry. Roots-oriented projects, like white artist Carlos Vives' (b. 1961) fusion of rock with traditional *vallenato*, have occasionally emphasized the African elements of the music. *Vallenato* has become the most popular local music in Colombia, and has made deep inroads in other countries, particularly Mexico.

Currulao

The traditional music of the rural southern Pacific coast, commonly called *currulao*, is among the most clearly African-derived in the country (figure 1). Its traditional format features a wooden *marimba* tuned to a scale found on African xylophones, bass drums called *bombos*, hand drums called *cununos*, tubular shakers called *guasás*, and the singing of elderly women called *cantadoras*. The genre was urbanized in the late 1960s, in particular by Enrique Urbano Tenorio (1920–2007; figure 2), known as "Peregoyo," and his group, the Combo Vacaná, from the city of Buenaventura, and to a lesser extent by the singer Tito Cortés, from the city of Tumaco. Peregoyo's band blended the cadences of *currulao* rhythms with the modern *cumbia*, and particularly the Afro-Cuban rhythms of the *mambo* and the Cuban *son*, in a format that included winds and electric bass and guitar. Singer "Caballito" Garcés, from Tumaco, and Petronio "Cuco" Álvarez, from Buenaventura, played guitar, sang, and composed songs, helping popularize the *currulao* as a guitar genre. The resulting style never attained the popularity of modern *cumbia*, but it has received more attention in recent years, as groups like Grupo Naidy and Grupo

Socavón have made recordings of traditional *currulao*. Some younger artists from the Pacific coast, particularly *marimba*-player Hugo Candelario González (b. 1967) and his Grupo Bahía, as well as the musicians in Grupo Orilla, Grupo Experiencia,

Figure 2 Currulao *pioneer Enrique Urbano Tenorio, "Peregoyo," Cali, 2002.*
Photo by Michael Birenbaum Quintero.

Figure 1 Members of the Torres family and the group Pura Sangre play *currulao* near Guapi, Cauca Province, Colombia, 2003. The instruments, *from left*: a *cununo* (hanging), two *bombos*, another *cununo*, and the *marimba*.
Photo by Michael Birenbaum Quintero.

and others—mostly black artists born on the Pacific coast and based in the city of Cali—have begun to fuse traditional *currulao* with Afro-Cuban dance musics such as salsa and *timba*, including the ancestral *marimba* alongside electric bass and keyboards and winds in a way that embraces innovation and the explicit recognition of traditional forms.

Chirimía

Chirimía, a genre developed in the northern Pacific province of Chocó, has been subject to similar processes of roots-conscious modernization. It is a brass-band music, including a bass drum (*tambora*), a snare drum, tin cymbals, and one or two clarinets, backed up by a small tuba called a euphonium. In the early twentieth century, this format replaced an older instrumentation, which featured percussion and homemade flutes. Beginning in the mid-1990s, artists from Chocó began to combine electric keyboards, basses, and drumsets with an expanded wind section, emphasizing more Caribbean-influenced local rhythms, such as *aguabajo* and *abosao*, and imported genres, like salsa, over the more archaic *polkas* and *mazurkas* that had entered the repertoire alongside the brass instruments. The result is the boisterous, bawdy, and eminently danceable genre *tecno-chirimía*, which has begun to enter the mainstream in the hands of artists like La Contundencia and Grupo Saboreo and more experimental groups like Bambazulú.

Hybrid and Cosmopolitan Forms

Cuban Influence: Son and Salsa

Afro-Cuban music has long influenced black Colombians. Beginning in the 1920s, musicians in the Caribbean and in Chocó Province began forming sextets (*sextetos*), featuring some combination of lead and backing vocals, bongos, clave, maracas, a *marímbula* (a box fitted with metal keys, like the African *mbira*), a scraper (like the *guacharaca* or the Caribbean *güiro*), and sometimes a large hand drum. Some of these groups, such as Sexteto Tabalá, from the Caribbean town of Palenque, and the Sexteto Murindó, from Chocó, continue to this day. More-modern forms of Afro-Cuban music were influential in Colombian cities with a large black population, such as Barranquilla, on the Caribbean coast, and Cali, which imported salsa through the nearby Pacific coast city of Buenaventura. Cali still identifies itself as the capital of salsa—a title it claims as the home of numerous salsa groups and as the originator of the buoyant and energetic Cali salsa dance-style. The Colombian salsa movement was spearheaded by

black groups such as Grupo Niche and Orquesta Guayacán (Cali-based, but of Chocó origin) and Joe Arroyo (b. 1955) of Cartagena, and is carried on by younger exponents, such as Jimmy Saa and Yuri Buenaventura (both of Buenaventura). These musicians have created a uniquely Afro-Colombian style of salsa, with references to black history, other Afro-Colombian musical styles, and the everyday lives of black Colombians.

African Pop in Colombia: Champeta

Another important Afro-Colombian musical form is the Caribbean coastal music called *champeta* and *terapia*. Its origins lie in a system of dueling sound systems called *picós*, which, as in Jamaican sound-system culture, compete for dancing audiences' loyalties on the basis of volume and songs only they possess. In their search for unusual records, sailors in Cartagena began bringing home records from other parts of the Caribbean and even Africa, introducing the Colombian Caribbean to such genres as Congolese *soukous*, South African *mbaqanga*, Senegalese *mbalax*, and Nigerian *juju* and *highlife*. [See Popular Music in the Congos, Black Popular Music in South Africa, and Yorùbá Popular Music in the Africa section.] Soon, local artists, such as the group Anne Zwing, Louis Towers, and Elio Boom, began to make Spanish-language covers of these musics, accompanied by the synthesizers that are part of the *picós*, to create a new musical form. Younger singers, such as Álvaro el Bárbaro, El Afinaíto, Sayayín, Mr. Black, Cándido Perez, and Mr. Boogaloo, have popularized *champeta* throughout the western Caribbean, from Venezuela into Central America. It continues to be, alongside *vallenato*, the music of choice of the black working class in the Colombian Caribbean.

Hip-hop and Reggaetón

Young black Colombians have been particularly inspired by hip-hop and *reggaetón*. In the 1990s, hip-hop became an important means for marginalized Afro-Colombian youth in the cities to protest their situation. The Panamanian dancehall reggae of the 1980s was popular in Colombia, but the boom of Puerto Rican *reggaetón* has inspired a new crop of artists, who have tended to be more dance oriented, though some artists slip easily between the styles and reference social and more-playful themes in their music. Many of the more-recent black exponents of rap and *reggaetón* are from the Pacific coast. They include Choc Quib Town (figure 3), from Chocó; Jr. Jeim and Element Black, from Buenaventura; Candyman, from Cali; and Leka el Poeta, Misterioso, and Master Boys, from Tumaco. Many

Figure 3 Choc Quib Town at the Rap al Parque Festival in Bogotá, 2003. *Photo by Christopher Dennis.*

of these artists consciously represent Afro-Colombian and specifically Pacific themes, musical styles, and slang in their work.

Progressive Fusion

As a direct result of a burgeoning Afro-Colombian political movement, the 1990s saw a sudden visibilization of Colombia's black population with the adoption of a multicultural national identity in the 1991 constitution and the legalization of certain rights for Afro-Colombian communities in the 1993 "Law of Negritudes." As multiculturalism grew, traditional Afro-Colombian music began to be represented more in national musical festivals and other important spaces. Colombian musicians, both black and nonblack, began to assimilate these folkloric musics, particularly traditional *cumbia* and *currulao*, into musical fusions involving cosmopolitan elements such as rock, jazz, funk, punk, reggae, rap, and electronic music. This trend toward fusion, exemplified by young, Bogotá-based, mixed-race groups like La Mojarra Eléctrica, Curupira, Kilombo, and Tumbacatre, and the all-black rap group Choc Quib Town of Chocó, explodes the boundaries among pop, avant-garde, and traditional musics.

The State of Afro-Colombian Popular Music

In the early twenty-first century, Afro-Colombian popular music is probably more prominent than it has ever been in Colombia; even traditional Afro-Colombian music has begun to be recorded commercially. Nonetheless, aside from those popular musics, such as *cumbia*, *vallenato*, and certain examples of Colombian salsa, in which black musical elements have been most diluted, the new trends in Afro-Colombian popular music are largely unknown outside of Colombia and indeed within much of Colombia itself. This is largely because the Colombian mass media tend to ignore black popular musics, which accordingly circulate in underground, avant-garde, or highly localized circuits. This situation makes obtaining the latest releases difficult outside Colombia, and makes the genres of Afro-Colombian popular music among the best-kept secrets of the musical world.

—*By Michael Birenbaum Quintero*

Bibliography

Béhague, Gerard, George List, and Lise Waxer. 2001. "Colombia." *The New Grove Encyclopedia of Music and Musicians*, edited by Stanley Sadie and John Tyrell, volume 6, 134–149. London: Macmillan.

Birenbaum Quintero, Michael. "Liner notes." *Arriba suena marimba, Currulao Marimba from Colombia by Grupo Naidy*, SFW 40514 Smithsonian Folkways Records (2005).

Child, John. 2001a. "Discographic Profile: Grupo Niche." *Descarga Journal*, http://www.descarga.com/cgi-bin/db/archives/Profile64?i7Nfd69e;;1752 (accessed on April 30, 2007).

———. 2001b. "Discographic Profile: Guayacán Orquesta." *Descarga Journal*, http://www.descarga.com/cgi-bin/db/archives/Profile65?i7Nfd69e;;1753 (accessed on April 30, 2007).

List, George. 1983. *Music and Poetry in a Colombian Village: A Tri-Cultural Heritage*. Bloomington: Indiana University Press.

Pacini Hernández, Deborah. 1996. "Sound Systems, World Beat, and Diasporan Identity in Cartagena, Colombia." *Diaspora: A Journal of Transnational Studies* 5(3):429–466.

Silva, Lucas. "Currulao: A Musical Gateway between Africa and Colombia." http://www.otrabandarecords.com/otb_05.html (accessed on April 30, 2007).

Wade, Peter. 1999. "Working Culture: Making Cultural Identities in Cali, Colombia." *Current Anthropology*. 40(4):449–471.

——. 2000. *Music, Race, and Nation:* Música Tropical *in Colombia*. Chicago and London: The University of Chicago Press.

——. 2005. "Colombia" In *The Continuum Encyclopedia of Popular Music of the World*. Vol. 3. *Caribbean and Latin America*, edited by John Shepherd, David Horn, and Dave Laing, 297–304. New York, London: Continuum Books.

Waxer, Lise. 2002. *The City of Musical Memory: Salsa, Record Grooves, and Popular Culture in Cali, Colombia*. Middletown, Conn.: Wesleyan University Press.

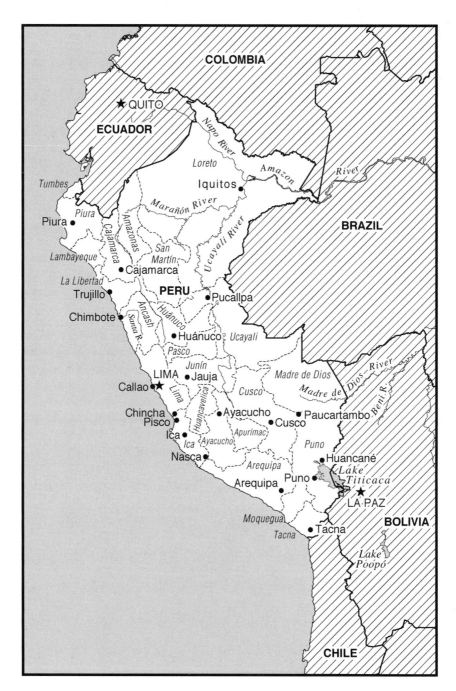

Peru

Peru

Peru is a country of diverse geographical areas, languages, races, and cultural traditions. It is the third-largest nation in South America, with more than 28 million inhabitants distributed within its coastal, Andean, and Amazonian areas. It borders Ecuador and Colombia to the north, Brazil and Bolivia to the east, Chile to the south, and the Pacific Ocean to the west. Spanish, Quechua (the official language of the Inca Empire) and Aymara are the principal languages spoken in Peru, along with numerous Amazonian languages.

The pre-Hispanic cultural heritage of Peru can be traced back to about 1400 B.C.E., when the Chavín culture surged in the central Andes of Peru. Throughout the centuries after its decline, there emerged successive and prosperous cultures, all of which the Inca Empire subdued in the 1400s. The Inca Empire stretched from northern Ecuador to central Chile. The Spanish incursion of the 1500s put an abrupt end to the autonomous development of indigenous cultures in coastal and Andean Peru. The colonial system introduced an era of economic exploitation of the Peruvian Indians through such institutions as the *encomienda*, a system by which land and peasants were governed by Spanish landlords, the *mita* (coercive labor for the colonial administration), and the collection of forced tribute (Indian contributions in kind to the Spanish crown). With these tactics, ideological struggles against indigenous religious practices, such as the extirpation-of-idolatries campaign conducted by the Spanish clergy in the 1600s, were enforced. These actions and the diseases brought by Europeans caused a dramatic depopulation of indigenous peoples.

Distinctive social and ethnic groups began to emerge soon after Europeans arrived. A solid difference was made between Spanish settlers born on the Iberian Peninsula and those born in the colonies; the latter, labeled creole (*criollo*), were considered socially inferior to the former. Early miscegenation between Spanish men and Indian women created a mestizo racial group, which during most of the colonial period occupied an ambivalent social position between Spanish and Indian. The importation of African slaves added another ethnic dimension to the colonial social framework.

The modern nation of Peru resulted from the political and economic independence of the creoles from Spanish jurisdiction in 1821, after which a new sector of rich and influential plantation owners replaced the *encomenderos*. The political and economic structures of the new nation remained in the same hands, and the subordination of Peruvian Indians and mestizos persisted.

In pre-Hispanic Peru, indigenous cultures had occupied the coast and the mountains, but during the colonial domination, Spaniards settled mostly in the coast, while the mostly Quechua Indian peasants (Aymara in the far south) inhabited primarily the Andean area. Coastal Peru became a bastion for white and creole culture (with the important presence of the black slaves, eventually liberated in 1854), whereas the Andes became a stronghold for Indian and mestizo communities. With massive migrations to the capital, Lima, beginning in the 1950s, and the economic and social consequences of the revolutionary régime of 1968–1980, which implemented radical agrarian reforms and structural changes crucial to the Peruvian economy, the geographical and cultural partition of the country began to blur. The Peruvian Amazonian area, the third important geographical area in the country, continued to be occupied by more than fifty scattered and seminomadic ethnolinguistic groups, which for centuries remained isolated from national affairs. This article discusses the musics of the Andean and coastal areas.

Musical Instruments

The Peruvian Andes
Many pre-Hispanic musical instruments, including a drum (*tinya*), flutes (*quena* or *kena* and *pinkullo*), and panpipes (*antara* and *siku*), are still played in the Peruvian Andes. European musical instruments—including the guitar, the accordion, the harp, and the violin—were introduced by Spaniards, but are often constructed from local materials. Since the 1890s, Andean peasants have adopted trumpets, saxophones, clarinets, and other European band instruments.

Drums (Membranophones)
Drums are named according to their sizes and localities. Local names include *tinya*, *wankara*, and the Spanish terms *bombo*, *caja*, and *tambor*. Drums range in size from a 20-cm-wide *tinya* to a 70-cm-wide *caja*.

Most are double-headed cylindrical drums. Contrasting with wind instruments (played only by men), small drums, like the *tinya*, are, as in pre-Hispanic times, played mostly by women, on any of several occasions, including music for marking animals in the central Andes. Bigger drums are played by men, mostly for accompaniment, in small or large ensembles.

Wind Instruments (Aerophones)

Traditional raft panpipes, such as the *ayarachi*, the *chiriguano*, and the *sikuri* (plural of *siku*), are always played collectively in the southern department of Puno. These panpipes, usually named after the ensemble of which they are part, are tuned to a diatonic scale. These are double-unit panpipes, designed to be played by pairing two halves, each half containing complementary pitches. One half is designated *ira* 'leader'; the other, *arca* 'follower'. The playing technique of these groups is complex. *Sikuri* ensembles consist of panpipes of different sizes. Some are tuned in octaves, whereas others (called *contras*) are tuned in fifths. An ideal orchestration would include eight different groups of instruments, but not all ensembles present all the possible combinations. Other panpipe traditions, such as those of the *ayarachi* and *chiriguano*, are subdivided in three groups, each of which is tuned to the octave. *Sikuri* and other panpipe ensembles perform intensively throughout the annual calendar of fiestas, in weddings, and at other lifecycle events, such as a child's first haircut (*corte de pelo*). In several traditions in the Puno area and in Lima among migrants from Puno, players of each half-panpipe play a drum at the same time (figure 1). Elsewhere, as with the *andara* (*antara*) in Cajamarca, a single-unit panpipe is played as a solo instrument.

Different vertical end-notched flutes (*quena*), vertical duct flutes (*pinkullo*, *tarka*), and side-blown flutes (*pito*) are widely disseminated in the Andes. The *quena* (*kena*) is usually made from cane, but sometimes from wood, and since the 1970s from plastic. Examples are usually between 25 centimeters and 120 centimeters long. They may have three to eight fingerholes. One of the most ubiquitous types, measuring 30 to 40 centimeters long, has six fingerholes in the front and a thumbhole in the back. The *quena* can be played as a solo instrument in private and contemplative situations, but in public performances it is usually played with other instruments, as in *conjuntos* in Cusco, and with large ensembles of instruments of the same type, as for *choquela* dances in Puno and carnival dances in the Colca Valley, Arequipa.

No archaeological evidence has been discovered in Peru for determining the origins of duct tubular flutes (although they existed in ancient Colombia and Mexico), but globular flutes with duct mouthpieces are found archaeologically. It is therefore generally considered that they originated during the colonial period. Today's duct flutes are most frequently made of wood or cane in sizes ranging from 30 to 120 centimeters long, and may have a variable number of fingerholes, to be stopped with the fingers of one hand or both hands. One of the commonest names for duct flutes (played with two hands) in the Peruvian Andes is *pinkullu* (also *pincullo*, *pinkillo*, *pinkuyllo*, and many other spellings), called *flauta* in many areas and *chiska* and *rayán* in Ancash. One of the most disseminated types is the three-holed

Figure 1 In a street in La Victoria, a *barrio* in Lima, a panpipe group consisting of migrants from the department of Puno and their descendants performs for an event. *Photo by Cathy Collinge Herrera, 1984.*

one-handed duct flute, played in a pipe-and-tabor mode. In northern Peru, pipe-and-tabor duct flutes are of two types, the *roncador* 'snorer', characterized by a rough sound (found in Ancash and Huánuco), and the *silbadora* 'whistler' (also *flauta*), with a mellower timbre (found in Cajamarca and La Libertad). Pipe-and-tabor players perform widely in public festivals (figure 2). They fulfill a central role in ceremonies associated with communal labor in the fields and in the construction of buildings in Junín and Ancash. In the Colca Valley, a six-hole *pinkuyllo* 120 centimeters long, played by one performer accompanied by a drum played by a woman, is used exclusively in fertility rituals. Duct flutes can be played in ensembles of instruments of the same type, including the five- and six-hole *pinkillo* in Conima, Puno; from eight to fifteen performers play them in unison, accompanied by drums.

The *tarka*, another popular duct flute, occurs only in Puno. The feature that distinguishes it from other duct flutes is that in cross-section it is hexagonal. Usually with six fingerholes, it is played in public festivals in large ensembles (*tarkeadas*), but it has been reported to be played as a solo instrument in private situations by shepherds in the mountains.

Stringed Instruments (Chordophones)

Since ancient Peruvians used no stringed instruments, it is reasonable to conclude that guitars, mandolins, *bandurrias*, harps, violins, and other European or European-inspired instruments currently in use were introduced during the colonial period. The *charango*, in certain localities also called *quirquincho* 'armadillo' and *chillador* 'screamer', is a small guitar, made of wood (figure 3) or armadillo shell. Common to southern Peru and Bolivia, it is from 23 to 45 centimeters long. It has diverse tunings and variable numbers of strings. The commonest tuning for the ten-stringed (five double courses) *charango* is the Santo Domingo (ee–aa–eE–cc–gg). The six-stringed variant usually duplicates the third string, one of which is tuned to the octave of the other. In Cusco, Andean peasants play *charangos* predominantly with a strumming style while a single string carries the melody; mestizo performers play in a plucked melodic mode, interspersed with strumming sections.

The design of the European guitar has undergone no drastic changes in its adaptation to Andean musical practices, though its tuning varies by area.

Figure 2 Two pipe-and-tabor musicians (*cajeros*) perform at the Huanchaco patronal festival in Los Baños del Inca, 1979.
Photo by Dale A. Olsen.

Figure 3 Nicanor Abarca Puma, a *charango* maker and player from Arequipa, plays a *charango de caja*, 1979. Resembling a small guitar, it has five triple courses of metal strings.
Photo by Dale A. Olsen.

Besides the standard system, tunings depend on locality, each of them with a specific name.

Spanish missionaries propagated European harps and violins throughout the Peruvian Andes, where today, both kinds of instruments are played individually or together as part of larger ensembles. In contrast with guitars and violins, harps have evolved in several ways, ranging from the triangle-shaped *arpa indigena* (figure 4) to the smaller *domingacha* type, with a pear-shaped soundbox. The Peruvian harp is diatonic, usually tuned to a C major scale. It uses from twenty-six to thirty-six metal or nylon strings and has no pedals. It is so light that it can be easily played upside down in a sling around the player's neck (thus extending high above the player's head) during processions and festivals.

Harp performance styles vary geographically. The harp can be played solo and in ensemble, where it provides bass and harmonic functions. In some areas, it is played as an accompanying percussion instrument by a *tamborero*, a person who beats his fingers on its body while someone else plucks the strings.

Figure 4 The late Fausto Dolorier Abregu, professional harpist and former professor of harp at the national school of folkloric arts, Lima, 1979.
Photo by Dale A. Olsen.

Ensembles

Andean music has adopted the accordion, widely used throughout the area but especially by *conjuntos* in Cusco, string ensembles in the Callejón de Huaylas (in Ancash), and the *estudiantina* group of stringed instruments in Puno. Wind instruments—clarinets, saxophones, trumpets, trombones, euphoniums, tubas—make up brass bands. Saxophones (alto, tenor, baritone), clarinets, harps, and violins form the basis of the typical orchestra (*orquesta típica*), the most popular ensemble in the central Andes department of Junín and neighboring areas (figure 5).

DISC
1
TRACK
7

Local instrumental ensembles play in various contexts. Ensembles combining a harp and violins pervade the Andres, as do the combination of flute and drum played by a single performer or by several, as in the *banda de guerra* of Cusco, which combines *quena* flutes, accordion, mandolin, harp, and a violin. The *banda típica* in northern Cajamarca mixes *quenas* and percussion instruments (snare drum and cymbals). Large ensembles of one instrumental type—for example, wind instruments such as *pitu*, *pinkillu*, and *tarka*—are common in the south. The *estudiantina* ensemble of Puno includes guitars, *charangos*, mandolins, and an accordion. The *herranza*, an ensemble that accompanies herding rituals in the central Andes, merges a violin, several *wak'rapuku* (coiled cowhorn trumpet), and a *tinya*. The string ensemble (*conjunto de cuerdas*) of Ancash combines a violin, a mandolin, and sometimes a harp or a *quena* and an accordion.

The Coast

After the lute (*laúd*) and the *bandurria* had disappeared from the urbanized coast, the guitar became the most important instrument in creole music there. It serves as a solo instrument or for voice-accompanying duos and trios, especially in the *vals criollo*. After the 1950s, when creole music began to be disseminated via commercial records and the mass media, the creole repertoire began to be performed by various musical instruments and ensembles. The guitar remained the most vital instrument in live performances, but percussion instruments—such as the *cajón* 'big box' and Iberian castanets (usually replaced by a pair of spoons in live performances)—were introduced. Afro-Peruvians commonly play the *cajón*, a variably sized wooden box with a hole in its back; the performer sits on it and strikes it with both hands.

In rural coastal areas, other instruments are played. Many of them—such as the *pinkullo* and the *caja* (played by a single performer, as in the highlands), the harp, the *chirimía*, and the instruments

Figure 5 An *orquesta típica* consisting of five alto saxophonists, three tenor saxophonists, two clarinetists, and (not visible) two violinists and a harpist, perform at the patronal festival of San Juan Bautista, Acollo, Junín, 1979.
Photo by Dale A. Olsen.

that form the brass band in Lambayeque—are also played in the Andes. For *marineras* (dance music in compound 6/8 and 3/4 meter, called *sesquiáltera* in Spanish), a *tamborero* beats on the soundbox of a harp while the harpist plucks the strings and sings. The banjo, introduced in parts of the north Peruvian coast around 1900, is now used to play *valses* and *marineras*.

The guitar is the most important instrument in the Afro-Peruvian tradition. Peruvian blacks incorporated it and the harp in street fiestas as early as the 1700s, but this tradition has been forgotten. Still in use are the *quijada* (or *carachacha*), the jawbone of an ass, mule, or horse, whose teeth rattle when the jawbone is struck against a hand. After the 1950s, when a process of revitalization of Afro-Peruvian music took place, Caribbean instruments (including congas, cowbell, and bongos) were incorporated into musical ensembles.

Musical Genres and Contexts

The Peruvian Andes

Current Andean musical expressions are revitalizations of pre-Hispanic indigenous genres, local developments based on colonial European models, or recent configurations derived from the encounter with national and transnational urban musical forms. Among the pre-Hispanic genres of song cited by early chroniclers and still persisting among southern Andean peasants is the *harawi*, a monophonic genre of song that consists of one musical phrase repeated several times with extensive melismatic passages and long glissandos. It is associated with specific

ceremonies and rituals, including farewells and marriages, and agricultural labor, including sowing and harvesting. It is usually sung in high-pitched, nasal voices by elder women called *harawiq*. In Cusco, this genre, known as *wanka*, is associated with the same ritual contexts. The *kashwa*, a pre-Hispanic genre usually associated with nocturnal harvest rituals, is performed in a circle by young, unmarried men and women. *Haylli*, a responsorial genre, is performed during communal agricultural fieldwork.

Among the Andean musical genres associated with specific contexts is the *carnaval*, a song and dance for carnival. The *walina*, a genre linked with the ritual clearing of irrigation channels in the highlands of the department of Lima, is customarily sung by men while a *chirimía* plays a countermelody.

Some genres have become dissociated from their original contexts. These include the *santiago* (originally a kind of song from the Central Andes, performed by a woman during the ritual marking of animals), the *huaylas* (once a ritual harvest song, also from the Central Andes), and the *carnaval* of the southern Andes. These genres became accepted beyond their villages, achieving local significance in traditional fiestas. Later, they began to be distributed by the record industry, achieving national coverage and eventually emancipating themselves from their original ritual contexts.

The most widely disseminated and popular song-dance genre in the Andes is the *huayno* (*wayno*). It has many geographic variants and goes by different names, including *chuscada* (Ancash), *pampeña* (Arequipa), *cachua* (Cajamarca), *chymaycha* (Amazonas and Huánuco), and *huaylacha* (Colca Valley). Usually in duple meter, it consists of two paired musical phrases (AABB). Like other Andean genres, it may have a closing section, called *fuga* or *qawachan*, which consists of a contrasting theme in a faster tempo. Today, it reflects the styles of the social and ethnic groups that perform it. As an autonomous expression of contextual and ritual constraints, it can be performed at any time and in various settings.

The *yaraví* is a slow, lyrical, mestizo genre in triple meter and binary form. Sung mostly in the southern Andes, it is usually associated with afflicted love affairs and nostalgic moods. Its melody has a minor tonality, is usually sung in parallel thirds, and has a flexible tempo. Having analogous musical characteristics is the *triste*, pervasive in northern Peru. In the central Andes, the *muliza*, though distinctive in style and form, resembles the *yaraví* and serves the same function. These genres are usually followed by a *fuga de huayno*, a *huayno*-like closing section.

Contrasting with fixed genres are nonfixed genres, organically linked to specific ritual contexts, including fertility rituals, agricultural communal work, the building of edifices, and lifecycle ceremonial phases (baptisms, courtships, marriages, funerals). In many cases, the accompanying music bears the name of the ritual, though in some cases a fixed musical form may be associated with the ritual.

In the Mantaro Valley in the department of Junín, the nocturnal harrowing of grain was until the 1950s accomplished by young unmarried men and women, who sang unaccompanied or with guitar accompaniment and danced on a mound of grain, separating the seeds from the husks. In the same area, the music of a *pincullo* and a *tinya*, played by one performer in pipe-and-tabor fashion, is reserved for times when the peasant community gathers to do fieldwork at specific points in the agricultural calendar, especially the first tilling of the soil and the harvest. Each musical repertoire pertains solely to its corresponding performance context, and although each tune has a descriptive name, the whole repertoire lacks a name other than that of the occasion for which it is intended. In Cajamarca in the northern Andes, the *clarín* is played during the *minka* (communal fieldwork), especially during the grain harvest.

The marking (*marcación*) of animals is one of the most ubiquitous fertility rituals in the central and southern Andes of Peru. Associated with the Andean mountain deities (the *wamani*, the *apu*, or the *achachila*, depending on the area), it is usually performed during specific seasons of the year. In the highlands of the Colca Valley in the department of Arequipa, a large *pincuyllo* and a *tinya* are played in the *tinka*, a ceremony during carnival when a llama is sacrificed and ritual offerings for the deities are buried. Music accompanies the steps of the ritual

and is played during rest periods when, after the ritual, the participants dance and relax. An ensemble of eighteen *quenas* or *chaqallos* accompanied by two *bombos* and a snare drum fulfills the same function during a similar ritual called *wylancha* in Puno. In the Mantaro River Valley, the musical ensemble of the marking of animals or *herranza* consists of one or two *wak'rapuku*, a violin, a singer, and a *tinya*. This ensemble's repertoire is strictly linked with each step of the ritual, and like the previously mentioned cases, is exclusively reserved for this occasion.

Ceremonial lifecycle phases are contexts for major musical repertoires. The role of music in courtship rituals is particularly solid in Cusco. In Canas, young unmarried men summon their chosen women by playing the *tuta kashwa* ('night dance', a particular melody) on their *charangos* during the fiestas of Saint Andrew (San Andrés) and the Holy Cross (Santa Cruz). Funeral music is usually sung by specialists at the wake or actual burial as in the festivity of the Día de los Muertos (Day of the Dead). In the Mantaro Valley, items in the repertoire of the funeral-song singers (*responseros*) have Quechua texts with strong musical-liturgical influence. In other areas, the relatives of the deceased may weep and grieve, combining spoken passages with musical cadences. When an infant dies in Puno, a lively *huayno* is sung with *charango* accompaniment because people believe that the dead baby goes to heaven in a state of grace; the death is therefore an occasion to celebrate, rather than grieve.

The annual festival calendar is the natural context for dance-dramas. The fiesta calendar, prolific throughout the Andean area, is the result of the blending of the pre-Hispanic agricultural calendar with the Christian calendar. Festivals are celebrated with greater or lesser intensity according to each locality. Some have achieved pan-Andean relevance. These include the Purification of Our Lady (Virgen de la Calendaria, 2 February), the Fiesta de la Cruz (3 May), the Nativity of St. John the Baptist (San Juan, 24 June), the Nativity of the Blessed Virgin Mary (8 September), and Christian seasonal observances, such as Christmas, Epiphany, Holy Week (especially Palm Sunday), and Corpus Christi. Carnival is celebrated throughout the Andes, often closely linked with the Purification of Our Lady.

Frequently, the actual fiesta lasts from three to five days, depending on the type of festivity and the area. The main events usually occur during vespers the evening before the central day, on the central day itself, and on the closing day (the farewell).

Music and dance are integral parts of the Andean fiesta (figure 6). The music for dance-dramas follows the structure of the dance-dramas themselves: a

Figure 6 On Sunday, the main day of the patronal festival of San Juan Bautista (Saint John the Baptist) in Acolla, Junín, dancers known as *tunantadas* and *chunginos*, representing Spanish nobility, perform to the accompaniment of an *orquesta típica* (only the upside-down harp is in view).
Photo by Dale A. Olsen, 1979.

multisectional form of two to six parts, each with different tempos and styles. Dance-drama choreography is usually fixed, and repeats itself year after year. Dance-drama music is unique, exclusively linked with the choreography of the dance from which it takes it name. Besides the dances in the fiestas, festive music includes music for fireworks, bullfights, horse races, processions, special offerings, and orchestral salutes (welcomes and farewells).

Music for dance-dramas can be performed by a single musician, several performers, or a large ensemble. The performers may be members of the community or hired musicians who play professionally in local markets. In many areas, mestizo sponsors of fiestas hire Indian performers to be closer to the tradition. In this sense, performers of music for dance-dramas may have a less conspicuous profile than the dancers. In some contexts, the latter usually dance to fulfill a religious vow to the Virgin, whereas musicians are usually hired. Brass bands, including winds, drums, and cymbals, became widely popular in the Andes in the beginning of the twentieth century, largely because military service had become mandatory, and few young men could avoid it. Brass bands remain one of the most popular vehicles for dance-dramas in the southern Peruvian Andes.

The Coast

The waltz (*vals criollo*), the most representative genre of the repertoire, is generally called creole music (*música criolla*), and many Peruvians consider it the foremost national music. A development of its European counterpart, it had acquired its local character by 1900. It developed from the Spanish *jota* and *mazurca* and the Viennese waltz, popularized in Lima by the mid-1800s. The Peruvian *vals* originated in the lower classes and neighborhoods of Lima. It was the genre the working classes in the *barrios* preferred, while the upper classes rejected it.

The *marinera*—until about 1900 known as *zamacueca*, *chilena*, *mozamala*, and *resbalosa*—is one of the most widely disseminated song-and-dance genres in the country. Originally from coastal Peru, it is widely performed in the Andes. In compound duple and triple meter (6/8 and 3/4), it has three distinctive parts: the song itself (three stanzas), the *resbalosa* (one stanza), and a closing *fuga* ('flight', not a fugue in the European sense). The *tondero*, a related genre, followed a parallel evolution in the northern coastal departments of La Libertad, Lambayeque, and Piura. In music and choreography, the *tondero* resembles the *marinera*, but it exhibits a distinctive harmonic structure: the first section (*glosa*) begins in the major mode, the second is in the relative minor mode (*dulce*), and the piece returns to the major mode in the third (*fuga*). Both genres are usually accompanied by guitars and a *cajón*. In northern Peru, the latter is replaced by a harp and a banjo.

Creole musical contexts in Peru are limited to the city of Lima and the adjacent coast. In coastal Lambayeque, dance-dramas (including *pastoras*, *margaros*, and *diablicos*) are accompanied by a *pincullo* and a *caja* (played in pipe-and-tabor style), brass instruments, and a *chirimía*.

The practice and performance of African-derived music, dances, and rituals by black slaves in Peru since the early years of the conquest is well-established in colonial and republican sources. The 1700s marked the beginning of creolization of the music of Peruvian blacks. With their integration into the dominant society, they began to accept and adopt creole cultural and musical expressions. During the 1800s, after the abolition of slavery, they intensified this process. By the 1950s, a small number of specialists remembered only a few genres of African-derived song, the repertoire had contracted to a minimum, and the choreographies of most were lost.

This repertoire was the subject of a revival and reconstruction that labeled it Afro-Peruvian, as put forward by the brother and sister Nicomedes Santa Cruz (1925–1992) and Victoria Santa Cruz (b. 1922), who performed, produced, and promoted Afro-Peruvian music and dances. The movement singled out black-associated genres that had previously been intermingled with the white creole repertoire. Genres such as the *festejo* (see boxed text), the *ingá*, the *socabón*, and the *panalivio* were commercially disseminated by the Santa Cruz family in the late 1950s. In the next decade, the *landó* (or *the zamba-landó*), the *son de los diablos*, the habanera, the *zaña*, the *samba-malato*, the *agua de nieve*, the *alcatraz*, and other genres were favored.

Andean Migrant Music in the City: *Chicha*

During the early 1960s, the popularity of the *cumbia* among Andean residents and migrants was boosted by the appearance of a new urban musical genre, *chicha* (also called *cumbia andina*), which blended musical elements from the *huayno* with the *cumbia*, achieved great approval among young people of Andean origins, and became especially important in its center of operations, Lima, though many of its principal performers came from the central Andes. Its style and the instrumental makeup of its musical groups reflect the influence that since the early 1960s

---

THE FESTEJO

Probably the most important Afro-Peruvian musical form is the *festejo*, whose rhythms occur in several genres. A typical *festejo* melody consists of short phrases with a surging rhythm, frequently interrupted at phrase-endings by a sudden pause, or by a tone of longer duration. The question-answer character of the melodic line in consecutive phrases is exaggerated in the final section (*fuga*), composed of melodic fragments sung responsorially by soloist and chorus. Considerable metric variety and even the simultaneous use of two different meters occur, but the underlying meter is essentially 6/8, with a stilted iambic rhythm.

A typical example (figure 7) has balanced four-bar phrases (repeated), rhythmic contrasts, the use of *fugas*, accent displacement, and calls and responses. The texts often have a strophic form. They usually treat a festive theme, often in a setting that evokes the days of slavery. Texts and melodies are sometimes interchanged between *festejos*, and texts may even be borrowed from another musical genre and set to a *festejo* melody and rhythm. This swapping of melodies and texts is common in the Afro-Peruvian musical tradition. The guitar, the *cajón*, and clapping provide the basic instrumental accompaniment. The use of the *cajón* in the *festejo* is an innovation of the 1950s, replacing the ceramic vessel or hollow log drums that were used previously, and most modern performances include the *quijada*, a lower jawbone of an ass, mule, or horse, stripped of its flesh and with teeth loosened so they rattle in their sockets.

cajón: a variably sized wooden box with a hole in its back; the performer sits on the instrument and strikes it with both hands.

The *festejo* was probably danced in free style. Several other genres of dance are based melodically and rhythmically on it. These include two novelty dances, the *alcatraz* and the *ingá*, and two competitive dances, the *zapateo* (*zapateado*) *criollo* and the *agua 'e nieve*.

The *alcatraz* is performed in a circle. One male–female couple at a time dances in the center. Either or both dancers carry a flaming stick or candle, with which he or she tries to light a paper streamer attached like a tail behind the partner, while the other makes such pelvic movements that the streamer flicks about, dodging the flame. To perform the *ingá* (also called *ungá*) and the *baile del muñeco* 'doll's dance', the dancers form a circle. In its center, embracing a large doll, pillow, or anything that could be used to represent an infant, one performer dances alone. After several minutes of dancing, the soloist passes the doll to someone of the opposite sex within the circle. This person takes a turn, and the sequence proceeds in that manner until all have danced.

The *zapateo criollo* (or the *pasada*) and the *agua 'e nieve* (or *agüenieve*) utilize *festejo* rhythms in a competitive demonstration of skill. *Zapateo*, from the Spanish term *zapateado* 'foot stamping', is a dance technique that involves rhythmic striking of heels and toes against the floor or against each other. The *zapateo criollo* is danced by a male who demonstrates his skill by improvising intricate rhythmic patterns with his feet, supplemented by rhythmic slapping. An element of virtuosity and even acrobatics is often present. The dance is usually performed competitively by two or more individuals, who take turns trying to impress onlookers or to score points with the person chosen to judge their contest. The *agua 'e nieve* is essentially the same, but based on *escobillada* technique, which is a brushing movement of the shoe or bare foot along the floor or ground.

Figure 7 Excerpt from "*Don Antonio Mina*," a typical *festejo*. Transcribed by William David Tompkins, from *El Festejo* (n.d.: B4). Translation: "They stabbed and killed / Sir Anthony Mina. / Up at the old ancient tomb / I saw the gentleman myself. "Throw it, throw it, throw it / from Lima to Lunahuana. "Mark of a blade. / A jar of water and a candy. / The candy maker."

international Latin American popular styles and American and British rock have had on young Andean migrants. A typical group consists of two electric guitars, an electric organ (replaced in the 1990s by a synthesizer), an electric bass, Latin percussion (*timbales*, congas, bongos, cowbell), and a vocalist, who performs in a style recalling that of Andean mestizo songs.

Chicha became a nucleus around which young unmarried men and women from first- and second-generation cohorts in Lima congregated every Sunday and holidays. Several *chichódromos* (locales for *chicha* events) opened in Lima, downtown and in the outskirts, and such groups as the Shapis, Alegría, and Chacalón y la Nueva Crema gained fame there. Though most *chicha* lyrics deal with romantic love, many feature themes directly linked to migrants' problems in Lima.

In rural areas, as in Paccha in Junín, *chicha* is usually played in public buildings at night in social dances (*bailes*) organized during the traditional fiestas. *Bailes* in Paccha gather young unmarried men and women together in the daytime without disturbing the normal development of the fiesta. In this setting, they may interact freely and independently in ways that they cannot during traditional festivities.

In the context of a social dance, *chicha* functions as a courting ritual, does not require heavy expenses, and may be enjoyed at any period of the year.

—Adapted from articles by Raúl R. Romero and William David Tompkins

Bibliography

Bolaños, César. 1981. *Música y Danza en el Antiguo Perú*. Lima: Museo Nacional de Antropología y Arqueología, Instituto Nacional de Cultura.

den Otter, Elisabeth. 1985. *Music and Dance of Indians and Mestizos in an Andean Valley of Peru*. Delft: Eburon.

El Festejo. N.d. Lima: Sono Radio LPL 9239. LP disk.

Olsen, Dale A. 1986–1987. "The Peruvian Folk Harp Tradition: Determinants of Style." *Folk Harp Journal* 53:48–54, 54:41–48, 55:55–59, 56:57–60, 57:38–42, 58:47–48, 59:60–62.

Romero, Raúl R. 1985. "La Música Tradicional y Popular." In *La Música en el Perú*, 215–283. Lima: Patronato Popular y Porvenir Pro Música Clásica.

———. 1989. "Música Urbana en un Contexto Rural: Tradición y Modernidad en Paccha, Junín." *Anthropológica* 7(7):121–133.

———. 1993. *Música, Danzas y Máscaras en el Perú*. Lima: Pontífica Universidad Católica del Perú.

———. 1994. "Black Music and Identity in Peru: Reconstruction and Revival of Afro-Peruvian Musical Traditions." In *Music and Black Ethnicity: The Caribbean and South America*, edited by Gerard H. Béhague, 307–330. Miami: North-South Center, University of Miami.

Stevenson, Robert M. 1960. *The Music of Peru*. Washington, D.C.: Organization of American States.

———. 1968. *Music in Aztec and Inca, Territory*. Berkeley: University of California Press.

Venezuela

When Spanish explorers encountered the Bay of Maracaibo, on South America's north coast, it reminded them of Venice; therefore, they called the land Venezuela 'little Venice'. Today, the country of Venezuela has a land area of 912,050 square kilometers—more than twice the size of California—and 2,800 kilometers of Caribbean coastline, and in 2006 had a population of roughly 25.7 million people. Its major cities are Caracas (the capital, founded in 1567), Maracaibo, Valencia, Maracay, and Barquisimeto. From the early colonial period through the first decades of the twentieth century, most of its inhabitants lived in rural communities, but today, more than 90 percent of its population resides in urban centers.

Traditional Venezuelan music derives from the cultures that have influenced most Latin American and Caribbean countries: the indigenous (aboriginal, Indian, Amerindian, native American), the European, and the African. Venezuela still manifests pockets of unacculturated indigenous music, but most of its traditional music is an assortment of genres and styles stemming from Spain and Africa.

In 1498, when European explorers arrived on Columbus's third voyage to the New World, about fifty thousand native Americans were thought to be living along the central Caribbean coast of Venezuela, an area no longer populated by indigenous peoples. Indigenous music survives primarily in the Amazon area, the Orinoco Delta, and the Guajira Peninsula. European and African influences predominate along the coast of north-central Venezuela, the most densely populated part of the country. Perhaps more than two-thirds of the Spanish who arrived during the first century of colonization came from Andalucía, in southern Spain. With colonization came Moorish influences; thus, when the term European is employed here, it is used in its broadest sense, including influences from Arabic, Islamic, and West Asian sources that informed Andalucían culture during the colonizing of the Americas.

In the Andes, Spanish influences predominate. Spanish-derived vocal forms and musical instruments form a plurality of Venezuela's existing folk music. Isabel Aretz has identified twelve families of song (cancioneros) in Venezuela's folk music, eleven of which she calls Spanish in origin; the remaining one is African-Venezuelan (personal communication). Likewise, though in any survey of musical instruments indigenous-inspired rattles and African-derived drums abound, the stringed instruments of Spanish origin are the most notable. The national instrument of Venezuela, a four-stringed lute (cuatro) closely resembling the ukulele, and Venezuela's next most prominent musical instrument, a harp (arpa), derive from Spain.

A Caribbean-island character is also apparent in much of Venezuela's music, linking this country musically to places such as Cuba, Curaçao, the Dominican Republic, Haiti, Puerto Rico, and Trinidad and Tobago. Much of this influence is African, and the influence of Africa on Venezuela as a whole is much greater than is often perceived.

Folk Music

Though elite and urbane individuals, from native American shamans and African princes to Spanish priests, have influenced traditional music in Venezuela, the main agents of this development have been peasants. European and African traits predominate in most folk-musical forms; indigenous phenomena are less apparent. Some Venezuelan folk music blends European and African music, but most of it comes from European or African sources. Some songs are obviously European in form; others feature the leader-response form of African music. Certain ensembles feature Iberian strings, but others feature African-style drums. Occasionally we find a juxtaposition of both, with European-derived lutes and African-derived drums in the same ensemble. Distinctions are sometimes obvious, sometimes subtle. Most of this music is associated with the fiestas that take place in Venezuela throughout the year.

The music of Venezuelan peasants of mixed ancestry is often called creole music (música criolla). In parts of Latin America and the Caribbean, this term identifies those of purely European ancestry; in Venezuela, it usually refers to the cultural trinity of indigenous America, Europe, and Africa. Likewise, creole often designates the traditional music of Venezuela. Even music sometimes called African-Venezuelan music is occasionally called creole music by those who perform it.

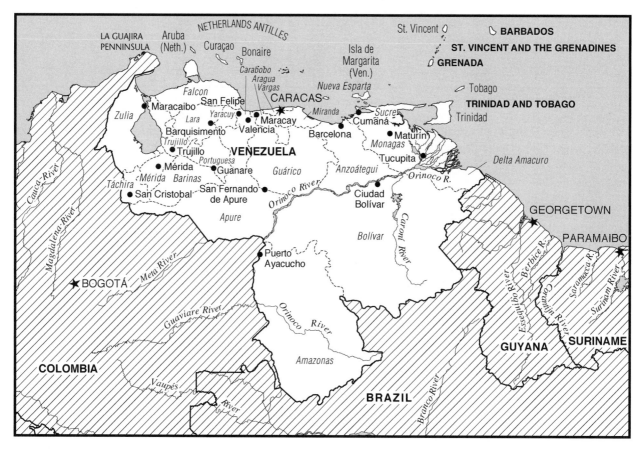

Venezuela

Traditional Musical Instruments

The roots of creole music in Venezuela can be traced in part through the study of musical instruments. Two important organological contributions to creole music from indigenous sources are rattles and wind instruments. The major instruments from Spain are stringed instruments, and African-Venezuelans are locally known for their drums and drumming.

Percussive Instruments (Idiophones)

Container rattles (maracas), usually in pairs, accompany just about every genre of Venezuelan folk music. Indigenous people commonly use a single rattle to accompany singing, but creole ensembles commonly employ a pair. (An exception is the use of a single rattle in some African-Venezuelan ensembles of the central coast.) Paired maracas are usually unequal in size and sound: one, usually larger, with more seeds, emits a deep, raspy sound; the other, with fewer seeds, emits a clearer and brighter sound. Often, a gender designation is assigned to each: the lower-sounding instrument is male, and the higher-pitched is female.

The most prominent idiophones of African derivation are the sides of wooden-bodied drums, struck with sticks commonly called *palos* and sometimes *laures* (figure 1). They embellish drummed rhythms, and children often play them while listening to drummed rhythms.

Another African-derived instrument, from the area of Barlovento, is an ensemble of stamped bamboo tubes called *quitiplás* (figure 2), an onomatopoeic word representing the rhythm of the two smallest tubes. The player holds one tube in each hand, striking the ground, followed by the other, and then striking both against each other, producing the last syllable of the word (*plás*), in a cyclic or continuous rhythm. Two or three other players each hold a larger tube, which they strike on the ground with one hand while using the other hand to accompany songs and dances of the *redondo* (drum) ensemble, using the same rhythms performed by these groups. Children often play *quitiplás* as a way of learning the rhythms of the drums.

Other African- and European-based idiophones commonly played in Venezuelan folk music are metal triangles, concussion sticks, bells, jew's harps (*trompa* or *birimbao*), and ridged instruments scraped with a stick (most commonly called *charrascas*). Steel

200

Figure 1 During the festival of Saint John the Baptist in Curiepe, Miranda (Barlovento area), two men beat sticks on the side of a drum. *Photo by Dale A. Olsen, 1974.*

Figure 2 On the street in Tacarigua, Miranda (Barlovento area), three men stamp bamboo tubes (*quitiplás*). *Photo by Max H. Brandt, 1973.*

drums are played in some urban centers and in the town of Callao in Bolívar State, where people from Caribbean islands have been relocating for decades.

Drums (Membranophones)

Though indigenous peoples of Venezuela used numerous kinds of drums, most drums used today are of African and European origin. From Europe came at least two double-headed drums, the bass drum (*bombo*) and the side drum (*redoblante*). The drum found most widely in the country, the *tambora*, may have been inspired by both traditions.

Africa is responsible for the greatest variety of drums. Barlovento (Windward), on the central coast in Miranda State, is famous for its African-Venezuelan drumming on three sets of drums: *minus*, *redondos*, and *tamboras*. Its stamped bamboo tubes, musically related to *redondos* and sometimes called drums themselves, are part of its heritage. Though multiple sets of drums commonly occur among ethnic groups in Africa (as among the Yorùbá of Nigeria, who have different families of drums), they rarely do in communities of the African diaspora in the Americas. Barlovento is an exception. Unlike in Africa, though, where a variety of composite rhythms or instrumental pieces can be played within the context of one family of drums, the drums of Barlovento feature only one composite rhythm. The only exception is the *malembe* rhythm and song form, performed for processions rather than dancing, primarily by *redondo* ensembles, but sometimes by *mina* ensembles.

Long, heavy log drums with a skin at one end—*burro, cumaco, mina, tambor grande*—are common in Venezuela. In performance, each most often sits on the ground. The main drummer straddles the end near the skin, and one or more other musicians beat the side of the drum with *palos* or *laures*.

Redondos and *tamboras*, two other kinds of drum on the central coast, have skins at both ends. The most common are *tamboras*, the main instruments that accompany all-night observances for honoring a saint or the Holy Cross. In Barlovento, they can be played alone, or in ensembles of up to four or five instruments, by performers who hold the drums between their knees while sitting. The physical traits of the *tamboras* and the rhythms played on them recall those of the *redondo* ensemble. The *tambora*, like the *redondo*, is played with one stick, which sometimes, depending upon the particular drum, strikes the side of the drum and the skin.

Redondos, found in a smaller area south and east of Caracas, are longer than *tamboras*, and are held between standing drummers' legs (figure 3). The three drums of the set are made from the trunk of a balsa tree (called *lano* in Barlovento), whose wood is soft and lightweight. Each drum, varying slightly in size, is hollowed to resemble an hourglass inside, and

is covered at each end with skins connected to each other with thin rope lacings forming W-shaped patterns. The drummer strikes the drum with a stick held in one hand and the fingers of the other hand. These drums have individual names, and are most commonly called *tamborcitos, tambores redondos*, or *culo 'e puya*. The only other musical instruments accompanying this ensemble are maracas.

Stringed Instruments (Chordophones)

The most important Spanish contribution to the instrumental music of Venezuela was the introduction of stringed instruments. Today, the four-stringed *cuatro*, found everywhere in Venezuela, even among indigenous groups, is considered the national instrument (figure 4). The diatonic or creole harp (*arpa*), though found in only two areas of Venezuela, is recognized as an important symbol of Venezuelan music (see figure 4), as attested to by miniature models in the gift shops of Caracas and other tourist-frequented communities.

In large cities, the *cuatro* is played as much as, or more than, in the countryside. It is often called a guitar (*guitarra*), since it is the most commonly used instrument of the guitar family in Venezuela, and it is known by diminutives—*guitarra pequeña, guitarrita, guitarilla, guitarillo*—and other names, such as *discante*. Primarily an accompanying instrument, it plays chords, mostly the tonic, dominant, and subdominant, but virtuosos such as Fredy Reyna include exquisite melodic techniques in their performances.

Small guitars with nylon strings are used primarily as accompanying instruments. Most, like the *cuatro* 'four', are named for the number of their strings.

Figure 3 During the festival of Saint John the Baptist in El Tigre, Miranda, three men play drums (*redondos*) with one stick and one hand, as a woman shakes maracas.
Photo by Max H. Brandt, 1973.

Figure 4 Accompanied by a *cuatro*, the Venezuelan musician Jesús Rodríguez plays a plains harp (*arpa llanera*) in Miami, Florida.
Photo by Dale A. Olsen, 1983.

They include the *cuatro y media* 'four and a half', *cinco* 'five', *cinco y medio*, *seis* 'six' (but smaller than the standard six-stringed guitar), *cuatro con cinco cuerdas* 'cuatro with five strings', and *cinco de seis cuerdas* 'six-stringed *cinco*'. In western Venezuela, the *tiple* 'treble' is common. Used as a melodic or chordally accompanying instrument, it most commonly has four double or triple sets of strings.

DISC
❶
TRACK
8

Plucked lutes (*bandolas* and *mandolinas*) serve as melodic instruments in Venezuela. The best-known *bandola*, from the plains, uses four gut or nylon strings. Barinas is the only plains state where the *bandola* is as popular as the harp—or perhaps even more popular. The *bandola* of the central coast has four courses of double strings, the higher-sounding ones from metal. The *bandola* of the eastern area (more commonly called *bandolín* or *mandolina*), smaller than the plains *bandola*, has four double courses of nylon strings. The *bandola* of the Guayana area (surrounding Ciudad Guayana, where the

Caroní River meets the Orinoco, in Bolívar State) borrows elements from the plains. The *bandola andina* (also known as a *bandurría*), found in the Andes in western Venezuela, has five or six courses of double or triple strings.

Of the stringed instruments used to play melodies, the violin (*violín*) is the most widely used instrument in Venezuela. It is a European model, like that used throughout the world.

The diatonic harp, once popular in Spain, is an important creole instrument in many countries of Latin America. The *arpa criolla* usually has between thirty and thirty-seven strings; thirty-three and thirty-four are the most common numbers. Its main performance styles in Venezuela are that of the plains (*arpa llanera*) and that of Aragua (*arpa aragüeña*, from the state of Aragua). Because the latter style also occurs in the federal district, the state of Miranda, and states closer to the coast than the plains states, it can conveniently be called the style of the central-coast harp. More commonly, it is specified by adjectives derived from placenames, including Aragua (*arpa aragüeña*), Miranda (*arpa mirandina*), and the Tuy River area (*arpa tuyera*).

The instruments differ slightly from one area to another. The plains harp has a narrower sound board than does the central-coast harp, and it now uses only nylon strings. The coastal harp sometimes has gut or nylon strings in its lower register, but metallic upper strings give it a more brilliant sound. Performance brings out an even more prominent difference between these harps (see below, in relation to the *joropo*).

The diatonic harp was taught to indigenous Venezuelans by Spanish priests during the early colonial period, and its music was fashionable in the salons of the urban upper class. The harp music heard today in Venezuela has roots in seventeenth- and eighteenth-century Spain, when the Renaissance modes had not yet been fully replaced by major and minor tonalities. Keyboard music was performed on diatonically tuned harps, then popular in Spain. The harp-playing styles of Venezuela closely resemble Spanish Baroque keyboard styles.

Wind Instruments (Aerophones)
Wind instruments are notable in the music of marginalized creoles such as the people of Falcon State, who dance to the music of an ensemble featuring *turas*, end-blown flutes, one male and the other female. Other flutes of this ensemble are *cachos*, made from a deer's skull with antlers attached; these are played in pairs, one large and one small.

Another popular Venezuelan wind instrument is the raft panpipe, locally called by several names, including *carrizo* 'cane' and *maremare* 'happy-happy', played by creoles in many parts of Venezuela. Especially well-known are the panpipes of Cumanacoa, in Sucre State, and those of San José de Guaribe, in Guárico State. Other creole wind instruments include cane and wooden flutes (vertical and transverse types) and conch trumpets (*trompetas de caracol*, *guaruras*). The last instruments play in drum ensembles of the Barlovento area.

Musical Contexts and Genres

Folk Roman Catholicism

Folk-religious music in Venezuela accompanies rituals that are apparently Christian, though many are not based on formal Roman Catholic teachings. Instead, this music has evolved with a creole version of Roman Catholicism developed from early colonial days to the present. The church was less influential in colonial Venezuela than in such places as Colombia and Mexico, and Spanish priests were not in abundance. Peasants (*campesinos*) observing native American, African, and Spanish beliefs and customs took the liberty of developing and conducting religious ceremonies, embellishing them with music, dance, costumes, and practices not always acceptable to visiting clerics. Even today, representatives of the official church frown on ritual aspects of Venezuelan fiestas.

Not all this music can be considered entirely religious in design. Much of it is dedicated to Christian saints, but texts and meanings are often interspersed with secular ideas and words. Some aspects of a particular fiesta (such as *salves*, sung at the beginning of a *tamunangue* in Lara) are traditional and acceptable facets of the Roman tradition, yet the music and dance known as *la perrendenga*, performed in front of the image of San Antonio later in the fiesta, has little to do with Christianity. Therefore, although the fiestas described below are Christian in name, creole Roman Catholicism plays a dominant role as they unfold. Furthermore, alcoholic beverages are almost invariably associated with these quasi-religious celebrations; it would be most unusual for the members of a participating music ensemble, usually men, not to share a bottle of rum or some other kind of spirits.

The combination of music and dance as tribute to deities is locally important, as is the concept of *la promesa*, the vow to honor a saint through music and/or dance in return for certain favors. The interplay and coexistence of beliefs and performances has produced a wealth of religiously inspired creole music and dance.

Velorios

Velorios, nightlong celebrations or night watches to honor a saint or the Holy Cross (not to be confused with wakes for a deceased person, also *velorios*) are common in Venezuela. In the plains, the music of *velorios* is primarily Spanish in origin, with stringed instruments predominating, but along the central coast the music is more African in origin, where *tamboras* accompany songs called *fulias*. Perhaps the *velorio* most widely celebrated in the Venezuelan plains is the wake of the Holy Cross (*velorio de cruz*) or May Cross (*cruz de mayo*). Table altars are decorated with flowers, and a chapel or a temporary roof is often constructed of fronds, papier mâché, flowers, or other materials to honor a cross, usually made of wood and decorated with the same materials. In and around the plains, especially in the states of Apure, Carabobo, Cojedes, Guárico, Lara, Portuguesa, and Yaracuy, the Holy Cross is venerated by performances of three-part polyphonic pieces (*tonos*), usually sung by men, sometimes unaccompanied, but more often accompanied by one or more *cuatros*. The music and texts came from Spain during the early days of the colony. Most harmonic singing in Venezuela is in two parts (usually at intervals of a third), but wakes in the plains use more-complex polyphony, unique in Latin America. The lead singer (*guía* 'guide') usually sings a solo phrase, and is then joined by two other men improvising a harmonic response—a higher part (*falsa*, also *contrato* and other names), and a lower part (*tenor*, also *tenorete*). In *velorios* of the central coast (especially in the federal district, the state of Miranda, and parts of the state of Aragua), vocal harmony is less important than melody. Here, the *velorios* are centered on the singing of *fulias*, accompanied by at least one *tambora* (but usually three or four), the scraping of a metal plate with a fork, a spoon, or other utensils, and usually one maraca or a pair of maracas. The *fulia*, the most complex of the drum-accompanied vocal genres of Barlovento, is found more widely dispersed in the central coast than are the songs associated with other drums. It has an alternating solo-chorus form of singing, like the other drum songs. The solo is sung by a man or a woman, and the choruses usually consist of male and female singers. The verses have fairly complex texts, but the choruses almost always include vocables or syllables, such as *o lo lo la lo lai na*.

The vigil continues until dawn, but *fulias* and the accompanying *tamboras* do not play constantly. The music is broken up every twenty to forty minutes with the recitation of *décimas*, ten-line stanzas of poetry brought from Spain in the early days of the colony.

Figure 5 During the feast of Corpus Christi in San Francisco de Yare, Miranda, the dancing devils of Yare (*los diablos danzantes de Yare*) perform. *Left to right*: an unmasked musician-dancer plays a single maraca, another plays a *redoblante* (military-style drum), and a masked man dances.
Photo by Max H. Brandt, 1973.

Men and women (usually men) recite this poetry after an order is given to the musicians to stop playing, usually with the words *hasta ahí*, suggesting that the musicians take a pause. Some people, even those who cannot read and write, are recognized as specialists in *décimas*. Dancing is never part of celebrations that employ the singing of *fulías* and the playing of *tamboras*. The *fulía–tambora* tradition is not limited to Barlovento; it occurs in more or less the same form in neighboring areas of the central coast.

Tamunangue

One of the most famous expressions of music and dance in Venezuela is the *tamunangue*, from the state of Lara in the northwest of the country. It is a suite of dances and music, usually performed in honor of San Antonio de Padua (Saint Anthony of Padua), the patron saint of Lara. It is regularly performed on 13 June, the saint's feast, but can occur during the weeks before or after.

The music for the *tamunangue* consists of singing accompanied by stringed instruments or maracas and a drum of African origin. Performances usually begin with the singing of *salves* dedicated to the Virgin Mary in a church or a chapel, outside which the dance of the *tamunangue* will be performed. The *salves* are usually accompanied only by stringed instruments—*cuatro, cinco, quinto, lira, cuatro de cinco cuerdas*, and *cinco de seis cuerdas*. The ensemble may have a minimum of two such instruments (one *cuatro* and one *cinco*), but many ensembles, often composed of musicians from diverse communities, have seven to ten.

The principal drum of the *tamunangue*—usually called *tamunango*, but also called *tambor grande* and *cumaco*—resembles the *tambor grande* and the *cumaco* from the central coast. With one head nailed in place, it is normally just more than one meter long, and sits on the ground during performance. In addition to the rhythms played by hand on the drumhead by a drummer who sits on the drum while playing it, sticks (*palos*, also *laures*) are struck against its side by one, two, or three men (*paleros* 'palo players'). On some occasions, and especially when the ensemble graces processions, the large double-headed drum known in most parts of the country as *tambora* is used.

The *tamunangue* begins with the piece "*La Batalla*" ('The Battle'), also called a game (*juego*). It is followed by distinctive dances and pieces of music that vary slightly from one community to another. "*La Batalla*" is a graceful stick dance accompanied by music. The stick (*palo*) or staff (*vera*), the size of a walking stick, is usually decorated. The battle, always between two men (regularly replaced), is elegantly executed with one stick hitting the other, never touching opponents' bodies. Four lines of verse are sung in 2/4 time.

Los Diablos Danzantes de Yare *'The Dancing Devils of Yare'*

Many central-coastal communities have organizations of masked devil dancers who perform during the feast of Corpus Christi. The most famous of them is San Francisco de Yare, in the upper Tuy Valley (figure 5). Music is less important in this tradition than in other Venezuelan festivals. The dancing devils of Yare are accompanied by a military-style drum (*redoblante*), single maracas carried by many masked dancers, and jingle bells attached to their clothing.

Secular Dance and Music: The Joropo and its Variants

Most creole music is associated with dance. Partly because of urbanization, contemporary Venezuelans are less skilled at folk dancing than were their ancestors, though Venezuelan folk dancing is taught in most grade schools; most recorded folk music heard today on public broadcasting systems and on private systems in homes and vehicles is played for listening, rather than for dancing. Nevertheless, most Venezuelans are aware of the association of dance with most of their folk music.

To most Venezuelans, the epitome of folk dance is the *joropo*, a music and dance influenced by Africa and Europe and known as the national dance of Venezuela. The term *joropo* refers to more than just dance: it denotes the genre of music and the event in which the music and dance are performed. A person can attend a *joropo* (event), request the performance of a particular *joropo* (musical piece), and execute a *joropo* (dance). Most often, the term names the dance. This is a couple dance, and each participant normally holds one or both hands of the partner, in the same dance position used by European couples to dance a waltz, for example. (Usually many couples dance at once.) The dance involves basic and intricate footwork. It is similar in style throughout Venezuela, but the musical ensembles that accompany it vary locally.

People in the countryside may speak of a particular *joropo* as an event that took place in the past, or one planned for the future. It can be on a small scale, organized by a family or a segment of a community, and may take place in a house. An excuse to have a modest *joropo* might be a baptism, a birthday party, or a visit by a special friend. Alternatively, it might be a more public event, perhaps as part of a communitywide fiesta coinciding with a national holiday or a religious celebration, such as that for the local patron saint. Such *joropos* usually take place in an outdoor public area or a community hall. Like many fiestas in Venezuela, they typically start early in the evening and last until sunrise. In the early 1920s, the genre was much more important than it is today. It included not only musical entertainment and dancing, but special food and drink, children's play, and courtship.

Joropo music is rhythmically sophisticated, commonly notated with a double-time signature of 3/4 and 6/8, producing polyrhythms and an always present polymetric sense of simultaneous duple and triple figures, which provide creative possibilities for instrumentalists and dancers. The tempo is always brisk: a common pace is 208 quarter notes per minute. Some vocal lines conform strictly to the accompaniment, but much of the singing demonstrates the "melodic independence" that Ramón y Rivera has often written about. This is a free style of singing, in which, except for the beginnings or endings of certain long phrases, much of the vocal line does not coincide rhythmically or metrically with the instrumental accompaniment.

The melodies are clearly Spanish in character; they have roots in Andalucía. The texts, sung in Spanish, relate to Spanish genres of early colonial days, such as the *romance* and the *décima*. Most pieces have fixed texts, but some texts are improvised. All this music is distinguished by having one musical note for each syllable of text.

The Joropo and the Plains Harp Ensemble

For accompanying *joropos*, the plains harp ensemble is probably the most famous in Venezuela. It is almost always an all-male ensemble, and can be purely instrumental or can have one vocalist, also usually male. It is often presented as the trademark of Venezuelan traditional music, partly because of the attractiveness of the instrumental combination and its repertoire. During the dictatorship of Pérez Jiménez (1950–1958), this music came to the fore as a national symbol, supported by the government.

The *arpa llanera* is the featured melody instrument of the ensemble, sharing the melody role with the vocalist, who does not usually play an instrument. The other two instrumentalists play a *cuatro* and maracas. Since the mid-1900s, a fifth musician, playing an acoustic or electric string bass, has been added to accentuate the bass, traditionally played by the lower strings of the harp. Perhaps the best-known harpists and advocates of this style during the second half of the twentieth century were Ignacio "Indio" Figueredo (1900–1995) and Juan Vicente Torrealba (b. 1917).

The *bandola*, a four-stringed, pear-shaped lute that takes the place of the harp in many ensembles (and which may have preceded the *arpa* in some Venezuelan communities), remains the melodic instrument of choice in the states of Barinas and Portuguesa, and is played in Apure and Cojedes; an eight-stringed version of it appears in Miranda, Sucre, and Anzoátegui. The virtuosity possible on it has been ably demonstrated by Anselmo López (b. 1934). The instrument is plucked with a pick, so the lower two strings provide an ostinato, much like that of the lower strings of the harp; the higher strings play the melody on alternate beats. Performances on the plains harp are usually dashing and impressionistic, but the plains ensemble is equally appealing to most listeners when the *bandola* is the leading instrument.

In the plains ensemble, the *cuatro* provides the basic harmonic framework and a strummed rhythmic pulse. One might expect the maracas to provide a basic rhythmic background, but a good player (*maraquero*) can steal the show with rapid rhythmic embellishments, a subtle shifting of accents from triple to duple meter, and a masterful visual display of arm-and-hand techniques.

Joropo *and the Central-coastal Harp Ensemble*

The *joropo* of the central coast (especially in the states of Aragua, Miranda, and the federal district, and in parts of Anzoátegui, Sucre, and Carabobo) is traditionally accompanied by two male musicians—one who plays the harp, and one who sings and plays maracas. The best-known musician to sing in this style was the late Pancho Prin, of the Tuy area of Miranda state.

An eight-stringed *bandola* (four double courses and similar in shape to the plains *bandola*) sometimes takes the place of the harp, which differs somewhat from that of the plains: its soundboard is slightly wider at the bottom, and its upper strings are metal, not nylon, though the lower strings are usually nylon or gut.

Central-coastal *joropo* music is less flamboyant than plains *joropo* music, and it is formally quite different. The vocal and instrumental melodies of the plains ensembles are songs with European-based harmonies and fixed texts, but the coastal style features shorter and more repetitive phrases, with melodies and texts likelier to be improvised. The harp makes complex melodic patterns.

The African cultural presence is more concentrated on the coast than on the plains. Because Barlovento is at the heart of this area, one would expect to find more African influences in this music than in plains *joropo* music. Indeed, the vocalist's improvisation recalls African musical traditions, as does the repetitiveness of themes and phrases—an important musical trait, not always appreciated by those who do not know African music.

Social Structure and Performance

Presentations of Venezuelan folk music in urban settings, at home and abroad, have since the 1960s often been organized and performed by university students and middle-class devotees of these traditions—citizens of ethnic and social backgrounds somewhat different from those who claim this music as their own. The core of this music remains in the countryside, performed by agricultural workers who, though not always having the educational and financial resources of their urban cousins, have access to the carriers and surroundings of traditional culture. It has been passed on to them orally by older relatives and neighbors. Since the 1980s, a revival of interest in creole traditions has produced hundreds of community-based performance groups scattered throughout the *ranchos* (poorer neighborhoods of Caracas), where few existed in the 1960s and 1970s.

—*Adapted from an article by Max H. Brandt*

Bibliography

Aretz, Isabel 1967. *Instrumentos Musicales de Venezuela*. Cumaná: Universidad de Oriente.

Brandt, Max H. 1994. "African Drumming from Rural Communities around Caracas and Its Impact on Venezuelan Music and Ethnic Identity." In *Music and Black Ethnicity: The Caribbean and South America*, edited by Gerard H. Béhague, 267–284. Miami: North-South Center, University of Miami.

Hernández, Daría, and Cecilia Fuentes. 1993. *Fiestas Tradicionales de Venezuela*. Caracas: Fundación Bigott.

Ortiz, Manuel Antonio. 1982. *Diablos Danzantes de Venezuela*. Caracas: Fundación La Salle de Ciencias Naturales.

Ramón y Rivera, Luís Felipe. 1969. *La Música Folklórica de Venezuela*. Caracas: Monte Ávila Editores.

——. 1971. *La Música Afrovenezolana*. Caracas: Universidad Central de Venezuela.

Salazar, Rafael. 1992. *Del Joropo y Sus Andanzas*. Caracas: Disco Club Venezolano. Book and compact disc.

——. 1994. *Caracas: Espiga Musical del Ávila*. Caracas: Disco Club Venezolano. Book and compact disc.

Mexico: One Country, Many Musics

Mexico is often seen as a land with a varied topography and at least three cultural identities—native pre-Columbian, Spanish colonial, and modern mestizo—but in reality it is much more complex and varied. Contemporary native Mexican groups speak more than fifty-four languages, and the twentieth-century emergence of a national identity embraced diverse strands of regional mestizo culture. Music has been a major signifier of these cultures. The large bass guitar shown opposite and known as the *guitarrón* is featured in mariachi groups that seem to typify Mexico by their presence in many Mexican restaurants in the United States. In reality, the instrument and mariachi itself are rooted in just one of Mexico's cultures—that of Jalisco and the surrounding states of western central Mexico, especially in the city of Guadalajara. The articles that follow depict Mexico's many musical cultures, beginning with those of the Mexica.

Francisco Castro of Guadalajara, a *guitarrón* player in a strolling mariachi orchestra, poses in a café.
Photo by Daniel E. Sheehy, 1984.

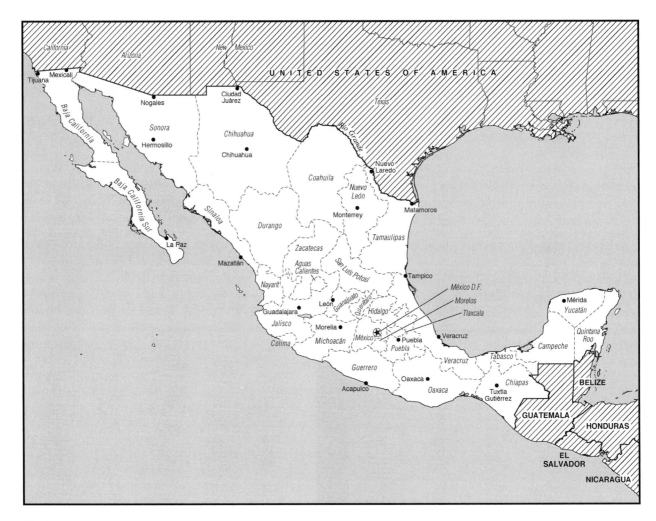

Mexico

Mexica (Aztec or Nahua People)

The oldest known version of Náhuatl, a language in the Uto-Aztecan linguistic family, was spoken by the Mexica people in pre-Columbian times. During the expansion of the Mexica (Aztec) Empire, it spread to other parts of Mesoamerica and served many native Americans as a lingua franca. Today, it has regional dialects. The Mexica were the bearers of a strong tradition of music and dance, particularly in the context of religious ceremonies, which they disseminated widely in many parts of what is now Mexico and Central America; like their language, these traits have regional variants in contemporary life.

Early Mexica Culture

Archaeological and historical evidence, the latter including chronicles written by Franciscan and Augustinian missionaries shortly after the Spanish conquest, indicates that people in the Aztec Empire during the early 1500s probably had no Nahua concept equivalent to the Spanish notion of music (though they did have a concept of beauty). This notion was introduced primarily by Roman Catholic missionaries, who taught European religious songs and hymns. Many terms in classic Náhuatl reveal indigenous concepts related to music, including singing (*cuica tlamatiliztli*), dancing (*netotiliztli*), sound or noise (*caquiliztli*), and the sound of trumpets (*tlatlazcaliztli*). Although it is unwise to explain Nahua music in terms of parallel musical concepts in other cultures, Nahua notions about the organized production of sounds were often expressed in terms of sound-producing actions and expressive movements of the human body, such as blowing through certain instruments that transmit sound like aerophones, using different manners of percussion, and creating sounds with the feet. From these facts, we may surmise that there was a strong link between music and dance.

Performances of music and dance occurred during the celebration of the ancient Aztec calendrical month Xocotl Huetzi (When the Fruits Fall), a festival among several dedicated to Xiuhtecuhtli (Yellow Face), the god of fire, one of the main deities of the Mexica pantheon. Other festivals with dances and music honored Xochiquetzali (Beautiful Flower), goddess of the moon. Two gods for music and dance were honored in the festival Xochilhuitl (Flower Festival). One of them was Xochipilli (Flower God), the solar deity of dance, music, flowers, games, love, pleasure, and poetry, whose counterpart was Macuilxóchitl (Five Flowers), the patron of dance and games.

Musical Instruments

Important musical instruments used for music and dance included struck objects (idiophones) and drums, plus certain wind instruments. Two idiophones—the *teponaztle* and the *huéhuetl*—were legendary in Mesoamerica. The *teponaztle* (also *teponaztli*) was a small, hollowed-out tree trunk with an H-shaped slit cut into it, producing two tongues. This instrument was positioned horizontally and struck with mallets. Each tongue produced a distinct pitch. Some ancient *teponaztle* preserved in the National Museum of Anthropology in Mexico City (figure 1) are of woods that produce a loud sound and are intricately engraved with important images, as of the deities Macuilxóchitl and Cuauhtli-Ocelotl (Eagle-Ocelot), and a serpent (*cóatl*). The *huéhuetl* was a single-headed cylindrical drum fashioned from a hollowed-out log (figure 2). Its size varied, but its dimensions reached a meter in length and 42 centimeters in diameter. Set in a vertical position with an animalskin head, it was played with the hands.

Pictographs in early colonial codices, particularly the Florentine Codex, offer important information about how the ancient Nahua played their percussion instruments in particular situations. The Codex Borbonicus describes the ancient calendars, rituals, cyclical celebrations, ceremonies commemorating the months of the Mexica (Aztec) year and other celebrations of the Aztec world. These codices offer ancient visual representations of Mexica culture and include many images of dancing associated with the sounds of the *teponaztle*, the *huéhuetl*, rattles, and conch trumpets. Allusions to the *teponaztle* and the *huéhuetl* frequently occur in sixteenth-century chronicles by Durán, Sahagún, and others, and in precolonial native paintings, such as those found in the Florentine Codex, the *Atlas Durán* (appended to Duran 1967), and other codices from the Mexica culture.

A description by Diego Muñoz Camargo (1947:146) tells how the *huéhuetl* and *teponaztle* were often played to accompany dances:

Figure 1 Two pre-Columbian Nahua slit drums (*teponaztle*), preserved in the National Museum of Anthropology in Mexico City. The upper instrument is wood engraved with an image of Cuauhtli-Ocelotl (Eagle-Ocelot); the lower instrument is ceramic, probably used for votive offerings.
Photo by Dale A. Olsen, 1970.

They had drums made with great beauty, tall ones, more than a half a man's height; and another instrument called *teponaxtle* [sic], made of a single log, rounded and hollowed out, whose sound carries more than half a league. Together with the drum they make strange and smooth sounds. With these drums, along with wooden trumpets and other instruments such as flutes, they produce a strange and admirable noise, and songs and dances so in rhythm that it is a sight to behold.

Modern Uses of Ancient Instruments

Today, the *teponaztle* is still in use and has various functions. In some Nahua pueblos in middle and west Mexico, certain patterns or sounds played on the instrument have a communicative function. In San Bernardino Contla, Tlaxcala, Nahua drummers play a pattern on a tall vertical drum of the *huéhuetl* type to announce a festival honoring the local patron saint; the sound of the drum is audible at a great distance. The Nahua of Pómaro, Michoacán, still play the *teponahuastle* (a version of the *teponaztle*) to announce Christian ceremonies.

In the valley of Puebla and Tlaxcala in central Mexico, the *huéhuetl* accompanies Christian ceremonies, calls people to Mass, and announces the beginning of patron saints' celebrations. In these settings, it is a member of the *conjunto azteca*, an ensemble that includes a *huéhuetl*-style drum, a snare drum, and a pair of *chirimías* (double-reed winds). This ensemble plays during Christian festivities in most Nahuatl- and Otomí-speaking towns in the Puebla-Tlaxcala Valley.

In relation to dance, the *teponaztle* and *huéhuetl* have been preserved mainly among *conchero* groups in Mexico City and in several other central Mexican

cities. The *conchero* dancers play armadillo-shell guitars while they dance in public displays tied to Christian traditions, especially the annual commemoration of the Virgin of Guadalupe (12 December). This is a principal occasion for such performances, when groups from many central Mexican towns congregate and perform to the accompaniment of *teponaztle* and *huéhuetl*.

In addition, in the north, west, center, and south of Mexico, indigenous people play musical instruments or in instrumental ensembles resembling those for the *teponaztle*. These include the *quiringüa* of the Purépecha of Michoacán state; the so-called *nokubson*, played by the Tenek of Hidalgo for the hawk (*gavilán*) and little tiger (*tigrillo*) dances; an instrument played among the Nahua people of Citlala and Quechultenango, Guerrero; and the *tunkul* of the Maya in Yucatán. The Wixarika people of Jalisco, Nayarít, and Durango play the *tepo*, which resembles the *huéhuetl*, for celebrations offering thanks to the gods for the firstfruits of their land.

Notwithstanding the indisputable Mesoamericanness of the use of *teponaztle* and *huéhuetl*, contact and fusion of indigenous and Spanish musical traditions occurred during the conversion of the indigenous peoples to Christianity, beginning in the early 1500s. This change coincided with changes in the Nahua people's values and worldviews, and has transformed the music. New European instrumental sources were adapted for and accepted in emergent musical ensembles. The instruments that significantly reflect the European musical tradition—violin, guitar, harp—have been those that most faithfully represent the preferred sound of indigenous peoples in contemporary times. It is hard to conceive of a

Figure 2 A pre-Columbian Nahua drum (*huéhuetl*) body fashioned from a hollowed-out log and preserved in the National Museum of Anthropology, Mexico City.
Photo by Dale A. Olsen, 1970.

traditional Mexican indigenous musical tradition that would not include bowed, strummed, or plucked stringed instruments. To a lesser extent, the *chirimía* (shawm) also found a place in many local indigenous communities.

These instruments were incorporated into the indigenous worldview, and most currently active ensembles are fusions, rather than reconstructions of European ensembles. These include Mesoamerican instruments such as rattles, usually played in ceremonially danced rituals associated with harvests that welcome the rains and bless the crops. Most of the stringed instruments are manufactured by indigenous people and mainly take the form of the four-stringed European violin, a small guitar (*jarana*, a high-pitched variation, with five strings or courses of strings), and a diatonic harp with twelve or twenty-eight strings.

Musical Contexts and Genres

Indigenous styles of playing musical instruments, formulating chordal progressions, and creating repertoires gave rise to the *son*, a musical genre that spread through much of the country. In the mestizo tradition, the word *son* is most often associated with regional musical styles performed on stringed instruments such as the violin, the *jarana*, and the harp. In indigenous music, however, especially Nahua music, the term *son* (pl. *sones*, diminutive *sonecito*) relates not to geographical locations, but to the relationship of the music with body movements and the symbolic representation of personages in ceremonial dances. In the Malinche dance (of Acayucan and Pajapan, Veracruz), a first group of musical pieces and a dance are formed by five *sones*, and a second group of musical pieces and a dance are formed by six *sones*. The Malinche dance begins with music and dance called *la cortesía* or *reverencia* 'the act of demonstrating respect for the dance', performed as the first encounter with La Malinche. This is an allegory of the native woman, Malinche, Cortes's concubine, adviser, and interpreter.

In this first group of *sones*, minor details in the dance receive local names. The first is the *son de cinco pasos y vuelta* 'son of five steps and a turn', the second is the *son de tres pasos y golpe de talón* 'son of three steps and a heelstroke', the third is the *son de la vuelta entera* 'son of a whole turn', the fourth is the *son de cuatro pasos al frente* 'son of four steps ahead', and the fifth is the *son de cuatro pasos* 'son of four steps'. A second group of *sones* indicates a change in attitude to that of a warlike confrontation, an allegory of the conquest of Mexico by the Spanish; it includes a sixth *son* (the *corrida del monarca* 'the monarch's run'), a seventh *son* (the *son de la guerra* 'son of war'), and an eighth *son*, with textual strophes about La Malinche.

Another example is the *danza de cuauileros* (or *danza de cuauilones*), found in the towns of Aquila, Coire, Maruata, Ostula, and Pómaro, near the Pacific Ocean in Michoacán. Also known as the *coloquio de la conquista de Hernán Cortés* 'colloquy of the conquest by Hernán Cortés', the dance represents the battle between native Americans and Spaniards. The performance is introduced with simulated combat using a wooden cudgel, Nahua warriors' favored weapon. The accompanying *sones* have different local Spanish names: the first one is *pata volando* 'flying foot'; the second, *cruzado* 'crosswise motion'; the third, *la cortesía* 'the paying of respect'; the fourth, *moviendo cadera* 'hip shaking'; the fifth, *primer paloteo* 'first attack with cudgels'; the sixth, *el brinquito* 'the little jump'; the seventh, *segundo paloteo* 'second attack with cudgels'; the eighth, *la cuchilla* 'the knife'; the ninth, *el engaño* 'the trick'; the tenth, *tercer paloteo* 'third attack with cudgels'; the eleventh, *pata ligera* 'agile foot'; and the twelfth (still with a Nahua name), *mochi nimochikahua* 'the leave-taking'. In addition to the cudgels, the dancers play rattles, coordinating their movements to the structures of the *sones*.

The titles of these *sones* indicate a display of skill in a simulation of battle. This display shows how the ancient Mexicans developed their military training. In addition, the attack with cudgels has to be precise and in accordance with the musical accents. The striking of the cudgels always occurs on the strong accents of every part of the musical piece; thus, there is no syncopation.

Some choreographies, such as those of the *cortesía* and *mochi nimochikahua*, are actually addressed to a saint. The movements in parts of the dance evoke religious attitudes; however, dancers' display of skill and competence earns high social status in Nahua society. Such dancers will gain prestige and will be recommended to other festival leaders.

The same towns in Michoacán have another dance, known by the Nahua terms *xayácatl* or *xaya-cates* 'the disguised men'; it parodies the famous Spanish dance *moros y cristianos* 'Moors and Christians', which reenacts the battles of the expulsion of the Moors from Spain. Men disguised as grotesque personages, wearing costumes made of coconut palms, leather masks, and tree branches, perform stylized simulated scenes of combat. Accompanied by violin and guitar, their dance has two sections: *xayácatl de pasultik* 'disguised men of the flat disguise', and *xayácatl alastik* 'disguised men of the curled disguise'. Both parts of the dance symbolize the victory of good over evil. Within the *xayácatl de alastik* occurs a representation of All Saints' Day, performed two days later, on the evening of 3 November, with four types of *son*: *niños disfrazados* 'disguised boys', in which disguised children enter with small canes, cowbells, and jingle bells; *quebrado* 'broken or turned motion'; *mihkuhika* 'the first change'; and *mihtutilo* 'the later change'. At the end of the *mihtutilo*, a new set of dancers, clothed in branches, thick grass, and other vegetation, enters, dancing and clapping their hands to the *son de pasultik*. The Nahua people of the Mexican Pacific Coast frequently allude to this event not as a dance, but as a game to frighten people (*mauiltic* 'to frighten, to play').

From the same Nahua area of Michoacán comes the dance of *corpus*, performed in mid-March to the accompaniment of a violin, a guitar, and rattles. The dancers are commanded by one male chief (*capitán*)

and two female chiefs (*capitanas*). The dancers interweave long ribbons attached to a long rope stretched out horizontally. Each dancer's role is to hold a ribbon, interweaving it with others, and then after a pause to undo the weaving through contrary movements. During this process, choreographed *sones*—including *la reata* 'the rope', *de rodillas* 'on one's knees', *el zapateado* 'the foot stamping', *el machetazo* 'the hit with a machete', *la cortesía* 'the paying of respect', and *la procesión* 'the pilgrimage'—are performed.

The most important musical trait of *sones* for Nahua dances is an ostinato bass in the harp, supporting a tonality that normally alternates between tonic and dominant chords. The meter does not change, and there is no prominent syncopation and no emphasis on improvisation, in contrast to the mestizo music of the nearby Michoacán area known as the hotlands (*tierra caliente*), where improvisation, syncopation, and changes in metrical emphasis are typical. With the use of harp and *jarana*, Nahua music shows a tendency toward isorhythm in its repetitive rhythms and short musical phrases. This is evidently the result of the link between the phrases of *sones* and the kinetic requirements of the dance.

Nahua *sones* for dancing are included in most important nonliturgical ceremonies within the Roman Catholic tradition, particularly in celebrations honoring patron saints. These celebrations are part of syncretized Mexican Christianity, which began to take shape in the 1500s by a substitution of divinities and an indigenous reinterpretation of Christian imagery and the Christian calendar. Out of this process came a native Christian tradition involving Náhuatl-speaking people in a system of ceremonial responsibilities such as *mayordomías* (the institution of having principals and elected native chiefs who organize rituals) and *pagar mandas, promesas*, or *ofrendas* (fulfilling religious vows, promises, or offerings, usually made in return for divine intervention). Among the Nahua along the Gulf of Mexico coast, the Christian personages with the most *mayordomías* and traditions of offerings are the Virgin of Guadalupe (celebrated 12 December), Saint Isidore the Farmer (between 14 and 17 May), Saint Joseph (17 May), and Saint Mary Magdalene (16 May). All these events include the performance of *sones* and the Malinche dance. Among Nahua people of the Pacific Coast, festive events include those honoring Saint Anthony (13 June), celebrated with *cuauileros* and *corpus*, and the Virgin of Guadalupe (locally, 12 December and Good Friday), celebrated with *xayácatl*.

—*Adapted from an article by Arturo Chamorro*

Bibliography

Anguiano, Marina, and Guido Munch. 1979. *La danza de Malinche*. México, D.F.: Culturas Populares, Secretaría de Educación Pública.

Dibble, Charles E., and Arthur J. O. Anderson. 1951. *Florentine Codex: General History of the Things of New Spain by Fray Bernardino de Sahagún, Book 2*. Santa Fé: School of American Research.

Durán, Diego. 1967. *Historia de las Indias de la Nueva España*. México, D.F.: Editorial Porrúa.

Hellmer, José Raúl. 1960. "Mexican Indian Music Today." *Toluca Gazette* (1 June). Toluca: Gobierno del Estado de México.

Landa, Diego de. 1959. *Relación de las Cosas de Yucatán*. México, D.F.: Editorial Porrúa.

Martí, Samuel. 1968. *Instrumentos Musicales Precortesianos*. México, D.F.: Instituto Nacional de Antropología e Historia.

Mendoza, T. Vicente. 1984. *Panorama de la Música Tradicional de México*. México, D.F.: Universidad Nacional Autónoma de México, Instituto de Investigaciones Estéticas.

Muñoz Camargo, Diego. 1947. *Historia de Tlaxcala*. México, D.F: Lauro Rosell.

Sahagún, Bernardino de. 1956. *Historia General de las Cosas de Nueva España*, vol. 1. México, D.F.: Editorial Porrúa.

Soustelle, Jacques. 1950. *La Pensée Cosmologique des Anciens Mexicaines*. Paris: Hermann.

Stevenson, Robert M. 1968. *Music in Aztec and Inca Territory*. Berkeley: University of California.

Mexico

In 1843, when Frances Calderón de la Barca, the wife of the Spanish ambassador to Mexico, wrote that for Mexicans, "music is a sixth sense," she joined a long line of distinguished observers who praised Mexican musical performances. Evidence of the musical achievements of Mexico's indigenous people is abundant. Archaeological remains bear witness to the complexity of musical instruments and performance in native American cultures more than a millennium before contact with Europeans. Sixteenth-century European chroniclers described the prestige and prominence of musical life among the indigenous peoples they encountered, and twentieth-century documentation revealed that many distinctive native musical traditions survived nearly five centuries after the Spanish conquistador Hernán Cortés defeated the Aztec Emperor Moctezuma.

During the colonial period, Franciscan, Dominican, Augustinian, Jesuit, and other Roman Catholic missionaries found European sacred music a valuable means of teaching the indigenous population the tenets and customs of Christianity. Many pre-Conquest indigenous musical practices were easily transferred to Roman Catholic contexts, so church music prospered. As deadly diseases and Spanish oppression diminished the indigenous population and as Amerindians, Europeans, and Africans intermingled, a new, mestizo ("mixed") population evolved. African peoples, most brought to Mexico as slaves, profoundly influenced the shaping of mestizo culture and music—an impact not yet fully understood or appreciated.

In the century after 1810, when Mexico achieved independence from Spain, many observers published accounts of regionally distinct traditions of music among rural mestizos. After the revolution of 1910, many of these traditions were officially promoted as symbols of national identity, or were popularized through national media. Also, from the adoring nineteenth-century accounts of visiting Italian-style opera singers, and from the strong following of nationalist composers in the twentieth century, we know that European secular fine-art music did not escape the Mexican attraction to music.

Many musical threads of Mexico's past have continued into the twenty-first century; however, rapid urbanization, the intensified commodification of music, an increasingly powerful and centralized media complex, and other modern trends, have worked to magnify and coopt certain musical styles, leaving others to languish in the shadow of neglect, and to introduce and promulgate new musical fashions from abroad, especially from the United States. [For a map of Mexico, see MEXICA (AZTEC OR NAHUA PEOPLE).]

The Historical Record

Music in the Colonial Period, 1521–1810

New Spain, as Mexico was called when it was a Spanish colony, enjoyed an active musical life. Most documentation surviving from the 1500s and 1600s tells of the learning, creation, and performance of European fine-art music, particularly that associated with the Roman Catholic Church. Missionaries relied on music as a means of enculturating indigenous peoples in the principles and ways of the Spanish Roman Catholic tradition. Native Americans responded by taking up European music in large numbers; many of them attained a high degree of musicianship in choral and instrumental performance. New Spain's church life was a rich vein of European musical production until its decline, in the 1700s.

Vernacular European and mestizo musics outside religious contexts seldom made their way into musical notation. Official documents suggest that musical performances occurred often; some attracted the reprimand of religious authorities on moral grounds. A violist named Ortiz was among the followers of Hernán Cortés. Locally made Spanish musical instruments were abundant soon after the Encounter. In the 1600s and 1700s, blacks gave profane musical performances (oratorios, escapularios) during religious festivities, ridiculing the sacred event. Colonial documents show that blacks played harps and guitars, danced publicly, and played important roles in shaping grassroots music.

In the late 1700s, as Spanish influence over the New World waned, the vernacular music of New Spain's criollos and mestizos took on a more local character. Spanish seguidillas, fandangos, sung verses called coplas and letrillas, and other folkloric genres were the models for the creation of new pieces called sones, first documented as such in 1766 in Spanish Inquisition records. Popular theater performed in the Coliseo in Mexico City around 1800 featured *tonadillas escénicas*—short, simple dramas, replete with new *sones* and other local melodies. The *jarabe*, a *son* intended especially for dancing, also emerged around 1800.

Music in the Independence Period, 1810–1910

Independence from Spain and the decline of ecclesiastical influence brought Mexican secular music to greater prominence. *Sones, jarabes*, and other melodies associated with political insurgence were honored as symbols of national identity. Writers of that time described a Mexican culture alive with musical activity marked by regional traditions and interregional sharing. Traditional Mexican melodies were arranged for piano and exalted in genteel society as national airs (*aires nacionales*) and little *sones* of the country (*sonecitos del país*). *Jarabes* flourished, especially in west and central Mexico, gradually evolving into potpourris of excerpts from *sones* and other popular melodies.

Independence led to the importation of music from Europe, especially Italy and France. Italian opera was imported, imitated, and emulated by Mexican musicians and composers. Outside the confines of the Roman Catholic Church, instrumental fine-art music was virtually unknown in Mexico until the first wave of foreign performers, after 1840. The piano became a standard piece of furniture in the homes of an expanding middle class. European fashions in dancing were adopted unchanged. The waltz (*vals*), introduced by 1815, met frequent condemnation as a "licentious" French import and was quite popular throughout the period. One of the most internationally renowned Mexican compositions of the 1800s was "*Sobre las Olas*" ('Over the Waves'), a waltz composed by the Otomí native American Juventino Rosas (1868–1894) in 1891. "*La Paloma*," the most popular song during the French occupation (1862–1867), had been written in the 1840s by the Spaniard Sebastián de Yradier (1809–1865) in the style of a Cuban habanera—a form that left a deep mark on Mexican music of later years. A voluminous repertoire of mazurkas (*mazurcas*), polkas (*polcas*), schottisches (*chotices*), waltzes (*valses*), and other pieces for dancing were composed in European styles by Mexicans in the late 1800s. In bandstands set up in town plazas across the country, brass bands (*bandas del pueblo*) performed *marchas*, European dances, *sonecitos*, and *jarabes*.

Music after 1910

With the Mexican Revolution, beginning in 1910, came a nationalist movement in cultural thought and policy. Intellectuals elevated and idealized Mexico's Amerindian past, and music scholars combed through archives and archaeological relics, recovering pre-Encounter musical achievements. Native American and mestizo songs and dances were collected and published. Mexico's centralized educational system codified and disseminated a select repertoire of music and dance. José Vasconcelos, Secretary of Public Education from 1921 to 1924, directed his agency, through its Aesthetic Culture Department, to encourage traditional dance; on the hundredth anniversary of the founding of the republic (1921), thousands watched as thirty couples danced "*El Jarabe Tapatío*" in a Mexico City ceremony unveiling the version to be taught throughout the country. Rural musicians representing locally distinctive mestizo styles migrated to Mexico City in search of professional musical opportunities.

In the 1930s and 1940s, the nationwide expansion of the radio and recording industries created a demand for local musics that possessed the potential for broad appeal. In the same decades, the Mexican film industry, while it created star entertainers singing in pseudo-folk styles, contributed to public awareness of certain styles of traditional music. These media were vehicles by which foreign music infiltrated local culture. For intellectuals, music from the United States was a major source of concern—a fear that led the music historian Gabriel Saldívar (1937:21) to promote national music as "a barrier of pure nationalism to the avalanche . . . of shabby [*quinto patio* 'slum'] songs" that had invaded Mexico. There are more than four hundred radio stations nationwide, most of them commercial. Although the media are the central force in shaping musical tastes, the fabric of Mexico's musical life, like that of most twenty-first-century large urban societies, is made up of hundreds of threads, commonly described in several ways: music of "ethnic groups," referring principally to Amerindians; regional musical culture (*música regional*); widespread genres of music, such as narrative ballads (*corridos*); folk-derived popular music; international pop-music fashions; and fine-art music.

Música Regional: The Mestizo Son

As mestizo culture took shape, the particular cultural blend, the shared life experiences over time, and the isolation of local communities led to considerable cultural diversity among mestizos. Musical life was more local and regional than it was national, and this tendency was reflected in the mestizo music that had evolved by the 1800s.

At the core of most regional musical styles that emerged with the formation of mestizo culture, particularly those of central Mexico, is the musical genre known as *son*. As the Spanish *seguidillas*, fandangos, *zapateados*, and secular forms widely known as *tonadillas* were accepted and reinterpreted by mestizos, new genres of music, based on Spanish predecessors, came into being. In the early 1800s, the Gran Teatro Coliseo de la Metrópoli in Mexico City and theaters in the provinces were clearinghouses for various genres of song and dance. Theatrical interludes featured Spanish and mestizo melodies and dances that were circulating throughout New Spain. These pieces, often called *sones*, took various forms, including that of *jarabes*, pieces documented as early as the late 1700s. Many extant *sones*, including "*La Bamba*," "*El Perico*," and "*El Palomo*," were documented in the early 1800s.

The mestizo *son* continues to be formally diverse, but a few generalizations are possible. It is oriented toward accompanying social dance, with vigorous, marked rhythm and fast tempo. It is performed most often by ensembles in which stringed instruments predominate, with notable regional exceptions. Its formal structure features the alternation of instrumental sections and the singing of short poetic units called *coplas*. The mode is usually major, with harmonic vocabulary mostly limited to progressions drawing from I, IV, II^7, V, and V^7. In contrast to the Amerindian *son*, the mestizo *son* is fundamentally secular, as is reflected in its textual amorousness and wit, its extraversion, and its performative settings.

When danced, the *son* is usually performed by couples, though some *sones* have special choreography that may call for other groupings. Triple meter (6/8, 3/4, or a combination of both) predominates, with many exceptions in duple meter. The performing ensembles include melodic instruments, such as violins and harps, and instruments that provide chordal and rhythmic accompaniment corresponding to specific regional styles, especially guitars. Singing is usually in a high vocal range, often in parallel thirds. Men predominate in public performances, but many women learn and perform *sones*, particularly in family settings. *Sones* are often performed at important lifecycle events (especially baptisms, birthdays, and weddings), in public commemorations of the civic-religious calendar (independence day, patronal saints' days), and in entertainment-oriented venues, including bars, restaurants, and theaters. Many government- and private-sponsored public concerts feature *sones* and other forms of folkloric music and dance.

Coplas performed for *sones* are short poetic stanzas that stand alone as complete thoughts, not linked together in a long narrative (as in some other Mexican genres). They usually consist of four to six octosyllabic lines. The even-numbered lines rhyme; the odd-numbered lines may end in consonance or assonance. The following is a typical *copla*:

> *Buenas noches, señoritas;*
> *muy buenas noches señores.*
> *A todas las florecitas*
> *de rostros cautivadores*
> *van las trovas más bonitas*
> *de estos pobres cantadores.*

> Good evening, misses;
> a very good evening, sirs.
> To all the little flowers
> with captivating faces
> go the prettiest verses
> of these poor troubadours.

Two major exceptions to this form are textual patterns derived from the *seguidilla* and the *décima*. In the former, seven-syllable lines alternate with five-syllable lines. The *décima* is a ten-line stanza, rhyming *abbaaccddc*. *Décimas* are present in certain *sones* of southern Veracruz, and in the *valonas*, a musical genre with several declaimed *décimas*, of the hotlands (*tierra caliente*) in southwestern Michoacán.

Regional Sones

These and other unifying traits make a case for a mestizo *son* "supergenre," but many regional styles of *son* are easily recognizable by the distinctiveness of their instrumentation, instrumental techniques, treatment of the *copla*, vocal nuances, repertoire, associated dances, and other factors. Many regional styles of Mexican music are distinguished by their forms of *sones* and several other styles in which the *son* has been historically influential, but not currently central to their identity. Seven principal kinds of *son* that mark regional musical styles are *son huasteco* of the northwestern geocultural area known as the Huasteca; *son jarocho* of the southern coastal plain of the state of Veracruz; *son istmeño* or *son oaxaqueño* of the Isthmus of Tehuantepec, mainly in the southwest portion of Oaxaca, overlapping with Chiapas; *chilena* of the Costa Chica, along the Pacific coast of Oaxaca and Guerrero; *son guerrerense* (*son calenteño*) of the Balsas River basin hotlands in Guerrero; *son michoacano* (*son calentano*) from the neighboring hotlands of Michoacán; and the *son jalisciense* of Jalisco. Four of these styles are described in detail below. Many regional styles in which the *son* is influential but not central are those of Yucatán and the northern border.

Son Jarocho

DISC
❶
TRACK
9

The *son jarocho* takes its name from a term of uncertain origin (possibly from *jaras*, clubs said to have been wielded by colonial militia) denoting the people of the southern coastal plain of Veracruz. Its most widespread typical instrumentation (figure 1) features the thirty-two- to thirty-six-stringed diatonic harp (*arpa jarocha*), a *jarana* (shallow-bodied guitar with eight strings in five courses), and a *requinto* ("*guitarra de son*," a four-stringed, narrow-bodied guitar, plucked with a 7.5-centimeter plectrum, fashioned from cowhorn or a plastic comb). The use of the *requinto* appears to be on the wane. In the south, near the border with Tabasco, the harp is rare, and smaller sizes of *jaranas* are found. In the central town of Tlacotalpan, a *pandero* (octagonal frame drum with jingles, like a tambourine) joins the ensemble. The harpist plays melody and bass. The *jarana* player employs patterns (*maniqueos*) to strum a rhythmic-chordal accompaniment appropriate to the meter, tempo, and character of the particular *son*. The *requinto* player (*requintero*) supplies an additional, largely improvisatory, melodic line, often interacting with the harpist's melody. Six-line *coplas* are most common and are the preferred medium for most textual improvisation, of which a great deal occurs.

It is often supposed that the *son jarocho*, more than any other regional *son* tradition, is of African origin. Most *sones jarochos* are based on a short, cyclical rhythmic-chordal pattern (*compás*) that drives the music through continuous repetition in the fashion of West African timelines (usually played on a bell) or African-Cuban beats (played on claves). Certain *sones*—"*El Coco*" and "*La Iguana*"—have a responsorial refrain. The style and degree of inter-action among musicians, dancers, and audience suggest a more African style. These factors, with the prominence of African and mulatto people in the area's ethnographic history, further support this notion.

Son Istmeño *or* Son Oaxaqueño

Customarily, unlike most regional *son* styles, the *son istmeño* is neither performed by string ensembles nor sung. Wind-and-percussion *bandas* follow the basic pattern of "sung" sections that alternate with instrumental interludes, though sections sung in other areas are performed instrumentally in a cantabile style. The *bandas* follow the models of European brass bands of the 1800s. Most *bandas* are composed exclusively of native Americans, the *banda* being a central social institution of many Amerindian communities; performances at civic and religious celebrations, however, are part of the musical life of mestizos and native Americans alike.

In the southernmost state of Chiapas and the southern edge of Oaxaca, the marimba (figure 2) is similar to the *banda* in its treatment of *sones*. It was probably modeled on African xylophone prototypes during colonial times, but it has been the domain of primarily mestizo musicians since at least the mid-1800s. An important icon of Chiapan identity, it is closely associated with the towns of Tehuantepec (Chiapas) and Juchitán (Oaxaca). It may be *sencilla* (a single instrument) or *doble* (a combination of a smaller and a larger instrument), and may be played by two, three, or more players. It is often accompanied by percussion and other instruments. It continues to consist of rectangular wooden slats of

Figure 1 A *conjunto jarocho* in Boca del Río, Veracruz, 1978. *Left to right*: Daniel Valencia on *requinto jarocho*, Rufino Velásquez on *arpa jarocha*, and Inés Rivas on *jarana jarocha*. *Photo by Daniel E. Sheehy.*

Figure 2 Near several restaurants in downtown Veracruz, a quartet plays a marimba and accompanying instruments. *Left to right*: two musicians playing the marimba, a drummer, and a *güiro* player.
Photo by Daniel E. Sheehy, 1978.

resemble the piano keyboard, with the black keys located above and set into the white keys. Marimba ensembles typically perform a wide-ranging repertoire, from pieces often called *sones* to a special repertoire for Amerindian events to current melodies spread through the popular media. The pieces most closely resembling the *sones* of other areas follow two main models: waltz-rhythm melodies, instrumental interpretations of songs; and fast-tempo *zapateados* cast in a 6/8 rhythmic mold with frequent shifts to 3/4.

Son Michoacano

In the neighboring hotlands of Michoacán, the *son michoacano* (*son calenteño*) is closely identified with a string ensemble consisting of a large diatonic harp (*arpa grande*), two violins, a *vihuela* (five-stringed guitar with a convex back), and a *jarana* (also known as *guitarra de golpe*, a deep-bodied five-stringed guitar). Like the *sones* of Veracruz and the Huasteca, the *son michoacano* uses instrumental interludes to separate the sung sections. Occasionally during these interludes, a violinist or guitarist kneels down and strikes the lower face of the harp with his hands as a percussive accompaniment (figure 3)— a practice that was apparently more widespread in earlier times.

The *son* is central to the repertoire of the ensemble, but two other traditional genres, *jarabe* and the *valona*, are distinctive of Michoacán. The *jarabe* formally resembles its counterparts elsewhere in west-central Mexico—a string of perhaps five to seven melodies performed instrumentally, each section corresponding to a particular pattern of

graduated lengths suspended over resonator tubes (each with a membrane that buzzes as its slat is struck), but its slatboard has been transformed to

Figure 3 A *conjunto de arpa grande* from the hotlands of Michoacán. *Left to right*: Ricardo Gutiérrez Villa, plays violin; an onlooker watches; a second violinist (name unknown) momentarily kneels and beats the harp with his hands; Rubén Cuevas Maldonado plays *arpa grande*; a musician (name unknown) plays *vihuela*; and Ovaldo Ríos Yáñez plays *guitarra de golpe* (*jarana*). *Photo by Daniel E. Sheehy, 1991.*

movement. The *valona* (the word is thought to derive from "Walloon," perhaps introduced during the presence of Flemish troops in the 1700s), more widespread in the 1800s, is a version of *décima*-based forms found in several parts of Latin America. Generally, a four-line *copla* precedes four *décimas*, the last line of each *décima* duplicating the first, second, third, and fourth lines of the introductory *copla*, in that order. A single basic melodic pattern functions as the introduction and as musical interludes between sections of text. The subjects are almost invariably witty or picaresque.

Son Jalisciense

The *son jalisciense* (*son* from the state of Jalisco) is perhaps the most widely known of Mexican *sones* through its performance by mariachis throughout the country. It is closely related to the *son michoacano* and to a lesser extent to other *sones* throughout territory stretching from southern Sinaloa to Guerrero. Before the introduction and standardization of trumpets in mariachis during the 1930s through 1950s, the accompaniment to it was one or two violins, a *vihuela*, perhaps a *guitarra de golpe*, and a harp or a *guitarrón*. Most *sones jaliscienses* are strophic songs in which *coplas* alternate with melodically fixed instrumental interludes. Some are rhythmically complex, with ornate patterns of guitar strumming and 3/4–6/8 metrical ambiguities.

Widespread Genres

Many regional musical customs, genres, and pieces are shared widely, especially by mestizos. Religious observances paying homage to the Virgin of Guadalupe or reenacting Mary and Joseph's journey to Bethlehem, songs sung by and for children, *corridos*, serenades (*serenatas*), the song "*Las Mañanitas*," and "national" music and dances derived from regional traditions are some of the most pervasive.

Religious Music

More than 90 percent of the Mexican population is nominally Roman Catholic. In addition to liturgical music and sacramental events that include secular music (such as baptisms, weddings, and funerals), there are specifically Mexican religious occasions with their own musical repertoires.

Among Mexican communities in Mexico and abroad, 12 December and the preceding weeks are a time of ceremonial devotion to the Virgin of Guadalupe. Special hymns and other songs of praise to the Virgin of Guadalupe are sung during processions, celebrations of the Mass, and late-evening or early-morning serenades in front of statues and images of her.

Early December is an important occasion for devotional performances by musical-choreographic groups often known as *concheros*, named for the guitar many of them play, fashioned from an armadillo shell. *Concheros*, whose performance also may be known as Aztec dance (*danza azteca*), are active in many parts of Mexico and the southwestern United States, but especially in the federal district (Mexico City) and the neighboring states to its north and east. Consisting mainly of blue-collar and lower-middle-class mestizos and Amerindians of both sexes and all ages, these groups take part in many saint's-day celebrations, singing, playing, and dancing while dressed in ornate costumes, evoking images of ancient Aztecs. Many carry out long-distance pilgrimages to the Basílica de Guadalupe at the foot of Tepeyac, where they perform tightly coordinated devotional choreographies.

In southern Veracruz and neighboring areas, the Advent tradition known as *la rama* involves groups of adults and/or children, who go from home to home asking for an *aguinaldo*, a gift of coins, candy, food, or drink. They typically carry with them a decorated branch (*rama*) and sing verses to the melody "*La Rama*" ('The Branch'). There are local variations of "*La Rama*," but it is distinguished by verses sung by individuals alternating with the refrain, beginning *Naranjas y limas, limas y limones, más linda es la Virgen que todas las flores* 'Oranges and lemons, lemons and limes, the Virgin is prettier than all the flowers'. The texts may refer to the birth of Jesus, or they may be entirely secular or picaresque in content.

The Corrido

The *corrido* is distributed widely throughout Mexico, but has been favored particularly by people in the north and west. Its historical roots are thought to be in the Spanish *romance*, a long ballad, structured in a series of *coplas*, and the nineteenth-century printed *décimas* distributed in the fashion of English broadsides as a means of spreading accounts of notable events. The revolution beginning in 1910 intensified the popular interest that catapulted the *corrido* to prominence, as it conveyed the events and often heroic exploits of such revolutionary figures as Francisco Madero (1873–1913), Francisco Villa (1878–1923), Emiliano Zapata (1879–1919), and many others.

It was in the revolutionary era (1910–1917) that the form and function of the *corrido* became relatively fixed. Structurally, the *corrido* most often consists of a simple melody the length of a *copla* cast in a I–V^7 harmonic framework and repeated for a variable number of *coplas*. The meter is usually 3/4, but 2/4 is common, particularly in renditions from later years, when *música norteña*, with its polka rhythm, came into fashion. The emphasis is on the text, sung straightforwardly, unfettered by musical complexities. Usually, the first *copla* is a formal introduction, and the final *copla* is a formal farewell.

The *corrido* continued in its function of memorializing current events, real or imaginary, long after revolutionary activity subsided. Battles between police and smugglers (*contrabandistas*), assassinations, horse races, and a wide range of tragic and comic stories provide fodder for the composers of *corridos*—on both sides of the Mexico–U.S. border.

Songs by and for Children
Children's game-playing songs are "probably one of the most traditional and persistent" musical repertoires in Mexico (Mendoza 1956:55). Most Mexican game-playing songs are clearly of Hispanic origin, though many variations on those Spanish prototypes have emerged over the centuries. Circular games (*rondas*), the most prominent, include jump-rope songs and clapping songs, in which the singing guides the movements of the game. "*La pájara pinta*," "*Amo ató matarile rilerón*," "*Doña Blanca*," "*A la víbora de la mar*" "*Juan Pirulero*," and many other such songs are heard on school playgrounds and in parks, streets, and other places where children play. The melodies and the texts vary, but most involve constant repetition and the use of nonlexical syllables.

Serenatas
Other musical practices widespread in Mexico include *serenatas*, the related song "*Las Mañanitas*," and songs and dances (usually associated with a particular cultural area) that have spread through the educational system or the popular media. *Serenatas* (apparently from *sereno* 'night watchman', referring to the early hours, when their performances traditionally occur) are courting, congratulatory, or devotional serenades. A man may contract or organize a group of musicians and unexpectedly serenade his lover outside her home. The recipient of the serenade may otherwise be a person celebrating a birthday or other happy event—or even an image of the Virgin of Guadalupe (particularly on 12 December).

The song "*Las Mañanitas*" is often the first song sung on these occasions. In earlier times, the term *mañanitas* 'early morning' was nearly synonymous with *serenata*, and included a range of songs that varied according to local custom. Currently, it often refers to a specific song, an arrangement combining portions of two different *mañanitas*— "*Las Mañanitas Mexicanas*" and "*Las Mañanitas Tapatías*."

Popular Music

Folk-derived Popular Music
Though the recording and broadcasting of regional musics had already been underway during the second and third decades of the twentieth century, the major explosion in Mexico's popular media history did not occur until the fourth decade. The powerful radio station XEW began broadcasting in 1930. It was followed by XEB and others, meeting a demand for live musical performances to fill the airtime. Seeking opportunities, musicians representing regional musical traditions flocked to Mexico City. In 1935, the Victor Talking Machine Company opened Mexico's first major record-production facility, expanding the availability of recordings of home-grown music. The Mexican film industry prospered in the 1930s and 1940s, and many influential films, such as "*Allá en el Rancho Grande*" (1936), "*Cielito Lindo*" (1936), and "*Ay Jalisco no te rajes!*" (1941) portrayed regional musicians, often to evoke an idealized sense of rural life. *Mariachi*, *jarocho*, marimba, and other kinds of typical music (*música típica*) were heard and seen throughout Mexico and abroad.

The dramatic growth of the radio, recording, and film industries during this time profoundly affected Mexican musical life. Professional composers proliferated, many building on the Mexican tradition of the nineteenth-century romantic song (*canción romántica*). Pseudo-folk and urban derivative styles of music emerged from rural predecessors. The communal character of regional music was displaced by a star system promoted by the commercial media. Foreign folk-derived genres, such as the Cuban bolero and the *cumbia* [see AFRO-COLOMBIAN POPULAR MUSIC], took hold at the cultural grassroots. American popular-music exports, from the foxtrot and blues to rock and rap, held sway over urban Mexicans' musical tastes.

Mexican Song: The **Canción Romántica** *and the* **Canción Ranchera**
Genres, structures, styles of interpretation, and accompanying instrumentation reflect the musical currents that have influenced the creation and performance of music in Mexico, particularly since the mid-1800s, a time of European romanticism, Italian opera, and the rise of the middle class, when

Figure 4 A mariachi in Mexico City poses in front of the historic cabaret Salón Tenampa, located on Plaza Garibaldi, where mariachis gather and perform daily. *Left to right*: two trumpets, two violins, a *guitarrón*, and a *vihuela*.
Photo by Daniel E. Sheehy, 1991.

sentimental and nostalgic composition emerged in Mexico. The terms *canción romántica* and *canción sentimental* described this musical strain, which remained in vogue into the early twentieth century and still constitutes a major thread of contemporary Mexican musical life. With Yradier's "*La Paloma*" (see above), Veracruzan composer Narciso Serradell's "*La Golondrina*," cast similarly in an *habanera* meter, was an important prototype for songwriters between 1870 and 1900.

In the first decades of the twentieth century, Yucatecan composers, influenced by the Colombian *bambuco* and Cuban parlor music, helped shape *canciones románticas*. The prolific Yucatecan songwriter Augusto "Guty" Cárdenas Pinelo (1905–1932) wrote many songs, such as "*Rayito de Luna*," that became embedded in the national musical repertoire. María Grever (1884–1951), based in New York for most of her musical career, created songs such as "*Júrame*," "*Cuando Vuelva a Tu Lado*," and "*Muñequita Linda*," and movie music with wide appeal in the United States, Latin America, and abroad. Agustín Lara (ca. 1897–1970) brought a new urban and more openly sensual sensibility to the *canción romántica* in more than five hundred compositions, such as "*Mujer*." His early prominence on Mexican radio and in films in the 1930s had a broad impact on musical tastes and contributed to the popularity of his music.

Typically, the *canción romántica* was, and continues to be, performed by a soloist or a duo or trio of singers, often accompanying themselves on guitars, perhaps with subtle percussion, such as maracas or *güiro* ('gourd' a scraped gourd idiophone with inscribed grooves or notches). One such

group, Trío Los Panchos, which became enormously popular in the late 1940s, furthered the prominence of the Cuban-derived, slow-tempo, romantic bolero. Its style of interpreting songs with suave, mellifluous voices singing in two- or three-part harmony strengthened the association of such groups with *canciones románticas* and the status of the romantic trio as a major Mexican musical stereotype.

The *canción ranchera* came about with the twentieth-century mass migration of rural people to urban areas, Mexico City in particular. Many urban Mexicans preserved a strong identity with their rural roots. The emergence of the *canción ranchera* paralleled the rise of the popular media and folk-derived ensembles such as the modern mariachi. Beginning in the 1930s and continuing through the century, popular singer-actor movie stars, such as Jorge Negrete (1911–1953) and Pedro Infante (1917–1957), portrayed idealized ranchers, Mexican cowboys (*charros*), and other rural stereotypes, singing country songs (*canciones rancheras*) with straightforward messages of love, romantic betrayal, and adventurous exploits. These songs, finding a niche in the commercial-music market, attracted countless songwriters. Among the most prolific and influential was José Alfredo Jiménez (1926–1973), who composed and recorded more than four hundred popular compositions beginning in the late 1940s. *Canciones rancheras* are typically in a simple binary form, in a slow duple or triple or fast duple meter and sung by a soloist in a direct, extroverted, passionate style, somewhat reminiscent of *bel canto*. The term is often extended to refer to any song sung in a *ranchero* style, and particularly such songs accompanied by a mariachi. The *bolero ranchero*, for example, is a version of the romantic bolero, interpreted in a more open-voiced, solo fashion.

Mariachi

Since the 1930s, the mariachi (figure 4) has been the most prominent folk-derived musical ensemble in Mexico. Postrevolutionary nationalism, which elevated grassroots cultural expression, and the rising radio and film industries, which disseminated it, contributed to its importance.

The old-time mariachi—one or two violins, a *guitarra de golpe* and/or a *vihuela*, and a harp or some form of string bass—still exists in some rural communities of Jalisco and Nayarít, where it plays a generations-old repertoire of *sones*, *jarabes*, and religious pieces called *minuetes*. Its presence has been eclipsed almost entirely, though, by the modern mariachi, which evolved largely in response to the success of Mexico City's commercial-music industry in radio, film, recordings, and later, television. The instrumentation was expanded to include sections called *melodía* (two trumpets and three to six or more violins) and *armonía* (a *vihuela*, a guitar, a *guitarrón*, and occasionally a harp). Since the 1930s, the evolution of the mariachi closely followed that of *música ranchera* and its star system.

The preeminent and archetypal modern mariachi since the 1940s has been Mariachi Vargas de Tecalitlán. Under the guidance of the Silvestre Vargas (1901–1985), Mariachi Vargas came to dominate commercial mariachi music. It appeared regularly in the major electronic media, accompanying the most prominent singers of *música ranchera*, and producing countless recordings. Its musical arrangements of traditional pieces and modern compositions set the standard for virtually all modern mariachis throughout Mexico and abroad. Since the 1950s, its close collaboration with the composer-arranger Rubén Fuentes (b. 1926), who joined Vargas as a musician in 1945, had a profound impact on mariachi music. His innovations brought the harmonic language of contemporary popular music and new instrumental techniques and rhythms into the canon of mariachi conventions.

—*Adapted from an article by Daniel E. Sheehy*

Bibliography

Béhague, Gerard. 1979. *Music in Latin America: An Introduction.* Englewood Cliffs, N.J.: Prentice-Hall.

Kaptain, Laurence. 1992. *The Wood That Sings: The Marimba in Chiapas, Mexico.* Everett, Pa.: HoneyRock.

Mendoza, Vincente T. 1956. *Panorama de la Música tradicional de México.* México, D.F.: Imprenta Universitaria.

Moreno Rivas, Yolanda. 1989. *Historia de la música popular mexicana,* 2nd ed. México, D.F.: Consejo Nacional para la Cultura y las Artes, Alianza Editorial Mexicana.

Saldívar, Gabriel. 1937. *El Jarabe, baile popular mexicano.* México, D.F.: Talleres Gráficos de la Nación.

Sheehy, Daniel. 2006. *Mariachi Music in America: Experiencing Music, Expressing Culture.* New York: Oxford University Press.

Stevenson, Robert M. 1952. *Music in Mexico: A Historical Survey.* New York: Thomas Y. Crowell.

Central America

Central America

Central America comprises seven nations: Guatemala, Belize, Honduras, El Salvador, Nicaragua, Costa Rica, and Panama. In pre-Columbian times, the region was the center of one of the world's most celebrated and musically complex civilizations: the Maya. Three centuries of Spanish colonial rule and independent evolution since 1821 have wrought differing national complexions from varied cultural roots. For example, most Guatemalans are Amerindians, most Costa Ricans claim European heritage, and nearly half the Belizean population is African. Musical cultures of the region reflect these differences. For instance, European-derived musical instruments, such as harps, guitars, and violins, are popular among native American and mestizo groups. To offer a sense of these musical cultures, we present articles on the Maya, the Garifuna of Belize, the marimba in Guatemala, and Panama.

A *garawoun* drummer plays the *primero*, a treble drum, during a *wanaragua* performance, Dangriga, Belize, 2005.
Photo by Oliver Greene.

Maya

Some 2.5 million Maya live in the southern Mexican states of Campeche, Chiapas, Quintana Roo, Tabasco, and Yucatán, and in Belize, Guatamala, and parts of El Salvador and Honduras. Most contemporary Maya live in towns and villages, practice subsistence cultivation of maize, follow traditional culture, wear distinctive dress, and speak one of twenty Mayan languages or dialects. Their worldviews, myths, and religious customs include elements of Christianity, which they have combined with their ancestors' religion.

Maya civilization developed and flourished roughly between 200 B.C.E. and C.E. 900 in the forested highlands and lowlands of southern Mexico and Central America. It reached its artistic and intellectual peak in the eighth century and then fell into abrupt decline. Pre-Columbian Maya musical life is known from Spanish records written in the early years after European contact and from Maya art and writings, which record history, genealogies, religious beliefs, and ritual practices. These records survive in murals, figurines, sculptures, and painted ceramic vessels. Three lowland-Maya books—the Dresden Codex, the Codex Paris, and the Codex Madrid (Tro-Cortesianus)—contain glyphic texts associated with pictures, some of which depict Maya instruments made of ceramic and bone. Instruments of perishable materials—cane, wood, and other organic products—have not survived.

Shortly after the initial Spanish contact, musical texts were written down in indigenous languages in the Spanish alphabet. These include texts in *Los Cantares de Dzitbalché* (*The Songs of Dzitbalché*) a manuscript from Campeche, Mexico, and in the *Popul Vuh* (*The Book of Counsel*), a mythology and tribal history of the Quiché. These and similar sources contain texts of ritual and calendric songs, lyric songs, and laments. Descriptions of the Maya left by Spanish colonists of the 1500s and 1600s contain scattered references to the music and instruments. No comprehensive, systematic study of the musical life of the ancient Maya exists, but some understanding can be gained from these sources.

The music of the ancient Maya was part of a unified cosmos in which all things had sacred significance and function. Certain gods—notably the sun god, for whose cult a log idiophone was played, and a monkey god, god of music and dance—were associated with music. Music and musical instruments played an essential role in communicating between people and spirits and were important in rituals and rites of passage. Scenes painted on ceramic vessels show musicians in attendance or playing in the presence of royalty and during rituals. A scene from the great murals at Bonampák in Chiapas shows an ensemble of musicians playing drums, trumpets, tortoise-carapace idiophones, and spiked vessel rattles at the ritual sacrifice of a captive or a slave. The tomb furnishings of kings and priests, outfitted with items needed for the journey to the afterlife, often included musical instruments. At a cemetery for priests and dignitaries on Jaina, an island off the north coast of the Yucatán Peninsula, virtually every excavated figurine is a rattle, drum, or vessel (globular) flute, and many figurines depict musicians.

Bonampák in Chiapas was once a principal Mayan city. Among its ruins is a temple in which extraordinary eighth-century murals are preserved. The murals depict a battle, a procession with instrumentalists, and other events, and have enhanced our understanding of Mayan society.

Survivals of musical instruments show that the Maya developed wind instruments, principally vessel flutes, of unique forms and acoustical properties. Double-duct or double-tube and triple-duct or triple-tube flutes evidence the use of paired and multiple tunings. Bone mouthpieces were probably used with trumpets, whose flared bells were made of basketry impregnated with wax or of wood, as depicted on some painted vessels and murals.

Maya idiophones included rattles, strings of shells or seedpods (draped on dancers or sewn to their clothing), spiked vessel rattles, and the hollow feet of ceramic offering bowls, which contained clay pellets or pebbles. Bone or wood rasps and struck wood or carapace idiophones were common. Maya drums included a waist-high single-headed wooden drum and smaller ceramic hourglass-shaped single-headed drums, sometimes joined in pairs. Murals and painted vessels reveal that the Maya combined instruments of different kinds to form ensembles. Stringed instruments were absent from ancient Maya music.

Maya culture has a perceptible homogeneity, but natural environments and historical developments have differentiated Maya musical life into two streams: that of the highlands of Chiapas and

Guatemala, and that of the lowlands of Belize, Guatemala, and southern Mexico. As the highland Maya are the better documented of the two groups, this article focuses on them.

The Highland Maya

The Maya who live in Chiapas and the Guatemalan highlands are among the least assimilated indigenous peoples in Mexico and Central America. Though surrounded by Ladinos (people of non-Maya culture whose first language is Spanish and who still function as semiautonomous groups in social, economic, political, and religious affairs), these Maya have resisted mestization. They share a common history as part of the Audiencia de Guatemala, a colonial administrative unit that tied Chiapas more closely to Guatemala than to the rest of colonial Mexico.

The Roman Catholic missionaries of the 1500s and 1600s fostered the Spanish musical education of indigenous people, particularly in styles practiced in Seville. They trained singers for choirs that sang plainchant and polyphony, and developed ensembles of strings and winds to accompany them. Spanish secular music too took root in the Maya colonies. In the 1800s, it became fashionable among the upper classes to collect Maya melodies and write them down in European musical notation, adjusting their details to conform to Western musical concepts.

In Chiapas, Mexico, the music of the Tzeltal, the Chol of Tojolabal, and the Tzotzil-speakers in the neighboring villages of San Lorenzo Zinacantán and San Juan Chamula (near San Cristóbal de las Casas) is the most extensively documented; in Guatemala, the music of Quiché groups, especially the Tzutujil-Maya of Santiago Atitlán, is best documented. Local styles and repertoires, details of the construction and tuning of instruments, and the components of ensembles differ from one language to another, and even from one town to another.

Musical Contexts and Genres

The traditional music of the highland Maya reflects the influence of colonial Spanish music, of which it contains some striking survivals, such as the singing of the texts of Tenebrae services (psalms and prayers of the Divine Office for Holy Thursday, Good Friday, and Holy Saturday) and late-sixteenth- and seventeenth-century style "falsobordone" settings, in which a plainchant melody is transposed to a higher octave and harmonized below in three or four parallel parts—a texture still cultivated in Santiago Atitlán, Guatemala. Survivals of Spanish folkloric and secular styles appear in pieces whose style and

form recall those of the chaconne and the sarabande, now played in Chiapas and Guatemala on instruments that conform to European models of the late Middle Ages and the early Renaissance. Examples are ritual songs frequently sung on a single melody (known as *bolonchón* in Zinacantán) and ancestral songs of the Tzutujil-Maya in Guatemala. In highland Guatemala, the term *zarabanda* denotes certain forms of popular music.

In the highlands, traditional Maya music is closely connected with events of the ritual calendar, in which indigenous and Christian cycles are intertwined. Little survives that has no European influence, but the least acculturated genres are shamanic songs, addressed to the ancestral gods by the shaman (*curandero*), a native ritual healer or maker of prayers. These songs cure illnesses and injuries, heal women after childbirths, bless new houses and fields, and enhance calendric rituals. They are freely sung to nonmetrical or (less frequently) metrical texts that contain standard material, improvised in what are known as Maya couplets, paired lines of poetic text in parallel construction, in which the second line repeats and varies the first. These are sung or declaimed mainly on a single tone, except for an occasional drop to a lower tone before the performer breathes or a rise at the end of a phrase, but they are sometimes sung to more complex melodies, which conform to formulas that govern melodic contours.

Stemming from Spanish colonial origins, yet thoroughly revamped by Maya musical style, are guitar-accompanied songs (*bix rxin nawal* 'songs of the ancestors') of the Tzutujil-Maya. Among them is a melody identical to the *bolonchón* of Chamula, performed in Chiapas instrumentaly or sung in unison without words.

The most frequent contexts for public musical performance in highland towns are fiestas, celebrations of feasts of local patron saints, according to the Christian calendar. For these celebrations, which may last from three to eight days, musicians from surrounding towns and villages join the throng and play in their own styles, often simultaneously with other musicians, creating a characteristic mix of multiple kinds of music. Typical of such festivities in Chiapas is the celebration of the fiesta in Zinacantán. In the central plaza on 20 January (the feast of Saint Sebastian), a local trio of harp, guitar, and violin plays the piece most typical of Zinacantán, the "*Canto de San Sebastián*" ('Song of Saint Sebastian'), a piece strongly reminiscent of the chaconne, with a sarabande-style rhythmic accompaniment. A similar ensemble accompanies ritual officials on their way to the church. Other musicians stroll with guitars, visitors from Chamula play button

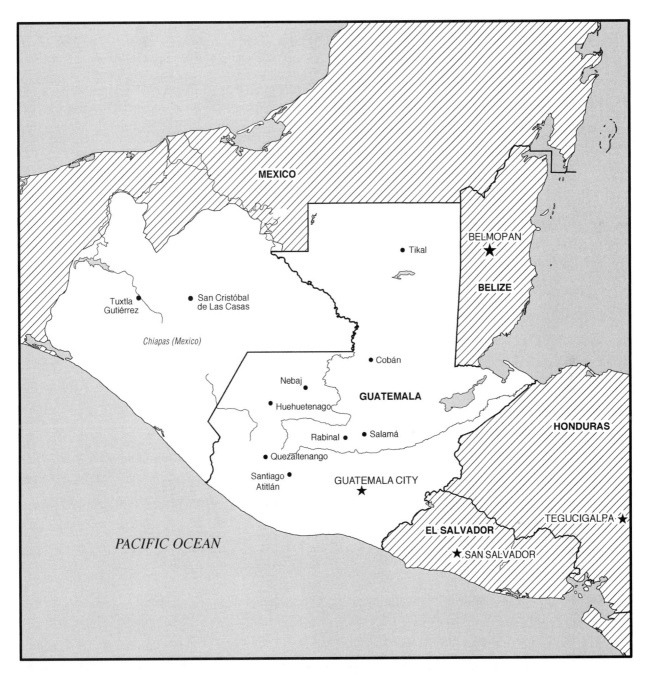

Chiapas, Mexico and Guatemala

accordions, and a wind band hired from out of town plays clarinets, saxhorns, and drums. Near the church, other ritual officials dance to the music of a three-holed flute and two large drums (*tambores*).

In Chiapas, a few melodies serve for many deities, so a single melody has many names. Similarly, the Tzutujil of Guatemala know a melody or a melodic formula by a broad title, such as "Song to Face-of-the-Earth," but may also call it "Rain Song" or "Song to Control the Winds" or "Song to Our Father the Sun," depending on the occasion or motive for its use and on the text, which the singer improvises.

All these songs come under the province of the god called Face-of-the-Earth. Apart from laments (sung during funerals and at the graveside), lullabies to children, and the occasional playing of the *tun*, no musical performance by Maya women of the highlands is documented.

In Chiapas and Guatemala, commercialized and media-dispersed popular music is pervasive. It is predominantly the popular music of Mexico, but also that of Latin America as a whole, and, to a lesser extent, the Caribbean. Recorded popular music—*canciones rancheras*, *corridos*, *cumbias*, or whatever is

231

currently broadcast on radio and television—is played on loudspeakers during the fiesta, sometimes drowning out the ritual music. Hymns of evangelical missionary churches, mostly from the United States (in Spanish or Mayan translation), are broadcast daily over loudspeakers in virtually every rural village and town, influencing popular musical taste.

Musical Instruments

The Tzutujil classify their musical instruments as male and female. Whether other Maya employ a similar taxonomy is unknown. Therefore, this overview follows the general system employed in the *Concise Garland*, rather than assuming all Maya have the same taxonomy.

Self-sounding Instruments (Idiophones)

An important Maya instrument is the log idiophone (*tun*, also *t'ent'en* and *c'unc'un*; Nahuatl *teponaztli*), a hollowed-out section of a tree trunk, into the side of which an H-shaped slit is cut, forming two tuned tongues, which players strike with sticks or dry corncobs. Typical is the *t'ent'en* of Zinacantán, constructed of two lateral sections: one of Spanish cedar and one of black cherry. This instrument is 62 centimeters long and 15 centimeters in diameter, but much larger sizes exist. Holes allow it to be suspended on a bearer's back with a tumpline passing around his forehead, while the player walks behind, playing it and a cane flute. Personifying the instrument by name (Our Holy Father *T'ent'en*) demonstrates regard for it as powerful, living, and preeminently sacred. When not in use, it is housed in a special chapel with the tumpline, the drumsticks, and two small sets of bow and arrows carried by the bearer and the player; in the chapel, these objects receive a daily offering of incense and candles. Before being used for the festival of Saint Sebastian or for the yearly rainmaking ritual (its only public appearances in Zinacantán), it is washed with water containing sacred herbs, reglued, and decorated with ribbons. It is sometimes played with gourd rattles and frame rattles.

In Guatemala, where log idiophones have the same names, they are treated with similar reverence. For rituals associated with rain and the sun, they are often played in pairs of a larger and a smaller instrument. In the town of Rabinal, Department of Baja Verapaz, they are in the ensemble *baile del tun* 'dance of the drum' that plays for the dance-drama *Rabinal Achí*.

Drums (Membranophones)

A cylindrical, double-headed wooden drum has deer-skin or dogskin, tensioned by cords laced through the hoop, to which the heads are fastened. The drum is known by many names: Tzotzil *tampor*, *tampol*, *cayobil*; Quiché *k'ojom*; Spanish *tambor*, *tamborón*. The diameter of the head and the height of the drum are about the same size, from about 38 centimeters to 1 meter. The player sometimes performs seated, using one or two padded sticks while holding the drum between the knees; in procession, the drum is carried on a bearer's back; the player follows, often playing the flute with one hand and beating the drum with a stick held in the other, in alternating phrases of rhythm and melody. In ritual contexts, the drum maintains a steady rhythm while the flute plays rhythmically free phrases that typically end with an ascending slide or the interval of a fourth or a fifth. Flute melodies come from the same repertoire as those of string trios, but the flute reproduces the melodic contour rather than the exact tones of the melody, and does so in a freer rhythm than a guitar or a harp.

A drum to which snares made of knotted leather cords have been added is smaller than the *tambor* and in Quiché languages is called *caj* (from Spanish *caja*). In some highland Chiapas towns (Magdalenas, Tenejapa, Venustiano Carranza), several drums combine with valveless trumpets and sometimes three- or seven-holed cane flutes. Their repertoire includes pieces in strict and rapid rhythms, plus melodies closely related to the European fife-and-drum tradition, imported from Spain during the early contact period.

Wind Instruments (Aerophones)

A Maya end-blown cane fipple (duct) flute, with one thumbhole and two to six fingerholes, is known by various names: Tzotzil *'ama*, *amael*; Quiché *xul*, *zu*, *zubac*, Spanish *pito*. It measures about 15 to 35 centimeters long, and 1.5 to 2 centimeters in diameter. A three-holed flute (*tzijolah*) produces tones by over-blowing. Because in this and other highland Maya styles exact pitch is less important than melodic contour, broad variations in flute-produced scales occur.

Stringed Instruments (Chordophones)

The Maya violin (*violín*) has a flat bridge, long f-holes, three pegs, and two or three strings. When played, it is held against the chest, not under the chin. The strings are stopped with the flats of the fingers. Each note is played with a full stroke of the bow, whose tension is adjusted with pressure from the player's thumb. Double-stopping is common. European prototypes of these violins probably came from the early 1600s.

The guitar (*ctar*) has several forms and sizes. The

Chamula guitar has four courses, the first double and the rest triple, with one unstrung peg. The Zinacantán guitar has five courses, the first triple and the rest double, with one peg unstrung.

In Chiapas, a large bass guitar (*kin*) has four strings widely splayed at the bridge, resembling its late-sixteenth or early-seventeenth-century European prototypes. Its playing-technique features chordal strumming, which makes all the strings sound with a single stroke of the nails. The number of instruments of each kind in a string trio may vary. Sometimes an accordion, drums, or maracas are added. Guitars provide chordal rhythm, a harp plays the bass and the melody, and a violin plays the melody. In unison falsetto, players may sing vocables, or texts in Maya couplets.

The Chiapan harp (*arpa*) is from 1.5 to 2 meters high, and has a straight pillar with incised decorations and a curved neck with a carved design. The design usually represents angels or birds facing each other, perhaps suggesting the ability of winged creatures to fly to a world above the earth and the power of ritual music to contact the gods. The back, made of five panels, is tapered, and the soundboard has three holes. The tuning pegs and feet are of wood, and the strings are of metal or nylon. It is leaned against the right shoulder; the right hand plays the upper register and the left hand plays the lower. Zinacantecos play with the fingernails of the right hand and fingertips of the left; Chamulas use fingernails only.

Ensembles

At highland Guatemalan fiestas, musical genres and ensembles are commonly mixed, though the marimba or the marimba band is practically universal, and string trios are rare. A principal difference in the musical practice of the areas is the importance and frequency of the use of marimbas: they are much more commonly played by Ladinos than by the Maya in Chiapas, where they are regarded as Ladino instruments; but in Guatemala, they are equally claimed by both cultures and are ubiquitous at festivities of all kinds. In Chiapas, they usually have chromatic keyboards and wooden, boxlike resonators; they are built by Ladino makers in the major municipal centers, including Tuxtla Gutiérrez and Venustiano Carranza. In Guatemala, gourd-resonated marimbas, built by Maya and Ladino makers, are still played, and diatonic and chromatic keyboards are common. Marimba players in Chiapas tend to play mestizo-style music, but Guatemala has a sizable repertoire of traditional Maya marimba music, some of which has African roots or early colonial origins.

Most widespread among the highland Maya is the ensemble of cane flute and drum. In highland towns, it heralds a ritual action or the event that follows it, often in procession. Thus, a flute and a drum lead participants into the center of town, musically telling of the nature of the ritual and of its commencement. This ensemble is reserved for sacred events. In general, each town has one such ensemble. The official position of flutist and drummer, often the same person, is passed through the male line and is usually a lifetime service.

Among the commonest ensembles in Chiapas is the string trio, which combines one or more guitars, harps, and violins. This ensemble plays for religious rituals, but may be hired to entertain at private parties. The instruments are locally made.

An important part of the musical spectrum at highland fiestas is the brass band, which may be hired from the Ladino community if no Maya ensemble is available. For fiestas in Chiapas, where the marimba is identified with Ladinos, a marimba band is usually hired from outside. Its main components are the *marimba grande*, a chromatic, six-octave instrument with boxlike resonators beneath the keys and played by two or three players; and the *marimba tenor*, with four or five octaves and two or three players. To these marimbas are added saxophones, trumpets, a string bass, drums, and claves, maracas, or güiros.

—*Adapted from an article by Linda O'Brien-Rothe*

Bibliography

Alfaro, Daniel. 1982. "Folk Music of the Yucatán Peninsula." Ph.D. dissertation, University of Colorado.

Franco Arce, Samuel. 1991. *Music of the Maya*. Guatemala: Casa K'ojom.

Gossen, Gary H. 1974. *Chamulas in the World of the Sun: Time and Space in a Maya Oral Tradition*. Cambridge, Mass.: Harvard University Press.

Martí, Samuel. 1968. *Instrumentos Musicales Pre-cortesianos*, 2nd ed. México, D.F.: Instituto Nacional de Antropología e Historia.

O'Brien, Linda. 1975. "Songs of the Face of the Earth: Ancestor Songs of the Tzurujil Maya of Santiago Atitlán." Ph.D. dissertation, University of California at Los Angeles.

Belize

Garifuna Music in Belize

Belize, formerly known as British Honduras, is the only English-speaking country in Central America. Located on the Yucatán Peninsula bordering Mexico to the north and northwest, Guatemala to the west and south, and the Caribbean Sea to the east, it has a land area of 22,965 square kilometers and divides into six major districts: Belize, Cayo, Corozal, Orange Walk, Stann Creek, and Toledo.

Belize has a population of 287,000, composed mainly of five cultural and ethnic groups: mestizos (of European and Amerindian descent); Creole (of African descent, with varying degrees or admixture from other ethnic groups); Maya (three Amerindian groups, including the K'ekchi, the Mopán, and the Yucatec); Garifuna (of African and Caribbean Amerindian descent); and East Indians. Other cultural or ethnic groups in Belize are Arabs, Taiwanese, Koreans, Mennonites, Rastafarians, Haitians, and West Africans.

English is the official language of the country, but Creole—a synthesis of English, African languages, and Spanish—is the lingua franca, especially in Belize City. The Garifuna of Belize (plus those of Guatemala, Honduras, and Nicaragua) are products of the genetic mixture of former West Africans and Carib, Arawak, and Taino who occupied the island of St. Vincent, in the Lesser Antilles. Garifuna ancestry can be traced back to the Yorùbá, Ibo, and Ashanti cultures of West Africa, in the lands that today comprise Nigeria, Ghana, Sierra Leone, and Mali. The genetic mixing began in 1635 (or perhaps earlier), when two Spanish vessels carrying West African slaves en route to Barbados were destroyed at sea during a storm; surviving Africans swam to St. Vincent Island and took refuge among the Amerindians there. Some sources suggest that the population of Garifuna on St. Vincent was augmented by runaway slaves from nearby islands: Maroons, also of West African origin, from groups including Ashanti-Fanti, Congo, Efik, Fon, and Yorùbá.

The Amerindian origin of the Garifuna is intricate. The Island Carib who intermixed with the West Africans were the offspring of the Arawak people known as Igneri and the Carib people known as Kallina or Galibi. During raids on Arawak (Taino) villages, Carib warriors would kill the men and take the women as wives; therefore, the Island Carib women spoke an Arawak language, whereas the men spoke a Carib language. Though Arawak prevailed as the dominant language of the Garifuna, numerous examples in which men and women used different words for the same object survive.

The Garifuna, also called the Black Carib by foreign observers, were defeated in battle by the British and exiled to Roatan Island, off the coast of Honduras, in 1797. The first Garifuna migrated to Belize from Honduras in 1802. To escape being massacred after the civil war in Honduras, another group left Honduras and settled in Dangriga on 19 November 1832, now recognized as National Garifuna Settlement Day.

Currently, many Belizean Garifuna reside in six communities in two districts in southern Belize: Dangriga, Georgetown, Hopkins, and Seine Bight in the district of Stann Creek, and Barranco and Punta Gorda in the district of Toledo. Most Garifuna live in Dangriga, and the next-largest numbers of them reside in Belize City, the most populous city in Belize.

Ritual Music and Musical Instruments

Garifuna ritual music displays elements of the music of West African ancestor worship and Amerindian shamanism. Religious practices, conducted by a shaman (*buyei*), include shamanistic healing and spirit-possession ceremonies, of which *adügürühani* (feasting the dead, the last of the postmortem rituals), also known as *dügü*, is the most elaborate. Rituals that follow the funeral and precede *dügü* are *beluria*, nine nights of family prayers, often concluding with communitywide participation in singing, drumming, and dancing; a mass for the soul of the deceased, with hymns sung to the accompaniment of drums; *amuyadahani* 'refreshing the dead', a private ritual, in which family members make offerings to their ancestors; *arairaguni*, an invocation to determine the cause of the fatal illness; and *achuguhani* 'feeding the dead' (also called *chugú*), usually a single day's ancestral-spirit-placating ritual that may or may not include singing and drumming. The influence of West African drumming and Amerindian vocal music and modality is apparent in the music of *adügürühani*.

Feasting the Dead (Dügü)

The most extensive Garifuna sacred music occurs in *dügü*, rites for supplicating and placating ancestral spirits. The term *gubida* generally refers to malevolent ancestral spirits; the term *ahari*, to benevolent ancestral spirits. When family members become ill and cannot be healed by conventional medicine, or when near-fatal accidents occur, a shaman is asked to determine the cause. With the assistance of spiritual helpers, the shaman conducts an invocation ceremony, *arairaguni*. With the shaman acting as a medium, the *gubida* reveals that it has caused the relative to become ill or allowed it to happen because it feels neglected. (The *gubida* is always a consanguineal relative of the patient.) The *gubida* may request an *achuguhani* or a *dügü*. The patient returns to good health if the ancestors invoked in the ritual and the officiating shaman consider the ceremony a success. The spirit may request that the patient's family build a new temple (*dabuyaba*), within which to hold the *dügü* and other religious rituals. Essential to all Garifuna communities, the temple symbolizes cultural and religious continuity (figure 1).

The primary function of music during the *dügü* is communication, mainly via songs and drums, with the ancestral spirits. The Garifuna do not believe that ancestral spirits literally reside in the drums; they believe that the sound of the heart drum (*lanigi garawoun*), the central and largest instrument of the three *segundas* (bass drums), has a calming effect on ritual participants, especially those who have become possessed by ancestral spirits.

The calming effect on participants may be attributed to the regularity and repetition of the drumming, a simple pattern in triple meter. Most instances of possession by ancestors occur during *dügü*, but instances of possession in other contexts have been reported. During ritual occasions, three drums are always used, though two are employed for secular dances and songs. The rhythm of the heart drum is thought to symbolize the heartbeat; with a shaman's rattle, it attracts the spirit from the mud floor of the temple. During the rituals, the chief shaman plays a container rattle (*sísira, maraga*) whose design is Amerindian, though similar rattles are found in Africa. It also serves in secular contexts.

In design and construction, *garawoun* reveal African and Amerindian traits. They consist of a hardwood log, usually mahogany or mayflower, that is hollowed out with a circular saw; the drumheads are made of skin (usually of deer, and sometimes of goat or peccary) and equipped with snares made of nylon or metal strings.

Traditional Garifuna music features two kinds of *garawoun*: *primero* 'lead drum' and *segunda* 'supporting drum' (figure 2). The *primero*, a treble drum about 30 to 45 centimeters in diameter and 60 centimeters high, provides rhythmic variety with syncopations and improvisatory passages. The *segunda*, a bass drum, about 60 to 90 centimeters wide and 90 centimeters high, maintains the steady pulse in duple or triple meter. During a *dügü*, three *segunda* play a simple unison beat in triple meter. In sacred and secular settings, the ensemble of drummers is called *dangbu*.

During the *dügü*, people perform several song-

Figure 1 A Garifuna temple (*dabuyaba*) in Dangriga, 2006. *Photo by Oliver Greene.*

Figure 2 Musicians play the *garawoun* drums, *from left: segunda, primero, segunda*, during a *wanaragua* performance, Dangriga, 2005. *Photo by Oliver Greene.*

and-dance genres: *abelagudahani, ámalihaní, ugulendu, awangulahani*, among others. *Abelagudahani*, a "bringing-in" song, is performed at the beginning of the ritual to escort fishermen to the temple from the sea, where they gather ritual food at the outlying cays. *Ámalihaní*, the central song-and-dance rite to placate specific ancestral spirits, is characterized by clockwise and counterclockwise progressions around the ancestor-temple, with stops at each cardinal point. Spiritual possession (*ónwehaní*) usually occurs during the conclusion of an *ámalihaní* and during a *chürürüti*, a period of drumming, singing, occasional *sisira* playing, and dancing that lasts thirty to forty-five minutes. During a *chürürüti*, participants move in circular patterns around the floor of the ancestor-temple. *Dügü* is primarily composed of alternate sessions of *chürürüti* and *ámalihaní*. Possession by ancestral spirits may occur during ordinary daily activities, and has even occurred during Christian church services.

Ugulendu, the fundamental sacred dance of the *dügü*, thought to be of Carib origin, is a tightly bound shuffle (legs and feet held close together), performed in a circular floor-pattern. *Awangulahani*, a song and dance for participants in pairs, celebrates the end of the *dügü* ritual proper. Three themes associated with this dance are the drawing of elder participants into the circle, the calming effect of the dance and its ability to make participants happy, and the circle as a symbol of completeness. Many songs for the *dügü* are composed in remembrance of a specific ancestor.

Secular Music and Dance

Traditional Garifuna secular music and dance display a synthesis of West African, Amerindian, English, Spanish, and Creole traits. The Garifuna use idiophones, drums, and stringed instruments to accompany many secular kinds of songs and dances. Drums are the most prevalent musical instruments of Garifuna traditional secular music, and rattles are often used with them to accompany some singing and dancing. Occasionally hollowed-out turtle shells of varying sizes, struck with wooden sticks, and blown conch shells are added to the ensembles; these instruments provide additional timbres, pitches, and rhythmic variety. The European harmonica is sometimes played, but the Spanish guitar is the only European instrument that has found a lasting place in Garifuna music, usually as an accompaniment for singing.

In secular Garifuna contexts, music serves for accompanying seasonal processions and mime-dances, as social commentary, at wakes and at work, as lullabies, and for entertainment. Specific rhythmic accompaniments and lyrics are associated with particular dances. Some secular genres are sung unaccompanied.

Processions and Mime-dances

Processions performed during the Christmas holidays are frequently accompanied by a combination of drums and winds, perhaps influenced by the British fife-and-drum tradition. Today, two types of processions and mime-dances can be seen in Belize: *wanaragua* and *charikanari*. Although they are traditionally performed by men at Christmastime, they are frequently performed by folk-dance companies. They are short dramas featuring stock characters who travel from yard to yard, collecting money for their performances.

Wanaragua, commonly known as *jankunú*, is performed on 25 December, 1 January, and 6 January ("Dia Rey," Three Kings Day). It is a masked, social commentary dance-song genre of mimicry composed primarily by men (figure 3). Related Christmas processionals and masked traditions are found in Jamaica (jonkonnu), the Bahamas (junkanoo), and other countries in the region. It was practiced in coastal cities in North Carolina in the United States until the late 1800s. It is a fusion of two ritual traditions: mummers' plays, introduced by the British during colonial times, and African harvest and ancestor rituals (perhaps the *egungun* ritual of the Yorùbá of Nigeria). Dancers wear tennis shoes, black kneestockings, white pants, shirts, and gloves, cowryshell knee rattles (representing an African retention), black or pink and green ribbons, colorful headwraps, and wire masks on which are painted a European face. Each dancer wears a headdress (*wababan*) made of long turkey feathers (symbolic of Native American ancestry), colored papier-mâché balls, and circular reflecting mirrors. A duple meter ostinato played on the *segunda* accompanies all *wanaragua* songs and dances: the drumhead is struck with both hands on the downbeat of every measure; the right hand anticipates the second beat by striking the membrane immediately before the left; the right hand then plays the second pulse of the subdivided second beat before repeating the pattern. *Primero* drummers interpret each dancer's move-

ments by drawing on an inventory of conventional rhythms.

Songs are performed in a call-and-reponse manner, one after the other without interruption, by a leader (usually male) and a chorus (usually women). Though the dance is festive, lyrics are typically about unrequited love, infidelity, the need for a wife, death, and other serious matters. Men occasionally dress as women and wear a white blouse and skirt, a mask, tennis shoes, and a communion veil, and women not uncommonly wear the male *wanaragua* costume.

Charikanari is a processional dance featuring stock characters, such as Two-Foot Cow, Devil, and numerous *hianro*—men and boys dressed as women. The Two-Foot Cow, typically a man wearing cowhorns, a cardboard mask, a trench coat, padded buttocks, and tennis shoes, chases onlookers, mostly youths and children. Devil, a man wearing a devil's mask, taunts observers and dances provocatively with the *hianro*. Music for dancing is provided by a *segunda*, a harmonica, a conch-shell trumpet, and rattles. A single melody is usually played on a harmonica, but comic songs are occasionally sung. Dancers are mute, as in *wanaragua*.

Christmas processions previously included two additional dances: *warini* and *pia manadi*. The former, last performed in the mid-1990s, features men wearing cardboard or wire masks and dried banana or plantain leaves. Dancers carried items such as an ax or an oar, and performed to the rhythmic accompaniment of *wanaragua* songs. *Pia manadi*, last seen in the 1970s, was a mimed play that involved the death and resurrection of one of the characters and displayed traits resembling those of English

Figure 3 Masked dancers perform *wanaragua*, Dangriga, 2000. *Photo by Oliver Greene.*

mumming plays. Accompaniment was provided by a wooden fife and a drum.

Songs of Social Commentary

Paranda is a folk-music genre for voice and guitar that is traditionally composed and performed by men as a serenade. A vehicle for social criticism, it shows the influence of Latin-American musical genres—perhaps an indication of the relationship maintained between the Garifuna of southern Belize and their nearby Guatemalan and Honduran neighbors. As with other Garifuna folksongs, *paranda* is both a rhythm and a musical genre. The duple meter rhythmic pattern repeated on the *segunda* is almost identical to the characteristic rhythm of *punta*, the most popular of the Garifuna song-and-dance genres. The *primero*, if used, improvises from a standard set of motives to add rhythmic variety to the ensemble.

Another social-commentary song-and-dance form, the most popular and best-liked Garifuna genre, is *punta*. In duple meter, dancers employ quick alternating movements of the hips and feet, keeping their upper torsos straight. As an expression of sexual politics, it is a variation of the cock-and-hen mating dance, common to many African-influenced cultures of the southern Americas and the Caribbean. Women's favorite form of social commentary, it provides an arena for exposing unacceptable behavior in personal affairs. *Puntas* are traditionally composed by women and are performed responsorially. The call, usually a phrase or two of a sentence sung by the leader, is followed by a choral response, often the completion of the sentence.

Popular Music: *Punta*-Rock

The most popular of the contemporary genres of dance-music in Belize, *punta*-rock, features the synthesis of electric instruments (as used in rhythm and blues, reggae, and numerous styles of popular Latin American music), traditional drums (*primero* and *segunda*), and rhythmic patterns of the *punta* dance. The creation of *punta*-rock, in the late 1970s, is attributed to Pen Cayetano, a musician and painter from Dangriga. Pen Cayetano and his band and the Original Turtle Shell Band were recognized as the first to add electric guitars and percussion instruments such as hollowed turtleshells, cowbells, *shakas* (rattles), and tambourines to the original rhythms of *punta*, as played on traditional drums. Cayetano's music is a fusion of Garifuna folksongs (mostly

puntas), indigenous rhythms, and Rastafarian ideologies. By 1980, the popularity of his band had spread from Dangriga to Belmopan, the capital, and to Belize City. Celebrated performers of *punta*-rock from Belize during the past decade include Mohobob Flores, Chico Ramos, Aziatic, Rhodee, Garifuna Legacy, Titiman Flores, Punta Rebels, Ugurau, and Supa G, with Andy Palacio, receiving the most international recognition. *Punta*-rock venues include nightclubs, sporting events, and blocked-off streets. The bands, though primarily Garifuna, may include creoles and mestizos. This genre has transcended its initial ethnic focus to become one the most popular forms of national music.

—*Adapted from an article by Oliver Greene*

Bibliography

Cayetano, Sebastian, and Fabian Cayetano. *Garifuna History, Language and Culture of Belize, Central America, and the Caribbean.* Bicentennial Edition. Belize City, Belize: self-pubished, 1997.

Foley, Kenan. 1995. "Garifuna Music Culture: An Introduction to Garifuna Music Practice with Emphasis on Abaimahani and Arumahani Songs." M.A. thesis, State University of New York at Binghamton.

Foster, Byron. 1994. *Heart Drum: Spirit Possession in the Garifuna Communities of Belize.* 2nd ed. Benque Viejo del Carmen, Belize: Cubola Productions.

Greene, Oliver N. 1999. " 'Aura buni, Amürü Nuni,' 'I am for you, you are for me': Reinforcing Garifuna Cultural Values through Music and Ancestor Spirit Possession." Ph.D. diss. Florida State University.

——. 2002. "Ethnicity, Modernity, and Retention in the Garifuna Punta," in *Black Music Research Journal* 22(2): 189–216.

——. 2006. "Music behind the Mask: Men, Social Commentary, and Identity in *Wanaragua* John Canoe)." In *The Garifuna: A Nation Across Borders*, edited by Joseph O. Palacio, 196–229. Belize: Cubola Press.

——. 2007. *Play, John Canoe, Play: The Garifuna Wanaragua Ritual of Belize.* Documentary film. Watertown, Mass.: Documentary Educational Resources.

Palacio, Andy. 1995. *Gimme Punta Rock . . . Belizean Music.* VHS. Distributed by Andy Palacio.

Palacio, Joseph O., ed. 2005. *The Garifuna: A Nation Across Borders.* Benque Viejo del Carmen, Belize: Cubola Productions.

Shepherd, John, David Horn, and Dave Laing, eds. 2005. *Continuum Encyclopedia of Popular World Music*, vol 3. New York: Continuum.

Taylor, Douglas. 1951. "The Black Caribs of British Honduras." M.A. thesis, University of Texas at Austin.

Valentine, Jerris J. 2002. *Garifuna Understanding of Death.* Dangriga, Belize: National Garifuna Council of Belize.

Wells, Marilyn. 1980. "Circling with the Ancestors: Hugulendii [*sic*]: Symbolism in Ethnic Group Maintenance." *Belizean Studies* 8(6):1–9.

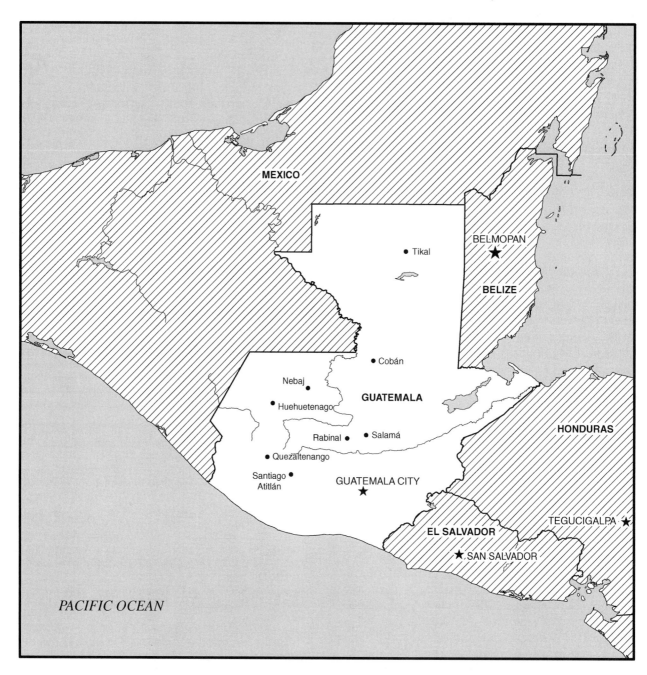

Guatemala

The Marimbas of Guatemala

The most popular Guatemalan folk-derived instrument is the marimba, a xylophone probably introduced from central Africa in the 1500s or 1600s. Guatemalan gourd-resonator marimbas resemble xylophones of central Africa, and the word *marimba* resembles *marimba* and *malimba*, African names for the instrument. There is no evidence of marimbas in pre-Columbian Mesoamerica.

The musical instruments and styles typical of Guatemalan music can be conveniently grouped into those commonly used by Maya and those more commonly used by Ladinos (Guatemalans whose primary language is Spanish), but the two cultures share the diatonic keyboard (or double) marimba.

The oldest known marimba was carried by a strap that passed around the player's neck or shoulders. In this form, called bow marimba (*marimba de arco*), the instrument had no legs. The keyboard was kept away from the player's body by a bowed branch (*arco*), which had its ends fixed to the ends of the keyboard. Later models, called table marimba (*marimba de mesa*), have legs and lack the bow.

The gourd marimba (*marimba de tecomates*) is a xylophone of diatonically tuned wooden slats (the "keyboard"), made from lowland hardwood (*hormigo* or *granadillo*) and suspended above a trapezoidal framework by a cord or string that passes through each slat at its nodal point, and through threading pins between the slats. Tuned gourds for resonation are suspended under the keyboard. Near the bottom of each gourd is a hole, surrounded by a ring of beeswax, over which a piece of pig's intestine is stretched; when the slat is struck, it makes a buzz (*charleo*). The gourd marimba is played by one, two, or three players, each using two to four mallets.

The diatonic keyboard (*marimba sencilla* 'simple marimba') has from nineteen to twenty-six slats that can be tuned by adding a lump of wax, sometimes mixed with bits of lead, to their undersides; a marimba tuned this way may be called a wax marimba (*marimba de ceras*). The slats are struck with mallets (*baquetas*) made of flexible wooden sticks wrapped with strips of raw rubber: larger and softer mallets are used for bass slats, smaller and harder ones for the treble range.

The marimba was first mentioned in Guatemala in 1680 by the historian Domingo Juarros (1953), who observed Maya musicians playing it in public festivities. During the 1700s, it became popular and was reported at religious and civil events. Its growth in popularity among Ladinos in the 1800s led to the extension of the keyboard to five, six, and seven octaves, and the addition of a fourth player. During the Guatemalan independence celebration of 1821, it became the national instrument. Later, the gourd resonators were replaced by harmonic boxes (*cajones armónicos*), wooden boxes fashioned to emulate the shapes of gourds, and the keyboard was expanded to about five diatonic octaves. This form retained the name *marimba sencilla*, referring to its diatonic scale. The *marimba de cinchos* (also called *marimba de hierro* 'iron marimba' and *marimba de acero* 'steel marimba') with metal slats also became popular, and even varieties with slats of glass or with bamboo resonators were developed. The gourd marimba and the diatonic keyboard, the forms most commonly played by the Maya, may be accompanied by a cane flute (*xul*), a shawm, a saxophone, or other band instruments and a drum (Quiché *k'ojom*, Spanish *tambor*, *tamborón*) or trapset.

The expansion of the marimba keyboard to include the chromatic scale is usually attributed to Sebastián Hurtado in 1894. Its names, *marimba doble* 'double marimba' and *marimba cuache* 'twin marimba', refer to the double row of slats that accommodates the chromatic scale. Unlike the piano keyboard, in which a raised semitone is found above and to the right of its natural, the sharp key of many Guatemalan marimbas is placed directly above its corresponding natural.

The repertoire of the double marimba is more popular and contemporary than that of the diatonic keyboard, though the former is often used to play the traditional *son guatemalteco* or *son chapín*, folkloric dance pieces typically in moderate to rapid 6/8 time that may be sung to four-line verses. Many local variations occur. The *son guatemalteco*, the national dance of Guatemala, is danced with stamping (*zapateado*). Music for the double marimba ranges from these traditional *sones* to light classics and popular music, often elaborately arranged, in which players display a high degree of virtuosity, precise ensemble playing, and expressive effects.

In villages and towns, the double marimba is often combined with saxophones, trumpets, trapset, bass viol with three strings (normally plucked), one or more male singers, and percussion instruments such as maracas, a shaker made of a thermos bottle with pebbles or pellets inside, and percussion sticks, to play music popularized in the media.

In larger towns and cities, double-marimba musicians are more often Ladinos than Maya. The instrument is commonly played in pairs: the *marimba grande* of six and one-half octaves (usually sixty-eight keys) played by four players, and the *marimba cuache* (also *marimba pícolo*, *marimba requinta*, *marimba tenor*), which has a range of five octaves (usually fifty keys), played by three musicians.

The traditional repertoire consists mainly of *sones*. When played in the context of Maya culture, these belong to a body of melodies reserved for calendric rituals of the saints and spirits, which are often danced but seldom sung. *Sones* played by Ladino musicians are drawn from the traditional folk repertoire of the *son guatemalteco* or *son chapín*.

—*Adapted from an article by Linda O'Brien-Rothe*

Bibliography

Chenoweth, Vida. 1964. *Marimbas of Guatemala*. Lexington: University of Kentucky Press.

Garfias, Robert. 1983. "The Marimba of Mexico and Central America." *Latin American Music Review* 4(2):203–232.

O'Brien-Rothe, Linda. 1982. "Marimbas of Guatemala: The African Connection." *The World of Music* 25(2):99–104.

Panama

From the sixteenth century, when Spanish conquistadors first landed on its Caribbean shores, to the nineteenth century and construction of its interoceanic canal, and finally political independence in the early twentieth century, the isthmus of Panama has served as the "Bridge of the Americas." It has been a stage upon which millions of people have played as they traversed the isthmus from the Atlantic Ocean to the Pacific and back; hundreds of thousands more have migrated through the canal from Africa, the Caribbean, China, Colombia, and the United States.

This narrow strip of land has served as a socio-political fulcrum and has provided the means for building empires in the Americas and Europe; yet rarely has it received attention for its beauty, diversity, and traditional culture. Few people beyond its shores appreciate the variety of its peoples, music, material culture, flora, and fauna, although in the twenty-first century tourism is expanding into a major industry. There is little recognition for the role that Panama has played in the development of other parts of the world, or even in modern history. For those who have had the occasion to spend time there and relish its everyday life, Panama presents an exciting and ever-changing social and cultural panorama, through which to enjoy the differences and similarities of the world's musical traditions.

Shaped in the form of a large recumbent "S," the country has nine provinces and four semiautonomous indigenous sectors (*comarcas indígenos*): the Kuna Yala (also written as Cuna) of San Blas, Emberá (within the Darién Province), Madungandí (between the Panama Province and Kuna Yala) and Ngöbe-Buglé (on the Atlantic between Veraguas and Bocas del Toro Provinces). Each province and *comarca* boasts of its traditions, food, music, festivals, and peoples. Folkloric customs and genres are associated with particular towns and provinces, though recent internal migration has fostered a dispersion of traditions across Panamanian territory and a concentration of peoples of different areas in the capital, Panama (Panama City).

History

Rodrigo de Bastidas, having received a royal license from Spain to explore in the New World, sailed from Cádiz in October 1501 and late in the year touched the easternmost sector of the Isthmus of Panama, near the Atrato River and the Gulf of Urabá, an area now part of Colombia. Columbus sighted the Caribbean coast of Panama only on his fourth voyage (1502), when he reached the western end of the isthmus and the Laguna de Chiriquí. The areas he explored and named—Portobelo and Bastimentos, later called Nombre de Dios (both now in Colón Province)—were to play important roles in the first wave of colonization and the economic boom that drew Europeans to the New World. With economic growth and prosperity, the cultural heritage of Andalucían Spain, especially Seville, was transported to Panama.

Andalucían Spain, from the eighth century to the fifteenth century, is the era of Muslim rule. This period is regarded as one of cultural flourish.

The movement and settlement of Spaniards, captive slaves, fugitive slaves, and indigenous populations during the colonial era set the stage for current Panamanian cultural areas and traditions. The strongest manifestations of Afro-Panamanian traditions appear on the Costa Arriba and the Costa Abajo (Colón Province) in the Darién area, and on the islands of the Gulf of Panama. The coast of the Caribbean province of Bocas del Toro, site of important banana plantations, is also an area of African descendants. Amerindian cultures include the Kuna, who reside in the San Blas Islands, the Choco in Emberá, and the Ngöbe-Buglé (formerly known as Guaymí and Teribe) in Ngöbe-Buglé. Climatically more temperate, the central provinces—Coclé, Herrera, Los Santos (Azuero Peninsula), and Veraguas—became the center of *mestizo* development and settlement with farmland and cattle ranches. Chiriquí, the westernmost province, has mountains and an extinct volcano with a mean altitude higher than most of the country; suitable for growing vegetables, it is the home of wealthy landowners and *mestizo* farmers.

In the mid-nineteenth century, a transisthmian railroad was constructed, mainly to accommodate gold miners traveling to California from the Caribbean and Atlantic regions, and in the late nineteenth century, the interoceanic canal was completed. The workforce needed to construct these wonders of engineering was not available in sufficient numbers on the isthmus, so thousands of contract workers

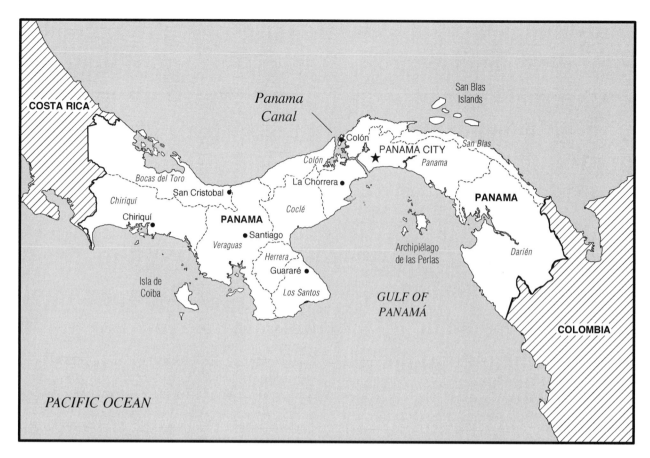

Panama

from many parts of the world were brought in. Chinese, Greeks, Lebanese, Italians, and others became a new wave of immigrants to cross the "Bridge of the Americas" in search of a better life. Communities of their descendants remain in Panama, still practicing ethnic cultural traditions. Among the most numerous contract workers and most visible today are Antilleans, people of African descent from English- and French-speaking Caribbean insular communities, including Antigua, Barbados, Haiti, Jamaica, Martinique, and Trinidad and Tobago.

Ethnic Populations and Regional Music

Self-identification in Panama does not follow regional lines and alliances to rural beginnings. For music, dance, and verbal traditions, associations and personal preferences are often based on ethnic origins and cultural traditions associated with a particular group. Every ethnic group that forms part of the fabric of Panamanian cultural identity has added something of importance to the mixture. Amerindians, Spaniards, and African slaves constituted the principal ethnic groups in colonial Panama;

their interaction and exchange in music, dance, and verbal folklore has taken forms that are singular to Panama.

Cultural influences cannot easily be ascribed to the relative numbers within colonial populations. In some parts of Panama, one group or another seems to have predominated in traditional music and dance, though musical instruments illustrate a totally different pattern of dispersion and origin. Officially, Spanish is the national language, spoken by peoples of all groups, but Amerindian groups maintain their cultural heritage, and within their own communities speak indigenous languages. Therefore, most verbal forms and vocal music within Panama utilize Spanish as the language of communication. Participants in African-influenced *congos* (see below) speak a dialect within their communities, though their songs are sung in Spanish. People of Antillean descent are essentially bilingual in Caribbean English and Spanish; however, they have had a strong incentive to assimilate, and few examples of Caribbean music and dance survive in their communities.

Archaeologists have searched for traces of Panama's pre-Columbian peoples. They have excavated many sites, though there are no large

Figure 1 Bone tubular flute from an unidentified ancient culture in Panama.
Photo by Dale A. Olsen, Museo de Sitio de Panama la Vieja, 2006.

pyramids or hidden cities to be found, as elsewhere in Middle and South America. Nevertheless, it is clear that for hundreds of years Panama was a major conduit between North and South American indigenous populations. Researchers have unearthed golden amulets and jewelry; bone, stone, and pottery artifacts; and ceramic tubular and globular flutes (figure 1). All these objects show that trade and exchange flourished among peoples of different areas over many centuries.

Among Amerindian peoples in Panama, the only one for whom any important study and documentation of music and dance exists is the Kuna. For years, Kuna expressive culture has attracted the interest of European and American researchers. The people

have continued to maintain a degree of independence from the center of Panamanian society; a large portion of their population remains in the San Blas Islands, Colón Province. Kuna musical performances and dances are uncommon outside of their own communities (figures 2 and 3). Kuna who reside in urban areas of Panama City or Colon, or in towns within the central provinces, maintain a somewhat separate existence.

Spanish influence in traditional Panamanian music is strongly represented by the language of lyrics and such instruments as the *guitarra* and *mejorana* (types of guitar), violin, and castanets. Many dances, especially for religious celebrations, owe their origins to European festivals. Among the most significant folkloric events are carnival, secular holidays that commemorate foundations of towns, and religious commemorations (including Corpus Christi, Holy Week, local patronal feasts, and regional holidays) when music, dance, traditional theater, costume, food, and traditional masks all mingle. It is often difficult to ascribe a dance or song to one ethnic origin in Panama, but the song form known as *décima* and dances such as the *cumbia, pasillo, punto,* and *vals* (waltz), are important representations of Spanish culture and cultural mixing. Music known as *música típica* 'typical music' does not usually distinguish among particular forms, and the most common *música típica* ensemble or *conjunto típico* includes a button accordion, a guitar (or a *mejorana*), a drum (usually a *tamborito*), and perhaps a rasp.

The influence of Africans and the traditions that characterized the cultures from which they came is best portrayed in the *congo* tradition and in such other danced genres as *los diablos de los espejos* of Garachiné (Darién Province), the music and dance of the people of the Pearl Islands, and genres such as *bullerengue, bunde, cuenecué, cumbia,* and *el tamborito,* the national dance. Most musical ensembles within Panama use African-derived drums, but their instrumentations differ, and each has a unique manner of playing.

The provinces of Colón, Darién, and Panama, plus the central provinces, have been the focus of important studies of Panamanian music and folklore. Varied musical customs occur in other areas of Panama, but there has been little systematic study. People born and raised in the interior of the country commonly preserve a lifelong identification and allegiance to their natal province. Frequently, those now living in the capital return to small towns in the interior to celebrate family occasions, local patronal feasts, national holidays, and local festivals.

Figure 2 Three Kuna female dancers playing rattles, Corti, Kuna Yala, 2006.
Photo by Dale A. Olsen.

Musical Instruments

Unlike the Maya in Guatemala, neither the indigenous people nor the later immigrant cultures of Panama have traditional systems for classifying musical instruments. Amerindian groups favor self-sounders (idiophones) and winds (aerophones), Panamanians of African heritage often employ drums (membranophones), and Panamanians of European descent and mestizos enjoy Spanish-derived stringed instruments (chordophones) and the button accordion. The following survey examines the instruments of the African- and European-derived musical traditions.

Self-sounders

The idiophones of Panama are associated with particular ensembles, genres, or occasions, adding an important percussiveness to the music and dance. Included within ensembles (*conjuntos*) are maracas and güiros, shaken and scraped idiophones, respectively. Dancers such as *los diablicos sucios* 'the dirty little devils' use castanets (*castañuelas*) as personal accompaniments, and big devils (*gran diablos*) often have jingle bells attached to their ankles or calves.

Though widely dispersed within Latin American customs, the most unusual among Panamanian percussive instruments is the *vejiga*, an inflated animal bladder worn by devils as part of their costume; when struck with a stick, it functions as a percussion instrument. Because of its material and construction, it is a both a membranophone and an idiophone,

being made from nonstretched skin. Devils' slippers or shoes (*cutarras*) also function as percussive instruments: the dancers, as they dance, articulate rhythms, with each foot parallel to the ground, accompanied by their castanets.

Drums

Drums are the most widespread instruments in traditional Panamanian musical performances. The shapes and sizes vary somewhat from town to town and area to area, but most are similar in construction and use. Few musical performances could take place without drumming and singing. The excitement created by drummers and the sonic punctuation of dancers' movements are the main source of the dynamism of performances. A drum ensemble may use drums of various kinds and sizes but usually consists of three or four instruments. The *caja* is played with two sticks, on one head and the side; most often it is placed on the ground and held with one foot while the performer plays. Other drums, played with the hands, may be held between the knees of a seated player or suspended from a cord around his shoulder or neck. Musicians use the latter method to move through streets in parades. All major musical genres and dances are supported by an individual drum with another instrument (such as a guitar or an accordion) or a drum ensemble. The national dance of Panama, *el tamborito*, is the most important drum-accompanied dance within the republic (figure 4); it is danced by couples.

Figure 3 Single Kuna male panpipe player, Corti, Kuna Yala, 2006. Kuna panpipes are always played in sets of two halves.
Photo by Dale A. Olsen.

The names of drums vary widely from one town or area to another, but they reveal something important. *Pujador* 'pusher', *repicador* 'chimer', *caja* 'box', *jondo* 'deep', and *seco* 'dry' are names that indicate relationships and timbral affinities within the ensemble, though they do not seem to make much sense in English translation. Each drum performs a role within the ensemble, and drummers must learn to listen to each other for cues and watch the dancers during a performance. The *caja* often provides a basic rhythmic pattern over which the *pujadar* and the *repicador* improvise complicated patterns. The higher-pitched drums often take turns in the role of soloist. The caller (*llamador*) might accompany *los diablicos sucios* of Chitré, the capital of the Herrera Province.

The *congo* ensembles share some of the naming conventions and playing techniques of drummers in other ensembles in Panama. Frequently, a *congo* drum receives a particular name, for example *Relámpago* 'Lightning', though the practice of baptizing drums [see AFRO-BRAZILIAN TRADITIONS] does not occur. Each group has three or four instrumentalists, a chorus of female singers, and a tradition of mimetic dances that recall colonial slavery.

Though far less commonly today, *conga* queens, their drum consort, and members of the court travel throughout the Caribbean coasts in visits (*visitas*) to other so-called kingdoms and palaces (*palacios*). Such visits can be made in cars on the highway, but in earlier days these journeys were quite difficult, as they had to be made in small boats or by walking through the forest.

Stringed Instruments

In most instances, stringed instruments provide melodies within instrumental ensembles. Traditionally, the violin, and in rustic communities the *rabel*, served in this capacity. The violin is still the instrument of preference for the *punto* (see below) because the sweetness and softness of its sound match the elegance and grace of the dance and its participants, but in rural and traditional Panama it has lost much of its importance.

More important is the *mejorana*, a small, five-stringed, fretted, guitarlike instrument, which in shape and size resembles the Hawaiian ukulele and the Venezuelan *cuatro*. Older instruments used animal material for the strings, but newer ones use synthetics, such as nylon. Its body is made of one piece of fairly soft wood. The front (*tabla* 'table'), with its round soundhole, is carved from another flat piece of wood, affixed to the body. Tuning pegs, carved from a harder wood, are placed in a pegbox at the end of a rather short neck. The *mejorana* is made by hand in rural Panama, though factory-made instruments are now on sale. The preferred instruments are those crafted by masters in the interior.

Panama has a set of commonly named *mejorana* tunings, though there does not appear to be any clear relationship between the names given to tunings and the notes that distinguish their configurations. The most common tunings are known as *por veinticinco* 'by twenty-five' and *por seis* 'by six'. Strings are named in a unique pattern: the two outer strings (1 and 5) are designated firsts (*primeras*), the next two strings on each side (2 and 4) are designated seconds (*segundas*), and the fifth string (3, in the middle) is called third (*tercera*). The *mejorana* is important within the musical traditions of mestizos from the

Figure 4 A *tamborito* ensemble; the *caja* player is in the center, with the *pujador* player to his left and *repicador* player to his right, province of Los Santos, 2006.
Photo by Dale A. Olsen.

central provinces and the capital. Performers (*mejoraneros*) accompany singers of *décimas* and the dance that bears the same name. Players learn from their friends, family, and relatives, and by observation within traditional contexts, and they must master a complex set of *torrentes* 'scales' for the accompaniment of *décimas*. The *mejorana* is played with the fingers and can yield single-line melodies, melodic-rhythmic patterns, and chords. Most players cannot read staff notation.

Wind Instruments

Within the mestizo tradition, a flute (*pito*) is sometimes heard playing with drummers and accordionists that travel the streets with the dirty little devils (see below). The *pito* is a small, high-pitched, side-blown flute made from cane. Its tone, being somewhat shrill, easily cuts through the din created by the dancers, other musicians, and the crowd.

The accordion (figure 5) has become an important melodic instrument within many ensembles of traditional Panama; in typical ensembles (*conjuntos típicos*), it carries the major share of musical performance. Imported from Germany and Austria during the 1800s, it has taken an honored place among musical instruments, often displacing the violin because of its loudness. The accordion used in Panama has buttons for left-hand chords and buttons or a keyboard for right-hand melodies. Though it functions, in most instances, as a melody instrument, it provides harmonic support. Accor-

Figure 5 An accordionist from the Department of Folklore, University of Panama, plays a Hohner button accordion, 2006.
Photograph by Dale A. Olsen.

dions appear in ensembles that play *cumbias*, *puntos*, *tamboritos*, and other popular dances.

Figure 6 A couple dance the *tamborito*, province of Los Santos, 2006. The female dancer's dress, known as a *pollera*, is Panama's national costume.
Photo by Dale A. Olsen.

Musical Genres and Contexts

Musical genres in Panama, as throughout Latin America, are usually linked to dance. Several Panamanian dances require no lyrics, although melodies may in fact have texts that members of the community know but do not sing while dancing. Each named dance is accompanied by a particular kind of ensemble, and is often associated with a specific ethnic group or area.

Among the most popular genres that is also a couple dance is *el tamborito* 'the little drum', a spectacular Afro-Panamanian drum-accompanied genre considered the Panamanian national dance (figure 6). Drums play an essential part in the choreography: they communicate with dancers and with each other, and they enter in rhythmic counterpoint with the dancers and their movements. In each area, specific steps (*pasos*) have names that elicit specific patterns from solo drummers. An important part of the performance, after the entrance of each new couple, is the couple's address to the drummers. The pair steps toward them, moves backward a few

steps, and approaches again. They make this gesture three times. The lead drum (*repicador* 'chimer' or *llamador* 'caller') then "chimes" specific beats (*los tres golpes*), making a high-pitched, bell-like sound on the drum, whereupon each couple makes a fast circular turn and begins the dance. Courtship is the theme, as it is of many dances in the Americas.

Close behind the *tamborito* in popularity is the *cumbia*, a music–dance genre featuring grouped couples, popular also among Panama's Colombian neighbors. It is distinguished by the dancers' counterclockwise movement, describing a circle. The group divides into couples, but men or women may dance as two circles moving in tandem, each partner facing the other. A typical ensemble provides music for the *cumbia* in Panama.

Other important traditional music-dance genres are the *mejorana* and the *punto*. The *mejorana* (which gets its name because it is accompanied by the *mejorana*, a small guitar) features 6/8 or 9/8 rhythms that oscillate between duple and triple pulses (*sesquiáltera*). The *punto*, though also using *sesquiáltera*, is slower. It is an elegant and graceful couple dance, found mostly in the interior of the country. It affords one of the few occasions where the violin finds a significant role within traditional musical ensembles; in the absence of a violin, an accordion is used.

The *bunde* and the *bullerengue*, both of Afro-Panamanian origin, are sung and danced in Garachiné, a small town on the gulf of San Miguel in the Darién Province, and in the towns of the area. The *bunde* is performed at Christmastime in honor of the baby Jesus, represented by a doll. Each of these genres is related to other Afro-Panamanian groups' traditions, especially *congos*, and each is accompanied by drums, a chorus of women, and clapping.

Most dances in Panama do not have an underlying or background story, but several important manifestations do—namely, *congos* and various devils (*diablos*), which can be conceived as dance theater.

Congos, Afro-Panamanian secret societies that originated in colonial times, today perform a dance theater featuring brilliant costumes, drumming, and responsorial singing by people of Afro-Hispanic descent. It is featured during carnival, folkloric festivals, and other celebrations. Most people see only the dance and hear the African-derived drums, experiencing the energy of movements and the rhythms. Among the *congos*, however, narratives retell oral histories of slave ships, the devil, the Virgin Mary, runaways (*cimarrones*), and everyday activities. The lyrics that accompany the songs during the dances do not always coincide with the background action, and the public must interpret the story and

Figure 7 Dario Lopez, a famous maker of devil masks and other artifacts, holds one of his masks in his home and workshop in Parita, province of Los Santos.
Photo by Dale A. Olsen, 2006.

understand what is happening from the dancers' movements and actions.

During the colonial period, liturgical dramas in spoken verse were common in Latin America; they instructed the illiterate population in the wonders and mysteries of biblical narratives. In Panama, the mirror devils (*diablos de los espejos*) and big devils (*gran diablos*), respectively from Garachiné and La Chorrera, portray variants of the Christian theme of the battle of good and evil. Garachiné is almost inaccessible except by air or water. The people and traditions of this area are related to descendants of runaways who fled to the jungles and the Pearl Islands of Panama (Archipélago de las Perlas). La Chorrera is in Panama Province, closer to the center of the country. Musicians accompany the mirror devils as they enact the defeat of the devil by the Holy Spirit. The big devils speak in verse, although what they are saying is virtually impossible to understand through their masks. As they move through complicated choreographic patterns, they act out a drama in which Lucifer, the fallen angel, does battle with the powers of good, personified by the Archangel Michael. Lucifer is vanquished and returned to the grace of God. The *diablos de los espejos* tradition is related to the *gran diablos* tradition, but the style of the mask is distinctive (figure 7), and

the theatrical subtext from which they perform their drama is quite different.

Vocal Music

Song and dance are intimately intertwined in the traditional musics of Panama, but song is probably the more important part of the equation. A typical vocal group consists of a lead singer (*cantalante* among most groups, *revellín* among *congos*) and a chorus of women (*segundas*), who sing and clap on major subdivisions of the pulse. Songs in this configuration are usually responsorial, as are most traditions in Panama. Singing loudly in a high register, the soloist often improvises and varies the text at will. A good voice is a powerful voice, which can rise above the chorus, the drums, all other instruments in the ensemble, and ambient noise.

A solo vocal tradition called *décima* is the province mainly of male singers. It is performed to the accompaniment of the *mejorana*. The singer (*decimero*) must have a powerful voice, but there is an emphasis on the clear and exact enunciation of the text. As a singer said, the textual message is the most important part of the *décima*. The *décima* is a poetic form that encompasses elaborate rhymes and melodic improvisation. The following text is an example of a vocal improvisation by the male singer Santo Díaz. It represents just a section of a longer piece, "Me duele tu corazón."

> *Me duele tu corazón.*
> *Tierra, tú me vas matando.*
> *Si acaso me oyes cantando,*
> *Yo no grito el mismo son.*
> *Voy llorando el pasión*
> *Que el recuerdo resucita,*
> *Saber que fuiste mansita*
> *Cuando yo te socolaba.*
> *Ay, amor, ¡cómo te amaba!*
> *Tierra, tierra, ¡qué bonita!*

> Your heart gives me pain.
> Land, you are killing me.
> If by chance you hear me singing,
> I don't shout the same song.
> I go crying the passion
> That memory revives,
> Knowing that you were gentle
> When I rocked you.
> Oh, my love, how I loved you!
> Land, land, how beautiful!

The *saloma*, a vocal melody of undetermined length, appears at the beginning and end of a *décima*. It is a subdued, deeply rhapsodic vocal line, often associated with the *torrente llanto*, used for performances of lyrical themes of sadness and intimacy. It exhibits a striking resemblance to the deep song (*cante jondo*) of Andalucían Spain. Sung almost like a recitative, it often uses vocables and closely follows the emphasis of spoken verbal rhythms. Most *salomas* are slow, and their major musical cadences coincide with significant textual phrasal endings. Some singers believe that individuals have characteristic *salomas* or manners of performance. They feel that one must sing a *saloma* at the beginning of a *décima* to "release the voice" and set the mood.

Shouts (*gritos*) ordinarily occur during agricultural activities when it is necessary to communicate in the field. For personal entertainment, men engage in such displays in homes, on the streets, and in bars. A measure of skill is needed to produce a *grito*, and a degree of stamina is needed to continue it for a concentrated time. It has more musical attributes when men exchange loud, high-pitched yodels. Two or more men sit face to face, or side by side, alternating their *gritos*. Often, after making four or five utterances, they stop for a rest and a drink. When they yodel, each man will often match the alternating pitches and duration of his counterpart in a sort of vocal duel.

Texts within musical compositions are important in Panama's traditional music. Declamations—dramatic recitations of poems, narratives, and *décima* texts—are often part of public celebrations and family occasions. Little has been collected of the texts of dance-theater presentations, and this is a fertile area for research.

Festivals

For many Panamanians, festivals (*fiestas*) are times of release and abandon—occasions to reestablish ties with the supernatural world, families, and areas, and to make public displays of faith. Some festivals, celebrated on a small scale, involve small numbers of people; others involve neighborhoods, towns, or areas. When a festival is shared by the national community, it permits even more possibilities for creative activity and expression. All festival occasions—religious, national, secular—are marked with singing and performances by instrumental ensembles.

Religious Festivals

In the interior of Panama on various occasions during the year, especially the Christian holiday of Corpus Christi, dirty little devils roam the streets in brilliant red and black striped costumes and musical ensembles. This is such a visually attractive tradition that it has been used to represent Panama—within the republic and outside it. Small companies of devils, accompanied by a guitarist and maybe a *pito* and a drummer, move throughout towns, performing for visitors. A special trait of their performance is the use of castanets, *vejigas*, and *cutarras*.

National Festivals

Independence Day, 3 November, occasions great musical activity, especially in the capital. Thousands of citizens crowd the streets in anticipation of parades that feature marching bands and drum-and-bugle corps from the secondary schools of the city and military units of the government. So many people march that the parades can last five hours. There are two routes, which the musical organizations exchange on the second day, so each has the opportunity of marching and performing for the maximum number of people and showing its prowess on the main street, Avenida Central. Newspapers publish the itineraries, organizational names, and pertinent information on each group. Though the bands are composed of instruments common to military bands in most countries, the percussion sections are greatly enlarged, and the rhythms used for the march are more related to *el tamborito* and other drum-accompanied dances of Panama than to those of John Philip Sousa. A marching band's line resembles a large group of dancers. To discover the more spectacular movements and playing styles, one has only to listen to and watch the bass drum: during each pattern, drummers vigorously lift their drums high in the air, rotating them back and forth so they can alternately strike the heads on opposing sides. Apart from carnival (celebrated in Panama and throughout much of Latin America), this parade is the most heavily attended musical event regularly presented in Panama.

Folkloric Festivals

In the early 1970s, Manuel F. Zárate (Panama's most prominent researcher in folklore) and Dora Pérez de Zárate were instrumental in helping promote an annual event in the former's natal province, Los Santos. For a week each year during the Festival de la Mejorana, performers from the province and cities throughout the country go to Guararé to perform and share their traditions.

—Adapted from an article by Ronald R. Smith
and Dale A. Olsen

Bibliography

Blaise, Michel. 1985. *Street Music of Panama*. Original Music OML 401. LP disk.

Carmona Maya, Sergio Iván. 1989. *La Música, un fenómeno cosmogónico en la cultura kuna*. Medellín, Colombia: Ediciones Previas, Editorial Universidad de Antioquia.

Cheville, Lila R., and Richard A. Cheville. 1977. *Festivals and Dances of Panama*. Panama: Lila and Richard Cheville.

Densmore, Frances. 1926. *Music of the Tule Indians of Panama*. Smithsonian miscellaneous collections, 77, 11. Washington, D.C.: Smithsonian Institution.

Drolet, Patricia Lund. 1980. "The Congo Ritual of Northeastern Panama: An Afro-American Expressive Structure of Cultural Adaptation." Ph.D. dissertation, University of Illinois at Urbana-Champaign.

———. 1982. *El Asentamiento cultural en la Costa Arriba: Costeños, Chocoes, Cuevas y grupos pre-históricos*. Panamá: Museo del Hombre Panameño, Instituto Nacional de Cultura, Smithsonian Tropical Research Institute.

Garay, Narciso. 1930. *Tradiciones y cantares de Panamá, ensayo folklórico*. Brussels: Presses de l'Expansion belge.

Hayans, Guillermo. 1963. *Dos cantos shamanísticos de los indios cunas*. Translated by Nils M. Holmer and S. Henry Wassén. Göteborg: Etnografiska Museet.

Izikowitz, Karl Gustav. [1935] 1970. *Musical Instruments of the South American Indians*. East Ardsley, Wakefield, Yorkshire: S. R. Publishers.

Lipski, John M. 1989. *The Speech of the Negros Congos of Panama*. Amsterdam and Philadelphia: J. Benjamins Publishing.

Llerenas, Eduardo, and Enrique Ramírez de Arellano. 1987. *Panamá: Tamboritos y Mejoranas*. Música Tradicional MT.O. LP disk.

Olsen, Dale A. 2007. *Music Cultures of the World: Panama as the Crossroads of the World*. Electronic book posted on the internet for the course MUH 2051, Florida State University.

Smith, Ronald R. 1976. "The Society of *Los Congos* of Panama: An Ethnomusicological Study of the Music and Dance-Theater of an Afro-Panamanian Group." Ph.D. dissertation, Indiana University.

———. 1985. "They Sing with the Voice of the Drum: Afro-Panamanian Musical Traditions." In *More than Drumming: Essays on Africa and Afro-Latin American Music*, edited by Irene Jackson-Brown, 163–198. Westport, Conn.: Greenwood Press.

———. 1991. Review of *Street Music of Panama: Cumbias, Tamboritos, and Mejorana. Latin American Music Review* 12(2):216–220.

———. 1994. "Panama." In *Music and Black Ethnicity in the Caribbean and South America*, edited by Gerard Béhague, 239–266. Miami: North-South Center, University of Miami.

Stiffler, David Blair. 1983. *Music of the Indians of Panama: The Cuna (Tule) and Chocoe (Embera) Tribes*. Folkways Records FE 4326. LP disk.

Zárate, Dora Pérez de. 1971. *Textos del tamborito panameño: Un estudio folklórico-literario de los textos del tamborito en Panamá*. Panamá: Dora Pérez de Zárate.

Zárate, Manuel F., and Dora Pérez de Zárate 1968. *Tambor y socavón: Un estudio comprensivo de dos temas del folklore panameño, y de sus implicaciones históricas y culturales*. Panamá: Ediciones del Ministerio de Educación, Dirección Nacional de Cultura.

The Caribbean

The Caribbean

The insular Caribbean region is centered on the islands of the Caribbean Sea, bordered by North, Central, and South America and the Atlantic Ocean, with a total landmass of about 235,700 square kilometers and a current population of about 38 million.

The heart of the region is the 3,200-kilometer-long arc-shaped archipelago called the Antilles or the West Indies, stretching between the Yucatán Peninsula and Venezuela. It consists, on the northern side, of the Greater Antilles and the large, mountainous islands of Cuba, Jamaica, Hispaniola, and Puerto Rico; and, on the eastern side, the double arc of the Lesser Antilles, comprising the Leeward Islands (northern group) and the Windward Islands (southern group). A southwestward extension of the latter includes Trinidad and Tobago, Aruba and the western Netherlands Antilles (Bonaire and Curaçao), and many small islands off Venezuela. The main islands and groups of the Lesser Antilles, north to south, are the British and American Virgin Islands, St. Martin, Antigua, Antigua and Barbuda, Monsterrat, Guadeloupe, Dominica, Martinique, St. Lucia, St. Vincent, Barbados, and Grenada; many small islands and islets join this chain. Another major group is the Bahamas, north of Cuba.

Contemporary Caribbean culture is best characterized as a hybrid that has evolved in the New World from Old World influences tempered by New World circumstances. Simultaneously, certain Old World cultural traits—from Europe and Africa—continue, especially in contexts of expressive culture. To offer a sense of this culture, we present articles on the musics of the Bahamas, Cuba, the Dominican Republic, Jamaica, Martinique, and Trinidad and Tobago.

An elaborately dressed dancer at carnival in Port of Spain, Trinidad, 1994. This extremely colorful and elaborate festival several weeks before Easter, like Mardi Gras in New Orleans and Carnaval in Brazil, is a time of merriment, cutting up, and letting loose. It is one of the most popular musical occasions in the Caribbean.
Photo by Carolyn J. Fulton.

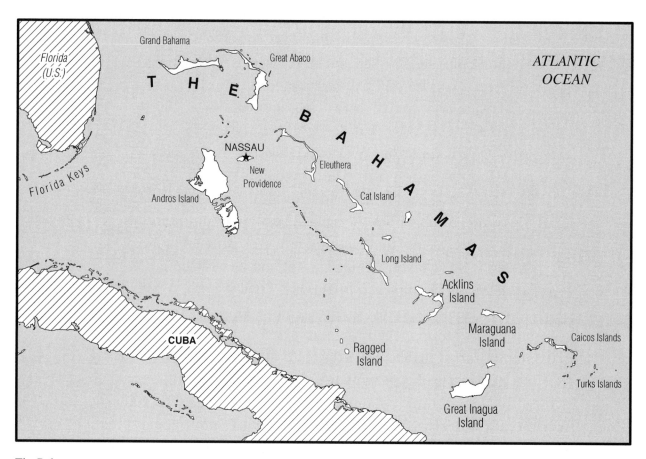

The Bahamas

The Bahamas

The Commonwealth of the Bahamas is an archipelago of some seven hundred islands and more than two thousand cays and rocks, situated in the Atlantic Ocean about 100 kilometers southeast of Florida. It stretches about 1,224 kilometers toward the northeastern coast of Cuba and the Turks and Caicos Islands. Only thirty of the islands of the Bahamas are inhabited; more than two-thirds of the country's 303,000 inhabitants live on New Providence, an island 11 kilometers wide and 34 kilometers long, on which Nassau, the country's capital, is located. Except for New Providence and Grand Bahama, the inhabited islands of the Bahamas are known collectively as the Family Islands. Eight-five percent of the country's inhabitants are of African descent; the remaining population is primarily of European heritage.

The principal industry of the Bahamas is tourism, which has greatly affected local music. Besides sun, sand, and sea, music offers diversion and entertainment to visitors at hotels constructed expressly to accommodate them. In the early years of tourism, these hotels were owned and operated by foreign concerns. Before 1949, most entertainers at these hotels came from the United States. Bahaman musicians performed in nightclubs outside the zones in which the hotels were located. In 1949, a musicians' union was formed; this entity, now known as the Bahamas Musicians Entertainment Union, protects Bahamian musicians' interests.

In 1967, the Bahamas achieved majority rule, and the new government bought many of the large hotels, enabling black musicians to obtain jobs, with the result that each hotel now has a resident group of black musicians.

Musical Instruments

Bahamians create their traditional musical instruments from simple, everyday materials. The dominant musical instrument is the *goombay* drum (figure 1), which Bahamian legend says received its name from the sounds made when its head is struck: the *goom* depicts the deep, resonant sound made when the head is struck near the center, and the *bay* (or *bah*) resembles the sound that occurs when the head is struck nearer the edge. However, the term *goumbé* is found in such West African countries as Senegal and Côte d'Ivoire: in Senegal, *goumbé* is a traditional women's dance associated with the planting season; and in Côte d'Ivoire, *goumbé* is a dance popular among young people. Both dances are accompanied by frame drums.

Figure 1 Goombay drummers from the Roots Junkanoo group perform, Nassau, 2004. The musician on the left plays a drum made from a 55-gallon oil drum; the musician on the right plays a factory-made tomtom.
Photo by Kenneth Bilby.

The *goombay* drum evolved from a frame drum similar to those used in West Africa and in some Caribbean countries. Rarely used in the Bahamas today, the frame drum is made by fashioning a strip of wood into a square or a circle and attaching a skin to one edge. Likewise, the *goombay* drum, which comes in various sizes, is made by stretching a depilated goatskin or sheepskin over one end of a cylinder. The drum is tuned by heating its skin over or near a fire—an action called bringing the drum up.

Lacking large trees from which to make drums, Bahamians had to be resourceful in finding materials. Before 1971, musicians made drums from wooden kegs that had held imported nails, cheese, or rum. With advances in technology and transportation, foreign manufacturers began shipping their goods in cartons, eliminating this source of material. Since 1971, Bahamians have used metal barrels to make their drums. The use of metal instead of wood has changed the tone of the drum, so that it is now slightly less resonant and mellow.

Bahamians have added new drums, used principally in junkanoo music. In 1985, junkanoo drummers began using tenor drums from Western trapsets. Lead drummers usually beat these drums, which they call tom-toms. They do not have to be heated, and consequently let the drummer perform without interruption. Drummers have introduced the bomber, a drum made by stretching a goatskin over one end of a washing-machine barrel, and the B-52, made from a 55-gallon oil drum. Smaller *goombay* drums can be used to play bass rhythms, but the bomber and the B-52 provide a more powerful sound.

Other instruments that might be included in a traditional Bahamian ensemble are cowbells, a carpenter's saw, a hair comb, a ridged bottle, shak-shaks, and a washtub bass. Cowbells, played in pairs, are shaken in a rhythmic pattern, or shaken and hit together. Cowbell players are known as bellers. In 1993, musicians introduced the concept of multiple cowbells: each bell has two or more heads and two or more clappers, reducing the number of cowbell players needed in an ensemble. Furthermore, since the heads are of varied shapes and sizes, these bells produce various timbres.

The carpenter's saw (figure 2) is a scraped idiophone. The player, holding the handle in one hand and placing its tip against his body, scrapes the serrations with a piece of metal held in the other hand. For tonal variety, he flexes the saw while playing it. The comb and the ridged bottle are scraped with a piece of metal. Sometimes a strip of paper is inserted through the teeth of the comb, over which the player blows to create various tones.

Shak-shaks are dried, seed-filled pods from the

Figure 2 Rake-'n'-scrape saw player Harold Chipman, Nassau, Bahamas, 2004.
Photo by Kenneth Bilby.

poinciana tree, or plastic bottles and tin cans filled with small stones. Both kinds of shak-shaks are shaken in the same manner as maracas. The washtub bass consists of a metal tub, usually turned upside down, to which a staff and a string are attached. Variations in sound are obtained by depressing the string near the upper portion of the staff.

Bahamian musicians utilize Western instruments, including banjos, guitars, accordions, pianos, drumsets, and modern electronic instruments. They sometimes incorporate them into ensembles that include the traditional instruments.

Religious Music

The religious music of the Bahamas has its roots in Africa and Europe. African influences are evident in layered voices and polyrhythms, and European influences are found in the sources of texts, primarily early Wesleyan and Baptist hymns. The major forms of traditional religious music are the anthem and the rhyming spiritual.

The Anthem
The Bahamian anthem is closely related to the spiritual of slaves and other blacks in the southern

United States. This relationship reflects the fact that enslaved Africans came to the Bahamas with whites loyal to Britain in the late 1700s, at the time of the American Revolution.

The Bahamian anthem, performed primarily in the Family Islands, tends to focus on biblical characters and in particular, their relationship to the sea. The anthem is optimistic, creating feelings of joy and celebration by emphasizing life after death. This contrasts with the African-American spiritual of the antebellum South, which was pessimistic and leaned more toward problems being encountered in mortal life.

The most common form of the anthem features a sequence of stanzas containing up to eight lines, held together by a single-line refrain that may be sung after each stanza or after each line in each stanza. It may comprise four-lined stanzas followed by four-lined choruses sung in multipart harmony. The tenor, which carries the melody, is typically placed between the other parts. Each voice is free to improvise melodically and textually, making the anthem highly textured and harmonically varied. The improvisation of the anthem leads to the production of unorthodox chords. Clapping and foot tapping usually provide accompaniment.

The anthem may be performed as a rushin' song. Rushin'—marching or dancing with shuffling steps—is associated with the junkanoo parade, but some congregations rush around their churches on New Year's Eve or during special services. During the rush, the participants sing anthems before performing responsorial chants. The rush recalls the ring shouts performed by slaves in the southern United States.

The Rhyming Spiritual

The rhyming spiritual, an outgrowth of the anthem, was closely related to the sponging industry, especially on Andros Island. Spongers often sang anthems while performing their tasks. Out of these anthems, they created songs that came to be known as rhyming spirituals. Since sponging is locally no longer a viable industry, the art of rhyming—the creation and recounting of sung verse—is gradually disappearing. Rhyming spirituals may sometimes be sung at wakes.

Rhyming spirituals are usually sung unaccompanied by at least two men, but women sometimes participate in performances. Rhyming spirituals involve singing in parts that may include alto, bass, and more than one tenor. The two most important singers are the lead tenor and the bass. The former, called the rhymer, sings the melody, provides the narrative of the song, and starts and ends each song; the latter, known as the basser, provides an eighth-note ostinato, which keeps time and serves as the foundation on which the other parts improvise. The other parts sing above the rhymer so that, as in the anthem, the lead tenor's melody is sandwiched between the other parts.

Though the rhyming spiritual is highly improvised, it is more harmonically restricted than the anthem, and singers tend to adhere to the tonic (I), subdominant (IV), and dominant (V). It consists of stanzas and refrains; each singer freely provides rhythmic improvisations in the stanzas, though the refrains are rhythmically uniform. Because of the improvisation in each part and the overlapping of phrases, the rhyming spiritual is performed without pauses.

The texts of the rhyming spiritual evoke biblical characters and stories, though a rhyming spiritual may recount the story of something that has happened in the community. One of the most famous Bahamian rhymers, Joseph Spence (1910–1984), was known for his brilliantly eccentric guitar playing. Contemporary performers of the rhyming spiritual include the Dicey Doh Singers.

Secular and Recorded Music

Before 1970, the secular music of the Bahamas was generically known as *goombay*, a name borrowed from the drum, the primary instrument for this type of music. Today, *goombay* is no longer used to define the entirety of Bahamian music. Instead, Bahamians divide their secular music into several categories, most accompanied by the *goombay* drum. These categories include rake 'n' scrape, goombay, and junkanoo.

Rake 'n' Scrape.

Historically, rake 'n' scrapes (figure 3) accompanied quadrilles. The current name, first used publicly in the 1970s by then radio DJ Charles Carter, derives from the raked and scraped idiophones used to perform this music. A basic rake-'n'-scrape ensemble typically includes a *goombay*, a carpenter's saw, and an accordion to provide melodic interest. The Western guitar, banjo, or harmonica may participate if no accordion is present, and a washtub bass, a hair comb, a ridged bottle, and shak-shaks may join in. More-modern rake-'n'-scrape ensembles often use electronic instruments; the bass drum replaces the *goombay*, the high-hat replaces the carpenter's saw, and the electronic keyboard replaces the accordion.

Figure 3 Rake-'n'-scrape band Franco and the Dogs, Cat Island, 2004. *Left to right*: Frank Williams, harmonica; James Levi Webb, goatskin drum; Glen Hanna, saw. On Cat Island, often regarded the home of rake 'n' scrape, musicians use the term *goatskin drum* to refer to the drum called *goombay* in Nassau. *Photo by Kenneth Bilby.*

The definitive trait of rake 'n' scrape is the rhythm usually produced by the carpenter's saw or ridged bottle. This rhythm of alternating eighth and sixteenth notes is sustained throughout the performance, providing a timeline. The timeline is provided by the high hat in modern rake-'n'-scrape ensembles. Rake 'n' scrape is dance music, but it can serve as the foundation for songs whose lyrics address local or foreign events, social problems, and cultural practices.

Goombay

The music now known as *goombay* is that which many non-Bahamians call calypso. It is primarily dance-music with lyrics that address current affairs or extol male sexual prowess or libido. Unlike in rake 'n' scrape (in which rhythm dominates), melody is important; consequently, melodic instruments such as the banjo, electric guitar, and piano are dominant. *Goombay* is the primary form of recorded music in the Bahamas, the music that visitors to the Bahamas are likeliest to hear. It features continuous strumming of the banjo or the electric guitar to complement the rhythm of the drums.

Famous *goombay* recording artists and performers include Alphonso "Blind Blake" Higgs, George Symonette (the "King of Goombay"), and Charles Lofthouse. Though these performers are deceased, their tradition continues, thanks to performers such as Ronnie Butler, Eric "King Eric" Gibson, and more recently Kirkland "K. B." Bodie and Cyril "Dry Bread" Ferguson.

Junkanoo

Junkanoo is traditional *goombay* performed by acoustic instruments within the context of the junkanoo parades at Christmastime. The number of instruments in each junkanoo group may range between ten and hundreds. The traditional instruments used in the parade include *goombay* drums, divided into three sections—lead, second, and bass. The lead drums play the more complex rhythm; the second drums match parts of the lead and bass rhythms; and the bass drums carry a steady, metronomic rhythm. The other traditional junkanoo instruments are cowbells, police whistles, foghorns (long black metal horns that emit a sound similar to that of a semitrailer), bicycle horns (which emit a higher-pitched sound) and conch shells. A horn blower may often play two or more foghorns together to make a fuller sound and give added reach. Sometimes foghorns and bicycle horns are combined to produce a mixture of textures and a contrast in timbers.

Junkanoo instruments are played rhythmically to satisfy the Bahamian aesthetic for a dense mosaic of textures, timbres, and rhythms. Through the use of these instruments, Bahamians continue an African orientation toward intensity in music performance through volume and noise.

Since 1976, junkanooers have used wind and brass instruments, including trumpets (figure 4), trombones, saxophones, sousaphones, and clarinets. The wind instruments, which play popular melodies, have replaced the traditional practice of singing during the junkanoo parade. A principal reason for the decline

Figure 4 Horn players from the Roots Junkanoo group, Nassau, Bahamas, 2004.
Photo by Kenneth Bilby.

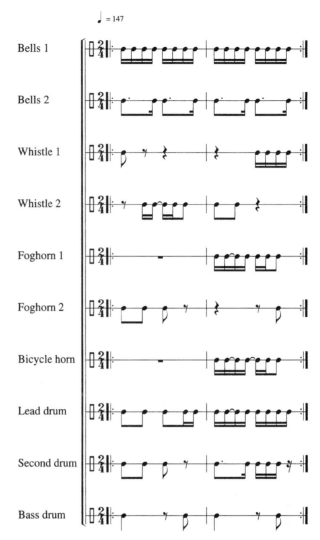

Figure 5 Typical rhythms and instrumentation of junkanoo music.
Transcription by Vivian Nina Michelle Wood.

of singing was that the junkanoo groups grew to such large numbers that it was impossible to hear human voices over the sounds of the instruments. The use of wind instruments has spawned controversy between those who feel that junkanoo should become a more modern cultural manifestation and those who believe the addition of such instruments removes junkanoo from its tradition and transforms it into an event that too closely resembles carnival in Trinidad and Tobago.

Junkanoo music is multilayered and polyrhythmic (figure 5). Each group of instruments has several rhythms, playable with many variations. There are two basic cowbell rhythms—one of repeated sixteenth notes, and the other of alternating dotted eighths and sixteenths. Each beller is free to play variations of these patterns by adding or deleting notes, or by hitting the bells together; the latter adds another timbre to the layers of music. The same process of variation applies to the foghorns, bicycle horns, and drums. Foghorns and bicycle horns sometimes play responsorially together. Bellers and drummers blow whistles in highly individualized rhythms that usually contrast with the cowbell and

drum rhythms, so that each musician simultaneously plays two rhythms—one on a drum or a cowbell, another on a whistle.

Junkanoo musicians stagger their entries into the overall music performance. In most groups, the leader of the drum section starts the music. Once he has set the tempo, the other drums start to play. After the drummers have settled into a steady rhythm, the leader of the bellers begins to play, followed by the other bellers. Once the drums and cowbells have jelled, the foghorns, bicycle horns, and whistles join in. The brass instruments do not usually begin to play until the entire rhythm section has come together and has established a steady tempo.

Junkanoo music is not limited to Christmastime parades. It is played in times of celebration or at other important times. Junkanoo bands accompany political rallies and beauty-pageant motorcades. In 1993, they accompanied the Davis Cup match in North Carolina, in which a Bahamian tennis team played against their U.S. counterparts, Junkanoo music broke out each time the Bahamian team scored a point.

Junkanoo and Recorded Music

Traditional junkanoo has strongly affected popular recorded music of the Bahamas, and the music has evolved from one in which basic rhythms undergirded calypsolike songs to a new form of highly electronic music called junkafunk. Junkanoo's influence was keenly felt around 1973, when a newly independent nation saw a return to what was perceived as authentic traditional Bahamian culture. Artists such as Tony "The Obeah Man" McKay and Eddie Minnis and Da Brudders released songs that married, in the case of McKay, traditional junkanoo elements (such as instruments and the imitation of the horns' dominant-tonic melodic intervals) to songs that depicted Bahamian culture. Minnis used an electronic rhythm section to duplicate traditional junkanoo rhythms. The music supported lyrics that addressed contemporary social problems or praised Bahamian traditions. In the early 1980s, a group of musicians led by Tyrone "Dr. Offfff" Fitzgerald and comprising a Western rhythm section, brass players, and traditional junkanoo instruments continued the use of junkanoo in recorded music.

The common denominator in Eddie Minnis' and Dr. Offfff's music was their rhythm section—a six-member group known as High Voltage, which, in 1992, changed its name to "Bahamen." It is responsible for transforming junkanoo music from music of the streets to music of the studio and dance floor. Bahamen has toured the United States, and its recordings have been released around the world. Promoted as junkafunk, its music reproduces traditional junkanoo rhythms on modern electronic instruments. *Goombay* rhythms are reproduced on a Western drumset and bass guitar, and whistle and horn patterns are produced by synthesizers. Performances sometimes involve traditional *goombay* drums and cowbells. Despite the use of electronic instruments, junkafunk retains the highly percussive, multilayered character of traditional junkanoo music. Its lyrics sometimes come from traditional *goombay* or rake-'n'-scrape songs.

More recently, junkanoo groups such as Roots have produced studio recordings of *goombay*-based songs undergirded by the junkanoo music that is performed during the junkanoo parades at Christmastime.

Festivals

Junkanoo

Junkanoo is a carnivalesque parade, in which costumed participants (called junkanooers) rush to the accompaniment of junkanoo music. The parade originated as a celebration by enslaved Africans, who received two days off for Christmas, and they often spent a portion of this time performing music and dances. After full emancipation (1838), they continued their celebrations. Those on New Providence Island later moved their celebrations to the downtown zone of the city of Nassau. The celebrations included the wearing of costumes and the provision of spontaneous music; they were principally the domain of the working class until 1958, when large numbers of middle-class persons began taking part in the parade.

The increased involvement of the government in the twentieth century and the widespread participation on the part of persons of all colors and classes have made junkanoo the premier cultural manifestation in the Bahamas. Junkanoo parades take place on 26 December and 1 January, between two and eight o'clock in the morning. Junkanoo may be seen on several of the islands, but the most elaborate performance takes place in Nassau. It is an intensely competitive event, involving music, dance, and elaborate costumes made from fringed crepe paper. Groups of up to a thousand persons vie for cash prizes and the acknowledgment of being the best performers. The latter acknowledgment is valued far more than the financial reward.

—Adapted from an article by Vivian Nina Michelle Wood

Bibliography

Bethel, E. Clement. 1991. *Junkanoo: Festival of the Bahamas*, edited and expanded by Nicolette Bethel. London: Macmillan Caribbean.

Edwards, Charles L. [1895] 1942. *Bahama Songs and Stories*. New York: G. E. Steckert.

Hedrick, Basil C., and Jeanette E. Stephens. 1976. *In the Days of Yesterday and in the Days of Today: An Overview of Bahamian Folk Music*. Museum Studies, 8. Carbondale: Southern Illinois University.

Wood, Vivian Nina Michelle. 1995. "Rushin' Hard and Runnin' Hot: Experiencing the Music of the Junkanoo Parade in Nassau, Bahamas." Ph.D. dissertation, Indiana University.

Cuba

About 11 million people inhabit the Republic of Cuba, a nation of more than sixteen hundred keys and islands located in the northwestern Antilles. The main island, Cuba, with a surface area of 105,007 square kilometers, is the largest of the Antilles. Before Europeans arrived, aboriginal groups occupied the archipelago. These groups died out as a result of exogenous diseases, forced labor, and mass suicide in response to this labor. Most of the current national population is descended from Spaniards (mostly from Andalucía and the Canary Islands) and Africans (mostly Bantu and Yorùbá). Small populations derive from French, Chinese, and Caribbeans of other islands. Spanish is the official language, but a few Cubans still speak African-derived languages. Local religions include several derived from African religions, but the largest in membership is Roman Catholicism.

Afro-Cuban Music

The most important African ethnic groups that participated in the amalgamation of the Cuban population were the Yorùbá, different groups of Bantu linguistic stock, and some groups from the former area of Calabar (Dahomey). There is little documentation of early African music in Cuba. The music of Africans and their descendants in Cuba was played on instruments that slaves built on the basis of African prototypes. African music found fertile soil for development, particularly as part of the slaves' reorganization of their religions and beliefs. Because all African religions have their own music, the religions brought by African groups to Cuba enriched the arts of the island. Even now, musical instruments, characteristic ways of playing them, songs, rhythms, dances, and even the use of music

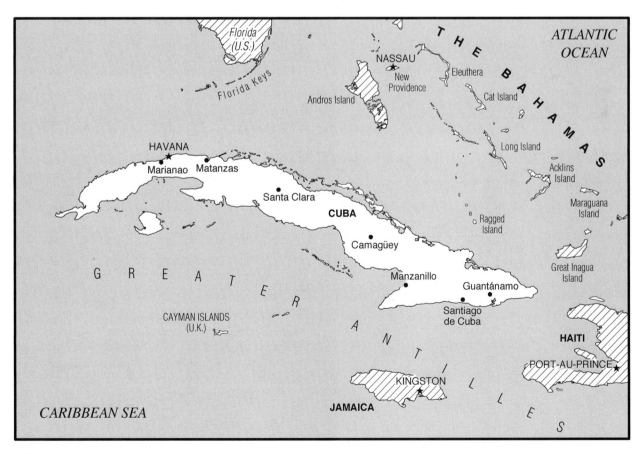

Cuba

for magical functions—are all practiced in ways resembling their New World beginnings, much as they must have been when Africans brought them to Cuba, hundreds of years ago.

Yorùbá Heritage and Santería

In Cuba, slaves of Yorùbá origin were generally known as Lucumí. Yorùbá music has remained, as a rule, more authentically preserved in western Cuba than in eastern Cuba, because most Yorùbá slaves were landed on the western coast, mainly in Matanzas, Havana Province, and the city of Havana. The survival of Yorùbá music and dance can be partially attributed to the fact that the Yorùbá arrived late in the slave trade, mostly during the first half of the nineteenth century.

Many African traditions were preserved in Cuba because masters allowed slaves to use their traditions of drumming and dance to worship as they had in Africa. Masters also allowed slaves to organize mutual-aid societies so they could better face their new way of life. These societies often had a king, a queen, and a complex social hierarchy with different levels, conferring prestige on the members of the group who held offices. This relative leniency, combined with compulsory baptism into the Roman Catholic Church, resulted in the syncretism of West African deities with Christian saints. In this sense, the Yorùbá-Cubans went so far as to name their religion Santería, in a frank allusion to the Christian saints. Many Yorùbá and their descendants congregated around temple-homes, headed by a religious godfather or godmother.

Musical Instruments

The most important musical instruments used in Santería rituals are two-headed *batá* drums (figure 1), always played in sets of three. These drums have retained the original hourglass shape of their African prototypes, but a clearer differentiation has been established in the diameter of the skins. The drum with the lowest pitch is the *iyá*, the middle drum is the *itótele*, and the smallest one is the *okonkolo*. The performer sits and holds a drum horizontally on his lap so he can strike either drumhead at will. The tension of the skin is fixed with tensors, usually made of rawhide. Sometimes bronze jingle bells (*chaworó*) are fastened around the heads of the *iyá*.

Also built by the Yorùbá in Cuba were the *iyesa*, a set of four cylindrical, different-sized double-headed drums. The tension of the skins is maintained with tensors that stretch from one skin to the other. Other Yorùbá drums in Cuba are the *bembé*, made in differing sizes from hollowed tree trunks. The skins

Figure 1 A famous *babalawo* adjusts the *chaworo* bells on his sacred *bata* drum. *Babalawo* is the highest rank for a priest; it is reserved for men, as it was in Africa.
Photo courtesy of the Archives of CIDMUC (Center for the Research and Development of Cuban Music), Havana.

are nailed on and tightened by heat from a fire. *Bembé* are not used for religious purposes.

Another group of instruments used by the Yorùbá in Cuba is a set of shaken idiophones, the *abwe* or *shekere*. These instruments are made from three large gourds covered with bead-studded nets. Each net fits loosely. When the instrument is shaken, the beads (made from seeds) strike the exterior of the gourd. This set of gourds is usually accompanied by a steel hoe blade (*hierro*), struck with an iron bar. In polyrhythmic music, the blade serves as a rhythmic guide.

Bantu Heritage and Congo Religion

The zone from which most Bantu-speaking slaves were taken is the Congo Basin and both sides of the Congo River. In Cuba, these slaves were known as Congos. It would be hard today to identify traits that would distinguish the ethnic groups of this linguistic complex, but the Loango, the Bavili, the Bacongo, the Mayombe, and the Ndongo have provided the greatest contributions to Cuban culture. Like the

Yorùbá, the Congos organized their religion in temple-homes, and they congregated around their godfathers' temple-homes, creating nuclei of godchildren.

Musical Instruments

The Congos brought not only their religion, but also their feasts, dances, and music. They reconstructed many African instruments in Cuba. Among these were several percussive wooden idiophones, of which the *guagua* (or *catá*) is the only survivor; it is a hollowed trunk, struck with two sticks. Drums introduced into Cuba by the Congo constituted the *ngoma* ensemble. *Ngoma* drums, made of wooden staves, are single-headed and barrel-shaped; they are usually played alone, but sometimes they are accompanied by the *kinfuiti*, another drum introduced into Cuba by the Congo. The Congo introduced *makuta* beats and dances, employed in a celebration that is no longer observed; the last record of that festivity is in the early twentieth century, around Sagua la Grande. The Congo instruments that had the greatest cultural impact were *yuka* drums, made from hollowed fruit-tree trunks, with a skin nailed to one end and usually played in a set of three. The largest is the *caja*, the middle is the *mula*, and the smallest is the *cachimbo*. These names seem to have come from ones used in the *ngoma* ensemble.

The Emergence of Cuban Music

In society, economics, and the arts, a distinctively Cuban nationality is thought to have emerged between 1790 and 1868, when there appeared musical genres that, despite having their roots in Spain and Africa, displayed elements of Cuban invention. There was a great surge of music played by Spanish musicians with academic training, who evidenced solid technical foundations in composition and in performance. Musical ensembles were organized around churches, particularly in Havana and Santiago de Cuba. This period witnessed the immigration of people of French descent from Haiti, and later from Louisiana.

Another important influence during this period was the introduction of opera and zarzuela companies from Italy and Spain. In urban areas, genres such as the Cuban *contradanza* and later the *habanera* were born. Traditional Cuban song took shape, as did *orquestas típicas* that played several types of dances. In rural areas, the musical genres that were later to be known as the *punto campesino* (in central and western Cuba) and the *son* (in eastern Cuba) emerged. In the chapels of Santiago de Cuba and Havana, Esteban Salas y Castro (1725–1803),

Juan París (1759–1845), and other musicians modernized the compositional techniques of Cuban ecclesiastical music.

The period 1868–1898 was marked by rebellions against Spanish rule. The Spanish government abolished slavery gradually in 1880 and definitively in 1886, freeing about a quarter of a million blacks, many of whom soon migrated to urban outskirts and margins. Before 1871, an estimated 150,000 Chinese laborers were brought over, mainly from Canton; though they eventually organized their own Chinatown in Havana and spread throughout the country, their tendency to stick together in closed groups limited their contribution to the common musical culture.

Important Cuban folkloric genres appeared on the urban peripheries during this period. Notable among these were the *rumba* and the *comparsa* (see below).

A vast migration from rural to urban areas, especially to Havana, contributed to the integration of many local traditions that had developed in different areas of the country. The effects of this migration were complemented by the movements of troops resulting from the wars for independence. Concert music, particularly piano music in Havana, changed considerably. Outstanding musicians appeared, such as Manuel Saumell (1817–1870), whose *contradanzas* for piano gave rise to Cuba's own concert music.

In 1898, during the last of the three wars for independence, U.S. intervention on behalf of the rebels helped free Cuba from Spanish rule. U.S. military occupation (1 January 1899 to 20 May 1902) brought North American capital investments in Cuba, and with them came the influence of North American lifeways on Cuban cultural expression.

The Republican Period, 1902–1959

Under the republic, a national consciousness based on Cuba's position as a politically independent nation began to arise. Cubans became increasingly aware of the need to develop a Cuban musical culture, and simultaneously the music of Cuba began to have influence outside Cuba. The early contacts of Cuban musical genres—particularly the *son*—with American jazz left marked effects on the Cuban genres and jazz, and on the popular music of the United States. In turn, the *rumba* and the *son*, and later the *cha-cha-chá* and the mambo, had an impact on Europe during this period. Cuban musical instruments such as the *tumbadora* (conga drums) and bongos began to be used in diverse instrumental ensembles in cultures outside Cuba.

Professional popular music, with deep roots among the population and intimate links to dance, left its mark too. It differed from folk music by the use of European technical elements in composition and interpretation. This music became easily commercializable because it was readily adaptable to radio and television, the media of mass communication. In turn, these media affected the development of Cuban folkloric ensembles. Dance music was by far the most popular, with roots deep in tradition.

Cuban music was nourished by waves of immigrants from the Caribbean, mainly from Haiti and Jamaica. These immigrants were attracted by a shortage of manpower in the sugar industry and in the growth of the railroads. The increased importance of radio, the introduction of television (in 1950), the appearance of several small record companies, and the construction of important musical theaters—all fostered a boom in Cuban music, mostly limited to Havana.

After 1959

The revolution of 1959 began the transition to a socialist society. The government instituted a free educational system, whose curriculum included the arts. The National Council of Culture was founded under the Ministry of Education, and in 1976, the council was elevated to the rank of Ministry of Culture. The National Council of Culture aimed to rescue Cuba's folklore. It allocated significant resources to the development of professional music and the Amateur Movement, which eventually produced many professional musicians.

A factory was established to mass-produce indigenous musical instruments, which until then had been produced only by individual craftsmen. Consequently, there was an increased availability of bongos, rattles (*chéqueres*), drums of the Abakuá secret society, and other Afro-Cuban musical instruments. Bongos, *tumbadoras*, guitar, *tres*, and other instruments that had been produced on a limited scale were turned out in greater numbers.

Professional popular music saw a marked development of the *son*, particularly in connection with *nueva trova*, a nationalistic movement, founded in 1962. The *son*, particularly its urban variants, became practically synonymous with Cuban popular dance music and had a far-reaching impact on the music later known as salsa. The influence of the *son* on the creation of salsa has been so far reaching that many specialists have mistaken one for the other.

Folkloric music became stronger in urban areas. People of central and western Cuba continued singing songs of the *punto guajiro* complex (see below), and the variants of the *son* (including the one called *changüí*) retained their predominance in the rural areas of the eastern provinces. The rumba remains a broadly practiced genre, particularly in Havana and in the Matanzas Province. Cuban musicians still compose boleros, *cha-cha-chás*, *contradanzas*, *danzones*, and *guarachas*, but none of these is as popular as the *son*.

Musical Genres

The history of Cuba's musical culture reflects a complex pattern of migrations and cultural confluences, leading to the emergence of widely differing musical traditions in remote areas of the country. These factors contributed to the development of a variegated national musical culture with local musical types. Communication among these areas and among the strata of the population has helped some local traditions gain national popularity and become typical expressions of a Cuban national identity.

The genres of Cuban traditional music divide into five complexes (*son*, rumba, *canción*, *danzón*, and *punto guajiro*), each comprising related musical genres based on common musical aptitudes and behaviors. These complexes are determined by style, instrumentation, and the makeup of traditional ensembles.

The Son Complex

The combination of plucked strings and African-derived percussion instruments gave birth to a musical genre called *son*, first popular among peasants of eastern Cuba. During the twentieth century, the *son* complex, because of its influence on dance music and its projection into practically all social and functional spheres of musical activity in the country, has been the most important musical genre in Cuba. Its earliest manifestations, perhaps dating as far back as 1750, were among the first Cuban musical genres or styles about which information survives.

The *son* took shape in rural easternmost Cuba. Its oldest genres include the *son montuno*, from the Sierra Maestra range in the southeast, and the *changüí*, from the area of Guantánamo. The formal structure of the oldest *sones* is the constant alternation of a soloist with a refrain, typically sung by a small choir. When the *son* emerged from rural areas, it acquired another important structural element: the inclusion of an initial closed structure in binary form, followed by the *montuno*, a section in which a soloist alternates with a small choir.

The instrumental ensembles (figure 2) that played *sones* always combined plucked string instruments—guitar, *laúd* (a type of guitar), *tres* (a variant of the

Figure 2 A *son* ensemble in the mountain area of Oriente. *Left to right: tres, tumbadoras, laúd, contrabajo, tres,* and *tres. Photo courtesy of the Archives of CIDMUC, Havana.*

guitar), and later the string bass—with percussive instruments such as bongos, claves, maracas, and the *güiro*. The vocal soloist is often the one who plays the claves, and the singers of the refrain are the other instrumentalists.

Within the context of the *son*, musicians exploited two important instruments for Cuban music—the *tres* and bongos (figure 3). The *tres* is a Cuban plucked stringed instrument that differs from the guitar mainly because of the way the strings are tuned. Three pairs of strings, each with a pitch and its octave, are plucked to build melodies as counterpoints to the main melodies of the singer.

The Rumba Complex

Another important generic complex in Cuba is the rumba, whose name probably derives from African-Caribbean words (such as *tumba, macumba,* and *tambo*) referring to a collective secular festivity. Originally, in marginal suburbs of Havana and Matanzas, the word meant simply a feast. In time, it took the meaning of a Cuban musical genre and acquired a specific instrumental format for its performance. It even gave rise to its own instruments: *tumbadoras* (often called congas), which have spread throughout the world.

In the beginning, the instruments that played rumbas were different-sized wooden boxes. Eventually, they evolved into three barrel-shaped drums, first called *hembra* 'female', *macho* 'male', and *quinto* 'fifth', and later called *salidor* 'starter', *tres-dos* 'three-two', and *quinto*. In African musical cultures, female drums, also called mother drums, are

Figure 3 A man plays bongos.
Photo courtesy of the Archives of CIDMUC, Havana.

tuned in the lowest registers. Male drums are in the mid-registers, and *quintos* are tuned in the upper registers. The *salidor* is the first drum that plays.

Tres-dos indicates that the drum will normally be beaten in a combination of three and two beats. These drums were genetically called *tumbadoras*. With their appearance, the instrumental format of the rumba was fixed. This ensemble is often complemented by a small *catá*, a hollowed tree trunk, struck with two sticks.

All genres of the rumba have the same structure. The lead singer starts with a section that *rumberos* (rumba players) call the *diana*. The singer then goes into a section of text that introduces the theme, and only after this does the rumba proper begin, with more active instrumental playing and a section alternating between the soloist and the small choir.

Of the genres that make up the rumba complex, the *guaguancó*, the *columbia*, and the *yambú* are the most popular in Cuba. The *guaguancó* has most deeply penetrated into other functional spheres of Cuban music, and is most generally identified with the concept of the rumba. The performance of *guaguancó* may include couple dancing, and the music and the dance have elements that reflect Bantu traits.

The Canción Complex

A third generic complex is the *canción* 'song', also embodied in Afro-Cuban forms and singing-styles. References to songs written by Cuban composers appear as early as about 1800. These songs, written in Italian styles of the day, had no features that could identify them as Cuban, but they gave rise to Cuban lyrical songs. The earliest appearance of Cuban elements took place in the texts. By about 1850, many songs of this type, such as "*La Bayamesa*" by Carlos M. de Céspedes (1819–1874), were in circulation.

Songs for two voices in parallel thirds and sixths and using the guitar as the instrument of preference have been in frequent use in Cuba since the 1800s. They laid the foundation for the emergence of the *canción trovadoresca*, a genre named after a collective term for its most important interpreters: *trovadores* 'troubadours'. José "Pepe" Sànchez (1856–1918), Sindo Garay (1867–1968), Manuel Corona (1880–1950), Alberto Villalón (1882–1955), and others decisively shaped the musical genre that has come to be known as the traditional *trova*.

The distinguishing feature of the *canción trovadoresca* in Cuba is how the song became closely associated with the singer, who moved around accompanying himself on the guitar, singing about things he knew or whatever struck his fancy. The word *trovador* was probably an attempt by these artists to establish a relation between themselves and the troubadours of medieval Europe. This genre developed greatly in Cuba after the 1960s, giving rise

to a new movement, *nueva trova*, which developed its own administrative structure and gained hundreds of members. Today, the movement has given way to boleros and other forms of romantic songs within salsa music.

Before the 1850s, this tradition was intended primarily for listening, not dancing. The situation changed with the rise of the important musical genre known as bolero, born in Cuba from antecedents in the Spanish bolero. Rhythms taken from those played by the Cuban percussive instruments of African origin were added to the traditional forms of the Spanish dance and melody. The creators of the new genre were *trovadores* from Santiago de Cuba who performed the *canción trovadoresca*. They gave the bolero stylistic elements and rhythms from the *son*, then popular only in rural eastern Cuba. José "Pepe" Sànchez is considered the composer of the first Cuban bolero, a genre cultivated by many songwriters and musicians abroad. In some Caribbean countries, it is one of the most important genres of popular music.

During the 1800s, societies whose only objective was to make music came into being. This is the case with *clave* choirs (*coros de clave*), which originated in Matanzas and Havana. These organizations had repertoires of songs called *claves*, composed by its members. They lost favor and disappeared early in the 1900s, but they contributed to the Cuban musical heritage a genre that preserves the original name.

Another musical genre of the *canción* complex is the *criolla*. It resulted from the continued development of the *clave*. The composer of the first *criolla* was Luis Casas Romero, who wrote his "Carmela" in 1908. *Criollas* are songs written in urban forms and style, with texts referring to rural themes. The tempo is slower than in the *clave*, and the meter is 6/8. The form is binary, and the harmonics are often modal.

With the *clave* appeared another genre, the *guajira*, written in 6/8 meter alternating with 3/4, and often including musical affectations evocative of rural peoples' plucked stringed instruments. Texts of *guajiras* celebrated the beauty of the countryside and pastoral life.

Cuban songs in general, but especially the bolero and the *Canción trovadoresca*, have joined with other Cuban musical genres, such as the *son*, to produce mixed genres that have influenced Cuban dance music.

The Danzón Complex

Large numbers of French people and Haitians with French customs reached Cuba at the end of the 1700s, when the character of the Cuban nation was taking shape. This migration gave rise to the fourth generic complex, the *danzón*, which had its origins in the early Cuban *contradanzas*, and projected forward in time to the *cha-cha-chá*.

The interpretation in Cuba of French *contredanses*—especially with the violin-piano-flute format—led to the development of a *contradanza* that may be considered Cuban, especially with the later introduction of percussive instruments taken from Afro-Cuban music. The earliest *contradanzas* were played by two different musical ensembles: the *charanga* (a Cuban popular music orchestra consisting of two flutes, piano, *pailas*, claves, *güiro*, two *tumbadoras*, four violins, and eventually a cello) and the *orquesta típica* 'folkloric orchestra'. The development of these ensembles, and the evolution and change experienced by the French and local *contredanses* in Cuba, gave rise to the *danza*, the *danzón*, the *danzonete*, the mambo, and the *cha-cha-chá*.

The *contradanza* acquired its distinctive profile during the 1800s and became the first genre of Cuban music to gain popularity abroad. It had four well-defined routines: *paseo* 'walk', *cadena* 'chain' (taking of hands to make a chain), *sostenido* 'holding of partners', and *cedazo* 'passing through' (as some couples make arches with their arms while others pass under them). Its structure is binary, and each section usually has eight measures.

Danzas cubanas were the result of the evolution of older *contradanzas*. Played by ensembles known as French *charangas* (*charangas francesas*), they evidenced greater contrast between the first and second parts of the overall binary structure. These pieces gave rise to the most important member of the complex, the *danzón*, of which Miguel Failde composed and premiered the first example, "*Las Alturas de Simpson*," in Matanzas in 1879.

Like the contradanza, the *danzón* was a square dance, but its figurations were more complex. The transformations brought about in it, particularly through the addition of new parts, gave it the structure of a five-part rondo. This might have been the origin of its name, since the addition of parts enlarged the piece, making it a "big *danza*" (the -*ón* suffix in Spanish is augmentative). The *danzón* is an instrumental genre usually written in 2/4 meter. Once considered the national dance of Cuba, it enjoyed enormous popularity during the late 1800s and early 1900s.

In 1929, another musician from Matanzas, Aniceto Díaz (1887–1964), combined elements from the *son* and the *danzón*, added a vocal part, and created a new style of *danzón* called the *danzonete*. His first composition in this style, "*Rompiendo la rutina*" ('Breaking the Routine'), established the

danzonete as a new musical genre. During the 1950s, further transformations of vocal *danzones* and the *danzonetes*, with the addition of new instruments to typical *charangas*, paved the way for Damaso Pérez Prado (ca. 1916–1989) and Enrique Jorrín (1926–1987) to create two new musical genres: the mambo and the *cha-cha-chá*.

The Punto Guajiro *Complex*

The *punto guajiro* and the entire complex of rural musical genres it embraces has developed largely within the framework of rural music in central and western Cuba, where country *tonadas*, *puntos fijos*, *puntos libres*, *seguidillas*, and other forms remain common. *Tonadas* are tunes or melodies sung to recite *décimas*. The *punto* can be *fijo* 'fixed' or *libre* 'free': if the accompaniment of the *laúd* and guitar is always present, then the *punto* is *fijo*; if the accompaniment stops to let the singer sing his melody and *décima* alone, the *punto* is *libre*. In the *seguidilla*, the singer uses verification that gives the impression of a never-ending strophe. The *zapateo* or Cuban *zapateo* is the dance used for the *punto*. *Guateques campesinos* was the name given to the typical parties of the farmers where the *puntos* were sung.

The transformation and modernization of the genres of this complex have been slower than in the other complexes of Cuban music, perhaps because it is limited to rural areas. Professional musicians have adopted some of these genres, usually in combination with elements of other generic complexes, as in the *son* and the *canción*.

Vocal and Instrumental Ensembles

The accompanimental requirements of certain musical genres fostered the creation of distinct types of musical ensemble. Plucked stringed instruments, with the guitar and the *tres* as the most central ones, produced the typical sound of most Cuban music. Also important were rhythmic patterns borrowed from the music of the Spanish *bandurria* and played by Cuban rural people on the *laúd*. The *bandurria* and the *laúd* are plucked stringed instruments brought by the Spanish settlers.

To the sound of the plucked strings was added that of African-derived percussion instruments. Ensembles took in bongos, *claves*, the *güiro* (and the *guayo*, its metallic counterpart), maracas, and the jawbone rattle (*quijada*), the *botija* (jug), and the *marímbula*. The *marímbula* is made from a large wooden box. Two metal bars fixed to the side of the box hold metal strips that serve as tongues (*languettes*), plucked with the fingers. Tuning is done by loosening the bars and adjusting the length of the tongues. The performer usually sits on the box, with his legs on either side of the *languettes*.

The most important percussive instruments that developed included *tumbadoras* (also called congas), *timbales* (big hemispheric drums played with two sticks covered with cloth or leather), and *pailas* (cylindrical metal drums played with two wooden sticks). Many variants of the cowbell (*cencerro*) developed. In performance, these instruments were often combined with instruments brought from Europe and assimilated into Cuban music in their original organological forms, as happened with the piano, the flute, the violin, the guitar, and other instruments.

This blend of instruments created the instrumental formats that give Cuban music a distinctive character. Some of the most important among them are the *dúo*, the *trío*, the *cuarteto*, the *septeto*, the *conjunto*, the *charanga típica*, the *estudiantina*, the *guaguancó* group, the *comparsa*, and the *gran combo* or *gran orquesta*.

The *dúo* consists of two guitars, or of a guitar and a *tres*. The performers sing two parts or melodic lines, called *primo* and *segundo*. This combination often serves for boleros, *canciones trovadorescas*, *claves*, *criollas*, and *guajiras*. In the eastern provinces, the *dúos* frequently perform *sones montunos*.

The *trío* retains the two vocal melodic lines, but a third performer often sings the *primo* while playing *claves* or maracas. The repertoire of the *trío* resembles that of the *dúo* because both are closely related to the *canción trovadoresca*. When this type of ensemble reached the cities, it took the *son* into its repertoire. Today, *tríos* appear throughout the nation. One of their most outstanding representatives was the Trío Matamoros, famous during the 1940s.

The *cuarteto* format includes two guitars (or guitar and *tres*), *claves*, and maracas. Sometimes, rather than *claves* or maracas, the fourth instrument is a muted trumpet. These groups retain the two melodic lines (*primo* and *segundo*), and base their repertoire on mixed genres such as the *guaracha-son*, the *bolero-son*, and the *guajira-son*. This ensemble was popular during the 1930s.

The instruments of the *septeto de son* are guitar, *tres*, trumpet (usually with mute), maracas, *claves* (played by the vocalist), bongos, and *marímbula* or *botija*. In its most recent version, a string bass replaces the *marímbula*. The *septeto* resulted from adding a muted trumpet to the *sexteto de son*. This combination crystallized in the 1920s, when the *son* was gaining popularity in the cities. One of the most important *septetos* in the history of Cuban music is

Ignacio Piñeiro's Septeto Nacional, a paramount example of a traditional Cuban musical ensemble.

The *conjunto*, another type of ensemble, consists of piano, *tres*, guitar, three or four trumpets, *tumbadora*, bongo, bass, and singers. The singers often play maracas and *claves*, or jawbone and *güiro*. The repertoire of the *conjunto* includes boleros, *guarachas*, and *cha-cha-chás*, and it sometimes plays mixed genres such as *guajira-son* and *bolero-son*. The Cuban *conjunto* enjoyed its greatest popularity in the 1950s, especially after the introduction of television in Cuba. Among the most outstanding representatives are the *conjuntos* of Chappotín, Pacho Alonso (1928–1982), Roberto Faz (1914–1966), and Conjunto Casino.

The *charanga típica* includes a five-key transverse flute, a piano, a string bass, *pailas*, two violins, and a *güiro*. It emerged during the first decade of the twentieth century; after 1940, it doubled the number of violins, and added a *tumbadora* and (later, sometimes) a cello. Some *charangas* have replaced the *pailas* with a complete set of drums and have included electric instruments such as electric bass, electric piano, and synthesizer. The term *orquesta* 'orchestra' has been commonly used since about the 1960s. Foremost in the repertoires of these orchestras was the *danzón*, but now the *son* is the most frequently played genre. During its popularity, these ensembles had no vocalists, but with the creation of the *cha-cha-chá* in the 1950s, they began to feature singers or a small choir. Arcaño y sus Maravillas and the Orquesta Gris are among the most important representatives of the instrumental phase of the *charanga*, and Orquesta Aragón and Enrique Jorrín's orchestra are probably the most important of the phase that included vocalists. One of the most successful *charangas* with electric instruments is Los Van Van.

In the late 1700s and early 1800s, the *estudiantina* was made up of two singers who sang *primo* 'first' and *segundo* 'second' while playing maracas and *claves*, plus others performing on a trumpet, two *treses*, a guitar, *pailas*, and a string bass. Some *estudiantinas* also included a *marímbula*. Their repertoire was based mainly on the *son*, but they also played *danzones*. Their tradition centered in Santiago de Cuba.

The *guaguancó* group has a soloist and a small choir, three *tumbadoras*, *claves*, and occasionally a small *catá*. Its repertoire includes the genres that make up the rumba: *guaguancó*, *Columbia*, and *yumbú*. One of the most important groups is Los Muñequitos, in Matanzas.

The instrumentation of *comparsas* has never been stable. They usually require instruments that can be carried and played at the same time. The most frequently used are *tumbadoras*, congas, bass drums, *galletas* 'cookies' (big drums in the shape of a cookie, played with a stick covered with cloth or leather), *bocus* (long, conical drums hung from the player's neck and shoulder and beaten with bare hands), cowbells, plowshares, steel rings, and other improvising instruments. In later phases, *comparsas* have included a trumpet as a solo instrument.

Comparsas accompany dancers who parade through the streets during carnivals. They had their origins in the celebration of Epiphany (6 January), during the colonial period. (The slaves were treated like children in many ways, and 6 January was Children's Day in the Spanish colonies.) Carrying lanterns and flags, slaves would take to the streets in the typical attire of their homelands. They would dance and parade to the governor's palace, where they would revel in African-derived dramatic presentations, songs, and dances.

Finally, the *gran combo* or *gran orquesta* is another important type of ensemble, influenced by jazz bands in the United States. Particularly after the 1950s, jazz bands began to be organized in Cuba, with repertoires that included *guarachas*, boleros, and *sones montunos*. The instrumentation of these bands consisted of trumpets; trombones; alto, tenor, and baritone saxophones; piano; bass drums; and Cuban percussion. They occasionally included a flute and a clarinet. It was with these bands that the mambo, an important musical genre, was born. One of the most important jazz bands was the Benny Moré Band, which became popular in the 1950s.

—Adapted from an article by Olavo Alén Rodríguez

Bibliography

Alén Rodríguez, Olavo. 1973. *Combinaciones instrumentales y vocales de Cuba*. La Habana: Editora Ministerio de Educación.

——. 1981. *Géneros de la Música Cubana*. La Habana: Editorial Pueblo y Educación.

Boggs, Vernon W. ed. 1992 *Salsiology*. New York: Excelsior Music Publishing Company.

Carpentier, Alejo. 1946. *La Música en Cuba*. Mexico: Fondo de Cultura Económica.

Grenet, Emilio. 1939. *Popular Cuban Music*. Havana: Ministerio de Educación, Dirección de Cultura.

Hernández, Clara, ed. 1982. *Ensayos de Música Latinoamericana*. Havana: Casa de las Américas.

Hernández Balaguer, Pablo. 1964. *Breve Historia de la Música Cubana*. Santiago de Cuba: Editorial Universidad de Oriente.

León, Argeliers. 1984. *Del Canto y el Tiempo*. La Habana: Editorial Letras Cubanas.

Linares, María Teresa. 1970. *La Música Popular*. La Habana: Instituto Cubano del Libro.

Manuel, Peter. 1990. *Essays on Cuban Music: Cuban and North American Perspectives*. Lanham, Md.: University Press of America.

Ortiz, Fernando. 1950. *La Africania de la Música Folklórica de Cuba*. La Habana: Ediciones Cárdenas y Cia.

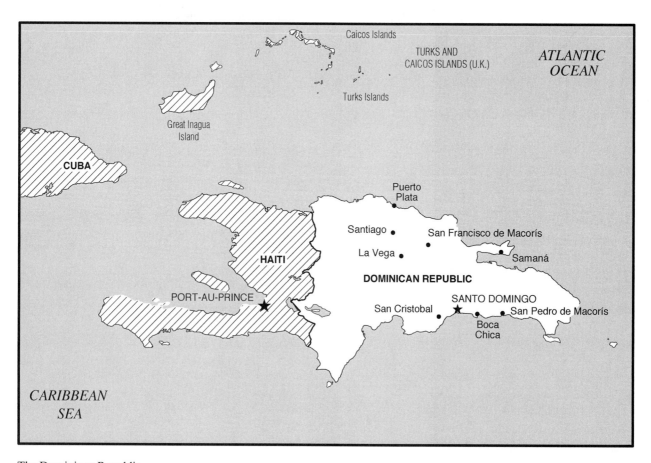

The Dominican Republic

The Dominican Republic

The Dominican Republic shares the island of Hispaniola with Haiti, but the two countries are culturally and musically distinct. A Spanish colony was founded as Santo Domingo on the southern coast in 1496 and began to flourish. However, Spanish explorers discovered the cultures and treasures of Mexico in 1519 and Peru in 1532, and by the mid-1500s, Spain shifted its attention away from Hispaniola and the island languished as a colonial backwater. This negligence allowed France to gain a foothold in the western part of the island. By about 1530, with the island's exploitable gold exhausted and the indigenous Taíno population drastically reduced, the basis for accruing wealth shifted to cattle ranching and agriculture, primarily sugarcane cultivation, carried out by African slaves. Those brought by the French developed a society more densely populated than and culturally different from Santo Domingo. In 1697, the Treaty of Rijswijk ceded to France the western third of Hispaniola, called Saint-Domingue as a translation of Santo Domingo. In 1804, a successful slave uprising led to the founding of the Republic of Haiti. In 1822, Haiti took over Santo Domingo to free it from Spain, but in 1844, Dominicans liberated themselves from Haitian and Spanish rule, founding the Dominican Republic.

History of Ethnic Composition

Native Taíno Heritage

The Taíno spoke an Arawak language. Arawak is one of four main language families of tropical South America. Seafaring Arawak-speakers from the Amazon and Orinoco River basins populated the Antilles, arriving at Hispaniola (which they called Haïtí or Quisqueya) more than four thousand years ago. When Europeans arrived, the Taíno of Borínquen (Puerto Rico) and Quisqueya were facing challenges from the bellicose Caribs, speakers of languages in another of the four main tropical South American language families.

Taíno musical culture is represented by little material evidence, since much of it was vocal. Bartolomé de Las Casas described the singing of large groups of Taíno women when they gathered to grate manioc for toasted flat cassava cakes (casabe). The most important Taíno instrument was a hollow log idiophone (mayohuacán; figure 1), struck for the

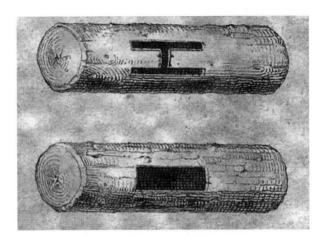

Figure 1 Mayohuacán, the native Taíno slit-gong (according to Fernández de Oviedo y Valdés 1526).

areíto (also areyto), a ritual in which dancers played maracas and may have worn rattles tied to their ankles. For signaling, the Taíno used conch trumpets (fotutos), which remain in use in some rural areas to announce danger, death, or meat for sale. They played flutes made of clay, bone, and perhaps cane, but few specimens survive. They had neither drums nor stringed instruments.

The areíto was the main musical event of Quisqueya, Cuba, and Borínquen. It was a large-scale song-and-dance rite that could last for hours or days, with a vocal or dance leader and a chorus or dance group of as many as three hundred men or women or both, accompanied by the mayohuacán. It varied by area and social occasion.

The chorus and dancers were positioned in a linear, circular, or arch formation, maintaining close contact with one another by holding hands or linking arms. The soloist and chorus moved forward and backward together in rhythm, the dancers playing maracas and perhaps wearing ankle rattles. The leader, a man or a woman (and probably a shaman), sang responsorially with the chorus, who repeated the leader's every line, but at a lower or higher pitch, while the leader kept dancing in silence. A soloist could be replaced, but no break would occur until the narrative song was finished; its performance could take three or four hours, or it could last from one day to the next. The tune and movements could alter when a new soloist took over, but the narrative had to continue; yet the tune for a new sung story could be the same as the former one.

Spanish Heritage

Spain itself was not monolithic at the time of the conquest of the New World; its culture represented the fusion of Sephardic Jewish, Arabic, and Celtic-Iberian elements. An impetus toward the New World was the Reconquest, with the final and definitive expulsion of Jews and Arabs from Spain in 1492, shortly before Columbus began his first voyage. One destination of their flight was the New World. Evidence of Jewish and Arab influence in Hispaniola appears in architecture, dialect, and the oldest surviving musical styles and genres. Other early Spanish immigrants included peasants from Extremadura and Andalucía. In the late 1600s, an important wave of immigrants arrived from the Canary Islands and others followed.

Like much Taino music, the first music that Europeans brought to Hispaniola was vocal. On the first voyage, when land was at last sighted, Columbus wrote that his sailors fell to their knees and sang the *Salve Regina*, a Marian antiphon, antedating the eleventh century. The *Salve Regina*, the sung rosary, and other prayers, music, iconography, and ritual procedures were introduced by Dominican clergy and then perpetuated by folk priests and other devotees in remote areas. The conservation of archaic liturgical practices in folk ritual demonstrates the importance of the oral tradition as a source of historical documentation.

The Dominican *salve* is the musical cornerstone of a saint's festival (*velación, noche de vela, velorio de santo; velar* is Spanish for 'to keep vigil'), the most frequent and ubiquitous event of Dominican folk Christianity. Rurally based and individually sponsored, the saint's festival is undertaken initially in fulfillment of a vow for divine healing, but it usually recurs annually as an inherited obligation. Its celebration lasts all night. After each of three rosaries (*tercios*), three sacred "*Salves de la Virgen*" ('Hails of the Virgin') are sung at the altar. In the east, the liturgical *salves* are followed by others in a style representing an African-influenced evolution of the genre; but in the southwest and north, the three sacred *salves* are followed by further *salves* of similar style, sung antiphonally or responsorially to any of a large number of melodies, until the next of the three rosaries in the event.

Other Dominican traditional musical genres of Hispanic heritage are also vocal, unaccompanied, unmetered, melismatic, and antiphonal. Sung high in male and female registers with tense vocal production, they are often in the minor mode or with a neutral third, but are unornamented. They include other types of ritual song of folk Christianity for saints' or death ceremonies: the (partially) sung rosary; altar and procession songs other than *salves* (generically called *versos*); songs for children's wakes (*baquiní*) such as the almost extinct *mediatuna* of Cibao, the northern region of the country; *romances* or Spanish ballads; children's songs and games; antiphonal, unmetered worksongs (*plenas*, not to be confused with Puerto Rican *plenas*); and various improvisatory sung conversations or debates (*desafíos* 'challenges'), performed within contexts of agricultural labor (such as the *chuin* of Baní, near the southern coast west of San Cristobal) for social commentary, expression of devotion, or courtship in a festive context, even at the periphery of a wake (such as the *décima*), or as ritual (such as the *tonadas de toros* of the east).

The **Cibao Valley**, the inland valley of the north, was settled in the earliest days of the colony, and its main city, Santiago de los Caballeros, is now the second largest city in the country. The Cibao boasts some of the best soil in the Caribbean and is the country's most densely populated area. Cibao people (*Cibaeños*) have a strong regional identity and their customs are highly Hispanic.

Instrumental Spanish-influenced music formerly accompanied largely creole social-dance genres with Spanish-derived stringed instruments: the now extinct treble guitar (*tiple*); the *cuatro*, with four double courses of strings (not to be confused with Puerto Rican and Venezuelan *cuatros*); the *tres*, traditionally triangular or guitar-shaped, now only the latter, with five strings tuned E–C–G, the top and bottom strings are double courses tuned in octaves; and the *guitarra*, the six-stringed Spanish guitar. All these were largely replaced about 1880 by the Hohner button accordion, introduced through trade with Germany, though the *tres*- and guitar-based merengue has been regaining popularity since the 1970s. Brass bands and dance bands (see below) represent another kind of European-derived ensemble; the former play marches, arrangements of art music, and creole dance music, bridging nonliterate and literate musical domains.

African Heritage

The native American population of Hispaniola—at least a million persons—was so rapidly reduced by warfare, disease, and suicide that its replacement by an African workforce began as early as 1502. The first Africans (*ladinos*) were Spanish-speaking Christians from Spain, present there in servitude for a century before 1492. They were soon joined in Hispaniola by *bozales*, direct imports from the African continent, starting with Wolof (*golofes*) from the Senegambian region. Later shipments embarked from increasingly southerly points on the West African coast until they were coming from the Congo-Angolan region. In 1822, the Haitian occupation ended the local slave trade. Before the 1540s, notable contact occurred between Taínos and Africans in their flight from bondage. In contemporary rural society, Afro-Dominican enclaves are important conservators of Taíno material culture.

The black population of the Dominican Republic was enriched in the nineteenth and twentieth centuries by immigration from North America, the Lesser Antilles, and Haiti. These components of the population have contributed to the fabric of contemporary national culture, especially nonliterate musical culture.

Instruments and Ensembles

Self-sounding Instruments (Idiophones)

A metal scraper (güira or guayo 'grater') is a modern version of the gourd (güiro) still played in Puerto Rico. The maraca is a small shaker with a wooden handle, filled with gourd seeds or pebbles and played in pairs or singly in the congos ensemble of Villa Mella, which may represent Taíno-African syncretism. A stick (catá) is beaten on the body of a longdrum in the northeast, including Samaná, where it is called maraca (not to be confused with the shaker of the same name). A pair of wooden idiophones (canoíta 'little canoe') resembles Cuban claves, but one is larger and hollowed out like a little canoe and of softer wood; these are played only with the congos ensemble.

> **Villa Mella** is a municipality located in the newly created Santo Domingo North Province, just north from the city of Santo Domingo. It is an Afro-Dominican enclave, characterized by its Brotherhood of the Holy Spirit and its *congos* drumming. The cultural region of Villa Mella extends beyond its municipal borders.

A recently introduced, definite-pitched, plucked idiophone is the marimba (also marímbula; figure 2), derived from the African mbira, but much larger and with fewer metal tongues. The player sits on its plywood box. It was probably imported in the 1930s with the popular sexteto of the Cuban son, and was adopted by the folk-merengue ensemble.

Drums (Membranophones)

Except in central Cibao, large drums include longdrums (palos, atabalesï), hand-played throughout the country. In all but two enclaves, these are

Figure 2 A man plays a *marimba* as part of a traditional merengue ensemble, 1977.
Photo by Dale A. Olsen.

hollowed-out logs with cowhide heads. All ensembles include responsorial singing by the drummers, plus, if for the saints, rather than the dead, a couple dance (baile de palos) symbolizing ritual pursuit, perhaps derived from the colonial calenda. The master drum (palo mayor), the largest and deepest, is the central drum in an ensemble of three (figure 3); the other drums are generically called alcahuetes ('pimps'). Regional variants of longdrum ensembles occur throughout the country except in the central Cibao Valley.

Smaller drums vary in length from some 25 to 75 centimeters and in diameter from some 23 to 38 centimeters, used as the key instruments in social-dance ensembles; the tambora of the northern folk merengue, the horizontal, heel-damped tacked head (balsié) of the priprí ensemble of the east and central south (the Caribbean juba drum); the vertical balsié (same name, different instrument, with a laced head); and the large, laced frame drum (pandero) of the priprí (same name, different ensemble) of the southwest. The nonliturgical salve ensembles of the central

Figure 3 A long-drum (*palos*) ensemble performs with a pair of maracas (lower right), and metal scraper (*güira*; left), Tierra Blanca, Cabral, Barahona, 2006. The central figure is the master drummer (*palero mayor*).
Photo by Martha Ellen Davis.

south and east use smaller membranophones: the cylindrical *mongó*, played singly with a polyrhythmic ensemble of round frame drums, and *panderos* (with tacked heads, some 23 to 25 centimeters in diameter and 4 centimeters high), similar to the tambourine but with few and irrelevant jingles, representing syncretism between Spanish (Arab heritage) and African instruments.

Descendants of British immigrants in the southeastern coastal city of San Pedro de Macorís have mummers (*momís*, *guloyas*) street-theater ensembles, consisting of a fife, a bass drum, and a triangle.

Stringed Instruments (Chordophones)

A Central African-derived instrument, the earth bow (*gayumba*, called *tambour maringouin* in Haiti, though almost extinct in the island) resembles the American gutbucket, but its resonating chamber is a palm-bark-covered hole in the ground. It plays any kind of music at festive, social occasions.

Wind Instruments (Aerophones)

The conch trumpet (*fotuto*), used for signaling, represents syncretism between a Taíno and an African instrument. Wind instruments used in the Haitian-Dominican ensemble of the *gagá* society (in Haiti: *rará*), which includes *petró* cult drums and an assortment of single-pitched bamboo trumpets (*vaccines* in Haiti, *bambúes* or *fotutos* in the Dominican Republic), whose players beat little sticks on their bamboo tube as they play, plus other metal wind instruments.

Traditional Dominican Music

Rural Music

Today's Dominican culture is best characterized as creole, the product of a process of adaptation and creative evolution that began in the earliest days of the colony. In recent decades, the evolutionary trend within the creole hybrid has been away from the Spanish heritage and toward greater African influence, marked by the gradual loss of acoustic stringed instruments, nontempered scales, antiphonal structures, and traditional vocal genres, including the *romance* and the *mediatuna*. Some genres, notably dance music and the nonliturgical *salve*, are the result of creolization; some contexts, genres, styles, and ensembles are New World continuities of Old World cultures. This musical phenomenon is epitomized in the saint's festival.

The Saint's Festival

In the religious context of the saint's festival, certain musical genres have been slow to change. These genres include the sung rosary, the sacred *salve*, and sacred drumming. This festival is thus a living museum of the most archaic practices of Spanish and African origin. It shows that "traditional" musical culture and its performers may be bimusical—a common Caribbean phenomenon.

Musical activities in the saint's festival have specific spatial and temporal placement, and they often have gender associations. The rosary and the *salves* are performed at the altar, the sacred European site (erected for the festival against one wall of the folk chapel, or of the sponsor's living room) and the domain of women's responsibility and authority. Men may participate, but the *salve* is essentially a women's genre in most of the country. Drumming (*palos*), a male activity, and the drum dance are situated in the center of the room around a center post (the sacred African site), temporally interrupted with *salves* (in the southwest), or outside in a covered patio, with the drums being hauled toward the altar for three sacred pieces after each rosary (in the east). If the festival of the east is a nightlong stop along a pilgrimage route, a separate room with a freestanding table is prepared for sung conversation (*tonadas de toros* 'bull songs') among members of a pilgrimage-associated brotherhood, who take donated alms and bull calves to Higüey, Bayaguana, and three other pilgrimage sites. If, as seldom happens, the sponsor of the saint's festival is a *vodú* medium, spirit possession by deities occurs, and while *palos* or *salves* are being played in public, spiritual consultations may take place there or in an adjacent private room.

Depending on the region of the country, social-dance music may be interspersed with drumming, played in a separate site on the festival grounds or played in the morning after the fulfillment of a vow. Rural social-dance genres practiced through the mid-twentieth century included variants of the Spanish *zapateado* called *zapateo* or derivatives of the English country dance: the *tumba dominicana*, displaced about 1850 by the merengue, the *carabiné* of the south; and the Haitian-derived *bambulá* in Samaná. In contemporary rural society, social dance includes the merengue from Cibao, the *perico ripiao*; the *merengue redondo* of the east (called *priprí* in the central-south); and in the south, the triptych of *carabiné*, *mangulina*, and *valse* (figure 4). The *carabiné* is a couple dance in duple meter, circular in formation, and with a caller who calls out the movements and changes of couples. The *mangulina*, a couple dance in 6/8, is traditionally danced unembraced and represents ritual pursuit; it is similar to other dances in the region, such as the *joropo* [see VENEZUELA]. The *valse* is a couple dance with music similar to the *mangulina*. The same genres may be danced outside the sacred site and on the occasion of the saint's festival. Secular venues of rural social dancing are bars and brothels. The nickname of the northern merengue, *perico ripiao*, is said to have been the name of a brothel in the 1930s in the province of Santiago.

The *Salve*

The *salve* has evolved into two coexisting subgenres: the Hispanic, sacred, liturgical Virgin's *salve* (*salve de la Virgen*) and a less sacred *salve* with added text (*salve con versos*). The latter (figure 5) exhibits an appended text and a different, African-influenced musical style: metered and rhythmic, instrumentally

Figure 4 Belí y Sus Muchachos, a southwestern *priprí* social-dance ensemble performs, Tierra Blanca, Cabral, Barahona, 2006. The group consists of a large hand-drum (*pandero*), a vertical drum (*balsié*), an accordion, and a metal scraper (*güira*) and plays the rhythmic triptych of *carabiné*, *mangulina*, and *valse*, as well as the *merengue*. Directed by accordionist Belisario 'Belí' Féliz, the ensemble may be the only active one remaining in the country.
Photo by Martha Ellen Davis.

Figure 5 Non-liturgical *salves* sung with *panderos* (hand drum), Santa María, San Cristóbal, 2006. *Photo by Martha Ellen Davis.*

accompanied, and responsorial, with a relaxed, mid-register vocal production. Its *versos* entail a secular response inserted between sacred phrases plus added quatrains at the end. It is accompanied by clapping and/or one small, vertical *mangó* (a drum typically played by a man), several small handheld drums (*panderos*, typically played by women), and a *güira* (played by a man). It reaches its most Africanized extreme in the *salve de pandero* of the central-south area, especially around Villa Mella and San Cristóbal, with the addition of many small drums played polyrhythmically and the elimination of a sacred text. Within the *salve de pandero*, the variant of the Province of Peravia (Baní) illustrates the coexistence of traditions of two origins within the musical subgenre, with the usual gender associations. Women sing the former positioned in a line in front of the altar, while men, in circular formation at the back of the chapel, accompany them with small drums.

Social Dance: The Merengue Típico or Perico Ripiao

Social-dance music, represented today by the folk merengue (*merengue típico* or *perico ripiao*) as a musical symbol of national identity, epitomizes the creolism of Dominican culture. The melodic instrument, formerly strings of the guitar family and since the late nineteenth century, a Hohner accordion, is European; the *tambora* has West African influence; the metal *güira* or *guayo* may represent Taíno-African syncretism; and the *marimba* is a Cuban-evolved version of the African *mbira*. The music is based on the quatrain, rendered partially in African responsorial form to African-influenced rhythms in accompaniment of a European-style couple dance with African influence in dance style, such as hip movement. This is the music-and-dance genre that dictator Rafael Trujillo (1891–1961) promoted as the national dance in ballroom adaptations. Though affirming *hispanidad*, he redefined national culture as creole culture, represented by his chosen musical symbol of national identity.

Urban Music

Since the rise of cities and of literacy, a dialectical relationship of musical exchange has bridged urban and rural traditions, as it does literate and nonliterate ones. Cities and towns have literate and nonliterate musical genres, the latter shared among virtually all social classes.

Dominican cities vary in their treatment of literate music. The larger cities and regional capitals have a sizeable educated elite and institutions that support fine-arts education and practice. The most musically active and prolific cities in the country are Santiago and Puerto Plata, and secondarily the capital (Santo Domingo), San Pedro de Macorís, and San Francisco de Macorís. Smaller and newer towns, especially around sugarcane mills, are largely conglomerations of peasants-turned-proletarians. Since 1961, large numbers of peasants have left the countryside, so the rural-urban dichotomy is now also found in the cities.

Figure 6 The *son*, an elegant urban social dance of Cuban influence, is danced by a couple, Santo Domingo, 2006. The *son* is practiced with recorded music or a live ensemble, typically the *sexteto*, which features voice, *claves*, bongos, muted trumpet, *tres*, and guitar.
Photo by Martha Ellen Davis.

Urban Social Dance

Social dances, concert bands, and dance bands are major vehicles of musical exchange among localities, social classes, and traditions. Since 1844 at the latest, dance-band musicians have served as conduits for introducing rural genres of dancing into the halls of the urban elite, and conversely, for transmission of urban fashions in social dancing, often of foreign origin, to rural areas.

The orchestrated merengue continues to evolve. Since the 1920s, band instruments have been added to the traditional ensemble, starting with the alto saxophone, the most characteristic instrument of the ballroom merengue band after the *tambora*. During Trujillo's time, the orchestrated merengue was adapted for the ballroom. An initial "stroll" (*paseo*) was added to situate partners on the dance floor. After Trujillo's fall, arrangers added other band instruments to the merengue and made stylistic changes in it, including a marked acceleration. The contemporary merengue bandleader Johnny Ventura (b. 1940) is credited with compositions and recordings intended for a broader, international audience. The modern orchestrated merengue is enjoying popularity throughout the Spanish-speaking world as one of the trendiest Latino dance

rhythms, but within Dominican musical culture, the ballroom merengue coexists with its unchanging progenitor, the folkloric *perico ripiao*. The vitality of the merengue bespeaks its role as a symbol of national identity. The folk merengue represents a rural, traditional identity, and the orchestrated merengue represents an urban, modern one.

The *son* (figure 6) is practiced in traditional lower-class Afro-Dominican sectors in the capital such as Villa Consuelo and the neighborhood of Borojol, and around the capital, most notably in Villa Mella, Manoguayabo, and Haina, and in the city of San Pedro de Macorís; it was and is practiced in Santiago, La Vega, and Puerto Plata, with live and recorded music.

Urban Song

Merengues were composed for dance bands by composers seeking inspiration in rural, nonliterate genres for the creation of songs and dances of the literate tradition with piano or band accompaniment directed toward urban audiences. Leading composer-conductors of this century included Julio Alberto Hernández (1900–1999) and Rafael Alberti (1906–1976). Several songs, including "*Quisqueya*" and danceable merengues such as Alberti's "*Compadre Pedro Juan*," have passed from literate to oral urban traditions, and are taken as collective musical symbols of national identity.

Another kind of urban music is the sentimental song of *trovadores*, crooners of serenades and parties, who strum acoustic guitars and sing amorous courtship songs in settings where alcohol is consumed. Their songs are transmitted largely orally, and more recently through recordings and broadcasts. Their medium and function, and certain of their genres (especially the bolero and the *valse*), are shared with their counterparts in other Latin American cities and towns. Other genres are Hispanic Caribbean (such as the Cuban-influenced *son*) or specifically Dominican (such as the *criollo*, a lyrical song in 6/8 time, also known in Cuba). The *son* tradition is maintained in Afro-Dominican sectors in the capital by the old Soneros de Borojols and ensembles of younger musicians in Villa Mella.

—*Adapted from an article by Martha Ellen Davis*

Bibliography

Austerlitz, Paul. 1997. *Merengue: Dominican Music and Dominican Identity*. Philadelphia: Temple University Press.

Coopersmith, J. M. [1949] 1976. *Music and Musicians of the Dominican Republic / Música y músicos de la República Dominicana*. Pan American Union, Music Series, 15.

Spanish translation republished by the Dirección General de Cultura, Secretaría de Estado de Educación, Bellas Artes y Cultos.

Davis, Martha Ellen. 1981. *Voces del Purgatoria: Estudio de la Salve dominicana.* Santo Domingo: Museo del Hombre Dominicano.

——. 1994. "Music and Black Ethnicity in the Dominican Republic." In *Music and Black Ethnicity: The Caribbean and South America,* edited by Gerard H. Béhague, 119–155. New Brunswick, N.J.: Transaction.

——. 2007. "Oral Musical Traditions of the Dominican Republic," and "Country Profile, Dominican Republic." In *Music in Latin America and the Caribbean: An Encyclopedic History, Vol. 2.: Performing the Caribbean Experience,* edited by Malena Kuss. Austin: University of Texas Press.

Fernández de Oviedo y Valdés, Gonzalo. [1526] 1986. *Sumario de la natural historia de las Indias.* Edited by Manuel Ballesteros. Madrid: Historia 16.

Garrido de Boggs, Edna. [1955] 2004. *Folklore infantil de Santo Domingo.* Santo Domingo: Sociedad Dominicana de Bibliófilos, 3rd ed. Musical transcriptions by Ruth Crawford Seeger.

Las Casas, Bartolomé de. 1958. *Apologética historia sumaria.* Madrid: Biblioteca de Autores Españoles.

Marks, Morton, and Isidro Bobadilla, ed. 1983. *Afro-Dominican Music from San Cristóbal, Dominican Republic.* N.Y.: Folkways Records.

Pacini Hernández, Deborah. 1995. *Bachata: A Social History of a Dominican Popular Music.* Philadelphia: Temple University Press.

Tejeda, Darío and Rafael Emilio Yunén, eds. 2006. *El merengue en la cultura domenicana y del Caribe.* Santo Domingo: Centro León, Instituto de Estudios Caribeños and Secretaría de Estado de Cultura.

Jamaican Traditional Music

In 1494, when Christopher Columbus made his second voyage to the New World, he found Jamaica inhabited by Arawak Indians. These people did not long survive Spanish colonization. Research has provided us with artifacts and knowledge of their era, but it has not unearthed evidence of their musical culture. As Arawaks dwindled in numbers (mainly from overwork and introduced diseases, to which they had little or no resistance), the Spanish began importing slaves from Africa. By the mid-1600s, the Arawaks had been virtually eliminated.

In 1655, a British expedition took Jamaica from the Spanish. Before fleeing the island, the Spanish released their slaves, many of whom went to the mountains and became known as Maroons. During the ensuing years, British settlers established sugar-cane plantations with the continued use of African slave labor. Some laborers were already in the system; others were newly imported; all were encouraged to produce children, who automatically inherited their parents' status as slaves.

The Emancipation Act of 1 August 1834 freed slave children born after that date and those under the age of six. Other slaves became apprentices for varying lengths of time. All were completely free by 1 August 1838. Not all freed Africans—by this time considered Jamaicans—chose to work on plantations. Slaves were replaced by indentured laborers, brought first from Central Africa, and then India, China, and Britain. Early on, Jamaica's African population far outnumbered its European colonizers; today, its nonwhite population remains the majority.

Circumstances in Jamaica dictated the development or the continuation of oral traditions in the arts and culture; many laborers on plantations could not communicate in their masters' languages. However, most Africans had come from societies in which oral tradition accounted for most learning. Many of the musical traditions passed along in this manner remain relevant today.

Principal Musical Traditions

Sacred Forms
Religious beliefs permeate all levels of Jamaican society. All its ethnic groups participate in religious

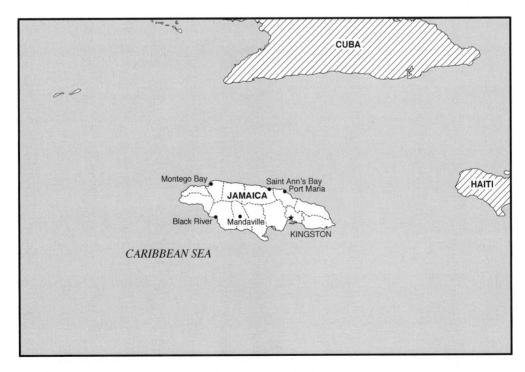

Jamaica

observances, whether adopted (as in the case of Christianity, which embraces people of European, African, and Asian origins), adapted (as with creolized forms), or traditional (as with Hindu, Jewish, or Muslim observances).

Christian

The music of Christian ecclesiastical traditions is prominent in Jamaica. Serving the Christian community are Anglican, Roman Catholic, Baptist, Moravian, Presbyterian, Methodist, and Seventh-Day Adventist denominations and their offshoots, plus American-influenced evangelical and Pentecostal churches. Music of the Protestant churches consists of Western traditional hymns and nineteenth-century gospel songs, composed by American hymn writers P. P. Bliss, Ira Sankey, and others. Organs and pianos are used in most churches that have a formal choir, and occasionally they are used in special instrumental pieces. Recitals of sacred music, especially around Easter and Christmas, are normal features of church calendars and often spill over into community activities. A growing trend in the evangelical and Pentecostal churches is the use of bands—drums, guitars, synthesizer or piano, and tambourines—to accompany exuberant singing in American popular gospel styles.

Christianity is the main religious influence, but Jamaican religions use concepts and practices inherited from African ancestors, sometimes mixing them with Christian beliefs. Judaism, Hinduism, and Islam are practiced by small numbers of Jamaicans. Music and movement are features of most religious services. Even in some churches from the European side of Jamaica's heritage (Roman Catholic and low-church Anglican), religious choruses and hymns are accompanied by bodily movements and clapping. Widespread sects are Revival, Maroon, Kumina, and Rastafari; far less common (and not addressed here) are Ettu, Nago, and Tambu. In many of these sects, drums are a significant instrument of musical expression, and they vary from sect to sect in their construction and style of drumming.

Revival Christianity

Revival is a blanket term that covers several Afro-Christian religions, including Revival Zion (or Zion Revival), Pocomania (usually pronounced "*pokominya*"), and other denominations, such as Zion Way Baptist. Each of these groups blends Christian and West African concepts and stresses the unity of the temporal and spiritual worlds. Revival Christian expression—which varies from church to church—can include singing, dancing, instrumental and percussive accompaniment, healing, divination,

and, sometimes, spirit possession. Revival activities may include street meetings to win converts, baptismal baths and fasting for purification, feasts for thanksgiving tables, mourning or memorial rites, and invocations of the spirit world for help.

Revival Christian music that sets the scene for and induces spiritual trance and possession is usually performed with melodic, harmonic, and rhythmic improvisations. Many of its songs are adaptations of Western-style hymns, but there is also chanting and responsorial singing. The music utilizes syncopation against contrasting rhythmic patterns provided mainly by a pair of drums (the larger known as "bass" and the smaller, played with sticks, as "side drum") and maracas, and by rhythmic body sounds such as clapping, stamping, moaning, and loud rhythmic breathing called "groaning" or "trumping." Many Revival Christian songs are based on gospel songs in old "Moody and Sankey" hymnals. Although less widespread than it once was, Revivalism continues to be central to the lives of thousands of Jamaicans.

Maroon

Jamaica has four communities of Maroons: one leeward (Accompong, located on the western side of the island) and three windward (Moore Town, Charles Town, and Scot's Hall, on the eastern side). Members of these communities are descendants of runaway slaves of various African "tribes" or "nations" (referenced today by terms such as *Kromanti*, *Papa*, *Ibo*, *Mandinga*, *Dokose*, and *Mongola*), who resisted enslavement and fought the British in a series of conflicts that resulted in two 1739 treaties guaranteeing their sovereignty; the accords remain in effect.

Maroons participate in a wide assortment of musical traditions found throughout Jamaica, but their cultural identity is largely based on a ritual complex called Kromanti Play or Kromanti Dance. (This name is taken from a historical Gold Coast slave port of the same name.) In Kromanti Play, participants turn for guidance to ancestral spirits, with whom they communicate largely through spirit possession (*myal*). Kromanti ceremonies are typically closed to outsiders, and are believed to be beyond the understanding of those who are not full-blooded Maroon. Among the Maroon territories, the Kromanti Play tradition in Moore Town is the most elaborate.

In Kromanti Play, several kinds of songs are performed. Some, like "Jawbone," "Sa-Leone," and "Tambu," are considered less spiritually powerful and sung in patois. These songs generally accompany recreational dancing. Others, including "Mandinga," "Papa," and "Kromanti" (or "Country") call to

Figure 1 Windward Maroon musicians and singers, Scot's Hall, St. Mary Parish, 1993. In the foreground, from left, are the *grandi* (supporting drum), the *gumbe* (lead drum), and the *kwat* (bamboo percussion instrument).
Photo by Kenneth Bilby.

mind archaic tribal distinctions, and are said to have great power. Used to accompany ritual specialists known as dancer-men or fete-men, they are an important part of invoking ancestral spirits.

In Kromanti Play, ensembles typically consist of a gendered (male–female) pair of long cylindrical drums (both called *printing*), a length of bamboo (*kwat*), beaten with two sticks, and a machete, struck with a piece of metal (*iron* or *adawo*). Often, a stick called *abaso* is used to play special rhythmic patterns on the head of one of the drums. The drummers in these ensembles are known as *okrema* 'printing-men'.

Another drum Maroons use is the *gumbe*, a square frame drum, said to have important spiritual power. Associated especially with Accompong, it is considered a symbol of the leeward Maroons; but it forms an essential part of the drum ensembles of the windward Maroon communities of Scot's Hall (figure 1) and Charles Town.

The instrument with greatest symbolic importance to all Maroons (and to many non-Maroons) is the *abeng*, a cow's horn, which came to the fore in the Maroon liberation struggles of the 1700s. Capable of passing on messages through a secret "*abeng* language," it has long been a part of strategic Maroon communication.

Kumina

Kumina is a religion and ceremonial tradition based on beliefs and lifestyles brought to Jamaica by indentured laborers from the Congo–Angola region of Central Africa between roughly 1840 and 1865. In Jamaica, Kumina is concentrated in the eastern parishes of St. Thomas and Portland, but is sometimes found elsewhere. Music and dance in Kumina

ceremonies honor, appease, and evoke the help of ancestral and other spirits for healing, thanksgiving, memorials for the dead, entombment, and celebrations such as weddings, births, and anniversaries.

Kumina ceremonies use two drums: the *kbandu* (or, more commonly, *bandu*) and *playing kyas*. Both drums are set on the ground, and drummers play facing each other at a distance of about one meter. Players straddle and sit down on the drums, which they beat using their palms and fingers; a drummer often uses his heel to change the drum's pitch. Usually, the beating of two sticks (*kata*) on the side or back of the *kbandu* helps build rhythmic excitement. The *kbandu*, the larger and lower-pitched of the drums, establishes the meter, while the smaller *kyas* plays complex lead patterns. In Kumina ceremonies, their combined rhythms control singers and dancers, invoke spirits, and sometimes induce spirit possession (*myal*).

There are two Kumina song categories: *country* songs, are sung in a ritual language combining features of several ancestral African languages (such as Kikongo and Kimbundu), typically heard in the more sacred sections of the rituals when communication with the spirits is sought; and *bailo* songs, sung in Jamaican Creole and usually heard before the onset of spirit possession or after it subsides, or at recreational events.

Rastafari

Rastafari is a millenarian religion and social movement rooted in the belief that Haile Selassie I (1892–1975), held to be a direct descendent of King Solomon, is a living god and the second coming of Jesus Christ. The political philosophy of Rasta is rooted in that of Marcus Garvey (1887–1940), who

Figure 2 Rastafarian drum-maker and musician Eric MacDonald (also known as Bro-Joe or Bongo Joe) in his workshop, with *nyabinghi* drums (a bass drum is on the left and funde and repeater drums are on the right), St. Andrew Parish, 2005. *Photo by Kenneth Bilby.*

preached pan-African unity and urged black people to look to Africa as their motherland. Selassie's coronation as emperor of Ethiopia (in 1930), making him the only African leader of an independent nation, motivated Rastas' subsequent development—a circumstance that Garvey, considered by Rastas a prophet, is said to have foreseen.

Interpreted in different ways, Rasta doctrine is based primarily on biblical verses, particularly the Old Testament's Book of Psalms and the New Testament's Revelation. Of particular importance is Psalm 137, which describes Rastas' commitment to Zion as an ancestral home (literally Ethiopia), and opposition to Babylon as the idea of all oppressive and corrupt world systems.

Dreadlocks, worn by many Rastas since the 1940s, have been seen as a way of preserving African roots by rejecting Western values and embracing black pride. Originally the fulfillment of a spiritual vow based on biblical verses, the wearing of dreadlocks today does not necessarily signify an adherence to Rasta belief. Many Rastas ritually smoke *ganja* (*Cannabis sativa*), which they regard as a vehicle for spirituality.

The music most closely associated with Rasta is *nyabinghi*, a neotraditional style of drumming generally credited to Count Ossie (née Oswald Williams, 1926–1976). *Nyabinghi* is a drum-based style, which consists of three drums borrowed from the Buru tradition (see below): the repeater, the funde, and the bass (figure 2). The funde plays a steady rhythm, often likened to a heartbeat, around which the lead drum, the repeater, improvises. The songs accompanying this music are often chanted adaptations of psalms, hymns, and local traditional songs, but original songs are sometimes sung. *Nyabinghi* music is most often performed at formal Rasta gatherings of the same name, and at less formal meetings held throughout the year.

In Jamaica, Rasta music and belief have had a substantial effect on the development of reggae (see text box p. 287). Through the music of reggae artists—most notably Bob Marley—they have had significant international influence.

Secular Forms

Secular musical forms in Jamaica are generally performed in social, ceremonial, and presentational contexts. Most often, secular music is meant to accompany dancing, but it accompanies music that encourages community participation. In special cases, it features cultural traditions that are otherwise considered sacred.

Mento

Mento is a rhythm, social dance and songform that many call "Jamaica's original music." A creolized genre, it emerged toward the end of the nineteenth century out of Jamaica's poorer classes, for whom New-World African traditions, European dance genres, and musical exchange via interregional migration were all influences. It is often associated with rural entertainment and recreation, and it became an important part of tourism in the 1940s, where it has since been marketed as calypso.

Virtually every mento band has at least one singer, but many have instrumentalists who sing (figure 3).

Figure 3 Freedom Mento Band, St. Catherine Parish, 2002. The musicians play, from left, banjo, bamboo flute, maracas, and drum and cymbal.
Photo by Kenneth Bilby.

Most mento bands consist of one or more guitars, a tenor banjo, maracas, and a large bass lamellophone, similar to the Cuban *marímbula*, and the Haitian *malinba*, called a rhumba box. To that, many bands add a violin, a clarinet, a saxophone or a bamboo flute or fife to play melodies. Other instruments—including a harmonica, an accordion, and a string bass instead of a rumba box—are less often used. Homemade instruments are common, and may include long bamboo trumpets called blow basses, plastic soda-bottle trumpets, or handmade drumkits; although once widespread, hand-built bamboo saxophones are now extremely rare. With amplification being a more important part of rural fêtes, many contemporary mento bands add an electronic keyboard and electric guitars and basses to round out their sound.

Almost always in major keys, mentos are made up of simple melodies that lend themselves to easy harmonization and sometimes complex improvisation. They are in quadruple time, with a composite of several interlocking parts. One instrument often plays a phrase accenting the second and fourth beats of a measure, while another simultaneously accents two three-count beats and then a short two-count beat (3+3+2).

Mento bands often have a large repertory of traditional, popular, and religious songs to maximize their opportunity to perform: they typically play for private and public parties, tourists in hotels or on beaches, state-sponsored festivals, all-night funerary events called nine nights and setups, or at rum shops, where musicians convene to play spontaneously.

Quadrille

As elsewhere in the Caribbean, Jamaica developed local variants of many European ballroom dances. Several such dances were common in the nineteenth and early twentieth centuries among all strata of Jamaican society. The most popular was the quadrille, a dance suite consisting of several figures, each associated with a distinctive step.

Jamaicans take two basic approaches to quadrille dancing. In the more formal, ballroom style, dancers are arranged in squares; the choreography is reserved, and the movements are restrained. The ballroom style is considered more refined, and dancers generally wear formal attire. In the camp style (sometimes said to be the creolized version), dancers are arranged in a variety of formations. The choreography is far less restrained: it emphasizes hip movements, and its general movements are freer. In staged performances, dancers wear traditional peasant costumes.

Quadrilles usually consist of no fewer than five figures, the content of which can be drawn from ballroom forms (including mazurkas, waltzes, polkas, and schottisches), but the fifth figure (and sometimes others) is often to a mento beat.

Historically, mento bands provided the music for quadrille dances. Today, fewer dancers learn how to dance quadrille, and as a consequence fewer mento

Figure 4 A fife and drum ensemble of the kind typically used to back Jonkonnu masquerade processions, St. Elizabeth Parish, 2004. *Photo by Kenneth Bilby.*

Figure 5 Buru drummers, St. Catherine parish, 2002. The musicians play, from left, funde, bass drum, and repeater. *Photo by Kenneth Bilby.*

musicians are learning how to play it. Although increasingly scarce, it is most often danced in (or in preparation for) Jamaica's annual National Festival for the Arts, held in August each year since 1962 to commemorate Jamaica's independence from Great Britain.

Jonkonnu

Jonkonnu—in many sources called John Canoe or junkanoo—is a neo-African Christmastime street festival, in which costumed revelers dance to music provided by bands of community musicians (figure 4). [To see how this festival is celebrated in another country, see THE BAHAMAS.] Originally practiced during the holiday that slaveholders gave their slaves around Christmas, it has been an element of slave culture since the eighteenth century. Though still found in local communities, it can be seen in staged performances and at national competitions, where it is presented as a symbol of Jamaican cultural identity.

MODERN JAMAICAN MUSIC

In addition to "social bands," which performed mento and calypso, the popularity of American swing led to Jamaican big bands. Sound-system operators, playing in the 1950s for "blues dances," specialized in imported rhythm-and-blues dance tunes on 45-rpm records—a style of music also heard on Radio Jamaica and Rediffusion and on WINZ in Miami. These operators, including Clement "Coxsone" Dodd (1932–2004), Prince Buster (b. 1938), and Duke Reid (ca. 1915–1974), competed on the strength of their systems and on the size and currency of their collections. Successors to earlier entrepreneurs, such as Stanley Motta and Ivan Chin, they formed the backbone of Jamaica's modern recording industry.

Locally, rhythm and blues developed an exaggerated backbeat and a quick tempo. This offshoot, ska, emerged around the time of independence (1962); the classic studio-ska band, the Skatalites, was born in 1963. In the latter half of the 1960s, vocal ska recordings lionized ghetto street culture, known as rudeness. Popular music became slower, and the bass and the drums rose to prominence. The newer sound, rock steady, was the immediate precursor of reggae. The influence of Rasta on the poorer classes, especially among musicians, showed clearly, not only in aural texture, but also in a preoccupation with biblical imagery and millenarian prophecy. Even non-Rastafarian performers widely copied Rastafarian beliefs, lifestyles, and patterns of speaking.

In the early 1970s, *Catch a Fire* and *Burning*, releases by Bob Marley and the Wailers, exported reggae to the world. Marley's synthesis of revolutionary ideology and Rasta spirituality appealed to disenfranchised people, especially those in the English-speaking Caribbean. Among Caribbean youths from Trinidad to the Virgin Islands, reggae promoted "dread talk," the colloquial Rastafarian version of Jamaican patois. Jamaicans living in London exposed English youths to ska and reggae, and in London pubs they developed a parallel ska-reggae scene, which appealed strongly to British punks and inspire Two-Tone, an antiracist movement and music, which united black and white musicians and fans.

Reggae's success in the United States and the United Kingdom—including reggae-style hits for Eric Clapton, The Clash, Debby Harry, and many others—inaugurated a new category of music for radio formats, record-store bins, and *Billboard* charts.

Today's Jamaican popular music is called dancehall (or, ragga, especially outside Jamaica). Growing out of the deejay practice of improvising lyrics over musical *riddims* (reusable rhythm tracks, usually consisting of a bass melody and a drum pattern), dancehall became an alternative to reggae for young Jamaicans in the early 1980s. Dancehall lyrics often address the problems many poor Jamaicans face and are often sexually explicit (or *slack*). One of the first hit records associated with this style was Wayne Smith's 1985 track "Under Mi Sleng Teng," which used a *riddim* created by producer King Jammy made completely from synthesized instruments. Contemporary dancehall artists include Shabba Ranks (b. 1966), Ninjaman (b. 1966), Beenie Man (b. 1973), Bounty Killer (1972), Lady Saw, Elephant Man (b. 1975), and Sean Paul (1973). In the 1990s and after, a new crop of artists (some of them active earlier) reintroduced socially conscious Rastafarian lyrics and concerns into dancehall music and achieved major success with this new "conscious" style; among these are Anthony B (b. 1976), Buju Banton (b. 1973), Capleton (b. 1967), Sizzla, Fantan Mojah, Warrior King, and I-Wayne.

Jamaican artists on the island and abroad have made substantial contributions to the technology of popular music worldwide through their efforts to develop dub tracks and versions, with some original tracks deleted and new tracks and sounds superimposed, and their extensive use of sampling. Jamaican styles of chanted poetry to musical accompaniment—which include toasting, dub poetry, dancehall, and, in Britain, ragga—have influenced North American rap and hip-hop vocals, and have found a substantial niche in world markets.

Members of jonkonnu bands are usually men, masquerading as male and female characters, each of which is associated with a particular dance. Bands typically include one or more of the following stock characters: King, Queen, Horsehead, Cowhead, Pitchy-Patchy, Devil, Actor Boy, Belly Woman, and Wild Indian. The music is most often instrumental. It consists of short and highly ornamented repetitive melodic lines, played on a fife (made of bamboo or plastic), accompanied by one or more snarelike side drums and a bass drum. Sometimes other instruments, including tambourines, conch shells (*conks*), cow horns, and graters, augment a band's sound.

Jonkonnu is generally considered a secular activity, but a few older versions of it maintain a spiritual dimension. In some parts of Jamaica, it is an aspect of an African-based religion called Gumbe Play. At Christmastime, trained builders (*myal men*) construct a house-shaped headdress called a *jangkunu* for a Gumbe Play healing ceremony. On Christmas day, it is paraded around the community, but once the seasonal spirit begins to fade (a matter of weeks), it is destroyed in another Gumbe Play ceremony. In this tradition, accompanying music includes songs with words. The square-framed gumbe drum plays a prominent role.

In other parts of Jamaica, a religious observance called Buru includes a masquerade festival that in some ways resembles the jonkonnu tradition. Buru—in secularized versions sometimes blended with a "Horsehead" character—includes music and dance as part of offerings to community ancestors. It is musically distinct from jonkonnu, however, in that it has its own repertory of often-ribald songs, and is accompanied by a set of three drums: the bass, the funde, and the repeater (figure 5), which were incorporated into the neotraditional style of Rastafarian *nyabinghi* drumming.

*—Written by Daniel Neely, Olive Lewin,
and Gage Averill*

Bibliography

Baxter, Ivy. 1970. *The Arts of an Island: The Development of the Culture and of the Folk and Creative Arts in Jamaica, 1492–1962*. Metuchen, N.J.: Scarecrow Press.

Bilby, Kenneth. [1995] 2006. "Reggae." In *Caribbean Currents: Caribbean Music From Rumba to Reggae*, edited by Peter Manuel, 177–215. Philadelphia: Temple University Press.

Bilby, Kenneth, comp. 1992. *Drums of Defiance: Maroon Music From the Earliest Free Black Communities of Jamaica*. CD (Smithsonian Folkways 40412)

——. 1999. "Gumbay, Myal, and the Great House: New Evidence on the Religious Background of Jonkonnu in Jamaica." *ACIJ Research Review* 4:47–70.

Katz, David. 2003. *Solid Foundation: An Oral History of Reggae*. New York: Bloomsbury

Lewin, Olive. 2000. *Rock It Come Over: The Folk Music of Jamaica*. Jamaica: University of West Indies Press.

Neely, Daniel T. 2001. "Long Time Gal! Mento is Back!" *The Beat* 20(6):40–42.

Stolzoff, Norman. 2000. *Wake the Town and Tell the People: Dancehall Culture in Jamaica*. Durham: Duke University Press.

Veal, Michael. 2007. *Dub: Soundscapes and Shattered Songs in Jamaican Reggae*. Middletown, Conn.: Weselyan University Press.

Waters, Anita M. 1989. *Race, Class, and Political Symbols: Rastafari and Reggae in Jamaican Politics*. New Brunswick: Transaction Publishers.

White, Timothy. 1989. *Catch a Fire: The Life of Bob Marley*. New York: Henry Holt

Martinique

Martinique, an island of the Lesser Antilles, supports a society formed by immigrants from the Caribbean, France, South Asia, and West Africa. Its population is about 400,000, consisting largely of descendants of West African slaves.

Martinique was a French colony since the 1600s, but in 1946 it became an overseas department of France. Its official language is French, but Martinicans use Creole (Kwéyòl) in everyday communication. This kind of bilingualism, in which a vernacular tongue remains in use without an official status, has encouraged the persistence of a parallel culture based on oral tradition. For Martinicans, the public use of Creole serves as a symbol of identification, a sign of contrast with the culture of metropolitan France.

Racial and cultural mixing has transformed Martinicans' daily life by creating multiple frames of reference for local identity. French, African, Asian, or creole elements may be present during a musical event, depending on where and when it occurs. The island's traditional and popular music contributes to a sense of local identity; for many Martinicans, it evokes the comforts of belonging. Like other Creole-speaking areas, Martinique reveals an interculturalism, and its musical practices are drawn from multiple sources, old and new.

Music and Creole Identity

Borrowing and reinterpreting different musical cultures, an integral part of the creative process, is a characteristic of creole cultures; thus was the term *creolization* born. Transforming original elements and substituting others, changing their function, attempting to retain ancestral customs, borrowing some expressions while denouncing others, reinterpreting and recreating certain musical genres—all these processes serve as reminders of how deeply Martinique is anchored in a creole identity.

Beguine, a Referential Genre

To identify an authentically Martinican musical genre, local discourse singles out the beguine (*biguine, bidjin*) because it comes down from early times and is performed frequently. Its music and dance are distinguished by a binary rhythmic pattern (figure 1a). *Mazouk*, another genre associated with

Figure 1 Referential Martinican rhythmic pattern: *a*, duple, as in the beguine; *b*, triple, as in the *mazouk*. *Transcription Monique Desroches.*

popular music in Martinique, is based on a rhythm similar to this, but in triple time (figure 1b).

Contemporary musical instrumentation favors two main kinds of Martinican beguine: drum beguine (*bidjin bélè*) and orchestral beguine. Each of these terms refers to contexts of a specific origin. The drum beguine comes from *bélè*, dances performed since early colonial times by the slaves who lived on the great sugar plantations. Musically, it can be distinguished from the orchestral beguine in four ways: its cylindrical single-headed drum (*bélè*) and rhythm sticks (*tibwa*), responsorial singing, soloistic improvisation, and a nasal vocal quality. The beguine figured in fertility rituals practiced in West Africa, the motherland of most Martinican slaves, but its ritual significance has disappeared in Martinique. The beguine could be regarded as a continuation of a value system that is in essence African, but with sugar plantations as its social platform. The late singers Ti-Émile, Ti-Raoul, and Eugène Mona remain symbols of the drum *bidjin*.

The orchestral beguine has taken a different route. Its ancestry goes back to Saint Pierre, an urban center that since the 1800s has harbored notable numbers of residents of French descent. It keeps the syncopations of the drum *bidjin*, but takes on an almost Dixieland flavor from its instrumentation (figure 2). Its melodies, sung in Creole, have a verse-refrain form, bespeaking an unmistakably French influence. The famous "*Mwen désenn Sin Piè*" and many other melodies popularized by Léona Gabriel (1891–1971), the Pierre Rassin Orchestra, Loulou Boislaville (1919–2001), and others, are orchestral beguines.

Kadans, *the Birth of a Creole Identity*

For most of the twentieth century, the musical ambience with which Martinicans identified was

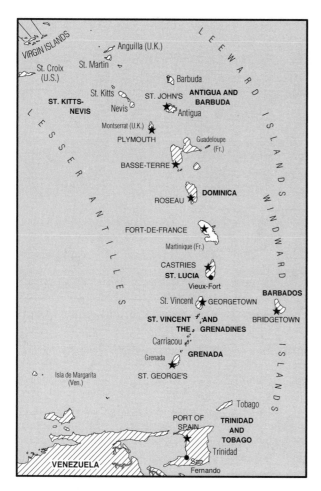

Martinique

Figure 3 Kadans rhythm.
Transcription Monique Desroches.

essentially defined by the two types of beguine, with the *mazouk* and the creole waltz, and only in the 1970s did this soundscape undergo substantial changes. The causes for the transformation were many, but one is supreme: the immigration to Martinique of Haitians fleeing their country for political reasons.

To the urban centers of the French West Indies, the Haitians brought the *kadans* 'cadence', a musical genre already familiar to Martinicans via radio. *Kadans* subtly uses musical accents, syncopation, and instrumental color, all derived from the small jazz orchestras of Haiti, which feature brass, lead and bass guitar, bell, and drums. One of its main features is a rhythm carried by the bell (figure 3).

The vocal technique of *kadans* contributes to its flavor by the use of onomatopoeia and long, drawn-out tones reminiscent of *bel canto* singing.

The arrival of this music upset the relationship that Martinicans had maintained with their music, their ties to island history, and their traditional music; however, it highlighted a sociocultural commonality between the cultures, with their shared history of slavery and a common language. So it was that the island's cultural landmarks were no longer based mostly on Martinican history and society, but became something vaster, embracing a larger part of the Caribbean.

Most music that had previously been produced in Martinique had come from groups formed on the spot at events of an equally spontaneous nature, but *kadans* set a new dynamic into motion, with new players, production values, and socioeconomic settings. Here were groups whose status approached the professional, among whom the majority had already recorded commercially and whose success had been transmitted by the media throughout the Creole-speaking Caribbean, setting a standard that local musicians aspired to meet.

Kadans swept the country, and most Martinican musicians turned to its performance and composition, recording on French and West Indian labels. For the first time, the Creole-speaking Caribbean moved to the same music. Singer David Martial and the group La Perfekta are examples of this development.

The result of this upheaval was that Martinicans' cultural identity had now to be considered internationally creole, not solely Martinican. In the early

Musical genre	*Bigin bélè*	Orchestrated beguine
Tempo	♩ = 280	♩ = 220
Dance type	circle and quadrille	couple
Formal structure	call and response (soloist improvises)	verse-refrain (8-m. phrases – ABA)
Instrumentation	*bélè* (drum) *ti-bwa* (sticks)	piano, trombone, clarinet, bass, drums, *chacha*
Context	rural (plantation)	urban
Influence	African	European
Basic rhythm		

Figure 2 The distinguishing traits of the drum beguine (*bigin bélè*) and the orchestrated beguine.

1980s, the founding of International Creole Day (Journée Internationale du Créole), held annually on 28 October, could be seen as the official manifestation of a sense of belonging, wherein music played, and still plays, a key cultural role.

Zouk, a Musical and Social Phenomenon

Kadans dominated the musical scene in Martinique until the mid-1980s, when *zouk* (perhaps glossable as 'dance party') arrived on the scene. Much more than a new concept or a fad, *zouk* reaches beyond the borders of the West Indies to the continents of Africa, Europe, and North America. Its essential expressive elements are drawn from French West Indian traditions, using the *bélè*, the Guadelupean *make*, or the *boulé* drums to maintain, with the *tibwa* (rhythm sticks) and the rattle *chacha*, a rhythm whose basic pulse comes from the drum beguine. Pierre-Edouard Décimus and Jacob Devarieux, the founders of Kassav' (the band that epitomizes the sound of *zouk*), added the festivity and release that mark the spontaneity of the street parade (*vidé*), integrating into the new music and dance some rhythmic elements of the old.

After the fashion of the *balakadri* (from the French *bal á quadrilles*) and the *bal granmoun* (old-time evening balls), a *zouk* then featured the new sound in alternation with dances such as beguines, "slows," and mazurkas to punctuate the evening's ambience. On top of this formula, the creators continued to creolize by slipping in the syncopation of calypso, putting the bass in the foreground (as in reggae), emphasizing guitar solos, and adding staccato brass, all solidly anchored in the ostinato figures of the drums as heard in the contemporary sound of Congo.

The popularity of *zouk* lay in its inventors' ability to engineer and balance its borrowed musical elements so effectively that an atmosphere of joy and release became associated with it. *Zouk* gave the region a second wind, perhaps even a new life, and became the common ground, the moment of exchange and synthesis, where all could meet. It could be seen not only as the reinterpretation, but as the creation, of a music that now expresses Martinican identity.

In addition, following the example of North American and European rock, Martinican musicians began to take an interest in the visual dimensions of performance, in which the stakes had become as important as those of the aural. Into Martinican musical experiences, they incorporated theatrical staging: choreography, costumes, lighting. They shifted the appearance of the presentation from that of a dance to that of a spectacle. When one compares the beguine of the 1950s to *zouk*, it is clear that a consequential transformation occurred, creating new relationships between the people and their music, where the latter is no longer simply intended to be danced to, but also to be watched.

Developments since the Early 1990s

Through its popularity and its worldwide recognition, *zouk* promoted a Martinican identity—but paradoxically, it fostered the appearance of revival movements. Since the 1990s, there have been several developments on the Martinican musical landscape, including post-*zouk* and the so-called rap and raggamuffin.

Post-zouk

Post-*zouk*, a return-to-the-past trend, can be seen as an extension of *zouk* stylistic aesthetics as described above, but with richer harmonies. It has more politically committed texts. In this regard, the local author Patrick Chamoiseau (b. 1953) is a common reference. The music always uses Creole as an identifying feature, although it interprets Creole through the lens of globalization; thus, migration and gender (feminine) became post-*zouk* issues.

Two names stand out for the role they played in shaping the post-*zouk* trend. One is Kali (b. Jean-Marc Monnerville, 1956), who at the beginning of the 1990s produced his recording *Kali: Racines*. This work met with instant success; it incorporates beguines, mazurkas, and creole waltzes played in the Saint-Pierre style (of the nineteenth century), with the traditional beguine instrumentation and an added synthetizer. Another important musician in this movement is Mario Canonge (b. 1960). A famous pianist, he draws from the traditional repertory like Kali, but adds jazz harmonies that show the inspiration of his teacher, Marius Cultier (1943–1985). Kali and Canonge have reinterpreted musical traditions, transforming their orchestration and harmonic language.

Hip-hop and Raggamuffin

French hip-hop (rap) and raggamuffin performers situate themselves in an international black community, one that goes beyond creole society, as in other Martinican musics. Raggamuffin is a mix between reggae and hip-hop. It features a syncopated rhythm (stressed second and fourth beats), played by the bass and sometimes also by the keyboards, alongside the rapid performance of a Creole text, often with edgy themes. Performers, mainly males, condemn the ghettoization of blacks in out-of-control urban environments and remind listeners that blacks are often left behind in the modern world.

—Adapted from an article by Monique Desroches

Bibliography

Desroches, Monique. 1985. *La musique traditionnelle de la Martinique*. Rapport 8. Montréal: Centre de Recherche Caraïbe, Université de Montreal.

——. 1989. *Les instruments de musique traditionnels à la Martinique*. Fort-de-France: Bureau du Partimoine, Conseil régional de la Martinique.

——. 1990 "La musique aux Antilles." In *La Grande Encyclopédie de la Caraïbe*, edited by Danielle Begot, 178–193. Italy: Sonoli.

——. 1996. *Tambours des dieux*. Paris and Montreal: Éd. L'Harmattan.

Guilbault, Jocelyne, with Gage Averill, Édouard Benoit, and Gregory Rabess. 1993. *Zouk: World Music in the West Indies*. Chicago: University of Chicago Press.

Popular Music in Trinidad and Tobago

The Republic of Trinidad and Tobago, a double-island nation of more than one million people, is a culturally diverse society. Its populations were recorded in 2000 as 40 percent East Indian, 38 percent African, 20 percent mixed, and 1 percent white. This cultural diversity has produced a variety of popular musics.

In Trinidad, the main occasion for the performance and development of African-derived popular musics has long been carnival, in which calypso, a topical genre called *cariso* in some nineteenth-century accounts, was sung by *chantwells*, a widespread term for singers in the French Creole Caribbean. The transition from French Creole to English occurred over several decades, starting about 1900; the English term *calypsonian* replaced *chantwell* some time later. The first commercial venues for calypso were tents, where calypsonians engaged in extemporized verbal duels (*picong*, from French *piquant* 'insult'), and performed topical songs to the accompaniment of Venezuelan-style stringbands [see VENEZUELA]. Early calypsoes used scales based on modes, locally called minor keys. Each took its name from the starting sol-fa note of the mode: *mi* minor, *re* minor, and *la* minor were commonest. Later, especially after 1930, most calypsoes were composed in major tonalities. Old calypsoes preserved vestiges of Creole, such as the formulaic cadential phrase *sandimanité*, from the French *sans humanité* 'without pity'. A portion of Lord Executor's "Landing of Columbus," published in 1926, illustrates the use of this tag (after Errol Hill, 1972:63):

Were you not told what Columbus saw
When he landed on Iere shore?
Were you not told what Columbus saw
When he landed on Iere shore?
He saw the Caribs so brave and bold,
The hummingbirds with their wings of gold.
He was so glad that he called the island Trinidad.
Sans humanité.

At times, the calypso deploys militant language against political oppression and social infringements, and it airs public and individual misdemeanors. It may offer lessons in ethnic pride, parody and shame exploitative acts, and influence social behavior by spreading scandal. Many of its texts are fun-loving *picong*; some belong to the genre known as the war, a battle of words; others employ metaphors to create sexual double-entendres.

For fifty years, the Mighty Sparrow (Francisco Slinger, b. 1935) has reigned as the most impressive and sophisticated modern calypsonian. Some of his songs exploit international and internal political events, and his musical and linguistic sensibilities have influenced pan-Caribbean calypso styles. His 1956 calypso "Jean and Dinah" is regarded a classic. Lord Kitchener (Aldwyn Roberts, 1922–2000), known as the "Grandmaster" of Calypso, had a similarly lengthy and consequential career, and recorded such hits as "Rainorama," "Pan in A Minor," and "Sugar Bum Bum."

Inventor (Henry Forbes), Roaring Lion (Hubert de Leon), Lord Invader (Rupert Grant) Atilla the Hun (Raymond Quevedo), Lord Executor (Phillip Garcia), Growling Tiger (Neville Marcano), Lord Pretender (Alric Farrell), Lord Beginner (Egbert Moore), King Radio (Norman Span), Lord Caresser, Small Island Pride, and Houdini are among the other great past practitioners. Titles such as "Lord" and "King" are avoided by younger artists, who choose noncolonial-sounding signatures, such as Black Stalin, Short Pants, and Chalkdust, or retain their own names, as has David Rudder.

Steelbands

Steelbands were invented in Trinidad and achieve brilliant applications there. They have roots in the carnival "road march." They started in the 1800s as neo-African percussion ensembles and were restructured after 1884, when the Peace Preservation Ordinance, as part of a long-standing campaign against lower-class and African cultural influence in carnival, banned drumming, stick fighting (*kalenda*), and the brandishing of burning cane. Tamboo-bamboo bands, which resulted, featured percussive and concussive lengths of bamboo, progressively augmented by metallic devices (dust bins, pots, brake drums). Around 1939, the vogue for metal sounds reached a peak with the appearance of an all-steel band, Alexander's Ragtime Band, named after a song by the American composer Irving Berlin. In the 1940s, a series of innovations led to the development of tuned, multipitched oil drums (pans), whose heads tuners hammered into discrete pitch sets. In each band, a percussion section (the "engine room")

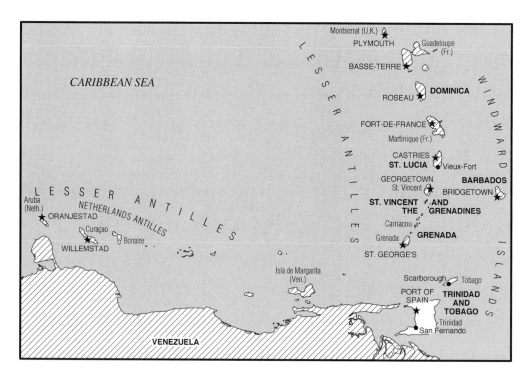

Trinidad and Tobago

featured trap drums, brake drums, and miscellaneous instruments.

Steelbands spread quickly through the English-speaking eastern Caribbean. Recordings from the late 1950s and the 1960s featured bands from Antigua, Anguilla, St. Kitts, Barbados, and Nevis; in all these places, bands entertained tourists and accompanied limbo dances. Steelbands are now based in countries all over the globe, and pans are increasingly found in ensembles other than steelbands, such as jazz combos.

Because of acoustic properties of the heads of the pans, the metal areas that produce individual pitches are not ordered according to a chromatic scale, but follow any of numerous distinctive arrangements. A player-tuner who has most effectively worked toward standardizing the patterns of pitches—into a circle of fifths—is Ellie Mannette (b. 1926), now a teacher of pan at the University of West Virginia. No national standardization has been agreed on, however, because makers prefer to put personal stamps on instruments they make. Other innovators include Winston "Spree" Simon, Bertie Marshall, and Anthony Williams.

Because the instruments have continued to develop, wide variations are evident in their construction and use. Today, ensembles are divided into sections determined by their ranges and roles. Melodic instruments include the tenor pan (formerly called the ping-pong, also known as lead, single tenor, soprano, and melody pan) and the double tenor (a set of two pans), though other pans will occasionally play the melody. Strumming pans, in imitation of the acoustic guitar, may include the double second, double guitar, quadraphonic, triple guitar, and cello (a set of three oildrums). The bass, formerly called tuned booms (a set of six to nine drums) and the tenor bass (a set of four drums) play the bass.

Using rubber-tipped sticks, musicians play single notes, double stops (two notes at once), and tremolos (rolls). A traditional parade style, "pan around the neck," gives players mobility, as each instrument is fixed to its player by a harness. For greater mobility in modern parades, the instruments are sometimes placed on car chassis, floats, or trucks. In concerts, all but the biggest are set on metal stands or racks. Music performed in Trinidad and Tobago is usually learned by rote, but sometimes from notation.

Efforts toward tonally enhancing, evolving, systematizing, and historically documenting the instrument continue. National industries sponsor steelbands and support biennial orchestral, solo, and composition competitions. The major competitions are the annual Panorama and the biennial Steelband Music Festival. As Trinidad's national instrument, pan is taught in some schools. As a result, the number of virtuoso panists is growing.

Soca

In the 1970s, a new style of party-dance calypso—soca (combining the first letters of *soul* and *calypso*), influenced by Indo-Trinidadian music and American funk and soul—emerged. It thrives in live performance and on recordings, made in Trinidad and other Caribbean countries and in diasporic Trinidanian communities, as in Brooklyn, New York. Soca singers from other Caribbean islands, especially Arrow (Montserrat) and Swallow (Antigua), have achieved market success, though nationalistic restrictions have prevented them from singing in Trinidad's carnival. Brass bands accompany soca and feature wind sections (saxophones, trumpets, trombones), synthesizers, electric guitars, electric bass, and trap drums, with strong bass-drum accents on downbeats, and lyrics that typically shun topical themes to set up a party ambience. The involvement of East Indians in Trinidadian popular musics has led to a variety of hybrid styles, such as chutney-soca. Fusions with Jamaican dancehall and American rap (ragga and other genres) are common.

Chutney

After the early 1990s, the popular songs of East Indian culture, known as chutney or Indian soca, set the scene at fetes (parties), competitions, and nightclubs. Songwriters mix the local Indian classical repertoire—a distinctive form, which developed in the early twentieth century—and traditional Indian instruments, such as the *ḍholak* (double-headed barrel drum), with calypso, soca, and other musical forms. Sharlene Boodram's 1994 competition-winning hit, "Chutney Time," is typical, with its driving intensity, rap style, and English text with occasional Hindi vocabulary:

Tie your *dhotī* [Hindu loincloth], man;
tie it up cause chutney down it extremely hot.
We say come down!
Form a little ring, man,
and I do a little thing, man,
and a wiggle of your body,
and I make your waist thin!

Chutney rap, *chutney jhūmar*, chutney lambada—the scene is alive with innovation as Caribbean styles are mixed with Bombay film music and American pop. Disco artists from India, notably the singer Kanchan and her husband, Babla, have made hit arrangements of Trinidad soca and chutney songs, such as Sundar Popo's "Chādar Bīchawo Bālma" ('Spread the Little Sheet Sweetheart'), adding studio techniques used in Hindi film songs. Today, the local recording industry in Trinidad is thriving, with many small private labels and one larger enterprise, Windsor Records in Port of Spain. East Indian recordings from Trinidad are readily available in the United States through various New York distributors, who provide prompt mail-order service for Trinidadian-Indian immigrants in North America.

—*Adapted from articles by Lorna McDaniel, Gage Averill, and Helen Myers*

Bibliography

Cowley, John. 1992. "Music and Migration: Aspects of Black Music in the British Caribbean, the United States, and Britain, before the Independence of Jamaica and Trinidad." Ph.D. dissertation, University of Warwick.

Elder, Jacob D. 1969. *From Congo Drum to Steel Band*. St. Augustine, Trinidad: University of the West Indies.

Herskovits, Melville J., and Frances S. Herskovits. [1947] 1964. *Trinidad Village*. New York: Octagon Books.

Hill, Donald R. 1993. *Calypso Colaloo: Early Carnival Music in Trinidad*. Gainesville: University Press of Florida.

Hill, Errol. 1972. *The Trinidad Carnival: Mandate for a National Theater*. Austin: University of Texas Press.

Quevedo, Raymond. 1983. *Atilla's Kaiso*. St. Augustine, Trinidad: University of the West Indies.

Myers, Helen. 1998. *Music of Hindu Trinidad: Songs from the India Diaspora*. Chicago: University of Chicago Press.

Stuempfle, Stephen. 1995. *The Steelband Movement: The Forging of a National Art in Trinidad and Tobago*. Philadelphia: University of Pennsylvania Press.

Warner, Keith. 1985. *Kaiso! The Trinidad Calypso*. Washington, D.C.: Three Continents Press.

3. The United States and Canada

The United States and Canada are home to people from nearly every nation in the world. The sheer variety and liveliness of their social and musical traditions reflect thousands of years of interactions, which continue to define their musical cultures. From centuries-old practices, such as performing mimetic dances at harvesttime, to newer ones, such as marketing popular music, and from the political performances of minstrel shows in the nineteenth century to the aesthetic experiments of modern compositions in concert halls in New York, Toronto, and Los Angeles, musicmaking in the United States and Canada has always been, and continues to be, a mixture of traditional and modern practices creatively blended to accommodate current social conditions and musical meanings. This section is a testament to the perseverance of individuals and communities that have kept their cherished traditions alive while creating new possibilities for their musical future.

Latin-flavored street music in New York City, 1981.
Photo by Terry E. Miller.

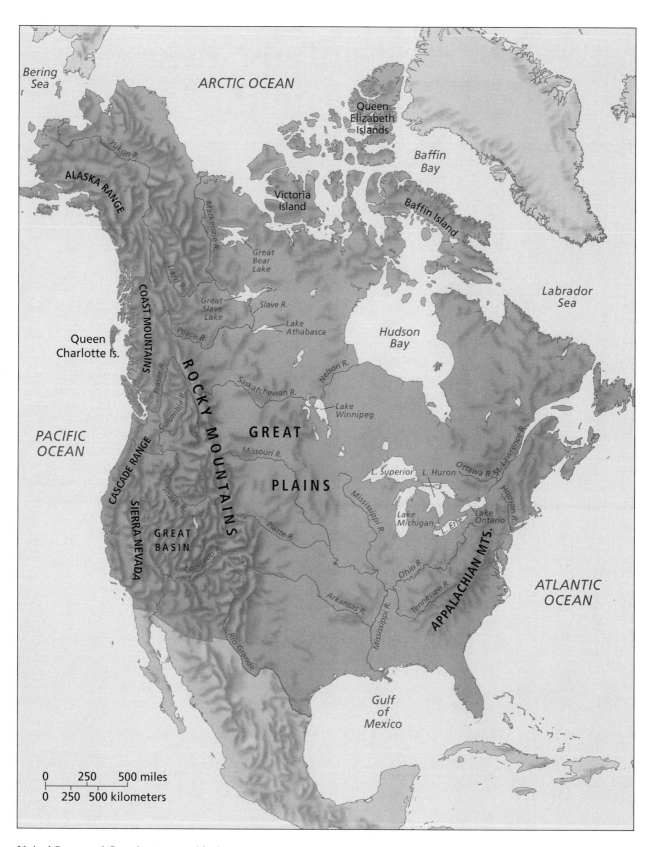

Bering
Sea

ARCTIC OCEAN

Queen
Elizabeth
Islands

Baffin
Bay

ALASKA RANGE

Victoria
Island

Baffin Island

Yukon R.

Mackenzie R.

Great
Bear
Lake

Labrador
Sea

COAST MOUNTAINS

Liard R.

Great
Slave
Lake

Slave R.

Lake
Athabasca

Hudson
Bay

Queen
Charlotte Is.

Peace R.

ROCKY MOUNTAINS

Fraser R.

Saskatchewan R.

Nelson R.

Columbia R.

Lake
Winnipeg

GREAT

St. Lawrence R.

PACIFIC
OCEAN

CASCADE RANGE

Missouri R.

PLAINS

L. Superior

L. Huron

Ottawa R.

Snake R.

SIERRA NEVADA

Lake
Michigan

Lake
Erie

Lake
Ontario

Hudson R.

GREAT
BASIN

Platte R.

Mississippi R.

APPALACHIAN MTS.

Colorado R.

Ohio R.

ATLANTIC
OCEAN

Arkansas R.

Tennessee R.

Mississippi R.

Rio Grande

Gulf
of
Mexico

| 0 | 250 | 500 miles |
| 0 | 250 | 500 kilometers |

United States and Canada, topographical

The United States and Canada as a Unified Musical Culture

Together, Canada—the modern world's second-largest country in area—and the United States—the fourth-largest—cover more than 7,384,000 square miles of land, approximately 90 percent of the continent of North America. From its highest points, Mt. McKinley in Alaska and Mt. Logan in the Yukon, to its lowest, in Death Valley, California, this land area (roughly 13 percent of the Earth's total) encompasses deserts, mountain ranges, polar ice caps, woodlands, rainforests, prairies, six time zones, and more than 330 million people of varying ethnicities, languages, and histories.

Unity in diversity is a common phrase often used today to describe the people and social contexts of the United States and Canada. It is an apt one, for although these two close neighbors share much in the way of geography, institutions, language, and music and therefore can be seen as a cultural and political unit, the people who live in these countries are highly diverse in expressing their social and musical identities, as nations and as nations within nations. Home to people of nearly all of the world's social, ethnic, religious, and language groups, the United States and Canada have embedded within their history, government, and national consciousness the twin ideals of democracy and equal human rights; although not always realized, these ideals have motivated much political, social, and musical activity within their borders.

The Earliest Inhabitants

The original inhabitants of the United States and Canada were ancestors of peoples believed to have emigrated from what is now the westernmost portion of Russia through the Bering Strait, possibly in two great waves (around 18,000 B.C.E. and 12,000 B.C.E.). Centuries before Europeans first arrived, American Indians and First Nations peoples had developed cultures based on hunting, fishing, and small-scale farming that were sustained by a traditional life infused with music and ritual activity.

Contexts for musical performance included ceremonies surrounding the yearly cycles of spring/summer and fall/winter activities (figure 1), including hunting songs (often revealed in dreams), planting (often including mimetic dancing) and harvesting (thanksgiving) songs and dances, and shamanistic practices, including individual and community healing ceremonies. Among the Plains Indians, song

Figure 1 Kwakiutl of the northwest coast, during their winter ceremony, 1914. Dancers wearing costumes and masks crouch in the foreground while others stand behind them. At the far left, the chief stands holding a staff. *Photo by Edward S. Curtis. Library of Congress, Prints & Photographs Division, LC-USZ62–49042.*

practices associated with medicine bundles and war dances were common. In the Northwest, among the Haida, Salish, and Athapaskans, potlatches (large feasts, characterized by gift-giving to all participants) were frequently held, as were ceremonies accompanying totem-pole carving and installation. Some music, such as gambling, game, and love songs, addressed daily social and communal life, while other kinds of music commemorated historical or mythical events. Social dance-songs, such as the women's shuffle dances of the Iroquois Confederacy in the northeast United States and southeast Canada, were also performed.

Many American Indians and First Nations peoples, such as the Inuit/Eskimo (living in harsh northern climates), remained fairly isolated and scattered from one another, while others, such as the Plains Indians in the central United States and Canada and the Woodlands Indians in the East, developed by the fifteenth and sixteenth century C.E. large and powerful hunting and trading networks, made up of independent communities tied together through elaborate exchange economies. The inter-tribal meeting, later to develop into the powwow, became an important context for the exchange not only of food and gossip, but also of songs and dances.

Traditional American Indian and First Nations song and dance was quite varied in its performance contexts and meanings, but it shared basic features: most of the music was vocal, monophonic (one line) or heterophonic (one line performed in different simultaneous variations), with frequent use of vocables (syllables that have no semantic meaning in the local language). No separate instrumental traditions existed, although instruments such as drums and rattles were frequently used to accompany song. Drums, especially, had deep power and significance for early communities, and became in later times a focus of much contention between aboriginal peoples and Christian colonists and other settlers, who regularly banned their use.

From Colonies to Nations: 1600–1800

There is archaeological and literary evidence for early Norse contact in Newfoundland around 990 C.E., but the first permanent European settlements were made by Spanish immigrants in 1565 at the site of modern-day St. Augustine, Florida; French immigrants at Port Royal in Nova Scotia in 1605; and British immigrants in Jamestown, now in Virginia, in 1607. Most early visitors were traders sent by governments and business interests in Europe in hopes of establishing ties with Indians who would help them make a profit in trading fur. By the early seventeenth century, American Indians and First Nations peoples in the East had developed skills that proved essential to European survival. With traders came notions of private ownership and a money-based economy. Missionaries from Spain and France arrived soon after, bringing a radically different spiritual worldview, based on the hierarchic principles of Christianity and on early modern European notions of class.

With the traders and clerics came music, musical instruments, and ideas of what music was and was not. By the mid-eighteenth century, English and French ballads and other popular secular pieces were commonplace, as were British regimental bands, fife-and-drum field or marching bands, and string orchestras playing the latest minuets and gavottes from Europe to entertain the landed gentry in the southern U.S. colonies, Newfoundland, New France (present-day Québec, claimed in 1607 for the French crown by Samuel de Champlain [1567–1635]), and Acadia (present-day Nova Scotia).

Various forms of hymns, psalmody, and Christian liturgical music became commonplace within European communities in the East, promoted in the United States by singing schools that sprang up especially in New England, and in Canada by the British Anglican and the French Roman Catholic churches, which controlled land ownership and much of the cultural life of New France. Gradually, as European-derived communities began to grow and social and musical institutions began to develop, new or newly adapted music, composed and performed within the Canadian and U.S. contexts, began to appear in the form of French *voyageur* ballads, Anglo-American ballads, theatrical music, and hymns composed and taught by singing masters and clerics.

Interactions between Europeans and American Indians and First Nations peoples were frequent especially in Canada, where the children of aboriginals and Europeans (especially the French) known as Métis began to develop a separate language and expressive culture. In the United States, as European settlements took more and more land, Indian lands began to shrink, and communities that had once roamed freely had to develop new forms of economy and social interaction, based on European models. Furthermore, disturbed by the drumming of many Indian groups with whom they had contact, Europeans began to ban its use in Indian ceremonies, describing it as sinful and primitive.

Many revitalizing movements, such as that of the Iroquoian Handsome Lake, who established the Longhouse religion in 1799, attempted to help Indian communities face the swift social, religious, and political changes (not to mention newly introduced diseases, such as tuberculosis and smallpox), and much Indian music developed at the time addresses the destruction of their traditional way of life. Some musical interaction took place, such as the development of the *katachina* ceremony (Indian/Spanish) and the Métis fiddling tradition (Indian/French/Celtic), but such interaction was limited for many reasons, not the least of which was that European concepts of music, especially secular forms, such as ballads, dances, and marching band music, and of notation whereby music was written down were initially unknown to the Indians, who viewed what they did as prayer, ritual, or ceremony—in other words, as religious and social, as well as "sounded," behavior.

Slavery was introduced into the United States in 1619 and into Canada in 1689; by 1800, more than a million blacks, of mainly West African and Caribbean descent, were living within these lands (about 95 percent of them in the United States). The majority of slaves in Canada were not imported directly from West Africa, but were brought in as property by Loyalists, who, remaining loyal to the British crown, emigrated from the United States in the late eighteenth century. Slavery as an institution was far less entrenched in Canada than in the United States, and was abolished somewhat earlier there, first in Nova Scotia in 1787 and in Upper Canada (present-day Ontario) in 1793. It would take another seventy years and the Civil War (1861–1865) for the United States to abolish slavery as a legal institution, and during that time, thousands of runaway slaves passed through the Underground Railroad, a system of interconnected hiding places that took them north via the Great Lakes from the United States into Canada, through cities such as Detroit, Buffalo, and Rochester. Frequently, African-American songs such as "Follow the Drinking Gourd" (the Big Dipper, shaped like a ladle) were used as musical–linguistic codes to give directions to runaways.

Slaves imported from West Africa and the Caribbean often brought small, portable musical instruments, such as drums and gourd rattles, and a vast and rich tradition of song, dance, ritual, and ceremony. Because they were frequently separated from their families, first in Africa and then again in North America, much of the integrity and cohesiveness of their musical cultures was lost. Furthermore, in constant fear of uprisings, slaveowners frequently banned, as they had with aboriginals, the use of drums and certain dances, regarded by the European gentry as indecent. Slave culture, especially in the United States, thus developed a uniquely "American" musical tradition, based on calls, cries, and other forms of vocal music that enabled slaves to perform their feelings while conveying vital bits of information.

In the eighteenth century, as a result of treaties negotiated in Europe between Britain and France after the Peace of Utrecht in 1713 and the French and Indian War (known in Europe as part of the Seven Years War, 1756–1763), France ceded to Britain most of its formerly claimed territory in Canada. Many French settlers in what was then Acadia (present-day Nova Scotia) were forcibly removed to the Louisiana Territory, a French-controlled portion of the southeastern United States, where they interacted with Africans and Indians primarily from the Caribbean, creating a new and vital Cajun culture, with its own dialects and musical traditions.

By the end of the sixteenth century, Spanish clerics had established a thriving mission culture predominantly in the upper Rio Grande Valley in New Mexico, bringing with them, directly from Spain or via Mexico, Spanish sacred music in the form of *alabados* (religious ballads related to plainchant) and religious theatrical forms, such as Christmas and Easter plays. They imported musical instruments from Europe, including organs, which they installed within newly built churches. Secular music traveled from Mexico and through Spanish-held territories in what is now the southwestern United States. As mestizo culture (a blending of Spanish, West African, and American Indian cultures) developed, new forms, such as the ballad (*corrido*) and ensemble music (*conjunto*) became popular along the Rio Grande and throughout the southwestern United States. European—predominantly German and Czech—immigration to Mexico introduced popular dances, such as the polka and the quintessential polka-band instrument, the button accordion, which became a mainstay of later Mexican ensembles.

Westward Expansion: 1800–1900

By the beginning of the nineteenth century, the United States of America and the two Canadas were established. (Upper Canada, present-day Ontario, and Lower Canada, present-day Québec, were united in 1840 and merged with other Atlantic provinces into the Dominion of Canada in 1867.) Boundaries between these nations were firmly drawn by 1850, with capitals in Washington, District of Columbia (1800), and Ottawa, Province of Ontario (1867).

The nineteenth century in both countries saw westward expansion to the Pacific Ocean; the immigration of European, Chinese, and Japanese groups;

the building of transcontinental railways; gold rushes of the 1850s in the United States and in the Yukon in the 1890s; policies, especially those of the U.S. government, surrounding the taking of Indian land, forcible Indian migration, and war; and discriminatory practices aimed at American Indians, First Nations peoples, and African Americans. Both countries expanded their landholdings through purchases from European and Mexican powers and through such business enterprises as the Hudson's Bay Company, which sold the land now known as the Province of Manitoba and the Northwest Territories to the newly formed Dominion of Canada in 1869.

By 1850, the United States had acquired most of its southeastern territory from France through the Louisiana Purchase (1803), Florida from Spain (1819), and much of the Southwest (Arizona, California, Nevada, New Mexico, Texas, and Utah, and parts of Colorado, Oklahoma, and Wyoming) from Mexico through the treaty of Guadalupe Hidalgo, signed at the end of the Mexican–American War in 1848. The last large chunks of land to be added to the United States were Alaska, sold by Russia in 1867, and Hawai'i, previously an independent kingdom and then a republic and annexed in 1898, but both would not become states until the middle of the twentieth century.

Sizable communities of Germans, Scandinavians, Italians, Ukrainians, and, in the mid-to late nineteenth century, Greeks, Hungarians, and Southern and Eastern Europeans, emigrated to the United States and Canada during this time, capitalizing on offers of inexpensive farmland and land grants in the prairie states and provinces. With these communities came their music, including Moravian hymns, Lutheran chorales, and Orthodox Russian, Greek,

and other Eastern Orthodox practices. German and Scandinavian communities, especially, modeled their musical activities after those they had enjoyed in Europe, and soon orchestras, town bands, choral societies, singing circles (*liederkranz*), and Ukrainian *bandura* 'long-necked chordophone' orchestras were established. Italians brought their musical culture to the New World in the form of opera and popular and folk-music traditions. Irish immigrants, escaping difficult economic conditions in their homeland, brought their rich folksong, fiddling, and dance traditions, primarily to Eastern cities.

As the major cities in the East and Midwest—New York, Philadelphia, Chicago, Toronto, and Montréal—began to grow, there developed communities that could sustain middle- and upper-middle-class European-derived musical institutions, such as concert halls, opera houses, theaters, and schools, modeled after their European counterparts. Classical concert music began to flourish, at first based on European models, but later taking on an "American" character, in part reflecting the adoption and adaptation of indigenous and newly arrived folk traditions.

In the rural U.S. South, other traditions slowly emerged: (1) the African-American spiritual and black gospel hymn, originally part of worship service, but later adapted for concert use by choirs such as the Wiregrass Sacred Harp Singers (figure 2); (2) white gospel songs, originally evolved from the shape-note tradition and the nineteenth-century camp meeting and produced in the thousands by composers such as Ira Sankey (1840–1908), Philip Paul Bliss (1838–1876), and Fanny Jane Crosby (1820–1915); (3) early blues, based on African-American field cries and hollers; and (4) country ("hillbilly") music, originally evolved from the

Figure 2 Wiregrass Sacred Harp Singers led by Henry Japeth Jackson, First Missionary Baptist Church, Ozark, Alabama, 1987. Henry Japeth Jackson is the son of Judge Jackson, author of *The Colored Sacred Harp* (1931).
Photo by Terry E. Miller.

Scottish and English ballad tradition that flourished there.

Westward expansion in the United States and Canada resulted in the shrinking of American Indian and First Nations lands and the continued destruction, especially in the United States, of Indian lifeways. In the 1880s, wars broke out between the United States and parts of the Sioux nation, for example. As in the East among the Iroquois a century earlier, Plains Indians developed new and creative ceremonies and rituals to counteract the destruction of their material and spiritual lives. Perhaps the best known was the Ghost Dance religion, which emerged in the 1880s and immediately traveled northward into Canada, espousing beliefs in the coming of a new world—free of whites, sickness, and hunger, and marked by the return of the buffalo. Misinterpreted as war dances, Ghost Dance ceremonies were banned; at Wounded Knee, South Dakota, in 1890, worsening relations between the U.S. army and the Sioux culminated in fighting in which several hundred people died, most of them Sioux, and the Ghost Dance religion never recovered.

First Nations peoples in Canada, though also facing discriminatory practices, were treated with somewhat more dignity than their U.S. counterparts. They were not forcibly removed and transported westward, as were some American Indians, such as the Seminole in the southern United States in the mid-nineteenth century, but emigrated on their own to find work and better living conditions. The Métis, who wished to separate themselves from the French community in Québec and the Prairies Indian communities, declared their own nationhood under the leadership of Louis Riel (1844–1885) in the Red River Valley of Saskatchewan, near Lake Winnepeg,

Manitoba, where they were ultimately defeated in the late 1880s. Certain musical fusions, such as the adoption and adaptation of the brass-band tradition by the Northwest Coast Indians, mark this period as one of continuous social and musical interaction.

In the mid to late nineteenth century, two events—the completion of the transcontinental railroad and the gold rushes (spawning their own repertoire of ballads) in both countries—established new patterns of immigration and social and musical exchange. Chinese and Japanese workers were brought to the United States and Canada in the 1850s to work as miners and later to help complete railways. They brought Asian religious beliefs and practices, with classical, theatrical, dance, and folk-music traditions. Cantonese workers, for example, established a community in Vancouver, British Columbia, one that soon supported several Chinese opera and theater associations. Never a majority in western Canada, the British worked with other Europeans primarily as farmers, performing agrarian-associated musical repertories, such as ballads, seasonal song cycles, and ceremonial music for weddings and Christian services.

Changing Patterns in the Twentieth Century

The major factors affecting the growth—and, occasionally, the demise—of musical traditions in the United States and Canada during the twentieth century included (1) the development of mass media and related technologies and the resulting commodification of folk, popular, and religious musics; (2) new patterns of immigration, resulting in the influx of large groups of people, predominantly from Southern Europe, Asia, and the Caribbean (figure 3),

Figure 3 Members of St. John's Spiritual Baptist Church in the Flatbush neighborhood of Brooklyn, New York, sing a hymn from the Church of England's *Hymns Ancient and Modern*. The Spiritual Baptist faith probably originated in St. Vincent Island in the east Caribbean, then flourished in Trinidad, but through immigrants it also thrives in New York City and Toronto. *Photo by Terry E. Miller, 1989.*

especially between 1880 and 1920, an influx that spurred new governmental policies concerning immigration, the status of citizens, and the construction of "ethnicity" and "multiculturalism" through revivals and other forms of cultural display; (3) the development of an American- and Canadian-defined classical-music tradition; and (4) the rapid growth of institutions that supported the collection, study, and teaching of U.S.- and Canadian-born musics.

The invention of the radio (in the late nineteenth century) and the rise of recording and broadcasting technology (in the late nineteenth and early twentieth century), with the completion of transcontinental railroads and highways, helped people and their musics travel and interact over greater and greater geographic, linguistic, and social distances. Now it was not necessary to make music oneself, or even to travel to a local concert hall, church, powwow, or fiddling festival to hear musical performances. By the mid-twentieth century, one could experience music from all over the world through recordings, and could even witness its performance in one's own living room through the medium of television. Perhaps one of the most profound social and musical changes that occurred when this technology was introduced was that for the first time in human history, musical sound itself (not just its abstraction in the form of notation) could be captured and materialized. This technology made new sounds possible and far more available to many more people and thus became a source of new creative techniques for composers, performers, and other musicians. At the beginning of the twenty-first century it is possible, through electronic media such as CDs, audiocassettes, videocassettes, computers, and other digital formats, for anyone (with the economic means to do so) to listen to, download, even edit any recorded music from any part of the world.

A major wave of immigration at the end of the nineteenth century through World War I (about 1880–1918) changed the face of the United States and Canada. Smaller communities had emigrated from the seventeenth century onward, but Ashkenazic Jews from Eastern Europe and Russia; Chinese, primarily from Canton; Doukhobors, a religious group from Russia, under the leadership of Peter Veregin; and Muslim Arabs from the Middle East began arriving in large numbers at that time, settling primarily in large urban areas, such as New York, Chicago, Edmonton, and Vancouver, or, as with the Doukhobors, in the farming communities of British Columbia. They brought not only their folk and dance traditions, but also liturgical, theatrical, and classical musics. Many Jews, for example, who had been cantors or instrumental musicians in Eastern

Figure 4 Cover illustration for the sheet music to Irving Berlin's "Alexander's Ragtime Band" (1911). The song, Berlin's first big hit, is a celebration of ragtime and became an icon of the era.
From the collection of the Music Department, New York Public Library for the Performing Arts, Astor, Lenox, and Tilden Associations.

Europe, joined newly established symphony orchestras. Others, such as Irving Berlin (1888–1989) and Al Jolson (1886–1950), quickly found their way to Tin Pan Alley (the colloquial name given to the New York City district where popular songs were written and sold) (figure 4), to the burgeoning film industry in Los Angeles, or to vaudeville stages. Still others, such as the Brooklyn-born Richard Tucker (1914–1975), became famous opera stars.

The first half of the twentieth century saw the development of African-American styles, such as gospel music (through the efforts of Thomas A. Dorsey [1899–1993] and others); the blues of Muddy Waters (1915–1953), Bessie Smith (1894–1937), and countless others; the ragtime of Scott Joplin (1868–1917); and early jazz forms performed and recorded by King Oliver (1885–1938) and Jelly Roll Morton (1890–1941), developed in large urban areas such as New Orleans, Chicago, Kansas City, and Montréal. In the white rural South, the popularity of "hillbilly," "cowboy," or country music, made popular by the recordings of Jimmy Rodgers (1897–1933), the

Carter Family, and others, would spread through radio programs such as *Grand Ole Opry* and ultimately merge with the blues in midcentury to form early rock and roll.

Hispanic music too began to emerge as a growing force, especially in the ballad tradition (*corrido*) and in popular dance music, as more and more people from Mexico and the Caribbean entered the United States and Canada and began to establish communities. Dances such as the *habanera*, the *son*, the rumba, the mambo and the cha-cha-chá—from Cuba, Puerto Rico, Haiti, and other Caribbean islands, performed in venues such as the Palladium Ballroom in New York City by bandleaders Xavier Cugat (1900–1990) and Tito Puente (1923–2000)—became wildly popular in the 1940s and 1950s, especially in urban areas such as New York, Los Angeles, and Toronto.

The new wave of immigration and newfound economic and social mobility for African Americans and African Canadians soon ushered in a wave of conservatism, in which laws such as the Chinese Restriction Act in Canada (1923–1947), the quota system in the United States (1921–1965), and the separate-but-equal doctrine (established in 1896 to keep public facilities such as schools, restaurants, and so on segregated by race; overthrown in 1954) in the United States, restricted the immigration and mobility of certain groups, most notably Chinese, Japanese, Jews, and African Americans, and discriminatory practices against these and other groups were common. American Indians and First Nations peoples became citizens through the 1942 Citizens Act in the United States and the Canadian Citizenship Act of 1947.

An outcome of a new ethnic and political consciousness in the United States and Canada at midcentury was renewal of interest in roots and old-time, Old World, or traditional musics. This interest crystallized in the 1950s and 1960s in the form of revivals, festivals, and other forms of cultural display in which people performed old musics in new settings for new audiences (figure 5), and largely white, young, middle-class audiences participated in group musical experiences, such as hootenannies and sing-ins, where governmental policies such as school segregation, the Vietnam War, and parental authority could be protested. Folksingers such as Pete Seeger (b. 1919), Joan Baez (b. 1941), Bob Dylan (b. 1941) and the Kingston Trio in the United States and Gordon Lightfoot (b. 1938), Joni Mitchell (b. 1943), and Buffy Sainte-Marie (b. 1941 or 1942) in Canada became not only national singing stars, but also national heroes to a generation of idealistic "flower children" (figure 6). In 1963, to implement ideals of ethnic diversity, Canada formed the Royal Commission on Bilingualism and Biculturalism and developed support for multiculturalism, eventually entrenched in the Multicultural Act of 1988.

Classical music traditions in the United States and Canada during the twentieth century developed in similar but slowly diverging ways. Both countries shared an interest in separating culturally from Europe and forming authentically North American forms and institutions. As early as the 1860s, "nativist" composers, including George Frederick Bristow (1825–1898) and Louis Moreau Gottschalk (1829–1869) in the United States and, in Canada, Calixa Lavallée (1842–1891), the composer of the present Canadian national anthem, "O Canada," and later Alexis Constant (1858–1918), were addressing a perceived need to establish independent national musical identities.

By the early twentieth century, U.S. composers such as Edward MacDowell (1860–1908), Henry F. Gilbert (1868–1928), Arthur Farwell (1872–1952),

Figure 5 A typical Appalachian string band, consisting of (*from left*) banjo, two guitars, fiddle, mandolin, and guitar, performing at the National Folk Festival near Cleveland, Ohio, 1984.
Photo by Terry E. Miller.

Figure 6 Woody Guthrie (1912–1967) spent most of his life traveling around the United States singing songs and playing guitar. Though he was hospitalized with a neurological disease from 1954 until his death, his songs, lifestyle, and populist politics were a primary influence on the folksingers and countercultural movements of the period.
Photo by Al Aumuller, 1943. Library of Congress, Prints & Photographs Division, NYWT&S Collection, LC-USZ62–130859.

and Charles Wakefield Cadman (1881–1946), were consciously incorporating American Indian and African American songs into their classical compositions; one example is Gilbert's symphonic poem, *Dance in Place Congo* (1906–1908), based on African-American tunes performed by southern blacks in the decades immediately after the Civil War. Perhaps the best-known U.S. composers in the 1920s and beyond whose works are most clearly defined as American are Charles Ives (1874–1954), Virgil Thomson (1896–1989), and Aaron Copland (1900–1990), who painted musical pictures of an idealized America. Examples are Ives's *Three Places in New England* (1904–1914) and the *Concord Sonata* (1911–1915), Thomson's music to accompany the film *The Plow That Broke the Plains* (1936), and Copland's ballets *Appalachian Spring* (1944) and *Billy the Kid* (1938). Truly revolutionary musics, notations, and technologies came later, generally between 1950 and 1970, in the electronic works of John Cage (1912–1992), Milton Babbitt (b. 1916), Elliott Carter (b. 1908), and Morton Subotnick (b. 1933).

Similar efforts were being made to assert a national aesthetic in Canada, but Canadian composers were likelier to study in England or France and to compose pieces based on preestablished European models. One such composer, Claude

Champagne (1891–1965), studied in Paris, but attempted to infuse his work with a Canadian consciousness, especially in works such as *Suite Canadienne* and *Images du Canada français*, in which he tried to depict musically the French Canadian countryside. In addition to prolific composing, R. Murray Schafer (b. 1933), perhaps Canada's best-known composer in the late twentieth century, established in the late 1960s the World Soundscape Project at Simon Fraser University.

As educational institutions began to develop and grow within the two countries, so did an interest in music scholarship, the collection and study of the musics not only of the great European masters through their own notations, but also of the people who had migrated to the United States and Canada, through ethnographic fieldwork based primarily on oral/aural traditions. Collectors such as Sir Francis James Child and Cecil Sharp (British-American ballads and folk materials), Frances Densmore (American Indian materials), Alan and John Lomax and Beth Lomax Hawes (early blues, ballads, and much else) in the United States; and Roy MacKenzie, Kenneth Peacock, Helen Creighton, and Edith Fowke (English ballad tradition, mainly in the Atlantic provinces), among others, in Canada contributed greatly to our understanding of music as both human social behavior and beautifully organized sound.

Differences in Musical Cultures

So far, this essay has concentrated on the shared social, political, and musical histories of the United States and Canada. But there is much that separates these countries into distinct musical cultures. Discussed here are some of these differences, such as the construction of separate, nationally based social and musical identities in each country; the relationships that the United States and Canada have maintained with Europe and each other; the role of government in the development of musical institutions and policies; and new ways to conceptualize music and social identity within the context of two pluralistic nations.

Separate National and Musical Identities
Differences in political and social histories between the United States and Canada have created musical stories that reflect these differences. Perhaps the most obvious difference between the countries is their geography: the contiguous United States shares a long southern border with Mexico, immigration from which, as from the countries of Spain (through Mexico), Central America, and the Caribbean, has

continued for centuries. Spanish, Mexican, and other Latin musics have long influenced the musics of the United States, first through missions in the South and West, later through border traditions (such as the *corrido* and the *conjunto*), and most recently through popular dances, songs, and styles (such as *salsa*) and musical elements (such as rhythmic complexity), that rock and jazz musicians have adopted.

On the opposite end of the continent, the northern coast of Canada faces the Arctic Ocean and the polar ice cap, and rugged, often hostile conditions there have made settlement difficult. The popular music industry of the Yukon has distinguished northern Canada, but Hispanic music until the late twentieth century was found less in Canada, with one major exception: Caribana, held in Toronto every summer and billed as one of the world's largest Afro-Caribbean festivals.

Another geographic consideration that has affected the development of distinct U.S. and Canadian musical personalities has been polarization of the coasts. In the United States, although an East–West distinction is present, especially in more recent times, the division between North and South is primary, having been solidified through centuries of difference in settlement patterns, economic institutions, and issues surrounding slavery. In Canada, the primary split has always been East–West, with the major cities of Toronto and Montréal being settled and "gentrified" long before the "rustic" western cities of Edmonton and Vancouver. These distinctions have been most apparent in the development of musical styles and institutions, such as performance halls and schools.

In constructing national identities over the centuries, the United States and Canada have frequently concentrated on, negotiated, or polarized different ethnic or racial groups—especially in relation to the overarching hegemony of western and northern European "mainstream" culture. In music festivals, and contests, this polarization served to highlight distinctive features of groups that distinguish them within the mosaic or rainbow of North American culture as a whole; more frequently, however, such discriminations have helped restrict and subjugate American Indians, First Nations peoples, African Americans, and others. These ethnic tensions have deeply affected the development of musical styles and genres within these countries, as many articles in this volume attest.

The major polarizations that have been used to construct positive or negative pictures of the unity of the United States and Canada have perhaps been the black/white (United States) and French/English (Canada) dichotomies, which have infused especially the written musical histories of both countries. In the United States, the racial divide has created barriers to musical interaction and the recognition especially of African-American and Hispanic contributions to a complete musical portrait. After-effects of slavery, in the form of discriminatory practices (such as those preventing black performers from playing in certain contexts), are still, albeit more subtly, affecting how black and white performers are received and accepted, though late-twentieth-century forms such as rock and rap have catapulted many black performers to international stardom.

In Canada, where slavery never became the settled institution it was in the United States, the French/English polarity has historically taken precedence. The original European settlers in Canada were French; the nation's first name, New France, reflected this influence until the mid-eighteenth century, when New France gave way to British-controlled entities known as the Two Canadas. The legacy of French control survives in Canada in the recognition of French as an official language, in separatist movements in Québec and elsewhere, in musical traditions (an example being *chansonnier*) that flourish in Canada but not in the United States, and in the growth of a separate culture, that of the Métis, descendants of Indians and French.

A final feature of U.S. and Canadian identities is their respective relationship to Europe. Though Canada, especially in more recent times, has begun to assert its musical "Canadianness," it maintains strong ties to Europe, especially to Britain and France, whereas composers and other musicians in the United States have made a more conscious turn away from Europe, attempting to construct uniquely "American"—that is, U.S.—musical identities.

Musical and Social Interactions

Another way of understanding how music and social identity work together in Canada and the United States is to see all forms of identity, even nationalistic ones, as constantly in flux and continuously negotiated in everyday and ritual life. For example, though we may conceptualize Canada and the United States as separate and distinct political entities (separated by a thick border on the map), ethnic, social, religious, and other kinds of groups freely cross such borders, creating fluid, permeable, and changeable cultural boundaries. Music, serving as a marker of aspects of one's identity at any given moment, is often used by individuals or groups to define themselves in relation to others and as a means for others to define them. A German-American brass band marching down the street during Oktoberfest, for example, may be an important way of demonstrating a German community's pride in its ethnicity, but each member of this community may have identities other than that of a German American—a Lutheran, a woman, a white person, and so on. Similarly, teenagers in the United States and Canada enjoy contemporary popular music, and one's whole identity as a "punk" or "nerd" can rest on the strength of which bands one prefers to listen to—but years later, those same teenagers may look back on those musical and identity choices as childish or silly.

Because we are all social and musical beings who interact with others, there is always the potential for identities and musics to intermingle and cross borders, creating new groups, new musics, and new interactions. Therefore, we should not be surprised to see new musical and social forms develop, such as Northwest Indian brass bands, French Indian blues, Celtic revivalists who are Jewish (and *klezmer* clarinetists who are not), African-American classical composers, and female percussionists, as well as unlikely musical combinations, such as Ukrainian country, American Indian gospel, or Christian rock, because these combinations are natural within the rich and complex contexts of social and musical plurality that define the United States and Canada today.

—*Adapted from an article by Ellen Koskoff*

Bibliography

Chase, Gilbert. 1987. *America's Music: From the Pilgrims to the Present*. Urbana: University of Illinois Press.

Chiswick, Barry R., ed. 1992. *Immigration, Language, and Ethnicity: Canada and the United States*. Washington, D.C.: AEI Press.

Crawford, Richard. 1993. *The American Musical Landscape*. Berkeley: University of California Press.

Diamond, Beverley, and Robert Witmer, eds. 1994. *Canadian Music: Issues of Hegemony and Identity*. Toronto: Canadian Scholars' Press.

Driedger, Leo, ed. 1978. *The Canadian Ethnic Mosaic*. Canadian Ethnic Studies Association Series 6. Toronto: McClelland and Stewart.

Hitchcock, H. Wiley. 1988. *Music in the United States: A Historical Introduction*. 3rd ed. Englewood Cliffs, N.J.: Prentice Hall.

Kallmann, Helmut. 1960. *A History of Music in Canada, 1534–1914*. Toronto: University of Toronto Press.

Kingman, Daniel. 1998. *American Music: A Panorama*. New York: Schirmer Books.

Koskoff, Ellen. 1980. *The Musical Self*. Pittsburgh: External Studies Program, University of Pittsburgh.

McGee, Timothy J. 1985. *The Music of Canada*. New York: Norton.

Slobin, Mark. 1993. *Sub-Cultural Sounds: Micromusics of the West*. Hanover, N.H.: University Press of New England.

Tawa, Nicholas E. 1982. *A Sound of Strangers: Musical Culture, Acculturation, and the Post-Civil War Ethnic American*. Metuchen, N.J.: Scarecrow Press.

Thernstrom, Stephan, et al., eds. 1980. *Harvard Encyclopedia of American Ethnic Groups*. Cambridge: Belknap Press of Harvard University Press.

Music of American Indians and First Peoples in the United States and Canada

Music of American Indians and First Peoples in the United States and Canada

American Indians and First Peoples comprise a variety of social, linguistic, and musical groups, from the Choctaw living in the swamps of the southeastern United States to the Inuit of the newest Canadian territory, Nunavut; from the six-nation Iroquois confederacy, located in western New York and southern Ontario, to scattered villages of the Eskimo (as the Inuit are called in the United States) of Alaska. First Peoples in Canada include the Métis, of Indian and predominantly French heritage, who form a separate social group, with their own language and their own cultural and musical identity. Despite a wide variety of languages, physical environments, and musical cultures, most American Indians and First Peoples share a history of interaction with outsiders and of rapid social and economic change, brought about by European immigration and expansion. Traditional musics address these concerns, as do musics and rituals developed since the nineteenth century, such as those associated with the Ghost Dance movement and the Native American Church. The articles that follow depict these and other cultural expressions.

Fancy dancer at the 202nd Omaha Nation Powwow in Macy, Nebraska, 2006.
Photo by Ben J. Smith.

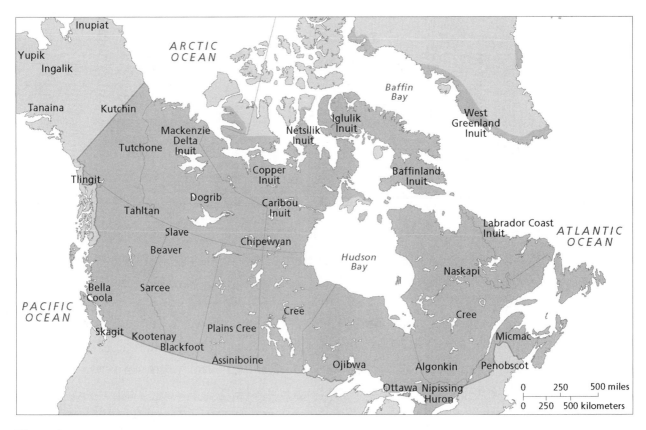

First nations

American Indians

Overview

For centuries, the aboriginal inhabitants of the continent—American Indians, Native Americans, First Peoples—have made music integral to their lives. Creation narratives, migration stories, magic formulas, and ancient ceremonial practices invoke music. Archaeologists have found North American musical instruments and pictographs of singing and dancing from 600 C.E. or earlier, and from places as far apart as the mounds of the Southeast and the cliff dwellings of the Southwest. Styles differ within tribal groups and among individuals, but the variety of the music is infinite, as people constantly recreate it in performance.

The migration of aboriginal peoples over time has encouraged musical interaction and exchange. Historically, North America was a great and open hunting, gathering, and fishing ground for many peoples, who gathered for agriculture, marriage, religion, ceremony, and trade, often ignoring political boundaries and formal tribal borders created largely after European occupation. In the nineteenth century, the U.S. and Canadian governments forced aboriginal peoples to leave their homelands and live on reservations, reserves, and allotments. In the twentieth century, individuals began leaving their reservations, migrating in the 1930s to work on commercial farms and in the 1940s to work in industries and join the armed forces. Starting in the 1950s, government agents urged many to relocate, and even moved them, for job training, to big cities in the U.S. West and Midwest. One way they made their lives happier in cities was to form powwow clubs and social dance clubs, often including people from different tribes. By the twenty-first century, individuals had begun to travel back and forth between cities and their homelands for events specific to their own tribes.

Sacred narratives, legends, music, and dances enable today's North American aboriginal peoples to maintain ceremonies and traditions critical to their lives. Their ceremonies—originating from a single creator, from deities, guardian spirits, and animal spirits, or from human storytellers and composers—are simultaneously ancient and modern. They rely on memory and reenactment, not written words, thus transcending generations and cultural boundaries. Even traditional apparel tells stories about the makers, wearers, and symbols important to nations, tribes, villages, clans, families, and individuals. The oral histories, songtexts, and sacred narratives—often called myths, creation stories, or Indian literature—are much more than extraordinary tales: they concern the land and the spirits of the land, important animals and plants, the history of the world and the people in it, and important religious and moral beliefs. The outlook embodied in these records reveal how Indians view their lives in relation to the rest of the world.

Musical Traits

In Indian music, the voice is the most important instrument. Vocal music includes solo pieces, responsorial songs (in which leader and chorus take turns), unison choral songs, and multipart songs, some with rattle and/or drum accompaniment. Many singers use a drum to set the beat and cue dancers, but rattles and sometimes whistles are common. Singers perform mostly in their native languages, but many songs convey their melodies in vocables—nonlexical syllables, such as *he, ya, ho, we,* and so on.

Songs usually begin with a soft, slow, stately drumbeat and get louder and faster as they go along. Hard and soft drumbeats, accented patterns, rattle-and-drum tremolos, and shouts enliven performances. These often signal important words, repeats, and changes of movement or direction for singers and dancers. Many such musical traits—the words, the number of repetitions, the instruments, the ways the singers work together—reflect a particular worldview and depend largely on the dance or ceremony being performed.

Songtexts

Many of the most ancient and least-changing songs are not intended to be sung in public or translated for the uninitiated. These songs are reserved for ceremonial occasions, which are often sacred and secret; they are usually not allowed to be recorded or made available for study. In contrast, ritual speeches performed at public ceremonies often sound musical because they employ rhythm and melody absent from everyday language; these are not usually secret, because any speaker of the language in which they are uttered can understand them. Often speakers refer to an event that is happening and explain its significance. For example, during a ritual speech preceding a stomp dance, a Cherokee speaker might discuss singing, dancing, being happy, and the all-night shaking of turtleshell rattles.

Songs often reference historical and current events. Probably the best-known Navajo song is "Shi' naasha'," composed in 1868 to mark the Navajos' release from internment at Fort Sumner, New Mexico (1864–1868), southeast of Albuquerque. The text expresses the people's joy in returning home. Unlike many other Navajo songs, it has a text of which almost every syllable is translatable. The words of the first stanza may be freely translated:

> I am walking, alive.
> Where I am is beautiful.
> I am still walking (lonely, sad, or nostalgic).

In "Shi' naasha'," vocables mark the beginning and ending phrase of each section; the same vocable phrase, *he ya he ne ya*, marks the end of the song.

Many tribes and nations have composed national anthems ("flag songs") in their own languages and styles. These are performed at the beginning of pow-wows and other traditional events. They are treated seriously: all people present stand, the men remove their hats, and no dancing occurs.

The subjects of songs reinforce important cultural elements. The first of nine San Juan Pueblo butterfly dances, a ladies'-choice partner-dance performed in the spring, tells how the corn is growing, starting from the sprout, and describes the green leaves, the red flower, and finally the white ear. It thanks Mother Earth, who produced that ear. The first section of the song is the entrance (*wasa*), sung entirely in vocables. The second section, the dance proper, includes vocables and Tewa words about growing corn.

Words can occur in songs in many ways: complete texts, isolated words sprinkled throughout, alternating phrases, verses with vocables, and words performed in improvisatory fashion. A Northern Plains rabbit dance with English words employs a typical placement for texts in Plains powwow songs:

A_1 = vocables (leader)
A_2 = vocables (chorus echoes leader)
B_1 = vocables (all)
C = text (all):

> Hey Sweetheart, I always think of you.
> I wonder if you are alone tonight, *hai yai*.
> I wonder if you are thinking of me,
> *Hai yai we ya hai ya*.

B_2 = vocables (all)

The song is then repeated, beginning with the second A section.

In the Cherokee stomp dance, the call–response style allows the leader freedom to improvise. After vocables establish each song in the cycle, the leader moves temporarily into a higher register and may improvise, adding Cherokee words or continuing in vocables; the chorus may then harmonize briefly, the melody may be altered, and the dancers may clap and add special hand-and-arm motions as they face the fire. The leader does not have to add words; the entire song is done with vocables if the leader so desires. The songs in the cycle are separated by shouts. One Cherokee song with words mentions the stomp dance, the song being used and its origin, the tobacco, and the group assembled at the stomp ground; another discusses the song itself, how quickly it starts, and how beautiful it is.

A few singers have incorporated popular tunes and words into social dance songs—pieces such as "Jambalaya" and "Sugar in the Morning" for the Navajo, "Dixie" for the Hopi, and "Amazing Grace" (in a buffalo-dance song) for the Jemez Pueblo in New Mexico.

Musical Origins and Sources

The origins of North American aboriginal peoples' music are many and varied. Some songs are described as coming from creation stories, individual inspiration, dreams, visions, personal or group experiences, purposeful composition, collaborative efforts, reworking time-tested models, buying, selling, inheriting, or misappropriating. Composers and singers cite many examples when music was taught or given supernaturally. For example, Changing Woman, a central character in Navajo mythology, the architect of creation, sings the world into being; accordingly, certain songs when sung by a Navajo ceremonial leader can reunite or restore the order of the universe and appease the forces of evil. The Lakota people trace their pipe ceremony and "Buffalo Calf Pipe Song" to White Buffalo Woman, who taught the ceremony to the people, and then departed and later transformed into a white buffalo. The warriors who founded the Lakota Fox Society followed the sound of singing to an old fox who taught them the first songs and rules for their men's association. On the Plains, songs were often described not as *taught*, but as *given*, by guardian spirits such as the fox; these songs were theoretically learned in one sitting.

Some aboriginal people still fast and seek visions that may include songs taught by animal or other guardian spirits. Songs can be inspired by natural sounds—from rivers, winds, and animals. Winnebago singers consider drums a source of songs, and believe that songs come from or exist in the air. Singers often talk about "catching" songs. In addition, songs are given, sold, or exchanged for many reasons, as when ceremonial activities and objects are transferred, people are initiated into societies, power is passed on, or honor and friendship are celebrated.

Some aboriginal American cultures encourage creativity, but others require exact duplication of music from performance to performance. Most recognize a need for new compositions and a desire to maintain as many old ones as possible. Improvisatory techniques, particularly in call-and-response songs, are a type of composition. The numbers of permissible verses and repetitions are often based on sacred numbers. When an old song or ceremony is revived, it is often renewed or updated in some fashion.

In some communities, musicians do not compose new pieces because of the revered origin of the age-old songs. The Cherokee provide an example. A Cherokee origin story concerns the cannibal monster Stonecoat, which introduced death to the Cherokee by eating unsuspecting villagers' livers. To weaken him, medicine men positioned seven menstruating women in his path (seven is a Cherokee sacred number). As he passed each woman in succession, he became weaker, and finally he was captured and burned. While he was burning, he sang all the songs that the Cherokee will ever need for dances, magic, and curing, and instructed the people as to the proper uses of the songs. Because music has a supernatural origin, the Cherokee do not formally compose songs, preferring to express their creativity through improvisation. The forms of music found in the stomp dance and in animal and agricultural songs, particularly the responsorial songs, allow for improvisation in words, melodies, and lengths.

Society and Gender

In many reservation or rural settings where tribal members live near each other, all or most community members are expected to participate in music-and-dance events, such as powwows, ceremonies, social dances, fiddle festivals, and hymn singings. Plains women often show approval by singing ululations (*lulus*). The lead dancer at a powwow sometimes blows a whistle, praising singers and calling for a repetition. If a Cherokee man does not lead the stomp dance well, or if he is of poor character, women will not dance behind him with their leg rattles, and he will have to leave the circle. By contrast, a young singer just learning to lead brings out all the people to dance with him and support his efforts.

Women can participate as singers, dancers, and instrumentalists in many events, but in others they must observe custom and not partake. Dances and songs for women are few. In the Northeast and Southeast, there are a few ceremonial and social dances for women. In these, one man or a few men provide the music—or, more recently, a women's singing group is featured. Ordinarily women may sing softly while they dance, accompanying themselves with leg rattles. In California and the Great Basin, there are hand-game songs for women alone, and in California and the Northwest Coast, many medicine songs, love songs, and other consequential songs are exclusively for women.

Dozens of ceremonies, songs, and dances throughout North America cannot be performed without women. Southeastern women provide accompaniment by shaking their leg rattles for animal, friendship, and closing dances, but they regularly have singing roles in the horse and ballgame dances. The Ojibwa women's dances in Wisconsin include a section in which the men drop out and the women sing alone, highlighting the words. Iroquois social dances require women's participation, particularly as dancers. Women's dance songs are the most popular type of song in singing contests, with all-female ensembles participating in recent times.

Tradition and Native American Music

North American Indians use the word *traditional* to refer to the languages, religions, artistic forms, everyday customs, and individual behavior that adhere to the oldest norms. They also use the word to refer to modern practices based on those norms. North American Indians organize and participate in festivals, social dances, games, special ceremonies, family and clan events, hymn singings, powwows, and medicine rites. Music pervades their lives, starting with creation stories and ending with death and memorial songs. North American Indian music emphasizes the traditions and values of Indian people, and has influenced American and Canadian society.

—Adapted from an article by Charlotte Heth

Bibliography

Amoss, Pamela. 1978. *Coast Salish Spirit Dancing: The Survival of an Ancestral Religion.* Seattle: University of Washington Press.

Bahti, Tom. 1970. *Southwestern Indian Ceremonials.* Flagstaff, Ariz.: KC Publications.

Cole, Douglas, and Ira Chaikin. 1990. *An Iron Hand upon the People: The Law against the Potlatch on the Northwest Coast.* Seattle: University of Washington Press.

Diamond, Beverley, et al. 1994. *Visions of Sound: Musical Instruments of First Nations Communities in Northeastern America*. Chicago: University of Chicago Press, and Waterloo: Wilfrid Launer University Press.

Gombert, Greg. 1994. *A Guide to Native American Music Recordings*. Fort Collins, Colo.: Multi Cultural Publishing.

Haefer, J. Richard. 1977. *Papago Music and Dance*. Tsalie, Ariz.: Navajo Community College Press.

Howard, James Henri. 1981. *Shawnee! The Ceremonialism of a Native Indian Tribe and Its Cultural Background*. Athens: Ohio University Press.

——, and Victoria Lindsay Levine. 1990. *Choctaw Music and Dance*. Norman: University of Oklahoma Press.

Keeling, Richard H. 1992. *Cry for Luck: Sacred Song and Speech among the Yurok, Hupa, and Karok Indians of Northwestern California*. Berkeley: University of California Press.

——. 1997. *North American Indian Music: A Guide to Published Sources and Selected Recordings (1535–1995)*. Garland Library of Music Ethnology, 5. New York: Garland Publishing.

McAllester, David P. 1964. *Peyote Music*. New York: Johnson Reprint Corporation.

——. 1973. *Enemy Way Music: A Study of Social and Esthetic Values as Seen in Navaho Music*. Milwood, N.Y.: Kraus Reprint Co.

Mishler, Craig. 1993. *The Crooked Stovepipe: Athapaskan Fiddle Music and Square Dancing in Northeast Alaska and Northwest Canada*. Urbana: University of Illinois Press.

Painter, Muriel Thayer. 1986. *With Good Heart: Yaqui Beliefs and Ceremonies in Pascua Village*. Tucson: University of Arizona Press.

Powers, William K. 1977. *Oglala Religion*. Lincoln: University of Nebraska Press.

——. 1982. *Yuwipi, Vision and Experience in Oglala*. Lincoln: University of Nebraska Press.

——. 1990a. *Voices from the Spirit World: Lakota Ghost Dance Songs*. Kendall Park, N.J.: Lakota Books.

——. 1990b. *War Dance: Plains Indian Musical Performance*. Tucson: University of Arizona Press.

Wyman, Leland Clifton. 1975. *The Mountainway of the Navajo*. Tucson: University of Arizona Press.

Musical Instruments

The term *musical instruments* is a misnomer for North American Indian cultures, as Indian languages did not have a word for *music*. Therefore, we must look to the cultures themselves to find terms used to specify items called musical instruments in English. Nearly every North American Indian culture has a term for song and a term referring to objects we call musical instruments. An example from the Tohono O'odham (formerly called the Papago; Tohono O'odham literally means *desert people*) of the American Southwest will illustrate this.

The Tohono O'odham call musical instruments *ñe'icuda* 'songmakers'. In O'odham culture, a gourd rattle, a basket drum, and scraping sticks are necessary to make or produce *ñe'i* 'song'. Without these instruments, song could not exist. When one learns or dreams a song, one learns what *ñe'icuda* to use, how to use it, and when and where to sing the song.

The O'odham call some musical instruments *piastakud*. The root *piasta* is borrowed from the Spanish lexeme *fiesta*; the suffix *kud* in the Piman language denotes a 'thing of' something, so the whole word means 'thing of a fiesta'. Instruments such as the saxophone, the guitar, the bass, and the drumset—used to perform what the O'odham call chicken-scratch music (*waila*)—are literally 'things of the fiesta', not *ñe'icuda*. They cannot be songmakers, as the music played at these dances is not *ñe'i* 'song', but polkas, schottisches, and two-steps, borrowed from nineteenth-century Mexico. Chicken-scratch music, though thoroughly incorporated into O'odham culture, is not conceived to be in the same class as O'odham music. Hence the O'odham have two distinct classes of musical instruments: songmakers and fiesta things.

North American Indians played and still play many kinds of musical instruments. They have abandoned the use of some, notably winds (the Plains flute being an exception), but they have borrowed instruments of non-Indian origins. This borrowing might better be called adapting, as illustrated in the O'odham use of instruments in chicken-scratch music.

Instrument Types

Several methods for the classification of musical instruments have been devised. Probably the most significant method for comparing instruments across cultures is the one proposed by Eric von Hornbostel and Curt Sachs in 1914. They based their classification on the method of producing sound in each instrument type: idiophone—in which the instrument itself vibrates; membranophone—in which a skin vibrates; aerophone—in which a column of air or air acting on the instrument vibrates; and chordophone—in which a string vibrates. Although this approach is easy for cross-cultural understanding, it is important to remember the significance of the cultural conceptions of musical instruments noted above.

Self-sounders (Idiophones)
This class of instruments, which includes rattles and clappers, is by far the largest in prehistoric and historic North American aboriginal cultures and is best discussed in regard to its subgroups.

Body Movements
The most readily accessible idiophone is the human body, though few reports of body movements as an intentional producer of music sound exist for North America. In the Northwest Coast and Northern California, handclapping accompanies singing. Body movements, especially those of dancers, may produce sound indirectly by the movement of clothing that may have jingles or bells attached. The stamping of feet may be considered a part of the body-sound continuum, especially in the South. The three predominant idiophones in North America are notched sticks and suspension and container rattles.

Notched-stick Rasps
The rasp is found predominantly in the Great Basin and the Southwest, and scattered through the lower Mississippi Valley, the Plains, and the Northeast. It usually consists of a length of wood or bone with notches or teeth cut along one side. It is scraped by another stick, or often by a scapular bone, to produce a grating sound. Resonators for it are made from inverted baskets, half-gourds, or even metal- or hide-covered holes in the ground. In some areas, especially the Pueblos of the Southwest, it is highly decorated, carried in dancers' hands, and used without resonators. In the southern Mississippi area, an alligator skin may serve as a rasp; inverted baskets are rubbed as rasps in Arizona.

Rattles

Suspension or Jingle Rattles Suspension rattles are made by suspending objects, usually from a stick, so that when shaken, the objects audibly strike one another. They are found throughout the United States, most densely from the Mexican border north along the west side of the Rockies and into Canada. The suspended objects include animal hooves (predominantly of deer or mountain sheep), claws (especially of bear), and bones, bird beaks, and tin jingles; hooves are the most widespread. These objects may be suspended from a stick, a cord, or a ring, or tied to a dancer's body or to clothing. They may hang from the ceiling, or from poles within a ceremonial structure, and small groups of them may be attached to other instruments, such as drums and whistles.

Container Rattles By far the most widespread and varied sound-producing instrument in North American Indian cultures is the container rattle (figure 1), found everywhere except in the Arctic. The major variable in the construction of container rattles is the material, which was traditionally taken

Figure 1 Container rattles used by Arikara Bear Medicine Men.
Photo by Edward S. Curtis, 1908. Library of Congress, Prints & Photographs Division, LC-USZ62–101186.

from local environments; at the beginning of the twenty-first century, many materials are widely distributed and sold from culture to culture.

Container rattles are made from gourds in the South (particularly the Southwest), from cow and buffalo hide (including the scrotum) on the Plains, wood in the Northwest, bark in the Northeast and the Great Lakes area, and turtleshells (box turtles in the South and terrapins in the Northeast). Local and less frequently used variants include coconuts (Southeast), baskets (Northwest Coast and Southwest), copper (Northwest Coast), cocoon shells (Southwest and California), bark (Great Lakes), small animal skulls (Northeast and Great Lakes), and pottery (Pueblos).

Drums (Membranophones)

Drums using a stretched skin are found in variations based on the number of heads, the shape and size (and in turn the number of people playing them), and whether or not they contain water. Examples of simple drums, consisting of a loose skin tied to four stakes (or held by people) and struck with a beater by a single person, are found in the central area west of the Rocky Mountains and on the Northern Plains.

Frame Drum

The most prevalent North American Indian drum is the frame drum with either a single or a double head (figure 2). Often erroneously called a hand drum or a tambourine drum, it is found throughout the entire continent except in lower California and parts of Arizona. Typically it has a circular frame, traditionally a bent stave of wood; in the late nineteenth century, cheese boxes became popular substitutes. When the frame supports a single head, the skin is usually knotted in the back to form a grip for the hand. Double-headed frame drums have a handle of hide thongs attached to the frame. Local variants include the Eskimo *someak*, which is single-headed with a short handle of wood, ivory, or bone on its lower side. The diameter of frame drums varies from four inches to more than thirty; on the Northern Plains, it is about fifteen inches. The depth of the frame varies from the one-inch Eskimo frame to three- or four-inch frames. The frame drum is normally held in one hand and struck with a beater held in the other hand.

The Log Drum

The so-called log drum consists of an instrument with one or usually two hide heads, which vary regionally in diameter and height. It is so named because it was traditionally made by hollowing out a log; similar instruments were made from barrel staves after contact with Europeans. In the Southwest, it

Figure 2 A drummer on Nunivak Island plays a frame drum. The skin from this instrument is made of walrus stomach or bladder.
Photo by Edward S. Curtis, 1929. Library of Congress, Prints & Photographs Division, LC-USZ62–46887.

usually has a diameter of about twelve to fourteen inches and a height of about twenty-four to thirty-six inches, and is normally played by one person.

On the Plains and in the Great Lakes and Northeast, the log drum usually has a diameter wider than its height, and is played by more than one person. It was traditionally made from a log, but the use of barrel staves is prominent today, and is sometimes considered "traditional," as are those made by the Ojibwa drummaker William Benishi Baker. This is the style of instrument that has become associated with the contemporary powwow, and so it is often called a powwow drum (figure 3). The Pueblos play log drums of either shape and size; their choice of instrument varies with the function or ceremonial activity.

Water Drums
Water drums vary from the oldest, traditional style, consisting of a pottery vessel used by the Navajo, to modern ones made from cooking pots. The Navajo instrument is an elongated vessel covered by a buckskin tied around the lip. In the Great Lakes area and the Northeast, wooden containers are partly filled with water and covered by skin, secured by an outer ring. The Ojibwa and Menominee use a hollowed-out log about fifteen inches tall, and the Iroquois use containers about four to five inches tall made from staves, probably devised from nail kegs brought from Europe. The Apache make a water drum from a cooking pot by removing the handle. A more specialized water drum, associated with the Peyote religion

(the Native American Church), is made from a metal cooking pot; its head is laced on in a star pattern, as prescribed by the norms of the religion.

Winds (Aerophones)
Instruments that use a column of vibrating air to produce sound include flutes, whistles, and bull-roarers.

Flutes
The most widespread wind instrument is the flute. Its traits, such as the number of soundholes and the type of material used in its manufacture, vary across the continent. North American flutes are of the internal duct type, with a hollowed interior tube containing a block, usually of the same material as the tube, that diverts the airstream to an exterior cap, which in turn directs air across a lip, causing the air column to vibrate. Flute stops (fingerholes) vary from one to nine depending on the culture—for example, three for the O'odham, four for the Yuman, and more among Northern Plains peoples. Flutes are made from cedar (Sioux and Northern Plains) and various other woods (like box elder), cane (O'odham, Yuman), bark (Northeast and Northwest), pottery (Rio Grande area), and even bone. Globular wooden flutes are found in the Northwest. Nearly all North American Indian flutes are end-blown, but side-blown instruments are reported for the Plateau, and a noseflute was apparently used in the Great Basin in the distant past.

Figure 3 A powwow drum is played by musicians at a powwow at Kent State University in Ohio, 2004. *Photo by Terry E. Miller.*

Whistles

Whistles are most commonly made from bone, usually the leg bone of an eagle on the Plains; cane and wooden whistles are found in California and the Northwest Coast. The interior deflector of whistles is normally a piece of pitch or resin, and the lower end of the instrument may be plugged with similar material. Bone whistles are commonly decorated with direct painting or etching, or (on the Plains) covered with quills or beadwork. In the Northern Plains, the distal end of wooden whistles is usually splayed and often carved as a bird's head; on the Northwest Coast, globular whistles may resemble human heads. More unusual are individual tubes connected in panpipe style.

Bullroarer

The bullroarer is used by many cultures in the American West. Consisting of one or occasionally two slats of wood attached to a long cord, it is swung in a circle overhead or beside the performer. The wood spins on its axis and creates a column of moving air, which has a typically humming, whooshing sound. The purpose of bullroarers varies from child's toy to ceremonial object; some are said to represent the sounds of wind, thunder, rain, and spirits. Whirling disks on cords produce sounds, but serve only as toys.

—*Adapted from an article by J. Richard Haefer*

Bibliography

Diamond, Beverley, M. Sam Cronk, and Franziska von Rosen. 1994. *Visions of Sound: Musical Instruments of First Nations Communities in Northeastern America.* Chicago Studies in Ethnomusicology. Chicago: University of Chicago Press.

Haefer, J. Richard. 1975. "North American Indian Musical Instruments: Some Organological Distribution Problems." *Journal of the American Musical Instrument Society* 1:56–85.

——. 1982. "Musical Thought in Papago Culture." Ph.D. dissertation, University of Illinois.

Vennum, Thomas Jr. 1982. *The Ojibwe Dance Drum: Its History and Construction.* Smithsonian Folklife Studies, 2. Washington, D.C.: Smithsonian Institution.

Musicmaking in Arctic Canada and Alaska

The Arctic encompasses an immense area, ranging from the Atlantic to the Pacific Oceans across the highest portion of North America. This area features a variety of ecosystems and landscapes and hosts several different cultural and linguistic groups. Two large and distinct musical cultures are discussed in this article: those of the Western Arctic and those of the Central and Eastern Arctic.

Culture of the Arctic

Arctic peoples belong to the Eskimo-Aleut linguistic family, which subdivides into three principal linguistic groups: Aleut, Yupik, and Inupiat. The Inupiat are by far the largest group, ranging from northern Alaska to northeastern Canada and Greenland. In Canada, Inupiat people call themselves Inuit. Thus, one may distinguish among the Mackenzie Delta Inuit, the Copper Inuit, the Netsilik Inuit, the Iglulik Inuit, the Caribou Inuit, the South Baffinland Inuit, and the Inuit of Québec and Labrador Coast. In theory, all Inupiat groups share a single language, but important dialectical and cultural differences exist.

Relationships to Other Culture Areas

Typical of the Arctic populations is relative isolation from non-Eskimoan cultures; however, North American Arctic populations share a circumpolar continuum with Siberian and Greenland Inuit. The southern margin of the Arctic is a no-man's land, the barrens, used sporadically by Arctic peoples for hunting and fishing. In the past, Inuit and Indian bands met in this zone, often at war with one another, but exchanging goods during peaceful episodes.

Musical Performance

Musicmaking in the Arctic primarily involves voices and drums. Many songtypes are exclusively vocal, and the use of one or several drums is mostly restricted to large gatherings. Even if songs have been composed expressly for the drum dance, they can be sung on intimate occasions without drumming and dancing, especially if they recount anecdotes concerning the singer's life, or if they express personal feelings and emotions. Drums are never played by themselves: they only accompany singing or dancing.

Figure 1 Drawing illustrating Arctic drumming performance techniques. Illustration François Girard. *Top left*: In the Western Arctic, Inupiat groups of drummers, usually seated, hit their drums from below, either the rim with the stick, or the center of the membrane in order to produce different timbres and volumes. They are singing for dancers in front of them. *Top right*: In the Western Arctic, Yupik groups of drummers, usually seated, hit their drums from above, always in the center of the membrane. They are singing for dancers in front of them. *Center*: In the Central and Eastern Arctic, the single Inuit drummer rotates his (usually) large drum so that his sticks alternately hit one, then the other underside rim. He dances as he is drumming to a song sung by a group of singers seated around him.

Drums and Other Soundmakers

With very few exceptions, the only drum-construction principle prevailing in Arctic areas involves stretching an animal skin over a relatively thin round wood frame. A handle is attached to the frame with lacing and a tongue-and-groove adjustment. There are important regional structural differences in performance practices between the Western Arctic and the Eastern and Central Arctic (figure 1). For personal pleasure, or to mark relationships with spirit-helpers, drummers freely decorate rims and handles with painted motifs. Only in the Western Arctic do people use another type of drum, the box drum, and then only for wolf dances.

Buzzers, bullroarers, and whistles existed in all Arctic regions, but did not figure prominently as musicmakers. Long ago in the Eastern Arctic, a metal jew's harp appeared, probably obtained from European fishermen and whalers. No doubt it became popular because it produced a louder sound than did the goose-feather quill. The creation of a crude box fiddle was probably inspired by encounters with sailors, who always included a fiddler on their expeditions.

Singing, Drumming, and Dancing

The term *personal songs* (in Central and Eastern Arctic, *pisirk*) designates songs that express a person's emotions and feelings or recount favorite anecdotes. These are composed singly or for drum dances. There are also songs to ask spirits for protection against dangers, illness, or evil. An individual's magic songs and formulas are used to influence events, such as wind and weather. Shamans communicate with spirit-helpers through their songs, and sometimes their drums, and thus effect cures and foretell events. Similar songs are in the Western Arctic drum-dance repertoire.

Numerous Inuit games—including juggling, hide-and-seek, rhymes, riddles, string games, and laughter-seeking games—require songs. Many games use sounds as the game element, requiring vocal abilities from a player, even though these sounds do not locally count as songs. The best-known of these games is the Eastern Arctic *katajjaq* (a word that lacks an exact English equivalent), in which two women face one another, almost touching, and repeatedly utter predetermined sound patterns—words, animal cries, or melodic fragments. Their voices, alternating among various vocal qualities—respiration patterns, registers, mouthshapes, voicedness, and voicelessness—follow each other as in Western contrapuntal imitation. The game requires rapid breathing, endurance, and quick reflexes, and it often becomes competitive. Most of the time, however, laughter and fun prevail over winning or losing. *Katajjaq*-type sounds are used in a similar game found predominantly in the Central Arctic (but not in the Western Arctic), in which words are part of a series (with narrative intent or not), rather than repeated.

Few songs are exclusively reserved for children; however, one children's song (*aqausiq*), typical of the Central and Eastern Arctic, symbolizes the special connection between a child and one or several close-kin adults. A child may own several such songs and cherish them throughout his or her life. These songs use diminutive forms of the child's name, or words pertaining to realities that warrant close attention.

The widespread tradition of storytelling—myth, legends, personal anecdotes—occasionally features songs. Songs often express dialogues between humans or animal characters, imitations of animal cries, and expressions of feelings and forebodings.

Drum Dancing in the Western Arctic

Drum dancing in the Western Arctic is an essential ingredient of annual rituals. Informal drum dances are often held at the end of festivals or interspersed with more formal events. Many festivals are held to appease the spirits of animals slain in the past year; deference to these spirits ensures that the species will allow more killing, therefore ensuring the group's survival for another year. The Yupik Bladder Feast and the Inupiat Whale Feast are the most elaborate and significant.

Another important feast complex concerns the relationship between the living and the souls of the deceased. A funeral ritual and a memorial ritual performed several years later are essential to this relationship. These festivals nearly always involve guests from other villages, to whom gifts are offered. Potlatching, a ritual form of giving gifts, involves costuming, masking, and feasting. Subjects of songs and their related mimetic dances pertain to the relationship among hosts, guests, and the deceased person (or group of persons) honored by the event.

As many drummers as are available sit or stand in a semicircle facing the audience. They sing songs composed and rehearsed for the occasion or chosen from an older repertoire. Dancers, both men and women, stand in front of them, forming a circle or a double semicircle facing the audience; they do not sing. In general, dancers stand in one spot, bouncing lightly, by flexing their knees in time with the drumbeats; arms and the upper body perform expressive movements. Men and women perform identical motions, but men move more vigorously. In some men-only dances, for example, performers leap and move around more freely, but still in synchrony with the drumbeats.

Drum dances and festivals are held in one of the large men's houses (*kasigi*) belonging to the host group. Informal dancing occurs, especially in summer, whenever small bands of performers simply want to enjoy themselves.

Central and Eastern Arctic Drum Dance

In the Central and Eastern Arctic drum-dancing tradition, a single drum dancer performs, surrounded by close relatives, who sing the songs he composed. This usually takes place inside a large snowhouse (*qaggi*), erected especially for the communal feasts, games, and dances that take place when nomadic bands gather for a long period of time. The drum dancer performs until he runs out of songs, or until he tires. He then is replaced by another, then another, and so forth. Thus, being a good drum dancer entails composing interesting songs, but also demonstrating strength and endurance. Dance motions, mainly performed with the upper body, are relatively free and adjusted to the swaying of the drum, which moves so that its rim meets the stick on one side, then on the opposite side. The drum dancer moves around inside the circle formed by the audience. He dances to songs telling personal stories, expressing the emotions engendered in him with body movements and with improvised cries and yells.

A partnership system exists in this region—usually two men ("song cousins") who dance and sing humorously to and about each other. Each man's songs publicize the other's idiosyncrasies, making people laugh. Such competitions may acquire grim meanings when a serious conflict arises between two people or two families. This must be resolved publicly, in a drum-dance duel. Songs of ridicule are then carefully prepared, and the singer-dancer who elicits the most laughter from the audience wins his case. In extreme cases, such as murder or theft, the loser may find himself in a life-threatening position if he is forbidden to participate in food-and-work-sharing networks, essential for survival in the Arctic. The drum dance thus functions in community life at several levels: as entertainment, as an expression of personal emotions, as an amusing competition, and as a means for resolving conflict.

Musical Styles

The vocal qualities of Arctic singing vary according to whether the performance is public or private: with the exception of the Eastern Arctic vocal games, context determines style. The soft, gentle voice used in private settings is sometimes transformed for character illustration in a story, but in public performances of drum dances, singers use a loud, resonant voice to compete with the booming drums. In the Western Arctic, loudness sometimes entails nasality. In the Eastern Arctic, the drum dancer punctuates his words and movements with cries of indeterminate length and tone, emphasizing emotion.

When men and women sing together, their singing is monophonic, with unison or octave doublings; however, in several communities of the West Coast of Hudson's Bay (Eastern Arctic), singers sometimes double melodies at the interval of a fifth or a fourth. Some scholars believed this to be an example of polyphony, but it is probably best regarded as an expanded form of unison, in which women's voices, higher than men's voices, sing in perfect parallel.

Texts

Different genres require different textual styles, of which there are many regional variants. In general, text settings are syllabic, with the occasional lengthening of a vowel on one or two tones or on a long-sustained tone, softly articulated with glottal pulsations. In many areas, consonants are somewhat softened, especially at the beginnings and ends of songs, making some words indistinct. Most of the time, meanings are conveyed through textual symbolism, imagery, and indirect references, using only a few meaningful words. Words are interspersed with vocables, of which the most typical throughout the Arctic are variants of the syllables ai-ya-ya or ai-ya-yanga. At times, these vocables emphasize feelings or fill in incomplete thoughts; they frequently begin and end phrases. They are used so consistently throughout the Arctic that songs typically called *pisirk* (the significance of which varies regionally) are often simply called ai-ya-ya.

Song Structures and Traits

With the exception of some through-composed game songs, Arctic song structures feature one or several melodic phrases that repeat with melodic and textual variation. Phrase length is determined by the number of words that need to be said, and sections made of one or several phrases are set off by lengthened notes on a single vowel.

The number of tones and their range varies widely by genre and area. Most songs use six different tones. Magical songs and story songs use fewer tones, smaller ranges, and more-frequent monotonic repetitions; game songs and drum-dance songs use the most tones and the widest ranges, sometimes as much as a twelfth. Songs typically have numerous textual repetitions, sometimes featuring two- or three-note melodic-rhythmic motifs (for example, Eastern Arctic game songs, magical songs, *aqausiq*) or four- or five-note melodic motifs whose rhythms derive from the nature of the text (for example, Alaskan drum-dance songs). In general, there is no metric regularity because rhythm is determined by word length and accentuation and thus has a recitativelike style. In drum dances, the drums beat a regular pulse of even-spaced single or double beats, the first being slightly shorter than the second.

—Adapted from an article by Nicole Beaudry

323

Bibliography

Beaudry, Nicole. 1978. "Le katajjaq: Un jeu inuit traditionnel." *Études/Inuit/Studies* 2(1):35–53.

———. 1986. "La danse à tambour des Esquimaux yupik du sud-ouest de l'Alaska: performance et contexte." Ph.D. dissertation, Université de Montréal.

Boas, Franz. 1888. *The Central Eskimo*. Sixth Annual Report of the Bureau of American Ethnology. Washington: Smithsonian Institution.

Johnston, Thomas F. 1976. *Eskimo Music by Region: A Comparative Circumpolar Study*. Canadian Ethnology Service paper 32. Ottawa: National Museums of Canada.

———. 1980. "Music of the Alaskan Eskimos." In *Musics of Many Cultures*, edited by Elizabeth May, 332–362. Berkeley: University of California Press.

Koranda, Lorraine. 1972. *Alaskan Eskimo Songs and Stories*. Seattle: University of Washington Press.

Sturtevant, William C., and David Damas, eds. 1984. *Arctic. Handbook of North American Indians*, 5. Washington, D.C.: Smithsonian Institution.

Métis

Métis peoples are those of mixed French and aboriginal ancestry; however, defining Métis identity and culture is far from simple. The word came into common use in the 1800s on the Canadian prairies to denote the children of French traders and aboriginal women, largely Cree and Ojibwa. These intermarriages spawned a syncretic culture, including distinctive languages, called *Mitchif* (or *Métchif*), and clothing, food, and music. But Métis peoples live in every province and territory of Canada and many of the northern U.S. states, roughly following the old east–west fur-trade routes, with some expansion northward and southward. It is therefore difficult to draw clear dividing lines between Métis, French, and aboriginal peoples, and aspects of Métis musical traditions extend into aboriginal, Inuit, and French communities.

Métis culture is perhaps best considered a complex of traditions with regional and even family variations. Given that numerous aboriginal cultures inhabited wide territories, it is surprising that recent studies reveal as much common ground as they do. What these studies show is a distinctive fiddle-and-dance tradition, which combines elements of Scottish, French-Canadian, American, and aboriginal cultures and shares common elements from Acadia to Alaska.

Fiddling and Dancing

Fiddling was so central to Métis culture and so identified with it at one time that players at Turtle Mountain, North Dakota, say, "There's no Métchif without no fiddle. The dancin' and the fiddle and the Métchif, they're all the same" (Leary 1992:27). Largely a male practice until recently, the fiddle tradition involves a style of playing and a core repertoire that can be traced to the fur trade in early Canada. This article examines what is known about it throughout its range, even as it occurs among peoples who identify themselves not as Métis, but as French or members of Saulteaux, Ojibwa, Cree, North Athapaskan, or other aboriginal cultures.

Athapaskan is a linguistic family that includes the languages of numerous tribal groups in Subartic North America and of the Navajo and Apache in the southwestern United States and northern Mexico.

Our knowledge of early Métis music comes from diaries, letters, and writings of non-Métis writers and from twentieth-century collections of oral traditions still active in Métis communities. By all accounts, fiddling for dancing became the mainstay of fur-trade culture in the nineteenth century. It was adopted by French, aboriginal, Métis, and Scots alike, and in many areas it replaced older indigenous musical traditions, especially in the late 1800s, when laws banning indigenous religious practices were passed. Evidence from Ontario suggests that many features of the older style survive in Cree communities in the north, but that more southern Métis communities are influenced by Ottawa Valley French and Irish practice; however, large gaps in our current knowledge remain.

Cultural Influences

The most noticeably distinctive feature of the older northwest Métis fiddle repertoire is highly asymmetric phrasing, a feature of much traditional aboriginal singing. Rather than the common two-section, four-phrase, thirty-two-bar form of Scottish tradition, forms vary widely from tune to tune, with no standard phrase length, number of phrases, or repeat patterns. In Manitoba, for example, a tune not uncommonly has phrases that vary in length between three and nine beats, which may or may not repeat, with phrases of five beats being especially common. The degree of formal irregularity varies from place to place, but current evidence suggests it is highest in communities where aboriginal languages are spoken.

Older fiddling exhibits other features of old aboriginal song, such as introductory and tag phrases, overlapping phrases, embellished cadences, and descending melodic contours. In this sense, it is not unlike the Mitchif language, which, in one version, is described as having a largely French vocabulary and an Algonkian-Ojibwa-Cree grammar. Similarly, the fiddle tradition can considered to have a largely Scottish and French vocabulary and an aboriginal structure. These features can be seen by comparing a Scottish version of a well-known tune with one of its Métis versions.

Indigenous influence is evident in attitudes surrounding fiddling. For example, there is often a sense of personal ownership of particular versions of tunes. Some people feel the tunes should not be

325

recorded, and there are stories that tapes have been erased, sometimes in mysterious ways, after their player has died. In Turtle Mountain, older players sometimes put rattlesnake rattles or other natural objects inside their fiddles; in Alaska, they decorate them with such symbols as feathers, ribbons, or beadwork. In Ontario, Vic "Chiga" Groulx, an elder of the Métis nation of Ontario, speaks of the fiddle as having a soul and the wood as being alive—a belief echoed on the prairies.

Aspects of Style

Clogging patterns involving both feet to accompany fiddling are common in Métis, aboriginal, and French-Canadian areas. A feature unique to North American fiddling, this seems to have developed in fur-trade culture. Whether it was of French-Canadian or indigenous origin we shall probably never know; however, there are interesting differences between Québécois and Métis–Native practice. Figure 1 shows the rhythms most commonly found in Métis/Native areas

In Québec, players do not generally clog in 6/8 rhythm, and though some use the 2/4 rhythm given here, Québécois players frequently fill in the pattern (figure 2). Some Québec players have a pattern for waltzes, and most Métis waltzes are played to a steady foot on every beat.

Altered tunings are used in Manitoba, Turtle Mountain, and Alaska–Yukon, most commonly (from lowest to highest) A–D–A–E and A–E–A–E. These are common in older Scottish traditions, in Québec, and in U.S. styles.

Bowing in the older style uses short, generally separate strokes, mixed with two-note slurs, as with French-Canadian bowing; however, there seems to be a stronger offbeat accent than in Québec, especially

Figure 1 Clogging patterns in 2/4 and 6/8 from Ebb and Flow Manitoba. *R* denotes the right foot, *L* denotes the left foot, though some patterns are reversed.

Figure 2 A standard Québécois clogging pattern for a reel.

in 6/8 tunes, resulting in two-note chords on accented notes. Some players practice what they call "double-stringing": playing extra open strings along with the melody. According to reports, this practice was much more popular in the past in all areas than it is now.

As in other North American fiddle traditions, older players tend to vary the tunes every time they play them, whereas younger players often have only one version of a tune. In Métis practice, variations can involve changes of phrasing, structure, and notes. Cadences, especially, frequently change length as players emphasize important notes by repeating and embellishing them.

The fiddle was generally unaccompanied until guitars came into use, in the mid-twentieth century. Sometimes a second fiddle was used, doubling the melody, playing in octaves, or playing drones or chords. In Turtle Mountain, one fiddler keeps time on the strings, playing a two-note chord on every beat with an off-the-string bow (lifted after each stroke); in addition, this technique, called "bucking" or "le boss," was used to teach.

Repertoire

Written descriptions of social events at fur-trading posts on Hudson's Bay and in the settlement of Red River (later Winnipeg) from the early 1800s report Scottish strathspeys, jigs, and reels, played by "Indian" fiddlers "to the vigorous accompaniment of the foot. We have known men to carry an extra pair of moccasins, so that when one pair was worn out on the rough floor they might not be at a loss" (Macbeth 1971:54). Strathspeys have largely disappeared, but jigs, marches, and reels of Scottish derivation, often called simply quadrilles or old Scotch reels, were still a mainstay of older players' repertoires in Manitoba in the 1980s. More than three hundred have been recorded from one player alone, Grandy Fagnan of Camperville, Manitoba. The Scottish forebears of some of these tunes are obvious, and further comparison with older Orkney, Shetland, and Scottish repertoire may reveal sources of others.

In all areas, older tunes are named for their dances: "Red River Jig," "Duck Dance," "Rabbit Dance," "Reel of Four," "Reel of Eight," "Hook Dance" (also called "Brandy" or "Drops of Brandy"), "La Double Gigue" ("Double Jig" in Alaska–Yukon), and "Handkerchief Dance" (or "Scarf Dance"). All these tunes are well-known on the prairies and in Alaska–Yukon. They appear to be related to dances from the Orkney and Shetland Islands. Each dance seems to have one particular tune associated with it everywhere in North America, but not always the same tune in every place. A few of the tunes are well-known ("Macdonald's Reel" for a "Reel of Eight," "Fisher's Hornpipe" for "La Double Gigue"), but others have proved elusive.

There are obvious Québécois connections in tunes and dances, further revealed by the use of the term *jig* in English for simple meter, corresponding to the French use of the word *gigue* for simple-time step-dance tunes. Thus, "La gigue de la rivière rouge" (in Québec, "La grande gigue simple") translates into "Red River Jig" and "La double gigue" into "Double Jig," with both being in simple duple time (though irregular), not in 6/8. Much of this Scottish-derived repertoire may have moved northwest from Québec. Some tunes, such as "Le brandy / Drops of Brandy" and "La grand gigue simple / Red River Jig," are regular in form in Quebec and asymmetric in Métis culture; others, such as "La double gigue," are irregular in both areas.

Step Dancing and the Red River Jig

West of Ontario, the Red River jig (figure 3) is considered a cornerstone of traditional Métis culture. Though still played in James Bay and northern Ontario, it is not common in more southerly Ontario Métis communities. The term *Red River jig* has become generic for step dancing in general (also called simply "jigging"), and the tune now almost universally played for it. There are reports in Manitoba of the former use of another "Red River jig" tune, known to some Acadian fiddlers. As with other tunes, fiddlers once took pride in having a personal version of "Red River jig," but the version recorded by Andy de Jarlis in the 1950s is most commonly heard today.

There are many regional variations in how and when the Red River jig is done, such as whether or not an individual, a couple, or several of either take to the floor simultaneously, the preferred posture, and whether the dance is done at a specific time (prairies) or whenever the dancers wish it (Alaska–Yukon), but some features are common throughout. The tune has two parts, a high-pitched one and a low-pitched one. The movements include a basic-time step on the high part and individual steps on the low part—steps that vary from person to person. Dancing is a test of endurance and skill; even in community settings, it has always been competitive in the number and complexity of steps. Some dancers claim to know thirty or more steps. In some areas, a straight posture with little movement besides that of the feet is prized (Winnipeg and Alaska–Yukon); in others, the body is bent over, almost to the floor (The Pas, Manitoba).

The Red River jig is danced by men and women. Many attest that the men's style and steps formerly differed from the women's, whose footwork involved smaller steps and less athletic movements, but the differences are less marked today. Though it is still a mainstay at social dances, it has been done in formal competitions since at least the 1930s in Manitoba. In competition, men and women, boys and girls usually compete separately and do only three fancy steps, being judged on each. At some contests, they preserve the circling movements common to community dances; at others, such as that held at Le Festival de Voyageur every winter in St. Boniface, Manitoba,

Figure 3 "Red River Jig," as played by Lawrence "Teddy Boy" Houle, 1985. *Transcription by Anne Lederman, field collection.*

each dancer must stay within a small square marked on the floor.

In most Métis communities, jigging is done throughout all group dances. Dancers usually do the basic-time step of the Red River jig, adapted to 6/8 when necessary, but in some northern areas, 6/8 is hardly ever played. Some dancers employ fancy steps during parts of the dances where they are not active. On the prairies, this practice of jigging constantly through all group dances is considered a way of distinguishing Métis communities from non-Métis ones.

—*Adapted from an article by Anne Lederman*

Bibliography

Bakker, Peter. 1992. *"A Language of our Own": The Genesis of Michif, the Mixed Cree-French Language of the Canadian Métis.* Amsterdam: University of Amsterdam.

Heth, Charlotte, producer. *Wood that Sings: Indian Fiddle Music of the Americas.* Smithsonian Folkways SF 40472.

Leary, James, ed. 1992. "Medicine Fiddle: A Humanities Discussion Guide." Booklet to accompany the film *Medicine Fiddle.* Marquette, Mich.: Northern Michigan University.

Lederman, Anne. 1984. "Fiddling in Western Manitoba." Hull, Québec: Audiotape Collection and Field Report, Canadian Centre for Folk Culture Studies, Canadian Museum of Civilization.

——. 1986. "Old Native and Métis Fiddling in Two Manitoba Communities: Camperville and Ebb and Flow." Master's thesis, York University.

——. 1988. "Old Indian and Métis Fiddling in Manitoba: Origins, Structure and the Question of Syncretism." *The Canadian Journal of Native Studies* 8(2):205–230. First published in *Canadian Folk Music Journal* 19:40–60.

——. 1989. "Dancing in Western Manitoba." Hull, Québec: Videotape Collection and Field Report, Canadian Centre for Folk Culture Studies, Canadian Museum of Civilization.

Loukinen, Michael. 1992. *Medicine Fiddle.* Marquette, Mich.: Up North Films.

Macbeth, R. G. 1971. *The Selkirk Settlers in Real Life.* Toronto: William Briggs.

Peterson, Jacquelin, and J. Brown, eds. 1987. *The New Peoples: Being and Becoming Métis in North America.* Winnipeg: University of Manitoba Press.

Whiddon, Lynn. 1993. *Métis Songs: Visiting Was the Métis Way.* New York: Gabriel Dumont Institute.

The Great Basin

The Great Basin Indians inhabited land that now includes much of Utah and Nevada and parts of Colorado, Wyoming, Idaho, Oregon, and California, plus the northern fringes of Arizona and New Mexico. The basin—a sunken area, also called a desert plateau—includes the mountains of the Humboldt Range of Nevada, the Wasatch Range of Utah, and the Rocky Mountains of Colorado, and other uplands, all of which provide forests and winter snows. The mountains block rainfall, however, creating an arid and harsh environment in most of the region. Over the ten thousand years of human occupation, large bodies of water, including the Great Salt Lake of Utah, have retreated in size.

The peoples occupying the basin today, whose ancestors arrived here from the South about 1000 C.E., include the Paiutes, Shoshones, Utes (Weeminuche or Weenuche), and Kawaiisu. The Washo, who live on land bordering California and Nevada, speak a common language with the Pomo and other, primarily northern Californian, groups. Distinct regional identities are claimed by the Northern Paiutes, the Owens Valley Paiutes, and the Southern Paiutes, who are linguistically closer to the Utes and the Kawaiisu than to the other Paiute groups. The Shoshones divide into Western, Eastern, and Northern groups, the latter traditionally associated with a Paiute group called Bannocks.

The introduction of the horse exaggerated regional tribal differences. Wherever the land sustained horses, as with the Northern and Eastern Shoshones and the Utes, buffalo hunting supplemented traditional lifeways. These groups adopted buffalo-skin clothing and tipis, and authorized chiefs to coordinate buffalo hunts and deal with enemies, who included the Nez Percé and the Flathead from the Columbia Plateau, the region north of the Great Basin. The Arapaho too were hostile, as were the Hidatsas, who became formidable after the 1700s, when they obtained firearms. Horses gave some Great Basin tribes an advantage over others, and some took Indian captives to sell as slaves to Spanish settlers.

The Ghost Dance

Beliefs in ghosts and a fear of the dead have always been common among American Indians. In the Great Basin, many believed that ghosts wanted to abduct the living. It is somewhat surprising, therefore, that the Ghost Dance gained as much momentum as it did. Many attribute this to the influence of Christian beliefs about heaven.

The Ghost Dance movement was preceded in the East by revivalist movements dating as far back as the 1760s. The Ghost Dance is believed to have been dreamed a century later by a Walker Lake–Walker River Northern Paiute prophet named Wodziwob. Another Paiute, Ta'vibo, from around Walker Lake, Nevada (southeast of present-day Carson City), spread Wodziwob's teachings, which included returning to the old ways of life and the resurrection of the dead. Around 1886, Ta'vibo's son Wovoka (Jack Wilson), a Northern Paiute medicine man, fused these teachings—now influenced by Mormon missionaries in Utah—with Christian ideas he had acquired when he had worked for a Presbyterian family named Wilson. Wovoka articulated a messianic promise: the Ghost Dance would restore life to what it had been, or better than it had been, before the Europeans had come: the buffalo would return, and the Europeans would disappear.

The movement quickly reached up to thirty-five nations, encompassing more than sixty thousand people. It was forbidden after the killing of about two hundred Lakota Sioux at Wounded Knee, South Dakota, in 1890, but Great Basin groups continued to sing its songs in association with a ritual for good health. Among the Wind River Shoshones, ethnomusicologist Judith Vander documented that Naraya songs rooted in Ghost Dance beliefs continued to be sung by some women for their own and others' physical well-being until the early 1980s, though most Shoshones had abandoned the beliefs and repertoire by 1940.

Music of the Ghost Dance

There exists a strong Great Basin influence in Ghost Dance songs, reflected in paired phrasing, the main stylistic identifier of this region. This involves simple melodic and textual repetitions of each of two or three phrases, for example (Mooney [1896]1973:963):

> E'yehe'! they are new—
> E'yehe'! they are new—
> The bed coverings,
> The bed coverings.

This song was received by a woman who, in her trance, was taken to a large camp where the tipis, beds, and interior furniture were made of new buffalo skins.

Songs were typically received in a trance induced by the Ghost Dance, in which hundreds of participants formed concentric circles, stepping to the left and dragging their right feet while the songs and dance got faster and faster. The stamping and dragging created a fine dust a few inches off the ground; every so often, someone would scoop some up and toss it into the air.

Traditional ideas held that ghosts took human and other forms, including that of a whirlwind. In the following song, the spiral of the whirlwind becomes Father, who wears crow feathers, recreating the spirit through which the dancers are to be borne upward to the new spirit-world (Mooney [1896]1973:970):

> Our father, the whirlwind,
> Our father, the whirlwind,
> Now wears the headdress of crow feathers,
> Now wears the headdress of crow feathers.

Contexts for Musical Performance

For the Great Basin groups, as for all American Indian nations (though not for First Peoples), music is integral to ceremony. Among the ceremonies that traditionally marked the ritual cycle were harvest festivals, birthing and naming ceremonies, puberty ceremonies, mourning ceremonies, war-related dances, the Bear Dance, and the Sun Dance among the Utes and Shoshones. Today, the prominent public ceremonies remain the Sun Dance and the Bear Dance. The Sun Dance in this region has never included the sacrificial practices of the Plains tribes' Sun dances, though it is accompanied by fasting and dancing in the sun and honors the sun. Formerly, stamping a buckskin-covered willow bough with deer hooves tied on top set the meter and tempo.

The Bear Dance

Disillusionment with the Ghost Dance brought changes in some ceremonies. The Bear Dance became focused on gaining good health, rather than on propitiating bears, aiding hunters, and making men and women successful in their sex lives. Participants began fasting for four days before the ceremony, often collapsing (as dancers had gone into trance during the Ghost Dance), to be revived by shamans with musical rasps. All the Ute groups adopted the Bear Dance, as did the Southern Paiutes, the Walapai

and Havasupai of what is now western Arizona, and Mojave peoples of the Southwest.

The ceremony seems to have been maintained with little change for hundreds of years. A celebration of spring and a new beginning for the people, the dance is performed in a specially constructed arbor, with an opening to the east and the singers positioned at the west. The dance is ladies' choice, but women cannot dance with their close male relatives: to dance with one's husband implies jealousy and invites bad luck. A "catman" with a long stick keeps the dancers in order; he uses the stick to "cut" the line, when couples start dancing back and forth together. If a dancer falls, a circle is drawn around the couple and they must sit there until a prayer is done for them. The dance goes on from late morning until midnight or later. The final song is a contest to see which group will outlast the other—the dancers or the singers. Formerly, a feast followed the dance; today's feast takes place at noon on a chosen day, and five or more cows are butchered to feed everyone present. The food is blessed by a Bear Dance "chief."

Elders consider Bear Dance texts referring to bears and deceased ancestors sacred, but most of the songs are more socially oriented. As in the past, they may carry images from the past year, including amusing gossip and commentaries on male–female relationships and notable events, but a somewhat standard repertoire appears to be emerging. Many contemporary Bear Dance songs rely heavily on vocables, with the use of *ya* or *heya* at the ends of verses and sometimes individual phrases. Figure 1 is a transcription of the first two verses of a Bear Dance song recorded and commercially released in 1974 by the Southern Ute Singers from Ignacio, Colorado. Subsequent verses, not seen in this transcription, are repeated exactly.

The Native American Church

Another Great Basin response to the disillusionment following the Ghost Dance was the more private pan-Indian ceremony of the Native American Church ("The Tipi Way"), in which prayers are offered to Jesus, God, Mary, and peyote, a hallucinogenic cactus, considered sacred medicine and a medium for communication with spiritual wisdom. The peyote cult (see textbox) arrived in the Great Basin around the turn of the twentieth century, but became the dominant religion only on the Ute Mountain Reservation in southwestern Colorado. The ceremony is basically the same everywhere, but variations reflect differences in traditional belief-systems among the basin groups.

Figure 1 Bear Dance Song No. 6, as recorded by the Southern Ute Singers in 1974.
Transcription by Paul Rudy.

PEYOTE RELIGION

The peyote religion, centered on the eating of peyote buttons, was introduced from Mexico to the southern plains around the 1880s and spread from there in all directions. It was formally incorporated in Oklahoma in 1918 as the Native American Church. A syncretic religion, peyotism combines indigenous beliefs and practices with Christian symbolism. Songs are a major and distinguishing portion of the ritual, which lasts all night, takes place in a special tipi, and includes sets of four songs sung by every person present (or by their designated representatives), each song repeated four times. Four special songs are sung by the ceremony leader at designated times: "Opening Song," "Night Water Song," "Morning Sunrise Song," and "Closing Song." The songs are sung by individuals who accompany themselves by shaking a gourd rattle decorated with characteristic motifs and colors; the person to the right of each singer adds a rapid, even drumbeat on a small water drum made from an iron pot. Between the songs in a set, the drummer may press a thumb into the moistened head of the drum, tightening it to raise its pitch. Peyote songtexts consist primarily of vocables, with a characteristic ending formula: *he ne ne yo way*. Like Ghost Dance songs, peyote songs typically have paired phrases; in many communities, they stand separate from secular songs.

Singing-style

Monophonic or unison singing is the rule in the Great Basin. The Ghost Dance texts above demonstrate the use of vocables and phrasing. Vocables connote "animal nations" in some instances; other-

wise, they preserve words from ancient languages, or represent an ingenious use of sounds for rhythmic or other musical effects. Their use may reflect pan-Indian ideas of the sacredness of sound, and they greatly ease singing among people who do not speak the same language. Thus, they reflect the free borrowing or trading of songs. Sung words in general are highly connotative, and their interpretation is difficult except for culture members and those with a clear understanding of the language and culture. The Paiutes and Utes related stories through songs, often using an improvisatory, syllabic style, in which a single syllable is set to a single tone.

Bear Dance songs make frequent use of syncopation, belying the general belief that there is little rhythmic variety in Great Basin songs. Movements such as the Ghost Dance and the Native American Church exposed Great Basin peoples to new and different repertoires and styles. Cross-tribal influences have continued to increase in importance as pan-Indian contexts have increased and developed through performance venues such as powwows.

Generally, Great Basin styles incorporate an open sound with an avoidance of high pitches, except for specific purposes. The loudness of singing depends on context. For example, Bear Dance songs require singers to sing loudly to balance the "growl" of multiple rasps (*moraches*). For this reason, singing for the Bear Dance is a test of stamina. Dynamics and other musical traits are most often in the service of emotional expression.

—Adapted from articles by Brenda M. Romero and Judith A. Gray

Bibliography

Jorgensen, Joseph G. 1986. "Ghost Dance, Bear Dance, and Sun Dance." In *Great Basin*, edited by William C. Sturtevant and Warren L. d'Azevedo, 338–367. Handbook of North American Indians, 11. Washington, D.C.: Smithsonian Institution.

Laubin, Reginald, and Gladys Laubin. 1977. *Indian Dances of North America: Their Importance to Indian Life*. Norman: University of Oklahoma Press.

Mooney, James. [1896] 1973. *The Ghost Dance Religion and Wounded Knee*. Reprint of the fourteenth annual report (part 2) of the Bureau of Ethnology to the Smithsonian Institution, 1892–93: *The Ghost Dance Religion and the Sioux Outbreak of 1890*. Mineola, N.Y.: Dover Publications.

Southern Ute Singers. 1974. Canyon Records CR-6113-C.

Vander, Judith. 1997. *Shoshone Ghost Dance Religion: Poetry Songs and Great Basin Context*. Urbana: University of Illinois Press.

The Plains

The Plains region of North America extends southward from Alberta, Saskatchewan, and Manitoba to Texas. Its western boundary follows the Rocky Mountains, and its eastern boundary loosely follows the Mississippi River Valley. Within it are two distinguishable environmental subregions, the Prairies and the High Plains. Tribes within it interacted with tribes outside it, blurring cultural boundaries.

The Prairie subregion, located in the eastern half of the Plains region, was historically home to semisedentary horticulturalist tribes, including the Pawnee, Arikara, Mandan, Hidatsa, Omaha, Ponca, Iowa, and Osage. This area was characterized by tall grasses and higher humidity and more rainfall than the High Plains to its west. The peoples of the Prairies relied on a diverse economic base of horticulture and hunting. The High Plains subregion was historically home to the Plains Indians, the nomadic buffalo hunters, including the Sioux, Assiniboine, Blackfoot, Sarcee, Plains Cree, Plains Ojibwa, Arapaho, Crow, Kiowa, Comanche, and Cheyenne. This area received less rainfall and moisture than did the Prairie region and was characterized by a variety of short grasses. Linguistically, the entire Plains region was diverse, including members of six language families: Siouan, Caddoan, Algonquian, Athapascan, Uto-Aztecan, and Kiowa-Tanoan, plus one language isolate, Tonkawa.

History and Culture

The history of Plains Indians and their music from first contact with Europeans (in the 1600s) to the present can be characterized as cultural florescence followed by cultural destruction followed by cultural regeneration. The history of the people of the region began to be documented with the arrival of Spanish, French, English, and, later, American explorers, travelers, traders, missionaries, and soldiers. During the early years of contact, what are often thought the classic attributes of Plains Indian cultures—large communal buffalo hunts, a horse-based culture, intertribal raiding and warfare, men's societies, and tribal ceremonies—formed and flourished. Yet there was greater variety among Plains cultures than these attributes suggest.

The Importance of Song to Early Plains Life

In the Plains region, singing accompanied all aspects of life, especially political life. Important rituals, known variously as the calumet or adoption ceremony, for example, were used to establish peace between groups. Governing organizations of Plains peoples employed song as a medium of expression and communication.

Music played a key role in Plains religions, both formally and informally. The dialogue between higher powers and individuals is expressed through song in many important Plains religious ceremonies, such as the Sun Dance, bundle ceremonies, and the vision quest.

Many of the economic aspects of Plains life were accompanied by music. Song was the medium used by many in asking for assistance in hunting, either in the communal buffalo hunts or individual occurrences, and was an integral part of the process of reaching trade agreements between groups through rituals, frequently being used as an object of trade.

Singing by women and men was important to the social life of the Plains peoples. From lullabies to memorial songs at funeral rites, the lifecycle was accentuated by song. Courting was assisted by the use of flutes, one of the few musical instruments used by Plains Indians. Various organizations, such as women's societies based on the production of beadwork or quill work, used singing as an entertainment activity. Many children's games were accompanied by songs, and singing was a popular activity by itself. Dancing was also a key social activity and was always accompanied by a variety of song forms.

Men's warrior societies relied on song for several purposes. Songs were used to document the successes of intertribal warfare as well as to recount individual exploits, known as coups. Many of these societies accompanied their social dances with songs particular to their groups.

Contact with the United States

At the beginning of the nineteenth century, a new presence came onto the plains—the Americans. With the Lousiana Purchase in 1803 and the expedition of Lewis and Clark beginning in 1804, this time of cultural florescence and the independent ways of life of Plains Indians was beginning to end. In the

1850s and 1860s, a series of treaties to establish early reservation boundaries was signed on the Plains. The confinement of Indian peoples to reservations on the Plains and cessation of intertribal warfare led to a decline of the warrior ethos, and warrior societies, which were key aspects of Indian culture, were divested of their power. However, America's involvement in World War I provided a new outlet for the warrior traditions of Plains Indians. Many young men joined the armed forces, and with their participation came a brief revival of warrior musical traditions. In the 1920s, Indian rights societies were organized in the United States in opposition to federal Indian policy. The Indian Reorganization Act in 1934 gave legal sanction to tribal holdings, encouraged the formation of tribal governments, granted religious freedom, and promoted the survival of arts, crafts, and other native traditions. In the 1950s, numerous revivals of secular and religious music and dance forms occurred. Today, Plains peoples are experiencing a new cultural florescence, one in which music plays a highly visible and important role.

Vocal Music

Plains music, which is primarily vocal, is integral to Plains cultures. In Plains singing, vocal quality is marked by tenseness, with pulsations on longer tones; it is influenced by the sound system of each language, such as the presence of nasal vowels. Glissandos grace the ends of phrases and songs. Musical texture varies between solo and group singing. Plains songs are typically monophonic, with women's parts approximately an octave above men's. The musical form is $A_1A_2B_1C_1B_2C_2$. Songs typically begin with a solo introductory line or phrase (A_1) that is repeated or sometimes interrupted by another soloist or the group (A_2); this is known as the "second." The song then moves into the main body, a chorus, divided into two verses (B_1C_1), which repeat (B_2C_2). In solo singing, a single introductory line (A) is followed by the main body of the song ($B_1C_1B_2C_2$).

Songtexts consist of words and vocables, separate or in combination. Vocables are formed from the sound system of the specific language of the singer and are primarily vowel sounds in combination with initial consonants. The melodic range typically exceeds an octave. The melodic contour is terraced and descending; each phrase begins lower than the start of the previous phrase. Five- and four-tone scales predominate, with the average range being a tenth. Major seconds and minor thirds are the commonest melodic intervals. Most Plains singing has a rhythmic accompaniment, provided primarily by a drum, but also by rattles and bells that dancers wear or shake. Drum rhythms vary according to the type of song or dance and range from an unaccented beat to an accented 1–2 beat to a steady tremolo.

Powwows

One of the most visible music-and-dance forms of today is the powwow (figure 1), a complex of features that originated in men's societies and centers on

Figure 1 Dancers at the 202nd Omaha Nation Powwow in Macy, Nebraska, 2006.
Photo by Ben J. Smith.

music-and-dance forms that have persisted in a historical continuum from the mid-1800s to the present. Developing on the Central Plains as a fusion of Ponca, Omaha, Pawnee, and Sioux forms, it adapted to the social, political, economic, and religious pressures that accompanied the breakdown of Plains cultures. In response to these pressures, it became a more strictly social form, allowing for prestige to be earned through dancing and singing, lessening the importance of warrior-society elements. It readapted as the United States and its Indian citizens entered the world wars, returning to the forefront the elements emphasizing honor. Since about 1950, it has retained elements from each of its functions: honoring, entertaining, achieving economic and social prestige, and expressing identity. As it spread throughout the Plains in the mid-1800s, each tribe contributed to it, or made some part of it uniquely its own. Today, powwows still express tribalism through individual dance outfits, language, singing, and traditions. The flexibility of powwows allows them to be interpreted on individual, tribal, and regional levels, and to remain culturally relevant as outlets for expressing tribal and generalized Indian identities.

There is a variety of powwow forms today, but the most distinctive difference is between those of the Northern Plains and those of the Southern Plains. With the relocation of tribal groups to Indian Territory (present-day Oklahoma) or reservations on the Northern Plains, two early versions of the powwow began to develop independently. Intertribal exchange within these regions in the late 1880s and early 1900s led to many local variations. In the mid-1900s, relocation policies, improved transportation, and other factors led to increased exchange and mutual borrowing between the regions.

Many elements are common to both Northern and Southern Plains powwows, but each version has developed from the influences of the tribal groups within its region. The structure of songs is basically the same in all versions, though the tonal range of songs varies. Songs of the Northern Plains are sung at higher pitches than those of the Southern Plains. Dance styles have been exchanged between regions, but each region has its own version. The movements vary according to tribal traditions, but dancers always circle the arena, clockwise or counterclockwise.

Contexts and Structures

Throughout the Plains, powwows have a basic form, regardless of their purpose and location. They can be held for recreation, competition, and honoring, on family, community, tribal, and regional levels. They may be held in temporary or permanent outdoor arbors, specially built structures, gymnasiums, and large modern arenas. They may last for only one evening, or they may be multiday events, sometimes beginning on a Thursday and ending late on Sunday night, or even early Monday morning. The following is a typical program of a powwow, listing the dances and their musical accompaniments.

Grand Entry or Parade

This dance leads off most powwows and serves as a way of bringing the dancers into the arena (figure 2).

Figure 2 Grand entry to the 202nd Omaha Nation Powwow in Macy, Nebraska, 2006.
Photo by Ben J. Smith.

The dancers enter in a predetermined order, beginning with flagbearers and followed by head dancers, royalty, male dancers, female dancers, and, finally, children.

Flag Song

This song functions similarly to the national anthem at sporting events and usually employs native-language texts. It usually precedes an invocation of some kind. It may be sung at sporting and special events, such as high-school graduations.

Veterans' or Victory Songs

These songs may be sung immediately after the invocation, or at any other time during a dance session, especially at the end of a dance. They tell of the actions of Native American soldiers and their military engagements.

Round Dance

Based on a basic side step, this genre of social dancing appears throughout the Plains. Each dance has a different connection to a particular society or origin, and the songs are derived from these sources.

Intertribal Dance

The most common dances at powwows are these simple dances, in which all can participate. They follow a basic toe-heel dance step and are dispersed between other dances, typically in groups, throughout dance sessions.

Two-step or Rabbit Dance

These are male–female partner dances in which dancers glide along while maintaining contact with each other, typically by holding hands or interlocking their arms. These dances are ladies' choice. Songs that accompany them are typically love songs, and are among the few texts sung from female perspectives.

Contest Dances

These are contests specific to each dance style. Men's dance styles include straight, traditional, grass, and fancy; women's dance styles include traditional, fancy shawl, and jingle. These styles vary among tribal groups and areas. Each style has specific songs for contest dancing. Typically, each style has two different contest dances: the first is known as a straight song; the second, as a trick song. Trick songs have elements that require dancers to perform certain trick movements, or to demonstrate the ability to follow unexpected starts and stops in the songs. Trick songs can be sung as exhibition dances, sometimes called specials.

—*Adapted from an article by Erik D. Gooding*

Bibliography

Black Bear, Ben Sr., and R. D. Theisz. 1976. *Songs and Dances of the Lakota.* Rosebud, S.D.: Sinte Gleska College.

Callahan, Alice A. 1990. *The Osage Ceremonial Dance I'n-Lon-Schka.* Norman: University of Oklahoma Press.

Giglio, Virginia. 1994. *Southern Cheyenne Women's Songs.* Norman: University of Oklahoma Press.

Gooding, Erik D. 1998. "Songs of the People: Plains Indian Commercial Recordings, 1968–1996." *Notes* 55:37–67.

Kavanagh, Thomas W. 1992. "Southern Plains Dance: Tradition and Dynamism." In *Native American Dance: Ceremonies and Social Traditions*, edited by Charlotte Heth, 105–123. Washington, D.C.: Smithsonian Institution.

Meadows, William C., and Gus Palmer Sr. 1992. "Tonkonga: The Kiowa Black Legs Military Society." In *Native American Dance: Ceremonies and Social Traditions*, edited by Charlotte Heth, 116–117. Washington, D.C.: Smithsonian Institution.

Mooney, James. [1896] 1973. *The Ghost-Dance Religion and Wounded Knee.* Reprint of the fourteenth annual report (part 2) of the Bureau of Ethnology to the Smithsonian Institution, 1892–1893: *The Ghost-Dance Religion and the Sioux Outbreak of 1890.* Mineola, N.Y.: Dover Press.

Powers, William K. 1990. *War Dance: Plains Indians Musical Performance.* Tucson: University of Arizona Press.

United States

United States, political

United States

Marveling at the cultural breadth of the United States, though its evident heterogeneity first impresses us, we may wonder about the core that creates a national identity. U.S. citizens view their musics in much the same way—marveling at its ethnicities, noting its various uses, exclaiming at its numerous types, and often wondering what makes them "American." The articles that follow discuss the four major groups of "recent" arrivals to the United States: African Americans, European Americans, Hispanic Americans, and Asian Americans. It examines the musics, musicians, instruments, and musical ideas they have contributed to the mosaic of American musical culture.

African-American Musics

Beginning in the early seventeenth century, Africans were taken from their home communities, mainly in West Africa, and brought to what would become the United States, where they and their descendants lived as slaves. Especially in the cotton- and tobacco-based economy of the rural South, slaves were frequently separated from families and supporting communities once they arrived. After slavery ended, in 1865, they continued to face harsh and demeaning discrimination. Much of their early music history reflects these social and economic conditions and the importance of Christianity in establishing strong communities and providing contexts for musical performance. Early forms, such as field cries and hollers, early blues, and other folk traditions, with spirituals and early musical theater, grew from a synthesis of predominantly West African and Western European musics, and developed over time into musical forms and styles that today permeate American music. This section documents four of the most influential of these forms and styles.

Oscar Pettiford and Junior Raglin perform in the Duke Ellington Orchestra at the Aquarium restaurant, New York City, ca. November, 1946.
Photo © William P. Gottlieb; www.jazzphotos.com.

Religious Music

Spirituals and gospel music are the musical genres that have long dominated the worship of black Americans in the United States. Scholars have documented the performance of lined hymns and psalms, traditional hymns, and songs from Western European classical music in black religious services, but spirituals and gospel music are the religious musical genres actually created by and for black people.

The breadth and depth of these genres represent the cultural legacy and therefore the cultural *identity* of African-derived people. The distinctiveness of African-American religious music reflects collective adaptation to ever-changing sociocultural and political situations, but continuities between spirituals and gospel hymns show the persistence of a self-defining core of cultural values among African Americans.

Spirituals

The earliest form of black religious music to develop in the United States was what is commonly called the folk spiritual, a genre that developed in the late eighteenth century. The designation *folk* distinguishes this genre from arranged spirituals—concert versions, which emerged after the Civil War.

The spiritual emerged in both the South and the North as a genre distinctively different from music that characterized European American musical tradition of the period. In both contexts, the critical factor that allowed blacks to articulate and advance a unique musical identity was that of autonomy. In the South, the invisible church—essentially worship hidden from the purview of whites—was the spawning ground. Whether in a ravine, gully, field or living quarters, African American slaves guarded their privacy, not merely out of fear of reprisal but out of their desire to express themselves in a way that was meaningful.

The character of worship among blacks during slavery is closely related to that of contemporary black worship. There was prayer, communal singing, testifying, and sometimes preaching. The most striking aspects of the worship were the manner in which these elements were expressed. Prayer was described as extemporaneous, typically moving from speech to song; congregational participation, in the form of verbal affirmations, was not only accepted, but expected and highly valued. Singing involved

everyone present, and was accompanied by clapping, body movement, and, if the spirit was particularly high, shouting and dance, peak forms of expressive behavior.

Ecstatic worship, in which participants expressed themselves through shouting, was commonplace. When spirits were high, services lasted far into the night, the length being determined only by the collective energy that fueled the group. Principles that governed the character of the worship also governed the character of the songs sung during the worship. In these spirituals, African-derived call-and-response patterns served on the one hand as an agent for stability, with the constant repetition of the chorus that encourages everyone to participate; but on the other hand, they served as an agent for musical change, with constant variation being provided through the solo. Throughout its history, African-American music has nurtured this tension between unity and diversity, individuality and collectivity.

The establishment of the independent African Methodist Episcopal congregation under the leadership of Richard Allen (1760–1831) set the stage for the autonomy that fostered the growth of the spiritual in the North. This congregation separated from the white Methodist parent church in Philadelphia in 1787, but it retained Methodist doctrines. Allen was satisfied with the "plain and simple gospel" of the Methodist Church—which, in his view, well suited his congregation because it was one that "the unlearned can understand and the learned are sure to understand" (Wesley [1935]1969:72). Allen's identification with Methodism was further evident in his decision to reject the standard Methodist hymnal; instead, he compiled his own, which included songs he felt had greater appeal for his congregation. He simplified texts and routinely added refrain lines and choruses. His goal was to generate congregational participation and assure freedom of worship for his members.

The songtexts and the aesthetic principles that affirmed musical and textual repetition—hand-clapping, foot-stamping, and body movement—met with great disapproval from the white Methodist establishment, to which it was especially disconcerting that secular songs were being used for sacred purposes. The practices that governed performance by these renegade Methodists were virtually identical to those of the basic folk spiritual, illustrating the ability of African Americans to transform genres that they themselves did not create into musical expressions of cultural relevance.

Arranged Spirituals

The next form of religious music expression to develop among blacks on U.S. soil was that of arranged spirituals. For many decades, spirituals were known and respected almost exclusively by blacks; however, with the formation of the Fisk Jubilee Singers in the early 1870s, spirituals assumed a character and a purpose that differed radically from their folk antecedents. The original group, eleven men and women, most ex-slaves, was established under the leadership of George White, the white university treasurer, who viewed musical concerts as a way of raising funds for Fisk University. According to black composer and Fisk professor John Work III,

> **Fisk University** was founded in Nashville, Tennessee, in 1866 several months after the Civil War ended. From its earliest days, the university has been one of the premier African-American educational institutions in the United States.

Mr. White decided on a style of singing the spiritual which eliminated every element that detracted from the pure emotion of the song. . . . Finish, precision, and sincerity were demanded by this leader. While the program featured Spirituals, variety was given it by the use of numbers of classical standard. Mr. White strove for an art presentation. (Work 1940:15)

The folk spiritual was now transferred to the concert stage. This change in function was accompanied by a change in performance practices: handclapping, foot-stamping, and individual latitude in interpreting melodic lines were replaced by predictability, controlled reserve, and the absence of overt demonstrative behavior. The aesthetic values that characterized George White's musical culture were being superimposed onto the spiritual.

Early recordings of the Fisk University Quartet document the continuing presence of unaccompanied syllabic singing, and the same use of calls and responses within the verse-chorus form as in folk spirituals. Folk-spiritual melodies served as a point of departure for arrangements grounded in Western European compositional techniques. The dialect of folk spirituals remained constant; however, the singers' vocal quality evoked European ideals of timbre. Heterophony yielded to clearly defined harmonic parts, and dancing was eliminated altogether. Folk spirituals could be repeated for indefinite durations, but performances of arranged spirituals were bound by the dictates of printed scores and the expectations of concert audiences.

The Fisk campaign was an overwhelming success. It inspired the formation of similar groups at other black colleges. Arranged spirituals now symbolize the best in the black college choir tradition. Generations of black composers developed folk melodies for performance on concert stages. Notable among many are John Work II (1873–1925), R. Nathaniel Dett (1882–1943), William Dawson (1899–1990), John Work III (1901–1968), and Undine Smith Moore (1904–1989).

DISC 1 TRACK 12

Transitional Gospel Music

By the time gospel music started its climb to acceptance and popularity, in the 1930s, folk spirituals had been in existence for well over a century. The advent of gospel music was precipitated by the migration of blacks from countrysides to cities during the years surrounding World Wars I and II. The migrants' natural predisposition to continue familiar patterns of behavior was evident in almost every aspect of their lives, ranging from favored clothing and food to favored styles of music and worship. One-room folk churches of the rural South became storefront churches of the urban North—a key setting for the emergence of transitional gospel music.

This new music presented a radical challenge to the religious status quo. From 1900 to 1930, three styles of it emerged: (1) the style pioneered by Charles Albert Tindley in Philadelphia; (2) rural gospel, the style that served as a sacred counterpart of the rural blues; and (3) the Holiness-Pentecostal style, which first rose to prominence in the Church of God in Christ.

The Tindley Style

The grandfather of gospel music, Charles Albert Tindley (1851–1933), was the minister of Tindley Temple Methodist Church in Philadelphia. Influenced by the doctrines of the holiness movement, he allowed services at Tindley Temple to continue all night long, filled with spirited congregational singing, extemporaneous prayer, and songs that Tindley himself had composed to complement his sermons. Tindley's church also included European anthems, which generated congregational response, even shouting.

The first of Tindley's gospel hymns was published in 1901. Among his output of forty-six songs are "We Will Understand It Better By and By," "Stand by Me," "The Storm Is Passing Over," and other enduring compositions. Considered representative gospel hymns, these are partly distinguished from folk spirituals by the use of instrumental accompaniment. They maintain a link to the spiritual tradition by successfully incorporating calls and responses into a verse–chorus structure.

Rural Gospel

A form of transitional gospel music emerged as a counterpart of the rural blues. Often sung by solo blues singers with guitar or harmonica accompaniment, this style was characterized by the minimal chord changes and variable rhythmic structures that typified rural blues around the turn of the twentieth century. Performers who represented it included Blind Willie Johnson (1897–1945) and Blind Mamie Forehand.

Holiness-Pentecostal Style

The third form of transitional gospel music evolved in the context of the newly formed Pentecostal denomination. In this setting, the character of folk spirituals are most evident. Congregations that evolved from the 1906–1908 Azuza Street Revival in Los Angeles, led by William J. Seymour, embraced a worship style that was uninhibited and highly demonstrative. Under the anointing of the Holy Spirit, congregants sang and danced with exuberance to the accompaniment of instruments shunned by the established denominations—trombones, trumpets, mandolins, and even jugs.

One of the most celebrated pioneers of the Holiness-Pentecostal style was Arizona Dranes (ca. 1905–1957), whose recording career spanned only two years (1926–1928). Her highly rhythmic, percussive ragtime piano style and her powerful, shouted vocal leads represent the epitome of the high-energy delivery that characterizes Pentecostal worship. She recorded with evangelist F. W. McGee (1890–1971), another pioneer, whose work is highly representative of this period and style.

Traditional Gospel Music

During the 1930s, the genre of traditional gospel music emerged, created by the meshing of the three styles of transitional gospel music. The man who figured most prominently in this merger was Thomas A. Dorsey (1899–1993), now often called the father of gospel music. He and other important gospel music pioneers, Mahalia Jackson (1911–1972) and Roberta Martin (1907–1969), for example, arrived in Chicago during the great migrations. Dorsey and Jackson brought with them a musical culture rooted in the sacred and secular traditions of the South;

northern contexts provided the impetus for the growth of something new.

Born in Villa Rica, Georgia (near Atlanta), the son of an itinerant Baptist preacher, Dorsey grew up playing the organ in church. As a boy, he worked selling soda pop at a vaudeville theater in Atlanta, where he regularly heard such blues performers as Ma Rainey and Bessie Smith. Before devoting his career to gospel music, he became a prolific composer of blues and jazz.

Like Dorsey, Mahalia Jackson (figure 1) embraced sacred and secular musics from childhood. A native of New Orleans, she was raised a Baptist, and found her place in the church choir at an early age. Her religious experiences included the Pentecostal Church, whose music she loved, located next door to her home. The aunt who raised her did not expose her to "worldly" music, but she listened to her older cousin's blues records whenever her aunt was not at

Figure 1 Mahalia Jackson, 1962. Known as the "Queen of Gospel," Jackson drew upon sacred and secular musics to create a style of religious song that had great influence on African-American religious music and brought her worldwide fame.
Photo by Carl Van Vechten. Library of Congress, Prints & Photographs Division, Carl Van Vechten Collection, LC-USZ62-109778 DLC

home. Her favorite performer was Bessie Smith, whose vocal quality she greatly admired and sought to imitate: "I remember when I used to listen to Bessie Smith sing 'I Hate to See that Evening Sun Go Down,' I'd fix my mouth and try to make tones come out just like hers" (Jackson 1966:36).

As did folk spirituals, gospel music in its formative years faced staunch opposition and criticism. When Dorsey began to promote his compositions, he faced rejection, in part because the music was viewed as having unacceptable links to secular music. Joining forces with Jackson, he initiated an audience-development strategy, which bypassed the black religious and musical establishment by taking the music "to the streets." He recalled:

> There were many days and nights when Mahalia and I would be out there on the street corners. . . . Mahalia would sing songs I'd composed, and I'd sell sheet music to folk for five and ten cents. . . . We took gospel music all around the country too. (Duckett 1974:6)

The music that Dorsey, Jackson, and other gospel pioneers promoted has risen to a position of prominence in the worship of African Americans of almost every denomination. It is sung by soloists and ensembles, choirs and quartets, men and women, young and old, black and white. In contrast to the simple accompaniment of piano and organ, which characterized the early years of gospel, there are now no limits to the types of instruments used to complement the singers—from saxophones to synthesizers to symphony orchestras.

—*Adapted from an article by Mellonee V. Burnim*

Bibliography

Boyer, Horace. 1992. "Charles Albert Tindley: Progenitor of African American Gospel Music." In *We'll Understand It Better By and By: Pioneering African American Gospel Composers*, edited by Bernice Johnson Reagon, 53–78. Washington, D.C.: Smithsonian Institution Press.

——. 1995. *How Sweet the Sound: The Golden Age of Gospel*. Washington, D.C.: Elliott & Clark Publishing.

Burnim, Mellonee. 1985. "The Black Gospel Music Tradition: A Complex of Ideology, Aesthetic and Behavior." In *More Than Dancing*, edited by Irene V. Jackson, 135–169. Westport, Conn.: Greenwood.

Burnim, Mellonee, and Portia Maultsby. 1987. "From Backwoods to City Streets: The Afro-American Musical Journey." In *Expressively Black*, edited by Geneva Gay and Willie Baber, 109–135. New York: Praeger.

Duckett, Alfred. 1974. "An Interview with Thomas Dorsey." *Black World*, July, 4–18.

Epstein, Dena. 1977. *Sinful Tunes and Spirituals: Black Folk Music to the Civil War*. Urbana: University of Illinois Press.

Jackson, Mahalia. 1966. *Movin' On Up*. New York: Hawthorn Books.

Harris, Michael. 1992. *The Rise of Gospel Blues: The Music of Thomas A. Dorsey in the Urban Church*. New York: Oxford University Press.

Hinson, Glenn. 2000. *Fire in My Bones: Transcendence and the Holy Spirit in African American Gospel*. Philadelphia: University of Pennsylvania Press.

Southern, Eileen. 1983. *The Music of Black Americans: A History*. 2nd ed. New York: Norton.

Wesley, Charles. [1935] 1969. *Richard Allen: Apostle of Freedom*. Washington, D.C.: Associated Publishers.

Work, John. 1940. *American Negro Songs and Spirituals*. New York: Bonanza Books.

——. [1949] 1983. "Changing Patterns in Negro Folk Songs." In *Readings in Black American Music*, 2nd ed., edited by Eileen Southern, 281–290. New York: Norton.

Blues

During the first decade of the twentieth century, the term blues began to be applied to songs emerging from black communities in the U.S. South. These songs were new and different, in their formal and musical characteristics and in the topics and attitudes their lyrics expressed. They are discussed in contemporary accounts of folklorists and other observers and in later reminiscences of people who were involved in music at this time. That blues songs seem to turn up everywhere in the South more or less simultaneously—in rural areas, small towns, and big cities—suggests that the genre had been developing for years, probably since the 1890s or before.

Historical Background and Contexts

Blues was not the only new musical development that emerged in the decades surrounding the turn of the twentieth century. It should be viewed as part of a wave of innovation in black American music—a wave that saw the first stirrings of ragtime, jazz, gospel music, and barbershop-style vocal harmony. This wave broke alongside important developments in literature, theater, the arts in general, and black political and religious life. The creativity behind it coincided with a hardening of white resistance to black social and economic progress in the form of Jim Crow laws and the institutionalization of racial segregation, the disenfranchisement of black voters, lynchings and other acts of terror, and the loss of jobs to swarms of immigrants from Europe. It was a time of the end of the dream that had once seemed attainable for black Americans following Emancipation. A generation that grew up seeing the erosion of its parents' freedoms had to create new responses to new situations.

Earlier black folk and popular music had consisted largely of folk and concert versions of spirituals, minstrel material, and instrumental dance-music played on the fiddle and other instruments, plus worksongs and children's game songs. Many black singers and musicians benefited from white patronage. The new musical genres exhibited a turning inward toward utilization of black folk-musical resources, an adaptation of Western forms, harmonies, and instrumentation to characteristically black styles, and a greater reliance on black audiences for monetary support and approval. Emphasizing performers, composers, improvisation, soloing, and self-expression, the new music became more introspective, self-absorbed, individualistic, serious, and worldly, while most whites were viewing blacks as an undifferentiated social caste with stereotyped mental and behavioral traits that cast them as ignorant, humorous, and carefree. The new musical genres challenged these stereotypes and led the way in the black struggle for freedom, justice, and equality throughout most of the twentieth century.

Of all the new genres of black music created at this time, blues was the most self-contained. Blues songs have mainly been sung solo, though duet and quartet performances and background vocalizing are not unknown. Singers, especially males, usually play an instrument, which in folk blues has usually been a guitar, a piano, or a harmonica. Many male folk-blues singers have preferred to perform solo, as have some female singers, though most of the latter have been accompanied by a single, usually male, pianist or guitarist. Even when other instruments are added, as in most kinds of popularized blues, emphasis is placed on individual expression and improvisation. Sometimes entire performances of blues—lyrics, melodies, and instrumental work—are improvised. Some performers are highly creative in this respect, but many are aided by a body of shared and familiar lyric and musical ideas and formulas that they recombine in ever-changing ways.

Contexts for Blues Performance

The geographical heart of the blues is the plantation country of the Deep South, stretching from the interior of Georgia to eastern Texas. Most blues singers were born and raised in this region. Music underwent a less intense, though still significant, development in Virginia and the Carolinas, and was even less developed in the border states and southern mountain regions and along the Atlantic and Gulf coasts. Within the geographical heart, certain areas, such as the Mississippi Delta and the river bottomlands of southeastern Texas, have proved especially important as places of innovation. Through the twentieth century, artists from these and other areas migrated to cities, within the region and outside it, especially in the Midwest and California, bringing rural styles with them and contributing to new urban musical syntheses. Over the years, blues has exhibited musical and lyrical traces of its origins and evidence of the desire of many performers and audience members to escape those origins.

Blues performance sometimes occurs as a solitary activity or in intimate settings, such as courtship, but it has always invited the presence of a public audience. It exists as music for listening and dancing, the two acts often occurring in the same context. In the rural South, the most common setting was a house party or an outdoor picnic. Another common institution, the jukehouse or juke joint, was a structure, often a residence, temporarily or permanently set up for music, dancing, drinking, eating, and other activities. In towns, blues musicians would gather and perform at cafés and saloons, on sidewalks and street corners, in parks, in railroad and bus stations, and inside and in front of places of business. In cities, blues were sung in vaudeville theaters, saloons, and cabarets, and at house parties, in parks, and on streets. Traveling tent and medicine shows often hired blues performers, providing opportunities for local and sometimes extended travel. Most of these settings persisted in black American communities until the end of the 1950s, but since then, the main locations have been clubs and auditoriums. Concerts and festivals, within and outside the black community, have provided additional settings for blues music in recent years.

Distinctive Traits

Many traits of the blues can be traced to antecedent musical forms. Several of these traits shocked and challenged the norms of Western music and American popular music: they entered the larger musical world for the first time through the blues and have come to be associated with blues ever since, though some are now commonplace in popular music. Four in particular have a special association with the blues.

Blues Texts

Blues lyrics are extremely frank and almost exclusively concerned with the self, placed in relation to others. They are sung primarily in the first person. When directed toward another person or about someone else, they deal with the interaction between the other person and the singer. Rather than telling stories in a chronological fashion, they express feelings and emotions, or describe actions based on them. These may be the real feelings and activities of the singer or those of a persona created by the singer, an exaggerated or dramatized self. The lyrics are realistic (as opposed to idealistic), nonsentimental, and serious (as opposed to light or frivolous). They

may incorporate exaggeration or boasting, but only as amplifications of essential truths. They may, and often do, convey humor, but usually as an expression of irony, cleverness, double or multiple meanings, or social commentary and criticism, not as an illustration of buffoonery or stupidity. Realism and seriousness, combined with the concentration on the self and a willingness to delve into sadness, deep feelings, emotions, and confessions, are probably responsible for the appellation blues, which became attached to this music at an early stage. Many blues songs express optimism, confidence, success, and happiness, but it is the melancholy or depressed range of emotions that has given the genre its familiar name.

The songs deal with the full range of human feelings and describe the ups and downs of daily life. The most prominent subject by far is love and sex. This is followed by travel; work, poverty, and unemployment; alcohol, drugs, gambling, and trouble with the law; sickness and death; magic and hoodoo, often in connection with these other themes; and current events. Many of these topics had rarely been discussed before in American popular song, except in a trivial, sentimental, idealized, or moralistic way. The highly secular content of the lyrics, the concentration on the self in the here and now, and the expression of certain emotions and subject-matter that are beyond the bounds of polite society have caused the blues to be viewed by many, within and outside the African-American community, as low-down, self-centered, or even "the devil's music." In contrast, a more positive view, expressed by some intellectuals and some blues singers, stresses the existentialism of blues lyrics, their emphasis on self-reliance and self-sufficiency, and their often outstanding poetic qualities.

The Role of Instruments

An instrument or group of instruments plays a necessary role in constructing and performing blues songs, rather than serving simply as a more or less optional harmonic and rhythmic background to singing. The instrumental part is, in fact, a second voice (sometimes several voices), punctuating and responding to the singer. It is therefore an integral part of the piece. The role of instruments as voices is well-known in most forms of African music and their New World derivatives, but seldom have instruments had as close a conversational dialogue with singers as in the blues. This sort of dialogue was uncommon in nineteenth-century American popular song, but through its use in the blues and the influence of blues on other popular genres, it has become commonplace.

The Blue Note

As the term suggests, blues introduced the concept of the blue note into American music. This term is used rather loosely, but essentially it means a note, sounded or suggested, that falls between two adjacent tones in the standard Western division of the octave into twelve equal intervals. Blue notes are thus sometimes described as neutral pitches, which can be notated by an upward- or downward-pointing arrow printed above a note, which functions in the same way as a sharp, flat, or natural sign.

Blue notes are easy enough to achieve with the voice. On many instruments, they can be produced by the use of special techniques to "bend" tones—for example, pushing the strings on the neck of the guitar; special tonguing and blowing methods on the harmonica, woodwinds, and horns; glissandos on slide trombones; and the slide or "bottleneck" technique on the guitar. On fixed-pitched instruments, such as the piano, blue notes can be suggested by the rapid alternation of adjacent tones, a flat grace-note before a natural, or the simultaneous sounding of a flat and a natural in a chord or in the separate melodic lines played by the hands. Pianists have been ingenious in turning the emblematic instrument of Western music into a blues vehicle.

Because blue notes are found in most blues, some observers use the term blues scale. There actually is no single scale for all blues. Many pieces are pentatonic; others are hexatonic and heptatonic, if one views the shading within the interval of a semitone as variations of a single scale step. The term blues scale, however, is a convenient designation for a scale that differs from a typical Western major or minor one by containing blue notes. Blue notes are clearly an extension of African musical practices and sometimes additionally an attempt to come to terms with Western instruments whose keyboards, fretboards, valves, and fingerholes are not designed to enable players to achieve them easily. Blue notes can thus be seen to represent symbolically a tension between an African musical legacy and a superimposed Western system, and a resolution of this tension.

Blues Forms

Most blues pieces utilize a twelve-bar AAB form or some variant of it. At its most basic, the stanza consists of a line of verse (A), the same line repeated, and a third line (B), rhyming with the first two (figure 1). Usually the B line explains, amplifies, comments on, or contrasts with the A line, rather than following from it chronologically. Each line occupies only slightly more than the first half of a four-measure section; the other portion consists of an instrumental response, though the instrumental part may be heard during the singing. The first line usually begins with the suggestion of a tonic chord, the second with a subdominant, and the third with a dominant, each of them resolving on the tonic by the time of the instrumental response. The third line usually passes through the subdominant on the way to the tonic. This form can be altered in many ways: through chordal substitutions, passing harmonies (serving to make the piece more harmonically complex), and simplification to two chords or only one (that is, a strictly modal piece without any suggestion of chord changes). The number of bars can be shortened or lengthened. In addition, there are eight-bar (two-line) and sixteen-bar (four-line) blues with their own typical harmonic patterns and variations, and some blues are conceived in a more or less freeform manner, without apparent reference to one of these patterns. The repetition of the A line, textually and often melodically, is a device typically found in much African music, whereas the use of a repeated multiphrase form with harmonic changes is more typically European. Another device that often occurs in the blues and links it to African traditions is the use of repeated short melodic-rhythmic phrases, often called riffs. A riff can extend the instrumental response to vocal lines and serve as a background behind the vocal lines, as an identifying marker for an entire piece. Usually, several different or variant riffs are used in a single blues where this concept occurs. The twelve-bar AAB form and the use of riffs entered the mainstream of American popular music through the blues and have now become so commonplace that they are seldom noticed.

Popularization

Even from the time of its origins, blues has been a commercial music in the sense that it has usually been performed with the expectation of monetary rewards. Unsurprisingly, therefore, blues quickly entered the world of popular entertainment and the mass media. During the first decade of the twentieth century, almost every black community in a city or a larger town, in the South and elsewhere, had a least

```
|    C    |    C    |    C    |    C    |
I'm going away, and I won't be back till fall.

|    F    |    F    |    C    |    C    |
I'm going away, and I won't be back till fall.

|    G    |    F    |    C    |    C    |
If my mind don't change, I won't be back at all.
```

Figure 1 A typical twelve-bar blues stanza in the key of C major with measure divisions and implied harmonies.

one vaudeville theater serving its entertainment needs. Traveling tent shows, minstrel shows, medicine shows, and circuses brought entertainment to these communities and many small towns that could not sustain a full-time theater. Thus, potential audiences had opportunities for supporting professional black singers, musicians, dancers, comedians, composers, and managers.

By 1910, there were reports of songs called blues being sung and played by vaudeville entertainers, and twelve-bar and other typical blues strains could be detected in published ragtime piano compositions. In 1912, four songs were copyrighted with the word blues in their titles; these included W.C. Handy's "The Memphis Blues." In the years immediately following, black-owned publishing houses, such as Handy's in Memphis (and later New York) and that of Clarence Williams in New Orleans, turned out dozens of blues (figure 2). Numerous Southern black vaudeville singers became closely identified with the blues and rose to the status of stars, among them Gertrude "Ma" Rainey (1886–1939), Butler "String Beans" May, and Bessie Smith (1894–1937; figure 3). They sang published blues hits, their own compositions, and adaptations of folk material. Many vaudeville and sheet-music creations that were called blues were actually popular songs or instrumental pieces in a ragtime style but incorporating one or more blues strains (for example, twelve-bar AAB) and blue notes. Blues were commercially recorded at this time by vocalists and dance and jazz bands, all of them white—indicating that blues had achieved a national popularity and identity as a distinct new genre of music.

Recordings

In 1920, vaudeville singer Mamie Smith (1883–1946) became the first black vocalist to record blues commercially: she had hits with "That Thing Called Love" and "Crazy Blues," compositions of fellow vaudevillian Perry Bradford. Her success led to recordings by many other vaudeville blues stars during the 1920s, most of them women, accompanied by small jazz combos. At first, the songs were compositions of professional songwriters in the multistrain format of ragtime music, but with blue notes and an occasional twelve-bar AAB strain. Representative singers in this style, besides Mamie Smith, were Lucille Hegamin (1894–1970), Alberta Hunter (1895–1984), Trixie Smith (1895–1943), Lizzie Miles (1895–1963), Ethel Waters (1896–1977), and Edith Wilson (1896–1981). By 1923, a new wave of singers had entered the studios, singing songs more often made up of variants of a single AAB

Figure 2 Sheet music cover to W.C. Handy's "Saint Louis Blues" (1914), one of the most popular blues songs ever written.
From the collection of the Music Department, New York Public Library for the Performing Arts, Astor, Lenox, and Tilden Associations.

strain and accompanied typically by a pianist, sometimes with one or two added jazz instruments. By this time, more of the songs were composed by the singers themselves. Some of the more prolific and successful artists in this style were Bessie Smith, Ma Rainey, Ida Cox (1896–1967), Rosa Henderson (1896–1968), Clara Smith (ca. 1894–1935), Viola McCoy (ca. 1900 to ca. 1956), Sippie Wallace (1898–1986), Sara Martin (1884–1955), Bertha "Chippie" Hill (1905–1950), and Victoria Spivey (1906–1976).

A few self-accompanied male vaudeville performers recorded in the early and mid-1920s, performers such as Sylvester Weaver, Papa Charlie Jackson (ca. 1880–1938), and Lonnie Johnson (1889–1970); but in 1926, a wave of folk-blues artists on record was launched by Blind Lemon Jefferson (1893–1929). Through the early 1930s, many recordings were made of solo guitar- or piano-accompanied blues singers, mostly male, presenting to a national audience the sounds typically heard at Southern jukehouses and barrelhouses and urban rent parties.

Figure 3 Bessie Smith began her career performing at theaters and in bars throughout the South. She made her first recording in 1923 and through the rest of the decade recorded with Louis Armstrong, Coleman Hawkins, Fletcher Henderson, Benny Goodman, and other jazz giants. She is widely regarded one of the greatest blues singers.
Photo by Carl Van Vechten. Library of Congress, Prints & Photographs Division, Carl Van Vechten Collection, LC-DIG-ppmsca-09571.

DISC
❶
TRACK
13

Some important singer-guitarists who followed Jefferson in this period were Blind Blake, Blind Willie McTell (1901–1959), Barbecue Bob (1902–1931), Sam Collins (1897–1949), Tommy Johnson (ca. 1896–1956), Charley Patton (1891–1934), Son House (1902–1988), Jim Jackson (1884–1937), Furry Lewis (1893–1981), Robert Wilkins (1896–1987), and Ramblin' Thomas (1902–ca.1945); barrelhouse pianists included Clarence "Pine Top" Smith (1904–1929), Speckled Red (1892–1973), Charles "Cow Cow" Davenport (1894–1955), Charlie Spand, and Henry Brown (1906–1981). Guitar duos, such as those of Memphis Minnie (1897–1973) and Kansas Joe (McCoy; 1905–1950) and the Beale Street Sheiks (Frank Stokes and Dan Sane), and the combination of harmonica and guitar, as in the work of Bobbie Leecan and Robert Cooksey, were popular at this time, as was the combination of piano and guitar, first popularized in 1928 in the recordings of

Leroy Carr (1905–1935) and Scrapper Blackwell (1903–1962) and those of Georgia Tom (Thomas A. Dorsey; 1899–1993) and Tampa Red (Hudson Whitaker; 1904–1981).

Blues musicians formed larger groups, made up of combinations of string, wind, and percussion instruments known as jug bands, skiffle bands, juke bands, washboard bands, stringbands, and hokum bands. Some of the better-known recording groups of this sort were the Memphis Jug Band, Cannon's Jug Stompers, Whistler's Jug Band, the Mississippi Sheiks, and the Hokum Boys. All these duos and small groups were prominent in urban centers of the South and the North, allowing rural migrants to find common ground in their solo performance styles, explore new musical directions, and compete with more established urban musicians.

The Great Depression, which began in the late 1920s, effectively killed the institution of vaudeville and the blues style associated with it. In the mid-1930s, as the recording industry began to recover, Chicago became the primary center of blues-recording activity, and studios concentrated on stables of reliable stars, who could sing, play their own accompaniment, help one another on records, and compose original songs to supply the increasing number of jukeboxes. This was a decade of consolidation and homogenization in the blues. The primary instruments of folk blues were brought into small ensembles (or made to suggest their sounds), as exemplified by the work of guitarists Big Bill Broonzy (ca. 1893–1958) and Robert Johnson (1911–1938), pianist Roosevelt Sykes (1906–1983), and harmonica player John Lee "Sonny Boy" Williamson (1914–1948). Other stars of this period, who sometimes performed on one another's records, were Washboard Sam (1910–1966), Bumble Bee Slim (1905–1968), Jazz Gillum (1904–1966), Peetie Wheatstraw (1902–1941), Walter Davis (1912–1963), Curtis Jones (1906–1971), Johnnie Temple (1906–1968), Georgia White (1903–ca. 1980), Lil Johnson, Merline Johnson, Rosetta Howard (1914–1974), Lil Green (1919–1954), Bill Gaither (1910–1970), Blind Boy Fuller (ca. 1908–1940), Kokomo Arnold (1901–1968), and Arthur "Big Boy" Crudup (1905–1974). In 1936, the Harlem Hamfats, a seven-piece group based in Chicago and made up of Mississippi blues and New Orleans jazz musicians, pioneered a type of blues combo sound that was a precursor of the modern blues band. Small combos continued to be popular into the 1940s; they gradually adopted a louder and more rhythmic style, known as jump blues.

Electric Guitars

Electric guitars were an important factor in the blues sounds that came to prominence in the late 1940s and 1950s. The guitar's role in small combos was enhanced by the louder volume and new timbres of the electric instrument, played alongside the piano and the harmonica, itself now played through a microphone and amplifier. Such recently arrived Southern musicians as Muddy Waters (McKinley Morganfield; 1915–1983), Howlin' Wolf (1910–1976), Little Walter (1930–1968), Jimmy Reed (1925–1976), and Elmore James (1918–1963) pioneered in small electric-blues combos in Chicago and other cities during this period. At the same time, a jazz-influenced hornlike-lead style of playing, featuring extensive string bending, was being developed in the cities of the West Coast and South by guitarists Aaron "T-Bone" Walker (1910–1975), Lowell Fulson (1921–1999), Clarence "Gatemouth" Brown (1924–2005), Pee Wee Crayton (1914–1985), B. B. King (b. 1925), and others, working usually with larger bands, containing winds ("horn sections"). Electric guitars gave new life to the tradition of solo-guitar-accompanied folk blues, as exemplified in the music of artists Sam "Lightnin'" Hopkins (1912–1982) and John Lee Hooker (1917–2001).

Soul Blues

During the 1950s and reaching full fruition in the 1960s, a melismatic, emotional, gospel-influenced singing style, known as soul blues, became popular, as one hears in the work of B. B. King, himself a pioneer in the modern lead-guitar style. Other early soul-blues singers were Bobby "Blue" Bland (b. 1930), Ray Charles (1930–2004), and James Brown (1933–2006). None of these artists or those who followed them restricted their singing to blues material. Their singing-style, with the introduction of the electric bass and organ toward the end of the 1950s, is perhaps the last major stylistic innovation in blues, whose popular contemporary sound is not much different from that of the 1960s.

—Adapted from an article by David Evans

Bibliography

Cohn, Lawrence, ed. 1993. *Nothing but the Blues*. New York: Abbeville.

Evans, David. 1982. *Big Road Blues: Tradition and Creativity in the Folk Blues*. Berkeley: University of California Press.

Harris, Sheldon. 1979. *Blues Who's Who*. New Rochelle, N.Y.: Arlington House.

Harrison, Daphne Duval. 1988. *Black Pearls: Blues Queens of the 1920's*. New Brunswick, N.J.: Rutgers University Press.

Kubik, Gerhard. 1999. *Africa and the Blues*. Jackson: University Press of Mississippi.

Lomax, Alan. 1993. *The Land Where the Blues Began*. New York: Pantheon.

Merwe, Peter van der. 1989. *Origins of the Popular Style: The Antecedents of Twentieth-Century Popular Music*. Oxford: Clarendon Press.

Oliver, Paul. 1969. *The Story of the Blues*. London: Barrie and Rockliff.

Titon, Jeff Todd. 1977. *Early Downhome Blues: A Musical and Cultural Analysis*. Urbana: University of Illinois Press.

Jazz: From Birth to the 1970s

Jazz is widely regarded as the pinnacle of African-American music in the twentieth century. It is distinguished by the originality of its improvisation and the virtuosity, erudition, professionalism, and artistry of its performers and composers. Many of its aficionados regard it as America's classical music, or African-American classical music, though this definition is sometimes contested. The respectability it acquired in the late twentieth century stands in stark contrast to the status of the music and its practitioners earlier in the century.

Several broad social forces have shaped the history of jazz and its cultural meanings in the twentieth century—forces including urbanization, racism, recording and broadcasting technologies, modernism as an aesthetic ideology, two world wars, and the civil-rights movement. The musical hallmarks of jazz are improvisation, syncopation, a rhythmic propulsiveness known as swing, a blues feeling, and harmonic complexity. Unlike in most other African-American musical genres, instrumental performance has been more prestigious and influential than vocal performance.

Jazz and Ragtime

Genres that contributed to the formation of jazz included ragtime, blues, marches, African-American religious music, European classical music, American popular song, and musical theater. These genres overlapped considerably, as the relationships among ragtime, musical theater, and jazz at the turn of the twentieth century illustrate. Ragtime today is most often associated with the piano compositions of Scott Joplin (1868–1917), but audiences of the 1890s associated it with song, especially so-called coon songs, which featured lyrics that stereotyped black Americans. Many examples of such songs emerged from the thriving African-American musical theater scene in New York. Among the most noted black American musical composers and performers of the day were Ernest Hogan (1860–1909; figure 1), Will Marion Cook (1869–1944), Bob Cole (1863–1911), the Johnson brothers (J. Rosamond [1873–1954] and James Weldon [1871–1938]), Bert Williams (1874–1922), and George Walker (ca. 1873–1911).

After the success of Ernest Hogan's "All Coons Look Alike to Me" (1896), which launched a fad for coon songs lasting until World War I, many of the

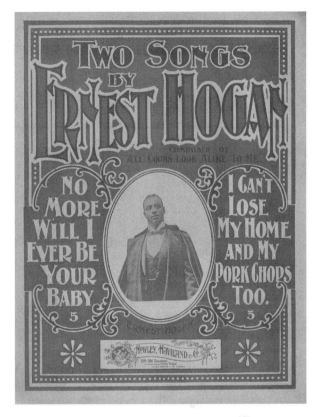

Figure 1 Ernest Hogan pictured on the sheet music to his songs "No More Will I Ever Be Your Baby" and "I Can't Lose My Home and My Pork Chops Too" (ca. 1899). Hogan was known as an exceptionally talented composer, actor, producer, dancer, and comedian.
From the collection of the Music Department, New York Public Library for the Performing Arts, Astor, Lenox, and Tilden Associations.

pioneers of mainstream American musical theater began composing ragtime songs, including George M. Cohan (1878–1942) and Irving Berlin (1888–1989). Images of African Americans in ragtime song were largely stereotypical—derived from representational conventions of minstrelsy and vaudeville—and contributed to a debate over ragtime's merits within both the black community and mainstream American society. Black elites objected to the denigrating racial images in the songs, while white society objected to the popularity of this "lowbrow" art form.

Ragtime made its initial impact on the musical stage, but instrumental ensembles including dance bands, brass bands, and concert bands soon incorporated it into their repertoires. Piano versions of ragtime songs were published, and in time, a distinctive piano repertoire emerged, one whose chief composers were Scott Joplin, James Scott (1886–1938), and Joseph Lamb (1887–1960). Perhaps the most famous piano rag, widely performed by pianists and instrumental ensembles, is Joplin's "Maple Leaf Rag" (1899).

The most common trait associated with ragtime is syncopation. To rag a piece was to syncopate its melody. Instrumental ragtime made extensive use of 2/4 meter and march form—sixteen-bar strains or themes. The most common formal arrangement consisted of two themes in the tonic key (AB or ABA), followed by a trio section, consisting of one or two themes in the subdominant key. March forms are widely found in early jazz. Musical innovations leading to the development of jazz as a distinctive genre occurred within instrumental ensembles that included ragtime as part of their repertoire.

New Orleans

Historians place the origins of jazz in New Orleans during the first years of the twentieth century, concurrent with the heyday of ragtime. Cornetist Buddy Bolden's band, which established a distinctive sound between 1897 and 1907, is often considered the first jazz band. Bolden (1877–1931) was known for improvisational elaboration of melodies, an ability to play loudly (legend has it that he could be heard across Lake Pontchartrain), and a deep feeling for the blues. Bands that competed with his in New Orleans featured marches, rags, and waltzes. Around 1900, brass bands, which had generally featured the careful execution of written arrangements, began admitting "ear" musicians ("routiners"), who created "head arrangements" and brought a more improvisational and blues-inflected style to the music. Brass bands were particularly important in transforming a straight march beat into the slow drag and up-tempo strut, the basic feels of New Orleans jazz style.

Hardening racial relations in New Orleans at the end of the nineteenth century shaped jazz. Increased contact between French-speaking Creole musicians and English-speaking blacks was a byproduct of the emergence of Jim Crow laws in the 1890s and the use of the "one drop rule" of racial classification. Under this rule, persons of as little as one thirty-second black ancestry (sometimes even less) were considered black, regardless of their appearance. The traditionally three-tiered New Orleans racial hierarchy—white, Creole, black—hardened into a two-tiered structure recognizing only black and white, especially after the Plessy v. Ferguson decision of 1896, the Supreme Court decision that established the doctrine of "separate but equal."

Creoles of color—predominantly Catholic, of French-speaking heritage, and generally of light complexion—resided "downtown" and had long cultivated instrumental virtuosity, musical literacy, and training in classical music. They considered themselves superior to their English-speaking and less musically literate black neighbors, who resided predominantly "uptown." Uptown musicians were noted for the blues, their improvisational abilities, and their abilities as ear musicians. The emergence of jazz as an instrumentally virtuosic, improvisational tradition that valued musical literacy emerged from a meeting of uptown and downtown. Among the Creole musicians most important to the development of jazz are pianist and composer Jelly Roll Morton (Ferdinand LeMothe, 1890–1941), clarinetist Barney Bigard (1906–1980), trombonist Kid Ory (1890–1973), and clarinetist and saxophonist Sidney Bechet (1897–1959). The pathbreaking soloists were uptown musicians, among them cornetist Joe "King" Oliver (1885–1938) and trumpeter Louis Armstrong (1901–1971).

Chicago

Despite the longstanding notion that jazz traveled up the Mississippi to Chicago (a legend that ignores that the river does not pass through Chicago), California—Los Angeles and San Francisco—was an equally important market for jazz before 1917. The bands of Freddie Keppard and Kid Ory were among many that brought jazz to California between 1914 and 1922. Chicago, nevertheless, holds a special place in the history of 1920s jazz, for it was there that Louis Armstrong's bold and virtuosic improvisational style became the talk of the town and set the direction for development.

In the summer of 1922, King Oliver asked Louis Armstrong to join his band in Chicago. Oliver's band played along "The Stroll," a thriving nightlife district on South State Street featuring several African-American-owned clubs: the Deluxe Café, the Pekin, and the Dreamland Café. These and other clubs became sites of racial boundary-crossing as interested young whites came to enjoy the music, among them saxophonist Bud Freeman (1906–1991), cornetist Jimmy McPartland (1907–1991), clarinetist Frank Teschemacher (1906–1932), and drummer Dave Tough (1908–1948). Many of Chicago's south-side clubs were black-and-tans, cabarets that presented African-American performers and catered to black and white audiences.

Between 1925 and 1928, Armstrong made recordings for OKeh (the music arranged by his wife and pianist Lil Hardin [1898–1971]) with groups known as the Hot Five and the Hot Seven. These are among his most celebrated recordings. They defined a bold, virtuosic improvisational style, which became the hallmark of early jazz. He moved away from melodic paraphrase to a more elaborate improvisational style, guided by the underlying harmonies, rather than the melody alone. Armstrong's solo on "Potato Head Blues" (figure 2) offers an excellent example of his classic style.

Armstrong's bandmates in the Hot Five were Lil Hardin, piano; Johnny Dodds (1892–1940), clarinet; Kid Ory, trombone; and Johnny St. Cyr (1890–1966), banjo—the last three, old friends from New Orleans. The Hot Seven added Baby Dodds (1898–1959), drums, and Pete Briggs, tuba. John Thomas, trombone, and Earl Hines (1903–1983), piano, were occasional sidemen. Though these recordings were made in Chicago and many earlier recordings by other bands included improvised solos, Armstrong's style set the standard for New Orleans jazz. The Hot Five and Hot Seven recordings established him as a cultural hero, especially in African-American communities, where his tremendous success contributed to a sense of communal pride.

Composers, Ensembles, and Big Bands

The emergence of improvising soloists was one hallmark of jazz, and the development of the jazz ensemble—large and small—was another. A particular sound produced through distinctive rhythmic, harmonic, melodic, and timbral vocabularies are just as crucial to defining jazz as improvisation is. Among the early jazz composers and arrangers who contributed to this sound were Jelly Roll Morton, Duke Ellington (1899–1974), Fletcher Henderson (1897–1952), and Don Redman (1900–1964).

Jelly Roll Morton's 1926 recordings for Victor illustrate the creative use of the ensemble in early jazz. Among the most highly regarded compositions from these sessions are "Black Bottom Stomp," "Grandpa's Spells," "The Chant," and "Smokehouse Blues." Unlike the Hot Five recordings, which omitted bass and drums, these recordings feature one of the best rhythm sections in early jazz: Morton,

Figure 2 Louis Armstrong's solo on "Potato Head Blues" (1988).

piano; John Lindsay (1894–1950), bass; Andrew Hilaire, drums; and Johnny St. Cyr, banjo. In "Black Bottom Stomp," Morton and his band, the Red Hot Peppers, deploy a dazzling variety of textures to energize the performance.

In New York of the 1920s, Fletcher Henderson and Don Redman developed a big-band sound by incorporating Armstrong, Coleman Hawkins (1904–1969), and other soloists into a dance band of larger instrumentation than that of typical New Orleans jazz ensembles. Henderson's band featured three trumpets, a trombone, three reeds, and a rhythm section. Henderson and Redman, working as a team, developed an arranging style that featured calls and responses between the brass and reed sections and the use of one instrumental choir as an accompanimental background for the other, often featuring a riff. Redman arranged ensemble sections in the style of improvised jazz solos. All these devices and techniques became staples of big-band arranging in the 1930s.

Duke Ellington developed a unique style for jazz ensembles in the 1920s. His style combined the "sweet" (that is, not blues-inflected) dance-band style with the exuberant New Orleans and blues-inspired trumpet style of New Yorker Bubber Miley (1903–1932) and Ellington's own stride- and ragtime-based piano style. Miley pioneered the growling trumpet sound that became a trademark of Ellington's so-called jungle sound. This sound had several elements: the use of a straight mute, an ordinary bathroom plunger to produce a wa-wa sound, a growl in the trumpeter's throat, and the trumpeter's simultaneous playing and humming of a pitch into the horn. Ellington's recordings of "East St. Louis Toodle-Oo" and "Black and Tan Fantasy" from 1926 to 1927 provide excellent examples of Miley's "talking brass" effect. Tricky Sam Nanton (1904–1946) adapted this sound to the trombone, and thereafter mastery of the growl sound was an essential for brass players in the Ellington band.

In 1927, Ellington got his first major break when he was hired at the Cotton Club, a Harlem nightclub catering to whites only and decorated in plantation motifs. The club featured shows combining music, exotic dancing (some performed in pseudo-African garb), and theatrical presentations. The Ellington orchestra, now expanded from six to eleven members, provided the clientele with the "primitive" ambience they were looking for, often through sophisticated musical means beyond their imagination. The club's regular radio broadcasts during Ellington's tenure there (1927–1932) brought his music into America's living rooms and made him a national figure.

Swing

Swing—jazz played mainly by big bands in a lively style suitable for dancing—came to the fore in the 1930s. The major big bands of the swing era served as important training grounds for younger musicians. Many improved their music-reading skills, understanding of harmony, and ensemble skills; some improved their composing and arranging skills under the tutelage of more experienced musicians. A hallmark of swing is the extensive use of riffs as ensemble textures, in at least four ways: as melodies; in calls and responses with other riffs or improvised passages; as a continuous supporting texture underneath a soloist or a written passage; and in layers. The artful use of repetition in a steady meter served as an anchor for dancers and was another hallmark of swing style.

In the 1930s, many virtuosic soloists emerged from groups of all sizes. Expanding on Armstrong's lead, musicians strove to extend the scope of solo improvisation. Among the most prominent soloists were Roy Eldridge (1911–1989), trumpet; Lester Young (1909–1959) and Coleman Hawkins, tenor saxophone (figure 3); and Art Tatum (1909–1956),

Figure 3 Coleman Hawkins performing at the Spotlite Club, New York City, ca. September, 1946. Hawkins' artistry on the saxophone helped make it one of the most prominent instruments of jazz.
Photo © William P. Gottlieb; www.jazzphotos.com.

piano. Vocalist Billie Holiday (1915–1959), whose paraphrases of melody and timing inspired many, including Lester Young, became prominent in the late 1930s, recording with members of the Count Basie Orchestra.

Bebop

During the war years, musicians frustrated with limitations on extended improvisation in big bands and dismayed by the dominance of white bands in the popular-music market forged an ambitious improvisational style that came to be known as bebop. (Musicians first called it modern music.) No longer content to be entertainers, younger jazz musicians demanded to be taken seriously as artists. The heroes of this movement were Charlie Parker (1920–1955; figure 4), alto sax; Thelonious Monk (1917–1982), piano; Dizzy Gillespie (1917–1993), trumpet; Kenny Clarke (1914–1985), drums; Max Roach (1924–2007), drums; and Bud Powell (1924–1966), piano. The legendary jam sessions that are said to have created the style took place in Harlem at Minton's and Monroe's Uptown House.

The musical innovations of bebop affected several dimensions of the music: instrumental virtuosity, harmony, phrasing, rhythmic feel, timbre, and tempo. Charlie Parker and Dizzy Gillespie reharmonized and/or wrote new melodies for standard jazz tunes, such as "Cherokee," "I Got Rhythm," and "What Is This Thing Called Love?" increasing the harmonic rhythm (the pace at which harmonies change) and

the tempo and improvising highly subdivided phrases, all of which set new standards for instrumental virtuosity. Drummers Kenny Clarke and Max Roach, picking up where Count Basie's drummer Jo Jones left off, transferred the standard ride rhythm from the hi-hat cymbals to the suspended ride cymbal, both altering the timbral color of the time-keeping pattern and increasing its volume. They began breaking up the time by inserting offbeat accents on the bass drum and snare, increasing rhythmic variety and dialogue in the rhythm section.

Among Parker's most celebrated recordings are "Koko" (1945), "Night in Tunisia" (1946), "Parker's Mood" (1948), and "Embraceable You" (1947). Among Gillespie's most admired recordings are several made with Parker, such as "Shaw 'Nuff" (1945), "Salt Peanuts" (1945), and "Hot House" (1953), and many under his own leadership, including "Woody'n You" (1946), "Night in Tunisia" (1946), "Manteca" (1947), "Cubana Be-Cubana Bop" (1947, a collaboration with George Russell [b. 1923] and Chano Pozo [1915–1948]), and "Con Alma" (1957).

In contrast to Parker and Gillespie, Thelonious Monk (figure 5) is recognized more for the originality of his compositions than for his virtuosity as a soloist. For the Blue Note label in 1947, he recorded many of his most famous compositions, including "Thelonious," "Ruby My Dear," "'Round Midnight," "Well You Needn't," and "In Walked Bud." Though greatly admired in the jazz world of the late 1940s (pianist Mary Lou Williams [1910–1981] was

Figure 4 Charlie Parker leads a quintet with Miles Davis on trumpet, Tommy Potter on bass, Duke Jordan on piano, and Max Roach on drums (both out of view), at the Three Deuces, New York City, ca. August, 1947.
Photo © William P. Gottlieb; www.jazzphotos.com.

Figure 5 Thelonious Monk performing at Minton's Playhouse, New York City, ca. September, 1947. *Photo © William P. Gottlieb; www.jazzphotos.com.*

among his earliest champions), Monk did not achieve broader prominence until the late 1950s and early 1960s. Monk's loss of his cabaret card in 1951 helped marginalize him, but perhaps a more important hindrance to his fame was the great difference between his aesthetic and that of mainstream bebop. Parker and Gillespie's music emphasized virtuosity, but Monk's music argued that less is more.

Cool Jazz and Hard Bop

Miles Davis's improvisational style also leaned toward an aesthetic that less is more. His solo career was launched by the celebrated "Birth of the Cool" recordings, made in 1949 and 1950. These recordings emerged from a think tank of composers and musicians who met in the apartment of arranger Gil Evans (1912–1988) in the late 1940s to explore musical ideas and theories and their potential application to jazz. The aesthetic that emerged from the group emphasized coloristic timbral effects, achieved through unusual instrumental pairings (French horns and tuba; alto sax and baritone sax; trumpet and trombone), no vibrato, and a seamless integration of written and improvised music, often disguising formal sectional boundaries of the music.

In the 1950s, the aesthetic of cool jazz, emphasizing lyrical melodic style and softer tonal colors,

became socially coded as a white sound, which contrasted with hard bop, coded as a black sound. Art Blakey (1919–1990) and the Jazz Messengers (the quintessential hard-bop band) often served to define the hard-bop alternative. Historians emphasize Blakey's and Horace Silver's (b. 1928) embrace of African-American roots through the exuberant expressive resources of blues, gospel, and rhythm and blues. Notable examples of this style are found on Blakey's "Moanin' " (1958). Mere opposition of black and white obscures the practice of some prominent white saxophonists associated with the cool sound (Stan Getz [1927–1991], Lee Konitz [b. 1927], Paul Desmond [1924–1977]) of imitating the lyrical swing of African-American artists such as Lester Young and Johnny Hodges (1906–1970). Also ignored by the black–white contrast is that one of the most prominent ensembles with a cool sound was the Modern Jazz Quartet, an African-American group.

The Civil-rights Movement and its Effects on Jazz

By the mid-1950s, the burgeoning civil-rights movement was exerting pressure on musicians to support efforts to end Jim Crow laws and customs. The black community expected musicians to demonstrate their commitment to the larger cause of racial justice and publicly shamed artists (such as Nat King Cole [1919–1965] and Louis Armstrong) who continued to accept engagements in performance venues that segregated audiences. The issue of audience segregation was more important to civil-rights organizations than whether or not a band had mixed personnel. Southern white audiences had long been comfortable with black and mixed entertainment as long as segregated seating remained. The activist climate emerging from the principal events of the civil-rights movement—the Montgomery bus boycott (1956), the desegregation of Central High School in Little Rock, Arkansas (1957), the independence of the African country of Ghana (1957), the student lunch-counter sit-ins in Greensboro, North Carolina (1960), the Freedom Rides throughout the South (1961), the campaign to desegregate Birmingham, Alabama, (1963), and the assassination of Malcolm X (1965)—had important consequences for jazz.

Jazz musicians reacted by performing benefit concerts, recording albums with political themes, attributing political meaning to particular jazz aesthetics, exploring African and other non-Western musical and religious ideas, and engaging in highly charged dialogues about race and racism in their industry. The emergence of several of the most revered figures in jazz and the aesthetics they represent—among them Miles Davis, John Coltrane (1926–1967), Charles Mingus (1922–1979), and Ornette Coleman (b. 1930)—took place against this historical backdrop.

Modal Jazz

Among the most important musical innovations in the 1950s and early 1960s was the development of modal jazz. Exemplified by Miles Davis's album *Kind of Blue* (1959), modal compositions reduced the number of harmonic changes, allowing soloists to improvise for an extended period of time over one or two chords. This harmonic background allowed soloists greater freedom to superimpose modes, scales, voicings, and melodic ideas over any particular sonority.

Modal jazz came to imply a more open-ended approach to form. Instead of observing a chorus structure, jazz musicians explored pieces that allowed soloists to play indefinitely over recurring chord patterns or rhythmic vamps. The vamp to John Coltrane's "My Favorite Things" (1960) as played by pianist McCoy Tyner (b. 1938) provides one example (figure 6); Charles Mingus's "Pithecanthropus Erectus" (1956) and Art Blakey's extended percussion solos on "Orgy in Rhythm" (1957) and "Holiday for Skins" (1958) provide additional examples.

In the early 1960s, John Coltrane shifted from a well-developed modern bebop style featuring harmonically dense compositions such as "Giant Steps" (1959) to an open-ended modal conception that explored African and Indian sources of musical and spiritual inspiration. His legendary ensembles—featuring McCoy Tyner, piano; Elvin Jones (1927–2004), drums; and Jimmy Garrison (1934–1976), bass (among others)—developed rhythmic and harmonic implications of open-ended modal approaches to improvisation—something that Miles Davis's quintet of 1963–1968 did also. Freed from the necessity of delineating frequently changing harmonies, bassists expanded their use of pedal points, pianists accompanied long sections with intricate

vamps and riffs, and drummers played with greater rhythmic density and cross-rhythms than had been customary in earlier styles. Among the recordings exemplifying this sound are Coltrane's *My Favorite Things* (1960), *Africa Brass* (1961), *India* (1961), *Crescent* (1964), and *A Love Supreme* (1965), and Davis's *My Funny Valentine* (1964), *Miles in Berlin* (1964), and *Live at the Plugged Nickel* (1965).

Free Jazz

A major aesthetic controversy erupted in the jazz world in early 1960, when alto saxophonist Ornette Coleman emerged on the New York scene. His dissonances and abandonment of chorus structures and fixed harmonic changes as means of organizing improvisation were claimed by some as *The Shape of Jazz to Come* (1959) (the title of Coleman's first release after his arrival in New York), decried by others as the destruction of jazz, and championed by still others as a music of social critique. Over the next seven years, an aesthetic community of jazz musicians committed to what was variously termed free jazz, the new thing, or avant-garde jazz emerged in New York. Among them were Coleman, Cecil Taylor (b. 1933), Albert Ayler (1936–1970), Archie Shepp (b. 1937), Sun Ra (1914–1993), and John Coltrane. Coltrane's turn toward free jazz gave considerable prestige to the free-jazz movement. The new approach fostered the creation of collective musical organizations such as Chicago's Association for the Advancement of Creative Musicians (AACM) (1965) and St. Louis's Black Artists Group (BAG) (1968).

The 1970s

The release of Miles Davis's *Bitches Brew* (1969) augured new directions for jazz, directions that embraced, rather than rejected, popular musical styles. Heralded for creatively synthesizing jazz improvisation and rock and roll, *Bitches Brew* used electrified rock and roll and many of the post-production techniques of popular music, including overdubbing and looping. Davis was particularly inspired by guitarist Jimi Hendrix (1942–1970), who reached a broad audience with his musical pyrotechnics. Later, Davis's fusion interests turned toward soul and funk in an effort to reach younger African-American audiences. His albums *A Tribute to Jack Johnson* (1970) and *On the Corner* (1972) illustrate this trend. Several other bands offering mixes among jazz, rock and roll, soul, rhythm and blues, and non-Western musics emerged in the 1970s, including, most prominently, Weather Report, John

Figure 6 The vamp to John Coltrane's "My Favorite Things" (1960), as played by pianist McCoy Tyner.

McLaughlin (b. 1942) and the Mahavishnu Orchestra, Herbie Hancock (b. 1940) and the Headhunters, and Chick Corea (b. 1941) and Return to Forever.

—*Adapted from an article by Ingrid Monson*

Bibliography

Berlin, Edward A. 1980. *Ragtime: A Musical and Cultural History*. Berkeley: University of California Press.

Blesh, Rudi. 1985. *Shining Trumpets: A History of Jazz*. 2nd ed. New York: Knopf.

Brunn, N. O. 1960. *The Story of the Original Dixieland Jazz Band*. Baton Rouge: Louisiana State University Press.

Budds, Michael J. 1990. *Jazz in the Sixties: The Expansion of Musical Resources and Techniques*. Iowa City: The University of Iowa.

Collier, James Lincoln. 1983. *Louis Armstrong: An American Genius*. New York: Oxford University Press.

——. 1989. *Benny Goodman and the Swing Era*. New York: Oxford University Press.

DeVeaux, Scott. 1997. *The Birth of Bebop: A Social and Musical History*. Berkeley: University of California Press.

Gillespie, Dizzy, with Al Fraser. [1970] 1979. *To Be or Not to Bop: Memoirs of Dizzy Gillespie*. New York: Da Capo.

Kmen, Henry A. 1977. *The Roots of Jazz: The Negro and Music in New Orleans 1791–1900*. Urbana: University of Illinois Press.

Longstreet, Stephen. 1965. *Sportin' House: A History of the New Orleans Sinners and the Birth of Jazz*. Los Angeles: Sherbourne Press.

Porter, Lewis, and Michael Ullman. 1993. *Jazz: From Its Origins to the Present*. Englewood Cliffs, N.J.: Prentice-Hall.

Stowe, David W. 1994. *Swing Changes: Big Band Jazz in New Deal America*. Cambridge: Harvard University Press.

Tirro, Frank. 1977. *Jazz: A History*. New York: Norton.

Hip-Hop and Rap: From Birth to the 1980s

Hip-hop, also called hip-hop culture, is a creative expression, aesthetic, and sensibility that developed in African-American, Afro-Caribbean, and Latino communities of the Bronx and Harlem, New York City, by the mid-1970s. Now an internationally recognized cultural phenomenon largely due to the popularity of rap, hip-hop encompasses four competitive performance expressions that often go unnoticed by the mainstream public. These elements are aerosol art (graffiti); b-boying/girling (break dancing); DJ-ing, or the art of using turntables, vinyl records, and mixing units as musical instruments; and MC-ing (rapping), the art of verbal musical expression. Those who consider their primary aesthetic to be shaped by hip-hop culture and/or claim a personal stake in its development form what is known as the hip-hop community. They are sometimes called hip-hoppers. Rap music, the most popularized manifestation of hip-hop, is a musical expression that emphasizes stylized verbal delivery of rhymed couplets—in other words, an AABB poetic scheme—typically over a prerecorded accompaniment (tracks). Rappers from hip-hop's beginning to the mid-1980s kept the literal interpretation of the rhyme scheme intact, with some syncopation.

Early History

Rap is rooted in cultural and verbal traditions from the United States and the Caribbean. Mainland traditions that remain visible in hip-hop include "jive-talking" radio personalities of the 1940s and 1950s and oral traditions of storytelling, toasting, and "playing the dozens," a competitive and recreational exchange of verbal insults. Jamaican traditions include toasting and mobile disk jockeys. Many hip-hop pioneers were Caribbean immigrants, who brought musical practices from their native countries and adapted them to new situations.

During World War II, Jamaicans heard African-American dance music on records and American radiobroadcasts and from soldiers stationed there. Rhythm and blues, bebop, and swing offered alternatives to the two government-run, British-modeled Jamaican radio stations, which broadcast calypso-styled mento and other styles that appealed primarily to economically higher classes. Imported African-American dance music grew in popularity, particularly at "blues dances," held mostly in economically

poor urban areas in the 1950s. Mobile disc jockeys (DJs), who provided music for social events, featured rhythm-and-blues records. They competed for the attention and patronage of social dancers using large sound systems ("sounds") in a battle of volume and song choices. These systems consisted of turntables, speakers, amplifiers, and a microphone. At the helm were Duke Reid (ca. 1915–1974) and Sir Coxone Dodd (1932–2004), who became legendary figures in the early era of mobile discothèques. DJs enlisted a paid crew of assistants and accrued loyal audience participants. Often, two DJs were booked to perform in the same space: they would engage in a battle of decibels and would select and order songs designed to elicit maximum responses from the audience.

DJs spoke "rhythmically over the music, [using their] voice as another instrument" on the microphone (Fernando 1994:34). Their comments, known as toasts, included praise for dancers' appearance and information on the next dance. With the development of the Jamaican recorded music industry in the 1950s, DJs began to record instrumental versions of songs, known as "dub" versions, on the B side of the vocal track versions, in response to the growing practice of DJs' toasting on the microphone at public dances. U. Roy, one of the most important figures in Jamaican toasting on record, was the first to record his style of rhythmic speaking over dubs in 1970. Both Jamaican and U.S. early rapping traditions were started by rapping DJs, who only later hired people to rap exclusively. Rappers became known as masters of ceremony (MCs) and were charged with motivating the crowd and delivering information about upcoming social events.

The mingling of Caribbean immigrant and native-born African-American and Latino communities in the United States set the stage for the development of rap music. A large Caribbean community had developed in New York, where the first rap musical dance events were said to have begun, as early as 1972 in the Bronx. The native-born African-American residents, many of whom were recent migrants from the South, had a vibrant verbal culture: they were familiar with toasting, albeit in the form of long, rhymed stories, often memorized and passed on orally. "The Signifying Monkey" is one such popular toast. Another, "Hustlers' Convention," was commercially recorded by The Last Poets, a spoken-word trio based in New York. For decades in America, to rap had meant 'to converse, to talk freely', and in the late 1960s it sometimes referred to the art of earnest verbal engagement, often meant to persuade listeners, and it did not necessitate rhyming. Rapping was perhaps most often associated with flirting, but it encompassed the rhetoric of political and social commentary. Popular rhythm-and-blues artists of the 1960s and 1970s rapped message-oriented sections toward the end of songs. Diana Ross (b. 1944) was well-known for her raps about love and relationships; Maurice White (b. 1941) of Earth, Wind & Fire rapped on the topic of inner beauty in a 1975 song, "All about Love."

Rapping as a distinct musical form developed in New York in the early 1970s as a cultural expression encompassed by hip-hop. Socioeconomic conditions in the Bronx and Harlem in the 1960s and 1970s profoundly shaped the aesthetics and activities of hip-hop culture. The construction of the Cross-Bronx Expressway, in 1959, speeded the deterioration of buildings and the displacement of people in south Bronx communities, and youth gangs and gang violence escalated there. Despite the turbulence of the 1960s and 1970s, Bronx youths developed and popularized expressions that eventually came to be associated with hip-hop culture, then primarily consisting of graffiti and competitive dancing. Hip-hop became a powerful cultural symbol of urban youth. Within a few years, it had spread beyond the Bronx.

1970s: The Era of Hip-hop DJs

The accessibility of rap music stemmed from several factors: residents who moved or traveled beyond the New York area; the local dissemination of rap music through the sale of home-produced cassette tapes of rap shows; and the non-Bronx residents who came to see live performances and reported or imitated them in their own neighborhoods. The primary mode of rap musical expression was then through live performances, held in parks, community centers, school gymnasiums, neighborhood clubs, private basements, and the like. Similarly, the dominant means of establishing one's reputation as a rapper was through performing at these events and trading in privately taped performances of the shows and locally pressed records. Taped rap music was sold from briefcases and the trunks of cars for as much as $15.00 per cassette. These tapes, which were often duplicated and passed on, contributed to the popularity of such acts as the Cold Crush Brothers, the Funky Four Plus One, and Kool Moe Dee and the Treacherous Three, several years before the advent of music videos.

DJs in the Bronx, including Kool DJ Herc (b. 1955), Afrika Bambaataa (b. 1957 or 1960), and Grandmaster Flash (b. 1958), are most frequently credited with developing hip-hop and rap music. DJs were acknowledged among New York hip-hoppers as the foundation of hip-hop culture, and in rap music DJs were a crucial defining element that distinguishes rapping from poetry and other types of oral performance. Though they provided music from prerecorded discs, taking the place of a live band, they made the musical practice equivalent to a live event through techniques of spinning, cutting, mixing, and scratching, the production of percussive sounds by moving a record back and forth rhythmically under a phonographic needle. Thus, they recontextualized the phonographs, turntables, and mixing units as musical instruments. As hip-hop became commercially recognized, the popularity of MCs overshadowed that of DJs.

Hip-hoppers acknowledge Kool DJ Herc as the father of hip-hop. Having arrived in the west Bronx from Jamaica in 1967 as an adolescent, he brought with him the practice of the mobile DJ, the Jamaican tradition of toasting, and competitive musical display. By 1973, he had begun providing music at social events in homes (house parties), public spaces (block parties), and community centers. By the disco era of the 1970s, he had become known not only for his selections of records, ranging from funk and rhythm and blues to Latin, but also for the manner in which he played them. Using two turntables with identical records, he would select the most percussive or rhythmically appealing sections ("the breakdown"), which often featured Latin instruments such as congas, timbales, and cowbells. Then he would switch back and forth between the turntables, finding the approximate spot where the section began. This resulted in an extended "break" section, which appealed strongly to dancing patrons. Hip-hop dancing, or b-boying/girling, became popularized as break dancing.

Kool Herc was recognized for his sound system, with its massive, bass-heavy speakers, which had a reputation for overpowering competitors, who included at that time fellow pioneer Afrika Bambaataa. Many DJs delivered rhymes to dancers at parties, but Kool Herc was known more for his musical choices and sound system. His musical speaking mostly consisted of letting people know where the next dance would take place. Later, he hired assistants to form his unit, the Herculords, who would rap as MCs. As in the Jamaican mobile DJ party scene, battling for dancing patrons' attention became a feature of the early New York hip-hop scene.

Afrika Bambaataa, an informal student of Kool Herc's style, by 1976 had emerged as his former mentor's competitor. He established his reputation as a DJ by mixing obscure and unusual records for his Bronx audiences, including rock, cartoon theme songs, and even excerpts from Western art music. Also of West Indian origin, he promoted hip-hop expression into the late 1990s through an organization known as the Zulu Nation. This organization began in the early 1970s as the Black Spades, a notorious Bronx gang. He redirected the gang's activities toward creative competition rather than violence, through b-boying/girling and graffiti writing.

Kool Herc and Bambaataa were known primarily for their musical choices and blending of songs, rather than for the turntable maneuverings, techniques, and tricks that marked later DJs. The Barbados-born, south Bronx resident Grandmaster Flash was one of several Bronx DJs who developed turntable manipulations into a distinct musical practice. He combined a background in electronics with his musical interests to become one of the most influential figures in hip-hop. His technological innovations with mixing units and the electronic percussion system came to characterize the hip-hop sound, particularly in the 1980s, of the electronic "beat-box."

1979–1985: Rap Music enters the Mainstream

The year 1979 marks rap music's first commercial release, "Rappers Delight," recorded by the New Jersey-based Sugar Hill Gang on an independent label owned by former rhythm-and-blues vocalist Sylvia Robinson (b. 1936). The song "King Tim III," recorded by the funk group Fatback Band, actually preceded Sugar Hill Gang's release as the first song featuring a hip-hop-style rapped section, but the song recorded by the latter group became the more popular.

The earliest recordings of rap music often featured a rapper rhyming over an instrumental version of a popular song played by a live band or a combination of simple synthesized percussion and live instruments. As in Jamaican dub tracks, the rapper would add his or her voice to the layer of live instruments. In 1982, recordings by Bambaataa's group, the Soul Sonic Force, defined the hip-hop sound of the 1980s by introducing synthesizers and electronic musical devices. Bambaataa and, later, Boogie Down Productions employed the technique of sampling—using snippets from previously recorded music as a basis for new material, part of a polyphonic layer, or a thematic reference. A popular Bronx DJ, Grandmixer D. St. (b. 1960), was featured on Herbie Hancock's "Rockit" (1983). This recording was the first recorded jazz and hip-hop collaboration and the first hip-hop-influenced record to win a Grammy award, extending the hip-hop audience beyond its local beginnings.

In the mid to late 1980s, rap music experienced a stylistic and economic shift, as its distribution means moved from local, predominantly black-owned labels to international conglomerates with greater resources to reach large audiences. By 1985, Queens-based group Run-D.M.C, under the business partnership of Russell Simmons (b. 1957) and Rick Rubin (b. 1963) (Def Jam), had sold over 250,000 copies of several recordings. This attracted the attention of Columbia Records, a major label, which struck a business deal with Def Jam worth approximately one million dollars; this was the largest business contract involving rap music at the time. Columbia became the distributor for Def Jam's other rap music arts, including the white hip-hop-influenced act the Beastie Boys, who sold over four million copies of their debut album *Licensed to Ill* (1986). Run-D.M.C. was also the first hip-hop group to commercially endorse a product, a popular sneaker. Other groups on the company roster that expanded hip-hop's popularity beyond the Bronx and Harlem were Queens-based LL Cool J (b. 1968) and Long Island's Public Enemy.

Women have been part of hip-hop expression from its early days, primarily as part of MC crews such as the Funky Four Plus One and Sugar Hill's female group, Sequence. For most of hip-hop's recorded history, however, women MCs were mostly seen as novelty acts, with a few exceptions. In the mid-1980s, some female artists were popularized momentarily through "answer" songs, which ridiculed popular songs by male acts. These answer songs included Roxanne Shante's "Roxanne's Revenge" (responding to UTFO's 1984 song "Roxanne, Roxanne") and Peblee Poo's "Fly Guy" (responding to the Boogie Boys' 1985 song "A Fly Girl"). Some of the most enduring female hip-hop acts released premiere albums in 1986. Salt-N-Pepa (Cheryl "Salt" James [b. 1964], Sandi "Pepa" Denton [b. 1969], and DJ Dee Dee "Spinderella" Roper [b. 1971]) was the most successful hip-hop group with its first album, *Hot, Cool and Vicious*. Queen Latifah (b. 1970) emphasized strong social messages and female empowerment in her first album, *All Hail the Queen*. MC Lyte (b. 1971) recorded her first album, *Lyte as a Feather*, at this time.

In the late 1980s, predominantly African-American and Latino communities of northern and southern California emerged as important new bases of hip-hop culture. In the West Coast style, the hip-hop traditions of hyperbole, self-grandeur, and storytelling stemming from the African-American popular toasts such as "The Signifying Monkey" and "Hustlers' Convention" blended in with themes influenced by popular black gangster movie characters such as Superfly and Dolemite. The result was a distinctive brand of hardcore known as "gangster" or "gangsta rap," exemplified in the music of Oakland's Too Short and Compton's Niggaz with Attitude (NWA). The often violent and drug-related activities of rival youth gangs such as the Bloods and the Crips, which had become highly organized by the mid-1980s, were familiar themes in West Coast street culture. Many West Coast acts claimed hip-hop authenticity because their lyrics reflected a California inner-city lifestyle—albeit often idealized, exaggerated, or conjectured—depicting guns, violence, peer allegiance, sex, drugs, and the exploitation of women. The popularity and record sales of other West Coast acts such as Ice-T (b. 1958), Compton's Most Wanted, and, in the early 1990s after the break-up of NWA, Dr. Dre (b. 1965) and Snoop Doggy Dogg (b. 1971) surpassed sales of the New York artists.

Since its start as youthful entertainment in the 1970s, hip-hop came to be considered the most important voice and vehicle for the expression of contemporary American urban youth in the last quarter of the twentieth century. At the beginning of the twenty-first century, it stands as one of the most influential cultural expressions worldwide.

—*Adapted from an article by Dawn M. Norfleet*

Bibliography

Fernando, S. H. Jr. 1994. *The New Beats: Exploring the Music, Culture, and Attitudes of Hip-Hop*. New York: Doubleday.

Hebdige, Dick. 1987. *Cut 'n' Mix Culture: Identity and Caribbean Music*. New York: Methuen.

Kochman, Thomas, ed. 1972. *Rappin' and Stylin' Out: Communication in Urban Black America*. Urbana: University of Illinois Press.

McIver, Denise L., ed. 2002. *Droppin' Science: Straight-Up Talk from Hip Hop's Greatest Voices*. New York: Three Rivers Press.

Norfleet, Dawn. 1997. " 'Hip-Hop Culture' in New York City: The Role of Verbal Musical Performance in Defining a Community." Ph.D. dissertation, Columbia University.

Perkins, William Eric, ed. 1996. *Droppin' Science: Critical Essays on Rap Music and Hip Hop Culture*. Philadelphia: Temple University Press.

Vincent, Rickey. 1996. *Funk: The Music, the People, and the Rhythm of the One*. New York: St. Martin's Griffin.

European-American Musics

European-American Musics

European immigration to the land that is now the United States began in the sixteenth century and has continued, with people of European descent then and now forming the majority of the country. British immigrants, who set up permanent settlements in the seventeenth century, donated to the New World their language, their political theories and governmental structures, and their musical culture—and their influence continues. European culture contributed music and dance to the American mix, and the entrance of southern and eastern Europeans, including large numbers of Ashkenazic Jews, in the late nineteenth and early twentieth centuries opened the United States to a wealth of religious and ceremonial practices. The articles that follow present a sample of European American musics and depict popular forms that grew out of them.

James Duff, fiddler, Hazard, Kentucky, ca. 1930.
Photo by Doris Ullman. Library of Congress, Prints & Photographs Division, LC-USZC4-4724.

Overview

Everyone living in North America with the exception of Native Americans, came from, or has ancestors who came from, somewhere else. Between 1820 and 1960, an estimated fifty million immigrants made the journey, the majority from Europe, in what has been described as the greatest migration in human history. Many formed ethnic communities that set them apart. At the same time, they joined a larger society, which created a culture of unity out of diversity. America has been called a melting pot, the theory being that immigrants from all over the world become Americanized to form a homogeneous whole. But a more accurate analogy might be that of a mosaic, with people of diverse ethnic backgrounds mixing together and coexisting. In a mosaic, each piece retains its individual integrity, but becomes an essential part of the complete picture. As Americans abandoned the melting-pot ideal, they came to value diversity, and even to celebrate it.

The dominant cultures of North America came from England, Spain, and France. The first immigrants established a culture and society into which subsequent immigrants would have to fit. From the beginnings, European immigrants differed from other Europeans. Immigrant communities were internally more heterogeneous. Individuals tended to set aside regional differences and coalesce into unified communities: regional identities gave way to ethnic identities. Because these groups were small in relation to the surrounding populations, they tended to have more tolerance for internal diversity. Non-English-speaking immigrants were often isolated by language, and they therefore tended to interact primarily with their own group. The music they listened to was what they had brought with them. These and other common cultural traits took on added importance in North America, becoming symbols of ethnic identity. As symbols, they sometimes had greater stability than before. Ethnic groups have tended to perpetuate customs, traditions, and music even after they have vanished in the lands of their origin. An example of this was the discovery of English and Scottish folksongs in the southern Appalachian Mountains by the folksong collector Cecil Sharp in 1916 to 1918. An even more extreme case is that of the hymns of the Amish, which are believed to be marginal survivors of monophonic German hymnody.

Hybridization

At the same time that some musical styles were being preserved in America, new musical styles were being created by a process of hybridization (or fusion). Multiple ethnic groups came into contact with each other and American popular culture. When different ethnic groups in close proximity had similar kinds of music, a performing ensemble from one group could cross over and play at the other group's social functions. Victor Greene (1992) and others have documented examples of such crossing over. A large proportion of the engagements of the Intihar Ensemble, a polka band from Johnstown, Pennsylvania, for example, were at weddings or other events that mixed ethnicities: a bride, for example, might be Polish, and the bridegroom Italian. The band's repertoire included Polish, German, Italian, Greek, Irish, and Mexican pieces, which reflected the ethnic makeup of its audiences. It performed music that could be appreciated by all, regardless of ethnic background, and had the overall effect of uniting its audiences despite their multiethnicity.

An additional force for hybridization has been the spreading of American popular culture by the mass media, which has led ethnic ensembles to adopt certain popular stylistic features, especially when performing in multiethnic contexts. One of the best examples of this hybridization is that of the Slovenian-style polka bands of the 1940s and 1950s. Their style, popularized by Frankie Yankovic (1915–1998), combined old Slovenian melodies played by two accordions, with popular rhythm provided by a bass, drums, and a four-string banjo. Its popularity stretched beyond the Slovenian community and even that of ethnic music in general.

All types of ethnic music discussed in this section have in common that at some point they moved from being performed just for a specific ethnic community to being performed in broader contexts. The style and repertory of the music became adapted to suit these contexts, to the point that the music was no longer associated with a single ethnic group. Some musics entered the mainstream of American popular music and were no longer considered ethnic. Sometimes older forms of ethnic music were revived, and the new champions of a given form came from a different ethnic background.

—Adapted from an article by Carl Rahkonen

Bibliography

Ferris, William, and Mary L. Hart, eds. 1982. *Folk Music and Modern Sound*. Jackson: University Press of Mississippi.

Grame, Theodore C. 1976. *America's Ethnic Music*. Tarpon Springs, Fla.: Cultural Maintenance Associates.

Greene, Victor. 1992. *A Passion for Polka: Old-Time Ethnic Music in America*. Berlekey: University of California Press.

Nettl, Bruno. [1949] 1960. *An Introduction to Folk Music in the United States*. 3rd ed., revised and expanded by Helen Myers (1972) under the title *Folk Music in the United States: An Introduction*. Detroit: Wayne State University Press.

——. 1973. *Folk and Traditional Music of Western Continents*. 2nd ed. Englewood Cliffs, N.J.: Prentice Hall.

Vernon, Paul. 1995. *Ethnic and Vernacular Music, 1898–1960: A Resource and Guide to Recordings*. New York: Greenwood.

English and Scottish Music

Seventeenth-century British settlements formed the nucleus of and a template for the institutions and culture of the United States and much of Canada. Native American teachings in hunting and agriculture helped the young colonies survive, but aboriginal music had too little in common with that of the colonists to mix with or even influence what was arriving. Colonial music at first consisted of British psalmody, ballads and other folksongs, dance music, and, by the end of the eighteenth century, popular music created in or funneled through Britain. The initial transfer of cultural materials differed little from their transfer from London to remote posts in the English countryside. As time passed and the population of North America increased, American cities could imitate London more closely, though the desire to do so waned. In the 1840s, when American blackface minstrelsy became the rage throughout the English-speaking world, the cultural flow began to reverse direction. Today, most British musicians who become popular in the Americas perform American-derived music.

Music for Worship

European immigrants brought with them two streams of music: military and religious. The first settlements in British North America—in Jamestown in 1607, at Plymouth in 1620, and at Massachusetts Bay in 1627—were founded largely for religious reasons, and musical life immediately focused on Protestant psalmody. The Pilgrims, a small, conservative group, which had broken away from the Puritans, brought psalm singing, for which they borrowed preexistent melodies. In theory, a tune could be employed at any time to set any text that was in a compatible meter, here meaning having a certain number of lines and syllables per line. For example, common-meter psalms had four lines of text, the first and third with eight syllables, the second and fourth with six syllables, matching many tunes already in religious use and many secular tunes. Tunes had names, some of which indicated an association with given psalms; for example, Psalm 100 was and is still sung to the tune "Old Hundred," in long meter, that is, four lines each with eight syllables.

Change in the English language meant that any translation of the psalms would in time seem clumsy and would be updated to achieve or restore whatever mix of grace and straightforwardness was desired. The first book printed in Britain's North American colonies was just such a revision: *The Whole Booke of Psalmes Faithfully* TRANSLATED *into* ENGLISH *Metre* (1640), which became informally known as *The Bay Psalm Book*. A small publication, which grew in subsequent editions, it quickly supplanted parallel publications throughout the colonies. Seventy editions were published in British North America through 1773, eighteen in England through 1754, and twenty-two in Scotland through 1759. The first edition did not contain musical notation; its authors recommended borrowing tunes from an earlier British publication. Thirteen two-part settings of psalm tunes appeared in a supplement to the book in its ninth edition (1698), these tunes drawn from John Playford's *Brief Introduction to the Skill of Musick*, printed in London; most later editions lacked music.

In a literal sense the first North American publication, *The Bay Psalm Book* should be considered a British book, successful not because of its place of origin, but because it presented an important body of literature in a fresh and accessible form. The early centuries of British-American life have left no documentation of any attempt to create region-specific tunes. Any regional, American quality that *The Bay Psalm Book* possessed would have to concern its populism, perhaps especially important in the colonies because of the arduousness of daily life there, which left little time for wrestling with abstruse language or tricky music—indeed, for learning to read music.

How did this early psalm singing sound? Widespread changes in church economics and responsibilities in Britain before the colonies were founded, plus a proscription of organs and choirs in many churches, made the tidy picture of musical performance offered by musical notation deceptive. The lack of musical notation in most of the books was not just a matter of ease of printing; few in most congregations read music. This situation spawned a fascinating manner of performance: lining out. A leader would sing a phrase to remind the congregation of the melody being used, and then the group would repeat that line. Next, the leader offered the second line, the group sang it, and so on. Contemporary American accounts of the results—positive reports in the mid-seventeenth century, but complaints by 1700—suggest a sound like that of twentieth-century survivals of this practice in southern Appalachia. The congregational answers took much longer than the leader's lining out, and were neither faithful copies of melodic contours, nor sung in unison: singers filled melodic leaps with intervening steps and put slides between adjacent tones; each performer managed these things idiosyncratically. Contemporary reports asserted that the results were a mess, though this practice can produce a rich heterophony (a musical texture in which variants of the same musical line are performed together).

Lining out answered by slow, varied responses, termed the usual, common, or old way of singing, began to be shunted aside by a return to singing by note—regular singing—beginning in the 1720s. In this reform, which remained vigorous for about a century, singing-masters (the first substantial body of native-born music professionals) taught music literacy in connection with sacred music in singing-schools, which lasted from a few weeks to a few months. The reform initially proceeded as it had (a bit earlier) in Britain, and took on an American cast with the flowering of shape-note singing and repertoires of music composed in the United States, especially in New England. In participating in each of these and many later developments in singing for worship, North American communities remained part of the complex of British culture. Some correspondence continues to this day, as religious organizations pay heed to national boundaries more as a matter of practicality than of conviction, but the continued differentiation in Protestant worship on both sides of the Atlantic has naturally entailed a gradual parting of the ways in associated musical practices.

Child Ballads and Other Folksongs

Late in the nineteenth century, Harvard English professor Francis J. Child (1825–1896) traveled to England and Scotland to seek out an old, substantial body of English-language poetry: ballads that still flourished in oral tradition. Lyrics and music proved appealing aesthetically, as centuries of revision by generations of singers had polished them. Scholars with a romantic and nationalist bent savored tunes and poetry endorsed by history and supposedly unsullied by industrialism and other unsalubrious modern trends. This was perceived to be purely Anglo-Saxon art. Child published 305 texts, many in multiple variants, in *The English and Scottish Popular Ballads* (1882–1898). Scholars following the lead of Briton Cecil J. Sharp (1859–1924) found that Child

had not been looking for surviving ballads in the best places. The tradition was actually more vigorous in North America than back in Britain. This body of song, still known as the Child ballads, became the focus of folk-music research in the United States and Britain: hundreds of collections and analyses made this the most studied body of folk music in the world.

Child ballads are strophic (with the same music for each textual verse), and are set to melodies that usually arch upward at the beginning of the verse, then downward at the end. Rather than melodramatically painting the often lurid stories, singers present these laconically. Rhythms are straightforward, but some singers dwell on given pitches. A majority are in major mode, though much scholarship deals with modes that contrast with major. In some contrasting modes, the two half-steps lie relative to the tonic (the so-called church modes); others use fewer than seven tones per octave. Indeed, pentatonic scales, more used in Scotland than in England, are employed frequently in the American South. Coffeehouse singers of the 1950s to the early 1970s often underlined the age of the Child ballads by performing ones with exotic topics and set in exotic modes; for example, "The Great Silkie of Sul Skerry," some forms of which are in mixolydian mode (like major, but with a lowered seventh scalar degree).

The texts tell stories, seldom tied precisely to time or place, partly through narration and partly through characters' voices. Verses—usually four lines long, sometimes with one or two repeated—range from a few to several dozen. Descriptive language often follows conventions: horses are usually dapple grays or milk-white steeds, and a maid's skin is lily white. The topics are venerable and enduring, though neither those explicitly tied to British history nor humorous ones haved fared well in America, with a few exceptions (Americans still laugh at "The Farmer's Curst Wife"). Many ballads relate bloody, perhaps supernatural tales, which offer titillation and moral instruction. In "Barbara Allen" (the only one of these ballads that frequently reached print in nineteenth-century America), a young man flirts clumsily, alienating the young woman he wished to impress; she spurns him, causing him to despair and die; filled with remorse, she herself pines away. The lesson: be considerate in expressing love. In "The Golden Vanity," a British ship is threatened by pirates; the captain convinces a boy to sabotage the approaching enemy despite great personal risk; if the plan succeeds, the boy will be rewarded with riches and social elevation through marriage to the captain's daughter; the valiant deed is done, but the boy is abandoned to drown. The lesson: do not trust those in power.

In comparison with Child ballads, broadside ballads are usually younger and refer explicitly to specific events in comparatively precise, though less poetic, language. Some began life as literal broadsides, that is, stories cast in verse sold as "extras," printed on one side of a sheet of newsprint, with the purchaser instructed to sing the tale "to the tune of" a song the author of the text felt was widely known. Of the tunes suggested in American nineteenth-century broadsides, two American tunes were common: "Kingdom Coming," by Henry Clay Work (1832–1884), and "Dixie," formerly attributed to blackface minstrel Dan Emmett (1815–1904), but more likely from a black middle-class family, the Snowdens. Perhaps the commonest tune for this purpose was a British broadside tune, "Vilikens and His Dinah," best known today with the text "Sweet Betsy from Pike." Such extras prevailed in Europe from the sixteenth through the mid-nineteenth centuries, but songs that match these in character continued to be made, for example, the turn-of-the-twentieth-century North Carolina murder ballad "Omie Wise."

Nonnarrative songs too came to North America from Britain. They were sung frequently and served as models for native composition. For example, a Scottish song, "The Cuckoo," flourishes in the American South and has verses that we can hear again in other well-known songs, such as "Stewball" and "Jack of Diamonds." It is especially hard to distinguish between distinctively British and American texts (or musical elements) in this repertoire.

Dance Music

Instruments and their music, apart from functional marches, arrived early in the British colonies, and they were employed in cultivated and casual settings. Many flutes, fifes, and especially violins arrived during the seventeenth century. Violins have flourished as concert violins and folk fiddles. Fiddling is marked not just by heavy reliance on oral tradition, but by customary functions, venues, repertoires, and, especially in certain parts of the South, playing techniques and some use of scordatura (tuning other than the usual low-to-high G-D-A-E, for example, A-E-A-E).

The violin and the fiddle still look alike, but the fiddle is less narrowly defined in quality and style of woodworking, varnish application, and range of desirable timbres. In many eras and locations, the nasal and cutting timbres associated with rough-and-

ready construction and cheap metal strings helped a solo fiddler be heard by vigorous dancers. Fiddles were the main instruments for performing British-American (and French-American) folk music from the late eighteenth century well into the twentieth century [see FRENCH-AMERICAN MUSIC IN LOUISIANA]. Fiddlers in the colonies that would become the United States drew primarily on British traditions (initially Scottish and English, later also Irish) for tunes, ways to compose tunes and shape repertoires, and playing styles. The young country spawned regional styles, with the northern United States following English models and retaining more music literacy. Southern substyles were more strongly linked to Scottish repertoires, transmitted through print and by ear, and they absorbed considerable African-American influence in performance styles. Imported and homegrown tunes on imported models were usually linked with dance genres. Through the early nineteenth century, fiddlers' repertoires supplemented these dances with vocal airs, marches, and other popular tunes. As decades passed and solo fiddlers, fifers, and flutists were replaced in cultivated circles by ensembles or keyboard instruments, fiddle music emerged as a repertoire containing older dances, descriptive airs, and hymn tunes. British hornpipes and reels became American hoedowns, just as other duple-time social-dance tunes eventually fit into the polka category and triple-time dances were reworked as waltzes.

As American fiddling became less British or French and more American, other instruments more frequently joined performances. Fifes, closely associated with fiddles since the Revolutionary War, were played in fife-and-drum corps (military and dance tunes were shared between fiddles and fifes). Fiddle-and-banjo duos burgeoned in the wake of the popularity of blackface minstrelsy and medicine shows, and became commoner when late-nineteenth-century mail-order catalogs helped disseminate newly cheap products, including instruments. Minstrel-style banjo playing, which survives as clawhammer and frailing styles in the upper South, included African-derived playing techniques, but the repertoire of Southeastern stringbands (fiddle, banjo, and supplementary stringed instruments, including guitar, upright bass, and perhaps mandolin) has always featured British-American dance tunes (figure 1).

The common-time reel and breakdown consists of two (or rarely more) eight-measure strains, which contrast in tessitura (emphasized tonal range). A typical performance in older, dance-oriented style consists of one strain twice, the other twice, the first twice, and so on until a few minutes have passed and the dancers have tired. A few Northern contradances

Figure 1 The Bog Trotters Band of Galax, Virigina, 1937. *From left*: Doc Davis plays the autoharp, Uncle Alex Dunford plays fiddle, Crockett Ward plays fiddle, Field Ward plays guitar, and Wade Ward plays banjo. The Bog Trotters synthesized a number of musical styles, including that of Irish string band music, but their oldest and primary influences were British. *Library of Congress, Prints & Photographs Division, Lomax Collection, LC-DIG-00412.*

preserve a formerly more common linkage of specific tunes with specific sets of dance figures, but many tunes serve interchangeably.

That certain tunes are often irregularly phrased or otherwise inapt for dancing shows that fiddlers have always played for their own and their peers' pleasure. Today's regional styles are characterized by their degree of melodic ornamentation and variation (primarily linear styles, such as those of Texas are commonest), their degree of affinity with older published models (New England style is commonest), and their amount of African- and Scottish-derived syncopation, bold and subtle, which is emphasized in the Southeast.

Most other dance genres have been assimilated into the breakdown, but the British hornpipe remains vital, especially in New England, and a few marches, jigs, and descriptive pieces have survived here and there. The most widespread alternatives to the breakdown are waltzes (in 3/4 time), which arrived in large numbers in British and British-based publications in the 1810s and 1820s, received new impetus around the turn of the twentieth century from the pop songs of Tin Pan Alley, and have returned as a standard ingredient in modern fiddle contests in most of North America. These contests represent a folk revival in which a blend of rural and urban brands of nostalgia, the modern luxury of plenty of practice time for players of all socio-economic backgrounds, and listening-oriented venues have produced legions of polished instrumentalists, again blurring the line between folk and art performance and between violins and fiddles.

Fiddling in the Southeast draws heavily on blackface minstrelsy, an essentially American entertainment. The first full evening of blackface entertainment was presented in 1843, and such evenings were taking place in Britain within a year. Minstrelsy took over the British stage so quickly because it stemmed from British theatrical models (non-Europeans were often imitated on stage there as early as the late eighteenth century) and contained enough British musical elements that the music was easily accessible. Many blackface songs were re-castings of British, especially Scottish, fiddle tunes and songs, sometimes with new texts, sometimes with new orchestrations and perhaps enlivened rhythms. Many such tunes were already widespread in oral tradition and, though repeatedly transformed, remain central in today's American folk music, particularly in the upper South. "Backside Albany," in 1815 among the earliest American blackface airs, borrows the melody of "Boyne Water," a British folk-song whose text mocked the ineptness of the British fleet and whose melody was frequently heard in the United States long before receiving its blackface text. "Old Zip Coon," one of the best-known minstrel songs, borrowed its contour from the eighteenth-century Scottish fiddle tune "Rose Tree" (which had first reached print in William Shield's ballad opera *Poor Soldier* in 1782), perhaps passing through an intermediate state as an antebellum fiddle tune, "Natchez on the Hill" (figure 2).

In addition to borrowing Scottish melodies directly (and a few Irish and English tunes), blackface minstrelsy drew on British, especially Scottish,

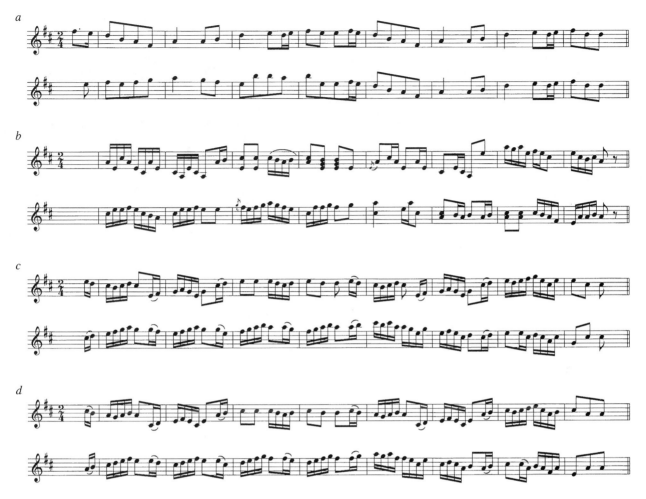

Figure 2 Ancestors of the American fiddle tune "Turkey in the Straw": *a*, "Rose Tree" is an eighteenth-century Scottish fiddle tune that was also a song in a ballad opera (*New and Complete Preceptor for the German Flute* 1824–1826:11); *b*, "Natchez on the Hill" is a fiddle tune adapted from "Rose Tree," one rare in the nineteenth century and today (Knauff 1839, 4:3); *c*, "Old Zip Coon," adapted from one of the previous tunes, became one of the most popular blackface minstrel songs (and instrumental melodies) (Howe 1851:43); *d*, it survived under that title into the twentieth century (Dunham 1926:6), but more often is encountered as "Turkey in the Straw."

models for harmonic and melodic formulas. Part of the motivation for adding a fifth string to the five-string banjo, the iconic minstrel instrument, may have to do with Scotland. During minstrel performances, this string was played unfretted, as a drone, just as in modern old-timey playing in the Southeast. This drone is played off the beat, producing syncopation, a feature that is generally and justly taken to reflect African influence, but the presence of a drone points less to any sub-Saharan musical tradition than to Scottish bagpipes and northern European dulcimers. Why did Scottish music influence this first important American entertainment so much? In the progressing industrial revolution, one refuge from soot, crowding, and alienation from the land was in a willfully rosy complex of memories of earlier rural life. For the British and other Europeans, Scotland embodied this ideal: its inhabitants were considered savage, crude, and generally inferior, but nevertheless possessed of an unthinking contentment and a handy folk wisdom, expressed in pithy sayings—qualities to be transferred to the images of American blacks acted out on minstrel stages.

—*Adapted from an article by Chris Goertzen*

Bibliography

Appel, Richard G. 1975. *The Music of the Bay Psalm Book, 9th Edition (1698)*. Brooklyn, N.Y.: Institute for Studies in American Music.

Bayard, Samuel P. 1982. *Dance to the Fiddle, March to the Fife*. University Park: Pennsylvania State University Press.

Bronson, Bertrand. 1959–1972. *The Traditional Tunes of the Child Ballads*. 4 vols. Princeton, N.J.: Princeton University Press.

———. 1976. *The Singing Tradition of Child's Popular Ballads*. Princeton, N.J.: Princeton University Press.

Chase, Gilbert. [1955] 1987. *America's Music: From the Pilgrims to the Present*. Rev. 3rd ed. Urbana: University of Illinois Press.

Child, Francis James. [1882–1898] 2003. *The English and Scottish Popular Ballads*. 5 vols. New York: Dover.

Coffin, Tristram P. 1963. *The British Traditional Ballad in North America*. Philadelphia: American Folklore Society.

Dunham, Mellie. 1926. *Fiddlin' Dance Tunes*. New York: Fischer.

Ford, Ira W. 1940. *Traditional Music in America*. New York: Dutton.

Hamm, Charles. 1979. *Yesterdays: Popular Song in America*. New York: Norton.

Howe, Elias. 1844. *The Musician's Companion*. 3 vols. Boston: Author.

Knauff, George P. 1839. *Virginia Reels*. 4 vols. Baltimore: George Willig Jr.

Lomax, Alan. 1960. *The Folk Songs of North America in the English Language*. New York: Doubleday.

Mellers, Wilfrid. [1964, 1965] 1987. *Music in a New Found Land: Themes and Developments in the History of American Music*. New York: Oxford University Press.

New and Complete Preceptor for the German Flute. 1824–1826. Albany, N.Y.: Steele.

Sharp, Cecil J. 1932. *English Folksongs from the Southern Appalachians*. London: Oxford University Press.

Stoutamire, Albert. 1972. *Music of the Old South: Colony to Confederacy*. Rutherford, N.J.: Fairleigh Dickinson University Press.

Temperley, Nicholas. 1979. *The Music of the English Parish Church*. 2 vols. Cambridge: Cambridge University Press.

Wolfe, Charles K. 1982. *Kentucky Country*. Lexington: University of Kentucky Press.

Traditional Irish Dance Music and Song

One of the largest groups in America today, Irish Americans live throughout the United States. Large communities thrive in New York City, San Francisco, Chicago, Boston, and Philadelphia. Irish immigration to the United States began in the eighteenth century and continues. New immigrants add to a rich legacy of folk and popular music. This transnational exchange is aided by international media, the commercial recording industry, and the back-and-forth migration of young Irish between Ireland and the United States.

Traditional Dance Music

Irish instrumental music originated centuries ago, primarily as accompaniment for dancing. Today, in Ireland and the United States, the music is played in informal community and familial contexts such as *seisiúns* (sessions), at *céilís* (group folk dancing), in concerts, and at Irish music festivals (figure 1). Playing styles and repertoire are usually learned through listening and imitating, tunes are composed more or less anonymously, and the music is, on the whole, crafted communally. Among the most commonly found instruments in traditional Irish music are fiddles, button accordions, wooden flutes, tin whistles, *uilleann* pipes (small, elbow-driven bagpipes), concertinas, mandolins, harps, and tenor banjos. Traditional Irish music is primarily melodic,

with a subtle but propelling rhythmic pulse. Because of this reliance on melodic lines, harmonic accompaniment is a development of the twentieth century, commonly provided by piano, guitar, and, since the late 1970s, multistringed instruments modeled after the Greek *bouzouki* and the medieval European *cittern*.

Countermelodies and harmonies are uncommon in what practitioners consider strictly traditional music, though many younger Irish ensembles incorporate them in performance. Dance tunes in duple time include lively reels (4/4 time) and polkas (2/4 time), and stately marches and syncopated hornpipes; tunes in triple time include jigs (6/8 time) and slip jigs (9/8 time). Also popular are waltzes (3/4 time) and slow airs and laments, largely unmetered. Regionalism plays a repertorial role: musicians from the northern counties feature tunes known as highlands (also called flings), mazurkas, schottisches, and barn dances, and players from the southwestern counties of Kerry and Cork are known for their upbeat slides.

Traditionally, playing styles were transmitted from player to player; recordings (and, more recently, tape recorders) have altered the process of dissemination. Between 1900 and the early 1930s, the demand for traditional Irish music in the United States was fueled by the arrival of hundreds of thousands of Irish immigrants. Major record labels, such as Decca

Figure 1 Informal Irish session at Furlong's Riverside Inn during the Catskills Irish Arts Week, East Durham, New York, 2006. The musicians in the middle play wooden flutes, the musicians on the ends play fiddles.
Photo by Paul V. McEvoy.

377

Figure 2 From left: Steve Brown plays fiddle, Tom Rota uilleann pipes, and Mike Jeanneau *bouzouki* at the Sunday jam session at Brian Boru Public House, in Portland, Maine, 2007. The *bouzouki* is a long-necked lute of Greek origin that was imported to Ireland and now appears in many traditional music groups. *Photo by Paul V. McEvoy.*

and Columbia, exploiting the market potential of this so-called Golden Age of Irish Music, made hundreds of 78-rpm recordings of outstanding Irish musicians residing in major U.S. cities. These recordings popularized and perpetuated specific playing styles and repertoires. The Sligo style, for example, remains one of the most popular among Irish-American players today, thanks to recordings of Michael Coleman (1891–1945), Paddy Killoran (1904–1965), James Morrison (1893–1947), and other fiddlers.

Irish Singing

Like Irish instrumental dance music, Irish traditional singing (*sean-nós*) has been passed down orally. Sung in Irish Gaelic, *sean-nós* songs are performed solo and unaccompanied, and feature intricate ornamentation. Once a means of recording local events and histories, they serve strictly as entertainment. Increasingly, contemporary *sean-nós* singers performing for American audiences select songs from the Irish- and English-language repertoires and eliminate verses to fit modern attention spans.

Sean-nós singing was largely inaccessible to many Irish Americans and the general public because of the language barrier, so it was bypassed in the revival of Irish music in the United States in the 1960s and 1970s. Songs in English, backed by guitars and banjo, took its place—a folksinging-style best exemplified by the Clancy Brothers and Tommy Makem (1932–2007), who, by capturing the attention of an international audience, spawned a new tradition. Eliminating most of the ornamentation found in *sean-nós* singing, they sang faster, with a driving beat, pri-

marily in unison—effects that gave them a group trademark and allowed audiences to participate, increasing their appeal. Their protest and political songs were well in keeping with the prevailing anti-war sentiment of the 1960s, and their appearances on television (then a relatively new medium) sparked an interest in Irish singing.

A new folk-based Irish singing-style emerged in the late 1970s, based largely on the music of the Clancy Brothers and Tommy Makem. It typically features a solo lead singer (sometimes with harmony vocals) and backup instrumentation, ranging from a single guitar to multifarious ensembles. Singers often deliver simpler *sean-nós* vocal ornaments; their repertoires, consisting of ballads, political songs, and original numbers, are typically in English.

Irish Traditional Music Today

The Irish traditional music community in the United States is thriving. Musicians of all ages and backgrounds—Irish immigrants, Irish Americans, and non-Irish—attend weeklong Irish music camps, play in Irish music sessions (figure 2) in large and small cities, and attend Irish music festivals. Major record labels and folk-music labels promote and produce Irish music; public and commercial radio programs give airtime to it; and concert venues, large and small, including Carnegie Hall in New York City and the Kennedy Center in Washington, D.C., regularly present it. With the more recent phenomenon of the Irish dance extravaganzas *Riverdance* and *Lord of the Dance*, its popularity seems to be growing.

—Adapted from an article by Rebecca S. Miller

Bibliography

McCullough, Lawrence E. 1974. "An Historical Sketch of Traditional Irish Music in the U.S." *Folklore Forum* 7(3):177–191.

Miller, Rebecca S. 1996. "Irish Traditional and Popular Music in New York City: Identity and Social Change, 1930–1975." In *The New York Irish*, edited by Ronald H. Bayor and Timothy J. Meagher, 481–507. Baltimore: The Johns Hopkins University Press.

Moloney, Michael. 1982. "Irish Ethnic Recordings and the Irish-American Imagination." In *Ethnic Recordings in America: A Neglected Heritage, 84–101*. Washington, D.C.: American Folklife Center.

Mullins, Patrick, and Rebecca Miller. *From Shore to Shore: Traditional Irish Music in New York*. 1993. New York: Cherry Lane Productions. Video.

O'Neill, Francis J. [1910, 1913] 1973a. *Irish Folk Music: A Fascinating Hobby*. Darby, Pa.: Norwood Editions.

——. [1910, 1913] 1973b. *Irish Minstrels and Musicians*. Darby, Pa.: Norwood Editions.

Power, Vincent. 1990. *Send 'Em Home Sweatin': The Showband's Story*. Dublin: Kildanore Press.

Country and Western

Country music is a vernacular form of American popular music that has traditionally been associated with the Southeast and with the rural Midwest. It features an emotive and highly ornamented singing-style, instrumental accompaniment that relies heavily on small ensembles of strings, and a repertoire derived from and influenced by older folk ballads and nineteenth-century popular songs. The term *country music* gained widespread acceptance only in the 1940s, but the music itself had emerged as a commercial artform between 1922 and 1927. The music has always been heavily involved with the mass media, especially radio and phonograph records, and many feel that mass media are essential features of the genre. The first center for the music was Atlanta, Georgia; but in later years, Chicago, Los Angeles, Cincinnati, Charlotte (North Carolina), and, finally, Nashville served as hubs. At times, starting in the 1940s, country music impinged on mainstream popular music, but it routinely became self-conscious about its identity and retrenched to reaffirm its traditional roots. It has been conservative in several ways: politically, musically, socially, philosophically, and even technically.

The Roots of Country Music

The roots of country music are found in the ballad tradition that accompanied Scottish and Irish immigrants into the Southeast in the nineteenth century [see ENGLISH AND SCOTTISH MUSIC; TRADITIONAL IRISH DANCE MUSIC AND SONG]. In this tradition, songs of love and death were sung unaccompanied, often unmetered, using so-called gapped scales, and often at full volume and the top of singers' ranges. A "high lonesome sound," it imbued country singing with a soulful stridency, as heard in performances by Roy Acuff (1903–1992), Bill Monroe (1911–1996), Dolly Parton (b. 1946), Hank Williams (1923–1953), and other major singers. Most modern singers had experienced firsthand contact with older, precommercial ballad singing. Another key stylistic element is what older singers called "snaking the melody," in which a word or syllable may be stretched over several notes, as heard in recordings by the Texas singer Lefty Frizzell (1928–1975) and the California singer Merle Haggard (b. 1937). Country vocal ornamentation includes the use of scoops and slurs; the use of "feathering" (a short slide up to a glottal stop) at the ends of lines; the deliberate dropping of a beat or a measure between lines; the use of falsetto as a high keening, or as a yodel; and an emphasis on nasality and head tones. Notions of vocal harmony came from Southern gospel-hymn singing-schools and songbooks; melodies were often sung an octave above the printed sources. At points in country music's development, major singers broke with older styles to favor newer, smoother styles, derived from mainstream pop singers like Bing Crosby (1903–1977), Red Foley (in the 1940s), Jim Reeves (in the 1950s), and Eddy Arnold (1950s–1960s).

The Instruments of Country Music

The instruments most associated with country music are fiddles, banjos, and guitars. Fiddles were a staple of Scots-Irish culture, and Americans were staging fiddling contests as early as the 1760s. Light and easily portable, fiddles soon found their way into the rural Southeast, with tunes carried across the Atlantic. Thus, "Miss McLeod's Reel" became "Did You Ever Did See a Devil, Uncle Joe," and dozens of new songs emerged as fiddlers performed at country dances, barnwarmings, county fairs, auctions, and political rallies. Unorthodox tunings emerged, like what many called "cross tuning" (A-E-A-E) to get harmonic drone effects. By 1900, fiddles had become the anchor of stringbands, and were being played solo less and less.

For decades, it has been accepted that the banjo was an African instrument brought to North America by slaves; we now know that its roots reach far into the culture of sub-Saharan Africa, with references to banjolike instruments dating as far back as thirteenth-century Mali. Through its use in minstrel shows in the 1840s, it made its way into Anglo-American musical circles and into the hands of rural Southerners, who subjected it to unorthodox, un-European tuning systems (especially complicated by the addition of a fifth drone string in the 1840s) and to tonal textures created by homemade skin heads and handcarved fingerboards. It was a favorite of Tennessee's Uncle Dave Macon (1870–1952; figure 1) and other country pioneers, but it declined in use in the 1940s, only to reemerge in the 1950s as the centerpiece of a new subgenre, bluegrass [see textbox], at the hands of innovator Earl Scruggs (b. 1924).

Figure 1 Uncle Dave Macon plays the banjo. Macon started playing the instrument as a boy, but didn't begin his professional career until in his fifties. He was also a talented singer, songwriter, and entertainer.
Photo courtesy University of North Carolina, Southern Folklife Collection.

The icon of country was the third and most recent addition to this trio, the guitar, which had been on the American musical landscape for most of the nineteenth century; but with gut strings and a soft sound, it was seen as a refined parlor instrument, suitable for young ladies to play. Around 1900, two things happened to change this perception. Guitarmakers began using steel strings and reinforcing the neck and tailpiece to accommodate the greater stress; these strings, often played with flat picks or fingerpicks, produced greater volume and brightness, and allowed guitars to join the stringbands of the day. The second important change occurred when the giant firms of Sears, Roebuck and Montgomery Ward began selling inexpensive guitars by mail. Unlike banjos, dulcimers, and other folk instruments, guitars were not easy for amateurs to make, and the cheap Sears Silvertones and Supertones went all over the South. As musicians became more proficient, they wanted better instruments. The best was the flat-topped Martin (originated in Pennsylvania before the Civil War) or the arch-top Gibson (dating from the 1890s); these models are still considered the standards for country. By the 1920s, guitars had made their way into rural Southern stringbands; some veteran country performers can remember the first time they saw a guitar and how it changed the music.

Major Figures

The 1920s–1940s

The commercialization of what would become country began in 1922 and 1923 with the first recordings by Texas fiddler Eck Robertson ("Sallie Gooden," Victor 1922) and Georgian Fiddlin' John Carson ("The Little Old Log Cabin in the Lane," OKeh 1923). With these releases, the big commercial record companies from the Northeast recognized that Southern audiences were a potential market for this kind of "hill-country" or "old-time" music, and they sent talent scouts into the area to set up temporary studios. One such studio, set up by artists and repertoire man Ralph Peer (1892–1960) in Bristol, Tennessee, struck paydirt almost immediately: it yielded a singing trio from nearby Maces Spring, Virginia, named the Carter Family, who had a knack for harmonizing old mountain songs and arranging them for guitar and autoharp accompaniment. Their recordings of songs like "Bury Me under the Weeping Willow Tree" (Victor 1928) and "Wildwood Flower" (Victor 1929) became standards. Their singing style and harmonies are still heard, as is the "thumbstroke" guitar style, perfected by Maybelle Carter (1909–1978). One day after the Carters were discovered, Jimmie Rodgers (1897–1933), a young singer from Mississippi, appeared before Peer. Rodgers offered a unique singing-style, heavily influenced by blues and cowboy songs; his forte was a pliant, expressive voice and an ability to break into falsetto on refrains—a technique that became forever associated with his careermaking song, "Blue Yodel" (or "Blue Yodel No. 1," Victor 1928). These two acts dominated early country: they sold more records than any other act, and had more influence. Rodgers died prematurely, but the Carters continued to work on records and radio until their breakup, in 1943. Other important first-generation performers included the banjoist and songster Uncle Dave Macon, the banjoist and singer Charlie Poole (1892–1931), the Georgia stringband the Skillet Lickers, and the ballad singer Bradley Kincaid (1895–1989).

During the second decade of country, the 1930s, performers found they could use radiobroadcasts and personal appearances to become fulltime professionals. Technical proficience increased dramatically, as did the number of original songs and styles. Innovations during this time often led to new subgenres within the music. One was the soft, plaintive close-harmony duet singing exemplified by groups such as the Blue Sky Boys (Bill Bolick, b. 1917; Earl Bolick, 1919–1998) and the Delmore Brothers (Alton, 1908–1964; Rabon, 1916–1952). Bestselling records in this style included "I'm Just Here to Get My Baby Out of Jail," "What Would You Give in Exchange for Your Soul?" and other sentimental pieces. When Texas yodeler Gene Autry (1907–1998) left his spot on WLS radio in Chicago to go to Hollywood to try his hand at films, he started a subgenre built on the image of the singing cowboy. Soon hundreds of singers, including many in the Southeast, were adapting a cowboy image and repertoire. The third major innovation, western swing, came from the Southwest. Popularized, though not invented, by Texas-born Bob Wills (1905–1975), it merged old-time fiddle breakdowns, blues, and *norteño* music with the uptempo swing style of bands such as Benny Goodman's and Jimmie Lunceford's [see TEJANO MUSIC: *CONJUNTO*]. During World War II, Wills transplanted his music to southern California, where it flourished and generated an entire musical scene.

By the 1940s, radio had become even more important, and powerful shows like WSM radio in Nashville's *Grand Ole Opry*, WLS's *National Barn Dance*, and WWVA's *Wheeling Jamboree* were attracting national attention for the music. During and after the war, the Armed Forces Radio Network recorded country programs and sent them around the world to GI outposts, spreading the music to new audiences. For a time, because it was full of smooth-singing Bing Crosby imitators, country seemed about to lose its identity, but it was rejuvenated by two rough-hewn but powerful stylists, Texan Ernest Tubb (1914–1984) and Alabaman Hank Williams, who, turning their back on idealized images of movie cowboys and on sentimental songs about death and children, addressed problems of modern-day working people: drinking, divorce, lost love, and money. Tubb's "Walking the Floor over You" (Decca 1941) and Williams's "Lovesick Blues" (MGM 1949) became emblematic of the new style and defined a direction that continues. Other country stylists of note during the late 1940s and early 1950s were Roy Acuff, Red Foley (1910–1968), Lefty Frizzell, and Faron Young (1932–1996). Women, discouraged from professional country by public opinion, had found an early role model in singing cowgirl Patsy Montana (1914–1996), who had a huge hit in 1936 with "I Want to Be a Cowboy's Sweetheart" (ARC).

Figure 2 Kitty Wells, 1943. The top female country star of her generation, Wells helped pave the way for Patsy Cline, Loretta Lynn, and other female country artists who came of age in the 1960s.
Photo courtesy University of North Carolina, Southern Folklife Collection.

In 1952, women found an even stronger model in Tennessean Kitty Wells (b. 1919; figure 2), whose "It Wasn't God Who Made Honkytonk Angels" (Decca) showed that a song from a women's viewpoint could become a bestseller.

By now, new instruments were helping define what was being called country and western music. Electric amplified guitars were featured on many of Ernest Tubb's recordings in the 1940s, and in many western swing bands; it soon became the lead instrument in country bands. In the 1920s, numerous musicians had adapted the acoustic Hawaiian guitar to country, and in the 1930s the Dobro guitar (a resonator guitar, played with a metal slide) resulted. Emerging in the 1940s was a solid-body amplified steel guitar called a "lap steel." In the late 1940s, players began to experiment with a pedal steel guitar, a flat steel guitar

382

DISC
❶
TRACK
14

BLUEGRASS

The American musical form known as bluegrass takes its name from the Blue Grass Boys (figure 1), the band of Grand Ole Opry star Bill Monroe (1911–1996). A Kentucky native, Monroe began developing this music in 1939, when he formed his band. He and his audiences viewed it as a modern country-music statement of the values associated with old-time music of the rural upland South. It included instrumental tunes associated with dances and frolics (figure 2), religious songs associated with Protestant hymnody, traditional ballads and lyrics, favorite old popular songs, and newly composed songs often modeled on older ones—all dealing with events and emotions, nostalgia for old rural homes, and stresses of modern urban life. The repertoire was set to a musical form that developed from earlier traditional stringband music, though more tightly integrated, faster, and demanding greater musical skills. It was presented in shows that featured select performers and covered topics in series—here the fiddle tune, there the bandleader's latest record, next the comedy routine, then the religious songs, and so on.

Figure 1 An early incarnation of the Blue Grass Boys. *From left*: Art Wooten plays fiddle, Bill Monroe mandolin, Cleo Davis guitar, and Amos Garren bass. Bill Monroe formed the group in 1938, and with well over one hundred different musicians, kept it going until 1996.
Photo courtesy Ben Car Archives.

Genres

Broadly speaking, bluegrass is divided into three genres: secular songs, sacred songs, and instrumentals. Each of these is subdivided according to its musical structures. For example, secular songs can be characterized in terms of the vocal parts used (duet, trio) or tempo (waltz, slow, medium, fast), and sacred songs can be "bass-led" or unaccompanied, have lyric content, or feature instruments or voices.

Vocal styles

Bluegrass vocalizing is influenced by Bill Monroe's practice of singing at the top of his range—often described as a "high, lonesome sound." Vocal textures are mostly clear, with a tendency toward the use of head tones; the most emulated singers have been those whose range is toward the high end. Stylistic influences have varied, with influence from mainstream American popular vocalists being reflected at

Figure 2 At the Smithsonian Folklife Festival in Washington D.C., couples dance to the Midnight Ramblers, a young bluegrass band from Virginia, 2007.
Photo by Jacob W. Love.

every point. Thus, early bluegrass lead singers like Clyde Moody (1915–1989) and Jim Eanes (1923–1995) showed smooth, "crooner" influences, but later singers have followed trends in mainstream country, rock, and other forms. In general, the details of earlier Southern folkstyles can be seen in recurrent details of vocal style, such as breaking final notes upward and ornamenting melismatically. Vocal harmonizing emphasizes blend and coordination: personal style is subordinated to the concept of a tight duet, trio, or quartet.

Instruments

Bluegrass instruments include guitars, fiddles, mandolins, five-string banjos, basses, and Dobro guitars. Strong emphasis is placed on acoustic (nonelectrified) instruments. With a few significant exceptions, the only electrified instrument heard in bluegrass has been the electric bass. Generally, each band uses one of each instrument, but two fiddles (playing in harmony) are occasionally used, as are two guitars (one playing rhythm, the other lead). Banjos and mandolins are rarely doubled for lead harmony, and then usually only on recordings or at jam sessions.

Bluegrass musicians seek instruments that have a broad dynamic range and can be played at great volume so as to "cut" (be heard) through the sounds of the other instruments or crowd noise. Players prefer certain makes and styles—in particular, the Martin D (Dreadnought) series guitars, Gibson Mastertone banjos of the type produced in the 1930s, and Gibson F5 Master Model mandolins, developed in the 1920s by acoustical engineer Lloyd Loar (1886–1943). Aficionados pay considerable attention to instruments that serve as icons within the music: old "original" guitars, banjos, and mandolins fetch high prices, and serve as models for modern recreations, manufactured and handmade. Fiddles and basses are chosen more on the basis of personal preference.

Performers

In addition to Monroe, who continued to perform with his Blue Grass Boys until six months before his death (at age 84), important bluegrass performers are Lester Flatt and Earl Scruggs (together from 1948 to 1969), Don Reno and Red Smiley (1952–1964), the Stanley Brothers (1947–1966), Ralph Stanley (since 1967), Jim and Jesse McReynolds (since 1947), the Osborne Brothers (since 1953), Jimmy Martin (since 1956), the Country Gentlemen (since 1957), Del McCoury (since 1968), the Seldom Scene (since 1971), Doyle Lawson and Quicksilver (since 1979), Hot Rize (1978–1990), the Nashville Bluegrass Band (since 1984), and Alison Krauss and Union Station (since 1984).

on a stand, attached to rods and pedals that allowed the performer to alter pitches and modulate chords. The pedal steel soon became country's most distinctive instrument: no other popular music genre utilized it. Early pioneers with it included West Coast studio musician Speedy West (1924–2003), Nashville session man Bud Isaacs (b. 1928), and Grand Ole Opry performer Buddy Emmons (b. 1937). Webb Pierce's hit recording of "Slowly" (Decca 1954), featuring Isaac's work, inspired hundreds of guitarists around the country and helped make the pedal steel the icon it remains.

The 1950s to the 1970s and beyond

By the early 1950s, Nashville had emerged as the geographical center of country music. One reason for this was that WSM's radio show *Grand Ole Opry* had emerged after the war as the nation's most popular country radio show, and many leading performers had moved to Nashville to be near it. The city was becoming a center for country-music publishing, with the formation of the first nationally successful firm, Acuff-Rose, in 1942. In addition to publishing the works of Hank Williams, Roy Acuff, the Louvin Brothers (Ira, 1924–1965; Charles, b. 1927), the Everly Brothers (Don, b. 1937; Phil, b. 1939), Don Gibson (1928–2003), and Roy Orbison (1936–1988), the company aggressively marketed its wares to pop-music producers. Nashville boasted a cadre of superior studio engineers; by 1946, two of them had set up the first permanent studio in town. In the 1950s, it attracted major record companies to town to record and maintain branch offices.

All of this eventually evolved into a phenomenon called "the Nashville studio system," which nurtured a generation of specialized musicians who did little but play in recording studios. Producers like Chet Atkins (1924–2001) and Owen Bradley (1915–1998), musicians themselves, set up an assembly-line system, in which performers would come into a studio without a band and would be given a studio band of crack technicians for backing on the record. (Among the best of these background musicians were guitarists Grady Martin (b. 1929) and Harold Bradley (b. 1926), fiddler Tommy Jackson (1926–1979), and steel player Jerry Byrd, 1920–2005.) While the music was clean and competent, the system left little room for innovation, and by the 1960s it was being blamed for a blandness that was infecting the music. Newer generations of session musicians have remedied that to some extent, and the session system remained in place.

Country's predictable musical settings of the 1950s were especially vulnerable to the rise of rock

Figure 3 Sheet music cover to Patsy Cline's version of "Sweet Dreams" (1963). Though just thirty years old when she perished in a plane crash, Cline is regarded as one of the top country singers of all time.
Courtesy of Ben Car Archives.

and roll. As young stars like Elvis Presley (1935–1977) and Carl Perkins (1932–1998) began to add a drumkit to their stage shows and added a heavy beat to the loud electric guitars, country bookings plummeted. Presley, from Memphis, began his career touring with country package shows, but teenaged record-buying fans had little interest in the established Opry stars. Some country stars, such as Marty Robbins (1925–1982), tried to accommodate the new sound by exploring the hybrid genre called rockabilly, a country sound with a strong beat. It helped weather the storm, and by the 1960s, a new generation of singers and songwriters was arriving in Nashville to rejuvenate the music. These included Willie Nelson (b. 1933), Waylon Jennings (1937–2002), Patsy Cline (1932–1963; figure 3), Don Gibson, Tom T. Hall (b. 1936), Kris Kristofferson (b. 1936), Harlan Howard (ca. 1927–2002), and George Jones (b. 1931). Writers like Hall, Howard, and Kristofferson were especially adept at turning away from the commonplace clichés of country lyrics and experimenting with new forms and subjects. Kentuckian Loretta Lynn (b. 1935), a protégée of Cline's, gave female fans a new voice in the country repertoire with songs like "One's on the Way" (Decca 1971). From the Bakersfield area in southern California came two of the most popular singer-songwriters of the 1960–1980 era, Buck Owens (1929–2006) and Merle Haggard. It was Haggard's songs like "Working Man Blues" and "Okie from Muskogee" that helped restore a social sensibility in the music. And from Fort Worth, Texas, came one of the era's most gifted songwriters, Townes Van Zandt (1944–1997). In "Pancho and Lefty," "To Live's To Fly," and other of his songs, Van Zandt's lyrics displayed a subtlety more characteristic of poetry.

Country has expanded beyond a niche music for a specific audience to become a nationwide phenomenon and a major international commercial success. Though still centered in Nashville, it has fans, media outlets, and concert venues all over the world.

—Adapted from an article by Charles K. Wolfe and Neil V. Rosenberg

Bibliography

Artis, Bob. 1975. *Bluegrass*. New York: Hawthorne.

Cantwell, Bob. 1984. *Bluegrass Breakdown*. Urbana: University of Illinois Press.

Horstman, Dorothy. 1975. *Sing Your Heart Out, Country Boy*. Rev. ed. Nashville: Country Music Foundation Press.

Kingsbury, Paul, ed. 1996. *The Country Reader*. Nashville: Vanderbilt University Press and Country Music Foundation Press.

——. 1998. *The Encyclopedia of Country Music*. New York: Oxford University Press.

Porterfield, Nolan. 1979. *Jimmie Rodgers: The Life and Times of America's Blue Yodeller*. Urbana: University of Illinois Press.

Rosenberg, Neil V. 1985. *Bluegrass: A History*. Urbana: University of Illinois Press.

Townsend, Charles, 1976. *San Antonio Rose: The Life and Times of Bob Wills*. Urbana: University of Illinois Press.

Wolfe, Charles K. 1976. *Tennessee Strings: The Story of Country Music in Tennessee*. Knoxville: The University of Tennessee Press.

——. 1999. *A Good-Natured Riot: The Birth of the Grand Ole Opry*. Nashville: Vanderbilt University Press and the Country Music Foundation Press.

French-American Music in Louisiana

Few French people immigrated directly to the United States; most French Americans came by way of Canada. Cajuns and Creoles, two major groups of French-speaking Americans, live in and around the Gulf Coast of Louisiana. Both groups have adopted a mixture of cultural elements, but each has a foundation in French language and culture. Today in southern Louisiana, French-speaking whites generally call themselves Cajuns, while French-speaking blacks call themselves Creoles. The groups have many interconnections in language, folklife, and music. With the blending of cultural elements over the years, it is not always a simple or clearcut matter to distinguish whether an individual is Cajun or Creole.

Cajun Music

The term *Cajun* derives from *Acadian*, the name of a group of French immigrants who settled along the coasts of what are now the Canadian maritime provinces of Canada and the U.S. state of Maine during the seventeenth century, forming one of the earliest colonies in the New World. Control of the area shifted between France and Great Britain. In 1755, after the Acadians refused to swear allegiance to the British crown, the British began to expel them (an action called Le Grand Dérangement). The Acadians went to several places, including New England, other parts of Canada, the Carolinas, and the French West Indies. By 1800, several thousand had found their way to southwestern Louisiana, where their culture had substantial influence.

Song

The roots of Cajun music may be traced to the original Acadian exiles. Cajuns continued the tradition of the evening party (*veillée*), where they sang songs, unaccompanied except for the rhythm of handclapping, foot-tapping, or banging on kitchen implements. They sang French ballads, humorous songs, and particularly the *complainte*, a long, melancholy story-song of their French heritage. Women sang lullabies; men, drinking songs; children, play-party songs. Cajuns learned these songs from aural tradition and printed sources; their themes included love and marriage, lovers moving away, animals, people and places, and the Civil War (Whitfield [1939] 1981).

Instrumental Music

Cajun instrumental music has always been closely tied to dancing. Originally, Cajun dances were small gatherings for family and friends (*bals de maison*), held in private homes where the furniture had been cleared from the front room or other large space. Eventually, these events evolved into larger public parties (*fais-do-do*, baby talk for 'go to sleep'); the term may come from the practice of putting young children to sleep in a special room while their parents attended the party. After World War II, Cajuns built larger, family-style dancehalls to hold *fais-do-do*, usually on Saturday evenings.

Early Cajun dance-music included mazurkas, polkas, reels, hot-steps, one-steps, two-steps, quadrilles (contradances), and waltzes; after a while, only waltzes and two-steps remained popular. The original Acadian exiles arrived without instruments, so they danced to *reels à bouche*, wordless music, made only with voices. Eventually, fiddles became the primary dance instrument. Dances were then played in arrangements for two fiddles: one carried the melody, and the other provided accompaniment. When German settlers brought accordions to Louisiana, in the late nineteenth century, accordions became the favored instruments of Cajun dance-music. Cajuns typically used diatonic one-row or two-row accordions, and developed a style of playing that combined traditional melodies with a push-and-pull rhythmic drive (figure 1). Traditional Cajun dance ensembles consisted of one diatonic accordion in the lead, one or two fiddles, and simple rhythm instruments, such as the triangle.

With the coming of the oil industry, improved transportation, and mass media, Cajun music absorbed influences from country and western, hillbilly, blues, western swing, and jazz. Dance ensembles began adding electrical amplification, guitar, steel guitar, bass, and drums. The use of accordions declined in the middle decades of the twentieth century, but made a comeback during the era of folk-music revivals, as the traditional sound of Cajun music came back into style (figure 2).

Creole Music

In eighteenth-century Louisiana, upper-class Spanish and French immigrants called their American-born descendants creoles. Later that century, when

Figure 1 Members of a Louisiana Cajun band at the National Folk Festival near Cleveland, Ohio. *Photo by Terry E. Miller, 1985.*

Figure 2 This type of old-fashioned button box accordion, whose bellows drive air through sets of metal free reeds to produce sounds is, along with the fiddle, an essential sound in Louisiana's Cajun music.
Photo by Terry E. Miller, 1990.

French-speaking blacks and mulattoes from the Caribbean and South America came to Louisiana as slaves for French planters or as "free men of color," they openly exchanged cultural elements with Cajuns. French-speaking blacks were called black Cajuns, black French, black Creoles, and creoles of color. Gradually the term *Creole* began to apply primarily to those in Louisiana French culture with an African heritage. Creole culture consists of a mix of elements, primarily African-Caribbean, Spanish, and French, which appear in their language, music, and cuisine.

Like the Cajuns, Creoles sang lullabies (*fais-do-do*) and songs of love and marriage, but they performed genres seldom heard in Cajun music: songs about food and songs of satire, mockery, and ridicule.

Like other French-speaking Americans, Creoles enjoyed evening house parties and dances. Creoles called such parties *la la* and *zydeco*. Zydeco draws from the same instrumental dance repertoire as Cajun music, but adds elements of African-Caribbean rhythms and African-American blues. The Creole version of the Cajun two-step, called the *la la*, is faster and more syncopated, as are Creole waltzes. The music has a greater emphasis on rhythm, a lesser one on melody, and frequently a blues tonality. Rural zydeco ensembles used instrumentation similar to that of their Cajun counterparts: the button accordion, the fiddle, and the *frottoir*, a metallic washboard played with thimbles, spoons, forks, or bottle openers. Urban zydeco groups tended to replace fiddles with electric guitars or saxophones and button accordions with piano accordions. For rhythm, they retained the *frottoir*, but sometimes added bass guitar and drums. Such groups could play traditional Creole tunes, rhythm and blues, soul, and other forms of African-American popular music.

Renaissance of French-American Music in Louisiana

Cajun music was first recorded in the 1920s, in the ethnic series of labels. By midcentury, national record companies sought music that would appeal to broader audiences, and Cajun groups of the time responded with a more popular Americanized sound. In the last half of the century, the traditional sound again asserted itself and was recorded by local and specialized companies.

Traditional Cajun and Creole musics are among the most widely popular ethnic genres in America. Their popularity stems from exposure at local and national folk-music festivals; tourism; increased public awareness through the work of scholars, performers, and cultural activists; direct promotion by the Council for the Development of French in Louisiana and the National Endowment for the Humanities; and foundation funding.

—Adapted from an article by Carl Rahkonen

Bibliography

Ancelet, Barry Jean. 1989. *Cajun Music: Its Origins and Development*. Lafayette: Center for Louisiana Studies, University of Southwestern Louisiana.

——. [1982] 1999. *Cajun and Creole Music Makers*. Jackson: University Press of Mississippi. New ed. of *The Makers of Cajun Music*.

——, and Philip Gould. 1992. *Cajun Music and Zydeco*. Baton Rouge: Louisiana State University.

Broven, John. 1987. *South to Louisiana: The Music of the Cajun Bayous*. Gretna, La.: Pelican.

Whitfield, Irène Thérèse. [1939] 1981. *Louisiana French Folk Songs*. 3rd ed. Eunice, La.: Hebert.

The Polish Polka

The Polish-American population in the United States consists mainly of fourth-generation descendants of nineteenth-century immigrants and post-Solidarity émigrés of the 1990s. Polish-American communities have numerous clubs, associations, churches with social halls and parochial schools, veterans' posts, Polish homes, and community centers with theaters, libraries, meeting rooms, and athletic clubs.

Polish Americans have had a central role in developing the polka tradition in the United States—a phenomenon involving many European-American ethnic communities: Czechs, Germans, Slovenians, Italians, Norwegians, Swedes, Ukrainians, Russians, Lithuanians, Finns, Mexican Americans, French Americans, and Anglo-Americans. In Polish communities, however, the term *polka music* is synonymous with *Polish music*. Most post-World War II immigrants from Poland came from more urban, well-educated backgrounds in comparison with earlier immigrants, and they tend to look down on polka music as being associated with negative, beer-drinking stereotypes of Poles, or of the American working class. They identify with European popular music, Polish composers in the Western classical tradition, or classically influenced polyphonic Polish-American choral groups.

Two polka traditions have existed in Central Europe since the 1830s: a rural folk tradition and an urban salon tradition. These traditions coexisted in Poland in the latter half of the nineteenth century and were brought to the United States by immigrants. A similarly dual tradition continues in the United States: the urban, "Eastern" style, and a revitalized and reconstructed rural, "Chicago" style.

Small instrumental groups with variable combinations—such as piano, bass, and sax; concertina, trumpet, and drums; and accordion, clarinet, violin, and bass—were common in Polish-American communities in Eastern and Midwestern cities since the 1870s, but organized polka bands of six or more members did not exist until the late 1920s, when a fusion of the rural string sound and the urban sound occurred. String-dominated bands gradually incorporated clarinet, trumpet, accordion, and drums, and the violin relinquished its lead role to these instruments.

In America during the 1930s and 1940s, Polish and Polish-American songs in duple meter were adapted as polkas by being performed in alternation with instrumental sections called drives. Later, songs were composed in this format. By the 1940s, Polish-American groups in Detroit and other cities were performing more and more for non-Polish audiences. This trend required them to incorporate mainstream American popular dance genres, such as the rumba, the cha-cha-cha, and the foxtrot. The Polish-American polka resulted from a syncretism of the *krakowiak* (a Polish regional dance), pan-European polka elements, and mainstream American popular dance-music.

Eastern-style Polka

Eastern-style polka was formulated by musicians such as Ed Krolikowski (Bridgeport, Connecticut) and Bernie Witkowski (New York City), both of whom were educated in Western classical music in Poland. Krolikowski absorbed musical influences from Dixieland, vaudeville, swing, jazz, Broadway musicals, and diverse European-American ethnic traditions. He and his peers created an Americanized, jazzed-up version of Polish music. His influence was increased by his fluency in six languages and his ownership of a music store. Witkowski, who had a background in classical and jazz clarinet, became a channel for the flow of ideas from big bands to polka bands in the 1930s. He expanded the role of improvisation in polka music, though most of it soon became carefully rehearsed variation. He emphasized precise playing by the melodic lead instruments.

Early urban-style groups that recorded in the 1920s and 1930s ordinarily used six or more of the following: clarinet, saxophone, trumpet, flute or piccolo, piano, concertina or accordion, banjo, xylophone, vibraphone, string bass, and drumset. Some of their recordings used non-Polish studio musicians. During the 1940s, many ethnic bands made the transition from neighborhood and home to hotel and ballroom, adapting themselves to the demands of mainstream American popular dance-music.

During the 1930s and 1940s, polka music became faster, with a brass-dominated, more brilliant timbre. Professional bands played pieces from "the Polish book" (polkas, waltzes, and *obereks*) and "the English book" (fox-trots, lindy hops, swing, ballads, tangos, rumbas, and hillbilly).

Urban-style ballroom polkas dominated Polish-American communities from the mid-1930s to about 1960. During this period, they incorporated rhythmic, melodic, and harmonic aspects of jazz, Latin, bluegrass, Cajun, country and western, and other popular musics. Classic Eastern-style bands were large ensembles that played technically precise, well-rehearsed variations with a continuous shuffling of lead instrumental combinations during performance. By the late 1950s, most of them had reduced their size and increased their amplification. Some, aiming to appeal to working-class audiences of mixed ethnic backgrounds, played rock medleys, country and western songs, Frank Sinatra and Tony Bennett classics, and Latin numbers; others focused on Polish-American dance music.

Chicago-style Polka

During the 1920s, village-style folk orchestras from Chicago rivaled the Eastern bands in popularity. Franciszek Dukla, a fiddler from rural Galicia living in Chicago, was the foremost exponent of a village-style Polish band (*wiejska*), in which a lead clarinet and violin played in heterophonic unison, accompanied by additional violins playing upbeat chords and a bowed bass. This style echoed the stringbands of the Podhale tradition of rural Poland.

During the 1950s, a revived rural style in Chicago began to challenge the popularity of the Eastern urban style. Chicago bands played at slower tempos, with fewer sections and key changes, and greater influence from Polish folksongs and *krakowiak* rhythms. The Chicago style became associated with more improvisatory, informal melodies, with irregular phrasing and syncopations. The instrumentation was simpler and less arranged than that of Eastern urban bands. The general feeling was of greater enthusiasm and emotionality, with an abandonment of complex arrangements and less reliance on notated music. By the late 1950s, Chicago-style polka was changing the sound of polka in the East.

Eddie Blazonczyk (b. 1941) exemplifies the multiple roles assumed by some of the better-known full-time professional bandleaders: singer, instrumentalist, host, emcee, promoter, producer, record company executive, disc jockey, composer, arranger, road manager, and studio engineer. His group, the Versatones, includes rock medleys with polkas, waltzes, *obereks*, and adaptations of country and western songs as polkas. These adaptations feature bluegrass fiddling in addition to the usual trumpet or clarinet duets during instrumental portions of the polka [see BLUEGRASS]. His songtexts often have a pattern of one verse in English followed by a translation into Polish. Nearly all of his polkas, waltzes, and *obereks* are new compositions, by himself or others.

A standard Chicago band has a trumpet lead, a clarinet playing harmony, a concertina and/or an accordion providing fill-in chords, a piano, a string bass, and a drumset. The bass, concertina, and accordion are amplified.

Figure 1 Marion Lush and the Musical Stars perform at the Aragon Ballroom, Chicago, 1962. *From left*: Gene Rydosz is on piano, Bob Bajek on trumpet, Marion Lush on trumpet, Andy Karsus owner of the Aragon, Ed Benbenek on clarinet, Mickey Lacny on accordion, Steve Jankowski on clarinet, Stanley Mikrut bass, and Chet Filipiak on drums.
Photo from the collection of Chester and Bernadine Filipiak.

Figure 2 The Joe Pasieka Band performs at the Polish Community Center in Binghamton, New York, 1975. Joe Pasieka is in the center holding a microphone. The band, from Mystic, Connecticut, featured two trumpets, accordion, and Pasieka's saxophone and clarinet playing.
Photo by Steve Litwin.

Polka Form and Instrumentation

Nineteenth-century European urban salon polkas had three or more purely instrumental sections, assigned to keys and often with contrasting instrumentation and texture. This style rarely had texts. The rural style, whether based on a song, a *krakowiak*, or a polka melody, usually had two sections, instrumental or alternating instrumental and vocal. These sections were either two different melodies or a single vocal melody rendered instrumentally with considerable melodic elaboration.

Contemporary Polish-American polkas are based on the two-section model. They begin with an instrumental section called the drive, the ride, and the push, followed by several sung verses alternating with the instrumental section. In general, a vocal melody is associated with a drive melody; a catchy drive theme may be rematched with other vocal melodies.

In all styles of polka, the melody is played by two or more lead instruments in unison or parallel thirds, supported by harmony instruments that provide a continuous chordal background, plus a bass line and drums. Lead instruments are generally clarinet, trumpet or cornet, or violin. The bass line is provided by a plucked or bowed stringed bass, an electric bass guitar, or the left hand on the piano.

Recent Polka Trends

In the early 1950s, a gradual merger of styles mixed Eastern tempos, Chicago ensemble sizes, and old-country qualities. Reduction in band size corresponded with a rise in the use of amplification. The resultant sound, developed in the late 1950s by

Marion Lush (figure 1) and called dyno style and push style, refers to the bright, brassy sound of two lead trumpets, amplified accordion, amplified bass, a large drumset, and a lively tempo (figure 2). This type of band may include electric guitar and/or electric keyboard and rock-influenced drumming, appealing to young people. In many areas during the 1960s, Eastern-style orchestras were replaced by smaller, neighborhood Chicago-style bands.

Contemporary songs composed by Polish Americans seldom refer to the immigrant experience. Some recapture the Old World rural past, but most focus on love, courtship, drinking, dancing, camaraderie, or pride in Polish heritage. Some songs, however, address the harsh realities of life, such as war. Walt Solek introduced English-language polkas in the mid-1940s; these show influences from country and western lyrics and rock and roll. Later bilingual polkas became popular. Today, the use of English coexists with the continued popularity of Polish-language songs.

—*Adapted from an article by Mark Levy*

Bibliography

Greene, Victor. 1992. *A Passion for Polka: Old-Time Ethnic Music in America.* Berkeley: University of California Press.

Keil, Charles. 1992. *Polka Happiness.* Philadelphia: Temple University Press.

Kleeman, Janice Ellen. 1982. "The Origins and Stylistic Development of Polish American Polka Music." Ph.D. dissertation, University of California, Berkeley.

Savaglio, Paula. 1996. "Polka Bands and Choral Groups: The Musical Self-Representation of Polish Americans in Detroit." *Ethnomusicology* 40(1): 35–47.

Early Jewish Pop Music

Persecution and need drove Jews from Poland, the Russian Empire, the Balkans, and Turkey to North America in a great wave of immigration from 1881 to 1924. For Eastern Europeans of the late nineteenth century, it was a musically complex period. An increasingly urbanized and proletarianized mass of Jews was inventing a Yiddish language-based popular culture (newspapers, pulp and art literature, theater, and popular song), so it was not carriers of a settled, ancient music culture who poured into New York, but modernizing members of a mobile and volatile generation of cultural experimenters and innovators. Yiddish-language popular songs tended to be penned in New York City's Lower East Side and exported to Europe.

The masses of immigrants sought relief from stringent working conditions and sordid housing in the entertainment district of New York or the theaters and halls of North American cities. Heavy urbanization of the Jewish population enabled Yiddish theater troupes to tour "the provinces" by going to Philadelphia, Chicago, and Detroit. The lively world of Yiddish theater fans and actors formed part of a sprawling scene that ranged from beer-garden vaudeville to upscale theater.

The energy displayed on stage spilled over into living rooms via the older medium of parlor pianos and the novelty of gramophones. On the Lower East Side, one could easily find music dealers who sold pianos and sheet music and arranged for music lessons on the premises. The songs heard on the stage moved quickly to the streets and into shop windows, and their history can only be sketched out here. The Jewish sheet-music industry was not the only such ethnic enterprise in America; there were German publications in the Midwest, for example. Yet because New York's Jews lived in the heart of America's music industry in concentrated numbers (perhaps 1,250,000 by 1914), they could produce an impressive in-group business. Composers could walk a few blocks uptown and offer songs in English to mainstream publishers in Tin Pan Alley, as Irving Berlin did around 1910.

The Yiddish-language sheet music of the immigrant age provides a glimpse into an age of transition, when Eastern European Jews were becoming Americans. As much as mirroring that process, the popular culture of the period—theater, music, newspapers, fiction, poetry—shaped it, creating an

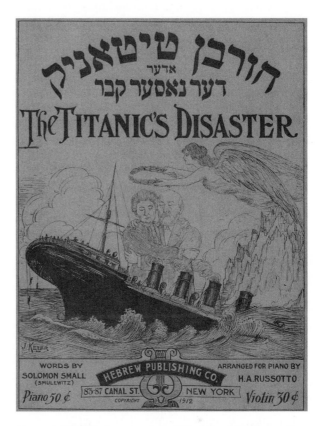

Figure 1 Yiddish sheet music to "The Titanic's Disaster" (1912), words by Solomon Small and piano arrangement by H.A. Russotto.
From the collection of the Music Department, New York Public Library for the Performing Arts, Astor, Lenox, and Tilden Associations.

Americanizing Yiddish language, music, and perspective that would influence the following generations. The cover art of sheet-music folios provides iconographic evidence, songtexts narrate the trends and tribulations of the community, and favored musical styles serve as a bridge from European to American taste. Shared concerns range from topics such as love to events such as the sinking of the *Titanic*, in 1912 (figure 1). In-group interests include the newly emerging social movement called Zionism, the need to observe Jewish holidays, the emergence of star celebrities (singers, songwriters, actors) within the ethnic boundary, and other such concerns. Like all newly arrived groups, Jews sang about the immigration process and of Old World. It is important not to think of Europe as "the Old World," because, until the destruction of European Jewry during World War II (1939–1945), Jews traveled back and forth, visiting relatives, finding spouses, and carrying songs across the sea. Nevertheless, the percentage of Jews who thought of America as a temporary home was far lower than among comparable immigrant groups, and the impact of Jewish-American music in Europe was much stronger than the reverse.

The music of this homegrown industry began in the 1880s with the creations of Abraham Goldfaden (1840–1908) and his colleague Sigmund Mogulesco (1858–1914), both of whom had emigrated to America, and a small circle of contemporary songwriters such as David Meyrowitz (1867–1943), Joseph Brody (1877–1943), Louis Friedsell (ca. 1850–1923), and Solomon Smulewitz (1868–1943), who changed his last name to Small. Their style was highly eclectic, drawing on everything from Italian opera and Romanian operetta to cantorial recitative. The standard structure for many songs of the period relied on a duple-meter verse moving to a waltz-time chorus, the stock American pop-song verse-and-chorus structure being a telling sign of modernization; yet many songs remained in a minor key, hardly an Americanism, and many dealt with issues of poverty and powerlessness far removed from Tin Pan Alley's concerns with love and comedy. "Mentshen-fresser" by Solomon Small/Smulewitz (1916) is constructed around the metaphor of the title, a common songwriting ploy of this repertoire. In the first verse, the man-eaters are the germs of tuberculosis, an endemic killer in the Jewish ghetto:

> Deeply buried in the lungs
> Lives the pale plague
> The bacilli and microbes
> Build their nest.
> They eat our bodies and lives
> And multiply greatly
> And we must fade away from the world before our time
> And we feel how we expire
> Quietly and slowly
> And the pains and the suffering
> Are terribly great
> And the dark thoughts
> Increase the pain.
> For years the Angel of Death
> Lives deep in our hearts.
> CHORUS: Microbes, bacilli, what do you want?
> Speak, whose errands are you fulfilling?
> You eat the victims mercilessly
> And aim only at blossoming life.
> You bathe in the tears of the weepers
> You extract the marrow from the bones
> Microbes and bacilli, what do you want?

This relentless imagery (rhymed in Yiddish semi-doggerel) extends, in subsequent verses, to other implications of the central metaphor:

> Crowned heads and diplomats
> To gain victory
> Force us to be soldiers
> Drive us to war.
> Young people by the millions
> Pay their price
> And their flesh
> Becomes cannon fodder
> And the crippled and the dead
> Fall here and there
> New lives are prepared
> To take their places
> And many corpses
> Are packed into big, deep graves
> And the rulers, the kings
> Play chess!

The "diplomats" verse ties the Jewish-American experience of tenement tuberculosis to the suffering inflicted on European Jewry by the ravages of World War I—of greater interest to Jewish immigrants in 1916 than to a general American public in the year before the United States entered the war.

Theater and Film Music

Music of the Yiddish theater grew more professional and more "American" in melodic line and choice of topic because of the impact of key individuals such as Joseph Rumshinsky (1881–1956), a prolific songwriter who set the tone in the 1910s and 1920s. He bridged the gap between the earlier style of the Goldfaden–Mogulesco era and the smooth, Broadway sound of later composers of the 1930s and 1940s, such as Abraham Ellstein (1907–1963), Alexander Olshanetsky (1892–1946), and Sholom Secunda (1894–1947). By the late 1930s, Secunda's "Bay mir bist du sheyn" could cross over to mainstream taste and become a standard of the pop repertoire. The growth of a Yiddish-language film industry, from silent movies of the 1910s to sound-movie production in the 1930s, created a brief but lively flourishing of soundtrack songs, some of which can still be heard at Jewish weddings.

As this in-group entertainment industry struggled to keep up with a changing cultural scene, some immigrant-era performers who had left the community for mainstream fame, such as the "red-hot mama," singer Sophie Tucker (1884–1966), kept their ties to a "home" ethnic audience. Perhaps the most compelling Jewish entertainer of this era was Al Jolson (1886–1950; figure 2). Born Asa Yoelson, a

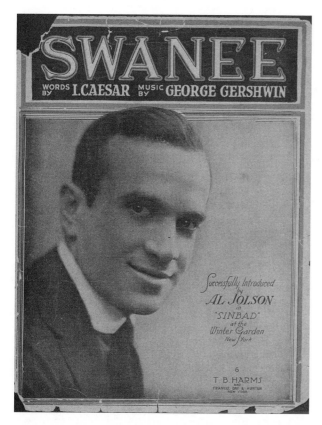

Figure 2 Al Jolson graces the cover of the vocal score to "Swanee" (1919), the music of which was written by twenty-year-old George Gershwin (1898–1937). Jolson incorporated the song into *Sinbad*, the show he was performing at the time, and it went on to sell a million copies of sheet music and over two million recordings. *From the collection of the Music Department, New York Public Library for the Performing Arts, Astor, Lenox, and Tilden Associations.*

cantor's son, he had a meteoric rise to highest-paid star, almost in a league of his own as an entertainer. Samson Raphaelson's 1925 Broadway hit play *The Jazz Singer* became the first successful sound film in 1927 on the strength of a movie audience's ability to see—and hear—Jolson perform on a film screen. Part of his incandescence must lie in the semiautobiographical quality of the plot, which shows a cantor's son being forced to choose between Broadway success and "the call of the race" as a successor to his father. Jolson's own success was partly attributed to "the tear in the voice," a supposedly Jewish trait, linked to Irving Berlin by non-Jewish show-business commentators and tied to the cantorial tradition.

Recordings

In parallel to the popularity of Yiddish theater music and the emergence of ethnically marked mainstream stars, talented and eclectic musicians such as Dave

Tarras (1897–1989), Naftule Brandwine (1889–1963), and Abe Schwartz (1881–1963) recorded dozens of 78-rpm recordings based on the repertoire of *klezmorim*, the wandering professional musicians of Eastern Europe. Just as tunes made their way from Jewish neighborhoods to the Polish gentry's drawing-rooms by way of *klezmer* ingenuity, melodies in New York traveled from downtown weddings to the studios of the major record companies, Columbia and Victor, and innumerable smaller labels. At the turn of the twentieth century, the Hebrew Disc and Cylinder Company issued what were familiar tunes of European origin for a New York public. These were generic dances, often based on southeast European styles common to several ethnic groups (Romanian, Greek, south Slavic, even Ukrainian, Turkish, and Armenian). For Columbia Records in the 1920s, Abe Schwartz and his backup musicians became a house band, which recorded the music of several ethnic groups under a variety of names. Schwartz was not the only crossover musician: David Medoff had a prolific, but short-lived, career in the 1920s singing Yiddish, Ukrainian, and Russian items, even including Christian Orthodox liturgical songs. Recordings of klezmer music declined during the Great Depression, even before the music had faded from the forefront of Jewish-American consciousness. By the 1940s, the music that wedding guests danced to in catering halls across America had yielded to more popular American-based styles, including swing and Latin music. The term *klezmer* became a sign of a musician's backwardness until the revival of the 1970s.

—Adapted from an article by Mark Slobin

Bibliography

Heskes, Irene. 1977. *The Resource Book of Jewish Music: A Bibliographical and Topical Guide to the Book and Journal Literature and Program Materials.* Westport, Conn.: Greenwood Press.

——. 1992. *Yiddish American Popular Songs, 1895–1950: A Catalog Based on the Lawrence Marwick Roster of Copyright Entries.* Washington, D.C.: Library of Congress.

Sapoznik, Henry. 1999. Klezmer! *Jewish Music from Old World to Our World.* New York: Schirmer Books.

Slobin, Mark. 1980. "From Vilna to Vaudeville: Minikes and Among the Indians." *The Drama Review* 24:17–26.

——. 1982. *Tenement Songs: The Popular Music of the Jewish Immigrants.* Urbana: University of Illinois Press.

——. 2000. *Fiddler on the Move: Exploring the World of Klezmer.* New York: Oxford University Press.

——, and Richard Spottswood. 1984. "David Medoff: A Case Study of Interethnic Popular Culture." *American Music* 3:261–276.

The Birth of Rock: A Musical Interaction

Musical interactions are a natural process of social and cultural exchange. People living side by side hear and experiment with each other's musics as with language, art, and other forms of expressive culture. In the United States, where social and cultural groups are extraordinarily diverse, and when new technologies are making the manipulation of sound increasingly possible, opportunities for musical borrowings, border crossings, fusions, and other forms of musical interaction abound.

The history of rock can be seen as a confluence of intersecting streams of musical styles and social interactions. Clearly divided into an early rock-and-roll period (heavily influenced by rhythm and blues), and later into a plethora of "rock" styles influenced by new technology and media, rock is the quintessential music of youth.

Rock and Roll

The term *rock and roll* historically has had three different but related meanings. First, it has commonly functioned, much like the word *jazz*, as an umbrella term for a range of postwar musical styles that have evolved from late 1940s styles of rhythm and blues, pop, and country. The overriding unifying factor has been the primary target audience for the music: white youth. In this sense, *rock and roll* is often used interchangeably with the short form *rock*, and is often understood in opposition to pop music, rock being considered by critics and fans alike as more "authentic." Rock and roll and rock have been routinely associated with youth disaffection, and, at various moments, each has served as the focal point for what can be termed moral panics within the hegemonic culture. Various definitions or usages of the term in the first sense subsume under the term *rock and roll* several rhythm-and-blues genres that have garnered a substantial white audience, such as black rock and roll, doo-wop, girl group, soul, funk, and rap, alongside genres produced and consumed nearly exclusively by whites, such as grunge, progressive rock, folk rock, punk, and heavy metal.

Second, *rock and roll* has commonly served to designate popular music styles that flourished from the late 1940s through the mid-1960s. By 1966 and 1967, new styles began to emerge that were different enough from the roots of rock and roll to be designated under the short form *rock*. The latter was assumed at the time to denote more "serious" music, which involved higher levels of musicianship (for example, the work of Cream, Jimi Hendrix (1942–1970), and the Mothers of Invention), borrowed features from Western classical and world musics (as on the Beatles albums *Revolver* and *Sgt. Pepper's Lonely Hearts Club Band* and the first two Velvet Underground albums), used much more complex formal structures and production techniques (for example, the Doors's "The End," the Beatles's "Tomorrow Never Knows," the Beach Boys's "Good Vibrations"), addressed deeper- and/or wider-ranging issues with more poetically informed lyrics (for example, the songs of Bob Dylan (b. 1941), the Band, and the Doors), and ceased to function only or, in the case of some groups, primarily as dance music and instead was designed for serious listening and contemplation. Part of the change to *rock* was a shift in designating the musicians; once called entertainers, they were now considered artists. The latter term was tied up with values derived from nineteenth-century conventions and included the notion that artists were special and thereby removed from everyday norms and constraints, and that rock musicians as artists were obliged to develop or progress over time. All these changes took place within the context of the development of FM radio, the full-length $33\frac{1}{3}$-rpm LP disk's becoming more important than the 45-rpm single, the publication of the first serious North American magazines dedicated to discussing these musics (*Crawdaddy* and *Rolling Stone*), and the publication of the first books on the subject: *Rock and Other Four Letter Words* (1968) by J. Marks and *The World of Rock* (1968) by John Gabree. The primary audience for rock and roll and rock under these definitions was again white youth.

Finally, rock and roll has been used, in a more strictly musicological sense, to designate a particular style of dance-oriented, high-energy, loud, up-tempo, blues-based music predicated on a "groove" in which bass drum and bass guitar (upright bass in the earliest recordings and live performances) accent beats one and three, a back beat (on beats two and four) is played on a snare (often in tandem with another instrument, such as a rhythm guitar or a piano), and a ride pattern, consisting of straight eighth notes, is played on the ride cymbal or closed hi-hat. One of the primary distinguishing features of this style is the use of rhythm guitar and/or piano to play an added sixth chordal pattern in straight eighth notes (root and fifth on the onbeats; root and sixth on the offbeats—derived from boogie-woogie piano playing) to accompany a vocal line that is also primarily sung in eighths. The typical performing force for rock and roll in this sense consists of electric lead guitar, electric rhythm guitar, bass and drums, and, at times, piano. In the 1950s, a tenor saxophone was used by virtually all black and some white rock-and-roll musicians as the primary lead instrument. Electric guitars and saxophones were often played in ways that distorted their timbre, adding to the primal energy of the music and its primary appeal to youth. Before the advent of punk (in the mid-1970s), rock-and-roll lyrics (as opposed to those of rock) were exclusively youth-focused, largely concerned with idealized, often sexualized boy–girl relationships (usually from a male viewpoint), rock and roll itself, cars, and skipping school.

The original recordings designated by the use of the term in the third sense were by Little Richard (b. 1932), Chuck Berry (b. 1926), Elvis Presley (1935–1977), and Jerry Lee Lewis (b. 1935). In the early and mid-1960s, British groups such as the Beatles, the Dave Clark Five, and the Rolling Stones, and American groups such as the Beach Boys, often played in this style: all four groups routinely recorded covers of Chuck Berry tunes on their earliest albums. In the late 1960s, Creedence Clearwater Revival and the Rolling Stones were the primary exponents of this style, though most groups of the time, including those as disparate as the Grateful Dead, the Byrds, the Velvet Underground, and Led Zeppelin, occasionally played in this style. Punk groups in the mid- and late 1970s such as the Sex Pistols and the Ramones, and later groups such as the Georgia Satellites in the mid-1980s and the Black Crowes in the 1990s, all continued playing music that fit into the style of 1950s rock and roll as originally articulated by Chuck Berry.

In all three usages of the term, *rock and roll*, in contrast to the earlier Tin Pan Alley tradition of white popular music, prioritizes performers over composers and recordings over songs. Further serving to demarcate rock and roll from earlier forms of white popular music in North America is that much of the music subsumed under all three definitions conveys a heightened sense of immediate and overt emotional engagement. All three usages of the term imply that rock and roll originated in the United States and spread throughout North America, into the United Kingdom and the rest of Europe, and eventually to the Middle East, South America, South Asia, and, in the case of soul, funk, and rap, into sub-Saharan Africa. This article discusses rock and roll as articulated in the second definition, limiting the discussion to the rise and development of the music from the late 1940s through the late 1950s.

Early Rock and Roll

Commentators have long argued over what should be considered the first rock-and-roll record. Sam Phillips (1923–2003), owner of Sun Records, and rock historian Robert Palmer (1945–1997) have argued for "Rocket 88," released on Chess in 1951 by Jackie Brenston and his Delta Cats. Others have suggested "It's Too Soon to Know" by the Orioles, first issued in 1948 by the tiny independent label It's A Natural and subsequently picked up by Jubilee Records. Still others have referenced "Cry" by Johnny Ray (1927–1990), released by Columbia in 1951. Such arguments are fruitless: it is impossible to establish what the first rock and roll record was, as criteria vary depending upon who is making the selection. It is useful, though, to look at the reasons why "Rocket 88," "It's Too Soon to Know," and "Cry" might be considered early prototypical examples of this music.

The Orioles are widely acknowledged to be the first rhythm-and-blues (as distinct from jazz and/or pop) vocal group. Their song "It's Too Soon to Know" reached number one on *Billboard*'s race jukebox chart, number two on *Billboard*'s race-sales chart, and, more important for this discussion, number thirteen on *Billboard*'s pop chart. (The race charts were designed to measure black consumption; the pop charts were designed to measure airplay on white-oriented radio stations and sales to white consumers). The Orioles were the first black artists recording in a new style to garner substantial airplay on white radio stations and to sell significant numbers of records to white consumers.

"Rocket 88" was also a number-one hit on the race charts, which in 1949 were renamed the rhythm-and-blues charts, but did not register on pop charts. Theoretically, the record was not consumed by a large number of European Americans; however, it was perhaps the first record to feature distorted electric guitar. This trait, combined with a lyric that consisted of a series of automotive or sexual metaphors, a frantic tempo, and an extended tenor sax solo involving overblowing, distortion, and cracked notes, makes the song, from a musicological point of view, an early recording containing many of the seminal features of rock and roll.

"Cry" was the first nationally successful record by a white singer to display a level of emotional outpouring that was completely foreign to the Tin Pan Alley aesthetic. It reached the top of all charts.

Taken together, these recordings articulate central tropes embodied in the earliest uses of the term *rock and roll*: the large-scale consumption of black popular culture by white youth; music that features distortion, fast tempos, and young people's lyrical concerns; and white performers' production of music that shows substantial debts to black music, especially in articulating overt emotional catharsis.

Rock and Roll Hits the Charts

The first black records to begin showing up regularly on pop charts, demonstrating substantial white consumption, were by black vocal groups: the Ravens in 1947, the Deep River Boys and the Orioles in 1948, and Billy Ward and the Dominoes in 1951. In 1952 and 1953, New Orleans rhythm-and-blues star Fats Domino (b. 1928) had two minor pop hits. New York-based singer Ruth Brown (1928–2006) and the vocal groups the Four Tunes and the Orioles also "charted pop" in 1953, but only in 1954 did a sizable number of black artists achieve hits on the pop charts, including the Crows ("Gee"), the Drifters ("Honey Love"), Hank Ballard and the Midnighters ("Work with Me, Annie"), and the Chords ("Sh-Boom"). Fats Domino was the only solo black male artist associated with rock and roll to achieve crossover success before 1955. Black vocal groups and female vocalists were less sexually threatening to white males and thereby more easily garnered white radio play and proved easier on pragmatic and psychological levels for white youth to consume.

The year 1955 marked the watershed, as black performers Little Richard, Chuck Berry, and Bo Diddley (1928–2008) enjoyed their first hits (for the Specialty and Chess labels), Fats Domino enjoyed his first top-ten pop hit (after twelve top-ten rhythm-and-blues hits between 1950 and early 1955, all released on Imperial), and white rock artist Bill Haley and the Comets reached the top spot for eight weeks straight with the rerelease of "(We're Gonna) Rock around the Clock," featured in the film *Blackboard Jungle*. By March 1956, Elvis Presley had begun to chart nationally. Equally telling is that in 1954, major labels released forty-two of the fifty top-selling singles, but in 1955, that number had dropped to seventeen of the fifty, as the pop charts became inundated with rock-and-roll records released on independent labels.

Early White Rock-and-roll Artists

It is unsurprising that the first examples of music made by white artists that was called rock and roll combined elements of country and pop music with rhythm and blues. Elvis Presley's first five releases on Sun Records, in 1954 and 1955, combined one rhythm-and-blues song with one country song. Presley modified the songs, adding substantial rhythm-and-blues elements to his recordings of country material and, similarly, adding country and pop elements to his versions of rhythm-and-blues songs. Subsequent white rock-and-roll artists, including Billy Lee Riley (b. 1933), Carl Perkins (1932–1998), and Buddy Holly (1936–1959), stated that it was hearing Presley's fusion of rhythm and blues, country, and pop that made them realize that they could combine the black music they had been hearing on black-appeal stations with the country and occasional pop material they had begun to play professionally. The new style was called rockabilly; the name was a hybrid of the terms for black rock and roll and white hillbilly music.

Presley was not the only artist experimenting with the cross-pollination of black and white styles. Many aspects of Chuck Berry's multistring guitar style can be traced to country guitarists such as Chet Atkins (1924–2001), and his predilection for text-heavy extended linear narratives resonates with long-standing country practices. Berry's first single and first hit, "Maybelline," was a rewrite of a country fiddle tune known as "Ida Red." By the mid-1950s, Tin Pan Alley songwriters had recognized that rock and roll was a combination of the two main tributaries of vernacular white and black musics. Max Freedman, author of several Tin Pan Alley chestnuts, including "Sioux City Sue," took the melody from Hank Williams's 1949 country hit "Move It On Over," added a riff section based on rhythm-and-blues star Jimmy Liggins's recording "Shuffleshuck," and wrote lyrics about rocking for what was seen by many as the clarion call of the era, "(We're Gonna) Rock around the Clock."

The Early Splintering of Rock and Roll

By the early 1960s, the major labels, aided by the tightening of radio playlists because of the payola scandal and the rise of the top-forty format, regained control of the pop market and began to promote and distribute a safer, softer, more pop-oriented version of the music, now performed by white teen idols such as Paul Anka (b. 1941), Ricky Nelson (1940–1985), and Johnny Burnette (1934–1964). A few American artists and producers, including Phil Spector (b. 1940), Link Wray (1929–2005), and the Beach Boys, pioneered new variants of rock and roll in this period, but it would not be until the British invasion in 1964, led by the Beatles, the Dave Clark Five, the Rolling Stones, and others [see BRITISH ROCK AND

Pop, 1950s to 1970s in the Europe section], that rock and roll would return in full force for a couple of years before mutating into new styles subsumed under the term *rock*.

Rock itself would mutate in myriad directions over the next decades, at points incorporating influences from folk, jazz, renaissance, baroque, classical, romantic, avant-garde, "new music," blues, *norteno*, tejano, Celtic, reggae, and world musics. Rock would continue to be produced and consumed primarily by white youth, but the age range of audiences would rise as the original fans of the music in the 1950s and 1960s aged. This expanded demographic produced tensions, as rock became heavily stratified in the late 1970s: many newer styles, such as punk, new wave, forms of heavy metal, grunge, rap, and dance musics were positioned in opposition to the music of the late 1960s and early 1970s, the latter now renamed "classic rock."

—Adapted from an article by Rob Bowman

Bibliography

Berry, Chuck. 1987. *Chuck Berry: The Autobiography*. New York: Harmony Books.

Broven, John. 1978. *Rhythm & Blues in New Orleans*. Gretna, La.: Pelican Publishing.

De Curtis, Anthony, ed. 1992. *Present Tense: Rock & Roll and Culture*. Durham, N.C.: Duke University Press.

Escott, Colin, and Martin Hawkins. 1991. *Good Rockin' Tonight: Sun Records and the Birth of Rock 'n' Roll*. New York: St. Martin's Press.

Gabree, John. 1968. *The World of Rock*. Greenwood, Conn.: Fawcett Publications.

Gillett, Charlie. 1970. *The Sound of The City The Rise of Rock and Roll*. London: Souvenir Press.

Guralnick, Peter. 1994. *Last Train to Memphis The Rise of Elvis Presley*. New York: Little, Brown.

Marks, J. 1968. *Rock and Other Four Letter Words*. New York: Bantam Books.

Tosches, Nick. 1984. *Unsung Heroes of Rock 'n' Roll*. New York: Charles Scribner's Sons.

White, Charles. 1984. *The Life and Times of Little Richard: The Quasar of Rock*. New York: Harmony Books.

White, George R. 1995. *Bo Diddley: Living Legend*. Surrey, Eng.: Castle Communications.

Latin Musics

Spanish immigrants were the first Europeans to establish a permanent settlement in what is today the United States—in St. Augustine, Florida (near present-day Jacksonville) in 1565. From then until the present, Spanish-speaking immigrants, Portuguese-speaking Brazilians, and mestizos (people of mixed heritage) have continued to arrive—via Mexico, the Caribbean, and Central and South America. They represent the second-largest and fastest-growing minority population in the United States. Hispanic musical communities, located primarily in Texas, New Mexico, California, and New York, have contributed vibrant rhythms, dances, instruments, and musicians to the American musical landscape. Genres such as the *son*, the *conjunto*, the mambo, the rumba, and the *cha-cha-chá*, from Mexico, Cuba, Puerto Rico, and other countries, greatly influenced popular music—especially African-American jazz and dances—in the mid- and late twentieth century, when dance crazes popularized by bandleaders such as Tito Puente were the rage. Latin musical elements are so pervasive that, like African and European elements, they are integral to American music.

An informal group of Puerto Rican *pleneros* playing different sizes of *pandereta* 'round frame drum' performs in a procession in Manhattan for a cultural festival, June 1979. *Photo by Daniel E. Sheehy.*

Overview

At the beginning of the twenty-first century, 40 million Latinos live in the United States, representing 13 percent of the population—about one of every eight residents. The U.S. Bureau of the Census uses the term *Hispanic*; however, *Latino* came to prevail as the most widely accepted label to describe a population of diverse national origins, cultures, and racial traits. Common terms of self-description point to national or regional origin—*mexicano* 'Mexican American', *puertorriqueño* 'Puerto Rican', *cubano* 'Cuban', *guatemalteco, boliviano, tejano, nuevo-mexicano*, and others—or those that emerged from sociopolitical movements, such as Chicano or Nuyorican (Puerto Rican New Yorker).

According to 2000 census figures, people of Mexican origin were by far the largest Latino group, comprising 58 percent of U.S. Latinos. Puerto Ricans followed, with 10 percent, and Cubans, with 4 percent. This section focuses on the musics of these groups.

Mexican-American Music

Mexican-American music includes all musics of Mexican origin that are practiced in the United States and musics created by communities historically associated with Mexico. The former means regional traditions of Mexican mestizo folk music, folk-rooted popular Mexican musics, and internationally popular urban musics. The latter means regional musical cultures from New Mexico (predating the existence of the Republic of Mexico, but strongly influenced by Mexican music), the Lower Rio Grande Valley of Texas, and California, and hybrid creations spawned by urban life.

The longest-lived musics in the United States are those of the Nuevo Mexicano and Tejano groups. Musical distinctions reflect broader cultural differences among Mexican-American subgroups, but certain unifying features are shared. Baptisms, birthdays, *quinceañeras* (celebrations for fifteen-year-old girls), and weddings are universally preferred life-cycle events for making music. *Cinco de Mayo* 'Fifth of May', commemorating the Battle of Puebla in the 1860s Mexican struggle against occupying French imperialist forces, emerged as the major annual celebration of Chicano identity, marked by performances of music and dance. Mexican Independence Day, 16 September, has similar importance, especially in communities with more recent roots in the Republic of Mexico. Mother's Day is another day for celebrations accompanied by music. The Roman Catholic feast of the Virgin of Guadalupe, on 12 December, is widely celebrated with hymns and other songs sung by congregations and, when possible, live mariachi music performing a post-Vatican Council II version of certain mass segments, known collectively as the Misa Panamericana. Social dances and concerts by touring Mexican superstar vocalists, such as Vicente Fernández (b. 1940) and Juan Gabriel (b. 1950), attract Mexican Americans of all backgrounds. The custom of the *serenata*—a short serenade to celebrate a birthday, Mother's Day, or a man's devotion to his beloved—continues in North American contexts. The Mexican song "Las Mañanitas," sung especially on birthdays, is known widely among Mexican Americans and other Latinos. The Mexican farmworker movement in the 1960s and 1970s occasioned performances of narrative ballads (*corridos*) that recounted strikes, praised leader César Chávez (1927–1993), and aimed to reinforce commitment to the movement (figure 1). Sparked by the civil-rights movement in the 1960s, the Chicano movement inspired interest in Mexican roots music as a cultural symbol. New musical compositions treating important Chicano leaders and events and calling for greater cultural pride came out of the Chicano movement.

Two folk-rooted musical styles—mariachis and *conjuntos*—are found throughout the United States and in Canada. Mariachis are based in most American states and in at least two Canadian provinces, and are widely recognized by non-Mexicans in the United States. Typically comprising two trumpets, two or more violins, a six-stringed, convex-spined bass (*guitarrón*), a five-stringed, convex-spined guitar (*vihuela*), and a six-stringed guitar, mariachis rose from regional roots in nineteenth-century west Mexico to become a twentieth-century pan-Mexican musical symbol. They are the principal ensemble for performing *música ranchera*, popular music often treating matters of unrequited love, evoking sentiment and appealing to pan-Mexican tastes. Songs such as "El Rey" ("The King") and "Volver, Volver" ("Return, Return"), composed and recorded by the late singer-songwriter Jose Alfredo Jiménez, are

Figure 1 Farmworker/musicians (*left* to *right*) Jesús Figueroa, Alfredo Figueroa, and Alfredo Figueroa Jr. pose in their home in Blythe, California, April 1999. *Photo by Daniel E. Sheehy.*

staples of their repertoire and are known by almost all Mexican Americans. Mariachis are sought out to perform at Roman Catholic masses, especially on the feast of the Virgin of Guadalupe. They frequently play at Mexican restaurants, Mexican-themed events, and celebrations of cultural diversity. Generally speaking, they are mobile, musically versatile, professional musical ensembles capable of performing a wide range of pieces, including many non-Mexican songs.

Large-scale mariachi festivals, numbering more than fifteen scattered throughout the Southwest in the 1990s, began in 1979 with the first San Antonio International Mariachi Conference, organized by Belle and Juan Ortiz. These festivals built upon two other trends that began in the 1960s. One was the emergence of programs of mariachi instruction and performance in schools in California, Arizona, and Texas (figure 2). The other was the development of nightclubs that present mariachi music on stage as a dinner show, reaching new audiences of highly assimilated, middle-class, urban immigrants and their offspring. The first such nightclub was opened in Los Angeles by bandleader Natividad Cano and his Mariachi Los Camperos in 1969.

Accordion-driven ensembles (*conjuntos*) have migrated with transient Mexican workers to all regions of the United States and to Canada. These groups may be of Mexican or Tejano origin. Mexican immigrant *conjuntos* of two or three musicians playing the Hohner or Gabinelli button accordion, the twelve-stringed *bajo sexto*, and, if available, the upright three-stringed bass (*tololoche*) are commoner outside Texas, reflecting the number and dispersal of Mexican immigrant workers. [See TEJANO MUSIC: CONJUNTO.]

Puerto Rican Music

The cession of Puerto Rico to the United States at the conclusion of the Spanish-American war, in

Figure 2 Mariachi bandleader/ violinist Natividad Cano (*left of center in white shirt*) and members of his group Los Camperos lead a workshop for high school students at the Viva el Mariachi Festival in Fresno, California, March 1997. *Photo by Daniel E. Sheehy.*

1898, began two processes that lasted throughout the twentieth century, especially after the end of World War I. First, the emerging influence of the North American popular-music industry, radio, and cinema bombarded the island with current musical vogues. Second, the northward flow to the United States—to New York City, in particular—of Puerto Rican professional musicians familiar with those vogues continued unabated. Internal economic shifts after the American takeover of the island displaced many workers, including musicians, and the hardships of the Great Depression accelerated the movement of musicians to New York, the hub of the entertainment industry. At the same time, the versatility gained by Puerto Rican musicians through exposure to Latin and North American musics worked to their advantage. These events contributed to the prominence of Puerto Rican musicians in the evolution of New York's musical life and the popular Latin musics it would spawn, especially Latin-Caribbean dance music. The multifaceted musical literacy of Puerto Rican musicians increased as Puerto Rican immigrants and their descendants became integrated into North American cultural life, borrowing from and contributing to important veins of popular music, such as jazz and rock and roll. Tito Puente (1923–2000), who made more than one hundred record albums and won many Grammy awards, was the most prominent example of Puerto Rican centrality to Cuban-derived popular Latin dance music and Latin jazz. Puerto Ricans such as singer-guitarist José Feliciano (b. 1945) and Metropolitan Opera singer Martina Arroyo (b. 1936) achieved national and international prominence.

Several popular forms of Puerto Rican traditional music are performed in the United States. The two principal strains of popular Puerto Rican folk music—*música jíbara* and the more African-derived genres of *bomba* and *plena*—enjoyed a revival in the 1990s. *Música jíbara* centers on the music and dance form called *seis*, and on the ensemble based on the ten-steel-stringed guitar (*cuatro*), the six-stringed "standard" Spanish guitar, and the gourd scraper (*güiro*). Puerto Rican *cuatrista* (*cuatro* player) Estanislao "Ladí" Martínez (1898–1979) was influential in forming the modern *jíbaro* ensemble (*conjunto jíbaro*), especially in the 1930s and after. He increased the popularity of the music by incorporating disparate musical genres into the repertoire and including more instruments in the ensemble: two *cuatros*, bongo drums, and even a bass and a conga drum. He was closely linked to Puerto Rican musical life in New York City through touring and recordings. In the 1990s,

several *jíbaro*-style ensembles, numerous individual musicians, and a few *jíbaro* instrument makers were active in the United States, especially in larger cities of the Midwest and Northeast, such as Chicago, New York, and Hartford, Connecticut. *Cuatrista* Yomo Toro's performances of traditional *seis*, Latin dance music, and Latin jazz gained him renown. As in Puerto Rico, *música jíbara* and the musical genre *aguinaldo* are most favored during Christmastime. The music is often associated with an idealized rustic past and the custom of *aguinaldo* singing, in which small groups go from house to house, perform, and ask for small gifts of money or food (*aguinaldos*). The texts, often improvised, evoke Christmas themes and ask listeners for a gift.

In the 1990s, the number of U.S.-based groups playing *bomba* and *plena* increased severalfold, in great measure the result of efforts by the group Los Pleneros de la 21 to reestablish the prominence of the music in the United States. Led by musician-teacher-bandleader Juan Gutiérrez, the Pleneros elevated the prestige of *bomba* and *plena* music in the United States through innovative instrumentation, frequent performances in the Northeast and upper Midwest, educational presentations, and emphasis on the importance of the music to Puerto Rican heritage. To multilayered interlocking rhythms of the *plena*'s two or three frame drums in graduated sizes (*panderetas*) and the *bomba*'s two single-headed barrel drums, the Pleneros added electrified bass, melody instruments such as piano and the *cuatro*, and additional percussion. Many other groups in the region emerged, modeled after the Pleneros. The popularity of *bomba* was reinforced by periodic performances by *bomba* groups from Puerto Rico, such as those of the Cepeda and Ayala families.

Cuban Music

In addition to Caribbean-derived music, Cuban musical traditions are practiced in the United States. In the Cuban community around Miami that resulted from the first wave of refugees (primarily of European background) from Cuba after 1959, when Fidel Castro's government came to power, a few musicians continue the rural folk tradition of the *punto guajiro*, singing often improvised poetic texts to the accompaniment of stringed instruments led by a six-stringed *tres*. The *son* is another important genre of this musical style; the basis of the popularity of the rumba during the 1930s (see below), it used Afro-Cuban rhythms such as the "anticipated bass," in which the bass line precedes the downbeat of a measure by one-half beat, and the *ritmo de tango*. In Cuba, *son* does not refer to a specific, formal musical structure: it describes a particular sound and instrumentation, characterized by a certain feeling. It originally emerged from the black population in rural districts of Cuba as a vehicle for entertainment at informal gatherings. In the early 1900s, it migrated to urban centers, and eventually affected all Cuban popular music. Though it was firmly based on African concepts, *son* guitar playing strongly recalled Spanish traditions.

Practiced much more widely is music of Afro-Cuban origin, predating, but arriving principally in the wake of, the Mariel boatlift, in 1980. Several Afro-Cuban religious musical traditions reflect the distinctive strains of African-derived identity in Afro-Cuban culture. Most prominent is the Yorùbá-derived *lucumí* tradition popularly known as *santería*. Central to the music of *santería* are three double-conical, two-headed drums of the *batá* ensemble. *Oru*, songs sung in the Yorùbá-based *lucumí* language, praise African deities such as Changó, Ogún, and Obatalá.

Many accomplished musicians and religious leaders in these traditions are based in large cities, particularly in New York, the mid-Atlantic region, southern Florida, and California. A few of the musicians, Francisco Aguabella (b. 1925), for example, have been active in the United States since before the Castro era. Some, like Aguabella, who performed with popular Afro-Cuban musician Mongo Santamaría (1922–2003), have been active in mainstream Latin popular music. Others, such as musician–instrument maker Felipe García Villamil (b. 1931), who arrived among the Mariel refugees, have devoted themselves mainly to religious activities. Afro-Cuban religion, ceremony, and music have attracted devotees from outside the Cuban community.

Other than the Cuban-derived music at the core of *salsa* (see textbox), the rumba is most central to secular Afro-Cuban music. It emerged in Cuba around 1900 and provided much of the rhythmic grounding for popular dance music that followed. A typical rumba ensemble may comprise three conga drums (*tumbadoras*), one of them being the smaller lead *quinto*; two *claves*, short concussed resonant sticks; and the *cajita musical*, a mounted hollow wood block played with two sticks. Principal types of rumba are the *guaguancó* and the *columbia*. Rumba music has attracted other Latinos and non-Latinos. In recent decades, instruments and rhythms have been borrowed from the sacred repertoire and incorporated into secular Cuban music. One example is the *batá-rumba*, an amalgam of sacred and secular rhythms and instruments. Carnival music of the *comparsa* is another important secular form of Afro-Cuban music (figure 3).

Jazz

Cuban influence in New Orleans can be clearly traced back to the 1880s, when the *habanera* first became popular, but Cuba's subtler impact—as heard in *tresillo*, *cinquillo*, and *clave* patterns, embedded in rhythmic and melodic ideas—is much older. This should be expected, for New Orleans was Spanish-controlled for two generations before the Louisiana Purchase of 1803, and movement between the city and Cuba was commonplace. Ferdinand "Jelly Roll"

Figure 3 Afro-Cuban ensemble Otonowa, based in Washington, D.C., performs *comparsa* music in a parade as part of the National Folk Festival in Johnstown, Pennsylvania, organized by the National Council for the Traditional Arts, July 1990. *Photo by Daniel E. Sheehy.*

406

SALSA

Salsa 'sauce' broadly denotes contemporary popular Latin dance music, which encompasses Cuban styles such as *son*, mambo, and *cha-cha-chá*, and incorporates ideas from Puerto Rico, the Dominican Republic, and to a lesser extent the rest of the Caribbean and Brazil, and black North American popular music.

Instrumentation reflects this mix. The typical salsa rhythm section consists of piano, bass, congas, bongos, *timbales, güiro*, maracas, *claves*, and often a drumset. Arrangements may add trumpets, trombones, and saxophones, and sometimes flute, violins, electric guitar, and synthesizers. Perhaps the first use of the term *salsa* in a musical sense goes back to Cuban composer Ignacio Piñeiro's 1933 song "Échale Salsita." Joe Cuba's recording of Jimmy Sabater's "Salsa y Bembé" (1962), Charlie Palmieri's recording of Víctor Velásquez's "Salsa Na Ma" (1963), and Cal Tjader's "Soul Sauce" were other early examples. The term *salsa* did not come into common usage until the early 1970s, when it appeared in *Latin New York* magazine and was adopted as a category for the 1975 Latin New York Music Awards.

From the mid-1970s into the early 1990s, the North American center for salsa was New York City, where, commercially empowered by the marketing of Jerry Masucci (1934–1997) and Johnny Pacheco (b. 1935), who founded Fania Records in 1964, salsa became the center of popular Latin musicmaking.

Salsa was early associated with the *barrio* district, working-class issues, Afro-Cuban religions, and an emerging Latino militancy. The music and lyrics were tough, provocative, and closely aligned to Afro-Cuban culture. Since the late 1980s, commercial considerations, in addition to an increasing Dominican presence in New York City, added new sensibilities. In the 1990s, the most commercially popular Latin music—led by Eddie Santiago (b. circa 1961), Louis Enrique, Willy Chirino, Jerry Rivera (b. 1973), and others—had a softer feel, and was often termed *salsa romántica*.

Many musicians who made their mark in earlier periods—including Tito Puente, Eddie Palmieri (b. 1936), Ray Barretto (1929–2006), Israel "Cachao" Lopez (b. 1918), and vocalist Celia Cruz (ca. 1929–2003)—continued to be important performers of salsa. Leading musicians who came of age in the salsa era include Louis Ramírez, Rubén Blades (b. 1948), Willie Colón (b. 1950), Héctor Lavoe (1946–1993), Gloria Estefan (b. 1957), and Sheila Escovedo (b. 1957?). Since the Mariel exodus from Cuba in 1981, the genre has received creative infusions from percussionist Daniel Ponce (b. 1953), drummer Ignacio Berroa (b. 1953), saxophonist Paquito D'Rivera (b. 1948), and trumpeter Arturo Sandoval (b. 1949).

Morton (1890–1941) claimed that a "Spanish tinge" was necessary for good jazz. W. C. Handy (1873–1958) traveled with his band to Cuba in 1900, where he heard numerous street bands.

Specifically traceable Cuban elements in jazz go back to Afro-Cuban flutist Alberto Socarras (1901–1987), who moved to New York in 1927, and Machito and his Afro-Cubans. Machito's orchestra, formed in 1940, combined traditional Cuban elements with jazz. Its rhythm section in its early years included piano, bass, bongo, and *timbales* (played by the young Tito Puente). In 1943, the same year that Mario Bauza (1911–1993) wrote "Tanga," conga player Carlos Vidal joined the group.

Afro-Cuban jazz gained a much larger audience in 1946, when Dizzy Gillespie (1917–1993), who had worked alongside Bauza when both had been members of the Cab Calloway Orchestra, began a brief collaboration with Chano Pozo (1915–1948), a Cuban drummer, *rumbero*, and Arará initiate. Although Gillespie and Pozo worked together for barely more than two years before Pozo's death, Pozo's introduction of the conga drum and complex Afro-Cuban rhythms associated with it brought new rhythmic energies to jazz and opened the door for conga drums to be used in this and other non-Latin styles.

—Adapted from articles by Daniel E. Sheehy, Steven Loza, and Steven Cornelius

Bibliography

Amjra, John, and Steven Cornelius. 1991. *The Music of Santería: Traditional Rhythms for the Batá Drums*. Tempe, Ariz.: White Cliffs Media.

Austerlitz, Paul. 1997. *Merengue: Dominican Music and Dominican Identity*. Philadelphia: Temple University Press.

Boggs, Vernon, ed. 1992. *Salsiology: Afro-Cuban Music and the Evolution of Salsa in New York City*. New York: Greenwood Press.

Camarillo, Albert. 1979. *Chicanos in a Changing Society*. Cambridge: Harvard University Press.

Figueroa, Frank M. 1994. *Encyclopedia of Latin American Music in New York*. St Petersburg, Fla.: Pillar Publications.

Glasser, Ruth. 1995. *My Music Is My Flag: Puerto Rican Musicians and Their New York Communities, 1917–1940*. Berkeley: University of California Press.

Herrera-Sobek, Maria. 1993. *Northward Bound: The Mexican Emigrant Experience in Ballad and Song*. Bloomington: Indiana University Press.

Manuel, Peter, ed. 1991. *Essays on Cuban Music: North American and Cuban Perspectives*. Lanham, Md.: University Press of America.

Pacini Hernández, Deborah. 1995. *Bachata: A Social History of Dominican Popular Music*. Philadelphia: Temple University Press.

Roberts, John Storm. 1979. *The Latin Tinge: The Impact of Latin American Music on the United States*. New York: Oxford University Press.

Tejano Music: *Conjunto*

Since the arrival of the first Spanish-speaking settlers in the early eighteenth century, people have come to Texas from many other states and parts of the world. They have brought with them ethnic cultures that, in turn, have acquired characteristics different from those of their homelands. They have contributed to the emergence of a regional Tejano culture. Some of their ancestors came with the original settlers; others arrived with later colonists: as one historian notes, all came "north from Mexico."

After 1845, when Texas gained its independence from Mexico, the *mexicanos* in Texas began to see themselves more and more as Tejanos. Since 1848, when the United States annexed Texas, differences between Mexicans in Mexico and Mexicans in the United States have become even more pronounced. Nevertheless, to this day, many Tejanos assert their claim to the label *mexicano*, though at some point they began to distinguish between *mexicanos* from Texas and *mexicanos* from Mexico by identifying themselves as *mexicanos de este lado* (Mexicans from this side of the Rio Grande) as opposed to *mexicanos del otro lado* (Mexicans from the other side).

Tejano cultural identity has been shaped by the historical conflict that has characterized relations between *mexicanos* and Texan Anglos, whom Tejanos still consider foreigners and interlopers. Perhaps the best example of a distinctly Tejano tradition born out of that clash of cultures are *corridos* of border conflict. Those composed in Mexico typically dealt with the Mexican Revolution (1910–1930), but in Texas the recurring theme was the longstanding conflict between Texas law-enforcement officers and Tejanos. *Corridos* depicted the Tejano man as a hero who, "with his pistol in his hand," always stood up to the "cowardly *Rinches de Tejas*" (Texas Rangers).

> A **corrido** is a Mexican folk ballad in strophic form, derived from the romance tradition.

Other noteworthy examples of Tejano culture are the Texas dialect of Mexican Spanish, which has contributed hundreds of Anglicisms to the Spanish language, and Texas-Mexican cuisine, without which Texas culture would be incomplete, but the best-known expression of contemporary Tejano culture is Tejano music.

The first genre to appear as an independent and identifiable type among Tejanos came to be called *conjunto*. In standard Spanish, the word *conjunto* means 'group'. In most Spanish-speaking areas of the world, it denotes any type of musical group or combo, but in Texas and northern Mexico, it has come to denote a group in which an accordion plays the lead and a twelve-stringed guitar (*bajo sexto*), an acoustic bass, and drums play background and rhythm. This combination of instruments evolved over about a century. Furthermore, Texas *conjuntos* and northern Mexican *conjuntos* (called *conjuntos norteños*) have had slightly different histories and characteristics.

The exact origins of *conjunto* music are impossible to determine because it is a folk music and, as such, was not notated; it was and continues to be learned by ear. Perhaps more important is that, for many years *conjuntos norteños* and Texas *conjuntos* were considered unworthy of formal study or propagation as important cultural forms in their respective countries. In Mexico, *conjunto norteños* were eclipsed long ago by mariachis and other regional forms considered more representative of Mexican national identity.

In Texas, *conjunto* music similarly had been a source of embarrassment to many Chicanos in the mid-twentieth century, especially to those in the emerging middle class, eager to shed their Mexican roots and Americanize themselves. In recent decades, however, interest in all aspects of *conjunto* music has proliferated, and it has enjoyed a resurgence in popularity among Chicanos and non-Chicanos.

Origins of *Conjunto* Music

The beginnings of *conjunto* music can be traced to the arrival in South Texas and Northern Mexico of the accordion. Invented in 1829 by Cyrillus Demian (1772–1847) in Vienna, it probably reached Texas and northern Mexico in the mid-nineteenth century. Evidently, it was introduced by German immigrants who came to south Texas and northern Mexico. They brought schottisches, waltzes, *redowas*, polkas, and mazurkas—music and dance genres historically identified with *conjunto* music. Whether *conjunto* music originated in Mexico and expanded into Texas, or was created by Texas Mexicans and spread south into Mexico, remains a topic of interest. The most plausible *conjunto*-origin theory is that Germans and their music arrived in the Rio Grande Valley (on both sides of the river) in the mid-nineteenth century, after which different traditions emerged on either side of the border.

Outstanding accordionists of the 1920s and 1930s were Pedro Ayala (1911–1990; figure 1), Narciso Martínez (1911–1992; figure 2), Santiago Jiménez (1913–1984), and Bruno Villarreal (d. 1976). These pioneers, using the single-row and double-row accordion, not only mastered those instruments, but learned the Germanic repertoire and composed tunes that became established in the south Texas *conjunto* tradition. They inspired generations of accordionists. They recorded with mainstream American labels

(CBS International and Decca, for example) as early as the 1920s.

Texas *Conjuntos*

In the late nineteenth and early twentieth centuries, Tejanos used several instrumental combinations, large and small. Perhaps the most popular type was the *banda típica*, which consisted of about eight members, usually local musicians who assembled to play for Saturday dances or special occasions such as weddings and debutante dances (*quinceañeras*). Because electricity was not readily available for

Figure 1 Accordionist Pedro Ayala known as *El Monarca del Acordeón* 'The Monarch of the Accordion', poses with Tejano bass player/guitarist Juan Viesca at the 1978 Smithsonian Folklife Festival in Washington, D.C.
Photo by Daniel E. Sheehy.

Figure 2 Pioneer *conjunto* accordionist Narciso Martínez (*center*) with bass player Juan Viesca (*right*) and unidentified *baja sexto* player (*left*) at the 1986 Smithsonian Folklife Festival.
Photo by Daniel E. Sheehy.

night-time illumination, dances were usually afternoon affairs (*tardeadas*). They were usually held outdoors, often in wooded areas, where large dance floors were built. Without inventions such as microphones, electric instruments, and amplifiers, these "brass bands" were the most appropriate to the context.

Smaller gatherings and venues afforded opportunities for smaller combos. A violin and *bajo sexto* combo was popular until the early twentieth century, but the accordion eventually replaced the violin and paired up with the *bajo sexto* to form the nucleus of the modern *conjunto*. Acoustics evidently played a part in the emergence of this combo. Of the venues, it was no doubt the honky-tonk (*cantina*), ubiquitous in rural and urban areas, that afforded the accordion and *bajo sexto*, two relatively quiet instruments, the opportunity to coalesce and thrive as a duo.

Completing the instrumentation of the modern *conjunto* were the drumset and the electric bass. The drumset, with its snare drum, bass drum, and cymbal, probably borrowed from the Tejano swing bands of the 1940s, was added to *conjuntos* during that decade. The electric bass, invented in the 1950s, became the last of the instruments to be added permanently to the ensemble. Before the 1940s, accordion and *bajo sexto* duos would sometimes add an upright bass and a *tambora* (a locally made bass drum).

The Accordion in Texas

Accordions with piano keyboards were invented soon after the button accordion, but folk musicians in Texas (and Mexico) have always preferred the button model, particularly the Vienna- or German-style button accordion. The earliest of these had a single row of ten treble buttons on the right side, on which only one scale could be played in three octaves, and two bass "spoon keys" on the left. In Texas *conjunto* music, accordionists do not use the bass keys. Instead, the bass line, played by the *bajo sexto* until the 1940s, is now played by the electric bass.

Since the mid-1940s, the typical Texas *conjunto* accordion has been the Hohner Corona II model, a triple-row, thirty-one-treble-button instrument; the Italian-made Gabbanelli is also typical. Each button on these accordions plays two notes: one when the instrument is stretched, and another when it is compressed. Each row of buttons plays one scale (in three octaves). A three-row instrument, for example, is built to play in three keys. Accidentals in one key may be found on one of the other two rows, but the fingering may be too awkward to reach them. To play in a wider variety of keys, professional accordionists must use more than one instrument, with additional keys included. Tonal variety may be achieved by using accordions, such as the Gabbanelli, which come equipped with tonal switches. Additional qualities may be added by changing the reeds in any given accordion, by using pickups, or by hooking the instrument up to electronic equipment.

As a lead instrument, the accordion is used for the melody in instrumental pieces such as polkas, and for introductions, background obbligato, and interludes or solos, especially as accompaniment to singing. Recordings indicate that the typical accordionist of the 1930s relied mainly on a simple melody, which resulted in a lively sound in faster tempos. By the 1940s, even average accordionists had mastered two- and three-line harmonies, which contributed to a fuller, more mature sound.

Other Instruments of the **Conjunto**

Since at least the early twentieth century, the standard guitar used in *conjuntos* has been the *bajo sexto*, a twelve-stringed Mexican guitar almost completely unknown to American musicians. The *bajo*, as it is commonly called, has steel strings and a deeper, more resonant sound than the classical guitar. It differs from the American twelve-stringed guitar in the type and size of the strings it requires, and in how they are placed and tuned. Unlike the American twelve-stringed guitar, which consists of six unison duplets (pairs) tuned like a six-stringed guitar (EE–AA–dd–gg–bb–e^1e^1), the *bajo* is tuned EE_1–AA_1–dD–bb–cc–ff; each of its three lower-register pairs consists of a bass string with a treble string placed above it and tuned an octave higher. The string pairs are placed in the following manner: a third string over a sixth string; a second string over a fifth string; and a first string over a fourth string. The pairing of treble-over-bass produces a more resonant sound than the large strings can produce alone. Pickups used for amplification have enhanced sound qualities and techniques.

For many years, the function of the *bajo* was to provide a bass line (with the three lower-register string sets) and strummed rhythmic chordal pulses (with the upper-register string sets). On waltzes, for instance, the bass would be played on beat one, and the chordal accompaniment on beats two and three. On duple-metered pieces such as polkas, it would play bass on one, chord on two. Since the introduction of the electric bass, *bajo* lower-register string sets (especially the fifth and sixth) have been rendered practically obsolete. Because the accordion is the lead instrument in *conjuntos*, the *bajo sexto* is rarely foregrounded, though many consider it to be the heart of the *conjunto*.

The electric bass is strictly limited to providing the beat (on one in 2/4 or 3/4 time; on one and four in 6/8 time; and on one, three, and four in four-beat Latin rhythms such as that underlying the slow *bolero*).

The drums consist of the same type of drumset used in Anglo-American dancebands and became an integral part of Texas *conjuntos* in the 1940s. The style of the drumming has evolved from those days, when the bass drum would be pounded loudly on the downbeat, the snare drum struck on the offbeat, and the cymbal hit occasionally, to one in which the bass drum is used sparingly and muffled, and the snare drum and cymbal are tapped much more lightly.

Modernization of *Conjunto*

In addition to incorporating modern accordions and adding the drumset and bass, other important developments have occurred in Texas *conjunto* music since the 1950s. In the 1950s, amplification of the *bajo*, bass, and accordion became standard.

Perhaps the most noteworthy characteristic of *conjuntos* since the 1960s is that the musicians have attained a remarkable degree of proficiency, stylization, and prestige. Their professionalism and the impact of the recording industry and of broadcasting are increasingly defolklorizing the *conjunto*. The standard ensemble described here is firmly established as a major genre of Tejano music tradition.

There have been countless groups since the 1940s, the best-known of which are Los Alacranes de Angel Flores, Chano Cadena, Los Cuatitos Cantú, Tony de la Rosa (1931–2004), Los Donneños, David Lee Garza y su Conjunto, Los Dos Gilbertos, Los Guadalupanos, Leonardo "Flaco" Jiménez (b. 1939), Santiago Jiménez Jr. (b. 1944), Estéban Jordán (Steve Jordan; b. 1938), René Joslin, Valerio Longoria

(1924–2000), Rubén Naranjo y los Gamblers, Los Pavos Reales, Gilberto Pérez y sus Compadres, Mingo Saldívar y sus Tremendos Cuatro Espadas, Rubén Vela (b. 1937), and Agapito Zúñiga. These groups, most of which were formed in the 1940s, not only learned the old German repertoire and the early Tejano accordionists' compositions, but introduced an entirely new instrument (the triple-row button-accordion), established the definitive Texas *conjunto* style, and carried the tradition to its zenith in the 1960s. They made original contributions to the Tejano tradition—contributions that distinguished Texas style from that of *conjuntos norteños* (from Mexico) and in turn led to greater variety in Tejano music in general.

Conjuntos played an important part in the genesis, prominence, and form of the other distinctly Tejano genres—*orquestas* (or *bandas*) and *grupos*. The *orquesta*, modeled after Anglo swing bands of the 1940s and 1950s, evolved into a distinctly Tejano big band. In the 1960s, there emerged the *grupo*, a keyboard-based hybrid ensemble, with roots in *conjunto* and *orquesta* instrumentation. *Conjuntos*, orquestas, and *grupos* remain popular.

—*Adapted from an article by José R. Reyna*

Bibliography

Burr, Ramiro. 1999. *The Billboard Guide to Tejano and Regional Mexican Music*. New York: Billboard Books.

Peña, Manuel H. 1985. *The Texas-Mexican Conjunto: History of a Working-Class Music*. Austin: University of Texas Press.

Reyna, José. 1976. "Tejano Music as an Expression of Cultural Nationalism." *Revista Chicano-Riqueña* 4(3):37–41.

———. 1982. "Notes on Tejano Music." *Aztlán: International Journal of Chicano Studies Research. Thematic Issue: Mexican Folklore and Folk Art in the United States* 13:1 and 2 (Spring and Fall). Los Angeles: Chicano Studies Research Center, University of California.

Asian-American Musics

Asian-American Musics

Asians, including people from the Middle East, South and Southeast Asia, and East Asia, are among the newest immigrants to arrive in the United States, beginning with the Chinese, and soon after, the Japanese, who came to work in mines during the gold rushes of the nineteenth century and to help complete the transcontinental railway. Settling primarily in California, Oregon, Washington, and British Columbia they brought classical music traditions hundreds of years old—ancient belief-systems, religious practices, and popular musics that they sometimes sought to replicate in their new homes. Chinese people in California still regularly perform Chinese operas. Instruments such as the Japanese *koto* and *shamisen* are regularly taught in Japanese-American communities in California, Hawai'i, and elsewhere. Immigrants from India and Pakistan, and late-twentieth-century arrivals, such as Vietnamese, Cambodians, Lao, and Indonesians, have established communities large enough to support traditional music and to join other Asian Americans who have ventured into Western popular and classical music.

Members of a Lion Dance troupe celebrate the opening of a new restaurant in New York City's Chinatown playing cymbals, gong, and drum, 1987. *Photo by Terry E. Miller.*

Overview

The presence of Asian musics in the United States is a multifaceted subject. Numerous Asian immigrant communities have coalesced in major cities, such as San Francisco, New York, Detroit, St. Paul, and Chicago, and in minor ones, such as Rockford, Illinois (Lao), Arlington, Virginia (Cambodian), Des Moines, Iowa (Thai Dam from Laos), and Fresno, California (Hmong from Laos). Some Asian communities, especially those composed of immigrants from China and the Philippines, have deep roots in the United States, but most Asian immigrants came after World War II as a result of changes in immigration laws and Southeast Asian wars. As the cultures they represent tend to be quite foreign to that of the mainstream European and British Isles–derived cultures, they are not easily assimilated, and the musics associated with them have usually remained hidden from mainstream view.

A second facet reflects how the non-Asian-derived population has assimilated Asian musics, often without direct contact. These contacts occur through popular recorded culture, occasional live concerts, the presence of ethnomusicology as an academic discipline, and world music ensembles that have sprung up on college and university campuses. Many such ensembles are directed by Asian musicians visiting as teachers or students; others are directed by non-Asian Americans who learned the music in the United States or abroad. In a sense, Asian musics may be divided into two categories: those that are self-expressions of specific communities, and those that have been appropriated by non-Asians. The former category is the focus of this article.

Asian Communities in the United States

People from almost all parts of Asia—East, Southeast, Central, South, and West—have come to the United States. Members of the earliest groups (Chinese and Japanese) came as laborers. Many Filipinos migrated to the United States during the period of American colonial rule (1898–1946). A significant number of Asians came as students and remained, usually in professional positions, after graduation. By far the largest numbers have come seeking asylum from economic and political upheavals. The most such refugees have come from mainland Southeast Asia, especially Vietnam, Laos, and Cambodia (figure 1).

As was true of earlier immigrant groups, people from Asia tended to cluster into communities, especially during the initial stages of settlement. Some of these communities have capitalized on their "exotic" appeal by attaining status as tourist attractions. "Chinatowns," most prominent in New York, San Francisco, Los Angeles, and Toronto offer more food and souvenirs than music, however. Los Angeles's "Little Tokyo" offers excellent restaurants and

Figure 1 Cambodian-American girls dance at the National Asian Heritage Festival in Washington, D.C., 1980. *Photo by Terry E. Miller.*

417

shopping. Orange County, California, site of the nation's largest Vietnamese community, offers shopping malls, supermarkets, and a freestanding popular music industry.

The nature of each Asian community offers insight into whether or not its music gains significance. Working-class Asians tend to have less interest in traditional music than do professional-class Asians, but this tendency may not apply if another factor, such as a strong religious center, brings people together to maintain old-country customs.

Economic Communities

The most cohesive Asian communities, those called "X-town" or "little X," include Chinese, Arabs, and Vietnamese and, to lesser extents, Japanese, Koreans, Lao, Hmong, and Filipinos. North America's Chinatowns were founded primarily by Cantonese-speaking immigrants from Guangdong Province (including Hong Kong) during the nineteenth and early twentieth centuries. Sharing a common language, the residents engaged in business, including restaurants, souvenir shops, and export-import companies, making these communities beehives of activity. Because of language barriers, few outsiders could appreciate locally produced or itinerant musical performances, such as opera troupes performing Cantonese opera, or performances by most silk-and-bamboo instrumental groups, sponsored by private organizations of amateurs. Later, Chinese immigrants from Taiwan (the Republic of China) and the People's Republic of China tended not to join the Chinatown community, because they spoke different languages and often came for professional

reasons. Beijing opera (*Jing xi*) in New York and Washington, D.C., for example, is not a Chinatown phenomenon. Therefore, Chinese communities have provided contexts for traditional performances, but these have attracted little notice from outsiders.

In Orange County's Little Saigon, a thriving music industry has developed. Because so many of the Republic of Vietnam's prominent popular singers and musicians escaped to the United States (and became concentrated in California), it is no surprise that they have been able to reestablish their careers within the Vietnamese communities of the United States. The Vietnamese music industry produces great numbers of audiotapes, music videos, and compact discs of popular songs, and artists perform live in concerts that attract large audiences. Traditional music, however, attracts little interest, though locally made DVDs of the popularized South Vietnamese theatrical genre called *cat luong* are widely available. Live performances are few.

Religious Communities

Where religion unifies a community, its religious center may provide contexts for traditional music. The religions of Asia represented through organized centers in North America include Hinduism, Islam, and Buddhism. Of these, Hindu temples have provided the most hospitable contexts for traditional music, almost exclusively that of southern India, the Karnatic tradition. Such music includes lay devotional songs (*bhajan*) and classical vocal genres. Festivals celebrating the sacred vocal compositions of St. Thyagaraja (1767–1847), southern India's greatest composer, often become successful by featuring local and visiting performing artists (figure 2). Because the

Figure 2 The renowned Smt. Jayanthi Kumaresh from southern India performs on vina at the Tyagaraja festival in Cleveland, Ohio, 2007. *Photo by N. Scott Robinson.*

people of northern India adhere to various religious systems, the impetus for Hindustani music has tended to come from Indian professionals or community organizations, such as cultural Indian Sunday schools, rather than from religious centers.

Chinese, Japanese, and Vietnamese Buddhist temples, all part of the Mahayana tradition, may maintain some forms of chant, but they have not offered significant contexts for other kinds of traditional music. The same is largely true of the Theravada Buddhist temples established by the Lao and Cambodian communities, but the Thai Buddhist temples in Chicago, Los Angeles, and New York have brought in Thai music teachers and developed traditional ensembles. Islamic mosques have not figured prominently in encouraging the traditional musics of immigrant groups from West and Central Asia.

Some Asian immigrant groups have founded Christian churches. Most prominent are Koreans, Japanese, Chinese, and Filipinos. As the practices of most Asian Christian churches are heavily Westernized, and many traditional musics are associated with non-Christian cultural beliefs and activities, churches are rarely associated with such musics.

Other Institutions

Some first-generation Asian immigrants were skilled musicians but few were able to continue their professional lives in the United States. Will their musics take root and be passed to younger generations? or will they cease upon the passing of their carriers? Arts councils in several states have established apprenticeships that, through financial incentives and public recognition, encourage traditional masters to find and train apprentices. Reviews of this process suggest mixed levels of success. Few wish to devote the time, energy, and money needed to learn traditional music if there are neither financial rewards nor ready contexts for its performance.

Classical Indian music and dance are likely the most systematically organized Asian traditions in the United States and Canada. A few masters work nearly full-time teaching classical Bharata Natyam dance, lutes (sitar and sarod), zither (vina), and drums (tabla and *mridangam*). These activities take place in private studios, under the auspices of Hindu temples, and in at least one established educational institution, the Ali Akbar College of Music in San Rafael, California. This training is available to non-Indian students as well as to those of Indian descent.

Asian-born musicians who play, compose, conduct, and teach Western classical music play an increasingly important role in American musical life. Although raised in Asia, they have devoted themselves entirely to Western music to the exclusion of their own traditions, and become Western musicians. Today, they are found performing in or conducting major orchestras, as faculty members in higher education, and as private teachers throughout the United States and Canada.

The Role of Music in Maintaining Unity and Preserving Identity

Popular genres—songs, film music, rock bands—outweigh traditional Asian musics in North America, but both play roles in maintaining unity and identity within immigrant communities. For example, to non-Indians, all people from India may be assumed to be of the same culture, but for Indians, the distinction between Karnatic (southern) and Hindustani (northern) usually remains clear, especially with regard to musical performances. St. Tyagaraja Festivals occur only where large populations of Karnatic Indians live [see THE TYAGARAJA FESTIVAL IN CLEVELAND, OHIO], and sarod concerts will attract large audiences only where large populations of Hindustani Indians live. Similarly, Cantonese opera attracts Cantonese-speakers, who tend to maintain an identity separate from Mandarin-speaking Chinese, who would likelier support Beijing opera. Concerts and other events offering music from the homeland reinforce the audience's identification with its native countries, and often subdivide audiences by geographical, linguistic, or religious origins.

In 1975, when refugees from Vietnam and Laos began arriving in North America, all were subsumed in one group. Before their arrival, all had clear notions of where they belonged in their homelands: Chinese-derived Vietnamese did not consider themselves to be Vietnamese in the same way that ethnic Vietnamese did, and few realized that some people from central Vietnam were in fact Cham, not Vietnamese. The Cham, who in Vietnam had to mute their ethnic identity, have reasserted it in the New World. Besides costume and language, a main ingredient used to invoke Cham identity is dance and music. People who had never paid much attention to these modes of expression in Vietnam now find them important in asserting a Cham identity, distinct from Vietnamese and American identities. Other so-called Vietnamese were in fact upland Mon-Khmer-speakers, unrelated to the lowland ethnic Vietnamese.

For North Americans, Lao constituted a single, if obscure, ethnic identity; but within Laos, distinctions are made between lowland, mid-upland, and high-upland groups, with most of the latter speaking non-Lao languages. The lowland Lao-speaking immigrants demonstrate their musical identity through (rarely heard) performances of *lam* singing (traditional Lao singing in repartee form), accompanied by a free-reed mouth organ (*khene*) and the more commonly heard rock band, which alternates traditionally derived dances and melodies with American line dances and whatever else is currently popular. Upland Lao, especially the Hmong, declare their distinctiveness in unaccompanied chanting of poetry and its realization on instruments, especially the free-reed mouth organ (*qeej, gaeng*).

A Multitude of Musics

The existence of Asian-derived musics within the United States can be explained from several viewpoints. These musics exist outside their original contexts, though immigrant communities often provide authentic but new contexts. This raises questions as to whether these musics should be heard as artifacts, or as part of an evolving process, which changes the musics and assigns them new meanings. These musics can be seen along a continuum from so-called pure survivals (brought from places where the original music has been changed or lost), to newly fused musics (created by stripping parts from world musical traditions and reuniting them in new ways).

Asian musics entered the United States through proliferating media—records, compact discs, audiocassettes, films, videos, CD-ROM, DVDs, television and radio shows, live concerts, performance courses—but most of these are experienced in new and often personal contexts (for example, the privacy of headphones or viewing rooms). They usually come in objectified form, stripped of their original meaning and awaiting the assignment of new functions and meanings. Asian musics may therefore be given meanings connected to novelty, liberalness, liberation, spirituality and the New Age, originality, exoticism, multiculturalism, cultural diversity, environmentalism, and a host of other thoughts, agendas, and desires. The users may know, but care little or nothing about, the original intentions, functions, or meanings of the music, but may harness them to express a contemporary American music here and now.

—*Adapted from an article by Terry E. Miller*

Bibliography

Morton, David. 1970. "Thai Traditional Music: Hot-House Plant or Sturdy Stock." *Journal of the Siam Society* 58(2):1–44.

Nguyen, Phong, with Adelaida Reyes Schramm and Patricia Shehan Campbell. 1995. *Searching for a Niche: Vietnamese Music at Home in America*. Kent, Ohio: Viet Music Publications.

Reyes, Adelaida. 1999. *Songs of the Caged, Songs of the Free: Music and the Vietnamese Refugee Experience*. Philadelphia: Temple University Press.

The Tyagaraja Festival in Cleveland, Ohio

The annual St. Tyagaraja music festival in Cleveland, Ohio (figure 1), is a ten-day gathering held in April, celebrating the death anniversary (*aradhana*) of the great South Indian saint-composer Tyagaraja (1767–1847) [see Karnatak Vocal and Instrumental Music in the South Asia section of volume 2.] It is the largest festival of its kind outside India. Similar festivals have been organized on smaller scales in Melbourne; Durban; Chicago; Washington, D.C.; Memphis; Tokyo; Toronto; and other cities where South Indians have settled. They gather at these festivals to pay musical homage to Tyagaraja. For many, it is an occasion to remember their cultural heritage and tradition through music and religious devotion (bhakti).

The Cleveland festival began in 1978—which makes it the oldest of these festivals and the most widely attended, with more than two thousand visitors from the South Indian community in Cleveland and other parts of the United States and Canada. It has been acknowledged by the U.S. House of Representatives, and the state of Ohio has formally designated its days as Tyagaraja Days. The government of India has taken notice of it by naming it an official pilgrimage site.

Currently, roughly 2,000,000 Indians live in the United States. In the mid-1960s, many of them formed urban communities in cities such as Atlanta, Chicago, Cleveland, Houston, and New York. Since then, nonresident Indians living in urban diasporas have maintained their cultural traditions in the form of festivals and other social customs and events.

Tyagaraja and the Festival at Tiruvaiyaru

The logistics of the festival are organized by the Aradhana Committee, South Indian volunteers living in Cleveland. Their aim is to recreate the atmosphere, music, and devotion present at the festival held in South India at Tiruvaiyaru, the composer's hometown. The Tyagaraja *aradhana* at Tiruvaiyaru takes place in January over a ten-day period, and is attended by devotees from all over South India. It is organized so that amateurs and professionals can equally express their devotion to Lord Rama, the seventh incarnation of Vishnu according to Hindu belief, in the form of bhakti and songs (*kritis*) composed by Tyagaraja. Whereas artists at Tiruvaiyaru are restricted to renditions of Tyagaraja's work alone, Cleveland performances occasionally include compositions by other revered South Indian composers, such as Syama Sastri (1762–1827), Muttusvami Diksitar (1775–1835), and Purandara Dasa (1484–1564).

Renowned for his pure devotion to Rama and his rejection of worldly possessions, Tyagaraja refused royal patronage on several occasions, claiming that his music was composed for no one but Lord Rama, whom his lyrics entreat to appear in a vision. Tyagaraja describes his helplessness as a mere human, and

Figure 1 The Carnatica Brothers from southern India perform at the Tyagaraja festival in Cleveland Ohio, 2007. Sri K. N. Shashikiran, on the right, is the senior vocalist and Sri P. Ganesh, on the left, is the younger vocalist. (The men are actually cousins.) To their left, Srimushnam Sri V. Raja Rao (front) and Thanjavur Sri Murugabhoopathy play the *mridangam*. At the right, Nagai Sri R. Muralidharan plays violin.
Photo by N. Scott Robinson.

begs Rama to release him from earthly concerns and prejudices. Tyagaraja sang for alms and refused to accept money from his students. The appeal of his *kritis* to mankind is manifested in his themes of moral uplift, spiritual direction, and fundamental truths in human life and existence. He believed that music is the path to salvation and the true medium for worship. The essence of South Indian culture is represented in his works through hundreds of accounts of episodes in Rama's life.

Tyagaraja's *kritis* are musically uncomplicated, and the lyrics are composed mostly in one of the South Indian vernaculars, Telugu, rather than in the more intellectual and ancient literary medium of Sanskrit. The most famous of his compositions is a group of five *kritis* called the *Panchamtna* 'Five Gems' *kritis*. These are usually sung in group songs (*bhajans*), rendered at the commencement of the Cleveland festival by a chorus of more than sixty amateurs and professionals. In all their simplicity and accessibility, *bhajans* can be rendered by amateurs who may be less able musically than the professionals, but wish nonetheless to participate in devotions during the festival. The composer believed that all devotees should have the opportunity to praise Rama through musical bhakti, regardless of their musical and intellectual abilities.

The festival at Tiruvaiyaru, on which the Cleveland *aradhana* is modeled, allows all devotees an equal chance to pay homage to Rama and Tyagaraja. Each performer, amateur or professional, is restricted to a single rendition of a *kriti* by the composer. No performer is paid, and entrance to the festival is free, though there is a charge for some concerts. The sole explicit purpose of the festival is devotion and musical homage to Tyagaraja.

Performance Practice

Despite the ideals of the festival in India, the main function of the Cleveland celebrations is to provide Indians living in the United States and Canada with a wealth of professional and inspirational music by inviting more than fifty world-renowned musicians from India to perform. Therefore, the element of audience participation—the singing of *bhajans*—is considerably limited, compared with that at Tiruvai-

yaru: it is reserved for weekend slots between professional concerts.

Two or three concerts a day are scheduled for professional musicians. World-acclaimed artists, such as violinist and singer Dr. M. Balumaralikrishna (b. 1930), flutist Dr. N. Ramani (b. 1934), and vocalist Smt. S. Sowmya, attract Indian music listeners from all over North America.

Professional concerts continue for up to four hours, sometimes until late into the evening—a common performance practice in South India. Tyagaraja's *kritis* are vocal works, but artists render them as instrumental compositions for violin, flute, vina, or *nadaswaram* solos, with accompaniment on instruments such as the South Indian double-headed drum (*mrdangam*), a supporting melody instrument such as a violin or a flute, and the *tambura* or *śruti-box*, which provides a drone (pedal point).

Soloists, whether vocal or instrumental, are expected to interpret and render the compositions according to their devotional content. Hence, knowledge of Telugu and the meaning of the *kriti* texts is essential for a true exposition of Tyagaraja's music. One of the festival organizers, Mr. Balusubramaniam, though he believes that a basic knowledge of the language is fundamental to an appreciation of Tyagaraja's work, estimates that only about 15 percent of the audience is familiar with Telugu. Nevertheless, many non-Telugu-speakers are sufficiently familiar with particular songs and their translations to minimize language as a problem. For them, the inspiration of the songs comes through.

—Adapted from an article by Claire Martin

Bibliography

Arnold, Alison. 1985. "Aspects of Asian Indian Musical Life in North America." *Selected Reports in Ethnomusicology* 6:25–38.

Ayyangar, R. Rangaramanuja. 1993. *History of South Indian (Carnatic) Music: From Vedic Times to the Present.* Bombay: Vipanchi Cultural Trust.

Farrell, Gerry. 1997. *Indian Music and the West* Oxford: Clarendon Press.

Jackson, William J. 1994. *Tyagaraja and the Renewal of Tradition.* Delhi: Motilal Banarsidass Publishers.

——. 1996. *Tyagaraja: Life and Lyrics.* Oxford: Oxford University Press.

Canada

Canada

Canada's people and music are as varied as its landscape. The second-largest nation in the modern world, Canada was originally inhabited by aboriginal settlers and later by European, African, Hispanic, and Asian immigrants. Its political history as a country first colonized and dominated by France and later by Britain has helped create a musical history that has been influenced by, but is strikingly different from, that of its neighbor to the south. Canadians frequently assert "the North" as a metaphor of nationhood, but paradoxically, its more than thirty million people are concentrated in communities along its southern borders. Complexity and diversity within and among Canada's cultural communities precludes comprehensive coverage in this section. The articles below offer a sense of the diversity of its music, moving regionally from east to west. The musical traditions of First Peoples are discussed in MUSIC OF AMERICAN INDIANS AND FIRST PEOPLES IN THE UNITED STATES AND CANADA.

John Gao plays a Chinese fiddle (*erhu*) for tips in the Toronto subway, 2006.
Photo by Christina Wong.

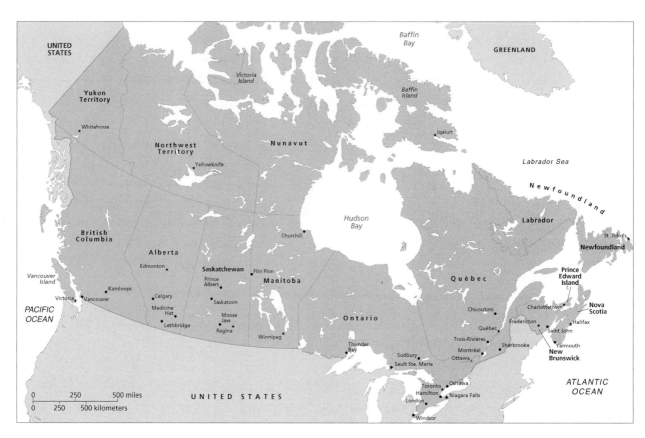

Canada, political

Anglo Music in Atlantic Canada

The region currently known as Atlantic Canada consists of the east-coast provinces of Nova Scotia, New Brunswick, and Prince Edward Island and the province of Newfoundland and Labrador. Nova Scotia, New Brunswick, and Prince Edward Island are called the Maritime Provinces or the Maritimes. People of British and Irish origin are the majority in all the provinces of Atlantic Canada, but Scottish Gaelic traditions thrive in Cape Breton and eastern Prince Edward Island. Atlantic Canada was historically dependent on the sea. Musically, these provinces share an Old World repertoire of traditional English and Scottish ballads, newer "broadside" ballads, and a fondness for comic and mocking songs, generally locally composed.

Nova Scotia, New Brunswick, and Prince Edward Island share a strong lumbering tradition with the northeastern United States and parts of Québec, Ontario, and the Prairies. Newfoundland was settled earlier and has always been culturally distinct; it is the oldest surviving British colony in North America, and has the largest repertoire of indigenous English-language folksongs of any area in Canada.

Story Songs: Ballads and Occupational Songs

Atlantic Canada was fertile ground for collectors throughout most of the twentieth century. Whether centuries old or recently composed, story-songs about historical, mythical, or local events have always been favored. Until the mid-twentieth century, these songs were mostly sung unaccompanied in homes, at sea, or in lumber camps, and were "characterized by a straightforward, undramatic solo performance with little dynamic variation from stanza to stanza" (Rosenberg 1992:473). High notes tended to be held and last lines spoken, revealing strong Irish influence. Some singers embellished the melody; others sang plainly. Songs were often associated with particular singers, so that others would not perform them.

The oldest songs are the ballads collected by Francis James Child (1825–1896), known in North America as Child ballads, with forty-four collected from Newfoundland, forty-seven from Nova Scotia, and thirty-eight from New Brunswick. However, Child ballads are a tiny part of the repertoire of male singers, from whom most of the collecting has been done. Musicologist Edward Ives notes that women

tended to know far more Child ballads, but often sang them only in private, so we may never know how widely they were known. According to the collections we have, the most popular in Newfoundland was "Sweet William's Ghost"; in all other areas, "Bonny Barbara Allen" was favored. Almost all of Child's comic and riddling ballads turn up, the latter featuring a devil-figure who asks a child riddles that he must solve to save himself.

Broadside ballads are more popular than Child ballads overall. Especially well-known were stories of separated lovers in which the man returns in disguise and tests his sweetheart's faithfulness. These turn up under many names: "The Pretty Fair Maid," "The Dark-Eyed Sailor," "The Mantle So Green," "The Plains of Waterloo."

More favored by male singers were songs related to work away from home: at sea, in lumber camps (Nova Scotia, New Brunswick, Prince Edward Island), and at seal and cod fisheries (Newfoundland). Older sea songs include shanties and stories of pirates and disasters, many featuring ghosts and other supernatural elements. Woods songs were frequently adapted from sea songs; certain elements, such as coming ashore after a long voyage, might change into coming back to town after a winter in the woods. Like disasters at sea, songs commemorated accidents on drives and in camps, but with far less supernatural content. Camps were known for their music. Ives reports: "I know of one man who went to work in the woods because he liked the singing, and several have told me how when they had come home from the woods, they would be asked if they had learned any 'new' songs" (1989:10). Sealing songs (swilin) in Newfoundland, stylistically similar to woods songs, relate details of work, tell stories of particular trips and hardships, and commemorate deaths.

Comic Songs

All provinces have a stock of comic songs, often called "ditties," most locally composed. Some woods songmakers became legendary for such songs—for example, Larry Gorman of Prince Edward Island, whose parodies and mocking songs were sung throughout the northeast. In Newfoundland, such songs typically make fun of individuals, or of people from certain places (figure 1).

'Deed I am in love with you Out all night in the fog-gy dew

'Deed I am in love with you, mus-sels in the cor-ner.

CHORUS: 'Deed I am in love with you
Out all night in the foggy dew
'Deed I am in love with you
Mussels in the corner

Ask a Bayman for a smoke
He will say his pipe is broke
Ask a Bayman for a chew
He will bite it off for you

All the people on Belle Isle
Don't get up 'til half past nine
Wash their face in kerosene oil
Paddy, you're a corker

I took Nellie to the ball
But she wouldn't dance at all
Nailed her up against the wall
Left her there 'til Sunday

Figure 1 "Mussels in the Corner," traditional Newfoundland song.
Transcribed by Anne Lederman from the singing of Henry Hibbs.

Figure 2 Don Messer's Islanders performing at station CFCY, 1948. On the left, Don Messer plays fiddle and around the microphone Marg Osburne sings and Charlie Chamberlain sings and plays guitar. The band was the most popular of its kind during the mid-twentieth century.
Photo by George Hunter. Credit: National Film Board of Canada / Library and Archives Canada.

Instrumental Music

Newfoundland is the only area of Canada where the fiddle is not the favored dance instrument. There, that honor goes to the button accordion. Known for fast tempos and simple chords (the standard one-row accordion could play only two chords), accordions pump out "singles" (2/4 tunes with generally two notes to a beat, also called polkas), "doubles" (6/8 or 9/8 tunes, also called jigs), and "triples" (2/4 tunes with four notes to a beat, also called reels or breakdowns) for group and step dances. Fiddles, tin whistles, and harmonicas are played, and dance tunes were frequently sung—a practice known as "gob," "mouth," or "chin" music, the last named after the practice of resting one's chin on one's hands while singing. Like the songs, the instrumental repertoire is heavily Irish-influenced, though much of it is unique to the island. There is a fair amount of asymmetric phrasing, resulting in "crooked tunes." Harry Hibbs (1942–1989) and Dick Nolan (1939–2005) popularized the accordion tradition with their recordings in the 1960s, which alternate instrumentals with sentimental Irish, country and western, and native Newfoundland songs. Two French Newfoundland fiddlers, Emile Benoit (1913–1992) and Rufus Guinchard (1899–1990), achieved national recognition, largely because of the support given them by younger revival players.

In the other Atlantic provinces, fiddles reign supreme. Gaelic and French Acadian areas have their own styles and repertoires, but English areas favor what has become known west of the Maritimes as the down east sound. Originally popularized by Don Messer and the Islanders of Prince Edward Island (figure 2) through national radio and television programs, it is a smooth, relatively unornamented distillation of older Anglo-Irish and Scottish repertoires. It favors waltzes, jigs, and reels, with some clogs, also called schottisches, for step dancing and some polkas and specialty dance tunes. The slow airs and strathspeys of Gaelic tradition are mainly done in down east style (though some survive as clogs); many Irish and American hornpipes have been sped up to the tempo of reels. Promoted through contests and recordings, this style dominates many parts of Canada. Well-known proponents of it, not all from Atlantic Canada, include Ned Landry (b. 1921), King Ganam (1914–1994), Ward Allen (1924–1965), Graham Townsend (1942–1998) and Eleanor Townsend (1944–1998), Peter Dawson of Ontario, and Ivan Hicks of New Brunswick, both still performing as of 2007.

—Adapted from an article by Anne Lederman

Bibliography

Creighton, Helen. 1966. *Songs and Ballads from Nova Scotia*. New York: Dover.
——. 1971. *Folksongs from Southern New Brunswick*. Ottawa: National Museum of Civilization.
——. 1979. *Maritime Folk Songs*. Toronto: The Ryerson Press.
——. 1992. "Folk Music: Nova Scotia and New Brunswick." In *Encyclopedia of Music in Canada*, 2nd ed., edited by Helmut Kallman, Gilles Potvin, and Kenneth Winters, 474–475. Toronto: University of Toronto Press.
Fowke, Edith. 1992. "Ballads." In *Encyclopedia of Music in Canada*, 2nd ed., edited by Helmut Kallman, Gilles Potvin, and Kenneth Winters, 70. Toronto: University of Toronto Press.
Ives, Edward D. 1989. *Folksongs of New Brunswick*. Fredericton: Goose Lane Editions.
——. 1992. "Folk Music: Prince Edward Island." In *Encyclopedia of Music in Canada*, 2nd ed., edited by Helmut Kallman, Gilles Potvin, and Kenneth Winters, 475. Toronto: University of Toronto Press.
Lehr, Genevieve. 1985. *Come and I Will Sing You: A Newfoundland Songbook*. Toronto: University of Toronto Press.
Rosenberg, Neil V. 1992. "Folk Music: Newfoundland." In *Encyclopedia of Music in Canada*, 2nd ed., edited by Helmut Kallman, Gilles Potvin, and Kenneth Winters, 473. Toronto: University of Toronto Press.

French Folk and Pop in Québec

The province of Québec (sometimes historically called New France) was explored by Samuel Champlain in the early seventeenth century. British colonists gained political control of it in 1763, but it continues to be dominated by French culture, institutions, and language.

Folk Music

The singing of folksongs and playing of traditional instruments by French settlers in Québec was an important part of the social fabric in the first centuries of European colonization. Folksongs were brought from France by settlers, many of whom originated in rural regions of Normandy and the Loire valley. Serving for entertainment and as a sustaining force in a harsh physical climate, music played a central role in peoples' lives. Scholarly attention has focused on collecting folksongs and studying forces of creativity and change, processes of oral transmission, and ideas surrounding origins and variants. Recent creative and performative trends reflect the blending of musical contexts: popular, traditional, First Nations, world music, and even concert music. Broadly considered, folk music in Québec continues to be a powerful symbol of regional—some would argue national—identity.

DISC
1
TRACK
16

Voyageur *Songs*

Of particular notice were the paddling songs of *voyageurs*, boatmen who traveled in canoes between trading centers in what was then known as Lower Canada (*le pays en bas*, Québec) and Upper Canada (*le pays en haut*, Ontario) and composed or adapted songs to the rhythms of paddling. First known as *coureurs de bois*, these men, many of whom were French or Métis, were crucial to the development of the fur trade in Canada.

The romantic image of the *voyageurs* appealed to European visitors, who were impressed by the extent to which singing was part of the *voyageurs'* work. On a visit to Canada in 1804, the Irish poet Thomas Moore (1779–1852) was so inspired by the sight of *voyageurs* on the St. Lawrence River that he composed the "Canadian Boat Song," the spirit and opening of which resemble the *voyageur* song "Dans mon chemin j'ai rencontré" ("On my way I met"). Early collections of *voyageur* songs include

Lieutenant George Back's *Canadian Airs*, a volume of melodies compiled during Back's work with Captain John Franklin's Arctic expedition in the early 1820s. Intended for commercial use and reflecting the popular taste of the period for salon entertainment, this book contained new words supplied by the editors and elaborate piano accompaniments. Another important early collection is that of Edward Ermatinger (1797–1876), a fur trader of Swiss and Italian descent. Gathered from 1818 to 1828, while Ermatinger worked for the Hudson's Bay Company, the collection contains eleven songs (texts and melodies). Edited and published by the Québec folklorist Marius Barbeau (1883–1969) in 1954, the Ermatinger collection demonstrates the pervasiveness of the *voyageur* repertoire (Québec, Ontario, and Manitoba) and is musical evidence of the substantial distances traveled by the *voyageurs*. A recent large compilation of *voyageur* songs is that of Madeleine Béland (1982).

Chanson and the *Chansonnier* Movement

Immediately after World War II, a new generation of popular performing artists emerged in Québec. Coinciding with the advent of television in the 1950s and major changes in popular music in that and the following decades, they extended the trend of combining folk and popular music idioms, especially in songs that reflected the cultural, spiritual, and political themes of emancipation and identity of the so-called Quiet Revolution in Québec, a movement dating from the 1950s and 1960s and arising from the repudiation of the historic domination of the Roman Catholic Church and other forces.

La Bolduc and the Beginnings of the Chansonnier Movement

La Bolduc (née Mary Travers; 1894–1941; figure 1) first recorded her own songs on the Starr label in 1929. Her earliest records sold more than twelve thousand copies—an unprecedented number in Québec during that time, given the newness of the technology and the poverty of French Canadians. She became known for boldly using vernacular lyrics, tackling economic struggles head-on (figure 2), and celebrating local rituals and daily life. In a career that lasted less than fifteen years and spanned most of the

Figure 1 La Bolduc with her fiddle. She also played the harmonica, accordion, and jew's harp.
Source: Madame Bolduc [musique]: paroles et musiques. *Compiled by Lina Remon in collaboration with Jean-Pierre Joyal. Montréal: Guérin, 1993: 45. Image downloaded from the Library and Archives Canada Web site.*

Figure 2 In "*Ça va venir découragez-vous pas*" (1930), La Bolduc sings about the hardships Canadians suffered during the Great Depression.
From the Library and Archives Canada/Music Collection.

Great Depression, she recorded more than forty 78-rpm records and performed regularly in Québec, Canada, and the United States. Her style and use of the French language offended the clerical sensibilities of the era and caused many to label her as a populist, but her songs continue to be associated with the origins of the *chansonnier* movement.

The Quiet Revolution

The decade of the 1960s was as turbulent in Québec as it was elsewhere in North America, though for somewhat different reasons. Profound changes known as the Quiet Revolution were harbingers of Québec's social, economic, and cultural modernization. Among the most striking of these changes was the secularization of Québécois society. The Roman Catholic Church had been as important a branch of government in the province as any elected body, and only in the second half of the twentieth century did it relinquish its stranglehold, particularly over education.

The musical tradition known as the *chansonnier* movement began in earnest in the 1950s and peaked during the 1960s. Songs (*chansons*) and songmakers (*chansonniers*) were seen as poetic voices of the people, whose aspirations were embodied in lyrical texts (both sung and in the form of monologues) and simple music. Thus, the vast majority of the artists associated with this tradition were young men who performed in song clubs (*boîtes à chansons*), the nightclubs that were the live venue of choice for performers during this period. These sprang up often literally overnight, all over the province. More often than not, the performers, including Félix Leclerc (1914–1988; regarded as the father of *chanson* in Québec), Georges Dor (b. 1931), Raymond Lévesque (b. 1928), Jean-Pierre Ferland (b. 1934), Sylvain Lelièvre (1943–2002), Pierre Létourneau (b. 1938), Claude Gauthier (b. 1939), Jacques Blanchet (1931–1981), Claude Léveillée (b. 1932), Robert Charlebois (b. 1945), and Gilles Vigneault (b. 1928), were the composers and lyricists of the songs they performed. As dominated by men as the rock tradition was in the

United States (there is indeed no equivalent word in French to designate a female *chansonnier*), the decade saw female artists perform as part of the movement—notably Clémence Derochers (b. 1934), Monique Miville-Deschênes (b. 1940), Monique Leyrac (b. 1928), and Pauline Julien (1928–1998).

The *chansonniers* spoke and sang the reality of Québec; its land (Leclerc's "Hymne au printemps" ["Hymn to spring"], Léveillée's "Pour quelques arpents de neige" ["For a few acres of snow"]); its climate (Vigneault's "Mon pays" ["My country"], Charlebois's "Demain l'hiver" ["Tomorrow, winter"]); its geography (Ferland's "St.-Adéle P.Q.," D'Or's "La manic"); its people (Vigneault's "Les gens de mon pays" ["The people of my country"], La Bolduc's "Nos braves habitants" ["Our brave people"]); and its cultural and political aspirations (Lévesque's "Bozo-les-culottes" ["Bozo-the-pants"] and Gauthier's "Le grand six pieds" ["The big six-footer"]). Audiences in Québec saw themselves, their histories, their daily struggles, and their hopes for the future through the *chansonniers'* music. For this and other reasons (the perceived originality of *chanson* as a genre, the status of *chansonniers* as artist-poets, and the consequent support they received from literary and other institutions), *chanson* was, and in many cases remains, lauded as the most important cultural emblem of Québec.

Félix Leclerc

Félix Leclerc is considered the father of *chanson* in Québec. The annual music awards in Québec bear his name (the Félix awards); the origin of Québec's motto, *Je me souviens* 'I remember', is usually attributed to a radio show he hosted in the 1940s; and there is scarcely a public performance in celebration of Québécois culture that does not feature a performance of one of his songs by a contemporary artist, regardless of the genre for which he or she is known.

Leclerc's career began in the 1930s in radio. During the 1950s, he became known as a performing musician, composer, and singer. After a series of successful performances in Paris, he became a star in Québec. The relationship between success in France and success in Québec—"if you can make it there, you can make it here"—continued into the 1980s.

The heyday of the *chansonnier* movement peaked at the end of the 1960s, when it ushered in changes that locally defined the more group- and rock-oriented 1970s. This is not to say that the figures popular in the 1960s were eclipsed: throughout the next four decades, many of them continued to compose, perform, and often be the centerpieces for live performances at such festivities as the annual free concert in celebration of Québec's national holiday. It was from among their ranks that a more diverse *chansonnier* tradition emerged.

—Adapted from articles by Gordon E. Smith and Val Morrison

Bibliography

Barbeau, Marius, and Jean Beck. 1962. *Jongleur Songs of Old Québec*. New Brunswick, N.J.: Rutgers University Press.

Barbeau, Marius, and Edward Sapir. 1925. *Folk Songs of French Canada*. New Haven, Conn.: Yale University Press.

Béland, Madeleine. 1982. *Chansons de voyageurs, coureurs de bois et forestiers*. Québec: Les Presses de l' Université Laval.

d'Harcourt, Marguerite, and Raoul d'Harcourt. 1956. *Chansons folkloriques du Canada*. Québec: Les Presses de l'Université Laval.

Giroux, Robert. 1984. *Les aires de la chanson québécoise*. Montréal: Editions Triptyque.

Kallmann, Helmut, Gilles Potvin, and Kenneth Winters, eds. 1992. *Encyclopedia of Music in Canada*. 2nd ed. Toronto: University of Toronto Press.

Thérien, Robert, and Isabelle D'Amours. 1992. *Dictionnaire de la Musique populaire au Québec 1955–1992*. Montréal: Institut québécois de recherche sur la culture.

The Development of Classical Music in Ontario

Of Canada's ten provinces, Ontario is the most populous, and Toronto, its capital, is the country's most populous city. The southern part of the province was called Upper Canada from 1791 to 1841, and Canada West from 1841 to 1867. The name *Ontario*—an Iroquoian word sometimes translated as 'beautiful water'—was first applied to the easternmost of the Great Lakes in 1641. It was adopted as the name of the province at the time of Confederation in 1867. [For a map of Canada, see ANGLO MUSIC IN ATLANTIC CANADA.]

The 1800s to Confederation

By 1840, the population of Upper Canada was about 400,000; the settlers were scattered in small communities from the Ottawa River to the head of the Great Lakes. Aside from British garrison bands, musicmaking was predominantly a matter of individual enterprise. It was becoming an important feature in churches, especially Protestant ones. Many settlers were Loyalists who had come from the United States and were familiar with singing-schools, the aim of which was to improve singing in church and to teach participants the basics of musical notation. The singing of moralistic texts to psalm tunes was a prominent feature of sacred music in Ontario.

As standards improved, church and community choirs would perform ambitious works for which an accompaniment might be provided by local bands, supplemented by whatever string players were available. Thus, in Toronto, the Musical Society was organized by 1835, and the Harmonic Society was giving concerts in 1840. In the years 1845–1850 and 1853–1855, organizations known as the Toronto Philharmonic Society gave six or so concerts a year. Original Canadian compositions were heard increasingly in Ontario parlors and concerts by the 1850s. Some Canadian content appeared in tunebooks and periodicals that often included one or two pieces of music in each issue.

About 1842, Abraham Nordheimer (1816–1862) settled in Kingston in southeastern Ontario, where he taught piano, voice, and violin privately and operated a music store. By 1844, he had moved to Toronto and was operating a music store and the first publishing firm in Canada that was dedicated solely to music (figure 1). His catalog included reprints of U.S. or European material and an ever-increasing number of piano and vocal works composed by Canadians, among them R. S. Ambrose (1824–1908); J. P. Clarke (ca. 1807–1877), the first Canadian to receive a bachelor of music degree, at Kings College, Toronto, 1846; William Horatio Clarke (1840–1913), father of the famed cornetist Herbert L. Clarke; W. O. Forsyth (1859–1937); Mrs. H. E. Gilbert (fl. 1870s); Edwin Gledhill (1830–1919); Henry Herbert Godfrey (1858–1908); Moritz Relle (fl. 1860s); Elizabeth H[arriet?] Ridout (dates unknown); Henry F. Sefton (fl. 1882); Henry Schallehn (1813?–1891?); Hattie Stephens (dates unknown); G. W. Strathy (1818–1890), the first Canadian known to have received the degree doctor of music, at Trinity College, Toronto, 1858; and Thomas Turvey (fl. 1860s–1870s). Some of

Figure 1 Front cover of a Nordheimer publication.
Source: Library and Archives Canada/Music Collection.

these works have been republished in the Canadian Musical Heritage volumes.

Famous musicians, including the singers Jenny Lind and Adelina Patti, the pianists Anton Rubinstein and Sigismund Thalberg, and the violinists Ole Bull and Henri Vieuxtemps, began to tour Ontario from the 1840s onward. The building of railway lines in the 1850s made for better traveling conditions for touring artists. When Lind performed at St. Lawrence Hall, Toronto, in 1851, more than a thousand people paid a minimum of three dollars to attend each of her two concerts. When the Germania Musical Society, an orchestra of twenty-two to twenty-five musicians originally from Berlin, gave concerts in Kingston and Toronto in 1850 and 1852, it had to repeat its program to meet the demand for tickets. Louis Moreau Gottschalk wrote vividly about his experiences performing in Kingston, Toronto, St. Catherines, and Ottawa in 1862 and 1864.

Until the 1860s, the building of instruments—mainly organs, pianos, and stringed instruments—was done by individuals such as Richard Coates (1778–1868), who made three organs for the community at Sharon. Even Theodor August Heintzman (1817–1899), founder of Canada's most important piano-manufacturing firm, built—in his kitchen!—his first instruments after moving to Toronto about 1858. In 1864, Robert and William Bell began turning out one melodeon a week in Guelph; within three years, they could not keep up with the demand for their instruments. The Bell Piano and Organ Company rapidly expanded its production of harmoniums or large cabinet organs, melodeons, and pianos that were shipped around the world. Customers included Queen Victoria and the Sultan of Turkey, and the company reported that 75,000 of its instruments were in use by 1895.

The Years of Rapid Expansion, 1867–1918

On 1 July 1867, Canada West (Ontario) joined Canada East (Québec), New Brunswick, and Nova Scotia to form the Dominion of Canada, the capital of which was to be Ottawa, a small lumber-industry town formerly known as Bytown. Within a decade, several bands were formed there, one of which, the Governor-General's Foot Guards, has remained active. Band concerts included marches, dances, hymn and folksongs, operatic selections, and the occasional locally composed work.

When Gowan's Opera House opened in Ottawa, in 1875, the Canadian-based Holman English Opera Company presented seven different works, including Bellini's *La Sonnambula*, Rossini's *La Cenerentola*, and Donizetti's *L'Elisir d'Amore*. Other new venues

were used for chamber-music concerts, such as those by the Canadian artists Frantz Jehin-Prume (1839–1899), Rosita del Vecchio (1846–1881), and Calixa Lavallée (1842–1891). Such events probably encouraged the formation of local organizations such as the Quintette Club, Musical Union, and miscellaneous choral groups.

The provision of better halls, the proliferation of musical organizations, and the drive for higher standards in musical education occurred in similar fashion in Ontario communities into the twentieth century. Choral groups predominated, employing instrumentalists as needed. The Toronto Mendelssohn Choir (figure 2), formed in 1894 by A. S. Vogt (1861–1926; figure 3), remains active and played a major role in establishing Toronto as the choral capital of North America in the early twentieth century. The Ottawa Orpheus Glee Club, formed in 1906, became the Orpheus Musical Theatre Society and still produces operettas and musicals; it is the longest-lived musical theater company in North America. In many communities, concert giving was initiated by a local women's musical club; the first such group in Canada was the Duet Club of Hamilton, founded in 1889 and still active.

Several teaching studios had been using the grand title of conservatory, but the first Canadian institution to offer instruction in a wide range of instruments and voice with basic training in theoretical subjects was the Toronto Conservatory of Music, formed in 1886. Offering both class and private instruction, it established syllabuses of required repertoire and initiated a graded examination system. It developed examination centers throughout Ontario and beyond. It became the Royal Conservatory of Music in 1947, and today is the largest national integrated music conservatory in the world. Other notable music conservatories in Ontario have included the Hambourg Conservatory of Music in Toronto (1911–1951) and the Western Ontario Conservatory of Music, established in London, Ontario, in 1891. The latter institution merged with the Western (Canada) Board in 1997 to become Conservatory Canada, which has an extensive national examination system.

Even though more-systematic musical education became available during this period, Ontario musicians who wished to pursue composition or international performing careers tended to go abroad for further education: W. O. Forsyth (1859–1937) went to Leipzig, Clarence Lucas (1866–1947) to Paris, and Gena Branscombe (1881–1977) to Chicago and later Berlin. These composers wrote in the larger genres and managed to have their orchestral and/or large-scale operatic or choral works performed

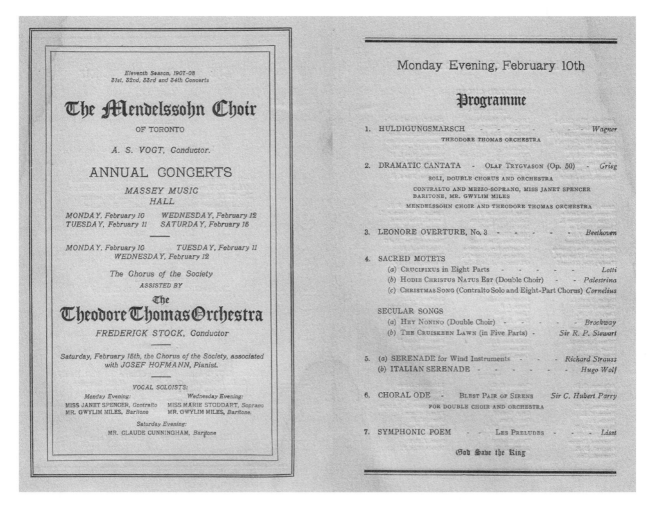

Figure 2 Program from the eleventh season of the Toronto Mendelssohn Choir, 1907–1908.
From the collection of Dr. Robin Elliott.

abroad. Homegrown operettas were occasionally seen on the stages of the opera house found in any Ontario town. One of these was *Leo, The Royal Cadet*, with music by Oscar Telgmann (1855–1946) and a libretto by G. F. Cameron (1854–1885), set in part at Kingston's Royal Military College. It premiered on 11 July 1889 in Kingston and by 1925 had been performed more than 150 times. Meanwhile, Torontonians from 1887 on could see the staple operas by Rossini, Verdi, Gounod, Massenet, and Wagner performed by touring companies.

Technology began to influence musicmaking in Ontario in the nineteenth century. In November 1879, a telephone was used to transmit the sounds of a concert taking place at St. James Hall, Ottawa, to persons sitting in the offices of the Dominion Telegraph Company. By the 1900s, telephone companies were often providing concerts of recorded music through the telephone to their subscribers on Sunday afternoons. Some Ontario piano-manufacturing companies by 1901 were making mechanical player

pianos, and between 1906 and 1925 every major piano manufacturer did so. Meanwhile, the production of grand and upright pianos was at its height in Ontario. The company W. Doherty of Clinton (north of London) began manufacturing organs in 1875; by 1900, it was making seventy-four types and had begun producing upright and grand pianos. The Sherlock-Manning Piano Company opened in Clinton in 1890 and was the last of the Canadian piano-manufacturing companies to close its doors in 1988. R. S. Williams, who made mandolins, banjos, guitars, violins, brass instruments, pianos, and reed and pipe organs, moved his factory in 1888 from Toronto to Oshawa, where it continued until 1932.

From World War I to 1960
World War I accelerated the emergence of Canada's sense of nationhood, but at great loss of human life. Many organizations that seemed to be well established early in the century faded away during the

Figure 3 A. S. Vogt. In addition to founding the Toronto Mendelssohn Choir, Vogt developed an international reputation as a conductor, published several books on music, was an administrator at the Toronto Conservatory of Music and the University of Toronto, and taught for over thirty years.
Photo by Moffett Studio, Chicago, date unknown. From the collection of Dr. Robin Elliott.

war because of a loss of personnel or leadership. Frank Welsman (1873–1952) formed the Toronto (Conservatory) Symphony Orchestra in 1906; it weathered the war years only to cease activity in 1918. In Ottawa in 1905, Donald Heins (1878–1949) formed an orchestra that thrice won the Earl Grey Orchestra Competition (created in 1907 and usually entered by four or five orchestras annually); it was once described by a New York critic as the finest community orchestra he had ever heard. The orchestra folded in 1927, when Heins moved to Toronto. Most instrumental musicians depended on playing for vaudeville shows and silent movies for a living. Even before the talkies arrived (in 1927), musicians wanting a respite from playing commercial theater music tried to organize orchestras. Thus was

the present Toronto Symphony Orchestra (TSO) formed; it gave its first concert on 23 April 1923. The young Toronto pianist Colin McPhee (1900–1964) performed his Second Piano Concerto with the TSO that year; this work was in a modern compositional idiom, but the score has been lost. By 1928, twenty-five TSO concerts were being broadcast annually on a trans-Canada network under the auspices of the Canadian National Railways. Many Ontario orchestras began as community ensembles and developed into semiprofessional or professional organizations, among them the London Civic Symphony Orchestra (founded in 1937), Kitchener-Waterloo Symphony Orchestra (1944), Windsor Symphony Orchestra (1947), Hamilton Philharmonic Orchestra (1949), Kingston Symphony (1953), International Symphony Orchestra of Sarnia and Port Huron (1957), and Thunder Bay (originally Lakehead) Symphony Orchestra (1960).

In 1936, the Canadian Broadcasting Corporation (CBC) was formed, creating employment for many musicians, especially in Toronto, the CBC's main English-language center. The CBC Symphony Orchestra (1952–1964) offered performances of contemporary works, many of which were commissioned from Ontario composers, including Harry Somers (1925–1999), Norman Symonds (1920–1998), and John Weinzweig (1913–2006). The orchestra participated in a famed series of performances and recordings of the works of Stravinsky and Schoenberg, frequently with the Festival Singers of Canada, founded by the conductor Elmer Iseler in 1954. The Festival Singers became Canada's first professional choir in 1968.

Other ensembles continued to be formed for chamber music. The most notable was the Hart House String Quartet (figure 4), formed in Toronto in 1924 as Canada's first fully subsidized chamber group. The quartet included works by Canadian composers in its repertoire and appeared throughout North America and Europe to high acclaim until its dissolution, in 1946.

Operatic productions by touring companies became fewer because of traveling expenses. More groups therefore formed to concentrate on operetta and opera production: at least half a dozen such groups were active in Toronto during the interwar years, but only with the establishment of the Conservatory Opera School in 1946 and the formation of the CBC Opera Company in 1948 did local professional opera production become firmly established. The Canadian Opera Company, which grew out of these organizations, is the leading producer of opera in the country, and moved into its new opera house, the Four Seasons Centre, in 2006.

Figure 4 Hart House String Quartet, ca. 1926. *Left to right*:
Harry Adaskin, Milton Blackstone, Geza de Krez, and
Boris Hambourg.
Credit: Library and Archives Canada/C-001395.

Before 1960, the foundation was laid for Ontario's
production of electro-acoustic music. Morse Robb
(1902–1992) of Belleville patented the world's first
electric organ in 1927. His experiments became
known to a young physicist interested in music, Hugh
Le Caine (1914–1977), who worked at the National
Research Council in Ottawa. By the mid-1940s, Le
Caine had developed the Sackbut, the first music
synthesizer. In 1955, he composed *Dripsody*, using
the sound of the fall of a single drop of water
manipulated by another of his inventions, the multi-
track tape recorder. His inventions graced the first
electronic music studio in Canada (and the second
one in North America) at the University of Toronto
in 1959.

Increased musical activity in Ontario during the
1940s and 1950s reflected in no small measure
the number of recently arrived immigrants from
Europe who were accustomed to having opportunities to attend chamber, symphonic, and operatic
performances. There was no consistent governmental
support for such activities, apart from the publicly
funded CBC and the National Film Board. With the
establishment of the Canada Council as a Crown
Corporation in 1957, funding for jury-approved projects of arts organizations became available. One of
the first funded projects in music was the Canadian
Music Centre in Toronto (established in 1959), which
provides a library of scores and an information
center for disseminating and promoting the music
composed by its associates.

Summer festivals began in the 1950s and proliferated thereafter. The Stratford Festival, founded
in 1953, became an important promoter of musical
and dramatic events before 1970.

Developments after 1960

A frequent performer at Stratford was Glenn Gould
(1932–1982), a Toronto-born and -trained musician
who established an international career as a pianist;
he was perhaps the best-known Ontario musician of
the century. Every aspect of musical activity has
flourished since 1960, and governmental support for
music has increased during this period. Greater
opportunities to study music at advanced levels have
become available as more universities (Toronto,
Western Ontario, York, Wilfrid Laurier, Ottawa, and
Carleton) have expanded their graduate offerings in
music disciplines.

An important classical-sized orchestra, the
National Arts Centre Orchestra, was formed in
1969, and is resident in a state-supported theater
and auditorium complex in Ottawa. Chamber-music
ensembles based in Ontario have included the Lyric
Arts Trio (1964–1983), the Orford String Quartet
(1965–1991), Canadian Brass (formed 1970), York
Winds (1972–1988), and Camerata Canada (1974–
1985). Ensembles active at the turn of the twenty-first
century include Thirteen Strings, the St. Lawrence
and Penderecki String Quartets, Amici, and the
Gryphon Trio.

Music festivals have proliferated. At Guelph in
1929, a festival was held in which Edward Johnson
(1878–1959), a Guelph native, leading tenor of his
day, and manager of the Metropolitan Opera (1935–
1950), had performed. The Guelph Spring Festival
began in 1968. Among the most highly regarded and
varied festivals are the Elora Festival and the Festival
of the Sound (Parry Sound), both founded in 1979.
The Ottawa Chamber Music Festival, within five
years of its founding (in 1994), had become the
largest festival of its kind in the world.

*—Adapted from an article by Elaine Keillor
and Robin Elliott*

Bibliography

Calderisi, Maria. 1981. *Music Publishing in Canada, 1800–
1867.* Ottawa: National Library of Canada.
*The Canadian Musical Heritage / Le patrimoine musical
canadien.* 1983–1999. Twenty-five volumes of pre-1950
Canadian notated music, each edition preceded by

an essay on the genre concerned. Website: http://www.cmhs.carleton.ca.

Gottschalk, Louis Moreau. 1964. *Notes of a Pianist*. Edited by Jeanne Behrend. New York: Knopf.

Green, J. Paul, and Nancy E. Vogan. 1991. *Music Education in Canada: A Historical Account*. Toronto: University of Toronto Press.

Jones, Gaynor. 1989. "The Fisher Years: The Toronto Conservatory of Music, 1886–1913." In *Three Studies: College Songbooks, Toronto Conservatory Arraymusic. CanMus Documents* 4:59–146.

Keillor, Elaine. 1988. "Musical Activity in Canada's New Capital City in the 1870s." In *Musical Canada: Words and Music Honoring Helmut Kallmann*, edited by John Beckwith and Frederick A. Hall, 115–133. Toronto: University of Toronto Press.

——. 1997. "Auf Kanadischer Welle: The Establishment of the Germanic Musical Canon in Canada." In *Kanada-Studien: Music in Canada*, edited by Guido Bimberg, 49–76. Bochum, Germany: Brockmeyer.

Kelly, Wayne. 1991. *Downright Upright: A History of the Canadian Piano Industry*. Toronto: Natural Heritage / Natural History.

Sale, David. 1968. "Toronto's Pre-confederation Music Societies." Master's thesis, University of Toronto.

Caribbean and Latin American Music

Caribbean and Latin American immigrants and their descendants have settled all across Canada. Most reside in urban areas in southwestern Ontario, particularly in the greater Toronto area (population about five million at the turn of the millennium), where Caribbean and Latin American and immigrants and their descendants comprise roughly 8 percent of the total population; elsewhere in Ontario, their concentration is much smaller. The first major wave of Caribbean and Latin American settlers arrived in the late 1960s and early 1970s.

The Caribbean-derived populace hails almost entirely from the former British West Indies, particularly Jamaica, Trinidad and Tobago, Barbados, and Guyana (on the northeast coast of South America, but nevertheless considered part of the British Caribbean). The Latin American–derived population hails mainly from the Spanish-speaking countries of Ecuador, Colombia, El Salvador, Chile, and Argentina. The Latin American and Caribbean immigrant populations in Ontario mirror the ethnocultural diversity of their homelands and have brought a broad range of musical practices to the province.

It is in North American Caribbean-style carnival festivities that the most radical departures from homeland practices are seen. In the homelands, carnival is a localized event, reaffirming and celebrating a national culture, be it Trinidadian, Barbadian, or whatever. In Caribbean-style carnivals in North America, however, the flavor is pan-West Indian or pan-Caribbean, and it sometimes extends beyond that. For example, the time frame of Toronto's Caribana festival spans not only the Trinidadian carnival core of calypso and *soca* music and the focus on elaborately costumed revelers, but events such as Reggaebana (a three-night showcase of Canadian reggae acts), AfriCaribeat (a four-night showcase of worldbeat acts), and Centre Island Music Fest (hip-hop and rhythm and blues acts). The Caribana Parade has occasionally had hip-hop and Latin American music floats. [For more on Caribbean and Latin American music, see the South America, Mexico, Central America, and the Caribbean section.]

Caribana

Caribana is a two-week-long festival of the arts that showcases expressive Caribbean traditions. Based primarily on Trinidad's carnival, it has become a centerpiece of Toronto's summer cultural fare. Begun in Canada's centennial year, 1967, as a small event celebrating the presence of newly arrived Caribbean immigrants in Toronto, the festival at the beginning of the twenty-first century attracted between 750,000 and one million people and poured considerable revenue into the local economy. It stands among the large and lucrative—for local businesses and entrepreneurs, though not for organizers and participants—carnival-type celebrations in major centers throughout the Caribbean diaspora, including London, New York, and Miami.

Caribana has tended to excel among its sister-festivals in attending to the masquerade element. Though beset in recent years by funding problems and other types of local-level political controversy, it has managed to go on as some forty masquerade bands (some with more than one thousand members) have delighted onlookers with lavish and spectacular costumes representing all manner of Caribbean flora, fauna, personages, and themes from world history and current events, local and global environmental issues, and flights of fantasy. Masquerade designers and players, who often spend a year laboring over their costumes, have several opportunities to display their talents during the festival, including the Junior Carnival, the King and Queen of the Bands Competition, and the Caribana Parade, the festival's highlight, in which masqueraders compete for the title of Band of the Year.

Propelling the parade, which lasts for more than eight hours, rain or shine, are the music bands and sound systems, which pump out calypso, *soca*, reggae, salsa, samba, and other familiar Caribbean and Latin-tinged rhythms at ear-splitting volume. Mounted on tractor-trailer trucks, musicians, deejays, and their towering equipment provide a riotous soundscape to accompany dancing masqueraders' and parade watchers' revelries. The Caribbean Cultural Committee once instituted a live-music requirement for the parade, but this requirement has given way to the pressures and popularity of technology. Live steelbands are nevertheless still an important component; their music can be heard not only in the parade, but also at the Pan Trinbago Panorama competition, part of the festival proceedings since 1995 and a further means to ensure that the Trinidad carnival tradition remains well-entrenched. Percussion groups (for example, East Indian–Trinidadian *tassa* drumming and Brazilian *batucada*) add variety to the soundscape.

Apart from the parade, festival events include calypso tents (shows), jump-ups (dances), fetes (parties), mas (masquerade) competitions, mas camp tours, fashion shows, craft sales, a junior carnival, pan blockos or blockoramas (steelband street parties), talk tents (shows featuring storytellers, comedians, and others expert in oral traditions), moonlight cruises on Lake Ontario, and a Caribana picnic on Toronto Island. Though Caribana is the official name for events sponsored by the Caribbean Cultural Committee, other organizations and individuals mount carnival-type events during the Caribana season. For example, the Organization of Calypso Performing Artists holds an annual Calypso Monarch of Canada Competition, featuring the talents of local calypsonians, who comment in witty and satirical fashion, often with the use of stage props and costumes, on local and international issues relevant to the Caribbean population.

The *Nueva Canción* and Andean Folkloric Music Scene

The newly arrived Latin American musical elements that were the most noticeable to the general populace in Ontario in the early years of Latin American settlement (1970s) were Andean folkloric music ensembles and the performers of *nueva canción*, the Latin American singer-songwriter movement that addressed the political oppression occurring in countries such as El Salvador and Chile with hard-hitting songs of social protest. In a related development, musical ensembles emulating traditional Andean highlands stylings and instrumentation were formed by urban middle-class youths, often university students, and became emblematic of a pan-Latin–leftist alliance. In greater Toronto, as elsewhere, *nueva canción* and Andean folkloric music have typically been presented in folk-music clubs and coffeehouses and at rallies, fundraisers, and other solidarity events. Andean folkloric ensembles became a fixture of the busking circuit and remain so, not always exclusively featuring Latin American musicians.

—Adapted from articles by Annemarie Gallaugher and Robert Witmer

Bibliography

Caudeiron, Daniel. 1992a. "Calypso." In *Encyclopedia of Music in Canada*, 2nd ed., edited by Helmut Kallmann, Gilles Potvin, and Kenneth Winters, 1118–1119. Toronto: University of Toronto Press.

——. 1992b. "Reggae." In *Encyclopedia of Music in Canada*, 2nd ed., edited by Helmut Kallmann, Gilles Potvin, and Kenneth Winters, 187–188. Toronto: University of Toronto Press.

Gallaugher, Annemarie. 1991. "From Trinidad to Toronto: Calypso as a Way of Life." Master's thesis, York University.

——. 1992. "Caribana." In *Encyclopedia of Music in Canada*, 2nd ed., edited by Helmut Kallmann, Gilles Potvin, and Kenneth Winters, 220. Toronto: University of Toronto Press.

——. 1995. "Constructing Caribbean Culture in Toronto: The Representation of Caribana." In *The Reordering of Culture Latin America: The Caribbean and Canada in the Hood*, edited by Alvina Ruprecht and Cecilia Taiana, 397–407. Ottawa Carleton University Press.

Jennings, Nicholas. 1996. "Some Like It Hot: Canadians Warm to the Sizzling Sounds of Home-Grown Latin Music." *Words & Music* 3(3):12–13.

Intercultural Traditions on the Canadian Prairies

The phrase *musical fusion* occurs most often in discussions of recent cross-cultural musical alliances. Sometimes these discussions allude to the late-twentieth-century demographic shifts that have resulted in unprecedented diversity in contemporary North American societies. Sometimes they relate to urgent postcolonial issues of appropriation and intellectual property rights. It is instructive to look at the topic with regard to earlier historical periods. As the multiculturality of North American society has existed since the sixteenth century and was recognized as distinctive by the late nineteenth century, musical interaction is a complex subject of inquiry. The label *fusion* suggests one type of interaction, but the topic cannot be addressed adequately without reference to other types of interaction, such as compartmentalization and parody—that is, to making borders as well as crossing them. This article examines several instances of musical interaction on the Canadian prairies since the 1920s. It considers genres and performance contexts that eased social interactions, whether or not the music embodied diverse stylistic references, types of cross-cultural commentary (including parodies of cultural stereotypes), and stylistic juxtapositions and/or syntheses.

In the prairies of the United States and Canada, the late-nineteenth-century encouragement of large-scale immigration from northern, eastern, and western Europe resulted in a society that effectively had no majority and no mainstream. The cultural diversity in architecture, religion, and foodways was already being represented as emblematic of the prairies in writings of the 1920s such as Victoria Hayward's *Romantic Canada*. The policy of block settlement, whereby all homesteaders of, say, Swedish or Icelandic descent settled in the same area, worked against cultural interaction. For many, the objective of language maintenance was another reason for discouraging interaction. Despite these factors, musical exchange and collaboration occurred, unevenly and in many forms. [For a map of Canada, see ANGLO MUSIC IN ATLANTIC CANADA.]

Genres and Performance Events that Eased Social Interaction

The performance of classical music and of folk music in classically influenced arrangements at concert venues attracted individuals from different ethno-cultural backgrounds. Hence, the *Encyclopedia of Music in Canada* reports that soloists in an oratorio performed in Winnipeg were "drawn from the Anglo-Saxon, French, Mennonite, and Ukrainian communities" (Kallmann, Potvin, and Winters 1992), but multiethnic involvement did not necessarily encourage musical fusion. Many choirs were established between the world wars, for instance, precisely to preserve repertoire in the language of their homeland. Male voices were especially popular, and separate Icelandic, Norwegian, Swedish, Polish, and Jewish choirs flourished in Winnipeg during this period. Increasingly after World War II, however, audiences for culturally specific performance became more diverse. The Yevshan Ukrainian Orchestra, established in Saskatoon in 1974, specializes in Ukrainian-Canadian works, but enjoys the patronage of a broader social spectrum. Similarly, large-scale music-and-dance shows became popular in western Canada, performed by Edmonton's Dnipro Ensemble (choirs, orchestra, dancers), Winnipeg's Hoosli Ukrainian Folk Ensemble, and other ensembles.

Potentially more conducive to social interaction were festivals. Extraordinarily forward-looking for their time were folksong and handicraft festivals of the 1920s organized by John Murray Gibbon (1875–1952) to celebrate the newly built hotels affiliated with the Canadian Pacific Railway. Organizers, including folklorist Marius Barbeau (1883–1969) and composer Ernest MacMillan (1893–1973), insisted on celebrating cultural diversity by inviting regional representatives of musical and craft practices and setting folk music for classical ensembles. Most of these festivals occurred in Québec City or on the prairies. The Winnipeg Festival of 1927, labeled the "New Canadian Folk Song and Handicraft Festival," featured performers and craftsmen of "European Continental extraction" from nineteen nations—a much more diverse representation than found in previous festivals. The Regina festival in 1928 featured thirty different ethnic groups.

Musical fusion was not the objective of the Canadian Pacific Railway Festival organizers (though the appropriation of folk music by composers such as MacMillan was fusion of a sort), but the juxtaposition of multiple musical traditions was a model that would continue to effect social interaction. It is unsurprising, then, that a 1949 anniversary concert in Winnipeg, organized by local Ukrainians, boasted of including Estonian, Hungarian, Latvian, Lithuanian, Polish, Ukrainian, and Yugoslav Canadians. Similarly, the spirit of cultural diversity was reinforced in multilingual radio programs such as those hosted by the Edmonton-based Czech musician Gaby Haas in the 1950s. By the 1980s, the Winnipeg Folk Festival (established in 1974) had become the largest event of its kind in North America.

More recently, musical juxtaposition has served to crosscut ethnic solidarities. For example, franco-phone artists in western Canada—entitled RADO, for Regroupement des Artistes Del 'Ouest Canadien—have produced two CDs featuring musicians of widely varying cultural backgrounds, including Acadians, Québécois, and West Africans; linguistic solidarity, in this case, facilitates ethnocultural border crossing.

Cross-cultural Musical Commentary, Borrowing, and Fusion

Relationships among ethnocultural communities varied enormously. As Robert B. Klymasz has observed, part of the variation relates to a rural–urban distinction: he characterized the former as "tight ethnic enclaves" (1972:373), the latter as having more dispersed populations. Additionally, one generation's friendships might not be maintained by the next generation. The custom of parodying ethnicities became entrenched in some musical practices. Even today, the French pop band Les Zed, whose members include individuals of French, Ukrainian, and English descent, parodies German polkas and fiddle ensembles. Cleaver's World performs regional and ethnic styles, one of which uses the parallel thirds of Ukrainian *bandura* ensemble arrangements. One of many early instances of consistent musical interaction is Ukrainian country music. For another such example, see Métis.

Ukrainian Fusions

After more than a century of residence in Canada, Ukrainian musicians have created fusions between the musics they hold in their memories or hear on contemporary Ukrainian recordings and North American popular music styles. Ukrainian fiddlers have maintained a culturally specific repertoire (the older genres of which include *kozatchok*, *kolomyka*, and *holub*) and distinctive styles of ornamentation. Ukrainian stringbands often include the *tsymbaly*, the Ukrainian hammered dulcimer.

The genre that has received scholarly attention, however, is Ukrainian country music. In the early 1970s, folklorist Klymasz (1972) studied 514 items from forty-two recordings by such artists as Mickey and Bunny [Sklepowich], Mae Chwaluk, Peter Hnatiuk, and the Semcuk sisters. He observed the extensive use of macaronic texts (in English and Ukrainian), the incorporation of *tsymbaly* in many recordings, and the canonization of a small subset of the most popular songs. English songs selected for adaptation often had features compatible with common patterns in Ukrainian folksong, such as the use of ten-syllable lines with a midline break. More recently, Ostashewski (2001) has studied musical fusion in the work of two western Canadian Ukrainian groups, the Kubasonics and Paris to Kyiv.

Other Fusions

The topic of musical fusion is generally addressed in Canada, as in the United States, with reference to musical practices that embody cultural diversity. In this framework, Native American blues or hip-hop artists, such as Murray Porter, Jani Lauzon, and TKO, collaborations between pop bands and symphony orchestras (for example, Spirit of the West and the Vancouver Symphony), Asian classical and jazz (for example, the work of Toronto *erhu* player George Gao), the folk rock of Ashley MacIsaac, the eclectic styles of music performed in the course of R. Murray Schafer's Wolf Project, and the host of world-music bands active in every major urban center are subjects worthy of study.

—*Adapted from an article by Beverley Diamond*

Bibliography

Hayward, Victoria. 1922. *Romantic Canada*. Toronto: The Macmillan Company of Canada.

Kallman, H., Gilles Potvin, and Kenneth Winters, eds. 1992. *Encyclopedia of Canadian Music*. 2nd ed. Toronto: University of Toronto Press.

Klymasz, Robert B. 1972. " 'Sounds You Never Before Heard': Ukrainian Country Music in Western Canada." *Ethnomusicology* 16(3):372–380.

Ostashewski, Marcia. 2001. "Identity Politics and Western Canadian Ukrainian Musics: Globalizing the Local or Localizing the Global." *Topia* 6 (Fall 2001):63–82.

British Columbia: An Overview

Canada's third-largest province is unique in its geography, history, and social demography. About 70 percent of the population resides in the Georgia Straits coastal area of the southwest (including the cities of Vancouver and Victoria, on Vancouver Island, and communities north of Vancouver). Residents of the north–south valleys, especially the Okanagan Valley, east of Vancouver interact with American neighbors along these north–south lines. The Peace River community of the northeast is more closely related to Albertan than British Columbian culture. In the far north, a community such as Atlin, which has an annual summer arts festival, relates closely to Yukon culture. [For a map of Canada, see ANGLO MUSIC IN ATLANTIC CANADA.]

Britain, for which James Cook claimed the land in 1778, had a dominant presence until the mid-twentieth century and still influences the character of Victoria, but the ethnocultural profile of British Columbia is distinctive. Inland and coastal First Nations (in eight distinct language families) are vibrant and diverse. In the south-central regions around Kootenay are Doukhobor communities. Asians have long been in British Columbia, beginning with Chinese miners in the Fraser Valley gold rushes of 1858 and the Klondike in the 1890s and laborers for the construction of the Canadian Pacific Railway. Japanese immigrants have made major contributions to the fishing industry. Since the 1970s, populations from Southeast Asia, South Asia, and the Pacific Islands have expanded rapidly. Asian citizens have suffered historically from severely discriminatory attitudes and policies. The Chinese Immigration Act banned Chinese immigration between 1923 and 1947, preventing family reunification and contributing to a downturn in the Asian population. Japanese citizens were forcibly confined in camps during World War II. In the 1980s and 1990s, Asian investors changed the architectural and social face of Vancouver, and have become community leaders.

Factors shaping British Columbian culture include the history of interactions between British and Asian communities, especially the earlier suppression and contemporary leadership of the latter, the richness of First Nations cultures in the province, and outsider interest in local visual arts and musical performances.

First Nations

As elsewhere in North America, the aboriginal people of British Columbia prefer their own names for themselves, though many are better known by names assigned (or misheard) by outsiders. Most First Peoples in British Columbia signed no treaties with colonial authorities. In the twentieth century, they struggled to control access to resources. A 1999 agreement between the Nisga Nation and provincial and federal governments, heralded as a model for intergovernmental relationships and the first modern land-claim settlement in British Columbia, provided a land base, resource control, self-government, and independent courts.

Haida, Tlingit, Tsimshian, and Wakashan cultures, in particular, have been extensively studied, photographed, and filmed. Often depicted are imposing carved heraldic emblems and crests on totem poles, housefronts, and ceremonial regalia; elaborate theatrical performance of traditional myth and clan symbolism by dancers in colorful button blankets, elaborately carved masks, and/or headdresses; and the validation of important events or relationships through feasting and gift giving at potlatches. The U'mista Cultural Center has played a significant role in rectifying museum representation and film production. Its film *Potlatch: A Strict Law Bids Us Dance* (1975) includes images of the 1921 potlatch given by Chief Dan Cranmer, after which forty-five prosecutions took place, and a 1974 event hosted by the Cranmer family.

More than many other forms of aboriginal creative work, Northwest Coast expressive traditions have been readily accepted as art by mainstream scholars. This treatment may partly relate to the visual impact of large pieces such as totem poles and housefronts, and partly to the unquestioned influence of Haida and Nootka artists on European-Canadian artists, such as Emily Carr (1871–1945), and partly to the complexity and abstraction of design. Chiefs' raven rattles are important examples of this complexity and abstraction. Artistic acclaim was earned by such artists as Mungo Martin (ca. 1880–1962) in the 1940s and Bill Reid (1920–1998), Robert Davidson (b. 1946), Lawrence Paul Yuxweluptun (b. 1957), Brian Jungen (b. 1970), and many others since the 1960s. With such extensive attention, there is widespread awareness of the problems of cross-cultural "translation" and interpretation.

Ceremonial life was organized around a bifurcation of the year, with spring-summer marked by extensive travel to ease fishing and hunting and fall-winter marked by residence in permanent villages, where ceremonial activity could best be conducted and song specialists were in high demand. In 1884, the Canadian government banned potlatches and the activities of associated dancing societies, and confiscated ceremonial objects, many of which entered museum collections. A wave of potlatch-related arrests was particularly intense in 1918–1920. The dances went underground. The antipotlatch law was repealed in 1951, after which time a renaissance of performance traditions has occurred.

On the northwest coast, complex aboriginal traditions of intellectual property have been negotiated differently in different eras. Some collectors have released recordings of traditional music for summer and winter ceremonials, clan songs, music associated with the myth of Baxbakwalanuxsiwae, which forms part of the chiefmaking ceremony (*hamatsa*), and mourning songs.

Coast and Interior Salish song and dance are distinct in many ways from that of the more northerly Wakashan-speaking communities. The complex of practices relating to guardian-spirit beliefs, renewed since the 1950s, and the more extensive influence of the Ghost Dance movement after the 1890s are historical differences. Information published about the music of interior communities is less extensive. Among several Okanagan cultural initiatives is a monograph by storyteller Harry Robinson (1900–1990) with Wendy Wickwire (1989). The Sen'klip Theatre Company, blending traditional and modern arts, is acquiring an international profile.

An unusually strong interest in brass bands emerged in British Columbia-based First Nations in the late nineteenth century. The earliest band was the Metlakatla community band, formed by missionary William Duncan in 1875. Nass River communities have had a longtime interest in band music: the Kincolith band and Nelson's [Silver] Cornet Band (named after conductor Job Nelson, who conducted at Kincolith for a while) flourished from the 1880s, and the former endured into the 1970s. In the late twentieth century, British Columbia-based musicians, including David Campbell and Fara Palmer, have had national recognition. Contemporary aboriginal music plays a major role on local radio stations.

European Musical Practices

Eighteenth-century British and Spanish interests in the area were in contestation; Spain, however, withdrew by 1795. Consequently, the cultural infrastructure of the region was developed and largely controlled by British settlers, whose musical practices, such as brass bands and English-language music theater, have been documented by Robert Dale McIntosh (1981, 1989). He shows that before 1900, Vancouver and Victoria supported several community-based ensembles and at least one military band, and Kamloops had three active bands. He documented more than a century of existence for the Nanaimo Silver Comet Band (established in 1872 and still active in 2007 as the Nanaimo Concert Band) and other ensembles, and traces their role in marches, parades, and concerts under William Haynes, Phillip Brandon, John Morris Finn, Arthur W. Delamont, and other bandmasters.

Choral music, often sponsored by Christian churches, enjoyed a similarly important role, with major choirs often predating their counterparts in Ontario, among them St. John's Choral Society, established in 1868 in Victoria, the Victoria Choral Society (1878), the New Westminster Choral Union (1882), the Vancouver Musical Club (1888), and the Arion Clubs Male Voice Choir (1893). The Vancouver Bach Choir, formed in 1930 with founding conductor Herbert Mason Drost, is the longest continuous choral organization in the province. Orchestras developed later; the earliest recorded by McIntosh was probably the Victoria Amateur Orchestra, founded in 1878. The "new" Vancouver Symphony Orchestra, directed by Allard de Ridder (1887–1966), emerged in 1930.

Musical theater and light opera have played an especially important role. The Vancouver Opera House (built in 1891) was one of many Canadian Pacific Railway-sponsored cultural projects. In the mid-twentieth century, a distinctive performance venue was Vancouver's Stanley Park, where from 1936 to 1963 the Theatre under the Stars produced summer shows. Outdoor venues remain popular in the mildness of the Vancouver and Victoria climate. Smaller communities were hardly left behind, however, as demonstrated by such groups as the Summerland Singers and Players and indigenous productions by companies in Salmon Arm and Cowichan.

Doukhobors

The Doukhobors are dissident Russian Christians, whose beliefs, which reject the authority of the Bible and the justice of secular government, and favor pacifism and social separatism, developed in the seventeenth and eighteenth centuries. In 1899, more than seven thousand of them fleeing persecution, immigrated to Canada, where they settled in south-central British Columbia and on the prairies. In communes where they have maintained their philosophy, they demonstrate commitment to ideals of justice, compassion for life, spiritual beauty, and social service, still questioning "the right of material and institutional power" (Mealing 1995:39). Their spiritual precepts were collected in the *Book of Life* and transmitted through unaccompanied choral singing.

Asians

The first wave of Cantonese-speaking Chinese arrived from Guangdong Province to work in gold mines in the 1850s and subsequently to build the Canadian Pacific Railway or seek their fortunes in the Klondike. They were almost exclusively men. Despite the hard labor, extreme cold, illness, and racism they met, their community, segregated in one neighborhood around Vancouver's Pendle Street, sustained their distinctive lifeways. This neighborhood remains the heart of the Chinese community in Vancouver. Photographic evidence proves the presence of Chinese orchestral and operatic performances by the 1890s. Early performances effected a sense of community and raised money for community projects and relief work in Asia. After 1947, when wives and families of many residents immigrated to Canada, an emphasis on family celebration developed for the first time. Under the umbrella of the Chinese Benevolent Society, many cultural—especially musical—associations developed.

In recent decades, the Chinese community has expanded exponentially and become more diversified and economically powerful. Products of this diversification are new opera associations and dance troupes, of which the Lorita Leung Dance Studio is one of the best-established. The Vancouver Chinese Music Ensemble (established in the 1980s) includes Cantonese and musicians from more northerly regions in China. The Vancouver Chinese Choir Association celebrated its tenth anniversary in 1995 with the production of a new self-titled recording, made live at the Orpheus Theatre. By the 1990s, the Dr. Sun Yat Sen Classical Chinese Garden hosted an annual summer series of Asian musics and served as a venue for the Vancouver Jazz Festival. New styles of popular music flourish in Vancouver, with artists such as Terry Watada and Sook-Yin Lee articulating Asian experiences in Canada.

The first Japanese immigrants reached Canada in 1877. By 1940, the Japanese-Canadian community around Powell Street in Vancouver was thriving. Many individuals were interned during World War II and subsequently dispersed across the country, and the community struggled to regain its stature and solidarity. Since 1977, the annual Powell Street Festival has commemorated the original community. Contemporary Vancouver-based performance groups include the Kokoro Dance Ensemble and several *taiko* drum ensembles, including the Katari Taiko Drummers and Uzume.

Figure 1 The CBC Radio Orchestra conducted by Alain Trudel at the Chan Centre, Vancouver, 2007. *Photo by Brian Hawkes. Courtesy of CBC Radio Orchestra.*

Sikhs constituted the largest South Asian population in British Columbia until the 1960s, when at least seven temples (*gurdwaras*) were in the province, some established as early as the 1920s (Qureshi 1972).

Concerts and Festivals

British Columbia's concert life is especially vibrant in Vancouver. The Vancouver Chamber Choir and the women's choir Elektra have international profiles and heavy recording schedules. The Vancouver Symphony Orchestra led in new directions, such as collaborating with Spirit of the West, a Celtic rock band. The CBC Radio Orchestra of Vancouver was the only radio orchestra in North America as of 2007 (figure 1).

Outdoor venues were mentioned earlier as particularly important during the Vancouver summer. The Vancouver Folk Festival (established in 1975), one of the oldest in the country, is based at Jericho Beach Park. Many venues for the Vancouver Jazz Festival are outdoors, as are those of the Merritt Mountain (Country) Music Festival, the Victoria Symphony Splash (at which the Victoria Symphony performs on a barge in the inner harbor), and the Caribbean Festival at Waterfront Park in North Vancouver.

—*Adapted from an article by Beverley Diamond*

Bibliography

Diamond, Beverley, and R. Witmer, eds. 1994. *Canadian Music: Issues of Hegemony and Identity*. Toronto: Canadian Scholars' Press.

Hoe, Ban Seng. 1989. *Beyond the Golden Mountain: Chinese Cultural Traditions in Canada*. Ottawa: Canadian Museum of Civilization.

Holm, Bill. 1983. *The Box of Daylight: Northwest Coast Indian Art*. Vancouver Douglas and McIntyre.

McIntosh, Robert Dale. 1981. *A Documentary History of Music in Victoria, British Columbia: Vol. 1, 1850–1899*. Victoria: University of Victoria.

——. 1989. *History of Music in British Columbia 1850–1950*. Victoria: Sono Nis Press.

——. 1994. *A Documentary History of Music in Victoria, British Columbia: Vol. II, 1900–1950*. Victoria: Beach Holme Publishers.

——, and Wesley Berg. 1992. "Edmonton." In *Encyclopedia of Music in Canada*, 2nd ed., edited by Helmut Kallmann, Gilles Potvin, and Kenneth Winters, 403–404. Toronto: University of Toronto Press.

Mealing, Mark F. 1995. "Doukhobor Psalms: Adornment to the Soul." In *Spirit Wrestlers: Centennial Papers in Honour of Canada's Doukhobor Heritage*, edited by Koozma J. Tarasoff and Robert B. Klymasz, 39–50. Ottawa: Canadian Museum of Civilization.

Qureshi, Regula. 1972. "Ethnomusicological Research among Canadian Communities of Arab and East Indian Origin." *Ethnomusicology* 16(3):381–396.

Reid, Martine. 1987. "Silent Speakers: Arts of the Northwest Coast." In *The Spirit Sings: Artistic Traditions of Canada's First Peoples* 201–236. Calgary: Glenbow Museum.

Robinson, Harry, and Wendy Wickwire. 1989. *Write It on Your Heart: The Epic World of an Okanagan Storyteller*. Vancouver: Talon Books / Thetus.

The Canadian Broadcasting Corporation

Radio has played a pivotal role in the history and dissemination of music in Canada, where the establishment of a professional apparatus for creating concert music came about only after the formation of the Canadian Broadcasting Corporation (CBC).

Between the founding of the CBC, in 1936, and the late 1950s, the CBC was the primary patron and commissioner of musical works in Canada. Because recording was negligible, private patronage minimal, touring prohibitively expensive, and concert audiences small, radio was central to forming a professional musical culture. Many ensembles and works were developed for radiobroadcasting, and radio became the dominant site of interaction among composers, musicians, and audiences. Most Canadians heard their first orchestras and bands live on the CBC. Access to radio time became more valuable—in money and prestige—than performance alone, and Canadian composers lobbied for it. Opera, choir, orchestral, and instrumental concerts simultaneously grew more distinct in organization and repertoire; their specialization broadened their repertoires to include lesser-known works by familiar composers and greater marginalization of works and styles outside the classical canon. Works written and performed by Canadians tended to retain stylistic traits out of fashion in their country of origin.

The CBC introduced many contemporary works when local performers remained reluctant to confront them. They introduced composers established in Europe, including Schoenberg and most notably Stravinsky, who guest-conducted his works with the CBC Symphony Orchestra from 1952 to 1964. Ten recordings of works conducted by him were released on record by the CBC, including "4 Études for Orchestra," "Scènes de ballet," "Symphony of Psalms," and "Symphony in C." This encounter encouraged commissions of Canadian compositions and performances. "No other single organization," the *Encyclopedia of Music in Canada* maintains, "has played so large a role in making Canadians and the outside world aware of Canadian cultural pursuits and in helping these to flourish. . . . No other organization is acknowledged as often as the CBC, whether as a performance medium, an employer, a sponsor, or a discoverer of talent" (Kallmann, Potvin, and Winters 1992:166).

Performances by Canadian performers were common through the 1940s and 1950s, and there was a higher proportion of original Canadian composition then than now. The CBC Symphony Orchestra broadcast classical and contemporary works weekly from 1952 to 1964. The greatest proportion of music broadcast on the CBC was "light music"; neither the CBC, nor its listeners, perceived the CBC as an alternative to commercial broadcasting. Its weekly schedule included jazz, folk and traditional, choral and religious, other light musics, and classical music. After television arrived and public radio took a narrower role in relation to commercial radio, "serious" drama and music continued on CBC radio—now unique in North America, but no longer buttressed by the popular appeal of programming "light music." Emphasis shifted from studio broadcasts to recorded music. By the 1970s, audiences for CBC's serious music programming had shrunk to a small percentage of Canadians.

CBC Radio One (primarily talk, with some concerts, interviews, and evening music programs) and Radio Two ("classics and beyond," with a postmidnight pop-experimental-alternative music program, modeled on community radio) remain free from the constraints of advertising and offer programs that do not have to compete with commercial radio for audience shares. The CBC has coproduction relationships with many Canadian arts organizations that save money and enable the CBC to make its tax-supported productions available as broadcasts and public events. Since 1945, the CBC has produced recordings of Canadian music performances for broadcasters worldwide, first under the label RCI (Radio Canada International) and, after 1966, under the labels CBC-SM and CBC-LM. These recordings distribute concerts by leading Canadian performers and ensembles and by top names in "light music," jazz, and pop in Canada, including Glenn Gould (1932–1982). Renowned not only for his award-winning piano recordings, Gould contributed to the emergence of a new genre of radio art. His 1967 *Idea of North*, produced by the CBC, employs fugal counterpoint to arrange voices and sounds of people traveling by train to northern Canada. This composition led to similar works, including explorations of urban and rural soundscapes, interior landscapes, montages, live performances, travels, and the political aesthetics of technology.

—*Adapted from an article by Jody Berland*

Bibliography

Augaitis, D., and D. Lander, eds. 1994. *Radio Rethink: Art, Sound and Transmission*. Banff: Walter Phillips Gallery, The Banff Centre for the Arts.

Berland, Jody. 1986. "Cultural Re/Percussions: The Social Production of Music Broadcasting in Canada." Ph.D. dissertation, York University.

——. 1994a "Radio Space and Industrial Time: The Case of Music Formats." In *Canadian Music: Issues of Hegemony and Identity*, edited by Beverley Diamond and Robert Witmer, 173–188. Toronto: Canadian Scholars' Press.

——. 1994b. "Toward a Creative Anachronism: Radio, the State and Sound Government." In *Radio Rethink: Art, Sound and Transmission*, edited by D. Augaitis and D. Lander, 33–44. Banff: Walter Phillips Gallery, The Banff Centre for the Arts.

Ellis, David. 1979. *Evolution of the Canadian Broadcasting System: Objectives and Realities, 1928–1968*. Ottawa: Minister of Supply and Services Canada.

Kallman, Helmut, Gilles Potvin, and Kenneth Winters. 1992. "CBC." In *Encyclopedia of Music in Canada*, 2nd ed., edited by Helmut Kallman and Gilles Potvin, 228–229. Toronto: University of Toronto Press.

MacMillan, Keith. 1992. "Broadcasting." In *Encyclopedia of Music in Canada*, 2nd ed., edited by Helmut Kallmann and Gilles Potvin, 162–167. Toronto: University of Toronto Press.

4. Europe

4. Europe

The music of Europe arose and flourishes within four distinct, but interconnected, social and cultural spheres. The aristocratic and educated elite patronizes classical music. Folk music sprang from the life and work of rural peasants. Religious institutions have fostered special genres for their liturgies and community celebrations. Cities—where all classes rub shoulders, and commercial goods and intellectual ideas are traded internationally—are the wellsprings of popular music.

Each of these European music worlds possesses a characteristic sound, recognizable across the continent and reflecting the social and cultural milieu in which it is created and practiced. Musicians from each sphere, despite their differences, have long borrowed musical ideas from their counterparts in other spheres. And the music within each sphere, despite the similarities, exhibits significant variation among communities—differences that depend on language, nationality, and local history.

A Ukrainian Cossack plays the *bandura* on the street in Gdansk, Poland, 2005.
Photo by Sean Williams.

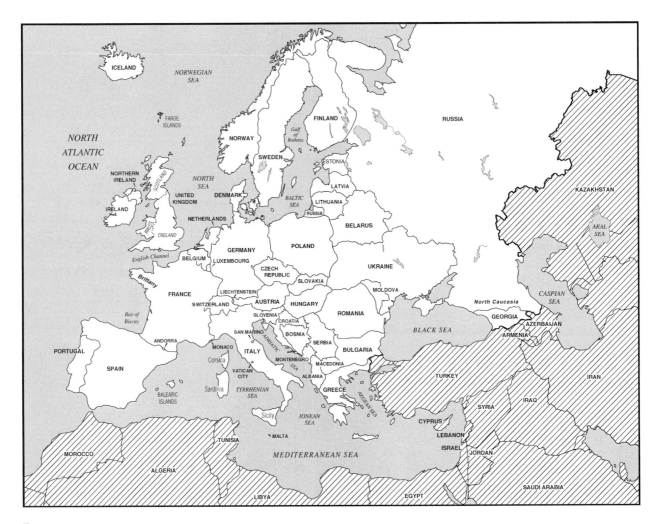

Europe

The Music of Europe: Unity and Diversity

Europe, though classified as one of the world's seven continents, is geographically a peninsula on the western end of the vast Eurasian landmass. Thus, its definition has always been cultural, rather than physical. Defying unity, however, the people of Europe have divided themselves by ethnicity, class, religion, language, and dialect. Each community has its own music and often believes this music to be a distinctive, even unique, representation of its identity. In 2007, Europe is divided into forty-five countries with a number of semi-independent areas. This fine geopolitical mosaic contained even finer subdivisions by ethnic and linguistic groups. Despite the daunting political problems created by ethnic, linguistic, and religious differences, many factors can be cited in arguing for the cultural—and musical—unity of Europe.

The music of Europe has typically been understood as falling into three large categories: folk, classical, and popular. Created by intellectuals, these categories began as markers of social class as much as musical style. The concept of *folk music*, credited to the German writer Johann Gottfried von Herder (1744–1803), stood for the music of rural peasants, who intellectuals believed bore the soul of a nation. An important, even defining, feature was its supposed transmission in oral tradition. *Classical music*, also known as *art music*, emerged as a category in the nineteenth century to label the work of a few supposed geniuses. Passed on in written form, it has come to be associated with urban, educated elites. The term *popular music* has been used to identify the music of the urban working and middle classes. Since the twentieth century, it has been transmitted primarily via electronic media—records, audiocassettes, compact discs, radio and television broadcasts, and computer files. These categorical distinctions, invented in Europe by Europeans, work better for European music than they do in most other parts of the world. But even here, they cannot contain the shifts in musical style, practice, and meaning created by musicians with the passage of time.

The invention of the term *folk music* coincided with the beginnings of the industrial revolution in Europe. By the early nineteenth century peasants were moving in large numbers from the countryside into cities and towns to find work in factories and shops and form a new working class. They brought their songs and music with them, invented new texts to suit new occupations, and adopted urban musical styles. Since the medieval period, trained musicians in churches and courts had incorporated the tunes of their country cousins, often with the goal of making their music more accessible and popular. In the nineteenth century, this practice became a crucial element of nationalism, as classical composers utilized folk melodies to create national styles of art music. The music popular with the new urban classes of the nineteenth century used the instruments and harmonies of classical music, sometimes applied to tunes and dance styles originating in the villages. In the twentieth century these categories continue to mobilize great aesthetic and ideological differences, while musicians take advantage of the possibilities for fruitful interchange among them.

Though classical music is the most prestigious and best studied of these three categories of European music, this section of the *Concise Garland* places folk music at the center of its story. It presents popular and classical music primarily in relation to traditional music and as social, more than aesthetic, practices.

The Shared Culture of Music in Europe

What factors contribute to the cultural and musical unity of Europe? First, ecologically most of the European continent lies in a temperate climatic zone. The length of growing and dormant seasons and the kinds of crops that can be grown vary significantly from south to north, but the continent has long been unified by similar patterns of summer agricultural work and winter rest. Common seasonal patterns have given rise to similar kinds of songs and dances for agricultural rituals and similar cycles of outdoor and indoor work and recreation. Though their musical forms differ, their functions are identical. In most of Europe, these functions have been lost, but the songs are remembered, especially in eastern and southern Europe, and are still sung at social gatherings and folk festivals. Because of their limited melodic ranges and short forms, many scholars regard them as belonging to the oldest layer of the European song repertoire. It is a tribute to the tenacity of tradition that they are still being sung at the beginning of the twenty-first century, when urbanization, mechanization of labor, and scientific agricultural techniques have virtually eliminated the need to sing them for their original functions: to assure fertility and lighten the burden of heavy manual labor.

A second factor unifying Europe has been the almost universal adoption of Christianity. Though many rituals and songs in Europe retain pre-Christian, pagan elements, such as worship of the sun and the moon, most of Europe was converted to Christianity by C.E. 1000. (The Lithuanians were the last to officially convert, in the 1300s.) Christian values and forms of worship have defined many aspects of life, including musical life, for Europeans ever since. The Christian calendar of holidays—Christmas, Lent, Easter, and others—overlays, but often retains, pagan fertility rituals. Christmas caroling during house-to-house visits is still known in many parts of Europe. The forty days of Lent were traditionally a period when most forms of traditional singing and dancing were prohibited, and other forms, such as song games, were substituted. Different national traditions share secular melodies derived from shared Christian liturgical music. The music to accompany the liturgy varies according to Christianity's main branches: Orthodoxy in the east; Roman Catholicism in the center, south, and west; and Protestantism in the north. Within a given branch, however, many aspects of musical style and musical life deriving from religious practice are shared across national and language boundaries. For example, Lutheran hymn tunes, some retained from Roman Catholic practice, are sung by Protestants throughout Europe.

Other common features of European cultural life derive from a shared history that includes widespread literacy, imperial and princely courts, the rise of an urban bourgeoisie from the sixteenth to the twenty-first centuries, and urbanization, industrialization, and the evolution of the nation-state as the primary unit of political organization since the nineteenth century. Though not all parts of Europe shared in this history in equal measure or at the same time, these processes have shaped a common European heritage. The invention of movable type and book printing in the 1400s enabled the spread of literacy and education, which, combined with musical notation and musical literacy, have defined musical life for the educated classes of Europe since the Renaissance. Literacy, coupled with a network of imperial and princely courts related by marriage and descent, created a shared European culture with many common features. Intellectual and musical ideas—and musicians—traveled with relative ease throughout most parts of Europe. Music from one country recorded in a shared notation was trans-ported to other countries, so that within a few years, or in some cases months, the newest developments in Italy, for example, became part of the musical life of France, Germany, and Poland. Thus, classical music forms an important part of Europe's shared cultural landscape. In the twenty-first century, mass media joined the book and the written score to aid the spread of musical culture, and shared forms of popular music gave the disparate cultures of Europe an awareness of their linked musical heritage.

Urban Folklore

The industrial revolution and the urbanization it spawned have created similar patterns in the decline and revival of folk music all over Europe. These processes began in England in the eighteenth century, spread through most of Europe in the nineteenth century, and reached the remotest areas of eastern and southern Europe in the twentieth century. As agricultural efficiency and populations increased in the nineteenth and twentieth centuries, many people left their villages to seek their fortunes in the cities. The story of village music in Europe is in some respects a story of decline everywhere, though at different times and at different rates in different places. In Bulgaria, for example, the traditional wedding celebration was reduced in the late twentieth century from a weeklong affair with elaborate ritual singing by participants to a day or a day and a half with hired professional musicians. In Finland, a typical wedding once lasted a day with hired musicians, but recently it has been shortened to a few hours, with a disc jockey or without any music at all.

Counterbalancing this decline of village musical life all over Europe has been the rise of new forms of urban folklore. New urban genres include occupational songs of the working classes that developed in the nineteenth century. In Finland political parties in the nineteenth century each had their own brass bands to accompany the singing of songs advancing their points of view. In Russia a new urban middle class populated the outskirts of cities in a transitional suburban zone between the city and its surrounding villages; in this zone, all manner of popular songs, including improvised ditties (*chastushki*) and an important genre of soldiers' songs, took root. While most of these developments retain only local importance, some urban popular genres have gained international recognition. For example, new forms of couple dancing from Central Europe (mazurka, polka, schottische, waltz) and their tunes spread throughout most of Europe in the nineteenth century. In the 1920s, Greeks from Turkey were repatriated in a forced population exchange. In

Athens and the port of Piraeus, they formed a new urban underclass, whose music, *rebetika* 'rebels' music', became internationally popular in the 1960s—as did the Portuguese urban genre, *fado*, which had a significant influence on the popular music of Brazil. The flamenco music of urban Gypsies in Spain has enjoyed similar international renown over an even longer period.

Throughout Europe, a less organic but still common response to the decline of village life and music has been the widespread support of efforts to preserve village folklore. In the nineteenth century, scholars, nationalists, and antiquarians initiated these efforts by collecting song texts (and more rarely, notated music) and publishing them in articles and books. In the twentieth century, preservationists' efforts took the form of grassroots "folk revivals," mainly in Western Europe, and state-supported performance troupes of professionals or amateurs, mainly in communist Central and Eastern Europe and the Balkans. These efforts at preservation and modernization of village traditions usually occur in urban settings and among educated youth, and are sometimes disparagingly called *folklorism*, or even *fakelore*; however, they have undeniably altered and reshaped the way music originally produced in rural areas is heard, understood, adapted and appreciated by modern audiences throughout Europe and the world (figure 1).

In some cases, the motivation for these preservation efforts has been a romantic nostalgia for supposedly lost ways of life by urbanites otherwise anxious to reject most other aspects of village life, such as its drudgery, illiteracy, and poverty. But even more importantly, these rural traditions are associated nearly everywhere in Europe with the nation itself, precisely because they are local and not supranational. In the nineteenth century, nationalists in Europe constructed an association between rural, village music and the people ("the folk") and soul of the nation. In the United States, the term *folk music* tends to retain the relatively innocent associations of the first meaning, that is, as rural, village, "old-time" music. In contemporary Europe, however, state interventions on behalf of folk music under all forms of government—democratic, fascist, and communist—have led to widespread disillusionment, particularly among youth, with this kind of music in many countries. The term *folk* has been tainted by these political and ideological associations, and some scholars have substituted other, possibly more neutral, terms to describe what they are interested in: *vernacular, traditional, village,* or *rural music,* for example. In this section, the decision about how to label this music has been left up to each author.

Musical Similarities in Village Music

Where traditional music is still vibrant, villagers often say that their music is unique, that the music of even the neighboring village is different. Similarly, many nations have striven in the last two centuries to define their rural music as a unique signifier of the nation in sharp contrast to the music of neighboring countries. Given these local views and national ideologies, which stress difference, can any common tendencies be found in the forms of European traditional music? There are a few.

Figure 1 Musicians and dancers from the Kashubia ethnic group in Pomerania, Poland, showcase their tradition in a folkloric performance for tourists, 2005.
Photo by Sean Williams.

Figure 2 The civil wind band Sociedade Artística Musical dos Pousos plays during the *peditório* of the feast of Our Lady of the Rosary (Festa da Nossa Senhora do Rosário), Alqueidão da Serra, district of Leiria, Portugal, 1995.
Photo by Salwa el-Shawan Castelo-Branco.

Performance Practice

Performance contexts are remarkably similar across Europe. In the past, calendric rituals, based on the agricultural cycle of work and Christian religious holidays (figure 2) provided important contexts for song and dance. The musical parts of the lifecycle included wedding celebrations and laments for the recently deceased. As traditional village culture waned, most calendric rituals and lamenting have tended to disappear, leaving the wedding as the most important traditional lifecycle ritual. Of course, informal social gatherings with song and dance as the main event continue nearly everywhere in the home, village square, and tavern. Since the second half of the twentieth century, concerts and festivals of rural music have been common throughout Europe.

Village music everywhere is passed on through oral tradition, though there are frequent reports of musicians and singers using notebooks to help them remember tunes and song texts. There is no traditional notation system, and subtle variations from performance to performance are the rule. Descriptive speech about music is limited, though scholars have been able to collect local terminologies that constitute a kind of native musical theory of a given tradition.

Most European traditional cultures maintain a fundamental division between vocal and instrumental music. The common form of vocal music in all of Europe is the strophic song, in which the lyrics are sung to a repeated melodic structure. A narrative song genre, the ballad, has proved especially fruitful for the study of pan-European musical trends. Common ballad melodies have been found in neighboring countries, and, perhaps surprisingly, certain ballad themes—such as the star-crossed lovers in the ballad known by its English title as "Barbara Allen"—have been documented in traditions as far removed as Scotland and Bulgaria.

Instrumental music in Europe seems to have its roots in the practice of shepherds: the use of flutes and bagpipes to pass the time, of horns for signaling, and of bells to identify animals. Instrumental music is also used nearly everywhere for dance music. The most common form consists of relatively short, repeated pairs of melodies (AA'BB'), but in some traditions it has been extended with succeeding pairs of lines (CC'DD' and so on) and improvisations. Musical instruments are important indicators of shared culture. The plucked zithers of Northern Europe and the double-reed oboes of Southern Europe unify territories of great linguistic and cultural diversity. And modern manufactured instruments, especially the accordion and the violin, give the sound of European traditional music a timbre that is similar nearly everywhere.

In the past, the most widespread performance style for song and instrumental music was probably the solo. The second most common practice for songs was unison or octave singing by a pair or group of singers. Unison performance by traditional instrumentalists, as in the violin section of a symphony orchestra, for example, was almost unknown until the early twentieth century. In Russia, Vasily Andreev experimented with orchestras of folk instruments, and this practice eventually spread throughout the Soviet Union and communist Central and Eastern Europe and the Balkans later in the century. About the same time, Swedish fiddlers formed societies that brought dozens of fiddlers together for festivals and competitions.

Other performance practices are widespread but not universal. Antiphonal singing by two soloists or groups is quite common, as is responsorial singing—solo call and choral response. Drone-based accompaniment in instrumental music is found virtually everywhere, but singing with drone accompaniment is common only in parts of Eastern and Southeastern Europe. The instrumental drone is often provided by a single instrument designed specifically to produce a melody plus drone, as with bagpipes, double-piped flutes, and bowed and plucked stringed instruments.

By the late twentieth century, village music everywhere in Europe had been influenced by urban music, with its chordal accompaniments primarily using triads built on the tonic (I), the subdominant (IV), and the dominant (V). Soloists and choruses are today typically accompanied by instrumentalists who play these chords, and instrumentalists form bands that double the melody in unison or play it in parallel thirds. Whatever drones might have existed in older practice are typically replaced by other instruments playing chords and a bass line.

Melody and Rhythm

One can make some generalizations about melodic and rhythmic structures. In many areas of Europe, an ancient layer of narrow-range (a fourth to a sixth) tunes that move diatonically by half steps and whole steps are still performed or were notated in the nineteenth century. More recent tunes extend the diatonic tendency over a wider range, to an octave or more. Pentatonic tunes, using five pitches within an octave, have a scattered distribution; not especially typical in Europe, they are important markers of regional or national identity where they occur [see HUNGARY].

Traditionally there were two treatments of rhythm: metrical, as in dance music; and nonmetrical, as in "table songs," by which guests were entertained while seated. Nonmetrical genres include Irish slow airs, the Russian *protiazhnaia pesnia* 'long-drawn-out song', the Romanian *doina*, and instrumental music such as the Greek *miroloyia* 'lament'. During the nineteenth century, whatever variety may have existed in European metrical constructions was reduced in most parts of Europe to duple and triple meters, influenced by emphasis on regular chordal harmonic rhythms and the spread of certain couple dances (especially the waltz, in 3/4 time, and the polka, in 2/4 time) and march rhythms (in 2/4 time). A small number of songs in irregular or added meters have been collected in Northern Europe, suggesting a once common European practice, but only a few traditions in parts of Central and Southeastern Europe consistently employ irregular, mixed, or additive meters (2 + 3, 2 + 2 + 3, and so on).

Distinctions in Music Style and Culture

Refracted through a kind of comparative wide-angle lens that takes in the whole continent's music, Europe appears fairly unified, whether we consider urban popular and classical, village, or religious genres; however, Europeans on the ground, who hear music in the surrounding villages or in neighboring countries, are much more inclined to talk about differences among their musical practices and the uniqueness of their local style than to regard these practices and styles as contributing to a European, or even a national, manner of musical performance. In fact, many historical and geographical reasons contribute to the variety of European music, and many ideological factors, especially nationalism, lead Europeans to emphasize their differences and thus the variety in their musical styles and practices, rather than their similarities.

Geography and Nationality

The European continent is broken up by peninsulas, islands, rivers, and mountain ranges—geographical features that tend to separate one group of people from another and have led over long periods of time to the development of metaphorical islands of local styles, some that transcend nationality. In southeastern Europe, for example, southern Albanians, Epirote Greeks, and western Macedonians share a possibly ancient three-part polyphonic singing style and pentatonic scale. Even in France, one of the oldest unified nations in Europe, regional languages and musical styles persist despite a long history of centralized education and industrialization.

In the nineteenth and early twentieth centuries, politicians created nation-states by unifying city-states and small principalities, as in Germany and Italy in the nineteenth century, or by dividing up the expired Austro-Hungarian, Ottoman, and Russian or Soviet empires. Partly because history has intervened to disperse and intermingle many ethnicities, the geographical distribution of ethnic groups and the boundaries of nations have never been as co-terminous as national politicians have hoped or claimed. The result since the early twentieth century has been a continuous series of wars between nations and within nations for national or ethnic rights and freedoms. In a more peaceful but nonetheless aggressive manner, musicians under the sway of nationalist politics have consciously used music as an important signifier of national and ethnic identity in these disputes. In a tragic instance, Bosnian music, once a cosmopolitan mixture has, since the 1991 war among Serbians, Croatians, and Muslims, differentiated itself as each ethnicity emphasizes musical elements with connections to Serbia, Croatia, or the Middle East.

Religious Differences

The image of Europe as a primarily Christian continent masks musically significant distinctions within Christianity and ignores the presence of other religions, especially Judaism and Islam. In Roman Catholic countries, the activities of religious brotherhoods provide important contexts for musical performance, especially in ritual processions. In Corsica and Sardinia, such brotherhoods preserve traditional styles of polyphonic sacred music. Protestants in some countries of Northern Europe perform religious hymns outside the liturgy for secular entertainment. Orthodox Christians believe the gravestone is a window on the other world, reachable through lamenting—a factor that has preserved lamenting into the present. Jewish wedding musicians (klezmorim) played for their non-Jewish neighbors, especially in Poland, Ukraine, and Romania, and their tunes have become part of national repertoires in those countries. With the assimilation of Jewish populations in the urban cultures of many countries of Central and Eastern Europe and the Balkans, Jewish musicians became and remain among the most esteemed performers of European classical music. Since the 1980s or before, neo-traditional and popular musicians in many parts of southern Europe—from the Balkans to southern Italy to Spain—have been reinvigorating their music with Middle Eastern elements.

Muslims still living in the Balkan Peninsula include Turkish minorities in Bulgaria, Cyprus, Greece, and Macedonia; minorities of Slavic-language-speaking adherents to Islam in Bosnia and Bulgaria; and the majority of Albanians. There are also Muslim groups in southern Russia, for example, Bashkirs, Chechens, Kalmyks, and Tatars. Since the 1960s, many Muslims have immigrated to western Europe—as "guest workers" in Germany (mainly Turks) and as the result of colonial collapse in France (mainly sub-Saharan and North Africans) and Great Britain (Arabs and Pakistanis). Besides a shared religious music and associated ritual occasions, such as Ramadan, many of these groups perform secular music with evident links to the Middle East—links that include stringed instruments such as short- and long-necked plucked lutes and melodic modes using augmented seconds and microtonal intervals.

Islamic rule in southern Spain from the ninth to the fifteenth centuries, and in the Balkans from the fourteenth to the early twentieth centuries, left its mark on the musical practices of Christians in Europe. Perhaps most importantly, the guitar and the violin, so important in contemporary European music, probably have their origins in Middle Eastern long-necked plucked lutes and bowed, pear-shaped fiddles, respectively. Early Christian religious music—some of whose melodies continue to resonate in modern religious and secular music—and some forms of Eastern Orthodox chant share features with Islamic and Jewish chanting. In Spain, flamenco retains elements of Arab music, especially in vocal style, ornamentation, and improvisatory practice. Many modes, meters, tunes and ornaments of Balkan urbanized traditional music have Turkish analogs.

Minorities

Europe is currently divided into forty-two sovereign countries, most so-called nation-states. A few—Andorra, Liechtenstein, Luxembourg, Monaco, San Marino, and the Vatican—are tiny principalities and city-states, and one, the United Kingdom, contains England, Scotland, Wales, and Northern Ireland. Switzerland has four official languages: French, German, Italian, and Romansch. In fact, such states have never been able to contain all the nationalities of Europe, few nation-states consist of a single nation, and no nation-state contains all members of its nationality. (Nationality in Europe in some respects resembles the American concept of ethnicity.) This inconsistency between the theory of nation-states—nationalism—and the on-the-ground reality of where people live has created conflicts between and within states: the Flemings and Walloons of Belgium, divided by language; separatist movements of Basques, Bretons, and Corsicans in France and Basques, Galicians, and Catalans in Spain; fighting between Albanians and Serbs in Kosovo Province, Serbia; and a host of groups seeking political autonomy in Russia and Georgia.

Whether in conflict or living peacefully, each minority has its own music, which it uses to articulate and express its distinctness from the majority in the nation-state. Such national minorities include the Saami in Norway, Sweden, Finland, and Russia; the Basques, Bretons, and Corsicans in France; the Sardinians in Italy; the Turks in Bulgaria; and many other cases. Such variety extends the musical differences implicit in the division of Europe into nation-states and confounds nationalistic attempts to bring all of a country's music under a unified cultural umbrella. Minorities and nationalities who live in different nation-states often have different music. For example, though scholars located some common features of the music of the Jews and the Roma (Gypsies), Europe's largest transnational minorities, Jewish and Rom music varies according to contact with majority cultures.

Urban-rural and Class Differences

At the local level, the social divisions among classes and the music associated with each constitute an important source of difference in European musical life. Perhaps the most important division exists between rural and urban forms of musical performance. Urban societies contain a class division between an educated elite that patronizes classical music and a working class that has spawned various forms of urban popular music. Each country's musical life is notably varied (figure 3), and many of the articles that follow describe that complexity.

The urban-rural and class divisions of Europe play themselves out differently in different countries of Europe—a historical process that contributes to the variety of musical styles in Europe. Great Britain and Ireland and most of Northern, Western, and Central Europe, for example, underwent industrialization and urbanization in the nineteenth century, much earlier than countries in Eastern Europe and the Balkans. In areas with the longest histories of industrialization and urbanization, traditional village music is declining or being influenced by urban popular or classical music. Germany provides perhaps the clearest case of a severely diminished rural music tradition, one that was subject to Nazi appropriation and distortion in the 1930s, to the

Figure 3 Two bassists play jazz and classical music on a street in Gdansk, Poland, 2005.
Photo by Cary Black.

point that scholars there have had to recast their notions of folk music to include urban and modern forms of music to find an object of study. By contrast, some industrialized countries (such as Ireland, Norway, and Switzerland) or somewhat isolated areas of such countries (such as Brittany in France) preserve flourishing traditions of what might be called neo-folk or neo-traditional music, often transplanted into urban environments through processes of revival, folklorization, and nationalism. In parts of southeastern Europe, the decline of rural music as a result of industrialization and urbanization began only after World War II; there, however, any negative effects of these processes on village music were mitigated by socialist governments' support of "people's music." As a consequence, many traditional practices unaffected by urban music, such as drone-based polyphonic singing and bagpiping, remain vital. At the same time, many rural practices in southeastern Europe, such as elaborate wedding music, have survived during the last fifty years by modernizing in line with developments in urban music.

Differences in Musical Style

At the level of musical style, each country, area, and village often seems anxious to assert its uniqueness, partly the result of nationalistic ideologies, but also of real experiences, such as the inability to dance to music from a neighboring village or valley. Examples of such uniqueness abound. The traditional, three- and four-part vocal polyphony of Georgia and the North Caucasus is known nowhere else in Europe, or indeed the world. Significant regional variations occur in traditional Bulgarian and Albanian part-singing. Though ornamented singing and playing is typical throughout Europe, each region seems to have a unique style of ornamentation that identifies it. The singing of lengthy heroic epics, once possibly widespread in Europe, is still found in only a small area of the central Balkans. Elaborate yodeling is limited to Europe's central alpine area although parallel types of high vocal tessitura are found in Norway and Sweden. A rhythmic device known colloquially as the Scotch snap (a sixteenth note followed by a dotted eighth), though hardly unknown in other music, is so pervasive in Scottish music that it is taken as a sign of Scottish musical culture. Instances such as these, multiplied thousands of times, create the impression of enormous variety and differentiation, rather than similarity, in European traditional musical culture. At the same time, a reading of articles on different countries in close succession reveals striking similarities in the social and historical processes affecting music across the continent.

—*Adapted from an article by Timothy Rice*

Bibliography

Buchan, David. 1972. *The Ballad and the Folk*. London: Routledge and Kegan Paul.

Entwhistle, William J. 1939. *European Balladry*. Oxford: Clarendon Press.

Grout, Donald Jay, and Claude V. Palisca. 1996. *A History of Western Music*. 5th ed. New York: Norton.

Karpeles, Maud. 1956. *Folk Songs of Europe*. London: Novello.

Ling, Jan. 1997. *A History of European Folk Music*. Rochester, N.Y.: University of Rochester Press.

Lord, Albert B. 1960. *The Singer of Tales*. Cambridge: Harvard University Press.

Wiora, Walter. 1957. *Europäische Volkmusik und abendländische Tonkunst*. Kassel: J. P. Hinnenthal.

A Guide to Pronunciation

This guide lists the approximate English pronunciation of the letters that appear in European languages.

General Guidelines

Unless otherwise noted, consonants and consonant clusters are pronounced roughly as their American equivalents. As in English, pronunciation of some letters varies with context, for example, *c* as in *coin* and *c* as in *cent*, and detailed guides for each language should be consulted.

Exceptions to American pronunciation and problematic consonants include:

r usually rolled or trilled
j usually pronounced like *y* in *yes* or the *h* in *hat*
w usually pronounced like the *v* in *van*
x usually pronounced like the *x* in *taxi* (exceptions noted below)
q usually pronounced like the *k* in *kite*
c like *ts* in *bits* (in Slavic and Baltic languages)

Commonly used diacritics include:

č *ch* in *chin*
ć *ch* in *chin*
dž *j* in *judge*
ñ *ni* in *onion*
š *sh* in *shine*
ś *sh* in *shine*
ž *z* in *azure*

Some distinctions marked by diacritics, such as those between *č* and *ć* or *š* and *ś* in some Slavic languages, have no equivalents in English.

Vowels are generally pronounced as follows:

a *a* in *father*
e *e* in *bet*
i *i* in *machine*
o *o* in *open*
u *u* in *rule*
æ *a* in *cat*
y *ü* in German *über* (in Finnish, Scandinavian)

Diacritics added to vowels usually indicate a long form, and the unmarked vowel is correspondingly shortened.

Individual Languages

Transnational Ethnic Groups

Basque
dd palatalized *d*; *dy* in *did you*
tt palatalized *t*; *ty* in *next year*
tx *ch* in *chin*
tz *ts* in *bits*
x *sh* in *ship*
z *ss* in *miss*

Celtic Languages (Welsh, Irish, Scottish Gaelic)
bh *v* in *van*
ch *ch* in Scottish *loch*; *h* in *help*
dd *th* in *they*
dh like French *r*; *y* in *yes*
fh [silent]
gh like French *r*; *y* in *yes*
ll similar to *hl*
mh *v* in *van*
s *sh* in *ship*
sh *h* in *hat*
th *h* in *hat*
w *u* in *June*
y *o* in *for*

Scandinavia, Finland, and the Baltic States

Icelandic
ð *th* in *the*
ll *ttl* in *battle*
rl *ttl* in *battle*
rn like *tn* or *n*
z *s* in *sell*
þ *th* in *thick*

Norwegian
qu *kv*

Finnish
z *s* or *ts* in *bits*

Western Europe

Dutch
g *ch* in Scottish *loch*

Europe

French
ç   c in *cedar*
ch   *sh* in *ship*
j   *s* in *pleasure*

Portuguese
ç   *c* in *cedar*
h   [silent]
j   *s* in *pleasure*
nh   *ni* in *onion*
x   *sh* in *ship*, *ks* in *books*, *z* in *zone*

Spanish
c   in Spain, *th* in *thick*; elsewhere, *c* in *cent*
v   between *b* in *boy* and *v* in *van*
´   accent changes stress, not pronunciation

Italian
z   *ts* in *bits*

Central Europe

German
v   *f* in *fight*
z   *ts* in *bits*

Polish
ch   *ch* in Scottish *loch* or *j* in Spanish *jota*
cz   *ch* in *chin*
dz   *ds* in *beds*
dż   *j* in *job*
ł   *w* in *will*
ń   *ni* in *onion*
rz   *s* in *pleasure*
sz   *sh* in *ship*
sczc   *shch* in *fresh cheese*
ś   between *s* in *sell* and *sh* in *ship*

Czech and Slovak
ch   *ch* in Scottish *loch* or *j* in Spanish *jota*
cz   *ts* in *bits*
gy   *j* in *job*
ŋ   *ni* in *onion*
ř   *rzh* in *Dvořák*
sz   *s* in *sell*
ý   *ie* in *field*

Hungarian
c   *ts* in *bits*
cs   *ch* in *chin*
dzs   *j* in *job*
gy   *dy* in *did you*; *d* in *adulation*
ly   *y* in *yes*
ny   *ni* in *onion*
s   *sh* in *ship*
sz   *s* in *sell* (not *s* in *rose*)
ty   *ty* in *Katya*
zs   *s* in *pleasure*
Double consonants are pronounced long

Eastern Europe

Russian
kh   *ch* in Scottish *loch* or *j* in Spanish *jota* or *kh* in *khan*
y   *wi* in *will*
´   palatalizes previous consonant: e.g., *ty* in *next year*

Ukrainian
ch   *ch* in Scottish *loch* or *j* in Spanish *jota*
z   *s* in *sell*
´   palatalizes previous consonant: e.g., *dy* in *did you*

The Balkans

Romanian
ă   *a* in *sofa*
j   *s* in *pleasure*
ş   *sh* in *ship*
ţ   *ts* in *bits*

Bulgarian
đ   *j* in *job*
ǵ   *gu* in *angular*
h   *ch* in Scottish *loch* or *j* in Spanish *jota*, or *kh* in *khan*
ḱ   *cu* in *cure*
ŭ   *u* in *but*

Greek
g   rolled *g*
h   *ch* in Scottish *loch* or *j* in Spanish *jota*

—Adapted from an article by Brian Patrick Fox

Song Genres

Europe has a wide variety of song genres in oral tradition. Precisely because these genres and their structures are oral and traditional they are often difficult to separate from the singing styles and contexts that give rise to them. Some genres, such as shepherds' or cowherds' cries, are closely connected to work or occupation; others, such as laments or wedding songs, are intimately connected to lifecycle events. Many surviving genres have their origins in the later Middle Ages; others stem from the modern period, especially the 1700s, with the growth of cities. Although much depends on how the cultural borders of Europe are conceived, some freely rhapsodic genres from outlying Saami, Uralic, or Mediterranean cultures make for a striking contrast with the picture of predominantly strophic (verse-form) melodies across the continent.

Song genres can be grouped by content, form, function, situation, and performance style. A broadly comprehensive grouping of songs by form distinguishes strophic and non-strophic types. The strophic type consist of songs in which the same music, usually two to four phrases with or without a refrain, is repeated for each new stanza (strophe) of text. Non-strophic songs are songs in which text and music are performed without the formal conventions of strophic songs. Strophic and non-strophic types have evolved in regional variations over many centuries since their original appearance, and they have subsequently been modified in local contexts.

Groupings of songs by content and situation can be arranged within the strophic-non-strophic scheme: lifecycle and calendrical songs (e.g., wedding and harvest songs); songs of work or occupation (e.g., mining songs, shanties, outlaws' songs); songs of domestic provenance (e.g., ballads, lyric songs); songs for public occasions (e.g., political and religious songs) and other varieties. Songs involving a special technique or form (e.g., falsetto cries, chants, yodels, epigrams, polyphony) can be enclosed within the above grouping on grounds of their purely musical features.

Non-strophic Song Forms

Non-strophic song forms are often rhetorical, involving communication over distance or with a different spiritual world: songs of the Vogul, Ostjak, and Saami peoples on the eastern and northern borders of Europe express a ritualized relationship with the natural world of animals; a woman's song after a bear hunt moves through a range of a sixth, with prominent leaps of a fifth. In his study of Saami folk music, Karl Tirén includes calls to shepherd dogs and reindeer. Open three-note or four-note structures form the basis for most shepherding calls in pastoral areas of Europe, such as the Alps, the Norwegian highlands, and the Carpathian chain.

Shepherd calls often involve virtuosic stretches of the voice: to a high F, E-flat, and D above the treble-clef staff. Others take the form of a dialogue song between herders. Before the arrival of twentieth-century technology, French plowmen signaled to their oxen in the recitative known as *briolage*, mentioned by the writer George Sand about 1850. The melismatic Swiss cattle calls (*Kühreihen*) were notated as early as 1545, and similar forms are found in pastoral contexts from Sweden to the Caucasus, with types such as the Romanian *hora lunga*, which has spun-out, repeated notes.

The solo yodel in pastoral societies is often cast in free form and develops the range between head and chest voice, sometimes in a range of up to two octaves. Multipart yodels, however, tend to construct regular groupings of four, eight, or sixteen measures. Laments for the dead, too, embody a significant group of open forms. Often narrow in range, they can encompass an octave, usually descending in an affective curve that is well documented in, for example, the Irish *caoine*.

Epic Songs and Singing

Stichic songs, often with an heroic theme, repeat in performance a single musical phrase corresponding to the single line of verse. They are composed in an open form, line by line, rather than in the rounded, closed form of the four-lined strophic song. Although no longer plentiful in Europe, stichic composition was a feature of epic songs, from Homer's *Iliad* and *Odyssey* to the French *Chanson de Roland*, the German *Niebelungenlied*, the Icelandic heroic songs, the Spanish epics of *El Cid*, the Russian *byliny* (sing., *bylina*), and the Ukrainian *dumy*, though epics had regional markings and were by no means uniform in theme or musical style. In modern times, stichic technique is chiefly known through the study of Yugoslav, and to some extent Greek, epic or heroic songs (see Bartók and Lord 1951; Notopoulos 1959). The stichic principle in Serbo-Croatian songs, with its ten-syllable line, allows the singer's free embellishment of the story and its episodes, and songs of two thousand to four or five thousand lines are not unusual. Some complete transcriptions of recorded performances have been made (e.g., Erdely 1994).

Epic singing in Russia has also been studied in regard to the *byliny* (or *stariny*, 'old songs', as the singers called them). About 2500 records of these (with about 120 topics) exist, dating from the seventeenth century, though most are from the late nineteenth century, when scholars published important collections. The first manuscript collection with melodies was made in the mid-1700s (by Kirsha Danilov); sound recordings were made at the end of the 1800s. Once widespread in the 1500s and 1600s, *byliny* have a diverse historical content: most surviving examples are from the Kiev or Vladimir cycle and tell of heroes such as Il'ya Muromets. *Byliny* were brought to Russia by itinerant musicians in the late Middle Ages and survived best in northern Russia, where peasants were less oppressed by serfdom; there too, the style was mainly one of solo singing. Choral singing of *byliny* was common in parts of the north and among the Don and Terek Cossacks of southern Russia. As an active form, the *bylina* gradually gave way to historical songs after the 1700s.

The melodies of *byliny* rework tunes popularly known by singer and audience, but they are distinctively compressed. This convention of form distinguishes the *bylina* from other songs with similar melodies: "I won't sing a song, but I'll sing you an ancient verse, a Kievan *bylina*," one singer said (Astakhova 1938–1951). Good *bylina* singers always had a "special talent" for this form, immersed themselves in their content, and made creative changes in the text.

In the Soviet period, when song themes were severely modified and *noviny* (new songs celebrating Soviet life) became the order of the day, women singers of *byliny* enjoyed fame: A. M. Krukova from the White Sea area had a repertory that included more than two-thirds of all Russian epic subjects, and an indigent peasant woman from the River Pinega, M. D. Krivopolenova, was brought to Moscow at seventy-two years of age to astonish audiences with her art. The latter would become excited just before singing, but when she began her beloved *byliny* before an audience of thousands, she felt free. At certain points in her "cheerful" *byliny*, she would represent specific episodes with gestures. But in serious *byliny*, quite another mood overtook her: for instance, she would weep as she sang "How Prince Roman Lost His Wife" (Sokolov 1971).

The epic singer in Greece and Yugoslavia, in contrast, was invariably male, and sang heroic songs for a male audience. This was especially true with the Muslim singers of Bosnia, whose repertoire frequently consisted of thirty songs, one for each night of Ramadan (holy month of fasting), when men of a community would gather in the coffeehouse from dusk to listen to epic singing. The repertoire in the former Yugoslavia consisted of songs about late medieval heroes, such as Marko Kraljevic, or after World War II, partisans fighting Nazi invaders. The singer would accompany his singing on a one-stringed bowed lute (*gusle*), taking care to engage his audience in the plot of the song. In Greece, the main heroic cycle concerns the late medieval figure Digenis Akritas, and in Crete, especially, the singer accompanies his fifteen-syllable lines on the bowed *lyra*. The melodic line in both traditions is almost always narrow, within the range of a fifth or sixth, and the singer plays ornamental interludes at pauses in his singing.

The American scholars Milman Parry and Albert Lord visited Bosnia in the 1930s to record and study the technique of composing epic songs in order to understand how the *Iliad* and *Odyssey* of Homer were composed and communicated. The result was a collection of more than 2000 recorded songs, the best of which have been published in the series *Serbo-Croatian Heroic Songs*. The different versions were conveyed to these scholars in three ways: through singing, reciting, and dictating. The absence of errors in the last medium led Parry and Lord to believe that the *Iliad* and *Odyssey* texts as they survive today were dictated.

Strophic Song Forms

Strophic songs by far outnumber non-strophic and stichic forms. Structurally, songs are found in long single lines and two-line strophes, such as in Faroese ballads or Lithuanian *dainas*. Strophes also result from the free repetition of three long lines, as in some calendric songs (e.g., Romanian *colinde*) and game, harvest, and wedding songs. Three-line melodies proper often have a close tie to religious or lifecycle events, such as the sacred song at weddings in Tesin, Silesia, at the turn of the twentieth century.

Four-line melodies form the largest class for several reasons. The danced forms of the late Middle Ages came to have a strong influence on song forms. Epic songs, closely associated with feudal society, gave way to the ballad with its more domestic concerns of an expanding bourgeoisie. Since the ballad was originally danced in parts of Europe (e.g., Denmark) and still is (the Faroes), the stanza structure, sometimes with separated or interlaced refrains, became a standard form. At the same time, the preference for a rounded four-line tune, usually with one note per syllable, is paralleled in the Gregorian antiphon and the Protestant chorale, especially in north-central Europe, though in Eastern Europe ornamental types can be found, such as the song of parting that Bartók recorded in Hungary (Bartók 1981 [1925]) and the recitative-style melody noted from Eastern European Jews (Idelsohn 1914–1932).

Ballads

Balladry as a song form came to dominate from about 1350, spreading from France and the Low Countries to the rest of Western Europe. Though narrative song types may have been already present in many areas, ballads emerged as the preferred form of the middle and lower classes in the period 1300 to 1500. Formulaic themes, situations, images and language are present in both ballad and epic as important structural elements; but these formulas make ballads concise and reductive, whereas epics are expansive. Some ballads are historical in content; others deal with the supernatural, or with tragic situations of rivalry in love. In French, German, and Italian traditions, the lyric element tends to dominate over the ballad narrative. Spain has a large body of ballads (*romances*), quasi-historical like the cycle surrounding El Cid, the eleventh-century warrior whose exploits against the Moors gave rise to songs. Few Spanish *romances*, however, show cross-cultural affinities in content; the form, too, does not adopt the stanza pattern and is usually cast in hexameter couplets with a caesura in the middle of each line.

In content and style, Hungarian ballads owe a great deal to French and Walloon influence, while in the Balkans, ballads in Slovenia are closest to central European ballad traditions. Ukrainian ballads frequently draw on a common Slavic epic tradition with its decasyllabic line and non-stanzaic patterns of versification. The ballad in Britain, influenced by French and Scandinavian types in subject matter and style, alternates four-stress and three-stress lines. Ballads, finally, have interacted with other genres: apart from organic ties to epic tradition in Spain and Eastern Europe, ballads have been found as lullabies, laments, or children's games, and parodies of well-known ballads are known in modern times.

The popular ballad melody has influenced the formation of the stanza structure, the tune's points of emphasis in a four-lined type being the cadence at the end of the second and fourth lines. The normal rhyme occurs at the same junctures. The most popular melodic pattern in the British ballads, and those North American ballads that derive from them, is the non-recurrent ABCD (and ABCDE), which avoids the repetition of other common forms (e.g., ABAB). The pattern ABAC is the next most frequent, phrase A being separated from its identical self by the more prominent melody lines B and C. The refrains and commonplaces reveal the powerful influence of melody (and dance) on the poetics and overall strophic form. If traditional ballads were at one time, like epics, recreated anew in performance, modern singers now "memorize" rather than freely paraphrase them since ballads are comparatively short.

The contexts of ballad singing have been variable—from humble cottage to drawing room, from marketplace to concert hall, from tavern to local festival. In rural Portugal, the harvest is a special time for singing ballads (*romanceiros*) in a collective setting. In Slovenia, an unusual ballad-singing context was during a wake, beside the corpse, when laments and religious songs would also be sung. Traditional ballad singing is still vigorous in pockets of Europe, but the folk revival after World War II again sparked interest in these songs. New ballads, more often than not political or satirical in thrust, have added to the repertoire, and the revival concert or folk club now provide revitalized situations for ballad performance.

The most remarkable aspect of ballad performance is the objective stance of the singer, who, though emotionally involved in the events of the ballad plot, avoids injecting subjective opinion. This stance is central to the ballad aesthetic. It is rare that a singer overtly expresses emotion while singing traditional ballads, since he or she normally allows the events to speak for themselves. In recent times, however, singers have been known to interject spoken elements between stanzas to continue a part of the tale they may have forgotten. In later ballad traditions, especially from 1700 to 1850, the broadsheets (broadsides) and chapbooks (pocket books) sold at fairs and in the city streets throughout Europe recycled older ballads and added new ones. Ballads with a more subjective cast and explicit moral content are found in great quantities in the 1800s, and political ballads, known since the eighteenth century, have again flourished since the twentieth.

Lyric Songs

This category covers many song types used for different purposes and occasions. Their generally non-narrative content sets them apart from ballads and

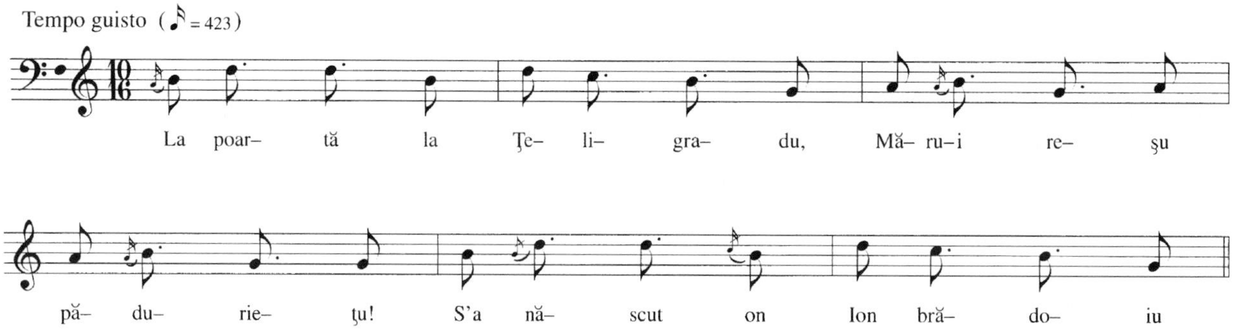

Tempo guisto (♪ = 423)

La poar– tă la Țe– li– gra– du, Mă– ru–i re– șu pă– du– rie– țu! S'a nă– scut on Ion bră– do– iu

Figure 1 A Romanian New Year's carol (*colinde*), a strophic, lyric song with verses of three lines set to three phrases of music in ABA form. After Bartók 1975: 142, #86a.

epics, and they may be embedded in rituals of the lifecycle or annual calendar. Wedding songs are especially important since the wedding alters the social structure of the community. Laments for the dead are often thought to be a separate genre because of contextual and stylistic features; but in Eastern Europe, laments were performed in the wedding to express the bride's fear of the perils ahead when she leaves her home. Before the 1917 revolution in Russia, professional weepers or criers—usually poor women, widows, or orphans—were specially invited to realize these fears in singing. Funeral laments, likewise, had parallels in the laments sung for departing soldiers or recruits. In modern times, Finnish Karelian singers have shown mastery of the older lament style. Albanians term the emotional lament "the lament by tears" and the more formal lament "the lament by voice." This conceptual division was observed in Ireland: the keen (Irish: *caoine*) beside the body was distinct from the poetic lament composed later.

Plowing, seedtime, and harvest provided the frame for many songs associated with seasonal activity. The symbols of fertility (seed, rake, threshing machine) entered songs of amorous and bawdy content. In France, plowing was accompanied by ritual *briolées*, farmer's cries urging on his team of horses, and plowmen may have felt the need to use protective magic in this formula. Harvest songs, however, suggest fertility. While reaping, female ballad singers (as in Portugal and Spain) sing ballads that include references to women's impregnation and pregnancy.

Seasonal songs such as carols sometimes incorporated older beliefs, like the English wassail at Christmastide (figure 1). But carols were once well known throughout the church year, at Easter as well as Christmas. The form of the medieval carol was related to continental forms such as the *rondeau*, *virelai*, and *ballade*, and to the Italian *laude spirituale*. The English carol is linked to the French *carole*, a dance song that was popular and courtly. From the 1300s, the carol seems to have become a festive song, as with boar's-head carols, in which the ceremonial carrying in of the head precedes ritual feasting; another type, like the *carole*, was associated with amorous games (e.g., "The Holly and the Ivy"). Religious carol texts may have been written by minor clerics who adapted their texts to popular melodies.

The carol in its older open, or processional, form is preserved in the May Day celebration of the hobbyhorse at Padstow, Cornwall. As the man inside an elaborately decorated hobbyhorse proceeds through the town, accompanied by a troupe who sing a "Morning Song" and a "Day Song," he and his companions stand still during the singing of stanzas and advance when the change to the burden (refrain) is made. The Padstow dance and song appear to be survivals of the medieval round dance and open procession, as the first lines of the chorus make clear ("With the merry ring, adieu the merry spring").

Love songs form the largest body of lyrical songs. Numerous as they are, they encompass a variety of themes: tragic and humorous, satirical and derisive, everything from the joys of physical love to the bitterness of betrayal. Almost every collection in Europe has a preponderance of such songs, though they have been less studied, on the whole, than narrative types. Because their forms are usually concise and flexible, lyric songs often merge with lullabies, wedding songs, and other types or genres. Many songs express a close or symbolic relationship with nature: with seasons (e.g., sun, moon, stars, wind, rain, snow), natural features (rocks, mountains, rivers, forests), birds (falcon, lark, nightingale, partridge, peacock, eagle, swan), animals (lion, bear, horse, wolf, fox, deer, fish), trees (oak, ash, holly, ivy, birch), plants (lily, rose, violet, rue, thyme, rosemary), and so on. But the symbols are not always interpreted in the same way. For instance, the swan in Russia symbolizes a bride; in Celtic countries, a supernatural creature.

Work songs split into two well-defined groups: those about a particular occupation (e.g., miners', soldiers', robbers' songs) and those accompanying actual labor (shrinking cloth, milking cows, rowing, hauling barges). The latter type has given way to the former as modern technology has assumed tasks formerly accomplished by hand. Scottish Highland *waulking* songs to accompany the shrinking of tweed had ritual aspects: no song could be repeated during the process, and the texts came from many quarters, including heroic lays and other work songs. Other such songs (e.g., milking songs) are meant to protect animals from supernatural forces. Of occupational songs that cover a wide range of types, miners' songs are among the oldest collected (the German *Bergreihen*, 1531).

Some song forms occur in a context of public competition among singers, such as the contests still known in the Basque country, Portugal, and Corsica. Other regional styles ask for command of a particular formal type: Portuguese *fado*, Spanish *cante jondo*, the Russian *chastushka*, or the Norwegian *stev*. Portuguese *fado*, resembling the song duels of Minho and the Azores, migrated from the countryside to city cafes in developing its somber themes, couched in musical arrangements showing strong Latin American influence. *Cante jondo*'s development is complex, but traditional performance demands a high degree of skill in singing, dancing, and guitar playing from members of the performing group (*cuadro*). The Russian *chastushka* is an instrumental-vocal genre in short, single-stanza couplets, usually with four lines and accompanied by accordion or *balalaika*. It can be performed solo, as a duet, or by a chorus. The *stev* in Norway (or *nystev*, 'new *stev*', originating about 1800) has four lines of nearly identical couplets and archaic melodies. The *stev* is performed in a parlando-rubato style with scope for variation, but has an asymmetrical rhythmic mode with a basic unit of one short beat followed by a longer one.

The musical features of lyric songs vary from region to region, context to context, and singer to singer. It is therefore difficult to reduce this mass of material to any single, unified, or convincing arrangement that covers the continent. Scholars have usually dealt with lyric songs within a study of a community's repertoire as a whole, or as falling within a particular context or occasion (e.g., wedding songs). The range of such songs across the sub-continent in music, text, context, and performance is astounding and is frequently dependent on local taste.

—Adapted from an article by James Porter

Bibliography

Astakhova, A. M., ed 1938–1951. *Bylini severa*. Moscow and Leningrad: Gos. izdatelstvo Karelo-finskoi.

Bartók, Béla. 1975. *Rumanian Folk Music*. Vol 4 ed. Benjamin Suchoff. The Hague: Martinus Nijhoff.

———. 1981 [1925]. *The Hungarian Folk Song*. Edited by Benjamin Suchoff. Translated by M. D. Calvocoressi. Albany: State University of New York Press.

Bartók, Béla, and Albert Bates Lord. 1951. *Serbo-Croatian Folk Songs*. New York: Columbia University Press.

Beissinger, Margaret H. 1991. *The Art of the Lautar: The Epic Tradition of Romania*. New York: Garland Publishing.

Entwistle, William. 1951 [1939]. *European Balladry*. Oxford: Clarendon Press.

Erdely, Stephen. 1994. *The Music of Four Serbo-Croatian Heroic Songs: A Study*. New York: Garland Publishing.

Idelsohn, A. Z. 1914–1932. *Hebräische-orientalischer Melodienschatz*. Leipzig: Breitkopf und Härtel.

Lineva, Evgeniia Eduardovna Paporits. 1893. *Russian Folksongs as Sung by the People and Peasant Wedding Ceremonies Customary in Northern and Central Russia*. Chicago: C. F. Summey.

———. 1905–1912. *The Peasant Songs of Great Russia as They Are in the Folk's Harmonization*. 2 vols. St Petersburg: Imperial Academy of Science.

Lord, Albert Bates. 1960. *The Singer of Tales*. Cambridge: Harvard University Press.

Notopoulos, James A. 1959. *Modern Greek Heroic Oral Poetry*. Notes, "Modern Greek Heroic Oral Poetry and Its Relevance to Homer." Folkways Records FE4468 LP disk.

Parry, Milman, Albert B. Lord, and David E. Bynum eds. 1953–. *Serbo-Croatian Heroic Songs*. Cambridge: Harvard University Press.

Sokolov, Y. M. 1971. *Russian Folklore*. Translated by Catherine Ruth Smith. Detroit: Folklore Associates.

Tirén, Karl. 1942. *Die lappische Volksmusik*. Stockholm: H. Geber.

Music Cultures of Europe

Only in the twentieth century was the political map of Europe divided consistently into nation-states. For most of history, parts of Europe were divided into hundreds of tiny principalities and city-states, while other parts were united into huge, multiethnic empires. This much longer history undercuts the simplistic view of European music as divided into many national musics. Some musical styles have a national character and are expressive of national identity. But others maintain local, regional, or minority identities. The same or similar musical styles, customs, and instruments can be common to ethnically distinct neighbors, reflecting long histories of shared cultural experience within far-flung empires. And some aspects of musical life—strophic songs, the structure of instrumental dance tunes, calendar and lifecycle customs, and professional art music—link many far-flung traditions in a pan-European web.

Piotr Parzyszek plays violin and Stanisław Ptasiński plays a three-row, folk treadle accordion (*harmonia trzyrzędowa pedałowa*), Mińsk Mazowiecki, Poland, 2004. *Photo by Jacek Jackowski.*

Transnational Ethnic Groups

The European political landscape consists of many small nation-states that tend to be viewed as ethnically homogeneous. In fact, few are, or ever were. They contain minority groups from neighboring countries, such as Swedes in Finland and Turks in Greece; a mix of ethnicities, as in Russia or Bosnia-Hercegovina; minorities lacking their own state, such as the Basques of Spain and France; and pan-European minorities, including Jews and Roma (Gypsies). For transnational ethnic minorities, music is a marker of ethnic and cultural difference. It expresses a distinctive cultural identity, which becomes highly meaningful when that identity is suppressed, censored, or persecuted by the mainstream. For certain minorities, including the Saami of the Arctic, the Basques of the Iberian Peninsula, and the Celtic peoples of northwestern Europe, singing songs gives new life to ancient languages in danger of being lost, and affords a sense of identity distinct from that of the nation-state in which they find themselves. Here we present articles on the music of two transnational groups: the Roma in Eastern Europe and the Basque in Western Europe.

A Romani musician plays a shawm at a market in Thessaloniki, Greece, 1993.
Photo by Terry E. Miller.

Romani (Gypsy) Music

For more than five hundred years, Roma in Eastern Europe have been professional musicians, playing for non-Romani peasants for remuneration in taverns and at weddings, baptisms, circumcisions, fairs, village dances, and other events. This professional niche, primarily for male instrumentalists, requires Roma to know and creatively interact with local repertoires. A nomadic way of life, often enforced upon Roma through harassment and prejudice, gave them opportunities to enlarge their repertoires and become multimusical and multilingual.

In addition to nomadic Roma, numerous sedentary Roma in major European cities professionally play urban folk, classical, and/or popular music. In Hungary, Russia, and Spain, certain forms of Romani music became national music, veritable emblems of the country. The music that professional Romani musicians play for their own people may or may not differ from the music they play for others. Many Roma are not professional musicians, but have their own music. All these groups have migrated within Europe, to varying degrees.

The noun *Rom* (plural *Roma*), rather than the more common English label, *Gypsy*, is used here because of its political connotations. The term *Gypsy* is usually an outsider's term, with strongly negative connotations, which derive from the false belief that these people's ancestors came from Egypt. Roma distinguish themselves by names describing region, occupation, religion, and dialect. *Roma* became a unifying term in the 1990s, as political consciousness was mobilized through unions, political parties, conferences, and congresses. In all these forums, music has played an important role in symbolizing Rom creativity and affirming Romani contributions to European culture.

Neither one worldwide nor one pan-European Romani music exists, despite an emerging awareness of ethnic unity. A Finnish Romani song may have more in common with an ethnic Finnish song than with a Greek Romani song, reflecting five centuries of coterritorial musical traffic. In contrast, some stylistic and performance elements, such as the propensity to improvise, are perhaps common to many European Romani musics.

Linguistic evidence shows that Romani ancestors migrated from northwestern India in the eleventh century. Romani, the language of Roma, is descended from Sanskrit and closely related to Hindi.

By C.E. 1500, Roma were established throughout Europe, where some settled and others remained nomadic.

In Europe, curiosity about Roma quickly gave way to hatred and discrimination. From the fourteenth to the nineteenth centuries in the Romanian principalities of Wallachia and Moldavia, Roma were slaves owned by noblemen, monasteries, and the state; they were sold, bartered, and flogged, and even their marriages were regulated.

This persecution continued through the twentieth century. In the 1930s, it escalated with the Nazis' rise to power. Roma faced a campaign of extermination only now being investigated: more than six hundred thousand—one-fifth to one-fourth of all Roma—were murdered. Beginning in the 1990s, harassment and violence toward Roma increased. In Eastern Europe, political and human rights activism among Roma has increased, particularly since the 1989 revolutions and the subsequent rise of scapegoating of Roma and violence against them. On a more positive note, since 1989 European Romani music festivals—some international—have been held in Austria, Bulgaria, the Czech Republic, France, Hungary, Poland, Macedonia, and Switzerland.

Hungary

There are three major groups of Roma in Hungary: 300,000* Romungre, who are urban and sedentary and speak Hungarian; 100,000 Vlach Roma, who were nomadic until the early twentieth century and speak Romani; 35,000 Boyash, who speak a dialect of Romanian. These groups neither intersocialize nor intermarry, and their musics differ markedly: Romungre music is professional and instrumental, whereas Vlach Romani music is vocal and nonprofessional; research on Boyash music is in its beginning stages.

Romungre are so famous in Europe for their professional string bands that many people mistakenly believe that this is the only type of Romani music. In the nineteenth century, they captured Western classical composers' attention, toured the best European concert halls, and became the representatives of

---

* Population numbers for Roma vary greatly depending on the source; the figures quoted in this article should be regarded as rough estimates.

Figure 1 A Romani string band performs in a restaurant, Bugak, Hungary, 1996.
Photo by Terry E. Miller.

Hungarian national music. In the eighteenth century, Panna Czinka (d. 1772) became the first well-known Romani violinist and bandleader, one of the few women to enter this profession. In her band, one violin played melody, and the other (the *kontras*) played harmonic accompaniment in a repeated rhythmic pattern; the other instruments were a double bass and a cimbalom (a trapezoidal struck dulcimer)—a combination still popular (figure 1). Ensembles like Czinka's, drawn from members of one family, were (and are) common, and players acquired their skills informally at home. Czinka's band had the patronage of a landowner who provided a house, land, and a red uniform every three years.

In the late 1700s, the *verbunkos*, a recruiting dance, became the characteristic Romungre genre. *Verbunkos* tunes, usually derived from folk songs, are distinguished by rich ornamentation, also a feature of European classical music, being partly improvised even in written works. Traditional song lines are elaborated with scalar patterns including augmented seconds between the third and fourth and between the sixth and seventh degrees of the scale. Augmented seconds are less evident in contemporary versions, in which major and minor scales are more common. The *verbunkos* scale has been termed the Gypsy scale—a gross generalization of a localized practice. The most famous Romani *verbunkos* composer, János Bihari (d. 1827), was a violinist and bandleader who played at royal military events and toured every important city in Central Europe.

From the mid nineteenth century to the early twentieth, Roma helped disseminate a new genre, the Hungarian popular art song (*nóta*). Songs of this genre were always harmonized, by piano on the printed page or Romani stringed ensembles in perfor-

mance. Texts reflected lyrical love themes. *Nóta* can be divided into two groups: the slow, rhythmically free *hallgató* and the 2/4 czardas (*csárdás*). Romani bands applied the *verbunkos* formulas to art songs, creating overnight hits, and the public clamored for their repeated performance. During this era, the populace accorded virtuosic Romani performers great respect. Aristocrats learned from them, made music with them, and even gave them their daughters in marriage. Because of their professional niche, Hungarian Roma creatively molded the popular repertoire and interacted dynamically with Hungarian folk music. The music became Romani just as much as it was Hungarian music and played by Hungarian Roma as their own.

The popularity of Romungre music remains strong. In the 1930s, a school for gifted Romani children was created, and by the 1960s, Romungre professional musicians numbered about eight thousand. The modern repertoire of urban bands includes popular art songs, folk songs, *verbunkos* and czardas music, selections from operas and operettas, international dance music (such as polkas and waltzes), international folk songs, and jazz. Ensembles string short tunes together, starting with the slowest and ending with the fastest. Their style of performance is so standardized that any good musician can sit in with any band, yet it is so individualized that bandleaders can easily distinguish among performers. What has been called the essential ants'-nest bustle in the music is achieved by heterophony, that is, two or more instruments simultaneously playing the melody with variant ornamentation.

Vlach Romani music is primarily nonprofessional and vocal, and is performed by men and women. Hungarians rarely perform or listen to Vlach Romani music. Songs are divided into two categories, slow and dance. Slow songs (*loki djili*) have a descending structure (perhaps an influence from Hungarian folk music), a range of more than an octave, major or minor tonality, and four-line melodies. They are performed parlando-rubato 'robbed speaking'—singing with a speechlike variable beat—and with interpolated exclamations, such as *hej*, *de*, and *jaj*. Unlike Romungre music, but like Hungarian folk songs, Vlach Romani songs do not have elaborate ornamentation. The melody of a song is highly variable; the singer has in mind an ideal tune, which may take a different shape from verse to verse. Vlach Roma compose songs from a limited stock of melodic formulas. Occasions for singing include in-group Romani events, such as weddings, baptisms, departures for military service, funerals, *mulatshagos* (drinking and singing celebrations), and daily life. Texts, usually in Romani but occasionally in Hungarian, are improvised and deal with the pain of life, poverty, imprisonment, and love, and make formalized statements about what it is to be a Rom. Romani singers still perform Hungarian ballads, which have died out in non-Romani contexts. Though these songs have been preserved during decades of industrialization and collectivism, texts, melodies, and performance contexts have undergone changes in the direction of the Romani *loki djili*.

Vlach Roma do not usually play instruments but dance to duple-meter songs (*khelimaski djili*), sung with sounds imitating instruments. Vocables are rolled (sung rhythmically) and backed up with oral double-bassing, short, exclaimed syncopated vocables, sung on upbeats. Singers make the bassing sound by blowing into their hands or buzzing their lips. They and sometimes the audience snap fingers, clap, drum on water cans, and tap spoons, creating a dense rhythmic texture.

As part of the urban revival of rural music in the 1970s, Romani youth formed bands such as Ando Drom, Fracilor, Kalyi Jag, and Romafolk and began performing for non-Roma. The most famous of the bands, Kalyi Jag, performs mainly Vlach Rom music with concert harmonizations and arrangements. The 1981 National Gathering of Romani Groups and the 1990 Ethnic Folk Music Gala have contributed to the popularization of Vlach Romani music.

Serbia

In the early twenty-first century, estimates of the Romani population in Serbia range from 100,000 to 500,000. The earliest evidence of Romani music in the region is found in the fifteenth-century archives of Dubrovnik, Croatia. In 1828, the most prominent musician at the court of Serbian Prince Miloš

Obrenović was a Romani *zurna* (keyless oboe) player. During the Ottoman period, Roma facilitated the spread of musical styles. Romani musicians in Vojvodina in the north primarily played violin and bagpipes until the 1930s, when they became heavily involved in *tamburica* (orchestra of long-necked, plucked lutes), formed on the model of Hungarian Romani string bands. Rural Romani musicians developed new performative techniques, which have become standard. The trend-setting Radio Beograd orchestra, formed in the 1930s, recruited the best Rom *tamburaši* (*tamburica* players) from the cafés and promoted musical literacy. Roma continue to play important roles in professional *tamburica* music, but since the 1960s, their repertoires have been affected by the popularity of newly composed folk music (*novokomponovana narodna muzika*), influenced by popular urban styles.

In the interplay of Turkish-influenced style, marketing, and Romani identity, Roma have played a vital role in facilitating interaction among distinct musical genres: village folk music, urban folk music, popular music, and *novokompanovana narodna muzika*. Serbian Romani singer Šaban Bajramović popularized the song "*Dželem, Dželem*" ('I walked and walked'), composed at the 1971 World Romani Congress by Jarko Jovanović; it became the Romani anthem. Perhaps because of its theme of travel, or because of its style—a combination of Turkish-influenced vocal improvisation, unpretentious emotionalism, and urban salon accompaniment typical of old city songs—it now exists in many variants throughout Europe.

In southern Serbia, the brass-band tradition arose in the 1940s. Romani bands are professional and play a Turkish-influenced repertoire. They are found throughout Serbia. Their instrumentation usually includes three flügelhorns, three or four euphoniums, one tuba, and one percussionist playing a bass drum with a cymbal mounted on top, though southern bands often employ clarinets, a *tapan* (double-headed cylindrical drum), and a *tarabuka* (goblet drum). Younger Romani musicians are increasingly playing modern instruments and adopting the *novokompanovana narodna muzika* style, and—like singer Šaban Bajramović and accordionist Bata Kanda—they are achieving popularity outside Gypsy communities.

Macedonia

Roma have a virtual monopoly of southern Balkan professional ensembles consisting of one or two *zurlas* (Macedonian *surla*, Bulgarian *zurna*), a double-reed conical-bore instrument, plus one or two *tapani* (Bulgarian *tŭpan*), double-headed cylindrical drums. Currently, *zurla* and *tapan* ensembles play at large public events, as in the former Yugoslav Republic of Macedonia, the Macedonian province of Greece, and the Bulgarian region of Pirin. *Zurla* and *tapan* ensembles vitally coexist with amplified modern bands because of their ritual function, their role in playing traditional dance music, and their symbolic association with Romani identity. In the 1960s in Macedonia, *zurla* and *tapan* players were even hired by radio and government-sponsored ensembles.

Zurla and *tapan* playing is reserved for men and transmitted along kin lines. In the villages around Galičnik, western Macedonia, most *zurla* players are from a single Romani family. Training takes place on the job, from elder to younger, and repertoire and technique are learned by listening and watching. Typically, one *zurla* has the melody while the other drones. Occasionally, both *zurlas* play in unison, in octaves or, more recently, in parallel thirds, and the lead *zurla* player does free rhythmic improvisations and metric improvisations. These devices alternate for varying lengths of times. Size of repertoire and technical virtuosity distinguish good *zurla* players. Ornamentation consists of rapid and even finger trills, mordents, and grace notes. Master *tapan* players improvise rhythmically and texturally, using the sounds of two drumheads to create complex polyrhythmic interactions between the *zurla* player and the *tapan* player.

Roma were the majority of performers in urban professional *čalgija* ensembles, which flourished until World War II playing Ottoman-derived vocal and instrumental music in a heterophonic style based on the *makam* system, emphasizing innovation and improvisation [For more on the *makam*, see TURKEY: AN OVERVIEW in the Middle East section of volume 2]. Each ensemble originally consisted of a violin, an *'ud* (plucked, short-necked, fretless lute) a *kanun* (plucked zither) a *dajre* (a frame drum with jingles) and a singer, but grew to feature a *džumbuš* (long-necked plucked lute with a skin face) a clarinet, a *truba* (trumpet) an accordion, and a *tarabuka* (goblet-shaped drum). Families of sedentary Roma have played *čalgija* for generations. Though the tradition is predominantly male, female professionals, usually relatives of male musicians, played for female guests in segregated Muslim events, and their ensemble consisted of a violin, a *dajre*, and sometimes an *'ud*, and the women accompanied their own singing. Women and young male Roma were hired to perform solo dancing in coffeehouses and at weddings. Currently, women are among the best singers, and Rom dance is almost exclusively female.

DISC
❶
TRACK
17

The *čalgija* repertoire included light Turkish classical pieces, rural folk music, and urban popular songs in the languages of the Ottoman city; it flourished in contexts such as coffeehouses, weddings, and other life-cycle celebrations, fairs, and saints-day celebrations. Profound changes in the 1960s, such as the migration of rural populations into urban centers, the spread of Western harmony and instruments, and the introduction of amplification, affected the style and texture of *čalgija*. Its tradition continues with electrified bands consisting of a clarinet and/or a saxophone, an accordion and/or a synthesizer, a guitar and/or a *džumbuš*, an electric bass, and a drum set and/or a *tarabuka*, plus a vocalist.

An important part of the repertoire is *čoček* in 2/4 (sometimes divided 3–3–2), 7/16 (3–2–2), or 9/16 (2–2–2–3), marked by *mane*, an improvised free-rhythmic exploration of the *makam*, using stock motifs and figures, played over a metric ostinato. The dance *čoček* is solo and improvised, and utilizes torso and hand movements. Until the 1970s, both men and women danced the *čoček*, but separately. Women danced in homes to the accompaniment of a female *dajre* player and women's singing; to dance for men was considered crude. By the 1980s, women were dancing *čoček* in public, and sexual segregation in dance was less pronounced.

The Rom singer most recognized by Roma and non-Roma alike is Esma Redžepova, born in Skopje. As part of the Stevo Teodosievski Ensemble (which included Rom clarinetist Medo Čun and ethnic Macedonians like Stevo), she was the first popularizer of songs in Romani among non-Roma, via concerts and recordings. In the late 1950s, her trademark song, "Čhaje Šukarija," took Yugoslavia by storm— heard via concerts, records, radio, and television. She toured the world, singing in packed halls and stadiums. Her renditions were fiery, emotional, and dramatic to the point of acting and dancing the text. In 1976, she and her husband, Stevo Teodosievski, were crowned "King and Queen of Romani Music" at the World Romani Congress in India.

Bulgaria

Currently home to about nine hundred thousand Roma (half Muslim, half Eastern Orthodox), Bulgaria has a musical history of Romani professionalism since the fourteenth century. Instrumental music is transmitted in the male line with informal on-the-job instruction. The most typical Bulgarian Romani instrumental genre, *kjuček*, can be found in two metric patterns: *Turski kjuček* (in duple meter) and *Ciganski kjuček* (in 9/8). Both sexes sing, but dancing is a female specialty. Unlike the situation in Macedonia and Serbia, Bulgarian Roma play traditional village instruments such as the *gŭdulka* 'bowed lute', the *gajda* 'bagpipe', the *kaval* 'end-blown flute', and the *tambura* 'plucked long-necked lute', in addition to Western European instruments. For example, Roma bear and monkey trainers in Bulgaria play a vertically held three-stringed pear-shaped bowed lute (*gŭdulka*, in Macedonia *ḱemene*). Many make their own instruments. In addition to playing dance music, to which the animal performs, they play and sing improvised historical ballads or humorous songs, sometimes providing social commentary. The Bulgarian socialist government strictly regulated animal trainers' travel and earnings, but since 1989, it has eased restrictions, and animal trainers now work in parks and playgrounds of major cities. Romani *gajda* players were and are well respected throughout Thrace and Strandža.

The most important genre of Romani-shaped contemporary Bulgarian music is wedding music, which developed along new lines in the 1970s, when amplification was introduced into village settings. In wedding bands, Roma often play with Bulgarian Turks and/or ethnic Bulgarians. What defines wedding music is a combination of instrumentation, repertoire, and style. Wedding music is also performed at baptisms, house-warmings, soldier-send-off celebrations, and other major ritual events in village and urban contexts. Instrumentation typically consists of a clarinet, a saxophone, an accordion, an electric bass guitar, and a trap-drum set. Less often one finds a violin or traditional village instruments. The repertoire consists mainly of songs and village dances with a Thracian emphasis. It also includes, especially at Rom events, *kjučeks*, whose tunes are composed by wedding musicians, inspired by folk and popular music from Serbia, Macedonia, Greece, and Turkey, film scores from the West, cartoon music, Middle Eastern music, Indian film music, and other sources. The emphasis is on originality and cleverness. Above all else, the ability to improvise is valued. The style of wedding singers emphasizes wide vibrato and extensive ornamentation. The unquestioned guru of wedding music is Ivo Papazov, a Turkish Rom, who founded the band Trakia in 1974. For two decades, he was the highest-paid wedding musician in the country, being in such demand that people waited for months to engage him. Now he tours internationally.

From the early 1970s until the 1989 revolution, all music specifically identified as Romani or in the Romani language was prohibited from media and public performance as part of the government's program to suppress minority ethnic identities. This prohibition included the playing and dancing of *kjučeks*. The *zurna* and the *tŭpan* were excluded from government-sponsored folk music schools. As part of the (anti-Turkish, anti-Muslim) Bulgarization campaign of the 1980s, *zurna* playing was prohibited in private and public settings. It survived, however, in unofficial contexts. Fines were levied, and licenses to perform were revoked, when violations occurred. Romani musical forms thrived anyway—in private settings and through cassette distribution. Since the 1989 revolution, Romani music has been revitalized and rehabilitated. Many new groups, such as Džipsi Aver, have formed, and annual festivals of Romani music have been held since 1993 in Stara Zagora. Romani influences are prominent in the commercially successful pop/folk fusion genre *chalga*. Compact discs with Romani music are being released by private companies, and experimentation with hybrid styles, such as rap, is strong.

France

The current French Romani musical scene is dominated by Manouch jazz, a style of playing that crystallized in the 1920s with the popularity of guitarist Django Reinhardt (1910–1953). Django's father led a family orchestra (violin, piano, guitar, and contrabass) that played popular music professionally for dances and in restaurants. The family was extremely poor, and Django, who was practically illiterate and never learned to read music, did not acquire his own instrument, a banjo-guitar, until he was twelve, when he began working professionally in dance halls. Badly burned in a fire in 1928, he lost the use of two fingers of his left hand. After two years of therapy, he devised a unique fingering system to overcome his handicap. In 1934, he and violinist Stephane Grappelli (1908–1997) founded the ensemble later known as Quintette du Hot Club de France, which recorded many albums. Reinhardt became an international celebrity and inspired numerous imitators. In 1946, he played in England and Switzerland and toured the United States as a soloist with Duke Ellington's band, playing amplified guitar for the first time. Called the genius of the guitar and blessed with an exceptional ear, he had a melodic and harmonic inventiveness that revamped the role of the guitar in jazz groups. His repertoire included blues, swing, waltzes, and rhythm and blues.

Despite his fame, Django remained a member of the Manouch community, a Romani subgroup. Some critics have condemned him for the Romani quality of his playing (usually labeled romantic), but others credit him with successfully blending Romani elements and jazz. Django's sons Lousson and Babik are also fine guitarists, and many other Roma—

including Bireli Langrene (b. 1966), Boulou Ferré (b. 1951), and Elios Ferré (b. 1956)—have followed in his style in Belgium, France, Germany, and the Netherlands. The Rosenberg Trio, consisting of Stochelo Rosenberg and his cousins, is popular in the Netherlands. Indeed, Manouch jazz has developed a following throughout Western Europe, and festivals of Romani jazz have been held regularly in France.

—Adapted from an article by Carol Silverman

Bibliography

Baumann, Max Peter, ed. 1996. *Music of the Roma: Ethnicity, Identity and Multiculturalism*. Special Issue of *The World of Music* 38(1).

Blau, Dick, Charles and Angeliki Keil, and Steven Feld. 2002. *Bright Balkan Morning: Romani Lives and the Power of Music in Greek Macedonia*. Middletown Conn.: Wesleyan University Press.

Dunin, Elsie. 1973. "Čoček as a Ritual Dance Among Gypsy Women." *Makedonski Folklor* VI(12):193–197.

Lemon, Alaina. 2000. *Between Two Fires: Gypsy Performance and Romani Memory*. Durham N.C.: Duke University Press.

Malvinni, David. 2004. *The Gypsy Caravan: From Real Roma to Imaginary Gypsies in Western Music and Film*. New York: Routledge.

Pettan, Svanibor. 2002. *Rom Musicians in Kosovo: Interaction and Creativity*. Budapest: Institute for Musicology.

Sárosi, Bálint. 1978 [1970]. *Gypsy Music*. Translated by Fred Macnicol. Budapest: Corvina.

Silverman, Carol. 2008. *Performing Diaspora: Cultural Politics of Balkan Romani Music*. New York: Oxford University Press.

Van de Port, Mattijs. 1998. *Gypsies, Wars, and Other Instances of the Wild*. Amsterdam: Amsterdam University Press.

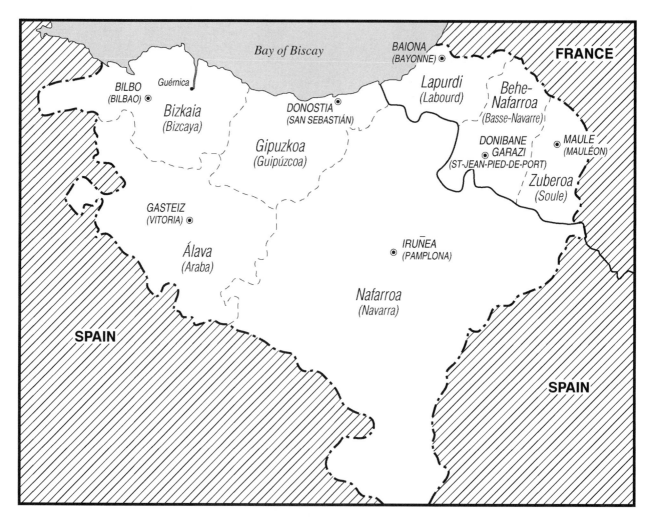

The Basques Provinces. Basque names are on top; Spanish and French names are in parenthesis.

Basque Music

Basque territory lies in southern France and north-western Spain along the Bay of Biscay and the western foothills of the Pyrenees. The origin of the Basque people, who number about one hundred fifty thousand in France and 850,000 in Spain, is obscure. Their language, Euskara, is not Indo-European, but derives from that of the Vascones and Aquitani of Roman times, groups whose successors resisted in turn Visigoths, Franks, Normans, and Moors. Historically important Basques include Saint Ignatius of Loyola (1491–1556), founder of the Jesuit Order, and Saint Francis Xavier (1506–1552), Jesuit missionary to India and Japan.

Basque national aspirations, language, and customs began to be recorded in the 1800s. During the Spanish Civil War (1936–1939), the German bombing and burning of the city of Guérnica—the original site of the Basque parliament until the late 1900s—inspired Picasso's famous painting of the massacre (now housed in the Centro de Arte Reina Sofía in Madrid). Many Basques emigrated to the Americas after World War II, and a Basque national government operates in Paris and New York.

Musical Structures and Styles

Diverse musical practices constitute Basque music. Most melodies collected in the nineteenth century—when the study of Basque music began—were tonal, with the majority in a major key, but about twenty-five percent were modal. The most popular dance-song type, *zortziko* 'made of eights', whose name refers to the eight steps of the dances it accompanies, has a meter consisting of two different asymmetric patterns—a duple one (2 + 3)/8 and a triple one (2 + 3 + 3)/8—whose combination creates an even more complex asymmetric meter. Jean Bergara, the famous Basque flutist of Saint Pée, said, "I don't know why, but I feel we are born with this rhythm." The rhythm has become symbolic of Basque identity, and the national anthem, José María Iparraguirre's "*Guernikako Arbola*" (1853) 'The Tree of Guérnica' is a *zortziko* (figure 1).

Song strophes have a three-part structure, ABA, often stretched to AABA. The stanza-and-chorus format, common in France and Spain, is rare in Basque country. The syllabic style, in which each syllable of the lyrics corresponds to just one note of the melody, allows many borrowings: the same words can be sung to different melodies and timbres, and the same melody can be put to different words.

Versifiers (*bertsulari*) take pride in their ability to improvise new verses (*bertsu*) for an existing tune. They improvise on informal social occasions and hotly contested organized competitions. They use four-verse structures, depending on whether the stanzas consist of four couplets (as in the *zortziko*) or five couplets (as in the *hamarreko*) and on whether the couplets contain thirteen or eighteen syllables. The former, divided into seven- and six-syllable hemistichs, are called *ttiki* ('small') lines; the latter, divided into ten- and eight-syllable hemistichs, are called *haundi* ('big') lines.

Another common form, *bederatzi puntuko*, consists of nine couplets or lines, all with the same rhyme, of varying numbers of syllables: 13 (7 + 6), 12 (7 + 5), 13 (7 + 6), 13 (7 + 6), 6, 6, 6, 6, and 12 (7 + 5). *Bertsulari* love to improvise on such formally complex structures and use subtle mnemonic devices to do so.

The role of musical improviser is becoming increasingly professionalized, and schools have been founded for the best improvisers to teach their techniques. The themes on which they improvise are quite varied. Some take the form of a dialogue—such as between two friends with opposing political views—which can be serious or satirical. When the *bertsulari* improvise alone, the theme is more literary. *Bertsulari* must sing in a throat voice and a declamatory manner, so the words can be understood. The syllabic character of the singing is indispensable for this purpose.

Musical Instruments

Most traditional Basque instruments are wind instruments. One of the most important, the *txistu*, is a three-holed duct flute, usually in the key of F, made of ebony, boxwood, or plastic, encircled by metal bands, with a metal mouthpiece. Flutists (*txistulari*) usually accompany dances solo, playing the *txistu* in the left hand while striking with a stick a snare drum (*danbolin*) suspended from the elbow. Groups of flutists may form bands. They also play in small groups of *txistu*, *silbote* (a side-blown wooden flute), and *atabal* (a drum larger than the *danbolin*). In Soule, the combination of *txirula*, a small, shrill

Figure 1 "*Guernikako Arbola*" 'The Tree of Guérnica', the Basque National Anthem, in *zortziko* rhythm and with piano accompaniment. Music and text composed by José María Iparraguirre in 1853.

wooden flute in the key of C, and *ttunttun*, a carved hollow wooden-bodied drum across which six strings are stretched and struck with a wooden stick, is considered an ancestor of the modern *txistu*-drum duo.

In addition to a single musician playing two instruments, duets of two musicians are also common. Since the 1980s, the *trikitixa*, a duet consisting of a diatonic accordion, a Basque drum, and singing, has been extremely popular. The musicians play for parades and chain dances, including *jotas*, fandangos, and *arinarins*, which everyone in Basque country knows. Another duet, from Alaba in Nafarroa, consists of a drum with a *gaita*, a double-reed instrument of Arab origin with eight finger holes. A third duet, played in Bizkaia, combines a frame drum (*pandero*) with *alboka*, two pipes each with a single reed and a horn at both ends, one acting as a bell, the other as a mouthpiece. Finally, the *txalaparta* is a percussion instrument made of two wooden boards about one and a half meters long and struck by two musicians with wooden sticks.

As with versifiers, playing traditional instruments is becoming a profession, and these instruments are gradually beginning to be taught in conservatories in France and Spain. Their use is governed mainly by

federations that organize annual contests, which declare one musician a champion and stimulate musical interest among other Basques.

Musical Contexts, Politics, and Identity

Traditional musicians are in great demand for carnivals, masquerades, *pastorales souletines* (popular theater of Soule), and village celebrations (figure 2). All the traditional instruments are present during Basque independence celebrations, which take place annually during October in Bilbao, attracting almost two hundred thousand participants, and for parades on behalf of the Basque language and the schools that teach it.

Numerous folkloric groups and many bands enliven local festivities. The Basque choral movement, one of the most active in Europe, takes the form of the *oxote*, eight unaccompanied male voices. In Gipuzkoa and Bizkaia, several vocal-harmony groups work with instrumentalists. In Soule, an entire village (different each year) presents a *pastorale*, a play accompanied by songs and dances. Supposedly descended from medieval mystery plays, they have been documented in performance since the 1500s.

Figure 2 Musicians play flutes and drums in morning preparation for the Festival of the Assumption, San Sebastián, 2005.
Photo by Sean Williams.

Every summer, more than five thousand people swarm into Soule's narrow valleys to participate in open-air, three-hour-long performances.

The versifiers' traditional improvisational art became popular in 1935, when Manuel de Lekuona published *Aozko Literature*, the first work devoted to the versifier's art, and Jose "Aitzol" Ariztimuño organized the first versifying championship. The contest was intended to be an annual one, but on 17 October 1936, Aitzol was shot by Francisco Franco's soldiers in Hernani (Gipuzkoa). Use of the Basque language was outlawed, as was any demonstration of Basque culture. But Basque music became synonymous with resistance: the Basque choral group Eresoinka sang throughout the world, and the dance group Dindirri performed throughout Basque lands, flouting the silence imposed on them. Singer Xabier Lete also defied Franco's censorship. For twenty-four years, despite the official cultural blackout, versifiers continued improvising in secret and in isolated villages. In 1960, a third championship occurred, organized just months after the birth in Bilbao in 1959 of Euskadi Ta Askatasuna (ETA, 'Basque Nation and Freedom'), a secret, armed group that fought the Spanish dictatorship for Basque independence. Versifiers reappeared in public as Basques reclaimed their identity, and versifying championships took place in 1962, 1965, and 1967.

In 1968, armed conflict between the Spanish Civil Guard and ETA resulted in further repressing and silencing versifiers, who could not organize championships until 1980. Since then, championships have occurred every four years. The competi-

tions reinforce the traditionally vital role of versifiers in the call to reclaim Basque identity. Versifiers regularly pay homage to Basque political prisoners—numbering about seven hundred—incarcerated in French and Spanish prisons. The *gaita* was heard in the Baigorri Valley at the burial of a member of Iparretarrak (the armed independence movement operating within France), and the *txalaparta* performs at the funerals of ETA militants.

The recording industry allows traditional singers like Peio Serbielle and Bena Achiary, and groups like Oskorri, to reach a wider audience, but it also puts out hard rock, trash, funk, and reggae-style music by Basque bands like Negu Gorriak and Hertzainak, who practice what might be called an art of citation. The renowned Basque accordionist Kepa Junkera uses a number of traditional instruments in his performances both inside and outside of Spain; in addition, he collaborates with traditional musicians from other cultures that have suffered political repression, such as the Irish.

Traditional music in this sense is not a reservoir of musical styles from times past. The frequent reuse of old forms in new guises feeds a Basque music that is not simply a collection of structural properties that have an academic stamp of authenticity. Instead, in varying situations, at particular times and places, and within shifting contexts, musicians perform music for listeners who recognize it as Basque music. In this way, Basque music is being made on the spot, within a partnership between listeners and performers.

—Adapted from an article by Denis Laborde

Bibliography

Arana Martija, Jose Antonio. 1985. *Basque Music*. Bilbao: Basque Government.

Aulestia, Gorka. 1995. *Improvisational Poetry from the Basque Country*. Reno: University of Nevada Press.

Azkue Aberasturi, Resurrección Maria de. 1919. *Música popular vasca: su existencia*. Bilbao: J. J. Rachelt.

——. [1923] 1968. *Cancionera popular vasca*. 2nd ed. Bilbao: Biblioteca de la Gran Enciclopedia Vasca.

Donostia, José G. de Zulaika Arregi de. 1994. *Obras Completas*. 9 vols. Donostia: Eusko Ikaskuntza.

Gascue, Francisco. 1913. *Origen de la música popular vascongada*. Paris: H. Champion.

Fagoaga, Isidore de. 1944. *La musique représentative basque*. Bayonne: La Presse.

Laborde, Denis. 1996. *Tout un monde de musiques*. Paris: L'Harmattan.

Landart, Daniel. 1988. *L'improvisation chantée en Pays Basque*. Bayonne: Centre Culturel du Pays Basque.

López, Aguirre Elena. 1996. *Del txistu a la telecaster: crónica del rock vasco*. Vitoria and Gasteiz: Edition Aianai.

Manterola, José. 1877–1880. *Cancionero vasco*. 9 vols. San Sebastian: J. Oses.

Sallaberry, Jean-Dominique-Julien. [1870] 1992. *Chants populaires du Pays Basque*. Nîmes: Lacour.

United Kingdom and Ireland

The United Kingdom and Ireland are musically linked mainly by songs in the English language, though other languages are also used. No matter whether from England, Scotland, Wales, or Ireland, many songs also have similar features, including a four-line form; the use of similar diatonic modes; and a relatively relaxed, unpretentious manner of singing. Today, instrumental dance music, often performed without dancers, seems more important in England, Ireland, and Scotland than in Wales (although Welsh music is undergoing a small but significant revival). The tunes possess similar structures (AABB) and meters (2/4, 6/8)—and the fiddle and melodeon are everywhere the most popular instruments.

Songs and instrumental music are mainly performed in informal settings among friends at home or the local pub, though a few calendar customs, especially Christmas caroling, include singing. Competitive festivals are another important context for performing and preserving traditional music. A folk revival, begun in the 1950s and 1960s, has helped invigorate once rural musical traditions threatened by urbanization and industrialization.

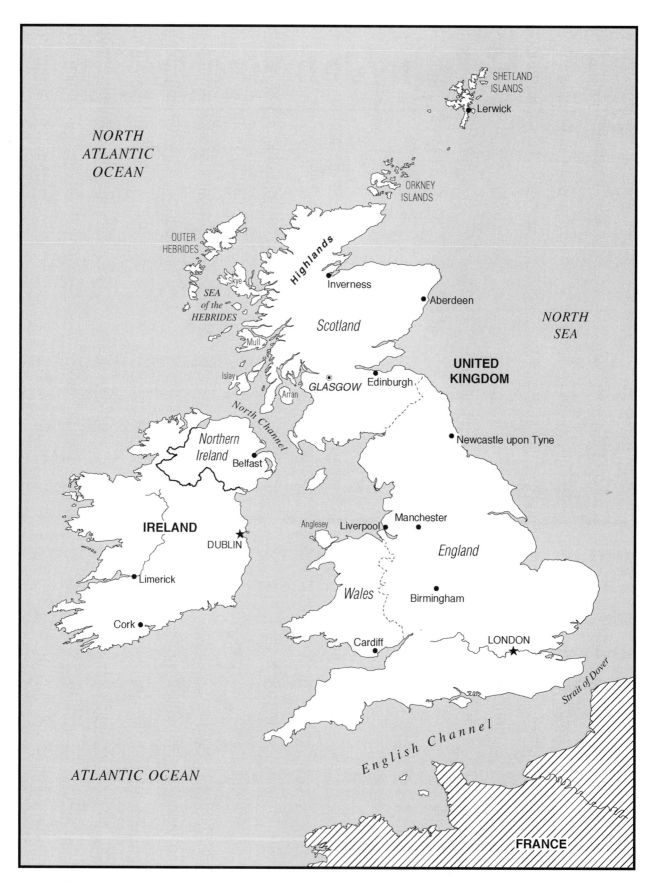

United Kingdom and Ireland

England

England is the largest of the four countries that constitute the United Kingdom and displays dramatic contrasts of population and topography. Geographically, it divides into a lowland south and east, an area of crop production and mixed farming, and the upland north and west, where sheep farming predominates. London, the old administrative and business center, and industrial cities such as Manchester and Birmingham have been transformed since World War II by multiethnic immigration, mainly from countries of the old British Empire. The country has long been ethnically mixed, with invasions and settlements by Celts, Romans, Saxons, Vikings, and Normans before C.E. 1100 and Welsh, Scots, Irish, Huguenot French, and Eastern European Jews in more recent centuries.

The present population of England is roughly 50 million, living in an area of 130,000 square kilometers. In the eighteenth and nineteenth centuries, England was at the forefront of the Industrial Revolution, a fact that brought benefits and disadvantages and marked the landscape permanently. Many areas now demonstrate contrasts between the declining old "heavy" industries (the manufacturing of metals and cloth, shipbuilding, and mining) and the developing newer manufacturing, service, and financial industries. In a country once described as the workshop of the world, only about 20 percent of the population are engaged in manufacturing.

Contexts for Music and Song

Singing of traditional songs regularly formed, and in some cases, still forms, part of social events and calendar customs such as hunt suppers, harvest homes (completion of summer harvest), friendly society feasts, and so on. Carol-singing and wassailing customs combined house visiting with the performance of specific songs. More often, people sang for simple enjoyment at home or in the pub. Some alehouses gained a reputation as singing pubs. Occasionally, a degree of formality affected pub singing, with one person acting as a chairman or master of ceremonies, but more often singing occurred informally.

Dance music in England is used in three important situations: for mixed social dancing (country dancing), for single-sex, and more recently mixed, display (ceremonial dancing), and socially without dancing. These contexts can intermingle. Music-only sessions might include solo step dancing, and social dancing might follow dancing for display. Dance music might be performed in different social spaces. Display dances by their nature were public, being enacted in streets and gardens normally at special times of the year. Social dancing took place at servants' balls, in dancing booths at fairs, in barns, on village greens, and in pubs and houses. In the twentieth century, the development of community and village halls, and of schools with large halls, provided for the continuation of country dancing. The performance of dance music, like singing, took place in public and private spaces, most commonly at home or in the pub.

The post-World War II folk revival gave rise to informal folk clubs, which usually met in rooms over pubs. At their height, in the 1960s, they numbered in the thousands. Though they still exist in most areas, their numbers have declined considerably since then. The music performed at these venues varied widely in type and quality, but the pubs provided a public platform for traditional performers. Festivals are the most prominent legacy of the later revival: to those with an interest in traditional music, festivals at Sidmouth and Whitby offer both a meeting place and a chance to hear traditional styles.

Singing Style and Song Types

The solo-singing style of English traditional singers is declamatory. Melody is a vehicle for words, and telling the story is most singers' prime consideration. Singing tends to be unemotional or stoical, in the sense that dramatic elements in the narrative are not stressed. English traditional singing is an art of understatement, but the singer's involvement with the song is total. Vocal production is full, open-throated, and sometimes nasal in quality, though there is considerable variety in vocal techniques used.

Most recorded English traditional song has been performed unaccompanied—a fact that has profoundly influenced singing style. Singers are free to vary the pace of delivery, to engage in metrical irregularity, and to vary the melodic line. They are also free to decorate the musical line, though the degree to which they do varies from singer to singer and region to region. Traditional songs are built on rounded structures such as four-line stanzas, with repeats that contain some element of variation. Sometimes variation is used to accommodate different syllabic line lengths and textual variations, but more usually it appears to result from singers' fancy and musicality.

English traditional song is not "pure melody" uninfluenced by harmony, however. Church and military bands played in harmony in the eighteenth and nineteenth centuries, and were widely heard. Traditional singing in harmony has been recorded extensively, notably in the performances of the Copper family of Rottingdean, Sussex, whose style has been explained as deriving from eighteenth-century glee singing, a form of amateur musicmaking in three or more unaccompanied parts, and from popular church music. Many traditional tunes have implicit harmony and are built on triadic structures (figure 1). Even tunes that are not in the major mode often seem to make use of triadic structures within their particular modality.

It is clear from early collectors' encounters with traditional music that much of it did not follow the conventions of the major-minor system of Western theory and practice. In an influential book, *English Folk-Song: Some Conclusions* (1907), Cecil J. Sharp characterized English tunes as being cast in the dorian, phrygian, mixolydian, aeolian, and ionian (major) modes, and occasionally in the minor. One year later, in 1908, the composer Percy Grainger (1882–1961) put forward a radically different explanation of the modality of English traditional song. For Grainger, there was but "one single loosely-knit modal folk-song scale" with certain unstable points, notably the 3rd, the 6th, and the 7th. The theories of Sharp and Grainger may not, however, be incompatible. Sharp's modalism works well enough as a classificatory scheme. Grainger's unstable scale appears to work at a deeper structural level and can explain how tunes change mode in the process of transmission. It can also deal with tunes that vary

particular intervals and with singers who employ flexible intonation.

Songs performed by traditional singers can be notated in common time, 4/4, 3/4, and 6/8 being the most frequent, with 5/4 also represented. Nine-eight and 7/4 are not unknown, and some songs display a marked irregularity in rhythm. Songs are normally set in four-line stanzas in common or ballad meter (4.3.4.3 as four-line alternating stresses) or long meter (8.8.8.8), with or without repeats or choruses, but a great variety of other metrical forms are found, some with interpolated chorus lines. Two- and eight-line forms are also encountered, and nineteenth-century songwriting, some of which was absorbed into popular tradition, took delight in more elaborate forms.

Melodic patterns are quite varied. Some tunes use internal repetition, sequence, and phrase transposition, while others draw their coherence from an overall structure that does not use such devices. Thus, ABCD is a common musical verse form for a song in ballad meter, but so too is ABBA for songs in long meter, and a wealth of other forms are found, including AABA, AABCD, ABB, ABACDEDF, ABCBC, and many more. The survival of a popular kind of church music known as *west gallery* (ca. 1750–1850) in oral tradition means that some elaborate fuguing tunes with highly melismatic melodies held a firm place in popular memory. Many examples of this type of material survive in the vigorous carol-singing traditions of South Yorkshire.

The repertory of English songs is made up of many layers. Versions of "The Miller and His Lass" can be traced back to the later Middle Ages, and "The Frog and the Mouse" and "The Three Ravens" are songs that were current in the Tudor period and survive into the present. Others were originated and sustained in tradition by the broadside press, which issued masses of cheap song sheets between about 1500 and 1900. Numerous songs by broadside poets passed into oral tradition and were reshaped by it.

Figure 1 A tune for the ballad "Lord Randal," sung by Mrs. Eliza Hutchings of Langport, Somerset, for Cecil Sharp in 1904. The tune outlines one octave of the major mode and emphasizes the notes of the G-major triad (g–b–d). Its four-line form is AABC. After Bronson 1959–1972:1:198.

Some of these were later collected and reissued in their reshaped form. Thus, broadside ballads, stage songs, music-hall songs, and popular songs from different periods contributed to the layering of the English traditional repertory.

Dance Music and Instruments

Like song texts and tunes, the English dance-tune repertory stems from various historical periods. Some seventeenth-century tunes have been played continuously since then, but much of the repertory seems to be eighteenth and early nineteenth century in origin. In the nineteenth century, traditional musicians began to assimilate new dance forms from the continent (like the polka and the waltz), and instrumentalists have readily incorporated twentieth-century dance tunes, provided these are adaptable to rhythmic and melodic conventions.

Dance tunes are typically more regular in shape than tunes not meant for dancing. A form of AABB (in which each letter represents an eight-bar strain) is the most common, though AABA and AABBCC crop up. An exception to this regularity is the music for Cotswold morris dancing, a central and south Midlands tradition, wherein the music often follows the dance closely. The pattern of sections can be complex, and many dances contain "caper" sections, which require the instrumentalist to play at a slower tempo, or at half speed (with note values doubled), while the dancers perform high leaps.

The time signatures and tune types of English dance music are hornpipes in 4/4, jigs in 6/8, polkas in 2/4, and waltzes in 3/4. The hornpipe, often used to accompany different types of step or clog dancing, is played either straight (with equal eighth-note values) or dotted (roughly, with the dotted eighth note followed by a sixteenth). In both cases, the tune typically ends with three stressed quarter notes. Marches in duple or triple time abound but often shade into other categories. The reel, a characteristic dance form of Ireland and Scotland, cast in 4/4 time with eight equal eighth-note pulses to the bar, is not much present in the historical record of English dance music.

English dance tunes are overwhelmingly major in tonality, though a few striking tunes make use of other modes. The repertory includes recognizably Scottish or Irish tunes, but the performance of English dance music differs strongly from that of Scotland and Ireland. English music has a contrasting rhythmic feel, is often slower in tempo, and uses up beats, syncopation, Scotch snap, and other devices. Each section of the music, usually four or eight bars, is clearly marked. When played by more than one instrumentalist, the tune is heterophonic, rather than unison. Bass parts were traditionally added to dance tunes by the use of a cello, bassoon, or serpent (a curved, wooden, lip-vibrated wind instrument, with six finger holes).

English fiddle playing distinctively places a great deal of emphasis on rhythmic thrust. The fiddle, however, seems to have suffered a relative decline in the nineteenth century, with the introduction of free-reed instruments, notably the melodeon (button accordion), the Anglo-German concertina (the "anglo"), and the mouth organ, instruments which produce different notes when bellows are pushed or pulled, or in the latter case, when reeds are blown or sucked depending on the direction of air over the reed. How much these instruments contributed to the development of traditional style and how much

Figure 2 A morris dance troupe performs in Pennsylvania, United States of America, 1997. *Photo by Terry E. Miller.*

they fitted with what already existed, are matters for conjecture: the particular jaggedness of sound produced by the push-and-pull bellows action (allowing no overlapping of notes) appears entirely appropriate for English traditional music. In the twentieth century, the widespread adoption of the piano accordion and the English concertina, instruments that produce the same notes whichever direction the bellows is played, has been seen by many as diluting and enfeebling the traditional style.

Fipple flutes are represented by various kinds of six-holed pipes. Early examples are made of wood, but in the nineteenth century, instruments such as the tin whistle or penny whistle were widely produced commercially. A related instrument is the three-holed pipe played with one hand only, leaving the other free to beat a small drum, called a tabor; the combination was called whittle and dub (whistle and drum). A primitive one-man band, used since the Middle Ages, it was a common accompaniment for morris dancing, a vigorous dance of central and southern England that is performed by costumed men wearing bells (figure 2). A parallel example of melody and percussion combined, at times, in one musician is the tambourine, sometimes played with the harmonica. Other percussion has come into play at various times: military drums, spoons, bones, or beer glasses. Some traditional bands incorporated modern drum kits into their combinations.

Traditional musicians play the instruments they can get their hands on or make; other instruments used by traditional instrumentalists include the hammered dulcimer, the clarinet, the piano, and the banjo.

—*Adapted from an article by Vic Gammon*

Bibliography

Atkinson, David, Vic Gammon, and Rikky Rooksby. 2007. *The Folk Handbook: Working with Songs from the English Tradition*. London: Backbeat.

Boyes, Georgina. 1993. *The Imagined Village: Culture, Ideology, and the English Folk Revival*. Manchester: Manchester University Press.

Bronson, Bertrand H. 1959–1972. *The Traditional Tunes of the Child Ballads*. 4 vols. Princeton: Princeton University Press.

Chappell, William. 1965. *Popular Music of the Olden Time*. New York: Dover.

Child, Francis James. 1882–1898. *The English and Scottish Popular Ballads*. 5 vols. Boston: Houghton Mifflin.

Grainger, Percy. 1908. "Collecting with the Phonograph." *Journal of the Folk-Song Society* 12:147–169.

Harker, Dave. 1985. *Fakesong. The Manufacture of British 'Folksong' 1700 to the Present Day*. Milton Keynes, UK: Open University Press.

Howes, Frank. 1969. *The Folk Music of Britain—and Beyond*. London: Methuen.

Karpeles, Maud. 1987 [1973]. *An Introduction to English Folk Song*. London: Oxford University Press.

Kennedy, Peter. 1975. *The Folksongs of Britain and Ireland*. London: Cassell.

Lloyd, A. L. 1967. *Folk Song in England*. London: Lawrence & Wishart.

Pickering, Michael. 1982. *Village Song and Culture*. London: Croom Helm.

Roud, Steve, Eddie Upton, and Malcolm Taylor, eds. 2003. *Still Growing: English Traditional Songs and Singers from the Cecil Sharp Collection*. London: The English Folk Dance and Song Society.

Russell, Ian, ed. 1986. *Singer, Song and Scholar*. Sheffield: Sheffield Academic Press.

Sharp, Cecil J. 1907. *English Folk-Song: Some Conclusions*. London: Novello, Simpkin.

Shepard, Leslie. 1962. *The Broadside Ballad*. Hatboro, Penn.: Legacy Books.

Van Der Merwe, Peter. [1989] 1992. *Origins of the Popular Style*. Oxford: Oxford University Press.

British Rock and Pop, 1950s to 1970s

Postwar Origins

The economically lean postwar years saw Britain's position as a world power recede and a powerful United States begin to exude its influence on British culture. As the pre-war importance of film and recording stars like George Formby waned and the appeal of wartime icons like Vera Lynn peaked, crooners such as Dickie Valentine ("All the Time and Everywhere," 1953) replaced them. Similarly, although big band artists such as trumpeter Eddie Calvert continued to have hits ("Oh Mein Papa," 1954), British youth increasingly turned to a reactionary and stripped down jazz that imitated New Orleans and Chicago bands of the 1920s, and called it "Trad." These sources would provide the springboard for British reactions to rock-and-roll.

Skiffle

The first American rock-and-roll song to have success in the United Kingdom, Bill Haley's recording of Big Joe Turner's "Shake, Rattle, and Roll" entered U.K. charts in mid-December of 1954. Earlier that year, the banjo and guitar player in Chris Barber's Trad band, Lonnie Donegan, recorded his imitation of Huddie Ledbetter's "Rock Island Line" when the producer ran out of things to record. In early 1956, as Haley's recording climbed British charts, Decca released Donegan's version of Ledbetter's story about railway life in the American Midwest hoping to capitalize on what they saw as a short-lived interest in guitar-accompanied songs. Donegan called what he did "skiffle," taking the word from a Paramount release in the United States called "Home Town Skiffle" (ca. 1920s), and describing a form which Americans might have called "jug-band music." The skiffle ensemble was primitivist: a guitar; a bass made from a tea chest, a pole, and a taut wire (the British equivalent of the American washtub bass); and a washboard. The musical and material simplicity of skiffle fit perfectly the musical skills and economic necessities of British youth in the mid-1950s.

Almost immediately, other British skiffle artists emerged including Chas McDevitt (who covered Elizabeth Cotton's "Freight Train" with Nancy Whisky singing) and the Vipers (with Wally Whyton). Skiffle flourished in the coffee bars that had sprung up all over Britain, but particularly in London where

the 2i's in Soho emerged as the most important. However, Donegan soon shifted his ensemble, dropping the improvised instruments in favor of an acoustic bass and a drum kit. Even more importantly, he added an electric guitar when he hired jazz musician Denny Wright for a proto-rock version of the American folk song "Cumberland Gap" (1957). American rock musicians continued to influence young British performers, particularly Buddy Holly, who toured the United Kingdom in March 1958. And during Gene Vincent and Eddie Cochran's 1960 tour of the United Kingdom, Cochran died in a car crash.

Early British Rock

Although several jazz bands, such as Tony Crombie's Rockets, attempted to recreate the sounds of American rock-and-roll, the first artist to have success preferred country music. Tommy Steele (b. Thomas Hicks, 1936) had been playing guitar and singing on American military bases in Britain and working as a cabin boy when skiffle became popular. Performing in the 2i's and other Soho night spots, he developed a comedic routine that parodied rock-and-roll: "Rock with the Caveman" (released on Decca in October 1956). One of his managers, Larry Parnes gave him his stage name (reminiscent of other pseudonyms like "Dickie Valentine") and created the story of an overnight sensation. Soon, others would follow. The most important of these was Cliff Richard (b. Harry Webb, 1940) and the Drifters, whose "Move It" (August 1958) many identify as the first example of British rock. Two years later, Johnny Kidd (b. Frederick Heath, 1939; d. 1966) and the Pirates recorded perhaps the best-known early British rock anthem, "Shakin' All Over" (June 1960). Parallel to their success was that of their backing bands. Richard's group, the Shadows (the name "Drifters" had already been taken in the United States), had a string of instrumental hits in the 1960s and one of Billy Fury's bands, the Tornados, had an international hit with "Telstar" (August 1962).

The Beatles

Emerging from the northern industrial port city of Liverpool, the origins of the most famous band of the 1960s lie in skiffle. John Lennon's (1940–1980) skiffle band, the Quarrymen, attracted the attention of another aficionado of American music, Paul McCartney (b. 1942). They almost immediately outgrew the simplicity of skiffle and moved to imitating Elvis Presley and Little Richard. With the addition of friend George Harrison (1943–2001), the band added a rockabilly flavor to their mix. After a few years of playing coffee houses, dances, and a stint in Hamburg clubs, they attracted the attention of entrepreneur Brian Epstein who offered to manage them and win them a recording contract. Adding drummer Ringo Starr (b. Richard Starkey, 1940), they had their first recording success with "Love Me Do" (October 1962) under the production of George Martin at EMI. Over the next year, their recordings of songs written by Lennon and McCartney began to dominate British recording charts, and by November of 1963, the British press proclaimed "Beatlemania." That success was followed in early 1964, when the Beatles appeared on Ed Sullivan's Sunday night television program in North America. Beatlemania became a global phenomenon.

Lennon and McCartney's songs and the way the band presented them reflected the Beatles' eclectic repertoire of rock-and-roll, rhythm-and-blues, rockabilly, show tunes, and girl-group pop. For example, "I Saw Her Standing There" combines a bass line from Chuck Berry's "Talkin' 'bout You," hand claps reminiscent of the Shirelles, and a guitar solo imitative of Carl Perkins. However, by 1965, songs like "Help!" (for their film of the same name) featuring contrapuntal responsorial lines and vocal harmonies, established a new benchmark for contemporary pop-music norms. In the wake of their success came numerous other pop and rock groups both from northern cities like Liverpool (Gerry and the Pacemakers, the Searchers) and Manchester (Herman's Hermits, the Hollies), as well as London (the Dave Clark Five, the Kinks, Manfred Mann).

British Blues

Just as British Trad jazz had provided a context in which Lonnie Donegan could explore Huddie Ledbetter's folk songs, other performers found the opportunity to celebrate contemporary blues musicians like Muddy Waters and Big Bill Broonzy. Indeed, both of these performers came to Britain and won fans, notably Alexis Korner (1928–1984) and Cyril Davies (1932–1964) who established a floating ensemble to celebrate and various clubs in which to hear this music. Korner and Davies' Blues Incorporated would feature many of Britain's 1960s rock stars, including Mick Jagger, Jack Bruce, Ginger Baker, and Charlie Watts. Of the various ensembles

that emerged from Blues Incorporated, the best-known are the Rolling Stones and Cream.

Formed by Brian Jones (1942–1969) with Mick Jagger (b. 1943) and Keith Richards (b. 1943), the Rolling Stones would celebrate a mix of American blues, rhythm-and-blues, and rock-and-roll. Initially, they latched on to the popularity of the Beatles, covering American recordings, such as Chuck Berry's "Come On" in June 1963, the way that most other British pop bands did at the time. However, one of their managers, Andrew Oldham, both convinced Jagger and Richards to begin writing their own songs and the band to adopt the posture as the anti-Beatles. Their first success came with the song "Last Time" (February 1965), which borrowed heavily from a Staples Singers gospel moan "This May Be the Last Time," accompanied by a recurring guitar riff and Jagger's snarled vocal presentation. They repeated this formula, notably with "Satisfaction" (August 1965) in which they combined complaints about a consumerist society with a driving and distorted guitar ostinato. Numerous other British blues bands surfaced in the era, including the Animals (featuring Eric Burdon from Newcastle), Them (featuring Van Morrison from Belfast), the Spencer Davis Group (featuring Steve Winwood from Birmingham) and London bands such as the Yardbirds (with Eric Clapton and later Jeff Beck and Jimmy Page) and John Mayall's Bluesbreakers.

Pop Art

The postwar population "bulge" combined with a decline in economic resources contributed to the ending of National Service in which young males were conscripted into the military after completing high school and the expansion of the post-secondary education system to accommodate them. An important feature of this era was the emergence of art schools, which many young musicians attended, including Pete Townshend (b. 1945) who applied academic concepts to his band's performances. The Who began by appealing to London's Mod sub-culture, and particularly the young, shorthaired males whose finely tuned sartorial sense helped establish Britain as a fashion leader. Townshend enunciated the violence of this scene through the concept of auto-destructive art, smashing his guitars and amplifiers as part of his act, particularly in tunes like "My Generation" (October 1965). Other mid-1960s bands, such as the Move, similarly built destruction and violence into some of their shows.

Townshend also applied his visual sense to the clothing he designed for the band, drawing in particular upon artist Peter Blake's notions about pop art. Townshend's search for relevancy directly contributed to his celebration of British culture. In parallel, his music began to capture a particular kind of British sensibility, taking up distinctly English subjects ("Happy Jack"). Similarly, other songwriters embraced their "Britishness," rejecting a pattern of copying Americans. Perhaps the most notable individual in this regard, Ray Davies (b. 1944) began his running commentary on British middleclass existence in songs like "Well Respected Man" (September 1965) and "Dedicated Follower of Fashion" (February 1966).

Subsequently, many British artists in the mid-1960s embraced the idea that one could take pop seriously and, consequently, the music grew distinctly more complicated. Again, the Beatles played an important role with their tape-loop psychedelic pastiche of "Tomorrow Never Knows" (August 1966) and recording Lennon's ode to his youth, "Strawberry Fields Forever" (released in February 1967). By the summer of 1967, their album *Sgt. Pepper's Lonely Hearts Club Band* set a precedent for pop music by presenting a complete work of integrated music and visual materials. That same year saw other groups reaching for new ideas, including Procol Harum's amalgam of Johann Sebastian Bach and Bob Dylan, "A Whiter Shade of Pale" (May 1967), and the Moody Blues integrated orchestral and pop creation, *Days of Future Passed* (December 1967).

Psychedelic Blues

Psychedelic culture, with its celebration of altered consciousness and vivid aural and visual elements, also influenced the British blues movement, particularly with the creation of so-called "super groups" that brought well-known musicians together into new performing entities. The two most notable of these were Cream, formed in 1966 by Eric Clapton (b. 1945), Jack Bruce (b. 1943), and Ginger Baker (b. 1940), and subsequently, Blind Faith, formed in 1969 by Clapton and Steve Winwood (b. 1948) and joined by Baker and Rick Gretsch. With the introduction of better amplification systems, these bands were now able to play larger venues and, consequently, to reap more income. Although their repertoire sprang from blues forms, Cream prominently featured the Skip James tune "I'm So Glad" in their programs, the technology and their focus on virtuosity helped drive the form into new musical territory. Their live shows featured extended solos and sometimes dueling personalities as musicians competed for the attention of their audiences. Perhaps most notable in this era was the appearance

of American Jimi Hendrix (1942–1970). Former Animal bass player Chas Chandler brought Hendrix to the United Kingdom in 1966, auditioned British musicians to accompany him (drummer Mitch Mitchell and Noel Redding on bass), and presented him as a British phenomenon.

Folk, Rock, and Beyond

As the British Empire dissolved, not only did British civil servants and their families return to the United Kingdom (e.g., Cliff Richard), but citizens from the British Commonwealth of Nations, who enjoyed immigration privileges, began arriving in Britain in significant numbers. Reflecting Britain's growing cultural diversity, Jamaican immigrant Millie Small had a hit with her ska tune "My Boy Lollipop" (March 1964), produced and promoted by a returned British expatriate, Chris Blackwell (who did the same for Bob Marley in the early 1970s).

In parallel with this diversification of the popular music, traditional British ballads and dance music found a voice in popular culture, first with performers like Donovan, and later with acoustic-electric combos like the Incredible String Band, Pentangle, and Fairport Convention. Two individuals in particular both championed British traditional music and incorporated non-Western musical ideas into their music. Guitarists Davy Graham and Bert Jansch (b. 1943) had a significant impact on other musicians when the former adapted North African *ūd* patterns for his instrument and the later integrated North Indian sitar ideas. The mid-1960s saw Indian musical ideas in particular appearing in recordings by the Kinks, "See My Friend" (July 1965), the Yardbirds, "Heart Full of Soul" (June 1965), and the Rolling Stones, "Paint It, Black" (April 1966). However, the most developed enunciations came from George Harrison with the Beatles with "Love You To" (August 1966) and "Within You Without You" (June 1967).

Progressive Rock

The eclectic mix of musical ideas that characterized British pop and rock in the late 1960s led to several significant stylistic innovations. Adopting an adventurous approach to musical form and eclecticism dramatically extended the length of recordings, and albums began to replace singles as the preferred mode of presenting recorded music. A heavier style of music also emerged with bands like Black Sabbath and Deep Purple who continued the tradition of bands like Cream. Led Zeppelin was formed in 1968 by former session musicians Jimmy Page (b. 1944) and John Paul Jones (b. 1946) with newcomers Robert Plant (b. 1948) and John Bonham (1948–1980), and began by combining a mix of blues and other genres into their music.

By the end of the 1960s, British popular music alternatively attempted to "Get Back" to rock roots, as the Beatles did with New Orleans homages like "Oh Darlin' " in 1969, and become even more complicated, as the Who did with *Tommy* in 1969. With the breakup of the Beatles in 1970, British rock and pop veered toward solo projects (George Harrison's *All Things Must Pass*, November 1970), the continued blossoming of existing stars (Led Zeppelin), and the beginnings of progressive rock. In 1966, Pink Floyd began the movement with shows combining extended instrumental improvisations and light projections, released *Piper at the Gates of Dawn*, in August 1967 and grew ever more theatrical through the 1970s. Perhaps the best example of their holistic approach to music and irrational symbolism, *The Wall* (1982) places in film the story of a disillusioned 1960s rock star that isolates himself from the world.

Progressive bands of the 1970s often chose abstract themes around the subjects of war, social repression, and insanity. Emerson, Lake, and Palmer's *Tarkus* (1971), for example, tells the story of a mythical war animal-machine. Genesis released their *The Lamb Lies Down on Broadway* (1974), in which Peter Gabriel (b. 1950) tells the story of a Puerto Rican youth searching for his brother in an underworld below New York. Even more musically complicated (if psychologically darker), King Crimson emphasized musical virtuosity and elements of jazz in their *In the Court of the Crimson King*, October 1969.

An important distinction in most progressive rock is the abandonment of the single and the embrace of the album. Adopting this format, progressive rock explored longer musical forms, the juxtaposition of the rock ensemble with other musical forces, such as the orchestra, and musical materials far more complicated melodically, harmonically, and metrically than rock and blues.

Reactions in the 1970s

As groups from the 1960s such as the Who and the Rolling Stones adopted stadiums and arenas as their primary concert venue and progressive rock artists sought intellectual sophistication, a new generation of audiences rejected these movements. As always, a core teen audience craved pop music and some bands modified their blues roots to become successful pop artists (e.g., Fleetwood Mac). Some audiences favored the social shock of glam (or glitter) rock,

with its themes of alien life, such as David Bowie (b. 1947) in his persona of Ziggy Stardust, and ambiguous sexuality. And, in some cases, audiences rejected outright all of the artificial theatricality and what they perceived to be the shallow commercialism of the era. Instead, they embraced musical simplicity.

British punk rock grew from American garage bands in general and Detroiter Iggy Pop (b. 1947) in particular. They eschewed virtuosity and the vague symbolism of 1970s singer-songwriters for aggressive and confrontational performances where they often had direct contact with their audiences. The short-lived Sex Pistols attacked the monarchy and British nationalism ("God Save the Queen," 1977), not to mention Britain's class system ("Anarchy in the UK," 1976). The Clash similarly championed disaffected British youth ("White Riot," 1977), but their approach was always more sophisticated and less dystopic ("London Calling," 1979) than the Sex Pistols. The Clash also began to enfold elements of Jamaican ska and reggae into their essential rock in what began to be known as 2 tone, reflecting the mix of white and black British musicians and the fast, rhythmically complicated music they created.

The Specials, who toured with the Clash as their opening act and may have inspired them to diversify their repertoire, put social issues in the forefront of their 2 tone songs ("Too Much Too Young," 1980) and continued a tradition of British bands mixing musical ideas. Similarly, the Police—formed by Sting (Gordon Sumner; b. 1951), Stewart Copeland (b. 1952), and Andy Summers (b. 1942)—combined reggae and ska in the music on their first album, *Outlandos d'Amour* (1978), but gradually grew more pop-oriented in the 1980s with songs like "Every Breath You Take" (1983).

British popular music in the second half of the twentieth century moved away from simple covers of American models to an eclectic mix of non-Western musics, traditional British folk music, Western classical music, and different kinds of jazz. The primary characteristic of British pop might be inclusion, with whatever new elements musicians have encountered grafted onto a stolid British approach.

—By Gordon R. Thompson

Bibliography

Davies, Ray. 1994. *X-Ray*. London: Penguin Books.
Everett, Walter. 1999. *The Beatles as Musicians:* Revolver *through the* Anthology. New York: Oxford University Press.
———. 2001. *The Beatles as Musicians: The Quarry Men through* Rubber Soul. New York: Oxford University Press.

Kozinn, Allan. 1995. *The Beatles*. London: Phaidon Press, Limited.

Leigh, Spencer, with John Firminger. 1996. *Halfway to Paradise: Britpop, 1955–1962*. Folkestone, Kent: Finbarr International.

Marsh, Dave. 1983. *Before I Get Old: The Story of the Who*. London: Plexus Publishing Limited.

Oldham, Andrew Loog. 2000. *Stoned: A Memoir of London in the 1960s*. New York: St. Martin's Press.

Palachios, Julian. 1998. *Lost in the Woods: Syd Barrett and the Pink Floyd*. London: Boxtree.

Thompson, Gordon. 2008. *Please Please Me: Change and Sixties British Pop*. New York: Oxford University Press.

Wyman, Bill, with Richard Havers. 2002. *Rolling with the Stones*. London: Dorling Kindersley Limited.

Yorke, Ritchie. 1990. *Led Zeppelin: The Definitive Biography*. Novato, California: Underwood-Miller.

Scotland

With a population of 5 million that has remained stable for a century, Scotland occupies the northern part of Great Britain and lies on the North Atlantic sea route between Ireland and Scandinavia. Historically, this position has affected its patterns of settlement and culture, though influences from the continent and even the Mediterranean are evident. Scotland's stormy past reflects invasions by Celts, Romans, Vikings, Normans, English, and others before and after the beginning of the Christian era. These invasions set up regions (in a land of almost 80,000 square kilometers) and religious affiliations critical to Scotland's cultural and political diversity: the Highland and Lowland division; northeast (conservative, Scandinavian-derived) and southwest (progressive, Celtic-inflected); Roman Catholic in the southern and Presbyterian in the northern Hebrides. Outside the industrial belt between the cities of Glasgow and Edinburgh, Scotland has large tracts of mountainous terrain (north and west) and agricultural land (east and southwest), as well as hundreds of offshore islands. [For a map of Scotland, see the one at the beginning of the UNITED KINGDOM AND IRELAND.]

In addition to English, Scotland maintains two languages, Gaelic and Scots. Gaelic has receded since the 1700s, but is still spoken in the Hebridean islands and pockets of the western mainland. Scots, in many regional dialects, is the vernacular language of the Lowlands. Both languages have given rise to musical genres that interact and overlap in melody and theme.

Song and Instrumental Music

Two distinct musical regions can be distinguished in Scotland: the Highlands and Hebridean Islands, and the Lowlands and Northern Isles.

Highlands and Hebridean Islands Vocal Music

Gaelic-speakers perpetuate musical genres attached to the lifecycle and the pastoral, clan-based society before 1700. Lullabies and laments, which often drew on related melodic material because of their social function and shared features in their refrains, can be related to two of three ancient divisions of Celtic music: those for sorrow (lament) and sleep (lullaby); that for laughter (dance music) was the third. As with many Gaelic songs, the refrain precedes the verses. Verbal and melodic formulas may stem from earlier times in suggesting magical or protective power; charms were recorded in the Hebrides during the twentieth century. The presence of history, in songs of clan warfare, and the overtones of natural magic have kept Gaelic songs alive despite the predicted demise of the language.

Hebridean labor songs accompanied milking, churning, dandling infants, rowing, and other activities integral to a pastoral society. Of special note are songs for waulking (shrinking) the tweed, a process performed by women until the introduction of technology in the twentieth century. The repertoire of waulking songs, which involves a call-and-response pattern, is enormous and drew its themes and melodies from diverse sources. Repetition of any song was considered bad luck, but the chorus is sung after every line to prolong the song, and repetition within text and melody is evident.

The themes of the lay, which was traditionally sung by male bards, deal with legendary heroic figures: Fionn, Fraoch, Ossian, and their adventures. The first lay to be written down ("*Laoidh Mhanus*," in 1784) was recorded as late as 1968 in the Hebrides with similarities in text and tune. The "Lay of Fraoch" illustrates the declamatory style of some singers (figure 1). The Gaelic text of stanza 1 shows the style.

Medieval bards employed meters based on the number of syllables per line (syllabic meters), but later came to use the stressed meters more common in Western Europe. Traditionally the province of male bards, in the twentieth century, women and men have been recorded performing lays.

Bards were patronized by clan chieftains and used music to praise or satirize the chieftain or his family. With the dispersal of the clans after the Battle of Culloden (1746), however, bards, along with harpers and pipers, lost their patrons. Many bards sailed with their clanspeople to the New World, where they coined heartfelt elegies praising their homeland. What evolved in their place, as a result of harsh anti-Gaelic laws and the emigration of the Highland Clearances, were local bards, singers, and composers. Such a local bard in recent times was Calum Ruadh Nicholson (1902–1978) of Skye, who composed satires and laments that were recorded in the 1960s.

Laigh éa— slain—te throm, throm Air nigh—ean Maigh— re nan còrn fi— al:

Sin 'nuair chuir i fios air fra—och 'S dh'fhios— raich a' laoch gu dé 'mi—ann.

A sore, sore sickness fell upon the daughter of Maighre of the bounteous goblets;

That was when she sent for Fraoch, and the warrior asked what was her wish.

Figure 1 The "Lay of Fraoch" employs a declamatory style characteristic of the genre. Recorded by P. McCaughery and Fred Kent, 1965.
Transcribed by James Porter.

Highlands and Hebridean Islands Instrumental Music

Pipers were also part of the clan retinue, and whole families (MacCrimmons, MacArthurs) evolved traditions of teaching and composition, e.g., by the use of mnemonic syllables, which influence pipers today. The Highland bagpipe chanter has a nine-note scale of ǵ–á–b–c♯″–d″–e″–f♯″–g″–a″ and the instrument has two tenor drones on *a* and one bass drone on *A*. A major form that emerged in the 1600s was *piobaireachd* (English pibroch, 'piping'), which may have evolved from clan-gathering tunes or laments. *Piobaireachd* (or better, *ceòl mór* 'great music') is a theme-and-variation form that can test a piper's mastery, especially in the cumulative effect of proliferating grace notes as the variations advance until the music returns to the theme or ground (*urlar*) at its conclusion. The singing of pibroch vocables (*canntaireachd*) was often linked to *port-a-beul* 'mouth music', used for dancing when no instrument was available, especially after the harsh laws imposed by the British government on the Highlands after the battle of Culloden. Realizing the powerful effect of massed bagpipers, the government enlisted pipers as part of its army, and still does. The dispersal of Scottish pipers over the British Empire spread the assertive sound of the instrument into countries that had bagpipes of their own, from continental Europe to India, displacing or dominating indigenous instruments through sheer volume of sound.

Bagpipe music includes song, march, and dance tunes (*ceòl beag*, or 'little music'), a suite of which forms the basis of modern piping competitions. Bagpipe and clan associations flourish throughout the Anglophone world, an index of the massive emigration of the 1700s and 1800s: the World Pipe Band Championship competition has been won by a Canadian band. Contemporary pipers of recognized skill who have also composed tunes include John D. Burgess, John MacFadyen, Robert Wallace, and Allan MacDonald.

The *clàrsach* (harp), obsolescent in Scotland and Ireland by about 1800, was revived in the 1890s. The fiddle, which had begun to displace the bagpipe in the more domesticated taste of the middle classes after 1700, eventually took over much of the piping repertoire and added more dance tunes. Niel Gow (1727–1807), the most famous Highland fiddler, composed tunes that imitate the bagpipe scale and the characteristic double-tonic device: figuration that is repeated a whole tone below or above.

Lowland and Northern Isles Songs

The Lowland tradition is noted for ballads and lyric songs (figure 2). The ballad focuses on a single incident and weds the plot and stanzaic form to a concise, rounded tune. Ballads arose in the late Middle Ages as the favored genre of a merchant class, but the genre itself is heterogeneous. Narrative content tends to the familial and domestic: many types work out, often tragically, a triangular love relationship; other topics are battles and historical events. Ancient tales appear in ballads recovered in modern times: that of "King Orfeo," collected in the Shetland Isles in 1880 and 1947, tells the classical legend of Orpheus.

The lyrics of songs of rural life often refer to plowing, seedtime, and harvest, metaphors for physical love. "The Shearin's No' for You" tells of a young woman whose pregnancy prevents her from bending to shear the wheat. Later nineteenth-century songwriters often sanitized such songs for middle-class taste; for example, "The Shearin'" became the genteel "Kelvingrove." Ploughmen in the reign of Queen Victoria (1819–1901) evolved the bothy song,

DISC
1
TRACK
18

495

Figure 2 Tina Stewart, Cameron Turriff, and Jane Turriff, traditional singers at their house in Fetterangus, Aberdeenshire, Scotland, 1972. *Photo by James Porter.*

Figure 3 Fiddlers at the Kinross Folk Festival, 1980. *Photo by James Porter.*

especially in northeast Scotland, where the bothy was housing for seasonal farm laborers. Though celebrating the all-male farmhand life, these songs cast a wry look at social mores, criticizing thankless toil and poor wages.

Ballads and songs are transmitted orally and by print. Hawkers sold chapbooks and broadsheets widely in the 1700s and 1800s, recirculating songs to rural and urban populations and adding topical items. Songwriters penned political ballads at the time of Union with England (1707) and continued with Jacobite, anti-Hanoverian songs in the 1800s. In the twentieth century, Ewan MacColl (1915–1989), Norman Buchan, Andy Hunter, and others renewed a tradition of protest or satirical songs. Political songs are largely pro-freedom, antiroyalist, and anti-Westminster, as the movement for national independence has grown since World War II.

Lowland and Northern Isles Instrumental Music

In the Lowlands and Northern Isles, the fiddle has been the instrument most favored since the 1700s. Regional tradition is strong in the northeast and especially in the Shetland Isles, where almost every house has a fiddle hanging on the wall. The whaling tradition of the 1800s led to the composition of many energetic and flowing Shetland tunes: ships from southern ports would take a fiddler on board as they steamed north to the whaling grounds.

The Folk Music Revival

Public awareness of vernacular musicmaking was assisted by a revival that began in the later 1800s and emerged again after World War II. The Edinburgh Reel and Strathspey Society was formed in 1881 with a reawakening of interest in old dances. Societies founded by Gaels living in exile (in Edinburgh, Glasgow, London) put on concerts and *ceilidh* 'evening entertainments'. In 1892 the National Mod singing competition was established. Choirs were formed and taught to use harmony; traditional singers were trained in voice production.

The Folklore Institute of Scotland began to record Gaelic songs in 1947. Broadcasting of traditional songs in Gaelic took a new and influential turn with singers such as Alasdair Fraser (Wester Ross), Flora MacNeil, and Calum Johnston (Barra). The School of Scottish Studies at Edinburgh University, founded in 1951, created an archive that houses an extensive collection of Gaelic and Lowland music.

After World War II, the Revival took on a more overtly political cast. Songbooks with antigovernment and antinuclear songs appeared, and folk clubs proliferated. Activist songwriters such as Thurso Berwick and Matt McGinn exploited the British government's neglect of Scottish affairs. Glasgow schoolteachers started folksong clubs at the classroom level. In 1965, the founding of the Traditional Music and Song Association of Scotland paved the way for annual folk festivals that still flourish (figure 3).

—*Adapted from an article by James Porter*

Bibliography

Alburger, Mary Anne. 1983. *Scottish Fiddlers and Their Music*. London: Gollancz.

Collinson, Francis. 1966. *The Traditional and National Music of Scotland*. London: Routledge and Kegan Paul.

Fiske, Roger. 1983. *Scotland in Music*. Cambridge: Cambridge University Press.

Johnson, David. 1972. *Music and Society in Lowland Scotland in the Eighteenth Century*. London: Oxford University Press.

——. 1997 [1984]. *Scottish Fiddle Music in the 18th Century*. Edinburgh: Mercat Press.

Kinnaird, Alison. 1992. *The Tree of Strings: Crann nan teud: A History of the Harp in Scotland*. Edinburgh: Kinmor Music.

Munro, Ailie. 1996 [1984]. *The Democratic Muse: Folk Music Revival in Scotland*. Rev. ed. Aberdeen: Scottish Cultural Press.

Purser, John. 1992. *Scotland's Music*. Edinburgh: Mainstream Publishing.

Sampson, Claude M. 1966. *The British Broadside and Its Music*. Piscataway, N.J.: Rutgers University Press.

Ireland

The Republic of Ireland occupies about 85 percent of Ireland's 84,431 square kilometers and is predominantly Roman Catholic, while the remainder is covered by Northern Ireland, a primarily Protestant part of the United Kingdom. More than 40 percent of the island's four-million inhabitants live in rural areas, where agriculture formed the economic base until industry began to expand, in the mid-1950s. English is the major language, but Irish Gaelic is also spoken by somewhat less than 20 percent of the population (of whom a much smaller percent are native Irish-speakers), mainly in the western parts of the republic.

Traditional Genres of Song and Styles of Singing

Irish traditional musical and poetic forms have much in common with those of Britain. Pentatonic forms common in Scotland recur in Ulster, and heptatonic modes are distributed in Ireland in much the same proportions as in England: more than half of the stock of tunes are major, and less than half are mixolydian, dorian, or aeolian, in that order of frequency. Irish songs are a thorough cultural mix; their texts and tunes are often recognizably of British origin, and Irish music uses the dance forms of England, Scotland, and the Continent.

Old Gaelic Genres

Certain old Gaelic genres, though no longer performed, were in use until recently. The death lament (*caoineadh na marbh*, anglicized as "keening"), a custom cited as early as the 1180s, involved both singing and spoken lament: melody mixed with speech heightened by emotion, in relatively free form. A striking traditional embodiment of the genre is the late-eighteenth-century "*Caoineadh Airt Uí Laoghaire*" ('Lament for Art Ó Laoghaire') (figure 1).

Another old genre, the Fenian or Ossianic heroic lay (*laoi Fiannaíochta*), is better preserved than the keen. Irish heroic songs, such as the lays of Fionn mac Cumhaill, with their narratives of hunts, invasions, extravagant battles, and otherworldly enemies, are slower than Scottish lays and have been sung almost exclusively by men. Lays continued to be sung until the mid-twentieth century, to music that most observers have called chant.

Figure 1 "*Caoineadh Airt Uí Laoghaire*" ('Lament for Art Ó Laoghaire'), a late-eighteenth-century death lament, sung by Máire Uí Chonaill, of Ballyvourney, County Cork. The widow is reacting to an assertion that she went to bed on the night of her husband's wake. Many features of this example are considered typical of the genre. The scale, which ranges over an octave, is missing the fourth degree, and the melodic phrases generally have a descending shape. De Noraidh 1965:28.

My love, my dear one!
Do not believe them
Nor the hint you got
Nor the hostile story
That I went to sleep.
Sleep did not come to me,
Your children were sore grieving,
And they needed
To be put at ease then. (Henry 1991)

Lyric and Narrative Songs and "Lilting"

Irish- and English-language lyric and narrative songs are less formally defined than lays, but quatrain form was practiced, early and late, in both languages, and after the Middle Ages verses of eight or four long lines have been common. ABBA form, borrowed more than two centuries ago from the British broadside ballad (figure 2), has been much commoner in English, though increasingly used in songs in Irish. The couplet rhyme and symmetrical musical repetition of English songs serve plain expression, while Irish uses the often more extended AABA form for more "difficult" expression (a term not usually depreciative in Irish), covering form and content and exemplified in lexical diversity and complicated rhyme. Despite such contrasts, cultural interaction has caused the introduction of features of each language and its song forms into the other.

The length of phrases helps make melody the most interesting musical feature of Irish song. An open cadence is usually followed by a closed one, and a low register by a high one. Airs, the conventional label for vocal melodies, may encompass a wide range, such as an eleventh or a twelfth—a trait sufficiently Irish for a melody of uncertain status, the "Londonderry Air," which runs to a fourteenth in its published form, to have become a world-renowned representative of the flowery, well developed, usually major, Gaelic tunes in AABA form.

Lilting (*portaireacht*), the singing of instrumental dance tunes to nonlexical syllables, is the only vocal music for dancing, but little used for that purpose today. Occasional verses of words may surface among the syllables of lilt, but they usually belong not to songs, but to a repertoire of verses used to amuse company.

Performance Styles and Practices

Singers usually modify strict meter by means of pauses or lengthening, not only at cadences, but at climaxes within lines. These modifications, known as rubato, vary in degree with the singer, the language, and the region. The slower and more rubato the song, the greater the opportunity for melodic ornamentation, used plentifully and traditionally in the Gaeltachts (native Irish-speaking areas) of Munster and Connaught, but not Donegal. This style, for which *sean-nós* 'old manner' is a recent label, is strongest in Connemara, where ornamentation embellishes notes, filling melodic intervals, and the extent of rubato contrasts in lingering and hurrying passages. Connemara *sean-nós* singing has influenced many young singers from all over Ireland and elsewhere, though its songs in Irish and their metrical verses recur in the other Gaeltachts, and the melodies are found throughout Ireland.

The underlying structure of singing is basically syllabic. Melodic ornamentation has its verbal

Figure 2 "Ann Jane Thornton," a narrative song, sung in English by Robert Butcher of Magilligan, County Derry. From the broadside ballad tradition, songs such as this, in quatrain (four-line) form, in this case ABBA, had come to Ireland by the eighteenth century. Shields 1964:42.

counterpart in the nonlexical syllables that singers insert freely into the words of songs. These syllables are also clearly intended as ornament. Big, sonorous voices are not favored, though a certain degree of pitch vibrato, far from the classical model, is at times audible. Traditional style is more inclined to diminish sonority in varied ways, as by emphasizing the voiceless sounds of in the verbal text. Though the rhythm is relaxed, a certain tenseness often leads to sharpening of pitch as the song progresses, so that it may end a step or two higher than it began. Songs may also end in speech, for it is old tradition to descend into speech in the concluding line, phrase, or word.

Traditional songs (and instrumental music) are transmitted and performed orally: performers do not countenance singing or playing from written music. "Help" in the performance of song may be supplied vocally by a second singer, and singing in duet is somewhat common, though it remains a monophonic variant on solo practice.

Irish music found more than temporary quarters in America, the chief destination of Irish emigrants since the late 1700s. Irish music has flourished there, and the exchange of players, more often than singers, between the homeland and what used to be called the New Island became common in the second half of the twentieth century. See TRADITIONAL IRISH DANCE MUSIC AND SONG in The United States and Canada section.

Instrumental Music

The instrumental repertory, traditionally played solo, but since the mid-twentieth century also in groups (figure 3), consists mainly of dance music. Though often played without dancing, it has experienced a renewal of its earlier function as a result of the revival of set dancing since the 1970s. It drew largely on native musical material to nourish a limited range of dance forms adopted from abroad: the jig, in 6/8 meter (with the slip jig in 9/8, and the slide in 12/8); the reel, in 4/4 or 2/2; the hornpipe, in 4/4; the polka, in 2/4; and the march, in 2/4 or 6/8. Dance music is played fast, with ornamentation, and today's technically skilled young players often take tempos as fast as possible.

Most players prefer reels, and some play nothing else. Dance tunes consist typically of two sections, traditionally called the tune (*fonn*) and the turn (*casadh*), each consisting of two four-measure phrases. The sections are usually repeated to make an AABB form. A few tunes with more than two sections may vary the order of their repetition (for example, ABCBAB). A performance conventionally consists of a series of two or more tunes in the same meter, even when not played for dancing, but items in different meters that are variants of one tune may be played successively.

Some instrumentalists also play slow airs taken from songs and played exclusively for listening. The basic meter is that of the song in question, which can bring in 3/4 meter, not otherwise represented in the instrumental repertoire, but the 3/4 or other song meter is played intentionally rubato. Some players successfully introduce considerable variation into their airs, and the flexible rhythm and melodic ornamentation resemble the Connemara *sean-nós* style.

Musicians usually provide interest by making rhythmic and melodic variations in successive repetitions and ornamenting notes somewhat as in the

Figure 3 A house session in Donegal, 2005. The musicians play (from left) the pennywhistle, a *bodhrán*, a piano accordion, and a guitar.
Photo by Sean Williams.

more ornate styles of singing, by adding single grace notes one or more degrees above the melody note, inserting trills and rolls (groups of three descending grace notes, the second of which is equal in pitch to the main note), and articulating successive main notes of identical pitch. These features enhance solo playing and the heterophonic group playing associated with a solo tradition.

Musical Instruments

The range of instruments played traditionally today is small—principally fiddle, wooden side-blown flute, tin whistle (a six-hole whistle flute), pipes (by which is meant bellows-blown bagpipes), concertina, and diatonic accordion. All these but the last two, if we take into account their respective precursors, have a long, even millennial, history. The contexts of their use are almost wholly recreational and without ritual significance.

In the eighteenth century, the violin (usually called fiddle by traditional musicians) enjoyed a boom in Dublin music publishing, and music for it was composed, or borrowed from popular tradition. The instrument is not played in a classical manner. It is held lower at a different angle, and the upper end of the bow is used most of the time. Fiddling was somewhat better sustained than piping until the late-twentieth-century revival.

The only traditional Irish instrument now in use that is of native elaboration is the *uilleann* pipes (figure 4). Like Scottish bagpipes, they now have three drones tuned in octaves, but to these were added a set of three pipes ("regulators"), each with a few metal keys depressed by the player's wrist to create limited harmonic accompaniment. The style of playing may be legato with open fingering, or staccato with closed ("tight") fingering. During the twentieth century, playing of the instrument declined to such an extent that its extinction seemed imminent, but revival since the 1970s has been impressive, and societies of players now exist, not only in Ireland, but also in Britain, Europe, America, and Australia. Today, the majority of pipers are men and the majority of harpers are women, though this has not always been the case.

The Revival of Irish Music

Music and dance were highly valued social practices in rural Ireland during the nineteenth and early twentieth centuries, when traditional instrumental music was usually played to accompany dancing. Contexts included crossroads dances, at which professional or semiprofessional itinerant musicians, usually a piper or fiddler, played outdoors for local residents, who danced and socialized, and the *céilí*, where friends and neighbors gathered to drink, sing, dance, tell stories, and play music for one another. Singing was traditionally unaccompanied, but instrumental music, though often solo, was played in unison by informal, impermanent groups of two or three musicians.

Traditional dancing and the rural *céilí* suffered a serious decline during the economic downturn of the 1930s. The Dance Hall Act of 1935 banned crossroads dancing, many dance halls closed, and the lack of employment at home led many rural musicians, with their neighbors, to leave the countryside to find work in Dublin, London, and the United States. The

Figure 4 Two *uilleann* pipers from the Vallely Family perform at the Smithsonian Folklife Festival, Washington, D.C., 2007. *Photo by Jacob W. Love.*

loss of traditional contexts for dancing led to a decline in the playing of traditional music throughout the country.

Although the dance-music tradition declined in rural Ireland, it was reinterpreted as the *céilí* band in urban contexts among Irish emigrant communities of Britain and America. Influenced by popular dance bands of the 1920s to 1950s and consisting of multiple fiddles, flutes, accordions, piano, and drum set, *céilí* bands presented dance tunes in a danceable style in which rhythm, harmony, and collective playing eliminated much of the ornamental subtlety of traditional solo playing. Initially a creation of the nationalist organization Conradh na Gaeilge (The Gaelic League) in the late 1800s, the *céilí band* was an early example of collective playing in Irish music, and by the 1950s it had become extremely popular throughout Ireland and in emigrant communities.

In the 1950s, an aesthetic reaction against *céilí* bands by intellectuals and the influence of commercialized American folk music, followed by an unprecedented increase in economic prosperity in rural Ireland in the 1960s, combined to form the basis for a so-called revival of Irish traditional music.

In 1951, members of the Pipers' Club formed the musicians' organization Comhaltas Ceoltóirí Éireann. They organized competitive local, regional, and national festivals each year, culminating in the Fleadh Cheoil na hÉireann (Festival of Music of Ireland). The competitions spurred interest among young people, who, in increasing numbers, began learning to play traditional musical instruments. Looking for opportunities to play informally, experienced and beginning musicians began to gather

in so-called pub sessions; in the process, they created a new tradition of collective playing. The repertoire is almost exclusively dance music, predominantly reels.

A second influence on the Irish revival came from the folk revival in the United States. The Clancy Brothers and Tommy Makem (1932–2007), emigrants from Ireland and aspiring actors in New York in the 1950s, began playing Irish songs in the folk-club scene in Greenwich Village, accompanying themselves on guitars and banjo and singing in unison, on the model of American groups like the Weavers. Their popularity and commercial success inspired similar groups in Ireland (the Dubliners and the Wolfe Tones) and Scotland (the Corries), and an active scene in pubs and folk clubs in Ireland and Great Britain.

Seán Ó Riada (1931–1971)—a classically trained composer—developed a fourth element of the Irish folk revival. In 1960 he organized traditional musicians into a group that became known as Ceoltóirí Chualann. Through his selection of instruments and his arrangements, he effectively invented a new tradition, a fusion of classical and Irish music. His choice of instruments included *uilleann* pipes, two fiddles, a flute, a whistle, a button accordion, a concertina, a harpsichord (which he played), and a *bodhrán*, a goatskin frame drum. He carefully orchestrated alternating solos and instrument combinations, and added countermelodies and chords in a way that highlighted the ornamental style of individual musicians and contrasted sharply with the *céilí*-band style. His group became extremely popular with the urban middle class and the artistic scene in Dublin. Affiliated musicians, under the leadership

Figure 5 The group Four Men and a Dog performs at the Smithsonian Folklife Festival, Washington, D.C., 2007. *From left*: Gino Lupari plays *bodhrán*; Cathal Hayden, fiddle; Donal Murphy, accordion; Gerry O'Connor, banjo; and Kevin Doherty, guitar. Formed in 1990, the group mixes traditional Irish music with a variety of other genres.
Photo by Jacob W. Love.

of the piper Paddy Moloney (b. 1938), became The Chieftains, who went on to become world-famous as performers of Irish music and a model for other touring bands, who perform at pubs, folk festivals, folk clubs, and formal concerts.

In the 1970s, celebrated bands such as Planxty, The Bothy Band, De Danann, and Clannad fused the traditional instruments of groups like The Chieftains with guitar-based ballad singing and influences from rock and jazz to produce complex instrumental accompaniments and virtuosic, hard-driving instrumentals.

The economic boom of the 1990s set the stage for a new kind of regional pride in Ireland and its musics. In the early twenty-first century, Irish music groups have ventured in many new directions (figure 5), including hard rock with Irish instrumentation, "Celtic-flavored" New Age recordings, and acoustic bands featuring world music instruments.

—Adapted from an article by Hugh Shields and Paulette Gershen

Bibliography

Acton, Charles. 1978. *Irish Music and Musicians*. Dublin: Eason.
Breathnach, Breandán, ed. 1971. *Folk Music and Dances of Ireland*. Dublin: Talbot Press.
Carson, Ciaran. 1986. *Irish Traditional Music*. Belfast: Appletree Press.
Cowdery, James. 1990. *The Melodic Tradition of Ireland*. Kent, Ohio: Kent State University Press.
De Noraidh, Liam, ed. 1965. *Ceol ón Mumhan*. Dublin: An Clóchomhar.
Henebry, Richard. 1928. *A Handbook of Irish Music*. Cork: Cork University Press.
Henry, P. L., ed. and trans. 1991. *Dánta Ban: Poems of Irish Women, Early and Modern*. Dublin: Mercier.
Ó Canainn, Tomás. 1978. *Traditional Music in Ireland*. London: Routledge and Kegan Paul.
Shields, Hugh, ed. 1964. "Some Bonny Female Sailors." *Ulster Folklife* 10:35–45.
——. "Popular Modes of Narration and the Popular Band." In *The Ballad and Oral Literature*, ed. Joseph Harris, 40–59. Cambridge: Harvard University Press.
——. 1993. *Narrative Singing in Ireland Lays, Ballads, Come-All-Yes and Other Songs*. Dublin: Irish Academic Press.

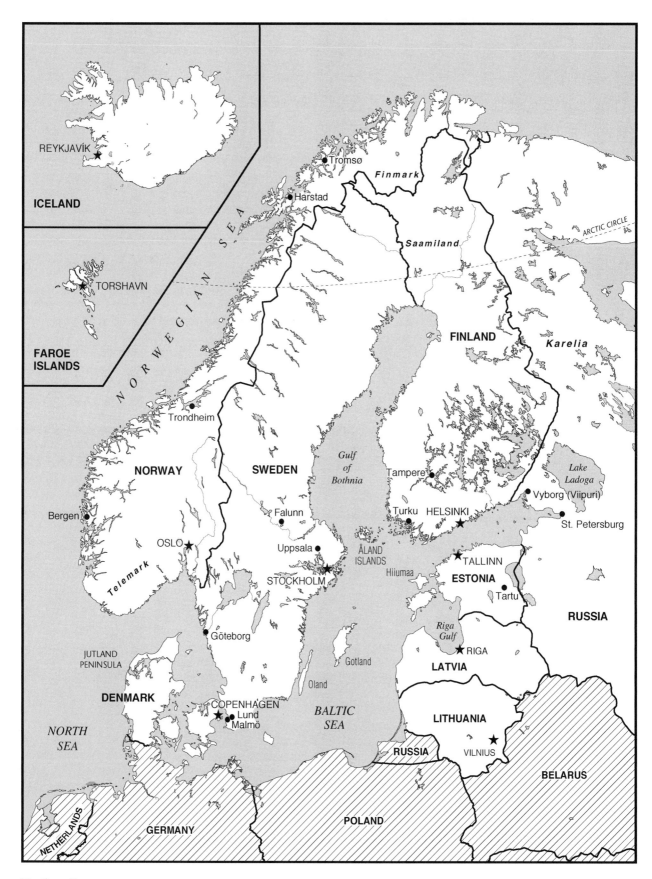

Northern Europe

Northern Europe

The people of Northern Europe speak languages in three families: Scandinavian, Baltic (Latvian and Lithuanian), and the non-Indo-European, Finno-Ugric languages (Finnish, Estonian, and Saami). Many countries of the region share the historical experience of Swedish or Russian rule. Protestant denominations are the norm, and as a consequence devotional singing has been a popular form of entertainment in many areas.

Epic poems and long historical ballads are still sung in Iceland and the Faroe Islands, and have been written down in Finland. Most singing is monophonic, but traditional forms of polyphony persist in Iceland. The most characteristic instrument of the region, the plucked or bowed zither, is found in nearly every country. The long mid-summer's eve is probably the most important calendar custom here. Many countries have contributed important composers and performers to the history of classical music. And several countries have internationally known popular musicians.

To offer readers a sense of the traditional music of this region, we present articles on Iceland, Norway, Sweden, Denmark, and Finland.

Iceland

Iceland lies in the North Sea, 240 kilometers southeast of Greenland, 800 kilometers northwest of Scotland. Geologically a new body of land, it seethes with geothermal activity, concentrating the population—sparse, at about 300,000—along the coast. At 103,000 square kilometers, it is Europe's second-largest island. More than 90 percent of the population live in cities and towns, and fishing and fish processing and aluminum manufacturing are the major industries.

Iceland was originally settled within a short span (C.E. 870–930), largely by immigrants from western Scandinavia. Some of these refugees came by way of Ireland and nearby islands, where they were joined by Celtic spouses, servants, and slaves, the degree and nature of whose influence has become a matter of interest to historians. Of the Nordic countries, Iceland has attracted the most interest among foreign historians, linguists, and social scientists—an interest dominated by a romantic-antiquarian perspective. Musicologists have tended to view Icelandic culture as static, dominated by a sense of history and mythology. Indeed, Icelandic musical culture has been remarkable, but this is because of active, not passive, causes.

Vocal Genres

Rímur

Rímur ('rhymes'; sing., *ríma*) are lengthy epic poems that used to be chanted informally when Icelandic family members gathered in the evening—occasions called *kvöldvökur* ('evening awakenings'; sing., *kvöldvaka*) that were an enormously popular means of cultural expression for almost six centuries. Though it no longer serves a function in contemporary life, *rímnakveðskapur*, the art of composing *rímur*, continues within the structure of clubs and other organizations more relevant to the urban milieu.

A strophic form, *rímur* combines a highly esoteric versification technique with a short, reiterated melody, traditionally intoned in a performance style between singing and speaking. The melody of a *ríma* may be of the simplest litany type, using as few as two pitches; other styles, however, manifest developmental subtleties and sometimes vie with the text in rhythmic intricacy. A more songlike, diatonic style is preferred by twentieth-century performers (figure 1).

Rímur were performed in various contexts, including sheepherding, fishing, and traveling, and they were a source of livelihood for itinerant performers. Characteristic of the tradition was the evening awakening, when a family gathered to hear legendary lore or history, read or recited by a chanter (*kvæðamaður*), who might be a family member, a neighbor, or an itinerant musician, renowned for special abilities.

The characteristic metrical shift at the beginning of each chapter (*ríma*) and the metrical manipulations within each chapter are a musical and textual device to sustain interest throughout a long narrative. A single *rímnaflokkur*—an entire cycle or a series of chapters—could consist of thousands of stanzas, using hundreds of metrical variations. The performance of a cycle of *rímur* includes the lengthening of the final note of each strophe; final tones are made prominent by an idiosyncratic ornament (*dilla* or *dillandi*), executed with vibrato. The characteristic timbre of the chanting has an intensity that heightens excitement as the recitation proceeds—an effect often enhanced by the abrupt raising in pitch of the last note of each stanza by a semitone. In traditional performances of *kvöldvaka*, the audience customarily joins in on the last note—a practice called *taka undir* 'to take under'.

No matter what the melodic style of *rímur*, the vocal timbre used by the chanter is an intense, guttural sound, and the performance is accomplished in a slow, dirgelike tempo. Records show that *rímur* were once associated with dancing, and perhaps dances influenced the metrical form of *rímur*. Melodies of *rímur*, called *bragir* and *stemmur*, may come from a body of existing tunes, or they may be newly created; a chanter who selects an existing melody may adapt it to various metrical configurations.

Tvísöngur

Iceland's other major indigenous vocal tradition is *tvísöngur* 'two-singing'. Usually thought of as a form, *tvísöngur* is more accurately described as a technique used to enhance the performance of sacred and secular vocal melodies, including those of *rímur*. This technique involves, in its simplest form, the

1. Lík- a- frón og lags- menn tveir, ljós- ið dags nær fá að skoð- a,
3. Fram- ar gnæf- a fjöll- in há; firð- a þreyt- ir leið- in hál- a

kveð- ja hjón og því- næst þeir það- an und- ir fjöll- in troð- a.
allt að kveld- i er þeir sjá á- kaf- leg- a mik- inn skál- a.

Stanza 1.	Stanza 3.
Líkafrón and his two companions,	Ahead, the high mountains tower;
as they see dawn break,	the slippery way tires the men
take leave of the couple and then	until the evening, when they see
walk from there toward the mountains.	an enormously big hall.

Figure 1 A *ríma* melody performed in the songlike, diatonic style preferred by some twentieth-century performers. Recorded and transcribed by Halldor Einarsson taped en route to Iceland on the freighter *Dettifoss*, 1965. *Translation by Hallberg Hallmundsson.*

Ljós- ið kem- ur langt og mjótt, langt og mjótt, langt og mjótt.

Ljós- ið kem- ur langt og mjótt, log'r á fíf- u stöng- um.

The light comes long and slender, long and slender, long and slender.

The light comes long and slender, flames glittering on stalks of cotton grass.

Figure 2 *Tvísöngur* 'two-singing' in parallel fifths. In the first phrase, the voices cross after the first two measures; in the second, the top voice leads a tritone and in stepwise motion outlines a high-pitched arch. After a transcription sent to Bjarni þorsteinsson by Benedict Jónsson about 1900 (þorsteinsson 1906–1909:212; see also Helgason 1980:114–115).

accompanying of one voice by another in parallel fifths; the melody is accompanied by an extemporized second part, which begins a fifth below the melody and crosses it to conclude a fifth above (figure 2). This procedure reflected a soloist's skill; the melody could be sung by multiple voices. More elaborate versions of *tvísöngur*, with doublings at the octave for other vocal parts, and a great variety of freer forms, were performed in sacred and secular settings. The *tvísöngur* has been applied in Iceland to a wide range of monophonic pieces, from flippant courting songs and the melodies of traditional *rímur* to Gregorian chants and psalm tunes.

Religious Singing

The first Icelandic printing of musical notation occurred in 1589, nearly six decades after the beginning of the Reformation in Denmark (1530); melodies were included in the *Psalma Bok*, compiled by Bishop Guðbrandur þorlaksson. The volume contained a diatribe against *rímur*, which the bishop called undesirable poems of giants and heroes and wicked and evil recitation. In 1594, he issued his Gradual (*Grallari*), containing Latin chants and Lutheran chorales. For more than two centuries, it functioned as a linchpin of Icelandic religious vocal tradition, and its influence is still felt. Danish imperial decrees aimed at enforcing standardization did not, however, succeed in supplanting indigenous Icelandic culture, musical or verbal.

Religious authorities also inveighed against the style of religious singing in the service. Even as late as the 1800s, the leading singers would not confine themselves to the notes as printed, but insisted on continuing the practice of applying ornaments and improvisation until the hymn tunes seemed utterly unrecognizable. Singing the notes was called singing the new way. Despite the ecclesiastical insistence on "correct" musical worship, the people viewed hymn singing as an integral part of their own domain, and continued informally, at least through the 1800s, to sing hymns in traditionally melismatic styles.

Musical Instruments

Two instruments, both bowed zithers, are unique to Iceland, though they share features with other northern European bowed lyres.

The *fiðla* has two or more horsehair strings (later, metal or gut), which run the full length of a slightly trapezoidal sound chamber. It is placed on a table-top, or laid across the knees of the player, who holds the bow like a pencil. The *fiðla* uses neither finger-board nor bridge, resulting in the production of a constant drone from simultaneously sounding strings. All strings but one are drones. The melody string is stopped from below, palm up. The technique employed on this instrument is similar to that used on the medieval bowed lyres typical of northern Europe and found in such extant examples as the Swedish-Estonian *talharpa* and the Finnish *jouhikantele*. The *fiðla*, which had almost disappeared from active use by the early 1800s, was revived in the twentieth century.

The other traditional instrument, the *langspil*, is also a bowed zither, usually with two to six strings (originally horsehair, later gut or wire) strung over a narrow, rectangular, box-shaped sound chamber, which has a sound hole at the lower end, where it flares out slightly. The fingers of the player's left hand press the melody string down onto frets, the drone strings are tuned in unison or to the fifth above the melody string, and the player holds the bow like a pencil. There is no bridge, and the bow actuates all strings simultaneously, producing a constant, thick-textured sound, typical of northern European bowed instruments of different categories: lute, lyre, and zither.

Trends in Traditional Music

In 1929 and 1930, two institutions devoted to *rímur* were founded: in Reykjavík, Kvæðamannafélagið Íðunn (Íðunn Chanters' Society, named for Íðunn, a Norse goddess), and in Hafnarfjördur, Kvæðamannafélag Hafnarfjardar (Hafnarfjardar Chanters' Society). Their purpose was to provide the opportunity to collect, perform, and create new *rímur* and *tvísöngur*, and in 1930 they established an annual field trip to further their goals. Since then, on the northern coast, another similar organization, Kvæðamannafélag Siglufjardar, has been formed.

More recently, a trio of traditional musicians—Njáll Sigurðsson, Bára Grímsdóttir, and Sigurður Rúnar Jónsson—have found themselves in demand for performances and lecture–demonstrations of Icelandic vocal and instrumental traditions, especially in Europe. Jónsson is one of the few Icelandic musicians to play the *langspil* and the *fiðla*, which he demonstrates on these programs. Since the 1950s, Anna Thorhallsdóttir has introduced audiences to the *langspil*, with which she accompanies her singing of hymns and other traditional material.

Traditional modes of expression have continued to persevere informally as well. The chanting of *rímur* always served multiple objectives: education, entertainment, protest, and competition—precisely the same purposes it continues to serve. A few *kvæðamenn* 'chanter-men' and *kvædakonur* 'chanter-women' still reside in rural areas. In the cities, founding members of *rímur*-devoted organizations tend to be persons brought up in rural traditions, and they participate in weekly walking clubs for the creation of *lausavísur* in new urban settings. Kvæðamannafélagið Íðunn, now with about 150 members, has always had a core of skilled musicians and versifiers. The organization continues to undertake field collecting and serves as a running documentary of the tradition itself.

Contemporary Iceland is alive with musical performance. Icelanders value the study and performance of music, so many children are given instruments to play from an early age. The towns and cities—especially Reykjavík—are home to a large variety of performing groups, including choirs, rock bands, and classical musicians. *Rímur* has even seen a small resurgence in a new guise: rap in Icelandic. Performers like *rímur* artist Steindór Andersen have made recordings that shift from *rímur* to rap, or otherwise play with traditional Icelandic musical forms in modern idioms. In addition, the international popularity of the singer-composer Björk (b. 1966) and the group Sigur Rós and the prevalence of live music in nightclubs has contributed to the growing popularity of Reykjavík as a musical destination, especially for other Europeans.

—*Adapted from an article by Pandora Hopkins*

Bibliography

Byock, Jesse. 1982. *Feud in the Icelandic Saga*. Berkeley: University of California Press.

Einarsson, Stefán. 1957. *A History of Icelandic Literature*. Baltimore: Johns Hopkins Press.

Hallberg, Peter. 1962. *Old Icelandic Poetry*. Lincoln: University of Nebraska Press.

Helgason, Hallgrimur. 1980. *Das Heldenlied auf Island: seine Vorgeschichte, Struktur Vortragsform: ein Beitrag zur älteren Musikgeschichte*. Graz, Austria: Akademische Druck und Verlagsanstalt.

Nielsen, Svend. 1982. *Stability in Improvisation: A Repertoire of Icelandic Epic Songs (Rimur)*. Translated by Kate Mahaffy. Copenhagen: Forlaget Kragen.

Ottósson, R. A. 1980. "Iceland: Folk Music." *The New Grove Dictionary of Music and Musicians*. Edited by Stanley Sadie. London: Macmillan.

Ryscamp, Charles. 1982. *Icelandic Sagas, Eddas, and Art*. New York: Pierpont Morgan Library.

Samsonarson, Jón, ed. 1964. *Kvæði og dansleikir*. 2 vols. Reykjavík: Almenna Bókafélagið.

þorsteinsson, Bjarni. 1906–1909. *Íslenzk þjóðlög*. Copenhagen: S. L. Møller.

Norway

From shortly before 1400 to shortly after 1900, Norway was ruled by non-Norwegian powers: first by Denmark, then by Sweden. The end of Danish rule (1814) inspired a nationalist movement to constuct a written Norwegian from diverse dialects, and the resultant language, *nynorsk* 'New Norsk', now enjoys equal status with older written Norwegian, *bokmal* 'Dano-Norsk', a form of Danish—reflecting a situation described as two nations within one. The indigenous Hardanger violin tradition was heralded as the national music of Norway. Since regaining independence as a constitutional monarchy (in 1905), Norway has continued to develop both strong regional and local affiliations and a sense of nationhood.

Norway occupies a 1,756-kilometer-long, narrow strip of land along the western coastline of the Scandinavian Peninsula. Fjords indent the (often mountainous) coast to create natural harbors, and a large percentage of the population of 4.6 million lives within 16 kilometers of the sea. Lengthy mountain chains divide the southern sector of the country into western and eastern regions, and distinguish the northern, arctic half from the broadened-out base in the southern highlands. Though these topographical features have inspired strong feelings of local identity, the ever-present waterways have provided exceptional opportunities for contact among valley communities and even with far-off countries.

About forty thousand Saami (formerly called Lapps) live in Finnmark, Norway's northernmost province. The Saami received their own parliament in 1989. Norway has three official languages: the two derivatives of Old Norse mentioned above, and Saami. The Hardanger violinist-composers Torgeir Augundson (1801–1872), called Myllarguten (The Miller's Boy), and Hårvard Gibøen (1809–1873), are two of Norway's most famous traditional musicians. Both from the county of Telemark, they achieved notoriety not only within the closely knit confines of indigenous music tradition, but throughout Norway. They established styles of playing that remain influential.

Vocal Genres

Sæter *Songs*

In Norwegian mountain communities during the most fruitful season of the year, women were in charge of the *sæter*, a summer farm for highland pasturing. Special sonic traditions grew up around farm activity: songs that accompanied the making of food, such as the butter-making song (*smørbon*); ornamented and individualistic animal calls, such as goat calls (*geitlokkar*), cow calls (*kulokkar*), and hog calls (*sauelokkar*); and elaborated shouts and hollers (*laling, huving*), which communicated from person to person across long distances. *Kulokkar*, generically animal calls, were highly idiosyncratic: yodeling, shouting, and singing were applied to an ornamented melodic line with microtonal inflections, often in a style between speaking and singing (figure 1). Variation in performance indicates that the genre offered scope for individual creativity within a traditional form.

Ballads

Ballads have been the primary means of transmitting historical narratives and legendary lore in Norway. They have been categorized according to subject matter: heroic songs (*kjempevisene*); knightly songs (*riddarvisene*), influenced by European romances; ancient, indigenous songs about the supernatural (*trollvisene*); sacred songs (*heilagvisene*), both Christian and pre-Christian; and animal songs (*dyrevisene*), which are humorous and often have a moral function. The heroic songs, still current in tradition-rich regions, stylistically resemble other epic-song traditions of northern Europe. In strophic form, each stanza is usually followed (occasionally preceded) by a refrain. Ballads are sung in a rhythm freely governed by speech accents in a vibratoless throat tone, a style of singing called *kveding*, which lets the singer control a high degree of ornamentation—a characteristic of much ballad performance in Norway.

The most famous sacred ballad, *Draumkvædet*, a medieval visionary poem, combines popular Christian (pre-Reformation) beliefs with mystic elements from earlier Norse religion. It tells of Olav Åsteson, who during a supernatural sleep from Christmas Eve to Epiphany receives a vision of heaven, hell, and doomsday. Four melodies are successively used in its fifty-two stanzas, each melody believed to be relevant to a particular portion of the story. In oral tradition, the melodic material is felt to be as old as the text.

Kom Su– mar– lauv, kom Sa– le, kom Bran– de– rygg og Sva– le. Kom

Lur– (re)–ve, kom Lar– ve og Li– ti– blom. Rek– kje og Snek– kje,

Skau– te og Rau– te. Et– te kje– me Sin– fak– se Sju– li– brand. Plu– lo, lu– lo– lo,

lu– lo lu– lo lu– lo lu– lo lo. Lu– lu– lu– lo.

Come, Sumarlauv! Come Sale! Come Branderygg and Svale! Come Lurve! Come, Larve and Little-Blossom! Rekkje and Snekkje, Skaute and Raute! After comes Sinfakse Sjulibrand.

Figure 1 A cow call (*kulokk*) with ornamented melody. A yodel-like refrain follows three texted phrases. Original pitch is a minor third lower. Sung by Hanne Kjersti Buen in Bø, Telemark, 1972.
Recording and transcription by Pandora Hopkins.

Stev *Tunes*

Older ballads, including *Draumkvædet* and most *kjempevisene*, use the old *stev* structure for each stanza:

/ u / u / u / u
/ u / u / u
/ u / u / u / u
/ u / u / u

This is a four-line stanza of trochaic tetrameter alternating with trochaic trimeter, with lines usually rhyming ABCB, though rhymes and meters are not standardized. The old *stev* tune, now virtually extinct, was a single stanza of popular poetry, a form that had its roots in the medieval period. It began to be supplanted during the nineteenth century by the new *stev* (*nystev*), which, though also containing four lines, differs in metrical construction and textual character. The text of the *stev*, old and new, has been the basis for vocal and instrumental improvisation. Singers have tended to regard the

> A stanza of **trochaic tetrameter** has four feet per line with each foot consisting of an accented syllable and an unaccented syllable (as in the word *tiger*).

> A stanza of **trochaic trimeter** has three feet per line with each foot consisting of an accented and an unaccented syllable.

stev as a way of singing, a basis for personal interpretation of text and melody, in contradistinction to songs that exist in songbooks or notated psalms.

Each of the four lines of new *stev* (*nystev*) contains four stressed syllables, and end rhyme links the first two and the last two lines. *Nystev* singing, with its uneven-beat patterning (sometimes reinforced with foot stamping), is sometimes associated with fiddle music; a *nystev* may have a ribald text, which frequently communicates an in-group joke or mockery. Fiddlers are usually adamant that the *nystev* grows out of the fiddle pieces, not the other way around (figure 2).

Religious Songs

As early as 1600, the Danish Reformed Church sought to impose the musical style and liturgy prevalent in Denmark on even the most isolated of Norwegian parishioners. This posed a serious threat to psalmodic improvisation, an integral part of popular religious observance at home and in church. However, instead of letting the existence of authorized texts destroy their creative performance tradition, performers used the printed chorale melodies as springboards for extemporizations that were melismatic, often modal, and rarely four-square in rhythm. In informal devotionals at home, parishioners successfully resisted the imposition of

Sov mi sø— te sul— le gjæ— va— re hell gul— le!

Bli lik snil— le pa— pa din, han er ful— la gut— en sin: og

han låg au i tul— le! Tral—la— la— lei, tra— la— lei,

tral— la— la— la lei— a.

Eveningtime brings shadows,
Mama embraces her baby,
Nothing dreadful can happen
To frighten her young one,
While Mama is rocking the cradle.

Figure 2 "Anne sit heime å tullar fe båne" (Anne sits at home singing [*tulling*] to her baby), a fragment of a vocal *nystev*, highly ornamented in the manner of instrumental music (after Buen et al. 1978:85).

central authority, perpetuating different styles of singing hymns, and improvising on the originals to create new material.

Musical Instruments and Instrumental Music

The most important instruments in use today are stringed instruments, though wind instruments are still used in pastoral settings.

The Langeleik

A slim, oblong, plucked zither, the *langeleik* 'long string' normally has eight steel strings, all but one are drones (figure 3). In performance, it lies on a table. The melody string runs over frets and is stroked by a plectrum held in the right hand. Between these strokes, the drones are plucked, being stopped by three left-hand fingers. The earliest evidence of the *langeleik* is a painting dated 1560.

The instrument has always been most closely associated with women. Sunday-evening concerts were regularly given by performers with a following

from the community. Pieces for listening (*lydarslåttar*) were played in early evenings, when *sæter* women did their weaving and embroidering; in late evenings, the *langeleik* accompanied social dancing. Today, Valdres continues to support an unbroken tradition of *langeleik* playing.

Bowed Strings

During the 1600s, members of the violin family began to be played in Norway, and the violin gradually took over the functions of the *langeleik*, which faded from view except in Valdres, where both instruments flourish. A second kind of violin also emerged, and two kinds of playing became associated with physically different violins; culturally, they divided up the country between them. The internationally known variety, called flat violin (*flatfele*) or usual or ordinary violin (*vanleg fele*), flourished in the northern, central, and eastern regions. The other variety, unique to Norway, was the Hardanger violin (*hardingfele* or 'Harding violin'), which held sway in the west and the south-central inner-mountain

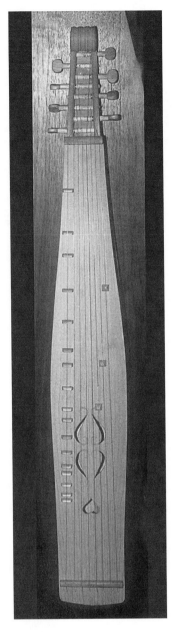

Figure 4 A *hardingfele* fiddle.
Photo by Terry E. Miller.

Figure 3 A *langeleik*.
Photo by Terry E. Miller.

valleys. This variation points to a larger issue within Norwegian music—the importance of regionalism. Whereas certain musical instruments are quite common in a particular area (the *hardingfele* in the south, for example), one rarely hears them in another area (the same instrument in the far north).

The Hardingfele

The *hardingfele*, which until the twentieth century was associated almost exclusively with men, is an elaborately ornamented violin with four or five sympathetic strings running beneath the fingerboard (figure 4). It must have been in existence by at least 1700, and has remained virtually unchanged since then. The instrument survived a period of intense religious persecution and increased in influence during the twentieth century—the same period that saw the disappearance of the pastoral-seafaring complex, to which it had belonged. The body of the *hardingfele* resembles the shape and size of a Baroque violin—smaller than the contemporary violin, with a more rounded body and a shorter neck. In addition to its most prominent feature, the sympathetic strings, it has a flatter bridge and fingerboard; elongated *f*-holes are so deeply cut into the belly that a protruding upper edge is formed; and its peg box, surmounted by a carved animal's head, is resplendent with gilt and reminiscent of the figureheads on Viking prows.

The *hardingfele* produces an unwavering background of upper-partial resonance created by the sympathetic strings. Other factors contribute to a thick texture, especially a seamless bowing technique applied to double and triple stopping, facilitated by the flatter bridge and alternate tunings (*scordatura*), which augment the number of open strings available for sympathetic resonance. The *hardingfele* produces its own melody and accompaniment and is primarily a solo instrument.

Aurally transmitted, traditional music for the *hardingfele* uses at least twenty different tunings. The instrument is normally pitched a whole tone to a tone and a half higher than standard A = 440 cps. A Hardanger fiddle piece is called a *slått* (pl. *slåttar*, from *slå*, 'to beat, to strike'). The tuning bound to any *slått* has extramusical connotations—for example, "Light Blue" is a tuning to be used at dawn, whereas "Troll Tuning" is used only between midnight and dawn. Though players no longer follow these rules strictly, they form part of the associations conveyed to knowledgeable listeners.

Slått music is not strictly tonal, but is usually constructed from disjunct tetrachords, often resulting in a scale not bounded by the octave, but including chromatic pitches. The musical structure can manifest an intricate melodic device that has been called inherent rhythms, single-line polyphony, and compound melodic line. Players have a special predilection for the tritone (a characteristic of music in other Nordic lands). *Slått* variations involve chains of motives, each slightly varied from its predecessor.

Rhythm is extremely complex; counterrhythms are heard against a firm backdrop of a repeating beat cycle; in a structure resembling that of the Indian *tāla* system, competing voices come together at periodic rest points. Performances also feature bowing across the beat and rhythmic alteration, the unequal performance of subdivisions of the beat. It is customary for player and audience to stamp their feet to the basic cyclical pattern throughout a performance. Sometimes the fundamental pattern is asymmetrical—that is, it consists of uneven beats.

Music for Dancing and Listening

Like the *langeleik*, the *hardingfele* has always served two functions, listening and dancing. It traditionally accompanies *bygdedansar*, the indigenous dances of Norway, which fall into two general categories according to their rhythmic makeup and type of step. Three dances in 2/4 or 6/8 meter—*gangar*, *rull*, and *halling* (*lausdans*)—are characterized by a slow and heavy, but flexible, gait. One dance—*springar*—is in triple meter, characterized by light, almost running steps or uneven, limping ones. The *halling* (*lausdans*) is an acrobatic solo dance, and the other three are couple dances.

Fiddler and dancers closely coordinate their actions in all these dances, the fiddler surrounded by the dancing couples. These dances are highly esoteric and difficult to perform; like *bygde* music, they are for trained specialists, not the general public.

In earlier times, at marketplaces, local courts of law, and informal gatherings, *slåttar* were played for listening. During the 1800s, fiddlers made names for themselves in formal concerts, and some even undertook concert tours to the United States. Today, the *hardingfele* appears in folkloric performances for tourists, and some people in the country regard it an anachronism, but the instrument is still widely performed in certain areas, particularly the southwest, and several contemporary popular musicians have begun to use it in their songs.

—*Adapted from an article by Pandora Hopkins*

Bibliography

Buen, Hanne, Agnes Buen Garnås, and Dagne Groven Myhren. 1978. *Ei Vise vil eg Kveda: Songar på folkemunn i Telemark*. Oslo: Tiden Norsk Forlag.

Goertzen, Chris. 1997. *Fiddling for Norway: Revival and Identity*. Chicago: University of Chicago Press.

Grinde, Nils. 1991. *A History of Norwegian Music*. Translated by William Halversen and Leland Sateren. Lincoln: University of Nebraska Press.

Hopkins, Pandora. 1986. *Aural Thinking in Norway Performance and Communication with the Hardingfele*. New York: Human Sciences Press.

Kortsen, Bjarne. 1975. *Norwegian Music and Musicians*. Bergen: Author.

Sevåg, Reidar. 1980. "Norway ii: Folk Music." In *The New Grove Dictionary of Music and Musicians*. Edited by Stanley Sadie. London: Macmillan.

Sweden

Geographically the fourth largest country in Europe, Sweden has about 9 million inhabitants, most of them clustered densely in a small part of an area of 449,750 square kilometers. The center and north of the country are heavily forested, with numerous lakes. The south supports an agrarian society, though most of the population lives in urban areas. The three major metropolitan areas—Stockholm (the capital), Göteborg, and Malmö—more than doubled in population between 1910 and 1970.

Evangelical Lutheranism claims about 90 percent of the population. Sweden's ethnic, linguistic, and religious homogeneity is modified by twenty thousand indigenous Saami and a post-World War II immigration from Finland, the Baltic countries, Italy, the Balkans, Iran, Turkey, and Latin America—immigration that accounts for about one-eighth of the population.

Regional Styles of Traditional Music

A common way to describe stylistic differences within Sweden is to speak of "musical dialects," as if musical styles were direct counterparts to linguistic dialects. At local levels, an abundance of dialects has been identified—in Dalecarlia, for example, one for each village. These dialects combine to form larger dialectal districts.

Another common way to divide Sweden, especially among folk musicians, is based on the character and distribution of instrumental tunes for the *polska*, a dance in 3/4 time, known in Sweden from the late 1500s and most popular before the early twentieth century. The dance has two parts: walking and turning. Freeform and improvisatory, it has many types and variants. It was the fiddlers' favorite genre. Tens of thousands of its tunes have been preserved, some of them primarily intended for listening, rather than dancing; the tunes also exist in many types, forms, and variants.

Until around 1650, parts of southern Sweden (Skåne, Blekinge, Småland, Halland, Gotland) belonged to Denmark, and proximity to Danish and German culture is clearly recognizable in local music there. An important part of the repertoire shows influences from the music of the upper classes of the 1600s and 1700s, but older styles are present. The south of Sweden, the east coast, and the islands of the Baltic sea (Gotland and Öland) reflect the economic boom in the 1700s, which, to even the remotest villages, brought new instruments, dances, musical forms, and styles. In Ångermanland, Hälsingland, and Gotland, violin music dominated dance-music in a style known as folk baroque. In southern and eastern Sweden, major modes are common, especially in tunes from the 1800s. There are many *åttondelspolskor* (*polska* in eighth-note rhythms), though the predominant type is *sextondelspolskor* (in sixteenth-note rhythms).

In central and western Sweden, many old-style tunes in minor modes survive and many new ones are composed. From Lake Mälaren northward, except for the eastern coast, *åttondelspolskor* are common; in western Sweden, triplet *polskas* (*triolpolskor*) proliferate. The folk music styles of western Sweden have traits similar to those of eastern Norway, and in many respects the territory of the Scandic Mountains forms a homogeneous culture area. Farther south, along the western coast, are many traces of contact with inhabitants of Britain.

Folk music in the far north reflects different waves of colonization in the seventeenth, eighteenth, and nineteenth centuries. Along the coast and east-flowing rivers are old and new styles, but farther north and west, in more recently colonized areas, popular idioms of the late 1800s predominate. Influences from Finnish folk music are perceptible in more populous areas along the border with Finland. The music of the Saami, scattered over vast expanses of northern Sweden, has left few marks on the music of the Saami's neighbors.

Musical Types and Structures

The oldest layer of music in Sweden, probably of medieval origin, consists of songs, ballads, herding music, and dance music—genres that share such traits as modal scales, narrow ranges, and short, repeated melodic formulas, heard in herding calls, lyrical songs, and melodies for flute, bagpipe, and violin.

In musical practice, the tones 1, 4, 5, and 8 of this scale are stable. The other degrees vary from one performance to another, within one rendition of a tune, or even within a given melodic phrase. Most collections and studies bear few signs of this musical practice, since the first generation of collectors and scholars often "corrected" the alterations on the grounds that they were mistakes or the result of poor intonation.

Ballads, many originating in the medieval period and once widespread throughout Sweden, have parallels throughout Scandinavia, Britain, and other European countries. Collected since the 1600s and praised by intellectuals as the most important folk-song genre, ballads mostly went out of oral currency in the 1700s. Broadside ballads (*skillingtryck*) and lyrical songs, which took over their function in the 1700s and 1800s, were preserved through a dialectical interplay between the oral versions and written or printed texts.

A second historical layer consists of dance music and songs of the 1700s, often deriving from popular dance music in Baroque style; the tunes have many formal and structural traits in common with the *galant* style: theme-development-theme form, sequential chains of sixteenth notes, a wide range (often over two octaves), and arpeggios or broken chords.

A third historical layer consists of music for the galop, the polka, the schottische, the waltz, and other dances, all introduced in the 1800s with newer instruments and ensembles: button accordions, mouth harps, and brass bands. This layer exhibits simple diatonic, stepwise melodies built on major or minor scales, with implicit harmonic progressions mainly in sixteenth-note rhythms (figure 1).

Other popular genres are drinking songs and erotic songs. Thousands of the former type still live in everyday practice, and many are known by almost every Swede. New versions, often of a burlesque character, are continually composed. A large number of erotic songs are still sung by teenagers. As with drinking songs, new variants are constantly appearing, often set to popular melodies.

Swedish folk songs are usually sung monophonically and in a fairly straightforward, unemotional manner: in a low or medium register and a slow tempo, with low volume and few ornaments; many folk songs have a solemn character, and have actually been sung as hymns. A few melismatic idioms do exist, however, as does singing at a high pitch—for example, cattle calls (*kulning*). Songs accompanying work, festivities, or dancing are sung in a more lively and rhythmic fashion.

Musical Instruments

Archaeological finds of flutes, bronze horns called *lurs*, and other instruments are evidence of musical activity from prehistoric times, much of it probably ritual. By the Middle Ages, Swedish musical culture was based on instruments found in other parts of Europe: the *hummel* (a plucked dulcimer), the *mungiga* (a mouth harp), the *spelpipa* (a duct flute), the *säckpipa* (a bagpipe), the *vevlira* (a hurdy-gurdy), the *nyckelharpa* (a keyed fiddle; figure 2), and the fiddle. All of these are still found in a variety of forms and are still played as folk instruments. To European instruments, Sweden contributed several prototypes, including the keyed fiddle, the Swedish lute, the Swedish clavichord (in use well into the 1800s), and the Swedish organ—all the result of a strong domestic instrument-building tradition that began to flourish in the 1700s.

The violin was brought to Sweden no later than the 1640s by French musicians hired to perform at the court of Queen Christina; in the 1700s, it conquered the rural population, among whom it soon became the most popular instrument. Musicians continued to play the same type of tunes as before, but they also learned styles related to virtuoso late Baroque music and pre-Classical violin music. Some musicians learned to play from musical notation.

The keyed fiddle was once played only in a small zone northeast of Stockholm, but after a vigorous revival in the 1970s and 1980s, it is played all over Sweden. The bagpipe enjoyed a similar revival in the 1980s. Though there are traces of at least three different types of bagpipes in Sweden from medieval times, it was probably never commonly played. A peculiar type—with a small stitched bag, one chanter, and a short drone—was played in villages in western Dalecarlia until the 1940s. This type, which provided the model for the revival, is now known as the Swedish bagpipe.

Figure 1 A typical nineteenth-century dance tune, with mostly diatonic stepwise melodic movement.

Figure 2 A woman plays a *nyckelharpa* on the street in Toledo, Spain, 2005.
Photo by Terry E. Miller.

By the late 1800s, the accordion had become popular, especially among urban working-class people. Because it became a symbol of progress, modernity, and industrialization, it was furiously opposed by spokesmen for supposedly authentic or original folk culture, most of whom belonged to the urban bourgeoisie and promoted the violin as the symbol of Sweden's folk heritage. Nonetheless, the fiddle and the accordion soon became an inseparable pair. The *gammeldans* 'old-time dance-music', a popular synthesis of old and new, is typically performed by bands consisting of accordions, fiddle, guitar, string bass, and drums.

DISC
TRACK
19

Folk music in Sweden was traditionally performed solo, or by two musicians playing in unison or octaves. In the late 1800s, specialized accompaniments became based on simple harmonic progressions or the improvisation of a second voice, using octaves, thirds, and sixths. In the mid-twentieth century, the latter way of accompanying spread, and is now the norm all over Sweden.

A popular ensemble that developed in the first half of the twentieth century under the influence of military brass bands and middle-class dance music is the fiddler's ensemble (*spelmanslag*). Early ensembles consisted of five to fifty fiddlers. Modern ones still consist mainly of fiddlers, but many include accordions, flutes, guitars, string basses, and drums. The ensembles perform folk music or *gammeldans*.

Contemporary Trends in Folk Music

Contemporary Swedish folk music consists of older styles and idioms consciously revived and reinterpreted for aesthetic or political reasons, plus newer forms and styles typified by enlarged forms, more and longer phrases, wider ranges, and more complex harmonic structures. Stylistic expansion is coupled to an expansion of instruments: Swedish folk music is played on older instruments (violins, keyed fiddles, bagpipes, and duct flutes), but many modern kinds have been introduced, including synthesizers, electric guitars, saxophones, and drum sets, often in combination with instruments from abroad, such as the *berimbau* (Brazilian musical bow), congas, and the *darbūka* (a Near Eastern vase-shaped drum). In turn, this expansion has furthered a search for new folk-music functions: on stage as chamber music, and in dance halls as popular dance music.

—Adapted from an article by Jan Ling,
Erik Kjellberg, Owe Ronström

Bibliography

Jacobsson, Stig, ed. 1993. *Swedish Composers of the Twentieth Century*. Stockholm: Swedish Music Information Center.

Jonsson, Bengt R., et al. 1978. *The Types of Scandinavian Medieval Ballad*. Stockholm: Svenskt Visarkiv.

Lundberg, Dan. 1998. "Folk Music: From Village Greens to Concert Platform." In *Music in Sweden*, edited by Susanne Concha Emmrich and Lena Roth, Stockholm: Swedish Institute. An updated version of this article is available online at http://www.visarkiv.se/en/folkmusic/index.htm

Lundberg, Dan, and Gunnar Ternhag. 2005. *Folkmusik i Sverige* (Folk Music in Sweden) 2nd ed. Stockholm: Gidlunds.

Lundberg, Dan, Krister Malm, and Owe Ronstöm. 2000. *Musik, Medier, Mångkultur: Förändringar i Svenska Musiklandskap*. Gidlunds: Hedemora. Translated by Kristina Radford and Andrew Coulthard as *Music, Media, and Multiculture: Changing Musicscapes*. Stockholm: Svenskt Visarkiv.

Ramsten, M., ed. 2003. *The Polish Dance in Scandinavia and Poland*. Stockholm: Svenskt Visarkiv.

Denmark

Denmark, a constitutional monarchy of 5.4 million people, occupies 43,069 square kilometers on the Jutland Peninsula (north of Germany) and six islands in the strait between the peninsula and Sweden. The economy, traditionally based on agriculture, shipping, and fishing, expanded after World War II to include manufacturing and services, including a furniture industry famous for its designs and craftsmanship. Lutheranism is the established religion.

Traditional Song Genres

The main genre of Danish folk song is the ballad—narrative, strophic song with end rhymes, with or without a chorus and a middle refrain. Medieval ballads consisted of two- or four-line stanzas with a special end-rhyme formation (*aa*, or *abcb*) and a chorus and possibly a middle refrain. They are categorized either as folk ballads (concerning persons of rank or encounters with the supernatural) or jesting ballads (concerning ordinary people, and often involving successful transgressions of religious norms and taboos).

Another, later category of ballad, echoing songs (*Efterklangsviser*), are known from written sources as far back as the 1500s. Similar to medieval ballads in text and content, they have a different metrical structure. Their content can be spiritual, secular, or historical. Ballads from the 1700s to the present—murder ballads, ballads of misfortune, and love, war, and sailors' songs—form a third major category. Parallel to the ballad genre is the popular singing of hymns with authorized texts, but with tunes that have been transformed.

The transmission of Danish traditional songs in the last 150 years has essentially taken place through broadsides (figure 1), prints that in the 1800s were sold in great numbers by balladmongers who appeared at markets or went from farm to farm. The tunes were often from already known ballads; if they were not, they were sung on the spot by the balladeer so people could learn them. The broadside served as a model that spread all over the country, causing later texts and tunes to display set forms and a certain standardization.

Musical Structure of Songs and Instrumental Music

When adults sing lullabies and dandling rhymes to children, and when children play their own singing

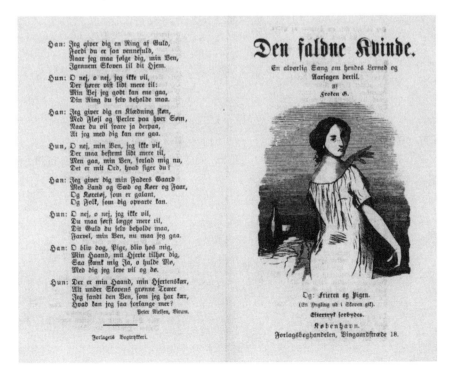

Figure 1 The cover and back page of a typical late-nineteenth-century broadside: "The fallen woman. A serious song about her life and the reason why." It contains words but no musical notation.

games and bantering cries, they freely link formulas related to hexachordal melodies—melodies with a six-tone pitch inventory—commonly found across Western Europe.

Most tunes for folk ballads, many jesting ballads, and a few nineteenth-century ballads belong to an early musical stratum that predates seven-tone modes. Individual tunes are structured as combinations of short melodic phrases, usually the length of a line in a diatonic scale with the range of a fourth, a fifth, or a sixth; a few pentatonic tunes also exist. Typical forms have two identical halves followed by a refrain—ABABC in four-line stanzas, AAB in two-line stanzas.

Ballad tunes and texts from the 1500s and 1600s were borrowed from Germany. The tunes usually have a more modal and metrical character than those discussed above, and are linked to particular texts.

During the 1700s and 1800s, numerous tunes marked by major-minor tonality appeared, often with an extended range. The influence of triadic harmony is evident in them, and their forms are more symmetrical than earlier tunes. The major mode became predominant during the 1800s. Two new musical forms account for about half the tunes: the ABCD form, with an overall arch shape; and the AABA form, with phrase B at a higher pitch than phrase A. The latter form is found in fiddlers' tunes and nineteenth-century love ballads.

Fiddle music can be divided into two historical strata. Old melodies, related to dances like the minuet and the *polska*, first appeared in music books before 1800 and are still performed in a few areas, such as Fanø and Lësø. In these tunes, the feeling of an underlying beat is stronger than that of a particular meter. The melody consists of one- or two-measure melodic and rhythmic motifs, repeated or transposed; phrases may include from five to nine bars. Newer melodies, the major part of the instrumental repertoire, are far more symmetrical and stereotypical, each phrase consisting of eight bars, normally repeated, and each melody, firmly based on major triads, evoking a tonic, a dominant, and a subdominant.

Folk Instruments

Around 1700, the *fedel*, a stringed instrument of the violin type, and the drum appeared as the most important instruments in rural music. The bagpipe, the hurdy-gurdy, and the mouth harp were undoubtedly used in this period, but their geographical distributions are uncertain.

In the early eighteenth century, the violin became the village musicians' predominant instrument, with the clarinet, the flute and, more rarely, the string bass. Accordions appeared in the late 1800s, and by about 1900 were competing with violins as the predominant dance instruments. More recently, musicians have come to use larger and more advanced accordions, but many accordion players' styles are still closely related to that of the two-row accordion.

Homemade instruments were fashioned in the nineteenth and early twentieth centuries. Clarinet-shawms are known in several forms made of pine, split, and hollowed out and bound or wedged together. A cow horn, possibly with one or more finger holes, was used as a bugle to call together the people of a village. The rumble pot, a friction drum made from a pot sealed with the skin of a pig's bladder and having a goose quill or a piece of reed attached to the middle, was used particularly in connection with New Year celebrations in Jutland and Fuen Island.

Music of Occupational, Social, and Religious Groups

Since the late 1950s, scholars have increasingly categorized Danish traditional music in terms of social groups and music's functions in society. The groups considered here include three main types of professional musicians—instrumentalists (fiddlers), who mainly play at dances in the country, street singers, and tavern musicians in towns—along with social groups marked by occupation, religion, political affiliation, age, and sex.

Instrumentalists

In rural areas, many instrumentalists played at dances, weddings, and seasonal celebrations, such as Shrovetide, Easter, Whitsunday, Midsummer Day, harvest festivals, and Christmas. They were also hired to mark the pace and rhythm of work, for example, the threshing of straw. Most often, they played the violin, but some used other instruments. Few earned their living solely by playing. They were usually artisans, blacksmiths, bricklayers, carpenters, small-holders, or farmhands, with music an important sideline.

Self-taught, many instrumentalists played by ear, having memorized their music. Others received instruction in childhood, or were apprenticed to an experienced instrumentalist who taught them dance tunes and how to read music. As a rule, only one musician played at a dance, and the instruments most often used were the violin and the accordion. Nineteenth-century dance ensembles included combinations of one or two violins, a clarinet or a flute, a trumpet, and a string bass. From the late 1800s, the accordion gained a foothold as an instrument for accompanying dancing; in the twentieth century, the piano and drums have also come into use.

Fiddlers play a variety of couple dances (fox-trot, *gammel vals*, i.e., 'old-fashioned waltz', galop, mazurka, polka, schottische, tango, waltz) and figure dances (*schottische anglaise*, minuet, and *polska*). Most instrumental dance tunes are played all over the country, but some—such as the figure dances in Thy and Sønderho and the *fannike* on Fanø—are specific to a certain area.

Street Musicians

Street musicians set up in the streets or backyards and sang or played for money; unlike professional or semiprofessional instrumentalists, they had no other occupation. Many came from a distinct social group, vagrants (*de rejsende*), who consist of families who have traveled around in house wagons since the early 1800s. Formal musical instruction was rare, but children learned to help at an early age, and thus acquired the trade.

The major part of street singers' repertoire was simply the music that was most popular. Before 1900, it consisted of broadside ballads and theatrical songs, and later it would include hits or dance music made popular by films or the radio. Apart from those examples, however, a few songs and tunes became associated with street singers; these included certain hits, broadsheet ballads about the dregs of society, prison ballads, and ballads about street singer's circumstances. The presentation, rather than the repertoire, is characteristic of street singing and street music: a fairly free and rather personal style allowed for rubato and melodic ornamentation with grace notes and glissandi. Street musicians might perform on their own; singing and playing at the same time, in pairs; or in larger ensembles.

In the 1800s, street musicians relied on the same group of instruments professionals used, but especially the guitar. In the twentieth century, the instruments were primarily the accordion, the banjo, the guitar, the saw blade, and spoons.

Tavern Musicians

Tavern musicians often belonged to vagrant families, and many street musicians were from time to time employed in taverns and beer gardens. Some, when they married and settled into a home, became tavern musicians. The tavern style resembles that of vagrants and street musicians, but its repertoire reflects the audience's demand to hear the most popular contemporary tunes.

Farmers' Songs

Well into the twentieth century, this group by far constituted the majority of the population. For the celebration of festivals such as New Year, Twelfth Night, Shrovetide, Easter, Whitsunday, and Mid-summer Day, villages had processions that used special songs. Some tunes are related to ballad tunes, but many are more recent.

Singing accompanied women's work (carding, milking, spinning), but the work is reflected less in the words or the tunes than in the style of singing, in which the rhythmical stress was evened out so the song could be sung independently of the rhythms of the work.

In rural areas, an important context for singing was twilighting—when young people sat in the dark, or did indoor work before lamps were lit, closely watched by a farmer and his wife. In the summer, they sat in roadside ditches, went for walks in groups, and met in farmhands' rooms, where the songs had a touch of eroticism.

Sailors' and Fishermen's Songs

During the era of sailing ships, sailors sang work songs, often English shanties in leader-chorus style, but also Danish and other Scandinavian shanties with tunes related to ballad melodies. The words were often heroic, but from time to time singers improvised satirical verses about onboard situations and individuals. The leader customarily sang the verse, and the others sang the middle refrain and chorus. In port and on watch below, narrative ballads (love songs) and ballads about the conditions on ships were sung. The tunes of these ballads derive from more recent musical styles.

Sailors' and fishermen's song traditions are closely connected. Fishermen sang work songs while hauling boats in, and cried work cries while hammering fishing stakes down. They also sang while not at work, as when storms kept boats in port, or when a whole family was mending the nets, or when fishermen went visiting in winter.

Religious Songs

Some religious movements have distinct musical forms. As late as the 1960s, Jutlanders employed a hymn-singing style that had been fairly common until the mid-1800s. Using *kingotoner*, tunes in a hymnbook compiled by Bishop Thomas Kingo (1634–1703), they sang in a slow tempo, with inserted passing tones and ornamentation.

The Home Mission, an evangelical branch of the Church of Denmark, strongly opposes public dancing, and as a result has retained the tradition of letting groups of engaged couples play singing games when they gather, after meetings or at private parties. Young people in the Home Mission used old traditional singing games, but they also invented new ones, often with words and tunes from official, patriotic songs.

The Folk Revival

In 1901, students and university graduates, taking their inspiration from Sweden, founded the Association for the Promotion of Folk Dance; local associations soon appeared all over the country. Its object was to preserve Danish folk dances and keep them alive in the manner in which they had been danced over the period from 1750 to 1850. To achieve this, members collected, taught, and performed dances. In 1946, the associations' musicians formed a subsidiary organization, Danish Folk-Dancers' Association of Fiddlers. By the late twentieth century, fifteen to twenty thousand people belonged to these associations.

In the mid-1960s—when the international folk-music revival reached Denmark—American, Irish, and English music prevailed, inspiring young musicians to incorporate foreign musical elements into their music. The interest in using Danish material then declined, except within leftist youth groups opposed to joining the common market. At the beginning of the 1970s, Thorkild Knudsen founded the first Folk-Music House, which started a movement that met the need for a physical and social setting for folk music activities. Folk-Music Houses were particularly interested in preserving ballad dancing. In them, young people who had no folk music tradition could meet the older bearers of folk music, learn from them, and continue the tradition. They could also learn to play an instrument and dance, and in some localities they collected folk music. The activities of the Folk-Music Houses ended in the early 1980s, but some associations still continue.

—*Adapted from an article by Svend Nielsen*

Bibliography

Abrahamson, Werner Hans Friederich, Rasmus Nyerup, and K. M. Rahbek. 1812–1814. *Udvalgte Danske viser fra Middelalderen.* 5 vols. Copenhagen: J. F. Schultz.

Bak, Kirsten Sass, Elsemarie Dam-Jensen, and Birgit Lauritsen. 1983. *Æ har høør . . . Sønderjyder synger.* Aabenraa: Institut for Grænseregionsforskning.

Berggreen, Andreas Peter. 1869. *Danske Folke-Sange og Melodier.* 3rd ed. Copenhagen: C. A. Reitzel.

Grüner-Nielsen, Hakon Harald. 1917. *Vore ældste Folkedanse, Langdans og Polskdans.* Copenhagen: Det Schønbergske Forlag.

——. 1920. *Folkelig vals.* Copenhagen: Det Schønbergske Forlag.

——. 1924. *Læsøfolk i gamle dage.* Danmarks Folkeminder, 29. Copenhagen: Det Schønbergske Forlag.

Holmboe, Vagn. 1988. *Danish Street Cries A Study of Their Musical Structure, and a Complete Edition of Tunes with Words Collected Before 1960.* Acta Ethnomusicologica Danica, 5 Copenhagen Forlaget Kragen.

Knudsen, Thorkild, and Nils Schiørring, eds. 1960–1968. *Folkevisen i Danmark: Efter optegnelser i Dansk Folkemindesamling,* no. 1–8. Copenhagen: Musikhøjskolens Forlag.

Koudal, Jens Henrik. *Rasmus Storms nodebog: En fynsk tjenestekarls dansemelodier o. 1760.* Copenhagen: Forlaget Kragen.

——. 1989. *Sang og musik på Dansk Folkemindesamling: En indføring.* Copenhagen: Forlaget Folkeminder.

Nielsen, Svend. 1978. *Glimt af dansk folkemusik: Tekster, melodier & kommentarer.* Copenhagen: Kragen.

——. 1980. *Flyv lille påfugl: Tekster, melodier og kommentarer til traditionel sang blandt børn.* Copenhagen: Kragen.

——. 1993. *Dansk folkemusik: en indføring i den traditionelle musik i Danmark.* Copenhagen: Dansk Folkemindesamling.

Finland

Finland (*Suomi* in Finnish) is a republic of 5.2 million people, of whom more than three hundred thousand are Swedes and other minorities. Finnish, one of the few non-Indo European languages in Europe, belongs to the Finnic branch of the Uralic language family, which includes Hungarian and Samoyed, a Siberian tongue. Other Baltic Finnic groups include Karelians, Veps, Votyans, Ingrians, Estonians, and Livonians; ethnic relatives also include the Saami of Saamiland, and the Mordvins and Maris of Russia's Volga basin.

A province of Sweden from 1150 to 1809, and of Russia from 1809 to 1917, Finland first became an independent country in 1917. Finland can be divided into three basic cultural zones: the west, influenced by Western Europe; the east, influenced by Eastern Europe and Russians via Karelia, an area in Finland and Russia; and the north, a zone of mixed Saami, Finno-Karelian, and Scandinavian elements. Older cultural elements survive mainly in the east, in the north, and in Russian Karelia; modern influence has entered primarily through the southern ports: Turku, Viipuri, and Helsinki.

Lutheranism, which came to Finland in the 1500s, had a profound effect on traditional music. Lutherans banned Kalevala singing as the main source of pagan culture. As people abandoned this tradition, they adopted new ones from western Finland, such as dancing to the accompaniment of violins, new rhyming stanzaic structures for texts, and a new tonal system.

Traditional Singing and Genres of Song

The oldest Finnish genres of song are the lament (*itku*, 'cry, weep') and the *runo* (or *laulu*). The underlying structure of both genres is a tetrachordal or pentachordal scale (C–D–E–F–G) with an unstable third degree, sung minor, major, and neutral, sometimes in the same song. The *runo* scale is sometimes expanded by the addition of a fourth below the tonic and a neutral sixth, a major seventh, and an octave above it. The *runo* and lament are sung syllabically.

The Karelian *itku* has no fixed textual meter. The singer starts on a high note and descends slowly to the tonic—a gesture repeated several times in improvised, heterometric lines. Containing mythic elements, laments convey symbolic expressions outside normal language. Lamenting was a socially

regulated way to express sorrow for weeks or months after death and a protection against destructive supernatural powers. Women also lamented departures, such as when a bride bade her home farewell and left for the bridegroom's house. Traditionally, the Karelian lament was restricted to women. All other genres were sung by men and women.

Strictly metric, the *runo* is the genre in which the text of the Finno-Karelian epic, Kalevala, was sung. Kalevala songs were used in all social occasions, from feasts and rituals to work and amusement. The textual meter consists of four trochaic feet: the first foot may have two, three, or four syllables, and the others have two syllables; hence, each line is composed of eight, nine, or ten syllables and melodic notes. The musical form was iterative: the singer repeated one isometric line (AAAA), or he would repeat two isometric lines that differed from each other (ABABAB). Since the 1700s, the basic unit of structure has become a four-line stanza (ABCB). In Finland, the musical meter used to be 5/4 or 5/8 and 2/4, but mixed meters were also usual, especially in Karelia. *Runo* texts in both genres employed alliteration, but not rhyme. Because the main stress in Finnish is always on the first syllable, upbeats are virtually nonexistent, and a stressed syllable tends to have a higher pitch than an unstressed one. Song texts in Kalevala meter have four feet per line:

Is-ki ker-ran, is-ki toi-sen.
He struck it once, he struck it twice.

Kalevala song texts include mythic, magical, and shamanic themes, sea adventures from the Viking age (ca. C.E. 800–1000), Christian legends, ballads, and dance-songs.

In the 1520s, when Sweden became a Protestant country, the Finns received from Germany new kinds of modal, and later tonal, songs with rhymed texts organized into stanzas. Many of the melodies, used as psalm tunes by the church, were borrowed from the popular love songs and ballads of the 1400s to 1600s. These new melodic principles combined with the structural principles of *runos* to form a new Finnish genre, *rekilaulu* (round-dance song), in which melodies are modal, major, or mixed. The musical meter is usually 2/4 or 4/4, the last two syllables sung with a double duration. Many genres originated in instrumental dance rhythms: the *polska*, for example, spawned corresponding *polska* songs with characteristic verse meter. *Reki* meter has seven feet per line, with a variable number of unstressed syllables per foot.

> *Kak-si mark-kaa mull on ra-haa,*
> *puo-let sii-tä on vel-kaa*
> *En-kös tyt-tö mam-mal-le-si,*
> *vä-vy-po-jaks kel-paa?*

> I've got two dollars in my pocket,
> half of it indebted.
> Ain't I quite a guy, my darling,
> to be a son-in-law to your mom?

Rekilaulu, whether lyric or epic, recount historical tales of people and events. Since the metric structure of *rekilaulu* was used to improvise texts, and since any text of *rekilaulu* could be applied to any melody in mazurka rhythm, mazurka songs became popular in the late nineteenth century. This poetic structure is still evident in popular music.

The Finno-Karelian style of singing is characterized by a relaxed voice in mid-register. The tempo is rather slow. The melody is not embellished, except in the singing of members of a Lutheran folk movement, the revivalists (*heränneet*), who decorate their performance of psalms. Singing used to be solo or in collective unison until the 1800s, when mixed four-part choirs became popular.

Musical Instruments

Traditionally, musical instruments were played mostly by men, although women working as shepherds played wind instruments such as animal horns. Only three native instruments are known to have been widespread among all Finns and Karelians: *torvi*, a trumpet made either of cow or ox horn, or birch or alder bark; *pilli*, a reed pipe or simple clarinet; and a duct flute made of willow wood. These were used for signaling, or for summoning people, and for the magical control of animals.

A fourth instrument, the zither known as *kantele*, may once have been widespread, but its practice ceased in western Finland after the 1600s (figure 1). Used mainly for improvisation and possibly for magical purposes, it disappeared in the west when Finns there learned social dances accompanied by violin (*viulu*). In the twentieth century, however, Finland and Karelia have experienced a significant *kantele* revival. Another stringed instrument, a bowed lyre (*jouhikko*), was mainly East Finnish and South Karelian, though it may have had a western origin. This was also eventually replaced by the violin (introduced into the east and north in the 1800s), after which the eastern Finnish Kalevala tradition

Figure 1 A *kantele* played by the musician and singer Timo Lipitsä, 1917.
Photo used with permission from the Folklife Archives, University of Tampere.

started to decline. Most *kantele* and *jouhikko* transcriptions are Karelian dance tunes.

Finland had no folk ensembles before the 1800s, when clarinet, violin, and later brass ensembles became popular. In the 1940s, a newer ensemble—two violins, plucked double bass, and school organ—developed in the western village of Kaustinen (figure 2). Since the late 1960s, it has become the model for many players of old fiddle tunes.

Twentieth-century Developments

In the mid-1920s, jazz (*jatsi*) and the tango became popular in Finland. In Helsinki, Turku, and Vyborg, youths played jazz (ragtime, foxtrots) in bands modeled on German groups and a Finnish-American group that visited Helsinki in 1926. In 1925, young workers founded a band, Dallapé (figure 3), that made recordings and traveled around the country into the 1930s. Dallapé spread their own version of jazz, mixing elements of American foxtrot, polkalike dances, *rekilaulu*, and Russian romances. This style is now known as *humppa*; because one of its major instruments was the accordion, it is also called accordion jazz. The Finnish tango employs slow, intimate movements, without the elaborate poses of the Argentinean original. *Humppa* involves lively movements taken over from the Charleston, the polka, and the two-step.

After World War II, the main trends have included the coming of rock and the strengthening of music education and of public support for music research with Tampere University as the main research center. Interest in folk music intensified after 1968, which is

Figure 2 The Kaustisen Pelimannit orchestra, 1956. *From left*: Eljas Kentala, violin; Mauri Salo, reed organ; Veikko Järvelä, bass; and Konsta Jylhä, violin.
Photo used with permission from the Folklife Archives, University of Tampere.

Figure 3 The Dallapé orchestra, 1927. *Photo used with permission from the Folklife Archives, University of Tampere.*

also the year the first Kaustinen International Folk Music Festival was held. Moreover, the highest education of folk music performers began at the Sibelius Academy in 1984. All kinds of musical instruments are now combined, and musical elements from different parts of the world have been joined with Finno-Karelian elements to produce a neo-folk music that is distinctly national in character. One professional folk-music ensemble, Tallari, performs practically all the Finno-Karelian genres of folk music. In the 1990s, the group Värttinä became popular at home and abroad. Consisting of four young female singers accompanied by a folk-rock band that adds *kantele*, violin, and accordion to the usual guitar, bass, and drums, Värttinä make their

own arrangements of songs they collected in Russian Karelia and among other Finnic groups in Russia. They also compose songs based on these styles and on Finnish archival collections.

—*Adapted from an article by Timo Leisiö*

Bibliography

Aho, Kalevi. 1992. *After Sibelius: Finnish Music Past and Present*. Helsinki: Finnish Music Information Center.

Granholm, Åke. 1974. *Finnish Jazz History, Musicians Discography*. Helsinki: Foundation for the Promotion of Finnish Music, Finnish Music Information Center.

Helisto, Paavo. 1973. *Finnish Folk Music*. Helsinki: Foundation for the Promotion of Finnish Music, Finnish Music Information Center.

Jaakkola, Jutta, and Aarne Toivonen, eds. 2005. *Inspired by Tradition. Kalevala Poetry in Finnish Music*. Helsinki: Finnish Music Information Centre.

Juntunen, Juho. 1990. *Finnish rock? Then it must B. Goode!* Helsinki: Finnish Music Information Center.

Komulainen, Orvokki. 1965. *Old Finnish Folk Dances*. Helsinki: Suomalaisen Kansantanssin Ystavat.

Konttinen, Matti. 1982. *Finnish Jazz*. Helsinki: Foundation for the Promotion of Finnish Music, Finnish Music Information Center.

Makinen, Timo. 1985. *Musica Fennua: An Outline of Music in Finland*. Helsinki: Helsingissa Kustannusosakeyhtio Otava.

Rahkonen, Carl. 1989. "The Kantele Traditions of Finland." Ph.D. dissertation, Indiana University.

Suojanen, Päivikki. 1984. *Finnish Folk Hymn Singing: Study in Music Anthropology*. Tampere: Institute for Folk Tradition, University of Tampere.

Virtanen, L. 1968. *Kalevalainen laulutapa Karjalassa* (The Kalevala song tradition in Karelia). Helsinki: Suomalaisen Kirjallisuuden Seura.

Western Europe

Western Europe

Western Europe

The predominant faith in Western Europe is Roman Catholicism, whose calendar of holidays, processions, and pilgrimages provides many occasions for making music. The languages of the region belong primarily to the Romance family of languages. Rhyming couplets form the basis for an important genre of song-dueling in Portugal, Spain, and the Mediterranean islands (Corsica, Sardinia, Sicily, and Malta). Narrative ballads are more prevalent north of the Mediterranean. Singing is mainly monophonic, but polyphonic styles exist in Sardinia, Corsica, and certain parts of Italy.

Tambourines and shawms, as well as a high-pitched, tense vocal production, are probably remnants of Arabic influence. The guitar is perhaps the instrument most associated with southwestern Europe, but diatonic accordions and violins are also found throughout the region. Municipal brass bands form an important part of musical life and play arrangements of popular pieces from the classical tradition.

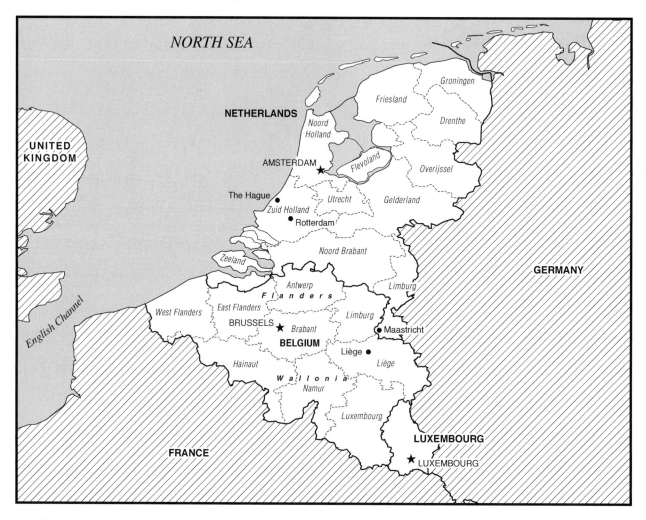

Low Countries

Low Countries

The Low Countries, so called because large parts lie below or just above sea level and on the deltas of major river systems such as the Rhine, include Belgium, the Netherlands, Luxembourg, and French Flanders. Tucked on about 74,000 square kilometers between France, Germany, and the North Sea, these countries have long been among Europe's leading centers of finance, commerce, sea trade, and industry.

The Netherlands' sixteen million people speak Dutch, though in the northern province of Friesland, Frisian (the Germanic language most closely resembling English) is an official language. Belgium, with ten million people, has three official languages: the Flemings of northern Belgium, known as Flanders, speak Dutch; the people in French Flanders also speak Dutch dialects; the Walloons are French-speakers from southern Belgium, known as Wallonia; and German is spoken in eastern Belgium.

The Low Countries are not separated from Germany and France by major natural borders, so they have always been open to cultural and musical influence from abroad. Only the Dutch-French language boundary in Belgium constitutes an ethnic frontier in some respects.

Vocal Music and Song Types

The traditional repertoire of songs in the Low Countries can be divided roughly into two groups, according to whether they originated first in oral tradition or in written form. Songs in oral tradition are generally cheerful. Dance-songs and game songs are sung by a group. As a rule, they are in binary measure and strict tempo. Particularly in Flanders, they are often sung in dialect. Each verse contains only one or two "new" elements or lines; the rest of the verse consists of repetitions of those lines and ever-returning fixed lines (refrains), among which are nonlexical syllables, such as *van falderadiere, van falderada* and *tradérira, luron, lurette*. Since these songs are constructed with mnemonic devices of this kind, they are hardly ever written down. Songs of this group are known in countless variants.

The second group includes songs whose lyrics were originally written down in manuscripts or broadsides. Their content relates positive and negative experiences, and they are usually sung solo. They can be in ternary measure, and the serious songs are often performed in parlando rubato. As a rule, the text is in a kind of standard French or Dutch. The verses contain four to eight or more lines, of which the last one or two are in some instances repeated. They were also transmitted orally, but this process usually resulted in a qualitative deterioration of the lyrics.

> **parlando rubato**, literally 'robbed speaking', is a singing style with a speechlike, variable beat.

In the Low Countries, folksinging is essentially monodic. Only rarely will a musical instrument provide accompanying harmony. Spontaneous two-part singing has been recorded sporadically, but this seems to be a nineteenth-century phenomenon. The melodic outline of traditional songs is usually undulating and fluent, with a marked preference for small intervals up to a fourth. Tunes, too, are essentially syllabic; melismas only occur exceptionally, and practically never exceed two notes to a syllable.

Tunes of more than four phrases are exceptional, and melodies often consist of only two phrases. One quarter of extant Dutch ballads have the form AB, the other most common forms being AAB, AABB, and ABC. Most melodies range between an octave and an octave and a fourth, and have a major heptatonic scale. About a third of the folk songs from the adult repertoire collected in Flanders in the 1800s and the early 1900s were in various modal scales; the rest are in major or minor keys.

The style of singing is sober, without grace notes, except in Volendam (Noord-Holland Province), where singers like to embellish their singing with turns on long notes, trills, and, less frequently, mordants on short notes. More common is the use of glissando; there is little variety in dynamics.

Context and Performance

Until the early 1900s, singing played an important role in everyday life, at work and leisure. Part of the repertoire is linked with important moments in human lives, such as conscription, marriage, or moving one's residence; hardly any songs, however, are connected with birth and death. Another important group consists of seasonal songs—luck-visit songs during carnival and Holy Week, on May Day, Midsummer, and Martinmas, and in the period from Christmas to Epiphany. Until about 1900, many luck-visit singers were handicapped or jobless adults, though they are now children and teenagers who go singing from door to door, and are given money or food, mostly biscuits, sweets, and fruits.

Market singers sang and sold broadsides from the 1500s until about 1900, and in Flanders even until about 1950. They were a familiar sight anywhere people gathered. Usually the singer would stand on a raised platform; with a stick or fiddlestick he would point at the main scenes of his song, depicted on a piece of cloth. Broadside singers accompanied themselves on the fiddle, and later on the accordion. Their repertoire dealt chiefly with love stories, and even more with sensational news (crimes, wars, disasters), with the odd religious song for variety. In the 1800s, the content of this repertoire was quite varied: bawdy and pathetic songs appeared side-by-side with anti-militarist topics. One of the last Flemish broadside singers, Hubert Geens (1917–2001) had a high opinion of his profession and its artistry, which he contrasted with that of the ordinary street singers, who begged from door to door as they sang.

Dance songs are now only to be found on the playgrounds of elementary schools, though until about 1900 they were performed by adolescents and adults. Instances of once popular sung round dances are *'t patertje* (a kissing dance from the Dutch language area), sung dances around the maypole or under the *rozenhoed* ('hat of roses', Dutch-language area), the *zevensprong* or *danse des sept sauts* 'seven-step dance', and dancing around bonfires during autumn and Lent, and at Midsummer and Easter. A repertoire of songs was linked with the *alion* ceremony in the Borinage area (Hainaut Province), held on Sunday in Lent, which included a big fire. A rich variety of songs also accompanied the *crâmignon*, an open-air chain dance performed until about 1960 in Liège, and still known in a few villages between Liège and Maastricht (Dutch province of Limburg), though now mostly accompanied by just a brass band.

Most songs collected since the mid-1800s are not older than the 1700s. However, the origin of some songs still known can be traced back as far as the 1500s. Some ballads even have medieval roots. Already in the 1800s, collectors were worried about the marked decline of traditional singing, and this decline was accelerated in the twentieth century by a combination of factors, the most important being the gradual loss of function.

Instrumental Music

Before the 1700s, folk musicians played by ear, and the nature of their repertoire can be derived only from iconographical sources and financial accounts. Though folk musicians did not leave written music, many traditional tunes found their way into collections printed for middle-class amateurs. For instance, a wealth of traditional music is found in the *Oude en Nieuwe Hollantse Boerenlieties en Contredansen* 'Old and New Dutch Peasant Songs and Country Dances', published in Amsterdam by Estienne Roger and Pierre Mortier (1700–1716). This is the largest collection of tunes ever published in the Low Countries. It contains more than a thousand folk-song melodies, marches, and dances known in Holland at that time, many of them foreign (mainly French and English) origin.

From these sources, it appears that until around 1700, there was no notable distinction between instrumental and vocal music in the Low Countries; tunes were often sung and played. The scarcity of bands points to the fact that, contrary to middle-class music, folk music of the region was essentially monodic, drones being the common form of accompaniment. Around the mid-1700s, popular music became predominantly tonal. It was still largely diatonic, but gradually moved away from vocal music. The drone accompaniment gave way to harmony. Country bands also adopted ensemble playing.

Shortly after 1815, the first waltzes, akin to the Alpine landler, appeared in the north of the Netherlands and the south of Belgium. The polka was introduced in 1844, and it immediately conquered even the remotest villages. Other couple dances imported around that time include the galop, the mazurka, the *redowa*, and the schottische. The quadrille was introduced in the mid-1800s. A descendant of country dances, it usually consisted of four to five figures, with different tunes in 2/4 or 6/8 time.

The instrumental tradition reached its greatest complexity in the second half of the 1800s. The handwritten scores of Belgian wind bands and mixed bands give a first and second part, offbeat chords, and a bass. Bands whose players were literate mostly played couple dances with the structure AABBACCAABBA, each unit consisting of eight or sixteen bars. Sections B and C (called *trio*) modulate to different related (mostly) major keys, usually to the dominant and subdominant, respectively.

Literate and illiterate musicians, however, continued to play older and simpler forms of instrumental music and dance until well into the 1900s. Old rounds, country dances, quadrilles, and pair dances were best preserved in the Twente area (Overijssel Province), the Achterhoek area (Gelderland Province), on the island of Terschelling, in the

West-Friesland area (Noord-Holland Province), in Antwerp Province, in the central part of Brabant Province, and in the Ardennes (Liège and Luxembourg provinces). Some communities have carried on the local tradition into the present day.

Musical Instruments

Though a large variety of instruments can be documented historically, many had disappeared from everyday practice by 1900, or are now played only in one or a few locales.

Drums

The friction drum (*rommelpot*) consists of a pot over whose lip a membrane—usually part of a pig's bladder—has been stretched. A stick is moved up and down through a central hole in the membrane, or, more commonly, tied into the membrane and rubbed with moistened fingers. The *rommelpot* usually accompanies luck-visit singing at Shrovetide or between Christmas and Epiphany—a tradition still alive in some villages.

Since its introduction at the end of the 1400s, the side drum has been one of the most important open-air instruments. From the 1700s on, it was also combined with other wind instruments than the fife. A high standard of drumming is achieved by the carnival drummers of Binche and surrounding villages (Hainaut Province), whose rhythms display a fascinating asymmetry.

Wind Instruments

Since the Middle Ages, the Low Countries have used a rich variety of duct flutes. Archeological research has yielded dozens of bone duct flutes. These flutes were often made from a goat's or sheep's shinbone or upper front leg bone. Most examples have two to four fingerholes and one thumbhole. The use of bone flutes seems to have died out around 1700. Six-hole duct flutes such as tin whistles were among the most popular traditional instruments of the Low Countries until the early 1900s, particularly in Belgium, where the last traditional players were recorded in the 1970s.

In the early 1800s, the manufacture of wind instruments underwent a revolution. From then on, brasses and woodwinds were made on an industrial scale, keeping pace with the rising popularity of wind bands. In the second half of the 1800s, wind bands made up of factory-made instruments were founded in almost every village. This form of organized ensemble playing naturally demanded a knowledge of musical notation, and numerous books

of music, written by literate musicians in the late 1800s or the early 1900s, have been preserved. The best musicians of the village wind bands formed small dance bands, which often consisted of a clarinet, a cornet, a trombone, and a tuba. There could also be a second clarinet, a flute, one or two flügelhorns, and a bombardon (a bass saxhorn or a bass tuba). Until the 1930s, wind bands were the most common type of band for large village dance halls.

The Accordion

The accordion was first introduced in Belgium just after 1840. It didn't become a truly popular instrument, however, until 1880, with the import of cheap, industrially made German models and the start of mass production in Belgium. In no time, the accordion dethroned the fiddle as the main folk instrument for all musical occasions except religious ceremonies. The accordionists often played alone, though some performers accompanied themselves on a drum set or a bass accordion, played with both feet. Frequently, the accordion also constituted the heart of dance bands. Clubs of amateur accordionists, which constitute an important social phenomenon, are still flourishing in Belgium.

Stringed Instruments

The Fiddle

The violin is first shown in popular contexts after about 1550; some fiddles made by rural musicians show archaic (Baroque) features. In the twentieth century, a classically inspired and a more archaic style of playing have been recorded. The latter survived until the 1970s, though only in the Walloon provinces of Liège and Luxembourg. The archaic style is characterized by nonlegato playing (single-stroke style), the use of drone strings, the absence of vibrato, economy of ornamentation, and some glissando. The fiddle can be used to play a second part or a rhythmic, generally offbeat accompaniment consisting of two notes, usually a third or a sixth, sometimes a fourth apart.

The fiddle was by far the most popular instrument for dancing in the 1700s and 1800s, until it was superseded by the accordion. Quite often it was accompanied by a bass or a cello; this duo survived in the provinces of Brabant and Antwerp until about 1920. Until about 1900, dance bands in the West-Friesland area (Noord-Holland Province) usually consisted of two fiddles and a bass. The fiddle was also often combined with brasses or woodwinds.

The Plucked Dulcimer

The plucked dulcimer (Dutch, *hommel*; French, *épinette*) was in use in the Low Counties at least as far back as the early 1600s. The instrument is usually placed on a table, and is occasionally also held across the lap or knees. In twentieth-century Belgium, the plucked dulcimer was exclusively played with a piece of cane or hardwood for fretting and a plectrum for plucking. Formerly in Noord-Holland and Friesland, the instruments with one or two melody strings were probably also played with a bow.

The plucked dulcimer was popular chiefly among farmers, craftsmen, bargemen, miners, and factory workers, and also among soldiers at the Belgian front during World War I; it was the only instrument often played by women. Occasionally it accompanied religious music. In Belgium in the early 1900s, a single plucked dulcimer often supplied the music for informal dances in pubs, or at family and neighborhood gatherings. Sometimes it was also played in bands, often with an accordion and one or more other stringed or woodwind instruments.

Though the plucked dulcimer was virtually extinct in the Netherlands by around 1900, in Belgium it peaked in popularity after World War I, and only went out of fashion in the late 1930s.

Revivals

Since around 1900, many traditional songs have been propagated in a cultivated form through schools, youth movements, and choral societies. Folk dancing was revived after World War I by youth movements of all kinds, many with educational goals, as a means to counter the growing popularity of couple dances of American origin.

The revival of native traditional instruments was started in 1968 by Hubert Boone's band, De Vlier. In Wallonia and the Netherlands, the revival of indigenous folk music began in 1973, largely under the influence of Flemish bands such as De Vlier and

't Kliekske, the quartet of folk music instrument maker Herman Dewit. At first, the revival caught on chiefly among university students and visual artists as a reaction to the alienating and leveling effect of the international commercial music business.

In contrast with older performers and organizations, revival ensembles have not limited themselves to the preservation of tradition in its most recent form, as it was collected among surviving mostly older musicians. Revival bands also go back in time by drawing from older, written sources, and by reconstructing and playing virtually extinct instruments. Another important tendency within revival bands aims at making traditional music relevant by means of arrangements, techniques, instruments, and instrumental combinations formerly unknown to tradition.

—*Adapted from an article by Wim Bosmans*

Bibliography

Boone, Hubert, 2003. *Traditionele Vlaamse volksliederen en dansen*. Leuven: Peeters.

Boone, Hubert, and Wim Bosmans. 2000. *Instruments populaires en Belgique*. Leuven: Peeters.

Bosmans, Wim. 1998. *Fijfer en Trom in het Vlaamse Land: The Fife and Drum in Flanders*. Peer: Alamire. (with CD)

——. 2002. *Traditionele muziek uit Vlaanderen*. Leuven: Davidsfonds.

——. 2007. *Pol Heyns en het volkslied*. Leuven: Peeters. (with CD)

Collaer, Paul. 1974. *La musique populaire en Belgique*. Brussels: Académie Royale de Belgique.

——. 1967–1997. *Dansen uit de Vlaamse gewesten*. 15 volumes. Schoten: Vlaams dansarchief.

Despringre, André-Marie. 1993. *Fête en Flandre: rites et chants populaires du Westhoek français 1975–1981*. Paris: Institut d'Ethnologie, Musée de l'Homme.

Rimmer, Joan. 1978. *Two Dance Collections from Friesland*. Grins: Frysk Institut oan de Ryksuniversiteit.

Thisse-Derouette, Rose. 1960. *Le recueil de danses manuscrit d'un ménétrier ardennais*. Arlon: Fasbender.

Van Duyse, Florimond. 1903–1908. *Het oude Nederlandsche lied*. The Hague: Martinus Nijhoff/Antwerp: De Nederlandsche Boekhandel.

France

France, a country of over sixty million people living in an area of 547,000 square kilometers, was, from the 1700s to the mid-1900s, one of the most influential cultural centers in Europe and the world. With 37 percent of its land arable and extremely fertile, its economy provided the basis for a rural, traditional music. Since World War II, however, the pace of industrialization has increased to the point where only 7 percent of the population engages in agricultural work.

The main traditional religion is Roman Catholicism, although a minority French Reformed Church continues to exist even after the absolutist expulsion of Huguenots (French Protestants) by Louis XIV in 1685. France is now essentially a secular state. However, the end of French colonialism has seen the immigration of peoples from West and North Africa, and non-European beliefs and religions followed with these immigrants. Extensive education has led to the dominance of standard French on the whole national territory, but there remain dialects (*patois*), other Romance languages (Provençal, Catalan, and Corsican), the non-Romance Breton, Basque, and Flemish languages, and the German dialects of Alsace and Lorraine—all still used, chiefly in rural areas and revival contexts. [For a map that includes France, see the one at the beginning of the Western Europe subsection.]

Songs and Singing

Most French traditional music is monophonic, with simple, short tunes, elaborated in strophic form or as dance tunes, usually of isometric phrases, repeated (in whole or part) without much use of new melodic material. The term *strophic* is used here to describe songs with a recurrent musical structure corresponding to a verse (*couplet*) or a verse with its refrain. Strophic songs have great formal variety, and only the main features can be outlined. The *chanson de danse* or *chanson en laisse* is well known from the Middle Ages onward. It consists of one or sometimes more series of discursive isosyllabic lines of six to sixteen syllables. A series of lines (*laisse*) is defined by its monorhyme assonance at line endings; a recurrent refrain combines with it to break it into regular strophes of one or two, occasionally three, lines. The *chansons de danse* originated as dance-songs, and some have continued to function, or have

been revived, as an accompaniment to dancing unsupported by instruments. The refrain may intervene within and outside the verse, and may contribute new (possibly preexisting) rhythmic or even melodic material. Rather than disunity, a sort of dialogue is thus established, reflecting the formerly more common solo-choral execution. The tune, embracing both parts, impresses unity on the whole by musical repetition or similitude. Dance songs make up a large part of the category of mainly recreative song, which may include religious ballads (*cantiques*).

The other strophic songs—of strophes formed not simply by subdividing a *laisse*, but by combining lines in a repeating verse structure—often have no refrain, or, if they have, give it less importance than it has in dance-songs. Among their forms, the commonest are verses of four and of three lines or—probably a later development of these—of eight or six short lines. Songs in these forms are usually isosyllabic, but variety arises from the popular songs of literate character, or their imitations, which have entered and remain in oral tradition. Some *enumerative songs*—a popular category in France—are recapitulative, augmenting the strophe progressively. Litanylike, the words newly interpolated repeat musical matter taken mainly from the tune as used in the first verse, which thus stretches out in lingering fashion. Other songs make similar use of simple repetition, especially if phrases are short (figure 1).

Aside from some "rhapsodic" pastoral songs, the common meters of French music are those of Western Europe: 2/4, 4/4, 3/4, 3/2, 3/8, 6/8, 9/8, sometimes 5/8, grouped in two-bar or three-bar units or multiples of these. Uneven rhythms arise from variations in the length of the units, especially from short sections of different meter—features that introduce contrasts into otherwise regular development. Most frequent are mixtures of duple and triple time: 3/4 occurring in 2/4, or 9/8 in 6/8. These effects are often associated with the presence of a refrain, but not exclusively, and they evidently have an ornamental quality, desired for its own sake. They belong mostly to an abundant repertory of fast tunes, in which other departures from strict meter are unlikely to go further than lengthening or shortening at the ends of phrases. In slow tunes, a certain amount of rubato is more general, but the long-drawn-out effects belong chiefly to some plowing

Figure 1 "*Le petit moine*" ('The Little Monk'), a song built on the repetition of short phrases. *Transcription by Hugh Shields.*

songs or other work songs, which do not admit of measured analysis.

Much French music has a narrow melodic compass; it is common to find hexachordal tunes or ones that develop almost wholly within a range of a fifth, including children's game songs, lullabies, plowing songs, some street cries, and what we know of medieval epics. Widest are some flowery tunes not associated with any specific social function, probably not of great age, but characteristic of sentimental songs on love themes: tunes extending to a tenth or an eleventh. Intermediate tunes, the majority, range from a sixth to an octave.

Melodic idiom can be plainly discerned as collectively diatonic. Scales coincide at times with the ecclesiastic modal tradition, but at others they differ from it by the absence or the variation of certain tones. Variation and absence are particularly common in the case of the seventh. When all seven tones are used, one may identify, in order of frequency, tunes in the ionian (home tone C), aeolian (A), dorian (D), and rarely mixolydian (G) or phrygian (E) modes, while pentatonic tunes are very rare. In a country productive of much medieval plainchant, religious song has naturally influenced the popular musical tradition as a source of melodic and idiomatic borrowings.

Performance

Centuries of classical polyphony have made little impression on the monophonic popular tradition and its realization mainly as solo performance. Nonetheless, monophony is not exclusive. Some ballad sellers and other singers have had instrumental accompaniment, usually fiddle. Singing to a fiddle recalls the *vièle* accompaniment that the medieval minstrel (*jongleur*) gave his heroic chant, and the ancient and modern practices have no doubt been largely heterophonic. Heterophonic also in varying degrees is the responsorial singing of dance-songs and of shanties, ceremonial choral performances such as the "*Bacchu-Ber*" in Dauphiné, collective bagpipe playing, general instrumental duets, and the technique of singing called *tuilage* (two voices alternate and slightly overlap) mainly in Breton, but also in French.

Two-part polyphony, striking in its dissonances, is an insular tradition that Corsica shares with Sardinia. In Corsica, *paghjelle* are polyphonic religious songs of wholly secular tradition; on the mainland, polyphonic practices exist in parts of the south. In the southeast (Haut-Dauphiné), semipopular songs in the eighteenth-century pastoral tradition have been provided with suitably mellow harmonic sections. This practice resembles the formerly widespread traditions of Christmas carols (*noëls*), often composed by church organists. In the southwest, an older tradition of two-part singing has its focus in the Basque country, but is also found in neighboring Romance-speaking Béarn.

Instruments and Instrumental Music

Accompaniment to melody on solo instruments is limited traditionally to the use of drones (*bourdons*) on violin, hurdy-gurdy, and bagpipes. A single player's drumming to a flute gives a kind of drone, or an actual drone of fixed pitch in the case of the string drum (*ttunttun*) of the southwest [see BASQUE MUSIC]. With the increasing availability of instruments and skill at reading music, however, playing in parts became more common in the twentieth century, however; certain regions have traditions of popular, literate bands: oboes, clarinets, and so on in Roussillon, brass in many places, notably Alsace. With these, we approach the playing in parts characteristic of classical music, or *musique savante* 'learned music' as the French often call it; vocal music, however, shows less tendency in that direction.

At first glance, the range of French folk instruments in the Musée des Arts et Traditions Populaires (Paris) seems to reflect a great variety of practice, but the limits of many of these instruments are geographically or historically narrow, and it would be of interest to know how many of those that are chiefly percussive, or tonally or acoustically primitive, would be considered musical in traditional terms. In a different way, the modern revival also implies abundance, but abundance that an anonymous copywriter no doubt justly attributed to *la boulimie instrumentale ambiente* 'the current hunger for instrumental novelty' (*Trad Magazine* no. 10:52). Evidence of traditional practice in recent generations gives a different picture, one in which only a small range of instruments was habitually used in every locality, each of them playable solo, or at times in small ensembles, whose music is essentially monophonic.

Certain paramusical agents of human elaboration contribute to the soundscape of France. The most obvious are bells. The churches of seventeenth-century Beauvais (in Picardy) had 135 great bells and a few dozen little ones, muted in time of epidemic out of consideration for the sick. Notably, in northern France, church bells remain a feature of urban life. On a smaller scale, cowbells (*clarines*) and sheep bells (*tintenelles*, *grelots*, in varying sizes) color the rural scene in the south.

Of instruments producing more elaborate music, the violin was the most widely used until relegated to second place by the accordion. The two continue in extensive use. Both are historical borrowings, one classical, the other conceived in a society of increasing factory production. This environment is perhaps what renders the accordion readily adaptable from traditional styles to urban *chansonnier* styles or innovating folk styles of today; the violin, however, had its traditional precursors from early times in France, and seems popularly to be associated with conservative tradition: the *crin-crin* 'fiddle'.

Neither the violin nor the accordion has any particular geographic association. While the chromatic accordion is more associated with France by foreigners, due to its use in urban cabaret music, the diatonic accordion is probably more common in traditional performance, and revival has once more accentuated its suitability to traditional monophony.

Two older instruments do have geographic associations: the bagpipe and the hurdy-gurdy. Known in French as vielle—or *vielle à roue* ('with wheel'), to distinguish it from the medieval fiddle-type vielle or *viele*—the hurdy-gurdy (figure 2) is firmly considered proper to Auvergne and Brittany, but chiefly the former. The same two provinces are also known for their native bagpipes: the Breton *biniou* (figure 3) and the

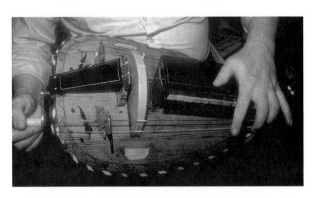

Figure 2 A hurdy-gurdy. A player turns the instrument's crank to rotate the wheel, which acts like a bow, continuously sounding the melody strings on the central part of the bridge and the drone strings on either side. The keys, pressed by the player's left hand, cause small wooden wedges (tangents) to press the melody strings at certain points on the fretboard. The continuous sound of the strings, especially the drones, gives the hurdy-gurdy a sound reminiscent of a bagpipe.
Photo by Terry E. Miller.

Figure 3 *Biniou* (bagpipe) and *bombarde* (oboe) players perform at the Festival Interceltique des Cornemuses, Lorient, Brittany, 1974.
Photo by James Porter.

Auvergnat (bellows-blown) *cabreta* (or Limousine *chabreta*).

Among other instruments used traditionally, the *épinette des Vosges*, a native plucked dulcimer, is the only notable stringed instrument, though revived only after near extinction. The rest are chiefly wind instruments that may conveniently participate in ensembles: clarinet, oboe, and trumpet in groups of two to four or more. Older are end-blown flutes, some of which may be played with a drum by a single performer—a practice already noted as southwestern in the sixteenth century. Three-holed flutes are played thus in Provence (*galoubet* with *tambourin*, a snare drum about 70 centimeters deep) and in the Basque country and adjacent Gascony (*chirula* with *ttunt-tun*). The drum in these areas is usually strung to produce rhythmic drones. Functionally dissimilar from all these is the harmonica, formerly appreciated for its mouth music (*musique à bouche*) and easy transportation.

Contexts for Music and Dance

Contexts for music, and especially singing, have been greatly formalized by French tradition. Opportunities for ceremony and song are often defined narrowly: the departure of a batch of conscripts to the army, or the making of reed or boxwood flutes at summer pastures (*en estive*). Such a narrow definition is especially characteristic of work songs, a plentiful category in France. The formalized contexts characteristic of traditional life are today greatly diminished, yet they were once familiar enough to attract to themselves songs not originally proper to them: flowing 3/4 ballads accompanying hand reaping, and songs on miscellaneous religious subjects sung by the customary *réveillez* beggars who go door to door on Easter. Among seasonal customs, the latter is probably the best preserved.

As for the lifecycle, no rituals pertaining to it have been so important as those of marriage, which have inspired so many contextually defined songs: songs sung by young men when visiting their fiancée; songs of mock abduction; songs with loose, sometimes bawdy, verses warning the bride of her duties and prospects; songs to sing at and after the banquet; others while visiting the bedded couple; others that tell what the bed says; and so on.

Among wedding songs, those that suit the banquet have the best chance of survival, for meals are a traditional focus of conviviality. The custom of singing after meals is a well-rooted one. Singing after meals, at least on special occasions, is likely now practiced more than singing at evening gatherings not associated with meals (*veillées*), whose demise, under the influence of television and other media, is much deplored in France. The *veillée* was undoubtedly the major context for recreative singing. Like other contexts, it often attracted suitable musical items, such as the march on the bagpipe, played to help the visitors walk home.

Music and Dancing

French traditions of dancing emerged from medieval ring dances and chain dances: *carole* and *tresche*, and later *branle*—closed in the *ronde*, open as in the *farandole*. They began to yield first to the contredanse, a figure dance that apparently was borrowed from the English country dance in the late 1600s, and in due course yielded to quadrilles; *branles*, however, are reported as popular even in the early 1900s. *Rondes* are usually sung and danced by the dancers, and their persistence in tradition has obviously sustained the link of singing with dancing. All the string and wind instruments popular in tradition seem to have accompanied dancing. Instrumental music for dance-tunes and marches is usually limited to two short phrases. The phrases are often repeated (*aabb*), with little variation unless in phrase *b* an open cadence is followed by a closing one.

—Adapted from an article by Hugh Shields

Bibliography

Arnaudin, Félix, ed. [1912] 1970. *Chants populaires de la Grande-Lande et des régions voisines: Musique, patois et traduction française*. Paris: Champion.

Arts et Traditions populaires. 1953–1970. 18 vols. Paris: Maisonneuve et Larose.

Beauquier, Charles, ed. 1894. *Chansons populaires recueillies en Franche-Comté*. Paris: Leroux.

Bénichou, Paul. 1970. *Nerval et la chanson folklorique*. Paris: J. Corti.

Béranger, Pierre-Jean. 1833. *Chansons nouvelles et dernieres*. Paris: Pérotin.

Bladé, Jean-François, ed. [1881–1882] 1967. *Poésies populaires de la Gascogne: Texte gascon et traduction française*. 3 vols. Paris: Maisonneuve et Larose.

Canteloube, Joseph, ed. 1951. *Anthologie des chants populaires français*. 4 vols. Paris: Durand.

Les Chansons de France. 1907–1913. 7 vols., nos. 1–28.

Coirault, Patrice. 1953–1963. *La Formation de nos chansons folkloriques*. 4 vols. Paris: Éditions Scarabée.

Cuisenier, Jean, Claudie Marcel-Dubois, and Maguy P. Andral. 1980. *L'Instrument de musique populaire: Usages et symboles*. Paris: Ministère de la Culture.

Davenson, Henri [Henri-Irénée Marrou], ed. 1944. *Le Livre des Chansons*. Neuchâtel: Éditions La Baconnière.

Decitre, Monique. 1960. *Dansez la France: Danses des provinces françaises*. 2 vols. Saint-Etienne: Éditions Dumas.

D'Indy, Vincent, ed. 1900. *Chansons populaires du Vivarais*. Paris: Durand.

Gastoué, Amédée. 1924. *Le Cantique populaire en France: ses sources, son histoire.* Lyon: Janin.

Hayet, Armand, ed. [1934] 1971. *Dictons, tirades et chansons des anciens de la voile.* Paris: Denoël.

Laforte, Conrad. 1973. *La Chanson folklorique et les écrivains au dix-neuvième siècle (en France et au Québec).* Montreal: Hurtubise.

———. 1976. *Poétiques de la chanson traditionnelle français.* Quebec: Presses Université Laval.

Laforte, Conrad, and Monique Jutras, eds. 1997. *Vision d'une société par les chansons de tradition orale à caractèrr épique et tragique.* Sainte-Foy, Que.: Université Laval.

Marzac-Holland, Nicole. 1983. "Folksongs of Bas-Maine: A Living Tradition." *Selected Reports in Ethnomusicology* IV:20–41.

Musiques d'en France: Guide des musiques et danses traditionnelles. [1984] N.p.: Centre National de l'Action Musicale.

Pécout, Roland. 1978. *La Musique folk des peuples de France.* Paris: Stock.

Tiersot, Julien. 1889. *Histoire de la chanson populaire en France.* Paris: Plon.

Trad Magazine. 1988, Nov.–, 1–. 62350 Robecq.

Vargyas, Lajos. 1967. *Researches into the Medieval History of Folk Ballad.* Budapest: Akademiai Kiadó.

Zumthor, Paul. 1983. *Introduction à la poésie orale.* Paris: Éditions du seuil.

Portugal

Portugal occupies a rectangular area of approximately 89,000 square kilometers at the southwestern edge of Europe, sharing the Iberian Peninsula with Spain. The Atlantic archipelagos of Madeira and Azores have been part of Portugal since their discovery and occupation, in the 1400s. Mainland Portugal is characterized by notable contrasts between the "Atlantic north" and the "Mediterranean south," and between the coast and the interior. Administratively, Portugal is divided into districts, each with a capital city.

Portugal emerged as a country in 1128, when the first Portuguese king, Afonso Henriques (r. 1139–1185), seceded from the kingdom of Castile; he later expanded his reign to the Muslim-dominated south. Afonso III (r. 1248–1279) established the boundaries that continental Portugal has had since.

Portuguese history was marked by maritime exploration and overseas colonization. During the 1400s and 1500s, the Portuguese were the first Europeans to conquer territories in Africa, Asia, and South America. To these lands, they carried Christianity and their language and culture, and they brought back trading goods, slaves, new crops, and cultural influences.

The Portuguese monarchy ended with the first parliamentary republic (1910–1926). A military coup in 1926 led to Antonio de Oliveira Salazar's dictatorship, which advocated a nationalistic ideology based on traditional values. The revolution of 25 April 1974 established democracy and ended colonial rule.

The population, of 10.6 million, is concentrated in the coastal areas—in Lisbon, the capital, and Oporto, the largest northern city. Large Portuguese emigrant communities exist in the Americas, France, and South Africa. Metropolitan Lisbon contains immigrant communities from the former colonies: Cape Verdians, Angolans, Mozambicans, Brazilians, Goanese, and Timorese.

Twentieth-century Portuguese Culture

The musical traditions of Portugal are highly diverse. Some styles and instruments including ballads, guitars, and vocal polyphony, partake of pan-European and pan-Hispanic traditions. Other styles and instruments were molded through Portugal's encounters with non-European peoples. Examples of

Figure 1 Maria Amélia Fonseca from the village of Monsanto, district of Castelo-Branco, accompanies her singing on the *adufe*, 1997.
Photo by João Tuna.

this include the *adufe*, a square frame drum (figure 1), adapted from the North African *deff*; modal structures with neutral intervals; and *fado*, which originated in nineteenth-century Lisbon from a synthesis of Portuguese and Brazilian genres and dances.

Until the 1950s, a few isolated rural areas preserved musical practices and styles documented around 1900; however, rural Portugal has undergone profound changes. The mechanization of agriculture at mid-century removed manual agricultural work as a context for making music. Emigration since the mid-1800s and migration to urban areas since the 1950s depopulated many areas, weakening traditions there. But migrant communities in urban areas have vigorously maintained their traditions, and through sponsorship returned emigrants have contributed to the continuity of practices, such as religious festivities (*festas*) and pilgrimages (*romarias*), and Portuguese communities abroad maintain traditional music through the activities of formally structured groups.

During the rule of António de Oliveira Salazar (1932–1968), his regime promoted their ideology through national and local institutions and controlled artistic activities. Within the domain of traditional expressive behavior, an ideologically charged concept of *folclore* was central. Numerous formally organized folklore groups (*ranchos folclóricos*) formed between the 1930s and 1950s, and competitions were established in which villages competed for a prize in recognition of their preserving local costumes, music, and dance. Since 1974, these *ranchos* have multiplied and become a local instead of a national phenomenon (figure 2). They are sponsored by municipalities and see themselves as representing their regions or locales. In many areas of Portugal, these groups have been the main repositories for traditional music and dance. Performances range from those adhering closely to local traditions to those presenting new interpretations.

Performance Contexts and Song Genres

In rural Portugal, singing, instrumental performance, and dance traditionally accompanied agricultural and domestic work, marked lifecycle events, entertained families and communities, and was a basic ingredient in sacred and secular rituals.

Before mechanization, agricultural labor was often accompanied by singing, by workers or hired musicians. Work songs are predominantly strophic, including songs accompanying plowing, threshing, harvesting, and olive gathering.

Ballads (*romances*) have been collected throughout Portugal. They are usually sung or recited by women without instrumental accompaniment. Their texts feature historical, religious, and social themes. Most ballads are strophic. The same text can be sung to multiple melodies, and the same melody can be used for multiple texts.

Throughout the district of Beja (southern Alentejo), agricultural workers of either sex formerly sang unaccompanied polyphonic songs (*modas*) while working. A *moda* consists of rhymed verses sung polyphonically in strophic form. These songs now thrive in contexts such as taverns, and in performances by the numerous formally structured choral groups formed since the 1930s (figure 3).

Monophonic or homophonic strophic songs marking lifecycle events—including lullabies, courting songs, wedding songs, and mourning songs—have been collected throughout rural Portugal. Today, most of this repertoire is no longer active outside of staged recreations.

Religious festivities and pilgrimages, complex community events that can last for several days, continue to provide vigorous contexts for making music.

Song Style

Vocal music, with or without instrumental accompaniment, is predominant in Portugal. Most vocal music is precomposed, but authorship is seldom known. (Some texts are attributed to local oral poets.) Throughout the country and in most genres, different texts are set to the same melodies. Since the 1970s, creativity in some genres has been practically limited to texts. Creativity with words is particularly valued in "improvised" vocal genres, known as *desgarradas*, *cantares ao desafio*, and *despiques*. These are song duels, usually between two or more singers with instrumental accompaniment. The words are improvised to a fixed melodic and harmonic pattern.

Metered strophic songs, with or without a refrain, predominate, and the quatrain provides the most

Figure 2 The Rancho Folclórico das Lavradeiras de Mosteiró, São Miguel de Matos, plays at the Harvest Fair (Feira da Colheita) of Arouca, district of Aveiro, 1995.
Photo by Salwa El-Shawan Castelo-Branco.

541

Figure 3 The Grupo Coral da Caixa Social e Cultural da Câmara Municipal de Beja plays during a parade of Alentejan choral groups in Lisbon, 1997.
Photo by Salwa El-Shawan Castelo-Branco.

common poetic structure. A musical phrase is usually set to one, two, or four lines of text, and singing is predominantly syllabic. Melismatic singing occurs primarily in the solo parts of the polyphonic modas in Beja, and in solo songs in the east-central districts.

Lyric songs with homophonic instrumental accompaniment are common in much of the country. Triadic vocal polyphony in two, three, and four voices occurs in various northwestern, eastern, and central districts, and in the southern district of Beja. Except for Beja, where multipart singing is primarily a men's practice, vocal polyphony is performed by women.

In much of the country, tonality is organized within the major and minor modes, and harmonic accompaniment centers on the alternation of tonic and dominant chords. Church modes and other modal structures that do not correspond to European common practice occur in areas that have preserved archaic practices, especially the districts of Castelo-Branco and Beja. Melodic ranges usually do not exceed a fifth or sixth beyond an octave. Duple and triple meters are most common in vocal music, including dance-songs.

Song texts deal with all aspects of rural life, past and present: agricultural work, nature, the local village or town, lifecycle events, love, emigration, religious themes, and historical and political events.

Instruments and Instrumental Ensembles

Diatonic and chromatic accordions are dominant in contemporary traditional music. Guitars of various sizes and types accompany vocal music and dance in many rural and urban traditions. The bagpipe, accompanied by a bass drum and a snare drum, has been central in religious festivities in the northeast and the coastal area from the north to the center. In the east-central area, transverse flutes are played by shepherds, and a sharply waisted guitar is used to accompany singing. Fewer instruments are used in the south.

Portuguese idiophones include castanets, a wood scraper (*reque reque*), a triangle (*ferrinhos*), a large clay pot (*cântaro com abano*), which the player holds below his left arm while hitting the opening with a straw or leather fan), and the *cana* (a cane tube about 60 centimeters long, cut vertically through the middle, creating two parts, which the player strikes together).

Of drums, the *caixa*, a snare drum with two skins and one or two sympathetic strings, is struck on the upper skin with two wooden drumsticks. It is played in ensemble with a bass drum (*bombo*). Other drums include two kinds of frame drums. The *adufe* is square, with two skins and interior metal jingles; it is played exclusively by women who hold it with the thumbs of both hands and the index finger of the left hand, leaving the remaining fingers free for playing the instrument. The *pandeiro*, a round frame drum with a single skin and metal jingles, is found mainly in the district of Évora, near the Spanish border. The *pandeireta*, a smaller *pandeiro*, is popular throughout the country as an accompaniment to informal singing and dancing and in string ensembles known as *tuna*. The northwestern friction drum (*sarronca*) is a clay pot with a narrow opening, covered with a skin that vibrates through the movement of a friction stick.

Stringed instruments constitute the richest, most varied category. Guitars (called *violas*), usually having five double or three double and two triple courses of metal strings, exist in many local variants. The term *viola* also denotes the "Spanish guitar" with six metal strings. The *cavaquinho* (figure 4), a small guitar with four courses of strings, is widespread in the northwest and Madeira, where it is called *braguinha*. Easy to transport and play, it was widely diffused by Portuguese settlers and emigrants—for instance, to Hawaii (where it is called *ukelele*), Brazil, and Indonesia (where it is called *kroncong*). The *guitarra*, also designated *guitarra Portuguesa* 'Portuguese guitar', has a pear-shaped soundboard and six double courses of metal strings. It is a local adaptation of the "English guitar," introduced to Portugal in the second half of the 1700s through the British colony in Oporto. It is used to accompany vocalists in the urban genre known as *fado*.

Fado

Of the various musical genres that developed in urban settings, the most significant is *fado*. It emerged in the poor neighborhoods of Lisbon

Figure 4 A *cavaquinho* player of the Rancho Folclórico de Viana do Castelo.
Photo by Elise Ralston, 1988.

between 1825 and 1850 as a synthesis of song-and-dance genres already popular in Lisbon and newly imported genres, many from Brazil. The subsequent history of *fado* passed through Lisbon's slums and salons, Portuguese vaudeville, the recording industry, and radio. During Salazar's dictatorship, *fado* was promoted as Portugal's "national song." Its texts were censored, its performers were required to obtain a license to practice their profession, and touristic restaurants (*casas típicas*) were instituted for its performance. Much of this period coincided with the careers of some of its most brilliant and celebrated figures: *fado* singers Amália Rodrigues (1920–1999) and Alfredo Marceneiro (1891–1992) and *fado* composers and guitarists Armandinho (Armando Augusto Salgado Freire, 1891–1846) and Martinho d'Assunção (1914–1992).

Today, *fado* can be heard in tourist restaurants, concerts in large auditoriums, neighborhood associations, taverns, and local restaurants. *Fado* performances involve a solo vocalist and instrumental accompanists. The vocalist (*fadista*) is the dominant figure. The first *guitarrista*, regarded as a second soloist, provides a melodic counterpoint and harmonic support to the main melody. When included, a second *guitarrista* furnishes a second melodic counterpoint and harmonic support. The *viola* is mandatory, and provides a harmonic and rhythmic grounding, allowing the *fadista* and the *guitarristas* to improvise. A *viola baixo* is occasionally used to provide bass progressions in a regular rhythm.

Fado practitioners classify their repertoire into *fado castiço*, 'authentic *fado*' (relatively old) and *fado canção* 'song *fado*'. *Fados castiços* have fixed rhythmic and harmonic schemes (usually I-V-I) and accompanimental patterns, but allow performers to use either precomposed or improvised melodies. The *fado canção* has a poetic and musical structure that alternates stanzas and refrains, more complex harmonic structures than those of *fado castiço*, fixed melodies, and a flexible accompanimental pattern developed within the basic harmonic scheme. *Fado* texts feature early *fado* performance contexts, such as houses of prostitution, Lisbon's old neighborhoods, *fado*-connected personages, specific events, feelings, the mother figure, and political struggle.

Popular Music since 1974

Musical expression central to the opposition of Salazar's dictatorship, contributed to the political process that culminated in the revolution of 1974 and the consolidation of revolutionary ideals. During three decades preceding the revolution, the *canção de intervenção* 'song of intervention' became an important vehicle for political protest. The songs of one of its main protagonists, the poet-composer-singer José Alfonso (1929–1987), were set to politically engaged poetic texts and integrated elements from the *fado* of Coimbra, Portuguese rural traditions, African music, and French popular song. His song "*Grândola Vila Morena*"—broadcast on the radio on the eve of revolution as a signal for insurgent troops to advance—became an emblem of the revolution.

For about a decade after the revolution, a movement for the revival of traditional music emerged among university students and young professionals. Inspired by the revolution, some groups were involved in political and social action in rural areas, where they collected traditional music with the purpose of salvaging disappearing practices by reproducing them on stage for urban audiences. More than a dozen groups that formed between the mid-1970s and mid-1980s typically performed traditional songs and tunes (reproducing rural repertoires) and recreations of those.

Increasingly various styles of urban music are produced and consumed in Portugal. Local pop and rock styles developed during the 1980s and 1990s, jazz performances by Portuguese and foreign artists increased considerably, and a local style of rap and varieties of African music thrive in Lisbon.

—Adapted from an article by Salwa El-Shawan Castelo-Branco

Bibliography

Brito, Joaquim Pais de, ed. 1994. *Fado: Voices and Shadows.* Translated by James Ormiston. Lisbon: Museum of Ethnology.

Castelo-Branco, Salwa El-Shawan, ed. 1997. *Portugal and the World: The Encounter of Cultures in Music.* Lisbon: Dom Quixote.

———, ed. In press. *Enciclopédia da Música em Portugal no Século XX.* Lisbon: Círculo de Leitores/Editorial Notícias.

Castelo-Branco, Salwa El-Shawan, and Jorge Freitas Branco, eds. 2003. *Vozes do Povo: A Folclorizção em Portugal.* Lisbon: Celta Editora.

Gallop, Rodney. 1936. *Portugal: A Book of Folk-Ways.* Cambridge: Cambridge University Press.

Graça, Fernando Lopes. 1974. *A Canção Popular Portuguesa*, 2nd ed. Lisbon: Publicações Europa América.

Holton, Kimberly DaCosta. 2006. *Performing Folklore: Ranchos Folcóricos from Lisbon to Newark.* Bloomington and Indianapolis: Indiana University Press.

Nery, Rui Vieira. 2003. *Para uma História do Fado.* Lisbon: Público.

Oliveira, Ernesto Veiga de. 1999. *Instrumentos Musicais Populares Portugueses*, 3rd ed. Lisbon: Fundação Calouste Gulbenkian.

Spain

With four spoken languages, several dialects, and seventeen culturally and politically distinct regions, Spain is a historically diverse nation. Its forty million inhabitants live in a 505,000-square-kilometer peninsula whose geography has isolated its people from the rest of Europe and served as a gateway between Europe and North Africa.

Once inhabited by Iberian tribes, Spain hosted Celtic, Phoenician, Hebrew, Greek, and Carthaginian cultures before a six-century occupation by the Romans (second century B.C.E. to the fifth century C.E.), followed by three hundred years of Visigothic rule. The invasion by Moors from North Africa (711–1492) led to the creation of the Arab kingdom of Al-Andalus, which ruled most of the Iberian peninsula, and left an enduring and distinctive imprint on Spanish culture. The Christian reconquest of Spain from the Moors led to the reactionary religious zealotry that fueled the Inquisition (1478), the expulsion of the Jews (1492), and the forced Christian conversion of the indigenous peoples of the newly conquered Americas.

The weight of traditionalism slowed Spain's democratization following World War II, when the rest of Europe underwent rapid political and social change. Spain approved its first constitution in 1978, setting the stage for reintegration into the modern European mainstream after nearly a century of isolation. About three-quarters of the population now live in cities, the largest of which are Madrid, Barcelona, Valencia, and Seville, but an enduring tradition is embodied in the persistent, though diminished, practice of traditional music in *pueblos*, the rural towns that many urban dwellers cite as home, even after generations in the city.

Personal connections to *pueblos* reinforce a regional identity in Spain, while the many mountain ranges that divide the country provide topological boundaries to its regions. Certain regions are famous for a typical musical form—Aragón for the *jota*, Castile for *seguidillas*, Andalucía for the fandango. Yet these forms have spread to local traditions throughout Spain.

Vocal Genres and Singing Styles

The *romance* 'ballad', the national Spanish poetic form, has roots in the epic narrative tradition, palace minstrel song, and fifteenth-century vernacular song. Its texts concern love, vengeance, history, legend, myth, crime, the supernatural, burlesque, and the Bible. *Romances* are still sung in rural areas throughout Spain, especially from Christmas to Lent. They are performed by a soloist or an unaccompanied unison choir, or are accompanied by a *rabel* fiddle or a violin in an Arabic-style heterophonic imitation of the vocal line, or by an ensemble of hurdy-gurdy (*zanfona*), guitar, and *vihuela* (a type of guitar).

Rondas 'round songs' comprise the largest, best loved, and least regionally varied part of the repertoire of collective songs. Their name refers to the tradition of rounding, in which young male musicians serenade the general public or, more likely, young women at the windows of their homes. Rounding can serve for the performance of Christmas songs (*aguinaldos*), *cantares de ayuda* for the gathering of alms, *auroras* to call people to the rosary, or wedding songs. The *ronda* form, usually of solo-chorus alternations of an octosyllabic quatrain, is most typical of traditional Spanish song. *Ronda* groups, though apparently casually formed, can be quite competitive, and serve to mark the territory of each group of young men.

May is the time for *rogativas*, prayer songs to local patron saints, asking for the crop's protection from drought and disease. Autumn is associated with a variety of vocal genres: *ramos*, songs for religious processionals; *romerias*, sacred and secular songs to accompany pilgrimages to local shrines; *exvotos*, songs of thanks for miracle cures and providential intercessions; *ánimas*, gory descriptions of the sufferings of souls in purgatory; and *gozos*, a semipopular medieval genre recounting the Virgin Mary's seven joys.

Christmas carols (*villancicos*)—at once sacred and secular, devotional and festive—are sung throughout Spain, accompanied by guitars, frame drums, friction drums, triangles, and brass mortars. Their texts, even as they narrate the birth of Christ, can be amorous, picaresque, or satirical, and their historical roots may go back to pre-Christian solstice celebrations.

Work songs divide into three groups. The first is for food-gathering tasks, such as hunting, fishing, threshing, and picking olives. Many of these songs demonstrate Mediterranean influence in *maqām*-like scales, supple meter, melisma, and descending melodies. The second group is for jobs such as milling, mining coal, and shearing sheep. These songs are often dialogues between two singers or a soloist and a chorus, utilizing repeated phrases with variations, wide tonal ranges, and rhythms keyed to the task. The third group is for domestic chores, such as cooking, cleaning, washing, and keeping taverns. Its repertoire shares musical traits with the second group.

Poetic Song Forms

Spanish song forms break down into two categories: the metric style brought from elsewhere in Europe by eleventh- to thirteenth-century troubadours, and usually containing verses and refrains with a degree of textual improvisation and instrumental interludes; and the free, unmetered songs of the Arabic tradition, which survive mostly in lullabies, work songs, and the Andalusian *cante jondo*.

Among the metric types, the *copla* ('couplet') is a common song form employing quatrains of octosyllabic lines with consonant or assonant rhymes in the even-numbered verses. The stanza can be followed by a refrain. The octosyllabic quatrain of *coplas* 'couplets' provides the poetic scheme for many lyric songs (*rondas*, *villancicos*, and others), most ballads (*romances*), and the *jota*, a widely known dance.

Another prevalent metric-song form is the *cuarteta* or *copla de seguidilla* (*seguidilla* quatrain or couplet). The *seguidilla* is a dance form that shapes vocal and instrumental songs throughout the country, demonstrating characteristic Spanish fluidity between dance and song genres. Quatrains of *coplas de seguidilla* alternate lines of five and seven syllables with rhymes linking the even-numbered lines, and are often followed by an *estribillo volante*, a tercet with lines of five, six, and five syllables. This form, known in Spain as early as the eleventh century, is widely dispersed (figure 1).

Given the formality of Spanish poetic structures and the refinement of lyric verses, the prevalence or *relinchidos* 'onomatopoeic shouts' might seem incongruous, but they are found everywhere. *Relinchidos* can be viewed as a relief from textual formality, or a typically Spanish juxtaposition

Figure 1 In triple meter and a major scale, a *seguidilla* alternates five- and seven-syllable lines. After Crivillé i Bargalló 1988:219.

of emotional exclamation with pious or solemn expression.

Melodic and Rhythmic Systems

In Spanish song, monody prevails, though there are exceptions. Many traditional songs employ descending, terraced melodies built on an E mode, with chromaticisms that may originate with Arabic modes. The raised third degree of this mode reflects the influence of the Arabic *maqām* "Hijaz Kar" or the Persian *dastgāh* "Tchahargah."

The Andalusian scale underlies melodies throughout the Iberian peninsula, but especially in Andalucía, Extremadura, Castile, and León. Such songs often conclude with four descending triads in parallel thirds—a distinctively Spanish cadential pattern. Other common modalities include the major mode, the minor mode, and alternations between the two within a song.

The solo vocal repertoire includes melismatic, asymmetric songs in Mediterranean-influenced free rhythm: work songs, lullabies, improvisations, and flamenco's *cante jondo* (see below). Most of the remaining repertoire is metric, in duple and triple meters. Spanish rhythms are often flavored with hemiola (*sesquiáltera*), which may involve alternation between 3/4 and 6/8 times or the insertion of a 3/2 bar in a 3/4 melody, creating polyrhythm against the accompaniment. Another rhythmic trait is *aksak*, the "limping" asymmetrical rhythms common to Turkish and Eastern European music. Usually *aksak* meters consist of five-beat measures grouped into three and two beats.

Musical Instruments and Instrumental Music

Much traditional instrumental music in Spain is monophonic. Though Spain is well known for the guitar, the Spanish instrumental tradition also relies upon flutes, shawms, and bagpipes, with rhythm provided by many types of frame drum and festive textural later added by a variety of metallic idiophones including bells and triangles. Many Spanish instruments bear evidence of Muslim influence. These include lutes, rebecs, psalteries, transverse flutes, shawm, trumpets frame drums, tambourines, and castanets.

Flute-and-drum duos, in which both instruments are played by a single musician, are widespread. Flutes are typically wooden with fingerholes; accompanying is a drum whose generic name is *tambor*. Similar to the flute-and-drum duo is that of the shawm or bagpipe with drum. The shawm is particularly popular in central Spain, the bagpipe, in northern Spain. Made of a goatskin bag, a tube for blowing into, drone tubes, and one melody pipe, the bagpipe is most frequently called *gaita*. The stridency of the shawm and bagpipe suit this ensemble for outdoor performances.

The prominence of the guitar in Spanish music is well known. Today, there is an extensive complex of guitars, from the large and low-pitched *guitarrón* to several small and high ones, including the *requinto*, the *timple*, the *vihuela*, the *guitarillo*, the *tiple*, the *triplo*, and the *tiplillo*. In central and southern Spain, the guitar often accompanies solo singing, as in flamenco; elsewhere, it is often played in ensembles, such as the *rondalla* bands, another widespread and important instrumental ensemble that accompany the singing of *rondas*.

Dance Forms

Spain's dances include the *jota*, the "mother dance" of the culture, with many variants; the *seguidillas*; and the fandango. All three are couple dances in quick triple time, encapsulating essential traits of Spanish music: dialoguing or solo-chorus vocal performance, small-group instrumental accompaniment, and evocative, poetic texts.

The *jota* has an instrumental introduction, followed by octosyllabic quatrains of *coplas* interspersed with refrains and instrumental interludes. The harmonies alternate between tonic and dominant chords. A complicating factor is that the four-line textual verse extends over a period of seven musical phrases, with the fourth, fifth, sixth, and seventh tending to group into two longer phrases, interrupted by held cadential notes—a pattern that, coupled with repetition of the fourth line of text, marks the dramatic high point of the verse. The cumulative effect of this musical-textual layering and repetition is of a nonlinear system that continues to loop back upon itself; surprise is heightened by the tendency to begin vocal phrases on the second beat of the measure, working against an emphatic downbeat in the accompaniment.

The fandango, most closely associated with Andalucía, is widely dispersed, with regional variations. It features sensual movements, laughter, and cries; these attributes combine with harmonic complexities to make it stylistically more expressive than the *jota*. The music begins with instrumental passages, followed by one or more chords to mark the beginning of the *coplas*. A stanza of five octosyllabic lines is sung over six musical phrases, with a complex harmonic progression.

Flamenco

Flamenco, the music and dance traditionally associated with the Gypsies (*gitanos*) of southern Spain, unites song, guitar, and dance in an emotional, deeply expressive art form. [Known as Roma elsewhere in Europe, Gypsies receive broader attention in the article ROMANI (GYPSY) MUSIC.] Flamenco music is the fusion of *gitano* musical traits and stylings with traditional and popular forms of Spanish music. Initially a *gitano* expression, it soon came to be practiced by non-*gitanos* (*payos*). Historically, its most important aspect is the *cante* "song," originally performed unaccompanied, with rhythmic accompaniment from a stick (*palo seco*) or sometimes claps. Later, in the era of the singing cafés (*cafés cantantes*), guitar accompaniment became a feature of the style.

The forms of flamenco can be divided into three groups: *cante jondo* 'deep song', *cante intermedio* 'intermediate song' (also known as *cante flamenco*), and *cante chico* 'light song'. *Cante jondo*, considered the oldest and most serious group, includes the important *palos siguiriyas* and *soleá*, both based on a complex, twelve-beat rhythmic structure (*compás*). *Cante intermedio* is a hybrid, created from the fusion of *cante jondo* and forms from Spanish folk and popular music styles, in particular the fandango, originally a dance of Arabic origin. The rhythmic structure of the *cante chico* is not so complex as that of the *jondo*, with the exception of the festive *bulerías*, also based on a twelve-beat structure. Primarily rooted in Andalusian folklore, it has assimilated Latin American musical traits.

DISC
❶
TRACK
21

History of Flamenco

The earliest accounts of flamenco, dating from the early nineteenth century, document parties in *gitano* homes and jam sessions (*juergas*), in taverns, bars, and brothels. The jam sessions were patronized by members of the wealthy, *señorito* class of Andalusian landed gentry, who sought entertainment among the lower rungs of the social ladder. *Cafés cantantes*, which appeared about 1840 in Madrid and Seville, offered flamenco artists regular contracts with fixed salaries and gave flamenco a reenergized, creative thrust. Purists have decried this period as the beginning of commercialization in flamenco, but it is now acknowledged as having been tremendously important in the artistic development of flamenco, particularly in the creation of new forms of *cante*, the addition of the guitar as an accompanimental instrument, and the growing importance of the dance.

After the *café cantante* era, flamenco was taken to the theatrical stage in the period known as flamenco opera (*operismo*). This period, which lasted through the 1920s, transformed more "authentic" styles of flamenco into the commercialized forms that held sway until the renaissance of older, more serious styles in the 1950s and 1960s. With sentimental songs, borrowings from Spanish zarzuela and popular South American song, use of sensational and melismatic vocal tricks, theatrical affectations, and florid lyrics, *operismo* came under attack by intellectuals, led by the composer Manuel de Falla (1876–1946) and the poet Federico García Lorca (1898–1936), who sought to restore popular respect toward flamenco as an art form.

In the early 1950s, a renaissance of serious, "pure" flamenco began, brought about partly by the influence of Spanish dance companies, whose touring resulted in the interest of international scholars and aficionados. In Jerez de la Frontera in 1958, the Cathedra de Flamenco (Institute of Flamenco Studies) was created. Nightclubs (*tablaos*) that offered performances of more "artistic" flamenco were opened in Barcelona, Madrid, and Seville. The 1960s saw the beginnings of small flamenco clubs (*peñas*), regional flamenco festivals throughout Andalucía, and the many contests (*concursos*) of *cante* and *toque*, in which important new flamenco artists got their first recognition.

Traits of the Genre

The guitar was introduced during the *café cantante* era, solely for accompaniment. The characteristic playing style—strumming (*rasgueado*), alternating with plucked melodic phrases (*falsetas*)—is an integral part of the ensemble of singer, dancer, and guitarist. The guitar style was soon expanded through the introduction of complex arpeggios, the four-finger tremolo, and more difficult left-hand work. The intense period of creativity and renovation that flamenco has enjoyed since the late 1960s is largely due to the work of young, innovative guitarists, whose incorporation of classical and jazz guitar techniques and Latin American rhythms and genres has influenced all aspects of flamenco, including the sung and danced elements.

In traditional flamenco contexts, onlookers played important roles. Their participation in the *jaleo*, a series of encouraging and admiring shouts from the audience added an essential element to the ambience. An audience of aficionados participates with claps and finger snaps. Flamenco *palmas* are rhythmic patterns based on the rhythmic structure of the *cante*. Members of the flamenco *cuadro* (dancers, singers, and guitarist) and skilled aficionados perform complex counterrhythms in the *compás*, complementing the guitar's rhythm and the dancer's footwork. The influence of the audience in the *jaleo* is less evident in concert and festival contexts, but it prevails in more intimate settings where flamenco is performed.

The texts of *cante flamenco* consist of "couplets" (*coplas*) three- to five-line stanzas. Most flamenco lyrics are sung in the Andalusian dialect of Spanish. Flamenco singers rely on traditional lyrics, which they enhance with variations. Some *coplas* are anonymous, but many were composed by famous poets, including Manuel Machado (1874–1947), Manuel Balmaseda, and García Lorca. The use of sophisticated flamenco lyrics has become common, reflecting the influence of García Lorca.

The lyrics of *cante jondo* communicate personal suffering with directness, simplicity, and lyricism, and evoke a deep sense of fatalism and nihilism. Death is a principal theme, as are the conflicts between hope and despair, love and the pains of love, guilt and atonement, and evil and divine protection. Verses of the *cante chico* tend to express humor and sarcasm, but they too reveal an underlying tragic or ironic sense. Since Franco's demise, some *coplas* have addressed overtly political themes.

—Adapted from an article by Elizabeth Miles and Loren Chuse

Bibliography

Chase, Gilbert. 1959. *The Music of Spain*. 2nd, rev. ed. New York: Dover.

Crivillé i Bargalló, Josep. 1988. *Historia de la música española*. 2nd ed. El folklore musical, 7. Madrid: Alianza Editorial.

García Matos, Manuel. 1958. *Spanish Folk Music and Dance*. Translated by Clover de Pertinez. Madrid: Inter Ministerial Organizing Committee for the Spanish Pavillion.

Livermore, Ann. 1972. *A Short History of Spanish Music*. New York: Vienna House.

Mitchell, Timothy. 1990. *Passional Culture*. Philadelphia: University of Pennsylvania Press.

———. 1994. *Flamenco Deep Song*. New Haven, London: Yale University Press.

Pohren, Don. 1992. *The Art of Flamenco*. 3rd ed. Seville: Society of Spanish Studies.

Ribera y Tarragó, Julián. [1922] 1970. *Music in Ancient Arabia and Spain*. English translation of *La Música de las Cántigas: estudio sobre la origen y naturaleza*, vol. 3. New York: Da Capo Press.

Schindler, Kurt. 1941. *Folk Music and Poetry of Spain and Portugal*. Edited by Federico de Onis. New York: Hispanic Institute.

Stevenson, Robert M. [1960] 1964. *Spanish Music in the Age of Columbus*. The Hague: Martinus Nijhoff.

Washabaugh, William. 1996. *Flamenco Passion, Politics, and Popular Culture*. Oxford and Washington, D.C.: Berg.

Italy

Italy's 58 million people have evolved traditions that share common elements with continental Europe and the Mediterranean. Consequently, some scholars have suggested that, while northern Italy is musically the south of Europe, southern Italy belongs to the north of Africa. The musical tradition of the Piedmont (in the north), for example, may relate more closely to the traditions of France, Spain, the British Isles, German-speaking countries, and Scandinavia than to those of Calabria or Sicily.

Along the peninsula, the transition from European to Mediterranean musical idioms occurs gradually, but on the basis of structure, manner of performance, and textual elements, Italy has four main regions of musical style: the Mediterranean (or south) and Sicily; the central region; the north; and Sardinia. Originally, the clearest division in musical, linguistic, and social styles was between north and south, bounded by the Apennines chain that links La Spezia and Pesaro. Heavy migration from south to north after 1945 further complicated the musical landscape.

Musical styles and practices vary from those reminiscent of Austrian folk music to others resembling Arabic melismatic singing. Linguistic enclaves, clearly related to traditions outside Italy, add to the variety: Albanian (in Calabria, Basilicata, and Sicily), Greek (in Apulia and Sicily), German (in Alto Adige, Trentino, and Veneto), Provençal (in Piedmont), and Catalan (in Sardinia). In these musical areas, little in the way of syncretism or acculturation has been observed. The Italian peninsula is thus a mosaic of local traditions, confined at times within a region, town, or family. From this point of view, there is no "Italian folk music." Rarely shared at the national level, folk song in Italy never became a national symbol. Instead, during the second half of the nineteenth and part of the twentieth century, opera and so-called Neapolitan popular song served such purposes.

Contexts and Genres of Traditional Song and Music

Singing in Italy, as elsewhere, has many uses, occasions, and associations. There are songs for life-cycle rituals (baptisms, weddings, burials), calendric carols (for Christmas, spring festivals, carnival), occupational songs (shepherds', soldiers', vendors', fishermen's), recreational songs (including dance songs), family songs (lullabies, children's songs), cattle calls, and so on.

Genres of Song

Two important types of Italian folk song are ballads (often called *canto epico-lirici*) and lyric songs (*canti lirico-monostrofici*). Ballads are found mostly in the north, where older dialects favored the spread of balladry, probably from France. Lyric songs are more common south of the Apennines, where pre-Latin languages were widespread. The north-south dichotomy holds true not only in the literary content of songs, but in musical style, including the type of vocal production, the mode of performance, and the compositional process.

Ballads

Ballads in Italy share some of their narrative themes with those of the Anglo-American canon established by Francis James Child (1825–1896). Even when narrative themes are close to those of the Child ballads, Italian melodies differ considerably from those of the Anglo-American tradition, where tunes frequently have modal features, often with flatted thirds or sevenths. In Italy, melodies for ballads usually have a clearly tonal character, at times resembling those of French-speaking territories.

Lyric Songs

Italian lyric songs exist in a bewildering variety, mostly in southern Italy and in the northeast. Some are *canzoni a ballo*, songs originally intended for dancing. Lyric songs function as lullabies, work songs, and serenades. They are also, to some degree, improvised. In performing, the singer draws on a repertoire of traditional versification and verbal formulas. Sometimes the singer will use ready-made stanzas that, with some variation, can be adapted to almost any theme. The text is coupled to a small number of melodic types, embellished and molded to the circumstance.

A lyric song can comprise a single stanza or, more often, several stanzas in which each unit expresses a complete thought. Whereas a single stanza from a narrative song would suffer from lack of context or completeness, a monostrophic *canto lirico* usually espresses a self-contained idea.

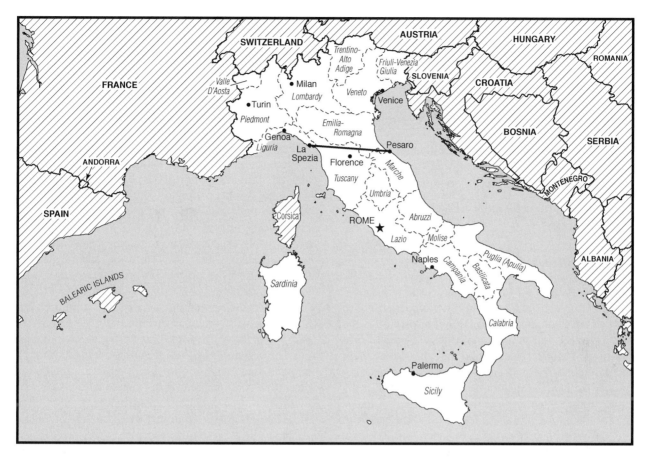

Italy

Seasonal Rituals

The most famous seasonal ritual is the *maggio* (May) celebration, still widespread across central Italy. Its associated songs (*maggi*), whose origins go back to the 1400s, have lost much of their ritual function. The *maggio* includes rituals such as offering of branches, flowers and eggs, choosing a May queen, planting a tree and dancing around it, serenading combined with the collection of alms, and the staging of drama with music and singing. This drama, the *maggio drammatico*, consists of scenes performed by peasant actors who sing songs with interludes on violin or accordion. Its subject matter is the life of a saint or a historical hero, the latter often derived from poetry by Ariosto, Dante, or Tasso and sometimes classical poetry (Virgil, Ovid) or chronicles of current events.

Begging songs (*canti di questua*) of various types are performed in conjunction with numerous seasonal and religious events. For example, the *canto della passione*, a begging song widespread in central Italy, is performed the week before Easter. It contrasts the devotional tone required by the subject—the trial, crucifixion, death, and resurrection of Jesus—with the *saltarello*, a dance that evokes joy and hope for the resurrection of Christ. A diatonic accordion (*organetto*) player and two singers, who accompany themselves on a hammered dulcimer (*cembalo*) and tambourines (*tamburini*), alternate stanzas.

Dances

The *tarantella*, a vivacious dance in 6/8, derives its name from the tarantula spider and its music from a dance-therapy ritual. Traditionally, people exhibiting hysterical or psychotic behavior were said to be spider-poisoned. To cure the "poisoning," musicians played a type of excited and incessant music, using fiddle, guitar, accordion, and frame drum (*tamburello*). The patient—most often a woman—danced to the music until she went into a trance and collapsed on the floor. The ritual is called *tarantismo* in the area of Apulia, where it occurred until the late 1950s.

The *tammuriata* (from *tammorra*, 'tambourine') of Campania is danced by man-woman, man-man, and woman-woman couples to syllabic lyric songs (*strambotti*), whose scale with an augmented fourth resembles the lydian mode. A tambourine accompanies the singing with a reiterated rhythmic formula that constantly undergoes microvariations, often joined by castanets, friction drum, mouth harp, and other noisemakers.

Many types of *saltarello* formerly existed all across central Italy. Still frequently encountered with variant names, they belong to a large group of courting dances. Dancing can be gentle and slow, though it is strenuous and acrobatic in the Marche. It is accompanied by the *organetto* in central Italy and a type of friction drum in the central-southern area.

Musical Style, Performance Practice, and Aesthetics

Tonal and Rhythmic Organization

The oral repertoires of Italy may be conceived as a tonal continuum. At one end, and by far the most conspicuous, are melodies that function according to the principles of classical functional harmony; at the other is music whose tonal material is organized into a variety of modal scales. Tonal melodies have a clear tonal center (or tonic), a dominant, and a leading tone (which in the melody seldom moves forcefully to the tonic). Neither vocal nor instrumental music in oral tradition follows the tempered scale, except in the case of instruments with mechanically fixed sound production: the accordion and its humble relative the *organetto* (small diatonic accordion), which has gradually replaced bagpipes in many areas.

Most of the nontempered diatonic scales in Italian folk music resemble the major scale. In modal tunes, there is always a tonal center of sorts, though functional notes such as the leading tone or the subdominant may be absent. Occasionally, "exotic" features occur, such as the modal formulas found in Sicily, which are reminiscent of the tetrachord of Middle Eastern classical music.

The Italian tradition contains both metric music in strict time or *parlando rubato* (with speechlike, variable beat), and nonmetric music. In the north, divisive meters predominate; in central and southern Italy, additive meters and other complex forms occur.

Binary organization is almost as common as ternary, except in the alpine area, where ternary meter is more common. Frequent shifts between binary and ternary are a trait of alpine style in Austria, France, and Switzerland.

The Organization of Performances

Italian performances include virtually all possible combinations of vocal, instrumental, and vocal-instrumental interaction. The range of vocal practices covers monophonic singing, drone-based polyphony, various kinds of heterophony, and choral polyphony. Antiphonal and responsorial performances are typical, especially in religious, quasi-liturgical songs. Perhaps the most famous responsorial performances are the tuna-fishing songs of Sicily, sung in unison or octave.

Choral singing belongs mainly to the alpine area and the north, where a variable number of singers sing two, three, or four parts. The accompanying part sings below the leading part or, less commonly, above it. This type of polyphony, structured in thirds or sixths, is widespread from the southern German territories to the valley of the river Po, and into Slovenia, Dalmatia, and northern Croatia (figure 1). In playfulness and intricacy of texture, the richest polyphonic forms include the *tiir*, from the town of Premana in Lombardy; the *trallalero*, in the area around Genoa, in which five vocal parts imitate various instruments; and the *bei* in Tuscany. These styles are neither song forms nor song types, but polyphonic procedures applied to different kinds of songs.

South of Naples, solo singing is predominant. Polyphony is seldom choral (in which participants join in and try to blend), but instead is unison singing that borders on heterophony, or two or three parts carried by single voices.

Textures cut across genres. Ballads, for instance, are performed solo or in chorus depending on the area and on the availability of singers; in the alpine area, choral performance is the most common. Lyric

Figure 1 "*Sul castel che 'l mira ben,*" an alpine song from the Trentino area, sung in parallel diatonic thirds and a major mode. *Transcription by Renato Morelli.*

songs like *cantu a vatoccu*, traditionally sung by two or three people at the most, are now sometimes performed chorally.

Vocal production differs sharply between the north and the south. In the north, especially the alpine area, choral singing of ballads is syllabic, the words are clearly intelligible, the tempo is strict, and the melody is unaffected by the content of the text; voices are full and relaxed, come from the chest, are free of vibrato, and aim at blending. Melodies are accordingly simple and unembellished, and the texture oscillates between homophony and heterophony. Southward from the Apennines, choral singing gradually disappears, the tempo becomes rubato, the meter shifts from divisive to additive, and a nonblending, strained, throat-and-head-centered vocal production predominates. In the Neapolitan area, vibrato is common in traditional and popular song. In Sicily, where the relationship of the Italian south to eastern and southern Mediterranean cultures goes back to antiquity, a nasal timbre and florid, embellished melodies resemble those of Arabic styles.

Musical Instruments

Though the use of most instruments remains confined to their local areas, some manufactured instruments enjoy nationwide use. The diatonic button accordion (*organetto*) has largely replaced many types of bagpipe. It typically plays the *saltarello*. Performers develop a virtuosic technique that they test in public competitions. Though the *organetto* still circulates widely in the central areas of the Marche, Lazio, Abruzzi, and Umbria, it has been replaced by the chromatic accordion in the north. Violins are still employed in many areas, but no repertory specific to them exists.

Many stringed instruments are found only locally. The harp exists in Viggiano, in southern Basilicata. The hurdy-gurdy (*ghironda*) was once confined to small areas in Piedmont, Lombardy, and Emilia, and today is found among revival groups. Variations of the *lira* of Calabria (a bowed, three-stringed fiddle, played on the knee) are played elsewhere in the eastern Mediterranean, especially in Crete and the Balkans. In the north, the guitar has the standard six-stringed form, but in central and southern Italy, the *chitarra battente*, has four or five courses of steel strings, tuned to suit rhythmic strumming. Traditionally, *chitarra battente* accompanies singing and dancing and is not a solo instrument. Other stringed instruments include zithers in the German-speaking Alto Adige and the one-stringed, bowed fiddle (*torototeld*) in the northeast.

Idiophones include crotals (clappers), *tricchebal-lacche* (the rattle of Naples, with three or five mallets inserted in a wooded frame, so the center one is fixed and the outer ones are free to strike against it), bells of various kinds, castanets, and *raganelle* (cog rattles). Church bells in Italy are played in complex and melodious rounds.

Wind instruments include a variety of flutes: the *firlinfeu* 'pan flute', single and double duct flutes, transverse duct flutes, open transverse flutes, and globular flutes. The double flute exists in Campania, Calabria, and Sicily. Reed instruments include single- and double-reed pipes (*ciaramella* and *piffero*, respectively), which can be played in sets of two or three, plus two distinct types of bagpipes. In the north, where bagpipes are now virtually extinct, they had one chanter and one or two drones. The central and southern Italian bagpipe (*zampogna*) features two chanters and one or more drones.

Literate Tradition

In the late Middle Ages and Renaissance, art music imitated traditional models. Some sixteenth-century madrigals and frottola melodies bear a strong resemblance to those still sung in oral tradition by poet-singers who improvise lyric songs. In the 1800s, the amount of art music patterned after traditional melodic types was small, whereas tunes belonging to the literate tradition were accepted and transformed in the oral environment: in Italy, where the phrase *art music* normally refers to opera, arias are heard in the villages.

It is hard to imagine the extent to which opera was a popular form of entertainment during the 1800s, and how widely it was disseminated through actual productions, transcriptions for brass bands and many other ensembles, itinerant groups of various sorts, and carillons and mechanical musical devices. Small villages that never had an operatic season saw the occasional production of works that had been successful in the large operatic centers. Such provincial productions helped reduce the distance that normally exists between urban music and rural music. At times, Italian traditional music shows the effect of contact with opera and with the popular-song tradition, a subsidiary stream of opera up until World War II. Indeed, tunes from famous and obscure works—including those of Mercadante, Meyerbeer, Donizetti, and Verdi—occasionally filtered into the oral tradition.

—*Adapted from an article by Marcello Sorce Keller*

Bibliography

Barblan, Guglielmo. 1941. *Musiche e strumenti dell'Africa orientale italiana*. Naples: Edizioni della triennale d'oltremare.

Barwick, Linda. 1991. "Same tunes, different voices: contemporary use of traditional models in the Italian Folk Ensemble's Ballata grande per Francesco Fantin (Adelaide 1990)," *Musicology Australia* 14: 47–67.

Bianco, Carla. 1973. *The Two Rosetos*. Bloomington: Indiana University Press.

Busk, R. Harriette. 1977 [1887]. *The Folk-Songs of Italy*. Musical examples by Giuseppe Pitre. New York: Arno.

Del Giudice, Luisa, ed. 1989. *Italian Traditional Song*. Los Angeles: Italian Heritage Culture Foundation and the Italian Cultural Institute.

De Simone, Roberto. 1979. *Canti e tradizioni populari in Campania*. Rome: Lato Side Editori.

Giuriati, Giovanni, ed. 1985. *Forme e comportamenti della musica folklorica italiana*. Milan: Unicopli.

Leydi, Roberto, ed. 1972. *Il folk music revival*. Palermo. Flaccovio.

———. 1973. *I canti populari italiani*. Milan: Mondadori.

Magrini, Tullia. 1986. *Canti d'amore e di sdegno*. Milan: Franco Angeli.

———. 1992. *Il maggio drammatico: una tradizione di teatro in musica*. Bologna: Analisi.

———. 2001. "Italy (Traditional music)." In *The New Grove Dictionary of Music and Musicians*, edited by Stanley Sadie, 12: 664–680. London: Macmillan.

Sorce Keller, Marcello. 1984. "Folk Music in Trentino: Oral Transmission and the Use of Vernacular Languages." *Ethnomusicology* 28:75–89.

———. 1986. "Life of a Traditional Ballad in Oral Tradition and Choral Practice." *Ethnomusicology* 30:449–469.

———. 1986. "European-American Music: Italian." *The New Grove Dictionary of American Music*. Edited by H. Wiley Hitchcock and Stanley Sadie. New York: Macmillan.

———. 1994. "Reflections of Continental and Mediterranean Traditions in Italian Folk Music." In *Music Cultures in Contact: Convergences and Collisions*, edited by Margaret J. Kartomi and Steven Blum, 40–47. Basel: Gordon and Breach.

Central Europe

Central Europe borders on all the other major geographical regions of continental Europe. The music of German-speaking countries (Germany, Austria, parts of Switzerland, Belgium, and Luxembourg) has some archaic features—such as the prominence of horns and trumpets and vocal cattle calls—with parallels in northern Europe. In the Slavic-speaking countries (Poland, the Czech Republic, and Slovakia), the ritual occasions for singing resemble ones in eastern and southeastern Europe, as do those of the Hungarians, who speak a non-Indo-European, Finno-Ugric language. As a center of literacy since the Middle Ages, the region has perhaps the longest and richest recorded history of folk and art music in all of Europe. Linkage among regional traditions is illustrated by the popularity of string bands and brass ensembles at all levels of society. The association of music with ideology and politics in this region has been particularly striking, whether the form of government was fascist in the 1930s and 1940s, communist from the late 1940s to 1990, or democratic.

Central Europe

Germany

One of the largest countries in Europe at 357,023 square kilometers, Germany was for much of its history a geographical term for an area of smaller states and principalities, politically unified from 1871 to 1945. From 1945 to 1990, it was divided into the communist German Democratic Republic and the democratic German Federal Republic. Highly urbanized, its population of 82 million is about 33 percent Protestant (mainly in the north and east), about 33 percent Roman Catholic (mainly in the south, in Rhineland and Bavaria), about 3.5 percent Muslim, and 0.1 percent Jewish.

Bordering on nine countries, Germany produced an influential music culture over several centuries with such composers as Heinrich Schütz (1585–1672), George Frideric Handel (1685–1759), members of the Bach family, Christoph Willibald Gluck (1714–1787), Carl Maria von Weber (1786–1826), Ludwig van Beethoven (1770–1827), Robert Schumann (1810–1856), Felix Mendelssohn-Bartholdy (1809–1847), Johannes Brahms (1833–1897), Richard Wagner (1813–1883), Richard Strauss (1864–1949), Paul Hindemith (1895–1963), Kurt Weill (1900–1950), Hans Werner Henze (b. 1926), and Karlheinz Stockhausen (1928–2007).

Song Styles

Knowledge about music in Germany in the first millennium is sketchy at best. Only indirect records of early German music exist before the first documented song, an Old High German song text of the ninth century. Unfortunately, the melody, written in neumatic notation without a staff, cannot be deciphered.

German song in the Middle Ages was marked melodically by its closeness to Gregorian chant. Most medieval German spiritual folk songs were derived from textual parodies of Gregorian melodies (primarily sequences), or syllabic settings (tropes) of previously melismatic melodies. Even dance melodies were modeled on forms borrowed from the structure of sequences. Secular songs in Gregorian modes, with rich melismatic material, flowery ornaments, and metrically unfettered melodies, closely parallel Gregorian chorales.

The dance-songs and rounds of the Middle Ages, typified through bar form (mostly AABA), had a different tonal and melodic orientation: pentatonic or triadic melodies. The rhythms of these melodies closely follow the meter of the verse. The same tendency can be seen in folkloric Christmas carols, particularly cradle songs (*Wiegenlieder*) in 6/8 or 3/4 meter with triadic melodies. But triadic melodies too were particularly characteristic of the alpine yodel, a nearly textless singing, which even today influences the melodies of Bavaria's secular and religious music.

Medieval documentation reports the existence of unaccompanied singing for dancing, drinking, magic, and cult singing, particularly at funerals and weddings. Christian music in the Middle Ages included pilgrims' and crusaders' songs, and the songs and religious dances of the fourteenth-century flagellants, which flared up intermittently in Germany, especially in times of plague. Such information demonstrates the existence of a widespread vernacular song culture associated with folk religion.

In German folk music of the Renaissance, major-minor dualism slowly yielded to the sovereignty of the major mode. All forms of singing and dancing, sacred and secular, followed this inclination. Singing became more and more bound to metrical organization in measures. Now and then, syncopation or metrical change relieved metrical rigidity.

Melodic modernization began in the late 1600s with more motivic unity, symmetrical phrasal periods, systematic shifts in modulation, phrasal repetitions (sometimes still based on the bar form of the Middle Ages), and conscious expressive use of major-minor polarity. During the 1700s and 1800s, these changes in sacred and secular folk song were harmonically supported within the limits of the tonic-subdominant-dominant cadential progression. German *Liederschulen* (song schools in Berlin, Leipzig, and Swabia) greatly influenced this development, as did the folkloric *Liederspiele*, a musical theater with spoken parts alternating with folkloric song.

The major mode proliferated in secular and sacred song in the 1700s and especially the 1800s. During the 1800s, melody evolved under harmonic influence but retained its periodic formal structure. Modulation became almost the rule, often with chromatic development, intervallic leaps, or suspensions of the fourth, sixth, and seventh scale degrees, and harmonically determined chordal melodies. This melodic type established itself speedily in song, folk music, and dance (especially the waltz). Patriotic songs, songs of the homeland or the Rhine, wine songs, students' songs, and church songs were disseminated through civic male choirs (mostly called *Liedertafel*), worker or factory choirs, and schools. This sort of melody still influences carnival songs and popular and commercial folk music.

In the early twentieth century, the German youth movement, initiated in 1896 by the creation of outdoor clubs (*Wandervogel*), quickly tired of such songs and dances, and began a countermovement by establishing its own repertoire. Hans Breuer's *Der Zupfgeigenhansl* (1908), the most famous songbook of the day, has been reprinted more than any other. It stimulated the composition of new songs for two reasons: first, through the revival of old German songs, and through the assimilation of little-known national and regional folkloric or "wander" songs. The movement's new songs were composed partly from historicized melodic, tonal, and formal models from the 1500s to the 1700s, and partly from new melodic types and songs with traits from Slavic, Balkan, and Scandinavian folk songs or marches.

After the Russian Revolution of 1917, emerging German workers' songs were greatly influenced by the Russian and Bolshevik heritage ("*Brüder, zur Sonne, zur Freiheit*," original Russian text by Leonid P. Radin, 1897; German text by Hermann Scherchen). Song texts by Bertolt Brecht (1898–1956) and Erich Weinert (1890–1953), set to music by Hanns Eisler (1898–1962) and Paul Dessau (1894–1979), led the field in the late 1920s ("*Solidaritätslied*"; "*Vorwärts, und nie vergessen*"; "*Einheitsfrontlied*"). These songs have a marchlike character, an upbeat nature, dotted rhythms, triadic melodies, signal motives, and modulatory multisectional forms, often marked by the alternation of a minor-mode strophe and a major-mode refrain ("In Paris, in Copenhagen, Zurich, Prague"). They were spread during the period of the Weimar Republic (1919–1933) by communist agitators and by wind bands and musical parades of the Roter Frontkämpferbund (Red Front-Line Society). Even more effective were the "brass shawm bands," whose instruments, developed from the automobile horn, produced penetrating tones by means of vibrating metal tongues.

After 1933, the Nazis abruptly ended the free development of music and youth song, and of socialist and communist singing. Hitler liquidated all political parties and their organizations, and banned nearly all youth groups, their songs, and songbooks. In their place, he offered Nazi-movement songs, circulated by schools, Nazi youth organizations (all adolescents were forced into membership), military,

government-controlled organizations, radio, recordings, and films. This repertoire encompassed not only retexted songs of the communists and socialists, but also older and modern military and marching songs, enlarged with traditional, politically neutral folk-song material, the latter tolerated thanks to a patriotic German folk ideology (*Blut und Boden* 'blood and soil'). Also, folk songs, dances, and instrumental music were pressed into service to shape the new "national-socialist person."

In November 1933, Germany's musical life fell under the control of the newly established Reichsmusikkammer (State Music Office). Directly supervised by "propagandaminister" Joseph Goebbels, this body tried to suppress all foreign or non-Aryan influences by regulating the work permits necessary for publicly practicing professional and amateur musicians. The purpose of this effort was to stanch the supposed subversion of the "moral strength of the people"—and beyond this, beginning five years later, after the terrible pogroms of "Crystal Night," by deportations and mass executions to destroy a flourishing old Jewish (especially Yiddish) German folk-music culture, with its fascinating folk songs and a vital—today by young German musicians partly renewed—klezmer music.

Newer Nazi songs, like "*Die Fahne hoch*" (the hymn of Hitler's combat group "SA"), "*Vorwärts schmettern die hellen Fanfaren*" (the hymn of the Hitler-Jugend, the Nazi youth organization), and the soldier's song "*Erika*," became ever more rigid and strict in rhythm, beat, tonality, and structure. Marchlike rhythms dominated, and the major mode expelled the supposedly non-Aryan minor mode. Hard, accented meters, short phrases, stiff dotted rhythms, triadic horn-signal melodies, ostinato motives, and the refrain form permeated this music. Paradoxically, these traits sometimes appeared in the work and protest songs of Hitler's opponents.

Banned and persecuted with other nonfascist organizations, members of christian churches (in the Protestant especially the "Confessing Church") and especially of their youth groups, sympathizers of the communists and socialists and other opponents of the Nazi Regime fought back also by songs. Singing by these groups in churches and secret meetings, in concentration camps or prisons became an effective means of political resistance or protest. A lot of songs, traditional and newly composed—and in this case often set to melodies in church or minor modes—as well as parodies of popular hit songs or forbidden Russian Cossack at times served as a code or a means of identification and became a medium for sometimes obvious, sometimes concealed, political or religious opposition. Especially the so-called

Edelweisspiraten 'edelweiss pirates', operating out of bombed-out cities along the Rhine and the Ruhr, specifically Cologne and Wuppertal, opposed Hitler most conspicuously also by songs.

By confiscating songbooks, sheet music, and instruments, by searching houses, by interrogating, torturing, and imprisoning individuals, by setting up special concentration camps for young political convicts and penal battalions, and by expelling students from schools and universities, the Nazis tried to suppress such activities. Swing-Jugend (Swing-Youth), a provocative opposition movement active in the cities and towns of occupied Europe, was an informal group of youthful enthusiasts of jazz and dance. Groups of young people mimed the clothing, hair, and lifestyles of their American contemporaries, opposing thereby the uniformed Nazi society and its conformist state youth groups. Nazi authorities mercilessly persecuted this movement.

In the post-World War II era, West German youth organizations regrouped and reclaimed songs forbidden during the dictatorship and those of earlier times. Schools endeavored to create a new repertoire, based on experiments in the 1930s with tonality, rhythm, harmony and irregular phrases and freed from traditional constraints. Postwar contact with the flood of African-American spirituals, blues, and jazz that swept through popular music radically changed the tone of German singing. Blues and jazz harmonies, and above all, jazz rhythms and phrasing, influenced popular singing, dancing, and instrumental music. In parts of Bavaria, however, older men still gather in the evenings at intimate beer houses after hiking and sing quietly in multi-part harmonies.

Instrumental Music

In the Middle Ages, instrumental music was played most often as an accompaniment for dancing, and it was sounded at parades, folk plays, markets, and celebrations. Important folk instruments included bagpipes, the hurdy-gurdy, the hornpipe, the trumpet, the animal horn, the mouth harp, the duct flute, the zither, the shawm, the friction drum, and later the alphorn. In town and country, traveling musicians, often itinerant clerics and students, disseminated instrumental and vocal music.

Urban musical culture, organized into guilds during the Renaissance, provided accompaniment to religious, vocational, and urban activities. On flutes, hammered dulcimers, shawms, crumhorns, trombones, and eventually trumpets and timpani (especially at tournaments) and stringed instruments, professional town musicians (*Stadtpfeifer*) performed music for religious and communal feasts, church services and festivals, receptions and jubilees, weddings and funerals, city-council meetings and market days. They also sounded daily hours from city towers, day and night, and at Christmas and New Year's. Their repertoire included not only signals and chorales, but also dances and songs. Enjoying regular employment, they were constantly under pressure from competing traveling musicians, organized into regional brotherhoods, the so-called piper's kingdoms.

Instrumental folk music and folk song attracted art musicians at this time. Suites of instrumental variations of songs and dances, and of arrangements of polyphonic songs, were based on dances and folk and community songs recorded in manuscript songbooks.

The practitioners of this vocal and instrumental culture included not only town musicians, cantors, and other professionals, but also school choirs, student *collegia musica*, and educated, noble amateurs or bourgeois dilettantes from the world of business and trade. The parts varied among vocal, mixed vocal-instrumental, and completely instrumental performance on instruments such as lute, organ, harpsichord, viola da gamba, and recorder. Improvisation figured prominently in performance, and performances took place in churches, schools, castles, city offices, dance halls, and coffeehouses.

Musical Instruments

A number of traditional German folk instruments have remained in use or been revived, such as the hurdy-gurdy, the hammered dulcimer, the alphorn, the zither (*Scheitholz*), the dulcimer, the psaltery, the cittern, the fiddle, the tambourine, musical spoons, the tenor drum, the shawm, and bagpipes. Nonetheless, the most significant instruments in contemporary folk music are modern and international.

The Accordion

Song-and-dance accompaniment in modern Germany is the domain of a relatively young, originally German, but now internationalized arrival: the accordion (vernacular German *Zieh-harmonika*). The incipient form of this instrument was invented in Berlin in 1821, but the musical dimensions of today's instrument have been extended through a highly developed system of buttons, keyboard, and register keys. Folk musicians were quick to recognize the accordion's potential as "the poor man's orchestra," an easily transported instrument that could play chords at the push of a button. Whether in solo playing or in accompanying songs or dances, it is the ideal partner for a one-man band. Consequently, at festivities and dances, in pubs, and at markets, numerous German traveling musicians of the nineteenth and twentieth centuries earned their living playing it with the harp, stringed, and wind instruments. It can also be found in large groups of orchestral dimensions.

The Mandolin

Comparable in function to the accordion is an older European folk instrument, the mandolin, which, especially in the Baroque era, was used in art music too, as in Vivaldi's concertos. It is mostly played solo, especially for accompanying songs; between the world wars and after 1945, however, German mandolins were built in various sizes, supplemented by other plucked instruments, and frequently grouped into mandolin orchestras.

The Guitar

The guitar was always both an art and a folk instrument. It remains a folk instrument in Germany partly because of its popularity in the 1800s. Nearly every pub in the alpine regions had an instrument at hand, and many people played it. The enthusiasm of the German youth movement for singing around 1900 is unimaginable without the guitar. Dangling on a neck strap, the instrument was the constant companion on outings, hikes, and camping trips. Though the number of youth groups has declined, the guitar's role in accompanying songs has prevailed. This result can be attributed to the prominence of the guitar in jazz, beat, and rock.

Marching Bands and Wind Bands

In enthusiasm for the Middle Ages, German youth groups in the 1920s rediscovered the mercenary's drum (*Landsknechttrommel*). After 1933, the tenor drum was revived in less sympathetic hands. The Music Corps of the Hitler Youth appropriated this instrument for their purposes, a tradition continued today by neo-Nazis; however, the marching bands of the annual, interregional, and nonmartial civil-militia "celebrations" (*Schützenfest*) employ the same drum as a rhythmic basis for their parades.

These parades are frequently accompanied by drum corps composed of transverse pipes and marching drums; both instruments have belonged to typical German military and march music ensembles since the late Middle Ages. Today, brass marching bands, successors of the eighteenth-century military wind bands, make up the most important component of these parades. Brass instruments and clarinets dominate these groups but are nearly always supplemented by saxophones.

A similar type of band participates in parades and processions. For example, the traditional songs of the St. Martin's Day children's procession by lantern light (*Fackelzüge*), especially popular in the Rhineland, are sometimes accompanied by wind bands, but without the usual cymbals. Similar ensembles participate in festivities, concerts, and assemblies, especially in Bavaria and Swabia, again during carnival and in South Germany's Shrove Tuesday (*Fastnacht*), functioning as a tourist attraction. Naturally, these activities have been commercialized and professionalized in a way that, to an increasing degree, undermines their "real-folk-music" status.

—Adapted from an article by Wilhelm Schepping

Bibliography

Brednich, Rolf Wilhelm. ed. 2001. *Grundriss der Volkskunde*. Berlin: Reimer.

Brednich, Rolf Wilhelm, Lutz Röhrich, and Wolfgang Suppan. ed. 1973, 1975. *Handbuch des Volksliedes*. 2 vols. München: Fink.

Bröcker, Marianne. ed. 2004. Das 20. *Jahrhundert im Spiegel seiner Lieder*. Bamberg: Universität Bamberg.

Deutsches Volksliedarchiv Freiburg. ed. 1935–. *Deutsche Volkslieder mit ihren Melodien*. 10 vols. to date. Berlin and Leipzig: Walter de Gruyter (vols. 1–4). Freiburg: DVA.

———. ed. 2000–. *Lied und populäre Kultur – Song and Popular Culture*. Jahrbuch des Deutschen Volksliedarchivs. Münster and New York: Waxmann.

Emsheimer, Ernst, and Erich Stockmann. 1966–1981. *Handbuch der europäischen Volksinstrumente*. Leipzig, Zürich, Freiburg: Deutscher Verlag für Musik.

Fackler, Guido. 2000. *"Des Lagers Stimme": Musik im KZ: Alltag und Häftlingskultur in den Konzentrationslagern*. Bremen: Edition Temmen.

Freitag, Thomas. 2001. *Kinderlied – Von der Vielfalt einer musikalischen Liedgattung*. Frankfurt and New York: P. Lang.

Gansberg, Ingeborg. 1986. *Volksliedsammlungen und historischer Kontext: Kontinuität über zwei Jahrhunderte?* Frankfurt and New York: Peter Lang.

Karbusicky, Vladimir. 1973. *Ideologie im Lied, Lied in der Ideologie*. Cologne: Gerig.

Klusen, Ernst. 1969. *Volkslied: Fund und Erfindung*. Cologne: Gerig.

John, Eckhardt. ed. 2006. *Die Entdeckung des sozialkritischen Liedes. Zum 100. Geburtstag von Wolfgang Steinitz*. Münster and New York: Waxmann.

Journal of the International Folk Music Council 1949–1968; continued by *Yearbook of the International Folk Music Council* 1969–1980; continued by *Yearbook for Traditional Music* 1981–.

Müns, Heike. ed. 2005. *Musik und Migration in Ostmitteleuropa*. München: R. Oldenbourg.

Niedhart, Gottfried, and George Broderick. ed. 1999. *Lieder in Politik und Alltag des Nationalsozialismus*. Frankfurt and New York: Peter Lang.

Noll, Günther. ed. 1994. *Musikalische Volkskultur und die politische Macht.* Essen: Die Blaue Eule.

Noll, Günther, and Helga Stein. 1996. *Musikalische Volkskultur als soziale Chance.* Essen: Die Blaue Eule.

Oetke, Herbert. 1983. *Der deutsche Volkstanz.* 2 vols. Wilhelmshaven: Noetzel.

Ottens, Rita, and Joel Rubin. 2001. *Jüdische Musiktraditionen.* Kassel: Gustav Bosse Verlag.

Otto, Uli, and Eginhard König. 1999. *"Ich hatt' einen Kameraden . . ." Militär und Kriege in historisch-politischen Liedern von 1749–1914.* Regensburg: ConBrio.

Potter, Pamela Maxine. 1998. *Most German of the Arts: Musicology and Society from the Weimar Republic to the End of Hitler's Reich.* New Haven, Conn.: Yale University Press.

Probst-Effah, Gisela: 1995. *Lieder gegen das Dunkel in den Köpfen. Untersuchungen zur Folkbewegung in der Bundesrepublik Deutschland.* Essen: Die Blaue Eule.

——— . ed. 2001. *Musik kennt keine Grenzen.* Essen: Die Blaue Eule.

Pulikowski, Julian von. 1933. *Geschichte des Begriffes "Volkslied" im musikalischen Schrifttum.* Heidelberg: Carl Winters Universitäts-Buchhandlung.

Rölleke, Heinz. ed. 1979. *Des Knaben Wunderhorn. Alte deutsche Lieder gesammelt von Achim von Arnim und Clemens Brentano.* 9 vols. Stuttgart: Kohlhammer.

Segler, Helmut. 1990–1992. *Tänze der Kinder in Europa.* Celle: Moeck.

Siefken, Hinrich, and Hildegard Vieregg. ed. 1993. *Resistance to National Socialism: Arbeiter, Christen, Jugendliche, Eliten.* Nottingham: University of Nottingham Press.

Stambolis, Barbara, and Jürgen Reulecke. ed. 2007. *Good-Bye Memories? Lieder im Generationengedächtnis des 20. Jahrhunderts.* Essen: Klartext-Verlag.

Stockmann, Doris. ed. 1992. *Volks- und Popularmusik in Europa.* Laaber: Laaber Verlag.

Austria

Austria, a land-locked nation of 83,849 square kilometers, is bordered on the west by Switzerland, the northwest by Germany, the northeast by the Czech Republic, the east by Hungary, the southeast by Croatia, and the southwest by Italy. Nearly all its 8 million citizens speak German (often in dialect); more than half are urbanites, and 75 percent are Roman Catholic. Physically and ideologically, the country centers on the valleys of the Danube River and its tributaries, valleys home to modern, productive agriculture. About 40 percent of the country is forested and mountainous. A common saying has it that Austria is not large, but tall. Its current borders date from the end of World War I. Before then, its capital, Vienna, was the seat of the Austro-Hungarian Empire. Prosperous and highly industrialized, modern Austria is now a federal republic.

Art Music

Most countries find national glory more in the past than the present, but Austrians have more than the average factual basis for such feelings, and thus an unusual predilection for respecting and liking music associated with the national (imperial) past. Many citizens, when asked to specify the most Austrian music, immediately recite a list of composers of art music, awarding special honor to Mozart (1756–1791), Schubert (1797–1828), and the Strauss family. The reasons behind the widespread respect for and knowledge of art music in Austria probably have much to do with the unarguable quality of the music itself. At the same time, this music evokes eras when Austria played a more prominent international role and perhaps suggests to many that the land that nurtured it must still be culturally powerful.

Folk Music

Austrian folk music is remarkably unified, though practitioners and scholars subdivide it into distinct regional repertoires. The common ground between these repertoires is largely in musical sound, especially mode, melody, meter, and rhythm, in addition to typical song topics, while vocal dialects and how instrumental ensembles are constituted are specific to regions. The yodel (*Jodler, Dudler*)—a family of song types that permeates alpine regions, within and near Austria—aptly illustrates connections and divergences in Austrian folk music. A typical yodel from the Tyrolian Alps (which spill into Italy) has a title and a text invoking its home through employing local dialect: *O du schiane, süasse Nåchtigåll* 'Oh you pretty, sweet nightingale' would be spelled *O du schöne, süsse Nachtigall* in formal German (figure 1). The theme, however, does not surprise. Light, cheerful, nonnarrative texts invoking the outdoors are ubiquitous.

No country in Europe has folk music more thoroughly wedded to the diatonic major mode and the fleshing out of harmony than Austria. A few songs are in some form of diatonic minor. In most yodels, harmonies are simple: in the first two measures, we hear a tonic chord, then, in the third measure, the dominant (including the seventh, as is common), which immediately resolves back to the tonic; the fifth measure goes to the subdominant, which will again return through the dominant seventh (ornamented by an appoggiatura in the third beat of the seventh measure) to the tonic. Such three-chord schemes dictate a body of melodies, many of which are strikingly disjunct. Frequent leaps of thirds, sixths, and even sevenths and tritones outline chords, and are easy to hear and to perform precisely because they do that.

This melody relaxes easily into triple meter, recalling a Ländler (the most common family of folk dances), just as many folk melodies can easily be classified as nineteenth-century social dances in meter, rhythm, and tempo. In addition to Ländler, songs that sound like waltzes (also in triple time), several types of polkas, and marches (both in forthright duple meter, but the latter at a slower tempo) can be found in much of the country. Many melodies feature dotted rhythms, but few include much syncopation. Most readers in Europe and the United States will find these melodies simple—a judgment based partly on fact, but reflecting widespread musical experience: centuries of mutual influence between art and folk music in Austria have produced folk repertoires that seem to ape the basic and most accessible features of the eighteenth- and nineteenth-century art music most often heard in European and American concert halls.

Regional Styles

The Tyrol, which has nurtured folk music with unusual persistence, adds Christmas and Easter carols, historical ballads, and songs about hunting to

Figure 1 "*O du schiane, süasse Nåchtigåll,*" a yodel from the Tyrol. The text reads: "Oh you pretty, sweet nightingale, come to me and sing a bit, come to me and sing really nicely, then you can go," followed by nonsense syllables.
Transcription by Franz Rattacher and Franz Friedrich Kohl. After Deutsch 1984:29.

a repertoire of yodels. It is difficult to distinguish between older yodeling styles and several recent waves of commercial yodels. Harps and a form of xylophone are still played. String ensembles survive in some areas, though the most common dance ensemble, dating from after World War II, features a chromatic hammered dulcimer, a zither, a guitar, a harp, and a bass.

The Salzkammergut, a region of mountains cradling chains of lakes, joins the province of Salzburg with Styria and parts of Upper Austria. Its most typical forms of vocal music respond to this geography. There are three- and four-part homophonic yodels, other multipart mountain pasture songs, and the *Almschroa*, a solo dairymaid's yodel. The most typical dance ensemble includes a pair of violins, a string bass, and a button accordion, which may also be played alone. Salzburg is home to a unique repertoire of songs for the Christmas season. Upper Austria (bordering on Germany and the Czech Republic) features numerous musical traditions of considerable antiquity. In addition to its own yodels, it is home to a contrasting form, the four-line song (*Vierzeiler*), and gives special attention to an elaborately performed and rhythmically complex form of the Ländler. Styria's most characteristic

dance is named for the province: the *Stierische* is a multipart sectional Ländler, the successive sections of which have an increasing rhythmic density that adds considerable excitement. The name is also used for the form of button accordion that often plays the genre. The local hammered dulcimer (*Steirisch*) is often played with that accordion and a bass, or, in a formerly more widely distributed ensemble, with fiddles and a bass. Yodels are common.

In the Vorarlberg, in the far west, older traditional music has largely given way to new forms. For instance, older dance ensembles focusing on clarinets and flügelhorns have in many places been replaced by groups featuring accordions, zithers, and guitars.

Vienna, the capital, is far to the east. In earlier centuries, its location placed it nearer the center of the empire. It is home to its own harmonically and chromatically enriched form of the waltz, and the artistic and nostalgically texted *Wienerlied* 'Viennese song'. Musical variety obtains in the geographically varied surrounding province of Lower Austria. Especially notable are the hymns of the wine country north and east of Vienna. In these hymns, lines for a pair of leaders alternate with lines for the congregation; the latter lines are still in two parts, but with each now doubled at the octave. Much Austrian folk music follows the yodel in belonging to the alpine stylistic category, but this hymn, like many Austrian religious folk songs, ballads, and soldiers' songs, fits into more general Germanic melodic style. Lastly, at weddings in the wine country, people dance the Ländler and polkas to ensembles led by clarinets or flugelhorns and including a button accordion and a bass flugelhorn.

Just as the Tyrol and its music are not entirely within the national boundaries of Austria (Tyrolian styles extend into Italy), two Austrian provinces include substantial ethnic minorities and their music. Burgenland, bordering on Hungary, nurtures quite a few typical (and some atypical) Austrian traditions, such as ballads, alongside the *tamburica* bands of the substantial Croatian minority (the term *tamburica* encompasses related and vaiously sized long-necked fretted lutes) and some Hungarian traditions. Last, Carinthia, bordering on Croatia, is home to the *Kärntnerlied*, a special Austrian love song, performed by choruses in four-part harmony. The Slovenian minority cultivates polyphonic songs sounding much like the *Kärntnerlied*.

—*Adapted from an article by Chris Goertzen and Edward Larkey*

Bibliography

Bloemke, Rüdiger. 1996. *Roll Over Beethoven: Wie der Rock 'n' Roll nach Deutschland kam*. St. Andrä-Wördern: Hannibal.

Brödel, Günter, ed. 1982. *Die guten Kräfte: Neue Rockmusik aus Österreich*. St. Andrä-Wördern: Hannibal.

Bronner, Gerhard. 1995. *Die golden Zeit des Wiener Cabarets—Anekdoten, Texte, Erinnerungen*. St. Andrä-Wördern: Hannibal.

Deutsch, Walter. 1980. "Austria, II: Folk Music." In *The New Grove Dictionary of Music and Musicians*. Edited by Stanley Sadie. London: Macmillan.

———. 1984. "Volksmusiklandschaft Österreich." In *Volksmusik in Österreich*, edited by Walter Deutsch, Harald Dreo, Gerlinde Haid, and Karl Horak, 9–44. Vienna: Österreichischer Bundesverlag.

Deutsch, Walter, Gerlinde Haid, and Herbert Zeman. 1993. *Das Volksleid in Österreich: Ein gattungsgeschichtliches Handbuch*. Vienna: Holzhauser.

———. 1995. *Lieder des Weihnachis Festkreises: Steirmark*. Vienna: Bohlau.

Horak, Karl. 1985. *Instrumental Volksmusik aus Tirol*. Innsbruck: Author.

———. 1988. *Musikalische Volkskultur in Burgenland: Ein Rückblick auf 60 Jahre Volksmusikforschung*. Eisenstadt: Bezirks Oberbayern.

———. 1989. *Ältere Zeugnisse zur Volksmusik des steinschen Ennsbereiches*. [Trautenfels]: Verein Schloss Trautenfels.

Lach, Robert. 1923. *Eine Tiroler Liederhandschrift aus dem 18. Jahrhundert*. Vienna: Holder-Pichler-Tempsky.

Larkey, Edward. 1993. *Pungent Sounds: Constructing Identity with Popular Music in Austria*. Austrian Culture, 9. New York: Peter Lang.

Seiler, Christian, ed. 1995. *Schräg dahoam—Neue Volksmusik und ihre Zukunft*. St. Andrä-Wördern: Hannibal.

Suppan, Wolfgang. 1981. *Das grosse stetrische Blasmusikbuch*. Vienna: Molden.

———. 1984. *Volksmusik im Bezirk Liezen*. Trautenfels: Verein Schloss Trautenfels.

Zoder, Raimund. 1950. *Volksleid, Volkstanz, Volksbrauch in Österreich*. Vienna: L. Doblinger.

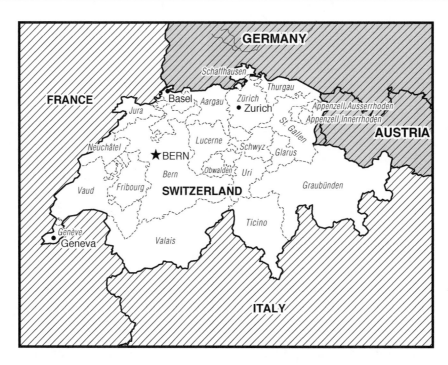

Switzerland

Switzerland

Switzerland was founded in 1291 as a confederation of the three *waldstätte* (today called cantons) Uri, Schwyz, and Unterwalden. In the following centuries, more cantons joined, until 1848, when the Swiss Confederation was established by the federal constitution, with twenty-five cantons. In 1978, the confederation accepted the French-speaking part of the canton Bern as the new, autonomous canton Jura. Switzerland comprises four distinct cultural and linguistic areas: Swiss-German, French, Italian, and Romansh, the last a collection of Rhaeto-Romanic dialects, spoken in canton Graubünden and adjacent parts of Italy. Although the country has 7.5 million inhabitants within 41,288 square kilometers and almost two-thirds of that area consists of sparsely inhabited mountains, distinct regions and many cantons or smaller areas have distinct musical traditions. Despite attempts to use folk music to forge a sense of national identity, many Swiss traditions are specific to certain isolated valleys or cities in which local history has created strong feelings of communal identity.

Traditional Musical Contexts

The rural economy of Switzerland gave rise to a repertoire of songs associated with agriculture, herding cattle, calendrical events, and lifecycle stages. Shepherds of the alpine regions preserved a large part of this repertoire, including songs accompanying milking, feeding animals, and blessing cattle. People believed they could entrance and control various animals with vocal music. This repertoire, maintained in isolated areas until about 1900, has been preserved in part. Its elementary forms include signal calls, yells, recitatives, a three-tone yodel, and melodic vocalizing.

Though archaic vocal styles have been widely replaced by newer ones, Switzerland's musical past maintains a presence, despite changed contexts. Musical traditions connected to calendrical events have been retained in cities and villages. Ancient beliefs in the power of so-called noisemaking instruments are at the core of many such events.

All kinds of bells are involved in most Swiss festivals occurring during midwinter (November through January). In many places, St. Nicholas Day (6 December), Christmas Eve, and New Year's Eve are marked by processions of men or boys, who around their waist or in their hands have a clapper bell or various types and sizes of jingle bells on a harness. In other places, the bell-ringing groups walk with groups of drummers or a brass band and with whip crackers.

In Urnäsch, Appenzell Ausserrhoden, on 31 December and 13 January (New Year's Eve in the Julian calendar) groups of men disguised as *silvesterchläuse* (*silvester* 'New Year's Eve'; *chläuse*, roughly, 'masks or masked figures') move from one farmyard to another and wish farmers a happy New Year, singing a polyphonic natural yodel (*zäuerli*). They accompany themselves with cowbells and large pellet balls, worn on their bodies. They form in two groups, the beautiful and the ugly. The beautiful ones are four masculine figures and two feminine figures. The masculine figures wear on their chests and backs a cowbell, each pair having a different size and tone. They make these sound by swaying their upper torsos. The feminine figures usually wear thirteen pellet bells that they make sound by hopping and moving around with tripping steps.

Another event—with an origin that predates the fourteenth century and has its roots in guild-based and military traditions—is the griffin pageant, which takes place in the second half of January in Basel. Drumming accompanies three mythical figures: a griffin (*vogel gryff*), a wild man (*wild ma*), and a lion (*leu*), which dance on a raft drifting down the Rhine and on the bridge that connects Grossbasel with Kleinbasel. This and other similar events are forerunners of the Swiss carnival traditions that begin in some places in January and end everywhere in the week after Ash Wednesday.

Fasnacht, the largest organized carnival in the country, takes place in Basel during the week after Ash Wednesday. Large fife-and-drum bands (*cliquen*) parade the streets in masks and costumes. Small ensembles travel from bar to bar singing *schnitzelbänke*, derisive songs, critiquing political and social events of the past year; the ensembles accompany themselves on guitars, accordions, or street organs.

Musical Areas

Stereotypical notions of Switzerland as a mountainous region of alphorns, yodels, cowbells, and brass bands fail to do justice to the country's local music practices, which differ significantly by language area, and even from canton to canton.

Swiss-German Areas

The most popular contemporary Swiss-German instrumental ensemble is the *ländlerkappelle*. The standard *ländlerkappelle* consists of clarinet, accordions (often the diatonic *schwyzerörgeli*), and a double bass; in central Switzerland the ensemble also includes a piano. When the ensemble plays for dancing, the clarinet may alternate with a saxophone, and in the 1990s, trombone sometimes joined the ensemble. A good *ländlermusig* is played *lüpfig* 'lifting', meaning the music must induce the audience to get up and dance.

The repertoire of folk music bands was always adapted to the fashions of the times. Since the 1700s, the bands have played in styles imported from Austria, England, France, Germany, Hungary, Poland, Scotland, and the United States. In genres such as the waltz, dancers added complicated mimetic figures to the steps and solo dancing, such as male footwork in central Switzerland and competitive heelwork in Appenzell. In the 1700s and 1800s, Northern and Central European dances were integrated into traditional dancing and were performed in cycles of dances.

The String Band

In the German-speaking canton of Appenzell and in the Toggenburg Valley, canton St. Gallen, a *striichmusig* 'bowed music' is a band consisting of a violin, a dulcimer, a bowed double bass, and a chromatic accordion or a piano. In the *original appenzeller striichmusig* 'original Appenzell string band' are two violins, a cello, a dulcimer, and a bowed double bass. This type of ensemble can be traced back to the early nineteenth century. About 40 percent of the stringband repertoire consists of waltzes and all other musical styles played by the *ländlermusig*. A specialty of this ensemble is the instrumental *zäuerli*, the polyphonic natural yodel, transposed for stringed instruments.

Yodeling

Yodeling can be heard in the Swiss-German language area from the north slope of the Alps into Appenzell and central Switzerland. The *jodel* is a vocal technique in which the singer alternates rapidly between chest voice and head voice.

In Muotatal, natural yodeling (*jüüz, jüüzli*) features a tense voice, falling glissandos, and zigzagging melodies. The intonational margin is wide and

dynamic accentuation is strong. Polyphonic performances include a bass (alternately sounding tonic and dominant), a second voice, and a soloist, who improvises in a higher register. Sometimes the second voice sings above the leader—a technique called *überjüüza*.

In Appenzell, natural yodeling (*zäuerle*, Appenzell Ausserrhoden; *ruggusserle*, Appenzell Innerrhoden) involves a lower vocal range, relaxed vocal quality, slow tempo, free rhythm, slides between notes, and a gradually rising intonation. On the tonic and the dominant, the soloist (*vorzäurer*) is accompanied by drones, which may be sounded above or below the soloist's pitch. These natural yodels are structured in two or three parts, each of which is repeated (in form, AABB or AABBCC).

Yodeling in Appenzell (as distinct from natural yodeling) has been famous since the 1600s and involves a tense vocal style, fairly rapid yodeling with a pulsating quality, and soloists accompanied by drones sung in triads or larger chords. Many ornaments are used, such as grace notes and trills. Accelerating yodels are called *schnelzer*. Yodeling competitions, which include telling jokes and demonstrating intricate footwork, are held in Appenzell.

Many distinctive local styles have been replaced by standardized repertoires and practices since the first "festival of singers," in 1825. The main agents of change were choral societies, yodeling clubs, and ecclesiastical choirs, which trained singers and provided a new repertoire of written music. Song structures were narrowed to strophic forms, Swiss-German dialect was sometimes replaced by standard German texts, and vocal style became standardized. Intonation conformed to tempered tuning, minor keys and modes were mostly replaced by major keys, descending melodic patterns fell into disuse, functional harmony and modulations were introduced, and yodels were incorporated as choruses into verse songs (*jodellied*).

The Romansh-speaking Area

Religious songs formed a large part of the folk repertoire in the Romansh-speaking area. Their texts, inspired by indigenous Romansh and German sources, were sung in German, Italian, Latin, and Romansh. Early themes included homesickness, the sadness of leaving, or archaic legends, as in "*Canzun da Sontga Margriata.*" Songs were used not only in church, but also in daily activities and events of calendrical cycles and individual lives.

For religious songs, a strong, high, metallic vocal quality was preferred, especially outdoors. Extremely high pitches were chosen for special occasions. This vocal timbre has been described as similar to the sound of an Eastern European vocal ensemble. Formerly, young adults were trained for vocal performance in singing societies (*cantaduras* or *cantadurs*) that performed in large groups, usually in two-to-four-part a cappella—a practice alive today, during pilgrimages, processions, and wakes.

Introduction of the organ and its repertoire into churches during the 1800s forced *cantaduras* out of churches and severely cut the Romansh folksong repertoire, though some of the songs are still known.

The French-speaking Area

Most popular songs in the French-speaking area can be traced to the French regions of Burgundy, Piedmont, Provence, and Languedoc and from Spanish Catalonia, from where they have been continuously imported by mercenary soldiers, merchants, and traveling musicians since the 1400s. Local individuals reworked this repertoire to fit contemporary situations, creating distinctive regional traditions. The texts of many songs feature historical events or patriotic feelings, and many versions of the same song appear throughout French-speaking Switzerland.

Pastoral songs (*pastourelles*) survived without being influenced by the poetry that transformed the parallel French tradition. Similarly, many old dance-song forms survive. The *riondâ*, a dialect word for singing and dancing, designated dances such as the *coraula*, during which two choruses answered each other; the *voeyesi*, performed around fountains during field burnings (*les brandons*); and a communal dance (*la grande coquille de Gruyère*), which involved the whole population of the area of Gruyère. Songs to accompany such dances were usually performed in 6/8 or 2/4 time, and made extensive use of the minor mode. Newer songs for dancing mostly accompany ring dances (*ronde*) in 3/4 time, make extensive use of the major mode, and involve onomatopoeic imitations of musical instruments (*turlututu*, *rantamplan*, *roupioupiou*, and others).

In French-speaking Switzerland, vocal music differs from Swiss-German styles in many ways. Rhythms tend to be in 4/4 (rather than 3/4) and songs are usually performed in alternation by a soloist and a chorus, with melodies sung in unison.

The Italian-speaking Area

Switzerland's Italian-speaking regions consist of three valleys in canton Graubünden and the whole of canton Ticino. Culturally, these areas belong to the alpine arch (reaching from the French Alps to the Slavonic Alps), but have more in common with the adjoining regions of Italy (especially Lombardy and Piedmont) than with the rest of Switzerland.

In this area, the guitar and diatonic accordion (*fisarmonica a nümar* 'figure-accordion') have been the main accompanying instruments for folksinging, but the violin, the mandolin, the hurdy-gurdy (*viula di orbi* 'blind man's viola'), and the mechanical piano (*il verticale*) have also been popular. In the mid-1980s, a bagpipe (*piva*) similar to those found in northern Italy was revived. Ensembles include the *bandella* (clarinet and four brass instruments), with a repertoire of polkas, mazurkas, waltzes, and schottisches.

Far from representing remnants of archaic traditions, the culture of the small, remoter valleys in the Alps has been influenced by foreign cultural traits, adopted and integrated into local ones; polyvocal singing in thirds, disseminated chiefly by organized alpine choirs, is the dominant model throughout the alpine region. This holds true for Ticino only as regards songs written by local composers, often the directors of such choirs. In Ticino, the most famous composer of this genre, Vittorio Castelnuovo (1915–2005), has written more than a hundred songs, many of them in local dialect and with easygoing melodies of the sort noted by the Italian ethnomusicologist Roberto Leydi (1928–2003). They were written with the feeling of a native who loves his home, and this is the reason many of his songs have been labeled authentic Ticinese folk song.

Brass Ensembles

Brass ensembles are found in nearly every village or precinct throughout Switzerland, and are an integral part of public activity. They perform at ecclesiastical festivities, public elections, and parades on national holidays. Modern brass ensembles came into existence in the early 1800s, when the German instrument makers Stölzel und Blühmel invented the valve system, allowing diatonic and chromatic scales to be played more easily than before.

Two types of ensemble are common: those with a *harmoniebesetzung* incorporate woodwinds and are usually found in larger localities; those with a *blechbesetzung* are composed of brass instruments with the addition of saxophones and occasionally other woodwinds, in the *fanfares mixtes* of the French-speaking area of Switzerland. In the 1950s, the band Musikgesellschaft Speicher from Appenzell introduced the English brass-band formation (brass instruments only, without trumpets) as a popular innovation. This formation is well established in Switzerland.

In Italian-speaking Switzerland, the *bandella*, a reduced version of the brass band, exists in Ticino, where it uses one or two clarinets, a trumpet, a tenor, and a baritone flügelhorn, a key trombone, and a bass tuba. Unlike the brass band, the *bandella* plays exclusively for public dances.

Musical Instruments

In addition to the noisemakers and bells found in great variety, and the widespread military drum, Swiss traditional music employs a variety of string and wind instruments. Modern, international instruments, such as harmonicas, accordions, guitars, clarinets, saxophones, and trumpets, have gradually been introduced into the traditional dance-music repertoire and form its main contemporary instrumentation.

Stringed Instruments

The use of stringed instruments in Swiss traditional music was first documented in 1447, when the nightly playing of trapezoidal hammered dulcimers (*hackbretter*) provoked a riot in Zurich. Today, the tradition of constructing and playing the *hackbrett*, once a popular instrument in Switzerland, survives only in Appenzell and the Goms Valley, Upper Valais. In Appenzell, the *hackbrett* is played in Appenzell string music (two violins, cello, double bass, dulcimer).

In the second half of the nineteenth century, two types of board zither were locally introduced: the *schwyzer zither* and the *glarner zither*, both named after the canton where they remain in use. In earlier times, the zither was played for small dance events, with a violin and a double bass. Now it is an instrument played mainly by women for self-entertainment.

Long-necked citterns are still made and played in the Toggenburg Valley, St. Gallen, and in Kriens, canton Lucerne. The *toggenburger halszither* has a flat body, shaped like half a pear, and it is performed as an accompanimental instrument. The *krienser halszither* resembles a guitar, and it is played with other citterns or in ensembles with guitars, lutes, and mandolins.

Today, the violin, the acoustic double bass, and the guitar are the most widely used stringed instruments. Mandolins are played as solo instruments and in small ensembles and orchestras with guitars, primarily in southern Switzerland. Mandolin and guitar duos and trios are preferred for accompanying local folk songs in the Italian-speaking canton of Ticino.

Alphorn

The alphorn, a wooden trumpet, is the most famous Swiss wind instrument. Its distribution stretches from Appenzell to Valais, in rural and mountainous areas, with significant regional variations. Archaeo-logical evidence in the form of bark trumpets indicates that its origins reach back to the Neolithic period. Old-style contemporary horns in the Bündner Oberland, Graubünden, and other relatively remote areas are handmade from wood (occasionally from metal pipes) and are about 2.5 meters long.

In Muotatal, two types of alphorn are found: the *grada büchel*, a straight, hollowed-out fir-tree trunk wrapped in birch bark, with a curved bell, is from 4 to 10 meters long; and the *büchel*, a smaller horn, whose coiled shape, first mentioned in 1820 in Grindelwald, seems to have been inspired by the modern trumpet. The *büchel* can be played at faster tempos and higher pitches than the *grada büchel*.

Until about 1900, the alphorn was played as a solo instrument to pacify cattle and send signals. Today, it is much played by amateur musicians in alphorn duets, trios, quartets, and larger ensembles. In the early 1970s, the alphorn made its entry into concert halls with compositions by the Swiss composers Jean Daetwyler, Étienne Isoz, André Besancon, Albert Benz, and others; then it entered pop music, and more recently, it and the *büchel* have appeared in jazz.

—Adapted from an article by Johanna Hoffman and Silvia Delorenzi-Schenkel

Bibliography

Alder, Arnold. 1995. *Die Geige in der Appenzellemusik: Anleitung für den Gebrauch der Violine in der Appenzeller Streichmusik*. Zurich: Mülirad-Verlag.

Bachmann-Geiser, Brigitte. 1999. *Das Alphorn. Vom Lock- zum Rockinstrument*. Bern: Verlag Paul Haupt.

Bendix, Regina. 1985. *Progress and nostalgia: Silversterklausen in Urnäsch, Switzerland*. Berkeley: University of California Press.

Gesellschaft für die Volksmusik in der Schweiz GVS, ed. 1985. *Volksmusik in der Schweiz. Herkunft und Geschichte, Instrumentale Musik, Volkstanz, Jodel, Volkslied, Chor- und Blasmusik, Liedermacher, Volksmusik und Brauchtum*. Zürich: Ringier.

Hürlemann, Hans. 1984. *Brummbass, Geige, Hackbrett. 100 Jahre Appenzeller Streichmusik Alder*. St. Gallen: VGS Verlagsgemeinschaft St. Gallen.

Leuthold, Heinrich J. 1981. *Der Naturjodel in der Schweiz*. Altdorf: Robert Fellmann-Liederverlag.

Mooser, Ueli. 1988. *Die instrumentale Volksmusik: Grundlagen und Musizierpraxis der Ländlermusik: Formen—Modelle—Beispiele—Anregungen*. Edited by Gesellschaft für die Volksmusik in Der Schweiz. Bern: Musikverlag Müller & Schade.

Peter, Rico. 1978. *Ländlermusik: Die amüsante und spannende Geschichte der Schweizer Ländlermusik*. Aarau: AT Verlag.

Ringli, Dieter. 2006. *Schweizer Volksmusik. Von den Anfängen um 1800 bis zur Gegenwart*. Altdorf: Mülirad-Verlag.

Weiss, Richard. 1946. *Volkskunde der Schweiz*. Zurich: Eugen Rentsch.

Wiora, Walter. 1949. *Zur Frühgeschichte der Musik in den Alpenländern*. Basel: Krebs.

Poland

A large lowland region of thick forests and fertile soil, Poland is bounded in the south by the Carpathian Mountains and in the north by the Baltic Sea. 38.5 million people, of whom 97 percent are Poles, inhabit its 312,000 square kilometers. Ethnic minorities include Belorusans, Czechs, Germans, Lithuanians, Slovaks, Ukrainians, and small groups of Gypsies and Jews. Between Germany in the west and Ukraine, Lithuania, Belarus, and Russia in the east, Poland's territory has been a battlefield throughout history.

Five main Slavic tribes populated the area: Polans (the most important), Vistulans, Silesians, Mazovians, and Pomeranians. They were converted to Latin Christianity at the end of the tenth century with the help of Czech missionaries. The absence of centralized authority from 1138 to 1314 contributed to the regional diversity of modern Poland. From the 1400s to the 1600s, the Polish kingdom, in union with Lithuania, was a great power, extending far eastward from Poland's present border. In the late 1700s, the country was partitioned among the Great Powers (Austria, Prussia, and Russia), and its sovereignty was not restored until the end of World War I. The German invasion of 1939 interrupted this period of independence and led to unprecedented material and human losses. Nearly fifty years of communist rule followed, ending in 1989 with the electoral victory of the labor movement, Solidarity. In the 1990s, Poland espoused a liberal, market-oriented economy, and in 2004, joined the European Union. Its economy is based on industry and small farming.

Singing Styles and Vocal Genres

Poland has major cultural and musical regions, three of which preserve the names of the Slavic tribes who settled there: Pomorze (Pomerania) in the north, Mazowsze (Mazovia) in the center and northeast, Małopolska (Little Poland) with the Carpathian area in the south and southeast, Wielkopolska (Great Poland) in the west, and Silesia in the southwest. Natural conditions in each region favor certain kinds of economy with implications for musical culture: hunting and fishing in the north, agriculture in the center, and sheep-farming in the southern mountains. During the nineteenth-century partition of Poland, cultural differences among Austria, Prussia, and Russia divided Poland into a more progressive west and a more traditional east.

Genres and Contexts

Traditional musical practice is organized in two cycles: an annual cycle (New Year's caroling, Lent, Easter caroling, midsummer, harvesting, and Advent) and a lifecycle (birth, childhood, wedding, marital life, death). The most important musical event, the wedding, has preserved the oldest strata of vocal repertoire.

Among the oldest vocal forms are women's calls (*wiskanie*) in the southern mountain area. These calls have a free rhythmic structure and descending melody, in which only the first and last note have definite pitch. Ancient spring songs dedicated to the end of winter and the coming of summer, once prohibited by the Roman Catholic Church and preserved mostly in western and southern Poland, are limited today to the children's repertoire and consist of short recited formulae of three or four notes on repeated rhythmic patterns. Old ritual songs from eastern regions, especially wedding songs and laments, are often free recitations. Funeral laments, which vanished long ago, have been replaced by a religious repertoire sung by professional performers. This repertoire plays a special role in Pomerania, especially in the Cassubia subregion, where group singing in the house of the dead during so-called empty nights (*puste noce*) is customary.

Folk-song Structures

Polish folk songs may be differentiated into short forms (dance songs) and long forms (narrative songs). The structure of vocal forms mostly depends on their function. In scales, rhythms, and content, ritual songs of the annual and lifecycles have preserved the oldest musical features, including remnants of pentatonic and narrow-range scales. Most Polish folk songs, however, are based on modal scales.

Most Polish folk songs have a strophic structure, with melodies consisting of two four-bar phrases. The most popular type is the *przyśpiewka* 'ditty', with a two-line text, often improvised, that refers to the performance context or contains playfully malicious remarks about other participants.

As a rule, Polish folk songs are syllabic, with occasional glissandi or melismas. Melismatic singing is typical of eastern regions and Kurpie. In northern areas (Kurpie, Mazuria, and Podlasie), an archaic performance manner, *apocope* 'whispering or omitting the last syllable of a song', was practiced. *Tempo rubato* is typical, especially of the central and southern part of Poland, where it combines with *mazurka* rhythms to create an oscillation between duple and triple time. In most regions, folk songs are performed monophonically, though heterophonic singing may have been practiced in the past. Only in the Carpathian area is polyphonic singing found. There, one singer initiates a song, and after a few notes others join in; some take the main melody while the rest add a voice below (figure 1).

Performance Style

Generally, singers sing in high registers, especially in Podhale in the Tatra Mountains, where men use strained voices on the fringe of screaming, while women sing quietly in low-pitched registers. In Kieleckie (in Little Poland), men and women sing in high tessituras. In the north, west, and east, registers are lower. The use of high, loud voices in Great Poland is sometimes explained as analogous to the sound of Polish bagpipes. In Mazovia, vocal timbres are more delicate.

In Kieleckie, songs often end with high-pitched shouts, and in Podhale, with women's calls. Vocal performances, especially those of Little Poland and the Carpathian area, are accompanied by spontaneous behavior like vivid gesturing, stomping, and shouting.

Musical Instruments and Instrumental Music

The oldest instruments found in the Polish area are drums, originating in the Neolithic period. In contemporary folk music, drums play an important role as rhythmic drones. The friction drum (*burczybas*),

for example, was used in carnival masquerades in Pomerania. The frame drum with jingles (*grajcary*, *cykace*) is typical of ensembles in central and eastern regions, where it is played with a certain virtuosity. In the 1920s and 1930s, it was replaced in some areas by a large two-headed drum (*baraban*), sometimes with an added cymbal or triangle.

The simplest wind instruments have signaling functions and vary in length from short clarinets (*bekace*) to long wooden trumpets and horns, known in Mazovia as *ligawka*, in Pomerania as *bazuna*, and in Silesia as *trembita*. In the Carpathian area, numerous flutes are used: end-blown, ductless shepherd's flutes without holes; duct flutes with six to seven holes; and a duct flute with a double pipe. Reed pipes are represented by the bagpipe, the only wind instrument traditionally used in folk ensembles.

Ensemble playing in Poland has been dominated by bowed stringed instruments. Traditionally, the most important melodic instrument was a fiddle (today a violin), popular all over the country (figure 2). A musical band could be created by a fiddle with only one accompanying rhythmic (drum), drone (bagpipe), or rhythmic-drone (bass) instrument. The importance of the fiddle is mirrored in folktales, many of which relate a common belief in the supernatural power of this instrument and of its player.

In newer types of ensembles with loud melodic instruments like accordion or saxophone, fiddlers use high violin registers to obtain more audibility. They play without vibrato and make extensive use of open strings. They prefer nonlegato bowing techniques and reserve pizzicato for special effects only, as in certain game-dances, in which switching from bowing to pizzicato indicates a change of partners.

Bass stringed instruments, used exclusively as accompaniment, exist in many regional versions varying from small local forms (like the two-stringed bass of the Kalisz area in the west) to standard double bass. Struck stringed instruments include the dulcimer (*cymbały*) known at least from the 1600s and today existing in two local versions: a large one

Figure 1 Carpathian polyphonic singing on a tune type called *nuta wierchowa*. After Sadownik 1971:275.

Figure 2 Piotr Gaca plays violin and Józef Iskrzyński plays frame drum, Rdzów, 2002. This is a typical small ensemble of central Poland.
Photo by Jacek Jackowski.

Figure 3 Bronisław Usinowicz plays the *cymbały*, Zgorzelec, 2002. Though Zgorzelec is near the German border in western Poland, this *cymbały* is the East-North kind. Usinowicz, originally from eastern Poland, settled in the west after World War II. His playing style is representative of the East-North.
Photo by Jacek Jackowski.

in the East-South (the area of Rzeszów), used mostly to play in ensembles as an accompanying instrument; and a smaller one in the East-North on the Lithuanian border, used as a solo melodic instrument (figure 3).

In some regions, bagpipes of various types play an important role as an ensemble instrument. Bagpipes from Great Poland and Silesia are equipped with a bellows; and in the Carpathian area (Podhale and Żywiec), with a blowpipe. All Polish bagpipes have single reeds and one drone pipe, though until the late 1800s, forms with many drones were documented. In Żywiec, an ensemble of bagpipe and violin is popular, but in Podhale, the bagpipe is a solo instrument.

Since the 1930s, other instruments have been adapted to folk-band use. These include the clarinet, the trumpet, and, above all, various accordions (figure 4), from the simplest concertinas to the piano accordion and an accordion with an air pump attached to the instrument by a long, thin tube. The bass, originally small and two- or three-stringed and used mostly as a rhythmic drone with no harmonic function, eventually became larger and four-stringed, and was used for playing harmonies. Nowadays, especially in large bands, the traditional homemade bass is often replaced by a double bass, which the player bows or plucks.

In Podhale, string ensembles are typical. They consist of one *prymista* (a melody-playing fiddler), two or more *sekund* (a fiddle that plays harmonic and rhythmic accompaniment), and a bass. Ensemble playing in Podhale is uniquely oriented toward chordal harmony (ornamented melody played against chords). The typical instrumental repertoire of the region consists of cycles of tunes starting with a moderate tempo but increasing in speed. A central

Figure 4 Marian Sikora plays the three-row folk accordion (*harmonia trzyrzędowa*), Rawa Mazowiecka, 2003.
Photo by Jacek Jackowski.

musical notion of Podhale is the tune (*nuta* 'note'), a concept of a certain harmonic structure identified by its name and often referring to the name of the musician who invented it.

Instrumental Music

As a rule, Polish folk-instrumental music is dance music. The only exceptions are signals played on wooden trumpets and horns and shepherds' tunes. Most instrumental dance tunes derive from vocal melodies, though the words are often forgotten. Instrumental versions differ from vocal ones in musical form (often phrases or single bars are repeated many times) and rich ornamentation, which consists of formulas typical of a given instrument. Typical traditional dance tunes of vocal origin are built of two phrases, each four bars long. The first phrase is repeated twice and the second as many times as desired. The melody is opened and closed by a special fiddle formula, the function of which is to inform other members of the ensemble and dancers of the type and tempo of the dance.

Triple-meter dances, namely mazurkas and other similar dances, are widespread and are considered particularly "Polish," because their rhythms echo the stress pattern of the Polish language. Polish words formerly had an initial accent, but today they have the accent on the penultimate syllable. This linguistic history contributes to the constitution of mazurka rhythms, which typically have measures of two sixteenth notes followed by two eighth notes. Such rhythms are typical of the family of dances known and dominant in Polish folk music from the Renaissance and Baroque period and consist of dances performed in different tempos: *oberek* (the fastest), *mazurek* (mazurka) *kujawiak, chodzony* (a walking dance) and, finally, the slowest one, *polonez* (polonaise).

Like the mazurka-type dances, the most popular duple-meter dance, the *krakowiak*, has entered the canon of Polish national dances. Regional dance tunes, *wiwat* (in duple or triple time), are popular in Great Poland, and the Carpathian area has preserved distinct local dances, including a couple dance (*góralski* 'highlanders' dance') and a men's dance (*zbójnicki* 'robbers' dance').

Social Processes of Making Music

As early as the 1700s, and especially during the 1800s, traditional music played an important role in the growth of a national consciousness and identity. An example of this process was the conscious stylization of folk dances, in which the mazurka, the polonaise, and the *krakowiak* were incorporated into a canon of so-called national dances. Even if these developments did not benefit Polish peasants directly, they resulted in the first serious attempts by intellectuals to document and preserve peasant music in written form. In the 1920s and 1930s, folk culture underwent a major transformation. New educational programs devoted to folk music were institutionalized. Many folk musicians attended schools, had contact with urban musicians, learned music notation, and were able to buy factory-made instruments.

Under communism after 1945, developments to some extent followed Soviet patterns. A large-scale documentation of folk traditions was undertaken, and folkloristic ensembles of professionals performing "embellished" folk music were promoted. Folk music was heard on radio and seen in concerts accompanying state ceremonies. The state's attempt to make folk music serve as an official musical emblem largely backfired, however. Many people rejected folk music, either as a symbol of difficult living conditions and poverty or as a tool of official policy.

In the post-communist 1990s, as in many Western European countries decades earlier, a trend developed to merge folk elements into popular music. Such experiments helped young people find an identity in an age of transnational music and provided a source of inspiration for new music. They have also changed the general attitude toward pure tradition, which is now more respected than when it was promoted by the state.

—*Adapted from an article by Ewa Dahlig*

Bibliography

Chybiński, Adolf. 1961. *O polskiej muzyce ludowej.* (On Polish folk music). Ludwik Bielawski ed. Cracow: Polskie Wydawnictwo Muzyczne.

Cooley, Timothy J. 2005. *Making Music In The Polish Tatras: Tourists, Ethnographers, and Mountain Musicians.* Bloomington and Indianapolis: Indiana University Press.

Czekanowska, Anna. 1990. *Polish Folk Music: Slavonic Heritage—Polish Tradition—Contemporary Trends.* Cambridge: Cambridge University Press.

Dahlig, Ewa. 1990. "Music and dance activities in Polish folk tradition: The problem of syncretism." *Dance Studies* 14. Jersey, 37–46.

——. 1991. *Ludowa gra skrzypcowa w Kieleckiem* (Fiddling in the Kielce region). Cracow: Polskie Wydawnictwo Muzyczne.

——. 1992. "Folk musical ensembles in central Poland and their music" *Studia Instrumentorum Musicae Popularis* 10, 56–60.

——. 1998. "Folk Music Revival in Poland and Northumberland." *East European Meetings in Ethnomusicology* 5. Bucharest, 45–50.

Dahlig, Piotr. 1993. *Ludowa praktyka muzyczna.* (Folk-musical practice). Warsaw: Wydawnictwo ISPAN.

Kamiński, Włodzimierz. 1971. *Instrumenty muzyczne na ziemiach polskich.* (Musical instruments in Poland). Cracow: Polskie Wydawnictwo Muzyczne.

Kolberg, Oskar. [1961] 1979. *Dzieła wszystkie* (Collected works). Vols. 1–57. Wrocław Poznań, Warsaw, and Cracow: Polskie Wydawnictwo Muzyczne.

Przerembski, Zbigniew. 1994. *Style i formy melodyczne polskich pieśni ludowych* (Style and form of Polish folksong). Warsaw: Wydawnictwo ISPAN.

Ryback, Timothy. 1990. *Rock Around the Bloc: A History of Rock Music in Eastern Europe and the Soviet Union.* New York: Oxford University Press.

Sadownik, Jan, ed. 1971. *Pieśni Podhala* (Folk Songs from Podhale). Cracow: Polskie Wydawnictwo Muzyczne.

Czech Republic and Slovakia

From C.E. 450 to 550, the Czechs settled in the Central European region of Bohemia (Čechy), with its gently rolling fields interspersed with forests, lakes, and rivers. Bohemia, ruled by the Premysl family for about four hundred years (895–1306), later became a semi-independent kingdom within the Holy Roman Empire. It reached its cultural and political peak under Charles IV, the Holy Roman Emperor, who ruled from 1346 to 1378, the period when Prague became the empire's leading city.

By the fifth century, the Slavic tribes who were to become the Slovak nation were well established between the Carpathian Mountains and the Danube River, with the Czechs and Moravians to the west, the Poles to the north, the Ruthenians to the east, and the Magyars (Hungarians) to the south.

Moravia, where certain Slavic tribes settled during the fifth century, lies between Bohemia and Slovakia. In the ninth century, these tribes united with other Slavic tribes to form the Great Moravian Empire, which Magyar invasions subsequently destroyed. In 1029, the Bohemian Kingdom formally incorporated Moravia as a separate territory, customarily ruled by a younger son of the Bohemian king.

Bohemia and Moravia became provinces of the Hapsburg Empire in 1526, when Ferdinand I, Holy Roman Emperor, was elected king of Bohemia. The throne of Bohemia became a hereditary possession of the Hapsburg archduchy of Austria, which from 1804 until 1914 was known as the Austro-Hungarian Empire. In October 1918, the first Czechoslovak Republic was formed as a result of the reorganization of the former Austro-Hungarian Empire. Industrialization and urbanization, already apparent in the nineteenth century, increased during the 1920s and 1930s. German expansion forced a temporary dissolution of the republic (1939–1945), and Bohemia and Moravia were formed into a protectorate of the German Reich. From 1945, Czechs, Moravians, Slovaks, and various minorities (more than fourteen million people altogether) lived in Czechoslovakia, a state renamed the Czech and Slovak Federal Republic in 1989. On 1 January 1993, the federation dissolved into independent Czech and Slovak republics. Both countries joined the European Union in 2004. In 2006, the Czech Republic (78,703 square kilometers) had an estimated population of 10.2 million people; Slovakia (48,845 square kilometers), an estimated population of 5.4 million.

Traditional Music

The Czech Republic and Slovakia have rich folk-music traditions, documented in more than a hundred thousand archived folk songs. The extent to which folk music remains a living tradition throughout both republics, however, is the subject of scholarly debate. In Bohemia, urbanization and industrialization have been blamed for the demise of the living tradition, with the daily performance of music and dance retained primarily in Chodsko, a small ethnographic district in the southwest. In general, the farther east through Moravia and Slovakia, the stronger is the living tradition; yet some occasions, including weddings, holidays, and festivals, require folk music and dance throughout Bohemia.

Historical, cultural, and geographic factors have resulted in substantial regional differences. Carpathian and alpine mountain ranges and valleys served to isolate certain peoples, resulting in the development of numerous musical dialects and the perpetuation of local traditions. Influences from surrounding peoples have also had their effects; for example, yodeling is found in Bohemia near the border with Bavaria, while strummed zither bands occur in southern Slovakia near the Hungarian border.

Commonalities

Despite regional differences, the folk music and dance of the Czech and Slovak republics share some common traits. Perhaps foremost is the relationship between music and dance. In several regions, as much as 80 percent of the music is intended to accompany dance. Some dance forms, including the "line dances" (*chorovod*) usually performed by young women, turning dances for couples (who rotate in place), and couple's round dances, occur throughout both republics. Everywhere each stanza of a song commonly alternates with dancing. In both republics, dances are punctuated with whistles, squeals, shouts, foot stamps, and slapping of the thighs and heels.

A second commonality is the relationship between language and music. Though Czech (spoken in Moravia also) and Slovak are different languages, both share two elements that bear on music: stress always falls on the first syllable of a word, and vowels are long or short in duration. Because of first-syllable

573

stress, pickup notes rarely occur, and phrases sometimes end on an unstressed beat or an offbeat to match an unstressed final syllable. Each line of a strophic song may display a unique rhythm, as long and short vowels fall on different beats. Vowel lengths and stresses distinguish Czech and Slovak music from that of neighboring peoples.

A third commonality is that in all three regions, some portion of the repertoire involves mixed meters, which, though they do not make up a large share of the Czech repertoire, are associated with some prominent dances. Duple and triple meter may alternate or occur simultaneously in several combinations; for example, a complete waltz section may alternate with a complete polka section. In the dance *zelenyj kúsek*, triple and duple alternate in one-, two-, or four-measure sequences (figure 1). The *furiant* has a basic triple meter throughout (written 3/4 or 6/8), but melodic accents result in alternating duple and triple two-measure patterns. The *furiant* dance figure includes two measures of duple hops followed by two measures of waltz steps. In eastern Moravia and Slovakia, songs not unusually have a duple rhythm in the accompaniment while the melody is written mainly in triplets, resulting in two against three.

Fourth, phrases may vary in length, more in some regions than in others. Though most Czech songs have balanced phrases, eight-bar phrases may be divided into 3 + 5 bars, or a combination of 4 + 4 + 6 bars or 6 + 6 + 7 + 7 bars may occur. Phrase length

often is closely related to the syllabic structure of the text.

Fifth, text is an important aspect of songs and covers a wide range of subjects, particularly those related to lifecycle and calendar-cycle events, work, the military, nature, and love. Most dance-tunes have texts. Even a solitary shepherd alternates between singing and playing tunes on the flute or bagpipes. Text setting is largely syllabic, with melismas used primarily for embellishment. Vocables are rare and tend to occur in refrains—*tra, la, la*, for example.

Sixth, traditional instrumental ensembles in both republics tend not to be large. Czech ensembles began when a violin and a clarinet joined a bagpipe (*dudy, gajdy*) in an ensemble known as *malá selcká muzika* 'small rustic band'. Later, an additional violin and clarinet and a string bass and a second bagpiper joined the ensemble to form the *velké muzika* 'large band'. In eastern Moravia and Slovakia, two types of small ensembles became prominent: the *sláciková muzika* (string band) of two to four stringed instruments and the *cimbalová muzika* (dulcimer band), generally consisting of two violins, one or two violas, one or two clarinets, string bass, and large hammered dulcimer (*cimbál*).

Seventh, vocal and instrumental musical styles bear a close relationship. Musicians comment on the similarity between vocal and instrumental timbres. Where the bagpipe is prominent, singers tend to imitate the bagpipe sound in their vocal timbre. Also,

Figure 1 "Zelenyj kúsek," a texted Czech dance from Chodsko, alternates sections in triple (3/8) and duple (2/4) meter. Two people sing the text in parallel thirds while two others sing the vocable *hó* on a drone at the interval of a fifth, imitating the bagpipe.

vocal range can be affected by instrumental pitch. String ensembles of eastern Moravia and northern Slovakia, for example, play in the key of D, forcing vocalists to sing in a high register. Czech bagpipes in E-flat do the same. Some singers even try to sing an octave above the bagpipe register, to be heard over its penetrating sound. Singers are praised for their ability to match instrumental styles, particularly in regard to the use of ornamentation, whether the grace notes and other embellishments of Czech bagpipers or the portamento and cadential formulas of eastern ensembles.

Eighth, improvisation is a common feature of folk music. Czech bagpipers are expected to develop their own variations on tunes and to change those variations with each performance. Variation techniques include the use of neighboring tones, passing and harmonic tones, grace notes, anticipations, turns, mordents and inverted mordents, trills, and rapid repetitions of a single tone. In protracted Moravian songs, elaborately embellished transitions occur from one phrase to the next on the parts of the first violinist, the clarinetist, and the *cimbál* player. Moravian dance-songs employ rhythmic variations. The same instruments in Slovak ensembles intricately ornament the melodies.

Ninth, polyphonic singing occurs to varying degrees throughout both republics, though it is more common in Moravia and Slovakia than in Bohemia. Polyphonic Moravian singing is primarily in parallel thirds and sixths, usually in two parts, but sometimes in three. Slovak singers tend to start with a solo voice intoning the first phrase, or the group beginning on a unison pitch, proceeding in parallel thirds, and ending in unison. In Bohemia, singing in parallel thirds and sixths has been popular in Chodsko. The lines of a duet may so intertwine that it is difficult to tell which has the melody.

Lastly, many of the same musical genres are found throughout both republics, with some more prominent in certain districts than others. In some districts, a given genre may still be performed as part of daily life, but in others it may occur only in staged festivals. Seasonal activities begin with songs and dances for celebrating the death of winter, children's spring game-songs in meadows, carnival, and Easter songs, and continue with songs for summer farm work, pasturing, herding, cutting timber, St. John's day, fall harvest activities, winter spinning and plucking down, and Christmas caroling. Wedding songs accompanying all ritual stages, from women's instructions to the bride, her farewell to her mother, the "capping" ceremony during wedding service (when she joins the ranks of married women), to the transportation of the bed to the new residence.

Lullabies, children's songs, and songs about love and nature are common in all districts.

Differences

Despite the shared characteristics of Czech and Slovak music, there are also many regional differences, between and within the two republics. On the broadest level is the distinction between western and eastern styles. Moravia, between Bohemia and Slovakia, is the transitional region. The dividing line between styles is roughly the Morava River, which flows through the center of Moravia. In music and dance, Bohemia and western Moravia are oriented toward the Western European style, whose music tends to be based on instrumental forms (waltz, polka); song texts consist primarily of metered poetry with regular, balanced phrases; the harmonic-melodic system is rooted in the major-minor structure, with the major mode most prominent; and, historically, triple meter predominated, though it no longer does. Melodies tended to originate with the bagpipe, with several different sets of lyrics for any given tune. The prominence of the bagpipe style resulted in legato melodies of stepwise motion, broken chordal passages, or a combination of the two. Though there are many lyrical songs, such as love songs, much of the music is based on dance forms, such as the triple-meter *sousedská* (a couple's round dance), the duple-meter *obkrocák* (a couple's turning dance), and the mixed-meter *zelenyj kúsek*.

In eastern Moravia and Slovakia, music tends to be based on vocal forms, in which stress falls on the most prominent words in the melody, rather than on the first beat of each measure. In nondance music, a parlando-rubato style with considerable rhythmic freedom is popular; the term *táhle*, meaning 'protracted' or 'drawn-out', is used by collectors to define this style. Uneven phrase lengths are common (5 + 5 + 4 + 5 measures, for example), as are the minor mode and duple meter. Dance forms have resulted in distinctive rhythmic practices, as with the uneven, offbeat-accented Moravian *sedlácká*, which increases from a slow to a rapid tempo, often in medleys of four tunes; women's circle dances of eastern Slovakia (e.g. *karicka*) with complex heel-stamping patterns; and variations of the *czardas* (*čardáš*), in which couples may compete with increasingly rapid, improvised steps.

Among the distinctive features of east Moravian music is melodic and harmonic coloration. Fluctuating tones (temporarily raised or lowered scalar tones) are used, giving rise to hybrid scales. Chord progressions are derived from modes, sometimes resulting in temporary shifts of the tonal center, with neutral chords (a chord that has one function in the temporary key and a different function in the primary key), secondary dominants, and dominants used to return to the original. Whether these shifts should be defined as modulations is the subject of scholarly debate, though the shift to the lowered seventh is so common as to be called the Moravian modulation by folk-music collectors and theorists.

Modern Processes of Folk-music Revival and Preservation

From the nineteenth century on, musicians, intellectuals, and others have taken special measures to preserve Czech and Slovak traditions. Two of these ways are described here.

Education

In some locations, folk musicians still learn their performance techniques and repertoires traditionally (figure 2). In mountain areas, children learn the game songs of pasturing and other seasonal activities by participating in them. Bagpipers learn their art as apprentices to a master piper; they listen to other pipers and develop their own variation techniques.

Folk songs have long been in the elementary-school curriculum. Students who show talent in music and dance at an early age attend a public school of the arts, where folk music and dance are supplementarily covered. At the secondary level, students may attend a conservatory of music and dance, where they follow a five- to six-year curriculum of study on one or more folk instruments or dance, and they perform in ensembles. In higher education, they study at an academy of music and dramatic art, or they pursue such fields as ethnography and folklore at a university. Graduates of conservatories and academies usually perform in a professional state or radio ensemble.

In the mid-twentieth century and later, numerous musicians left their villages to study at conservatories in the classical field, then returned home to learn to play folk music "in the tradition." They not only learned the local repertoire but went to archives to draw additional materials from collections. Often their knowledge of performance styles allowed them to incorporate these pieces with appropriate inflections, but sometimes their recordings showed they were playing the notation exactly as written and did not reflect the traditional style. This result seems to occur particularly where a break in the tradition had lasted for several years.

Festivals

Festivals have been a major factor in the preservation and revival of folk music and dance traditions. They grew out of the lifecycle and calendar-cycle festivities of feudal times. On completing the fall harvest, peasants expected landowners to reward them with food, drink, and money, which they celebrated during harvest feasts with songs, dances, and rituals. Other festive occasions included religious observances, the death of winter, the awakening of spring, carnival, and weddings.

Figure 2 To the accompaniment of recorders and a keyboard instrument, members of the children's folklore ensemble Vysočánek dance. The ensemble, founded in 1965 at the grammar school in the town of Hlinsko, welcomes children from ages four to fifteen. It has become well-known in the Czech Republic and beyond for maintaining the songs, dances, and customs of its region. *Photograph by Adrienne L. Kaeppler, 1996.*

With industrialization and the decline of such traditional activities, the concept of special public performances of folk music and dances began to take hold in the late nineteenth century and spread during the 1920s and 1930s. A major impetus, the Ethnographic Czech-Slovak Exhibition in Prague in 1895, led to the formation of local exhibits, museums, and performances. Especially after World War II, annual festivals were established in numerous locations, of which some of the most important were Strakonice in Bohemia, Strážnice in Moravia, and Vychodná in Slovakia. In addition to the major festivals, annual regional, district, and local festivals now feature traditional folklore.

The Strážnice Festival
The growth of the festivals, and issues that arose around them, may be illustrated by the example of the Strážnice festival. It began in 1946 as Czechoslovakia in Dance and Song, a celebration of liberation after World War II. It was sponsored by the Institute of Folk Arts in the town of Strážnice and authorized by the Czecho-Slovak government as the first all-state ethnographic festival. Performers from eight districts participated in competitions of fiddlers, singers, dancers, and ensembles. They were judged on technical merit and stylistic purity. Before long, changes and issues emerged. Though organizers of the festival aimed to contribute to the survival of ethnographic traditions, the Regional National Committee tried to influence the foundation of new ensembles in villages and the formation of youth ensembles in cities and on collective farms. In 1949, the university ensemble Lúčnica, from Bratislava, introduced new technical standards that led to new criteria for evaluating ensembles at these festivals.

By 1964, programs were divided into three categories: authentic folklore, featuring seasonal traditions and family customs; stylized programs with unified themes, such as "From My Homeland"; and foreign ensembles. Groups participated by invitation, and local programs began to be featured.

Since the 1970s, the festival has continued to focus on authentic folklore and public entertainment. From the outset of the festival, the programs have been recorded. Recordings have been issued from Strážnice and other festivals.

Jazz and Popular and Underground Music

After 1948, jazz was considered a bourgeois product and strongly discouraged. In the 1970s, jazz musicians, working without official approval, staged performances, published jazz bulletins, and supported multigenre underground music. The publication of the important journal *Rock 2000* (now known as *Art Forum*) began, and the music scene witnessed a synthesis of jazz and rock.

Because the government opposed jazz, dance music, which had been based on jazz music since the 1920s, was profoundly affected. In response, folk music was substituted in a popular format (*lidovky*), introduced primarily by the Polatov Wind Band; however, only the older generation accepted this change. Reacting to public pressure, swing was restored during the early 1950s. A pioneering performing group was the dance orchestra of Karel Vlach, who, with Gustav Brom and his band, worked for Czechoslovak Radio.

In popular entertainment, perhaps the most important performer was Jiří Suchy, who sang for the theatrical company Divadlo na zabradli, and with entertainer Jiří Slitr started the famous Semafor Theater. Performances at the Semafor were known for criticizing the communist regime. Musicians often escaped censorship and consequently developed unofficial, nontraditional, avant-garde, underground music.

The late sixties ushered in a new symbiosis between popular folk singers (*písničkáři*) and rock musicians, resulting in *folkníci*, who dominated the musical scene of the 1970s and 1980s. In Prague, *folkníci* included Vladimír Merta, Petr Lutka, Dagmar Andrtová-Voňková, and Jaroslav Hutka. In the 1970s, the center of folk activities was a Prague organization, *Malostranska beseda*, under whose auspices jam sessions, performances, seminars, and publishing centers were organized. Supraphon, a national record company, released singles and long-playing records by many of these musicians, who fought the political system. Many were constantly at odds with the law—for which they were periodically prohibited from working. Their compositions were not published, and they were often interrogated by the police.

The only musicians to be imprisoned were members of the rock band Plastic People of the Universe. Established in 1969 and soon the most influential pop-music phenomenon of its time in Czechoslovakia, the band provided ideological leadership for the younger generation.

Between 1968 and 1989 musicians labored under systematic restrictions. Their attitudes ranged from refusing to collaborate to using the system for personal gain. The most important figure in Czech alternative rock of the 1970s and 1980s was Mikoláš Chadima, a performer-composer-ideologue, who postulated that rock is not only entertainment, but a unique multimedia art which reflects individuals' feelings. A member of Rock and Jokes Extempore

Band, led by folksinger Jaroslav Jeroným Neduha, Chadima composed music that incorporated elements of rock, jazz improvisation, and the experimental avant-garde—genres linked to political criticism. In 1979, this band's performances featured black humor and violence, in which musicians used jazz or rock structures with new-wave and punk elements.

In Slovakia during the 1960s, neofolkloristic tendencies strengthened, as artists took their inspiration from jazz, popular, and non-European musics. One of the most active musicians in Slovak rock was Ján Baláž from Nitra, who cofounded the band Modus, which performed at home and abroad with a repertoire based on Western contemporary hits. The period of the mid-1970s to the mid-1980s represents the height of Slovak popular music. Leading the way were vocalists and composers Peter Nagy from Prešov, Marika Gombitová from Turany nad Ondavou, and Miroslav Zbírka from Bratislava.

—Adapted from an article by Magda Ferl Želinská and Edward J. P. O'Connor

Bibliography

Bartoš, František. 1901. *Národní pisně moravské* (Moravian folk songs). Revised ed. Brno.

Černy, Jaromir, Jan Kouba, Vladimír Lebl, Jitka Ludvová, Zdenka Pilková, Jiří Sehnal, and Petr Vit. 1983. *Hudba v česk'ych dějinach* (Music in Czech history). Prague: Supraphon.

Elschek, Oskár, ed. 1985. *Slovenská l'udová nástrojová hudba a l'udové piesne* (Slovak folk-instrumental music and folk songs). Musicologica Slovaca, 10. Bratislava: Veda, vydavatel'stvo Slovenskej académie vied.

——, ed. 1989. *L'udové hudobné a tanečné zvykoslovie* (Folk music and folk dance customs). Musicologica Slovaca, 15. Bratislava: Veda, vydavatel'stvo Slovenskej académie vied.

——, ed. 1996. *Dejiny slovenskej hudby najstarších čia po súčasnost'* (History of Slovak music from its beginning to the present). English summaries to chapter 8 ("Slovak Folk Musical Culture," "Slovak Folk Song," by Alica Elscheková) and chapter 9 ("Folk Music Instruments and Instrumental Music," by Oskár Elschek). Bratislava: Ústav hudobnej vedy SAVASCO.

Elscheková, Alica, and Oskár Elschek. 1980, 1982. *Slovenské l'udové piesne a nástrojová hudba—Antológia* (Slovak folk songs and instrumental music—an anthology). 2 vols. Bratislava: Osvetový ústav.

Erben, Karel J. 1984–1990 [1842, 1862–1864, 1886–1888]. *Prostonárodní české písně a říkadla* (National Czech songs and proverbs). Prague: Panton.

Helfert, Vladimír. 1946. *Czechoslovak Music*. Prague: Orbis.

Hudec, Konštantín, and František Poloczek. 1950–1964. *Slovenské l'udové piesne* (Slovak folk songs). Bratislava: Vydavatel'stvo Slovenskej akadémie vied.

Newmarch, Rosa. 1942. *The Music of Czechoslovakia*. London: Oxford University Press.

Ryback, Timothy. 1990. *Rock Around the Bloc: A History of Rock Music in Eastern Europe and the Soviet Union*. New York: Oxford University Press.

Slovenska spevy (Slovak songs). 1973–1983 [1880–1926]. 6 vols. Bratislava: Opus.

Hungary

Hungary (Magyarország), with a population of slightly more than ten million, occupies 93,030 square kilometers in the Carpathian Basin. Predominantly a plain known to the Romans as Pannonia, it is bisected from north to south by the Danube River. Ninety-two percent of its population are Magyars, four percent are Roma (Gypsy), and smaller minorities include Croats, Germans, Jews, Serbs, and Slovaks. Hungarians are significant minorities in the neighboring countries of Slovakia, Romania (especially in Transylvania), Serbia (especially in Vojvodina), and Croatia.

The Magyars, originally a Finno-Ugric people, who speak one of the few non-Indo-European languages in Europe, took control of Pannonia in the tenth century and converted to Christianity under the rule of the country's first king, Saint Stephen (ca. 977–1038). During the Middle Ages and the Renaissance, until the Ottoman occupation (1526–1686), Hungary was an important power within feudal Europe. For part of the sixteenth and seventeenth centuries, Hungary fell under Ottoman suzerainty, and in the eighteenth century under Hapsburg rule. Since the Counter-Reformation, the majority of the population, including the high aristocracy, has been Roman Catholic. A smaller part, though Protestant (Calvinist, Lutheran, Evangelist), has included a politically and culturally important segment of the middle nobility. In 1867, a dual monarchy, Austria-Hungary, was declared. Hungary became a republic for a few months in 1918–1919, then a constitutional monarchy with right-wing political leadership, until the communist takeover in 1949. Since 1989, Hungary has been a multiparty republic.

History of Folk Music

During centuries-long migrations from Asia, the Magyars encountered many ethnic groups. For centuries after the conquest of the present Hungarian lands, the Magyars continued to interact with the groups that coexisted in the Carpathian Basin. Because of this history and dramatic changes in Hungary's political, economic, religious, and social life in the past millennium, Hungarian folk music is a repository of multiple cultural resources. Historical and linguistic evidence, notated monophonic art songs since the sixteenth century, and recorded oral traditions since about 1900 allow for the proposal of a possible history for the parts of the folk-music tradition that survived into the era of recording.

The oldest layer of folk music consists of so-called old-style songs—fifth-shifting, pentatonic types, the "psalmody" style, and the "lament" style—and certain children's songs, ritual songs, and funeral laments. These styles may have retained Finno-Ugric musical elements, or at least may derive from genres that existed before the Hungarian conquest. During the first centuries of the Hungarian kingdom (established shortly after the conquest, in 1000), Magyars came into contact with European melodic styles and Gregorian chants. In the countryside, chant singing was widespread up to the Reformation. Though no piece in the surviving repertoire can be considered representative of what may have been sung centuries ago, scholars consider these old styles to contain Finno-Ugric, Turkic, and medieval European folk and chant elements.

It is unclear how the century-and-a-half-long Ottoman domination influenced Hungarian folk music. The presence of the Turkish aristocracy may have facilitated the spread of professional Romani (Gypsy) musicians, though Romani ensembles were insignificant in Hungary before the nineteenth century. This period, which coincided with the beginning of the Reformation, brought a new wave of Hungarian monophonic music and vernacular poetry, much of it preserved in manuscripts and print. Its most important genres were Hungarian-texted religious songs based on Gregorian chants; historic-epic songs; humanist, metric songs; and lyric songs, including those called flower songs (virágének). These classifications are based on the texts, not the music: the same melody appeared with various texts.

The second half of the eighteenth century witnessed the development of the verbunkos 'recruiting dance', an instrumental dance-music style. It probably originated with the "Hungarian dances" found in manuscripts and printed collections from the Renaissance and Baroque eras and which had national connotations. The eighteenth-century verbunkos shared certain features with much European music of the period (periodic structure, tonic and dominant triads, melodic turns), but it had unique traits, including characteristic figures of dotted rhythms, triplets, descending note-pairs, cadential syncopations, and ornaments attached to long notes. The *verbunkos* appears to have been known to all strata of society and was soon recognized as "national music"; it is unclear, however, with which segment of society or in which geographical area it originated, and how much of a role the growing number of professional Romani musicians had in its evolution.

The popularity of the *verbunkos* reached its peak in the nineteenth century. Several modern dances derive from it, and its characteristic ornamentation and rhythmic and melodic figures are recognizable in virtually all forms of instrumental music among Hungarian folk musicians. It penetrated into Hungarian Romantic art music, influencing piano pieces, symphonies, and chamber music. The nineteenth century also brought a new wave of song composition, which soon divided into two repertoires: one, known among the peasantry, is called, in scholarly writing, the new style folk song; the other, composed mainly by amateurs of the urban middle class, is today usually called art song, folklike art song, or Hungarian song. Stylistic differences notwithstanding, the two branches were related to each other and to older folk and art music, and the social distinction was not absolute, as some new-style songs circulated among all social classes. Unlike the old-style folk songs (typically performed solo in rubato rhythm), the new songs are mostly in metric rhythm and performed chorally.

The rise of the *verbunkos* and the creation of new song styles coincided with the development of instrumental string ensembles and the spread of professional Romani musicians. Roma were employed first by the aristocracy and the lesser nobility, but because of the rising standard of living among villagers, more and more of them could afford to pay a professional ensemble. By the end of the nineteenth century, Roma were the primary professional musicians, even in smaller villages; in Hungarian usage, however, "Gypsy music" normally connotes not all the music Roma play, but the repertoire and style they play in taverns and restaurants. [For more on Romani music, see ROMANI (GYPSY) MUSIC.]

The situation of folk music in Hungary today differs from one region to another. In more developed areas, many elements of the traditional way of life, including old rituals and songs, became extinct, the repertoire became more limited, and popular styles broadcast on radio became dominant. Certain instruments (e.g., bagpipe), performing styles (old style, ornamental singing), rituals (funeral lamenting), and genres (night-watchman songs) became rare or died out; nevertheless, genres and idioms thought to have disappeared by the 1970s can be still found in the less industrial areas, or wherever Hungarians are a minority. Musicians of the revival movement in the 1970s could study older instrumental styles (known from historical recordings) and learn dances directly from Roma or folk musicians of the Hungarian minority in Transylvania.

The urban revival started at the end of the 1960s among university students in Budapest, who composed, taught, performed, and organized regular dance meetings, called dancehouses. New compositions, often to texts by modern Hungarian poets, were inspired by various styles, including those of old-style folk songs (e.g., psalmody style), modern popular music, and Balkan folk music.

Though regions of Hungarian folk music show differences in their political, economic, ethnic, social, and cultural development, the folk musics of all Hungarian regions share some basic features. Vocal music, whether solo or choral, is uniformly monophonic, typically strophic, and performed in either rubato or *giusto* rhythm (see below), and it includes a wide variety of musical and textual substyles. Instrumental music manifests a distinction between solo-amateur-"peasant" style and ensemble-professional-Romani style. The virtuoso instrument is the violin, the core of the professional ensemble is the string family, most of the professional repertoire is dance-music, and most of the amateur-solo repertoire is based on vocal music.

Vocal Music

In peasant society, singing is a form of personal and social expression, an inherent part of community life. The performers of vocal music are not professionals, though good voice and musical ability is recognized and, in certain functions, required. But even the best singer is "untrained"—meaning that the art of singing is not transmitted in a guild, nor is it considered a profession. Unlike professional instrumentalists, who provide music for patrons, most singers in traditional contexts do not perform for an audience, but sing to themselves or act out their role in a ritualistic setting; in exceptional cases, the ritual may become an occasional performance, as in the Bethlehem play, whose performers rehearse and receive remuneration.

Vocal pieces may or may not be associated with ritual, and many songs occur in more than one context. Rituals are basically of two types: those of the lifecycle and those of the yearly cycle. The most important lifecycle rituals are funerals and weddings, both of which last for several days, containing series of ceremonies accompanied by vocal and instrumental pieces. The yearly cycle, based on the Roman

Catholic calendar, emphasizes Christmas, Easter, Pentecost, and about two hundred other Christian holidays. Tradition has preserved fragments of religious and secular customs of the Middle Ages and the Renaissance and elements of paganism and shamanism—all of which are now merged into integral ceremonies associated with a Christian holiday. The Bethlehem play (at Christmas) and the fire-jumping ceremony (on 24 June, St. John the Baptist's Day) are in several parts, with dramatic action and a series of musical items. Smaller rituals may consist of only one song ("Saying," "Greeting"), performed by a small group going from house to house.

Most vocal pieces do not directly relate to ritual, but they are not entirely "free of context" either. Participants agree on which songs are appropriate for a given situation or mood, how they should be performed, and by whom. What is considered appropriate or beautiful depends on the genre of the song, the age, gender, and number of performers, the ritual or social context, and the occasion. For example, it is inappropriate for older women to sing songs in some areas, yet this restriction does not apply to all genres, and not at all to the funeral lament, which is not considered "song."

The most important song genres are children's songs, *párosító* 'pairing songs', dance-songs, bagpipe songs, beggars' songs, drinking songs, ballads (*ballada*), *keserves* 'bitter songs' (i.e., lamenting songs), shepherds' songs, and soldiers' songs. Musical traits may or may not be relevant in defining a genre; in most cases, various elements—text, music, performance, and mood—are equally important. For example, in Transylvania and Moldavia, old-style songs, performed in a parlando-rubato manner and having sad texts that relate to love or prisoners' lives, are known as *keserves*.

parlando-rubato, literally 'robbed speaking', is a singing style with a speechlike, variable beat.

These songs do not always have a fixed form; combining existing poetic lines and stanzas with their own invention, singers improvise them to express their sorrows. For many listeners, it is the sad mood, the free performing style, and the personal content that primarily define this genre.

Genre, Style, and Performance

The only Hungarian vocal genre that calls for extensive textual and melodic improvisation is the funeral lament (*sirató*). Lamenting is a moral obligation, a service to the deceased, carried out by the dead person's closest female relative(s). The ritual and melody of lamenting seem to derive from pre-

Christian practice and possibly relate to commemorative heroic epics. Lamenting is done beside the bier and during the funeral, but a lament may be sung apart from the ritual, even years after the funeral, as a token of remembrance. Texts are improvised on the spot for the occasion, making use of traditional textual patterns. The melody, performed parlando-rubato, is roughly an extended descending line, whose fragments are repeated, varied, and rearranged in performance. Laments fall into two melodic styles: the diatonic style, which used to be performed all over the country; and the pentatonic style, known only in Transylvania.

Children's music includes counting songs, games, dance-songs, rhymes, and greetings for various occasions of everyday life and holidays. It is usually metric, with each item composed of loosely related poetic-musical lines. Some words and phrases may have no apparent meaning, but they often turn out to be textual fragments referring to extinct customs, shamanistic rituals, and pagan beliefs.

The core of Hungarian vocal music consists of strophic songs, usually composed of four isosyllabic six-, seven-, eight-, eleven- and twelve-syllable lines; within this framework, however, songs show great melodic and rhythmic variety. Collected Hungarian folk songs amount to several tens of thousands, not counting variant performances of the same song. The old-style songs alone number more than fifty-five thousand pieces, representing more than eighteen hundred melody types.

Songs are performed in either of two rhythmic styles: parlando-rubato and *giusto*. Theoretically, the term *parlando-rubato* refers to a manner of performance that follows the natural rhythm of the spoken text; such a definition, however, does not entirely hold true. Some performances follow the natural rhythm of the text more than others, but all have an underlying rhythmic pattern, repeated in all strophes. In all instances, the music reflects poetic rhythm, rather than the natural accentuation of phrases. In some performances, the syllables flow in a series of undifferentiated, even eighth notes; in others, the rhythm approximates metrical line-schemes. Asymmetrical rhythmic formations may recur and become fixed patterns within the performance; Béla Bartók called this phenomenon frozen rubato.

In *giusto*, the rhythm is executed according to a metric framework, yet there is slight and subtle flexibility in the durational values. Like parlando-rubato, *giusto* is a generic term for various performing styles, of which some may emphasize metric accents, others may have a somewhat blurred metric structure, and again others may be nearly as flexible as parlando-rubato though with a feeling of regular pulsation.

Parlando-rubato performance is almost exclusively solo, and choral performance is typically *giusto*. Since a melodic type may be used with different texts, it can be performed in various rhythmic styles, having parlando and *giusto* versions. A metric song may become parlando-rubato when performed by one person; nevertheless, some melodic and textual types occur almost exclusively in one or the other style: for example, psalmody style and *keserves* are almost always parlando-rubato, but bagpipe songs are always *giusto*.

In general, Hungarian vocal melodies can be called syllabic, but ornamentation is often substantial, and older recordings suggest that ornaments may have been much longer and structurally more important before the twentieth century. In contemporary performances, ornamental notes are usually distinguished from the "main" melodic notes: they are usually shorter, often reduced in dynamics, and performed with a different vocal quality. Styles of ornamentation show considerable regional differences: for example, north Hungary has a unique tradition: in contrast with general practice, new-style songs are performed with ornaments.

Melodic Types

Hungarian scholars conceive of folk songs in terms of thousands of related melodic types (*tipus*), which form about ten type-groups (*tömb*), also called melody styles. The history of some type-groups can be well established; for others, however, there is merely structural similarity among pieces. Some styles are the product of the nineteenth century; in this sense, the distinction between new and old styles is still meaningful. The new style proper continues to be the most popular: it contains about eight hundred melody types. Songs in this style are usually of a wide range, often with an arch shape (ascending-descending), and within the strophe, the last line is the recapitulation of the first. New-style songs are typically in *giusto* rhythm and performed chorally (figure 1).

The oldest surviving melodies are those of the psalmody and lament styles. Songs in the former style, known only in Transylvania, are tonally related to pentatonic laments: their performance is almost always a recitativelike parlando-rubato; their texts belong to so-called lamenting textual genres, such as ballads, *keserves*, prisoners' songs, beggars' songs, and soldiers' laments (and their related parody texts). Songs in the latter style appear to have originated with the diatonic lament, whose melodic motives and

typical lines they share. Their melodies, found among seventeenth- and eighteenth-century notated monophonic art songs, are often related to heroic, epic, and religious texts in the art and folk traditions. Texts thus provide contextual links between psalmody- and lament-style songs and funeral laments: the essence of laments and epic poetry is commemoration.

Instrumental Music

In Hungarian instrumental music, two categories can roughly be distinguished: solo-amateur-peasant and ensemble-professional-Romani music. Among amateurs, solo instrumental music is a form of private entertainment; its use in rituals and social ceremonies, if it exists at all, is secondary to the use of vocal genres and professional instrumental music. Solo instrumentalists are not professionals, but laborers, who earn their living from agricultural work. They have no formal training, and learn to play the instrument rather late in life, for their own enjoyment. They might be asked to play at lesser social occasions, and they normally do so, without expecting remuneration. They are rarely called to play at weddings, dancehouses, or important rituals.

Béla Bartók, Folk Song Collector
The phonograph was invented independently by Thomas Alva Edison in the United States and Charles Cros in France (1877), and this invention led inevitably to the desire to capture manifestations of oral tradition with greater fidelity. In the decades that followed, numerous pioneering recordings were made of European folk music. Bela Bartók was an important collector and editor of folk music in Central Europe and the Balkans during this period. He produced editions of Hungarian (1924), Romanian (1913, 1923, 1935), Slovakian (1959–1970), and Yugoslavian (1951, 1954) musical traditions in addition to studies he made in North Africa and Asia Minor, and was the major force in comparative field-based studies (1934). No other scholar accomplished as much as he in this period, an incredible feat when one considers his brilliant achievements as a composer. His systematic analysis of each tradition goes beyond simple identification of scale or meter, and takes structural scrutiny and classification to extraordinary lengths. The influence of his methods, formed in the climate of positivistic science, has not always been beneficial: academies of science, especially in Eastern Europe, have tended to stress classification and structure to the point where many of the essential features of musicmaking, such as affective communication or intonation, were minimized or lost. It could be argued that Bartók's best analyses of folk music are found in his arrangements, which synthesize many performative elements of folk music.

Figure 1 The new-style folk song "*De Nekem is volt édesanyém . . .,*" as performed by Istváan Gömbér, age 65 of Felsővály (Gomor). Like many songs in this style, this one has a pentatonic scale, the second line repeats a fifth above the first, and each phrase has an arch shape. After *Anthology of Hungarian Folk Music II: The North* 1986:2:4.4.c.

Solo instrumental music is almost entirely based on the vocal repertoire. Typically, the amateurs play what they can also sing, and in some performances the instrumental rendition hardly differs from the vocal model. Nevertheless, the more skilled performers alter the songs considerably: they not only add ornaments but transform melodic lines and rhythms with great creativity. In fact, the virtuosity and imagination in the best of such performances differ in no essential way from what may be produced by the leading violinist of a professional ensemble.

To make musical sounds, amateurs use signal instruments (bell, cow horn), professional implements (whip), and improvised devices, such as leaves and spoons. Traditionally, even the more developed solo instruments were homemade, though today factory-made substitutes are also used. These solo instruments include various flutes, the *tárogató* 'Hungarian clarinet', the cane pipe, the zither, the *tambura*, the harp, types of cimbalom, the ocarina, the mouth harp, and, for rhythmic accompaniment, friction drums and the *gardon* (see below). Among more modern, factory-made instruments, the most popular are the orchestral flute, the clarinet, and the accordion.

Unlike these instruments, two other solo instruments were associated with professionalism. In preceding centuries, the bagpipe (*duda*) was a professional instrument, and bagpipers were occasionally hired by aristocrats. The hurdy-gurdy (*tekerő*) has traditionally been a beggar's instrument, having a less prestigious "professional" role. In recent times, the duo of hurdy-gurdy and clarinet has been used to accompany dancing. Players of these instruments tended to be outsiders, or even outcasts, in relation to the society whose members paid them.

From the early nineteenth century, the bagpipe was gradually replaced by the modern string ensemble. At the beginning of the twentieth century, bagpipers and the hurdy-gurdy-clarinet duo were still called to play at poorer weddings, or to perform for parts of the ceremony. The genuinely amateur instruments survived the growing popularity of the string ensemble, but the bagpipe died out, precisely because it was a professional instrument and as such depended on its market. Today's professional folk ensemble is the outcome of almost two centuries of development. First a solo violin, then a violin duo was used. At the end of the nineteenth century, the violin duo was still sufficient at social occasions. When only two violins play together, both may play the melody, each with different ornamentation, together producing a heterophonic-sounding, dissonant, but expressive style—a performing practice that survives only in the so-called instrumental *keserves*. In what appears to be a more modern practice, the violins have different roles, and their parts are called accordingly: *príma* 'lead melody' and *kontra* 'rhythmic-harmonic support'. The players are thus the *prímás* and the *kontrás*.

The basis of today's string ensemble is *príma*, *kontra* (played by a violin and a viola or a three-stringed viola), and bass (cello or double bass). To these instruments, another violin or viola, a clarinet, a cimbalom, and occasionally an accordion may be added. Because of the popularity of the instrumental-ensemble repertoire and the outstanding Romani player Aladár Rácz, the modern Schunda cimbalom gained national recognition among classical instruments.

The violin and *gardon* ensemble is known in only a few regions, particularly Gyimes, Transylvania. Normally, a man plays the violin while a woman, often his wife, accompanies him on the *gardon*. The *gardon* has roughly the shape and size of a violoncello and serves as a percussion accompaniment; a factory-made cello or a homemade imitation of it can be used. The player beats the strings, located in one plane, with a wooden stick, and combines the beat with plucking, picking up the thinner, side string and letting it strike the fingerboard, thus producing extremely complex rhythms, often in asymmetrical meters (*aksak*).

Unlike most other instrumental styles, string-ensemble music is flourishing in the villages and has served as the basis of the urban revival movement. Since only remnants of the once-virtuoso bagpipe repertoire were recorded, we will never know how closely the virtuosity of the violin resembled that of the bagpipe, which it replaced in the same function. Some structural traits—for instance, the alternation of strophes and interludes—appear to be similar.

In villages, string ensemble music is primarily for dancing. The contexts for dancing are most importantly weddings, but there are regions with regular dance parties (*táncház* 'dancehouses', referring to the location and the event). In Szék, each section of the village has its own dancehouse and musicians. Dancing takes place sometimes two or three times a week; dancing at weddings may last for thirty hours. The success of the dancehouse depends largely on the musicians, primarily on the *prímás*. Each individual has a favorite piece, and the *prímás* is supposed to know it and play it specifically to him or her. The musicians decide the final form of each dance, the dance cycle, and to some extent the entire event.

The tempo and rhythmic outlines of individual pieces are defined primarily by the dance type, but this framework permits ample opportunity for improvisation. Hungarian dances are usually in duple meter. The most important distinction is between slow and fast dance types: they differ in rhythm, performing style, and accompaniment. In most dances, traces of old Hungarian dances and *verbunkos* music can be discovered. Typically, the "melody" is played by the *prímás* in a freely ornamented style; the *kontrás* and the bass play repetitive rhythms, almost always with major chords, regardless of the modality of the melody. Slow dances are often accompanied by *dűvő* rhythm, a regular rhythm with slurred, offbeat accentuation. Fast dances are almost always accompanied by even eighth-note chords.

Most Hungarian dances are couple dances, but men's solo dances, women's (young girls') chain dances, and dueling war dances can still be found in some regions. Hungarian dance-music is cyclic: three to six dances follow in series in a regionally typical traditional order. Dance cycles show great variety regionally, and there may be variant traditions even in one village.

—*Adapted from articles by Judit Frigyesi and James Porter*

Bibliography

Anthology of Hungarian Folk Music I: Dance Music. 1985. Selected from the collection of the Musicological Institute of the Hungarian Academy of Sciences by György Martin, Istvan Nemeth, and Erno Pesovar. Hungaroton LPX 18112–16. 5 LP disks.

Anthology of Hungarian Folk Music II: The North. 1986. Selected from the collection of the Musicological Institute of the Hungarian Academy of Sciences by Lujza Tan and László Vikar. Hungaroton LPX 18124–28. 5 LP disks.

Bartók, Béla. 1931. *Hungarian Folk Music*. London: Oxford University Press.

Frigyesi, Judit. 1998. *Béla Bartok and Turn-of-the-century Budapest*. Berkeley: University of California Press.

Kodály, Zoltán. 1960. *Folk Music of Hungary*. Translated by Ronald Tempest and Cynthia Jolly. London: Barrie & Rockliff.

Martin, György. 1988. *Hungarian Folk Dances*. Budapest: Corvina.

Sárosi, Bálint. 1970. *Gypsy Music*. Budapest: Corvina.

———. 1986. *Folk Music: Hungarian Musical Idiom*. Budapest: Corvina.

Sebők, János. 1983–1984. *Magya-Rock*. 2 vols. Budapest: Zeneműkiadó.

Szendrei, Janka, László Dobszay, and Benjamin Rajeczky. 1979. *XVI–XVII századi dallamaink a népi emlekezetben* (Sixteenth- and seventeenth-century melodies in the folk tradition). 2 vols. Budapest: Akademiai.

Vargyas, Lajos. 1983. *Hungarian Ballads and the European Ballad Tradition*. Translated by Imre Gombos. Budapest: Akademiai.

Eastern Europe

Eastern Europe

Eastern Europe

For most of the last two hundred years, the peoples of Eastern Europe were part of the Russian Empire (1800s) or the Soviet Union (most of the 1900s). More than other regions of Europe, the musical cultures of Eastern Europe feature singing in general, and traditional polyphonic singing in particular, over instrumental music. The Slavic-speaking people of Russia, Ukraine, and Belarus share similar styles of two-voiced singing, some related to Slavic-language polyphonic singing in southeastern Europe. In North Caucasia and Georgia, where non-Indo-European languages are spoken, people sing in unique, rather complex, three- and four-voiced polyphonic styles.

During the Soviet period, folk-music practice came under nearly complete state sponsorship and control. The state's ideology fundamentally changed traditional soloistic and small-group practices by remolding them into large orchestras of folk instruments and choruses. Musical scholarship has been rather sophisticated in this region but, because of language barriers, little known outside of it.

To offer readers a sense of the rich village music traditions of Eastern Europe, we present articles on Russia and the Ukraine.

Russia

Though 80 percent of Russian territory is in Asia, the historical and cultural heart of Russia—between the Karelian peninsula in the west and the Ural Mountains in the east—is in Eastern Europe. The population grew from 10 to 12 million people in the seventeenth century, to 55 million in 1897, and to 142 million people in 2006.

The European part of contemporary Russia is a multiethnic territory whose geographical position has brought ethnic Russians into constant contact with other ethnicities, including Finno-Ugric, Baltic, and Turkic peoples, all of whom have left their mark on Russian music. The area between the Volga and Oka rivers, where Slavic and Finnic tribes interacted as early as the ninth or tenth centuries, is considered the historical core of Russia. By the twelfth century, it had given rise to 224 cities, which attracted Russian immigrants from elsewhere.

The northern area, Pomorie, consisted of the delta of the North Dvina, Onega, and Pechora rivers, and included many aboriginal peoples (Karels, Komi, Lopars, Nenets, and Veps). This area was colonized by two streams of Russians, first from Novgorod and then from Rostov and Suzdal. A third area, the middle Volga, known as Povolzh'e, was formed in the sixteenth and seventeenth centuries, and was the only area that supported fishermen. The other two areas supported the cultivation of grain, whose various types figure prominently in folk-song texts.

Musical Dialects and Genres

Not surprisingly, there is no pan-Russian tradition. Every region has its own system. In the north, the dominant genres are epic songs and laments; in the southwest, calendric songs, with characteristic yells (*gukania*); in eastern Vologda, laments; in the south, circle dances. Some regions have unique ritual genres, including certain Easter songs, carnival (Shrovetide) songs, and Christmas carols.

Calendric Songs

Calendric songs linked to the yearly cycle of agricultural work exist in European Russia only in areas bordering other ethnic groups. Most are no longer performed in their original contexts. The richest area for such songs is in western Russia, on the border with Belarus, historically linked to a tribe known as Krivichi, whose people lived around Briansk, Smolensk, Pskov, and Tver. The second area is the border with the Ukraine, especially around Kursk and Belgorod. The third is the upper Volga area on the ethnic border with Mordvinians around Riazan, Vladimir, and Lower Novgorod. Wherever these songs exist, they constitute the core of the local song tradition. The only really widespread calendric song ritual is *koliada*, caroling on Vasil's Day (New Year's) and Christmas in the orthodox Christian calendar. Yet, there are many types of songs associated with a host of seasonal rituals.

The first songs of spring are sung in March at the Annunciation, when chanted invocations to spring birds substitute for songs proper, which custom forbids at that time of year. The next cycle consists of songs for St. George's Day (23 April), when cattle are led to summer pastures. Easter is marked by *volochebnye pesni* 'trudging songs', named for the singers' manner of walking from village to village on roads muddied by spring rains. Their festive melodies are unique in the calendric cycle. On the first Sunday after Easter in the Kostroma region near the Volga, carolers go to newlyweds' houses to sing newlywed songs (*viunishnye pesni*).

Summer rituals are celebrated mainly in Krivichi territory. The first ritual is *troitskie* (Whitsunday)—normally the fiftieth day after Easter, between the beginning of May and the middle of June. The summer-solstice songs, *kupalskie pesni*, are sung in western areas on Midsummer's Day (23 June), the eve of St. John's Day, as villagers holding a scarecrow (*kupala*) leap over a fire. The texts are ballads about the magical origin of plants, and melodies show links to many other agricultural ritual songs for spring and for the harvest and the melodies of refrains are even reminiscent of *koliada* songs. After St. Peter's Day (12 July), haymaking (*senokos* or *pokos*) begins, and fieldwork is accompanied by special songs. During the harvest, each village gathers to help one family, which in return for the work provides a big meal, at which collective-help songs (*tolochnye pesni*) are sung. Harvest songs and associated rituals differentiated the harvest into beginning, middle, and end. Though harvest songs do not belong to events in the calendric cycle itself, they demonstrate many musical links to other genres of calendric songs and help establish the musical unity of the entire yearly cycle.

Calendric rituals unite speech, heightened speech, song, movement, and dance. They are performed outdoors with loud, shouting voices and unusual vocal timbres, addressing nature, spirits, birds, and heaven. Their scales are untempered and difficult to notate. A typical stanzaic structure of calendric songs repeats the text of the first phrase in the second phrase, but compresses it into a shorter time span with new music. The third phrase then contains a new line of text and new music.

Weddings

Nearly two-thirds of all songs collected during fieldwork are wedding songs, which continue to be performed. No two villages share the same music for wedding songs, even when they share the texts and the general order of rituals. A given village has five to twelve tune formulas, but a few villages have just one or two. The songs accompanying the main events of the wedding are sung forcefully, with each syllable stressed and accompanied by foot stomping, tapping on the table, and ecstatic shouting.

The main genres are lyric songs, farewell songs to the bride, songs praising the groom and other guests, teasing songs, taunting ditties (*draznilki*), short ditties (*chastushki*), ritual-bread songs, processional songs, laments by or for the bride, and songs that describe each wedding event. These last songs, which resound during the entire sequence of events, are unique to weddings and, unlike the other nuptial genres, have no structural parallels in other genres. Songs detailing the protocol of the wedding and wedding lyric songs have musical features unique to the Russian song tradition and distinct from those of neighboring traditions.

Russian culture has developed two kinds of weddings: joyful weddings and funereal weddings. The former are typical of the west and south; the latter, of the north. Songs for the former are stylistically related to calendric songs; songs for the latter, to funeral laments. Joyful weddings link Russian wedding rituals to those of other Slavic peoples. They feature "song wars" and other forms of ritual antagonism between the two families. Funereal weddings feature the bride lamenting while her girlfriends sing, or lamenting while others dance or vocally imitate instrumental music. In some areas, the bride engages in ritual crying without text on vocables, such as *u-u*, *ha-ha*, and *oi-oi*. In other areas, the bride laments by improvising texts as she addresses the guests at the wedding.

Laments and Dirges

The Russian tradition has many kinds of laments (*prichitaniia*, *vopli*). The funeral lament proper provides the model for all others (figure 1), which include laments at memorials, laments for soldiers being sent to war, widows' laments, and laments over fires, floods, crop failures, epidemic animal diseases, and forced separation from relatives. The texts of funeral laments, addressed to the dead person, contain incantational formulas that suggest a magical power to raise the dead.

Performers improvise using formulaic structures or models. The core of this tradition is in the Russian north. In performance style, which often invokes crying, they are clearly distinguishable from all other genres; in structure, however, they are clearly linked to other song genres.

Figure 1 A funeral lament (*prichitaniia*), performed in a style resembling epic or liturgical singing, with a wide melodic range and in a free rhythm. After Zemtsovsky 1967a:61.

Epic Song (Bylina)

Sung epics are known either as *bylina* 'what it was' or *starina* 'old song', and have about a hundred different plots. The average *bylina* is about a thousand lines long. Some stories reflect Russian history from before the first medieval state, in the tenth century; others reflect more internationally known themes, such as the husband returning home to remarry his wife (known from Homer's *Odyssey*, for example) and the father fighting with his unrecognized son; yet others reflect mythological and fairy-tale themes.

In Russian education and intellectual life, the *bylina* occupies the highest position in the hierarchy of traditional culture. In the nineteenth century, epics were unknown to most Russian peasants, limited as the genre was to the north, but mass propaganda promoted the *bylina* as the true source of a pan-Russian tradition.

Epic singers are held in high regard for their memory and skill. Their traditions are passed on within families known as epic dynasties, the most famous of which is the Riabinin family. Most solo epic singers are male, but group singing can mix male and female singers, often from the same family. The last recordings of this tradition were made in the 1970s, but its themes and heroes continue to enjoy a second life in literature, schoolbooks, classical music, films, paintings, and other forms of popular culture.

The recordings of the last hundred years are exclusively vocal, but most scholars assume a distantly past tradition of epics accompanied by a *gusli* (zither) and a *gudok* (bowed lute). Epics have three main performance styles: rhapsodic singing, alternating with recitation that uniquely combines fast speech with hints of exact pitch; ensemble performance without real polyphony, but more melodic than the first type; and group polyphonic singing in song style (figure 2). Each epic text does not have its own tune; rather, tunes belong to the performer, who may have one or two tunes to which he sings all the epic texts he knows. The structure of stanzas is flexible and can change, for example, to a simpler structure as the singer tires. During a performance, the pitch often rises.

Epic tunes are structured around short melodic motifs (*popevki*), which can be made to accommodate three main types of stanzaic structure: twelve to fourteen syllables per line, with three main accents; eight to eleven syllables, with two main accents; and irregular stanzas, set to regular musical phrases of twenty rhythmic beats, with three held notes to mark a three-syllable cadence in each line. Generally, each line of text is set to a single melodic phrase.

Lyric Songs

Lyric songs, perhaps more than other genres, are found among all elements of society, from villages to suburbs to cities: peasants, seasonal and factory workers, servants, students, soldiers, prisoners, homeless people, thieves, and ethnic minorities, such as Gypsies. They are performed at a variety of occasions and in different musical styles. The most archaic surviving style is limited to a range of four or five diatonic tones, and is most typical of the western Russian tradition.

The most elaborated forms of peasant lyric songs are the so-called long-drawn-out songs (*protiazhnye pesni*), known practically everywhere in Russia and featuring extended melodic motifs (*popevki*) on selected syllables, effectively creating two rhythms: one based on the duration of syllables and one the result of intrasyllabic melodic rhythms. The favored locale is outdoors, where lyric songs are performed with an open, loud sound; in contrast, lyric songs that have come to villages from cities are typically performed in houses at social gatherings.

Lyric songs can be performed by a soloist or a chorus of people gathered to socialize or work together, and until the 1930s were frequently performed by trios of professional singers. Scholars

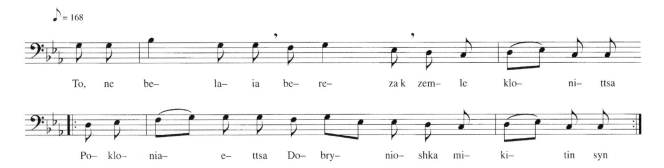

Figure 2 Excerpt from an epic song (*bylina*) about the epic hero Dobrynia of the Onega region, performed by an ensemble with distinct pitches but without polyphony. After Astakhova 1951: no. 3.

distinguish two performance styles: a strict style and a free style, with virtuoso embellishments and expressivity.

The most popular instrument for accompanying city lyric songs after about 1800 was the seven-stringed guitar. So popular was this guitar that it became a symbol of Russian city culture. Perhaps the most creative performance style involves taking printed lyrics and improvising a melody over standardized chord progressions. This manner, still especially popular among student hikers and mountain climbers, has given birth to a new genre, after-ski songs, which, in the post-Stalinist period, were revived with new texts, having a strong political, even anti-Soviet, cast. The most popular performers—Bulat Okudzhava (1924–1997), Vladimir Vysotskii (1938–1980), and Aleksandr Galich (1918–1977)—had their songs circulated via samizdat (self-published) cassette tapes (*magnitizdat*), and their songs were widely sung by young people.

Musical Instruments and Instrumental Music

Russian instrumental music underwent two historical crises, in which authorities tried to annihilate important parts of the tradition. In the seventeenth century, Tsar Aleksei Mikhailovich, the father of Peter the Great, became vehemently Orthodox and ordered the destruction of the stringed instruments of secular minstrels (*skomorokhi*), including the *gudok* (bowed fiddle) and the *gusli* (plucked zither), neither of which ever fully returned. In the 1920s and 1930s, Stalinist authorities collected and burned villagers' homemade violins and other stringed instruments, which they considered symbols of bourgeois culture; instead, they promoted military band instruments as the ideal of a new society.

Aside from minstrels, the best performers of instrumental music were traditionally shepherds and wedding musicians. Shepherds played mainly wind instruments. A duct flute (*dudka, sopel, pizhatka*) had five or six finger holes. Single reeds were placed in one or two pipes with a horn bell (*zhaleika, pishchik*); one pipe might have three holes, the other pipe, six. A shepherd could play two contrapuntal melodies. In the morning, pipers played the tune "The sun rises; the shepherd goes crazy"; in the evening, they played the tune "The sun sets; the shepherd enjoys himself." A wooden trumpet (*rozhok*) of various sizes had five finger holes and one thumbhole. In the Vladimir and Yaroslavl districts, the *rozhok* tradition called for ensembles of up to 120 players, who often imitated vocal polyphony.

The most popular Russian traditional instrument is the balalaika, a three-stringed strummed lute with a triangular sound box. Played solo, or since the 1930s in ensembles, it accompanies songs, *chastushki*, and dances.

The oldest Russian bowed stringed instrument was the *gudok*, a three-stringed pear-shaped fiddle made from one piece of wood; its successor, a violin (*skripka* 'to squeak') homemade from glued pieces of wood, also had three strings. The center of this tradition was west Russia, where the violin was exclusively a wedding instrument, traditionally played seated. Today, most violinists play four-stringed manufactured instruments. Since the 1920s, violin and accordion duos have been used for weddings.

The diatonic button accordion (*garmoń, garmoshka, garmonika*) was widespread in Russia by the 1840s, and from the 1860s to 1880s it was the most popular Russian folk instrument. Many European dance tunes were introduced to Russia via the accordion and then passed on from Russian to minority groups. A fully chromatic button accordion (*bayan*), introduced in the early twentieth century, became extremely popular. Its earliest versions had chords present on the buttons of the left, while the right hand played the melody. Later versions had individual notes on the left hand.

Folk Music in the Early Twentieth Century

At the beginning of the twentieth century, three main trends profoundly affected Russian musical life: staged interpretations of Russian folklore, cheaply printed and widely sold songbooks, and gramophone records.

Staged Performances
Staged concerts of Russian, Ukrainian, and Gypsy choirs, balalaika orchestras, solo and duo accordionists, instrumental and vocal combos (balalaika and mandolin, singer and accordionist), and dancers who acted out the content of folk songs were enormously popular in Moscow, St. Petersburg, and Kiev, and toured provincial cities. In 1913, Andreev's orchestra celebrated its twenty-fifth anniversary, to great acclaim. In his honor in 1921, this orchestra was renamed The State Great Russian Orchestra Named after Andreev.

The most popular genre of stage music, especially with prominent members of the Russian intelligentsia, were Gypsy romances, performed by soloists and choirs in restaurants on the outskirts of Moscow and St. Petersburg. The choirs, always composed of Gypsies, sang in Russian and Romani in a characteristic Gypsy style [see ROM (GYPSY) MUSIC]. Except for a few famous singers, such as the legendary Stesha (1787–1822) from the Gypsy choir of Ilya Sokolov (1777–1848) and Varvara Panina (1872–1911), the soloists were usually non-Gypsies, attracted to the genre by its popularity and the possibility of making good money. The biggest star, an Armenian from Tbilisi who moved his audience to tears with his singing, took the stage name Sasha Davydov (1850–1911).

Songbooks (Pesenniki)

The second trend began about 1900, when inexpensive songbooks containing popular folk songs from the stage repertoire, many with texts only, flooded markets in Moscow, St. Petersburg, and Kiev. Each of about ten publishers produced about twenty thousand copies per year; this publishing peaked in 1911, when 180 new books were published. Most of the songs were so-called cruel romances about unhappy love affairs, suicides, and murders. A subcategory of these books included songs of thieves, convicts, and hobos. About a dozen were produced by a Swede, Wilhelm N. Garteveld (1862–1928). These books helped spread newly composed folk songs, creating the first folk songs known throughout Russia and not limited to a particular region. Even today, Russian ethnomusicologists find these songs the best preserved and easiest to collect in Russian villages.

Hundreds of thousands of individual songs were published as sheet music; in Moscow, the Iambor Company systematically published in pocket-size editions music of virtually every kind: popular, folk, student, Gypsy, music-hall, and even favorite classical songs, marches, and dances, including waltzes and the two-step. Russian folk songs in popular arrangements and with singers' photographs were also published by Semyon Iambor between 1907 and 1914.

The Gramophone

The third trend at the beginning of the century was the boom in the production and sales of the gramophone, a machine that, like the songbooks, helped join city culture with village culture. From 1900 to 1907, half a million gramophones were sold in Russia. By 1915, Gramophone and Pathé, English and French companies, respectively, were selling up to twenty million phonograph records (*plastinky*) of Russian stage performers annually, in addition to sales from their international catalog. Other gramophone companies included Sirena Record, Stella Record, Orpheon, Lirophone, Ekstraphone, and Zonophone Record.

Listening to recordings on the gramophone became a part of everyday social life, not just among urban elites, but in provincial areas. During World War I, so-called gramophone concerts became popular, especially on ships and in hospitals. On the street, in parallel with phonograph recordings, barrel organs played cylinders of the stage repertory.

—*Adapted from an article by Izaly Zemtsovsky*

Bibliography

Asaf'ev, Boris. 1953. *Russian Music from the Beginning of the Nineteenth Century.* Translated by Alfred J. Swan. Ann Arbor: J. W. Edwards, for the American Council of Learned Societies.

Astakhova, Anna. 1951. *Byliny Severa* (The Bylinas of the North). Vol. 2. Moscow-Leninigrad: Akademiya Nauk S.S.S.R.

Bailey, James, and Tatyana Ivanova. 1998. *An Anthology of Russian Folk Epics.* New York: M. E. Sharpe.

Beregovsky, Moshe. 1982. *Old Jewish Folk Music: The Collections and Writings of Moshe Beregovski.* Edited by Mark Slobin. Philadelphia: University of Pennsylvania Press.

Brill, Nicholas. 1980. *History of Russian Church Music: 988–1917.* Bloomington: Indiana University Press.

Campbell, Stuart, ed. and trans. 1994. *Russians on Russian Music, 1830–1880: An Anthology.* Cambridge and New York: Cambridge University Press.

Cushman, Thomas. 1995. *Notes from the Underground: Rock Music Counterculture in Russia.* Albany: State University of New York Press.

Feigin, Leo, ed. 1985. *Russian Jazz: New Identity.* London and New York: Quartet Books.

Geldern, James von, and Richard Stites, eds. 1995. *Mass Culture in Soviet Russia: Tales, Poems, Songs, Movies, Plays, and Folklore, 1917–1953.* Bloomington: Indiana University Press.

Lineva, Evgeniya, ed. 1905–1912. *The Peasant Songs of Great Russia as They Are in the Folk's Harmonization.* St Petersburg: Imperial Academy of Science. London: D. Nutt.

Porter, James, ed. 1997. *Folklore and Traditional Music in the Former Soviet Union and Eastern Europe.* Los Angeles: Department of Ethnomusicology, University of California, Los Angeles.

Ryback, Timothy. 1990. *Rock Around the Bloc: A History of Rock Music in Eastern Europe and the Soviet Union.* New York: Oxford University Press.

Schwarz, Boris. 1983. *Music and Musical Life in Soviet Russia: Enlarged Ed., 1917–1981.* Bloomington: Indiana University Press.

Smith, Gerald. 1984. *Songs to Seven Strings: Russian Guitar Poetry and Soviet "Mass" Song.* Bloomington: Indiana University Press.

Starr, S. Frederic. 1994. *Red and Hot: The Fate of Jazz in the Soviet Union, 1917–1991.* New York: Limelight Editions.

Swan, Alfred. 1973. *Russian Music and Its Sources in Chant and Folk-Song.* London: J. Baker; New York: Norton.

Warner, Elizabeth, and Evgeny Kustovskii. 1990. *Russian Traditional Folk Song.* Hull, U.K.: Hull University Press.

Zemtsovsky, Izaly. 1967a. *Russkaia protiazhnaia pesnia* (The Russian long-drawn-out song). Leningrad: Muzyka.

——. 1967b. *Toropetskie pesni: pesni rodiny M. Musorgskogo* (Songs of Toropets: Songs from M. Mussorgsky's homeland). Leningrad: Muzyka.

——. 1972. *Obraztsy narodogo mnogogolosiia* [Examples of (Russian) folk (song) polyphony]. Leningrad: Sovetskii kompozitor.

——. 1978. *Fol' klor i kompozitor* (Folklore and the composer). Leningrad: Sovetskii kompozitor.

——, comp. and ed. 1982. *Narodnaia muzyka SSSR i sovremennosť* (Folk music and current lifestyles in the U.S.S.R.) Leningrad: Muzyka.

——, comp. and ed. 1995. *Russkaia narodnaia pesnia: neizvestnye stranitsy muzykaĺ noi istorii* (The Russian folk song: The unknown pages of musical history). St Petersburg: Institute for History of the Arts.

Ukraine

Ukraine, the second largest country (603,700 square kilometers) in Europe after Russia, consists of forests in the north, steppes in the south and east, and mountains (the Carpathians) in the southwest. Until the 1970s, the northwest was a marshy area, which has since been drained. From roughly the late 1600s, much of central and eastern Ukraine was part of the Russian Empire and then the Soviet Union. Western Ukraine, known historically as Galicia (in Ukrainian, Halychyna), was part of Polish or Austrian states from the 1300s until 1939. At the time of the disintegration of the Soviet Union (in 1991), more than 96 percent of the Ukrainian population voted for independence. In 2006, much of the population of more than 46 million worked in industry, mining, aeronautics, metals, service, and agriculture.

Village Vocal Music before Collectivization

In peasant Ukraine before collectivization (in the 1930s), most village musical life was formally organized around the Christian calendar of feasts and fasts, or longstanding institutions of civil society such as weddings, funerals, seasonal or agricultural celebrations, and ritual and nonritual evening social gatherings of various kinds. Church choirs and the occasional military band in a market town were the only socially organized music practices not primarily local or regional in character.

The Social Organization of Singing

Genres, repertories, and other performance practices were divided between women and men. Most ritual vocal music was performed by women and girls, though men also participated; most instrumental music was played by men and boys, though women also participated. Women and men or girls and boys shared numerous nonritual vocal genres and certain musical instruments more or less equally. Women and men and girls and boys performed some nonritual genres, such as lyrical ballads, love songs, and soldiers' songs, sung informally by anyone at any time.

Most ritual musical performances in villages were specific to certain contexts and people. Wedding ceremonies were acted out in a sequence of events over the course of three to seven days. Most wedding rituals required songs, some of which were realized in groups, some rendered solo, still others a combination of group and solo singing. The singing lasted for hours, as hundreds of ritual texts were rendered, mainly by women acting in specific roles: the bride, the bridesmaids, an older woman acting as a sergeant-at-arms for the women, the bridegroom's sisters, the bride's mother, and the bridegroom's mother.

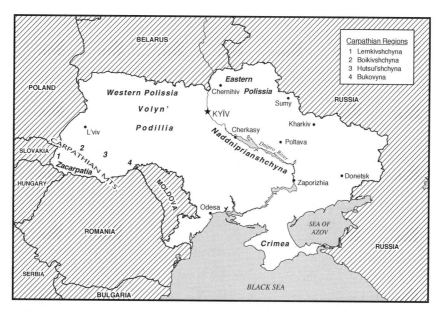

Ukraine

Women had to learn hundreds of ritual texts, numerous melodies, and the sequence of events that included ritual dances. Most men knew far fewer texts, for, with only a few exceptions (e.g., the *boiary* 'groomsmen'), men did not customarily have ritual wedding roles to fulfill. The music of the wedding sequence was part of a series of social obligations into which a woman was born. Not knowing these texts and melodies would have been a breach of custom. Ritual songs could be extremely long, with hundreds of strophes. Each village sometimes had only ten or twenty melodies to which the texts were sung. Some melodies, those with a range of a fourth or a fifth, were among the oldest elements of local music culture.

Music practice reflected village social structure. Girls from one place (a *kutok* or 'corner' of the village) and one generation shared a common aesthetic and musical knowledge. Large villages could have five or even ten corners, and a small village might have two or three. In wedding and other ritual contexts, specific people sang specific songs. As girls entered young adulthood, their roles, ritual obligations, and music practices changed. As they aged into mature women, their roles and music practices changed again, but it was still among their musicosocial group, based on generation and corners, that these practices were realized. Each stage in life required a different set of ritual songs for a given generation of a particular corner.

Though ritual wedding music may have been known to all women, all women did not know it equally well. Some were leaders, to whom others looked when no one else could remember a line of text or which melody or ritual came next. The best local singers were expected to lead the ritual life of the village. Whenever possible, they were invited to weddings. Though not paid cash for their services, they were greatly admired for their skill and memory. In contrast to instrumental musicians, who had an ambiguous status bordering on the lowly, the best female singers' status was high, and they were respected individuals.

Women vocalists' artistry was still evident in the 1990s, when folkloric ensembles in Ukraine and most of Eastern Europe contained perhaps ten times more women than men; thus, this gender-specific role survived as a folkloric element. Village women's prominence as vocal musicians reinforced their social power. They controlled most aspects of village ritual and the social calendar—which in turn put them in a position to influence social activities and relationships.

Another context for singing dominated by women was *dosvitky*. Between late September and Lent,

virtually all girls from the age of ten until they became engaged had for their primary social activity the participation in *dosvitky*, for which they gathered nearly every evening (and some days) to sew, weave, embroider, make hemp rope, sing, and dance. The girls usually sang while they worked at the home of a widow or childless adult woman, whom the girls paid in labor, food, and firewood.

Singing Styles

Vocal music among peasants in Ukraine varied by region and genre. A succinct regionalization of vocal practice is hard to formulate because practices overlapped from region to region in ways that defy easy description and classification. As a result, the ethnographic and musicological literature about Ukraine includes no detailed study of regionalism in vocal music.

A few generalizations are possible, however. In most regions vocal production is with an open throat, with higher registers resonated in the head, especially in women, giving the sound a slightly nasal quality. This nasality is more pronounced in eastern regions and Polissia, and less pronounced in lowland Halychyna. Differences in vocal practice between eastern and western Ukraine provide the most obvious basis for regional differentiation. In eastern regions (including Chernihivshchyna, Kharkivshchyna, Poltavshchyna, and Sumshchyna) and many central regions (Cherkashchyna, most of Kyïvshchyna, eastern Polissia) two- and three-part harmony is more prevalent than in western Ukraine.

In most of western Ukraine, monophony is common for certain genres, notably the narrow-range wedding melodies known in most of lowland western Ukraine as *ladkana*; however, in some locales certain of these melodies are sung in two voices.

Village Instrumental Music and Musicians before Collectivization

In Ukraine, four types of instrumentalists existed before collectivization: part-time specialists, who played in regionally specific ensembles for weddings and various social events; specialists found only in certain regions; *kobzari* and *lirnyky*, blind peasant minstrels; and nonspecialists, who played for their own amusement or to accompany singing at informal social gatherings

Part-time Specialists

Part-time music specialists performed instrumental music for weddings, *dosvitky*, baptismal parties, and other evening gatherings, and in some regions in village inns. They were farmers who relied for their

Figure 1 A fiddle and a bass play an excerpt of a *kolomyka* from the Boikivshchyna region of the Carpathians. The bass part contains a rhythmic drone on two notes a fifth apart. After Khai 1989:8.

livelihood primarily on agricultural labor and home industries. Instrumental music was a part-time service or craft, and professionals rarely lived in villages. Instrumental musicians were not different from the local blacksmith, wheelwright, or miller, all of whom farmed the land and organized most of their family labor around agricultural activities. Most musical instruments were handmade by local masters who supplemented their agricultural income by selling them to local specialists or minstrels.

With few exceptions, the instruments of village specialists in Ukraine resemble those of most of Eastern Europe. In the 1800s, the violin or fiddle (*skrypka*) was widely made by village craftsmen, usually on the model of the classical violin. The bass (*bas*), about the size and shape of a violoncello, seems to have had three strings in most areas, with variant tunings (1–5–8 or 1–4–8 or 1–4–m7) that enabled the performer to play two sets of rhythmic drones (figure 1). In the twentieth century, this instrument was often replaced by a contrabass.

In Ukraine, Poland, and Belarus, peasants played the trapezoidal hammered dulcimer (*tsymbaly*). Not a typical Gypsy instrument as in Romania, Moldova, and much of Hungary since the early 1800s or before, it was widely distributed among Jews, and can be regarded as the main Eastern European Jewish instrument until about 1900. In village practice among Christians and Jews, it was small, usually with triple, quadruple, or quintuple courses of strings, and was played in a range of about three and one-half octaves. At the time of collectivization, it was still common in western Boikivshchyna and Hutsul'shchyna, but rarer elsewhere.

The single-headed frame drum (*bubon*) is characteristically played with a small wooden mallet. The double-headed field drum or side drum (*baraban*) has been known over all lowland Ukraine since at least the early twentieth century and in some regions perhaps from as early as the 1700s. Until the

mid-twentieth century, most village drums were made by local masters, but since then they have often been replaced with small bass drums purchased in stores. Since World War I, the bass drum has often had an attached metal cymbal. Since the 1930s or so, but especially after World War II, local musicians sometimes called the drum-cymbal combination *dzhaz* 'jazz'.

Specialists on these instruments performed for weddings, *dosvitky*, and other evening gatherings, and in some regions in the village inn. They performed in regional ensembles that differed over time and space. The following ensembles were some of the more common ones between 1890 and 1920: In lowland western Ukraine (Halychyna), one or two fiddles with a *bas*, or one or two fiddles and a *bubon* or *baraban*, with or without a *tsymbaly*; in the forests and swamps of northwestern Ukraine (western Polissia and parts of Volyn'), one or two fiddles and a *bubon*; in central and eastern Ukraine (Chernihivshchyna, Kharkivshchyna, Kyïvshchyna, eastern Podillia, and Poltavshchyna), a box fiddle and *bas* with or without *tsymbaly*, or one or two fiddles and a *bubon* or *baraban*. These ensembles had dozens of variations, including those with wind instruments, which were increasingly common from after World War I until the 1960s and 1970s, when the electrification of village ensembles began.

A free-reed, button accordion (*harmoniia*) entered peasant practice in Eastern Europe at the turn of the twentieth century and gained favor among villagers throughout the twentieth century. By the mid-twentieth century it was known in varieties widely dispersed throughout Europe, as was the piano accordion, a larger instrument. As ensemble instruments in Ukraine, accordions were at first used in groups that included a fiddle, *bubon* or *baraban*, and sometimes *tsymbaly*, but by the end of World War II the fiddle had declined in many regions, and the *tsymbaly* even more so. By the 1960s, the fiddle was still in decline, and the *tsymbaly* was nearly defunct in most lowland regions. In the 1990s, the most common village ensembles that were not electrified consisted of *harmoniia* or accordion or the Russian variant known as *baian*, with *bubon* or *baraban* and wind instruments. The fiddle remained in use in some locales, but was often played only by elderly musicians who were rarely requested to perform. In the 1990s, the most obvious regional exception to these changes was Hutsul'shchyna, where younger performers played fiddle and regional instruments. In virtually all regions, it was common in the 1980s and 1990s to find a mixture of electrified instruments (guitars and keyboards) and a standard percussion trap set used in combination with acoustic instruments from the village past.

Blind Minstrels

Ukraine's blind peasant minstrels were named, after the instruments they played, *kobzari* 'kobza players' and *lirnyky* 'lira players'. (The *kobza* was a plucked bowl lute; the *lira* was a standard European hurdy-gurdy.) Most blind minstrels had families and homes. They were not vagabonds or beggars, as they are frequently—but incorrectly—portrayed. They are better thought of as traveling musicians who worked on the road for part of the year and spent the other part at home. They traveled through villages and small towns, stopping and performing near or in markets, fairs, monasteries, and village houses. From singing and playing, they earned cash and foods. They took most of the money home and pooled it with other family income.

The main part of their repertory was not the heroic epic genre of Cossack Ukraine known as *dumy*, but Christian songs known in most regions as *psal'my*. Few minstrels knew more than two or three *dumy*, but they generally knew twelve, twenty, or more *psal'my*. They routinely performed satirical songs and dances. Until collectivization, they were apparently most often requested to perform, and earned the most money from, *psal'my*, which could be strophic or recitativelike, and treated themes such as "The Last Judgment," "Jesus, my great love," and "Lazarus."

The *kobza* (called *bandura* by some researchers), a plucked bowl lute, has a complex history made confusing by contradictory or unreliable information in the historical ethnographic literature. In the late 1800s, the strings normally numbered from eight to about thirty, and were tuned to produce different scales, but especially those with a minor third, raised fourth, and minor seventh. Most strings were made of sheep gut in the 1800s, until copper and steel strings replaced these. In the 1800s, most performers sounded the strings only in open position. Both

DISC
❶
TRACK
23

hands were used to pluck open strings. *Kobza* and *lira* were usually played solo. In one style, a performer sang and played simultaneously. In another, a performer sang unaccompanied, sounding the instrument only during interludes between sections of the text.

Village Music after Collectivization

Village musical life in Ukraine and research about that music changed in profound ways in the 1930s, when the Soviet Union under Joseph Stalin instituted collectivization of land and industrial production, mass deportations and executions in villages, purges of the intelligentsia (including music researchers), proscriptive and prescriptive administrative controls over music performance in villages, and administrative control over music-research methods, aims, and content. These changes, which have continued to influence village musical practice and music research in Ukraine, can be described as part of a "modernization program," the "destruction of the peasantry," the "repression of Ukrainian culture," or the "repression of traditional culture," but however characterized, they represent an important turning point in village musical life and its research. Evaluation of current music practice cannot be reasonably undertaken without considering the institutional changes in music practice early in the Soviet period.

In rural Ukraine, many musical activities associated with this turning point took place in each village "club," a building or even a house in which Soviet cultural activities were organized. At the club, many social activities—including plays, reading circles, a choir, *komsomol* 'communist youth' meetings, and the like—were organized.

The clubs were also the primary performance context of a then recently invented Soviet music culture, one distributed widely to the village population, often including an instrumental ensemble. Such ensembles had little to do with village musical life before collectivization. Their repertory, instruments, and performance practices were derived from mass activities designed, controlled, and distributed through a network of governmental institutions, far removed from village practice and civil society. In most villages, the directors of music ensembles were not native to the area. They were professionals trained in the special urban institutions of Narkomos (Narodnii Komisariiat Osvity, People's Commissariat of Education) and sent to villages to teach this mass musical activity, sometimes using music notation, in other cases teaching by rote. Especially common were instrumental ensembles of plucked lutes, homogeneous groups of a mandolin, a guitar, a balalaika, or a *bandura*, or combinations of these. Other ensembles consisted of so-called folk instruments (*narodni instrumenty*) with fiddles, end-blown flutes, a hammered dulcimer, drums of various kinds, and one or more of the plucked lutes mentioned above. They performed a mixed repertory, arranged or composed in styles consistent with state policy. Many of these ensembles became massive in size—"the bigger, the better," according to the prevailing ideology.

This repertory was controlled through "repertory lists" published in journals and provided to village music directors. Under threats of repression, state ensembles could not usually deviate far from these lists, which included stylized folk songs and dances, revolutionary marches, selections from the European classical music repertory, popular urban Soviet (mostly Russian) music, and arrangements accompanying hymns in praise of Lenin, Stalin, the Red Army, and war heroes and songs about tractors, collectivized agriculture, and the war against so-called class enemies. The state provided most of the components necessary for this music: the music institutions (village clubs), the social organization of the music (directors sent to villages to organize music activities, including music ensembles), the repertory (contained in the repertory lists), and special performance contexts. In villages, these contexts included gatherings sponsored or demanded by local party officials, Soviet holidays, and (somewhat later) elections. Some of these ensembles participated in vast competitions (*olimpiady* 'Olympics'), held periodically from 1931. Here, participants in Soviet music culture gathered locally, regionally, republic-wide, or even federally, to perform on stage for an audience and a jury of party activists, who gave awards to performers who played in a highly virtuosic style. Village music practices, not normally a featured part of the program, seem to have been considered primitive and therefore undesirable.

Not all instrumental music practices changed immediately with collectivization and the state's effort to alter music performance. In some regions, the instrumental practices of village wedding ensembles continued at least into the 1960s. In the mid-1990s, some instrumental ensembles not associated with state-funded or controlled collectives routinely performed at weddings a repertory that was at least in part regional or even local, as they had throughout the Soviet period. In some locales, these ensembles continued their grandparents' and great-grandparents' performance practices, mixing older local or regional genres, melodies, and dances with those of the 1950s, the 1960s, and the late twentieth century. This result particularly occurred in Hutsul'shchyna, Boikivshchyna, and parts of Bukovyna, as in various locales scattered throughout Ukraine.

—*Adapted from an article by William Noll*

Bibliography

Beregovsky, Moshe. 1982. *Old Jewish Folk Music: The Collections and Writings of Moshe Beregovski*. Edited by Mark Slobin. Philadelphia: University of Pennsylvania Press.

Hrytsa, Sofia. 1990. *Ukrainskaya pesennaya epika*. Moscow: Sovetskii Kompozitor.

———. *Muzychnyi fol'klor z Polissya v sapysach F. Kolessy ta K. Moshyns'koho*. Kyïv: Muzychna Ukraïna.

Humeniuk, Andrei I. 1967. *Ukraïns'ki narodni muzychni instrumenty*. Kyïv: Naukova Dumka.

———. 1972. *Instrumental'na muzyka*. Kyïv: Naukova Dumka.

Khai, Mykhailo. 1989. "Narodnoe muzykal'noe ispolnitel'stvo Boikovschchiny." Candidate's dissertation, LGI TMIK.

Kolberg, Oskar. 1964–. *Dzieła wszystkie* 35, *Przemyskie* [first published in 1891]; 36, *Wołyń* [first published in 1907]; 52, *Białoruś-Polesie*; 54, *Ruś Karpacka*; 56 1; *Ruś Czerwona*; 57: 2: 2, *Rus Czerwona*. Cracow: Polskie Wydawnistwo Muzyczne et al.

Kolessa, Filaret. [1910, 1913] 1929. *Narodni pisni z halyts'koï lemkivshchyny*. Etnohrafichnyi Zbirnyk, 39–40. L'viv: Naukove Tovarystvo im. Shevchenka.

———. [1910, 1913] 1969. *Melodiï ukraïns'kykh narodnykh dum*. Kyïv: Naukova Dumka.

Kvitka, Klyment. 1924. *Profesional'ni narodni spivtsi i muzykanty na Ukraïni*. Kyïv: Zbirnyk Istorychno-Filolohichnoho Viddilu Ukraïns'koï Akademii Nauk.

———. 1971. *K. V. Kvitka: Zbrannye trudy v dvukh tomakh*. Edited by Volodymyr Hoshovs'kyi [in Russian, Vladimir Goshovskii]. Moscow: Sovetskii kompozitor.

———. 1985–1986. *Vybrani statti*. 2 vols. Edited by Anatolyi Ivanyts'kyi. Kyïv: Muzychna Ukraïna.

Lysenko, Mykola. [1894] 1955. *Narodni muzychni instrumenty na Ukraïni*. Kyïv: Mystetstvo. First published in *Zoria* 1 and 4–10.

———. [1874] 1978. *Kharkterystyka muzychnykh osoblyvostei ukraïns'kykh dum i pisen' u vykonanni kobzaria Veresaia*. Kyïv: Muzychna Ukraïna. First published in *Sbornik Iugo-zapadnogo otdela russkogo geografischeskogo obshchestva* 1.

Noll, William. 1994. "Cultural Contact through Music Institutions in Ukrainian Lands, 1920–1948." In *Musical Cultures in Contact: Convergences and Collisions (Australian Studies in the History, Philosophy and Social Studies of Music)*, ed. Margaret Kartomi and Stephen Blum, 2:204–219. Sydney: Currency Press.

———. 1994. "The Social Role and Economic Status of Blind Peasant Minstrels in Ukraine." *Harvard Ukrainian Studies*. 17(1–2): 43–71.

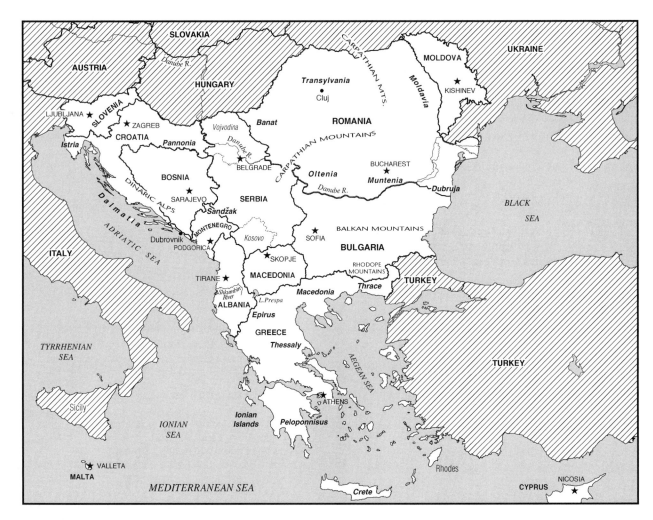

The Balkans

The Balkans

The Balkan Peninsula in southeastern Europe is home to an astonishing variety of ethnicities, languages, religions, regions, and musical styles. Despite this diversity, a number of common threads tie together Balkan musical life. Calendar and lifecycle rituals, especially weddings, are still vibrant occasions for musical performances. Narrow-range melodies, some sung in drone-based polyphonic styles, are sung in many rural areas. Traditional homemade instruments, especially flutes and bagpipes, figure prominently in musical life, often played in additive meters unusual in the rest of Europe.

A part of the Ottoman Empire for many centuries, the region features Middle Eastern instruments and performance genres, especially in towns. Gypsies (Roma) play an important role as professional musicians in all these cultures. Most of the region came under communist rule after World War II. These regimes supported staged, arranged, and choreographed versions of folklore as symbols of national identity and political ideology—a process that bolstered rural traditions threatened by industrialization and urbanization.

To offer a sense of the diverse musical cultures of the Balkans, we present articles on Romania, Bulgaria, and Greece.

Romania and Bulgaria ethnographic regions

Romania

Romania, with the Danube River to the south and the Black Sea to the east forming natural boundaries, has an area of nearly 238,000 square kilometers and a population of 22.3 million. Romanians trace their ancestry and language to the Romans, though their ethnic origins include a mixture of peoples. Romanians form the majority of the population at 89 percent; other ethnic groups include Hungarians, Germans, Ukranians, Serbs, Croats, and Roma (Gypsies). About 86 percent of Romanian citizens belong to the Romanian Orthodox Church; the rest are Roman Catholics (Uniate) or Protestants, or have no religious affiliation. Widespread industrialization and urbanization of a previously rural, agricultural economy and way of life began only after World War II.

Ancient Romania was inhabited by the Dacians, a northern branch of the Thracian tribes. The Roman conquest, of C.E. 105–106, gave way to Goth, Hun, Avar, Slav, Bulgar, and Hungarian invaders, from the fourth to the tenth centuries. The feudal principalities of Transylvania, Moldavia, and Wallachia (which included present-day Oltenia and Muntenia) emerged in the eleventh through the fifteenth centuries. In the first half of the sixteenth century, they became vassal states of the Ottoman Empire. The Austro-Hungarian Empire annexed Transylvania in 1699. Moldavia and Wallachia united under a single prince in 1859, adopted the name *Romania* in 1862, and achieved independence from the Ottomans in 1878. With the defeat of the Austro-Hungarian Empire in 1918, Banat, Bucovina, and Transylvania united with Romania.

Romania's royal sovereignty, established in 1881, was abolished in 1946, and a Romanian Peoples Republic was proclaimed, emphasizing industrialization, the formation of agricultural cooperatives, education, and culture. The communist era ended violently in December 1989.

Contexts for Music

Most performances of Romanian folk music, song, and dance are directly tied to rituals and other traditional occasions: winter customs (Christmas and New Year), agrarian rites and feasts (planting and harvesting), and social and ritual events (weddings, burials, work parties). While some have historical roots in antiquity, many have lost their initial magical meanings and today are performed primarily for spectacle.

Winter Rituals

Since Roman times, the winter solstice has been celebrated with ritual songs, masked dancers, and ritual greetings. Caroling (*colinde*), the most important winter custom, begins on Christmas Eve or the day before, and lasts until Epiphany. Boys, girls, teens, and adults, six to twelve in number, go from house to house, singing in unison or occasionally accompanied by instruments. Their songs express hope for prosperity, good crops, health, and happiness; the hosts, in turn, treat the carolers with hospitality, gifts, food, and drinks. Sometimes the festivities conclude with dances involving hosts and singers.

On New Year's Day or New Year's Eve, children or young men go through the village carrying a colorfully decorated plough. Accompanied by a friction drum (*buhai*), a shepherd's flute, or other instruments playing nonmetrical melodies, they deliver long recitations depicting fieldwork. Jokes, shouts, the crack of whips, and bells punctuate the text and the instrumental tunes. Variants of this custom survive in Transylvania, Moldavia, and Maramureş.

Masked dancing recalling Dionysian festivals occurs during winter feasts. Among the most remarkable are *capra* 'goat', found in Transylvania, Maramureş, Bucovina, Moldavia, and Muntenia; and *ursul* 'the bear' and *calul* or *caiuti* 'hobby horses', found in north-central Moldavia and Bucovina. Some instrumental melodies are unique to these rituals, and musical instruments such as drums, bells, friction drums, cog rattles, alphorns, and horns add to the uproar with which the new year is greeted. During the communist era, festivals of masked dances were organized in Hunedoara, Maramureş, Bucovina, and Moldavia, and during the post-communist era, they are still flourishing (figure 1).

Spring and Summer Rituals

Spring and summer rituals relate to agriculture and sheepherding. The beginning of the agricultural and pastoral seasons are often marked by feasts involving the entire community. In Maramureş, the first farmer to plough his fields is honored in a festive ceremony, *plugarul* 'the ploughman'. In Banat, Transylvania,

Figure 1 A parade of winter customs and rituals in Sighetu Marmaţiei, Maramureş, 2006.
Photo by Valeriu Apan.

and Maramureş, the taking of sheep to mountain pasturage is also ritually celebrated. Requests for rain are sung or chanted by children, the most important being *paparuda* 'raincaller' and *scaloian*.

Harvest rituals include *drăgaica* in Muntenia, where on 24 June (St. John's Day) girls between eleven and fifteen years old perform a ritual song in asymmetrical meter, a circle dance (*hora*), or a suite of dances. In Transylvania, *cununa* 'the wreath' has survived as a significant traditional feast at the end of the harvest. It unfolds in several stages: the harvester's departure, making a wreath, carrying and watering the wreath, and a communal feast with dancing and music. A slow, ornamented, lyrical song accompanies the solemn procession. Some of the songs retain mythological elements, such as the dispute between the sun's sister and the wind's sister over their brothers' qualities.

The *căluşul* 'little horse', a ritual dance performed at Whitsuntide (the fifth week after Easter) to create fecundity, or to heal or prevent illness, is practiced in Oltenia, Mutenia, and parts of Dobruja. The *căluşari*, a group of seven, nine, or eleven young men, dance intricate virtuosic figures in a circular promenade to the accompaniment of vigorous dance-music played on one or two violins and sometimes other instruments (figure 2).

Lifecycle Rituals
In the human lifecycle, marriage and death are marked by the most elaborate rituals and musical expressions.

The most important moments in the wedding ritual, each accompanied by specific songs or instrumental tunes are *cununa* 'the wreath', *steagul* 'the flag', *îmbrăcatul* 'the dressing of the bride', *iertările* 'the forgiveness', *cununia* 'the church ceremony', and *masa mare* 'the grand feast'. Wedding music is vocal (songs dedicated to the bride, groom, mother-in-law, godfather, godmother, and so on) and instrumental (dances, marches, and music for the feast). Traditional wedding melodies are sung by the guests, who are accompanied by paid instrumentalists and, in some areas, professional folksingers.

Burial rituals employ two main categories of music: ceremonial songs (*cîntece ceremonale*), found in northern Oltenia, Banat, and some areas of

Figure 2 Dancers (*căluşari*) perform the spring healing ritual (*căluşul*), Oltenia.
From the collection of Valeriu Apan.

Transylvania; and laments (*bocete*), practiced everywhere. In both categories, the singers or lamenters evoke the deceased's momentum toward transition, recall the deceased's life, and express relatives' and acquaintances' grief. The ceremonial songs, sung by women not closely related to the deceased but hired for this purpose, are performed in unison or antiphonally with narrow-range, slow-moving melodies. Ceremonial songs include "*Cîntecul Zorilor*" ('Dawn Song'), sung at sunrise as an announcement of the death; and songs accompanying each part of the ritual such as "*Al Drumului*" ('On the Road') and "*Al Gropii*" ('At the Grave'). The laments are improvised narratives sung by female relations or friends of the deceased. They begin at the moment of death, continue through the burial, and reappear at commemorative dates after the burial. Their poetry combines elements from the deceased's life and the sentiments of those left to mourn. The solo singing (occasionally, group singing) is mingled with weeping, usually at the cadence, and in Bucovina may be accompanied by the shepherd's flute. The alphorn (*bucium*) is often used for burial services, especially when the deceased is a young person or a shepherd.

Dances

The basic Romanian dances—*hora* (a circle dance) and *sîrba* (a line dance)—are found, with variations, in most of the country. Each region also has unique dances.

Polyrhythm, resulting from an overlapping of music, steps, shouted verses, calls, interjections, cries, whistles, and clapping, is quite common. Some dance tunes have fixed forms comprising two or three sections; others involve the varied repetition of one or a few motifs. Meters are binary or asymmetrical; triple meter is largely absent. Instrumental accompanists vary from soloists (almost always men) to small bands using a variety of instruments: violin, duct flutes (*fluiere*), panpipe (*nai*), *taragot* (a wooden conical-bore, single-reed wind instrument), cimbalom, accordion, guitar, and bass.

Vocal Genres

The most prominent vocal genres performed during rituals and social occasions are the *doina*—improvised lyrical song—and the *cîntec*, strophic song.

Doina

Unique to Romania, the *doina* is found throughout the country under various names: "long song" (*hora lunga*), "song of the forest," and "song of sadness."

Doina may be vocal or instrumental, and are performed by men and women, solo or with accompaniment. Their texts relate to themes of love, nature, longing, sorrow, and grief. Lullabies (*cîntece de leagăn*) are sung to *doina* tunes. Their texts concern love, nature, longing, sorrow, and grief. The musical form is freely improvised, but the textual meter is octosyllabic, except when extended by *noduri* (glottal sounds), though this is very rare.

Three types of *doina* may be distinguished. The first type, found in Maramureş, Năsăud, Bucovina, and northern Oltenia, has a narrow melodic range, and so most scholars presume it to be the oldest. The melodic line is typically diatonic major, with the fourth degree raised or natural. Singers begin with an introductory recitative, which is succeeded by an improvisatory section involving repeated ornamental melodic variations. The concluding formula is usually a recitative on the tonic.

The second type is found in the previously mentioned zones and some parts of Transylvania, Muntenia, and Moldavia. *Doina* of these types have a wider melodic range within a simple, less ornamented structure.

The third type, *de dragoste* 'of love', appears much newer, possibly of professional minstrel origins, and is found in the southern part of the country. *Lăutari* (professional musicians, many of them Roma) perform it during social occasions with romantic and sometimes erotic texts. Musicians and singers show off their expressive abilities in wide-ranging, highly ornamented, rubato melodies (figure 3).

Cîntece (*Strophic Songs*)

Strophic songs are used as ceremonial songs in wedding and funeral rituals and fertility rites, and serve as laments, epic songs, and lullabies. *Cîntece* have a regular strophic form with two to seven melodic lines and vary regionally in structure and style. Singers modify the basic structure with each repetition: they may repeat or omit a melodic line and vary the pitches and rhythms. Songs use major and minor modes and various approaches to rhythm. The poetry touches on a wide range of emotions and is organized as a succession of octosyllabic (or sometimes hexasyllabic) lines, with or without stanzaic organizational principles.

Instrumental Music

Romanian instrumental music perhaps has its origins as the pastime of shepherds, though song and dance accompaniments are its other important functions.

Figure 3 A *doina* of love (*doina de dragoste*) from Muntenia, sung, after the opening descending melisma, in a spoken (parlando) rhythm. The curved lines over a note indicate a slight shortening of the duration as a way to capture the freedom in the rhythm. After Oprea and Agapie 1983:317.

Shepherds' Music

Shepherds' instruments include the *bucium* 'alphorn' and the *tilinca* (an end-blown flute, without a duct or holes for fingering), which produce notes based on overblowing the harmonic series. The richness of melodies depends on the player's skill. Shepherds also play widely various duct flutes (*fluier, caval*).

Some shepherds' melodies are variants of *doina* tunes and have long phrases and wide ranges. Others consist of repeated melodic motifs. Shepherds play numerous signaling melodies on the alphorn to gather sheep to the fold and prepare them for the trip to summer pasturage or winter homes.

A particularly elaborate item in the shepherd's repertoire is "*Mioritsa*," an instrumental rendition of a tale about a shepherd losing his flock. Usually played on the *fluier*, it has many variants around the country. The piece portrays a shepherd's feelings while he searches for his flock in a series of episodes: a sad song, usually a *doina*; a lively melody, typically a dance tune; another sad song, the initial or another selection; and a lively melody. In some areas, the tale is amplified with episodes explained through recitation and illustrated by music.

Vocal-instrumental Music

Romania's epic genre, *balade* ('ballads', also called *cîntece batrinsti* 'oldtime songs'), flourished in the feudal period between the sixteenth and nineteenth centuries. Most describe the conflicts, manners, and aspirations at the that time, and though some are still performed in many parts of the country, they are gradually being replaced by other genres.

In the past, peasant-bards sang ballads at different social occasions and accompanied themselves on the shepherd's flute, bagpipe, or other instrument. In contemporary times, professional singers, accompanied by violin or a small ensemble of two violins, *cobza*, *ţambal* (cimbalom), and bass, sing them at weddings or other social gatherings. The musicians play a prelude, interludes, and a postlude and occasionally double the voice. The instrumental accompaniment consists of a continuous rhythmic figuration of the basic chords. The musicians conclude with a lively instrumental dance piece. The sung parts are interwoven with the instrumental solos and passages of spoken narrative. The performers may use mimicry and other dramatic effects to stress actions recounted in the text. The performance is free and improvisatory. The same ballad will be condensed or amplified according to the listeners' interest and the performers' disposition.

Musical Instruments

In Romania today, many folk instruments continue to be played, though the accordion, the clarinet, and the guitar are more and more replacing the traditional accompanying instruments.

Percussion Instruments (Idiophones)

Two idiophones that can vary their pitches include the mouth harp (*drîmba*) and bells (*clopote* and *zurgălăi*), cast in many sizes and used in New Year's ceremonies and weddings (decorating the nuptial banner) and hung around the necks of cattle and sheep as signal devices. The *toaca*, a wooden plank or metal plate struck with one or two wooden hammers, produces different percussive pitches depending on where it is hit. Monks and nuns use it in monasteries to announce Mass and other offices, and children play it during Lent in Oltenia, Banat, and Maramureş.

Drums (Membranophones)

Drums are widespread and are used most often in rituals. They include the friction drum (*buhai*; figure 4); various one-headed frame drums (*dairea*, *dara*, *vuvă*), about 25 centimeters in diameter (Oltenia and Muntenia), and *doba*, 80 centimeters in diameter (Moldavia); and double-headed drums (*tobe*, *dube*), with a diameter between 20 and 25 centimeters (Hunedoara, Banat, Bihor, and Arad). In some parts of the country, a snare drum (*darabana*) and a bass drum (*toba mare*), borrowed from military bands and jazz bands, and a cymbal are used alongside other instruments to accompany dancing.

Stringed Instruments (Chordophones)

Stringed instruments, especially important to professional musicians, include the *cobza* (a short-necked plucked lute), the *ţambal* or cimbalom (a trapezoidal hammered dulcimer), and the violin.

The *cobza*, a pear-shaped, bent-necked lute resembling the Middle Eastern *ʿūd*, is probably the oldest stringed instrument in Romania (figure 5). Professional musicians use it to accompany melody instruments. It has eight to twelve gut or metal strings arranged in four courses of two or three strings each. Common tuning follows a pattern of fifths and fourths. Once widespread, it has largely been replaced by the guitar and the cimbalom.

The *ţambal* is used as an accompaniment and a solo instrument. It was first mentioned in Romania in 1546. Originally played in the castles of the nobility,

Figure 4 Boys from Moldavia play the friction drum (*buhai*).
From the collection of Valeriu Apan.

Figure 5 Young musicians from Moldavia play a lute (*cobza*), a panpipe (*nai*), an accordion, and other instruments.
From the collection of Valeriu Apan.

it passed into the hands of professional, mainly Roma, folk musicians and was common in the nineteenth century. These zithers are tuned in three ways: "Romanian" (chromatic succession), "Hungarian" (diatonic succession), and "transport" (chromatic-diatonic succession). The strings are struck with two mallets, wrapped in cloth or cotton to soften the sound.

The violin (*viora*), the mainstay of professional musicians since the 1700s, is found all over the country, sometimes modified, as in Vrancea, where up to eight sympathetic strings are added to the four that play the melody. Though the typical tuning in fifths has become standard, more than thirty *scordaturas* (tuning variations) ease the playing of certain fast dance melodies or the obtaining of special sound effects.

Wind Instruments (Aerophones)

Wind instruments were the mainstay of the rural, peasant tradition. The Carpathian Mountains still echo with the powerful sound of the alphorn (*bucium*), an ancient pastoral instrument made of wood or (in northern Romania) metal. Functioning primarily as a signaling instrument and in funeral processions, alphorns are blown in the manner of trumpets and can produce harmonics from the third to the sixteenth.

Flutes are the most common folk instruments: researchers have identified seventeen types. The most widespread is the *fluier*, a variously sized six-holed duct flute, usually made of wood. The scale is diatonic, with a range of almost three octaves. Chromatic tones can be obtained by half covering the holes or using cross fingerings. It is played solo and in orchestras.

The most famous of all Romanian flutes, however, is the *nai* (figure 5), a type of panpipe that has existed in Romania since ancient times. The standard *nai* consists of a slightly concave row of twenty cane, bamboo, or wood pipes of different lengths and diameters, arranged according to size in the shape of a wing. Sound is made by blowing across each pipe separately, enabling the musician to play a diatonic scale from b^1 to g^4 with f♯s. Chromatic pitches are produced by tilting the instrument. Since the 1960s, the lower register has been expanded by adding up to seven more pipes. The *nai* is employed in a great variety of musical genres, from free-form melodies to the most intricate dances. Professional musicians play it solo or in an orchestra.

The most important reed instrument, a bagpipe known as *cimpoi*, was once widespread and played at weddings, but has now been largely replaced by other instruments. It is made of a large goatskin bag, equipped with two wooden pipes—fitted with cane or reeds—and a blowpipe. The drone pipe is usually made of three sections without holes for fingering, but the melody pipe has five to eight holes. The scale of the instrument is usually diatonic, with a range of one octave. Dance melodies make up the bulk of its repertoire.

The *taragot*, a keyed, conical-bore instrument with clarinet mouthpiece and reed played in Banat and Transylvania, is an idealization of an older double-reed *zurna* instrument, invented at the end of the nineteenth century. It is well suited to *doina*, though it is played for fast dance melodies with astonishing virtuosity.

Performance Practice

Most Romanian folk music is performed monophonically, but polyphony and harmony occur in some vocal, instrumental, or vocal-instrumental group performances. These polyphonic and harmonic forms, which result from superimposed melodic lines or a drone or the use of chords, are typically rudimentary when played by villagers and more developed in professionals' practice. In the vocal genres, antiphonal performance results in rudimentary forms of heterophony and polyphony.

In instrumental and vocal-instrumental performance, instrumental harmony as accompaniment appears in various forms and depends on the instruments used for accompaniment, the musical region, the genre, and the musicians' skill. For example, the

DISC
1
TRACK
24

cobza, the *chitara* (guitar), and the *zongora* (the guitar of Maramureş) play simple harmonic forms. *Cobza* players strum *ţiituri* 'rhythmic formulas', differentiated and named after dance type and musical form (fixed or free) and using bichords (fifths and fourths) and major and minor triads (tonic, dominant, and subdominant).

Urban musicians have adopted traditional melodic-rhythmic formulas, but use a harmonic language strongly influenced by Western harmony. Concert bands and orchestras employ a more compact, complex, and richer harmonic style than is used in traditional folk ensembles—a result of their formal training. Their style, heard in recordings and broadcasts, has influenced many village musicians around the country.

Musical Life in the Communist Period

During the communist period, the government highly valued folk music and folk arts as symbols of national identity. "Cultural houses" and other organizations popularized folk music and dance within the country and abroad. Suites, rhapsodies, symphonic dances, ballets, and choral pieces inspired by folk-song melodies and folk-instrument sonorities were especially popular. Operas drew their texts from national epics, ballads, and other folk genres.

From 1976 to 1989, new emphasis was placed on the highly politicized National Festival of Political Education and Socialist Culture, which included unending tributes to Nicolae Ceaucescu, the national and Communist Party leader. These festivals were aimed at constructing an idealized image of village life. Folk-music performance became static and artificial, as if preserved in a museum.

During the last years of the communist regime, when the national TV channels broadcast only two hours per evening, the only cultural treat that continued to be offered was a weekly folk-music program. Such official support in fact alienated many people from traditional culture and folk music, which they came to hate more and more. During the same period, a dynamic, underground folk-music culture emerged in rural and urban areas, ignored by scholars, officials, and the state media. This music was an amalgam of Serbian-influenced "Banat music," Turkish music (by way of Serbia), and some Roma-influenced music, and was disseminated via privately recorded cassettes.

—*Adapted from an article by Valeriu Apan*

Bibliography

Alexandru, Tiberiu. 1980. *Romanian Folk Music*. Bucharest: Musical Publishing House.

Apan, Valeriu. 1994. "The Panpipe (*Nai*) in Contemporary Romanian Folk Music." Ph.D. dissertation, University of California, Los Angeles.

Bartók, Béla. 1967–1975. *Romanian Folk Music*. Edited by Benjamin Suchoff. The Hague: Mouton.

Cosma, Viorel. 1982. *A Concise History of Romanian Music*. Bucharest: Editura Ştiinţifică şi Enciclopedică.

Kligman, Gail. 1981. *Căluş: Symbolic Transformation in Romanian Ritual*. Chicago: University of Chicago Press.

——. 1988. *The Wedding of the Dead: Ritual Poetics and Popular Culture in Transylvania*. Berkeley: University of California Press.

Oprea, Gheorghe, and Larisa Agapie. 1983. *Folclor Muzical Românesc* (Romanian musical folklore). Bucharest: Editura Didactică şi Pedagogică.

Pennington, Anne E. 1985. *Music in Medieval Moldavia*. Bucharest: Editura Muzicală.

Popescu-Judetz, Eugenia. 1979. *Sixty Folk Dances of Romania*. Pittsburgh: Tamburitzans, Institute of Folk Arts, Duquesne University.

Bulgaria

Though small, economically poor, and historically isolated, Bulgaria has produced a musical tradition that has won international respect for its traditional music and brilliant singers. In classical music, Bulgarian singers, including Nikolai Ghiaurov (1929–2004), Boris Christov (1914–1993), Raina Kabaivanska (b. 1934), and Ghena Dimitrova (1941–2005), have achieved fame in the world's finest opera houses. Women's, children's, and mixed choirs routinely win international choral competitions, such as the International Eistedfodd in Llangollen, Wales. Béla Bartók was only the most prominent of many outsiders to notice Bulgaria's vivid asymmetrical rhythms. In the 1960s, the colorful dancing, singing, and instrumental music of the National Ensemble for Folk Song and Dance, commonly known as the Philip Kutev Ensemble, made a vivid impression in Western Europe and North America, with its arrangements of folk songs sung with a chest-voice intensity by village singers trained to perform in three- and four-part harmony.

Such international recognition and success represent the tip of an iceberg of lively, rich, musical practice within a country of 7.3 million people and 110,994 square kilometers in southeastern Europe. [For maps that include Bulgaria, see the ones at the beginning of the Balkans subsection and at the beginning of ROMANIA.]

Bulgaria has absorbed various cultural influences over its history. Slavic settlers from the north displaced the Thraco-Illyrians in the 500s. In the 600s, the Bulgars, a tribe of military horsemen from Central Asia, assumed political control of the local Slav agriculturalists, but left few traces besides their name and the large states they established in the Middle Ages to battle the Byzantine Empire. Two Bulgarian Empires dominated large parts of the Balkans for much of the period from 800 to 1385, when the Ottoman Turks conquered the Bulgarian lands. Bulgarian culture was preserved mainly in oral village traditions until the 1800s, when a "national renaissance" began. Bulgaria reemerged politically as an independent principality in 1878 and an independent kingdom in 1908, under German and Austrian political and cultural influence. From 1944 to 1989—a period characterized by active state support of music and art and a move away from a primarily agriculture-based economy to an urban, industrialized one—Bulgaria was ruled by the Communist Party as one of the Soviet Union's most loyal allies. Since 1989, Bulgaria has become a multi-party democracy, and state support of the arts has declined.

Musical Style

Some broad points can be made about Bulgarian village musical style—though it should be remembered that regional variation confounds nearly every generalization. Strophic songs, sung metrically or nonmetrically, provide the basis for vocal performance and instrumental music. Instrumental dance tunes often begin with song tunes before launching into instrumental variations, and nonmetrical instrumental tunes are usually improvisations based on nonmetrical song tunes.

Most metrical songs and tunes originally accompanied dancing and were sung antiphonally by two pairs of singers near the head of the dance line. Dance-songs typically consist of two phrases of four measures each, structured AA, AA^1, or AB. Songs with pairs of three-, five-, and six-measure phrases are common, as are pairs of unequal-length phrases. Each phrase is typically set to an eight-syllable line of text, but six- and ten-syllable lines are also common. Sometimes refrains replace text, or are added at the end, unbalancing the symmetrical structure and requiring one or more measures of melodic material. The commonest meter is duple and transcribed in 2/4 time. The melodic range is usually narrow, extending to a fifth above and a second below the tonic. Major, minor, and Phrygian diatonic tetrachords are common, as are ones with augmented seconds. Some tunes include major and minor thirds or major and minor seconds and various ornaments are typically applied to the basic tune.

Although duple meter provides the metrical foundation for most songs and dances in Bulgaria, the culture is justly famous for its so-called asymmetrical, additive, unequal-part, *aksak* (Turkish for "limping") meters, which add variety to the music. These meters, performed at fast tempos, combine or add groups of two and three pulses to form meters of five, seven, nine, and eleven pulses, grouped into "beats" of unequal length. The typical Bulgarian dance form, generically called *horo*, consists of an open or closed circle of dancers holding hands.

In addition to metrical dance tunes, the Bulgarian repertoire of song and instrumental music consists of many nonmetrical songs typically sung while seated at wedding-banquet tables, at spinning bees, when guests gather in the home, or while resting from work in the fields. Formal principles of metrical songs include the use of two phrases of similar length, modal variety, narrow range, and ornamentation. These songs allow for each of these features to be expanded in some way—for example, to three-phrase structures, slightly wider melodic ranges up to an octave and occasionally even more, correspondingly greater modal possibilities, and even richer ornamentation, especially on long-held notes. Though song performances are constrained by the demands of the text, instrumentalists often use song tunes as the basis for extended improvisations.

Musical Instruments

Traditional instruments, once made primarily by the players (each using rules of thumb of his own invention), answered to few general rules or notions of absolute pitch, and varied significantly from region to region. During the socialist period, the professionalization of folk music, the creation of ensembles, and a growing sense of a national style led to an increasing standardization. A small set of instruments, basic to the new folk orchestra (*narodni orkestri*) and constructed to an absolute pitch standard, strive to play a tempered scale and are widely distributed in the country.

Traditionally, only men and boys played musical instruments. One of the first opportunities to learn to play was while herding cows, sheep, goats, and pigs in pastures outside villages. Boys' and shepherds' typical instruments were homemade flutes: the *duduk*, a short, end-blown whistle-flute with six finger holes; and the *svirka*, a short, end-blown, fippleless flute with six finger holes and perhaps a thumb hole. Also known was the *lokarina*, a clay, globular flute with eight finger holes and two thumb holes. All three flutes play diatonic melodies over a two-octave range.

The most advanced instrument in the flute category is the *kaval*, now standardized as a national instrument—a long, end-blown, rim-blown flute with seven finger holes and a thumbhole. The finger holes are placed to produce a chromatic scale over three or more octaves, each register with a distinctive timbre. Many Bulgarians regard the *kaval*, with its wide range, honey tone, and rich ornamentation, to be the most expressive Bulgarian folk instrument.

The most widespread reed instrument is the bagpipe (*gajda*; figure 1), a favorite instrument at

Figure 1 The *gajda* demonstrated by ethnomusicologist Alan Thrasher.
Photo by Terry E. Miller.

outdoor celebrations, like weddings, fairs, and village dances because of its loud sound. The bag consists of a whole goatskin. Wooden stocks, tied into the front-leg and neck holes, receive the melody pipe, drone pipe, and blowpipe. The melody pipe, with a single reed, has seven finger holes and a thumbhole and a range of a major ninth, and can play chromatically with cross-fingerings. In the southwestern region, the *zurna* (a double-reed, conical-bore oboe) is played by Rom musicians.

The main bowed-stringed instrument is the *gŭdulka*, a pear-shaped lute with three or four metal playing strings, played with a horsehair bow. The *gŭdulka* was used to accompany dancing and singing, in some cases with the musician playing and singing simultaneously. It was a favorite of blind beggars, and is still used by Rom beggars with trained bears or monkeys on chains. The modern *gŭdulka* has about eight sympathetic strings lying underneath the playing strings and tuned to important notes in the scale, creating an instrument with an unusually loud, resonant, full-toned quality.

The traditional plucked stringed instrument is the long-necked lute (*tambura*). Undoubtedly a local descendant of the Turkish *saz*, it was originally popular where Turkish and Muslim influence was strongest and was used mainly to accompany male singing. The oldest forms were made from a hollowed-out, pear- and bowl-shaped piece of wood, covered with a wooden face with a few small holes for resonance. The instrument typically had four strings arranged in two double courses, tuned a fourth or a fifth apart. Using a plectrum, the player played the melody on one course and sounded a drone on the open string.

The most common drum, *tŭpan* (barrel-shaped, double-headed drum), was the specialty of Romani (Gypsy) musicians. Slung over the left shoulder and struck with a hefty stick on one head and a thin wand on the other, it was traditionally most popular in the southeastern and southwestern parts of the country, where it accompanied bagpipes and oboes at outdoor celebrations. During the socialist period, it became a fixture in folk orchestras. Two other drums, the vase-shaped, single-headed *darabuka* and the single-headed frame drum (*daire*), are played mainly by Turkish and Romani minorities.

Village music began to change after 1878, as men served in the military and learned to play instruments in army brass bands. Small ensembles with clarinet, trumpet, trombone, baritone horns, and *tŭpan* with an added cymbal became popular at village and town weddings and fairs in many parts of the country, where they competed with and sometimes replaced traditional instruments. Later, the accordion and violin were added to ensembles, whose instrumentation has never been standardized. In all areas of the country, accordion and clarinet became extremely popular, and many fine virtuosi developed to play them.

Songtexts

Songtexts are constructed of a series of lines (abcde . . .), each with the same number of syllables, but no additional verse structure, rhyme, or poetic rhythm. In a typical performance of a two-phrase song, the second line of text in a verse often becomes the first line of the next verse, yielding the performed structure ab bc cd de . . . The most common number of syllables per line is eight, but songs with lines of six, seven, and ten syllables are typical. The texts are constructed using the same formulaic principles detailed for Serbo-Croatian epic ballads in Albert

Lord's *Singer of Tales* (1960). Common formulas (cliché-like word clusters) recur in every song for bodily attributes (black eyes, white face, thin figure) and objects in the environment (cold water, white rock, well-fed horse). Though communal rather than solo singing and shorter-than-epic texts probably reduces the amount of variation, each performance varies according to the memory of the singers and the circumstances in which they sing. In many contemporary contexts, and especially on recordings, only a portion of the text is sung; listeners in principle know what happened or are content to guess.

The language used in song texts varies slightly according to regional dialects, but the contents of the songs are remarkably consistent across the country. They are usually told by a narrator in the third person and consist in large part of dialogue between a mother and her son or daughter, two lovers, a Turk and a Bulgarian, a mother-in-law and daughter-in-law, or a circle of friends. Some ritual songs and work songs simply describe the action they accompany (the bride goes to church with her family, the sun casts no shadow at noon, we are entering the host's home). Most are lyrical songs about human relationships or historical songs detailing the unhappiness caused by war or oppression. Rather than monologues pouring out inner feelings, the third-person, dialogic nature of the texts tends to leave feelings to be inferred or imputed empathetically, as situations are described or opinions stated rather matter-of-factly. One of the most common evocative techniques, usually at the beginning of a song, invokes an image from nature and then switches to a person, implicitly linking his or her feelings to something in nature: "the Vardar River [of Macedonia] flows with mud" signals the emotional turmoil of a bride at a wedding; "a thick fog fell" represents the feeling of the bride's parents as the groom's family arrives to take their daughter; "the sun shone in the meadow" turns out to be the joyful sighting of a beautiful girl. Some songs depict joking relations between lovers and happy unions between attractive couples (often he is a good musician, and she is a good singer or dancer), but most detail the trials and tribulations of life: interference from parents, infidelity and betrayal, untimely sickness, death, or even murder, unhappy family relations caused by marriage and remarriage, and suffering during the five hundred years under Ottoman Turkish occupation.

Traditional Contexts for Music

In every region and village of the country, musical life once moved to the larger rhythms of the seasons and their associated work. Many songs, instrumental tunes, and dances could be performed at any time or "whenever guests gathered together," but a substantial portion of the repertoire consisted of a lengthy music-and-song cycle performed over the course of a year, each piece performed only during the appropriate period or ritual. Not every ritual occurred in every region, but some of the most widespread ones are described here.

Calendric Rituals

The most important winter ritual is *koleda*, a still-performed Christmas or New Year's caroling ritual, in which boys go from house to house singing songs and saying a blessing for the family's health, fertility, and happiness in the new year. The *koledari* (carolers) know twenty or more songs, each addressed to a specific class of person in the household: a land-owner, his wife, an eligible bachelor, a young girl, a pregnant woman, a new baby. The songs often have refrains (*koledo le*), and many are in asymmetric meters.

The Saturday before Palm Sunday, called *lazarovden* (Lazar's Day), featured young girls caroling from house to house with a set of lyrical love songs and wearing, in the Shop region, elaborate headdresses. A special dance, often in 7/8 and performed by four girls arranged in a square pattern, was performed in each yard. In exchange for the girls' good wishes, performers received gifts symbolizing fertility, such as flour and eggs. Easter, called Velikden (Great Day), ended Lent and was celebrated with three days of dancing in the village square to a set of love songs reserved for the occasion.

The heavy fieldwork of summer was relieved by frequent Sunday saint's day celebrations. People and musicians gathered to visit friends and relatives, show off musical and dance skills in the village square, and perhaps attend a wrestling match accompanied by music on *tŭpan* with bagpipes (*gaidi*) or double-reeds (*zurni*). The huge repertoire of instrumental dance-music and summer dance-songs testifies to the importance of summer saints' days as a performance context.

Fieldwork involving hoeing and harvesting was once accompanied by songs, sung nonmetrically solo or in pairs of singers in antiphony while bent over at work, during rest periods, and on the way to and from the fields. A few texts contain mythical themes, anthropomorphizing the relations between the sun, the moon, and stars.

In autumn, unmarried girls gathered at a neighbor's house for communal handwork, accompanied by *sedyanka* songs that treat historical and love themes and are often nonmetrical, with the largest ranges and most extended forms in the repertoire. These gatherings attracted bachelors, some with musical instruments, to an evening of flirting and dancing. The girls tease one another about boyfriends in short *pripevki*, dancelike songs.

Lifecycle Rituals

The wedding cycle (*svatba*), in addition to the church ceremony and celebratory feasting, was a kind of folk drama evoked in song, with all the emotions associated with transferring the bride from her home to her groom's family's home with each ritual event accompanied by instrumental music, traditionally on bagpipes and now by a small band of Western or traditional instruments. The songs—sung by unmarried female relatives or close female friends of the bride while braiding her hair and veiling her as she bids farewell to her mother on the way to the church—describe the bride's feelings, especially her fears, as she bids her youth, family, and friends good-bye, and the joy of her new family as they accept her. The first stages of the wedding—the shaving of the groom, the procession of the groom's party to the bride's house, and the presentation of the veiled bride—are accompanied by nonmetrical instrumental tunes (*svirni*); then, after "taking" the bride, the youth of the wedding party dance a lively *rŭchenitsa* (line or solo dance in 7/16) during the procession to the church and later to the groom's house. Nonmetrical *sedyanka* songs with texts about engagements and marriages were sung at the wedding banquet.

Besides weddings, the only other lifecycle rituals are those associated with births and deaths, and in Bulgaria these are rarely accompanied by music or song per se, but with genres possessing some musical characteristics, particularly the lament (*oplakvane*), which incorporate non-metrical recitative-like melodies; lullabies take the form of sing-song recitations. Laments are performed by close female relatives of the deceased.

Contemporary Contexts and Performance Practices

After 1944, the economic, social, and educational conditions in villages changed dramatically, ending many traditional practices and causing the decline of others. At the same time, the Communist Party and its propaganda organs, recognizing the value of the existing folk traditions and seeking to support them in new forms suitable for the new society it was creating, had an enormously rich store of village singers, musicians, and dancers and a huge repertoire of songs, dances, instrumental tunes, and ritual contexts to draw on. The government began creating new national institutions to replace the family, the village, and the local region as supporters of folk music.

In the early 1950s, two professional ensembles were created: the National Ensemble of Folk Songs and Dances, under the direction of the composer Philip Kutev; and the Ensemble for Folk Songs, at Radio Sofia. Both held extensive auditions of village performers, collected their repertoires, harmonized their songs for three- and four-part a cappella female choirs, and arranged instrumental tunes and song accompaniments for a small orchestra of folk instruments: one or more bagpipes, two or more *kavals*, six or so *gŭdulkas*, two *tamburas tŭpan*, cello, and bass. To their music and song arrangements, the Kutev ensemble added choreographies of village dances, weddings, and other customs.

To perform the new choral and orchestral arrangements effectively, musically illiterate villagers in professional ensembles were taught to read musical notation, and in the 1960s and 1970s high schools and post-secondary "higher institutes" were founded to teach repertoire, performance style, and the notational and conceptual skills necessary to arrange and choreograph folk music.

The Kutev ensemble's harmonizations of traditional songs stimulated the formation of thousands of amateur choirs in villages, towns, and factories, and its choreographies influenced to varying degrees amateur village folk ensembles, whose repertoire and style of performance were organized by the Ministry of Education and Culture. As the larger ensembles in the main provincial towns improved in quality and mastered the complicated presentational style, many became professional, "national" ensembles, funded by the provincial government to tour and entertain villagers in the local province, around the country, and even abroad.

Somewhat independent of the state apparatus supporting folk-music presentation, music for family celebrations—weddings, engagement parties, and sending sons off to the army—continued to flourish. Families poured enormous amounts of money into food, drink, and music for these events; musicians, especially those playing Western instruments (like clarinet and accordion) not supported by folk-music ensembles could make substantial livings in this market, and ensemble musicians supplemented their state income. Unlike the truncated, short, preservation-oriented performances presented on stage by the ensembles, these events lasted a day or more, demanded nearly continuous playing, and inspired innovation and technical display to attract clients. In this environment, technique became more virtuosic, and the repertoire grew in complexity through improvisation, some of it by musicians trained in music theory at the new schools for music. By the 1980s, the vibrant wedding music tradition had produced "stars"—the most famous of whom was the clarinetist Ivo Papazov—whose popularity, technical brilliance, and improvisational skills seriously challenged the conservative aesthetics of the state-sponsored ensembles.

In the wake of *glasnost* in the 1980s, bands, musicians, and singers experimented with "folk-jazz" fusions and more complex mixes of avant-garde classical music with folk, jazz, rock, and Latin music. In the late 1980s, Bulgarian folk-song arrangements, under the title *Le mystère des voix bulgares*, and the virtuosic clarinet playing of Papazov graced the worldbeat charts in Europe and North America.

—*Adapted from an article by Timothy Rice*

Bibliography

Buchanan, Donna. 1991. "The Bulgarian Folk Orchestra: Cultural Performance, Symbol, and the Construction of National Identity in Socialist Bulgaria." Ph.D. dissertation, University of Texas at Austin.

——. 1995. "Metaphors of Power, Metaphors of Truth: The Politics of Music Professionalism in Bulgarian Folk Orchestras." *Ethnomusicology* 39(3):381–416.

——. 1996. "Wedding Musicians, Political Transition, and National Consciousness in Bulgaria." In *Returning Culture: Musical Changes in Central and Eastern Europe*, edited by Mark Slobin, 200–230. Durham, N.C.: Duke University Press.

Ivanova, Radost. 1987. *Traditional Bulgarian Wedding*. Sofia: Svyat Publishers.

Kachulev, Ivan. 1978. *Bulgarian Folk Music Instruments*. Pittsburgh: Tamburitza Press.

Katsarova, Raina, and Kiril Djenev. 1976. *Bulgarian Folk Dances*. Cambridge, Mass: Slavica.

Kolar, Walter, ed. 1976. *The Folk Arts of Bulgaria*. Pittsburgh: Tamburitzans Institute of Folk Arts, Duquesne University.

Kremenliev, Boris A. 1952. *Bulgarian-Macedonian Folk Music*. Berkeley: University of California Press.

——. 1976. "Bulgarian Folk Music: Some Recent Trends." In *Bulgaria Past and Present*, edited by Thomas Butler, 373–392. Columbus, Ohio: American Association for the Advancement of Slavic Studies.

Krŭstev, Venelin. 1978. *Bulgarian Music*. Sofia: Sofia Press.

Rice, Timothy. 1994. *May It Fill Your Soul: Experiencing Bulgarian Music*. Chicago: University of Chicago Press.

Greece

Greece (*Hellas* in Greek) occupies 131,944 square kilometers in the southeastern corner of Europe, one fifth on islands in the Aegean and Ionian seas. Poor in natural resources, the country has an economy dominated by agriculture, shipping, and tourism. The ancient architecture, philosophy, and politics of Greece have had an unparalleled influence on Europe and the rest of the world. Ancient Greek music has been less influential less for its sound, which is almost impossible to reconstruct, than for giving Europeans the very name *music*, the idea of musical notation, basic concepts of music theory and terminology, and beliefs about the nature and meaning of music.

A turbulent history of warring city-states in the pre-Christian era was succeeded by a series of powerful empires: the Roman after 146 B.C.E., the Byzantine from the sixth century, and the Ottoman from 1453 to 1912, although Greece was an independent kingdom for most of the nineteenth and twentieth centuries. Greece's contentious politics have inspired and led to the censoring of many songs in urban and rural traditions.

In an overwhelmingly Orthodox nation of 10.6 million people, Greeks share a legacy from Byzantium in their ecclesiastical music. Secular music, while manifesting the social and cultural variability of the Greek Orthodox world, echoes the modes, melodies, and vocal style of religious hymns. Its variability stems partly from accidents of landscape and history. Before extensive road-building programs after World War II, treacherous, mountainous terrain on the mainland separated regions and, often, nearby villages. Unpredictable seas isolated Greece's fourteen hundred islands. These barriers enabled dozens of distinct local traditions to thrive in close proximity. At the same time, Greeks have long been passionate travelers. Shared regional cultures were nurtured at country fairs, where people of neighboring villages or islands exchanged songs. Even before the late 1800s, when massive waves of emigration began, generations of young men had left to travel—as soldiers, seafarers, merchants, traders, and craftsmen—to the rest of Europe, North Africa, and the Central Asian hinterland.

The variety of regional music-making styles shows the traces of specific local histories. Mellifluous *kantadhes*, romantic popular serenades of the Ionian Islands, reflect a former Venetian colonial presence, while the Macedonian Romani (Gypsy) ensemble of two shawms (*zournadhes*) and a drum (*daouli*) recalls four centuries of Ottoman rule. Greek musical encounters with East and West reach back to a time before the 1400s, when these cultural spheres shared many musical traditions. When Western musical forms and practices began to follow the path leading to the Renaissance, Greek music remained a collective tradition, in which innovation was constant, but the formal recognition of individual authorship was downplayed. As a consequence, classifying Greek music as a branch of Near and Middle Eastern music makes musical and historical sense. Ecclesiastical and secular Greek musics have become imbued with tonalities that sound "oriental" to Western ears, though they may also bear witness to more archaic systems, which predate the separation of East and West.

The contemporary array of distinctive folk, classical, popular, and ecclesiastical musics reveals the position of Greece as a geographical and ideological crossroads between Europe and Asia. Orthodox liturgical music, folksongs (*dhimotika*) of the peasantry, and twentieth-century urban popular songs (*rebetika* and *laika*) are clearly, though no longer exclusively, marked by an Eastern musical sensibility. In contrast, Western music, though well known in the islands, was first introduced to the mainland, initially in the form of Italian operas and military bands, only in the early years of the struggle for Greek independence (after 1805), by composers and politicians who wanted to Westernize Greek musical tastes. Since the late-nineteenth century when operettas became popular with Athenian bourgeois society, urban Greeks have embraced the harmonies, instrumentation, and dance styles of European popular music.

Folk Music

Greek folk music as a whole exhibits certain general traits: a modal melodic structure; a tendency toward vocal monophony and instrumental heterophony; uneven (Turkish *aksak*, 'limping') meters, including 5/8, 7/8, and 9/8, in dance songs; an emphasis on ornamentation; and a common body of poetic images and sung formulas. Within this stylistic unity, distinctive regional musics and local styles within regions have developed. The increase in commercial folk-music recordings and of folklore programs on radio and television has accelerated the movement of songs across regions as folk musicians borrow—or as they say, "steal"—and rework new tunes, as they always have, to expand their repertoires. This tendency has diluted the purity of regional and local musics while leading musicians to exaggerate unique regional features. Even with newly borrowed elements and the addition of new instruments (like the now ubiquitous electronic synthesizer), regional musics remain recognizable.

On historical and stylistic grounds, folk music can be divided into two major classes: music of the mainland and music of the islands. On the mainland, nearly all of which the Ottoman Empire once controlled, wind instruments—the *zourna*, the *karamoutza*, and the *pipiza*, all double-reed shawms; the *gaida*, a single-reed, single-drone bagpipe; the *klarino*, a clarinet; and the brass *korneto*, a horn—dominate instrumental ensembles. Meters are usually asymmetric, and rhythms can be complex. Dances often feature upright postures and leaps.

Island musics, by contrast, show the influence of French, Genoese, and especially Venetian colonizers, and of the cosmopolitanism of the Orient. In ensembles, a wide array of stringed instruments takes center stage. These range from the plaintive violin and shimmering *sandouri* (a trapezoidal dulcimer, struck with wooden beaters) to the Cretan lyra, a bowed fiddle. Melodic lines and the movements of the dances they accompany are supple and lilting. Duple meters predominate, though uneven asymmetric meters—the *karsilamas*, a dance in 9/8, and the *zeibekiko*, a dance in 9/4, both originally from coastal Asia Minor—occur.

The distinction between mainland and island musical styles is also evident in folk-song texts, whose range of themes is extremely wide; however, only on the mainland, in areas that experienced Ottoman domination, does one find heroic songs describing the exploits of the *klephts*, the bandit-heroes of the resistance against the Turks. Island songs, by contrast, are predominantly erotic, and are notable for their florid imagery. Structural distinctions are also apparent. Throughout Greece, the most common verse structure is "political verse," a fifteen-syllable verse in iambic meter, comprised of two half lines, the first having eight syllables and the second having seven. The half line is the basic unit from which folksongs are constructed. It is also the unit of the formula, a group of recurring words, recognizable by conventional syntax, imagery, or sense. Folksongs composed of political verses are found in mainland and island communities, but the rhyming couplet, unique to islands historically under Frankish control, differs in two ways: it uses rhyme, as virtually no

other Greek folk-song genre does, and each verse is a self-contained semantic unit, an epigram, rather than a fragment of a larger song.

Traditional Contexts of Folk-music Performance

Singing, playing instruments, and dancing were central activities of communal life in rural communities throughout Greece until the late twentieth century. Mothers soothed babies with lullabies (*nanarismata*), farmers hummed tunes as they walked to their fields, shepherds lazily whittled, then musically mused, on the bevel-edged flute (*floyera*), and in the coolness of late-summer afternoons, adolescents courted through swing songs (*tis kunias*), couplets teasingly exchanged while boys watched girls ride the neighborhood swing. To pass winter evenings, neighbors regularly gathered around someone's hearth, singing, telling stories and jokes, and gossiping.

Elaborate collective rituals and celebrations punctuated the peasant calendar to commemorate crucial moments in individual lives (baptisms, marriages, deaths) and high points of the agricultural and religious year: the twelve days of Christmas, carnival, Easter, and the feasts of the community's patron saint(s)—events that in their most resplendent guise, the *paniyiri*, might include a bazaar, beggars, wrestling matches, and other accoutrements of a country fair. These celebrations involved the exchange of gifts, the preparation and consumption of prodigious amounts of food and drink, and the hiring of musicians.

In many places, wedding festivities lasted from Sunday to Sunday, and associated rituals for weeks afterward. Day after day, around the table in the early morning, hours of feasting and dancing led to more pensive, usually nonmetrical singing.

Contemporary Rural Contexts

Making music remains an important collective activity within many rural communities, and in a few is flourishing as never before, but on the whole its traditional forms and contexts have been dramatically attenuated. Since the late 1800s, and particularly since 1945, the transformation of Greece from a predominantly rural society to an urban one (most of the population living in the conurbation of Athens) has had undeniable consequences for music making, as for every other aspect of rural life. With the gradual exodus of young, able-bodied adults and their families seeking better jobs in the cities, countless villages have become "old peoples' homes," with no viable future, save as a holiday destination. As joyful communal events like weddings diminish in frequency, celebratory singing and dancing are superseded by the sounds of women lamenting their loved ones' deaths and the loss of a way of life. Radio and television have altered local patterns of recreation. Rather than spending winter evenings singing and telling stories, each family is more likely to sit at home in front of a television set, and as children learn songs and dances, not from their elders, but, in supposedly correct versions, from school lessons (a phenomenon imposed on some communities since the mid-1800s, on others much later), a once supple tradition becomes rigid and artificial.

Urban Music

In Greek, the word *laika* has two meanings: it refers both to the general category of urban popular songs, and is used in a more restricted sense to denote urban popular music of the postwar era. Largely ignored by scholars, urban *laika* are a rich and continuously evolving musical universe; indeed, the *bouzouki* (figure 1), the instrument outsiders most strongly associate with Greece, is used only in urban musical ensembles.

Rebetika

Rebetika constitute the most distinctive genre within urban music. Sometimes compared to American blues, *rebetika* are songs of the dispossessed, living on the margins of society—songs of love, loss, poverty, jail, and hashish, composed and performed from about 1900 until the early 1950s. Though initially confined to members of a small subculture, *rebetika* eventually became known through commercial gramophone records—made in Turkey, Piraeus, New York, and Chicago, as early as 1904, but particularly from the 1920s onward—which disseminated them within Greece and to Greek emigrants living abroad.

As a result of associations this music had with the urban underworld and Turkish culture, critics from all sides derided it. The conservative establishment condemned it as immoral, and especially during the regime of Ioannis Metaxas in the late 1930s, systematically harassed musicians and censored recordings that referred to hashish. Left-wing authorities, for their part, considered *rebetika* politically unenlightened, and thought the peculiar mix of defiance and resignation conveyed in *rebetika* lyrics inhibited workers' formation of class-consciousness. In the late 1960s, however, young people began to see *rebetika* as a symbol of resistance to repression, and the genre experienced a surge in popularity that shows no sign of abating.

The etymology of the term remains obscure, but *rebetika* are rooted in the traditional singing of the poorer urban classes, who began to migrate to the towns and cities in the 1700s. Though the structures and themes of many *rebetika* show clear links to rural

Figure 1 Bouzoukis hang in a shop window in Thessaloniki.
Photo by Terry E. Miller.

folk traditions, this music was shaped by, and came to be the quintessential expression of, a different social world. In the urban centers of the Aegean coast, *rebetika* developed within two distinct, if connected, cultural settings: musical cafés, and jails and hashish dens (*teké*).

Musical cafés, humble establishments serving wine and simple food, sprang up in Aegean ports after 1900. One end of the room was usually free for street musicians, many of them Roma, to gather and play music for tips. After the influx of refugees, including professional musicians, from Asia Minor into Athens and Piraeus after 1922, such cafés typically hosted their own small orchestra (*koumpania*), comprising a *sandouri*, a *laouto* (a long-necked, plucked lute), and an *outi* (a bent-necked, plucked lute) or a *saz*, (the Turkish long-necked plucked lute). A female singer, accompanied by *defi* (frame drum), *koutalia* (spoons), or *zilia* (metal finger cymbals), often did the belly dance. Audiences of refugee women and men came to hear Smyrna-style songs—emotional, ornamented pieces, whose lyrics, interlacing Greek, Turkish, and occasionally Judeo-Spanish, proclaimed grief at losing their beloved homeland.

Though the music of the cafés had a sophisticated urban pedigree, another stream of *rebetika* developed in underworld haunts. In jails of the mid-1800s to the early 1900s, petty thieves, crooks, and political dissidents developed a unique musical culture. Prisoners carved from bedposts the necks of tiny *baglamadhes* (originally part of the family of Turkish *sazes*) and composed songs of fate, love, and defiance, peppered with jailhouse slang. Out of jail, in the poor neighborhoods of Piraeus, such men gathered in the hashish den, smoking hashish (officially tolerated until 1936) from Turkish hookahs while one of their number quietly strummed a *bouzouki* or a *bağlama* and another stood up to dance an introspective *zeibekiko*. With interpreters like Markos Vamvakaris (1905–1972), the Piraeus style flourished in the 1930s, when it replaced the lavishness of the *koumpanies* with a male vocalist and a spare *bouzouki* accompaniment. Though the *teké* was primarily a male setting, certain "free" women (*derbiderissa*), who made their own living and their own rules, were attached to it.

Laika

By the early 1950s, *rebetika* had ceased to be a creative form. After that, *laika* (understood in its restricted sense as postwar urban music) came into its own. *Laika* had its roots in *rebetika*, but took on a more respectable and westernized form. Ensembles grew to include new instrumental combinations: a piano, a guitar, drums, and an accordion joined the *bouzouki* and the *baglamadhes*. Composers increasingly replaced Turkish modes, known in Greece as *dhromi* 'roads', with the diatonic major and minor scales of European popular music promulgated by popular dance bands. Eastern sensibilities, which had once permeated *rebetika*, became a conventionalized orientalism, the new middle-class and nouveau-riche audiences began valuing technical virtuosity more than soul, and Manolis Hiotis (1920–1970), the most famous *bouzouki* player of the 1950s, added a fourth string and changed the tuning to play faster and produce a more European sound. Dancing in respectable establishments (*bouzoukia*) and their shabbier counterparts (*skiladhika*, 'dog's dens'), patronized by the working classes, differed greatly from those of cafés and hashish dens. Dancing became an acrobatic, exhibitionist display, complete with ostentatious "gifting" to the musicians, and admiring friends' ritualized smashing of plates at the dancer's feet.

Record companies have continued to produce recordings of *laika*, in its light (*elafrolaika*) and heavy (*varialaika*) styles, with crooning lead singers, accompanied by electrified *bouzouki* and other instruments, performing songs with European harmonies and *rebetika* rhythms.

Except as old 78-RPM records scoured from the flea markets of Monastiraki, *rebetika* did not survive in the conservative postwar climate. The military junta that seized power in 1967 jailed Elias Petropoulos for publishing his landmark book, *Rebetika Tragoudhia* (1968). Its publication was influential, however. By the early 1970s, many young people were rediscovering in *rebetika* lyrics and subcultures the symbols of resistance to repression. After 1974, when democracy returned, record companies began to reissue old 78s on long-playing disks. The Center for the Study of Rebetic Song, established in Athens during the period of revival, has produced impressive reissues, which, released on the Falirea Brothers label, contain extensive album notes of the songs' social and historical contexts.

—*Adapted from an article by Jane K. Cowan*

Bibliography

Alexiou, Margaret. 1974. *The Ritual Lament in Greek Tradition*. Cambridge: Cambridge University Press.

Anoyanakis, Fivos. [1965] 1979. *Greek Popular Musical Instruments*. Athens: National Bank of Greece.

Beaton, Roderick. 1980. *Folk Poetry of Modern Greece*. Cambridge: Cambridge University Press.

Butterworth, Katharine, and Sara Schneider. 1975. *Rebetika Songs from the Old Greek Underworld*. Athens: Komboloi Press.

Chianis, Sotirios (Sam). 1980. "Greece, Folk Music." In *The New Grove Dictionary of Music and Musicians*. Edited by Stanley Sadie. London: Macmillan.

Cowan, Jane K. 1990. *Dance and the Body Politic in Northern Greece*. Princeton: Princeton University Press.

Danforth, Loring M. 1982. *The Death Rituals of Rural Greece*. Princeton: Princeton University Press.

———. 1989. *Firewalking and Religious Healing: The Anastenaria of Greece and the American Firewalking Movement*. Princeton: Princeton University Press.

Georgiades, Thrasybulos. 1973. *Greek Music, Verse, and Dance*. New York: Da Capo Press.

Holst, Gail. 1977. *Road to Rembetika: Music of a Greek Sub-Culture: Songs of Love, Sorrow and Hashish*. Limni and Athens: Denise Harvey and Co.

Keil, Charles, and Angeliki Vellou Keil. 2002. *Bright Balkan Morning: Romani Lives and the Power of Music in Greek Macedonia*. Photographs by Dick Blau, soundscapes by Steven Feld. Middletown, Conn.: Wesleyan University Press.

Leotsakos, George. 1980. "Greece, After 1830." In *The New Grove Dictionary of Music and Musicians*. Edited by Stanley Sadie. London: Macmillan.

Petrides, Ted. 1975. *Folk Dances of the Greeks*. Jericho, N.Y.: Exposition Press.

Tragaki, Dafni. 2007. *Rebetiko Worlds*. Newcastle, U.K.: Cambridge Scholars Publishing.

Watts, Niki. 1988. *The Greek Folk Songs*. Bristol: Bristol Classical Press.

Wellesz, Egon. 1949. *A History of Byzantine Music and Hymnography*. Oxford: Clarendon Press.

Winnington-Ingram, Reginald Pepys. 1980. "Greece: Ancient." In *The New Grove Dictionary of Music and Musicians*. Edited by Stanley Sadie. London: Macmillan.

5. Oceania

In Oceania, music is not just for listening, but for seeing and feeling. Music is sung, played, danced, and acted as part of social, religious, and political events. In the world at large, fantasies and stereotypes about Oceanic peoples and their musics compete with knowledge and understanding, though millions of individuals have traveled to the Pacific—as tourists, missionaries, scientists, or warriors, or for medical, economic, or political reasons.

Today, Oceanic music is performed in sacred spaces, on festival stages, in urban clubs, and at family gatherings. But above all, musical performances are markers of cultural and ethnic identity. The music of Oceania engages insiders and outsiders alike with its meaningful complexities and simplicities, its purposeful elegance and abandon.

Kiwai dancers compete at the Port Moresby Show in Papua New Guinea. In the Kiwai dance, male and female dancers move in parallel lines, apart from male and female singer/instrumentalists, who play kundus, rattles, and small bamboo garamuts.
Photo by Don Niles, 1982.

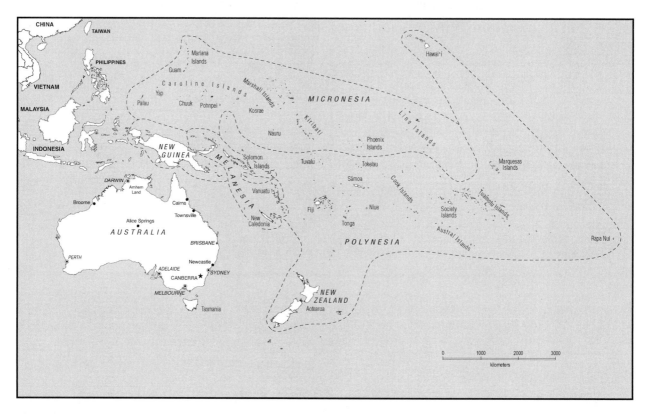

Oceania

Profile of Oceania

The Pacific Ocean covers one-third of the earth's surface, and its lands are inhabited by hundreds of cultural groups. Oceania includes some twenty-five thousand islands, ranging in size from tiny specks of coral to the Australian continent. About fifteen hundred of the islands are inhabited by diverse peoples, many of whom have mixed and intermixed over time. Environments range from snowy mountains to raging volcanoes, from steaming forests to searing deserts, from sparkling beaches to sheer cliffs (figure 1).

Some thirty million people inhabit Oceania. Many once lived in separate groups of only a few hundred individuals, while others were part of islandwide chiefdoms with populations in the tens of thousands. Today, traditional living arrangements coexist with large ports and cosmopolitan cities. The people speak hundreds of dialects and languages—some mutually intelligible over wide expanses of ocean, others unintelligible to the residents of adjoining hamlets.

Prehistory and History

People probably began moving eastward from Southeast Asia about fifty thousand years ago. Exactly when they began to do so, why, in what numbers, where they came from, and how they traveled are matters for conjecture and research. The physical conditions of lands they found differed from those of the same locations today. During the last Ice Age, sea levels throughout the world were lower than they are now; the sizes and shapes of islands were larger and more varied, and the distances between them were shorter.

At the eastern end of the Indonesian chain of islands, a continent lay athwart the passage to the Pacific Ocean: Sahul Land, as it is called, spanned what are now New Guinea, Australia, and Tasmania. Migrants and accidental voyagers from the west reached its coasts to become its earliest inhabitants. Succeeding millennia saw other contacts and arrivals, who brought pigs (possibly ten thousand years ago), dogs, fowl, and probably Asian bananas, breadfruit, taro, and yams. These they disseminated by trade and migration.

Much later, peoples with an archaeologically defined cultural tradition, now known as the Lapita cultural complex, spread from the Bismarck Archipelago (mainly New Britain and New Ireland), along the coast of New Guinea, throughout Melanesia, and finally into Polynesia. The Lapita complex, named after the site where it was first identified in New Caledonia, is distinguished by earthenware ceramics with distinctive decorations. It is the most important cultural tradition for understanding the prehistory of much of Oceania.

Over time and space, ancestral cultures diversified. They eventually formed the historic cultural complexes usually grouped together under the terms Australia ('southern land'), Melanesia ('black islands', including New Guinea), Micronesia ('small islands') and Polynesia ('many islands').

The spellings of non-English terms

Most languages of Oceania use fewer distinct sounds than English. In careful pronunciation, many Oceanic vowels and consonants have approximately the sounds of their unmodified letters in the International Phonetic Alphabet.

Many languages of Oceania use a glottal stop, usually represented by an inverted comma, as in the word *Hawaiʻi*, which, as pronounced in the islands, has a catch in the voice between the last two vowels. A notable instance of this convention is the word spelled *ʻukulele* in texts on Hawaiʻi, but *ukulele* elsewhere. Some writers keyboard the glottal stop as an apostrophe, and French orthographic tradition adds French accents—so the spellings *ʻAreʻare*, *ʾAreʾare*, *ʻAreʻare*, and *ʾAréʾaré* name the same people.

A macron lengthens its vowel and may change the meaning of a word. Lengthening has many functions, as in pluralizing (Sāmoan *fāfine* 'woman', *fāfine* 'women'). Some orthographies show extra length by doubling the written vowel, but others may use a macron or no sign at all. Because of certain word processors' limitations, some authors print macrons as umlauts—so *ö* in one text might represent *ō* in another. Some authors mark lengthening with a colon.

In some orthographies, *g* specifies the phoneme /ŋ/, usually spelled *ng* in English, as in "singer." For the same sound, other languages use *ng*. This inconsistency makes cognates less apparent—as with the word pronounced /toŋa/ and spelled *toga* in Sāmoan but *tonga* in Tongan. In languages that use prenasalized consonants, *b* may stand for /mb/, *d* for /nd/, and *q* for /ŋg/. These conventions cause confusion with languages like those of Malaita, where *g* is /ŋg/ (like Fijian *q*, unlike Sāmoan *g*), but *ng* is /ŋ/ (like Tongan *ng*). A standard orthography of the Solomon Islands uses *ḡ* to represent plain /g/.

623

(a)

(b)

Figure 1 Oceanic environments: *a*, tropical island paradise in Haʻapai, Tonga; *b*, view from Kalalau Lookout, Kauaʻi Island, Hawaiʻi. *Photos by Adrienne L. Kaeppler, 1967.*

Oceania in the Larger World

In addition to indigenous differences that existed in precontact times, colonial encroachments in Oceania included those of Britain, Chile, France, Germany, Indonesia, Japan, the Netherlands, Russia, Spain, and the United States of America, unilaterally and in various combinations.

Outsiders' influence on Oceanic societies has been uneven, ranging from areas of New Guinea where the primary contact has been with patrol officers, missionaries, anthropologists, and film crews, to lands that serve as overseas provinces of major outside powers, including the Society Islands (part of France), Papua (formerly known as Irian Jaya, a province of Indonesia), and Hawaiʻi, the fiftieth state

of the United States. Between these extremes are Tonga, an independent kingdom, which, though extensively influenced by Britain, was never completely a colony, but only a protected state; newly independent states, including Fiji, Kiribati (formerly the Gilbert Islands), the Solomon Islands, Tuvalu (formerly the Ellice Islands), and Vanuatu (formerly the New Hebrides); islands related to a larger political power, such as the Cook Islands, in association with New Zealand; and Guam, a territory of the United States.

Cultural Identity

Oceanic societies were extremely varied. The social systems within each part of Oceania—Australia,

New Guinea, Melanesia, Micronesia, Polynesia—share core traits, but some societies do not easily fit into one of the major groups. New Caledonia has many elements in common with other Melanesian societies, but has hereditary chiefs (more typical of Polynesia), and Fiji is in some ways a transitional area between Melanesia and Polynesia. Many Oceanic cultures are as different from each other as they are from other cultures in the world.

In the last decades of the twentieth century, separate peoples of Oceania came to feel that they had more in common with each other than with outsiders. These feelings were not trivial or artificial, but arose from real concerns. What these societies have in common is the colonial experience, as varied as it may have been, and the love-hate relationship that has emerged with the colonizing power in the wake of efforts toward, and in some instances the achievement of, political independence.

An important dilemma of independence is the necessity of interacting with other nations in international arenas, such as meetings of the United Nations and UNESCO, and the maintenance of embassies and other consular activities in foreign metropolitan areas, while maintaining cultural individuality and forging a national identity. Though politicians are usually not artists, performers, or sociologists, they legislate cultural policy. Throughout Oceania, cultural identity expressed through the performing arts has political and social value.

PACIFIC FESTIVALS OF ARTS

Since 1972, Pacific Islanders have had an international venue for their performances: the Pacific Festivals of Arts, planned to be held every four years in a different nation. Nine festivals have been held: Suva, Fiji, 1972; Rotorua, Aotearoa, 1976; Papua New Guinea, 1980; Tahiti, French Polynesia, 1985 (rescheduled from 1984); Townsville, Australia, 1988 (figure 2); Rarotonga, Cook Islands, 1992; Apia, Western Sāmoa, 1996; Nouméa, New Caledonia, 2000; and Palau, Micronesia, 2004. Though these events have become increasingly political, they emphasize preservation and development in the performing arts. Troupes borrow from each other—and festival borrowings have appeared at later festivals.

Figure 2 At the Pacific Festival of the Arts in Townsville, Australia, Banabans now living in Fiji perform a segment of the Fijian program.
Photo by Adrienne L. Kaeppler, 1988.

Yesterday and Today

Descriptions of Oceanic music, dance, and performative contexts were made by Europeans during the late 1700s, and especially the 1800s, when Christianity reached most areas of Oceania and became part of the literature of exploration. Ethnographic collections of Oceanic objects, including musical instruments and costumes, were collected, and some of these treasures are now in Pacific metropolitan centers, including Auckland, New Zealand; Honolulu, Hawaiʻi; Nouméa, New Caledonia; Papeʻete, Tahiti; Vila, Vanuatu; Suva, Fiji; and Sydney, Australia. Many books, manuscripts, and objects survive in collections in libraries and museums overseas, especially in Britain, France, Germany, and the United States.

The peoples of Oceania have discontinued some of their musical traditions, but have continued others. Modern Oceanic music has borrowed from abroad, but ongoing musical systems use intercultural borrowings to shape artistic products into locally meaningful forms. New works depend on knowledge of traditional aesthetic systems in which musicians have immersed themselves. Modern composers and performers do not slavishly copy old products and processes: instead, they draw from their backgrounds and experiences to create artworks that make old Oceanic themes understandable anew.

—By Adrienne L. Kaeppler

Bibliography

Bellwood, Peter, et al., eds. 1995. *The Austronesians: Historical and Comparative Perspectives.* Canberra: Australian National University.

Finnegan, Ruth, and Margaret Orbell, eds. 1995. *South Pacific Oral Traditions.* Bloomington: Indiana University Press.

Goodenough, Ward H., ed. 1996. *Prehistoric Settlement of the Pacific.* Philadelphia: American Philosophical Society.

Irwin, Geoffrey. 1992. *The Prehistoric Exploration and Colonisation of the Pacific.* Oakleigh, Victoria, Australia: Cambridge University Press.

Johnson, L. W. 1983. *Colonial Sunset: Australia and Papua New Guinea 1970–1974.* St. Lucia: University of Queensland Press.

Linnekin, Jocelyn, and Lin Poyer. 1990. *Cultural Identity and Ethnicity in the Pacific.* Honolulu: University of Hawaiʻi Press.

Siikala, Jukka, ed. 1990. *Culture and History in the Pacific.* Helsinki: Finnish Anthropological Society.

New Guinea

New Guinea

Rhythmic sounds from percussive logs, hourglass-shaped drums, whirled slats, paired flutes, shaken rattles, and leaves are complemented by the visual impact of costumes with moving parts, while bodies of men and women move up and down or side to side. Sounds and movements imitating waterfalls and other natural phenomena and learned from birds and other animals pervade the traditional musics of New Guinea.

Success in life depends on working with spirits, nature, and kin. Musical sounds are spirits' voices. Performances validate the identities of individuals and families, and affirm communal feeling in gender relations, trade, warfare, and parliamentary debate. Traditional musics are transformed into modern ones, while modern musics are transformed into traditional ones.

Performers from New Guinea play *kundus* and dance at the Pacific Festival of the Arts in Apia, Sāmoa, 1996.
Photo by Adrienne L. Kaeppler.

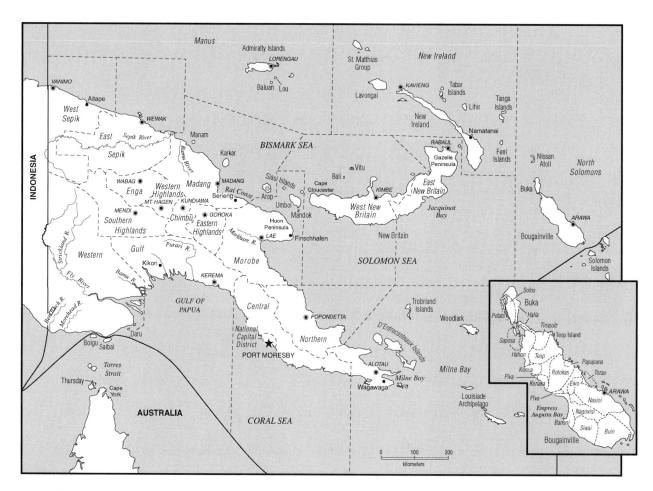

Papua New Guinea

The Music and Dance of New Guinea

The landmass of New Guinea supports numerous sociocultural groups, with a long prehistory of cultural challenges and a checkered history of colonial influences. Global politics of the 1800s and 1900s resulted in political boundaries that do not match cultural and social boundaries. Papua (West Papua), the western part of the island, is politically a province of Indonesia. Papua New Guinea includes not only the eastern part of the island of New Guinea, but large and small islands—New Britain, New Ireland, Manus, the Trobriand Islands, Bougainville, and others—whose cultures are in some cases only distantly related (map). When dealing with the arts, it is appropriate to use cultural boundaries, yet political divisions influence how people construct their past.

Many societies of New Guinea have features in common, including social organizations centered on leaders who attain power and renown primarily by individual or family achievement. Each tribal grouping, and in some cases each village, differs in important ways from others. This diversity manifests itself in hundreds of dialects and languages, details and underlying concepts of political structures and social relationships, the fabrication and use of material culture, the use and exploitation of the natural environment, religion and ritual, clothing, lore, poetry, music, and dance.

The people of many areas favored elaborate rituals and dramatic ceremonies, often connected with the building of men's houses (structures in which men spent time and kept ceremonial objects), rites of initiation and puberty, wars, and funerals. These were occasions for spectacular displays: dressed in showy costumes and painted in characteristic designs and colors, participants wore or carried carved and painted figures and ceremonial boards. To the accompaniment of singing, drumming, and dancing, huge masks—representing spirits, totems, and ancestors—made their appearance. In stylistic details and underlying concepts, each area, tribe, and even village differed from others.

Papua New Guinea is one of the most linguistically complicated nations on earth; current estimates range between seven hundred and eight hundred distinct languages. At present, three languages are widespread in the country: English, promoted by the educational system; Tok Pisin, also called New Guinea Pidgin; and Hiri Motu, also called Police Motu. It is uncertain how the distribution of indigenous languages relates to the distribution of musical styles, instruments, rituals, and other musically important aspects of human experience. Linguistic diversity does not mean that neighboring groups did not communicate: people learned neighboring languages; they married, fought, and traded with their neighbors. In coastal and inland areas, extensive trade-based networks helped diffuse and popularize musical instruments and dances.

History and Government

European contact with Melanesia began in the 1500s with visits by Portuguese ships; Indonesian and Chinese contacts may have occurred earlier. In 1884, Germany proclaimed a protectorate over northwest New Guinea and the Bismarck Archipelago (mainly New Britain, New Ireland, and the Admiralty Islands), and Britain proclaimed a protectorate over southeastern New Guinea and adjoining islands. In 1906, the federal government of Australia took responsibility for British New Guinea. In 1914, at the outset of World War I, Australian troops occupied German New Guinea; later, the League of Nations gave Australia a mandate for its administration. From 1921 to 1942, Australia administered separately the Australian Territory of Papua (formerly British New Guinea) and the Mandated Territory of New Guinea. During World War II, Japanese troops conquered part of the former and much of the latter; after the war, Australia again became the controlling authority. In 1945, the two territories administratively merged, forming the Territory of Papua and New Guinea. The first nationally elected legislature met in 1964. On 16 September 1975, Papua New Guinea attained independence as a sovereign state within the British Commonwealth.

Cultural Regions

For descriptive convenience, Papua New Guinea divides into four regions: Papua, Highlands, Mamose, and Islands. Among these regions, cultures overlap; within these regions, much cultural variation occurs. Several provinces make up each region. Provincial distinctions and boundaries more often reflect colonial policy than ethnographic reality. The geographical untidiness of cultural diversity makes any nationwide overview of music and dance difficult. To give a sense of this diversity, though, groups from each region are described in the articles that follow.

Musical Instruments

The distribution of musical instruments in New Guinea reflects distinctive ethnological patterns. Some of the present-day distribution of instruments is attributable to trade, geography, and environment, just as these factors figure in the distribution of languages and other cultural traits. Some instruments correlate with musical contexts and genres.

The Garamut

The *garamut*, a hollowed percussive log, takes its name from a common indigenous name for the tree from whose wood men commonly hew the instrument. Societies in much of the Mamose and Island regions use it. In addition to accompanying songs and dances, it often serves for intervillage communication. Men play *garamuts* with either of two techniques: jolting, when they hit the instrument with the end of a stick; and striking, when they hit it with the side of a stick. By far the more common technique in New Guinea is jolting.

The Kundu

A widely distributed instrument is the *kundu* (figure 1), a drum, most widely played by men, but in some areas played by women. It is absent in certain inland areas of the mainland, and in much of the Island Region. Because it is widespread, its absence is possibly more revealing than its presence.

The *kundu* has the shape of an hourglass, or sometimes a cylinder or a cone. One end is open, and the other holds a membrane. In one hand, a player holds the instrument (sometimes by a handle), and with the other, strikes the head. Materials of construction vary: the body is normally wood; bamboo and clay variants occur. In lowland areas, the membrane is usually from a monitor lizard or a snake; in mountainous areas, it may be the skin of species of cuscus, ringtail, wallaby, or other marsupial; in some areas, it may be the skin of a megapode, a bird that lays eggs in mounds of debris.

Players often tune the *kundu* by attaching to the membrane blobs of beeswax (from stingless bees) or gum from trees. Tuning involves heating the membrane over a fire, adjusting the blobs, and testing the sound. Some peoples along the Rai Coast and in inland areas tune the instrument by pasting clay onto the membrane.

A common accompaniment to singing, *kundus* usually serve nonreligious purposes. Their rhythmic

Figure 1 A Boazi man holds an exceptionally large *kundu*, Western Province.
Photo by Don Niles, 1984.

patterns often give clues about the performers' geographical origins. Researchers distinguish between peoples that play *kundus* synchronously (with obvious coordination in sonic motion) and those that play *kundus* asynchronously (with little or no such motion). The former peoples are more numerous; they subdivide into those that use repeating, unvarying rhythms, and those that use different rhythms to structure music sectionally.

Other Instruments and their Social Implications

Probably the most widespread musical instrument in New Guinea is the *susap*, an orally resonated jew's harp, usually played by males, though seldom associated with male religious activity. Its ordinary use, as an instrument of self-entertainment, gives it less social importance than other, less widely distributed, instruments. For signaling, men in coastal areas sound conchs or *garamuts*. Flutes and trumpets, voice-modifying tubes, rattles, and miscellaneous percussion instruments also occur in New

Guinea; the forms and materials used for their construction vary widely.

The distribution of sound-producing instruments conspicuously parallels the distribution of languages. The number of linguistic groups increases from south to north on the mainland, and so does the variety of instruments: in the Mamose Region, ensembles of variously sized and pitched flutes, *garamuts*, trumpets, and voice-modifying tubes are typical, but in much of the Papuan Region, typical musical instruments are a rattle, a *kundu*, a conch, and an end-blown flute. Besides the mere presence or absence of an instrument, other factors—indigenous names, constructional materials, performative usage, distinctive rhythms—prove useful in understanding relationships among cultural groups. Comparative work along such lines has focused on why the *garamut* is absent from the Papuan Region.

Musical Contexts

A useful Tok Pisin term for which English has no convenient word is *singsing*. This term can refer simply to any performance of a song, but it often denotes an important context: purposeful singing and dancing by decorated performers. Purpose, song, dance, and decoration intertwine: particular occasions demand particular dances, which, in turn, require appropriate decorations and preparatory rituals. Dancers, singers, and instrumentalists may perform separately, but *singsings* require their simultaneous participation.

Music and dance highlight various occasions: birth, initiation, first menstruation, courting, mourning, first haircut, construction of a house or a canoe, exchange-related ceremonies, religious activities, welcoming, farewelling, fighting (before, during, after), séances, communication, games, and general amusement. Such contexts vary by culture and area. People often regard "dance" as an integral part of a performance; to separate it from "music" is often a Westernism, foreign to local concepts of effective performance.

Sounds highlight events. In many areas, sounds appease ancestral spirits by proving that traditions are continuing according to familiar notions of correct procedure. But sounds also serve other purposes: sending messages between lovers, evoking emotional states, ordering uninitiated persons away, and so on.

Male Initiations

Music in New Guinea importantly occurs in association with male initiation. Instruments often play a prominent role, either as creators of a spirit's voice, or as objects that even males must not play or see until they have undergone the rituals that transmit or authenticate esoteric knowledge and guarantee social responsibility. Uninitiated persons—boys and females—fear the sounds, and must not learn that men create them. For learning this secret, women have been put to death, despite widespread belief in myths that women once held such knowledge, which men took from them. Paired, side-blown Sepik (northern lowland) and Highland flutes are the most thoroughly studied examples of secret instruments, but men employ other instruments, including voice-modifying tubes and vessels, whirled slats, end-blown flutes, piston flutes, vessels inserted into water or mud, rubbed idiophones or "self-sounding" instruments, and ensembles of trumpets or side-blown flutes.

These instruments often produce continuous sounds, rather than sounds subject to interruptions (such as inhalation), or they change the quality of human vocalizations. By setting sounds apart from ordinary experience, acoustic continuity fosters the illusion that the sounds emanate from nonhuman sources. Continuous sounds may inhere in the instrument (like whirled slats), or result from a specialized technique (like playing in alternation, common with flutes and trumpets). Men modify their voices by singing through bamboo, gourds, and conchs.

Christian Missions

In the 1800s and early 1900s, missionaries reacted harshly against indigenous music, especially music associated with non-Christian religious practices. Most missionaries, in the light of their own morality, considered indigenous music and dance the results of moral darkness.

A desire to make Christian substitutions fostered new styles of singing and dancing, dependent in part on the music of the local missions. Some missionaries banned indigenous dancing completely; others allowed dances to be modified, or Polynesian styles to be substituted. Some missionaries made Christian men prove their faith by disrespecting the old ways, particularly by revealing to women and uninitiated youths the secret instruments. Missionaries everywhere banned dances that promoted sexual activities.

In the second half of the twentieth century, most churches with long histories in Papua New Guinea championed some aspects of local culture and sought out indigenous contributions to Christianity. Since it was neither possible nor worthwhile for many peoples to revive abandoned practices, revised versions have been created.

STRINGBANDS

An important musical development occurred in Papua New Guinea when songs began to be accompanied by guitar-based ensembles, often with the addition of ukuleles. These instruments were available before the 1940s, but only after 1945 did they became widespread. By the 1990s, some bands were using portable loudspeakers (figure 2).

Figure 2 Surrounded by onlookers, a Porgera string band (of Enga Province) performs; a portable loudspeaker amplifies the sounds of the guitar on the left.
Photo by Don Niles, 1991.

Local styles began to develop, and styles such as Central, Tolai, Manus, New Ireland, Buka, Sepik, Highlands, Gulf, and Oro, are obvious to many listeners, whose criteria for differentiating them include guitar-playing methods, vocal harmonization, melodic contour, lead-guitar line, instrumentation, form, and linguistic details. In addition to such distinctive features, much popular music uses only tonic, dominant, and subdominant chords. Formerly, the tuning of guitars and ukuleles varied from standard Western norms; tunings had such names as *Sunset*, *Five-Key*, *Sāmoan*, and *D-Key*. By the 1990s, the use of nonstandard tunings had become less frequent.

In language, instrumentation, and locale, acoustic stringbands contrast with electrically amplified bands, variously called electric bands, power bands (*pawa ben*), and live bands (*laiv ben*). Stringbands often sing original compositions in local languages and are associated with villages. In contrast, power bands often sing in English, add bass guitars and drums, and are associated with towns. Their rise began in 1962, when drinking was legalized for nationals, and mixed-race bands began playing in hotels and taverns. By the 1980s, with the greater availability of electric instruments, such contrasts were less valid. In some villages close to towns, power bands have usurped the position of stringbands, and sing in local languages.

Stringbands and power bands remain popular. A thriving, highly competitive, local cassette-recording industry supports them. Since most bands sing in local languages, few can become popular outside the areas where their language is spoken. Successful exceptions are bands like Helgas and Paramana Strangers (both of Central Province), and Barike and Painim Wok (both of East New Britain). Some bands have tried to overcome linguistic barriers by including songs in Tok Pisin, Hiri Motu, and English. Shortly after Papua New Guinea gained independence, the focus for popular music was Central Province, which supported many bands and studios; but the mid-1980s saw a shift to Rabaul, because the studios there competitively promoted bands. In September 1994, volcanic eruptions in the Rabaul area devastated studios there.

Several bands have tried to incorporate elements of indigenous music into popular music. Most of these bands, especially Sanguma, Tumbuna, and Tambaran Culture, have resulted from experimental work done at the National Arts School, now the Faculty of Creative Arts of the University of Papua New Guinea. Other bands have explored these lines in subtler ways, and the music of many bands reveals indirect influences from indigenous music. In the 1980s, gospel bands became important; these ensembles are a stringband or a power band, but their songs, usually in English, are often covers of overseas religious songs, associated with fundamentalist or charismatic Christian movements.

Words in Musical Settings

Texts often employ archaic terms. Metaphoric language, different from everyday speech, is common everywhere. Songs provide an aural representation of myths and legends—a striking feature where stories of ancestors' actions are taught to youths during initiation, especially in the Sepik or northern lowland area.

An important metaphoric process is the use of singing to map ancestral actions and migrations. Places cited in musical texts often evoke nostalgia for individuals, events, or eras. The order of songs, which can determine the correctness of performances, may play out against segments of day and night.

The Papua New Guinea Music Collection (1987) contains more than three hundred examples of music, from every province. The largest and most representative collection of indigenous recordings, it provides a foundation for future research. Many local cultures, with hundreds of languages and millions of people, still await their first musical recordings and their first systematic writings on music.

Dance

New Guinean structured-movement systems, though having elements in common, differ from area to area. Throughout New Guinea, they have an elemental basis in rhythm. This feature contrasts with Polynesian dancing, whose elemental basis is poetry.

Traditionally, ritual movement was often the province of men. Women might perform at the end of a line, or near the men, or as observers. Whether part of rituals or social activities, dancing is usually participatory, rather than presentational. Performances may not have a specific facing: performers arrange themselves in a circle, or in lines or groupings. These positions may be static, or may shift as performers move. At some occasions, two or more groups perform different dances simultaneously; each group focuses on itself, rather than on any spectators who may be present, and they do so even when ranged in a single line or column. Dancers often form a moving group, which takes participants from one area to another.

When performers are arranged in a circle, each may move in a circular direction, or the whole circle may move in one or another direction. A common choreographic pattern is arrangement in two columns, which move in one direction by pairs. The first pair, followed by the others, makes a half-turn outward, and then moves in the opposite direction until two lines are formed going in that direction; then they reverse again. Or dancers may be arranged side by side in one or more long rows facing in one direction for one sequence of movements, and then, perhaps, facing the opposite direction for another (figure 3). In many cases, dance is realized as movement only after the introduction of a regular rhythm set by the beating of *kundus* (or occasionally *garamuts*) or the jingling of rattles. Changes in instrumental rhythms may trigger changes in movements. In some areas, melodic instruments, such as panpipes, furnish the aural dimension.

The most characteristic movements are up-down bouncing of legs and body. The torso typically serves as one vertical unit: the hips do not usually move separately or break at the waist, even when a dancer sways from side to side. The body may be held

Figure 3 Papua New Guinea dancers at the Pacific Festival of the Arts. *Photo by Adrienne L. Kaeppler, 1980.*

Figure 4 In the *ida* ritual of Punda Village, West Sepik Province, men play end-blown wooden trumpets while masked dancers perform. *Photo by Don Niles, 1986.*

DISC
1
TRACK
25

straight, or it may be inclined forward slightly at the hips. The vertical movements are often created by alternately bending the knees and lifting the heels in place, or by step-bend-step-bend progressing, forward or backward. Performers often carry *kundus*, sometimes carved or painted or both. Singing may involve vocables (such as *yo-o yo-o*) or short texts, which may or may not convey narrative meaning.

A leader begins by bending and straightening his knees. The others down the line join in or circle until the whole group moves up and down together, in place or in a prearranged choreographed pattern. Costumes emphasize this rhythm. They consist primarily of attachments, most of which are mobile. Bird-of-paradise plumes and other feathers extend from headdresses, backs, bustles, or arms. Hanging rattles of seeds or shells are attached to legs or costumes, or are held in the hand. Cuscus skin ripples like vertical waves, and shredded leaves and fibers cascade and bounce. In some areas, penis coverings (of gourd, shell, or bark) emphasize the up-down movement of the penis (figure 4). All accoutrements of dress contribute to making a mass rhythmic statement, and it is difficult to discern if costumery aims at emphasizing rhythm, or if rhythm is a way of showing off costumery.

These are not the movements of everyday life elaborated for a stage: they are movements of the supernatural and the ceremonial world, or movements to project hostility, warfare, and leaders' rise and fall. The visualization of rhythm manifests underlying equivalence-based cultural principles: villages are equivalent, tribes are equivalent, individuals are equivalent; yet, like leaders, they all rise and fall, each having equal access, each in its own time.

—*Adapted from articles by Adrienne L. Kaeppler and Don Niles*

Bibliography

Chenoweth, Vida, ed. 1976. *Musical Instruments of Papua New Guinea.* Ukarumpa: Summer Institute of Linguistics.

———. 1979. *The Usarufas and Their Music.* Publication 5. Dallas: Summer Institute of Linguistics Museum of Anthropology.

Feld, Steven. 1990. *Sound and Sentiment: Birds, Weeping, Poetics, and Song in Kaluli Expression.* 2nd ed. Philadelphia: University of Pennsylvania Press.

Harrison, Simon. 1982. *Laments for Foiled Marriages: Love-Songs from a Sepik River Village.* Boroko: Institute of Papua New Guinea Studies.

McLean, Mervyn. 1994. *Diffusion of Musical Instruments and Their Relation to Language Migrations in New Guinea.* Kulele: Occasional Papers on Pacific Music and Dance, 1. Boroko: Cultural Studies Division, National Research Institute.

Schieffelin, Edward L. 1976. *The Sorrow of the Lonely and the Burning of the Dancers.* New York: St. Martin's Press.

Waiko, John D. D. 1993. *A Short History of Papua New Guinea.* Melbourne: Oxford University Press.

Papuan Region of Papua New Guinea

The Papuan region includes the provinces along the southern coast: Western, Gulf, Central, Milne Bay, and Oro (Northern). Port Moresby, the capital of Papua New Guinea, lies in this region, within the National Capital District.

Much of the region lies south of the central mountains. Large expanses of lowlands and plains gradually narrow toward the east. The largest river in the country, the Fly, dominates Western Province. In Gulf Province, the Purari River has an extensive delta at its outflow into the Gulf of Papua. Farther east, foothills often reach down to the sea. By the ratio of height to width, Goodenough Island (Milne Bay Province) is one of the most mountainous islands in the world.

South of Western Province is the Torres Strait, which separates New Guinea from Australia. Until about six thousand years ago, this strait was dry land. Trade has occurred extensively throughout the strait, sustaining many cultural relations and products, including rattles, songs, and dances. The presence of the *kundu* in the Cape York area of Australia probably reflects influence from New Guinea.

The Motu of Central Province

Central Province surrounds the National Capital District. Both entities share the administrative center of Port Moresby. About forty thousand Motu live in villages around the district and along the nearby coast. They occupy seven western villages, four eastern ones, and three independent of the rest and each other.

The western and independent villages formerly engaged in *hiri*, an activity that has become a symbol for the Motu people. In large vessels, Motu men sailed 400 to 500 kilometers northwest to exchange arm shells and pottery for sago, an edible starch, to supplement their food between yam harvests. *Hiri* voyages occurred in October or November, with the southeast trade wind; the men returned in late December or January, with the northwest monsoon.

As the *hiri* has become an icon of the Motu generally, so each vessel was an emblem of the clan whose men planned its construction and voyage. The most important men worked in pairs. During the planning, building, and voyaging, the crew abstained from certain activities of ordinary life, including sexual relations. Each vessel bore its clan's name; if a vessel represented two clans, half the vessel bore one name, and half the other. The signs of these names were badges that decorated the vessels.

Music of the Hiri

The *hiri* were occasions for performing *ehona*, songs sung by men to the accompaniment of a bamboo percussion instrument (*sede*). One node was left intact, the other removed. A tonguelike projection, cut out of the side of the bamboo and extending beyond the open end, was hit with a stick. Men returning from a successful voyage stood on the vessel and sang while hitting their *sede*. *Ehona* were also sung at wakes; hence, they seemed suitable for times of danger or grief, as when men were facing death, or had just died.

Back in the village, women have their own songs and dances. They perform *upara* to strengthen people remaining in the village and those on the *hiri*, keep the *hiri* leaders' wives from worrying, save the voyaging men if their vessel is overdue, and welcome the men home.

The Motu have not made *hiri* voyages since the 1970s, but during the annual Hiri Moale Festival in Port Moresby, they reenact the building and sailing of their vessels. Aside from the display of Motu traditions, this festival has become an occasion for peoples of other parts of the country to present dances.

The Motu and Missionaries

The Motu were one of the first peoples in Papua New Guinea to undergo a sustained missionary presence. In 1872, missionaries from the London Missionary Society (LMS) made first contact. Soon the base for their effort in the Papuan Region was near Port Moresby. They fretted about Motu dances, which they thought occasioned adultery, so people who performed the old dances could not belong to the church.

LMS missionaries introduced hymns in Motu sung to Western melodies. The first hymnal printed in a Papua New Guinean language was published in Motu (1877). Eventually local choirs developed. Formed in the early 1930s, the Poreporena Village Choir, led by John Spychiger of the LMS and performing in Motu and English, was, before World War II, one of the first choirs to be locally broadcast on radio.

Missionaries recognized a need for substitutes for music they decried. LMS Polynesian teachers working in Motu villages introduced Christian singing based on their own traditions. Songs in the introduced style, now known as prophet songs (*peroveta anedia*), feature unaccompanied independent melodic parts for women (*pere* 'treble') and men (*maru* 'bass')—terms with Polynesian roots. Texts were originally in Polynesian languages, but new ones were composed in Motu. Texts often allude to biblical stories. Today, *peroveta* are a strong Motu tradition. They have spread to other areas of the region, where they are performed at church functions and the Hiri Moale Festival.

Because the Motu have been living near the national administrative center and have long had contact with missionaries and other outsiders, they participated in the early development of stringbands. With the assistance of studios based in Port Moresby, Motu-language songs spread widely throughout the region and remain influential.

Angan Peoples of Gulf Province

Gulf Province occupies an area bounded by about 300 kilometers of Papua New Guinea's southern coast. Its northern boundary lies in mountainous terrain 50 to 150 kilometers inland. In the west, the mouths of the Purari, Kikori, Turama, and other rivers form an alluvial fan, with sloughs and inlets on which people have built villages and camps, accessible only by canoe. A virtually uninhabited coastal plain ranges from less than 20 kilometers wide (near Kerema), to more than 110 (northwest of Kikori); especially in the east, this plain has kept mountain peoples, such as the Angan, culturally separate from coastal peoples. About thirty languages are spoken in the province.

After about 1960, mountain people's contacts with outsiders intensified. Apart from persons who lived near government stations, the population (of about ten thousand) maintains customary marriage, religion, medicine, and other contexts.

The sharpest musical contrast between the mountains and the coastal areas is that most of the young people in the mountains know and perform their music. As travel to urban centers becomes easier, more young people leave the villages, and the proportion of those who know only indigenous music decreases. Indigenous music remains dominant in the mountains.

Inland, the groups most available for study have been those of the Angan family of languages, of which four (Akoye, Ankave, Tainae, Kamea) appear in the province. Each of the first three languages has

a thousand or fewer speakers, spread out in fewer than a dozen villages per group. The Kamea number more than thirty thousand, living in hamlets from Kerema to Wau (Morobe Province).

Angan Singsings

Angan singsings mark the end of mourning. As host and honoree, the closest male relative of the deceased goes to dry meat for distribution on the last day of the event. When he returns from that work, families from neighboring hamlets, and even neighboring languages, begin preparing for the singsing, which fills each night for a week to a month. Men prepare headdresses; women prepare the incidentals needed for the journey. Each headdress is a 2-meter-long pole, topped with a bird-of-paradise effigy and strapped to the dancer's back. A plank of wood tied with a headband or rope braces and anchors it above his forehead. Halfway up the pole, a sprig of leaves protrudes forward and upward. Attached just below the bird of paradise, a cape drapes over the dancer's head and shoulders, giving the effect of a man's torso with an oversized conical head. Also attached below the bird of paradise is a pair of meter-long poles; on the end of each, one large cockatoo feather protrudes parallel to the ground. An hourglass drum completes the outfit. Women in attendance may carry branches of a tree whose leaves serve in magic; they wear "grass" skirts, but no special decorations.

Most performers arrive, usually grouped by clan, after about 10:00 P.M. Performers sing and dance idiosyncratically. Men bob their heads, bending their knees in time with their drumming, so the movement of the cockatoo feathers describes a semicircle from above the headdress almost to the ground. Women may hold branches in either hand while swiveling their hips—a motion their skirts exaggerate. Early in the night, women walk in a circle, exaggerating the motions of their hips. As the performers' energy dissipates, men sing less frequently and dance less vigorously, until, near dawn, the remaining dancers are plodding or simply standing in place. The walk provides an opportunity for girls to flirt by stepping behind favored boys. At sunrise, the party breaks up.

The day after the last night of the feast, the host rehydrates, cooks, and distributes the dried meats; the distribution discharges debts incurred during bereavement. At sundown, after he has distributed the meats, he dons ceremonial belts. For about ten minutes, he dances—first alone, then with his wife or wives. People toss green stalks of bamboo onto a bonfire; the stalks explode with a bang. The celebrants then shoo away the spirits of the deceased, and the singsing ends.

Angan Musical Style

An Angan chorus is a large group of soloists, simultaneously singing their own melodies at idiosyncratic tempos. They base their melodies on a shared tonal center. Solo singing is by far the most common Angan music. The Akoye have two styles: *ayaake* is spontaneous, often improvised singing; *oimae* is music for singsings, usually accompanied by a steady beat on a drum.

Inside houses, where traditional singing occurs spontaneously, a husband and wife often sing duets, consisting of differently texted melodies in the same style, sharing one tonal center. Angan phrases end in long notes. Often, as one singer holds a note, the other singer begins a new phrase: when the second singer reaches a cadence, the first begins a second phrase; and so on. Sometimes the duet resembles the choral style, with the performers simultaneously singing different songs.

—Adapted from an article by Don Niles and Virginia Whitney

Bibliography

Dutton, Tom, ed. 1982. *The Hiri in History: Further Aspects of Long Distance Motu Trade in Central Papua*. Pacific Research Monograph 8. Canberra: Australian National University.

Fischer, Hans. 1986. *Sound-Producing Instruments in Oceania*. Edited by Don Niles. Translated by Philip W. Holzknecht. Boroko: Institute of Papua New Guinea Studies.

Kunst, Jaap. 1967. *Music in New Guinea: Three Studies*. Translated by Jeune Scott-Kemball. Verhandelingen van het Koninklijk Instituut voor Taal-, Land- en Volkenkunde, 53. The Hague: Martinus Nijhoff.

Highland Region of Papua New Guinea

This region, deriving its name from its altitude in the central mountains, includes Enga, Western Highlands, Southern Highlands, Chimbu, and Eastern Highlands provinces. With only 13 percent of the country's area, it contains 36 percent of the population, but has fewer languages than the other regions because some of its languages are spoken by tens of thousands of people.

The highest point in Papua New Guinea, Mount Wilhelm (4,509 meters), lies in the region. About three hundred to four hundred years ago, the introduction of sweet potatoes permitted gardening at higher altitudes, the domestication of more pigs, and the rise of pork-based feasts, replacing feasts of ceremonial puddings.

The Melpa of Western Highlands Province

Western Highlands Province, in the center of the region, is the most populous province in the region and the second most populous in the country. The province contains numerous broad valleys, where the main population lives.

Just outside the provincial capital, Mount Hagen, is Kuk Swamp, where archaeological research has uncovered a network of drainage ditches dating back about nine thousand years and suggesting that horticulture developed here about the same time as in southeastern and western Asia—making New Guineans among the first gardeners in the world. Local societies have leader-based organizations and elaborate exchange ceremonies.

About eighty thousand Melpa-speakers live around Mount Hagen township. Intensive horticulturists, they grow sweet potatoes as their staple and coffee for cash. For compensation payments, ceremonial exchanges, and brideprice presentations, they rear pigs. Men dominate politics—as orators, settlers of disputes, and legislators.

Europeans entered the area in 1933, searching for gold. They brought colonial controls, economic and political changes, and Christian denominations: Roman Catholic, Lutheran, and Seventh-Day Adventist; later, charismatic evangelical sects arrived (Baptists, Apostolics, Assemblies of God). Despite much cultural change, the Melpa still perform many of their precontact genres of music and dance. Pastors have translated Christian songs into Melpa, and participants in the church compose guitar-accompanied songs, but the indigenous genres are expressively unmatched by the introduced genres.

Social Contexts

The Melpa most commonly voice their feelings in songs of courtship and songs based on melodies and images similar to these but directed toward kin, friends, or enemies. Public songs are composed for and performed at dances, which accompany ceremonial exchanges (*moka*) (figure 1). Funeral songs, sung solo or in concert, lie midway between the personal and the public; composed by individuals of either sex, they emerge in the process of grief and mourning.

Courting

Since about 1980, courtship songs and the occasions on which people perform them have become a casualty of radios, cassettes, and the introduction of Christian music and values. Traditionally, people

Figure 1 A female Melpa performer wears finery of feathers, shells, paints, plaited fibers, and beads.
Photo by Andrew J. Strathern.

sang these songs at night. Decorated with feathers, marsupial furs, and facial paint, suitors would visit a house where one or more girls were expecting them, chaperoned by a senior woman. To encourage the girls to emerge from the sleeping compartment, the suitors would begin singing. After a while, a girl would come out and kneel, facing the fire. A suitor would sit at her side. Accompanied by spectators' singing, he would sway his head toward the girl until his forehead touched hers. After a few quick rotations of the neck, with noses pressed together, the pair bobbed their heads in unison to the floor three times or so, and then brought them up for a fresh round. After a while, another suitor would replace him beside the girl, who during one evening might "turn head" with half a dozen youths. An evening of courting could lead to elopement, but the seriousness of paying a high brideprice, with its attendant risk of failure, always loomed.

Ceremonial Exchanges (Moka)

To partners in allied groups, men give pigs and Papua New Guinean currency. By surpassing gifts received earlier from the other side, they try to display superiority. A crowd of spectators gathers to rate the wealth handed over and the dancers' decorations. For these exchanges, leaders compose songs that hosts perform for guests. The texts comment on political relations, subtly revealing states of hostility or alliance, ironically deprecating the collective strength of their singers, and obliquely announcing intentions to fight or make peace. Men and women dance in separate companies, each with its own song. On the same occasions, young people of both sexes convene informally to perform dances and songs that have humorous or sexual connotations.

Dancing among the Melpa is a rhythmic analogy of human and bird-of-paradise lives. The birds mature by growing the famous tail plumes, lost by molting after their sexual display. Men's dances at festivals of exchange demonstrate the maturity of the leader holding the festival. Men dance for the climax of the event; they then molt their dance, putting it away until the next festival.

Most men dance the *mörl*, for which they wear feathered headdresses; black, white, and red facial paint; long-stringed aprons, netted by women; and at their backs, bunches of fresh cordyline leaves. They face the spectators in a long row, holding spears or *kundus* (*nditing*). Their song wafts up and down the line, as lead drummers and singers take it up in turn and simultaneously bend their knees to the drumbeats. Rather than expressing triumph over their competitors, *mörl* often evoke feelings of loss on the deaths of clansmen, whose absence from the dancers'

line reduces its length. Most texts have just one stanza, which performers repeat many times, sometimes singing of themselves collectively in the first person singular: *Ndekene moklp noint ndop a | Kant mel a. | Kana rapa kröu ronom. | Ang nim elpa mak rolna, | Rokl e kawa ndonom* 'Here at Ndekene, I look / Across the river. / The men's house at Kana is cold. / My brother, you made another mark, / And our tall man is missing'. Here, to one of their tribesmen, they impute wrongdoing that resulted in the death of a tall, handsome man. Concealed intentions to pursue revenge underlie such sentiments of grief and loss. They add counterpoint to the formal speeches made after the dancing ends—speeches that usually proclaim alliance and peaceful intent.

For *moka*, married women perform *werl*, slow dances in place. Wearing ornaments and feathers, they keep time by beating *kundus*. Their songs repeat the topics of *mörl* or detail the activities of young men of the community into which they have married. One begins by recalling that for tethering pigs, women weave ropes: *Okla ndop kant e, o e, | Kora Manda wi, o, | Weng kan kanem, o e: | Werl ro* 'I look up and I see, o e, / Up there Manda from Kora, o, / Is weaving a rope, o e: / Strike *werl*'. In the second stanza of this song, the women recall that to decorate their heads for dancing, they mount scarab beetles within orchid fibers: *Noint ndop kant e, o e, | Kora Korlopi noi | Morok rom ronom: | Werl ro* 'I look across and see, o e, / Over there Korlopi from Kora / Sings to the scarab beetle: / Strike *werl*'.

Funerals

For funerals, people compose and teach *ka*, highly stylized and expressively simple songs, which praise the dead or accuse them of deserting the living. This example honors a Mokei man who died in 1971 in a car accident: *Mbarat o rokl nile | Kokela ond o. | E e e ye e. | Wö kuki ndaep nile nga, | Korop nint o. | We e e e* 'I have just come / Along the road. / E e e ye e. / My fine-skinned man, / I search for him, I say. / We e e e'. Smeared in orange or yellow clay, a massed choir of male mourners performed the song. They marched onto the arena where the body was on display, circled it counterclockwise many times, and sat at the edge of the grounds. Other *ka* receive similar performances.

Recreational Music

For casual entertainment, persons of either sex play *susaps* (*tembakl*) or four-holed end-blown flutes (*koa pela ming*), in both cases using melodies associated with tales. A flutist may accompany a singer or sing the song after playing the melody. Because of the

Oceania

availability of radio and cassettes, skill at playing these instruments is declining. Individuals of the same sex may play them in duets. The words of recreational songs might evoke warfare, pose a question to creatures of the forest, or express a philosophical point.

Ballads

Ballads (*kang rom*) are important items of sung entertainment. They are performed mostly by men, though some women know them. Often using archaic forms of expression, they tell stories (also preserved in certain tales) of the doings of heroes and heroines. Performing them is a challenge, because the singer should complete a piece without a break—inhaling at the end of each couplet, but continuing to sing—for hundreds of lines. Singers perform at night, mostly in men's houses, for a circle of kin and visitors. In payment, listeners present small gifts.

The Enga Peoples of Enga Province

About two hundred thousand Enga, the most numerous people of Papua New Guinea, live in scattered hamlets in the mountains and valleys north and west of Mount Hagen. They speak a single language, differentiated into nine dialects. Throughout the province in the late twentieth century, singsings became a business, especially at Christmas. Hosts charge admission and sell food and drink. Attendees pursue politics and social affairs: they may arrange marriages, negotiate trades, exchange pigs, and pay compensation to a murdered man's relatives.

Musical Styles

For eight social settings, the Enga maintain distinct styles of singing. To meet evolving cultural needs, they have modified some of them. The musical style of songs for courting serves for newly composed songs, whose subjects include astronauts, nationhood, and Christian themes. Informal activities invite the performance of songs. Journeys, men's work (like building houses), and women's work (like gardening) are typical themes. The songs are mostly improvised, though examples called *pindita wee* have retained popularity for generations.

Dancing

The Enga perform dance-songs (*mali lyingi*) at singsings. Enga dancing is famous for its line of men with interlocked arms. Standing in place, dressed in long skirts, they bend their knees to a slow and steady drumbeat, making their skirts flip in unison, like a waving curtain. On offbeats, they hiss.

Another famous trait of the costume is a wig, circular and black, worn by each dancer to symbolize strength and handsomeness. Speakers of each dialect use a distinctive style of wig. Each man's wig is made of cuttings of his own hair, kept since adolescence. Inserted in it, bird-of-paradise plumes or long, black feathers evoke an imposing height. On noses and foreheads, men often wear paint, which identifies clan and status. They wear kina shells as breastplates. Girls and women occasionally join the line, standing beside a relative or friend.

The Enga have two other dances. In semicircles, three or four singer-dancers link arms over their shoulders, performing unaccompanied. Larger ensembles, with individuals not touching, focus the performance on a prospective spouse.

Courting

Adolescents meet at parties organized by adolescent girls, with married aunts or sisters as hosts and chaperones. Invited boys approach the designated site, announcing in songs that they will see the girls at sundown. They pass by, singing. At dusk, they return, joking and singing. They enter silently and sit on the men's side. The hostess and her husband serve them food, and the husband and his sons then leave. The girl who organized the party goes to get her girlfriends; in her absence, the boys sing songs of courtship (*enda lakungi*). The girls arrive and sit on the women's side. They too begin to sing. Boys, a few at a time, go over to them. As the singing continues, each boy whispers into the ear of one girl. Girls' songs alternate with boys' songs. Near dawn, both sides sing jointly. Then, while the girls sing, the boys leave.

Initiation

Male initiation formerly prepared adolescents for manhood. Five to ten males retreated to a secluded part of the forest, where respected elders taught them magical techniques to counter women's contaminating influences. The elders encouraged them to dream about the clan's future. Emerging from these rites, the initiates celebrated maturity. Standing shoulder to shoulder with eyes closed, bodies oiled, faces blackened, and wigs adorned with special plumes, they sang initiatory songs, whose texts metaphorically related a boy's love for a girl whom he hoped to marry and told of his aspiration to clan-based leadership. With rapt attention, relatives strained to hear each nuance of the sacred lyrics, for they forecast the clan's future.

Poetry

Many Enga lyrics are direct. One, sung by the clan of the deceased to the people who have given compensation, says: "We are brothers, and we thank you for the pigs from Wabag." Others common at singsings in the 1990s included these: "We gathered feathers for decoration; now we are singing; some of the feathers will be broken"; and "Though some of our people have died, we still have a healthy community, and we have young men who are growing up."

Other texts have hidden meanings. The text "When I went to *sanggai*, it was cold near the gate; I throw away my things and come home" might mean "You jilted me; you accepted gifts from another." The text "The house shines; when I see it, I want to come: why don't you hide the shining?" might mean "Your body is beautiful; it attracts me: why don't you cover it?" Dance-songs praise one's clan, citing pigs, cassowaries, and kina shells.

The Music System

The Enga recognize that certain people have an ability to compose, and prefer that performers have strong, resonant voices. Skilled singers, usually elders, strategically position themselves in the line of dancers. A clan's reputation and influence in part depend on the quality of the music it performs. The Enga admire composers who can improvise imaginative lyrics.

Men's songs have a narrow range and distinctive glides. Informal songs are responsorial, with a leader and a chorus; each phrase varies the initial one. A typical text is a women's song about building houses: "Now I am working; someday I will sleep in a good house; now I am not concerned about these things." Young women sing this before their marriage. These songs have in common an inventory of four essential tones, C–D–E–F or D–E–G–A, of which the lowest is the tonal center.

Musical Instruments

The most important Enga instrument is the *kundu* (*laiyane*). With hot coals and knives, men hollow out a hardwood log, scraping away the excess until a shell of about 1.5 centimeters remains. The drumhead is the skin of a lizard or a pig, wetted and stretched onto the rim, and sealed there by sap. Tuners stick several pellets of heated resin to its center. In dance-songs, each man grasps his drum at its middle, steadily beating its head with his free hand.

Informally, Enga soloists play end-blown bundle panpipes (*pupe*) and bamboo flutes (*kululu*). The latter have three to five holes for fingering, and measure some 40 centimeters long, with a 3-centimeter bore. Both instruments are commonest in the Kandep area. For amusement, young men play bamboo *susaps* (*olaiyole*).

The Huli of Southern Highlands Province

Southern Highlands Province lies in the southwest of the region. Mendi is the provincial capital. Colonial powers joined part of the province to Papua, to the south. Its northern and central cultures have many ethnographic parallels with other upland cultures; peoples along its southern and western borders share some traditions with lowland cultures.

Culturally and linguistically homogeneous, the Huli inhabit the Tagali River Basin and surrounding areas. Their land covers roughly 5,200 square kilometers, mainly at altitudes of 1,500 to 2,400 meters. Sweet potatoes are the Huli staple.

Huli society is egalitarian, with cognatic descent expressed in the formation of clans. Males and females occupy separate houses in scattered settlements. Young men withdraw to the forest to develop survival skills and grow their hair, symbolizing masculine strength and purity. Some join the organization of celibate bachelors,

> **cognatic descent**
> A mode of tracing ancestry that regards a person as being equally related to his or her father's and mother's family.

receive magical ginger plants, and wear crescent-shaped ceremonial wigs. After passing tests, they receive common, rounded wigs and panpipes. Some remain bachelors, but most marry.

Sweethearts show affection through poetic stanzas articulated with a two-stringed musical bow (*gáwá*) and a *susap* (*híriyùla*). A man marries by paying his in-laws about fifteen pigs. The couple postpone consummating the marriage for months, but begin gardening and raising pigs. Spouses occupy separate houses, but meet in their gardens. Most marriages are monogamous. Polygynists court additional wives at nocturnal gatherings (*dáwanda*), which only married men and single women attend; the men sing clan-identifying songs (*ú*, *dáwanda ú*), enabling the women to choose their partners.

Huli spirits include God, departed human spirits, and demons. Myths record Huli history, including the development of language, yodeling, and musical instruments. Ritual practices include mass sacrifices of pigs to avert catastrophes and promote healthy crops, animals, and humans. In the *màli*, a ritual celebrating successful sorcery, *kundu*-playing men dance; by the 1970s, this genre was commemorating Independence Day and religious celebrations.

Music Systems

The Huli have no term for any comprehensive concept of "music." Most perform many vocal and instrumental genres, mostly solo; performers spontaneously compose pieces. Besides magic-controlling recitations (learned from older practitioners), aspiring musicians receive no instruction; to develop skills, they watch and practice.

In musical expression, language is paramount. Apart from drumming (*bà* 'hit'), all vocal and instrumental performance employs the mouth, and is signified by *là* 'speak', as in *híriyùla là* 'speak with the *susap*, play the *susap*'. Poetic articulation characterizes all performances on the double-stringed musical bow and the *susap*: while the vocal cords remain inactive, the oral cavity reshapes the acoustic energy of the instrument. When men play long panpipes, they often whisper phrases.

Huli poetry develops the imagery of parable words. Stanzas typically consist of multiple repeated lines, each containing a changing noun. Alternating names of places and clans identify individuals or express yearning for one's homeland. The Huli say thoughts form in the heart, rise in breath from the lungs to the mouth, and roll off the tongue as words. Language determines musical structure: linguistic tones affect melodic tones, and linguistic articulation determines musical pace and rhythm. Where context or instrumental technique disallows linguistic articulation, music imitates yodeling—the precursor of human speech, according to Huli myths.

Pitch is described as *dìndiha* 'underneath', *dòmbena* 'in-between', or *dāliga* 'above'. Various expressions—*lō pòdo íri dāli* 'break the speaking up and down' and *lōpodopoda* and *lōpodalu* 'going up and down'—describe melodies. *Lō pòdo* (also *lō pòda*) 'breaking the speaking' denotes pauses and codas. Another expression, *gilinine òre pōdolene* or *pōdolene*, implies breaking a decorated length into pieces. *Gīlini*, *gīli*, and *gīligili* (zigzag patterns in using cane to bind artifacts) suggest movement up and down. Men's singing on a level pitch below melodies, the continuous sound of the outer *gáwa* string below inner-strand melodies, and the underlying pitch of the longest bundle panpipe blown in passing to surrounding tubes, are denoted *lā āmuhà* 'speak, stand toward *āmu* direction'. This direction lies along a valley, or horizontal; musically, it means 'going along straight'.

Vocal Music

Huli vocal music encompasses solo and collective yodeling, solo laments of love, collective singing, laments, storytelling, legal declamations, and magic-controlling recitations. Descriptions of two of these genres follow.

Yodeling

Yodeling is an important Huli musical activity. People differentiate two main types of men's yodel-ing: solo (*ú*), and collective (*ìwa*). Solo yodeling helps people communicate across mountainous terrain. Men yodel whole statements; each ends with a high-called *ú*. Purely yodeled signals include *à–ú–à–ú* 'Where are you?' and *háko–háko* 'I'm here'.

Collective yodeling occurs when men work together. It synchronizes individual actions, informing listeners of the activity in progress. It has several genres, each based on patterns of interlocking calls: the high-falling *ú* begins all collective yodeling, is usually started by one man, and can spring from a low pitch on the vowel /a/, the same level to which it falls; *pēge*, *pēbe*, *hēbe*, *pēbo*, or *bēbo* is a level, lower-pitched call; the level *kē* is the highest falsetto call; *ī*, a medium-level call, follows *kē*; *gèla* is a rising call, yelled in a medium range; *púlu* or *úlu*, the lowest call, resembles a falling exclamation. The Huli have six main genres of collective yodeling; descriptions of three of them follow.

Nògo ú 'pig yodel' is performed by men carrying cuts of butchered pigs to the *hòmanogo*, a feast held after mourning a death. It is based on the pattern *ú–gèla*, which pivots on the piercing call *ú*. It signals that the death has been compensated for, so mourning must cease.

Gèla is the name of the *ìwa* yodeled in public processions of the fertility rituals *tēge* and *gáia tēge*, and in *tēge púlu* initiations, as the initiates run to the culthouses with their guardians and during rituals inside the house. It follows the *ú–gèla–púlu* pattern, where *púlu* often overlaps *gèla*. Boys sometimes cry the *kē* call above the men's *gèla* and *púlu*. The call *gèla*, with its syllables a major second apart, has a clearer melodic structure than that of the pig yodel; the syllable *kē* lies an octave above the syllable *là*. The *gèla* coordinates collective movements, summons spirits, and frightens younger initiates to toughen them.

Women have solo and collective calls. In rage or excitement, a woman shouts *hèagola!* Peaceful groups of women walking to their gardens in fine weather call out *hēao*.

Magic-controlling Recitations

People of either sex learn magic-controlling recitations (*gāmu*) from older practitioners or spirits. Context allows for wide stylistic variations, from secret mumbling to loud performing. Women use *dàgia gāmu* to help their daughters obtain desirable husbands; when painting girls for dances, this is named *hàre gāmu* (from *hàre* 'ochre facial paint'). Mothers with sickly babies can pay an older practitioner to perform *wāneigini gāmu* ('children magic'). After removing a child from its mother's hearing, the old woman mutters her *gāmu* while rubbing clay and spittle on its body. Women perform *húbibi gāmu* to make men appear invisible to their enemies in battle; *húbibi gāmu* also protect a husband from another woman's charms.

Men also use magic. Bachelors perform *mānda gāmu* to make their hair grow and perform *iba gìya gāmu* to receive their ginger plants. Both genres use falsetto, with melodic structures that resemble those for telling stories. During initiation rituals, specialists loudly perform *lìruali āwa* for healthy crops, pigs, and initiates. Male exorcists perform *bílogua* while performing farewell *dáwe* (*dáwe bílogua*) and hitting their long *dìndanao tàbage* drums.

Musical Instruments

Huli instruments include a *susap*, three drums, three musical bows, and three panpipes. Apart from drumming, which accompanies men's dancing, these instruments are played solo.

Susap

The *susap* is cut from wild bamboo and shined by being passed through ashes. Twine is affixed to the basal end. Holding the instrument between the lips, the player jerks the twine to vibrate the tongue of the instrument. Men and women play *susaps* in contexts used for the musical bow. The performance features poetic articulation. Inarticulate interstanzaic sections imitate Huli collective yodeling. The stanza in figure 2 uses cloud imagery punctuated by the phrase *àyago nēdò* 'I am in a state of having experienced sorrow'.

Drums

Kundus have undecorated, somewhat hourglass-shaped bodies of *làyano* wood, with single heads of cuscus skin. Held in the left hand, they are hit with the right open palm. The *tòmbena tàbage* sounds *dòmbeni* or *tòmbeni* 'in-between'; the long *dìndanao tàbage* sounds *dìndiha* 'underneath'.

Male dancers play the common *tòmbena tàbage* at *màli* celebrations. In two facing rows, wearing ceremonial costumes with crescent-shaped red or black wigs, they jump sideways while hitting their drums in a simple syncopated rhythm.

Only male mediums play *dìndanao tàbage*. During exorcisms, two or three exorcists, wearing feathered headdresses and women's skirts, run around a bonfire beating their drums; they stop periodically to perform *bílogua* into the fire. Their comical attire and running supposedly make malevolent demons laugh, and *bílogua* stanzas suggest the demons should go far away. Exorcists sometimes use the rare decorated *yūlu málai* (or *málai*), which sounds *dàliga* 'above'; with a fishtail-shaped body and a lizard-skin head, it was formerly imported from Papuan Plateau peoples.

The Two-stringed Bow

The *gáwa* is a two-stringed, orally resonated, strummed bow, through which performers articulate spontaneously created poetry. Played by both men and women, the instrument has a soft, clear, shimmering sound. The Huli consider its performance the supreme artistic achievement.

Figure 2 Excerpt from Amele's performance on a Huli *susap* at Bebenete in 1978. *Transcription Jacqueline Pugh-Kitingan.*

Makers pass a strong, flexible piece of wood through hot ashes. The bowstring and plectrum are traditionally *tùgubili*-vine root; from the 1970s, makers have also used wire, strummed with *ígibu* cane or bamboo. The bow is mouthed at its shorter end. The left hand holds the longer end, while the right hand strums the bowstring with a plectrum near the mouth. The inner string sounds a major third higher than the outer; when stopped by the left thumb, the inner pitch rises a semitone.

Performance on two-stringed bows features the articulation of poetry. Texts are figurative: a text expressing a woman's love for her husband is: "I am being wetted by rain from Ìbai, Àluya, Àndama, Gúrubu, Gàngabu, and Màndalo"—her husband's clans.

Bundle Panpipes

Huli men play bamboo bundle panpipes of three kinds: the common, medium-sized, seven-tubed *gúlupòbe*; the rare, longer *gùlungùlu*; and the short, eight-tubed *púlugèla*. Their sound is soft and breathy. Men play common *gúlupòbe* and *púlugèla* on long daytime journeys; they keep *gùlungùlu* at home for playing at night. They play *gúlupòbe* and *gùlungùlu* upon reaching adulthood and wearing wigs. They carefully tune and personally label the pipes. The longest pipe of a *gúlupòbe* measures about 60 centimeters; that of the *gùlungùlu* reaches about 90 centimeters. Both instruments have seven pipes, the shortest closed by a bamboo node. Pipes are cut from *bè háraya*, bundled with the longest pipe in the center, and bound with twine or grass.

Men sometimes whisper courtship-related words as they play. The lyrics are short fragmented statements, unlike those of other Huli sung poetry.

A man plays the short *púlugèla* only after he has fathered children. Its performance imitates *màli ìwa* and *gèla* styles of yodeling. Consisting of four open and four closed pipes, about 25 centimeters long, it is held in the right hand with the three longest (closed) pipes against the fingers and the three shortest (open) pipes against the thumb. Its tuning varies. Discordantly breathy timbre enhances the imitation of yodeling.

—Adapted from an article by Don Niles,
Andrew J. Strathern, Vida Chenoweth,
Paul W. Brennan, and Jacqueline Pugh-Kitingan

Bibliography

Brennan, Paul W. ed. 1970. *Exploring Enga Culture: Studies in Missionary Anthropology: Second Anthropological Conference of the New Guinea Lutheran Mission.* Wapenamanda: New Guinea Lutheran Mission.

——. 1977. *Let Sleeping Snakes Lie: Central Enga Religious Belief and Ritual.* Adelaide: Australian Association for the Study of Religions.

Chenoweth, Vida. 1976. *Musical Instruments of Papua New Guinea.* Ukarumpa, Papua New Guinea: Summer Institute of Linguistics.

Feil, D. K. 1987. *The Evolution of Highland Papua New Guinea Societies.* Cambridge: Cambridge University Press.

Pugh-Kitingan, Jacqueline. 1977. "Huli Language and Instrumental Performance." *Ethnomusicology* 21:205–232.

——. 1979. "The Huli and Their Music." *Hemisphere* 23:84–89.

——. 1981. "An Ethnomusicological Study of the Huli of the Southern Highlands, Papua New Guinea." Ph.D. dissertation, University of Queensland.

——. 1992. "Huli Yodeling and Instrumental Performance." In *Sound and Reason: Music and Essays in Honour of Gordon D. Spearitt,* ed. Warren A. Bebbington and Royston Gustavson, 64–120. St. Lucia: Faculty of Music, University of Queensland.

Strathern, Andrew J. 1971. *The Rope of Moka.* Cambridge: Cambridge University Press.

——. 1972. *One Father, One Blood.* Canberra: Australia National University Press.

——, ed. 1974. *Melpa Amb Kenan.* Port Moresby: Institute of Papua New Guinea Studies.

Mamose Region of Papua New Guinea

The Mamose Region includes the provinces along the northern coast of New Guinea: West Sepik, East Sepik, Madang, Morobe. Its name derives from parts of the names Madang, Morobe, and Sepik. With 31 percent of the national area, it supports 16 percent of the population.

Most of the region is north of the central chain of mountains. The Sepik River, the second longest in the country, drains the western part of the central depression. To the east of its mouth is the Ramu River; farther east, near Lae, is the Markham River. The Torricelli Mountains, near the border with Indonesia, run west to east, in West Sepik Province. On the border of Madang and Morobe, the Finisterre and Saruwaged ranges rise to about 4 kilometers.

The Abelam of East Sepik Province

The administrative headquarters of East Sepik Province is Wewak. The peoples of this province live along the river and its tributaries, in the Torricelli and Prince Alexander mountains to the north, and the Hunstein Range to the south. The fame of wooden carvings made in the province attracts tourists.

There are about sixty thousand Abelam. The Samukundi Abelam, on whom this sketch concentrates, densely populate the foothills of the Prince Alexander Mountains.

Abelam musical performances usually occur in either of two places: for male initiations, within the ceremonial house; and for public rituals and social occasions, on the ceremonial ground in front of it. At the center of this ground lies the moonwoman, a smooth, roughly spherical white stone about 20 centimeters in diameter, on which social dancing, to songs called *bira*, focuses. A ring of men, each carrying a *kundu* in one hand, circles it counterclockwise; with the palm of the free hand, they strike the drumheads. Drummers take turns, but the best play longest. The meters are irregular, in patterns that mark out sung phrases. The tempo starts slow, and repeatedly accelerates and decelerates.

Dancers of both sexes, often with linked arms or hands, circle the drummers counterclockwise in a normal gait. A chorus of women stands inside this circle, facing the moonwoman. Performances are casual; individuals come and go at will. Each event lasts all night, with only short interruptions; it ends at daybreak. At large celebrations, singing and dancing may fill several nights.

Festivals involving long yams are momentous occasions. Male prestige hinges on success in growing large tubers, which may exceed 3 meters long. Men display their finest tubers, which intervillage rivals inspect and measure. Later, the growers give the tubers to the rivals, who try to return yams as large as or larger than those received. (Returning a like-sized yam ends the rivalry; returning a larger one continues it.) After the inspection and measuring, men take turns walking the ceremonial ground, brandishing spears, giving brief speeches, and performing songs called *minja*. When the yams are unusually large, initiated men hold a *kaangu* ceremony, which non-initiates may not attend; texts of its songs focus on sacred ancestors.

At the singsing after the judging of the yams, pairs of male dancers cluster around several singer-drummers. In time to the drumbeats, some dancers bend their knees; others shuffle one foot forward (left, right, left, right); younger ones kick a foot high off the ground as they bring it forward. A second dance then begins. The tempo quickens. The drummers face each other in parallel lines. Other participants follow randomly behind them. With a quick, prancing step, the lines back away from each other, only to reconverge; they continue this oscillation until the song ends. Singsings of many types accompany male-initiation ceremonies. In stylized and symbolic motifs, costumes combine shells, feathers, flowers, and paint. Particularly distinctive are men's headdresses, woven from split cane and adorned with colorful feathers. At successive initiatory stages, headdresses increase in size. For the final stage, they tower 3 to 6 meters above dancers' heads.

Musical Instruments

Most Abelam instruments serve ceremonial functions. Two percussion instruments, the *susap* and the *garamut*, are exceptions. People play *susaps* infrequently, according to whim; the instruments do not have high cultural significance. *Garamuts* (*mi*) have utilitarian and ritual functions. Hollowed from hardwood logs, they adorn most main Abelam hamlets, summon people to meetings, signal important occasions (deaths, harvests, feasts), and accomplish certain tasks (calling home a person or a lost pig, warning a rainmaker or sorcerer to desist). Intricately carved *garamuts* stay hidden inside the ceremonial houses, where only initiated men may see them. These instruments form trios: the lead *garamut* (*maama mi*) has the lowest pitch; the second (*kwaté mi*), an intermediate size and pitch; the third (*nyégél mi*), the highest pitch.

In ritual contexts, people play several wind instruments: whirled slats, vessel flutes (carved from nuts), conch trumpets, and bamboo wind instruments. With carved wood and other objects, these instruments form a class of sacred items, displayed to initiates during initiations and called spirits' voices.

The only Abelam drum is the *kundu* (*kaang*), carved from one piece of wood. Stretched lizard skin covers one end of it. To control the pitch and timbre, the center of the head bears waxy pellets.

Musical Genres

The Abelam have two basic genres of song: *minja*, normally performed solo by men; and *bira*, performed by mixed-sex ensembles. Solo singing ordinarily occurs during yam festivals, village meetings (to resolve conflicts or help heal individuals), and the performance of myths and tales. Typically, men perform in turn, each singing one song.

In the context of yam festivals, the performances of *minja* become musical duels. Texts recount incidents in veiled, metaphorical diction: a leaf floating on water may represent the body of an enemy, killed near a river. The performer may sing of birds or flowers, but most adult listeners grasp his hidden messages. These songs, routinely meant to insult, are frequently answered with rejoinder *minja*, relating other incidents.

An important genre of solo song, the *ngwayé kundi* 'stopping talk', can interrupt fighting or warfare. The singer hoists in the air a leaf of the *naaréndu*, a symbol of peace. He sings the song and gives a short speech. While he is performing, people must suspend hostilities. *Ngwayé kundi* also herald the settlement of disputes.

Mixed-sex singing, *bira*, associated with yam festivals and male-initiation ceremonies, occurs typically at night. At yam festivals, *bira* have polyphony in two parts: one for male singer-drummers, and one for a chorus of women. Vocal lines alternate and overlap. Melodies, which usually descend about an octave, freely repeat, with bridges between statements. The most distinctive features of the music are the extent of its repetition and the irregularity of its rhythms.

—Adapted from an article by Don Niles, Richard Scaglion, and Alice Pomponio

THE *SIA* OF THE SIASI ISLANDS

The *sia*, the trademark singsing of the Siasi Islands, symbolizes the region. Nationwide, children perform it at school festivals, and it has spread throughout Morobe, coastal West New Britain, and parts of Madang.

The Siasi Islands lie 40 or more kilometers off the mainland of New Guinea, with a population of about twelve thousand. The main islands are Arop to the northwest and Umboi to the southeast. Siasi Islanders are famous as maritime entrepreneurs, who connect participants as far apart as Madang, Kilenge, and Finschhafen in a system wherein people trade goods, services, and important knowledge, including songs and dances.

The *sia* originated on Arop. Its origins have been recorded in a sacred myth, and in genealogies. The name *sia* comes from the Arop word for bird. The dancers' movements often imitate the motions made by birds, especially in the principal dance, that of the golden-crested cockatoo. Performances occur at night. (Dances performed by day are called *kai*.) A *sia* performance usually honors firstborn children at their first singsing. It is the most melodic and colorful Siasi dance. For these reasons, Siasi Islanders often choose to perform it at regional shows and teach it to schoolchildren as part of their curriculum. It serves as a context for arranging trysts—a trait that has elicited comment from all sorts of outsiders, from the first missionaries to mainland New Guineans. For this and other reasons, early missionaries tried to eradicate all dance-related feasts, and Siasi Islanders who converted to Lutheranism did abolish them. Of the small islands of the archipelago, only Mandok maintains its feasts; its people became Roman Catholics because the priests of that religion did not insist on abolishing cultural practices of this kind. Aromot Island, partly Lutheran and partly Roman Catholic, is divided on the subject.

The *Sia* of Mandok Island

Men, the featured dancers, demonstrate their talents for style, motion, and endurance. They move in different formations at different periods of the day, following a complex sequence over many days. After they perform, village elders clear the central plaza to make way for dancers who imitate scenes from nature in popular skits that include a man hunting a wild boar, a cockatoo crossing an open space to peck at bananas, and two birds traveling together along a branch to a desired location. The most talented dancers wait until nightfall to perform solos. While they perform, they hold pigs' tusks in their teeth. In the dark, their white hats and other white decorations, picking up the soft light from fires and pressure lamps, seem to glow.

From the sidelines, women sing in tense falsetto, soaring above the male voices' melodic lines. Women dance in twos and threes, arms linked in a rhythmically bouncing walk, swinging special pandanus baskets in their hands. For *kai*, women hold the baskets high; for *sia*, women swing them from a lower position. Women scrutinize the men, perhaps to slip a betelnut into a dancer's basket as he passes—an invitation for a tryst.

The *Sia* as an Index of Change

Over time, to accommodate individual creativity and current fashion, songs have been added to the *sia*, and costumes have been altered for it. Its form, function, and meaning have remained core features of Siasi life, and stand as testimony to the continuity of Siasi Islanders' values and culture.

When performed for firstborns, the *sia* can last for years, at a cost of thousands of dollars. The primary objects of exchange were formerly pigs and locally carved bowls, up to 1.2 meters long. The child's parents and grandparents gave these valuables to a ritual-exchange partner in the village, or to their overseas-trade partner, as appropriate. The partner's family distributed the pork and other valuables, with food for the feast—betel, manioc pudding, sweet potatoes, taro pudding, and tobacco. After persistent European contact, and especially the introduction of a market economy and industrially manufactured goods, the processes and functions of exchange and feasting remained, but the actual goods in play changed to reflect the hosts' financial means, including resources from urban relatives and wage employment.

In addition to goods for distribution, sponsors give gifts to relatives and present special gifts to kin who help them with stages of the feasts. Often these latter gifts are responses to specific requests, or to their recipients' known desires. They might include wristwatches, pressure lamps, cassette radios, tapes, batteries, saucepans, pots, nails, can openers, vegetable peelers, bedding, towels, clothing, children's toys, running shoes, soccer balls, guitars, guitar strings, and other merchandise.

Costumes have changed while maintaining the themes of the dance. Precontact male dancers wore barkcloth obtained from New Britain through trade partnerships; today's dancers may or may not have this cloth, but they do wear shorts, and possibly a wristwatch or sunglasses. The materials of men's hats have changed from real feathers to white paper, with the occasional cereal-box logo when available. An important part of the costume is white armbands and legbands, today supplied by sterile gauze—a fact that becomes a source of contention with medical dispensaries, whose personnel view this use as wasteful. Women's costumes have changed to include 2.5-meter saronglike strips of cloth, bras, baby powder, face-and-chest splash, and store-bought paint and colored feathers for the hair.

Bibliography

Fischer, Hans. 1986. *Sound-Producing Instruments in Oceania*. Edited by Don Niles. Translated by Philip W. Holzknecht. Boroko: Institute of Papua New Guinea Studies.

Harrison, Simon. 1982. *Laments for Foiled Marriages: Love-Songs from a Sepik River Village*. Boroko: Institute of Papua New Guinea Studies.

Niles, Don. 1992. "Flute and Trumpet Ensembles in the Sepik Provinces." In *Sound and Reason: Music and Essays in Honour of Gordon D. Spearritt*, edited by Warren A. Bebbington and Royston Gustavson, 49–60. St. Lucia: University of Queensland.

Pomponio, Alice. 1992. *Seagulls Don't Fly Into the Bush: Cultural Identity and Development in Melanasia*. Belmont, California: Wadsworth.

Scaglion, Richard. 1997. "Abelam: Giant Yams and Cycles of Sex, Warfare, and Ritual." In *Asia and Oceania*, edited by Melvyn Ember and C. R. Ember, 253–276. Portraits of Culture: Ethnographic Originals, 4. Englewood Cliffs, N.J.: Prentice Hall.

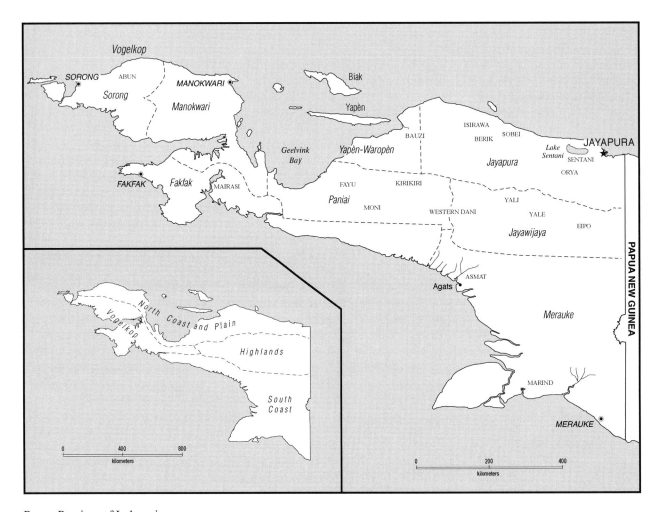

Papua Province of Indonesia

Papua Province of Indonesia

The easternmost province of Indonesia, Papua (formerly known as Irian Jaya) covers the western half of New Guinea Island. Its central mountains ascend more than 5 kilometers, but much of its land is swamp. Its two million inhabitants are clustered in more than 250 distinct groups. Most interior peoples had first contact with the outside after 1945; even in the late 1990s, the southern slopes of the central mountains, the northern border with Papua New Guinea, and the Wapoga (Owa) River watershed had experienced no direct contact.

Politically, the province divides into eight regencies, clustered in four cultural regions (map): the highlands (Jayawijaya, Paniai), the north coast and plain (Jayapura, Yapèn-Waropèn), the south coast (Merauke), and the Vogelkop (Sorong, Manokwari, Fakfak). Since provincewide studies of music have not been carried out, available information remains scattered and sketchy.

A Lowland People: The Asmat

The Asmat inhabit part of the southwestern coastal swamp and forest of Merauke Province, an area which, though visited by Captain Cook (1728–1779) and technically controlled by the Netherlands through 1962, has known continuous outside contact only since the early 1950s. Formerly hunter-gatherers, the Asmat have settled mostly in villages. Music informs their culture, as revealed in the myth of Fumeripits, the creator, who carved the first Asmat people from wood and drummed them to life.

Musical Contexts and Genres

The most important Asmat music enhances rituals, which demarcate seasons and lifecycle stages, placate and communicate with ancestral spirits, brace villages for battle, and consecrate feasts. Music is part of a sacramental whole, organized by experts who occupy inherited positions of status. Among the most important rituals are *bis*, *warmoran* (sending spirits of the dead to "the other side"), men's initiations (*emak cem*), sago-palm feasts, longhouse feasts, headhunting raids, shieldmaking festivals (*salawaku*), ceremonies of masks and adoption, peace-and-reconciliation feasts, warrior's funerals, canoe-dedicating feasts, and *basu suangkus* ("making visible" the heads of men killed in battle).

Bis, the central ritual, lasts for weeks, when men carve and set up poles, 4.5 to 9 meters high, portraying dead ancestors. Believing death to be the work of enemies, both spiritual and human, people sing songs pledging revenge. Painted, dressed in fur or feather headdresses, boar's-tooth or dog's-tooth necklaces, and bone or shell nasal ornaments, and carrying spears, men sing and dance during breaks from carving. Women perform simultaneously but apart. The music includes songs celebrating the carving (sample text: "Now I am carving your mouth"), commemorating dead individuals, and recounting history and mythology. In the longhouse at night, men present the nucleus of ritual music: epic cycles lasting up to twenty-four hours. The cycle *Bowep* narrates the villagers' origin, deeds, and journeys. When men haul the trees felled for poles, women attack, in a mock skirmish. Only women sing the myths *Bokpim* and *Cawor*. *Bis* formerly ended in a headhunting raid, beginning with embarkation to the sounds of the headhunting trumpet (*fu*).

Initiations formerly followed headhunting rituals. Paddling home from a successful raid, men sang songs and sounded *fu*. They ritually washed and scorched the freshly severed head; old men then ate the brains and decorated the skull. Men smeared a mixture of blood and ashes onto the initiate, who contemplated the skull for three days while listening to songs of history and genealogy. Each night, all villagers celebrated, singing with drums and festively eating sago, furnished by women, their arrival announced by trumpets used in the context of head-hunting.

In evenings, parties gather around a fire and sing. Women sing lullabies and nursery rhymes. While working, paddling canoes, gathering wood, fishing, and collecting sago, people sometimes sing or whistle. They use music in courtship and for expressing thanks and appreciation. To commemorate a villager's death, women improvise a lament and throw themselves into mud. Songs of sorrow and complaint provide women with humiliative power, commonly regarding mistreatment, social missteps, failure in battle or hunting, and sexual problems.

Music in the Mind

The Asmat believe music to be powerful: a given piece can appease spirits, drive away disease and suffering, cause death, facilitate a sexual seduction, brace a village for battle, and protect canoeists and the inhabitants of new homes. Many songs are available for all to sing. In ritual performances, men and women have separate roles, songs, and leaders. Each important ritual song belongs to an individual, who controls its performance. This copyright is heritable and transferable. The Asmat acknowledge ancestors' musical contributions but do not attribute the source of music to spirits. Few compositions have an identifiable composer, and spontaneous composition has value in songs of grief, derision, and courting. Some people compose and perform personal songs, such as pieces recalling a loved one. Many Asmat villages share specific pieces, with associated notions about where and when to perform them.

Asmat musical timbre is relaxed, with unchanging volume. Melodies normally descend, developing motives through thematic repetition. Meter is unvarying, but tempo sometimes accelerates. Choral textures are usually responsorial; at the end of sections and pieces, shouts punctuate cadences. Sometimes a lead singer sustains a major third above a chorus. Large forms have discrete sections, and certain songs chain together into suites. All songs have poetry, sometimes in long, highly organized texts. Most ritual texts employ an ancient, secret, ceremonial language, which has symbolic, magical, and spiritual significance and occurs only in song. Musical elaboration focuses on words, not melodic or rhythmic material.

The Asmat learn music informally, through observation and imitation. Promising boys and girls are trained, usually by their kin, to be musical leaders. In the 1990s, schools (run by Christian missions or the government), churches, and mosques taught or sponsored musical performances.

Musical Instruments

Asmat carvers hew hourglass drums from ironwood or hibiscus, with heads made from dried iguana skin. A mix of a drum-owning family's blood and ground clamshells attaches the head to the rim, around which is braided a rattan strip. Players tune a drum by heating its head over a fire and attaching resinous or waxy blobs to it. Meant to last, drums become heirlooms.

Asmat head-hunting trumpets are end-blown straight trumpets without a mouthpiece. Made of wood or bamboo, covered with symbols, they are not always carvers' work. The Asmat consider them signaling devices. Far inland, people play conical trumpets, jew's harps, and whirled slats; children use leaves as buzzers.

Music in Transition

Most Asmat have been in continuous contact with outsiders since 1953. Traders, missionaries, officials, teachers, and corporations have brought outside musics. In 1979, government-sponsored tourism began. Indonesian popular music and non-Asmat indigenous music now reach most villages. Issues of introduced language and instruments concern Asmat elders, but young people enjoy music heard on radio and cassettes.

The government and some missionaries have tried to suppress Asmat rituals. The last authentically complete *bis* occurred in 1974. By Indonesian law, musical performance for a *bis* can lead to criminal prosecution; persons wishing to hold a major ritual must seek permission from the government, which views ritual efforts as nonproductive. Some villages perform rituals secretly or in the jungle. Revitalization movements, in which music plays an important part, have appeared, notably in 1976. An important annual celebration is Christmas. Introduced instruments, especially ukuleles, guitars, and harmonicas, are popular.

A Highland People: The Eipo

The Eipo live in the valley along the upper course of the Eipomek River. The climate is cool and wet: trails and paths hardly ever dry off. Larger animals and reptiles seldom visit this altitude; nor do mosquitoes, so malaria is unknown. Eipo villages have twenty to 250 inhabitants, mostly dwelling in round huts. The social order is egalitarian, organized into clans. Because local life is ruled by the struggle for food, adults have little leisure: they spend time carving arrows, making axes, building huts, and braiding nets or ropes. Most evenings, rain and cold disfavor public activity. People huddle beside fireplaces, women and children in family houses, and men in men's houses. Only rarely does somebody sing. Intervillage feasts resulting from marriage, friendship, and trade are highlights of Eipo culture.

The only indigenous Eipo musical instrument is a jew's harp (*bingkong*), which, in construction and playing, resembles those found generally in New Guinea. Since bamboo does not grow at Eipo altitudes, instruments are made from *fina*, a local reed. Boys and men play. In scattered areas, rarely at *mot* (see below), men play hourglass drums, imported from lowlands.

Research documented life in the southern part of the valley in 1975–1976. Since then, disasters have challenged the Eipo world. In 1976, two earthquakes destroyed local villages. Christian missionaries began restricting the performance of *mot* to Christmas, or banning them altogether.

Musical Contexts and Genres

Feasts

Mot are ceremonial songs and dances performed by men at feasts held to mark an alliance, the end of a war, or the payment of duty or compensation. Men perform them after having cleared an area of the forest and cultivated a new garden. Feasts occur about every five years when the stock of pigs, having been reduced by slaughter for the previous feast, has replenished itself. Men perform *mot* on a sacred ground in front of the men's house, usually in a central location within a village, where women and the sick may not venture, though women may dance on the edge of this space.

The formal structure of the music reflects the choreography, which divides into four sections: position A, static; position A, dynamic, moving counterclockwise to position B; position B, static; and position B, dynamic, moving back to position A. The song is performed only in the static sections. In the dynamic sections, the dancers utter alternating rhythmic shouts on the syllables *ae, ha, hu, lo, uh, wo, ya, ye,* or *yui,* or make in-breathed whistling (*kwasekokna, fotfotana*) or gasping (*kolkolana*).

A *mot* is started by a lead singer (*mot winye*), who normally stands at the head of a semicircular row. He improvises a short syllabic phrase. The chorus adds stereotyped melodic movements, sung on vocables (*mot dem wine gum* 'empty *mot* without a story'). Standing side by side, the men form a line; the first dancer starts running and shouting, and the others follow. They glide like a serpent, coming at last to a standstill, the lead singer now among them. The singing resumes, and the queue unfolds in the opposite direction.

Lead singers' words are cryptic. They may hint at the names of hills, forests, dead people, mythical ancestors, cultural values, plants, animals, or events. They may joke or ironically comment on the guests or the missionaries' introduction of new animals (like fowls or ducks); mock unsuccessful hunters, people afraid to fight, or the hosts; mention hunting, mythical ancestors, mythical creators, bringers of culture, spirit voices, or scenes from war, nature, friendship, and trade; or make joyful expressions. About fifteen kinds of *mot*, with specific names and tonal structures, exist among the Eipo.

Gossip

In the morning before going into the gardens, women sometimes gossip, mainly about sexual liaisons, while men make implements. People may sing *dit* during these activities. The occasions behind the creation of many *dit* and the name of the composers, usually women, are known. Most *dit* derive from sexual liaisons; all have an underlying story, though texts may merely evoke natural images or describe sites. A subgenre, *kulub-kulub dit*, hints at sexual intercourse. Some texts concern researchers' arrivals, airplane-dropped goods, and the building of an airstrip; others mock individuals. *Yaltapenang dit* recount the mythical origin of the Eipo. Content-based categories do not differ from each other musically: standard melodic patterns serve for old and new lyrics.

Laments

Laments (*layelayana*) are spontaneous expressions of mourning, interspersed with weeping or crying. They begin emphatically and loudly; after some minutes, they end quietly. In 1975, a Munggona man about twenty-two years old died, and his brother lamented his death: *Nun-de kurunang-anye mirin bol bobobbin-namume. / Dibnamum-ate / Neik-ak mabnanam abmanumwe. / Na niye-o, fi ubninbinamalak / Na niye, na niye, gum yanamal-ak-e*! / 'You wore dark skin, but you were our light. / You departed from us just now. / We just had agreed to sleep side by side [in the men's house]. / Oh, my father, he went irreversibly from us. / My father, my father, he will not come back to us, woe!'

—Adapted from an article by Vida Chenoweth, Kathleen Van Arsdale, and Artur Simon

Bibliography

Kunst, Jaap. 1967. *Music in New Guinea: Three Studies.* Translated by Jeune Scott-Kemball. The Hague: Martinus Nijhoff.

Simon, Artur. 1978. "Types and Functions of Music in the Eastern Highlands of West Irian." *Ethnomusicology* 22(1):441–455.

Van Arsdale, Kathleen O. 1982. "Music and Culture of the Bisman Asmat of New Guinea: A Preliminary Investigation." In *An Asmat Sketchbook,* 8:17–94. Agats, Irian Jaya: Asmat Museum of Culture and Progress.

Van Arsdale, Peter W. 1975. "Perspectives on Development in Asmat." In *An Asmat Sketchbook,* 5. Agats, Irian Jaya: Asmat Museum of Culture and Progress.

Van Arsdale, Peter W., and Kathleen O. Van Arsdale. 1991. "Asmat." In *Encyclopedia of World Cultures,* 2:19–21. Boston: G. K. Hall.

Australia

A cosmopolitan nation with musics of indigenous peoples coexisting and intermingling with musics of immigrants is the destiny of Australia in the twenty-first century. From didjeridus to beer-cap rattles, from clapsticks to symphony orchestras, from island songs to urban reggae, from wallaby mimes to the postmodern dances of Pina Bausch, Australian music encompasses the expected and the fantastic.

Secret rites of Aboriginal men and women are performed in songlines of the Dreaming. The Sydney Opera House hosts hometown operas and Russian ballets. Greek songs, Brazilian sambas, and Vietnamese instruments grace performing spaces inhabited by *trompe-l'oeil* Parthenon fragments and dot-painted murals. Australia mixes old and new, global and local, with music at the heart of a creative nation. In the article that follows, these elements are explored in the musics of its indigenous peoples.

The Bangarra Dance Theatre, an indigenous dance company, performs *Ochres*, choreographed by Stephen Page, using modern-dance-inspired movements to evoke the Dreaming. *Photo by Adrienne L. Kaeppler, 1996.*

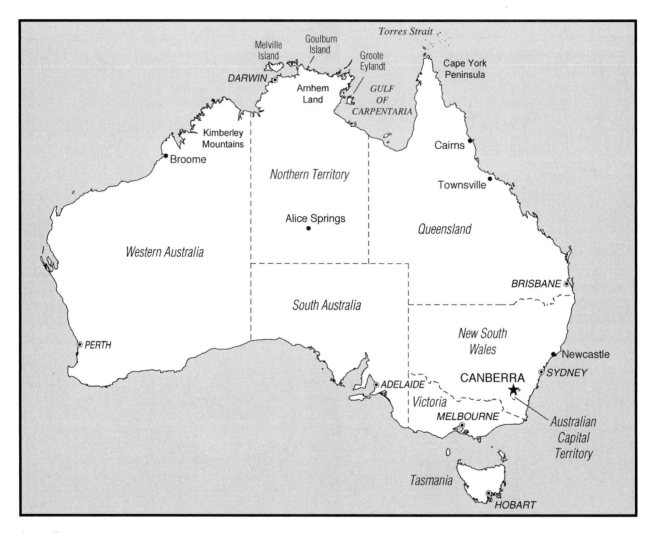

Australia

The Traditional Music and Dance of Australia

Australia is home to a multicultural population of twenty million people. The first Australians migrated from Southeast Asia more than forty thousand years ago. They spoke more than two hundred languages, and occupied ecological zones varying from a vast continental desert to small tropical islands. The modern history of Australia began in 1788, when representatives of the British government established a penal station at Port Jackson (now Sydney). The people of this settlement, mostly convicts and soldiers, were outnumbered by the indigenous population, and this imbalance probably continued for decades. Social interactions between the original inhabitants and the newcomers were inevitable. These interactions included the hospitality some indigenous people extended to the newcomers in the form of invitations to entertainments of music and dance.

The earliest accounts of indigenous performance were recorded in settlers' and explorers' diaries and drawings. In an indigenous language spoken around Port Jackson, the word for a performance of music and dance was documented as a term that in the form *corroboree* was widely adopted by immigrants and indigenous peoples who spoke other languages.

Little is known of indigenous performances in the 1700s and 1800s. By the 1900s, when serious musical research began, the music of southern Australia, the region of most intense European settlement, had changed substantially. In the northern half of Australia and in the center, outsiders' values intruded less, enabling old practices to continue. Regional differences in indigenous musical styles and cultures of longer standing than the last two centuries remain.

Indigenous Australian music is mainly vocal. Sung texts are the primary locus of indigenous literature. Specially sung languages employ poetic techniques and vocabularies that do not occur, or occur in altered forms, in ordinary spoken language; special knowledge is required to interpret their words. The lyrics of genres primarily consisting of vocables are uninterpretable.

Vocables: A spoken or sung wordlike sound that has no meaning.

Most indigenous songs are sacred, or refer to sacred realms. Performances often occur in restricted contexts, where only women, only men, or only the initiated may be present. Some songs are intended purely for entertainment, or to accompany dancing, or to comment on scandalous behavior. The indigenous uses of songs include initiation and mortuary ceremonies, ceremonies for managing conflict, religious ceremonies that link communities over a wide area, healing and bewitching, attracting a desired member of the opposite sex, and inducing rain.

The most spiritually powerful songs are believed to have been created by ancestral spirits at the beginning of time, in the period known as the dreaming. The texts of such songs are inviolate, since they record the spirits' utterances. Strong sanctions, including the threat of death, have been invoked to prevent their alteration. Performance puts these texts into appropriate rhythms and melodies, interlocked with designs and movements. Correctly performed, such songs are believed to release ancestral power. Except as performance involves exploring the oral-compositional processes that will yield a correct "fit," such songs cannot be said to be composed.

Dreaming: The realm of the spirits and totems of Aboriginal Australians, a realm accessible in dreams.

Other kinds of song believed to have been created in the dreaming involve freer processes of oral composition, ensuring that no two performances of a song, though similar, will be exactly the same. For any given subject, singers draw on a set of stock epithets, adjusting their overall structure to fit that of danced structures. Performances involve complex negotiations between one or two singers, a didjeridu player, and (where present) dancers.

Indigenous Musical Instruments

Indigenous songs in Australia are typically accompanied by musical instruments, mostly idiophones. Various concussion sticks, locally called clapsticks, are used over most of Australia; the most noteworthy are paired boomerangs. Holding the center of a boomerang in each hand, a player taps the extremeties of the boomerangs together, usually simultaneously, but sometimes rapidly alternating the taps at each end. Boomerang clapsticks may be played by many performers in unison, creating stunning effects.

Idiophones: Instruments, such as clapsticks or a rattle, that sound "of themselves."

Drums in the form of waisted or cylindrical open-ended wooden drums, held horizontally and struck by hand, occur only on Cape York Peninsula and in the Torres Strait Islands. Most drums used in the strait are made in Papua New Guinea.

The remaining instrument of note is the didjeridu, a conical wooden trumpet with no fingerholes, usually measuring between 1.5 and 2 meters long. Technically simple, it can demonstrate considerable musical virtuosity in a skilled performer's hands. In the late twentieth century, often played solo, it became a widespread symbol of aboriginality.

DIDJERIDUS

Didjeridus are usually made from termite-hollowed branches of eucalyptus trees. Men strip the bark and clear the internal bore. They may smooth both ends of the tube with a file. To give a better seal between lips and instrument, and to protect the lips, players may add beeswax or eucalyptus gum to the blowing end. With wax, they seal any cracks in the tube. They sometimes soak instruments, further sealing the tube; for the same effect, they may blow water through the tube during a performance. They often paint didjeridus with elaborate designs.

Trees commonly used in making didjeridus include stringybark, woollybutt, red river-gum, bloodwood, and ironwood. In Western Arnhem Land, the trunks of pandanus trees are frequently used; because pandanus instruments are quite porous, they are thoroughly soaked before being played, or sealed with oil-based paints or plastic tape. Bamboo was formerly used, and plastic and metal piping have recently been used.

Distribution

DISC
❶
TRACK
26

The didjeridu primarily accompanies public songs in northern Australia, most notably *wangga* and *lirrga* of Western Arnhem Land and the Kimberley Mountains, and the clansongs *bunggurl* in Central and Eastern Arnhem Land, including Groote Eylandt (figure 1). An exceptionally large didjeridu was used in *ubar*, a ceremony not performed since the 1950s or earlier. A large wooden trumpet is used in *djungguwan*, a ceremony of Eastern Arnhem Land, where it has a representational, rather than a musical, function. Didjeridus were widely reported in northern Queensland around 1900, but now are seldom heard there.

The instrument became established in the Kimberleys during the twentieth century, with the genres *wangga* and *lirrga*. By the 1970s or before, it was widely played throughout the continent (especially in the southeast and the southwest), where in the local revival of Aboriginal culture it became a symbol of aboriginality. Its use in popular music of the 1990s extended its performance overseas.

Figure 1 In the Nauiyu Nambiyu community, Daly River, Northern Territory, Jimmy Numbertwo performs a *lirrga*, accompanied on a didjeridu by Robert Ilyerre Daly.
Photo by Linda Barwick, 1995.

Technique

Differences in didjeridu technique are important elements in defining the musical styles and substyles found in northern Australia. Most importantly, didjeridu-accompanied genres of Central and Eastern Arnhem Land use an overblown "hoot" not found in genres of Western Arnhem Land.

Performers blow into the didjeridu with loose lips to sound the fundamental as a drone. In Central and Eastern Arnhem Land, by tightening the lips and increasing the air pressure, players sound an overblown note. Except in some metrically free styles in Central Arnhem Land, the drone on the fundamental articulates rhythmic and metric patterns through the mouthing of vocables into the instrument. Some of these vocables—*didjeridu-didjeru, didjemro-didjemro, didjeramo-rebo didjeramo-rebo*—suggest how the instrument may have acquired its English name.

Further patterning of the drone occurs as a result of circular breathing: the player snatches breaths through his nose while expelling air held in his cheeks. The expulsion of air creates pulsations, tonal variations, and slight rises in pitch, further patterning the drone. Perhaps the most spectacular patterning is found in Eastern Arnhem Land, where complex patterns involving lightly spat overtones are produced in virtuosic displays. To mark structural points (such as the beginning or end of sections of a song), or to produce variant patterns that mark off internal formal divisions, players produce sustained overtones. In unmeasured styles, the didjeridu sustains unpatterned notes of irregular length, and introduces overblown hoots at important structural points.

Songs of Central-Eastern Arnhem Land use overtones in both ways described above, but *wangga* and *lirrga* make no use of overblowing. There, a major technical element is the humming of a tone near the pitch of the second harmonic to produce a complex chord, rich in harmonics. With this technique, performers articulate rhythmic patterns typical of Western Arnhem Land. Special patterns may cue metrical changes in *wangga*; in Western Arnhem Land, where the didjeridu stops playing before the voice, players use terminating formulas with their own mouth sounds. In Western and Central Arnhem Land, the pitch of the drone normally coincides with the final of the singer's melody. Didjeridus used in *wangga* and *lirrga* are usually shorter and higher in pitch than those used in clansongs of Central Arnhem Land. Longer, deeper-pitched instruments are used in Eastern Arnhem Land, where players apparently do not try to match the pitch of the didjeridu with that of the singer's voice.

Players may perform standing or sitting. For parts of ceremonies that involve procession, they often stand or walk. Postures while sitting vary between Western and Central-Eastern Arnhem Land: in the west, where the didjeridu is shorter, the player holds the far end of the instrument off the ground, or supports it on his foot, resting his right arm on his raised right knee, supporting the didjeridu on his wrist or holding from below; in Central-Eastern Arnhem Land, the player rests the far end on the ground, or places it in a resonator (such as a bucket or a large seashell), and in time with clapsticks may tap the tube with his fingernail or a stick.

Northern Australia (Arnhem Land)

Arnhem Land occupies north-central Australia, a region that supports two musical-cultural areas: Central-Eastern Arnhem Land and Western Arnhem Land. Only the former area lies wholly within the geographical and political boundaries of Arnhem Land. The border between these areas roughly tracks the western boundary of the Arnhem Land Reserve, set aside to protect Aboriginal people from outside interference. A high degree of cultural interpenetration occurs between these areas, particularly near their borders.

Solo singing accompanied by clapsticks and a didjeridu is the predominant musical ensemble. In the whole of Arnhem Land, singers are specialists who travel around the country performing for ceremonies. All traditional Aboriginal artistic performances in Northern Australia—singing, dancing, executing visual designs—are associated with religious rites. They may occur in nonceremonial contexts, but ceremony remains their most potent context. Ceremonies that celebrate ancestral beings' creative activities bear restrictions on who may perform or witness them: many of their songs, dances, and visual designs are secret, never heard outside ceremonial contexts. Public ceremonies, whose songs and dances are associated with spirits of lesser potency than ancestral beings, are common throughout Northern Australia, and performances of their songs often occur in nonceremonial contexts. In the frequency of ceremonial performances and the diversity of artistic forms associated with them, Northern Australia is unusually rich.

Central-Eastern Arnhem Land

The music of Central-Eastern Arnhem Land (including Groote Eylandt) differs from that of Western Arnhem Land on the basis of the genre, genesis, song ownership, and structure of songs and associated dances and designs. The people of this area divide their universe between two moieties, Dhuwa and Yirritja. Through affiliation to a moiety, people are associated with the set of totemic species (spiritually connected animal figures) belonging to that moiety. A principal moiety-specific ceremony named *madayin* celebrates the activities of ancestral beings who in the dreaming traveled through Central-Eastern Arnhem Land naming countries and languages, creating clans and waterholes, distributing sacred objects, and singing the songs of this ceremony.

> **Moiety:** One of two basic complementary subdivisions of a group of people.

Each moiety owns unique ceremonies and has a set of clapstick-accompanied songs, usually called *madayin*. Such ceremonies include love-magic songs, which occur in series restricted to either men or women, and secret religious ceremonies.

The principal elements of social organization in Central-Eastern Arnhem Land are clans. They belong to either of two moieties. Within a moiety, certain clans may share some totems, but no two clans share identical sets. Each clan owns defined tracts of land and ritual property associated with them, including the songs, dances, paintings, and sacred objects that invoke clan-linked totemic species and natural phenomena.

Musical Contexts

Clansongs celebrate the activities of totemic spirits. They are sung primarily in three public ritual contexts: mortuary ceremonies, the principal contexts; ceremonies of ritual diplomacy; and ceremonies associated with initiating pubescent boys. They may be performed in the public parts of otherwise secret ceremonies and in nonceremonial contexts for entertainment. All three ceremonial contexts require singing and dancing, with visual representations of totemic beings in several media: totemic designs painted on special poles, coffins, and dancers' bodies; carvings; sculptures in sand; and objects made from feathers or leaves.

Another public genre, extremely popular in northeastern Arnhem Land, consists of *djatpangarri*, didjeridu-accompanied songs sung by young unmarried men, often called fun songs in writing. The texts are formulaic, mainly nonsense words, but the songs are associated with everyday topics, including the first Disney cartoons seen locally. Most *djatpangarri* follow the same melodic pattern.

Musical Ownership

In Central Arnhem Land, series of clansongs are known by proper names specifying the subject of the series, or by the name of the owning clan. In East Arnhem Land, these series appear to be named by reference to the owning clan and the subject. Since clan-owned totemic species vary from clan to clan, the totemic spirits about which songs are sung vary from clan to clan. The Murlarra (Morning Star) series, belonging to the Rembarrnga-speaking Balngara clan of Central Arnhem Land, covers sixteen subjects: four birds (brolga, ibis, lotusbird, snipe), four fish (perch, saratoga, longtom, shark), three other animals (butterfly, python, wallaby), two plants (stringybark, yam), two forms of spiritual beings, and the morning star. Other clans also own Murlarra, but their subjects differ. The Murlarra of one Djinang-speaking clan shares five subjects (brolga, ibis, butterfly, wallaby, morning star) with that of the Balngara clan, but has fourteen other subjects. In Central Arnhem Land, each clan normally, though not exclusively, owns just one series of songs, but in East Arnhem Land, clans appear to own more than one: men can sing the songs of their clans, their mother's mother's clan, and any clan having the same series.

Musical Performance

Clansongs are sung by one or more men accompanying themselves on clapsticks with a didjeridu. Any performance thus has three main musical elements: song, clapsticks, and didjeridu. Women do not perform alongside men, but in funerals and related circumstances may engage in ritual wailing. Men and women's dancing may accompany the performance of clansongs; such dancing affects the musical performance.

In a typical performance, a particular subject is sung several times, followed by the singing of another, and so on. Throughout the area, subjects involve two environments: dryland and wetland. In Central Arnhem Land, subjects of both types occur in one series; in East Arnhem Land, songs associated with the sea often form a series different from those associated with the land. In Murlarra, the implied environment plays an important role in structuring performances: several subjects from one environmental type are sung; and then, if the performers wish, they move to subjects from the other, often making a comment such as "We'll go down (or up) now." They never interweave subjects of the two types.

In Central Arnhem Land, subjects may be sung in several styles. A major distinction is between performances featuring no fixed metrical relationship among voice(s), clapsticks, and didjeridu, and those in which these elements follow the same meter. Rembarrnga-speaking owners of Murlarra cite these styles respectively as *ngarkana* and *djalkmi*. Only nine of Murlarra's sixteen subjects are sung in *ngarkana*, but all subjects may be sung in *djalkmi*. Dance, too, falls into these categories. In *ngarkana*, structured movements are unmetered and uncoordinated with musical elements; dances continue through several musical items. In *djalkmi*, dancers perform in time with the music; each dance corresponds to a single musical item. In northern Central Arnhem Land, a similar distinction appears to apply to the series Djambidj. An "elaborate dance," in which several musical items whose sounded elements display complex metrical relationships accompany a single dance, contrasts with "formal dance," in which each dance is performed in time with a single song in the same meter.

Djalkmi show a distinction between musical items in which the tempo of the clapsticks is fast and those in which it is slow. Certain subjects may be sung with fast and slow beating. The fast mode represents the adult phase or a large manifestation of a subject; the slower mode, an immature phase or a small manifestation of the subject. Performance realizes any such subject as one or more items in the fast mode, followed by one or more in the slow mode. When musical items are realized in *ngarkana*, they precede those in *djalkmi*.

Song Structure

Throughout Central-Eastern Arnhem Land, measured songs commonly have three parts: an introductory section, the body of the song, and an unaccompanied coda. The introductory section may present each of the components. The lead singer establishes an appropriate clapstick pattern. He may quietly sing a few vocables, convey to other performers information about the song, comment on something unrelated to the music, or begin singing lines of the musical text. Other singers present begin tapping their clapsticks in time with his. The didjeridu enters, typically on two or three short tones, after which it sets up a rhythmically patterned drone. In the introductory section, it may add overblown notes.

The body of the song consists of sung text, accompanied by clapsticks and didjeridu. At the start, the singer usually leaps to the highest note of the first of several vocal descents that form the main melodic material of the item. In Central Arnhem Land, one melody sometimes serves for all items in the series; for other series, such as Djambidj, several melodies serve. A clear relationship apparently exists between the melody or set of melodies and the series. The relationship between melody and clan is clearly defined: in East Arnhem Land too, each of a clan's series has its melody or melodies, though for some songs singers may use other clans' melodies. As a singer performs, he draws from a memorized pool of apt textual phrases. He fits these to the melody improvisatorily. Textual units are measured in relation to clapstick and didjeridu patterns. Textual units frequently consist of a semantically meaningful word, followed by vocables to fill out the meter. The order in which textual units occur varies from performance to performance, so the texts of no two performed items are likely to be identical.

Clapsticks and didjeridu articulate the metrical framework of songs. To articulate internal divisions within songs, each may vary. Each series normally has a range of associated clapstick patterns. Particular subjects often use contrasting alternatives.

The beginning of the coda is signaled by a cadential pattern from the didjeridu, ending on the overtone and variant clapstick patterns. A short hiatus frequently occurs before the singers begin a coda. Two singers performing together often differ markedly in text and melody.

Western Arnhem Land

In Western Arnhem Land, the principal public genres are *wangga* and *lirrga*, which mark celebrations of the social dimensions of life. Singers sometimes give proper names to a set of songs. In the east, where this area borders on Central Arnhem Land, *wangga* and *lirrga*, more commonly known there by the Gunwinguan term *gunborrg*, are often performed in ceremony alongside *manikai* and *bunggurl*. In the west (around Port Keats), and in the eastern Kimberley Mountains, they may be performed alongside public series (like *djanba*) that extend into the Kimberley Mountains, or even with series from Central Australia.

The principal criterion for distinguishing between *wangga* and *lirrga* appears to be the language and the tribal affiliation of the songman who owns them. Songmen who speak Batjamalh, Marrisyebin, Marritiyel, or Ngalkbon sing *wangga*, but speakers of Marrengarr, Mayali, or Ngan'gityemerri sing *lirrga*. The two genres share many formal features, but the key to formal differences between them lies in the movements associated with them.

Musical Performance

Some texts of *wangga* and *lirrga* consist solely of vocables. Primarily a vehicle for rhythmic, timbral,

WANGGA

Wangga, public dance-songs, are performed in ceremonial contexts and for entertainment. At ceremonies, they are often performed alongside examples of other genres, including *lirrga*, with which they share many features, and *djanba*, a genre from the Kimberley area. The details of a performance vary by location, song, and occasion. The following discussion focuses on *wangga* owned by Marrisyebin people, whose country lies at Nadirri, near the mouth of the Moyle River.

Structure and Style

Nadirri *wangga* have three kinds of movement: men's, women's, and textually accompanied actions. One dance serves for the lyrics of all *wangga*. Movements derive their connection to songs through actions depicting the spirits from whom the songs came. Vocal and instrumental sections of *wangga* alternate. Men's and women's dancing usually coincides with instrumental sections; the actions coincide with vocal sections. Elsewhere, mimetic dancing and other formal arrangements of vocal and instrumental sections occur.

In Nadirri *wangga*, men's dancing, the most elaborate, has four phrases: a preparatory walk, in step with the rhythm of the sticks; a run, when dancers establish their positions on the central part of the ground; a stamped phrase; and a terminal phrase of idiosyncratic movements, when performers display exceptional agility.

Dances can begin when dancers choose to join with instrumentalists, but they end when the beating of clapsticks ends. Women dance during instrumental and vocal sections. They define the space by moving slowly along its circumference. During the singing, they perform an undulating side step, taking the rhythms in their bodies and arms; alternatively, some travel a few steps, stop, and perform digging-like motions to the side. As clapstick beats begin, they stop traveling, and to each beat perform a sharp bounce with their legs and arms, the accents down and in toward the torso. Sometimes during vocal sections, senior men perform solo actions, including approaching people and looking for footprints on the ground. Such actions may recall the behavior of the spirits from whom the songs came.

Structured Movements of Wangga

Wangga posture for men and women is bent slightly forward at the hips, legs rotated outward, knees relaxed. Women gaze at the ground; men look toward the singers or other dancers. Women's dynamics are more fluid and rhythmic than men's, but men's steps, even their runs, are light and agile, with sharp, discrete movements. The apparent simplicity of the actions, as in other Aboriginal dances, masks agility in the dynamics of movement.

Wangga stamps include even steps, using alternate legs; a sharp rebound from the ground; no bouncing of the body, the head remaining at a constant height; legs folded close under the pelvis, especially by expert dancers; and stamping in place. Stamps connect the dancers to the ground, but the action is light, with an energetic rebound. This lightness results from how the feet contact the ground: curled, so soles can scoop up sand as they lift, raising a cloud of dust. Arms do not perform specific actions or patterns, but follow the energy and rhythm generated by the stamps.

Relationship of Dancing and Singing

To herald the beginning of a dance, male dancers often form a tight, inwardly facing circle. A senior dancer initiates a one-syllable call, which the other performers join. The circle breaks up, the dancers fill the space, and clapstick beats begin. Calls punctuate the performance, usually as dancers' and singers' signals cue the ends and beginnings of phrases. The dancing and musical phrasing are tightly intertwined. Phrases of the dance and the music coincide only at the terminal phrase, which begins within a five-beat break at the end of the clapstick phrases. The beating and the dancing end together.

and melodic interplay, these texts are not used like those of dreaming-originated songs, whose correct interpretation is controlled by knowledgeable performers. Other texts resemble statements that could be made in spoken registers, perhaps more than in any other traditional Aboriginal Australian songs.

Wangga and *lirrga* are performed by one to three male singers. Women rarely perform alongside men. Singers accompany themselves on a pair of clapsticks, accompanied by a didjeridu and singing either to accompany dancing or without dancing. *Wangga* often have accompanied sung sections that alternate with purely instrumental sections. Their melodies consist of descents that cadence on a final whose pitch corresponds to that of the didjeridu. Some singers use widely varying melodies, but others maintain the same basic melody for all songs in a set. Some descents may be unstable; some consist almost entirely of a vocal glide.

Singing is accompanied by a didjeridu and the metrical beating of sticks, or by didjeridu alone. Singing unaccompanied by sticks is often unmetrical, though variations of timbre and amplitude in the didjeridu may articulate a metrical framework. Most singers can perform metrical and unmetrical songs.

Musical Ownership

Wangga and *lirrga* are given to songmen (and occasionally to women, who pass them on to male singers) by spirits, usually when recipients are dreaming, often in association with a picture reflecting a textual theme. These spirits take various forms, including the ghosts of deceased songmen, animals, or semihuman beings (such as the dwarflike *walakanda* of the Daly area).

Songs may be inherited from a father or an uncle; a few popular songs by deceased singers continue to be performed. How songs come into being—and the way in which no effort (comparable to that made to maintain dreaming songs, or even *manikai* and *bunggurl*) is made to preserve them after a singer's death—reflect a stronger association of these songs with the everyday world than with the dreaming.

Wangga and *lirrga* are performed by one, two, or three male singers. Women rarely perform alongside men. *Wangga* melodies consist of descents that end on a pitch corresponding to that of the didjeridu.

Queensland

The second-largest state in Australia, Queensland consists of 1,727,200 square kilometers of land, including arid desert and lush forest. Of more than a hundred indigenous languages locally spoken before 1788, only fifteen are thriving.

Two major indigenous cultures meet in Queensland: Torres Strait Islanders to the far north and Aboriginal people on the mainland. Throughout indigenous Queensland, music is a vocal art; instruments function as accompaniments only. Percussion instruments are featured on the mainland, while drums are used in Cape York. Peoples of the eastern Torres Strait favor flutes, panpipes, and a single-reed instrument of New Guinean origin.

Torres Strait

More Torres Strait Islanders live along the coast of Queensland than in the islands themselves, and their music and dances are known throughout Queensland. Island dances—music and movement—came as early as 1871, when London Missionary Society missionaries from West Polynesia began teaching their hymns, songs, and dances to replace indigenous traditions. European administrators and church officials favored island dances because their lack of a mythological base made them a safe alternative to premissionary arts. Island dance music is in two- or three-part harmony, cadencing in unisons or octaves, and its melodies have a range of an octave or more. Its instruments may be guitars or ukuleles, drums, and rattles made of strung segments of the matchbox bean.

Dancers sing as they dance, either in a massed, military formation, or as one or two soloists, moving more or less in synchrony. Sometimes members of the audience march between rows of dancers, sprinkling talcum powder on the backs of certain dancers, showing relationship and support. Dancers decorate themselves with palm-leaf strips and usually wear headbands. For some songs, seated singers gesture from the waist up. Topics include historical events (such as the landing of the supply boat *Cora*) and the performers' wishes, sorrows, and aspirations. Island dance plays—featuring processionals, a game, and recessionals—are popular.

Traditional music of Torres Strait had mostly been replaced by music for island dances by 1898, when the Cambridge Expedition to the Torres Strait recorded and filmed in the strait. Secular dance songs often employed a five-tone scale, laments employed sustained notes with ornamental flourishes, and the melodies of religious songs occasionally included microtonal wailing.

Dances consisted of highly stylized movements, some of which were mimetic. Dancers, usually male, performed secular works in a semicrouching posture, skipping on the tips of their toes. In varying sequences, they performed fifteen or more named variants of their basic step. Decorations, including animal and humanlike masks, accentuated their movements. The Cambridge Expedition filmed a segment of dancing in which a performer wore a halolike white-feather headdress (*dhari*), which now graces the Torres Strait Islander flag.

Cape York

This area is unique in how people use percussion instruments. In western Cape York, singing is performed by a solo singer in a tense style and a narrow vocal range, sometimes on a single tone, punctuated by a chorus of clapsticks, rattles, claps, shouts, and calls. Eastern Cape York belongs to the region of *bora*—initiatory songs and rituals—which extends down the east coast, where singing is more relaxed and melodic ranges are wider.

Music of Cape York can be divided into cult-owned, clan-owned, and individually owned songs. Cult-owned songs are for special rites; clansongs belong to specific totemic groups; and individually owned songs often require virtuosic dancing, known as shake-a-leg, an energetic solo dance, in which the (male) performer holds his legs wide apart and moves forward without lifting his feet off the ground. Excluding *bora*, ceremonial songs are sung in a strained timbre within a melodic range as narrow as a major second, often punctuated by calls. *Bora* melodies, performed with a more relaxed quality, often in a low vocal register, have a wider range. Accompaniment, from clapping, boomerang clapsticks, or a drum, consists of strictly even beats. If two nonmelodic instruments perform together, they relate in the proportion of one to two. The people of Cape York also perform island dances, country, and popular music.

Songs and dances in Cape York relate to the land, often to specific sites, and must be performed by the proper persons. Placing performers and spirits into juxtaposition, they express identity in terms of historical, mythological, and proprietary acts. *Wanam* is danced within a tight circle by carefully designated participants. The Kugu-nganhcharra (of western Cape York) see songs as potentially less dangerous than dances. Singing invokes a spirit, but dancing demonstrates its presence; therefore, old men say they must protect initiates or newcomers from the power of the dancing. Ceremonial owners offer this protection by invoking spirits and rubbing onto initiates the scent of their armpits.

Cape York dancers may wear humanlike masks. An area is carefully prepared with props, such as carved totemic objects or massed leafy branches. Since the mid-1960s, festivals for dancing have drawn Aboriginal people from Queensland and other areas, and have changed by incorporating competitions and attracting tourists.

The Kimberley Region

North of the Great Sandy Desert in Western Australia, the Kimberley region is bounded on the east by the Ord River Basin, and on the south and west by the Fitzroy River Basin and the Dampier Land Peninsula. Considerable trade of ritual and material goods occurs eastward into Western Arnhem Land and southward into the Western Desert. Linguistically, Kimberley languages are distinct from Western Desert and Arnhem Land languages.

The distribution of musical genres differs by area. Central Australian genres occur along the southern edge of the Kimberleys, from La Grange to Halls Creek; at the eastern boundary, Northern Australian genres entail different practices. Kimberley genres are most strongly present from Dampier Land to Kalumburu; through ritual exchange, they have spread into contiguous areas of Northern and Central Australia.

Singing, a feature of rituals accompanying major personal events (including initiation and burial), serves important roles in maintaining lands and species and entertaining audiences. Many ceremonies, especially those dealing with the dreaming, bear restrictions on who may participate in and witness them, restrictions that apply especially to the most powerful dreaming performances, including the major traveling-dreaming cults and so-called love-magic ceremonies. Many restricted genres form part of a ritual-exchange complex with neighboring groups in Central and Northern Australia.

Dreaming-related ceremonies are commonly owned by moieties or otherwise defined descent groups, but many public genres are individually owned. Public genres, bearing no restrictions on who may witness them, are performed for entertainment, and they accompany public sections of rituals, including initiations and mortuary ceremonies. Some public genres may be performed by mixed-sex groups.

The most widely documented public genre is known by different names in different locations. In southern Dampier Land, it is called *nurlu*. Spirits of deceased kin or agents of conception reveal *nurlu* and associated dances to dreaming individuals. Men's boomerang clapsticks and women's clapping or thigh slapping accompany the songs, whose texts are set to a flexibly descending melody and convey a Central Australian musical style. Men and women may sing, but only men dance.

Balga are distinguished from *nurlu* by being owned by moieties, rather than individuals, and accompanied by clapsticks, rather than boomerangs. *Balga* are mainly performed in the central-north parts of the Kimberleys. The cognate genre, *djanba*, accompanied by clapsticks (men) and slapping or clapping (women), occurs in the south and east Kimberleys, and has extensions into Western Arnhem Land.

Lilydyin (also called *ludin*), individually owned topical songs performed by men of northern Dampier Land for entertainment and without dancing, are said to be individually composed. Of similar origin and treating similar subjects, *dyabi* (also called *yabi*), performed in southwest Kimberley, have a unique accompaniment: serrated sticks, producing a rasping sound when rubbed together.

The performance of didjeridu-accompanied *wangga* generally conforms to that in Western Arnhem Land, where the genre originates and whence performers frequently travel into the east Kimberleys for ceremonies. Songs are performed by one or two men accompanying themselves on paired clapsticks to the accompaniment of a didjeridu. Another genre originating in Western Arnhem Land performed in the east Kimberley is the didjeridu-accompanied *djirri djirri*.

Musical Performance

A west Kimberley performance of a *nurlu* illustrates important aspects of musical performance. The series named Bulu consists of seventeen songs and three dances owned by George Dyunggayan, a Nyigina-speaker, who lived on pastoral stations near the lower Fitzroy River, east of Broome. Many *nurlu* originated around 1925 from Dyunggayan's dreamed experiences with the spirit of his deceased father, Bulu, and several agents of conception (*ray*); the songs describe a journey undertaken by the group through Nyigina and Warrwa country, around the lower Fitzroy River basin. The other songs, which appeared after 1925, also describe events in the spiritual world, but do not reenact a dream-spirit journey. Frequent references to the weather, especially to rain and clouds, reflect Dyunggayan's status as a doctor, believed to hold special powers in relation to spirits and the weather. In 1985, Raymond D. Keogh recorded several performances of Dyunggayan's *nurlu*. On one occasion, Dyunggayan sang with the Nyigina singer Butcher Joe Nangan.

In the first text in the Bulu series (figure 2a), the beating—by boomerang clapsticks and clapping, the former twice as fast as the latter—has a set relationship to the text, whose linguistic structures illustrate common features of Aboriginal lyrics: the words mix everyday Nyigina, suffixes added for rhythmic purposes, and one term of unknown meaning. The suffixes -*mirri* and -*dyina* occur only in musical texts, where they end everyday words for

rhythmic purposes. The meaningful parts of this phrase are *Wanydyal*, the name of a waterhole, and *yingany*, meaning in everyday Nyigina 'he was there'. In the second phrase, the word *mindi* has no known meaning, and the word *yarrabanydyina* in everyday Nyigina means 'we (exclusive) saw him'. A gloss given by George Dyunggayan and Paddy Roe clarifies the text: Bulu and his *ray* come out from the waterhole Wanydyal and contemplate where they will go; Dyunggayan is with them, dreaming. Subsequent songs in the Bulu series name other sites passed in the journey, aurally mapping it. The singers may begin and end at any point in the textual cycle, which over the course of an item repeats up to seven times; in figure 2b, they begin in the middle of the first line and end in the middle of the second.

Central Australia

In the center of the continent, singing is primarily vocal. Throughout the desert, the preferred style is unison singing, sometimes in octaves to accommodate male and female ranges. Departures from unison are usually understood as mistakes, but in some areas these variants are optional, or occur accidentally, through slightly different timing of intervallic leaps. Women and men have separate musics and musical occasions, in addition to jointly performed ones. Commonly, male singers accompany themselves by beating clapsticks; women accompany themselves by striking their bodies.

Central Australian melodies move in a series of terraced descents from a high pitch to a low pitch, with upward leaps to begin new descents; melodies end quietly on a tonic, with reiteration of the lower pitch for several cycles of the text. Melodic ranges extend from an interval of a second to more than an octave. The sequence of higher and lower notes must remain constant throughout any song that maps an ancestral journey, regardless of the performed lengths of texts related to each site being sung. Strict rules, known by good performers, govern the interlocking of text and melody.

Melodic ornamentation includes elaborate glides and microtonal oscillations of pitch, deliberate overemphasis of certain pitches, and anticipatory slides, all in solo and collective singing. To achieve unison, women commonly sing at the low end of their range, and men sing at the high end of theirs. Vocal timbres range from low and sonorous to high, harsh and nasal. Women use ritualized wailing as a vocal mechanism for expressing grief.

Ancestral personalities are represented in music mainly through scent or taste. The sensory essence of an ancestor reveals itself in the sounds of a song the

a

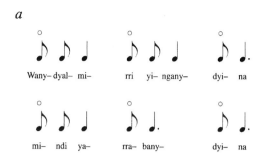

b

Figure 2 Verse 1 of the Bulu series: *a*, text and rhythmic setting (after Keogh 1990:92, 165); *b*, performance of George Dyunggayan and Butcher Joe Nangan in 1985 (after Keogh 1990:215–218). The circles represent accompanimental clapping or slapping of the thighs. Boomerang accompaniment typically occurs at twice this speed.

ancestor composed. Each ancestor has its own scent, embodied in musical structure. By correctly performing an ancestor's songs, a descendant can reproduce the ancestor's sonic signature. Differentiation among ancestral scents reflects partly the pitch-based distance between the pivots in the descent, and partly the length of time spent at each of these points. Specific locking of text to melody may affect this

identification, as may exact or proportional duration within identifying melodic sections.

Texts and Syllabic Rhythm

The texts and rhythms of individual songs are fixed and can be varied only in minor ways. Because the songs follow an ancestor's track, they must follow the same order on each occasion. Most are believed to have originated anciently, but provisions for receiving new songs from spirits exist.

Texts usually have two lines, which make similar statements with minor differences, or say the same thing in different dialects; or the second line may balance the first, making a fuller statement. Because syllabic patterns closely connect with given texts, rhythms sometimes acquire textual meanings. The structure of rhythmic patterns resembles that of texts, with two main sections corresponding to the verses.

Sung language is perceived differently from spoken language: highly symbolic, it gives mere suggestions of meaning. Texts can therefore be interpreted on different levels, depending on the listener's level of knowledge. Rhythm is important, since common rhythmic structures, such as rhythms using three adjacent short notes, often convey related meanings. By stressing phonemes and morphemes (units of sound and of meaning, respectively) not ordinarily stressed in speech, combining and splitting words, and adding the second half of one word to the beginning of the next, performance disguises words and their meanings.

Adults never tell children the secret meanings of texts, but teach simplified versions. The ceremonies in which children take part involve their community; participants perform and understand the music at their own level. In closed ceremonies, the esoteric meaning of texts gradually unfolds to appropriately initiated adults.

Women's Dancing

Women's dancing of Central Australia has two major classes: formal, subdivided into painted dances and painted closing dances, and informal. During formal performances, dancers' bodies bear painted designs relating to the dreaming being celebrated. Informal dancing can occur outside the formal framework, rendered as introductory sections and interludes, which require no paint.

Women may perform informal dances spontaneously in front of singers, but formal dancing requires strict control in hiding painted dancers until the singing begins, creating a simultaneous revelation of structures of songs, dances, and painted designs. During breaks in the singing, the dancers turn their (usually unpainted) backs toward the singers. On the ground, dancers' tracks create designs believed to hold prodigious power; women conclude important secret ceremonies by obliterating these tracks, lest a man see them and sicken.

Musical Accompaniments

In Central Australia, the main accompaniment of singing is concussive or percussive. Boomerangs, predominantly weapons of hunting, serve in pairs as clapsticks for musical concussion. In some areas, people discard clapsticks after musical use; in others, they keep them specifically as percussive instruments. Forms of rhythmic accompaniment include clapping, stamping, beating a mound of earth with a rounded stick, rapid beating of alternate ends of a pair of boomerangs, and slapping the thighs, an exclusively female practice.

Other musical instruments of Central Australia are the whirled slat and the *ulbura*, a wooden trumpet made from a hollow log about 60 centimeters long and 5 centimeters in diameter. In ceremonial settings, these instruments symbolize ancestors' voices. The didjeridu is not indigenous to Central Australia.

Functions of Songs, Roles of Performers

Within ceremonies, songs have several functions. Singers sit apart from where dancers are being painted, but they must sing certain songs while the paint is being applied. In specific songs, the singers and the painters communicate on the dancers' state of readiness. Early in the process, a leader sitting with the singers starts these songs; as the time for dancing nears, the painters start songs until the dancing starts.

Special songs accompany dancing; others are for returning power to the soil after performances. Some dances are fast, with percussive accompaniment; other dances are slow and unaccompanied. During a ceremony, women responsible for preparing the ceremonial ground sing special songs. A performance ends with a song to return to the soil the power raised by the ceremony.

Differing roles of ceremonial participants reflect differing ownership and ritual responsibility, and distinguish classes of performers, such as lead singer, singer, and dancer. People can access the power inherent in these songs only by performing them correctly; consequently, leaders must maintain the accuracy of their songs. By ensuring that songs are sung in their correct order, starting and finishing each song, introducing the correct beat, and understanding deeply the symbolism and power of each song, the leader controls the singing. The leader usually opens each item with a short solo; and when others are sure of the text and the beat, they join in. Many young people need to follow the melodic contour given by the leader until they know it for themselves. The leading of the group by an unknowledgeable singer will not produce the desired effects.

In ceremonial contexts, singers present the words spoken by the ancestor at the creation of the ceremony, while dancers, by portraying the ancestor's actions, present the parallel physical manifestation.

Whenever possible, songs are performed at the sites through which the ancestors passed at the beginning of time. The major role of the owner of a ceremony is to portray the ancestor. No ceremony can be performed without the owner's presence and permission. The hereditary owner of some women's secret songs is a man, who may not sing the songs in public, but has the right to grant women permission to sing them. The manager prepares the site, paints the dancers, provides food and gifts for the owner, shouts instructions to the singers and the dancers, and cleans up afterward.

Southeastern Australia

Southeastern Aboriginal Australia comprises what is now New South Wales, southern Queensland, Victoria, southeastern South Australia, and Tasmania. The reasons for treating it as a distinct musical region are the shared consequences of a similar colonial history more than the shared features of indigenous musical pasts. After 1788, when British colonization began, the major cities of what became the most densely populated part of Australia— Adelaide, Brisbane, Melbourne, Newcastle, and Sydney—sprang up along the southeastern continental rim. All but Newcastle became state capitals, extending urban influence inland in a widening fan. In most of the region, indigenous people faced new forms of disruption and death earlier and often more intensely than elsewhere. Aborigines of Tasmania experienced a genocidal invasion. Each of these states today has a vigorous population of people of mainly southeastern Aboriginal descent. New South Wales and Queensland have the largest Aboriginal-identifying populations in Australia. Each has about 25 percent of the total.

Evidence for "The Old Songs"
The only recorded performances of Tasmanian vernacular songs are Fanny Cochrane Smith's wax-cylinder recordings, made in 1899 for the Royal Society of Tasmania. In 1972, Smith's granddaughter recorded what she remembered of one of these songs, but the meanings of the words have been lost. Southeastern Aboriginal recordings housed in the Australian Institute of Aboriginal and Torres Strait Islander Studies (AIATSIS) consist largely of solo songs performed by elderly people, often sung incidentally in the course of nonmusical projects, such as recording languages. These singers remembered songs as keepsakes of customs and gave limited information about earlier musical meanings and contexts.

Early twentieth-century accounts of singing and dancing come from anthropologists and travelers. There are pictures of performances by the nineteenth-century Aboriginal artists Barak, Tommy McRae, and Mickey of Ulladulla, and pictures by outsiders. There are also photographs of ceremonies. Available evidence leads to certain conclusions about the range of performative elements, participants' roles, musical instruments, painted designs, and so on. Commonly, women beat a possum-skin pillow resting in their laps, men clicked paired boomerangs, and male dancers wore leaf rattles tied to their legs.

Ceremonial and other Special-purpose Songs
Throughout New South Wales by 1905, regular ceremonial activity, which continued longer in the north of the region, was drawing to a close. Only a handful of recorded songs are ceremonial in origin or have powers to heal, control weather, and the like. Even those who remembered them would have been reluctant to sing them out of religious contexts or in the absence of authority to invoke their powers. In the 1950s, George Dutton, reportedly the only surviving ritual leader of the extreme north and west of the region by the 1930s, recorded initiation-related items.

Corroborees and Occasional Songs
Long after ceremonial life had ended, secular occasional and informal songs continued to be composed in some languages of the region. The texts of such songs in the AIATSIS archive consist mainly of evocative words, phrases, and sentences, conveying scenes, characters, and events. The songs are often so allusive as to permit multiple interpretations. As songs traveled from one language to another, meanings and interpretations were often learned separately from texts.

Many short solo fragments are described by their singers as corroboree songs. *Corroboree* originates in a Sydney-area word denoting a particular dance. It entered English via pidgin to mean any Aboriginal dancing. This meaning raises two questions: Were full performances of these songs longer? If so, what were the conventions for extending them?

Reactions to Introduced Music
Southeastern Aboriginal people have long welcomed, and even traveled large distances in search of, new songs and languages, so their enthusiasm for introduced music is unsurprising. In 1794, when Goethe was remarking that "the French tune of Malbrook" was pursuing travelers wherever they went, coastal Aborigines were singing it while paddling their canoes.

As gatherings for ceremonies declined, and with them singing and dancing at corroborees, other forms of recreational music grew up in the communities where Aborigines lived. Claypan dances, on riverine flats or banks, became popular. Instruments played included fiddles, accordions, harmonicas, zithers, banjos, and guitars. A highlight of the new music was gumleaf bands, which flourished in the 1920s and 1930s [see text box].

Since the people of what is now Sydney first began adopting songs from Europe, Aboriginal people in the southeast have responded to and appropriated various vocal and instrumental music. Their main kinds of songs have been hymns and gospel songs,

GUMLEAVES

Some Aboriginal peoples once played single-reed aerophones made from the leaves of local eucalyptus trees or shrubs. These leaves served as hunting and bird-calling devices, signaling instruments, and musical toys. Responding to Christian evangelization in the late 1800s, detribalized Aboriginal peoples of southeastern Australia developed these instruments into bands, which played European hymns, American gospel songs, popular music, and classical music.

The earliest documented gumleaf band appeared in 1892, when Salvation Army officers recruited tribesmen to play gumleaves in their street procession through Bordertown, South Australia. This band may have had precedents, since the missionization of Aboriginal people began in the early 1850s, when conventional instruments were unavailable on the frontier. Gumleaf bands became nationally popular in the 1920s. No women belonged to major gumleaf bands, but women played gumleaves in church, and sometimes whole congregations played.

Early Twentieth-century Bands

The Wallaga Lake Gumleaf Band from the south coast of New South Wales used a large kangaroo-skin drum to mark time. From the 1920s through the 1950s, apart from hymns, this band played popular and patriotic songs and dances. Bandsmen were known to play gumleaves in counterpoint while dancing. In the late 1920s, the fourteen members spent months walking around the coast to perform at a ball in Melbourne; along the way, they did casual work, fished for food, and slept in the open. Some members marched at the opening of the Sydney Harbour Bridge in March 1932, and during the same decade collaborated with the Cummeragunga Concert Party on the Murray River to tour the Goulburn Valley and Riverina District. The Lake Tyers Gumleaf Band of Victoria performed for tourists. During World War II, leaders of army-recruiting drives employed its members in publicity stunts.

Gumleaves joined other instruments, including bones, spoons, ukuleles, fiddles, harmonicas, and accordions. In the 1920s and 1930s, several Aboriginal vaudeville troupes toured the eastern seaboard. For paying audiences, they played in theaters, incorporating into their acts the sounds of jazz and the movements of clowning, corroboree-style stepping, and the Hawaiian hula. Virtuosos played gumleaves "no hands"—while playing an accordion with their hands or a harmonica with their nose.

From Ensemble to Solo Tradition

By the 1960s, gumleaf duos, trios, and quartets came into vogue, overshadowing larger ensembles. The causes of this change included the Aboriginal urban drift, the rising popularity of guitars, the effect of rock, and the spread of television. Since 1977, informal and localized traditions have yielded to a national solo competition, open to Australians of any descent.

The leading Aboriginal exponent of the instrument is Herbert Patten (b. 1943), who as a child near Orbost, Victoria, observed the techniques of his great-uncle Lindsey Thomas. Like Thomas, Patten produces the deep, strong gumleaf tone of the open-air tradition, sometimes ornamented by wobbles (trills), vibrato, and "wawa" effects. Recordings of his performances, ranging from Aboriginal and European songs to jazz items like "Birth of the Blues," are held at Monash University, Victoria. Dedicated female performer Roseina Boston (b. 1935) plays frequently on radio in Australia; she is descended from Possum Davis, former conductor of the Burnt Bridge Gumleaf Band of New South Wales.

ballads, popular songs, American popular and country music, rock, and reggae. Aboriginal people often marked introduced songs as theirs by translating the texts into their own languages and including foreign-language words in their own compositions in new styles.

—Adapted from articles by Stephen A. Wild, Allan Marett, JoAnne Page, Grace Koch, Linda Barwick, Catherine J. Ellis, Tamsin Donaldson, Margaret Gummow, Robin Ryan, and Herbert Patten

Bibliography

Barwick, Linda, Allan Marett, and Guy Tunstill, eds. 1995. *The Essence of Singing and the Substance of Song: Recent Responses to the Aboriginal Performing Arts and Other Essays in Honour of Catherine Ellis*. Oceania monograph 46. Sydney: University of Sydney.

Berndt, R. M., and E. S. Phillips, eds. 1973. *The Australian Aboriginal Heritage: An Introduction Through the Arts*. Sydney: Australian Society for Education through the Arts and Ure Smith.

Breen, Marcus, ed. 1989. *Our Place Our Music: Aboriginal Music: Australian Popular Music in Perspective*, 2. Canberra: Aboriginal Studies Press.

Clunies Ross, Margaret, and Stephen A. Wild. 1982. *Djambidj: An Aboriginal Song Series from Northern Australia*. Canberra: Australian Institute of Aboriginal Studies.

Clunies Ross, Margaret, Tamsin Donaldson, and Stephen A. Wild. 1987. *Songs of Aboriginal Australia*. Oceania Monograph 32. Sydney: University of Sydney.

Elkin, A. P., and Trevor A. Jones. 1953–1957. *Arnhem Land Music (North Australia)*. Oceania monograph 9. Sydney: University of Sydney.

Ellis, Catherine J. 1964. *Aboriginal Music Making: A Study of Central Australian Music*. Adelaide: Libraries Board of South Australia.

———. 1985. *Aboriginal Music: Education for Living*. St. Lucia: University of Queensland Press.

Fischer, Hans. 1986. *Sound-Producing Instruments in Oceania*. Edited by Don Niles. Translated by Philip W. Holzknecht. Boroko: Institute of Papua New Guinea Studies.

Jackomos, Alick. 1971. "Gumleaf Bands." *Identity* 1(1):33–34.

Jackomos, Alick, and Derek Fowell. 1993. *Forgotten Heroes: Aborigines at War from the Somme to Vietnam*. Melbourne: Victoria Press.

Keogh, Raymond D. 1990. "*Nurlu* Songs of the West Kimberleys." Ph.D. dissertation, University of Sydney.

Marett, Allan. 1991. "Variability and Stability in Wangga Songs of Northwest Australia." In *Music and Dance of Aboriginal Australia and the South Pacific*, edited by Alice Marshall Moyle, 194–213. Sydney: Oceania Publications.

Marett, Allan, and JoAnne Page. 1995. "Interrelationships Between Music and Dance in a Wangga from Northwest Australia." In *The Essence of Singing and the Substance of Song: Recent Responses to the Aboriginal Performing Arts and Other Essays in Honour of Catherine Ellis*, edited by Linda Barwick, Allan Marett, and Guy Tunstill, 27–38. Oceania monograph 46. Sydney: University of Sydney.

Mitchell, Ewen. 1996. *Contemporary Aboriginal Music*. Port Melbourne: Ausmusic.

Neuenfeldt, Karl William. 1996. *The Didjeridu: From Arnhem Land to Internet*. Sydney: Perfect Beat and John Libbey Publications.

Ryan, Robin. 1997. "Ukuleles, Guitars or Gumleaves? Hula Dancing and Southeastern Australian Aboriginal Performers in the 1920s and 1930s." *Perfect Beat* 3(2):106–109.

Sullivan, Chris. 1988. "Non-Tribal Dance Music and Song: From First Contact to Citizen Rights." *Australian Aboriginal Studies*, 1:64–67.

Sutton, Peter, ed. 1989. *Dreamings: The Art of Aboriginal Australia*. Ringwood, Australia, and London: Viking Penguin.

Wild, Stephen A., ed. 1986. *Rom: An Aboriginal Ritual of Diplomacy*. Canberra: Australian Institute of Aboriginal Studies.

Melanesia

Melanesia

Orchestras of log percussion instruments or panpipes give melodic and rhythmic meaning to public events; hourglass-shaped drums, friction blocks, and whirled slats give sounds of fear and wonder; flutes whisper songs of love; spectacular displays of masks and massed bodies bespeak life-crisis feasts and secret-society rituals. Melanesians have created, and still use, a sensational variety of accoutrements and musical instruments to complement their singing and dancing.

Influences from the outside world—explorers, missionaries, merchants, immigrants, and media—have expanded the array to include stringed instruments, which have sparked the rise of pan-Pacific pop amid familiar local forms. From ritual to reggae and rock, contemporary performances in Melanesia mix old and new—at work, during ceremonial events, in festivals, and for tourists.

Dukduks, masked spirits, perform at Beru Hamlet, Mapiri Village, Nissan, North Solomons Province, as men playing kundus provide rhythmic sounds. *Photo by Steven R. Nachman, 1971.*

The Music and Dance of Melanesia

Melanesia (from Greek, meaning 'black islands') encompasses an area of the Pacific Ocean roughly west of the International Dateline, south of the equator, and east of New Guinea. The French explorer Dumont d'Urville used the term to describe the skin of the people he encountered; their physical traits, however, are as varied as their cultural traits. Melanesian societies range from those where power lies in the ability to create a following, to those where power comes from the inheritance of chieftainship. Though the term Melanesia is anthropologically unhelpful, no term has satisfactorily replaced it.

Melanesia, here excluding New Guinea, includes four regions: a series of islands that are part of the nation of Papua New Guinea, the Solomon Islands, New Caledonia, and Vanuatu. The current political boundaries do not necessarily match any sociocultural entities of the past. The peoples of these nations have developed distinct musical practices.

Traditions particular to parts of Melanesia include elaborate dances and panpipe ensembles (figure 1) (sometimes joined by wooden trumpets), voice-modifying instruments, and horizontally and vertically placed log percussion instruments.

Performances in much of Melanesia involved spectacular displays made in times of crisis and rituals associated with secret societies and advancement to higher grades in them, warfare, construction of men's houses, funerary and memorial ceremonies, the making and consecrating of log percussion instruments, and reactivating social relationships. Performances often included large masks and other-worldly costumes, set into motion by performers moving to sounds from struck logs, hourglass drums, flutes, panpipes, or singing.

—*Adapted from an article by Adrienne L. Kaeppler*

Figure 1 Carrying weapons and playing raft panpipes (*takamasi*), men of Kukurina Village, North Solomons Province, Papua New Guinea, dance.
Photo by Don Niles, 1982.

675

Island Region of Papua New Guinea

The Island Region of Papua New Guinea includes Manus, New Ireland, East New Britain, and West New Britain provinces. With North Solomons Province, it contains 12 percent of the area of Papua New Guinea and 16 percent of the national population. It contains islands within the Bismarck Archipelago: the Admiralty Islands, New Ireland, St. Matthias Group, Lavongai (New Hanover), and New Britain. Austronesian languages are spoken throughout the region; non-Austronesian languages occur on New Britain, New Ireland, and Bougainville. For a map of this region, see the one at the beginning of the New Guinea subsection.

Baluan in Manus Province

Manus Province, in the northwest of Papua New Guinea, borders the Federated States of Micronesia in the north and Indonesia in the west. In the east are the Admiralty Islands: Manus and numerous smaller islands, including Los Negros, Rambutjo, and Baluan. In the west are several groups of small islands. The administrative headquarters, Lorengau, lies on the eastern part of Manus Island. Some of the western peoples display Micronesian physical and cultural features.

Baluan, a volcanic island of about 23 square kilometers, lies about 50 kilometers southeast of Manus. It has a population of about four hundred, living in patrilineally exogamous clans. The fertility of the soil enables the people to get cash from growing fruits and vegetables.

Composing means producing new texts stimulated by events while using and modifying old musical patterns. The proper composition of songs is possible only if the composer has inherited magical powers, enhanced by the use of ginger, cinnamon, and betel. "Anyone who wants to influence things and events through magic," says Konda'i Lipamu, "has to follow all the rules related to the kind of magic he wants to practice." Performing songs or recitations, some men exercise magical power.

Good singers and instrumentalists are treated as specialists. For providing musical services, they receive dogs' teeth, shell money, food, and round wooden dishes filled with meat, fruits, turtles, and seasonal goods. At festivities, a specialist may func-tion as master of ceremonies. In *garamut* ensembles and multipart vocalizing, Baluan music is polyphonic. Flutes, panpipes, and *susaps* serve only for expressing soloists' moods and aiding love-controlling magic.

Dance

Women's costumes for dancing formerly consisted of fine skirts, made from dyed, braided, fringed, knee-length, raffia strings, held at the waist by a braided belt, covering the front and back to leave the hips free. Preferred colors were red, yellow, and brown. A woman would wear a braided, dyed, raffia headband about three centimeters wide. A similar braid circled upper arms, upper calves, and ankles. Women wore dogtooth necklaces, which were replaced in the late 1990s with beads of plastic and glass. They carry a woven fringed shoulder bag. At Christmas, they decorate their heads and necks with leaves, flowers, or baubles. Most enjoy exposing bras and petticoats.

In all simply structured dances, women stiffly hop up and down on both feet, which they point outward, parting their legs. Then they shuffle their feet backward and forward. They shake leaves in their hands, turn their shoulders in counter-movement to their hips, puff out their chests, and swing their breasts. Christian churches have censored many of these movements.

Men traditionally danced wearing headbands, armbands, legbands, and dogtooth necklaces. Each attached to his penis a white shell, which his father or another close relative had given him at initiation. Performers waggled their penises and made coital movements. Christian missionaries and directors of the Paliau movement prohibited these dances on Baluan; nowadays, men rarely perform them.

Vocal Music

Baluan musical classification focuses on user and function. Each vocal activity has a context-related term. The term *wokwok* can be glossed 'call out loudly for an announcement' and 'recital of a ritual text'. For some kinds of singing, the term *w(e)ii* denotes the main women's ritual song and men's work-accompanying songs. Used as a verb ('sing'), it is gender-neutral and does not cover all kinds of singing. Older persons say [uii]; younger ones, [uei]. Hence the spelling *w(e)ii*.

Throughout the province, a unique style of vocal polyphony is an important element in religious beliefs. Some songs have more power than others. Songs stand in a hierarchical order: *kolorai*, of highest value; several kinds of *w(e)ii*; and *polpolot*, songs for entertainment, with no ritual value.

Baluan vocal texture has two parts: a lead (*yaret* 'call out') and a second (*isiol* 'join'). For *kolorai*, the lead stands on the left of the second; for *w(e)ii* and *polpolot*, the lead is a soloist, but more than one person may sing the second. Singers of *polpolot* position themselves side by side in a line, sitting or standing. By the 1980s, because indigenous social structures were no longer intact, *polpolot* had become the most important genre. *Kolorai* and *w(e)ii* were moribund; older musicians regretted that young people no longer understood Baluan's ancient ritual language used in those genres.

The Performance of Kolorai

Only important and wealthy persons can afford to sponsor *kolorai*. Performances formerly commemorated deceased persons; specialists performed inside the men's house between sunset and sunrise. The texts have a heroic character. Sections in the old ceremonial language are unintelligible; specialists now improvise new texts. The textual rhythm dominates the musical rhythm; interpolated exclamations, sighs, and vocables occur. The performance proceeds expressively. To intensify emotion, singers sometimes raise a hand. The lead usually starts with the exclamation *oi*, expressing grief at the loss of the person commemorated; it also "opens the voice," as singers say. The second repeats the initial phrase, changing it slightly; it then aids the soloist by singing the main referential notes as a drone. The lead uses cadential formulas, crossing below the tonic and returning above it. This crossing forms the most important simultaneous interval of the style. *Kolorai* follow and precede performances by *garamuts*.

The Performance of W(e)ii

The term *w(e)ii* denotes something smooth and quiet; musically, it specifies ritual songs shorter than *kolorai* and having three dependent sections and a coda, without antiphonal features. Specialist singers are women; men sing one solo genre. There are five main varieties of *w(e)ii*: those sung by women at commemoration rituals, outdoors during the day; those sung by women at other functions, such as bride-price-paying ceremonies and canoe-carving ceremonies; those sung by women as laments after the loss of a loved one; those sung by either men or women in worry or nostalgia; and those sung solo by men while working.

W(e)ii follow and precede a piece performed by *garamuts*, the *kileŋ w(e)ii*, to which women usually dance, making restricted spatial movements within scattered formations. They hop, shifting their feet back and forth. Slowly they progress forward. They first move their arms, but then hold them close, repeatedly twisting the torso.

The Performance of Polpolot

Without restrictions of place or time, people perform *polpolot* for entertainment, introduced by rhythmic patterns borrowed from *w(e)ii*. Texts are in colloquial speech, without ritual value.

Instrumental Music

Throughout Manus Province, *garamut* ensembles are the most important form of instrumental music. Each language names the instruments differently, but the numbers and functions of the instruments within an ensemble mostly remain the same. At high-ranking leaders' weddings, players double every instrument but the lead instrument.

A *garamut* ensemble has six instruments in four sizes: three *san(t)san*, one *kipou*, one *lolop*, and one *kil*. The *san(t)san*, the smallest, is about 80 centimeters long, with a diameter of 25 centimeters. The *lolop* is about 110 centimeters long and 36 in diameter; in performance, it takes the lead. The *kipou* is 140 centimeters long and 46 in diameter. The most revered instrument is the *kil*, about 2 meters long, with a diameter of 66 centimeters; it rests on the floor. The *kil* may lean against a post or a solid wall or rest on a wooden stand.

Men hew *garamuts* from *sinal*, a tropical laurel. Rituals mark selecting and felling a tree, transporting the trunk to a sacred area, and finishing the log, which men cut to size and hollow with fire. Some stages of the process are secret. Finally, men polish and paint the instruments. Unplayed *garamuts* "have no voice." Especially at Christmas and Easter, men adorn new instruments with leaves and flowers, and carry them on special beds to the feast, where men knock them against a previously played instrument.

Each performer strikes a *garamut* with wooden sticks. A secret magic spell protects against evil spirits: performers chew ginger, cinnamon bark, and secret herbs (sometimes with betel), and spit the mixture into their hands; murmuring the spell, they rub it onto the sticks.

Rhythmic formulas (*kileŋ*) are fast, long, and complex. They never accompany singing. Before and after songs, they accompany dancing. They serve as signals and summonses. In the early 1980s, eighteen patterns were extant. Descriptions of five of these *kileŋ* follow.

1. *Kileŋ pame(k)*, related to the ritual use of betel, is performed during a major feast to remind leaders to cut the nuts; *kileŋ kolorai* introduces and concludes *kolorai*.
2. *Yalyal*, for one instrument (*lolop*), is performed immediately after someone has died. Repetitions of the pattern tell the status and sex of the deceased.
3. *Samari* regulate meals at certain festivities; they occur in four patterns, each of which usually repeats four times.
4. *Kileŋ boy* is addressed to a much-appreciated fish. When people bring ashore a catch of this fish, the ensemble performs this pattern.
5. *Purui* marks the sunset during a festivity, after which the feast takes a different course.

Other Musical Instruments

Several wind instruments serve for private expression and love-controlling magic. The *yui*, a raft panpipe, consists of four bamboo tubes, tuned E–F–F-sharp–G-sharp. Blowing two adjacent tubes simultaneously yields a narrow second. The *yui* is suitable for performing two-part songs, mainly polpolot; only males play it. A notched bamboo flute (*ruŋ*) is about 35 centimeters long, open at both ends, with three equidistantly spaced holes near the far end. Men play it for recreation and love-controlling magic. From bamboo tubes 15 to 25 centimeters long, people of either sex make and play *susaps* (*kupu-(w)uk, kubu(w)uk*).

Music in Transition

Baluan supports five churches: Roman Catholic, Lutheran, Seventh-Day Adventist, United Church, and Baha'i. Hymns are similar in all. Based on four-part harmony, they are sung in as many parts as available voices permit; improvised harmonies result in chains of six-three chords. The texts of most Baluan hymns are in the Tolai language. From 1946 to 1954, John Paliau, a charismatic local politician, imposed on the inhabitants of Baluan a modernizing movement, which, by interrupting indigenous sociocultural activities, drastically changed local customs and obliterated much of the people's religious heritage.

Young people informally play guitars and ukuleles, sometimes in bands. Instrumentalists may sing popular songs; others may join in, singing, clapping, humming, and whistling. Many such songs came with missionaries, sailors, and other visitors; some came when local persons returned from work on other islands. Structurally, most resemble hymns.

People of the Tabar Islands, New Ireland Province

New Ireland Province is in the northeast of Papua New Guinea. Its largest island, New Ireland, is a long, narrow landmass. Other islands important in the province are Lavongai (New Hanover), the St. Matthias, Djaul, and the Tabar, Lihir, Tanga, and Feni groups. The administrative headquarters, Kavieng, lies at the northwestern tip of New Ireland Island.

Tabar consists of three islands—Simberi, Tatau, Big Tabar—that lie off the northeast coast of New Ireland. The people cultivate sweet potatoes, catch fish, and operate important ritual ceremonies. Before 1884, when a German administration arrived, residents had a reputation for repelling outsiders—renown enhanced by reputed skill in the arts of death. But trade was an intrinsic part of the people's place in the world: Tabar joined a network that linked the coastal islands to villages on the mainland.

Songs of the Malanggan Traditions

In ritualized contexts in northern New Ireland, songs are used most notably in the *malanggan* complex of ceremonial activity, centered on funerary rites and the commemoration of dead relatives. Other ritual contexts that use songs include the removal of broken taboos, sorcery, hunting sharks, and the relationship between a person and his or her totemic shark. Songs induce supernatural assistance during medical treatments, for gardening, and in fishing.

In Tabar, songs are an integral part of more than twenty *malanggan* traditions, each of which has its own character, ritual sites, ritual behavior, history of ownership and context, names, and music. Each tradition can include forty or more songs, which all owners of *malanggan* may perform in a ritual context related to the song's specific tradition.

Malanggan songs can be sacred, sung only by men in the *malanggan* ritual site, or secular, sung by all owners of *malanggan* (men, women, children) during *malanggan*-related activity held in the open. Non-sacred songs are most usually sung at funerals while the participants are sitting on the ground in the village plaza. These songs are part of the traditions to which the deceased person belonged. If he or she had owned *malanggan* rights in, for example, Valik, Deŋenasi, and Kulepmu, then during the night after the death, mourners would sing the entire known corpus of secular songs of those three traditions.

Most sacred songs accompany *malanggan* activity or mark sections within a ceremony. During the construction of a ritual house, activity-specific *malanggan* songs serve for hauling logs, attaching sago leaf to laths, attaching laths to the framework, and so on. These songs are sung by all the participating men and boys, who may be sitting, standing, or even hanging eight meters up in the rafters. Other sequences of songs recount the history of the *malanggan* copyrights being used. The first song in the Malagacak tradition travels from one ritual site to the next; bringing each location to mind, it presents the circumstances when the ownership of that set of *malanggan* had changed hands. The second song in this tradition closes the gate of the ritual site, breaking the connection between the sacred *malanggan* world and the secular world.

Musical Instruments

Unique to northern New Ireland, the three- or four-tongued friction block is used in ritual contexts as a dominant feature of the *malanggan* tradition called Lunet (or Lounet) on Tabar. This instrument is colloquially called a bird (*ma*) because its cry is bird-like and much of the ritual in the Lunet tradition involves bird-related imagery. But in central New Ireland, where the instrument was apparently invented, it has been documented by other names (see textbox). According to current belief, it was originally made in the image of a bird by men living high in the forest plateau of central New Ireland. A man initiated into the Lunet tradition would hide in a conical "nest," suspended from a tree over the grave-yard, or resting on a table made from an inverted trunk with its roots forming the platform. Hidden inside this nest, at night and in the early morning before the *malanggan* ritual, he would rub both hands and the instrument with leaves of cordyline (*Taetsia fruticosa*), and then play the instrument by rubbing the tongues in sequence. Women and the uninitiated were told that its sound was the voice of spirits of the dead.

Another instrument locally restricted to the ritual context of *malanggan* is the whirled slat, made from segments of bamboo and sounded during funerary ceremonies. Conch trumpets (*tavuri*, *tuwir*) are restricted to certain types of *malanggan* ritual. They formerly announced success on shark-hunting expeditions. Other wind instruments used on Tabar include an end-blown bamboo flute (*katoŋuŋu*) and bamboo panpipes (*potoviso*), both of which serve in breadfruit-fertility ceremonies and other secular activities. Men use panpipes to attract and seduce women.

Tabar Islanders use three percussive instruments: *garamuts*, bamboo instruments, and *kundus*. Garamuts are used in sacred contexts at ritual sites, and in secular contexts, such as the social event called rounding the *garamut*, which occurs in the village plaza at night. The bamboo instrument is much lighter; women use it during their fertility rituals and in other ceremonial activities where women play a dominant role. *Kundus*, evidently an import from elsewhere in Papua New Guinea, mainly accompany vigorous dances.

Rattles, used in ritualized and secular contexts, include the *leŋaleŋa*, made from seed cases or shells and played mainly during *malanggan* rituals; and the *tobo* (which evidently originated on mainland New Ireland), resembling the *leŋaleŋa* but having dog's-tooth clappers.

—Adapted from an article by Don Niles, Gerald Florian Messner, and Michael Gunn

679

FRICTION BLOCKS

These instruments have three tongues (seldom four or five) that when rubbed make a piercing sound. Only in the late twentieth century, when the instrument lost its deeper spiritual significance, could its background be explored. Its production, use, and playing remain secret and concealed from noninitiates.

The instrument comes in three sizes. A small version (12–20 centimeters) produces a shrill, penetrating squeak. Some of its names are Nalik *karao* 'lizard', Kara *qatqat* 'small frog', and Tabar-Mandar *kulekuleng* 'tiny night-active bird'. A medium version (25–35 centimeters) produces a smoother, high-pitched sound. Some of its names are Nalik *manibobos* 'night-active bird', and Kara *paleseqau* 'smaller bird'. A large version (40–65 centimeters) produces a medium-high-pitched sound. Some of its names are *launut*, *lounut*, and *lounuat* (from Tabar *lunit*, probably the generic name of the instrument).

Larger versions are said to sound like a bird; smaller ones, like geckoes, frogs, or squeaking birds. Bird-related names prevail. The legend of the origin of the *lounuat* says a woman discovered the instrument upside-down in a cave on the beach, where waves were pushing it to and fro, making it cry. Afraid, she ran home to tell her husband. He seized it and tried to make it work. In vain he knocked it, and then blew air onto it. Finally, by rubbing it, he made it cry. In *lounuat*-using societies, all important customary objects originated with women, who yielded them to men.

Manufacture and Learning

The *lounuat* is made from the wood of the tree *savaf*, which also serves for canoes, masks, and sculptures. Knowledge of its manufacture, restricted to the men of a few subclans, passes down through maternal moieties. This copyright is valuable cultural property.

A *lounuat* master accepts only adepts displaying appropriate behavior and customary knowledge. He initiates apprentices into its secrets by making them reenact the legend. Starting with silent observation, they move stepwise through its plot.

Players rank high. Their office, kept for life, requires them to behave perfectly. In return for playing, they receive prestigious gifts, including the most highly valued parts of butchered pigs, other high-prestige foods, and shell money. Formerly, when a performer died, his instruments would be cremated with him, or thrown with his body into the sea.

Tuning and Playing

The tongues are tuned relatively. Each instrument has a unique tuning, but all feature a sequence of low–medium–high. (One exception shows a medium–low–high pattern.) The intended sound is a piercing, beating cluster, with a frightening effect for noninitiates. *Lounuat* are played in different sizes simultaneously, in ensembles of twenty or more. At grand occasions, like funerals, they join an ensemble of reeds and whirled slats.

Players hold small instruments in one hand. They address medium and large ones in either of two ways: sitting with the instrument between their thighs, and standing with the instrument between their legs. To get enough friction, they moisten their palms and fingers with the sap of rubber or breadfruit trees. Each player rubs the tongues in the direction of his body, from the farthest (with the lowest pitch) to the nearest. While hearing the sound of the instruments, noninitiates may not look at the players or the instruments.

Most of the music has been forgotten. It served for signaling (as did that of log percussion instruments), when it announced the deaths of important men or women. Only three ritual pieces survive. Their structure is intricate: a rhythmic series of low, medium, and high pitches, in slow and fast modes. In Nalik, these pieces are "*Di Vozi*" ('A Gasping Man Climbs the Hill'), "*Di Buak a Rangana Urima*" ('Pluck a Branch from the *Urima*'), and "*A Vel(e) Sikau Ina Gom i Varakaum*" ('Two Singing Birds Alternate').

Acoustics

Played indoors, one instrument was measured at a sound-pressure level of 115 decibels, almost painfully loud. (The human threshold of pain is about 130 decibels.) The *lounuat* produces a quasi-sinewave tone, mixed with friction-produced noise. This pattern is unusual among percussion instruments. In culturally conditioned noninitiates, the sound of several of these instruments being played at once may indeed arouse fear.

Bibliography

Fischer, Hans. 1986. *Sound-Producing Instruments in Oceania*. Edited by Don Niles. Translated by Philip W. Holzknecht. Boroko: Institute of Papua New Guinea Studies.

Hesse, Karl, with Theo Aerts. 1982. *Baining Life and Lore*. Boroko: Institute of Papua New Guinea Studies.

Laade, Wolfgang. 1998. *Music and Culture in Southeast New Britain*. Bern: Peter Lang.

Messner, Gerald Florian. 1983. "The Friction Block *Lounuat* of New Ireland: Its Use and Socio-Cultural Embodiment." *Bikmaus* 4(3):49–55.

Niles, Don William. 1980. "The Traditional and Contemporary Music of the Admiralty Islands." M.A. thesis, University of California at Los Angeles.

Schwartz, Theodore. 1963. *The Paliau Movement in the Admiralty Islands, 1946–54*. Anthropological papers, 49. New York: American Museum of Natural History.

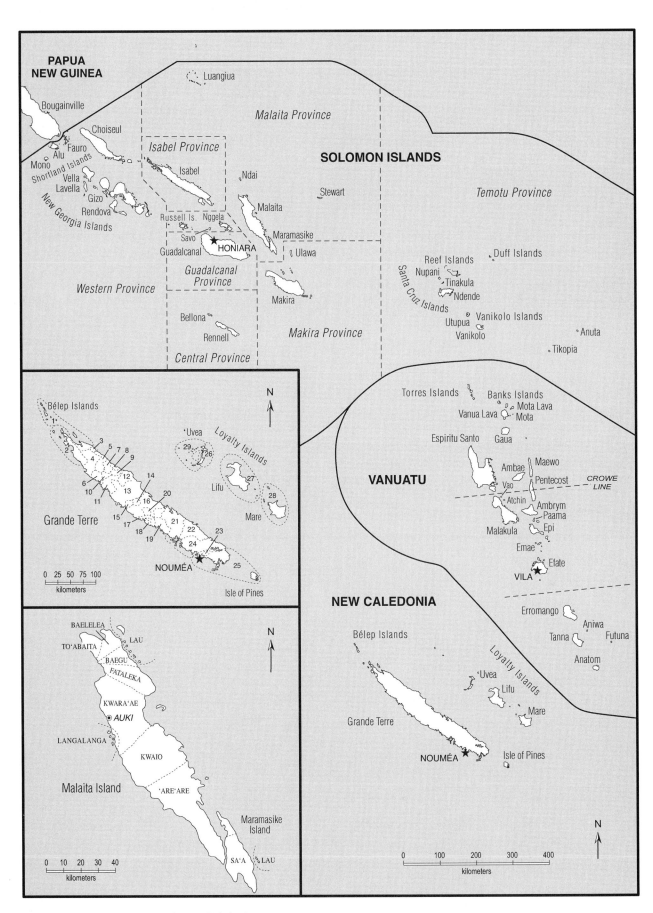

Solomon Islands, Vanuata, and New Caledonia

Solomon Islands

In 1568, hoping to find gold to rival that of the biblical King Solomon's mines, the Spaniard Álvaro de Mendaña (1541–1596) visited and named the Solomon Islands. Louis de Bougainville (1729–1811) in 1768 determined the extent of the archipelago, and gave his name to its largest landmass.

Bougainville, Buka, and several small islands form the North Solomons Province of Papua New Guinea, home to some 130,000 people. The rest of the archipelago forms the independent nation of the Solomon Islands, with a population of about 260,000. Several Polynesian outliers are located in the Solomons. The archipelago saw fierce combat between Japanese and American forces during World War II.

Musically, the Solomons are known for their panpipe ensembles, still used in traditional styles, including polyphony in several parts, sometimes doubled, tripled, or quadrupled at the octave. Details of this polyphony vary geographically. Panpipe ensembles may form into contemporary bands, which play Western-inspired pop. A famous dance, in which men in lines carry wicker shields, is said to derive from Nggela Island, but is performed by men of Guadalcanal.

The Halia of North Solomons Province, Papua New Guinea

The culture of the North Solomons Province of Papua New Guinea has strong cultural affinities with that of the rest of the Solomon Islands. In both areas, panpipe ensembles are important, and the absence of the *kundu* in Buka and Bougainville, in contrast to most other parts of Papua New Guinea, is a strong parallel with the Solomon Islands. Most peoples of Buka and Bougainville practice polyphonic singing as the norm. They consider the *susap* a men's instrument and the musical bow a women's instrument; in a given language, both instruments usually share one name.

Probably the most distinctive musical context in Buka and Bougainville is dancing to the music of wind instruments. An ensemble commonly consists of several differently sized double-row panpipes (one row with distal ends closed, one row with open ends), several end-blown bamboos tied together like a raft, and an end-blown conical wooden trumpet. While performers dance in a concentric circle, this ensemble accompanies polyphonic singing with vocables.

About thirteen thousand Halia-speakers inhabit the east coast of Buka Island. Rainfall is scarce. The people sometimes move from coral-cliff villages to camps on the beach, 60 meters below. There, when the tide is out, freshwater springs well up from under the coral. The Halia grow food in gardens, and get fish and shellfish from the sea. They buy imported food in Buka Town.

The Halia have had contact with outsiders for about a century. Some of their music is no longer current, but singsings remain important. Local schools educate children in their own language. In the mid-1980s, the people were beginning to seek outside help in finding ways to preserve their music.

Musical Contexts

Halia people sing in many contexts. On the water, rowing from Buka to the Carteret Islands, they sing while waiting for the sun to set; at daybreak, they sing when light permits going ashore. Women traditionally performed brideprice songs and laments. Current songs treat subjects like Christian faith and soldiers at war.

By organizing and hosting a singsing, a Halia man gains prestige. The evening before the event, he sponsors a rehearsal. In a counterclockwise-moving circle, men play pipes and bamboo trumpets. Songs are accompanied by *garamuts*, pipes, or both. Girls dance in a line, arms hooked together, rocking forward with their weight on the left foot, then leaning back with weight on the right foot while tilting the pelvis. As the night progresses, all other participants circle in a walking step; only the girls perform formal steps.

A singsing held in the 1980s featured nine songs. The first song celebrated the host. It had three parts: the first part included singing with pipes and trumpets, the second featured instruments only, and the third returned to the first part. The second song celebrated the singers; it was performed with the wind instruments and repeated three times. One group sang the third song to overpower the music of another, singing simultaneously; people sang it three times unaccompanied, then twice with wind instruments. The fourth song, sung with wind instruments, was repeated. Five songs followed. People sang song five for enjoyment; it was accompanied by two *garamuts* and repeated five times, with a text of vocables only. Song six sometimes expresses jubilation at catching tuna; people sang it five times unaccompanied, then twice more with *garamuts*. People sometimes sing song seven when going to the garden. It was accompanied by *garamuts*, and repeated once. Song eight expressed happiness about singing in front of the *garamuts*; it was repeated nine times. Guests sang song nine as they departed; accompanied by *garamuts*; it was repeated three times.

Musical Instruments

In communal dancing and singing with wind instrument accompaniment, singers take their pitches from the wind instruments, two kinds of which accompanied dance-songs: bamboo panpipes, bound in rows of four; and bamboo trumpets, bound in rows of three, the longest of which extended about a meter. At the beginning of a song, a low E-flat sounded. The players, all men, were all but hidden in the crowd. Occasionally, they raised the long pipes skyward as they sounded them, their cheeks puffing. Some pipes played G-flat and A-flat somewhat sharp, but the consensus in vocal and instrumental parts was G-flat and A-flat unsharped. Voices entered contrapuntally: first the instruments, then the singers (figure 1). Men may play *garamuts* singly or in pairs, accompanying singing and dancing.

Music System

Phrasing in Halia songs consists of two to eight types, which derive from three minimal prototypes: A, AB, and ABC. Variations consist of slight modifications: melodic substitution, expansion, and contraction.

Halia performances are polyphonic. A typical *garamut*-accompanied song has no text. A male leader sings an introduction on the vowel /o/ until a men's chorus enters singing /oa/, and then women enter, singing /ae/. Three beats before the women begin singing, two *garamuts* enter. This is a simpler

pattern than that of other songs in the cycle, which insert eighth-note pairs, plain or dotted, between triplets.

The Blablanga of Isabel Province, Solomon Islands

Santa Isabel is a long, narrow island. The interior has forested mountains; along the coast, coral reefs jut into the sea. Outside a few lagoons, coastal waters are rough. About once a week, an interisland freighter calls at Buala, the port. Several times a week, planes land on a nearby coral atoll, from which cargo and passengers go by canoe to Buala.

On the central northeastern coast live about six hundred Blablanga. They subsist on sweet potatoes and other garden crops, supplemented by imported foods: rice, tea, biscuits, canned meat. A few local coconut plantations produce copra. People earn cash from collecting trochus shells; ships take burlap bags full of these to Honiara, where Japanese traders buy them for making buttons, jewelry, and paint. Blablanga houses have bamboo walls, verandas, and sago-leaf roofs. A village in the foothills may have a related village on the edge of the lagoon. In 1982, musical data were obtained at Hovukoilo and its related village, Popoheo.

Musical Contexts and Genres

On the water, Blablanga women sing unaccompanied songs. Other songs include a song of welcome, plus songs dealing with the familiar, such as sea turtles and dogs. Choirs of mixed voices sing in contrapuntal textures, but only men sing songs that originated in warfare.

War-related Dance

As performed by men of Hovukoilo, war-related dances (*ragi māgana*) display physical grace and control. Singing, the men move slowly and serenely.

Figure 1 Excerpt of Halia singing with wind instruments, Hanahan Village, 1984.
Transcription by Vida Chenoweth.

Back and forth, keeping in tempo, each man swings a shield supported on his left arm. In his right hand, he holds an ax, which he leans against his right shoulder. As the leader calls out instructions, the dancers' bodies rotate to the right and left. When each body rotates leftward, its right leg slowly lifts, kicking to the left; when the body rotates rightward, the left leg slowly lifts, kicking to the right.

The leader cues every change in choreography. At a given call, the men crouch; in synchrony, they may bob up and down. Simultaneously, each man continues to swing his shield, but now holds it flat on the forearm, instead of vertically. At another cue, they rise and begin to step forward, one leg crossing in front of the other. Before weight goes onto the foot in action, the foot gently taps the ground several times. Throughout, the knees bend in time with the beat.

A typical dance begins with men in three columns, facing forward. A leader sings a musical introduction (figure 2). As some men join his vocal part, others sing a countermelody above it. The only text sung is the vocable *e* or *he*. After introductory intervals, the pitches stabilize. The melody, derived from a scale whose tones are alternately a major second and a minor third apart (G–A–C–D–F–G), has a wavy contour.

Dances with Wind Instruments (Gragi Nifu)

Men may dance while playing bamboo trumpets (*bubu*) and panpipes (*nifu*). Each man wears a loincloth or shorts, white designs painted on his face, chest, and back, and a shell disk through his nasal septum. A large slice of shell in a half-moon shape hangs from his neck.

The music begins with trumpets. When the panpipes enter, the dancing begins. Facing inward in a circle, players slowly step left and bend the knee. By pivoting on one foot while lifting the other, they turn to face outside the circle. They continue playing. The circle gradually turns in a clockwise direction, as they again step left. Dancers with midsize trumpets begin a movement that resembles scooping the earth with their trumpets, while the bass trumpets continue to sound.

Performances in 1982 used thirteen trumpets, of two sizes. Eleven were of medium length, about five decimeters, and sounding a pitch lower than F a

Figure 2 The start and basic pattern of a Blablanga war-related dance, performed by men of Hovukoilo in 1982. *Transcription Vida Chenoweth.*

twelfth below middle C. Men played the long trumpets in alternation, acting as drones. The melody and tonal inventory of ceremonial dances draw from the same scale as warlike songs, but with E-flat as tonal center. They have no vocal parts, but each dancer plays a wind instrument. In addition to the trumpets, men play three sets of panpipes: small, medium, large, two of each set. The small instruments have about eleven pipes, the longest about 13 centimeters. The large instruments consist of about twelve pipes, the longest about 50 centimeters. The texture is harmonic, though the performers conceive the parts linearly. Harmonic seconds sometimes occur as voices cross. All phrases end on the same tone, with octave duplications. A pattern that emerges at phrasal endings strengthens the sense of a greater tonal center in association with a lesser one, reminiscent of a tonic-dominant relationship.

Women's Songs

Women sing as they travel by canoe, and musically welcome visitors. Often when they sing, a man positions himself as their leader. In a song performed in 1982, the vocal parts were rhythmically identical. Each part is equally prominent, so the tonal center is less obvious. Variation comes from minimal melodic substitution.

Musical Instruments

Only the men of the Blablanga play panpipes and trumpets. The people of Buala have one log instrument, which sits in a cradle about a meter off the ground. Instrumentalists stand to play, using short, thick sticks, one in each hand. Its call develops two patterns, used only for signaling.

The Fataleka and Baegu of Malaita Province, Solomon Islands

Malaita Province consists mainly of the islands of Malaita and Maramasike. Its people are mostly Christians. The administrative capital is Auki, at the northern end of Langalanga Lagoon. The main exports are copra and timber. The distinctive musical instruments of Malaita are bamboo panpipes, made and played in varying sizes and sets, in sacred and secular contexts. The musical scale most frequently used by panpipe ensembles divides the octave into seven equal intervals.

The Fataleka and Baegu inhabit northern Malaita. Their most highly valued ceremony is the funeral series (*maome*), organized after an important person's death and consisting of an eight-year-long set of rituals. Panpipe ensembles perform during

particular rituals; in some, men perform narrative songs, to the accompaniment of concussion sticks.

The Fataleka play solo bundle panpipes (*tala 'au, susuku*) only during the funeral series, but the Baegu also use *susuku* for entertainment in nonritual contexts. The Baegu instrument has seven pipes in a bundle; the Fataleka instrument has nine pipes in a trapezoidal bundle, in rows of two, three, and four pipes. The Fataleka associate rattle-accompanied songs (*uunu* in both languages) with divinatory sessions, but the Baegu sing them at festivals and ceremonies including those of the funeral cycle.

Songs

Fataleka divinatory songs (*uunu*) form a subgenre of *'aukwee*, items that include *nguu 'oio*, songs associated with warriors. Characteristic of *'aukwee* is singing in two parts, *na'o* and *buli*, performed by a men's choir seated in two facing rows, each singer holding a rattle. One man flicks his wrist to sound his rattle continuously; the others sound their rattles on downbeats. The men hum, but sometimes take up the lead singer's words. They perform on nights when they must make big decisions. They believe their leader sees lights representing ancestral spirits, whose appearance he interprets.

Narrative songs, relating myths and histories, are sung at night during certain rituals of the funeral series, and at weddings. Some continue for hours. Sitting in two facing rows, men beat concussion sticks as they hum in two parts, *buli* and *bola nguu*. In the middle of the *bola nguu* row sits a soloist (*sili*), who alone sings words. When he stops for breath, the singer of the *tali nguu*, seated on his left, relieves him, singing without words. These songs divide into sections, each of which has a melody, sung several times to accommodate its words.

Before playing panpipe music, Fataleka and Baegu musicians sing an introductory song (*mae'au*). Sitting in two facing rows, they sing in two parts. With a sudden crescendo, they stand up. They repeatedly stamp their right feet on the ground, sounding rattles tied to their ankles.

Women and girls sing *roiroa* in unison for entertainment; the singer who best knows the melody and the words leads while the others hum. A child's older sister may sing lullabies (*rorogwela*). The words of a typical example refer to such a situation: the elder sister asks the baby not to cry, saying its parents are dead and no one else is around to hear it.

Musical Instruments

Struck and blown tubes (*sukute*), played for private entertainment by Baegu women and girls (and

Figure 3 At a chief's installation, Baelelea men carry flat, painted carvings of hornbills and other birds. Panpipe players form a cluster behind the dancers. The Baelelea live in northern Malaita and have musical traditions that resemble those of the Fataleka and Baegu.
Photo by Adrienne L. Kaeppler, 1976.

sometimes boys), consist of two pieces of bamboo, 25 and 28 centimeters long and open at both ends. The lower end of a tube held in the right hand is tapped against the left thigh. The other tube is held in the left hand, its upper end tapped alternately against the left cheek and the right palm; between these movements, the player blows into it. The player may use the left tube alone.

The musical bow (*kwadili*), played only by Fataleka and Baegu women, has two strings attached to a bamboo tube open at both ends. The player holds the bow in her left hand, puts the tube between her lips, and plucks the strings with a plectrum or the end of the fiber from which the strings are made, obtaining two fundamental sounds. She sometimes presses her left thumb on the strings to shorten their vibrating length, raising the tone. Resonance of her oral cavity amplifies select harmonics.

The Fataleka bundle panpipe consists of nine variously sized bamboo tubes, open at both ends. Holding the tubes in place, the player moves his head to blow into specific pipes.

The Fataleka panpipe ensemble (*'au sisile*) has six musicians, who play for the funeral series. Four like-sized instruments—*safali, ufi buri, sui, sili*—have fifteen pipes each; the other two, *life na'o*, have three pipes, pitched lower. The musicians stand in two facing rows, with the players of three-pipe instruments in the middle of each row. On their right ankles, musicians wear rattles made of dried husks.

The Fataleka ensemble *'au sango*, with the same instruments as *'au sisile*, involves dancers, wearing rattles on their right ankles and standing on each side of the musicians. It plays four pieces: *Safali Fuli 'Au, 'Ae 'Au, Faa Sungu,* and *Faa Sasaka*. Between pieces, dancers change sides. During the fourth

piece, instrumentalists change places while playing. Dancers carry in their right hands flat carvings painted black, white, and red, depicting a hornbill (figure 3). One dancer shakes a rattle, whose sound is brighter than that of the ankle-tied rattles.

The end-blown flute (*sukwadi*), played only by Fataleka and Baegu women, is a bamboo tube open at the lower end, with a circular mouthpiece in the node that closes the upper end. It has no holes for fingering. The player opens and closes the lower opening with her right forefinger. In addition to two fundamental sounds, she obtains harmonics by overblowing.

The panpipe ensemble (*'au ero*) ordinarily consists of twelve musicians, but the number varies. Each musician plays a nine- or ten-pipe instrument. Complementary sets of pipes produce a scale of seven equidistant tones: odd-numbered tones from the *buli* "behind" instruments, and even-numbered tones from the *na'o* "front" instruments. The musicians arrange themselves in two facing rows, the *buli* on one side and the *na'o* on the other. *Na'o* and *buli* are also the names of the two main polyphonic parts.

Adapted from an article by Adrienne L. Kaeppler, Don Niles, Vida Chenoweth, J.W. Love, and Hugo Zemp

Bibliography

Chenoweth, Vida. 1972. *Melodic Perception and Analysis: A Manual on Ethnic Melody.* Ukarumpa, Papua New Guinea: Summer Institute of Linguistics.
——. 1979. *The Usarufas and Their Music.* Dallas: Summer Institute of Linguistics Museum of Anthropology.
——. 1984. *A Music Primer for the North Solomons Province.* Ukarumpa: Summer Institute of Linguistics.
Ivens, Walter G. [1930] 1978. *The Island Builders of the Pacific.* New York: AMS Press.

Richardson, Susan. 1986. "An Analysis of Halia Music." Document in ethnomusicology, Wheaton College.

Stella, Regis. 1990. *Forms and Styles of Traditional Banoni Music*. Boroko: National Research Institute.

Suri, Ellison. 1980. *Ten Traditional Dances from the Solomon Islands*. Honiara: Solomon Islands Centre, University of the South Pacific.

Thurnwald, Richard. 1971. "Instruments de musique de Malaita (I)." *Journal de la Société des Océanistes* 30:31–53.

Vatahi, Albert. 1989. "Panpipe Ensembles of the North Solomons." Manuscript. Institute of Papua New Guinea Studies Music Archive.

Zemp, Hugo. 1972. "Instruments de musique de Malaita (II)." *Journal de la Société des Océanistes* 34:7–48.

——. 1981. "Melanesian Solo Polyphonic Panpipe Music." *Ethnomusicology* 25(3):383–418.

——. 1995. *Écoute le bambou qui pleure: récits de quatre musiciens mélanésiens*. Collection "L'aube des peuples." Paris: Éditions Gallimard.

Zemp, Hugo, and Daniel de Coppet. 1978. *'Aré'aré: un peuple mélanésien et sa musique*. Paris: Éditions du Seuil.

New Caledonia

The New Caledonian archipelago includes Grande Terre (the mainland) and surrounding islands: to the south, the Isle of Pines; to the east, the Loyalty Islands; to the north, Belep. Extending over 80,000 square kilometers, it has reef constructions (lagoons, atolls) and a mountain range that divides Grande Terre into a narrow, heavily rainwashed, coastal strip on its east side, and broad, dry coastal plains on its west. The prevailing climates are tropical and temperate. A hot season with deep atmospheric depressions alternates with a cool winter. The natural vegetation—mangrove, shrub, savanna, forest—supports many endemic species. [For a map of New Caledonia, see the one at the beginning of SOLOMON ISLANDS.]

About thirty-five hundred years ago, a people whose descendants call themselves Kanaks first settled New Caledonia. A few Polynesian migrations, of which the last reached Uvéa in the 1700s, contributed to the process of linguistic diversification. In the late 1700s, when European explorers reached the archipelago, more than thirty languages were locally spoken. The French government claimed the territory in 1853. Waves of European immigrants followed, and Kanak life underwent violent changes.

Twenty-nine aboriginal languages are spoken in the archipelago. In contrast to linguistic diversity, however, cultural practices (including music) exhibit comparative unity. The largest difference occurs between Grande Terre and the outer islands, which have absorbed cultural traits from Polynesian settlers.

Musical Contexts and Genres

Vocal genres of music divide into two classes: a body of more intimate music, linked to the household; and a body of communal music, performed at major ceremonies of exchange. The first class includes lullabies, games of noisemaking and singing, melodies for flutes, and curative and religious invocations. The second class includes rhythmic speeches, men's songs, mimetic dances, and since the end of the 1800s, the music of mixed choirs, cast in the mold of Protestant hymns—a European musical genre, which New Caledonians call *pilou-pilou*, denoting any kind of Kanak communal music. Descriptions of two of these communal styles appear below.

Since the Europeans' arrival, the islands appear to have adopted more flexible musical practices, and have accepted the modification of certain musical elements of old forms, such as the tendency to use the tempered scale and sing in unison. The musical life of Grande Terre, however, seems to have been more rigid, more secretive, and less equipped to face the vectors of change: censorship by Christian priests, broadcasting on radio, and recording on tape.

Singing on Grande Terre

On Grande Terre, two-part men's singing is held in higher esteem than other kinds of music. The accompanying dances are called round dances or outdoor dances, according to the area. The pattern is that of a human wheel in motion. Two singers stand at the hub, surrounded by a dozen musicians, who stamp bamboo tubes on the ground, clash bark-clapper beaters, or scrape palm spathes. With rhythmic shouting, calling, whistling, and hushing, they urge the singers on. Finally, everyone attending, dances counterclockwise around the orchestra, joining in the medley of sounds with jokes and exclamations. The dance itself is simple: people sway along, stamping, walking, or trotting, depending on how close they are to the center. It lasts all night, sustained at the center by successive pairs of singers.

All over Grande Terre, the tempo of any single song is constant and unchanging, but the paces of different songs may differ. For rhythm, the ensemble splits in half. Each half has the same number of musicians and the same combination of instruments, power, and pitch. One half is said to mark the main beat; the other, to "cut" or "pierce" it.

The first singer leads each repeat, setting pitch and tempo. After a short segment, the second singer answers, as the ensemble joins in. The paired singers share each melody, divided into three or four segments, which sometimes cross and meet in true counterpoint. The effect of this duo is that no silence occurs. The orchestra supports the singers, maintaining the tempo and vigor of the ensemble. The singers do not strictly follow the beat of the clappers. By the accuracy of the melodic interweaving, singers brook no interruption or slackening in phrasing. These qualities make up the main aesthetic criterion for this song, which "must be spirited," or "must not drop"—literally, "must be sung pushing ever higher, as if two men were chasing each other up a hill."

Intensity of phrasing comes from simple counterpoint, where the two voices alternate or double each other in parallel. One of the voices supports the other with marked stresses or short elaborations on one syllable, or again, prepares the tension of the liaisons between the melodic segments by a progression of tones independent of the other voice. The themes often build on small intervals, but the overlapping of long and short segments enhances melodic contrast. Rather than producing an alternation of the voices themselves, the intertwining favors close and rapid alternation in the mutual support and autonomy of the parts.

Drawing widely on the names of places, lyrics recount historic events, such as interclan wars, alliances, or colonial episodes; they define social areas and relations with the natural world; they sometimes tell stories of love. The singers often perform borrowed songs, the words of which they do not understand. During most of the performances, because of the noise, the crowd dancing around the singers cannot hear the sung words; with coded gestures, the singers cue them. Thus, in performance, the words are secondary.

Figure 1 A dancer from New Caledonia performs at the Pacific Festival of Arts.
Photo by Adrienne L. Kaeppler, 1996.

Mimetic Dances

According to tradition, birds taught Kanak people how to dance. In certain regions, the gray fantail, which hops ceaselessly (elsewhere, the *notu*, a big and beautiful pigeon, which struts powerfully) gave the inhabitants a love of rhythmic movements. This kind of dance tells a story through figurative and stylized gestures, performed by a company in synchrony; it consists of a series of segments, each executed twice.

The choreographic narrative of dances in the north of Grand Terre (area of Hoot ma Whaap) may be a legend, or it may recount historical events, or describe the building of chiefs' houses or the cultivation of yams. In the rest of Grand Terre, the main subject of dances is warriors' exercises, such as attacking and defending with traditional weapons. The dancers arrange themselves in rows or lines while one or two leaders dance at the side, or weave among the rows. In the Loyalty Islands and on the Isle of Pines, these dances are more often led by a mixed choir of men and women, who simultaneously and rhythmically strike leaf parcels and bamboo tubes. On the mainland, an ensemble behind the dancers accompanies them; the Paicî area uses no instrumentalist at all.

Painted black, the dancers hold bunches of pandanus root or straw, emphasizing their movements. The basic action, from which all the actions evolve, is a series of vigorous stamps, broken up by a light hopping on the supporting foot. The main rhythm of mimetic dances in the north of Grande Terre is a repeating pattern of eight eighths, of which the second and sixth are stressed.

On Grande Terre, as each troupe of mimetic dancers makes its entrance into the center of the village, it is ritually shielded by accompanists carrying branches while a leader dances in front, to divert spectators' attention. These acts, which supposedly protect the magic powers that favor dance, prevent accidents. Before starting, the dancers offer a gift of allegiance to the male representatives of the maternal line in the ceremony. These dances are transmitted through formal apprenticeship.

Dancers of the district of Wetr on Lifou in the Loyalty Islands have asked themselves how to present an old legend in a dance so that everybody understands it. In their dances *Capenehe e Hlemusese* and *caee* (both created between 1992 and 1994), the performers become actors, for their dance is a music-accompanied skit. Before these dances receive off-island performance (figure 1), a participant expains the legend in the language of the audience.

Until the early twentieth century, each hamlet had its own dance. Imbued with a strong sense of communal ownership, these dances are inherited patrilineally. After the changes of around 1900 and the tendency to "globalize the Kanak," the search for cultural identity in the 1980s led to a more local, more differentiated characterization of Kanak culture, and the resurgence of mimetic dances has strengthened this tendency. The dances are spectacular productions, and for that reason are most subject to self-conscious change and folklorization.

Musical Instruments

Musical instruments of New Caledonia fall into two main classes: instruments of entertainment, including musical toys; and instruments associated with dances and ceremonies. These classes overlap: during dances, certain toys (whistles, jew's harps) sometimes punctuate sequences, or highlight the rhythm and excite the dancers; and under the censorship of Christian missionaries, ceremonial instruments (such as panpipes) have become children's toys.

Most of these instruments are still in use. Instruments of European origin, sold commercially, include metal whistles (*vesel*) and harmonicas (popular in the early 1900s), played during dances in the islands. Guitars turn up everywhere, usually in young people's hands.

Instruments of Entertainment

These are various small objects, easy to make and nonpermanent. On the east coast of Grande Terre and in the Loyalty Islands, jew's harps are made from a strip of coconut foliole and held between the musician's teeth or lips, with a segment of the midrib of a green foliole, which twangs the leaf when hit by the hand. A whirring disk is made from *Cycas* fruit, pierced by two strings. A coconut-leaf whizzer resembles one found in Vanuatu.

A piston flute is usually made from rose laurel, but sometimes from a native shrub. In the water-struck flute of the Loyalty Islands, "smaller pieces of cane, made up at one end, and filled with water, according to the pitch of the tone desired, were blown; these hoho produced a sound resembling that of Pan's pipes" (Hadfield 1920:134).

An obliquely played end-blown flute comes from the petiole of the papaya; open at both ends, it is roughly 30 centimeters long. Played mainly in gardens and on the paths leading to them, it is often associated with courtship.

A side-blown flute found on the mainland is made of a reed, or of a thin, native bamboo. Closed at both ends, it has a fingerhole at the end opposite the hole

for blowing. It is curved, about 1 meter long, with a diameter of 2 centimeters.

Ceremonial Instruments

Self-sounding Instruments (Idiophones)

Stamped bamboo tubes—*wau* 'bamboo' in the Xârâcùù and Ájië languages of the central mainland, and *duu hyavic* 'real bamboo' in languages of the north—are primarily instruments of the mainland. They contribute to the rhythmic support of two-part men's songs and mimetic dances. They measure from 1 to 1.5 meters long, and are between 7 and 25 centimeters in diameter. They are normally made from a thin native bamboo. (In the Loyalty Islands, where bamboo does not naturally grow, musicians use tubes brought from Grande Terre, or, as a substitute, plastic pipes.) Women sometimes stamp tubes, but in important ceremonies, only men do. Stamped tubes also appear in the Loyalty Islands.

Two-part men's songs follow a rhythmic beat set mainly by concussive clappers made from fig bark, stuffed with dried grass and melaleuca bark. Clappers are usually about 30 centimeters long, one held in each hand. This instrument is called *cinfwe* 'fig-tree bark' in the north, where people say it was originally made of crab shells. Apparently an isolated instrument in Oceania, it occurs only in Grande Terre. As part of the most important musical context, these clappers are highly valued, and they bear important connotations of ceremonial exchange and competition: old people say that when the clappers "are well played, the force of their rhythm causes a strong wind to arise, lifting coconut fronds, and causing coconuts to fall"—which could well be a metaphor for aggression against the chief hosting the ceremony. Alternatively, it might be an image of pleasure, the enthusiasm of the chief who dances and gives his fruits (offers his daughters). In response, the hosts may fill their clappers with magical leaves, which, as they say, "will awaken everybody, lift the dance, bring down the opposing singers, and calm the guests' greed and aggressiveness."

Wind Instruments (Aerophones)

Throughout New Caledonia, the conch is the most symbolically charged instrument. The shell is usually the larger triton, less frequently the smaller. With one exception, these are end-blown trumpets without a mouthpiece; exceptionally in Oceania, one observed side-blown conch has the hole for blowing on the side opposite the opening of the shell.

An instrument of the chieftainship, the conch summons people to meetings and ceremonies. After being turned into a trumpet, it must undergo ritual washing with magical plants, which give it the power to summon; then, for safekeeping, it goes into a special basket, high in the chief's house.

Each hamlet formerly had its own conch, with its own rhythm: "the conch is the chief's voice," people would say. Set as a sculptural element atop the pole of the chief's house, it becomes a symbol of the chief's power and alliances. It once had a religious meaning: men blew it to call and petition gods, and its sound marked important steps of agrarian rites. A northern myth links it with the aerial power of thunder and the mineral power of mountains.

—Adapted from an article by Jean-Michel Beaudet and Raymond Ammann

Bibliography

Ammann, Raymond. 1997. *Kanak Dance and Music: Ceremonial and Intimate Performance of the Melanesians of New Caledonia, Historical and Actual*. Nouméa: Agence de Développement de la Culture Kanak. Book with compact disc.

Fischer, Hans. 1986. *Sound-Producing Instruments in Oceania*. Edited by Don Niles. Translated by Philip W. Holzknecht. Boroko: Institute of Papua New Guinea Studies.

Hadfeld, Emma. 1920. *Among the Natives of the Loyalty Group*. London: Macmillan.

Tjibaou, Jean-Marie. N.d. *Kanaké: The Melanesian Way*. Translated by Christopher Plant. Pape'ete: Éditions du Pacifique.

The Upright Log Instruments of Vanuatu

Vanuatu comprises scores of islands with a population of about 170,000, speaking more than 100 languages. First visited by the Portuguese Pedro Fernandez Queiros in 1606, these islands remained little known to the wider world until the late 1700s, when Captain Cook (1728–1779) surveyed them and named them the New Hebrides. [For a map of Vanuatu, see the one at the beginning of SOLOMON ISLANDS.] The performance of music and dance featured masked rituals and the sounds of log percussion instruments (idiophones), which often gave voice to ancestral spirits, represented by human images carved in stones and tree ferns. These spirits issued commands: through conventional rhythms, they incited the living to dance. Their placement reflected social structures: in areas that traced descent through the mother's line, they sometimes lay horizontally, but in areas that traced descent through the father's line, they often stood upright.

These upright log instruments are unique to central Vanuatu. Rising up to six meters above the ground and vertically planted, they were once used in an area defined on the north by the Crowe Line and on the south by the strait between Efate and Erromango. Nineteenth-century pictures often show them in groups. Specimens from Efate, Malakula, and Ambrym have reached museums worldwide, featured as artistic carvings, not as musical instruments. Despite widespread interisland voyaging, the idea of making such instruments was not pursued outside central Vanuatu, neither in the neighboring northern islands, nor in the southern ones, where log idiophones are not used and the only struck instruments are handheld bamboo tubes.

In border areas in the north of the distribution, some longish log instruments may be used horizontally and then propped up for specific ritual purposes, as for women's ululations in South Pentecost circumcision ceremonies. In central Vanuatu, the wooden, upright, planted instruments are usually played alongside smaller, portable ones oriented horizontally. An exception to the north of the Crowe Line is Maewo, where for certain ritually special purposes performers hold portable wooden instruments upright while playing.

For manufacturing log idiophones, the relative hardnesses of the trees determine the selection of species. For the upright instruments, trunks are dressed to the shape of regular cylinders; through a slit, they are hollowed out, and their surfaces are ornamentally carved.

—*Adapted from an article by Adrienne L. Kaeppler and Peter Russell Crowe*

Bibliography

Bonnemaison, Joël, Kirk Huffman, Christian Kaufmann, and Darrell Tryon, ed. 1997. *Arts of Vanuatu.* Bathurst, Australia: Crawford House Publishing.

Deacon, Arthur Barnard. 1934. *Malekula: A Vanishing People in the New Hebrides.* Edited by C. H. Wedgwood. London: Routledge.

Layard, John. 1942. *Stone Men of Malekula: Vao.* London: Chatto & Windus.

Lindstrom, Lamont. 1990. *Knowledge and Power in a South Pacific Society.* Washington, D.C.: Smithsonian Institution Press.

Micronesia

Singing and moving for gods of the sea, storms, sacred creatures, and spirits of the deep; conveying aural assistance to guide tattooers' hands and lessen the pain of tattooing; performing for welcomes and farewells; dancing to ensure fertility—all gave aesthetic enhancement to Micronesians' lives.

Some of these traditions are only memories; others have been culturally reconstituted in original and altered forms: modern gods require new styles and sites of musical performance; musical ideas and concepts are imported from colonial and influential countries. During generations of change, Micronesians have transformed old and new into musical traditions specific for each community, yet ready to meet the challenges of the twenty-first century.

Men of Namoluk Atoll perform with bamboo sticks while Kameol (1901–1971), a choreographer, looks on.
Photo by Mac Marshall, 1971.

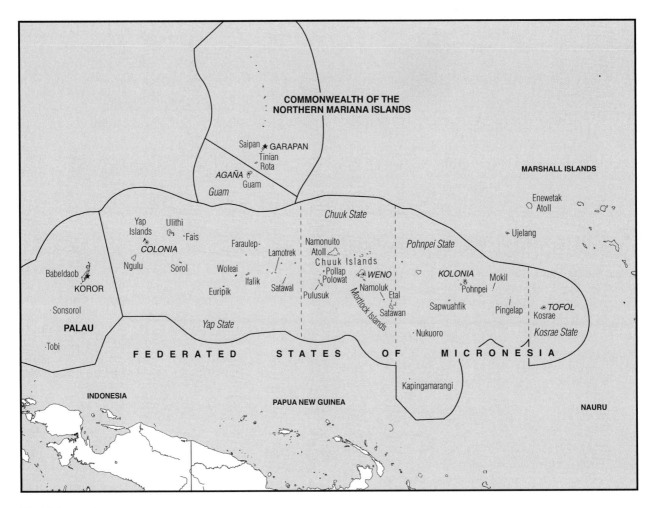

West Micronesia

The Music and Dance of Micronesia

The name *Micronesia* (from Greek, meaning 'tiny islands') was first used by Europeans in the 1830s for mapping the islands that lie east of the Philippines, north of Melanesia, and west of Polynesia (see maps). When political self-determination led to the establishment of the Federated States of Micronesia (often abbreviated to *Micronesia*), islanders and foreigners began using the distinction to specify that government and the islands and the peoples of its states. The name is an appropriate description for more than two thousand islands having only about 3,000 square kilometers of land. Micronesia includes three archipelagos (the Caroline, Gilbert, and Mariana islands), two parallel chains (the Marshall Islands), and two solitary islands (Banaba [Ocean Island] and Nauru).

Geologically, Micronesia contains three kinds of islands. Its high islands—the Marianas and five insular complexes in the Carolines (from west to east, Palau, Yap, Chuuk, Pohnpei, Kosrae)—are mostly volcanic in origin, with extensive natural resources. Its low islands—most of which lie in seventy-two coral atolls in the Carolines, Marshalls, and Gilberts—are smaller, with limited land-based resources, but bountiful marine resources in atoll lagoons. Its raised coral islands—Banaba, Nauru, and some scattered elsewhere—are intermediate in size, but have, or formerly had, phosphate deposits, useful to foreign interests.

Politically, Micronesia includes the Commonwealth of the Northern Mariana Islands, the Federated States of Micronesia, Guam (an unincorporated U.S. territory), and four republics (Kiribati, the Marshall Islands, Nauru, Palau). Some boundaries correspond roughly to indigenous settlement at the time of European contact; some resulted from foreign involvements; and Kiribati's resulted, in part, from twentieth-century geographic expansion to accommodate the growth of the population.

The population of Micronesia is less than five hundred thousand, but its density in some urban centers is high: on Majuro, capital of the Republic of the Marshalls, it is about fifteen hundred persons per square kilometer; Ebeye, an islet in Kwajalein Atoll, has nearly twenty times that density.

Origins, Settlements, Cultures

The roots of the Micronesian peoples lie in Southeast Asia, but Micronesians were, and are, diverse in physique, social organization, language (at least twelve mutually unintelligible languages are still spoken), and many other aspects of culture, including music and dance. Their diversity can be attributed to differences in routes and dates of migrations, accommodations to the natural resources of the islands on which they settled, postsettlement contacts with other Micronesians and other peoples of the Pacific, and internal changes during periods of isolation, which, as for Nauru, were of long durations.

Some high islands in western Micronesia (Guam, Palau, Yap) were settled more than three thousand years ago by Austronesian-speaking peoples from island regions now known as the nations of the Philippines and Indonesia. Some eastern Micronesian islands (the Gilberts, Kosrae, the Marshalls, and Pohnpei) were settled more than two thousand years ago by peoples of a branch of Austronesian-speakers from Melanesia, probably some directly from the islands now known as Vanuatu and others progressing through West Polynesia. The central Carolinean atolls were probably settled last, by peoples who had sailed westward from the eastern Carolines until they reached Palau and Yap, which had already been inhabited.

By the time of European contact, the people of some high islands no longer made long voyages, but the peoples of the low islands continued to sail, not only among islands of an atoll, but among atolls. Central Carolineans regularly voyaged to the Marianas, and occasionally—sometimes unintentionally—to the Marshalls and the Philippines. The central Carolineans are the world's only people with an unbroken tradition of open-ocean, noninstrumental navigation, a skill that in the 1970s a respected navigator from Satawal shared with Hawaiians eager to replicate ancient Polynesian voyages.

Ceremonial musical performance preceded departures for long voyages; feasting and dancing welcomed voyagers on their return. Sometimes when visiting an island for peaceful purposes, voyagers and hosts performed for each other—a custom that continues in new contexts. Occasionally, new songs with dancing recounted the events of a voyage.

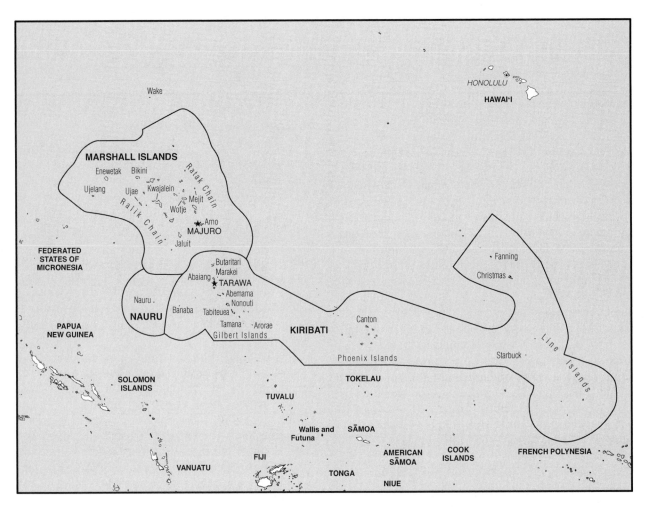

East Micronesia

Micronesians had many reasons to undertake long voyages, among them war (to expand a chief's domain or exact revenge for a battle), refuge (after a typhoon or a drought had devastated local resources), and trade. The most extensive interisland trade flourished before the 1800s within the so-called Yap Empire. People from the atolls west of Chuuk periodically voyaged to Yap, where, as an item for exchange, usually called their tribute, they gave a dance to the chief of a Yapese village. That item became highly valued property of that village, was learned by an appropriate group of villagers (the text maintained in the language of origin), and was performed when the chief required.

Musical Instruments

Throughout Micronesia, the human voice was, and continues to be, the predominant musical instrument. In the language of musical texts and some aspects of musical style, the vocal musics of each Micronesian culture differed from the others. The genres of each culture were differentiated by textual content, musical style, and manner of performance—whether solo or collective, and if collective, whether in unison or in multiple parts. Most vocal music was, and much still is, owned by a specific person, clan, or village, and was performed only in specific contexts for specific purposes.

Percussion involving the human body—stamping feet, clapping hands (with flat or cupped palms), clapping one hand over the hollow formed within the bent elbow of the other arm when pressed against the chest, slapping hands on thighs or chests—is a major auditory component of many Micronesian musical performances. Skill in dancing the most highly valued genres was essential to attaining adulthood. Except, perhaps, for food at feasts, synchronized performances by groups of men or women (in most Micronesian cultures, not together), were the principal presentations on prestigious occasions. Other genres were performed in less formal contexts; and in some islands, young men and women danced together while courting.

Instruments external to the human body served for music, signaling, and other purposes. With rare exceptions, they were percussion or wind instruments, made from a single material, used for a single purpose, and limited in geographic distribution. Important exceptions included the conch trumpet, used throughout Micronesia primarily for signaling. Sticks were widespread as implements used in dancing (figure 1). In some cultures, they were of bamboo; in others, of wood; in a few, they featured plaited leaf or feather ornaments. Most stick dances were stylized enactments of combat. A few were training exercises for combat: warriors in parallel-facing lines rhythmically and vigorously executed complex stick-clashing patterns, and frequently interchanged positions within and between the lines.

The only Micronesian drum was single-headed, resembling drums of some Melanesian peoples. In the eastern Carolines (where only men played it) and the Marshalls (where only women played it), it was shaped like an hourglass. In Nauru, its body was more nearly cylindrical.

DISC
1
TRACK
28

Two indigenous instruments are of special interest. A reed flute with an external duct—similar to those of some Filipino peoples, but different from the other flutes of Micronesia and elsewhere in Oceania—was played in Palau and Yap. A stone instrument, valued in Pohnpei for its sonority, was used in preparing the ceremonial beverage *sakau*: striking fist-sized stones against large, sonorous, differently pitched basaltic slabs, young men pounded kava roots in prescribed sequences of interlocking rhythms.

A few easily made instruments serve as children's toys. The conch trumpet serves for signaling in Kiribati, and occasionally in theatrical presentations.

Only sticks remain essential to the performing arts. Micronesians abandoned drums and other instruments when missionaries proscribed their use, and reed flutes and other instruments when they adopted Western instruments.

Responses to Christian Missionaries

For Christian missionaries who went to Micronesia to convert the islanders, the music of their particular denomination was intrinsic to the practice of their faith. The music they introduced, and the songs composed by Micronesians in these styles and styles derived from them, are major components of music in Micronesia.

The Chamorro, the indigenous people of the Marianas, converted to Roman Catholicism and adopted the music of Spanish Jesuits, who in 1668 established a mission on Guam. The peoples of Yap and the western Carolinean atolls rejected early-eighteenth-century efforts at conversion, but in the late 1800s began accepting Roman Catholicism and its music. The Yapese, while incorporating Christianity into their heritage, retained their dancing, and set biblical texts to the music and body-movement style of an indigenous genre of dancing. Dances with indigenous movements are performed in Roman Catholic churches in Kiribati.

The peoples of eastern Micronesia (eastern Carolines, Gilberts, Marshalls) had their first experience with Christian missionaries in the mid-1800s, when the American Board of Commissioners for Foreign Missions (Congregational) expanded its work in the Pacific, westward from Hawai'i. These missionaries abhorred not only the liquor and

Figure 1 Yapese women perform a stick dance in a space bordered by stone valuables (*rai*). Photographer and date unknown.
Courtesy of Hamilton Library, University of Hawai'i.

behaviors that whalers had introduced, but all customs integrated with indigenous beliefs. In their view, dancing was sinful, and performing music—except Christian hymns—was a waste of time, so they prohibited their converts from participating in these activities.

The missionaries quickly learned local languages, translated hymns, and taught the islanders to sing. In schools, they taught musical notation. Micronesians soon began composing religious songs in hymnodic styles (later also in gospel-music styles), and choral singing became a communal activity, within and without churches. Choral competitions and festivals, which became major events, continue in some islands. Kosrae has village-choir competitions, and Kosraeans from the whole island and several overseas communities gather at one church every four years to celebrate Christmas. Musics of other denominations—the London Missionary Society, the Liebenzell Mission, the Congregational Church of Japan—as adopted and adapted, added to Micronesian styles and genres.

During the colonial period, nativistic religious movements arose among several Micronesian peoples. Of these, Modekngei, which originated in Palau during the Japanese administration, contributed to the perpetuation of the precontact Palauan heritage through its songs in indigenous musical style. Musics of Shinto and Buddhist rituals, introduced during the Japanese administration, made little or no continuing contribution to local music.

Of the sects and denominations that entered Micronesia during the latter part of the American administration, the Church of Jesus Christ of Latter-Day Saints (Mormons) has proselytized most successfully and extensively. Throughout Micronesia,

it uses the same hymns (with texts translated into local languages), favors a "sweet" vocal timbre (in contrast to the intense vocal production favored by some islanders of other denominations), and relies on the accompaniment (or, more accurately, support or leadership) of Japanese-made electronic keyboards.

In a few islands, locally composed hymns and religious songs remain the predominant music and collective singing remains a major public activity; but in other islands, especially those in which the population divides among competing faiths, these songs and their singing have lost much of their former importance.

Music and Dance in the Early Twenty-first Century

Popular songs, foreign and locally composed, are heard extensively on radio, and as live or recorded commercial entertainment in urban centers (Guam, Majuro, Palau, Saipan). In addition to performing for local people and tourists, Micronesian performers and composers seek fame and money by distributing cassettes of their music. Many contemporary songs about love, personal and environmental problems, and other topical concerns have texts in an indigenous language, with musical features that identify them and specific places or people; others, especially those with English-language texts, sharing enough traits to be enjoyed beyond political boundaries, are considered pan-Micronesian. This identity does not embrace the popular music of Nauru or Kiribati; apparently, popular musics have not bridged a long-standing boundary between foreign administrations.

Traditional arts, especially dancing, have enjoyed a renaissance (figure 2). To negotiate relationships with

Figure 2 At the Pacific Festival of the Arts, performers from the Northern Marianas Celebrate their past. Little is known of the indigenous arts of the Marianas, including music and dance, and, few objects are found in museums. For this festival, performers often present plays based on reconstructed traditions and performances based on the manipulation of sticks.
Photo by Adrienne L. Kaeppler, 1996.

other peoples and governments, each new government needed to define its people. A powerful statement of sociocultural identity—and of collective commitment to a village, an island, or a nation—can be made by a large troupe of performers in a rehearsed presentation, whether of an old dance or of a new one with genre-specific movements, set to a text newly composed for a particular event. Because Micronesian cultures value dancing highly and the visual components of dancing are readily recognized (even if the text is not understood), dancing is a particularly effective cultural identifier. Therefore, teams of dancers often represent Micronesian peoples and governments, abroad (as at the Pacific Festivals of Arts) and in civic events at home. Some Micronesians have recreated what they appreciate as ancient music to identify themselves more closely with their natural environment and neighboring islanders, and to represent themselves in civic, national, and international events.

In some islands, to build self-esteem and pride in cultural identity, schools teach traditional dances to children, often with less limitation to clan affiliation than in precontact times. For twenty-first-century Micronesians, as for their ancestors, indigenous performing arts are not merely reflections of culture (as many outside writers describe their own arts and those of other peoples), but active determinants of people's places in the world. To offer readers more detail on the indigenous arts of Micronesia, the pages that follow provide accounts of them in Yap and Kiribati.

Yap in the Federated States of Micronesia

The Federated States of Micronesia (FSM) is a multicultural nation with a population of about 110,000. From 1947 through 1986, it was administered by the United States as part of the U.N.-designated Trust Territory of the Pacific Islands. In 1986, the FSM, as a sovereign republic with a constitutional government, entered into a compact of free association with the United States, to be in force through 2001. This compact was amended and renewed in 2004.

The FSM consists of four states: Yap, Chuuk, Pohnpei, and Kosrae. The last contains only the island of Kosrae, a high, volcanic island. The others include high islands and atolls. Land areas in the FSM range from Pohnpei's 334 square kilometers to atolls of less than 1 square kilometer.

Yap State comprises the closely grouped islands known as Yap and the atolls of Ulithi, Fais, Ngulu, Sorol, Euripik, Woleai, and Lamotrek. The Yap Islands are distinct from the others, which, despite strong historical and political ties with Yap, have cultural affinities with Chuuk. Yap first experienced contact with European cultures in the mid-1800s. From 1886 to 1979, contact took the form of colonial administration.

In 1979, Yap joined the FSM. Under self-government, the preservation of Yapese culture became an important concern. On Yap Day (1 March), celebrations feature dance-songs, which cultural-awareness classes study in municipal elementary schools. WSZA, the local radio station, airs local genres, especially *teempraa* and dance-songs. It features local bands (which cultivate a popular keyboard-and-vocal idiom) and transmits the Voice of America.

Vocal Music

All surviving Yapese music is vocal. It falls into two classes, each with a distinct context: performances of personally expressive songs (*tang*) occur in private; rehearsals and performances of dance-songs (*churuq*) occur in public, including Christmas Eve celebrations of Mass. Yap is in the diocese of the Caroline Islands, whose see is on Pohnpei; most of its priests and deacons are from Yap and the outer islands.

Instrumental music is not highly featured in Yapese culture. The earliest surveys cited wind instruments: *ngal*, end-blown bamboo flutes; *uchif*, leaf oboes, made from rolled coconut leaves; and *yubul*, conch trumpets. These instruments are no longer in use.

Private Songs

From precontact times, two genres of *tang* have survived: songs of love (*dafael'*), dealing with lovers' personal experiences, and songs of abuse (*t'aay*), recounting situations in which one party has supposedly injured another. Songs of abuse are a culturally legitimate means of social retaliation. Typical recipients of musical abuse are chiefs and former lovers. The word *t'aay* can also be interpreted 'rust, filth, bilge, excrement'—senses that well describe the content of the texts. By local criteria of propriety, the subjects of *tang* made them unsuitable for public performance. Because the singer often sat under a pandanus tree, the songs became known as *taan e chooy'* 'under the pandanus'.

During the Japanese period, a new genre developed: *teempraa utaa* (or *teempraa*) 'songs in mixed languages' combined Japanese melodies with Yapese and Japanese words. After 1945, this genre included songs based on American and European melodies, with mixed Yapese and English words.

Public Songs

Churuq are monophonic, strophic songs, with narrow ranges. Melodic phrases curve upward. Most are in duple time. Older texts are about historical events, wars, and mythology, but newer texts frequently have biblical themes. Melodies and texts are often interchangeable.

Yapese dancing and singing are inseparable. Men dance only with men; women, only with women. Children learn from adults of their own sex. Performances begin with a solo introduction, whose text apprises the audience of the story or sense of the dance.

Of the musical genres performed on the island, dance-songs are the most valued. As a social and communal obligation, their performance reinforces the sense of belonging to the community and helps confirm and define relationships, satisfying individual and social needs. In contrast, Yapese regard solo performances as personal expressions, which do not meet public needs.

A group rehearses privately for several weeks. For approval, it then performs for its village. When the planned occasion has passed and the group has performed, the group performs again for the village. That performance is the *penga lan* 'hanging up'—a term that refers to the hanging up of valuables (including shell money) in the rafters of the meeting-house (*pebai*). These practices hark back to the 1800s, when villages danced competitively.

Yapese *churuq* include dances by seated or standing performers, dances with bamboos, and marching dances.

Dances

DISC ❶ TRACK 29

Par-nga-but are line dances by seated performers wearing grass skirts and arm-and-head decorations made from coconut leaves and flowers. Movements of the upper body and arms illustrate the texts, which usually deal with events or people. Dancers' clapping accompanies a solo vocal introduction. A call from a soloist cues the start of unison singing, marked by another round of clapping.

Dances by Standing Performers

Many Yapese recognize four genres of dances by standing performers. For one, called *barug* by women and *tey* by men, dancers perform in a row. Among the oldest *churuq*, they are rarely performed. In style and subject, they resemble the dances by seated performers.

Tam' are funeral dances, whose movements resemble those of *barug*. Only women perform them, in honor of the dead.

In *täyoer*, women may proclaim a person's good deeds, reminding that person of his or her social duties; for the proclamation and performance, the dancers request payment. After a line whose meaning is unknown to the translator, an example goes: *Padre Thall, o, gamade, / Liyol e kogbod, / Ningad fangicho gadi / Kefel!* 'Father Thall, oh, we / The girls are here, / For us to say / Farewell'. The text is in short phrases, set to music that uses a scale transcribable as E–G–A♭–B.

An erotic dance, *kuziol* (women's version) and *gasalaew* (men's version), has movements that suggest coital positions and techniques. The texts cite the erotic shortcomings of the opposite sex. The dance is also called *umman*, a term that denotes the thrusting of hips.

Other Dances

In *gamal'*, paired dancers face each other in sets of four. On downbeats, each strikes a meter-long tube of bamboo against her partner's tube. When the dance becomes too vigorous for the performers to keep singing, a separate singer or group backs them up. Yapese believe *gamal'* traveled as payments of tribute from Woleai to Ulithi, and then to Yap. The texts are not in Yapese. Marching dances (*maas*, from English 'march') may have come from Pohnpei after 1945. No comprehensive study of these dances in the Carolines has been done.

Kiribati

The Republic of Kiribati—thirty-three scattered islands with an area of 811 square kilometers—encompasses the Gilbert, Line, and Phoenix Islands and Banaba. Most of the country's seventy-six thousand people live in the Gilberts, sixteen low coral islands known as Tungaru; a third live in the urban center of Tarawa, an atoll. The Gilberts were under British rule from 1872 to 1975, united with the Ellice Islands (Tuvalu). In 1979, they gained independence as a member of the British Commonwealth.

The culture of the Gilberts shows Polynesian influence resulting from ancient Sāmoan contacts and joint colonial administration. The Gilbertese (I-Kiribati) are renowned for indigenous skills and customs, including music and dance. Traditionally, the nine northern islands divided into several stratified societies under chiefly control; the southern islands, more egalitarian, were ruled by councils of male elders. Through the 1800s, warfare and factional fighting appear to have been common except on the two northernmost islands, Butaritari and Makin.

Musical Contexts

Many old genres are still performed, as are new and syncretic styles of sound and movement. Important social activities and discussions occur in meeting-houses (*maneaba*), affiliated with churches, schools, civic organizations, and performing troupes. Social gatherings include farewell parties, ceremonies associated with a new *maneaba*, gatherings to welcome or entertain visitors, and newer celebrations, including civic holidays and festivities associated with schools and churches. Rooted in custom and etiquette, such gatherings require feasts and artistic performances, as of oratory, music, and dance.

Singing often occurs when family and friends gather or travel, and for individual relaxation. "Island nights" are social dances, which feature live or recorded Kiribati and other Oceanic music, rock, or country. Hymns and religious songs are important to all religious sects; special presentations occur on Christmas and Easter. While cutting toddy in coconut trees, men sing to coax sap from the tree—and to announce their presence to unwary people below.

Social Groups and Music

Music and dance are important markers of I-Kiribati identity. Traditionally, all the singers and dancers of any troupe came from one descent group, a body that, with its associated lands and heritage, defines its members' social place. Skills associated with musical composition and performance (*kainikamaen*) were valuable clan property, as were ancestral spirits and historical narratives. Performances in *maneaba* were the most public and communal display of the strength of this knowledge.

In the late 1800s, beliefs and social concepts introduced by missionaries and the colonial government challenged the vigor of descent groups and brought changes in the structures of music and dance. Performance now marked events relating to governments, churches, schools, and holidays. On Tarawa, groups developed solely for singing and dancing; now serving a quasi-kinship function, they include resident outer-islanders and Tarawans, and vie to be chosen to perform at public events.

Competition in Musical Performance

Competition filled Kiribati life. It permeated games, musical performance, rivalries between descent groups, and warfare. Before battle, to encourage warriors, communities sang and danced. Victories in battle and in dance had similar effects: both proved the superiority of a clan's knowledge of supernatural powers. At least in the southern islands, I-Kiribati connect one's (lineage-determined) seat in the *maneaba* with one's role in fighting and dancing: people who defended the village in battle took the leading positions in performance.

Formal competitions included contests (*kaunikai*) between rival troupes and matches (*uaia*) between individual dancers. Both called for supernatural intervention and psychological motivation through public and private rituals. Ostensibly a contest of singing and dancing, *kaunikai* were actually competitions between bodies of knowledge. Apart from social occasions and entertaining guests, performances were not merely for enjoyment. When more than one troupe performed, people seethed with antagonism and tension, as the rivals, ritually strengthened and protected, faced each other from opposite ends of the *maneaba*. At stake were the health and lives of the composer, his assistants, and the lead singer.

A contest began with a challenge, frequently the result of gossip about the abilities of a musically specialized priest (*tia-kainikamaen* 'skillworker'). Protective words and phrases guarded against one's own inadvertent errors and one's rivals' dangerous phrases. In a song that begins *Tabekan toa nikunau aio Rurubene ma Nareau, te riki teuana* 'The raising of my song is from Rurubene and Nareau, who are united', attributing the text to prominent deities gives it strength and vitality. A declaration like *E I tabukibuki ngai ao I taebaeba* 'O I am hilly and like a gust of wind' asserts the composer's invincibility. *N na katea rabanau te nang roro* 'I will build my defense of thick dark clouds' is a protective phrase, symbolizing a wall of protection against enemies, as dark clouds block the burning rays of the sun.

Supported by supernatural power, songs made rivals falter, sicken, or die. In the text *Ti ibeia baani kana natin bakoa* 'Hammer the distant rocks into pieces for the food of baby sharks', the beginning invokes an opposing group's turmoil; the reference to sharks adds insult. Through the imagery of slumber with a deity, the phrase *be anoiko Nei Tinanimone ba ko na matu ma ngaia* 'for Nei Tinanimone sees you and you will sleep with her' threatens a composer with death. To harm or kill selected targets, participants surreptitiously pointed ritually prepared sticks at them.

Musical contests required ritual preparations, which encouraged spirits to work through the singers and dancers, making them fit, inspired, exciting, and safe. Ceremonies protected troupes and individuals, and enhanced the protective power of costumes. *Mamira*, ceremonies not limited to competitions, bestowed blessings on a song to enhance its appeal and its composer's fame (figure 3).

Pressure from the colonial government and missionaries, who considered the passion of competitions unhealthy and unproductive, resulted in modifications. The goals of competition became less malevolent, as rivals tried merely to undermine the success of each other's performance. With decreased emphasis on the descent group has come a change of name: from *kaunikai* to *kaunimaneve* 'competition with musical texts' (*maneve*). With proclamations of superiority in artistic skill, songs tease and provoke rivals. Involving village or social groups rather than lineages, formal competitions are more closely associated with choral singing (*kuaea*) than with dancing (*maie*). This change probably resulted from suppression of dance-associated rituals; eventually, ritual aspects resurfaced in more efficient forms. Choral singing as a genre became institutionalized in the 1960s in tandem with a resurgence of interest in artistic skill. Outstanding performances display forceful singing, with precision in diction. A trend of the 1990s and 2000s is that competitions are advertised—and winners receive cash prizes.

Despite these changes, competition still frames Kiribati dancing, and awareness of its impact guides rehearsals. Competitions are judged on the precision of singing and dancing, the attractiveness and appeal of songs and choreographies, and the excitement experienced by the audience. Occasionally, composers conduct *mamira* for dancing and choral singing, though large communal rituals are rare. On radio and cassettes, successful songs carry composers' fame throughout the nation and beyond: to I-Kiribati settlements in Fiji, Nauru, and the Solomon Islands.

The Power of Performance

A dramatic potential of performance is an ecstatic state (*angin te maie* 'the power of the dance'), brought on by the event in combination with psychological factors of social identity, sexuality, and shyness. This state is shown by dancers' labored breathing, vigorous movements, trembling, and screaming, and by singers' vocalizing more loudly, increasing the tempo or tonal level of the song, and moving with greater force. Transferred from the dancing, this state can be seen in singing when participants vocalize and play instruments fervently, often with their eyes closed.

I-Kiribati believe the ecstatic state displays the power of *kainikamaen*, as spirits work through the performers. Participants ensure that performers not lose control and cry, faint, or make mistakes. Elements of the music and dance are consciously structured to create tension. One or more exciters (*tani-kaunga*) roam among the singers to encourage them to sing enthusiastically, inspiring the dancers.

Musical Systems

Indigenous Kiribati dances are usually called *ruoia*. They vary slightly from island to island, but usually include the *kawawa*, a warm-up dance; the *arira* or *katika ne bee*, dances for men to fasten their mats; the *wanibanga*; the *wantarawa*; the *bino*, performed seated; the *kamei* or *kabuti*; and in some areas, more obscure forms, *tie*, *tarae*, and *kamaototo*. On Butaritari and Makin, battles between chiefs were celebrated with danced suites, such as *ietoa* and *nantekei*, in which the performers divided into opposing groups, named after legendary canoes. Each dancer

Figure 3 At a *mamira* ceremony on the beach at Betio Islet, Tarawa Atoll, the troupe ItitinKiribati performs a Polynesian-influenced dance, accompanied by log instruments and a bass drum.
Photo by Mary E. Lawson Burke, 1985.

carried a stick decorated and tapered at each end, representing a weapon.

Ruoia are performed by a line of one to six dancers, who execute choreographed sequences of flowing movements, interspersed with poses and abrupt movements of head, hands, and arms. Stylized walking, swaying of the hips (for females), and bending of the knees are features of certain dances. Dancers in a single line are of the same sex and approximate age, but mixed dancing formerly occurred. Movements and positions are based on actions of birds, fishing, martial arts, sailing, and canoes. Dancers do not interact with onlookers, but maintain a fixed aloofness (figure 4).

Located behind the dancers are the singers, arranged in lines, or more traditionally, in a canoe-prow formation. With rehearsed precision, they sing, clap, and move with the principal dancers, stamping their feet and slapping their skin. Dancers and singers alike sing initial dances.

The music uses a five-tone scale, roughly analogous to the tempered tones D–E–G–A–B. Melodies are syllabic, conjunct, and through-composed in one to three sections, each of which may immediately repeat. Within each section, rhythmic activity often goes from free meter to duple meter. In free-metered sections, the chorus performs choreographed movements accented with clapping; in metered sections, it provides steady stamping, clapping, and slapping. Concluding the song and the dance is a climactic cadence (*motika*), often shouted.

Each dance has its music. *Kawawa* may use from one to three pitches, but *wantarawa* and *wanibanga* often consist of melodies on one tone, which gradually rises through the performance. The *kamei*, danced by men or women, consists of two or three sections, as does the *kabuti*, an analogous women's hip-shaking dance. The music in each section begins with a freely rhythmic melody centered on the minor third E–G, and ends in a *ruruo*, a passage in duple meter, centered on A, and accompanied by choral clapping. Each succeeding section has proportionately lengthier *ruruo*, and often the last consists almost entirely of *ruruo*.

DISC **1** TRACK 30

The *bino*, considered by many I-Kiribati to be their most elegant dance, is also sectional. Based on a five-tone scale, the first section is rhythmically free; a seated chorus mirrors the dancers' movements. The second section is in duple meter with choral clapping.

Each section of a *ruoia* has a distinctive solo cue, which gives the starting pitch of the melody. The lead singer then begins; at a designated spot, the chorus joins in. Though the music may contain passages of harmony in thirds, fourths, or fifths, the singing is usually in unison, with men and women an octave

apart and simultaneous variants provided by the lead singer.

Musical Instruments

Indigenous Kiribati musical instruments were few. Bodily percussion was the main accompaniment to singing, and conch trumpets (*bu*) served for signaling. Percussion on *baoki*, a large, flat, wooden box borrowed from Tuvalu, supplements bodily percussion as accompaniment for *ruoia* and *bātere*. Since the early 1980s, some troupes have used bass drums and small log percussion instruments. Electronic keyboards, acoustic guitars, and ukuleles often accompany *kuaea*, and guitars or ukuleles may accompany the casual singing of *anene*. Bands that provide music at social dances often use electric instruments and Western drums.

New and Borrowed Genres

The term *maie* denotes dancing and associated singing. *Maie* and *bātere* also denote dances that incorporate traits of outside music or dance, and *bātere* denotes the Tuvaluan *fātele*, from which the term derives. The *kateitei*, the *kaimatoa*, and the *buki* are *ruoia*-derived dances with percussion-box accompaniment. Their melodies, and those of contemporary dances from the northern islands, have Western musical traits, including diatonic major scales, functional harmonies, and duple meters. Typical patterns of clapping (different from those of *ruoia*), steady acceleration of tempo (borrowed from *fātele*), and costume are hallmarks of several of these dances, which probably developed around 1900. *Kakibanako* and twentieth-century *bino* incorporate sections of older and later musical styles. *Ruoia*-derived dances have a different starting cue; the chorus, seated, provides only rhythmic clapping or percussion-box accompaniment. *Ruoia*-derived dances include most recent compositions, but new movements are sometimes composed for a *ruoia* song.

Vocal genres include *kuaea* ('choir') accompanied by guitars and ukuleles (occasionally electronic keyboard), using functional tonal harmonies, duple meter, narrow melodic range, monotonic passages, and typical cadences. *Kuaea* are associated with youth, civic, or religious organizations, but unaffiliated groups have formed since the early 1980s. Though usually comprising males and females, some *kuaea* are for males only, with the highest one or two of the (four to six) vocal parts sung in falsetto. An important genre, the *kuaea* incorporates many rituals and compositional methods of the *kainikamaen*.

Songs called *anene* are sung informally in a late-twentieth-century local style, incorporating Western

(a)

(b)

Figure 4 Solo dancers in characteristic poses: *a*, seated with diagonal arms, a Kiribati dancer performs a *bino* in Tanimaiaki Village, Abaiang Atoll (*photo by Mary E. Lawson Burke*, 1985); *b*, standing, with typical positions of the arms in northern-movement style, a Kiribati dancer performs in Nanikai Village, Tarawa Atoll.
(*photo by Mary E. Lawson Burke, 1981*).

musical elements. Lacking the drive of *kuaea*, they are in the repertory of amplified bands, which entertain at weddings, social dances, and other events. "Te katake," a historical song, is sung by one or two individuals as informal family entertainment.

—*Adapted from articles by Barbara B. Smith, Eve C. Pinsker, Deirdre Marshall, and Mary E. Lawson Burke*

Bibliography

Born, L. 1903. "Einige Bemerkungen über Musik, Dichtkunst und Tanz der Yapleute." *Zeitschrift für Ethnologie* 35:134–142.

Browning, Mary. 1970. *Micronesian Heritage*. Dance Perspectives, 43. New York: Dance Perspectives Foundation.

Burrows, Edwin G. 1963. *Flower in My Ear*. Seattle: University of Washington Press.

Fischer, John L. 1970 [1957, 1966]. *The Eastern Carolines*. Revised edition. New Haven, Conn.: Human Relations Area Files Press.

Grimble, Arthur Francis. 1989. *Tungaru Traditions: Writings on the Atoll Culture of the Gilbert Islands*. Edited by H. E. Maude. Pacific Islands Monograph Series, 7. Honolulu: University of Hawai'i Press.

Grimble, Rosemary. 1972. *Migrations, Myth and Magic from the Gilbert Islands: Early Writings of Sir Arthur Grimble*. London: Routledge and Kegan Paul.

Hijikata, Hisakatsu. 1995. *Gods and Religion of Palau*. Edited by Hisashi Endo. Collective Works of Hisakatsu Hijikata. Tokyo: Sasakawa Peace Foundation.

——. 1996. *Myths and Legends of Palau*. Edited by Hisashi Endo. Collective Works of Hijikata Hisakatsu. Tokyo: Sasakawa Peace Foundation.

Maude, Honor. 1971. *The String Figures of Nauru Island*. Adelaide: Libraries Board of South Australia.

O'Connell, James. [1836] 1972. *A Residence of Eleven Years in New Holland and the Caroline Islands*. Honolulu: University Press of Hawai'i.

Pinkser, Eve C. 1992. "Celebrations of Government: Dance Performance and Legitimacy in the Federated States of Micronesia." *Pacific Studies* 15(4):29–56.

Walleser, Sixtus. 1915. "Die Tanzgesänge der Eingebornen auf Jap." *Anthropos* 10:654–659.

Polynesia

Poetry, sung and danced; chiefs, honored and entertained; families, made and defined; the creation of gods, islands, and people; the celebration of love, the joy of birth, the solemnity of war, the dignity of death—this is Polynesian music.

At the core of Polynesian music lie words, for music is primarily a vehicle for conveying poetry. Words are the basic and most important feature of Polynesian musical performance. Rendered melodically and rhythmically, words impart hidden meanings through metaphors, whose allusions can be interpreted on multiple levels. Performers are storytellers, who sing to communicate messages by moving their hands and arms while keeping the beat by moving their hips, feet, and legs.

At the Pacific Festival of Arts, the Cook Islands National Dance Company performs.
Photo by Adrienne L. Kaeppler, 1985.

The Music and Dance of Polynesia

Polynesia (from Greek, meaning 'many islands') comprises a large number of islands mapped roughly as a triangle with Hawai'i at its northern apex, Rapa Nui (Easter Island) at its southeast, and Aotearoa (New Zealand) at its southwest. Culturally, Polynesia has three subdivisions: West Polynesia, East Polynesia, and Polynesian outliers west of the triangle. Ancestors of the Polynesians originated many generations ago in Asia or Southeast Asia. They developed a maritime culture as they migrated through eastern Melanesia to West Polynesia and beyond.

Traditionally throughout Polynesia, prestige and (usually) power resided in chiefly offices. Political regimes were long and enduring, and succession to chiefly office was by genealogical rules. Rank, based on descent from gods, was a distinctive social feature, which often resulted in pyramidal social structures, with the highest chief at the top and commoners at the base; relative rank within the pyramid influenced social relationships.

Music and dance paid allegiance to rank-based sociopolitical systems by validating and helping construct systems of social distinctions and interpersonal relationships. Specialists composed poetry, added music and movement, and conducted rehearsals. Music and dance were, and still are, composed to be performed for audiences, which bring to performances a critical aesthetic appreciation. The order of pieces within a performance, and performers' placement, clothing, and accoutrements imparted important information about the performers, the occasion, and the sociopolitical system.

Music and Dance

Poetic texts, based in metaphor and allusion, formed the basis of most Polynesian music: formally, music and dance were aural and visual vehicles for conveying oral literature. Rendered melodically and rhythmically, words suited the contexts in which they were performed, and were often accompanied by movements that contributed to the telling of stories.

Indigenous ceremonial contexts included investitures, weddings, funerals, and celebrations of historic and contemporary events. Social structure and religion often motivated aesthetic productions, but performances, though serious in intent, were often occasions for entertainment. Other music included work, game, and love songs, and songs deriding or praising people and places. Functions included celebrating persons, places, and events, criticizing social institutions (as with the 'arioi of the Society Islands, with performers breaking ordinary social rules), and paying allegiance (as with Tongan faiva, in which performers honored chiefs).

To understand Polynesian music and dance, performers and audience members must understand the spoken language, have an aesthetic appreciation of the rhythmic and melodic rendering of the poetry, grasp the allusions of the texts and the movements, and fathom relevant sociopolitical contexts and cultural philosophies.

Music was, and still is, primarily vocal. Nonvocal sounds, including claps and slaps, emphasized rhythm, often with contrasting timbres; but they seldom emphasized melodies. The only distinctive Polynesian melody-producing instrument was the nose-blown flute, made from a joint of bamboo and played by blowing through a nostril. With the introduction of European-derived instruments, especially ukuleles and guitars, instrumental melodies became more important, though a primary function of these instruments was often rhythmic.

Polynesian meter is usually duple; any change of tempo is usually acceleration. Songs often end in a downward trailing off. Intensity or loudness is not varied for effect, as such changes would inhibit understanding the poetry. This trait confirms the nondramatization of storytelling, a trait also visible in the movements of Polynesian dance: performers do not become characters in a dramatic interchange, and stylized gestures do not correspond to words or ideas put together in a narrative sequence.

Performers and Audiences

Performances are usually given by groups, large or small, in which all performers do the same sequence of choreographed movements at the same time. Sometimes, men's movements differ from women's movements. Many performances occur seated (figure 1). When standing, the legs and hips add rhythmic and aesthetic dimensions, but do not usually advance a story. Most important are the movements of the hands, wrists, and arms. The rotation or turning of the lower arm, flexion and extension of the wrist, curling of the fingers, flexion at the knuckles, and

Figure 1 Singing and movements of arms and hands are important dimensions of Polynesian music and dance. Lapaha, Tonga, 1975. *Photo by Adrienne L. Kaeppler.*

placement of the upper arm in space are significant dimensions. The combination of two bodily complexes—the amount and velocity of movements of the hips and legs, and the interplay of movements and placements of the hands, wrists, and arms—gives each Polynesian movement tradition its distinctive style.

Polynesian audiences were interested in hearing stories and accepting a composer's challenge to understand the deeper meaning embodied in the poetry and movements. Without knowledge of the language and conventionalized text-and-movement allusions, the lack of dramatization makes following a story impossible, and some audience members nowadays may not realize that a story is being told. Though melodically, polyphonically, and rhythmically engaging, the rendering of the poetry made the musical dimensions secondary and often repetitious. Similarly, Polynesian dance was the visual dimension of this poetry, with metrical lower-body-movement motifs and text-tied arm movements. Postcontact Polynesian music has changed in the direction of more melodic and rhythmic variation, and dance has become more pantomimic; nevertheless, poetic texts remain the basis for most music and dance.

KAVA

In most of Polynesia, people traditionally prepared, served, and drank kava, an infusion of the basal stems, stump, and roots of *Piper methysticum*, a tropical pepper, which grows more than three meters high. Researchers have not fully explored the psychoactivity of kava and its neurological effects, but they classify it as a soporific, a drug that enhances feelings of happiness and sociability.

Kava is almost everywhere ceremonial and social. In Tonga, Sāmoa, and Fiji, its public consumption makes a political display, validating chiefly status. During less ceremonious occasions, people may drink kava with intoxication in mind. The physiological effects of kava, and the range of its political and religious functions, shape in important ways its interface with music.

Music Associated with Kava

Formal Settings

In much of Polynesia, kava validates political relationships. Preparers, orators, apportioners, servers, and drinkers follow culturally prescribed strictures of etiquette, covering placement, posture, gesture, and sequence. Protocol may require poetry or music, often performed at set junctures in the process, as in eighteenth-century Hawai'i, when Captain Cook (1728–1779) observed singing during the preparation of the beverage.

As men strain kava in Fiji, seated male choruses do a song-dance that recounts the origins of the beverage or chronicles local histories. A text from Taveuni begins: "Sleeping at night; the day dawns; / The sun is on the warpath in the sky. / They go and pull up the kava to bring it" (after Hocart 1929:64–65). Associated movements include synchronized clapping and gesturing. Three claps mark the end of the preparations, and again when each drinker empties the cup. As preparers finish straining kava in Sāmoa, the apportioner declaims a *soloʻava*, a poem recounting the origins of the beverage, or alluding to other myths or legends. A short formula declares the readiness of the beverage. Those who will drink applaud with slow handclaps. Loudly intoning apt epithets, the apportioner calls each party who will drink. On hearing one's call, one may clap several times, expressing delight.

As individuals drink kava, etiquette may require that others be silent, or dancing and singing may continue, or participants may converse, depending on the society, who is present, and what the purposes of the occasion are.

Informal Settings

Informal drinkers often entertain themselves musically. In old Sāmoa, young drinkers challenged one another to intone poems; the penalty for misstatement was to dance alone, sometimes naked. In Tonga, during young people's informal kava-drinking parties (*faikava*), drinkers sing to the accompaniment of guitars, and women may dance. Female dancers also perform in the kava-drinking circles that serve as rotating credit associations among Tongans living in Honolulu: drinkers contribute to an association's funds by decorating the dancer with dollars. Some cities have kava bars.

—Adapted from articles by Adrienne L. Kaeppler,
J. W. Love, and Lamont Lindstrom

Bibliography

Burrows, Edwin G. 1936. *Ethnology of Futuna*. Bulletin 138. Honolulu: Bernice P. Bishop Museum.

——. 1945. *Songs of Uvea and Futuna*. Bulletin 183. Honolulu: Bishop Museum.

Highland, Genevieve A., Roland W. Force, Alan Howard, Marion Kelly, and Yosihiko H. Sinoto, eds. 1967. *Polynesian Culture History: Essays in Honor of Kenneth P Emory*. Special Publication 56. Honolulu: Bishop Museum Press.

Hocart, A. M. 1929. *Lau Islands, Fiji*. Bulletin 62. Honolulu: Bernice P. Bishop Museum.

Lindstrom, Lamont. 1987. *Drugs in Western Pacific Societies: Relations of Substance*. ASAO monograph. 11. Lanham, Md.: University Press of America.

Love, Jacob Wainwright. 1991. *Sāmoan Variations: Essays on the Nature of Traditional Oral Arts*. New York, London: Garland.

Marshall, Mac, ed. 1979. *Beliefs, Behaviors, and Alcoholic Beverages: A Cross-Cultural Survey*. Ann Arbor: University of Michigan Press.

Mead, Margaret. 1969. *Social Organization of Manua*. Bulletin 76. Honolulu: Bernice P. Bishop Museum.

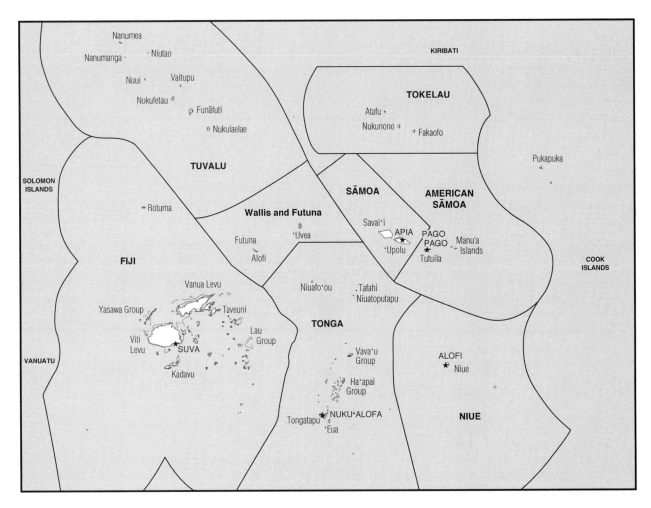

West Polynesia

West Polynesia

West Polynesia includes Fiji, Tonga, Samoa, ʻUvea, Futuna, Niue, Rotuma, Tokelau, and Tuvalu. Each archipelago is socially distinct, but all share basic cultural and linguistic patterns. Research on the prehistory of West Polynesia shows that the Lapita cultural complex, derived from Melanesia and marked by distinctive dentate-stamped pottery, was locally important. West Polynesian voyagers maintained interarchipelago trade-based networks, which included the import and export of chiefly spouses and prestige items. The movements of certain raw materials linked utilitarian necessities (such as hardwood for canoes and basalt for adzes) to ritual necessities (such as colored feathers and special plaiting materials), and to marital partners and warfare.

During the 1400s to 1600s, Tonga dominated West Polynesia, under what is known as the Tongan Empire. Tongan overlords and warfare were tied to fertility-oriented rituals associated with the Tuʻi Tonga dynasty, whose originator was a descendant of Tangaloa, the sky-god. These rituals required the presentation of firstfruits and other tribute, but they served as outlets of exchange, including the sexual unions that introduced variety into local gene pools.

Musical instruments important in West Polynesia are hollowed logs, stamped bamboo tubes, struck wooden plaques, mats, noseflutes, and conch trumpets. Contemporary instruments include ukuleles, guitars, electrically amplified stringed instruments and keyboards, and the wind instruments used in brass bands.

An analysis of West Polynesian dance reveals a torso usually upright, shoulders that do not move, and an emphasis on hand-and-arm motifs that enhance poetic texts. Within these conventions, movements vary with gender: men perform "virile" movements, often with the legs parted, open to the sides; women perform "graceful" movements, with the upper legs parallel and close together. Hip movements—subdued, often hidden by voluminous costumes—are not a significant dimension. Distinguishing features are the complexity of the interplay among turning the lower arm, bending the elbow, extending and flexing the wrist, and curling the fingers. Dance implements, such as paddles, clubs, and long staffs, are found throughout the region; sometimes struck, they may make artistic patterns in space.

Fiji

An independent nation of about 320 islands in eight groups, Fiji lies at the confluence of Melanesia and Polynesia, sharing cultural and physical affinities with both. Its performing arts, however, are considered Polynesian because of their similarities with West Polynesian performing arts.

The main islands, Viti Levu and Vanua Levu, show distinct cultural differences between the coast and the interior. Most villages recognize lineage-based distinctions between "land people" and "sea people." Even the smaller islands in the Lau Archipelago, on the eastern reaches of the nation, observed this distinction. Other main groups are Kadavu to the south, and the Yasawa Islands to the west.

Indigenous Music

The mainstays of Fijian music are *meke*, sung narrative texts with instrumental and dance accompaniment, performed in ceremonial and social contexts by men or women (rarely mixed) in lines or blocks, standing or sitting (figure 1). Movements, usually synchronous, emphasize collective excellence, rather than individual achievement. Men's movements are vigorous; women's, graceful and controlled.

Fijians subdivide *meke* into named genres, distinguished from each other by the dancers' gender, position (sitting or standing), movements, and accoutrements. Genres include men's dances with spears (*meke wesi*) and clubs (*meke i wau*), dances with fans (*meke iri*), a standing women's dance (*seasea*), standing men's dances (*ruasa*, *liga*), and the popular *vakamalolo*, done by seated men or women. The *meke ni yaqona* is a ceremonial song, performed by men while making ritualized movements of their arms and clapping their hands during formal kava-drinking ceremonies. The genres of *meke* are performed with varying frequencies in different areas. On Taveuni and Kadavu, the *vakamalolo* predominates.

The significance of performance has changed with the society, but *meke* remain a feature of important occasions, such as religious conferences, weddings, and official visits by political dignitaries. Some genres, including *vakamalolo*, are more popular than others. Some support competitive dancing. Some survive by altering their functions; for example, men's dances with spears and clubs have become vehicles for entertainment on festive occasions and in *meke* competitions.

Vocal accompaniment for Fijian *meke* usually comes from singers who sit in a tight circle, with the leaders near the center. The most important person in the performance of any *meke* is the composer, who creates or supervises the creation of the poetry, the music, the dance, the accompanying instrumentation, and the costumes. The composer of the lyrics, male or female, is usually known by name. Composers teach their *meke*, and may lead the singing.

Performances of *meke* exhibit the usual Polynesian emphasis on the primacy of a text. Lyrics usually divide into stanzas, each of which may repeat. The number of lines in a stanza, and the number of words in a line, vary. The ends of lines usually rhyme on an identity of two vowels, regardless of any associated consonants. Recounting historical events, lyrics often use archaic words and structures.

Some *meke* have a prelude (*ucu*), sung without dancing; the meke proper consists of several stanzas, and often includes a refrain, sung after a series of stanzas. *Meke*-style singing without dancing is called *vucu*. Usually in three or more vocal parts, vucu may chronicle events, praise deeds or individuals, or lament a death. They are usually sung by men for relaxation at night, with or without instrumental accompaniment.

Fijian musical theory distinguishes vocal parts or roles by name. The *laga* 'to sing' usually leads, closely followed by the *tagica* 'to cry, to chime in', sung at higher pitches than the *laga*. Parts called *druku* 'bass' are sung in several levels. In effect, *laga* and *tagica* are high solo parts, and *druku* constitute a harmonizing chorus.

Vakalutuivoce 'dropping the oar', an ancient style of unaccompanied Fijian singing, survives in some areas. Formerly, two people rowing or rafting down a river sang songs in this style. Their voices moved in close counterpoint, emphasizing the harmony of a major second.

Apart from *meke*, *vucu*, and *vakalutuivoce*, the principal forms of musical expression in old Fiji were lullabies, game songs, and work songs. Like *meke*, these genres survive in Fiji, but their frequency of performance has decreased, and some are moribund. Lullabies, sung to children by parents, or more commonly, grandparents, have narrow melodic ranges. Game songs include juggling songs, sung by women, and various children's songs. Men's javelin-throwing songs are almost extinct. Special songs formerly accompanied fishing, planting, and other kinds of work.

Christian Religious Music

Fijian biblical songs (*same* 'psalms') bridge the precontact and Christian periods. They are sung in Methodist churches by mature women. Their texts are based on Fijian-language biblical passages, of which the Song of Solomon and the parable of the prodigal son (Luke 15:11–32) are favorites. Musically, they derive from *meke* and owe little to outside influence. Their vocal parts are *laga*, *tagica*, and *druku*, as in *meke*.

The catechism, another unaccompanied religious genre, is usually sung responsorially from the Fijian hymnal, with the leader speaking the questions and the congregation answering in a musical style like that of *same*.

Choral polyphonic singing of religious texts is extremely popular in Fiji. These pieces, *sere ni lotu*,

DISC
1
TRACK
31

Figure 1 Backed by a male chorus, seated Fijian women perform a *meke* at the Pacific Festival of Arts. *Photo by Adrienne L. Kaeppler, 1992.*

range from simple hymns to ambitious choral arrangements, using common-practice tonal harmonies.

Musical Instruments

The most common musical instruments that accompany *meke* are *lali ni meke*, small struck logs, played with two wooden sticks, and *cobo*, clapping with cupped hands. To these, the performers in some areas add bamboo tubes (*derua*), which they stamp against the ground.

Other indigenous musical instruments are large struck logs (*lali*), often used in pairs for summoning people to church, and a conch trumpet (*davui*), used for signaling. In a performance by two large *lali* filmed in Baidamudamu (Kadavu) in 1986, one instrument played an ostinato while the other played interlocking patterns. The playing of panpipes and bamboo noseflutes, once common in Fiji, is now almost extinct.

Introduced musical instruments mainly include guitars, ukuleles, and mandolins. These instruments may occasionally accompany modern-style *meke*, but their primary use is for popular music.

Pop Music

Fijian popular music (*sere ni cumu* 'bumping songs') developed since the mid-1920s under the influence of European and American popular music. The genre relates to styles that developed elsewhere in Oceania under similar influences, most of which retain elements of their pre-European musical traditions.

At first, Fijians borrowed Western melodies and fitted them with Fijian words. They still do, but a more important development was the indigenous composition of Fijian popular music. Though words and melody are Fijian-composed, these songs take inspiration from Western or Westernized music, including music from other Pacific Islands and the Caribbean.

Fijians distinguish between village-style *sere ni cumu* and more sophisticated, commercial brands of Fijian popular music, found in towns. On Taveuni Island and elsewhere, singers call the village style *sere ni verada* 'veranda songs', in reference to their typical context. Informal and laid back, this style is said to be the oldest popular music current in Fiji. Village-style *sere ni cumu* are traditionally sung by men only, mainly because only men ordinarily participate in extended kava-drinking sessions. (Occasionally, these sessions include women.) Many lyrics of *sere ni cumu* concern love, human relationships, and the beauties of nature and homeland.

Musical Style

Songs may be sung unaccompanied, or accompanied by slow and steady strumming on guitars and ukuleles. Village-based groups are renowned for tuning their instruments distinctively. As with Hawaiian slack-key guitars, individuals and ensembles tune their guitars and ukuleles in special ways, developed to suit their styles of playing.

Ensembles sing in three- or four-part harmony, using progressions that usually follow Western models, mainly on tonic, subdominant, and dominant triads. Typically, the vocal lines are closely spaced, but the bass tends to be spatially separate and dynamically prominent. Its importance possibly relates to that of the bass drone, which harmonically anchors the singing of *meke*.

Though set in Western melodies and harmonies, many village-style *sere ni cumu* exhibit elements that link them to pre-European musical traditions. Some have narrative texts that contain the poetic imagery and symbolism typical of old *meke* and pre-European lyrics elsewhere in Oceania. Other features reminiscent of old *meke* include a triple subdivision of the basic beat and men's falsetto singing. Most examples are sung by performers sitting in a tightly bunched circle, with the leaders in the middle; this format is typical also of *meke*.

Most cultures of Oceania value collective performance more highly than solo performance. Similarly in Fiji, polyphony, albeit in Western tonality, is the prevailing texture for collective singing. Most *sere ni cumu* are merely songs (with or without instrumental accompaniment), not ordinarily associated or performed with dance. The *tarālalā* is an exception. A social dance, it enlivens festive occasions. Its music resembles that of other *sere ni cumu*, but with livelier rhythms. People usually dance it in a line, taking several slow steps forward and then backward. Methodist missionaries introduced it as an entertainment for kindergarteners.

In urban centers, professional bands produce more up-to-date *sere ni cumu*, featuring electric instruments, upbeat rhythms, and varied harmonies. Modernized songs accompany Western-style dancing. Village-based bands copy these styles, including Fijian adaptations of the major international varieties of rock. Reggae, in particular, has had a big impact on Fijian music.

Tonga

The kingdom of Tonga consists of 172 islands, totaling 748 square kilometers; thirty-six are inhabited by about 100,000 people. Tongan society is rooted in a genealogically stratified social structure. As a British-protected state, it easily absorbed the British monarchical mystique. Titles bestowed on certain chiefs came to define hereditary nobles with landed estates. These concepts codified ideas that had been present in precontact times.

Music is, and probably always has been, an important element in the life of the Tongan people. No event is complete without music, and what is remembered about an event is often the music performed in it. Music defines an event by giving voice to its purpose.

New compositions were, and are, composed for any important public or private event. Major compositions, such as *lakalaka*, are often restaged for contemporary events. The restagings commemorate the event for which the *lakalaka* was composed, and may recall other events at which it has been performed. Analyses of musical compositions help decode cultural ideas about values; rather than simply reflecting these ideas, however, Tongan musical compositions help construct and restructure them.

Thinking about Tongan Music

Modern Tongan music is a composite of multiple strands of sound and movement, evolved from precontact Tongan performances under a variety of influences: from other Pacific islands, from the Western world, and in the late twentieth century, from the Caribbean.

Indirectness (*heliaki*), a concept through which Tongans construct meaning in their lives, finds its most important outlet in music, where metaphors emphasize the centrality of oratory to social activity and hierarchy. Using metaphors, composers choose ideas and information that will be sung, remembered, and usually accepted by the populace, especially if the composer is a genealogically important person or a member of the royal family.

Poetry

An important activity in Tongan life is the performance of oratory and poetry. Rendered melodically, and sometimes accompanied by percussive instruments and sounds and movements made by human bodies, poetic texts are often complex. Their functions are primarily secular: composed mainly for specific occasions, they honor individuals, social groups, villages, and events. They chronicle the history and values of the Tongan people.

Poetry is basic and composed first. Lyrics receive a melody, often a preexisting one; or a composer invents a new melody, or improvises a melody. When performed for a subsequent occasion or event, melodies may undergo major changes, but Tongans believe poetry in such settings should undergo only minor changes. Adding music to a new poetic composition, composers often take melodic motifs from old songs, or combine parts of melodies of several old songs. Composers may borrow other Polynesian or Western melodies, altering them to fit local tastes and needs.

Polyphony

Vocal and instrumental polyphony has long existed in Tonga. Ensembles of stamped bamboo tubes and struck log instruments accompanied danced poetry. Eighteenth-century accounts report that voices were harmonious and melodious, and state that Tongans sang in parts. Singing in parts, though no longer the same as that described by eighteenth-century visitors, remains conceptually similar. The most important part is the *fasi*, the leading part or melody, often conceptualized as fitting with a lower part (*laulalo*), a movable drone. These parts may receive decoration from others.

According to elderly and knowledgeable musicians in the 1960s, precontact Tongan singing had up to six parts. Men usually sang the leading part (*fasi*). Two women's parts were described as high and low. *Lalau* was described as a men's part that could cross above the melody. *Ekenaki*, another men's part, was sung lower than the melody. Finally, *laulalo* was a low men's part, conceptually like a drone. According to Tongan views, *fasi* and *laulalo* were the essential parts; the others were decorative.

This six-part texture seldom occurs in contemporary Tongan performance, having been replaced by Western-derived harmony. In the newer texture, men and women may each sing a *fasi* (the women's *fasi* is sometimes known as *solo*, the Tongan word for soprano) on the same melody an octave apart. Women have one or two lower parts (*kanokano* and *'oloto*), similar to a high and low alto, though some singers say these parts are the same. Some men sing bass (*laulalo*), and others sing tenor (*tenoa*), which may cross above the *fasi*.

Though the evolved style of singing in parts resembles the old, its tonal intervals are based predominantly on those of Western music. The bass is more melodic, and women have an added soprano part (*fasi* or *solo*), sung an octave higher than the men's *fasi* or a separate part. In the older and the evolved styles, the parts are inconsistent, and often collapse into two or three: *fasi*, *laulalo*, and a decoration of the *fasi*.

Sung poetry is primarily a group activity, rendered in several parts. A leader may sing a few introductory notes to set the pitch and tempo, and then others join in. On each repetition, the parts and ornamentation may differ slightly.

Polykinetics

Tongan structured-movement systems are based on three parts of the human body. The legs and feet serve primarily to keep the rhythmic pulse, often a series of side-to-side steps, executed nearly in place; in seated dances, one foot may keep a metrical pulse. For women, movements of the feet and legs are small, in keeping with the stricture of always having the upper legs parallel and close together. Men's movements are larger, with more actions, including kneeling on one knee, striking the ground with feet or hands, and even lying or rolling on the ground.

Hand-and-arm movements are most important and form complex motifs, which have three functions: to allude to selected words of the text, or to concepts arising from the poetry; to form beautiful movements, which decorate or complete textual and musical phrases; and to form dividing motifs, which separate stanzas or sections of poetry. Arm motifs involve flexible wrists and lower-arm rotations with various movements of the fingers and positions and facings of the palms, occurring in a limited number of arm positions. These motifs are known by the general term *haka*. Some motifs have specific names, such as *milolua*, a movement that derives from the wringing of kava. Women's arm movements are soft and graceful, but men's involve stiffer wrists or clenched fists. A tilt of the head to the side, though sometimes choreographed, is primarily an aesthetic element, added by the performer to express *māfana*, an inner feeling of exhilaration.

Musical Contexts and Genres

Based on context, function, musical setting, bodily movement, and textual structure, Tongan sung and moved poetry can be categorized into six main performative types: laments and eulogies, work songs, game songs, narrative songs, sung speeches, and *hiva kakala* 'sweet song, fragrant song'. Descriptions of two of these types follow.

Sung Speeches with Choreographed Movements (Faiva)

Though the word *faiva* basically denotes the application of skill or cleverness, it can denote, in a more restricted sense, genres describable as sung speeches with choreographed movements. These *faiva* usually occur during ceremonial occasions known as *kātoanga*, featuring the performance of music and structured movements as complex verbal, rhythmic, and visual theater. Village-, community-, or school-based *faiva* in the current repertory include *lakalaka*, *māʻuluʻulu*, *meʻetuʻupaki*, *faʻahiula*, *sōkē*, and *kailao*.

The most important of these genres, a key to understanding Tongan cultural and social values, is *lakalaka*. Here, history, mythology, and genealogy influence contemporary events, and the values that *lakalaka* imparts primarily concern social structure and the people of rank through whom that structure operates. Though this genre is considered a late-nineteenth-century innovation, it appears to be an evolved form of the *meʻelaufola*, an indigenous genre.

The poetry of a *lakalaka* is a series of concepts and references, rather than a complete story, and is usually composed for performance at a specific event. Poetic allusions often evoke mythology and genealogy, usually in roundabout ways. Many of the allusions are understood by everyone, but others are understood only by other poets, and the desire is often to take old allusions and transform them into something new. The references are often common knowledge, but observers must make associations to proceed to an understanding of successive allusions. The figurative language and allusive movements elevate the king and the chiefs, paying them honor while honoring the dancers and their villages.

The performers of a *lakalaka* are men and women, often two hundred or more, arranged in two or more rows facing an audience. The men stand on the right side (from the observer's viewpoint), and the women stand on the left. Men and women perform different sets of movements, consistent with the Tongan view of what is suitable and appropriate for each. The movements of the arms allude to the lyrics.

Each *lakalaka*, in a structure derived from that of formal speeches, has three sections: an introductory *fakatapu*, which acknowledges the important chiefly lines relevant to the occasion; the main section (sometimes called *kaveinga*), which conveys information about the occasion, genealogies of relevant people, the history or mythology of the village performing, and other information; and the closing *tatau*, a counterpart of the *fakatapu*, in which the performers say goodbye, again deferring to the chiefs. One stanza may be a *tau*, a section that expresses the essence of the performance, during which the performers do their best to compel the audience to pay strict attention.

This structure forms the outline of a *lakalaka*. The overall design, and thus the meaning of any specific composition, however, need not be apparent until the end. The meaning reveals itself as each verse—through verbal, musical, and visual allusions—builds on those that have gone before, mediated through the aesthetic principle of indirectness or *heliaki*.

Hiva kakala

Hiva kakala 'sweet song, fragrant song' is one of the major Tongan musical genres of the twentieth

Figure 2 A *tauʻolunga* accompanies a *hiva kakala* in Tonga. *Photo by Adrienne L. Kaeppler, 1967.*

tauʻolunga need not make consistent allusions to the poetry, but may focus on the creation of beauty. They have been composed and choreographed by some of the most famous choreographers of the twentieth century—Queen Sālote, Vaisima Hopoate, and Tuʻimala Kaho.

The sentiment expressed by the poetry of *hiva kakala* usually focuses on an individual or a place. Movements may occur spontaneously (figure 2). They are widely known motifs, which in other performing genres often serve as fill-in motifs. The *heliaki* of the poetry and the movements may allude to the performer, the text, or the overall concept of the composition.

Most modern examples have stanza-refrain alternation. Sometimes each stanza is sung twice before the refrain, and sometimes the refrain precedes the first stanza. Melodies and their accompanying harmonies may come from hymns, Western secular songs, and earlier *hiva kakala*.

Musical Instruments

Several important indigenous Tongan percussive instruments served to accompany danced poetry. Indigenous Tongan melodic instruments were noseflutes, panpipes, and conch trumpets; Western contact brought instruments used in brass bands and stringbands.

Self-sounding Instruments (Idiophones)

Two kinds of jew's harps—the *ʻūtete*, made of a coconut-leaf midrib, and the *mokena*, made of bamboo—served as toys. In the 1960s, the former were remembered by older people, who recalled having played them as children, obtaining myriad sounds by playing two or more at the same time.

Human bodies also serve as sound-producing instruments. Skin strikes skin in several named movements: a high-pitched flat clap (*pasi*); a low, cupped clap (*fū*); clapping the back of one hand to the other open palm; snapping the fingers (*fisipā*); and slapping the thighs (*pāpātenga*), and other parts of the body.

Wind Instruments

Raft panpipes (*mimiha*) served mainly for amusement, but are important because they provide clues for understanding Tongan musical aesthetics. No aboriginal panpipes remain in Tonga; several survive abroad, in museums. Most were collected in the late 1700s (figure 3). Bound with twisted coconut fiber, most of these consist of ten bamboo pipes (some have nine or five), closed on the lower end by a node and open at the top. Both sides of the top are beveled, probably to facilitate moving the instrument

century, the musical genre most often composed and sung. Its thousands of compositions are evidence of the thoughts and values of the Tongan people. It evolved from *pō sipi*, poems recited spontaneously during informal kava-drinking gatherings. *Pō sipi* consisted primarily of allusions to the (female) mixer of the kava, made on behalf of one of the young men in attendance, either by one of his friends, or by a ceremonial attendant (*matāpule*). Place names and allusions to flowers referred to the individual without naming her. During the 1800s, melodies were added to the poetry, often in the form of verse-chorus alternation, borrowed from the structure of Protestant hymns.

Hiva kakala are usually played and sung by gatherings of men or women or both, forming stringbands of ukuleles and guitars; sometimes a bass, electronic keyboards, violins, and accordions are added. Movements are then added; the word that describes them, *tauʻolunga*, is the word Tongans use for the English word *dance*. The movements of

along the lips while blowing, and to control the direction of the airstream.

The surviving instruments show a pattern with three important intervals. A nine- or ten-pipe instrument had two sets of four pipes each. A set consisted of three tones, with a repetition of the middle tone. One of the sets was slightly higher in pitch than the other. Finally, there was a high note, and sometimes a low note; these notes do not seem to have been essential, but varied from panpipe to panpipe, and may have been considered decorative.

Conch trumpets (*kele'a*) served for amusement and signaling. Fishermen sounded them when returning to shore, announcing that they had caught fish. Others sounded them to announce the approach of an important person. Today, when the king approaches, a fanfare on brass instruments replaces the blasts from *kele'a*.

DISC
❶
TRACK
33

Noseflutes (*fangufangu*) may have provided musical amusement, as a pastime at the end of the day. A primary use of the noseflute was to awaken a high-ranking person. To awaken chiefs was bad manners, except with a noseflute. In 1953, during the Tongan visit of Queen Elizabeth II (b. 1926), *fangufangu* roused the slumbering monarch. Today, they are seldom played, but they can be heard each day at the radio station's opening and closing.

Sāmoa

The Sāmoan archipelago divides into two political units: Savai'i, 'Upolu, and two small inhabited islands, Apolima and Manono, united as the independent nation of Sāmoa; and Tutuila and a cluster of little islands known as Manu'a, united as a territory of the United States of America.

Thinking about Sāmoan Music

Verbalization, intonation, and movement combine to create many Sāmoan genres. The union of words, music, and motion is evident in songs designed for public presentation; but even in private, performers may spontaneously move their arms, or rise to involve their legs. A narrator may gesture to enhance critical actions or moments in a tale.

Sāmoan musical genres do not fit into a tidy hierarchical structure, but the language has names for select kinds of singing and dancing. In reaction to Christianity, genres of indelicate dancing disappeared, and the ordinary processes of cultural change have led to such a turnover that few musical genres popular in the mid-1800s are performed today, at least under the same names.

Sāmoan lyrics bind words (*'upu*) into lines (*fua'i'upu, fua'itau*), which usually end in rhyme. The

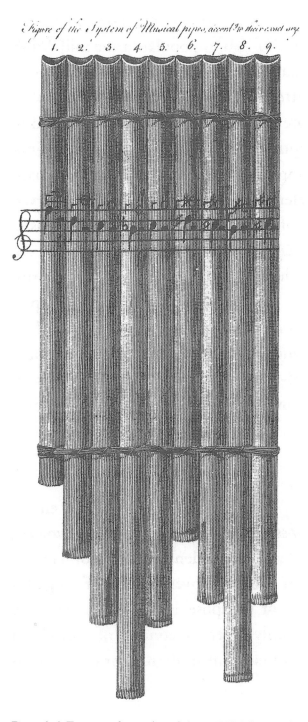

Figure 3 A Tongan raft panpipe of about 1770 (after Steele 1771:76).

words once had a meter (*fua*) possibly based on the length of vowels, which, in some genres, percussive stress may have overridden. The basis of Sāmoan music is the human voice (*leo*).

Most singing in Sāmoa is choral. Leaders (*usu*) are the few singers who begin phrases; the chorus (*tali*) are the many singers who finish them. Sometimes these parts engage in dialogue, as in a song popular

Figure 4 A Sāmoan melody popular before the twentieth century, showing the division into *usu* and *tali.*
Transcription by J. W. Love.

before the 1900s (figure 4), shown with *tali* phrases indented:

> *Aue, toli mai pua mōtoe!*
> > *Tala lava ʻoe.*
> *Aue, toli mai pua mātala!*
> > *Tala i le vasa.*

> *Aue*, O pluck and bring budding gardenias!
> > Open them yourself.
> *Aue*, pluck and bring opening gardenias!
> > Open them at the groin.

Texts transcribed in the 1800s show that the singers of the *usu* launched into the refrain, cueing and sometimes overlapping with the *tali.*

Polykinetics

Sāmoan structured-movement systems combine the activity of three parts of the human body, roughly seen as legs, arms, and head. The torso is inactive, with the back straight and the hips not making large movements. The feet and legs follow the beat. In a typical men's stance, the knees are bent, the body's weight is on the balls of the feet, and the heels metrically move outward and inward. Seated dancers may use their feet or knees to keep a metric pulse. Women's foot-and-leg movements are small; men may make larger movements, with more muscular involvement. In the excitement of dancing, men and women may seize and wave objects, and shake or bounce against furniture, houseposts, and walls; men may kneel, strike the ground with their forearms and hands, and roll on the ground.

The hands and arms make complex movements (*tāga*), which have multiple functions: to allude to sung words, comment on implied concepts, and decorate and connect musical phrases. *Tāga* use flexible wrists. Movements and positions of fingers and palms occur in a limited number of arm positions. Men's and women's hand-and-arm movements may be soft, but men's may use stiffer wrists or clenched fists, and may be faster and freer.

The head and face mask or express emotion. When a ceremonial virgin performs the last dance (*taualuga*), she fixes her facial muscles into a weak smile, maintaining an aloofness that onlookers interpret as dignity. Men and women clowning around featured soloists may show animation, including frequent tilts and turns of the head, variable facial expressions, and darting eyes; they may grunt, shout, and whoop.

Musical Contexts and Genres

Artful performances grace many aspects of Sāmoan life. Chiefly councils feature intonationally and rhythmically marked orating and poetical reciting. Services in churches have several kinds of singing, sometimes with instrumental accompaniment. Weddings, visits, and wakes require singing, and some events invite dancing. Because music helps define occasions, performances need apt music, and newly composed pieces are much in demand. Highly important, however, are older items: some are the points of departure for new compositions; others, by metaphorically linking the present to the past, lend historical authenticity to an occasion, and so are performed intact, or as close to bygone styles as modern interpretation allows. Descriptions of three of these genres follow.

Storytelling

Storytellers entertained children and adults with tales (*fāgono*), many of which contained sung sections (*tagi* 'cries'), usually representing a character prominent in the plot. Skilled storytellers received fame beyond their own villages. Since the late 1800s, the classical repertory has become diffuse, accommodating prosaic narratives (*tala*), whose characters may have nonindigenous names, undertake nontraditional activities, and recount biblical stories.

Performing a *fāgono*, a narrator takes standard plots, and within limits that vary from tale to tale and from moment to moment within a tale, improvises the diction. The sung sections have structures more set and less variable than the words of the narration. They often take the form of an outburst, when a character expresses emotions. In response to exciting events in the plot and stirring moments in the sung sections, an audience freely exclaims the word ʻaue, and may add other conventional responses.

Many *tagi*, especially short ones, have lines of approximately equal length, arranged in regular succession. In some tales, short *tagi* repeat. Older examples set simple rhyming phrases to simple melodic formulas, concluding in a nonformulaic section. In some *tagi*, the refrain begins and ends each line or stanza. An excerpt shows how the refrain stretches the story out.

> *Īlae, Īlae,*
> 'Ua 'ou fāifai mao lava,
> *Īlae, Īlae*
>
> *Īlae, Īlae,*
> 'Ona 'ua sui 'o lona suafa:
> *Īlae, Īlae,*
>
> *Īlae, Īlae,*
> " 'O Sugaluga-opea-mai-vasa,"
> *Īlae, Īlae,*
>
> *Īlae, Īlae,*
> 'Ua fānau ai la'u nei tama.
> *Īlae, Īlae,*
>
> *O Ila, O Ila,*
> I've really acted by chance,
> *O Ila, O Ila,*
>
> *O Ila, O Ila,*
> Because he changed his name:
> *O Ila, O Ila.*
>
> *O Ila, O Ila.*
> "Driftwood-floating-from-sea,"
> *O Ila, O Ila,*
>
> *O Ila, O Ila,*
> By whom I've borne this my child.
> *O Ila, O Ila,*

Through a skilled singer's voice, the ponderousness of the plot, slowed by the repetitions of the refrain, can evoke an entrancing atmosphere. More practically, these repetitions give the singer time to recall or plan upcoming lines.

Some texts have multiple refrains and achieve a higher degree of structural complexity. In one pattern, some *tagi* have stanzas that gain lines, one by one, until, by the end of the piece, the structure severely tests singers' faculties of recall and listeners' powers of concentration.

Exchanging Women's Goods

Certain goods manufactured from natural objects by women are known as *tōga*. Their formal bestowal, accompanied by a range of performed language (orating, citing conventional phrases, singing), has important social implications, some of which involve music. At weddings, funerals, the paying of civil penalties, and other contexts that imply reciprocity, ceremonial mats ('*ietōga*) are the cardinal medium of exchange. Etiquette requires the recipient of such a mat, or even a person who catches sight of one, to respond, especially with the formula *sāō! fa'alālelei!* To plait mats, women work for months, usually in cooperative associations. On completing an association's mats, the weavers, helped as necessary by their kin, parade the mats around the village, receiving refreshments served by chiefs. This parade authenticates the mats so they may enter the system of exchange. On catching sight of the mats along the route, onlookers spontaneously shout *sāō! fa'alālelei!* and join the singing.

Visiting

Intervillage visiting (*malaga*) is a longstanding institution, with cognate activities elsewhere in Polynesia. In varying numbers, but ideally in tens or scores, people travel for overnight visits, sometimes circling an island and stopping at receptive villages en route. These events may involve the youthful affiliates of a church, or the women of a village or neighborhood, or members of other groups. Interactions may involve competitive activities, like orating and the playing of games. The hosts provide food and lodging, and the guests provide entertainment.

The distinction between guests and hosts plays itself out in the orating, playing, feasting, singing, and dancing associated with the visit. Usually, the drinking of kava (with its attendant oratory and poetry) precedes the feast, and the musical performance follows. Inside a house, the guests take one side and the hosts the other, forming seated choruses, facing each other. Between the choruses, individuals or small groups from one side stand to dance while the rest of their company sings. One side performs and then yields to the other, and the sides alternate repeatedly. Set phrases mark the shifts: these include sung statements, such as '*ua alu atu le afi* 'the fire has gone to your side', recalling the practice of illuminating performers by torchlight. The last number of an event is the *taualuga*, the dance of the hosts' ceremonial virgin. Formerly, when unmarried men went on *malaga*, this dance paired the ceremonial virgin with the guests' ceremonial beau. Before the late nineteenth century, the event might then have broken down into lascivious dancing, but Christian prudery ended most such enjoyments.

Musical Instruments

Musical instruments enhance Sāmoan vocal performance. The action of the human body is a primary musical instrument. Skin strikes skin in several named movements: a high-pitched flat clap (*pati*), a low-pitched cupped clap (*pō*), the snapping of fingers (*fiti*), and the slapping of other parts of the body. These and other actions occur in *fa'ataupati* and *sāsā*, songless movements performed by a

DISC
1
TRACK
32

company in synchrony. Their sounds combine with stamps and vocal clicks and grunts to make a favorite aural mix. Formerly, putting one hand under the opposing armpit and moving the opposing bent arm up and down (the action called *sāsāfiʻa*) augmented movements of *sāsā* and possibly other genres. The collective rubbing of palms (*mili*) makes a sound used mainly in introductory sections.

Old Sāmoa had several percussion instruments. A common accompaniment to dancing was percussion on a rolled-up mat (*fala*), sometimes with a bamboo tube inserted into its hollow, when the instrument was called a *tuʻituʻi*. Another percussion instrument, the *faʻaaliʻi lāiti*, also called *pulotu*, was a slat loosely fitted into a board, which the performer hit with two sticks. For private amusement, individuals played jew's harps (*utete*).

Ukuleles and guitars commonly furnish accompaniment for private, informal singing by individuals and groups. Ukuleles are available for purchase, but boys take pride in making their own. Indigenous wind instruments included conchs (*pū*), whistles or pipes (*faʻaili*, a term based on the verb *ili* 'blow'), and a noseflute (*fagufagu, siva-a-ʻofe*).

—Adapted from articles by Adrienne L. Kaeppler, David Goldsworthy, and J. W. Love

Bibliography

Collocott, Ernest Edgar Vyvyan. 1928. *Tales and Poems of Tonga*. Bulletin 46. Honolulu: Bishop Museum.

Kaeppler, Adrienne L. 1983. *Polynesian Dance, With a Selection for Contemporary Performances*. Hawaiʻi: Alpha Delta Kappa.

Kubuabola, S., et al. 1978. "Poetry in Fiji: A General Introduction." In *Essays on Pacific Literature*, edited by Ruth Finnegan and Raymond Pillai, 2:7–19. Suva: Fiji Museum.

Love, Jacob Wainwright. 1991. *Sāmoan Variations: Essays on the Nature of Traditional Oral Arts*. New York and London: Garland.

Martin, John, ed. 1818. *An Account of the Natives of the Tonga Islands*. 2 vols. London: Constable.

Moyle, Richard M. 1987. *Tongan Music*. Auckland: Auckland University Press.

———. 1988. *Traditional Samoan Music*. Auckland: Auckland University Press.

Quain, Buell Halvor 1942. *The Flight of the Chiefs: Epic Poetry of Fiji*. New York: J. J. Augustin.

Steele, Joshua. 1771. "Account of a Musical Instrument, Which was Brought by Captain Furneaux from the Isle of Amsterdam in the South Seas to London in the Year 1774, and Given to the Royal Society, and Remarks on a Larger System of Reed Pipes from the Isle of Amsterdam, with Some Observations on the Nose Flute of Otaheite." *Philosophical Transactions of the Royal Society* 65:67–68.

Thompson, Chris. 1971. "Fijian Music and Dance." *Transactions and Proceedings of the Fiji Society* 11:14–21.

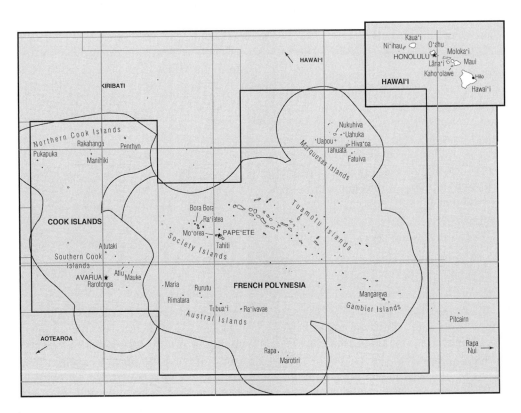

East Polynesia

East Polynesia

East Polynesia includes the Cook Islands, the Society Islands, the Austral Islands, the Tuamotu Islands, Gambier Islands (including Mangareva), the Marquesas Islands, Hawaiʻi, Rapa Nui, Aotearoa, and the Chatham Islands. Aotearoa and the Chatham Islands form an independent nation, New Zealand. Rapa Nui (Easter Island) is a dependency of Chile. Hawaiʻi is a state of the United States of America. The Cook Islands have a special political relationship with New Zealand. The Marquesas, Societies, Australs, Mangareva, and Tuamotus constitute an overseas territory of France known as French Polynesia.

East Polynesians share with their West Polynesian and outlier cousins similarities in musical concepts and contexts, especially the importance of sung poetry. Polyphony took different forms, and in some areas (including Hawaiʻi and Aoteroa) was absent from indigenous practice. After European contact, thickly textured harmonic forms became typical, especially of French Polynesia and the Cook Islands.

The inventory of musical instruments differed greatly from that of West Polynesia. Drums of different sizes, made of a sharkskin-covered hollow wooden cylinder and called *pahu*, replaced or supplemented log instruments; mouth-resonated bows were found in the Marquesas, Australs, and Hawaiʻi; mouth-blown flutes and wooden trumpets are known from the Marquesas and Aotearoa; rattles and clappers were used in Hawaiʻi, the Marquesas, and Aotearoa; *poi* (weighted balls, attached to strings) create visual designs and audible rhythms as they strike the body.

East Polynesian movement systems emphasize arm-and-hand movements, upright torso, lack of shoulder movements, restricted locomotion, and linear formations. Various combinations of wrist flexion and extension and the rotation of the lower arm result in characteristic movement motifs. Lower arm rotations in conjunction with a rather stiff wrist are characteristic for Tahiti, while a hand quiver with a stiff wrist is characteristic of New Zealand. In Hawaiʻi, a flexion and extension of the wrist in conjunction with bending at the knuckles and curling the fingers are characteristic. In East Polynesia, lower-body movements have been elaborated into complex motifs that differ by gender. The lower-body motifs usually keep the time, while the arm movements convey the poetry. A combination of two main elements—the arm-wrist movements and the interplay of leg-and-hip movements—gives each Polynesian dance tradition a distinctive style.

Society Islands

The Society archipelago includes windward islands (Tahiti, Moʻorea, Maiʻao, Tetiaroa, Mehetia) and leeward islands (Raʻiatea, Tahaʻa, Huahine, Bora Bora, Tupai, Maupiti, Maupihaʻa, Manuae, Motu One). The term *Tahitian* applies to the shared language and culture typical of the archipelago. In referring to the language and revived customs, the term *māʻohi* 'indigenous' is increasingly popular.

Beginning in the 1950s, French Polynesia experienced intense, accelerated social transformation. Islanders responded by adapting their performances to common artistic values, expectations, and aesthetics. Outsiders sometimes reproach Tahitians for commercializing the arts during this period; Tahitians, however, portray these years as ones when they restored the beauty and dignity of their music and dance, established these traditions in a global world, and searched for authenticity.

Musical Instruments

Musical instruments in Tahiti are associated with specific forms of singing and dancing. Guitars (electric and acoustic), drums, electric bass, and synthesizers accompany songs for entertainment, religious songs in popular styles (played by young people), couple dancing at local hotels and bars, fashion shows, and theatrical events. Guitars and ukuleles, a requisite for informal music, accompany large groups of dancers. Around 1993, locally made eight-stringed ukuleles in unusual shapes came into vogue.

Instruments that accompany Tahitian-style dancing include a log percussion instrument, *tōʻere*, played with one stick (two-stick playing, *tāʻiri piti*, is an importation from the Cook Islands); the one-headed *faʻatete*, a short drum, played with two sticks; and the two-headed *pahu*, with origins in the European bass drum. In the mid-1980s, performers began to use the *ihara*, a bamboo instrument in which raised lengths of the bark are struck with sticks; by 1995, it had become a regular member of several instrumental ensembles. Noseflutes (*vivo*), played until the early 1900s, made a quiet comeback after an appearance in a Heiva performance (1976) by the troupe Te Maeva. At the same performance, Te Maeva resurrected the one-headed *pahu tupaʻi rima*, a tall, hand-struck drum, which gained popularity during the 1980s and is now an accepted addition to the standard ensemble (of *tōʻere*, *faʻatete*, and *pahu*). The conch trumpet (*pū*) is often sounded to accent the start of a dance.

The reappearance of, and renewed interest in, such instruments as the *ihara*, the *vivo*, and the *pahu tupaʻi rima* emphasize issues of identity. The disappearance of these instruments caused a break in the tradition; their revival reflects contemporary views, and provides a model for revalidating aspects of their history. A key to understanding is not to look for a pure, unchanged tradition, but to enjoy how Tahitians bring tradition into the present.

Choral Music

British missionaries arrived in the Society Islands in 1797. To describe introduced Christian hymns, they transliterated the English term *hymn* into a Tahitian form, *hīmene*. By the late 1800s, the term *hīmene* denoted all choral singing, Christian or not. It adjectivally specifies choirs (*pūpū hīmene*) and describes events (like *tātaʻuraʻa hīmene* 'choral competition') in which choral singing is a major component.

Tahitian choral singing is comprised of named styles differentiated by musical criteria, and of named repertorial categories differentiated by non-musical criteria, such as poetic content, the performers' ages, and whether or not the text appears in a printed hymnal. At the broadest level, Tahitians differentiate two categories of musical performance: styles of reputedly indigenous origin are *hīmene māʻohi* 'true *hīmene*'; styles of reputedly foreign origin are *hīmene pōpaʻa* 'foreign *hīmene*'. Musical traits differentiate five styles: *hīmene nota*, *hīmene puta*, *hīmene rūʻau*, *hīmene tārava*, and *hīmene tuki*. The first two are of foreign origin, the last two are of Polynesian origin, and the third, originally of foreign origin, is considered indigenous. Descriptions of two of these genres follow.

Hīmene tārava

Singers agree that the term *tārava*, a verb meaning 'to lie horizontally', denotes the drawn-out cadence at the end of stanzas. *Hīmene tārava* are indigenous in origin. They flourish in French Polynesia in three regional styles, whose differences appear in the number of named vocal parts and their musical content. *Hīmene tārava Tahiti*, the style practiced in the windward islands, usually has five to seven vocal

parts. *Hīmene tārava raromataʻi*, the style practiced throughout the leeward islands, averages seven to nine or ten parts. Society Islanders collectively call the styles practiced in the Austral Islands *tārava Rurutu*.

Hīmene tārava have a detailed vocabulary, by which singers distinguish the vocal parts and articulate various aspects of singing procedures. The number and musical contents of vocal parts vary among choirs. In general, each vocal part takes one of three ascribed functions: textual declamation, melodic decoration, and rhythmic punctuation. Some are for women, and some are for men. Vocal melodies are narrow, and the melodic configuration that results from combining individual parts is the musical basis for locally distinguishing *hīmene tārava*.

In a typical *hīmene tārava*, a female lead singer (*faʻaaraara* 'to awaken') commences, giving out the first line in a strong, confident, often piercing voice. Other singers find their own niches at their own pace, some entering almost simultaneously with the leader, others taking as long as the entire first line of text. A successful start is described as rising (*maraʻa*); conversely, when singers fail to catch (*haru*) onto the leader, the *hīmene* is said to fall (*topa*). Once the performance is underway, at least one soloist (usually a woman) ascends to the perepere, the high decorative part. At the back of the choir, young men and teenaged boys perform grunting (*hāʻū*). At the end of the stanza, the singers coalesce on the tonic. There is a moment of anticipation while they hold the tonic in unison. If someone restarts the stanza, the cycle repeats, either until everyone is exhausted and no one gives out the beginning line, or (in the case of presentational performances) until the end of the final repetition of the final stanza.

Though no evidence on the birth of *hīmene tārava* has turned up, the genre undoubtedly has links to the local establishment of Protestantism in the early 1800s; travelers' accounts document its practice since the 1870s. Its music probably emerged from indigenous styles, revitalized in the 1830s and 1840s, for some of its traits correspond to those of performances reported by eighteenth-century explorers.

Hīmene tuki

Tahitians describe the *hīmene tuki* as a Tahitian rendition of the Cook Island equivalent of *hīmene tārava*. The word *tuki* is the Rarotongan term for the guttural grunting performed by the men in short periods near the ends of phrases or stanzas. This style is sometimes called *hīmene rarotoʻa*, referring to the Rarotongan-language texts and to Rarotonga, principal island of the southern Cook Islands. The texts come from two sources: the current Cook

Islands Protestant hymnal and Cook Islanders living in the Society Islands.

Hīmene tuki are through-composed, and each normally consists of three or four sections of music. Tahitians observe the conventions of repetition by repeating the final one or two lines of text within a section and then repeating the entire section, but they like to combine different sources into one *hīmene tuki*. As performed in the Society Islands, *hīmene tuki* have two vocal parts, named by gender: women sing the primary melody in unison; men dwell on grunting, to an extent that Cook Islanders find excessive.

Singers in the Society Islands perform *hīmene tuki* only on special occasions, not normally in regular Sunday worship. Women sit on the floor, in straight or semicircular rows. Older men sit behind them. Younger men, who stand around the others in a horseshoe-shaped row, bend inward and outward in synchrony, and perform scissorlike movements of the legs (*pā'oti*) during the grunting.

Performance Venues

Choral singing in the Society Islands flourishes in two contrasting domains: Christian worship and civil celebrations. It emerged out of Tahitian Protestantism, established by 1819. Christian denominations established in later decades have adopted musical styles associated with Protestant worship and devotional activities. *Hīmene* are an integral part of the two major devotional activities: worship and Bible-study meetings.

During worship on Sundays, *hīmene* separate major components of the service: confession of sins, biblical readings, a sermon, an offering, and, on the first Sunday of each month, communion. The congregation sings the opening and closing *hīmene*, and set *hīmene* during the confessional and the offering. The other *hīmene* are performances prepared by the choirs within a parish.

Bible-study meetings are held in *fare putuputura'a*, halls maintained by parochial groups, whose membership is determined by locale within the parish. Each meeting is devoted to interpreting one assigned biblical verse, delivered within a Tahitian oratorical framework. The singing of *hīmene tārava* occurs between spoken remarks. The texts are short, four to eight lines in a stanza, and normally only one stanza; they usually paraphrase biblical episodes relating to the verse under study.

Choral singing is an integral part of civil festivities for the French national holiday, observed annually since 1881, following French annexation of the Society Islands, with precedents in festivities commemorating the birthday of the French Emperor Napoleon III in 1859 and 1875. In the 1880s, these festivities featured choral-singing competitions. Participants emphasized *hīmene tārava*, for which judges awarded the largest prizes.

Dance

In Pape'ete and its environs, people attend presentations of Polynesian dances. They recognize differences in dances of the Society, Tuamotu, Marquesas, and Austral Islands. They see Western dances, including contemporary popular styles, ballet, and modern dance. Occasionally, they see Chinese dances. They see the national styles of visiting troupes, participate in school, church, district, and professional troupes, take formal classes in imported and Tahitian dances, and dance the night away at hotels and bars.

Beyond the cosmopolitan life of Pape'ete, dance participation consists of couple dancing using imported or Tahitian movements and group dancing. Couple dancing is participatory, improvisatory, and spontaneous; dancing in groups is presentational, choreographed, and rehearsed. In Pape'ete, dancing occurs nightly; in outlying districts and on the other islands, it is less frequent, and may consist of a weekly Tahitian show at a hotel and weekend couple dancing to a local band's music. Communal and ecclesiastical events that include dancing dot the calendar and animate village life.

Group Presentational Dance

Group dancing has roots in traveling companies of *'arioi*, sacred, privileged, ceremonially initiated musicians, dancers, and actors, consecrated to the god 'Oro, and dedicated to pleasure and entertainment. The arrival of the *'arioi* began a period of festivity, with feasting, athletics, oratory, and performances by elegantly costumed performers.

Protestant missionaries, deprecating the worship of 'Oro, encouraged legislation that restricted dancing, and even forbade it. Penalties for dancers and audiences did not stop surreptitious performances, which included nighttime entertainments in valleys far removed from missionaries and administrators. Choreographed Tahitian dances were introduced to the Marquesas in the 1880s, confirming a continuity that neither the government nor the church approved.

Because of the drunkenness and impropriety of bar-girl dancers in Pape'ete, dance from the 1920s to the 1950s had a stigma that prevented widespread participation, particularly for women. In 1956, to restore beauty and dignity to Tahitian dance, schoolteacher Madeleine Mouā created a professional troupe, Heiva. Several of her dancers started their own troupes, of which the most famous was Te Maeva, formed by Coco (Jean Hotahota) in the late 1960s. Judged the best male dancer in the Bastille Day competitions, Coco became the most important creative force in twentieth-century Tahitian dance.

'Ōte'a

Danced in "grass" skirts (*more*) to drummed rhythms, the *'ōte'a* is, for outsiders, a stereotypical image of Pacific dance (figure 1). For Tahitians, a well-done *'ōte'a* crowns a presentation, and displays the choreographer's creativity, the dancers' and drummers' stamina, the troupe's knowledge and understanding of appropriate interplay between drumming and movement, and the physical beauty of dancers and costumes.

As performed in the twentieth century, *'ōte'a* represents a possible mixing of two genres. Though early sources describe dances for which females displayed hip movements, the term *'ōte'a* as the name of a dance does not appear until the late 1800s, when it was described as a men's dance and a warriors' dance. Since the 1950s, *'ōte'a* have been choreographed for mixed groups. Remnants of the older practice remain in the inclusion of separate dances for men and women.

'Ōte'a may develop a theme, such as the mythical Hina's clam, a fan, or a star; or they may relate legends or incidents. The movements are mostly abstract. Movements of the arms, hands, head, and upper torso function in isolation from movements of the legs and lower torso, as if an invisible line horizontally divides the body at the waist. Symmetrical and asymmetrical usage of the arms occurs; asymmetrical positions or movements usually repeat on the opposite side. Women revolve their hips, with legs slightly flexed and feet flat on the ground; men open and close their legs with knees bent and feet close together.

The basic formation consists of parallel same-sex columns, or formations that relate to a chosen theme. By the 1920s, changes of formation had become features. Since the late 1970s, they have occurred more frequently, with greater emphasis on variety of patterning.

An ensemble of male musicians provides musical accompaniment: three *tō'ere*, one *fa'atete*, and one *pahu* are standard. Important occasions call for many dancers and an expanded orchestra, adding hand-struck, one-headed membranophones (*pahu tupa'i rima*), a bamboo struck instrument (*ihara*), and additional *tō'ere* and *fa'atete*.

Musical accompaniment draws from a repertory of repeating rhythmic patterns (*pehe*): the lead instrument (*tō'ere 'arata'i*) introduces the initial pattern, one or more *tō'ere tāmau* provide the basic rhythm, and a smaller, higher-pitched *tō'ere tāhape* improvises. The *pahu* provides the basic pulse, coordinating the other performers; the *fa'atete* plays rapid subdivisions of this pulse, interjecting dotted rhythms and syncopation. The ending may use a standardized formula (*toma*).

'Ōte'a costumes worn on important occasions exemplify the creativity of local handiwork with fibers and shells. *More*, skirts made from strips of the inner bark of the *pūrau* tree, are topped with fibrous belts ornamented by shells, seeds, mother-of-pearl, and feathers. Skirts are also made of *'autī* leaves and other plant materials, or strings of flowers or shells. A large headdress and an upper-body covering (fabric, fiber, shell, or coconut bras for women; shawls or sashes for men) coordinate in color and

Figure 1 Students from the Society Islands perform a Tahitian *'ōte'a* at the Polynesian Cultural Center. *Photo by Adrienne L. Kaeppler, 1964.*

design with the belt. Necklaces of shells or flowers and optional whisks of *pūrau* fibers complete the costume. For ordinary events, crowns, garlands, and belts of flowers, ferns, or leaves, provide fragrant and pretty costumery. Dancers may carry spears, fans, torches, or other props relating to the theme of the presentation.

ʻAparima

Performed by large groups, *ʻaparima* tell stories through an expressive use of hands. They are of two basic types: *ʻaparima vāvā* 'mute storytelling dances' and *ʻaparima hīmene* 'sung storytelling dances'. The former tell a story by miming everyday activities, such as making *poʻe* (a pudding of cooked fruit or root vegetables), grating coconuts, and fishing, and are sometimes described as dances done *i raro* 'in a low position'—kneeling or sitting. A percussive ensemble accompanies them, the rhythms differing subtly from those of *ʻōteʻa*. Rather than serving as a force that shapes the choreography, the drumming underscores the mime with less virtuosic, more repetitive patterns, intended to coordinate the dancers' movements.

ʻAparima hīmene have texts and stringband music. The texts exploit many topics, but many express love (for a person or place), or describe the physical features and beauty of a favorite locale. A text of greeting or formal acknowledgment of those present is commonly the first dance. The final dance is often slow and peaceful, closing the presentation with a feeling of repose. Dancers and instrumentalists sing the melody and improvise inner parts, guitars and ukuleles provide the chordal structure, and the *pahu* reinforces the pulse.

ʻAparima emphasize arm-and-hand movements. Lower-body movements include sideways steps, taps of the heel, and slowly revolving hips. Gestures underscore key words in the text: a hand to the eyes conveys the idea of looking. Hands over the navel symbolize the homeland, referring to the Tahitian practice of burying a newborn's placenta under the house. Ornamental gestures include waves, decorative claps, and other nontextual movements, added for sight or sound. Performers may also make mimetic gestures.

ʻAparima may alternate with *ʻōteʻa*, or can occur as a series of items in a separate portion of a program. Separate segments of *ʻōteʻa* and *ʻaparima* allow dancers to change costumes and perform the *ʻaparima* in *pareu* (a wraparound cloth, tied into pants for males and a skirt for females), with garlands for the neck and head. As in the *ʻōteʻa*, dancers may carry story-related props, including fishing poles, hats, and fans.

PERCUSSIVE ENSEMBLES OF THE COOK ISLANDS

The fifteen Cook Islands are widely scattered, with only 241 square kilometers of land, spread over thousands of square kilometers of ocean. The official language is Cook Islands Māori (Rarotongan), but each island cultivates a different dialect or language; English is spoken widely. Music has a highly public role in Cook Islanders' lives. It enhances ceremonial, ritual, and festive occasions, including the investiture of leaders, religious ceremonies, children's christenings, marriages, and funerals.

Percussive ensembles are an important part of the national identity. The drumming of traveling Cook Islands entertainers—Araura, Betela Dance Troupe, the Cook Islands National Arts Theatre, the Cook Islands Youth Council—is admired by attentive audiences.

Typical ensembles use three struck log instruments (*tōkere*, *pātē*, and *kaʻara*), combined with two drums (*paʻu* and *paʻu mangō*). The *paʻu* keeps a basic one-one beat, interrupted by the *paʻu mangō*, which, because its pitch is higher, gives out distinctly perceptible rhythms. The *pātē* sets a basic rhythmic pattern, which the high-pitched sound of the *tōkere* plays against. To that, the *kaʻara* adds percussive complexity by stressing offbeats.

The *tōkere* is ideally made from a straight hardwood branch about 50 centimeters long and about 12 centimeters wide, free of smaller branches. The carver sets the wood lengthwise on the ground, and along one part of the surface cuts a 5-centimeter longitudinal slit, leaving about eight centimeters uncut at both ends.

Through the slit, the carver hollows the interior. Parallel to the first slit, he cuts a second slit from one end, working 2.5 centimeters inward, leaving five centimeters of unremoved wood between the slits. He cuts the other end the same way, and then hollows out the end slits, taking care not to break the septum of unremoved wood. The amount of wood hollowed out from the center slit determines the pitch and timbre of the instrument.

The *tōkere* is played with two 30-centimeter sticks, usually made from ironwood roots. Each stick is five centimeters in diameter at one end, tapering to a point at the other. Holding the thicker end, a player strikes the side of the central slit; for special effects, he hits the end slits. Players sometimes strengthen and weight the sticks by soaking them in mud for days before a performance.

Carvers cut the *pātē* from a branch of a hardwood tree, and occasionally from the trunk. The carving resembles that of the *tōkere*, but the ends are often left intact. The length of a *pātē* varies from 70 to 90 centimeters, depending on the pitch and timbre desired. If three pitches are needed, a carver makes three *pātē*, of varying sizes. Players ordinarily use one 30-centimeter stick, hitting the side of the central slit or the side of the body of the instrument.

The *ka'ara*, made from a tree trunk, is about twice the size of *pātē*. A carver hollows the instrument by a process resembling that of the manufacture of *pātē* and *tōkere*, but giving the slits the form of a triangular figure eight. The top of the *ka'ara* has decorative cross-hatched lines, sometimes with painted patterns in black. The size and shape of the slit give the instrument at least three different pitches. The triangular openings are connected by a middle narrow slit. When struck, each triangular side and the central narrow slit produce a specific tone.

A player uses two 30-centimeter sticks, which vary from those used in playing the *pātē* and the *tōkere*. Instead of hardwood, the wood is cut from a coconut frond. Softer, it has the effect of eliciting from the *ka'ara* a haunting, mellow sound.

The *pa'u* and the *pa'u mangō* are usually made from the trunk of a tree or from a large round piece of wood. Carvers hollow them out and cover their opening or openings with the skin of an animal or a shark.

Pa'u are made from several kinds of wood. The trunk is cut to the desired length, ranging from 1.8 to 2.4 meters. The maker hollows out the inside of the log, leaving a circular outer strip at least seven centimeters thick. The work of hollowing out large drums formerly involved many people, who burned out the interior with fire; alternative techniques are now available, but the task remains arduous. The openings are covered with dried skin and bound with rings and cords. The cords were formerly lengths of coconut fiber, passing from holes in the skin down to slots, through which they were fed for tying around the woodwork between the lower corner of the base and the bottom of the slot. Players use a round, 30-centimeter beater, usually of wild hibiscus. Many villages formerly had communal drums. For playing, these were hung from trees. The diameter of such drums reached one meter.

The *pa'u mangō* has a tongue, carved on the inside of the top portion. It is not usually hollowed out completely: the carver leaves a septum between the top and bottom sections. One old kind of *pa'u mangō*, hollow throughout, with skin covering one end, has gone out of use. Another kind, with the tongue, is in common use; it has one skin, ideally of shark. A third kind, resembling the second, bears carved figures for religious, decorative, or historical reasons. Players use two thin, 30-centimeter beaters, or strike the drumhead with their hands. To improve the sound of the instrument, players often heat the drumhead with fire or in the sun. The skin commonly used today is goatskin.

Hawai'i

The Hawaiian archipelago includes eight high volcanic islands and a chain of more than two hundred uninhabited atolls stretching more than 320 kilometers from southeast to northwest. The original settlers were Polynesian seafarers from the Marquesas Islands, as early as about C.E. 650; settlers from the Society Islands followed, beginning about 1150.

Indigenous Hawaiian society had three classes: chiefs (*ali'i*), believed to have descended from gods; commoners (*maka'āinana*), unable to trace descent from gods; and slaves and untouchables (*kauā*). At the heart of the beliefs that guided social practices was the concept of *mana*, sacred power, manifested in varying degrees in animate forces (including people) and inanimate objects.

In January 1778, two ships of a British expedition of discovery led by Captain James Cook (1728–1779) were the first European vessels to visit Hawai'i. Within two decades, the resources of the islands were attracting American and European traders, hundreds of whom, in the wake of whaling and commerce in sandalwood, took up residence.

Missionaries of the American Board of Commissioners for Foreign Missions began Christian evangelization in 1820; within five years, conversion of the populace was effectively accomplished. By the mid-1800s, laborers were coming from China and Japan to work on sugar plantations; by 1900, laborers were also coming from the Philippines and Portugal.

The Hawaiian constitutional monarchy, established after King Kamehameha I (d. 1819) had brought the islands under unified rule, was overthrown in 1893 by American businessmen, who formed and controlled a republic until 1898, when the United States annexed the islands. In the twentieth century, tourism was a major source of economic development, and many Hawaiians pursued assimilation as a social goal. Hawai'i attained U.S. statehood on 21 August 1959.

Traditional Music

Despite missionaries' attempts at suppression and periods of Hawaiians' neglect, indigenous musical traditions that flourished at the time of European contact survive, coexisting with Western musical styles and repertories. During the past two centuries, they have experienced multiple revivals of interest and popularity.

Indigenous Style

Categories of Poetry The term *mele* denotes a poetic text and its performed vocalization. The *mele* is the basis of all performance; without it, no performance can occur. Poetic texts are named in either of two ways: by topic and by style or styles of recitation (the choice of which usually stems from the topic).

Numerous named categories of Hawaiian poetic texts can be arranged on a continuum from sacred to secular. The most general categories are as follows; each includes additional subcategories (not listed).

1. *Mele pule* are prayers dedicated to gods. The most sacred are prayers that ritual specialists (*kahuna*) performed for rituals associated with state religion. For family gods and personal supplications, households used separate prayers. Prayers specific to occupations, often within the purview of trained specialists, concerned medicinal specialists' work, canoemaking, and dancers' training and performance.

2. *Mele ko'ihonua* and *mele kū'auhau* are genealogical songs, typically tracing lineages from humans back to gods. The most celebrated, *Kumulipo*, traces human history back to the origin of the universe.

3. *Mele inoa* 'name songs' honor people. This category has several important subcategories.

Mele ma'i are genital songs, whose function is to celebrate procreative ability. Animal-oriented songs, individually named by species (such as *manō* 'shark', *pua'a* 'pig') are usually addressed to individuals, or to animal forms of ancestral gods. Laments and funerary dirges (*mele kanikau*) are composed and performed during periods of mourning, to honor the deceased.

4. *Mele ho'oipoipo* 'lovemaking songs' (also called *mele ho'oheno* 'cherishing songs') are dedicated to specific, though often unnamed, individuals. This poetic emphasis is predominant among *mele* composed in the twentieth century.

5. Assorted texts for informal occasions, performed and occasionally composed spontaneously. These include texts of welcome (*mele kāhea*), admiration (*mele aloha*), and criticism (*mele nemo*).

Styles of Vocalization Hawaiians distinguish between mele accompanied by dance and mele not accompanied by dance: the former are usually called *mele hula*; the latter, *mele oli*. A musical distinction lies in the presence or absence of metered pulse, a requirement for synchronizing dancers' movements: the pulse in *mele hula* occurs in sets of even numbers of beats, with duple subdivision of beats.

Vocalizations include six named styles of vocal delivery, of which five are used in *mele oli* and the sixth in *mele hula*. Each has particular poetic associations: *kepakepa*, speechlike vocalization with a crisp and rapid delivery of syllables, particularly suited for reciting long prayers and genealogies; *kāwele*, speechlike vocalization with a clearer sense of pitched contour, also suited for reciting genealogical texts and prayers; *olioli*, vocalization with sustained pitch, using one principal tone (which may occasionally receive embellishment from auxiliary tones, usually lower) and applicable to the full range of poetic types, except laments and funerary dirges; *ho'āeāe*, vocalization with prolonged sustained pitch and elaborate patterned vibratos, appropriate for lovemaking songs; *ho'ouwēuwē*, vocalization with extremely prolonged sustained pitch and wailing, appropriate only for laments and funerary dirges; and *'ai ha'a*, vocalization for *mele hula*, using regular patterns of pitch with metered pulse.

Vocal Ornaments On the most detailed level, vocal ornaments are associated with vocal styles. These ornaments involve articulatory techniques related to pronunciation; many of them are associated with particular styles of vocal delivery. The most prominent ornament is vibrato (*'i'i*), used extensively in *olioli*, *ho'āeāe*, *ho'ouwēuwē*, and *'ai ha'a*.

Musical Instruments Most indigenous Hawaiian musical instruments are associated with dancing. Anciently, a conch (*pū*) served for signaling, especially in battle; it continues to be used, at the beginning of concerts and pageants. Lovers communicated by playing noseflutes (*'ohe hano-ihu*), whose repertory especially included courting songs. Instruments used for dancing fulfill one of two basic functions, depending on who plays them.

For standing dances, musicians play any of three instruments and vocalize the *mele*. The function of these instruments is to provide a pulse that guides the dancers' lower-body movements. A pair of drums—the *pahu* (a sharkskin drum, struck with bare hands) and the *pūniu* (a fishskin coconut-shell drum, on a stand or tied to the musician's right thigh, and struck with braided leaves or a cord)—are most often played in combination. The *ipu* is a struck gourd instrument; two gourds glued together at the neck are *ipu heke*. The *pahu* and the *ipu* have a basic inventory of named rhythmic patterns. Those for the *pahu* are named after specific textual passages in the dances in which they occur; for example, the pattern *kaulilua* derives its name from the first word of the piece "Kaulilua," and the pattern *e uē* derives its name from the phrase "*e uē*." For the *ipu*, the rhythms are not textually specific, but are universally applicable. The player grasps the gourd by its neck and alternately thumps it on the ground and slaps it on its side.

For sitting dances, the dancers themselves play instruments and vocalize the *mele*. The instruments include the *'ulī'ulī*, a seed-filled gourd, with an attached handle and feathers; *pū'ili*, a length of split bamboo, closed at the end of the handle; *'ili'ili*, water-worn pebbles, one pair held in each hand; and *kālā'au*, a pair of hardwood sticks. In addition to acoustically enhancing the performance, these instruments function as an extension of the dancers' hands.

Mele Hula Among *mele* composed for dancing, *hula pahu* and *hula 'āla'apapa* show important distinctions in the accompanying instruments and the format of the poetry. *Mele hula pahu* are composed for *pahu*-accompanied performance. These *mele* are through-composed, with no regularly recurring melodic or rhythmic patterns, though in a given *mele* identifiable rhythmic motifs may occur, with specific sequences of movements at particular points. About ten *hula pahu* are known to exist.

DISC
❶
TRACK
34

Mele hula 'āla'apapa are composed for *ipu*-accompanied performance. These *mele* are also through-composed, but share two structural attributes. First, the text is arranged into sections (*paukū*), of which some *mele* contain only one. Though *mele* may have multiple *paukū*, these sections may not be identical in length, melody, or number of gourd-marked beats; thus, despite the appearance of having stanzas, these *mele* are not, strictly speaking, strophic. Second, each *paukū* precedes a sequence of movements associated with a specific set of rhythms, as in figure 2, from a *mele* dedicated to Hī'iaka, sister of Pele, goddess of volcanoes. The *paukū* of the text, as taught by the late Zaneta Ho'oūlu Richards and translated by Amy Ku'uleialoha Stillman, reads:

> *No luna e ka Halekai, o ka ma'alewa,*
> *Nānā ka maka iā Moananuikalehua lā,*
> *Noho i ke kai o mali'o mai*
> *I kū a'e lā ka lehua i laila lā.*
> > *'Ea lā, 'ea lā, 'ea.*
> > *I laila ho'i.*

From above at Halekai, from the mountain-ladder
The eyes gaze upon Moana-nui-ka-lehua,
Sitting in the calm sea
Where the *lehua* blossoms stood upright.
> Tra la, tra la.
> There, indeed.

Dance

Hawaiian poetry is conveyed through vocalized rhythmic and melodic motifs and movements of the human body. Ancient Hawai'i had two structured-movement systems: *ha'a*, ritual movements performed on outdoor temples; and *hula*, formal or informal entertainment. Movements visually enhanced vocalized texts by objectifying them in *ha'a* or alluding to them in *hula*. Today, these systems have coalesced into one: *hula*.

Aesthetics, Composition, Performance
An important Hawaiian value is indirectness (*kaona* "hidden or layered meaning"), a concept that pervades Hawaiian life. Indirectness and skill (*no'eau*) are important elements in Hawaiian music and dance. A poetic text incorporated its initial *kaona* through the composition of melodic-rhythmic contours by one or more verbal artists (*haku mele*). A movement artist then choreographed the text, using motifs from the Hawaiian structured-movement system. The movements suggested or depicted certain words, or enhanced the text through veiled or hidden meanings. Especially in relation to words and their

HULA KU'I

In the 1800s, Hawaiian society underwent turbulent changes, including the rejection of the indigenous state religion, the acceptance of Christianity, the widespread embracing of Western goods, customs, and government, and the loss of national sovereignty. Among the changes relevant to the practice of music was a major revival of *oli* and *hula* in the 1870s and 1880s.

The reign of King David Kalākaua, lasting from 1874 to 1891, holds special significance for Hawaiian traditions. After decades of censure, Hawaiian customs became revitalized when Kalākaua encouraged their revival. He summoned master-teachers (*kumu hula*) to the court at Honolulu and gave them royal patronage. Out of this atmosphere, a new style of dancing emerged, that of the *hula ku'i*.

The term *ku'i*, meaning 'to join old and new', refers to the mix of old and new components of poetry, music, dance, and costume. Traditional conventions gained a new format: texts became strophic, and each strophe consisted of a couplet. Indigenous vocal styles and ornaments were added to melodies based on tempered tones and simple harmonies. Each couplet was uniform in length, most commonly eight or sixteen beats. The format mandated the repetition of the melody for each couplet, and each couplet was commonly performed twice. An instrumental interlude separated the stanzas; in dances by seated performers, this interlude is called *kī'i pā*. New sequences of movements joined preexisting, named, lower-body motifs. Locomotive lower-body motifs were emphasized over stationary ones, favored in earlier dancing. The shredded-grass skirt brought to Hawai'i by Gilbertese laborers came to be favored. Male dancers wore long-sleeved shirts and slacks, with a skirt over the slacks. Ankle-length Victorian gowns, especially the white gown worn at academic commencements, also became a costume for dancing.

The defining distinction of the *hula ku'i* was accompaniment from guitars and ukuleles. For dances by standing performers, *mele* composed in the new format added the accompaniment of *ipu* or other indigenous percussive instruments. In the twentieth century, performances of those *mele* came to be called either ancient *hula* or *hula'ōlapa*, referencing the division of labor between dancers (*'ōlapa*) and musicians (*ho'olapa*). The same, or other, *mele* performed with the accompaniment of stringed instruments were called *hula ku'i*—a term that in the twentieth century more commonly became replaced by modern *hula*.

combinations, *kaona* had a power that could harm as well as honor. From cultural knowledge, observers had to deduce the meaning of *kaona*-laden texts.

Traditional interpretation was a kind of storytelling. The performer never became an actor or a character in a drama, but performed a story audibly and visually, telling about persons, places, and events. Performances were not dramatic in any Western sense: they had no conflict, nor did they express emotions. The introduction of characterization distinguishes later Hawaiian dances from earlier ones: performances became more pantomimic, and storytellers became like actors telling stories to audiences that did not fully understand the language.

Structures and Movements

The vocalization of *mele hula* is akin to that of *oli*, though it has less vibrato (*'i'i*). The rhythm, in 2/4 or 4/4 time, is more regular, permitting people to perform together as singer-instrumentalists (*ho'opa'a*) and dancers (*'ōlapa*), who might number one or more.

Hula are performed standing or seated. In the seated position, the body's weight is supported on the knees and lower legs, folded under the upper legs or at the sides; the knees are far enough apart that the buttocks can be placed on the ground between the feet. This position may strain the upper leg muscles, as some movements require that the body be raised and lowered and the torso make circling movements that can place the back on or near the floor. Seated performers may play percussive instruments and sing. In the standing position, the lower body conveys the rhythms or furnishes the rhythmic environment for arm-and-hand motifs. Lower-body motifs have names, and include the interrelated movements of feet, legs, and hips. The feet are close together, flat on the floor, with knees bent. The amount of flexion of the knees and turnout of the ankles varies according to teachers' and performers' preferences. The back is straight, and the shoulders do not usually move, except as required by movements of the arms. The head, and especially the eyes, follow the hands. If both arms are not doing the same movement, the eyes usually follow the hand farther away from the body, usually the one alluding to the text.

The structure of a *hula* begins with a *kāhea*, a recitation of the first line of its text. A percussive

Figure 2 Beginning of "*No luna e ka Halekai,*" a *mele hula ʻālaʻapapa*, in the version taught by Zaneta Hoʻoūlu Richards. *Transcription by Amy Kuʻuleialoha Stillman.*

instrument then sets the rhythm, and movement-accompanied poetry (through-composed or in couplets) follows. Between stanzas, a short instrumental phrase may occur, and one performer may recite part of the succeeding line of text. The dance concludes with an ending motif; a final *kāhea* announces the name of the honored person, place, or event. A set of dances follows an entrance dance (*kaʻi*), and precedes an exit dance (*hoʻi*). Lower-body motifs, with arm-and-hand movement, are choreographed—combined simultaneously and sequen-

tially—as meaningful imagery, based on a text. Through a specific choreography, a sequence of motifs has meaning as one component of a larger social activity.

Categories of Hula

The most important danced *mele* were *mele inoa*, honoring a god or a chief, and *mele hoʻoipoipo*, songs of a topical or endearing nature. *Mele inoa* were *ʻālaʻapapa*, texts composed in sections, sung with the

Figure 3 At the Festival of American Folklife, three generations of Zuttermeisters perform a *hula 'auana*. In 1984, Kau'i Zuttermeister (*center*) became the first recipient from Hawai'i to be awarded the National Heritage Fellowship by the U.S. government.
Photo by Adrienne L. Kaeppler.

playing of a gourd idiophone. Movements alluded to words of the text, with often only one allusion per line. In the 1800s, *mele inoa* evolved into *hula ku'i*, joining the old and the new, or *'ōlapa* (depending on the music), composed in usually repeating couplets. Movements interpret texts. Usually, couplets are performed first to the right side of the body and then to the left. *Mele ho'oipoipo* were less formal, sometimes extemporaneous, about people, places, and current events. *Mele ma'i* are a subdivision of *mele inoa*. Usually performed last in a set, *mele ma'i* honor the physical means of perpetuating the royal lines, alluding to nature; today, the movement references may be explicit.

Mele hula are categorized according to the musical instrument with which the sung poetry is integrally related. The poetry for *hula pahu* is performed with a *pahu*, a drum; *hula pā ipu*, with a struck gourd; *hula kāla'au*, with sticks (*kala'au*), and sometimes with a treadleboard (*papa hehi*); *hula 'ulī'ulī* are performed with a gourd rattle; *hula pū'ili*, with a slit bamboo rattle; *hula 'ili'ili*, with stone clappers; and *hula pa'iumauma*, with open palms striking chest and thighs. Since the 1960s, additional categories have been introduced, especially for festivals (figure 3). Thus, old *hula* (*hula kahiko*) include *hula* performed with any traditional musical instruments and less melodically variable vocal contours, and *hula 'auana* include *hula* performed with introduced musical instruments and Western harmonies.

Aotearoa (New Zealand)

Primarily composed of two large islands of about 260,000 square kilometers, and with a population of about 3.5 million, Aotearoa is isolated from its neighbors by large expanses of ocean. Its endemic plants and animals evolved into many species, but included no mammals. Distance was a factor in Māori settlement, the final major migration of Polynesian people, which occurred before A.D. 1000. To British observers, Aotearoa looked like the antipodes, the farthest place on the globe. They called it New Zealand and colonized it.

Topographical extremes—high mountains, rugged hills, an extensive plain—encouraged settlers and their descendants to concentrate in small communities, which developed unique flavors. Māori tribal dialects developed, and woodcarving, tattooing, music, and dance acquired localized traits. In and after the 1800s, patterns of settlement preserved the musical styles of some European immigrants: Scots in Dunedin, English in Canterbury, Dalmatians in Northland. The twentieth-century concentration of Pacific Islanders in Auckland and the cosmopolitanism of Wellington continue this diversity.

Musical Instruments

In the late twentieth century, important work in music scholarship and performance included the revival of Māori flutes (*nguru*, *kōauau*, and others), traditionally associated with birth, death, fertility, and healing. Under Christian missionaries' influence, the use of these instruments had waned, and after the mid-1800s it had died out. Mrs. Paeroa Wineera, the last surviving *kōauau* player who had learned in the traditional fashion, died in the 1960s. Because owners readily traded Māori flutes to European explorers, the world's museums possess many superbly carved specimens.

The *pūtōrino* is an unusual wind instrument because it probably served as flute, bugle, and megaphone. Other Māori instruments include bone castanets (*tōkere*); a mouth-resonated bow (*kū*); a whirring disk (*kōrorohū*), into which priests sang incantations; a whirled slat (*pūrerehua*), gourd (*poiawhiuwhiu*), and ball (*poi*); a tapped whale's rib (*pākuru*); and a jew's harp (*rōria*). These instruments present many sounds, drawn from a wide variety of materials: jade, wood, whales' teeth, and avian and human bones.

By copying museum specimens, makers reconstruct instruments; by experimenting with sounds, performers try to recapture old techniques of playing. Māori elders' memories of the contexts in which flutes were played, and their assent to the validity of experimental sounds, permit the revival of the traditions.

Mōteatea: *Māori Musical Poetry*

Mōteatea is a multipurpose compositional and performative tradition of the Māori people. Neither simply music nor simply poetry, a single *mōteatea* may employ a single form (such as that of the lullaby), and it may be an important educational tool, used to impart to children important information about history and philosophy. *Mōteatea* can take any of numerous forms appropriate to a particular situation: trivial and profound, sacred and profane, instructive and amusing. Forms of *mōteatea* include laments for the dead, lovers' songs, songs to answer marriage proposals, songs in reply to taunts and slander, ancient songs, songs for birds, songs about making peace, surfing songs, cursing songs, songs about coveting guns, daydreaming songs, and songs for presentation at a feast.

Māori composers did not create music purely as sonic entertainment, though they did develop criteria for appraising the qualities of a performance. With dance, oratory, and other arts, *mōteatea* were cherished for reaching into the spirituality of people's lives. Māori looked for the revisitation of spirit—the juxtaposition of time, place, and people, and the melancholy reminder of past events and their meaning for present circumstances.

A Lament by Te Rauparaha

In the early 1800s, Te Rauparaha (d. 1849), a leader of the Ngāti Toa people, lived at Kāwhia, on the western coast of Te Ika-a-Māui. In the 1820s, he led his people southward, seeking new lands. Before leaving, he composed a ceremonial farewell, which, in the Ngāti Toa version, became his lament for Kāwhia, the land long inhabited by his people. It begins: *Tērā ia ngā tai o Honipaka, / Ka wehe koe i au,*

ē! / He whakamaunga atu nāku / Te ao ka tākawe / Nā runga mai o Te Motu. / Ka mihi mamao au ki te iwi rā ia: / Moe noa mai, i te moenga roa 'Those waters of Honipaka, / I leave you now, *ē!* / But my spirit still clings / To that cloud floating / Above Te Motu. / I pay respect to those distant people: / Sleep on, in the great sleep' (after Ngata 1928:92). To enunciate grief on leaving, Te Rauparaha used classical Māori associations of spirit and land. He linked his spirit to the clouds floating above Te Motu, an island in Kāwhia Harbor, where people would go to present songs and stories to one another. The migration of Ngāti Toa tells an epic story of enterprise common in Māori history. To Māori, the beauty of this text arises not just from the sounds of its words, but from knowledge of its composer. Brought together, words and knowledge multiply in meaning. As in this lament, composers use beautiful elements in the natural world—birds, clouds, spirits, tides, and so on—as symbols of their exploits and their lives.

Musical Contexts and Functions

Texts are one component of Māori music: the circumstances of performance are another. Ritual meetings, where performances of classical Māori music most often occur, involve performers' and listeners' formal interactions in prescribed ways. Historically, music reinforced, challenged, and sometimes disparaged interpersonal and intertribal relationships.

The Legacy of Mōteatea

Mōteatea traditions persist. They underpin and ornament Māori society with exquisite expressions and philosophical explanations. Māori composers are acute witnesses of human acts and the circumstances that surround them; they often provide alternative interpretations of critical events, supplementing the historical record.

Māori society is undergoing reconstruction and redevelopment. In this process, *mōteatea* perform an important function: from ancient literature and traditions, tribes preparing for the future are seeking guidance. Their endeavors attest to the endurance of certain features of the human condition and the *mōteatea* that discuss them.

The revival of *mōteatea* has paralleled a revitalization of tribal systems and institutions. Māori people are reworking and reestablishing traditional institutions, such as whare *wānanga*, traditional schools of higher learning. Literature is a large part of the curriculum, and *mōteatea* have aided the philosophical empowerment of those institutions. Re-examining traditional theatrical institutions, many tribes are giving attention to *mōteatea* and musical instruments. Identifying theater as a vehicle for development, young Māori attend schools dedicated to drama and other arts, and represent their experiences by reworking traditional forms of making music.

Dance

Within Māori cultural contexts, dance is a powerful message-bearing expression. The significance of any aspect of it cannot be dissected from that expressive purpose, any more than from the language of its texts, the music of its delivery, or the customs surrounding its performance. There are three main types: *haka*, *waiata-a-ringa*, and *poi*, two of which are described below.

Haka

Haka peruperu and *haka taparahi* are vigorous, awe-inspiring, spirited, bellicose dances. Scores or hundreds of angry-acting men raise a storm of elemental force. To lift morale, inspire warriors before battle, and terrorize enemies, *haka taparahi*, performed without weapons, required the body's committed involvement. *Peruperu*, performed with weapons, was the classic battle-line *haka* (figure 4).

Foot-and-leg movements set the pulse by repeated rhythmic plantings of feet on the ground, establishing the body's weight and balance. The footfall portrays warriors holding their ground while displaying alertness and focusing on their opponents. Feet move swiftly to new positions, deliver attacks, warn with threats, alter the body's alignment, and defend by dodging or parrying. A proverb warns that "slow feet are wet feet"—wet with blood. That proverb seems danced out when the legs bend swiftly up underneath the body as if to avoid an enemy's weapon. By contrast, other jumps, begun with feet wide and legs bent, may land on the knee, emphasizing occupation of the land.

Textual messages are delivered in a sequence of arm gestures, thrust in particular directions. Fists may be clenched, or open palms may forcefully strike the torso, chest, shoulders, hips, or thighs. Some gestures are directed toward the body, some away from it, some downward, some upward, and some at the enemy (the audience). Most emphasize textual themes and moods, but a few may serve as rhythmic or patterning links, providing contrast to interpretive gestures. Performers move in synchrony, but individuals have considerable scope for individuality, particularly in facial expression.

Wiri, the rapid quivering or rotating of arms and hands, is said to bring Māori dance to life. The distinctive quivering crosses back and forth between what can be seen and what can only be felt. Connecting overt and trace movements signals that the performer's body and mind are on the same continuum. At times, warriors seem to internalize *wiri* into minuscule vibrations of the torso, neck, head, and limbs, bringing the body to a feverish standstill, preceding an explosion of rage. *Wiri*, *whakapī* (contorting the facial features), *pūkana* (a fixed glare, rolled or

Figure 4 At the Pacific Festival of the Arts, Māori men, members of Ngāti Rangiwewehi, perform a *haka peruperu*. *Photo by Adrienne L. Kaeppler, 1996.*

protruded eyeballs), *te arero* (a protruded tongue), belligerent snorts, and other vocalizations combine to deliver warnings, threats, and challenges.

Haka poi

Performances with *poi* involve the rhythmic tossing, hitting, and catching of a ball or several balls, traditionally made from bulrushes and attached to strings, either about 15 centimeters long or about 120 centimeters long. In each hand, skilled performers may hold one or two short *poi*, or one or two long *poi*. Warriors formerly used *poi* actions to maintain wrist flexibility, but *poi* have developed as a women's dance. Classic *poi* dances and songs are reputed to have been those of the people of the Taranaki, Rotorua, and Whanganui tribal areas, but *poi* are now performed everywhere in Aotearoa. The dancers' singing sets the rhythm for the movements. The sounds of the *poi* hitting parts of the body and the rustling of the skirts provide distinctive accompanimental elements.

—Adapted from an article by Adrienne L. Kaeppler, Jane Freeman Moulin, Amy Kuʻuleialoha Stillman, Takiora Ingram, Jon Tikivanotau M. Jonassen, Allan Thomas, Te Ahukaramū Charles Royal, and Jennifer Shennan

Bibliography

Andersen, Johannes C. 1933. *Maori Music with Its Polynesian Background*. Polynesian Society Memoir 10. New Plymouth, New Zealand: Thomas Avery & Sons.

Barrère, Dorothy B., Mary Kawena Pukui, and Marion Kelly. 1980. *Hula: Historical Perspectives*. Pacific Anthropological records, 30. Honolulu: Bishop Museum.

Davey, Tim, and Horst Puschmann. 1996. *Kiwi Rock: A Reference Book*. Dunedin: Kiwi Rock Publications.

Dix, John. 1988. *Stranded in Paradise: New Zealand Rock 'n' Roll 1955 to 1988*. Wellington: Paradise Publications.

Elbert, Samuel H., and Noelani Mahoe. 1970. *Nā Mele o Hawaiʻi Nei: 101 Hawaiian Songs* Honolulu: University of Hawaiʻi Press.

Emerson, Nathanial B. 1909. *Unwritten Literature of Hawaii: Sacred Songs of the Hula*. Washington, D.C.: Bureau of American Ethnology.

Handy, E. S. Craighill, and Jane Lathrop Winne. 1925. *Music in the Marquesas Islands*. Bulletin 17. Honolulu: Bishop Museum.

Jonassen, John. 1991. *Cook Islands Drums*. Rarotonga: Ministry of Cultural Development, Cook Islands.

Kaeppler, Adrienne L. 1993a. *Hula Pahu: Hawaiian Drum Dances: Volume 1: Háʻa and Hula Pahu: Sacred Movements*. Bishop Museum Bulletin in Anthropology 3. Honolulu: Bishop Museum Press.

Kanahele, George S. ed. 1979. *Hawaiian Music and Musicians: An Illustrated History*. Honolulu: University of Hawaiʻi Press.

McLean, Mervyn. 1996. *Maori Music*. Auckland: Auckland University Press.

McLean, Mervyn, and Margaret Orbell. 1979. *Traditional Songs of the Maori*. Auckland: Auckland University Press.

Moulin, Jane Freeman. 1979. *The Dance of Tahiti*. Papeʻete: Christian Gleizal/Les éditions du Pacifique.

Ngata, Apirana T. 1928. *Nga Moteatea*. Vol. 1. Wellington: Polynesian Society.

Oliver, Douglas L. 1974. *Ancient Tahitian Society*. 3 vols. Honolulu: University of Hawaiʻi Press.

Roberts, Helen H. 1926. *Ancient Hawaiian Music*. Bulletin 29. Honolulu: Bishop Museum.

Shennan, Jennifer. 1984. *The Maori Action Songs*. Wellington: New Zealand Council for Educational Research.

Stillman, Amy Kuʻuleialoha. 1982. "The Hula Kuʻi: A Tradition in Hawaiian Music and Dance." M.A. thesis, University of Hawaiʻi.

Tatar, Elizabeth. 1982. *Nineteenth Century Hawaiian Chant*. Pacific Anthropological Records, 33. Honolulu: Department of Anthropology, Bernice P. Bishop Museum.

———. 1993. *Hula Pahu: Hawaiian Drum Dances: Volume II: The Pahu: Sounds of Power*. Bulletin in Anthropology, 4. Honolulu: Bishop Museum.

Thomson, John Mansfield. 1991. *The Oxford History of New Zealand Music*. Oxford and Auckland: Oxford University Press.

Glossary

Produced and compiled by Jesse Reiswig

abakkabuk An old Tuareg **rhythm**, used in the creation of music for light entertainment and dancing.

a cappella 'as in a chapel': without **accompaniment**: i.e., referring to solo or choral vocal music sung without instrumental accompaniment.

accompaniment A part or group of parts in a piece of music that serves as **harmonic** or **rhythmic** support to the main, melodic (see **melody**) part or parts.

accordion A portable, handheld **wind instrument** that has a large, flexible **bellows** in the middle, used to force air through small reeds inside, producing **tones**. One hand plays a keyboard that controls a higher-pitched set of reeds for melodic parts; the other hand presses buttons controlling lower-pitched reeds for **accompaniment**. The instrument is a German invention of the early nineteenth century and today is played throughout the world.

adhan (also *adhān, azān, ezan*) An Islamic call to prayer, performed five times per day by a solo vocalist from the mosque.

aerophone A musical instrument whose principal sound is caused by the vibration of air enclosed within it or agitated immediately around it.

afoxé Contemporary Afro-Brazilian carnival music.

Afro-Beat A Yorùbá musical genre originating in the late 1960s as a mixture of **highlife**, **jazz**, and **soul**, and influential in *jùjú* and *fújì*.

Afro-Cuban music A catchall term for modern African-influenced Cuban music. Secular genres with the most pervasive African influence include the *rumba* and the *comparsa*. However, most of today's Cuban music shows clear and pervasive African influence, particularly in **rhythm**.

aggu (plural *aggutan*) A Tuareg professional storytelling musician of the artisanal caste.

agídìgbo (1) A large box-resonated Yorùbá **lamellaphone** that resembles a Cuban analog; (2) The Yorùbá version of *konkoma* music, brought to Lagos by Ewe and Fanti migrant workers.

agogo A struck clapperless bell of the Yorùbá of Nigeria.

agua 'e nieve (or *agüenieve*) A competitive Afro-Peruvian dance genre that utilizes *festejo* rhythms.

aguinaldo In Puerto Rico, a genre of **strophic** song particularly associated with Christmastide. It takes its name from the small Christmas offering of the same name, often handed out to people who travel door to door, entertaining with songs.

ahal A Taureg courtship gathering that features love songs, poetical recitations, jokes, and games of wit.

ahidus (also *haidous*) A Berber dance of the middle and eastern High Atlas.

ahwash A Berber dance of the western High Atlas.

'ai ha'a A Hawaiian style of vocalization for *mele hula*, using regular patterns of **vibrato** and a **metered** pulse.

ajísáàrì Yorùbá music customarily performed before dawn during Ramadan by young men associated with neighborhood mosques.

aksak The "limping," asymmetrical **rhythms** common to Turkish, Greek, and Eastern European music. These rhythms, performed at fast **tempos**, combine groups of two and three pulses to form **meters** of five, seven, nine, and eleven pulses. *Aksak* is also found in music in Spain, where typical *aksak* meters consist of five-beat **measures** organized into groups of three and two beats.

alphorn Any of various wooden trumpets, grouped in several subtypes. It is played prominently in Switzerland and other areas of Europe; it is the most famous Swiss **wind instrument**.

ámalìhaní A complex dance of the Garifuna *dügü* ritual in Belize, characterized by movement in a circular pattern and reversals of direction.

anacrusis A **note** or series of notes that precedes the downbeat of a **measure** or **phrase**; it can be known as a "pickup," a "pickup note," an "upbeat," and a "pickup measure."

anene A genre of informal Micronesian songs incorporating Western musical elements. Lacking the drive of *kuaea*, they are in the repertory of amplified bands, which entertain at weddings, social dances, and other events.

anhemitonic Featuring an inventory of **tones** with no **semitones** (minor seconds).

anhemitonic pentatonic scale A five-tone **scale** that does not contain **semitones**.

animism A belief-system emphasizing the personification or divinity of animals, plants, or other natural elements.

antiphonal (in vocal music) Characterized by the alternation of two or more **choirs** or other vocal groups.

antiphonal singing A vocal performance in which two or more **choirs** or other vocal groups alternate.

anzad (also *anzhad* and *imzad*) A Tuareg one-stringed fiddle.

anzad n-asak Tuareg music for the *anzad* and human voice.

àpálà A Yorùbá musical genre that originated in the Ijẹbu area, probably in the early 1940s.

'**aparima** A Tahitian dance in which large groups of performers tell stories through an expressive use of their hands.

'**aparima hīmene** The sung version of 'aparima, which has text and **stringband** music.

'**aparima vāvā** The silent version of 'aparima, which tells a story by miming everyday activities.

aradhana A South Indian death-anniversary commemoration celebrated in many immigrant Indian communities in the United States and Canada.

areito (also **areyto**) A pre-Columbian celebratory event of the Taino Indians of the Caribbean that includes music and dance.

'**arioi** Eighteenth-century professional traveling entertainers of the Society Islands.

arpa 'harp': a **diatonic** harp without pedals, played in many areas of Hispanic America, especially Chile, Ecuador, Mexico, Paraguay, Peru, and Venezuela.

aṣíkò A Yorùbá dance-drumming style of the early years of the **jùjú** musical style, performed mainly by Christian boys' clubs.

atabaque A conical single-headed drum of Brazil and Uruguay.

atonal Without **tonality**; without **key**.

'**aukwee** A song genre of the Fataleka people of northern Malaita. Characteristic of 'aukwee is singing in two parts, **na'o** and **buli**, performed by a men's **choir** seated in two facing rows, each singer holding a rattle.

ayaake Spontaneous, often improvised solo singing in Angan music of New Guinea.

ayarachi A Peruvian **panpipe** tradition, whose instruments are subdivided into three different groups. The instruments of each group are tuned to the **octave**.

backbeat (or **back beat**) A sharp emphasis on beats two and four in music with four beats per **measure**. It is usually associated with **rock and roll** and related styles of music, such as **rhythm and blues**.

bağlama (plural, **baglamadhes**) (1) A plucked **lute** of the Turkish **sāz** family, used among various cultures of the Eastern Mediterranean; it is the central instrument in Turkish folk music. (2) A distinct but related **lute**, essentially a half-sized version of the **bouzouki**, used in Greek **rebetika**.

bagpipe (often referred to in the plural, as **bagpipes**) A reed instrument consisting of a flexible airbag into which air is blown by mouth or a **bellows**, and fitted with a **melody** pipe and one or more accompanying **drone** pipes.

Bahamian (or **Bahamanian**) **anthem** A genre of religious music of the Bahamas, closely related to spirituals sung by slave and free blacks in the southern United States. This relationship reflects the fact that enslaved Africans came to the Bahamas with whites loyal to Britain in the late 1700s, at the time of the American Revolution. Exemplars of the genre tend to focus on biblical characters, and in particular, on their relationship to the sea.

baião A social dance music from Northeast Brazil, typically played by trios of **accordion**, triangle, and **zabumba** drum.

bailados A general term for Afro-Brazilian dramatic dances. These dances include processions and actual dramatic representation, with numerous characters, spoken dialogues, songs, and dances, accompanied by small instrumental ensembles.

baile pastoril A Christmas cycle that is a subgroup of a genre of "dramatic dances" (danced folk plays), common on the northeastern coast of Brazil.

bajo sexto A guitar with six double **courses** of steel strings, used in Texas–Mexican **conjunto** music.

bala (or **balafon**, **balanji**) A **xylophone**, prominent among the **jeli** of Sierra Leone, with wooden keys, arranged in consecutive **pitch** order and fastened to a frame of gourd resonators.

balabolo A basic musical pattern for a Maninka **xylophone** player.

balalaika A Russian stringed instrument with a distinctive, triangular-shaped body. It usually has three strings or three pairs of two strings each—a total of six strings.

balga A vocal genre of the Kimberley area of Western Australia, distinguished from **nurlu** by being owned by **moieties**, rather than individuals, and accompanied by **clapsticks**, rather than boomerangs. **Balga** are mainly performed in the central-north parts of the Kimberleys.

ballad Any **strophic** song that tells a narrative.

banda 'band': usually either a **brass** band (a large ensemble of mixed European-derived **wind instruments**), or any ensemble of **aerophones** and **percussion instruments**.

bandella A small ensemble of the Italian-speaking areas of Switzerland, consisting of one or two clarinets and four or five **brass instruments**.

bandola A four stringed, pear-shaped plucked **lute**, serving as a melodic instrument in Venezuela.

bandoneón An Argentine concertina, whose popularity was spread by **tango** music.

bandura A Ukrainian plucked bowl **lute**: an alternate name, used by some researchers, for **kobza**.

bandurria (1) Guatemalan twelve-stringed **lute**; (2) sixteen- to twenty-stringed **chordophone** shaped like a mandolin.

baraban (1) A large two-headed Polish drum. (2) A Ukrainian field drum.

bas A Ukrainian string bass, typically with three strings, about the size and shape of a cello.

basesa A popular music of the east coast of Madagascar.

bàtá A Yorùbá ensemble of conical, double-headed drums, associated with the thunder god, Ṣango.

batá drum The most important musical instrument used in **Santería** rituals. It is a two-headed drum, always played in sets of three, and retaining the original hourglass shape of the drum as used by the Yorùbá in Africa. One bulb of the hourglass is larger than the other, and each bulb is crowned with a drumhead (see **bàtá**).

bātere A Kiribati song with interpretive movements, adapted from the Tokelauan **fātele**.

batuque (1) An Afro-Brazilian religion and dance in Pará, São Paulo, and Rio Grande do Sul states; (2) An Argentine variant of the Afro-Brazilian religion.

bebop (or simply **bop**) The initial style of modern jazz, which grew prominent in the early 1940s, typified by quick **tempos** and **improvisation** based on **harmonic** structure, rather than **melody**. The name **bebop** comes from nonsense syllables used in the improvisatory so-called "scat" singing, which the short melodic bursts typical of bebop melodies often resembled.

beguine (or *biguine, bigin*) A social dance-music genre of Martinique and Guadalupe, with West African influence, and today an internationally known dance.

bélè (1) A dance style performed since colonial times in the French Caribbean, especially Martinique; (2) A cylindrical single-headed **membranophone** of Martinique used in the *bigin bélè* genre.

bellows A collapsible container with air inside. When the container is collapsed, the air inside is forced through an outlet nozzle of some kind. Many musical instruments use a bellows to produce sound.

bendir A Tunisian single-headed **frame drum**, played with the *mizwid* to accompany praise songs.

bepha Visits by groups of youthful Venda and Tsonga performers, sent by one chief to another.

bertsulari Basque "versifiers," who improvise new **verses** (*bertsu*) during informal social occasions and hotly contested organized competitions.

bhajan A Hindu genre of lay devotional songs from the Karnatak musical tradition of southern India. *Bhajan* have continued to be an important genre in Hindu centers throughout North America.

bhakti 'Religious devotion': an Indian concept that has been incorporated into many immigrant Indian communities in the United States and Canada.

bigin (see **beguine**)

bigin bélè 'drum beguine': one of the two main types of Martinican **beguine**, deriving from the *bélè* dances.

bino A dance considered by many I-Kiribati to be their most elegant; it is broken up into sections. Based on a five-tone **scale**, the first section is **rhythmically** free; a seated **chorus** mirrors the dancers' movements. The second section is in duple **meter** with choral clapping.

bira (1) A Shona spirit-possession ceremony in which participants seek assistance from their deceased ancestors; (2) One of two basic vocal genres of the Abelam of New Guinea, performed by mixed-sex ensembles, which accompanies social dancing.

bis The central ritual of the Asmat people of New Guinea.

bloco afro A genre of contemporary Afro-Brazilian carnival music.

bluegrass A hybrid of Appalachian "old-time" or "hillbilly" music (with roots in traditional music of the British Isles), and the classic **country music** of the Carter Family, Jimmie Rodgers, and others. Bluegrass was developed by Bill Monroe in the late 1930s in Kentucky. It is usually performed by four to seven people singing and accompanying themselves on acoustic stringed instruments including guitar, mandolin, fiddle, banjo, and bass.

blue note A **note** that is lowered (relative to the standard **pitches** of a Western **diatonic scale**) for expressive purposes in **blues** and blues-influenced music (including **jazz** and **rock and roll**), and in older genres thought to be ancestors or relatives of the blues (e.g., **waulking** songs of Scotland).

blues A musical genre and structure originating in African-American communities in the U.S. South in the early twentieth century. It evolved from other forms of secular and sacred song. The usual blues lyric is organized in a three-line **stanza**, with the second line being a repeat of the first. A blues is typically characterized by **blue notes**, often flatted thirds and sevenths.

blues scale A **scale**, commonly used in **blues** music, incorporating a flatted third, fifth, and/or seventh scalar degree (see **blue note**).

bodhrán A traditional Irish handheld **frame drum**.

bolo gbili The "heavier," older songs of a praise-song repertoire, which evoke the past through allusion to history and myths.

boîtes à chansons 'song clubs': the nightclubs that were the live venue of choice for performers during the period of the **chansonnier** movement of the 1950s and 1960s in Québec.

bola nguu One of two hummed parts (the other being *buli nguu*) sung by men during the performance of Fataleka narrative songs.

bolero A Cuban dance (based on an earlier form of the dance originating in Spain) and songform, characterized by distinctive, interlocking **rhythmic** patterns. It developed in Cuba in the 1850s and later spread to Mexico and elsewhere.

bomba A genre of Afro-Puerto Rican music and dance centered on *bomba* drums.

boogie-woogie A genre of fast tempo **blues**, originally performed on solo piano, that became popular in the 1930s. In later developments, it came to be played in full band contexts. Its distinctive shuffle is thought to be one of the main ingredients in the later **rock and roll**.

boomerang clapsticks An Australian **concussion** stick. Holding the center of a boomerang in each hand, a player taps the extremities of the boomerangs together, usually simultaneously, but sometimes rapidly alternating the taps at each end.

bòorii (also *bori*) Any of several Hausa groups organized around possession-trance performances.

bora Initiatory songs and rituals of the eastern Cape York area of Australia.

bossa nova A genre of Brazilian popular music developed in the late 1950s. While drawing on various traditions, the mellow sound of the guitar and the soft **percussion** highlighted complex principles of **rhythmic** organization, rather than visceral qualities.

bouzouki A long-necked plucked **lute** of Greek origin, usually having three or four pairs (**courses**) of strings. It is the principal instrument of the Greek *rebetika*. Since the 1960s it has been incorporated into Irish traditional music, both in Ireland and among Irish communities elsewhere.

branle A French courtly dance popular from the sixteenth to the late nineteenth centuries.

brass instrument A class of **aerophone** in which air is pushed into the resonating areas of the instrument by the vibration of the player's lips against each other, and often against a mouthpiece at the **proximal** end of the instrument. The instruments, despite the fact that they may be made of any number of different alloys, are called brasses, since in the European classical tradition they were usually made of brass.

break In **rhythm and blues**, disco, funk or **hip-hop** music, an instrumental interlude that focuses on **rhythmic** aspects of the music. As breaks are often the most rhythmically dynamic sections of a song, urban **DJs** in the 1970s, especially in the Bronx, began to isolate breaks on a given record and repeat them continuously—an important innovation leading to hip-hop music.

bubon A Ukrainian single-headed **frame drum** played with a small wooden mallet.

büchel A small Swiss **alphorn**, shaped in a coil (see also *grada büchel*).

bucium A Romanian style of **alphorn**.

buli A name for one vocal part in Fataleka **polyphonic** vocal music.

bullroarer A musical instrument found throughout the world. It is typically a wooden slat tied to a string or leather thong and whirled in the air to produce a sound like rushing wind.

Bulu series A *nurlu* series that consists of seventeen songs and three dances and is owned by George Dyunggayan, a Nyigina-speaker, who lived on pastoral stations near the lower Fitzroy River in Australia.

bumba-meu-boi A dramatic Afro-Brazilian dance that is the last dramatic dance of the *reisado* cycle.

bunggurl A public genre of song in Western Arnhem Land, Australia. The genre is often performed in ceremony alongside *wangga* and *lirrga* (see *manikai*).

buraambur A genre of classical Somali poetry of the *gabay* class.

Buru (or Burru) A traditional Jamaican drumming tradition. The individual drums used in Buru drumming are called Buru drums.

bylina (plural, *byliny*) (also *starina*, plural *stariny*) A Russian epic song, of about a thousand lines, using any of about a hundred different plots. *Byliny* were brought to Russia by itinerant musicians in the late Middle Ages and survived best in northern Russia. The style was mainly one of solo singing, but **choral** singing of *byliny* was common in parts of the north and among the Don and Terek Cossacks of southern Russia.

caboclo Music of the Brazilian **mestizo** culture of Native American and Portuguese heritages, especially in northeast Brazil.

cadence A **melody** or a sequence of **chords** that functions as the close of a musical section or **phrase**. It typically fosters a sensation of resolution, and in **tonal** music is typically a technical resolution of a **harmonic** progression back to the **tonic**.

cadential Characterized by the presence of a **cadence**.

café cantante 'singing café': any of numerous bars in Spain featuring performances of **flamenco**, found prominently in Madrid and Andalusia.

caixa A medium-sized drum commonly used in Afro-Brazilian and Roman Catholic traditions of dramatic music and dance.

cajón 'big box': a variably sized wooden-box **idiophone** with a hole in its back, commonly used by Afro-Peruvians. The performer sits atop the instrument and strikes it with both hands.

Cajun music A music developed by descendants of French-speaking settlers deported to Louisiana from Acadia, the Canadian Maritimes, during the eighteenth century. The word Cajun evolved from *Acadian*.

čalgija (also *çalgi*) A Macedonian, Albanian, and Serbian Romani urban professional ensemble.

calypso A genre of Afro-Caribbean music that evolved in Trinidad starting in the nineteenth century. It is typically vocal, and is today internationally prominent and well known.

canción 'song': (1) A general term for all kinds of vocal-based song throughout the Spanish-speaking world. (2) A complex of a wide variety of forms of Cuban song.

cancioneros A term used for various families or subcategories of folksong in Venezuela, the majority of which have a dominant Spanish influence.

canción ranchera A type of Mexican *son* linked to the rise of the popular media and to the popularity of folk-derived ensembles, such as the modern *mariachi*; sometimes informally called, "Mexican country songs."

canción romántica (1) A genre of nineteenth-century Mexican romantic song; (2) A genre of romantic popular song featured at the annual Gastón music festival in Managua, Nicaragua.

canción trovadoresca A Cuban genre created by singer-composers of Santiago de Cuba.

cantaduras (or *cantadurs*) Historic singing societies of the Romansh-speaking area of Switzerland.

cante chico 'small song': one of three types of Spanish **flamenco** singing, with a **rhythmic** structure less complex than that of the *cante jondo*.

cante intermedio 'intermediate song': one of three types of Spanish **flamenco** singing, a hybrid of *cante jondo* and forms from Spanish folk and popular music styles, especially the **fandango**.

cante jondo 'deep song': one of the three types of Spanish **flamenco** singing, considered the oldest and most serious.

canto epico-lirici A genre of Italian **ballad**, found mostly in north Italy.

canto lirico-monostrofici A genre of Italian **lyric song**, common south of the Apennines.

cantoria (1) A genre of Brazilian secular song of the northeast, sung by singer-bards; (2) Brazilian folksinging usually involving an improvised duel, also known as *desafio*.

capoeira An Afro-Brazilian game-dance. From a game-fight believed to have been practiced by slaves during resting periods in the fields, it developed into a martial art with subtle choreographic movements and rules.

carib-berie (see **corroboree**)

carnaval (English: 'carnival') A secular celebration before Lent in Brazil and throughout most of Hispanic America, and an occasion for the performance and development of many musical styles.

carole A French dance tradition that emerged from medieval ring dances and chain dances.

cassuto A musical scraper, played particularly by Kumbundu-speakers of Angola.

cayaar A major class of Somali poetry and performance that includes dance-songs, often with topical subjects.

céilí Irish domestic evening entertainment and visiting, when friends and neighbors gather to drink, sing, dance, tell stories, and play.

céilí band A large Irish dance band with fiddles, **flutes**, **accordions**, piano, and drum.

cha-cha-chá (or *chachachá*) A Cuban dance-music genre created during the 1950s. The term imitates a **rhythm** prominent in the music, the sound of dancers tapping their shoes on the floor.

chanson (1) 'Song', in French; (2) A Québécois genre of vocal music, usually sung by men, which was extremely influential in the 1950s and 1960s. It treated subject matters associated with a rising sense of national, cultural, and secular Québécois identity.

chanson de danse (also *chanson en laisse*) A French **strophic** song, consisting of one or more lines of six to sixteen syllables.

chanson en laisse (see *chanson de danse*)

chansonnier 'Song-maker': a singer, usually male, of *chanson* with lyrics closely associated with a rising sense of national, cultural, and secular Québécois identity in the 1950s and 1960s.

charanga (also *charanga típica*, or *charanga francesa*) (1) A Cuban ensemble combining piano, violin, and **flute** with **percussion**; (2) (or *charanga-vallenato*) A subgenre of Colombian *vallenato*.

charango (1) In the Andes of Argentina, Bolivia, and southern Peru, a small guitar made of wood or an armadillo shell with eight to fifteen metal or nylon strings tuned in five **courses**; (2) Bolivian small plucked **lute** with four or five double courses; (3) Ecuadorian small six-stringed plucked lute with double courses.

charikanari A Garifuna processional dance of Belize featuring stock characters.

chastushka 'short ditty': a Russian instrumental-vocal genre in short, single-stanza couplets accompanied by an **accordion** or a *balalaika*.

chegança Brazilian dances celebrating Portuguese maritime exploits.

Chicago-style polka A continuation of the more rural tradition of **polka** from Eastern Europe (compare **Eastern-style polka**), as fostered and nurtured in a Chicago-based North American tradition.

chicha (also *cumbia andina*) A distinctly Peruvian variant of *cumbia* that joined Colombian *cumbia* rhythms to highland *huayno* melodies.

Child ballad Any of a repertoire of popular English and Scottish traditional **ballads**, first systematically collected by Francis James Child (1825–1896). Child ballads typically have short, usually four-phrase **melodies**. The term *Child ballad* encompasses American variants, and among the original collection were American songs originating ultimately from the British Isles.

chimurenga 'song of liberation': any **mbira**-derived song related to the uprising in Rhodesia (now Zimbabwe) or to modern Shona political processes in Zimbabwe.

chiriguano A large Peruvian **panpipe**.

chitarra (or *chitara*) 'Guitar', in Romanian and Italian.

chitarra battente 'Beaten guitar' (Italian): a central and southern Italian guitar, played with a **plectrum** to accompany singing.

choir (or **chorus**) An ensemble of singers.

choral Having a musical texture that includes a **choir** or choirs.

chord A set of three or more distinct **tones**, performed simultaneously or in rapid succession. Chords are conventionally thought of as simultaneously performed tones that are at consonant **intervals** to each other (see **consonance**).

chordophone The general category of musical instruments in which a string or strings stretched tightly over a rigid support vibrate, thus creating sound.

chorões 'weepers': strolling Brazilian street musicians.

chorus (1) The repeated section of a **strophic** song, which often (but not always) has identical text, **melody**, **rhythm**, etc., during each repetition. It is often known as the **refrain**, and is conventionally considered to be the central component of a strophic song, with the **verses** serving as elaborations; (2) (or **choir**) An ensemble of singers.

chromatic Consisting of **semitone** intervals; i.e., based on the *chromatic scale*, a **scale** consisting of twelve semitone intervals to the **octave** (compare **diatonic**).

ch'unchu A Bolivian caricature dance.

churuq A vocal dance-song genre of the Yapese.

chürürüti In Garifuna ritual and performance, a thirty- to forty-five-minute period of the drumming, singing, occasional playing of a *sisira* (container rattle), and dancing.

cimbál A large hammered **dulcimer** of eastern Moravia and Slovakia.

cimbalom The informal name for a trapezoidal struck **zither**, of Hungary and Romania, used for **accompaniment** and as a solo instrument. Its more formal name is *ţambal*. The instrument is thought to be a possible ancestor of the modern *hammered dulcimer* (see **dulcimer**).

cîntece Any of numerous Romanian **strophic** songs with two to seven melodic lines that vary regionally in structure and style.

circular breathing A technique in which a performer inhales through the nose while exhaling through the mouth so as to produce a continuous stream of sound; used primarily by players of **wind instruments**.

clansong A song owned by a clan; in Aboriginal Australia, a song created by totemic ancestral spirits (see **totem**) and performed publicly to celebrate the spirits' activities.

clapsticks In Aboriginal Australia, a concussed pair of sticks or boomerangs (see **concussion**).

clave 'key': (1) A basic Afro-Cuban **rhythmic** pattern underlying a great majority of **Afro-Cuban music**; (2) In Cuba and other Latin American areas, two hardwood dowels struck together to make a sound (i.e., to mark the *clave*, the basic underlying **rhythm**); (3) A nineteenth-century song genre composed by the members of "clave choirs," organizations devoted to the production of new music.

cobza A Romanian plucked short-necked **lute**.

čoček A dance of south Serbian and Macedonian Gypsies.

coconut A dance of poorer people in northern and northeastern Brazil.

743

comparsa A characteristic Cuban dance and its accompanying music, with a strong symbolic and **rhythmic** origin in Afro-Caribbean slaves' rituals, performed during *carnaval*.

complainte A **Cajun** genre of long, melancholy story-songs inherited from the Acadian people, sung particularly at evening parties called *veillées*.

composition (1) A musical piece whose primary form is predetermined, not improvised, often written down; (2) The process of creating a musical piece.

conchero A Nahua dance accompanied by an armadillo-shell guitar, also called by the same name.

concussion The act of striking one part of an object against another part of itself, or one of two paired similar objects against the other (e.g. two similarly sized wooden blocks), thus producing a sound (compare **percussion**).

concussive idiophone An **idiophone** made to sound by the action of one part against another, as with **clapsticks**, paired stones, and castanets (compare **percussive idiophone**).

conga (also *tumbadora*) A tall, barrel-shaped, single-headed Cuban drum of African origin. Perhaps the central drum in **Afro-Cuban music**, it is now used throughout Latin America and the world.

conjunto 'combo': (1) A general term used throughout the Spanish-speaking world to denote musical ensembles that play any of many musical genres; (2) In Texas, synonymous with *conjunto tejano*, the accordion-driven Texas–Mexican ensemble.

conjunto jíbaro A Puerto Rican ensemble principally for performing *música jíbara*, with instruments including the ten-steel-stringed *cuatro* guitar, the six-stringed "standard" Spanish guitar, and the *güiro* 'gourd scraper'.

conjunto norteño A northern Mexican ensemble, similar to the Texan *conjunto*.

conjunto típico The Panamanian ensemble that performs *música típica*, music with a Spanish influence.

consonance (1) An **interval** that is conventionally considered to be stable and sonorous, with no need for resolution; (2) The general presence of sonority or **harmonic** stability in a piece of music.

container rattle A rattle that contains seed or other small objects that produce sound when the instrument is shaken.

contradanza (1) A Cuban genre with French origins, belonging to the *danzón* family; (2) A Guarijio song-dance in duple **meter** with a triple subdivision (6/8).

cool jazz A restrained form of **jazz** that emerged in the late 1940s on both coasts of the United States but became associated primarily with the West Coast. With its fluid character, mellow **dynamics**, and intricately contrived **harmonic** structures, it came to be heard as an antidote to the wild, fast, energetic **improvisations** of bebop.

copla 'couplet': (1) A short poetic unit in Spanish, often of three-to-five lines; i.e. a **verse** or **stanza**; (2) A genre of Spanish poem or song (typically of a narrative nature) with eight-syllable lines; (3) A Spanish-derived genre of sung poetry that became, in Mexico, one of the bases for *son*.

copla de seguidilla (also *cuarteta*) A Spanish metric songform.

corrido A Mexican folk **ballad** and **strophic** song stemming from the Spanish *romance* tradition, with lyrics structured in the format of the *copla* song (i.e. featuring sets of *coplas* (stanzas) with eight-syllable lines).

corroboree (also *carib-berie*) An Aboriginal Australian nocturnal festivity with singing and dancing.

counterpoint The relationship between multiple lines of music that may be **rhythmically** independent from one another but are **harmonically** interdependent.

country music A form of U.S. popular music associated with the Southeast and rural Midwest. It is generally characterized by an emotive and highly ornamented singing-style, an instrumental **accompaniment** that relies heavily on small ensembles of stringed instruments, and a repertoire that has been derived from and influenced by a **ballad** tradition that accompanied Scottish and Irish immigrants into the Southeast in the nineteenth century (compare **bluegrass**).

course (of strings) In a **chordophone**, a group of two or more strings placed closely together and designed to be played simultaneously. They are typically tuned to the same **note** or in **octaves** in such instruments as the twelve-string guitar (which has six courses of two strings each).

Creole (1) Affiliated with a Louisianan culture and people of an origin that is both French-speaking and racially mixed; (2) (*creole*) A hybrid language that emerges as a new and distinct idiom from two or more distinct source languages.

Creole music A loose affiliation of musical styles practiced by French and Caribbean settlers in the U.S. gulf-states, characterized by syncopated **rhythms**.

criolla 'Creole': (1) Cuban urban genre with rural themes, belonging to the *canción* family; (2) *criollas*, Uruguayan societies whose principal objective is the preservation of traditional rural festivals.

csárdás (see *czardas*)

cuarteta (also *copla de seguidilla*) A Spanish metric songform.

cuatro 'four': (1) A four-stringed small guitar originally from Venezuela and diffused to Colombia, Grenada, Trinidad, and other areas near Venezuela; (2) A Puerto Rican guitar with five **courses** of two strings each; it is Puerto Rico's national instrument.

cumbia The best-known Afro-Colombian popular music. Modern popular cumbia is a synthesis of Caribbean traditional musics, featuring complex **polyrhythms**, voices, and **flutes**, including the traditional, folkloric *cumbia*. Modern cumbia has proved immensely popular in Colombia and other Latin American countries, particularly Mexico, the Andean nations, and Argentina.

cununa 'the wreath': (1) A traditional feast at the end of the harvest in Transylvania, Romania; (2) A song genre that is an important accompaniment to portions of a wedding ritual in Romania.

cyas A Jamaican Kumina ceremonial drum.

czardas (or *csárdás*) A Hungarian dance in duple **meter** in which dancers start slowly and finish in vivacious whirls.

dafael' A Yapese song of love, and a genre of *tang*.

dajre (also *daire*) An Albanian, Macedonian, and Bulgarian single-headed **frame drum**.

dāliga 'above': a Huli term used to describe relative **pitch**.

danbolin A Basque snare drum.

dancehall A Jamaican popular music that developed around 1979, featuring a vocalist (or **DJ**) **rapping** (or "toasting") and singing over a dance-oriented, typically electronic **rhythm**. Though it is often considered a form of **reggae** (and is often called "dancehall reggae," especially by people outside Jamaica), purists debate whether it should be so considered (see *ragga*).

dandi A stick- and hand-beaten drum in a **mbira** ensemble that plays **improvisations**.

danzón A Cuban instrumental dance genre; the national dance of Cuba.

décima (1) A Spanish and Hispanic-American song containing ten-line **stanzas**, eight syllables per stanza, and a set **rhythmic** scheme; (2) A sung genre for courtship or expression of religious and social commentary.

desafío An Iberian song duel (see *cantoria*).

dhaanto A class of Somali poetry and song performance that varies highly in meaning depending on the area of the country. In some areas *dhaanto* is synonymous with the larger class of **cayaar** poetry, while in other areas the term is more accurately seen as a sub-class of *cayaar*.

dhikr (also *zikr*; and, in Turkey and some portions of North Africa, *zikir*) A portion of **Sufi** acts of worship: the regular chanting of a sacred phrase (usually a name or description of Allah), typically accompanied by regular body movements. It involves what Western ears hear as musical elements, but the emphasis is on the repetition of divine names and the recitation of sacred texts.

diatonic A term describing music that utilizes the **tones** found in a **diatonic scale**.

diatonic scale Any seven-note **scale** (eight counting the **octave**), with either a whole-tone or **semitone** interval between consecutive **pitches** (and always including both whole-tone and semitone intervals), used commonly in Western music. In a diatonic scale, each letter name is used for only one **tone** (for example, the C major scale is C–D–E–F–G–A–B–C). The major scale and the natural minor scale are examples of diatonic scales.

didjeridu A wooden trumpet, usually about 1 to 1.5 meters long, played mainly by Aborigines of northern Australia.

dìndiha 'underneath': A Huli term used to describe relative **pitch**.

dìndanao tàbage The long-shaped Huli **kundu** that sounds *dìndiha*, or 'underneath', and is played only by male mediums.

disc jockey (*DJ*) A person who selects, announces and/or plays prerecorded music over the radio, at a discotheque, or at an outdoor party or other event. In modern **hip-hop**, **reggae**, party, and club contexts, the DJ's art has evolved far beyond the simple playback of recorded material and now may typically involve manipulation and interaction with pre-recorded music, to create a performance.

dissonance (1) An **interval** that is conventionally considered to be unstable, unpleasant or unharmonious, with a need for resolution to a more aurally pleasing interval, or **consonance**; (2) The general presence of unpleasant sonority or **harmonic** instability in a piece of music.

distal Far from a point of reference: in particular, the portion of a musical instrument farthest from the sound-making source. For instance, in the case of **brass instruments**, the distal end is the "bell" out of which sound exits the instrument (compare **proximal**).

dit A song genre sung in the morning by the Eipo women of New Guinea. The texts are stories, often involving sexual liaisons, but may treat other subjects.

DJ (see **disc jockey**)

djalkmi A **clansong** style of Central Arnhem Land, Australia, in which voices, **clapsticks** and **didjeridu** follow a fixed **meter** (compare *ngarkana*).

djanba A public genre of song and dance that originated in the Kimberley area of Australia. The genre is often performed alongside such other common genres as *wangga* and *lirrga*.

djatpangarri (also *djedbangari*) Often called "fun songs," these are **didjeridu**-accompanied songs sung by young unmarried men, especially in Northeastern Arnhem Land, Australia. The texts use mainly "nonsense" words or syllables, but the songs are associated with everyday topics. Most *djatpangarri* follow the same melodic pattern.

djembe A goblet-shaped hand drum originating in West Africa and popular throughout the world.

doina (also *hora lunga*) A Romanian improvised lyrical song genre.

dòmbena (or *tòmbena*) 'In-between': A Huli term used to describe relative **pitch**.

dosvitky A Ukrainian social gathering for unmarried girls to sew, embroider, sing, and dance.

Draumkvædet The most famous sacred Norwegian **ballad**. A medieval visionary poem, it combines popular Christian (pre-Reformation) beliefs with mystic elements from earlier Norse religion.

dreaming (also *dreamtime*) The realm of Aboriginal Australians' ancestral and totemic (see **totem**) spirits, accessible in dreams.

drone A sustained musical **tone**, chord, or pattern of tones, against which one or more melodic parts may move.

druku In a **meke**, a **choral** bass part that harmonizes with the high solo parts *laga* and *tagica*.

dub A genre of music of Jamaican origin that consists of, essentially, instrumental versions of vocal recordings, typically with extra instrumentation and effects added. Dub versions began to appear on the B-sides of single records in the late 1960s in Jamaica, which generally featured the vocal version of the song on the A-side. Dubs were an important component in the prehistory of **hip-hop**, as Jamaican **DJs** playing dub records in public began to improvise words over the records (see **toasting**).

duct flute (also *fipple flute*) An end-blown **flute** in which air is blown across the blade-like edge of a hole.

dügü (also *adügürühani*) A Garifuna funereal ceremony, and an occasion for the most extensive Garifuna sacred music.

dulcimer Either of two types of folk **zither**: (1) The Appalachian lap dulcimer, a slender strummed instrument with three or four strings (see also the related **plucked dulcimer**); (2) The much rarer hammered dulcimer, a trapezoidal stringed instrument with several dozen pairs of strings and played with light, handheld hammers, descended from the Persian-Indian *santūr* (see glossary for volume 2) or Hungarian *cimbalom*.

dumy A genre of Cossack Ukrainian heroic epic songs.

dùndún A double-headed, hourglass-shaped, Yorùbá pressure drum, which can reproduce the glides of Yorùbá speech; a symbol of pan-Yorùbá identity (compare *gángan*).

duru A Yorùbá two-stringed plucked **lute**.

dynamics The relative loudness or softness of volume in a piece of music.

Eastern-style polka A continuation of the more urban tradition of **polka** from Eastern Europe (compare **Chicago-style polka**), as fostered and nurtured by musicians throughout the U.S. Eastern seaboard.

ehona Songs sung by men to the **accompaniment** of a bamboo **idiophone** on the occasion of a *hiri*.

enda lakungi Songs of courtship sung at courtship parties by adolescent boys of the Enga people of Papua New Guinea.

erhu A low-pitched two-stringed Chinese fiddle.

escobillada An Afro-Peruvian dance technique in which the foot is brushed along the floor or the ground.

fa'atete A short Tahitian drum, played with two sticks, used to accompany dancing.

fadista The vocal soloist in Portuguese *fado* music, and the dominant musical performer.

fado A genre of urban vocal song performed by a solo vocalist accompanied by one to four guitarists. It emerged in the poor neighborhoods of Lisbon between 1825 and 1850 as a synthesis of song-and-dance genres already popular in Lisbon and newly imported genres, many from Brazil.

fado cançãdo 'song fado': modern *fado* whose songs have a structure of **stanzas** and **refrains**, more complex **harmonic** structures than those of *fado castiço*, fixed **melodies**, and flexible patterns of **accompaniment**.

fado castiço 'authentic fado': the older genre of *fado*. Its songs have fixed **rhythmic** and **harmonic** schemes (usually I–V–I) and patterns of **accompaniment**; performers, however, usually perform composed or improvised **melodies**.

fāgono A Sāmoan tale, performed by a storyteller. Sung sections (*tagi*) have more rigorously defined structures than spoken sections.

faiva A genre of sung speech with choreographed movements prominent in the Polynesian kingdom of Tonga. *Faiva* usually occur during ceremonial occasions featuring the performance of music and structured movements as verbal, **rhythmic**, and visual theater.

fakatapu The introductory section of a *lakalaka*.

falsetto A singing technique designed to enable a singer to produce **pitches** higher than those of his or her normal range (though pitches in the normal range may also be sung in falsetto voice). It is lighter and less powerful than the normal "chest voice."

fandango An animated Spanish, Portuguese, and Basque music and dance form in triple time, closely associated with the Spanish province of Andalucía. The dance is typically performed by a woman and a man. Many scholars believe it to be derived from the *jota*.

fangufangu A Tongan nose **flute**, used for recreation and to awaken a high-ranking person.

fasi In Tongan **polyphony**, the leading part or **melody**, usually sung by men; first described in the eighteenth century, and often conceptualized as fitting with a lower part (*laulalo*).

fātele A Tokelauan song with interpretive movements, adapted in Kiribati as the *bātere*.

festejo An Afro-Peruvian musical form, often interrupted at **phrase** endings by a sudden pause or a long, held **tone**.

final The **tone** on which a **melody** ends.

fiðla An ancient Norwegian **lyre** or **harp** (see *harpa*).

fipple flute (see **duct flute**)

flamenco A music-and-dance tradition originating in Andalusia in Southern Spain, typically featuring guitars, singing, and distinctive, stomping dance. It is traditionally associated with the Roma of Southern Spain (see *Rom*) but may also have an Arabic influence.

flügelhorn A **brass instrument** with three valves. It resembles a trumpet or a cornet, but has a shorter body than either instrument. It has wider tubing and produces a fuller, more mellow sound than a trumpet or cornet.

fluier A Romanian six-holed **duct flute**.

flute A generally high-pitched, reedless **wind instrument**, in which sound is produced by air blown by the player across a soundhole.

folk spiritual The earliest form of black religious music to develop in the United States; a late-eighteenth-century creation.

forró (1) A Brazilian social dance-music; (2) A *caboclo* dance parry of Brazil; (3) An accordion-based dance music of northeast Brazil, derived from *baião*.

fotuto An archaic Colombian gourd, shell, or wooden trumpet.

frame drum A drum in which membrane(s) are stretched over a light, usually circular frame (see **membranophone**).

free jazz A movement among **jazz** musicians that commenced in the early 1960s and was inspired by the work of Ornette Coleman, John Coltrane, Cecil Taylor, and others. The music of free jazz featured a dissonant **harmonic** style (see **dissonance**) and the abandonment of fixed harmonic changes as a means of organizing **improvisation**.

frequency The number of times that a complete vibration occurs per a unit of time (typically seconds). In sound, frequency is the primary element that determines our perception of **pitch**.

frevo (1) Brass-band carnival march-music and dance-music from Recife, Pernambuco, Brazil; (2) An electrified version of same in Salvador, Bahia.

frevo-canção A kind of *frevo* song developed for middle-class carnival balls in private clubs in the 1930s in Recife, Brazil. It features an instrumental introduction inspired by the *frevo de rua*, followed by a solo song with choral **refrains**.

frevo de bloco A form of Brazilian *frevo* music, catering to a middle-class sensibility, which was developed around 1915 as a response to the unfavorable, violent reputation of the *frevo de rua* among the middle and upper classes. The *frevo de bloco* is distinguished from the *frevo de rua* by lighter instrumentation, the inclusion of a female **chorus**, slower **tempo**, frequent use of the minor **mode**, and lyrical textual sentimentality.

frevo de rua 'street frevo': a kind of *frevo* music that originated in the early 1900s in carnival clubs of urban laborers in Recife, Brazil. It was a loud street-band music, heavy on **brasses**, winds, and **percussion**, typically in a fast duple **meter**.

friction block An **idiophone**, found in Melanesia and other areas, having usually three tongues that when rubbed make a piercing sound.

frottoir A metallic washboard played with thimbles, spoons, forks, or bottle openers, that is an essential **rhythm** instrument in **zydeco** music. It and instruments like it are also used in **Cajun music**.

frottola (plural, *frottole*) Any of numerous northern Italian secular songs of the late fifteenth and early sixteenth centuries. It was an important and widespread predecessor of the **madrigal**.

fu Trumpet played during and after headhunting raids by the Asmat people of Merauke Province, Papua New Guinea.

fuga (or *qawachan*) 'flight': a coda or closing section found at the end a number of Andean musical genres. It consists of a theme that contrasts with that of the main body of the piece, and is played at a faster **tempo**.

fújì The most popular Yorùbá musical genre of the early 1990s, using a lead singer, a **chorus**, and drummers; a development from *ajísáàrì*.

fulia A drum-accompanied Venezuelan **responsorial** song genre.

fundamental The component of a musical sound having the lowest **frequency** and upon which a series of **overtones** may be based.

fundeh A Jamaican single-headed **membranophone** played with the hands.

furiant A triple-**meter** Bohemian dance with alternating duple and triple accentual patterns.

gabay Somali poetry that deals with politics, war, peace, and social debate; the term may refer to a class of poetry, with numerous subclasses, and is the name of one of the subclasses itself.

gaita A **bagpipe** of northern Spain.

gajda A Bulgarian and Macedonian **bagpipe**.

gamal' A Yapese dance characterized by sets of four paired dancers, who face each other and sing until their movements become too vigorous, at which point another singer or group supplements or replaces them.

gammeldans 'old-time dance-music': music that developed as Swedish urban folklore in the 1920s.

gāmu Magic-controlling recitations performed by male and female Huli, people of the Southern Highlands Province of Papua New Guinea.

ganga (plural, *gangatan*) (1) A double-headed cylindrical drum played in Niger to herald the beginning and end of Ramadan; (2) A small, double-headed, handheld Tuareg drum.

gángan A Yorùbá "talking drum" (compare *dùndún*).

garamut A class of hollowed **log idiophone** played especially in the Mamose and Island areas of Papua New Guinea.

Log idiophones are played elsewhere in Oceania, but are not called *garamuts* in those places.

garawoun A Garifuna single-headed cylindrical drum in Belize, in a set with distinctions **primero** and **segunda**.

gáwa A two-stringed, orally resonated, strummed bow, through which Huli performers (of Papua New Guinea) articulate spontaneously created poetry. Played by both men and women, the instrument has a soft, clear, shimmering sound. The Huli consider its performance the supreme artistic achievement.

gèla A Huli *ìwa* (**yodel**) performed in the public processions of fertility rituals and initiations.

ghaita A Moroccan and North African oboe.

Ghost Dance A revivalist movement that sprang up among the Paiute people in the 1880s, in which believers received songs while in trancelike states induced by a rapidly accelerating dance. It spread rapidly, particularly across the Great Plains, as some native Americans eagerly believed that participation in it would bring back the world as it had been before the white invasion: the buffalo would return and whites would disappear.

glissando (plural, *glissandi*) A sliding movement made through a succession of ascending or descending **pitches** to a final **tone** or **chord**, with pitches in between also clearly sounding. With keyboard instruments, the effect is produced by sliding one or more fingers rapidly over the keys. A similar effect can be produced on a **harp** and some other stringed instruments by sliding the fingers across a succession of strings.

glottal stop (1) During vocalization, the interruption of the breath by closure of the glottis (the space between the vocal cords); (2) A typographical symbol representing this action.

goje (also *goge*, *gòjé*) (1) A one-stringed Hausa bowed **lute** with a resonating hole in the membrane, not the body; (2) A single-stringed Yorùbá bowed lute, made of a calabash and covered with skin.

goombay (1) A primarily sung dance-music of the Bahamas, with lyrics that address current affairs or extol male sexual prowess or libido; it is often confused internationally with **calypso**; (2) A Bahamian single-headed **frame drum**, associated with the music of the same name.

Goombeh (1) An African-based Jamaican cult; (2) *goombeh*, Jamaican square goatskin **frame drum** played with the fingers, considered male.

gora A Khoikhoi bow instrument of southern Africa in which a musician blows onto a feather to vibrate the string attached to the bow. Variations in blowing make the instrument bring out different **tones** of the **harmonic** series (compare *lesiba*).

gospel music A specific genre of predominantly vocal music with lyrics based on Christian scripture and evangelical ideas developed by African Americans. It evolved out of such genres as the **folk spiritual** in the early twentieth century and is associated with increased urbanization. It uses musical structures and styles associated with the **blues**, **country music**, and many other historical and contemporary genres.

grace note A melodically inessential **note** added as an embellishment. In written music, a grace note is printed in small type to show that it is not counted as taking up any time in relation to the current **measure**; when played, it must necessarily take time from the note that it embellishes.

grada büchel A long Swiss **alphorn** with a curved bell, carved from a fir-tree trunk and wrapped in birch bark (see ***büchel***).

griot A West African musical specialist, usually a custodian of important historical and cultural knowledge.

groaner A male solo bass singer, typically backed by a female ***simanjemanje*** in South African ***mbaqanga*** music.

grupo A keyboard-based hybrid Tejano ensemble that emerged in the 1960s. It had roots in both ***conjunto*** and ***orquesta*** instrumentation.

guaguancó A Cuban couple-dance genre belonging to the ***rumba*** family.

guajira A Cuban genre of the ***canción*** complex. The texts of the ***guajira*** center on the beauty of the countryside and pastoral life.

gudok (also ***guduk***) A Russian three-stringed, pear-shaped, bowed **lute** made of one piece of wood.

gudulka (in Macedonia, ***kemene***) A Bulgarian pear-shaped bowed **lute** with three or four metal playing strings and about eight sympathetic strings.

guitarra de golpe (see ***jarana***)

guitarra portuguesa A Portuguese guitar with a pear-shaped soundboard and six double **courses** of metal strings.

guitarrista 'Guitarist', in Spanish and Portuguese.

guitarrón 'large guitar': (1) A Mexican bass guitar with rounded back, used in ***mariachi*** groups; (2) A low-pitched, large-sized Spanish guitar.

gùlungùlu (also ***ngùlungùlu***) A rare, long, seven-piped variety of Huli bamboo bundle **panpipe**, whose longest pipe may reach up to 90 centimeters (compare ***gùlupòbe***, ***pùlugèla***).

gùlupòbe A common, medium-sized, seven-piped variety of Huli bamboo bundle **panpipe**, whose longest pipe measures about 60 centimeters (compare ***gùlungùlu***, ***pùlugèla***).

gumleaf An Australian single-reed **aerophone** made from the leaves of local eucalyptus trees or shrubs.

gumleaf band A musical band created as a response to Christian evangelization in the late 1800s among detribalized Aboriginal peoples of southeastern Australia. The bands used gumleaves as an instrument to play European hymns, American **gospel** songs, popular music, and classical music.

gusli A Russian plucked **zither**.

ha'a A system and collection of structured movements of ancient Hawai'i. It was utilized to perform ritual movements in outdoor temples. Today it has been subsumed into the modern ***hula*** system.

habanera A nineteenth-century Cuban song form and dance form, featuring a slow to moderate duple **meter** and a characteristic **rhythm**. Its name reflects its origins in Havana, from where it spread to Spain, Europe, and throughout Latin America.

hackbrett (plural, ***hackbretter***) A Swiss and northern Italian trapezoidal struck **zither**, mainly of Appenzell and the Goms Valley, Upper Valais.

hadra A large North African ceremonial celebration of Muhammad's birthday or any other appropriate

occasion; though the ***hadra*** takes many forms, it typically includes special songs and **rhythms**, rigorous dancing, and an element of the supernatural.

haka One of three main kinds of Māori dance.

haka peruperu A vigorous, bellicose ***haka*** of the Māori people of Aotearoa, performed with weapons.

haka poi A dance of Māori women of Aotearoa, performed with a ball (***poi***) attached to a string. Swinging, whirling, and catching the ball demonstrates the performers' agility. Each performer may manipulate multiple ***poi***.

haka taparahi A vigorous, bellicose ***haka*** dance of the Māori people of Aotearoa, performed without weapons.

harawi (or ***hamui***, ***wanka***) A pre-Columbian Incan nostalgic **monophonic** love song genre that still persists among Andean peasantry. It consists of one musical **phrase** repeated several times with extensive melismatic (see **melisma**) passages and long glissandi (see **glissando**).

hard bop A **jazz** style that developed out of **bebop** in the mid-1950s. Where hard bop differed from bebop was in its greater incorporation of **rhythm and blues**, **blues** and **gospel** influences.

hardingfele A Norwegian violin, modified to have four sympathetic strings.

harmoniia A Ukrainian free-reed, button **accordion** (see ***baian***).

harmonic (1) An **overtone** whose **frequency** is an exact multiple of that of the **fundamental**. Any fundamental has a series of harmonics: the first harmonic, the second, and so on; (2) Functioning as a harmony, particularly when accompanying a **melody**.

harmonium Keyboard instrument of Western origin. Air pumped by a **bellows** through freely vibrating reeds generates the sound; the player pumps the bellows with one hand while playing the keys with the other. Earlier versions of the instrument used foot pedals to control the bellows.

harmony That aspect of music which is concerned with the simultaneous performance of distinct tones and their relationships to each other. Often conceived of as one of the three main components of music, with **melody** and **rhythm**.

harp A **chordophone** with plucked strings perpendicular to the soundboard. There are many varieties of harp found all throughout the world.

harpsichord A Western European keyboard instrument, dating from as early as the late Middle Ages. It has strings plucked by plectra (traditionally quills), engaged by the action of the keys. The instrument, still in use today, is one of the predecessors of the modern piano.

heello Youth-controlled Somali poetry, often treating political themes.

hees A Somali work-accompanying song.

heliaki In Tongan verbal expression, indirectness or veiled meaning, considered by Tongans a desirable aesthetic quality (compare ***kaona***).

hemiola The performance of two sounds of equal duration in the time occupied by three metrical pulses, or the performance of three sounds of equal duration in the time occupied by two metrical pulses.

hera (or *munyonga, matepe, madhebhe*) A **mbira** played by the Korekore people of Zimbabwe. This instrument has about twenty-nine narrow keys, played with both thumbs and both forefingers. In comparison with other forms of mbira, its music is much faster and has lower bass **notes** but a lighter sound, and its **rhythms** are more complex.

heterophony The musical texture characterized by the simultaneous performance of variations of the same **melody** (compare **polyphony**).

hexachord A sequence of six **tones** that function as a **scale**, which served as the basis of much music theory in Europe during the Middle Ages. The two middle **tones** are separated by the **interval** of a **semitone**, while all other intervals in the scale are whole tones. Hexachords have been widely used in modern twelve-tone theory.

highlife A genre of West African popular music that originated in present-day Ghana in the early 1900s. It features clarinets, trumpets, cornets, baritones, trombones, tuba, and parade drums.

hīmene (or *hīmeni, īmene, ʻīmene*) From French *hymne* or English *hymn*, a class of East Polynesian **choral** singing, originally combining indigenous musical textures with European harmonies and now perceived as an original cultural expression.

hīmene tārava A genre of French Polynesian **choral** singing, distinguished by a drawn-out **cadence** at the end of **stanzas**. The number and musical contents of vocal parts vary from **choir** to choir.

hīmene tuki A genre of **choral** singing that Tahitians identify as originating in the Cook Islands. As performed in the Society Islands, *hīmene tuki* have two vocal parts, the **melody** performed by women, and a gruntlike part performed by men.

hip-hop (1) Beginning in the early 1970s, a primarily black and Latino street culture comprising **rap** music, **break** dancing, graffiti, a distinctive mode of fashion, and more; (2) A form of primarily African-American spoken-word music; one element of hip-hop culture. Also known as **rap**.

hira gasy An **improvisational** theatrical form most representative of the Malagasy highlands in Madagascar.

hiri An occasion in which men of the Motu people of southern New Guinea engage in a long-distance voyage for the purpose of trading goods.

hiva kakala A genre of Tongan popular song, the Tongan musical genre most often composed and sung. Examples of *hiva kakala* are usually played and sung by gatherings of men or women or both, forming **stringbands** of ʻukuleles and guitars; sometimes a bass, electronic keyboards, violins, and accordions are added. The genre may be accompanied by dance.

hoʻāeāe A Hawaiian style of singing with sustained **pitch** and patterned **vibratos**, locally deemed appropriate for love-making songs.

hocket A musical technique in which a **melody** line is performed by several voices or instruments in such a way that, while one voice or instrument plays, the other(s) is (are) silent. In this way, the melody proceeds, performed by one voice/instrument at a time.

homophonic Characterized by **homophony**.

homophony Multipart music that features a **melody** supported by an **accompaniment**. In homophonic music, the accompanying voices usually have weak melodic identity and little independence from the melody they accompany. Homophony is distinct from **polyphony**, in which each part retains independence as a separate melodic line.

hoʻouwēuwē A Hawaiian style of singing with prolonged sustained **pitch** and patterned **vibrato** locally deemed appropriate for laments and funerary dirges.

hosho A Shona seed-filled gourd rattle that accompanies singing, *mbira dzavadzimu* ensembles, and **panpipes**.

huayno (also *wayno*) A popular central Andean song-dance genre. Usually in duple **meter**, it consists of a pair of musical **phrases** in periodic form (AABB). Like other Andean genres, it may have a closing section, called *fuga* or *qawachan*, which consists of a contrasting theme in a faster **tempo**.

huéhuetl A large Nahua single-headed cylindrical hollowed-out **log idiophone** of ancient origin, also used by the Maya.

hula ʻālaʻapapa (see *mele hula ʻālaʻapapa*)

hula ʻauana (see *mele hula ʻauana*)

hula kahiko (see *mele hula kahiko*)

hula kuʻi (see *mele hula kuʻi*)

hula pahu (see *mele hula pahu*)

humppa A style of Finnish music for dance that mixes **jazz**, fox-trot, **polka**, *rekilaulu*, and Russian romances.

hurdy-gurdy (also *wheel fiddle*) A **chordophone** of medieval European origin, resembling a violin and sounded by a cranked wheel which pass over the strings. **Pitch** is altered by keys that change the strings' vibrating length. Hurdy-gurdies typically have **drone** strings and **melody** strings.

idiophone A musical instrument (such as a rattle or chime) whose principal sound is the vibration of the primary material of the instrument itself.

ihara A bamboo struck **idiophone** of Tahiti.

ijexá Style, **rhythm**, and dance in Brazilian *afoxé* and Candomblé music.

improvisation (also, *extemporization*) An act of musical creation that occurs during performance, as opposed to the performance of content that is strictly determined (**precomposed**) in advance.

ingá An Afro-Peruvian novelty circle dance.

interval The distance in **pitch** between two different **tones**, measured in **semitones**.

ipu A Hawaiian gourd **idiophone**. The player grasps the gourd by its neck and alternately thumps it on the ground and slaps it on its side.

isicatamiya The step dancing of **choirs** of male Zulu workers. The term later became a standard name for the music and dance of Zulu workers' choirs.

itku 'cry, weep': the lament, one of the oldest Finnish song genres.

iwa A general name for all varieties of collective Huli **yodeling** performed by men.

jabâ A Tuareg **compositional** formula of recent origin, which serves for light entertainment and dancing, and praises youth and youthful pleasures.

jaleo The encouraging and admiring shouts of the audience in a Spanish **flamenco** performance.

Jamaican quadrille The most popular of the Jamaican variants of European ballroom dances in the nineteenth and early twentieth centuries. Historically, *mento* bands provided the music for quadrille dances.

Jankunú (see *wanaragua*)

jarabe 'Syrup': A Mexican *son* intended especially for dancing.

jarana A name for various Mexican and Nahua guitars (some of which are also called *guitarra de golpe*), encompassing a variety of shapes, sizes, **courses**, and strings.

jauje A Hausa double-headed hourglass-shaped tension drum.

jazz A music developed in the United States, primarily from **ragtime** and **blues**, probably in New Orleans around 1900. It quickly became a popular dance music, ultimately resulting in the big-band **swing** era of the 1930s. Jazz music gradually came to be defined as an **improvisational** music, dominated by instrumentalists who took turns improvising entire lengthy solos. Today, *jazz* encompasses a wide variety of styles, with **diatonic**, **pentatonic**, **chromatic**, and **atonal** harmonic structures.

jeli (plural, *jelilu*) A male verbal and musical praise-singing specialist of Sierra Leone, often employing the *bala* or the harp-lute for **accompaniment**.

jeliba A player of the *bala*.

jelimuso (also *jelimusolu*) Any Maninka woman who sings praise songs.

jig A lively Irish dance and musical genre, reflecting a Scottish influence.

jiifto A genre of Somali classical poetry, of the *gabay* class.

jodel (see *yodel*)

joropo A European-derived "national" couple-dance of Venezuela.

jota (1) An Aragonese couple-dance in quick triple time, accompanied by a castanet; (2) A Basque chain dance.

jouhikko A Finnish bowed **lyre**.

jùjú (1) A Yorùbá tambourine; (2) A Yorùbá musical genre originating in Lagos around 1932 that features a singer-banjoist, a *ṣẹ̀kẹ́rẹ́*, and a *jùjú*.

junkafunk The Bahamian musical group Bahamen's musical innovation of using *junkanoo* rhythms on modern electronic instruments.

junkanoo In the Bahamas, *goombay* music performed by acoustic instruments in *junkanoo* parades at Christmastide.

ka Highly stylized and expressively simple funeral songs of the Melpa of Western Highlands Province, Papua New Guinea.

ka'ara A **log idiophone** of the Cook Islands, made from a tree trunk.

kabary An important Malagasy ceremonial oration, which involves formulaic speech commonly addressed to the living and the ancestral dead, and made often at the outset of a ceremony.

kabosa (also *kabosy*) A plucked Malagasy **lute** played in Arabia from about 500 C.E. to about 1500 C.E.

kabuti A women's hip-shaking dance of Kiribati, consisting of two or three sections.

kachacha A Central African dance accompanied by the music of single-headed goblet-shaped drums and sometimes a two-note **xylophone**.

kadans A Haitian-derived musical genre of Martinique. Kadans makes subtle use of musical accents, **syncopation**, and instrumental color, derived from the mini-jazz orchestras of Haiti.

kāhea A recitation of the first line of text of a *mele hula*, which begins its performance.

kai The daytime dance equivalent to the *sia*.

kaiamba The most common percussive shaker played to accompany ceremonial Malagasy music.

kalangu A double-headed Hausa hourglass-shaped tension drum, associated with butchers and recreation.

Kalevala A Finno-Karelian epic, whose text historically was sung at social occasions from feasts and rituals to work and amusement.

kalon'ny fahiny An elite Malagasy musical form based largely upon European opera, yet still distinctively Malagasy. It uses dramatic themes from everyday experience, and in aural terms, incorporates a unique highly exaggerated vocal **vibrato**, especially in the upper register of women's voices.

kamei A Kiribati dance, performed by men or women and consisting of two or three sections.

kang rom A **ballad** of the Melpa people of Papua New Guinea.

kantele A Finnish and Karelian plucked **zither**, whose practice ceased in western Finland after the 1600s.

kaona Indirectness, an important Hawaiian aesthetic value. In poetry, *kaona* may involve layers of veiled or hidden meaning (compare *heliaki*).

katajjaq An Inuit game played in the eastern arctic, in which two women standing face to face repeatedly utter predetermined sound patterns—words, animal cries, or melodic fragments. Their voices—alternating among a variety of vocal qualities, including producing sung sounds while inhaling—follow each other in sequence.

kaunikai A formal competition of singing and dancing between rival troupes within Kiribati society (see *kaunimaneve*).

kaunimaneve A modern variant of *kaunikai*. The goals of competition are generally less malevolent, and rival troupes are organized less around descent group.

kava An infusion of the crushed roots or stems of the plant *Piper methysticum*, served as a beverage, consumed formally in some societies to mark the making or affirmation of social structures or alliances.

kaval A Bulgarian and Macedonian end-blown **flute** with seven fingerholes and a thumbhole, now standardized as a national instrument. Many Bulgarians regard the *kaval* as the most expressive Bulgarian folk instrument.

kayamba A rectangular reed box, filled with stones or seeds and played in coastal communities of Kenya.

kbandu A Jamaican single-headed cylindrical **membranophone** played with the hands during the Kumina ritual.

kele'a A Tongan conch trumpet, used for signaling (as in fishing, or announcing the presence of an important personage) or for entertainment.

ḱemene (see *gǔdulka*)

keserves 'bitter songs': Hungarian laments with improvised lines (see **improvisation**).

key The principal **tonality** of a piece of **tonal music**. It identifies a **tonic** note (represented by a letter and sometimes a sharp or flat symbol) and the **modality** of **the tonic triad**. (Examples of keys are C major and B-flat minor.)

kil The largest of four instruments used in *garamut* ensembles of Manus Province, Papua New Guinea. It is about 2 meters long, with a diameter of 66 centimeters; it rests on the floor (compare *kipou*, *lolop*, *san(t)san*).

kileŋ Fast, long, and complex **rhythmic** formulas played by *garamut* ensembles of Manus Province, Papua New Guinea. They accompany dancing, before and after singing.

kipou One of four instruments used in the *garamut* ensembles of Manus Province, Papua New Guinea. It is about 140 centimeters long, with a diameter of 46 centimeters (compare *kil*, *lolop*, *san(t)san*).

kjempevisene A genre of Norwegian heroic song.

kjuček A Bulgarian Romani instrumental genre.

klezmer An ensemble music of Eastern European Ashkenazi Jewish origin, with lyrics typically in Yiddish. Historically, the term referred to any musical instrument used in the genre, and later to any musician playing the music. Only in the latter half of the twentieth century did the term take on its modern meaning, referring to the musical genre itself.

koa pela ming A four-holed end-blown **flute** of the Melpa people of Western Highlands Province, Papua New Guinea, played for recreation.

kōauau A Māori **flute**.

kobza A Ukrainian plucked bowl **lute** (also *bandura*).

kobzar (plural, *kobzari*) Historically, Ukrainian blind peasant minstrels who played the *kobza* (see *lirnyky*).

koliada A Russian caroling ritual at Christmas and St Basil's Day.

kolorai A **polyphonic** Baluan vocal genre, which people of Baluan regard as their most highly valued vocal music.

kontra The rhythmic-harmonic support part played by one violinist in a Hungarian folk-violin duo, accompanying the **melody** played by the other violinist.

kontrás In a Hungarian folk-violin duo, the violinist who plays the rhythmic-harmonic support part (*kontra*) and accompanies the *prímás*.

kora A harp-lute of the Manding, with nineteen or twenty-one strings; accompanies singing of praise or historical songs.

kotso A single-membrane hourglass tension drum of the Hausa.

koumpania A Greek ensemble of instrumentalists and vocalists, often featured at the musical cafés that sprang up around Aegean ports after 1900. The *koumpania* came to prominence starting in the 1920s, performing *rebetika* starting in the 1920s. The players often hailed from Asia Minor.

kponingbo A twelve- or thirteen-keyed Zande log **xylophone**, accompanied by a struck hollow **log idiophone** (*guru*) and a double-headed drum.

krakowiak A popular Polish regional dance and a genre of Polish folksong that became an element of the fusion of styles resulting in the modern Polish-American **polka**.

kriti A kind of musical **composition** typical of Karnatak Indian classical music. Its style has been incorporated into the music of many Indian communities in the United States and Canada.

kuaea A Micronesian vocal genre accompanied by guitars and *'ukulele* (and/or occasionally an electronic keyboard), using functional **tonal** harmonies, duple **meter**, a narrow melodic range, and typical **cadences**.

kukuma A Hausa small one-stringed bowed **lute**.

kulokkar A highly idiosyncratic cow-call genre of Norwegian mountain communities. **Yodeling**, shouting, and singing are applied to an ornamented melodic line, often in a style between speaking and singing.

kululu An Enga bamboo **flute**, with three to five fingerholes and measuring about 40 centimeters long.

kundu A drum played in most of New Guinea. It is shaped like an hourglass, cylinder, or cone. One end is open, while the other is closed with a membrane. It is played most widely by men, but sometimes by women.

kuomboka A ceremony performed by the Lozi to mark the retreat from the floodplain as the river rises seasonally.

kwaito A new style of South African popular music, which flourished after the release of Nelson Mandela from prison in 1990; it combined the beat of American "house," slowed down and blended with local African vocal tonalities, with **rapping** in mixed African and township argots.

kwat A length of bamboo beaten with two sticks by Jamaican Maroons.

kwela A style of street **jazz** that sprang up in southern Africa in the 1940s and 1950s and featured pennywhistles; the precursor of *mbaqanga*.

là 'speak': a Huli term that designates all vocal and instrumental performance employing the mouth (which accounts for all Huli musical performance save drumming).

laga In the *meke*, the leading vocal part, usually answered by the higher-pitched *tagica* and harmonized by the bass, *druku*.

lagatoi A trading vessel of the Motu people of Papua New Guinea.

laika (1) A general category of Greek popular urban songs; (2) In a more restricted sense, Greek urban popular music of the postwar era.

laisse A type of **stanza** or **strophe** that featured prominently in varieties of French poetry and song of the Middle Ages, notably the *chanson de danse* (aka *chanson en laisse*).

lakalaka The most important Tongan *faiva*. Its poetry conveys a series of concepts and references, rather than a coherent story. Usually composed for performance at a specific event, it is performed by men and women, often two hundred or more, arranged in two or more rows facing an audience.

lali A large Fijian **log idiophone**, often used in pairs for summoning people to church.

lamellaphone (also *linguaphone*) Any musical instrument whose sound is result of the vibration of a long, thin, movable plate or plates affixed to one end. The **mbira** is an example of a **lamellaphone**.

ländlerkappelle The most popular contemporary Swiss-German instrumental ensemble, typically consisting of a clarinet, **accordions**, and a double bass.

langeleik A Norwegian plucked **zither**.

langspil An Icelandic bowed **zither** with two to six strings.

laouto A Greek long-necked plucked **lute**.

laúd A type of Cuban guitar.

laulalo A vocal part in a style of Tongan **polyphonic** vocal music (as analyzed in the eighteenth century) that is low in **pitch** and functions as a movable **drone**. It and the *fasi*, locally considered the most important vocal parts in this style of music, interacted with each other. Other voices were considered further decoration of these components.

layelayana A lament of the Eipo people of Papua (formerly Irian Jaya), a province of Indonesia on the western half of New Guinea Island. The genre is a spontaneous expression of mourning, interspersed with weeping or crying. A *layelayana* begins emphatically and loudly, after some minutes ending quietly.

lesiba (or *lisiba*) A southern Sotho musical bow, adapted from the *gora* of the Khoikhoi, played by blowing onto a feather to vibrate the string.

lied (plural, *lieder*) 'song', in German.

likembe An East African **lamellaphone**, played in ensembles of up to fifteen (also known as **mbira**).

lira A Ukranian **hurdy-gurdy**. It traditionally has one **melody** string (with a keyboard to adjust **pitch**) and two **drone** strings.

lirnyk (plural, *lirnyky*) Historically, a Ukrainian blind peasant minstrel who played the *lira* (see *kobzari*).

lirrga One of the two principal public genres of song in Western Arnhem Land, Australia (the other being *wangga*). Performances of *lirrga* mark celebrations of the social dimensions of life.

litungu An eastern African eight-stringed **lyre**.

llamador A time-keeping drum used in Afro-Columbian *cumbia* music.

log drum Musical instrument constructed from a wooden log that is beaten with a stick; although called a drum, it is really an **idiophone**.

log idiophone A hollowed log, branch, or other piece of timber, played by being struck (with the side of a stick or sticks) or jolted (with the end of a stick or sticks), often in ensemble.

loki djili Slow songs of the Vlach Romani of Hungary; they have major or minor **tonality** and four-line **melodies**.

lolop One of four instruments used in *garamut* ensembles of Manus Province, Papua New Guinea. It is about 110 centimeters long, with a diameter of 36 centimeters (compare *kil*, *kipou*, *san(t)san*).

longo A central African portable, gourd-resonated **xylophone**.

lō pòdo 'breaking the speaking': a Huli phrase denoting pauses or codas.

lounuat (also, *launut*, *lounut*) A Tabar **friction block** about 40–65 centimeters long. It produces a medium-high-pitched sound when rubbed.

lute Any member of a family of plucked stringed instruments played in many areas of the world and having many variations. Lutes often have pear-shaped bodies, usually fretted fingerboards, and heads with **tuning** pegs often angled backward from the neck.

lyra A pear-shaped three-stringed bowed fiddle common in Greece and Crete (see *kemenje*).

lyre A **harp**-like instrument of Greek origin, which, in antiquity, though held vertically on the lap, was strummed with a **plectrum** as with a **zither**, rather than plucked as with a harp.

lyric song In the original meaning of the term, a song suitable for **accompaniment** by the **lyre**. Lyric songs are generally non-narrative songs, often expressing emotions or describing the ritual action they accompany.

madayin A set of **clapstick**-accompanied songs owned by each **moiety** in Central-Eastern Arnhem Land, Australia.

madrigal Any of several types of usually unaccompanied vocal **polyphony** employed especially in the **Renaissance** and most often set to secular Italian poetry.

maggi Songs associated with the *maggio* (May) seasonal ritual, widespread in central Italy.

maie Dancing and associated singing within the context of Kiribati performance; also, Kiribati dances that incorporate traits of outside music or dance.

makam (plural, *makamlar*) (1) Any of various Turkish melodic **modes**; the **scales** of the Turkish melodic, or *makam* system; (2) A musical composition or performance based on one of the *makam* modes. In Europe, *makam* are used in parts of the Balkans and North Caucasia (see *maqām* for an analog in Arabic).

makwaya A Black South African popular **choral** music style, developed at the end of the nineteenth century as a blend of African and European musical styles.

malaga A ceremonial Sāmoan visit, often solemnized by formalities including orations and *kava* and sometimes celebrated with singing and dancing.

malanggan A dramatic commemorative rite of northern New Ireland, involving masked performers who often voice their messages through the sounds of musical instruments.

mali lyingi A dance-song of the Enga people of Papua New Guinea.

mambo A modern Cuban music and dance form that came to prominence in the 1940s, developing out of the *danzón* genre. The name *mambo* derives from a specific *danzón* written by Orestes and Cachao López, itself called "Mambo" (meaning 'conversation with the gods'), which prominently used African folk **rhythms**.

mamira Kiribati ceremonies that, in pre-colonial times, bestowed blessings on a song to enhance its appeal and its composer's fame.

mandolina (1) An alternate name for the *kabosa* (also *kabosy*), played in southern Madagascar. This instrument often has moveable frets made of fishing line, and only the upper part of the neck, near the peghead, is commonly fretted. Unlike the Merina *kabosy*, which has metallic strings (often bicycle brake-cable strands), the *mandolina* usually has nylon strings; (2) (or *bandolín*, *bandola*) A plucked **lute** of Venezuela that has four double **courses** of nylon strings.

maneaba A Kiribati meetinghouse in which important social activities and discussions take place.

manikai A public genre of song in Western Arnhem Land, Australia. The genre is often performed in ceremonies alongside *lirrga* and *wangga* (see *bunggurl*).

manza A Zande **xylophone** of Central Africa, tuned **pentatonically**, and associated with royalty.

maqām (plural, *maqāmāt*) Any of various melodic **modes** in the repertoires of today's Arab musicians. According to theoretical sources, each maqām is a melodic framework with a **tonic** note (*qarār*) and a **scale** of one or two **octaves**. *Maqām*-like scales appear in Spanish worksongs because of longtime Arab influence in southern Spain. (See *makam* for a Turkish analog.)

marabi A South African hybrid of indigenous and urban music, dance, and context.

marake A Wayana cycle of ceremonies that constitute a boy's initiation ritual.

mariachi The most nationally prominent folk-derived Mexican musical ensemble since the 1930s, usually consisting of guitars, *vihuela*, *guitarrón*, violins, trumpets, and singers.

marimba A box-resonated **xylophone** of African origin (a version is played in the islands of Zanzibar and Pemba and on the nearby mainland). It is played in Central America, Colombia, Mexico, and Venezuela.

marinera One of the most widely disseminated song-and-dance genres in Peru. Originally from coastal Peru, it is widely played in the Andean area. Its **meter** is a combination of duple and triple time and features extensive use of **hemiola**.

maro vany 'many strings': a regional name for the *valiha* used by the Antandroy, a southern group of Malagasy, and some other peoples primarily of southern Madagascar.

maròokaa (plural, *maròokii*) (also *maroka*) A Hausa singer of praise songs.

maru 'bass': the male vocal part in unaccompanied Christian vocal music of Polynesian origin as introduced in Papua New Guinea in the early twentieth century (see *peroveta anedia*).

maskanda A popular South African Zulu electric guitar band style, featuring male and female dancers, that was developed from both Zulu traditional folk guitar music and *mbaqanga*.

mazurka A popular nineteenth-century European couple dance in moderate triple time.

mbaqanga A South African **jazz** idiom that took its name from a stiff corn porridge.

mbira (or *marimbula*) A class of African **lamellaphone**, varieties of which are particularly prominent among the Shona. Mbiras are plucked by thumbs and forefingers, and played solo or in ensembles. Its use has spread internationally.

mbira dzavadzimu 'mbira of the ancestral spirits': a Shona **lamellaphone** with twenty-two or more wide keys. Players use the forefinger of the right hand and both thumbs.

mbube A style of predominantly male Zulu singing in South Africa, so named because of the popularity of the song *Mbube* ('lion') by Solomon Linda (later recorded in the United States as "Wimoweh" by the Weavers and "The Lion Sleeps Tonight" by the Tokens). Traditionally an **a cappella** choral music, the style is often loud and powerful. It has been popularized internationally by the group Ladysmith Black Mambazo.

MC (sometimes spelled "emcee") An acronym for *master of ceremonies*. Originally a person who announced records or live musicians in front of an audience, in the early years of **hip-hop** music, **DJs** began to use individuals calling themselves *MCs*, or "crews" of multiple MCs, to announce records and heighten the party atmosphere by **rapping** party lyrics over instrumental **breaks** played by the DJ. The role of the MC (or **rapper**) in hip-hop gradually expanded to the point of eclipsing that of the DJ.

measure (or *bar*) A unit of musical time consisting of a regular grouping of beats determined by the music's **meter**. In musical notation the boundaries of a measure are denoted by *a bar line* on either side of the measure.

meke A Fijian sung narrative text with instrumental **accompaniment** and dance, performed in ceremonial and social contexts by men or women (rarely in mixed groups).

mele A Hawaiian poetic text and its vocalization, of which there are two major categories: (1) *mele hula*, singing with dancing; (2) *mele oli*, singing without dancing.

mele hoʻoipoipo A genre of *mele*, or sung poetic text, often called a lovemaking song, which typically functions as an informal topical song and is sometimes directed at a specific individual.

mele hula (or simply *hula*) A sung Hawaiian poetic text (*mele*) accompanied by dancing.

mele hula ʻālaʻapapa A *mele hula* accompanied by the *ipu*, a Hawaiian gourd **idiophone**, and arranged in sections called *paukū*.

mele hula ʻauana (or simply *hula ʻauana*) 'modern hula': a *mele hula* incorporating newer movements, with harmonized sung text accompanied by plucked stringed instruments of Western origin.

mele hula kahiko (or simply *hula kahiko*) 'ancient hula': a *mele hula* incorporating older movements, with **monophonically** recited text accompanied by indigenous instruments.

mele hula kuʻi (or simply *hula kuʻi*) A *mele hula* that is accompanied by guitars and *ʻukeleles* and was developed in the late nineteenth century.

mele hula pahu (or simply *hula pahu*) A *mele hula* accompanied by the *pahu*, a sharkskin drum, struck with bare hands.

mele inoa A genre of danced *mele* honoring a god or chief.

mele maʻi The *mele inoa* usually performed last in a set to honor the physical means of perpetuating the royal lines.

mele oli A sung Hawaiian poetic text (*mele*) not accompanied by dancing.

mele pule A sung Hawaiian poetic text (*mele*) that functions as a prayer to gods.

melisma (plural, *melismata*) In vocal music, the technique of singing several **notes** to any one syllable of text. Music that utilizes this technique is said to be *melismatic* (as opposed to **syllabic** music, in which each syllable of text is set to one note of music).

melody A succession of single **tones** occurring through time that produces a distinct **phrase** or idea; often conceived of as one of the three main components of music, along with **harmony** and **rhythm**.

membranophone A musical instrument whose principal sound is created by the vibration of a stretched skin. Skin instruments are often called *drums*, a term otherwise used for the body or chamber. Confusion arises when *drum* is used for skinless items, such as oil drums and steel drums—the former not a musical instrument, the latter an **idiophone**.

mento A genre of traditional Jamaican music, with some similarities to **calypso**. It has greatly influenced commercial Jamaican genres, including *ska*, **rock steady**, **reggae**, and **dancehall**.

merengue A lively traditional and popular music and dance genre that has become a symbol of national identity in the Dominican Republic. It typically alternates **verses** and **refrains**, with **responsorial** singing. The genre is popular throughout Latin America, especially in Venezuela.

merengue típico (also, *perico ripiao*) The "folk merengue." Its music and dance, an amalgamation of African and European traits, was promoted in the Dominican Republic as the national dance, thus defining the national culture as a **Creole** culture.

mestizo In its original meaning, a person of mixed European and Amerindian descent. The term now applies to other mixed populations in other parts of the world.

metallophone A **percussion instrument** composed of a series of metal bars that sound successive **pitches** of a **scale** when struck; i.e. a metal-keyed **xylophone**.

meter The regular pattern of strong and weak **rhythmic** pulses underlying some music. Each repetition of the pattern is a **measure** (compare **rhythm** and **tempo**).

metered Having an underlying **meter**.

microtone Any **interval** that is smaller than a **semitone** (a minor second).

mimesis The imitation or representation of some aspect of nature or human behavior in an art form.

minja One of two basic vocal genres of the Abelam of Papua New Guinea. Minja are usually performed solo by men (compare *bira*).

minu A drum of the central Venezuelan coast.

mizwid A Tunisian **bagpipe**, used with the *bendir* to accompany songs of praise.

moda 'fashion': a **metered**, unaccompanied, **polyphonic**, Portuguese **strophic** song sung by persons of either sex in any of various contexts.

modality The aspect of a given musical piece that is determined by its use of a musical **mode**, as distinguished from **tonality**, which is characterized by the use of the major or minor **scales**.

modal jazz A style of **jazz**, developed in the late 1950s, that based its **melodies** and improvisations on musical **modes** instead of the major and minor **scales**. The effect was a more **harmonically** open backdrop for soloists, with a more ambiguous **tonality**, allowing new freedoms of **improvisation**.

mode (1) Any series of **tones** that forms the basic **tonal** material used in **composition** or **improvisation**; (2) Any of a set of fundamental **rhythmic** templates or guidelines used for composition and improvisation.

modulation A change from one **key** to another within a **composition**.

moiety One of two descent groups in a society, in cases in which the given society can be subdivided into precisely two descent groups when studying kinship and ancestry.

moka A Melpa ritual for the ceremonial exchange of goods.

monophonic Characterized by **monophony**.

monophony Music that contains only a single melodic line or **melody** without harmonic **accompaniment**. A piece of music may be considered **monophonic** even when performed by multiple voices, as long as they all play an identical melodic line, or the same line duplicated at the **octave** (compare **polyphony** and **homophony**).

morache A rasp played by Utes in the Bear Dance.

mörl A Melpa men's dance, performed in place in a line during a *moka*, with each man holding a spear or playing a *kundu* and singing words usually evoking feelings of loss on a clansman's death.

morpheme Any of the smallest units of spoken sound in a given language that are capable of conveying meaning. Morphemes are often thought of as being reducible to still smaller units, called **phonemes**.

mot An Eipo ceremonial song and dance, performed by men at feasts held to mark an alliance, the end of a war, or the payment of duty or compensation.

mōteatea A multipurpose **compositional** and performance tradition of the Māori people of Aotearoa.

motif In music and dance, a short theme or idea that recurs as a unifying thematic element.

motive A short melodic **phrase** or idea, which often recurs or reappears throughout a piece of music.

mukupela A drum associated with Luba-Lunda chieftainship and kingship in central Africa.

Murlarra A **clansong** series of Central Arnhem Land, Australia.

música criolla 'Creole music': (1) In Venezuela, music of Venezuelan peasants of mixed ancestry; (2) Roman-Catholic-Spanish, Arab-Andalusian, and Chilean foundations of Chilean musical and poetic practice; (3) A coastal Peruvian music of Afro-Peruvian influence.

música jíbara A musical tradition associated with rural Puerto Rican communities and sometimes performed in the mainland United States. It centers on the music and dance called *seis*; stringed instruments dominate, and improvised texts are common.

música ranchera A form of Mexican "country" music, associated particularly with the *mariachi* band (see *canción ranchera*).

música típica A general name for various Panamanian musical genres with a Spanish influence.

nai A Romanian **panpipe** that has been played in Romania since ancient times.

na'o A name for one vocal part in Fataleka **polyphonic** vocal music.

ñe'i 'song': the name for all the song-styles originated by the Tohono O'odham, native Americans of the southwestern United States. Styles originated by other cultures and played by the Tohono O'odham are not called *ñe'i*.

ñe'icuda 'songmakers': a name for musical instruments of mostly indigenous origin among the Tohono O'odham, native Americans of the southwestern United States.

ngarkana A **clansong** genre of Central Arnhem Land, Australia, in which there is no fixed metrical (see **meter**) relationship among voices, **clapsticks**, and *didjeridu*.

ngoma (1) A single-headed, barrel-shaped **Afro-Cuban** drum; (2) An ensemble including *ngoma* drums (see *ng'oma*).

ng'oma A drum used among royal ensembles of the Lozi and Nkoya of southern Africa, which has a paste added to the head to deepen its sound.

ngongi Double bells, played only by royal ensembles of the Lozi and Nkoya.

ngwayé kundi 'stopping talk': a genre of Abelam solo song (in Papua New Guinea), important because it can interrupt fighting or warfare and herald the settlement of disputes. The singer hoists in the air a leaf of the naaréndu, a symbol of peace; he sings the song and gives a short speech. While he is performing, people must suspend hostilities.

njari A **mbira** that had its origins in the Zambezi River Valley of Zimbabwe in the 1700s.

nògo ú 'pig yodel': A Huli **yodel** performed by men carrying cuts of butchered pigs to the *hòmanogo*, a feast held after mourning a death.

norteño A northern Mexican style of music, distinguished by the use of the **accordion**.

notched stick rasp An indigenous North American musical instrument, found predominantly in the Great Basin and the Southwest. It consists usually of a length of wood or bone with a series of notches or teeth cut along one side. This is scraped by another stick, or often by a scapular bone, to produce a grating sound.

nóta A genre of Hungarian popular art song, disseminated largely by Roma (see *Rom*).

note (1) A **tone** occurring as part of a musical piece; (2) A symbol used in written music to represent such a tone or any other musically significant sound. Placing the note in a specific location on the musical staff indicates the **pitch** of that note.

novokompanovana narodna muzika 'newly composed folk music': a song genre, influenced by popular urban style, that has been prominent in the former Yugoslavia since the 1960s.

nueva canción A genre of urban song and its accompanying instrumental music, often drawing from South American folk elements and representing some form of social protest.

nurlu A **dreaming**-related Australian dance and song genre. Spirits of deceased kin or agents of conception reveal nurlu and associated dances to dreaming individuals.

nyabingi drumming Neo-traditional Rastafarian drumming, whose **rhythms** have influenced rhythms in more commercial Jamaican musical forms.

nystev 'new stev': a new form of *stev*, with a form somewhat different form that of the older version, which began to replace old stev structures as a main structural element in Norwegian **ballads** during the nineteenth century.

oberek A Polish dance in fast triple **meter**, with two-against-three cross-rhythms and energetic leaping and stomping.

octave (1) A musical **interval** encompassing eight degrees; (2) The **interval** between a **pitch** and a sound of twice or half its **frequency**.

ògìdo A Yorùbá bass *conga*, developed from Latin American prototypes.

oimae Angan **polyphonic** vocal music for **singsings**, usually accompanied by a steady beat on a drum.

okoma A large Wayana ceremony that is part of the boys'-initiation ritual (*marake*).

olaiyole An Enga bamboo *susap*.

olioli A Hawaiian style of vocalization characterized by the use of one principal sustained **tone** (which may occasionally receive embellishment from auxiliary tones, usually lower).

operismo A genre of Spanish "flamenco opera" that flourished in the early twentieth century. The genre transformed more "authentic" styles of **flamenco** into the commercialized forms that held sway until the renaissance of older, more serious styles in the 1950s and 1960s.

organetto An Italian small **diatonic** button **accordion**.

orixá 'deity': in Yorùbá (Brazilian spelling): a theological feature of Brazilian Candomblé.

oro A Yorùbá secret society of night hunters, symbolized by the playing of a **bullroarer**.

orquesta (or *banda*) A Tejano ensemble that was modeled after the Anglo **swing** bands of the 1940s and 1950s, and gradually evolved into a distinctly Tejano big band.

orquesta típica 'typical orchestra': (1) An Argentine *tango* ensemble of the 1920s; (2) An ensemble of the central Peruvian highlands, consisting of saxophones, clarinets, violins, and **harp**; (3) An instrumental ensemble characteristic of Cuban music.

ostinato A short musical pattern repeated continuously throughout a musical piece or a section of a musical piece.

'ōte'a A Tahitian dance, performed in "grass" skirts (*more*) to drummed **rhythms**.

outi A Greek bent-necked, unfretted plucked **lute**.

overblowing A technique of playing a **wind instrument** that emphasizes a **harmonic** or harmonics rather than the **fundamental**, usually accomplished by increasing the force of air passing by or into the **proximal** end of the instrument.

overtone Any of the high, quiet **pitches** produced by a sound, that have a higher **frequency** than the **fundamental** of a given **tone**. Overtones, together with the fundamental, comprise a complex tone.

pagode A form of *samba* that became popular in the 1980s and grew out of the intimate, backyard forms of samba, but added new instruments to the mix. Its lyrics tend to be clever and humorous, and suggest solutions to life on the margins of society.

pahu An East Polynesian hand-struck footed drum having a shark- or rayskin head and a body usually carved from coconut or breadfruit wood, ranging from about 20 to about 110 centimeters high.

pahu tupa'i rima A tall, one-headed, hand-struck Tahitian drum, which fell out of use, but was revived in the late 1970s.

palos A kind of drum played in the Dominican Republic.

pandeiro (also *pandeireta*) (1) A Portuguese round **frame drum** with metal jingles, originally a medieval instrument; (2) A handheld frame drum of Brazilian origin, similar to a tambourine, but distinct primarily in having a tunable head (a more modern descendent of the medieval Portuguese *pandeiro*.

pandereta A Puerto Rican round **frame drum** found in various sizes.

pandero A large, laced **frame drum** common in the southwestern Dominican Republic, and closely related to the *pandereta*.

panpipe (often plural, as *panpipes*) A set of differently **pitched** end-blown **flutes**, usually bound in a bundle or a row (the latter called *raft panpipes*).

parlando rubato (or *parlando-rubato*) Literally, 'robbed speaking': a singing style with a speechlike, variable beat.

partial (short for *upper partial tone*) Any **overtone** of a given **tone** (i.e., not the **fundamental**).

pastorale A Basque play accompanied by songs and dances and supposedly descended from late medieval mystery plays dating from the 1500s.

pātē A small **log idiophone** played by percussive ensembles typical of the Cook Islands; its use spread to Sāmoa in the nineteenth century.

pa'u A drum played by percussive ensembles typical of the Cook Islands.

paukū An individual section of a *mele hula 'ala'apapa*. Each *paukū* precedes a sequence of movements associated with a specific set of rhythms.

pa'u mangō A drum used by percussive ensembles typical of the Cook Islands. Its **pitch** is higher than that of the *pa'u*.

pentatonic Having a **pitch** inventory of five **tones** to the **octave**.

pentatonic scale Any five-note **scale**; varieties of pentatonic scales are used in **composition** and **improvisation** all over the world.

percussion The striking together of two dissimilarly shaped or sized objects, producing a sound or vibration (e.g. beating a block with a stick) (compare **concussion**).

percussion instrument A musical instrument sounded by being struck, scraped, or plucked by another object.

percussive idiophone An **idiophone** made to sound by the action of a beater, as with **log idiophones**, wooden plaques, and **xylophones** (compare **concussive idiophone**).

pere A melodic women's vocal part in Motu *peroveta anedia*.

perico ripiao (see *merengue típico*)

peroveta anedia 'prophet song': A twentieth-century Motu genre of vocal music, whose **melodic**, **rhythmic**, **harmonic**, and textural style and original language were brought to Papua New Guinea by Polynesian Christian missionaries.

pesenniki Inexpensive published Russian songbooks containing popular folksongs, whose production became widespread about 1900.

pesni 'songs', in Russian.

peyote religion (or *peyotism*) An indigenous North American religion centered on eating of hallucinogenic peyote cactus. It originated in Mexico and spread to the southern plains of the United States in around the 1880s. It features a combination of indigenous beliefs and practices with some added Christian symbolism. Songs are a major and distinguishing portion of ritual.

phoneme Any of the smallest linguistically distinctive units of sound in a given language (compare **morpheme**).

phrase A short to medium-length section of a larger piece of music that has an internal coherency, and can be thought of as a musical "sentence." It often leads, at its end, to a place of **harmonic** resolution, or **cadence**.

piastakud In the O'odham language, a word that refers to musical instruments of a primarily non-indigenous origin. It literally means 'thing of the party', the root *piasta* being borrowed from the Spanish word *fiesta*, 'party, celebration'. The term encompasses instruments—such as the saxophone, guitar, bass, and drumset—used to perform *waila*, or "chicken scratch" music (compare *ñe'icuda*).

pibroch The English-language adaptation of the Gaelic Scottish term *piobaireachd*.

pickup (see **anacrusis**)

pinkullo (or *pinkullu, pincullo, pinkillo, pinkuyllo, pincuyllo, pinkuyllu*) A central Andean, vertical, end-blown **duct flute**, with three to eight fingerholes, widely disseminated in the Andes.

piobaireachd A classical Scottish **bagpipe** tradition that emerged in the 1600s (see *pibroch*).

pisirk In the central and eastern arctic, songs that express emotions and feelings or recount favorite anecdotes. They are composed singly or for drum dances.

pitch (1) The perceived "highness" or "lowness" of a sound. Pitch is actually a function of the **frequency** of an acoustic wave—the higher the frequency, the higher the perceived pitch; (2) A **note** or a **tone** of a precise frequency.

pitu A side-blown six-noted **flute** of the Q'eros people.

plectrum A small, thin piece of metal, plastic, or other material, held between or worn on a finger or fingers and used to pluck the strings of a guitar, **lute**, **lyre**, or other stringed instrument. Often known colloquially as a "pick."

plena A genre of **strophic** song with percussion **accompaniment** rooted in African-derived communities of coastal Puerto Rico.

plucked dulcimer (Dutch, *hommel*; French, *épinette*) A fretted instrument of the **zither** family, related to the Appalachian hammer dulcimer (see **dulcimer**) of the United States. It was in use in the Low Countries at least as far back as the early 1600s. The instrument is usually placed on a table, and is occasionally held across the lap or knees.

polka A lively couple dance or piece of music of Bohemian or Polish origin in duple **meter**.

polpolot A Baluan song for entertainment, having no ritual value.

polska A Scandinavian improvisatory dance in triple time, known in Sweden from the late 1500s. In Finland, the dance spawned a corresponding vocal genre with a characteristic verse **meter** based on the dance **rhythms**.

polykinetic Having multiple movements, as a dance in which individuals or groups perform movements that differ distinctively from those of other individuals or groups, or in which movements of some of an individual's body parts differ from those of the same individual's other body parts as they move together.

polyphonic Characterized by **polyphony**.

polyphony Music that simultaneously presents two or more distinct and independent melodic lines (or "parts" or "voices").

polyrhythm A set of two or more simultaneously performed, distinctive **rhythms**.

popevki Short melodic turns, **motifs**, and models for traditional Russian **melodies**.

portamento A melodic slide between two **pitches**.

pō sipi A Tongan poem recited spontaneously during informal **kava**-drinking gatherings.

potlatch A ceremonial feast held by certain native American peoples of the northern Pacific coast of North America, in which the host gives away gifts in a display of his wealth. Sometimes hosts will publicly destroy valuable items to show the degree of their wealth. The events serve a more general social function: a chance for attendees to solidify social connections with others and foster new ones.

precomposed With performed content firmly and precisely established in advance.

príma The lead melodic part played by one violinist in a Hungarian folk-violin duo and supported by the *kontra* part.

prímás In a Hungarian folk-violin duo, the violinist who plays the **melody** part (*príma*), and who is accompanied by the *kontrás*, the violinist who plays rhythmic-harmonic support.

primero The "lead drum" version of the Garifuna *garawoun*. A treble drum, about 30 to 45 centimeters in diameter and 60 centimeters high, it provides **rhythmic** variety with **syncopations** and **improvisational** passages.

proximal Close to a point of reference: in particular, refers to the portion of a musical instrument closest to the source of sound making vibration. For instance, in many **wind instruments**, the proximal end is the mouthpiece (compare **distal**).

psaľmy Christian songs, the main part of the *kobzari* and *lirnyky* repertoire.

Pukllay taki Carnival songs performed at an all-night "song competition" by leading men of Q'eros hamlets. The dominant song at the upcoming carnival festivities is chosen from the songs performed.

púlugèla (also *wélagèla*, *gèlagi*) A short, eight-piped Huli bamboo bundle-panpipe (compare *gùlungùlu*, *gúlupòbe*).

punta A social-commentary song-and-dance form, the most popular Garifuna dance-song genre. Puntas are traditionally composed by women and are performed **responsorially**. The call, usually a **phrase** or two of a sentence performed by the song leader, is followed by a **choral** response, often the completion of the sentence.

punta-rock The most popular of the contemporary genres of dance-music in Belize; it features the synthesis of electric instruments, traditional drums (*primero* and *segunda*), and **rhythmic** patterns of the *punta* dance.

punto fijo (also, *camagüeyano*) A genre of Cuba's *punto guajiro* complex, originally from the central provinces of Cuba. In it, the **accompaniment** of *laúd* and guitar is always present.

punto guajiro A Spanish-derived complex of rural musical genres from the western and central provinces of Cuba, marked by improvised song texts and accompanied by an ensemble consisting mainly of stringed instruments.

punto libre (also, *pinareño*, *vueltabajero*) A genre of Cuba's *punto guajiro* complex, originally from the western provinces of Cuba. In it, the **accompaniment** of *laúd* and guitar ceases when the vocalist begins singing his **melody** and *décima*.

pupe An Enga bundle **panpipe**.

pututu A Q'eros conch trumpet, played by communal authorities as a sign of their rank.

pwita A friction drum of Central Africa.

quadrille A square dance of European origin performed by four couples; also, the musical **accompaniment** for the dance.

quena (or *kena*) A vertical end-notched **flute** of the Andes, generally made of cane, but sometimes of wood or plastic.

ragga (short for "ragamuffin," a derogatory term describing the music's creators) A subgenre of Jamaican **dancehall** music in which **accompaniment** is typically electronic or synthesized. Sometimes also thought of as a synonym of **dancehall**.

ragga-muffin A Martinican mix between **reggae** and **hip-hop** musics. It features a syncopated **rhythm** combined with a rapid performance of a **Creole** text often with social themes.

ragtime A musical **rhythm** and genre popularized in the early twentieth century and characterized by a syncopated **melody** placed against a steady **accompaniment**.

rake 'n' scrape A Bahamian secular music that accompanied **quadrilles**. The name derives from the raked and scraped **idiophones** used to perform it, instruments that include such household objects as carpenter's saws, hair combs, washtubs, and ridged bottles.

rancho folclórico Any of numerous Portuguese folklore groups, prominent between the 1930s and 1950s, dedicated to an ideologically charged concept of *folclore*. Competitions were established in which villages competed for a prize in recognition of their preserving local architecture, costumes, music, and dance.

rap (also, rap music, hip-hop music) A form of primarily African-American spoken-word music; one element of **hip-hop** culture.

rapper (see **MC**)

rapping The process of **rhythmically** speaking a composed or improvised lyric (or occasionally even syllables with no attributable meaning). It is performed with or without **accompaniment**, and is a major component of **rap** music.

rebetika (or *rembetika*) An urban Greek popular music, developed by Greeks expelled from Turkey in the 1920s and popularized internationally in the 1960s.

redondo (usually used in plural form, as *redondos*) Any of several long drums, held between standing drummers' legs. The three drums of a set of redondos are made from the same trunk of a balsa tree. The drummer strikes the drum with a stick held in one hand and the fingers of the other hand.

reel A couples dance, and its accompanying music, in duple time at a moderate **tempo**, originating in Scotland and Ireland. It spread throughout northwestern Europe and to the United States.

reel à bouche 'mouth reel': A musical genre developed by early Acadian settlers who arrived in North America without instruments. It was wordless vocal music for dancing a **reel**.

refrain The line or lines of text and/or music that are repeated in a poem or a song. In songs, a refrain is often equivalent to a **chorus**.

reggae (1) A specific music of Jamaican origin, influenced by many styles, including **mento**, traditional Afro-Caribbean drumming, and North American **rhythm and blues** and **soul**. Now extremely popular throughout the world, it arose as a distinct musical genre in the late 1960s directly out of **rock steady**; (2) An umbrella term to cover a wide variety of Jamaican musical forms, including **dancehall**, **ragga**, and others.

rekilaulu A genre of Finnish dance song. *Rekilaulu* recount historical tales of people and events.

relinchidos (from *relincho*, the sound of a horse's whinny) High-trilling vocal cries in Spanish music.

repartee A sung debate that pits one performer against another.

requinto (also, *guitarra de son*) A four-stringed, narrow-bodied Mexican guitar, used in the **son jarocho**.

responsorial Having the quality of a call-and-response pattern. In responsorial music, a singer or singers enunciate a **melody**, which another singer or other singers "answer."

réveillez The French custom of begging for eggs and other gifts while singing religious songs at Easter.

rhyming spiritual An outgrowth of the Bahamian anthem. Songs of this genre are usually sung unaccompanied by at least two men, but women sometimes join them. The texts usually center on biblical characters and stories, but sometimes recount the story of something that has happened in the community.

rhythm Any pattern of long and/or short **notes** occurring over a certain duration of time. Rhythm is often conceived of as one of three main components of music, with **melody** and **harmony** (compare **meter** and **tempo**).

rhythm and blues A style of urban African-American music that came to prominence just after World War II, arising out of the big band **swing** era, as larger bands became for difficult to maintain in the changing market. A primarily vocal music featuring pianos, horns, drums, and guitars, rhythm and blues was one of the primary styles that engendered **rock and roll**.

rhythmic (1) Having or involving **rhythm**; (2) Characterized by a pronounced rhythm.

rímur Icelandic **ballads**, sometimes having up to one hundred **stanzas**.

rock An umbrella term that is used to describe a wide variety of postwar popular U.S. and international musical styles that evolved out of the original **rock and roll**, in combination with other influences.

rockabilly A fusion of **country music** with **rhythm and blues**, which came to prominence in the mid-1950s and was performed predominantly by young white people in the Southern United States. One of the earliest styles of **rock**

and roll, it retained many stylistic elements of its predecessor, hillbilly boogie, but strengthened the **backbeat** and deemphasized such traditionally country instruments as the steel guitar.

rock and roll (or *rock 'n' roll*) A style of popular music of U.S. origin, which gained recognition as a distinct music from its parental genres in the mid 1950s, when it became highly popular among white youth. At its simplest level, it was a fusion of **rhythm and blues** with **country music**, set to the **rhythmic** pattern established in the 1920s **by boogie-woogie** music. It is a dance-oriented, high-energy genre.

rock steady (or *rocksteady*) A Jamaican popular musical genre that had a brief period of popularity in the mid to late 1960s. A descendant of *ska* and a predecessor to **reggae**.

Rom (plural, *Roma*) Any individual within a pan-European minority, traditionally known as the Gypsies.

romance A long, often epic **ballad** of Spanish and Portuguese origin, structured in a series of *coplas*. In Latin America, it is thought to be a major historical root of the *corrido*, and is also sung by Sephardic Jews in Bosnia-Herzegovina.

rommelpot (1) The European term for a Khoikhoi drum of southern Africa, which is made by placing skins over a pot (a different instrument than the European *rommelpot*); (2) A European friction drum of the Low Countries.

Romungre music The music of the Romungre, one of the major groups of Roma (see *Rom*) in Hungary. Romungre stringband music is so famous that many believe it to be the only type of Romani music, despite the great variety in existence.

ronda The best loved and mostly pervasive genre of collectively known songs throughout Spain. Their name refers to the tradition of rounding (serenading).

ronde A French and French-Swiss closed ring dance, sung and danced by the dancers.

rozhok A Russian wooden trumpet with five fingerholes and one thumbhole.

rubato (see *tempo rubato*)

rumba Any of several music and dance genres created by Afro-Cuban slaves using specific **rhythms** that originated in Africa.

runo An ancient, strictly metric, Finnish genre in which the text of the Finno-Karelian epic, *Kalevala*, was sung.

ruoia The most commonly used name for indigenous Kiribati dances.

ruruo A musical passage performed in duple **meter**, found in both the *kamei* and *kabuti*, Kiribati dances.

sákárà (1) A Yorùbá single-membrane clay **frame drum**; (2) A Yorùbá musical genre for dancing and praising, performed and patronized mostly by Muslims.

salegy A popular music that originated in northern Madagascar, but is currently performed in most areas of the island.

salsa 'sauce': any of a wide variety of popular Latin music-and-dance genres. The sound of salsa genres not only encompasses a variety of Cuban styles, such as *son*, *mambo* and *cha-cha-chá*, but incorporates ideas from

Puerto Rico, the Dominican Republic (and to a lesser extent the rest of the Caribbean and Brazil) and black popular music from North America.

salve The musical cornerstone of a saint's festival, the most frequent and ubiquitous event of Dominican folk Christianity. In today's *salve*, musical elements of different historical origins coexist and have become merged.

salve con versos One of two coexisting subgenres of the *salve*. The *salve con versos* is less sacred than the *Salve de la Virgen*. It has a text (the *versos*) that entails a secular response inserted between sacred phrases. It also has an African-influenced musical style: **metered** and **rhythmic**, instrumentally accompanied, and **responsorial**.

Salve de la Virgen The strictly liturgical, purely Hispanic, traditional subgenre of the *salve*.

salve de pandero The most Africanized variety of *salve con versos*. It features the addition of many small drums playing **polyrhythms** and the elimination of a sacred text.

samba (1) The best known of Brazil's musical forms. Considered internationally to be Brazil's national music, it has become something of an umbrella term to designate a range of popular styles, all of which have elements that at some level can be traced to African origins; (2) A quadrangular, wooden **frame drum** introduced by Brazilian returnees to Africa and played in churches.

samba-canção 'song samba': a generally slowed-down, romantic *samba*.

samba de gafieira A form of *samba* that became popular in the 1980s and made its home in *gafieiras*, large dance halls patronized by the urban working class (see also *pagode*).

samba enredo A *samba* genre with a narrative text.

same 'psalm': a Fijian song with texts based on a Fijian-language biblical passage.

sandouri A Greek trapezoidal struck **zither**.

Santería An Afro-Caribbean religion that fuses traditional West African Yorùbá and Roman Catholic elements, resulting in a unique hybrid. It took root in Cuba and Brazil and spread throughout South America, the Caribbean and beyond.

san(t)san One of four instruments used in the *garamut* ensembles of Manus Province, Papua New Guinea. It is about 80 centimeters long, with a diameter of 25 centimeters (compare *kil*, *kipou*, *lolop*).

sāsā A Sāmoan genre of songless movements performed by a company in synchrony.

sāz (or *s'az*) A long-necked, fretted, plucked Turkish **lute**, imported into the Balkans and Georgia during the Ottoman period and still played by Muslim minorities in some areas of Europe. It commonly has twelve to seventeen frets, and two or three **courses** of strings.

scale Formally, a series of **tones** placed in order either from the lowest to the highest **pitch**, or from the highest to the lowest. Compositionally, scales, like melodic **modes**, are often used as the melodic raw material of a piece of music.

sean-nós song 'old style song': an unaccompanied solo song, with melodic ornamentation, performed in Irish (Gaelic) or English. Especially prominent in the Irish-speaking areas of Munster and Connaught, the genre is also performed among Irish-American populations.

sede A Motu bamboo **idiophone**.

sedyanka 'sitting bee': Bulgarian autumnal social gatherings for spinning or embroidery, accompanied by singing.

seguidilla (1) A fast-paced dance and folksong of Spanish origin in triple time. The form has been assimilated and transformed by **mestizo** culture in Mexico, becoming a major point of influence in the creation of Mexican *son*; (2) In Cuba, a genre of Cuba's *punto guajiro* complex of rural musical styles, distinct from other styles of punto guajiro in that the end of **phrases** within the accompaniment do not fall at the same place as the end of phrases in the vocal lines, giving the impression of a never-ending **strophe**.

segunda The 'supporting drum' version of the Garifuna *garawoun* drum. It is a bass drum, about 60 to 90 centimeters wide and 90 centimeters tall, and maintains a steady pulse in duple or triple **meter**.

seis A Puerto Rican music-and-dance form, related to the *décima*, originating from Spain. Its simple **accompaniment** is typically played by *cuatro*, guitar, and **percussion**.

sèkèrè (1) A Yorùbá melodic shaker, consisting of beads or shells wound around a gourd. (2) A traditional Yorùbá musical style, accompanied by the *dùndún*, *agídìgbo*, *agogo*, other instruments, and a **chorus**.

semitone An **interval** whose size is determined by the division of the **octave** into twelve equal-tempered intervals (see **temperament**). It is the smallest interval in common use in Western music.

serenata A Mexican courting, congratulatory, or devotional serenade. A man may contract or organize a group of musicians and unexpectedly serenade his lover outside her home. The recipient of the serenade may otherwise be a person celebrating a birthday or other happy event—or even an image of the Virgin of Guadalupe; (2) Among professional *mariachi* musicians, a short performance of several songs.

sere ni cumu A genre of Fijian popular music that developed in the twentieth century under the influence of European and American popular genres.

ser-i An old Tuareg **compositional** formula or **rhythm** used to create music for light entertainment and dancing; it is a traditional pattern, played for the enjoyment of members of the artisanal caste, to which the musicians belong.

siku (plural, *sikuri*) A traditional **panpipe** of Peru.

sia A nocturnal mimetic (see **mimesis**) dance that originated in the Siasi islands and spread to become a cultural icon of the Mamose Region of Papua New Guinea; the trademark **singsing** of the Siasi Islands.

simanjemanje The soft female **choir** that backs up a male **groaner** in South African *mbaqanga* music.

singsing In Papua New Guinea, the performance of a song or songs, especially in public, with dancing by decorated performers.

ska A Jamaican musical genre that arose in the late 1950s, combining elements of **mento** and **rhythms** of traditional Jamaican drumming with American **rhythm and blues**. Its "inside-out" beat is also characteristic of its descendents, **rock steady** and **reggae**.

skiffle A British adaptation of American folk music. It rose to commercial success in the mid 1950s, and inspired a major craze of homemade music among British youth.

759

Instruments included such household objects as a washboard (for **percussion**) and a primitive bass made by pulling a wire tight over a pole stuck into a tea chest.

slått A Norwegian *hardingfele* piece.

sodina A Malagasy **wind instrument**, traditionally a bamboo end-blown **flute** with six fingerholes and one thumbhole; more recently *sodina* have been constructed from metal or plastic piping. The instrument has no mouthpiece of any sort: sound is created by forcing air at an angle across the open tube—a difficult technique to master.

solfège A system of verbal syllables that represent relative **tones**.

solo (1) A Sāmoan rhyming poem, especially one suitable for recitation in a *kava* ceremony. (2) An alternate name for the leading vocal part (*fasi*) in Tongan vocal **polyphony**, when that part is sung by women.

someak An Inuit or Eskimo single-headed **frame drum** with a short handle of wood, ivory, or bone.

son (plural, *sones*) (1) In Mexico, a **mestizo** genre of traditional dance music that arose out of native styles of playing instruments. It usually has a vigorous **rhythm**, simple **harmony**, and **strophic** form; (2) (also, *son cubano*) A genre of strophic song and dance originally native to rural Cuba, combining elements of European and African origin. An urbanized version became practically synonymous with Cuban popular dance music and had a far-reaching impact on the music later known as *salsa*.

son chapín A traditional Guatemalan dance piece and its accompanying music.

son cubano (see **son**)

son guatemalteco The national dance of Guatemala, a traditional dance and its accompanying music, performed with *zapateado*, 'stamping' (see *zapateados*).

son istmeño (also, *son oaxaqueño*) An unusual Mexican regional *son*, which, unlike other genres, utilizes wind-and-percussion *bandas*.

son jalisciense A Mexican regional *son* from the state of Jalisco. It is performed by *mariachis* throughout the country and is perhaps the most widely known of Mexican *sones*. Its traditional **accompaniment** (before the introduction of trumpets in mariachis) was one or two violins, a *vihuela*, perhaps a *jarana*, and a **harp** or a *guitarrón*.

son jarocho A southern Mexican regional *son*, traditionally featuring a **harp** and two kinds of guitars: a *jarana* and a *requinto*.

son michoacano A regional Mexican *son* from the hotlands of Michoacán. It traditionally features a large **harp**, two violins, a *vihuela*, and a *jarana*.

soul A music of African-American origin that developed in the United States as a hybrid of **rhythm and blues** and **gospel**. The gospel influence is seen notably in many soul singing styles, which emulate the intensity and sanctity of church singing, despite the secularism of the lyrics.

spike fiddle A fiddle or violin whose neck goes completely through the body of the instrument and out the other end; it is held vertically, not rested on the shoulder.

stanza (also, **verse**) A subdivision of a poem, usually characterized by some pattern, such as a common **meter**, rhyme, or syntax.

starina (plural, *stariny*) (see **bylina**)

stev A four-line **stanza** used as a main structural element in Norwegian **ballads**.

strathspey A Scottish **reel** performed at a slow, stately **tempo**.

strüchmusig A Swiss band consisting of a violin, a **dulcimer**, a bowed double bass, and a **chromatic** accordion or a piano, in a German-speaking area of Switzerland.

stringband (in Tok Pisin, *stringben*) A Polynesian musical ensemble formed mainly of stringed instruments, usually guitars, sometimes incorporating 'ukuleles and rarely banjos.

strophe A component section of a poem, distinguished by a particular rhyme scheme, **meter**, and/or length (see **stanza**).

strophic A descriptive term for poetry made up of smaller segments, or **strophes**, all of which are identical to each other in **meter**, rhyme, and length. When strophic poetry is set to music, the music itself is said to be strophic if the musical setting is identical for each strophe of the poem.

strophic song A song in which the musical setting is identical for each **strophe** of the text it accompanies.

Sufi A member of an ascetic order of Muslim mystics (see **Sufism**).

Sufism A mystical tradition that makes up a major part of the belief-system and practice of a **Sufi** Muslim.

susap An orally resonated **lamellaphone** of New Guinea, possibly the most widespread musical instrument in New Guinea. It is often played for private entertainment by males.

suspension rattle A rattle made by suspending objects from a stick or other device so that when shaken, the objects strike one another and produce sound; also called a jingle rattle.

swing A feeling of **rhythmic** momentum common to playing techniques in the **jazz** idiom.

swing music (also, *big band music*) A **jazz** style that emerged in the 1930s and was an extremely popular dance music in the United States and, later, elsewhere. It is typified by a strong **rhythm** section, a large band, and medium to fast **tempos**.

syllabic Characterized by a vocal presentation in which no more than one syllable of text is set to each **note** of music (compare **melisma**).

syncopation Within a musical passage, a shift of accent relative to the underlying metrical pattern of strong and weak pulses (see **meter**). Beats falling on a normally unstressed pulse within a **measure** will be accented, while beats falling on a normally stressed pulse within a measure will not be accented. For instance, in meters with four pulses per measure, beats one and three are the normally stressed pulses; a **rhythm** within that meter which stressed beats two and four would be considered syncopated.

taarab A popular coastal East African music that traditionally accompanied Swahili love-related poetry, often played at weddings.

taarabu Swahili Arab-influenced music that has been popular since the 1970s in Kenya and other East African coastal communities; it employs electric and electronic instruments, including guitars and organs.

t'aay A Yapese song of abuse, recounting situations in which one party has supposedly injured another.

tàbage A word used to describe various kinds of Huli *kundu* drums.

tāga In Sāmoan dance, certain movements made by a performer's hands and arms, which allude to sung words, comment on implied concepts, and decorate and connect musical **phrases**.

tagi A sung section of a Sāmoan narrative tale (*fāgono*).

tagica In a Fijian *meke*, a higher-**pitched** vocal part, which typically responds to the leading part (*laga*).

tahardent (1) A Tuareg three-stringed **lute**, resembling the Mauritanian *tidinit*; (2) A Tuareg musical genre that has become popular in Niger.

takəmba A recent Tuareg genre in which seated listeners respond to **rhythms** with undulating movements of the torso.

tali 'response': (1) The singers making up the **chorus** in Sāmoan **choral** music, who end **phrases** begun by one or more leaders (*usu*); (2) The music sung by them.

ṭambal (or *cimbalom*) A trapezoidal struck **zither** used for **accompaniment** and as a solo instrument. It is prominent in Romania and Hungary. The instrument is thought to be a possible ancestor of the modern *hammered dulcimer* (see **dulcimer**).

tambor (1) Any drum (Spanish-language); (2) A specific, double-headed wooden drum played by the Maya in Central America.

tambora A bass drum with heads on both sides of the instrument, used in the Venezuelan central coast. It is also used prominently in Dominican *merengue*, in Columbia, Cuba, and elsewhere.

tambura A Middle Eastern fretted long-necked **lute** imported into the Balkans during the Ottoman period. Undoubtedly a local descendant of the Turkish *sāz*, it was originally popular where Turkish and Muslim influence was strongest, and mainly accompanied male singing. It subsequently spread through Eastern Europe and among the Roma (see **Rom**).

tamburaši Players of the *tambura*.

tamburica (1) An orchestra of long-necked, plucked **lutes**, common in 1930s Serbia, and featuring many Romani musicians (see **Rom**); (2) A term encompassing several related and variously sized long-necked fretted **lutes**, found, for instance, among the Croatian minority in Austria in *tamburica* bands.

tamunangue One of the most famous expressions of music and dance in Venezuela, from the state of Lara in the northwest of the country. It is a suite of dances and music, usually performed in honor of San Antonio de Padua, the patron saint of Lara. The music for the *tamunangue* consists of singing accompanied by stringed instruments or maracas and a drum of African origin.

tang A personally expressive and usually privately performed Yapese song.

tango A genre of music and dance with a nostalgic and melancholic character that became prominent in the late 1800s, and is centered on one city, Buenos Aires. Its popularity peaked in the 1940s, then declined, but in the 1980s began to rise again, nationally and internationally.

tapan (plural, *tapani*) (Bulgarian, *tŭpan*) A barrel-shaped, double-headed drum, prevalent in Bulgaria and throughout the southern Balkans, and a specialty of Romani musicians (see **Rom**).

tarabuka A goblet-shaped drum of Middle Eastern origin played in the Balkans (see *darabuka*, in the glossary of volume 2).

taualuga The finale of a Sāmoan performance of singing and dancing, usually featuring a distinguished woman and her attendants.

tau'olunga A Tongan dance performed by women. The word is a borrowing from the Sāmoan *taualuga*.

tazammart (also *tasansagh* and *tasensigh*) A Tuareg four-holed **flute**, made of a reed or metal tube.

teempraa utaa (or simply *teempraa*) A genre of Yapese *tang* that evolved under Japanese influence, and combined Japanese **melodies** with Yapese and Japanese words. After 1945, this genre included songs based on American and European melodies, with mixed Yapese and English words.

tembakl A Melpa *susap*.

tempered (see **temperament**)

temperament In the **tuning** of an instrument, the adjustment of acoustically natural **intervals**, so that the instrument can be played in any **key** without retuning. Temperament is fundamental to Western performance practices.

tempo (plural, *tempos* or *tempi*) The perceived speed of a musical performance; it can be regarded as the amount of time that passes between the regular metrical pulses of the music (compare **meter** and **rhythm**).

tempo rubato Rhythmic flexibility, or the relaxation of strict adherence to time. **Tempo rubato** (or simply *rubato*) typically involves an alternation between increased and decreased tempos for expressive purposes, and done at the discretion of the performer(s).

tende (also, *tindi*) A Tuareg term referring to a single-headed mortar drum, the music that accompanies it, and the social event that features it.

tende n-əmnas Any of several events where the mortar drum is typically played and that feature personalized references to camels.

teponaztle An ancient Mesoamerican **idiophone** made from a hollowed-out tree trunk, with an H-shaped slit cut into it, producing two tongues. It was positioned horizontally and struck with mallets. Each tongue produced a distinct **pitch**.

ternos Ensembles of dramatic music and dance in central and southern Brazil.

tesîwit A pastoral Tuareg **strophic** poem sung solo to formulaic **melodies** or **motifs**.

tessitura The most comfortable or general range of a voice or instrument.

tetrachord A series of four **diatonic** tones, in which, in ancient Greek music theory, the first and last in the sequence were separated by the **interval** of a perfect fourth. Ancient Greeks used the tetrachord as the fundamental means of determining **tuning**, and as a fundamental series of **tones** for determining the melodic identity of a **composition**. In modern usage, the term may refer to any series of four diatonic tones, whether or not the first and last are separated by the interval of a perfect fourth.

through-composed In vocal music, having distinct music for each distinct section of text; i.e., there is music accompanying all text, and none of it is repeated from section to section.

tidinit A Mauritanian **lute**.

timbales Big hemispheric drums played with two cloth- or leather-covered sticks, ubiquitous in **Afro-Cuban music**; also prominent in some Afro-Brazilian music.

timbre (also, *tone color*) The particular quality—of a musical performance, voice, instrument, or ensemble—that distinguishes it from another even when producing identical **pitches**.

tinya A small Peruvian drum, played mostly by women.

toasting A practice of Jamaican mobile sound system **DJs**, beginning in the 1960s, in which they spoke **rhythmically** over the records (often **dub** records) that they were playing. The subject matter included praises for dancers on their appearance and information on the next dance. This practice was an important precursor to the **rapping of MCs**.

tō'ere A **log idiophone** of the Society Islands, beaten with one stick.

tōkere A **log idiophone** of the Cook Islands, beaten with two sticks.

tololoche A Mexican-style string bass, often with three strings, rather than the four strings typical of the symphonic string bass.

tòmbena tàbage A common variety of Huli **kundu**, which sounds *dòmbena* (or *tòmbena*), "in-between." It is played by male dancers at celebrations.

tonada In Cuba, a tune or **melody** sung to recite *décimas*.

tonal Characterized by **tonality**.

tonal center In any **melody** of **tonal music**, the **tone** that serves as a point of **harmonic** resolution or repose; **tonic**.

tonality (1) The system of **tonal** organization that may exist in a given piece; (2) In **tonal music**, a specific system of tonal organization. It is characterized by the use of a single **key** as the basis of each **composition**. The keys are conceived of by reference to a **tonic** (or root) note and a **mode** (which in tonal music typically refers to the major or minor **modes**). Examples of key therefore would be C major or A minor.

tonal music Music that uses a specific system of **tonality** (see **tonality**, definition 2).

tondero A Peruvian musical genre closely related to the *marinera*, but exhibiting a distinctive **harmonic** structure.

tone (1) A **pitch**, with a definite **frequency**; (2) A pitch or range of pitches treated within a musical system as a sonic identity, and often analyzable as a constituent unit of a musical **scale**; (3) The character or quality of the sound produced by a specific instrument, group of instruments, voice, or group of voices.

tonic (or *tonic note*) The root **note** of any given **scale**. Also, the note that is the **tonal center** of any given **key**. May also be seen in the context of the **tonic triad**, which is a **chord** based on the tonic note in a given key.

tonic triad (or *tonic chord*, *root chord*) The **triad** in any **key** that is based around the **tonic** note of that key.

totem A living being, natural object, or human representation of a natural object, which serves as an emblem of a family, clan, or larger societal group.

tres A six-stringed plucked **chordophone** of Cuban origin, differing from a standard guitar mainly in its **tuning**: three pairs of strings, each with a **pitch** and its **octave**, are plucked to build **melodies** as counterpoints to a singer's melodies.

triad A **chord** made up of three **pitches**. In formal use, the term specifically refers to a three-**note** chord in which the **interval** between each pitch is a third.

tritone The **interval** otherwise known as an augmented fourth or diminished fifth, generally perceived as having a dark and dissonant character.

tromba A Malagasy ceremony that involves ancestor reverence and worship, and possession of spirit mediums by ancestral spirits. Each tromba spirit has her or his own favored musical **composition**, and the tromba is thus an important context for ceremonial music in Madagascar.

trovador A crooner of serenades and parties who sings sentimental songs, strums acoustic guitars, and sings courtship songs in urban settings; found in Cuba and the Dominican Republic, and throughout Latin America.

tsaba-tsaba An urban popular dance-song genre, drawing from South African **choral** music.

tsaboraha A Malagasy ceremony that is an important context for ceremonial music.

tshikona The national music of the Venda, produced by an ensemble of pipes, each of which produce only one **pitch**, played in **hocket**.

tsymbaly A trapezoidal hammered **dulcimer** of the Ukraine, Poland, and Belarus.

tulon bololu "Play" songs of various ethnic groups of northern Sierra Leone that are relatively light in subject matter.

tumbadora (also, *conga*) A tall, barrel-shaped, single-headed Cuban drum of African origin; perhaps the central drum in **Afro-Cuban music**, it is now used throughout Latin America and the world.

tumbuizo A genre of song performed by women in Kenya, singing in Swahili.

tuning (1) The act of adjusting the sound-making mechanism(s) of a musical instrument to set the **pitches** that it can produce; (2) The array of **tones** to which a given instrument is customarily or currently tuned.

tŭpan (see *tapan*)

tvísöngur 'two-singing': an Icelandic vocal form and technique of accompanying another voice in parallel fifths.

txalaparta A Basque **idiophone**, consisting of one or more wooden planks beaten by two players to create different **rhythmic** patterns.

txistu A Basque three-holed **duct flute**, typically played by the left hand while the right hand plays a drum.

ú, dáwanda ú A Huli clan—identification song.

uilleann pipes A traditional Irish **bellows**-blown **bagpipe**. Like Scottish bagpipes, they now have three **drones** tuned in **octaves**, but to these were formerly added three pipes ("regulators"), each with a few metal keys depressed by the player's wrist to create limited harmonic **accompaniment**.

'ukulele (or *ukulele*) Hawaiian name given during the 1880s to the *braguinha*, a small four-stringed Portuguese musical instrument of the guitar family. This name and the instrument are now commonly recognized worldwide.

unison (1) The **interval** created when two or more musical instruments or voices perform the same **tone** simultaneously (i.e., an interval of zero **semitones**). (2) The simultaneous sounding of two or more instruments.

usu The leader or group of leaders who function as choral leaders in Sāmoan **choral** music. They begin **phrases** that are finished by the **chorus** (*tali*).

uunu A Fataleka rattle-accompanied divinatory song.

vakalutuivoce 'dropping the oar': an ancient style of unaccompanied Fijian vocal **polyphony**, performed by two people while rowing or rafting, with their voices emphasizing the **harmony** of a major second.

vakamalolo A genre of Fijian *meke* performed by seated men or women.

valiha A wire-stringed tube **zither**, the best-known instrument of Madagascar, also played in Tanzania.

vallenato An Afro-Columbian music dating from the beginning of the twentieth century; its lyrical style is inherited from archaic Spanish oral poems and work songs, but its **rhythmic** elements show prominent African influences.

valonas A Mexican musical genre with several declaimed *décimas*, of the southwestern part of the state of Michoacán.

vals criollo The Peruvian waltz, generally called **Creole music** (*música criolla*); many Peruvians consider it the foremost national music.

vandumbu A ritual of Ngangela-speaking peoples of Central Africa, commemorating dead kings or chiefs; also, the principal musical instrument of the occasion, a megaphone.

veillée An evening gathering that was once the major occasion for French recreational singing not associated with meals. *Veillées* are rarely held in contemporary French culture.

velorio A nightlong celebration or night watch to honor a saint or the Holy Cross, common in Venezuela. In the Venezuelan plains, the music of the *velorio* is primarily Spanish in origin, with stringed instruments predominating, but in the central coastal area, the music is more African in origin.

verbunkos A Hungarian military-recruitment dance.

verse (1) A line of poetry or text; (2) A group of lines of poetry that together form a segment of a poem, often separated from the other groups by a pause or, in written poetry, spacing or punctuation. In songs with a verse–chorus structure, verses may be separated by a recurring **refrain** (see **stanza**, **strophe**).

vibrato The tremulousness given to a musical **tone** by rapid variations in its **pitch** or intensity, often for expressive effect.

vihuela (1) A sixteenth-century Spanish guitar, typically with twelve paired strings; (2) A five-stringed Mexican guitar with a convex back, used in the *mariachi* ensemble and in the *conjunto de arpa grande* ensemble.

villancico A Spanish Christmas carol.

viola A Portuguese and Brazilian guitar, related to the Spanish *vihuela*, and having varying numbers and **courses** of strings. In Portuguese *fado* music, the viola is mandatory, and provides **harmonic** and **rhythmic** support, allowing the *fadista* and the lead *guitarristas* to improvise. It is also one of the most common stringed instruments in central and southern Brazil.

viola baixo A large bass guitar that plays the bass line in a performance of Portuguese *fado*.

viola caipira The most common *viola* in southeastern Brazil. It is smaller than a guitar, and has five double **courses** of metal strings. In contrast with the *viola de cocho*, it has a full, metallic **timbre**.

viola de cocho A form of *viola* found in Mato Grosso do Sul in Brazil. It has five single **courses** of strings, made of animal gut or fishing line. It produces a deep, hollow sound, more percussive than **harmonic**.

violão The common Portuguese-language term in Brazil for a standard guitar.

vivo A Tahitian nose **flute**.

vocable A spoken or sung syllable that carries no lexical meaning; used to vocalize music, as in *fa-la-la*. Despite its lack of lexical meaning, it may produce an emotional meaning or elicit an emotional response.

voyageur songs Songs composed by boatmen who in the eighteenth and nineteenth centuries traveled in canoes between trading centers in what was then known as Lower Canada (Québec) and Upper Canada (Ontario) and composed or adapted songs to the **rhythms** of paddling.

vucu Fijian *meke*-style singing without dancing.

wanaragua (also *Jankunú*) A procession and mime-dance of Belize.

wangga One of the two principal public genres of song in Western Arnhem Land, Australia (the other being *lirrga*), usually deemed to have been received from spirits in dreams. Performances of *wangga* mark celebrations of the social dimensions of life.

wanibanga An indigenous Kiribati dance, which, like the *wantarawa*, often consists of one-tone **melodies**.

wantarawa An indigenous Kiribati dance, which, like the *wanibanga*, often consists of one-tone **melodies**.

water drum An indigenous American drum that is partially filled with water. Many varieties are found elsewhere in the world.

waulking song A genre of Scottish folksong, traditionally sung by women while waulking cloth (beating newly woven cloth to soften it). The repertoire of waulking songs, which involves a call-and-response pattern, is enormous and drew its themes and **melodies** from diverse sources.

w(e)ii A term which, as a noun, denotes the main Baluan women's ritual song and men's work-accompanying songs. Used as a verb ('sing'), it is gender-neutral and does not cover all kinds of singing. Older persons pronouce the word as [uii], but younger ones pronounce it as [uei]; hence the spelling *w(e)ii*.

werl A Melpa married women's slow dance, performed in place in a line during a *moka* with each woman playing a *kundu* and singing words resembling those of a *mörl* or detailing young men's activities.

whirled slat An **aerophone** consisting of a thin, lens- or rhomboid-shaped wooden slat attached to a string and made to hum by being whirled through the air.

wind instrument A musical instrument whose principal sound is the vibration of air enclosed within it or agitated immediately around it (see **aerophone**).

wiri A rapid quivering of arms, hands, and fingers that is a feature of Māori dance. Performers sometimes transfer *wiri* into minuscule vibrations of the torso, neck, and head.

xayácatl (or *xayacates*) A Nahua dance of the Michoacán area; it parodies the famous Spanish dance *moros y cristianos* 'Moors and Christians', which reenacts the battles of the expulsion of the Moors from Spain.

xylophone A **percussion instrument** that consists of a set of bundled tuned bars that are struck by a mallet.

yaraví A slow, lyrical, **mestizo** musical genre of the southern Andes; it is usually associated with afflicted love affairs and nostalgic moods.

yodel A vocal technique in which the singer rapidly alternates between **falsetto** and full-voiced singing while generally alternating between **pitches**.

yui A Baluan raft **panpipe**, consisting of four bamboo tubes.

zabumba A double-headed Brazilian bass drum.

zapateados An up-tempo dance of Spanish origin, popular in Mexico and Central America. Its **rhythms** are accented by a dancer's shoes, in a technique analogous to tap dance of the United States.

zapateo criollo (also *zapateado criollo*) A competitive Afro-Peruvian dance genre that utilizes *festejo* rhythms. It is danced by a solo male who demonstrates his skill by improvising intricate **rhythmic** patterns with his feet, supplemented by rhythmic slapping.

zikr (see *dhikr*)

zither Any **chordophone** in which the, usually numerous, strings are strung over the body of the instrument and run the entire length of the body. The instrument is typically set on a horizontal surface, and the strings may be struck in any of numerous ways.

zortziko 'made of eights': the most popular Basque dance-song type, in asymmetrical **rhythm** and consisting of eight steps.

zouk A musical and social phenomenon that arose in the mid 1980s in Martinique and spread beyond the West Indies to Africa, Europe, and North America. Its essential expressive elements are drawn from French West Indian traditions.

zurna (also, *zurla*, *surla*) A double-reed, conical-bore oboe played by Romani musicians (see *Rom*) in southwestern Bulgaria.

zydeco A **Creole** musical genre developed after World War II as a synthesis of traditional **Creole music**, **Cajun music**, African-American musical influences such as **rhythm and blues** and **jazz** as well as some Afro-Caribbean **rhythms**.